NO
LONGER
HUMAN

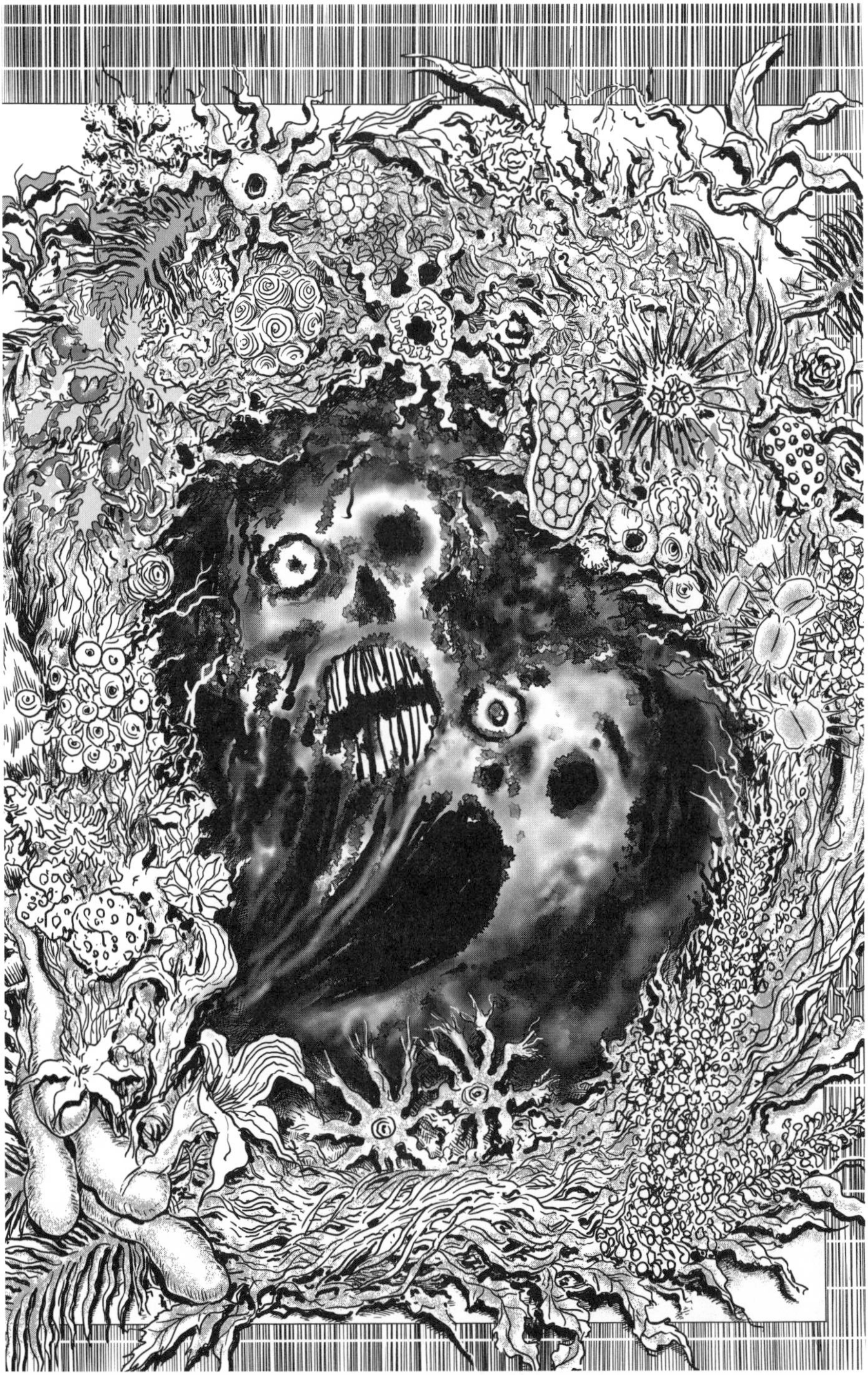

Junji Ito

NO LONGER HUMAN

Original novel by Osamu Dazai
Based on English translation by Donald Keene

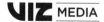 **MEDIA**

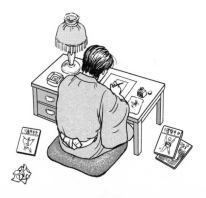

CONTENTS

CHAIN No. 1: Yozo Oba

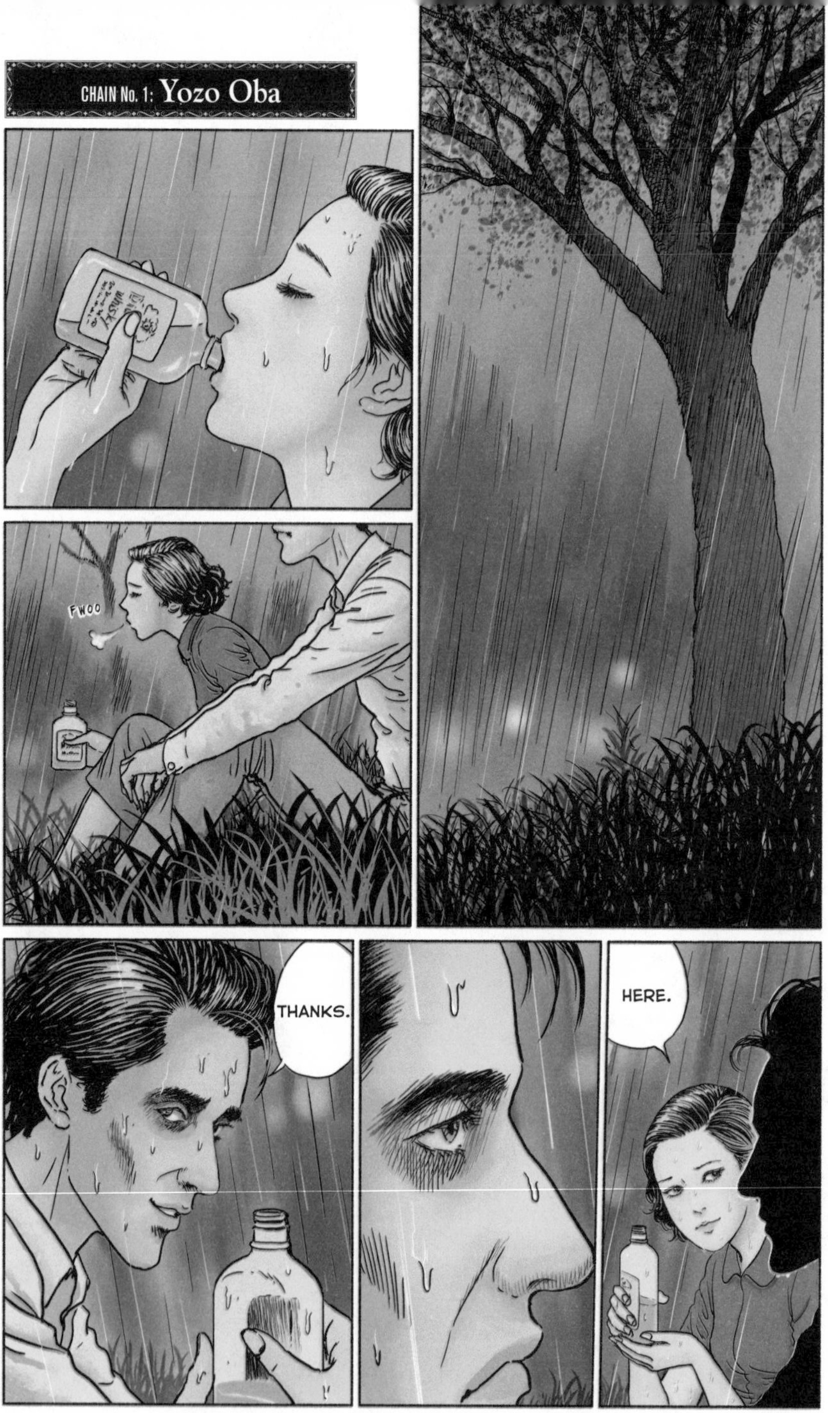
FWOO
HERE.
THANKS.

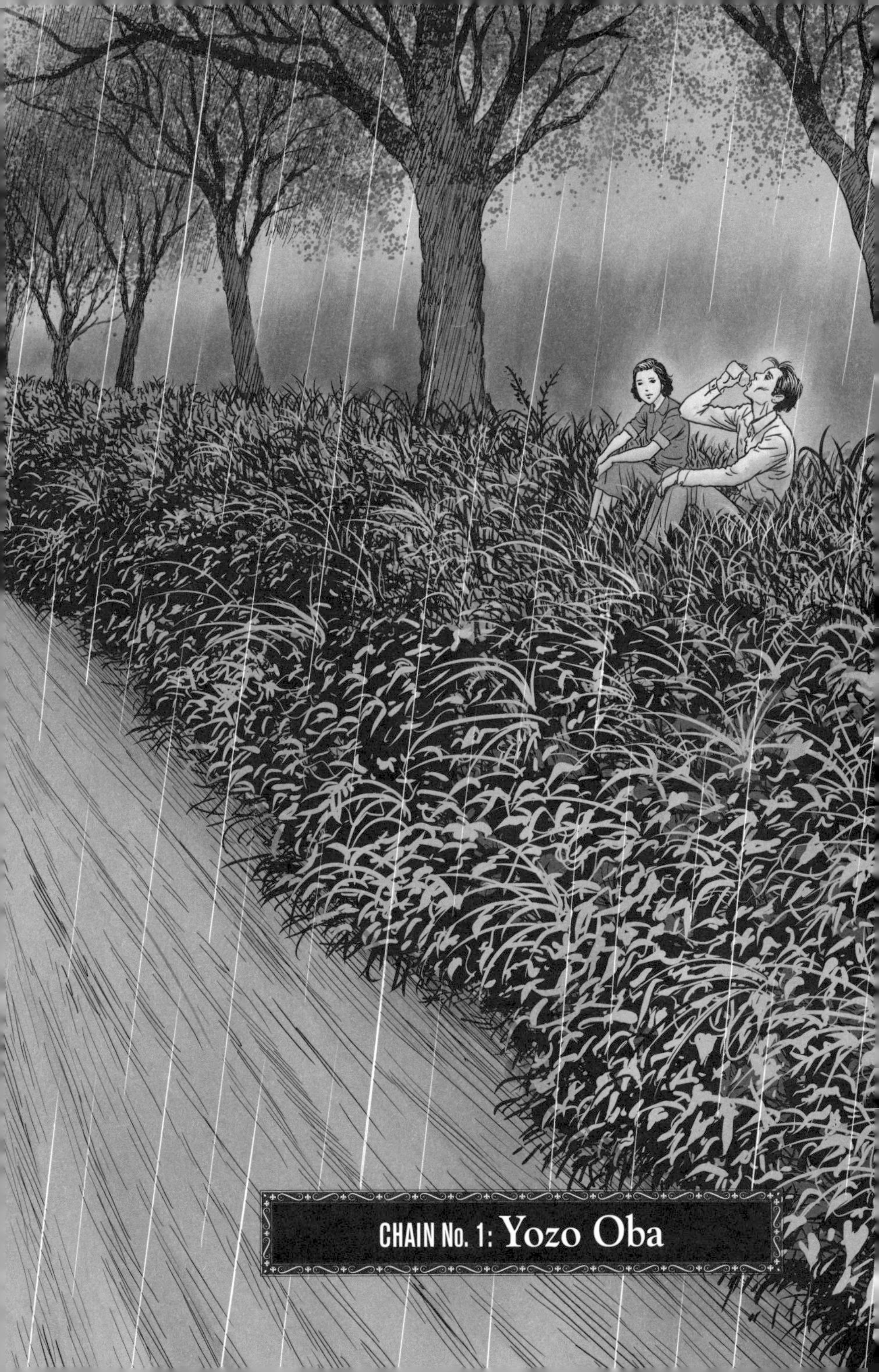
CHAIN No. 1: Yozo Oba

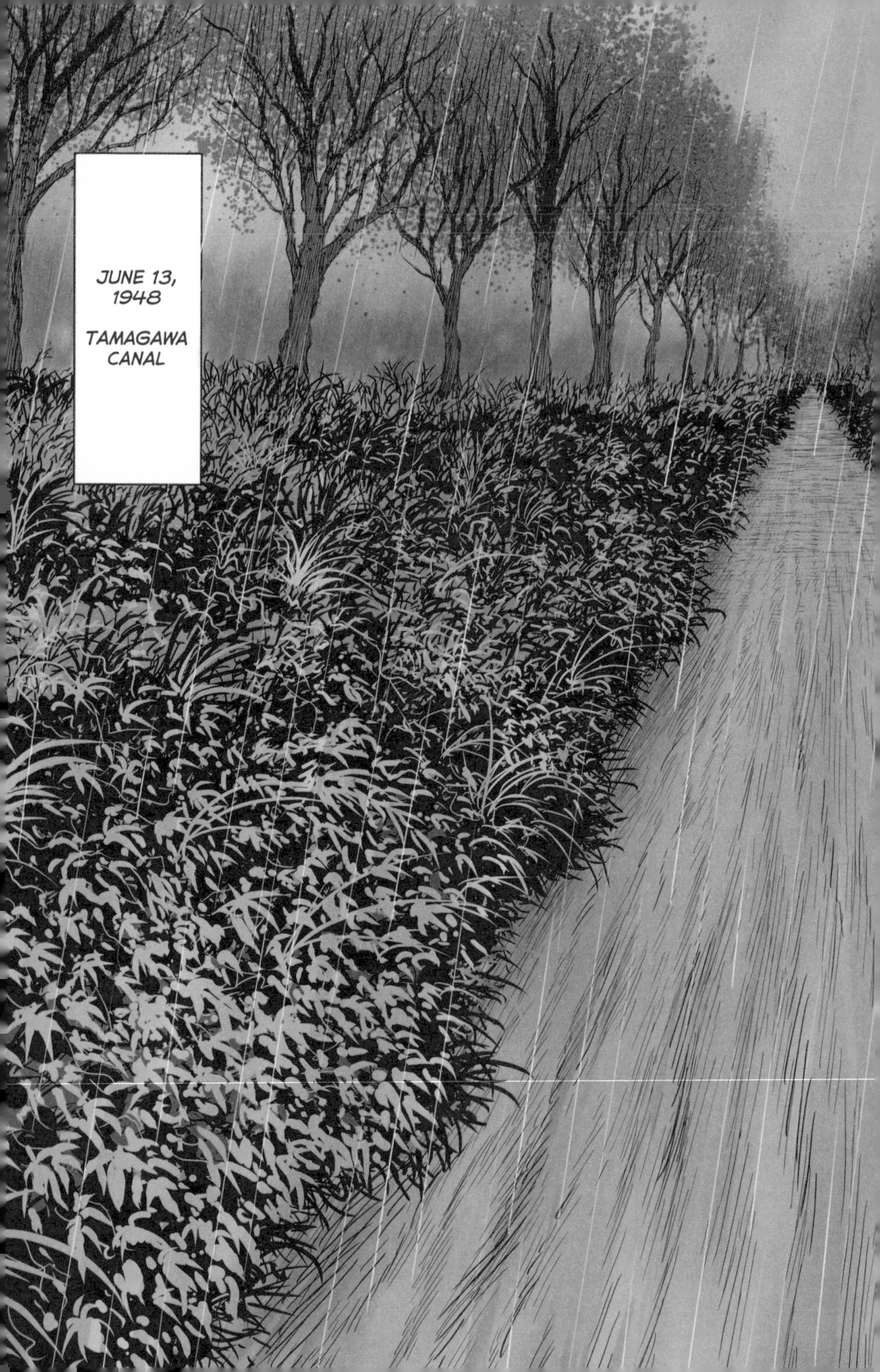
JUNE 13, 1948
TAMAGAWA CANAL

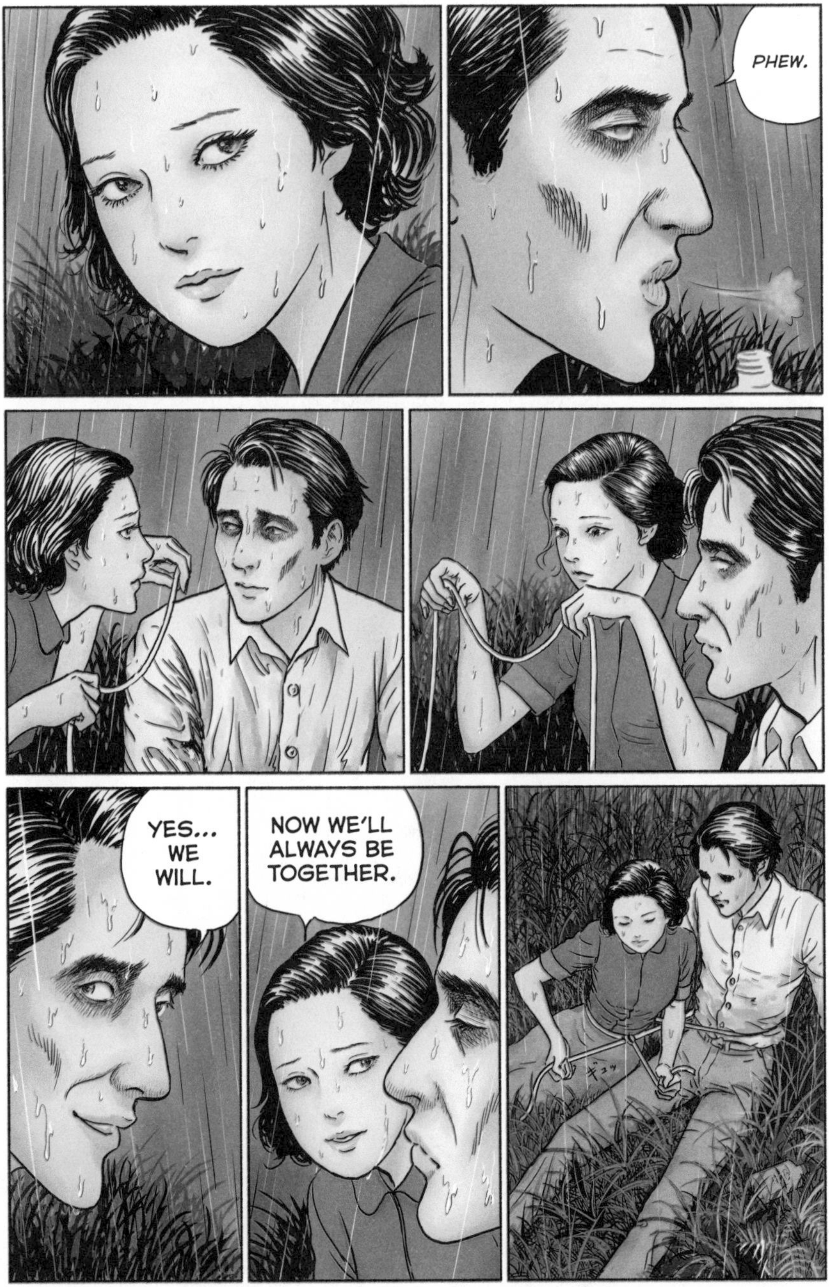
PHEW.
NOW WE'LL ALWAYS BE TOGETHER.
YES... WE WILL.

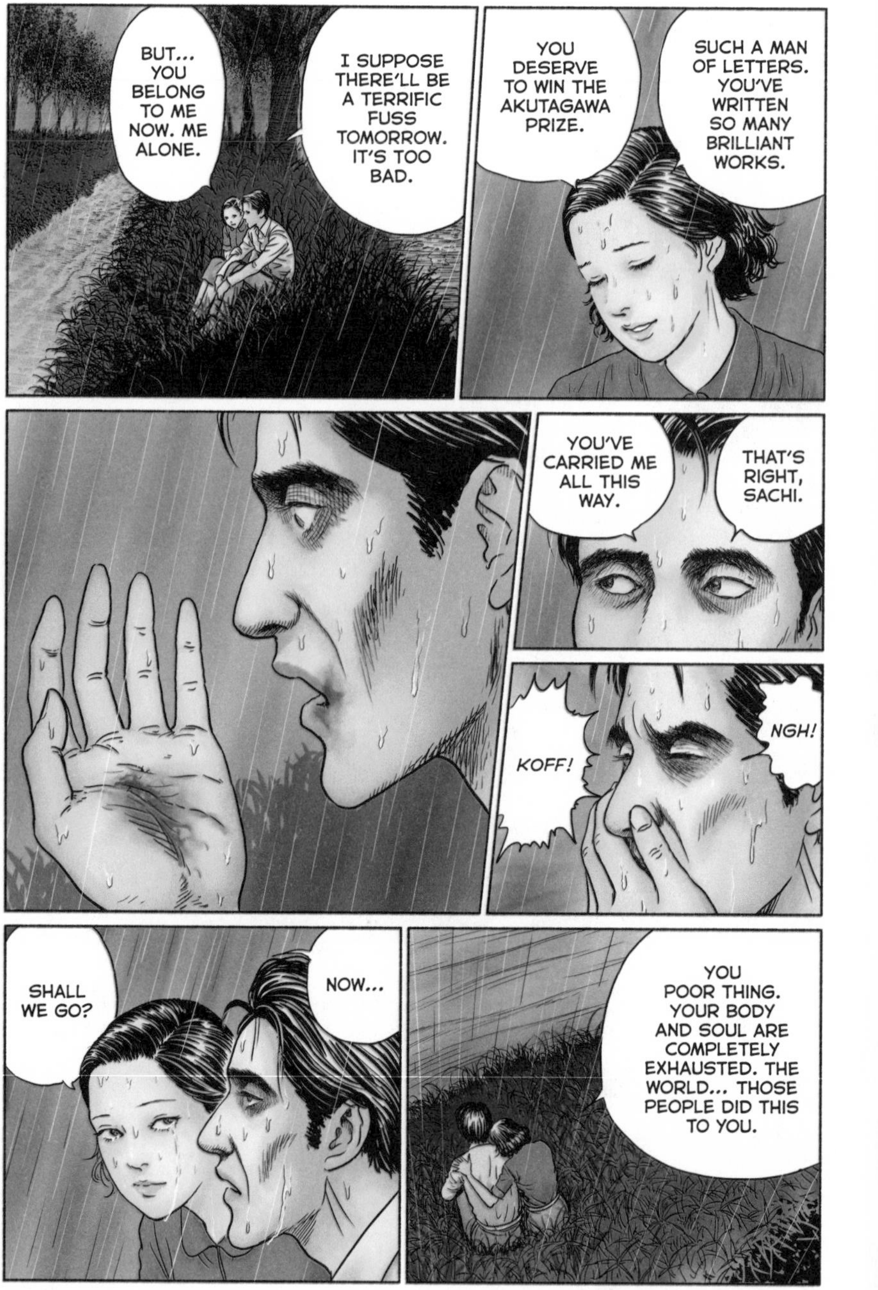
SUCH A MAN OF LETTERS. YOU'VE WRITTEN SO MANY BRILLIANT WORKS.
YOU DESERVE TO WIN THE AKUTAGAWA PRIZE.
I SUPPOSE THERE'LL BE A TERRIFIC FUSS TOMORROW. IT'S TOO BAD.
BUT... YOU BELONG TO ME NOW. ME ALONE.
THAT'S RIGHT, SACHI.
YOU'VE CARRIED ME ALL THIS WAY.
NGH!
KOFF!
YOU POOR THING. YOUR BODY AND SOUL ARE COMPLETELY EXHAUSTED. THE WORLD... THOSE PEOPLE DID THIS TO YOU.
NOW...
SHALL WE GO?

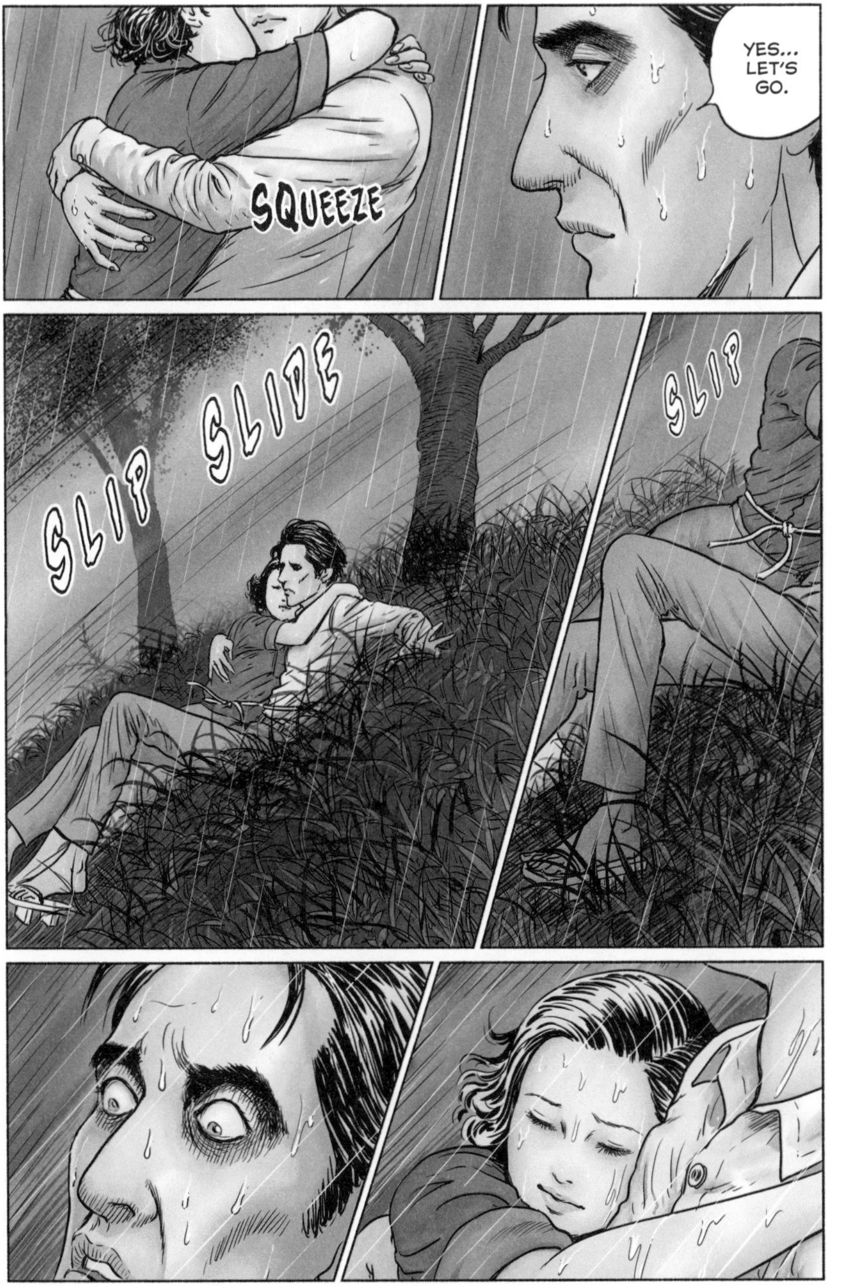
YES... LET'S GO.
SQUEEZE
SLIP
SLIP SLIDE

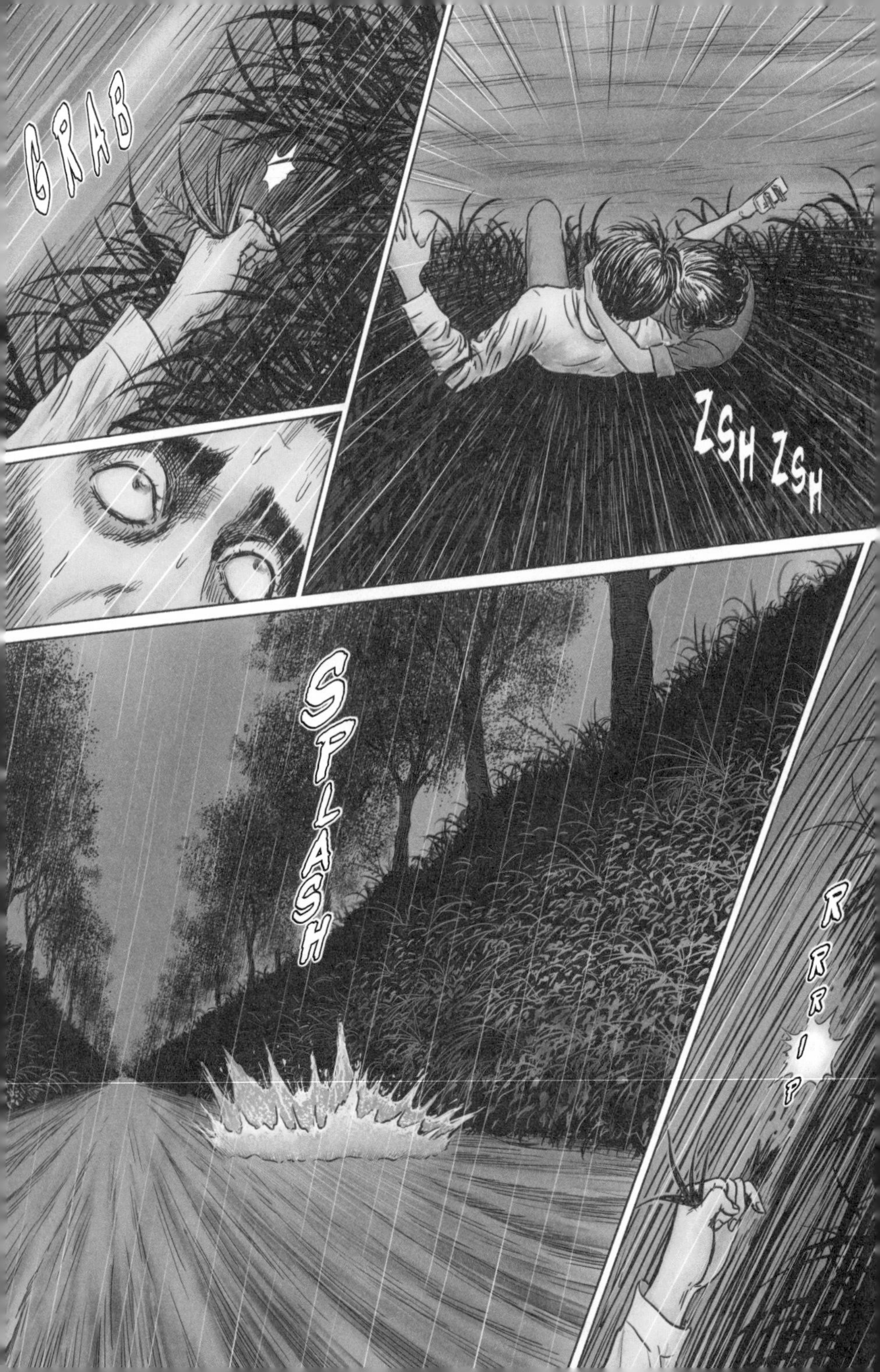
ZSH ZSH
GRAB
RRRIP
SPLASH

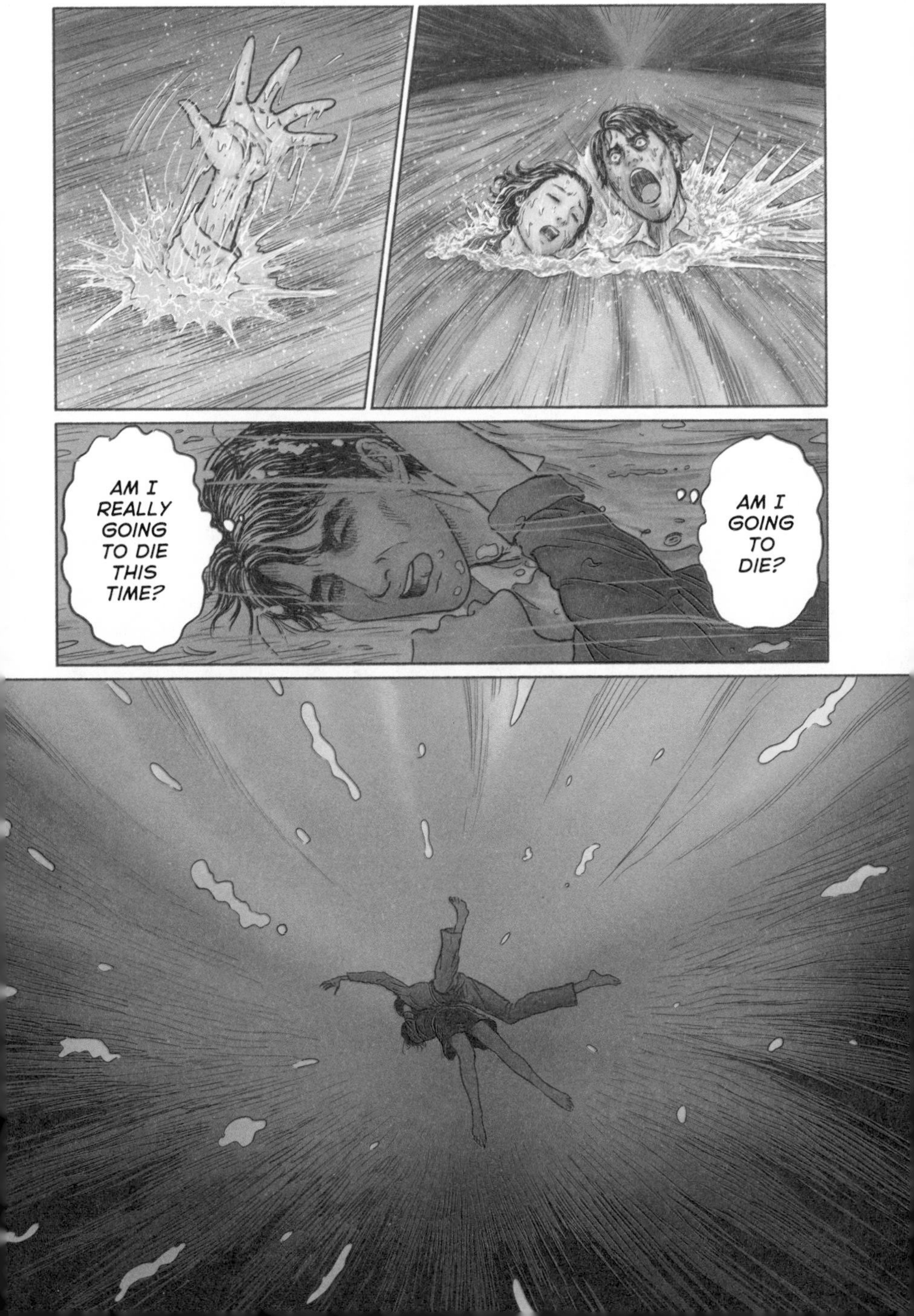
AM I GOING TO DIE?
AM I REALLY GOING TO DIE THIS TIME?

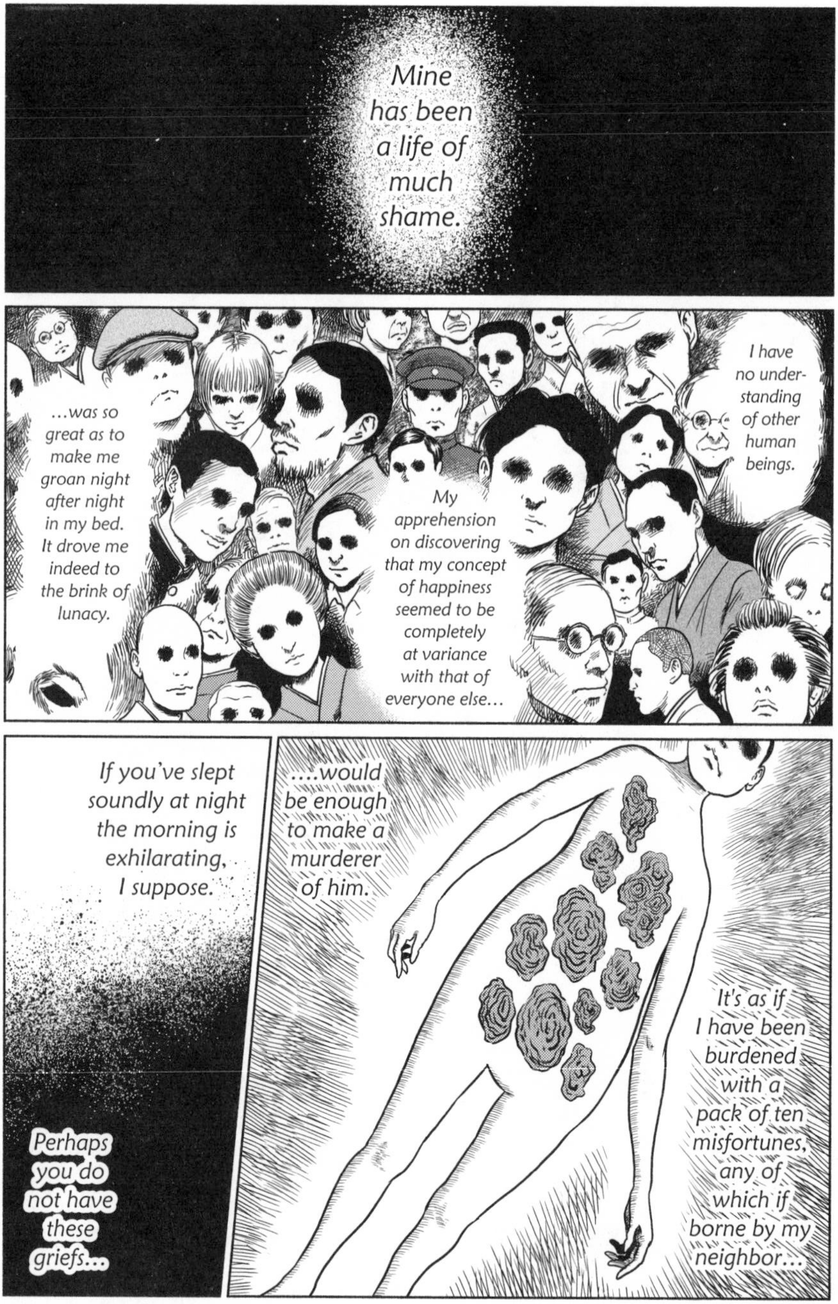
Mine has been a life of much shame.
I have no understanding of other human beings.
My apprehension on discovering that my concept of happiness seemed to be completely at variance with that of everyone else...
...was so great as to make me groan night after night in my bed. It drove me indeed to the brink of lunacy.
It's as if I have been burdened with a pack of ten misfortunes, any of which if borne by my neighbor...
....would be enough to make a murderer of him.
If you've slept soundly at night the morning is exhilarating, I suppose.
Perhaps you do not have these griefs...

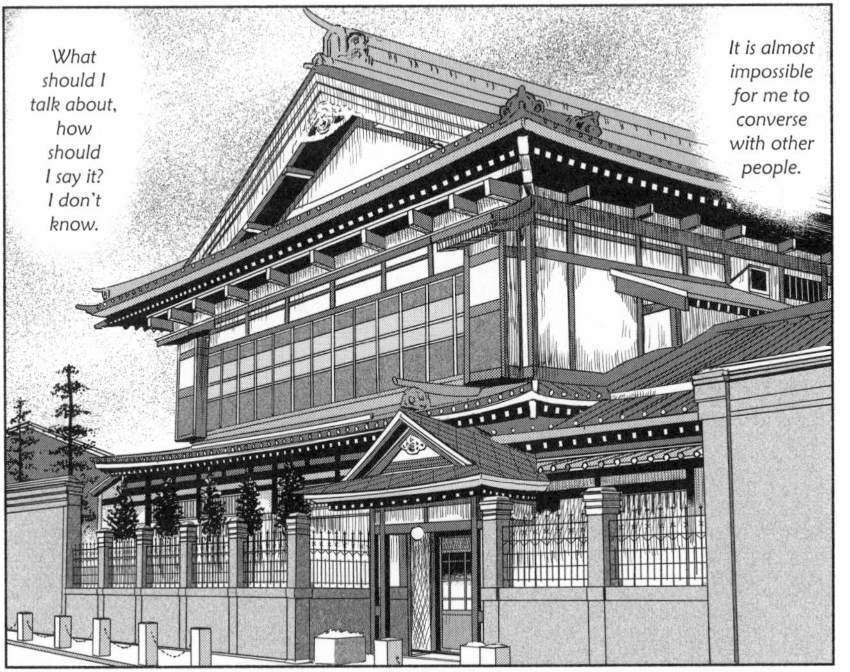
It is almost impossible for me to converse with other people.
What should I talk about, how should I say it? I don't know.

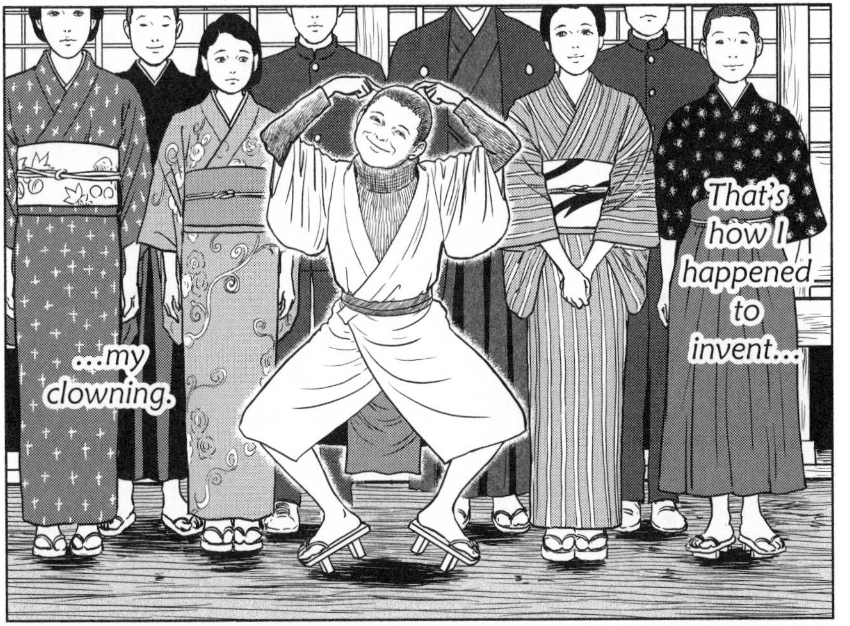
That's how I happened to invent...
...my clowning.

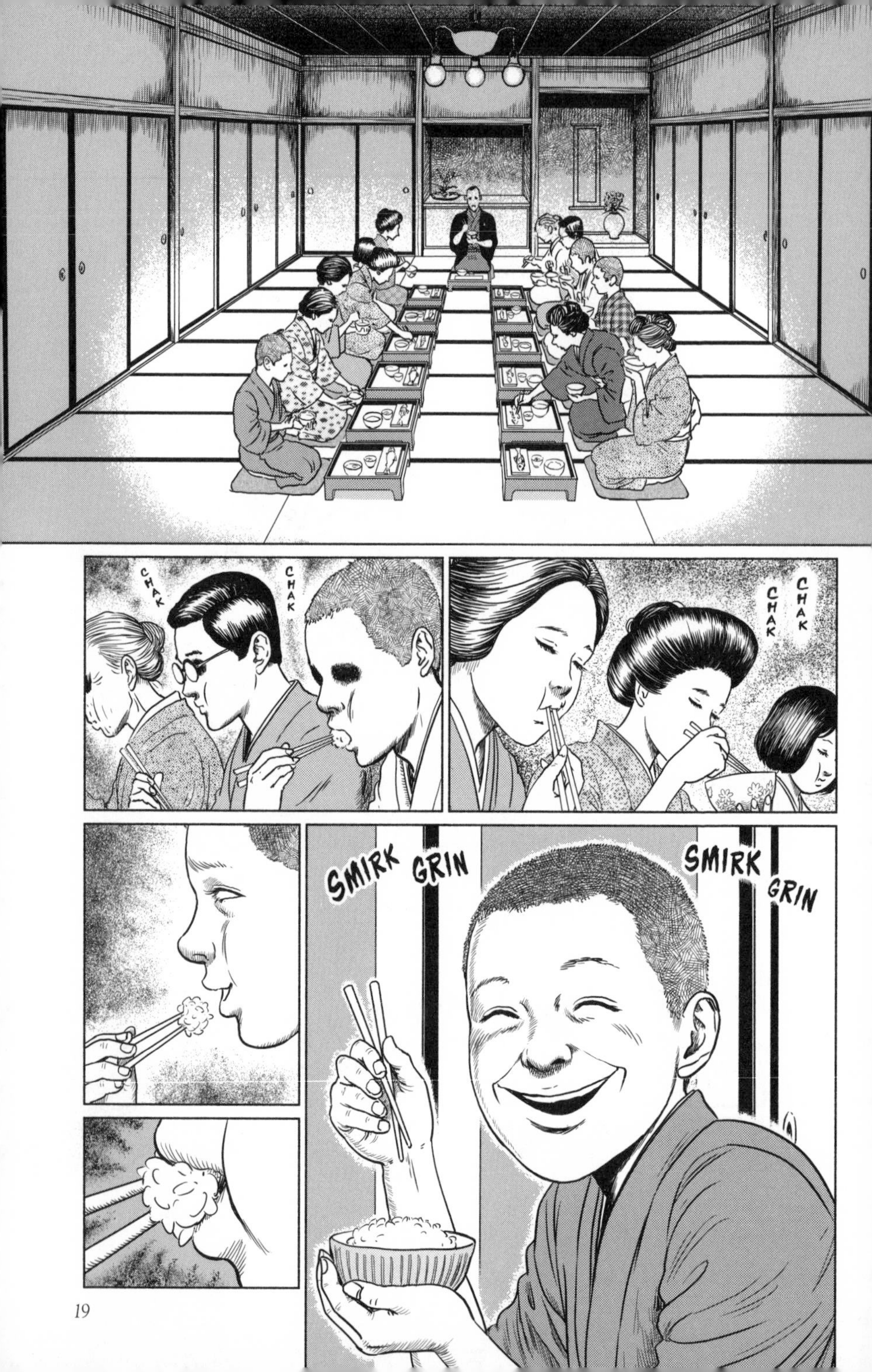
CHAK CHAK
CHAK
CHAK
SMIRK GRIN
SMIRK GRIN

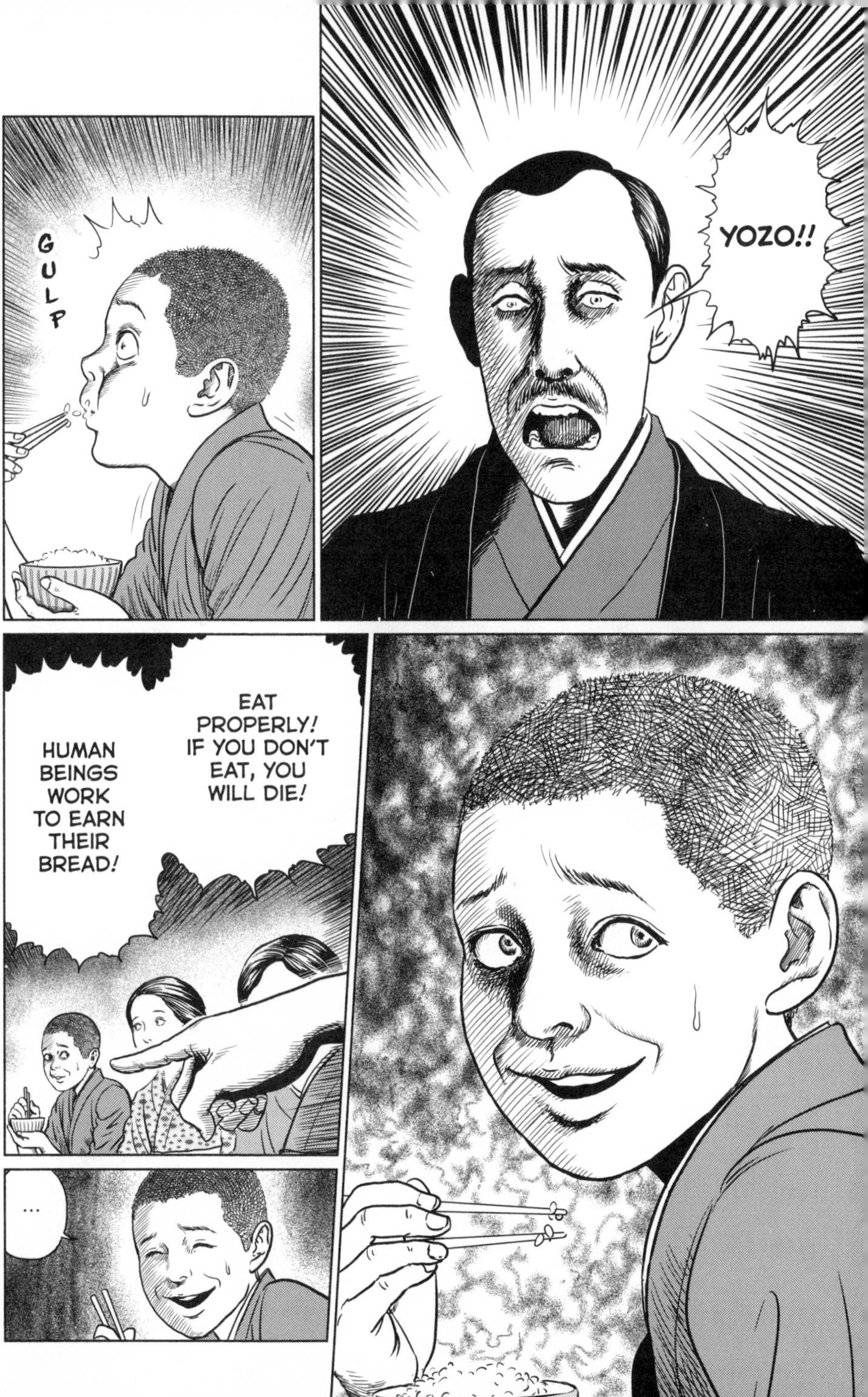
YOZO!!
GULP
EAT PROPERLY! IF YOU DON'T EAT, YOU WILL DIE!
HUMAN BEINGS WORK TO EARN THEIR BREAD!
...

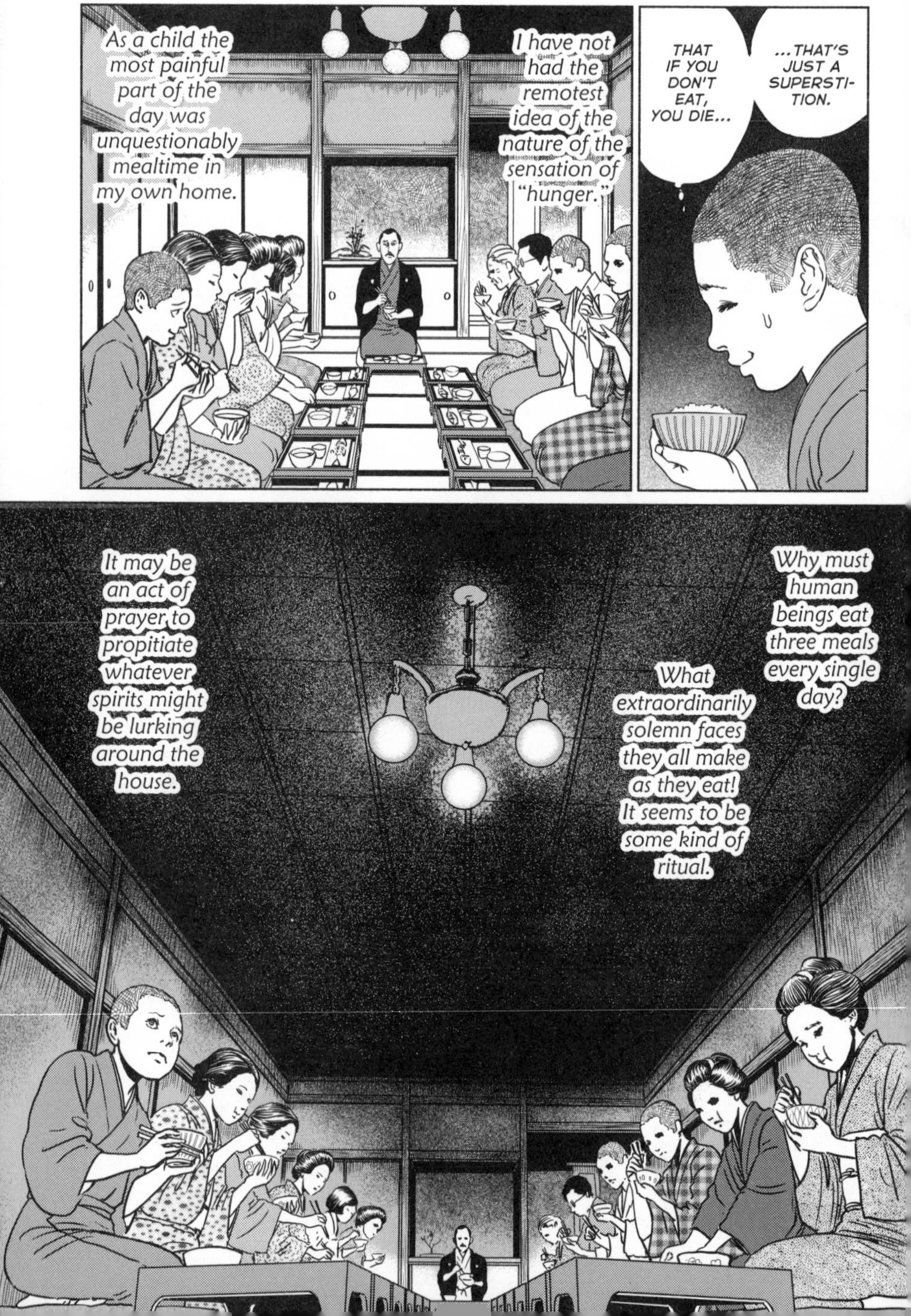
THAT IF YOU DON'T EAT, YOU DIE...
...THAT'S JUST A SUPERSTITION.
I have not had the remotest idea of the nature of the sensation of "hunger."
As a child the most painful part of the day was unquestionably mealtime in my own home.
Why must human beings eat three meals every single day?
What extraordinarily solemn faces they all make as they eat! It seems to be some kind of ritual.
It may be an act of prayer to propitiate whatever spirits might be lurking around the house.

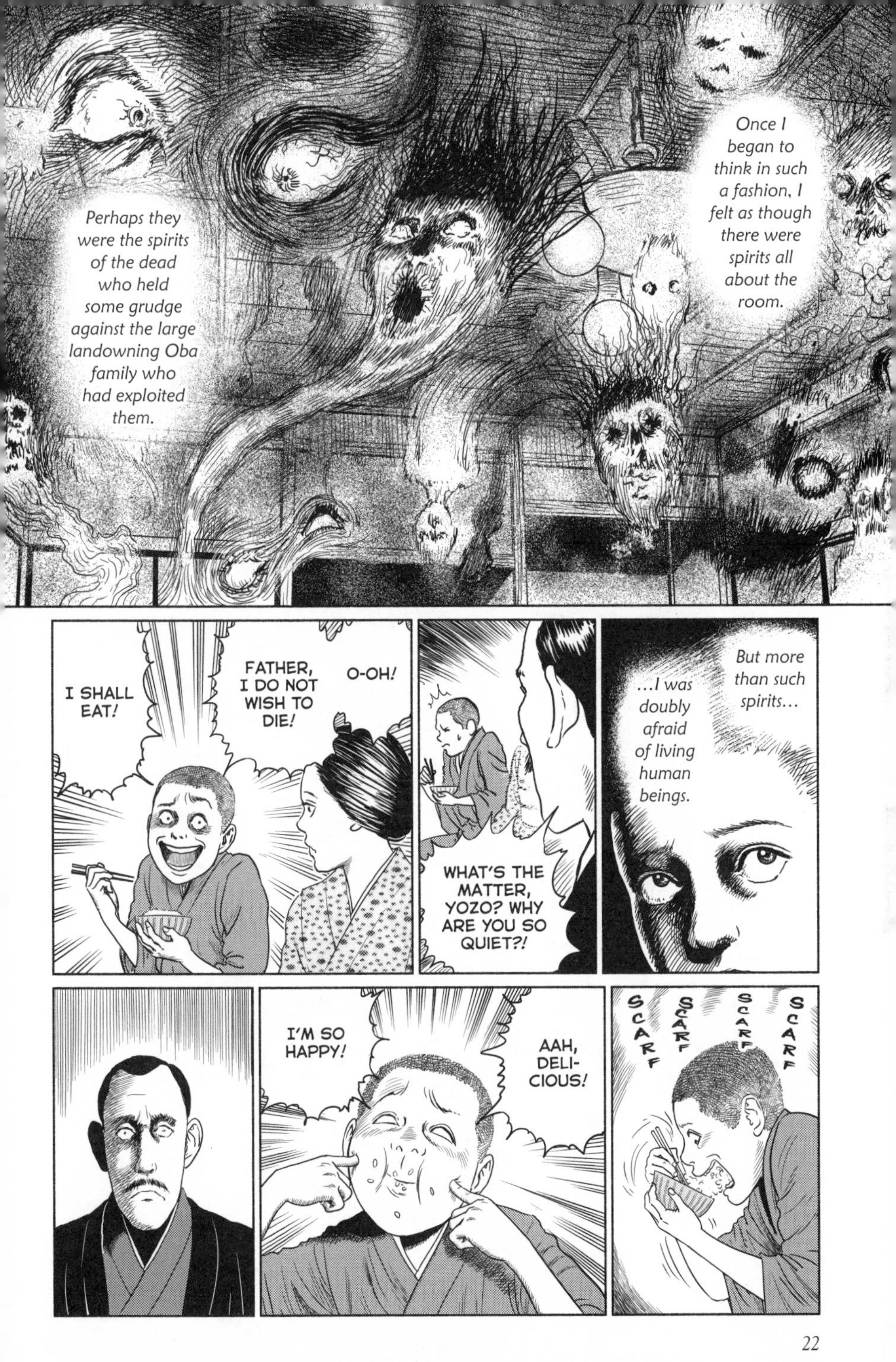
Once I began to think in such a fashion, I felt as though there were spirits all about the room.
Perhaps they were the spirits of the dead who held some grudge against the large landowning Oba family who had exploited them.
But more than such spirits…
…I was doubly afraid of living human beings.
WHAT'S THE MATTER, YOZO? WHY ARE YOU SO QUIET?!
O-OH!
FATHER, I DO NOT WISH TO DIE!
I SHALL EAT!
SCARF
SCARF
SCARF
SCARF
AAH, DELICIOUS!
I'M SO HAPPY!

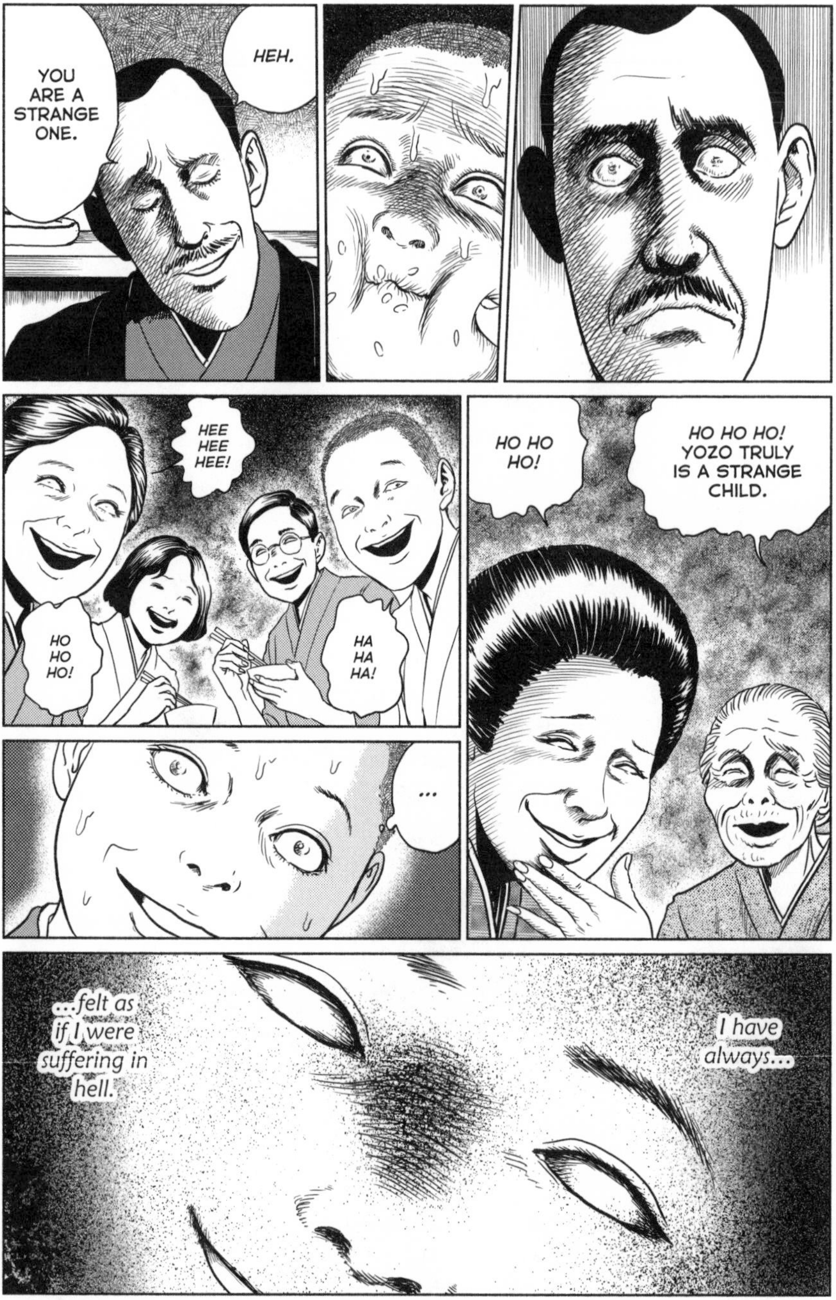
HEH.
YOU ARE A STRANGE ONE.
HO HO HO! YOZO TRULY IS A STRANGE CHILD.
HO HO HO!
HEE HEE HEE!
HA HA HA!
HO HO HO!
...
I have always...
...felt as if I were suffering in hell.

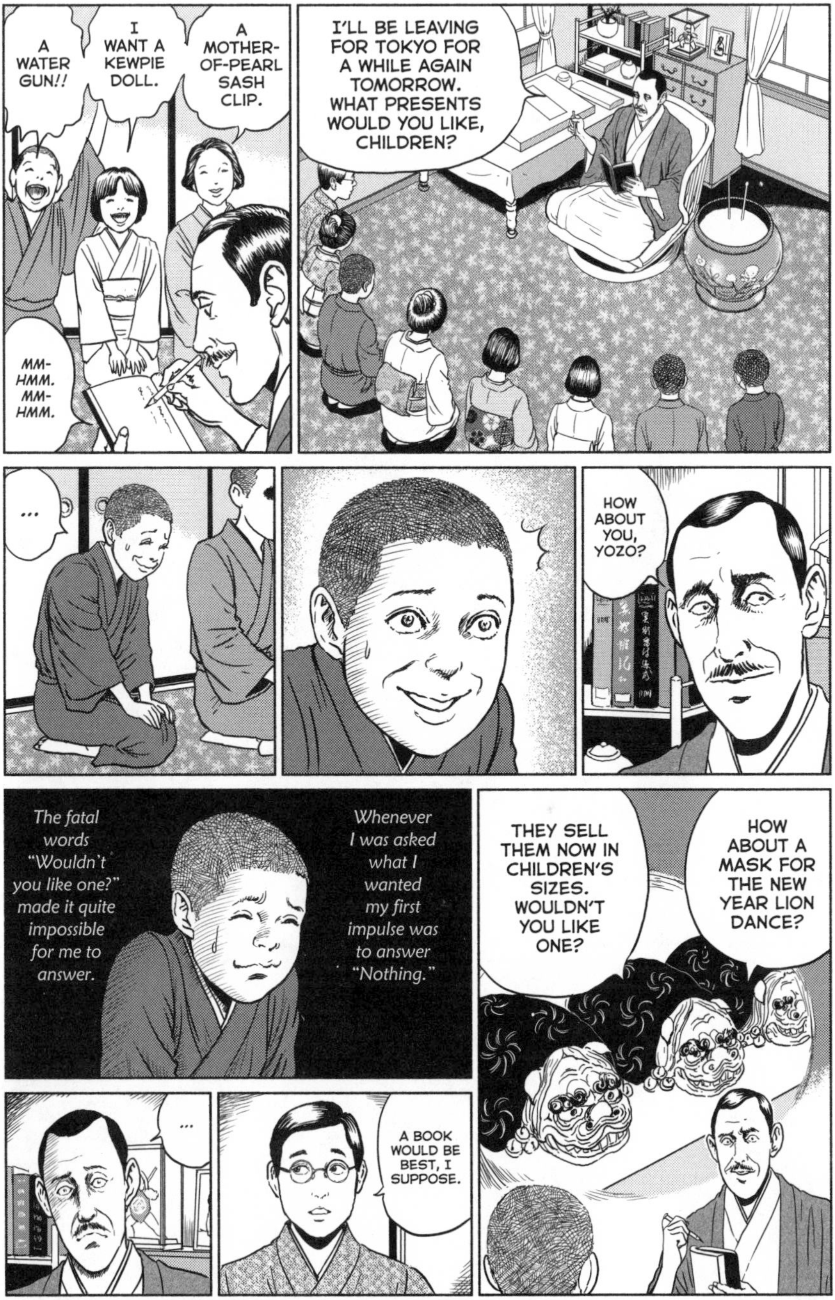
I'LL BE LEAVING FOR TOKYO FOR A WHILE AGAIN TOMORROW. WHAT PRESENTS WOULD YOU LIKE, CHILDREN?
A MOTHER-OF-PEARL SASH CLIP.
I WANT A KEWPIE DOLL.
A WATER GUN!!
MM-HMM. MM-HMM.
HOW ABOUT YOU, YOZO?
...
HOW ABOUT A MASK FOR THE NEW YEAR LION DANCE?
THEY SELL THEM NOW IN CHILDREN'S SIZES. WOULDN'T YOU LIKE ONE?
Whenever I was asked what I wanted my first impulse was to answer "Nothing."
The fatal words "Wouldn't you like one?" made it quite impossible for me to answer.
A BOOK WOULD BE BEST, I SUPPOSE.
...

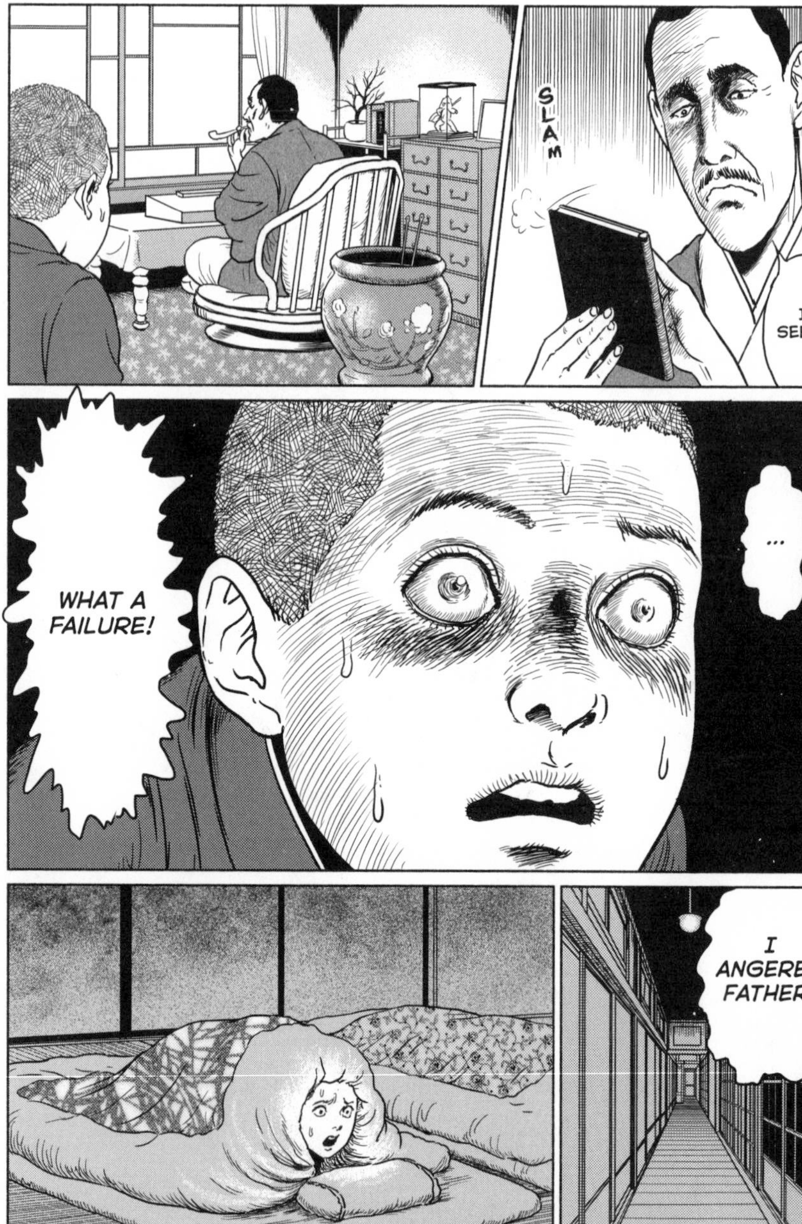
SLAM
I SEE...
...
WHAT A FAILURE!
I ANGERED FATHER.

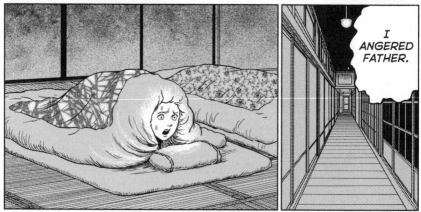

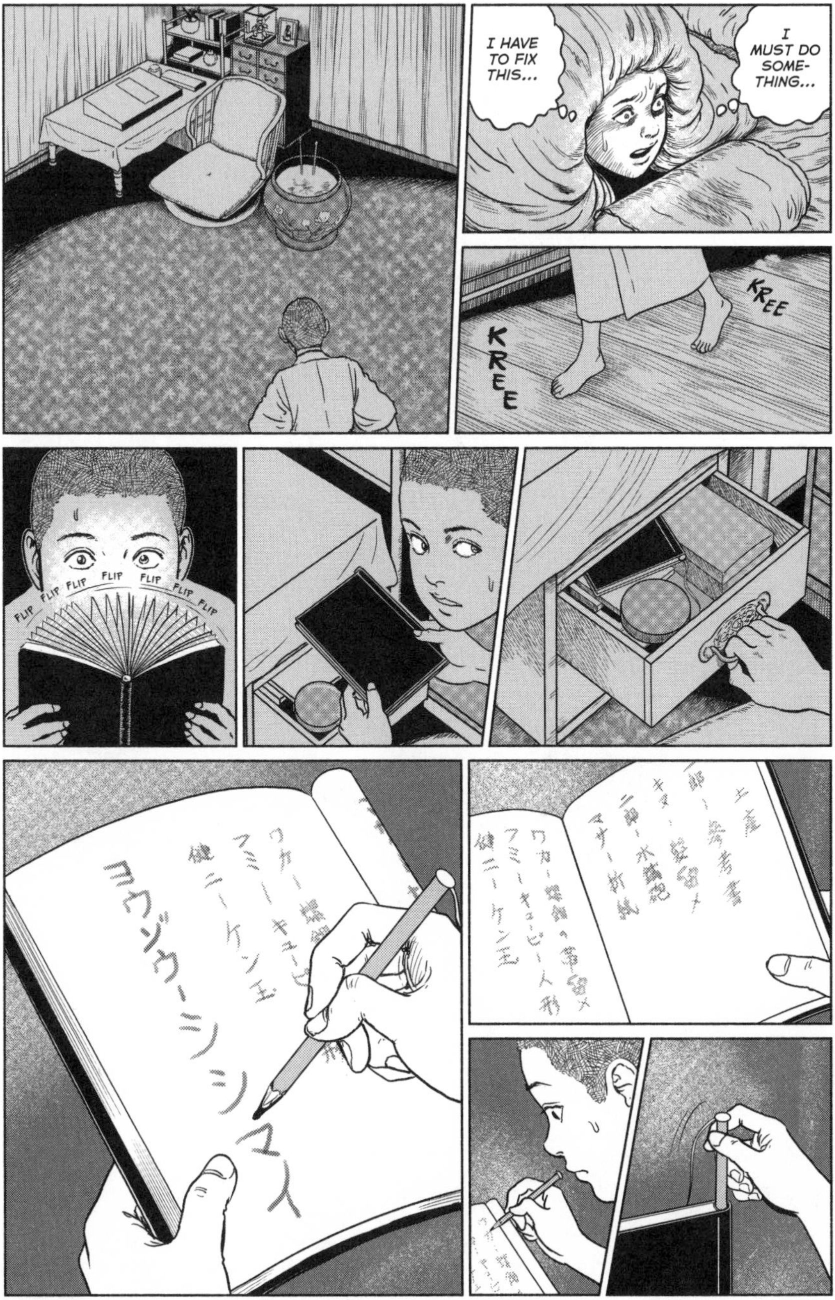
I MUST DO SOME-THING...
I HAVE TO FIX THIS...
KREE
KREE
FLIP FLIP FLIP FLIP FLIP FLIP FLIP
ヨウゾウーシシマイ

*Yozo: Lion mask

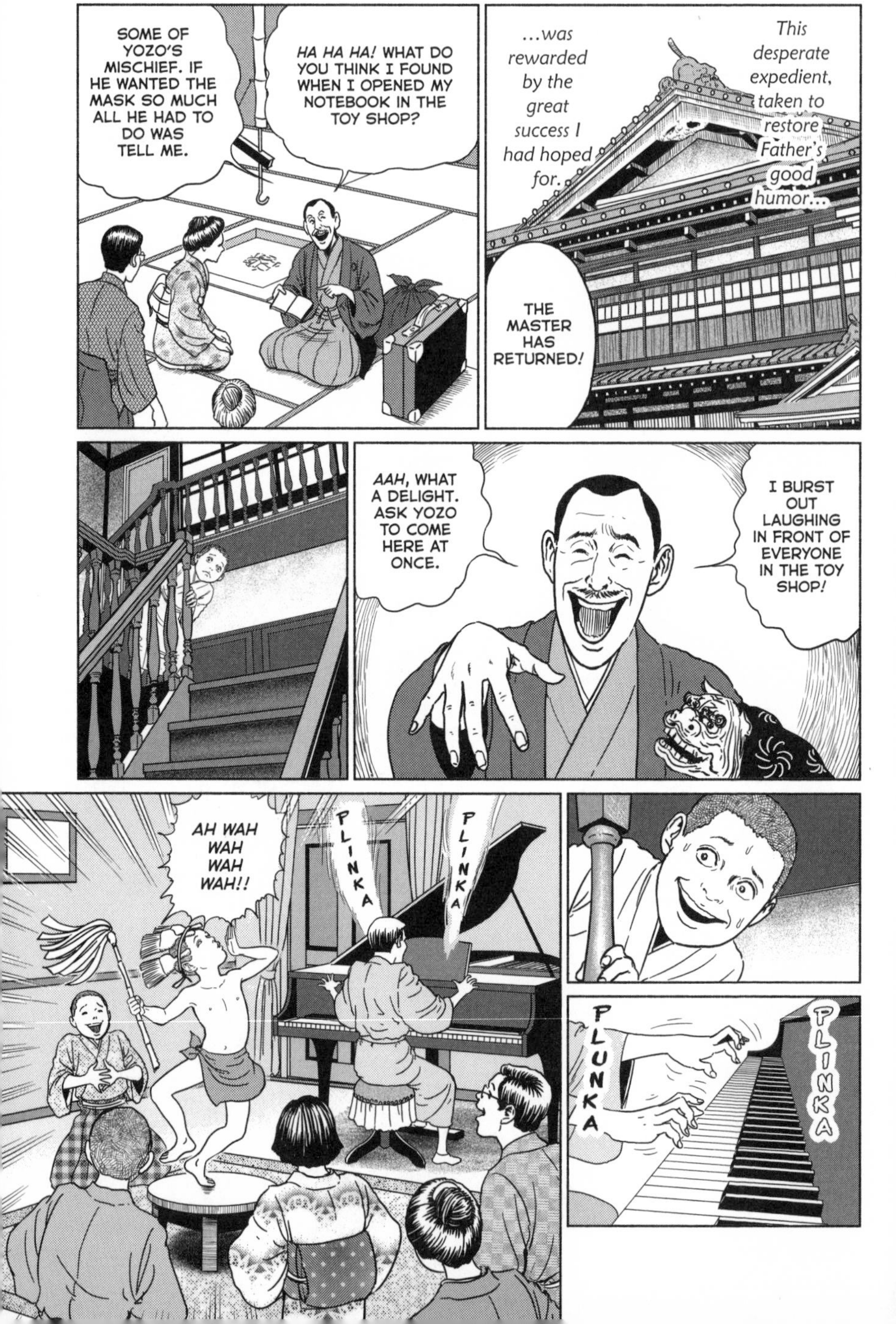
This desperate expedient, taken to restore Father's good humor…
…was rewarded by the great success I had hoped for.
THE MASTER HAS RETURNED!
HA HA HA! WHAT DO YOU THINK I FOUND WHEN I OPENED MY NOTEBOOK IN THE TOY SHOP?
SOME OF YOZO'S MISCHIEF. IF HE WANTED THE MASK SO MUCH ALL HE HAD TO DO WAS TELL ME.
I BURST OUT LAUGHING IN FRONT OF EVERYONE IN THE TOY SHOP!
AAH, WHAT A DELIGHT. ASK YOZO TO COME HERE AT ONCE.
PLINKA
PLUNKA
PLINKA
PLINKA
AH WAH WAH WAH WAH!!

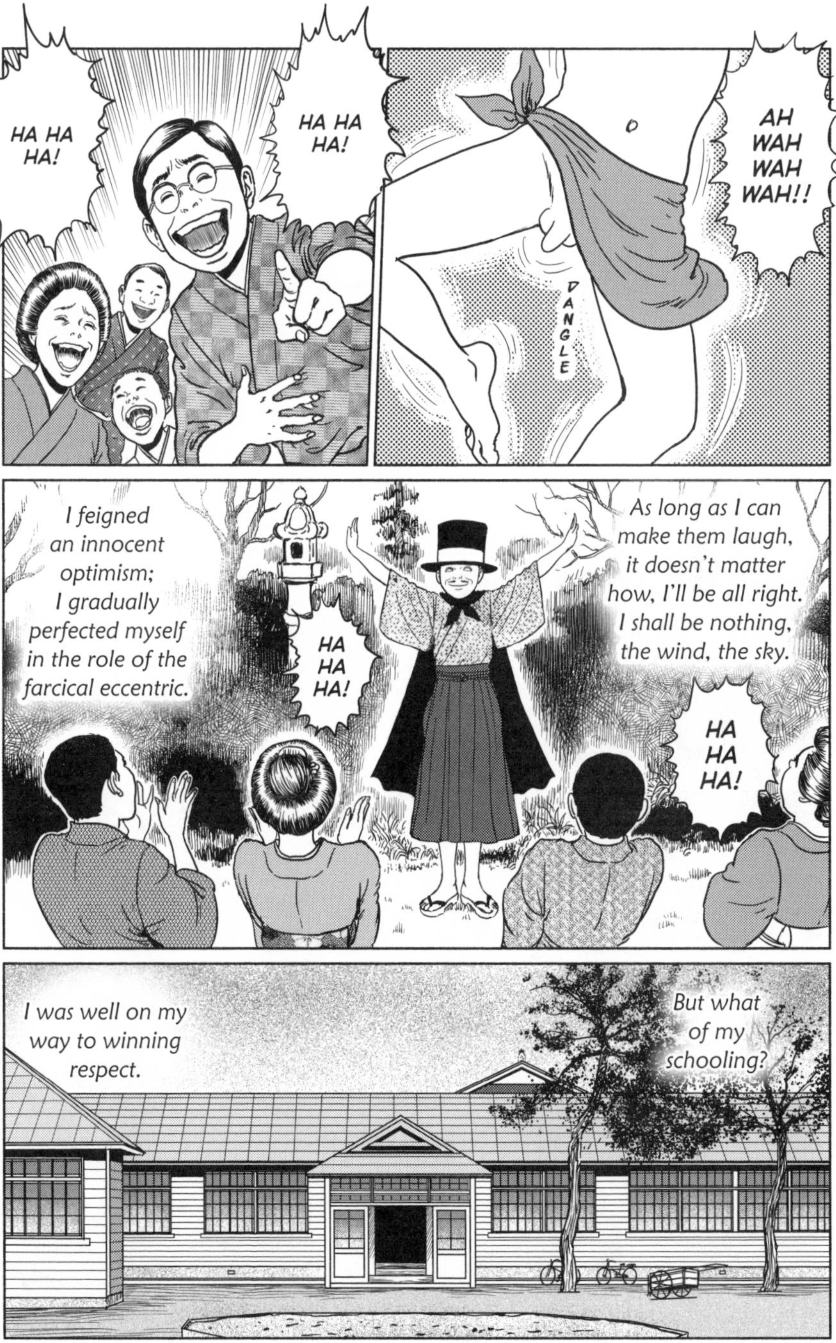
AH WAH WAH WAH!!
DANGLE
HA HA HA!
HA HA HA!
As long as I can make them laugh, it doesn't matter how, I'll be all right. I shall be nothing, the wind, the sky.
I feigned an innocent optimism; I gradually perfected myself in the role of the farcical eccentric.
HA HA HA!
HA HA HA!
But what of my schooling?
I was well on my way to winning respect.

*Final exam results 1. Yozo Oba

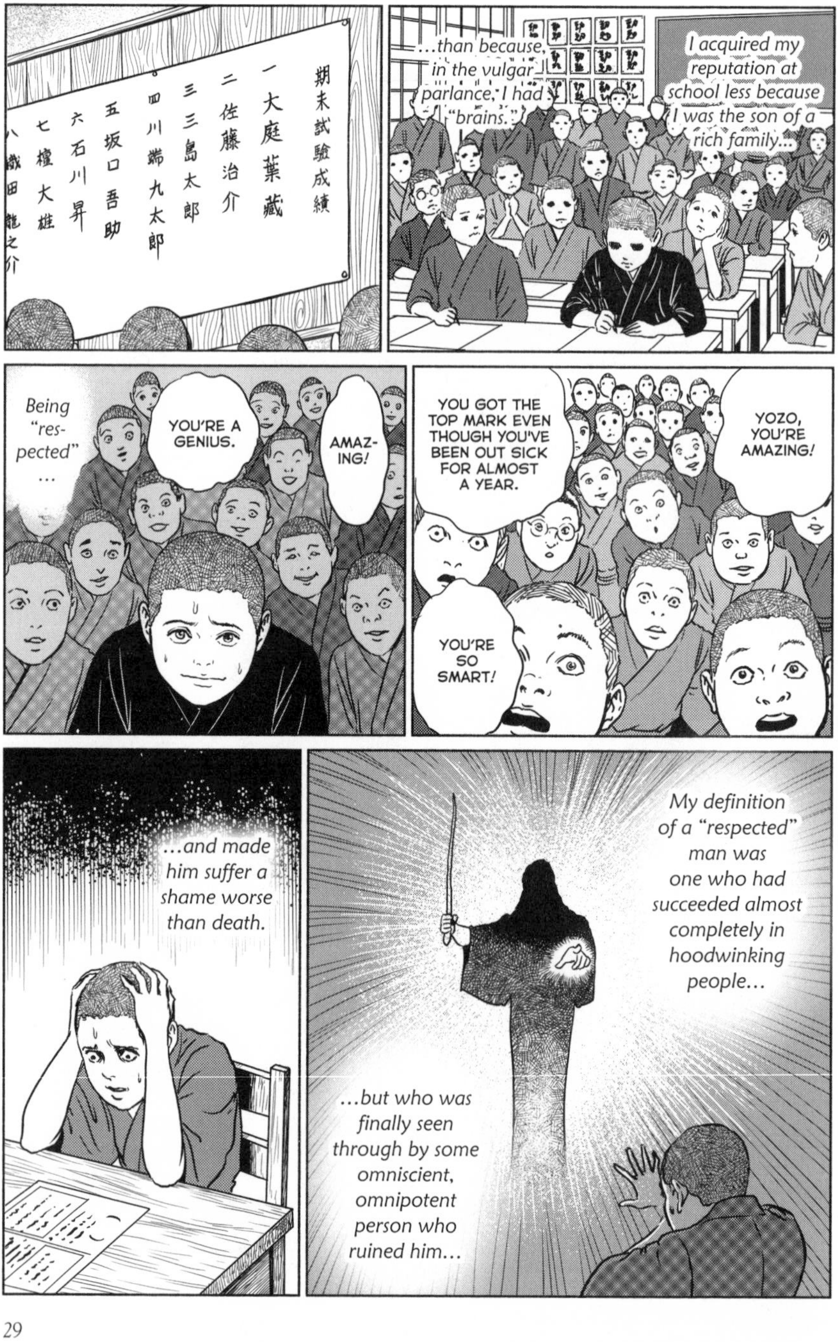
I acquired my reputation at school less because I was the son of a rich family...
...than because, in the vulgar parlance, I had "brains."
期末試験成績
一 大庭葉藏
二 佐藤治介
三 三島太郎
四 川端九太郎
五 坂口吾助
六 石川昇
七 檀大雄
八 織田龍之介
YOZO, YOU'RE AMAZING!
YOU GOT THE TOP MARK EVEN THOUGH YOU'VE BEEN OUT SICK FOR ALMOST A YEAR.
YOU'RE SO SMART!
AMAZ-ING!
YOU'RE A GENIUS.
Being "res-pected"...
My definition of a "respected" man was one who had succeeded almost completely in hoodwinking people...
...but who was finally seen through by some omniscient, omnipotent person who ruined him...
...and made him suffer a shame worse than death.

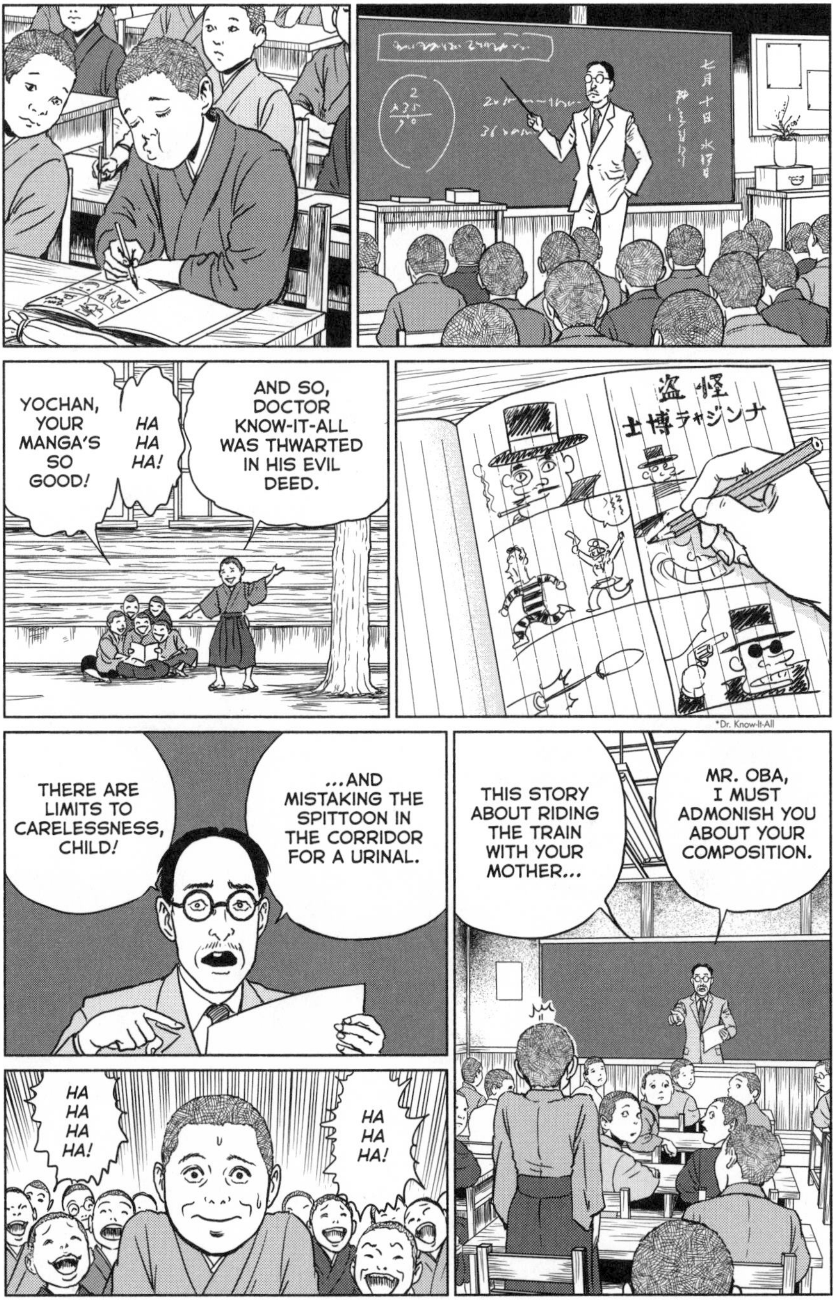
盗怪
士博ラャジンナ
AND SO, DOCTOR KNOW-IT-ALL WAS THWARTED IN HIS EVIL DEED.
HA HA HA!
YOCHAN, YOUR MANGA'S SO GOOD!
MR. OBA, I MUST ADMONISH YOU ABOUT YOUR COMPOSITION.
THIS STORY ABOUT RIDING THE TRAIN WITH YOUR MOTHER...
...AND MISTAKING THE SPITTOON IN THE CORRIDOR FOR A URINAL.
THERE ARE LIMITS TO CARELESSNESS, CHILD!
HA HA HA!
HA HA HA HA!

*Dr. Know-It-All

*Faculty Room

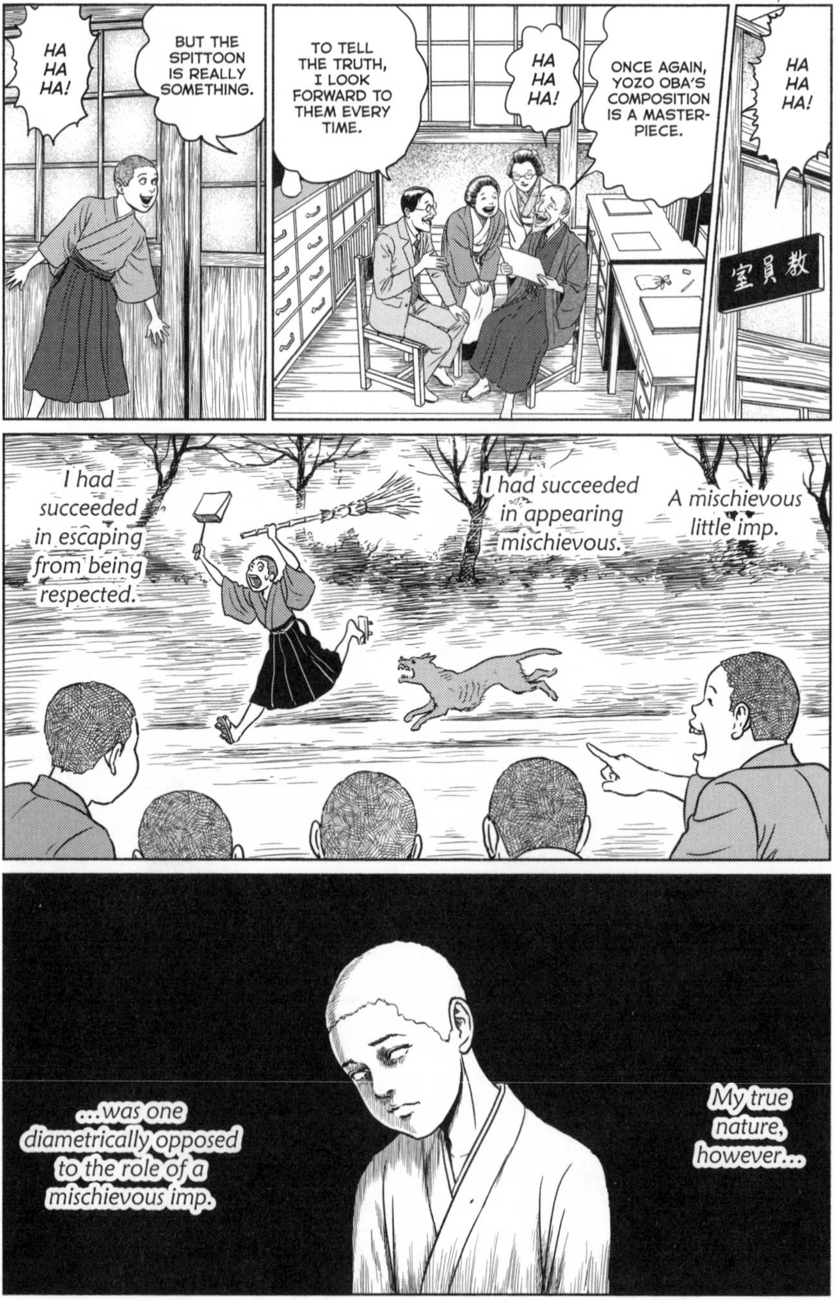
HA HA HA!
教員室
ONCE AGAIN, YOZO OBA'S COMPOSITION IS A MASTER-PIECE.
HA HA HA!
TO TELL THE TRUTH, I LOOK FORWARD TO THEM EVERY TIME.
BUT THE SPITTOON IS REALLY SOMETHING.
HA HA HA!
A mischievous little imp.
I had succeeded in appearing mischievous.
I had succeeded in escaping from being respected.
My true nature, however...
...was one diametrically opposed to the role of a mischievous imp.

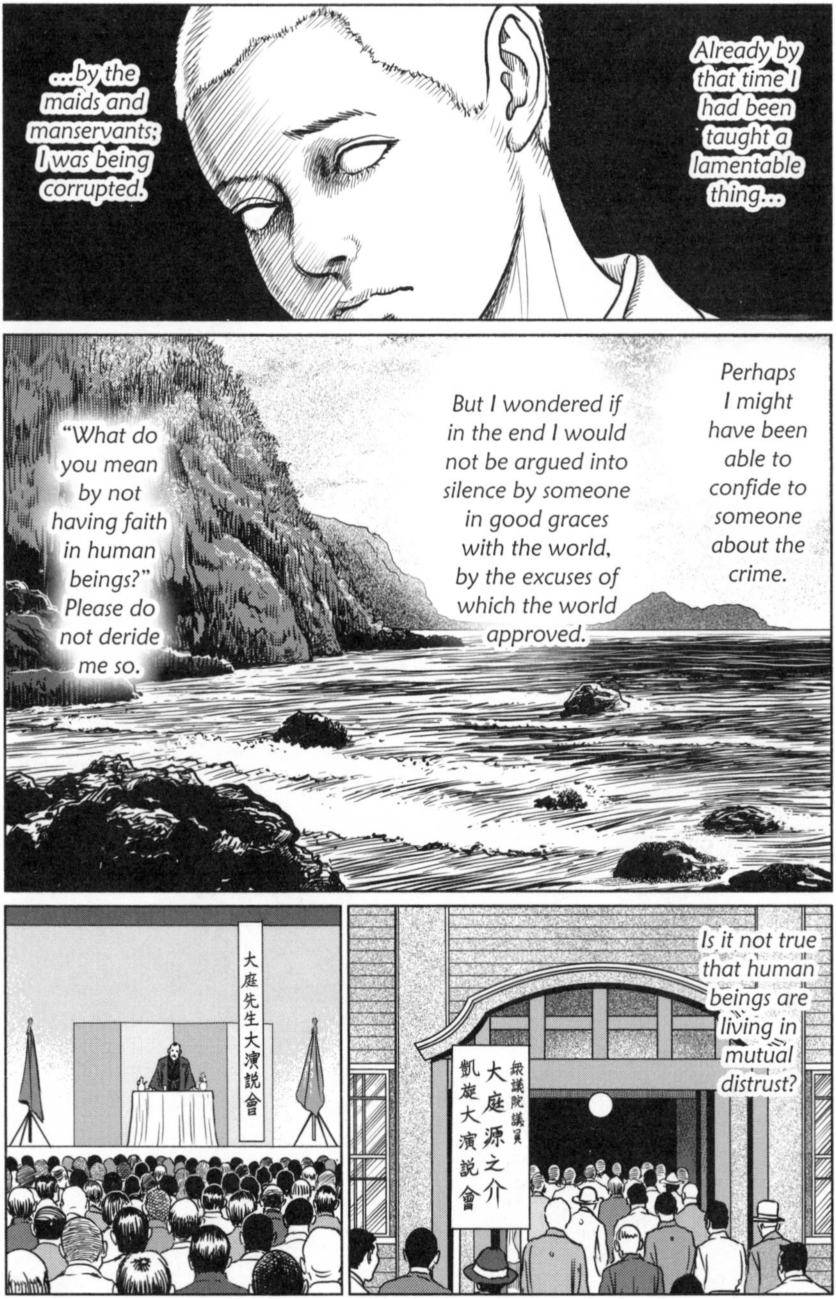
Already by that time I had been taught a lamentable thing...
...by the maids and manservants; I was being corrupted.
Perhaps I might have been able to confide to someone about the crime.
But I wondered if in the end I would not be argued into silence by someone in good graces with the world, by the excuses of which the world approved.
"What do you mean by not having faith in human beings?" Please do not deride me so.
Is it not true that human beings are living in mutual distrust?
衆議院議員
大庭源之介
凱旋大演説會
大庭先生大演説會
* Congressman Gennosuke Oba, Victory Speech

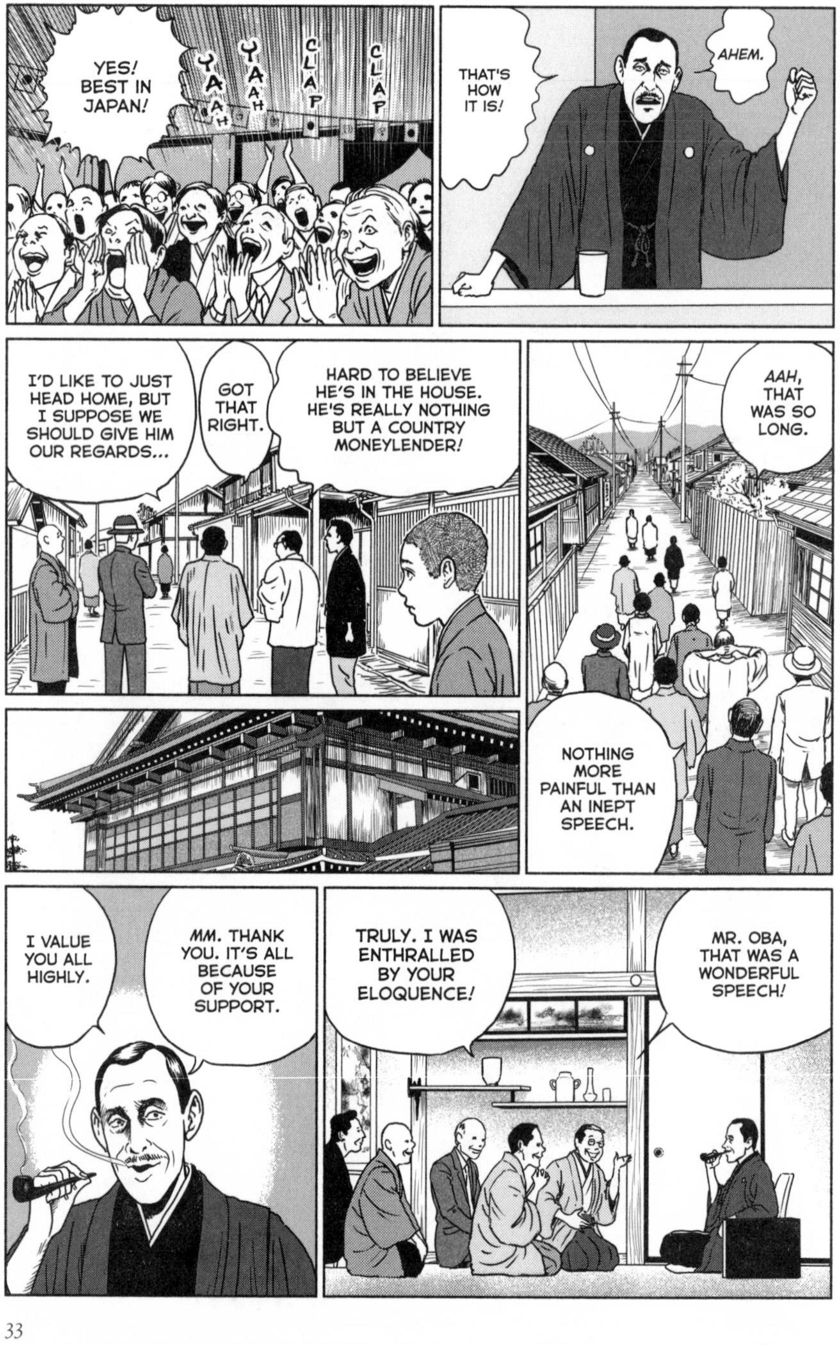
AHEM.
THAT'S HOW IT IS!
CLAP
CLAP
YAAAH
YAAAH
YES! BEST IN JAPAN!
AAH, THAT WAS SO LONG.
NOTHING MORE PAINFUL THAN AN INEPT SPEECH.
HARD TO BELIEVE HE'S IN THE HOUSE. HE'S REALLY NOTHING BUT A COUNTRY MONEYLENDER!
GOT THAT RIGHT.
I'D LIKE TO JUST HEAD HOME, BUT I SUPPOSE WE SHOULD GIVE HIM OUR REGARDS...
MR. OBA, THAT WAS A WONDERFUL SPEECH!
TRULY. I WAS ENTHRALLED BY YOUR ELOQUENCE!
MM. THANK YOU. IT'S ALL BECAUSE OF YOUR SUPPORT.
I VALUE YOU ALL HIGHLY.

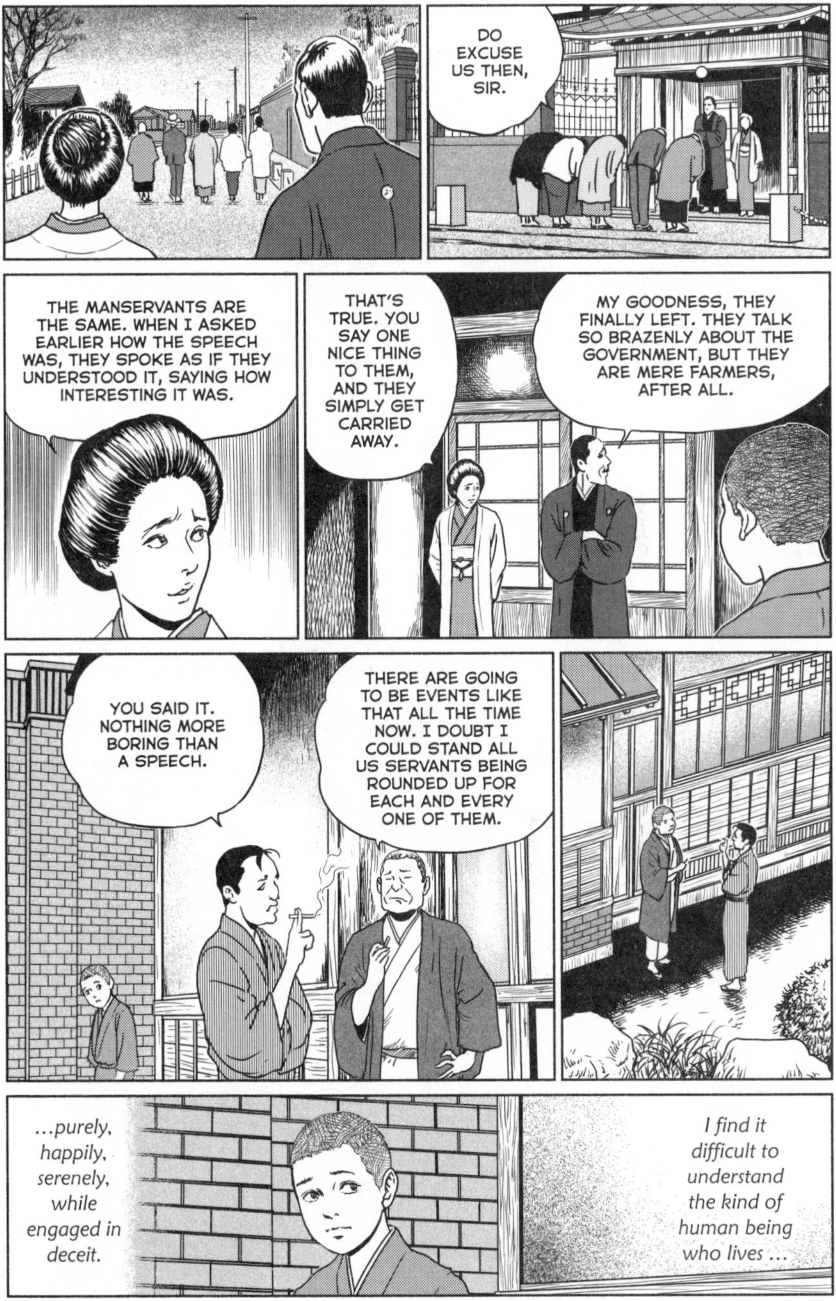
DO EXCUSE US THEN, SIR.
MY GOODNESS, THEY FINALLY LEFT. THEY TALK SO BRAZENLY ABOUT THE GOVERNMENT, BUT THEY ARE MERE FARMERS, AFTER ALL.
THAT'S TRUE. YOU SAY ONE NICE THING TO THEM, AND THEY SIMPLY GET CARRIED AWAY.
THE MANSERVANTS ARE THE SAME. WHEN I ASKED EARLIER HOW THE SPEECH WAS, THEY SPOKE AS IF THEY UNDERSTOOD IT, SAYING HOW INTERESTING IT WAS.
THERE ARE GOING TO BE EVENTS LIKE THAT ALL THE TIME NOW. I DOUBT I COULD STAND ALL US SERVANTS BEING ROUNDED UP FOR EACH AND EVERY ONE OF THEM.
YOU SAID IT. NOTHING MORE BORING THAN A SPEECH.
I find it difficult to understand the kind of human being who lives ...
...purely, happily, serenely, while engaged in deceit.

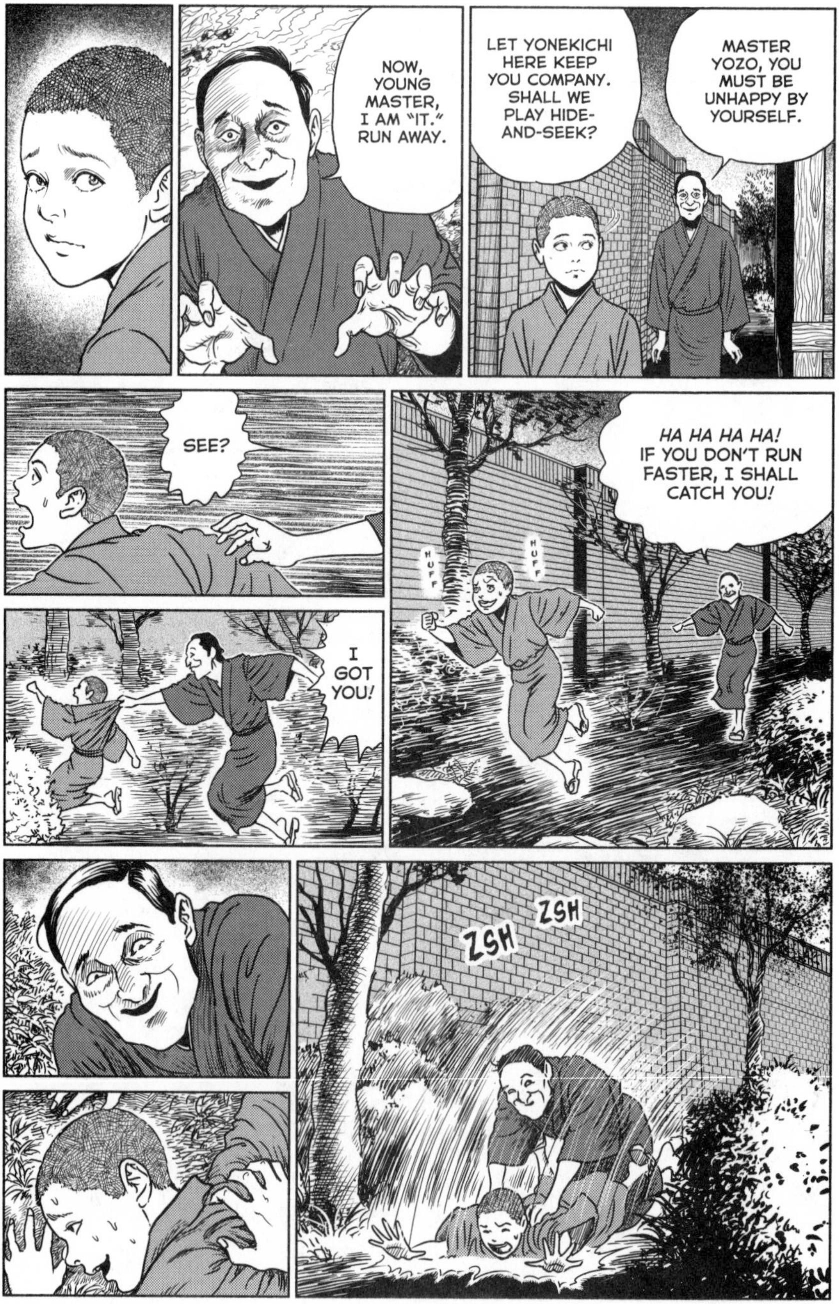
MASTER YOZO, YOU MUST BE UNHAPPY BY YOURSELF.
LET YONEKICHI HERE KEEP YOU COMPANY. SHALL WE PLAY HIDE-AND-SEEK?
NOW, YOUNG MASTER, I AM "IT." RUN AWAY.
HA HA HA HA! IF YOU DON'T RUN FASTER, I SHALL CATCH YOU*!*
HUFF
HUFF
SEE?
I GOT YOU*!*
ZSH
ZSH

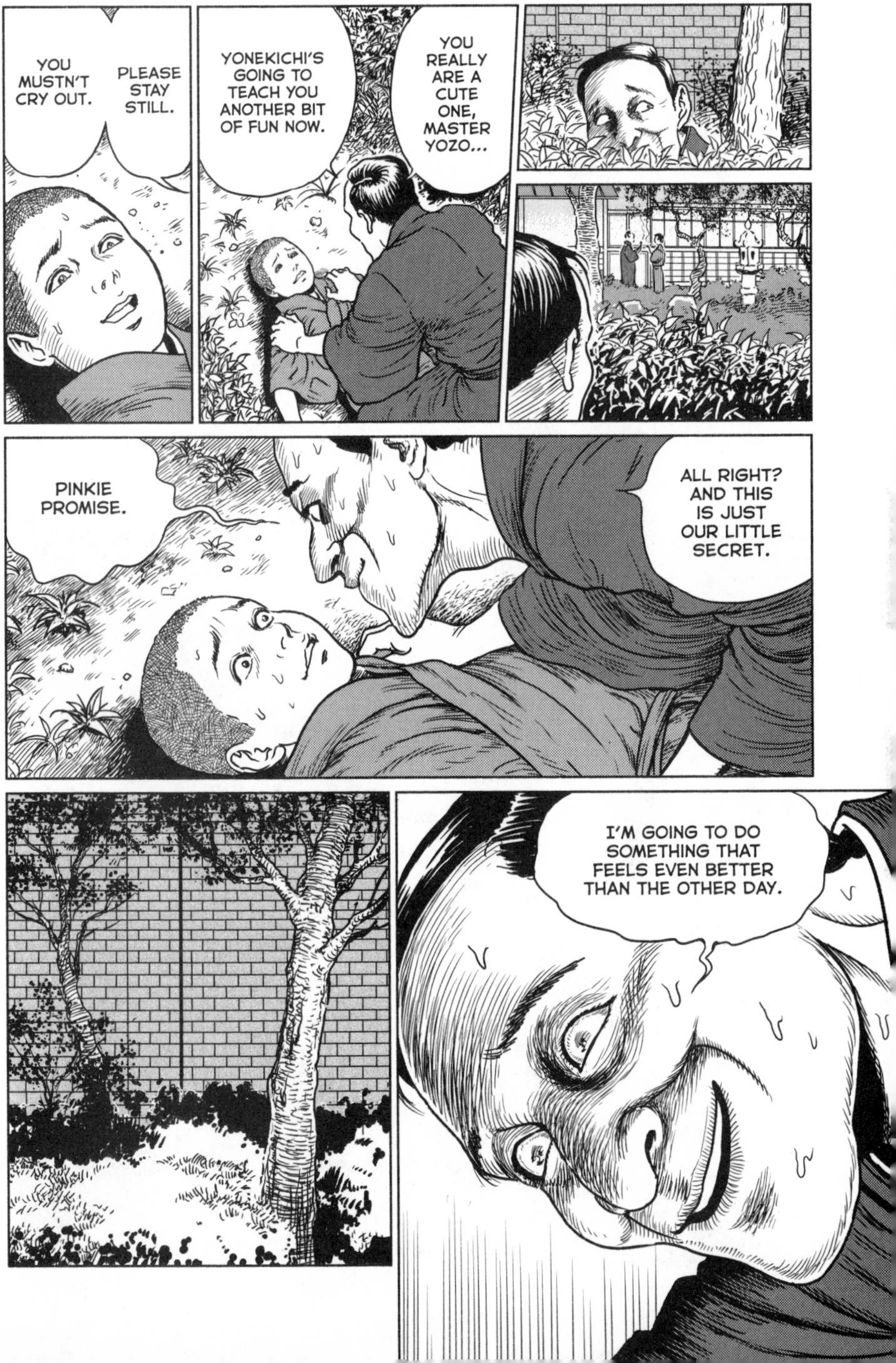
YOU REALLY ARE A CUTE ONE, MASTER YOZO...
YONEKICHI'S GOING TO TEACH YOU ANOTHER BIT OF FUN NOW.
PLEASE STAY STILL.
YOU MUSTN'T CRY OUT.
ALL RIGHT? AND THIS IS JUST OUR LITTLE SECRET.
PINKIE PROMISE.
I'M GOING TO DO SOMETHING THAT FEELS EVEN BETTER THAN THE OTHER DAY.

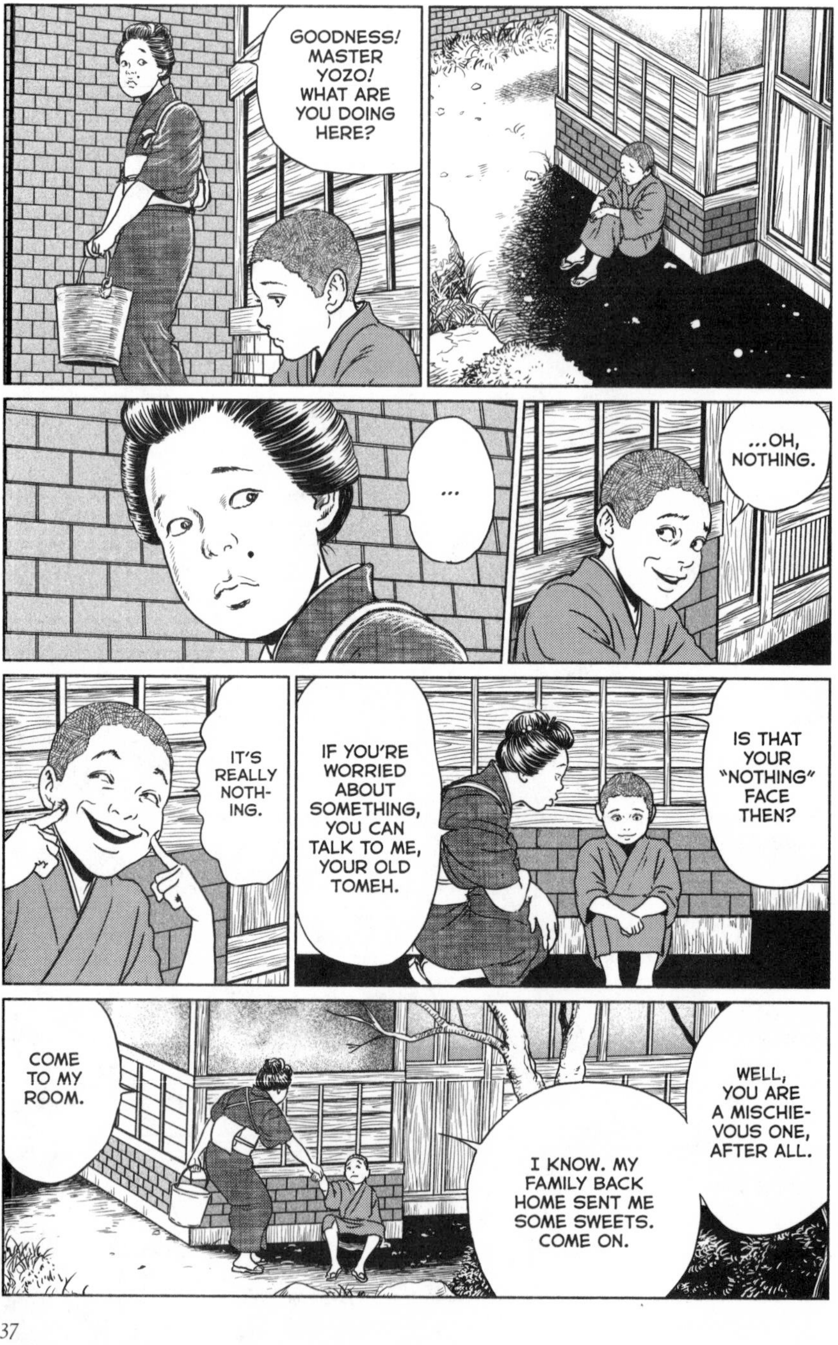
GOODNESS! MASTER YOZO! WHAT ARE YOU DOING HERE?
...OH, NOTHING.
...
IS THAT YOUR "NOTHING" FACE THEN?
IF YOU'RE WORRIED ABOUT SOMETHING, YOU CAN TALK TO ME, YOUR OLD TOMEH.
IT'S REALLY NOTH-ING.
WELL, YOU ARE A MISCHIE-VOUS ONE, AFTER ALL.
I KNOW. MY FAMILY BACK HOME SENT ME SOME SWEETS. COME ON.
COME TO MY ROOM.

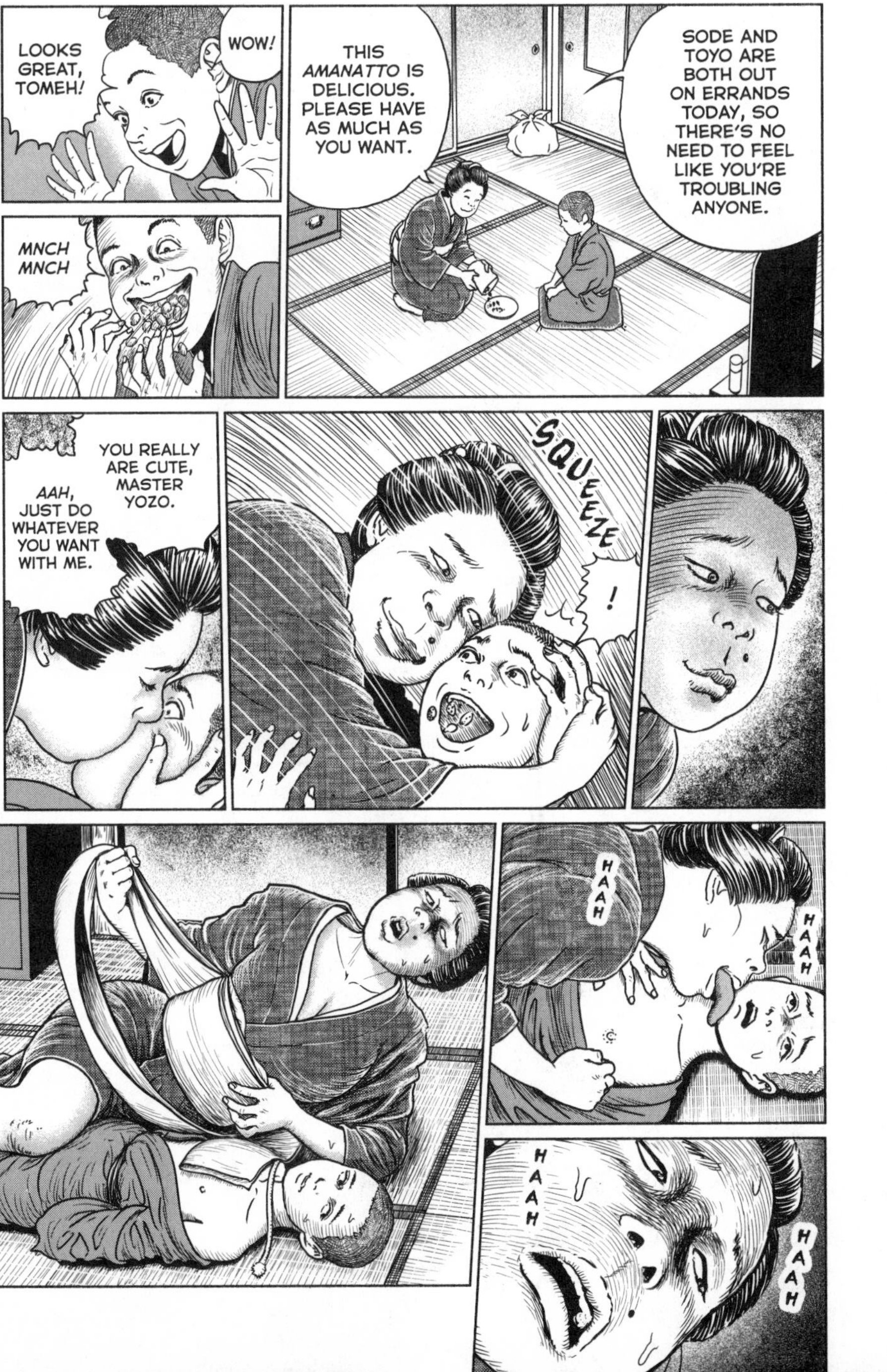
SODE AND TOYO ARE BOTH OUT ON ERRANDS TODAY, SO THERE'S NO NEED TO FEEL LIKE YOU'RE TROUBLING ANYONE.
THIS *AMANATTO* IS DELICIOUS. PLEASE HAVE AS MUCH AS YOU WANT.
WOW!
LOOKS GREAT, TOMEH!
MNCH MNCH
SQUEEZE
!
YOU REALLY ARE CUTE, MASTER YOZO.
AAH, JUST DO WHATEVER YOU WANT WITH ME.
HAAH
HAAH
HAAH
HAAH

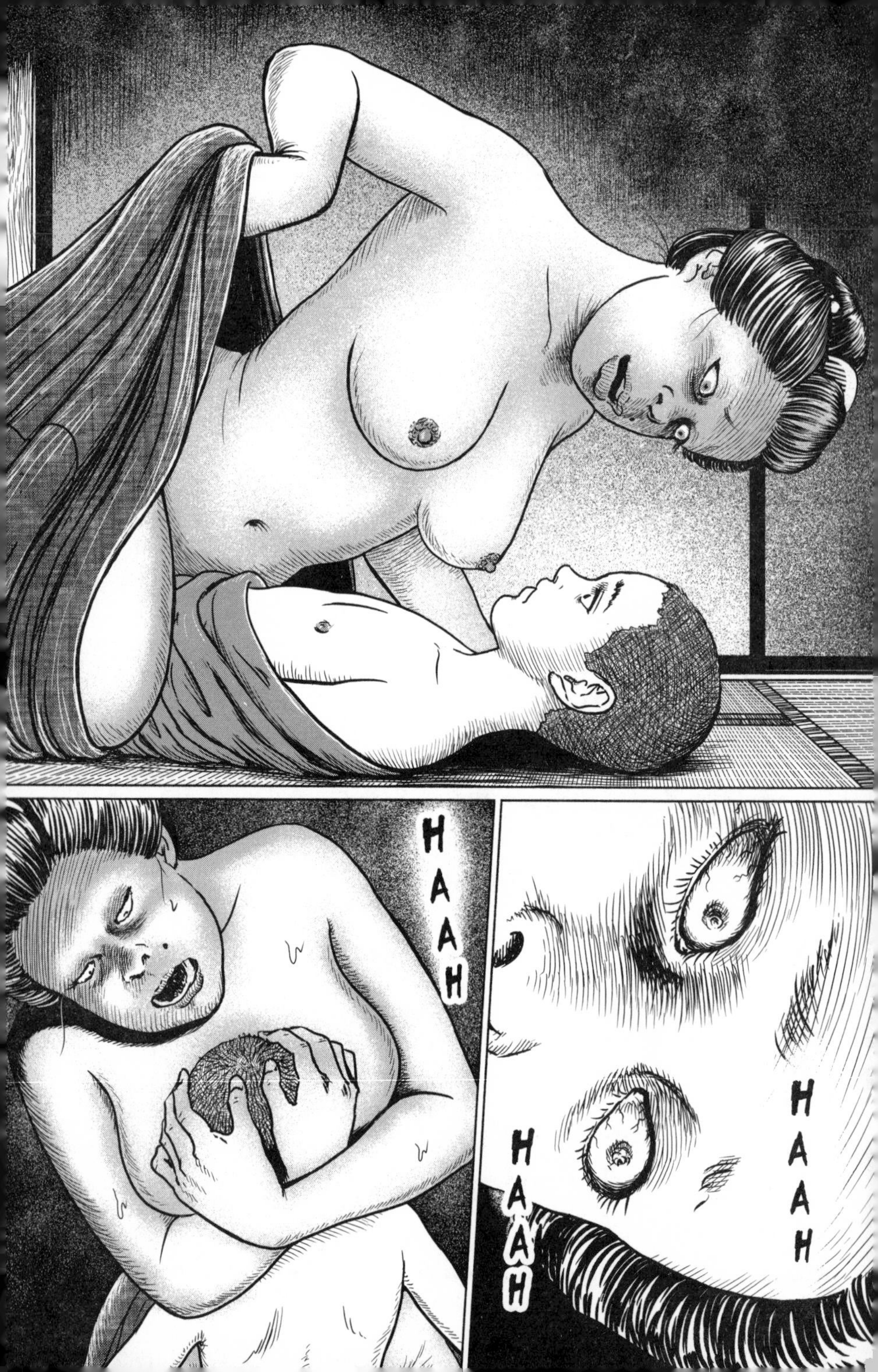
HAAH
HAAH
HAAH

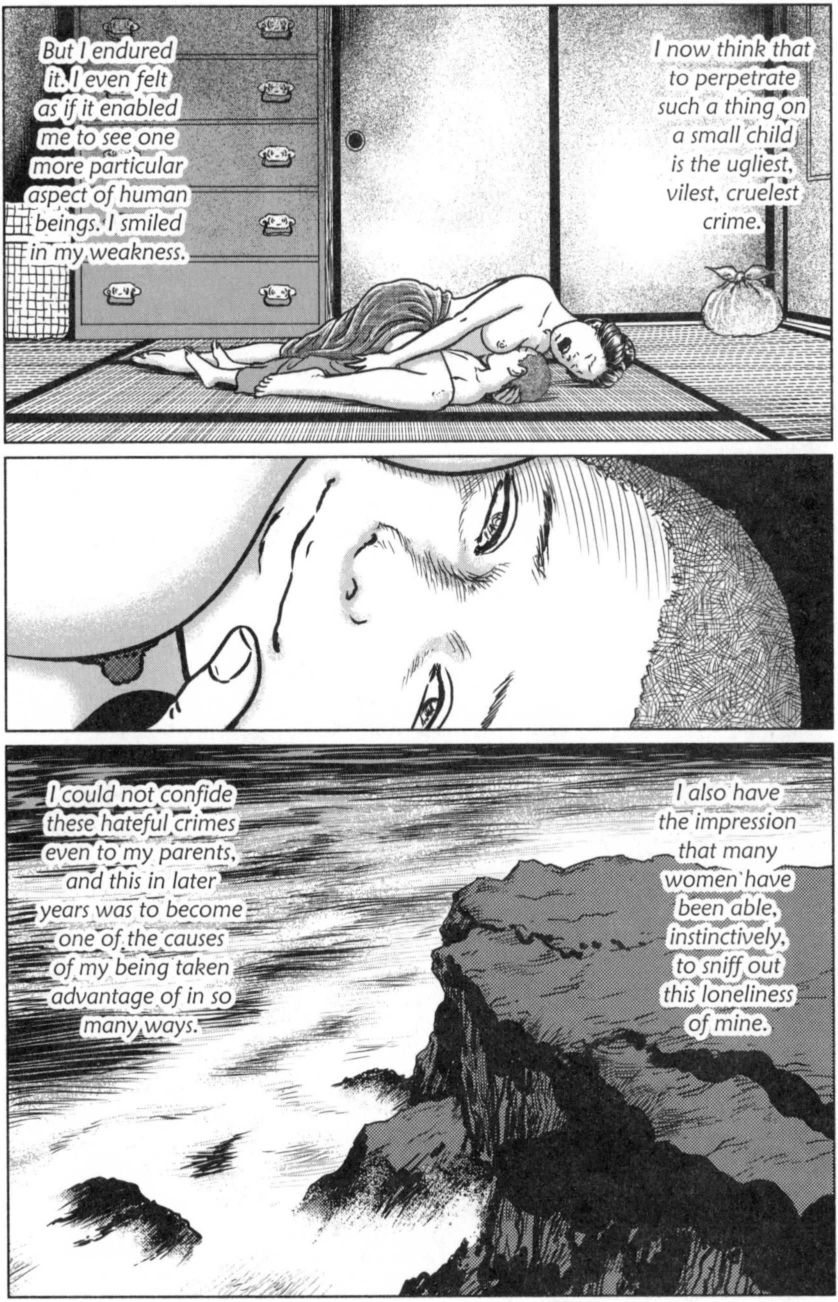
I now think that to perpetrate such a thing on a small child is the ugliest, vilest, cruelest crime.
But I endured it. I even felt as if it enabled me to see one more particular aspect of human beings. I smiled in my weakness.
I also have the impression that many women have been able, instinctively, to sniff out this loneliness of mine.
I could not confide these hateful crimes even to my parents, and this in later years was to become one of the causes of my being taken advantage of in so many ways.

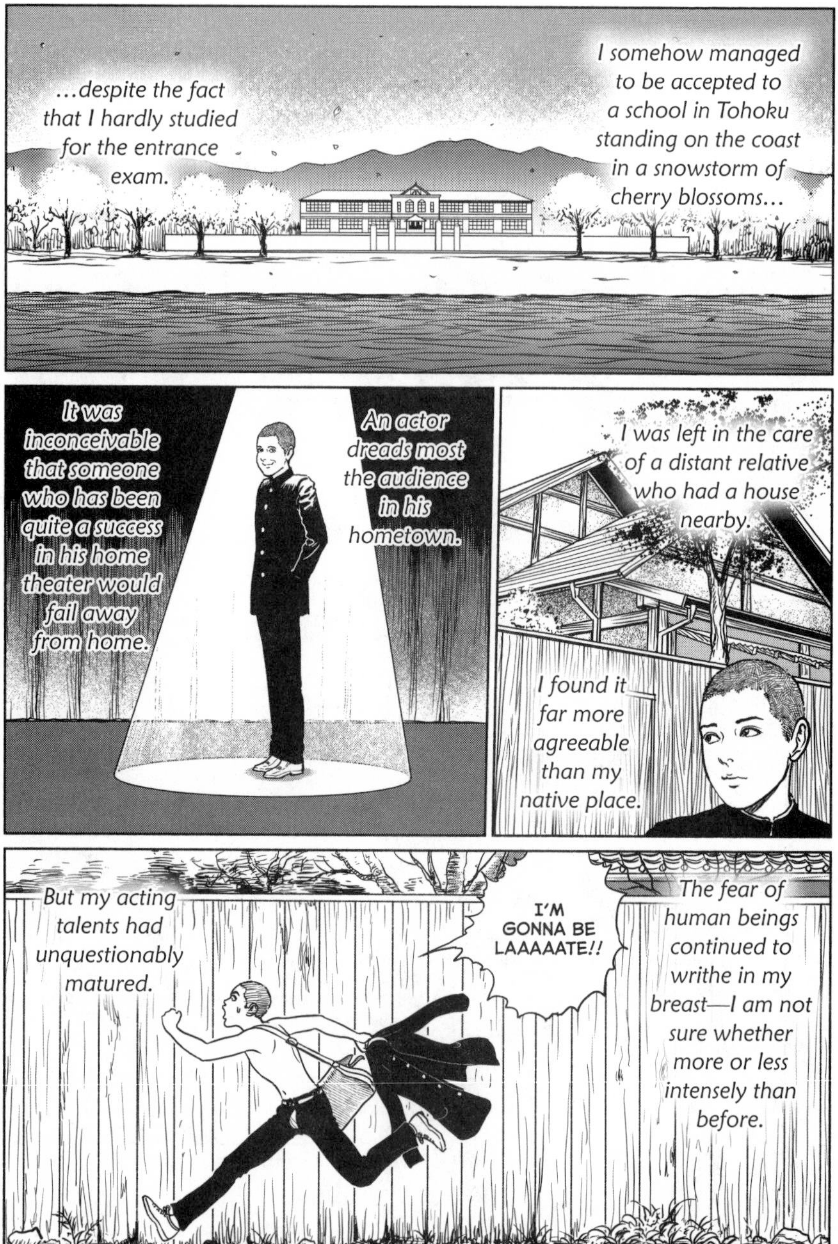
I somehow managed to be accepted to a school in Tohoku standing on the coast in a snowstorm of cherry blossoms…
…despite the fact that I hardly studied for the entrance exam.
I was left in the care of a distant relative who had a house nearby.
I found it far more agreeable than my native place.
An actor dreads most the audience in his hometown.
It was inconceivable that someone who has been quite a success in his home theater would fail away from home.
The fear of human beings continued to writhe in my breast—I am not sure whether more or less intensely than before.
I'M GONNA BE LAAAAATE!!
But my acting talents had unquestionably matured.

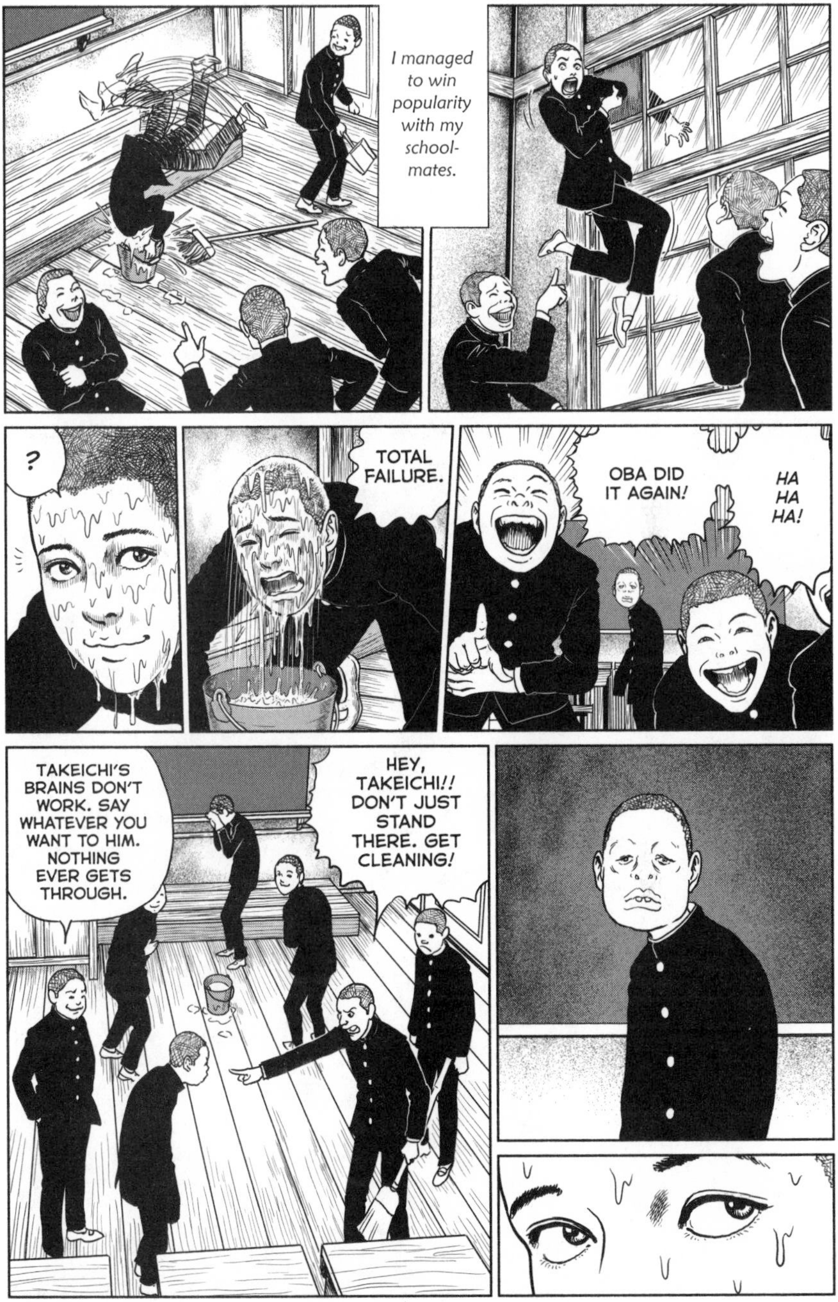
I managed to win popularity with my schoolmates.
OBA DID IT AGAIN!
HA HA HA!
TOTAL FAILURE.
?
HEY, TAKEICHI!! DON'T JUST STAND THERE. GET CLEANING!
TAKEICHI'S BRAINS DON'T WORK. SAY WHATEVER YOU WANT TO HIM. NOTHING EVER GETS THROUGH.

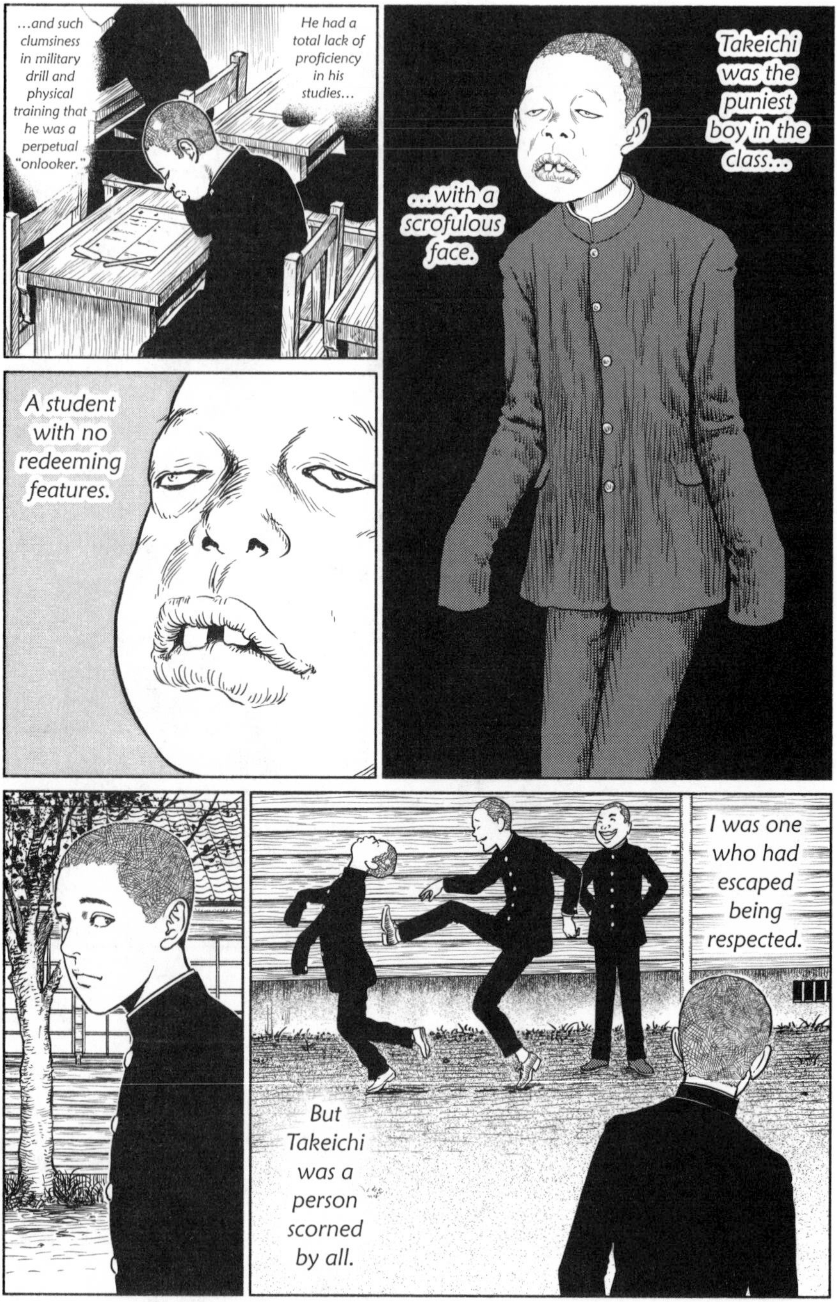
Takeichi was the puniest boy in the class...
...with a scrofulous face.
He had a total lack of proficiency in his studies...
...and such clumsiness in military drill and physical training that he was a perpetual "onlooker."
A student with no redeeming features.
I was one who had escaped being respected.
But Takeichi was a person scorned by all.

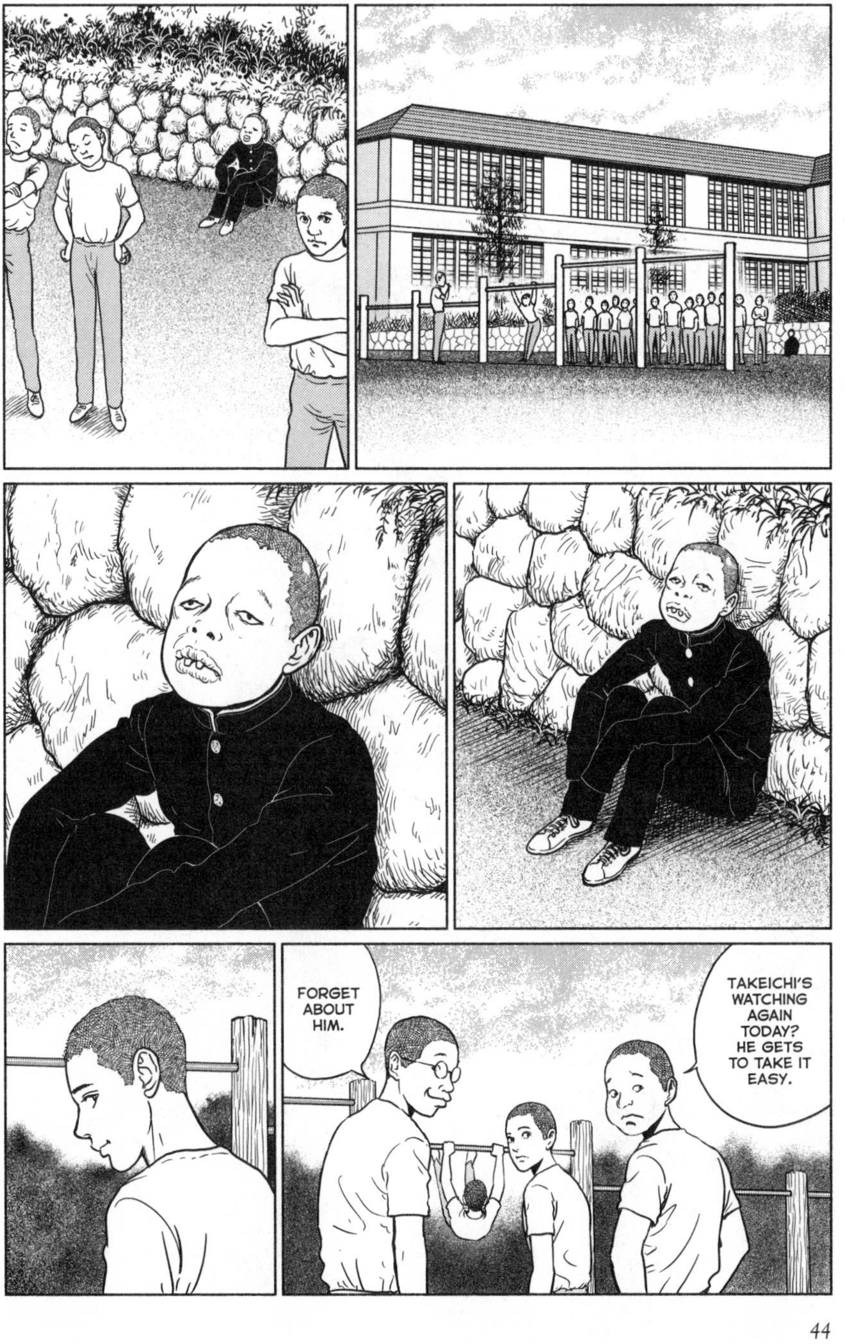
TAKEICHI'S WATCHING AGAIN TODAY? HE GETS TO TAKE IT EASY.
FORGET ABOUT HIM.

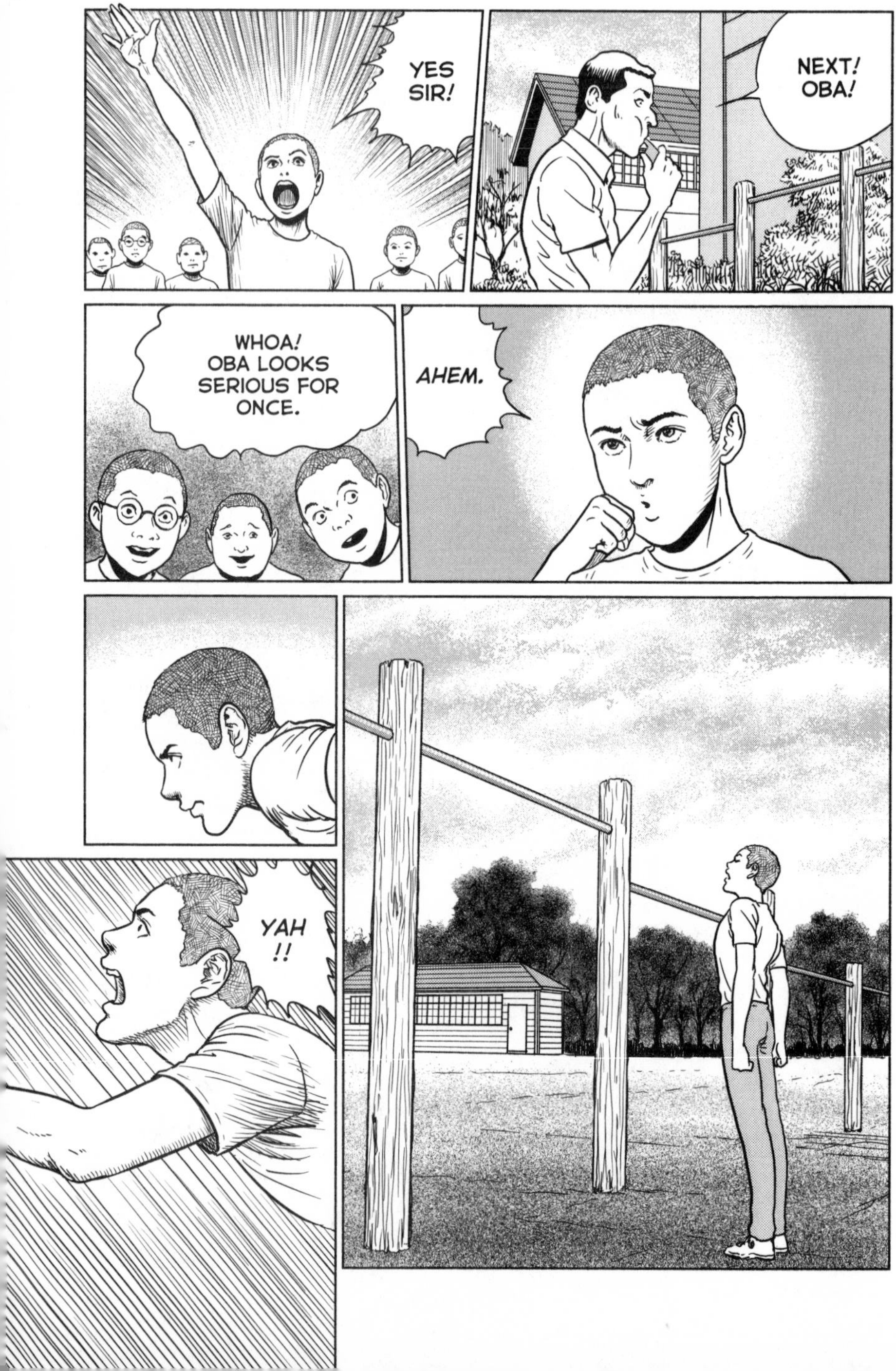
NEXT! OBA!
YES SIR!
AHEM.
WHOA! OBA LOOKS SERIOUS FOR ONCE.
YAH !!

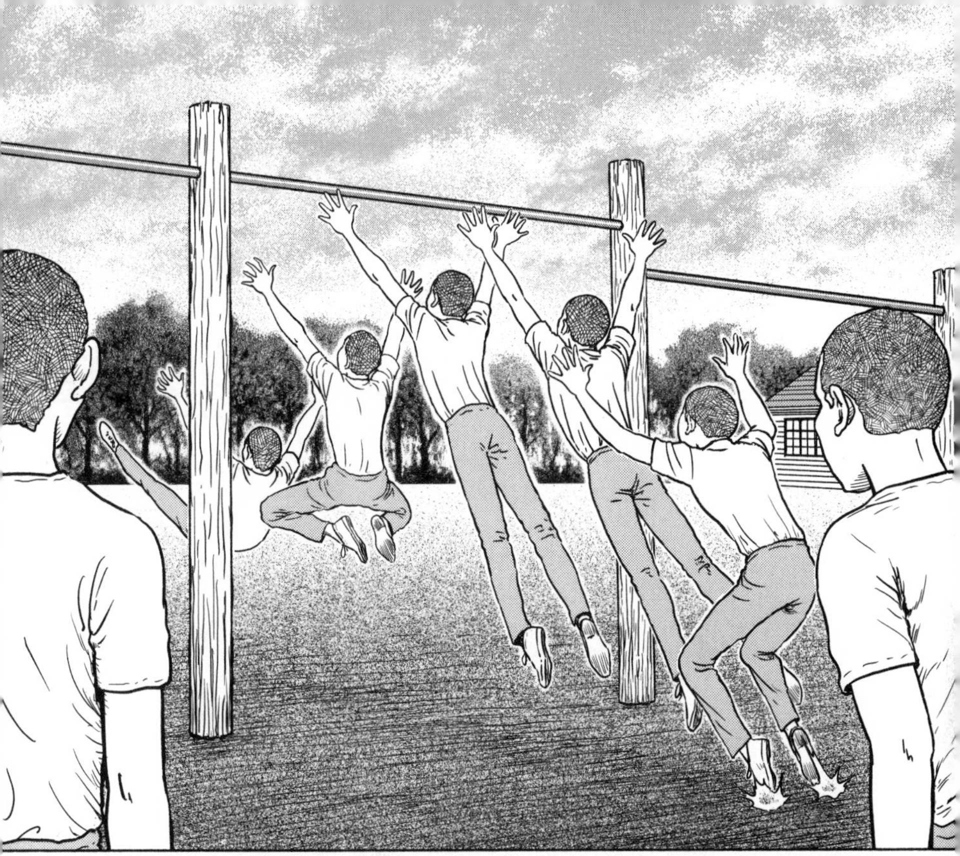

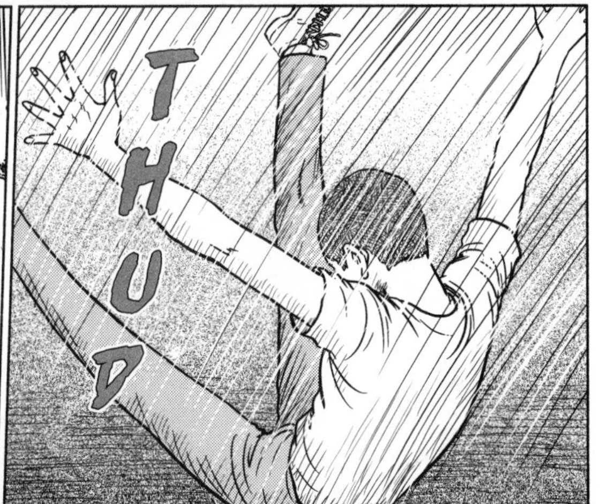
THUD

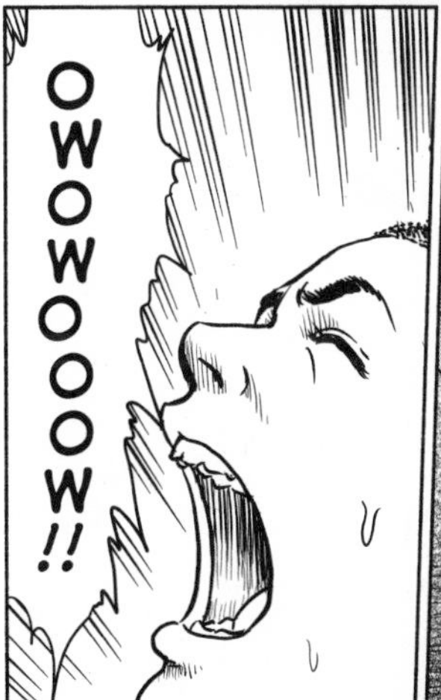
OWOWOOOOW!!

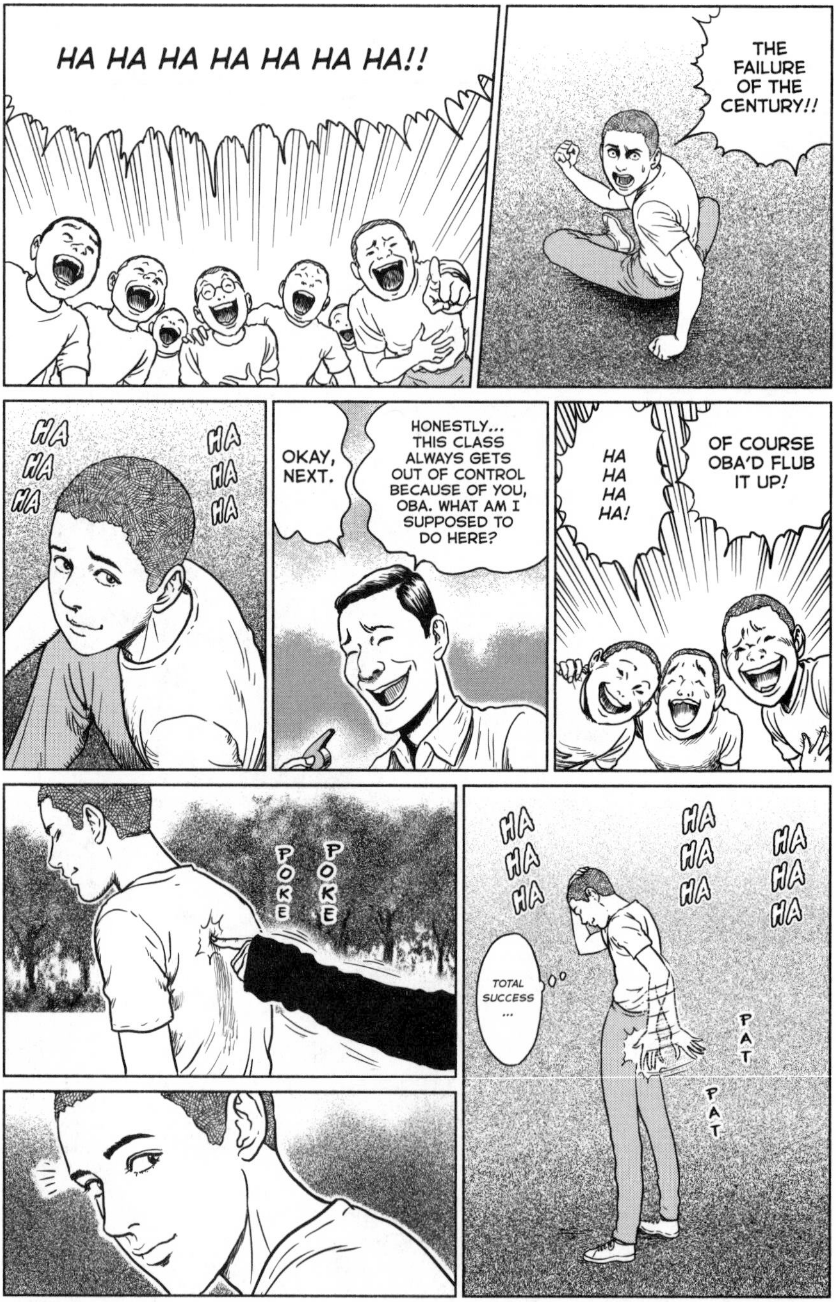
THE FAILURE OF THE CENTURY!!
HA HA HA HA HA HA HA!!
OF COURSE OBA'D FLUB IT UP!
HA HA HA HA!
HONESTLY... THIS CLASS ALWAYS GETS OUT OF CONTROL BECAUSE OF YOU, OBA. WHAT AM I SUPPOSED TO DO HERE?
OKAY, NEXT.
HA HA HA
HA HA HA
HA HA HA
HA HA HA
HA HA HA
TOTAL SUCCESS ...
PAT
PAT
POKE
POKE

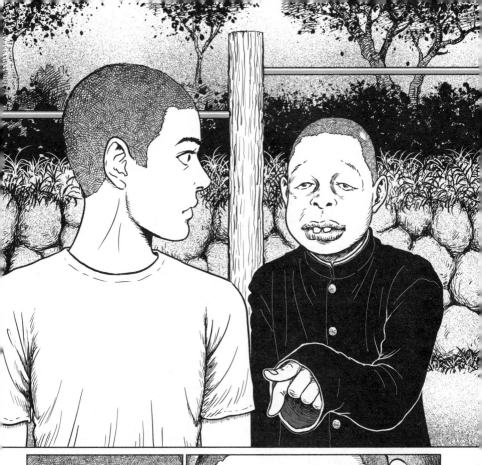

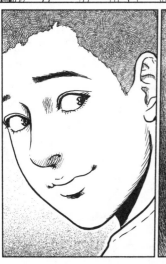

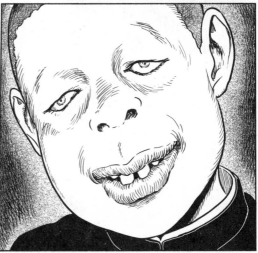

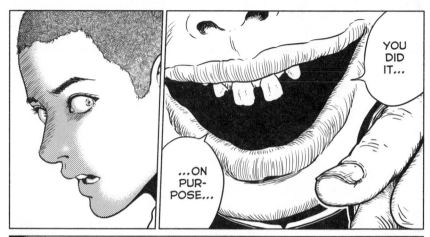

YOU DID IT...

...ON PUR- POSE...

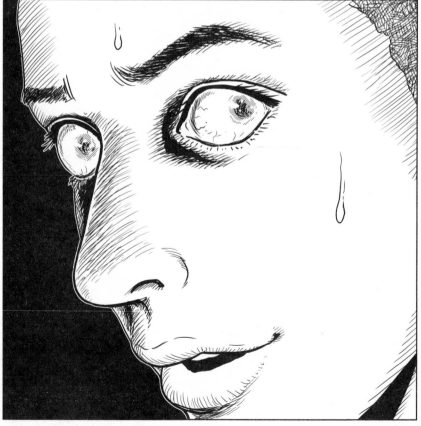

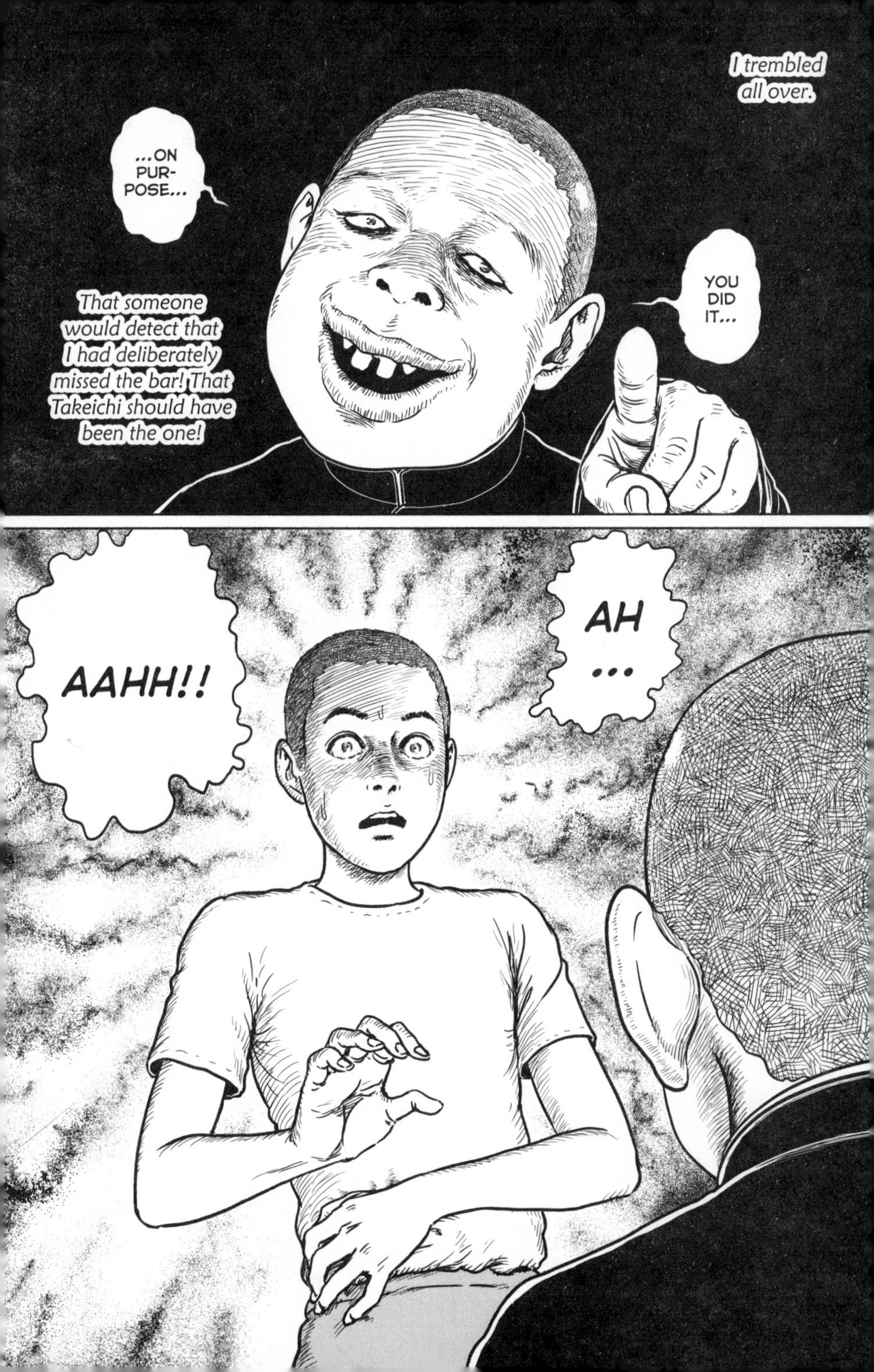
I trembled all over.
YOU DID IT...
...ON PURPOSE...
That someone would detect that I had deliberately missed the bar! That Takeichi should have been the one!
AH ...
AAHH!!

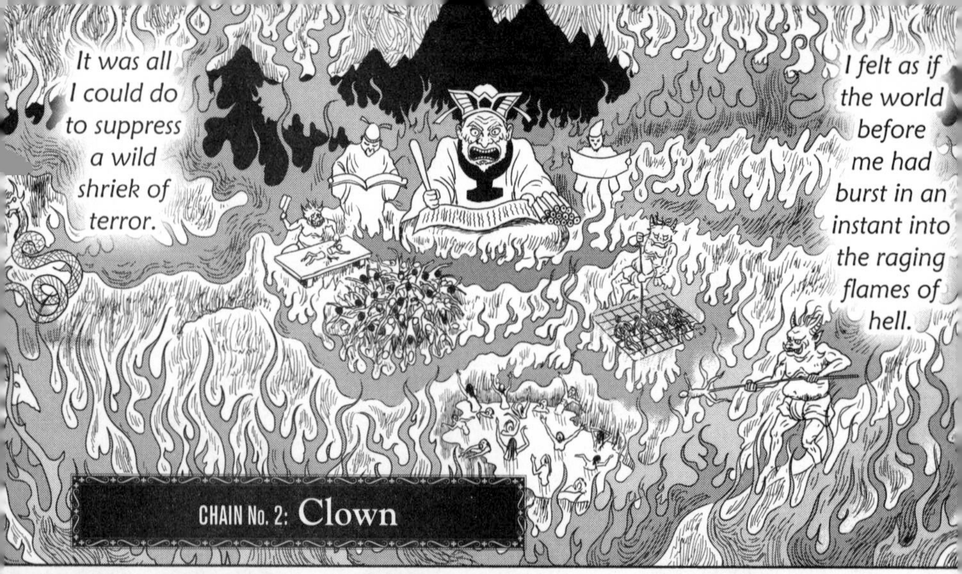
I felt as if the world before me had burst in an instant into the raging flames of hell.
It was all I could do to suppress a wild shriek of terror.
CHAIN No. 2: Clown

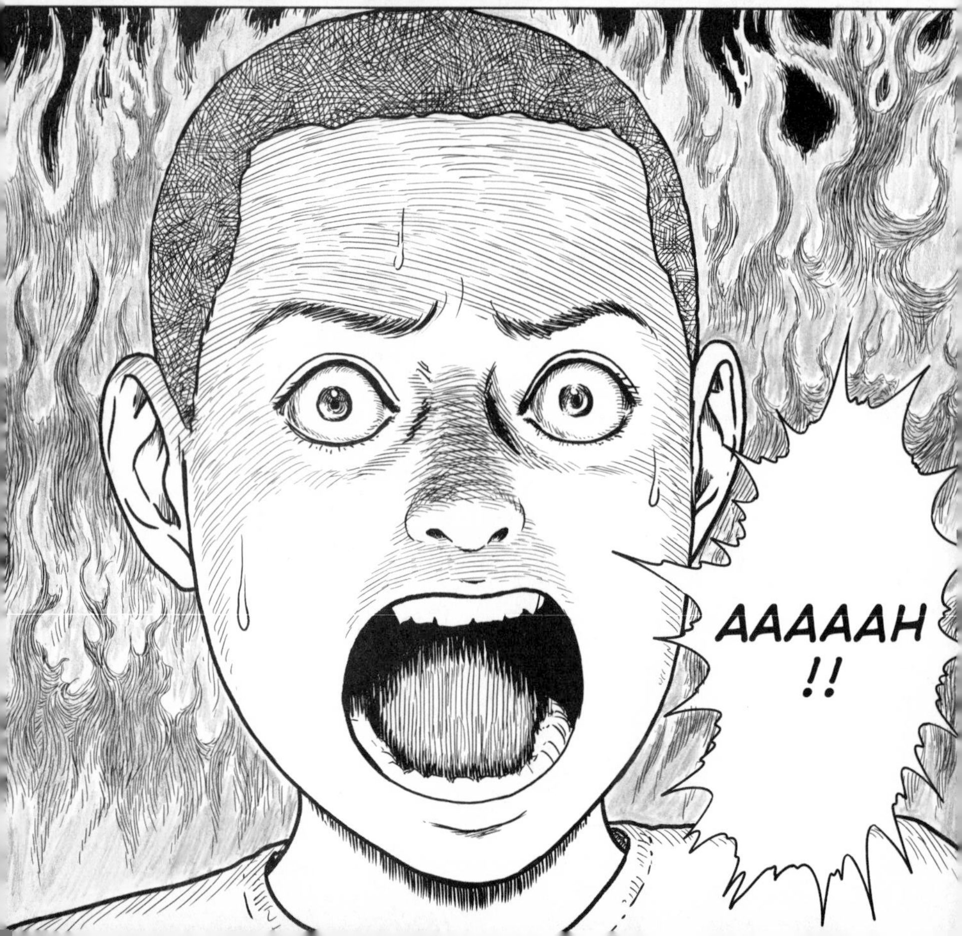
AAAAAH !!

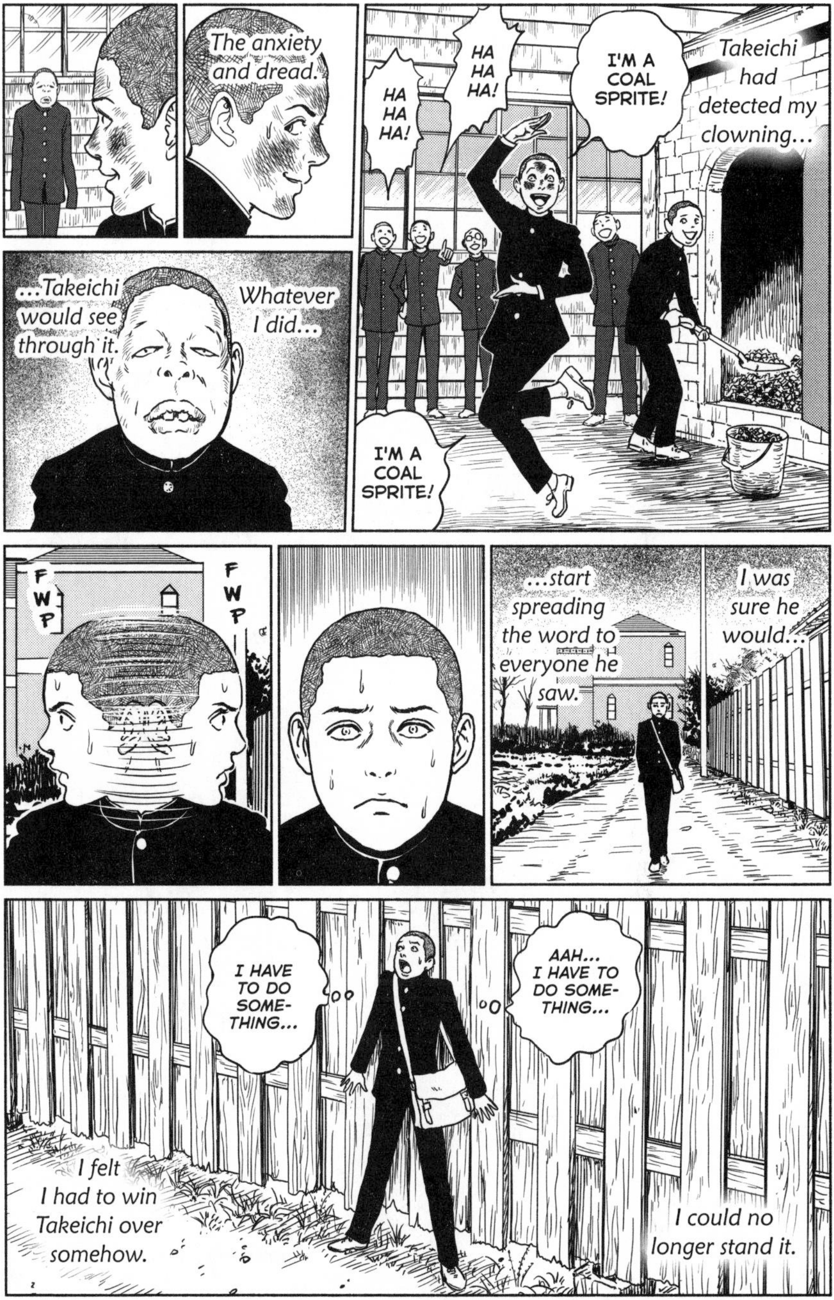
Takeichi had detected my clowning…
I'M A COAL SPRITE!
HA HA HA!
HA HA HA!
I'M A COAL SPRITE!
The anxiety and dread.
Whatever I did…
…Takeichi would see through it.
I was sure he would…
…start spreading the word to everyone he saw.
FWP
FWP
I could no longer stand it.
AAH… I HAVE TO DO SOME-THING…
I HAVE TO DO SOME-THING…
I felt I had to win Takeichi over somehow.

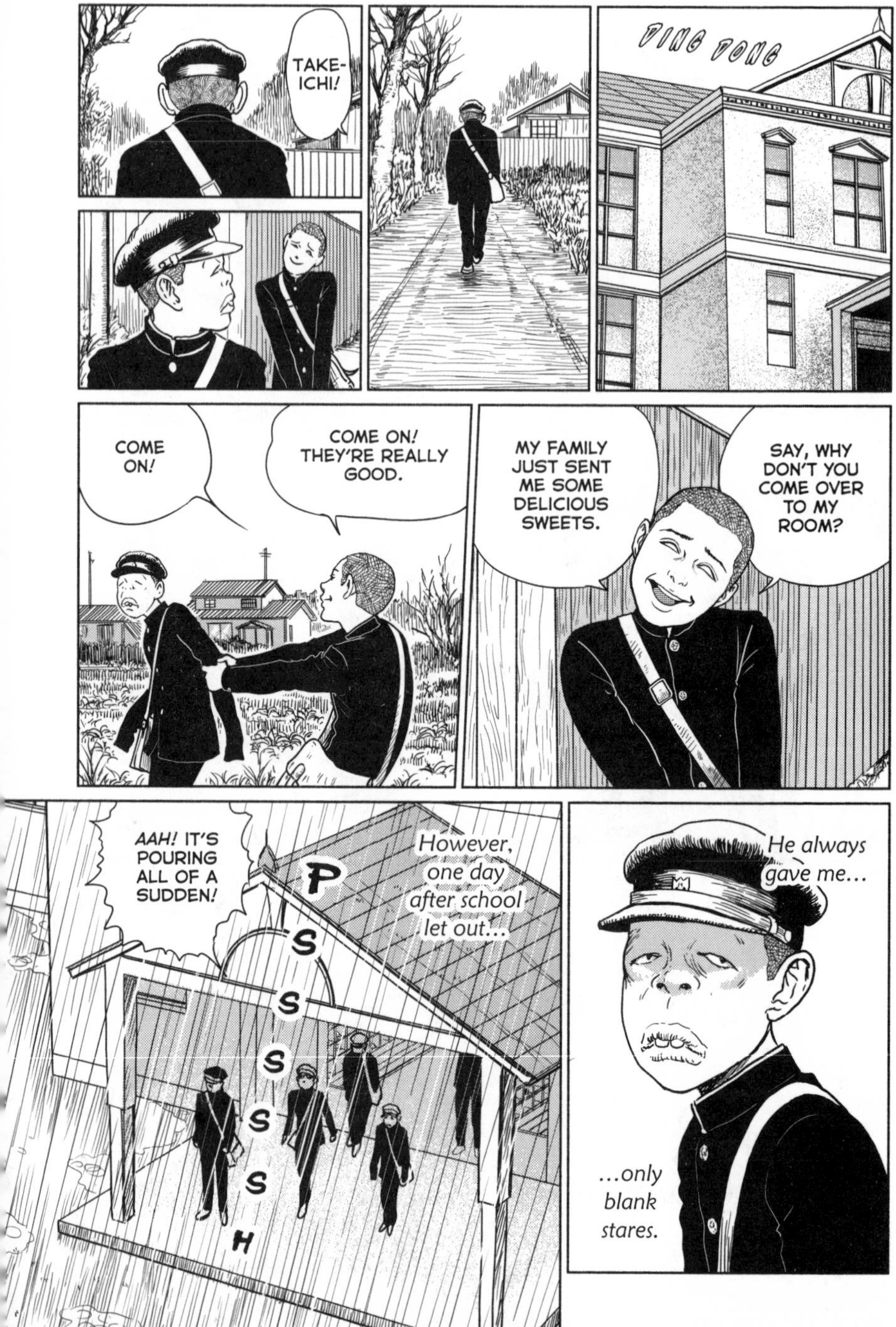
DING DONG
TAKE-ICHI!
SAY, WHY DON'T YOU COME OVER TO MY ROOM?
MY FAMILY JUST SENT ME SOME DELICIOUS SWEETS.
COME ON! THEY'RE REALLY GOOD.
COME ON!
He always gave me…
…only blank stares.
However, one day after school let out…
AAH! IT'S POURING ALL OF A SUDDEN!
PSSSSSH

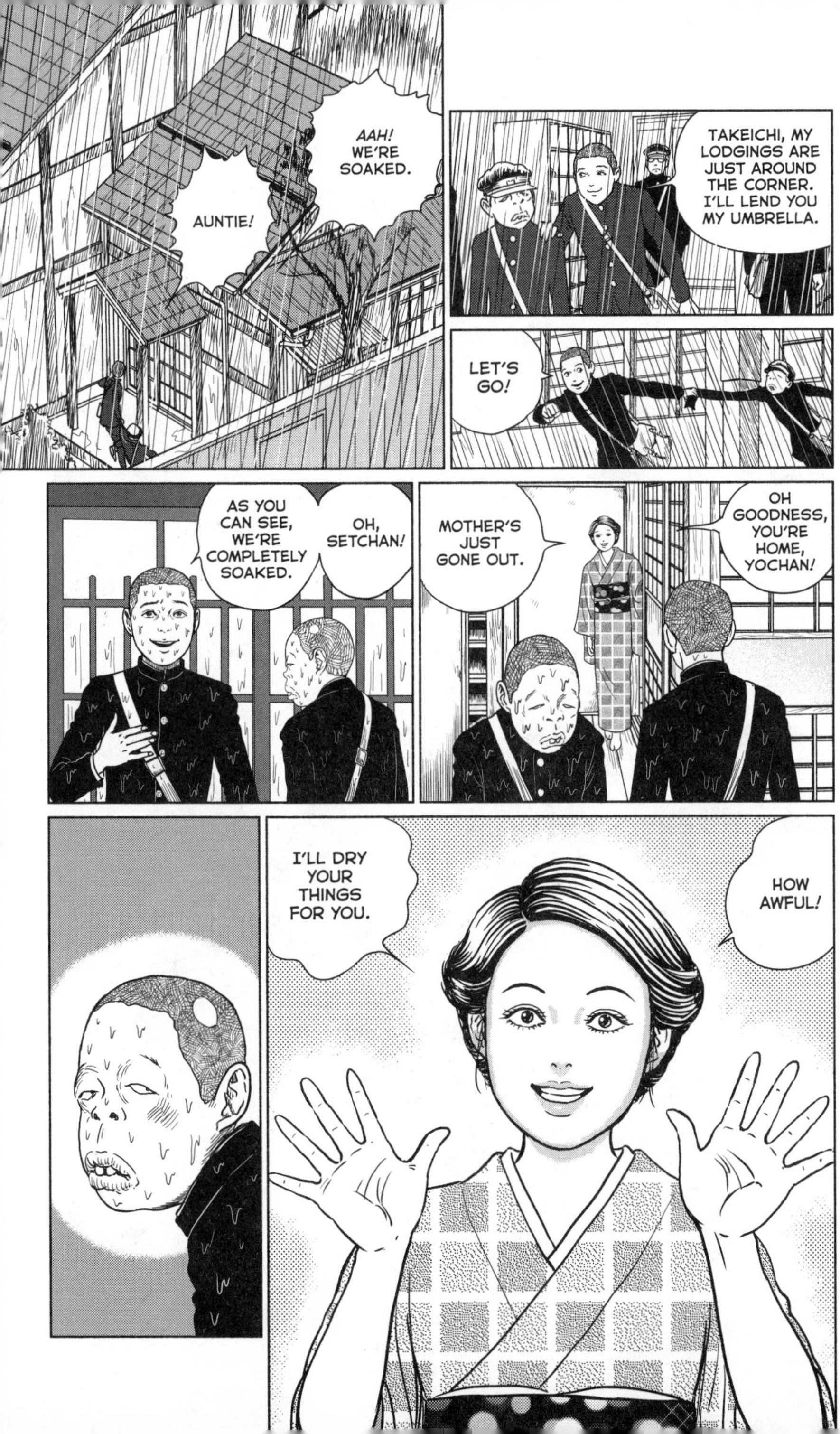
TAKEICHI, MY LODGINGS ARE JUST AROUND THE CORNER. I'LL LEND YOU MY UMBRELLA.
LET'S GO!
AAH! WE'RE SOAKED.
AUNTIE!
OH GOODNESS, YOU'RE HOME, YOCHAN!
MOTHER'S JUST GONE OUT.
OH, SETCHAN!
AS YOU CAN SEE, WE'RE COMPLETELY SOAKED.
HOW AWFUL!
I'LL DRY YOUR THINGS FOR YOU.

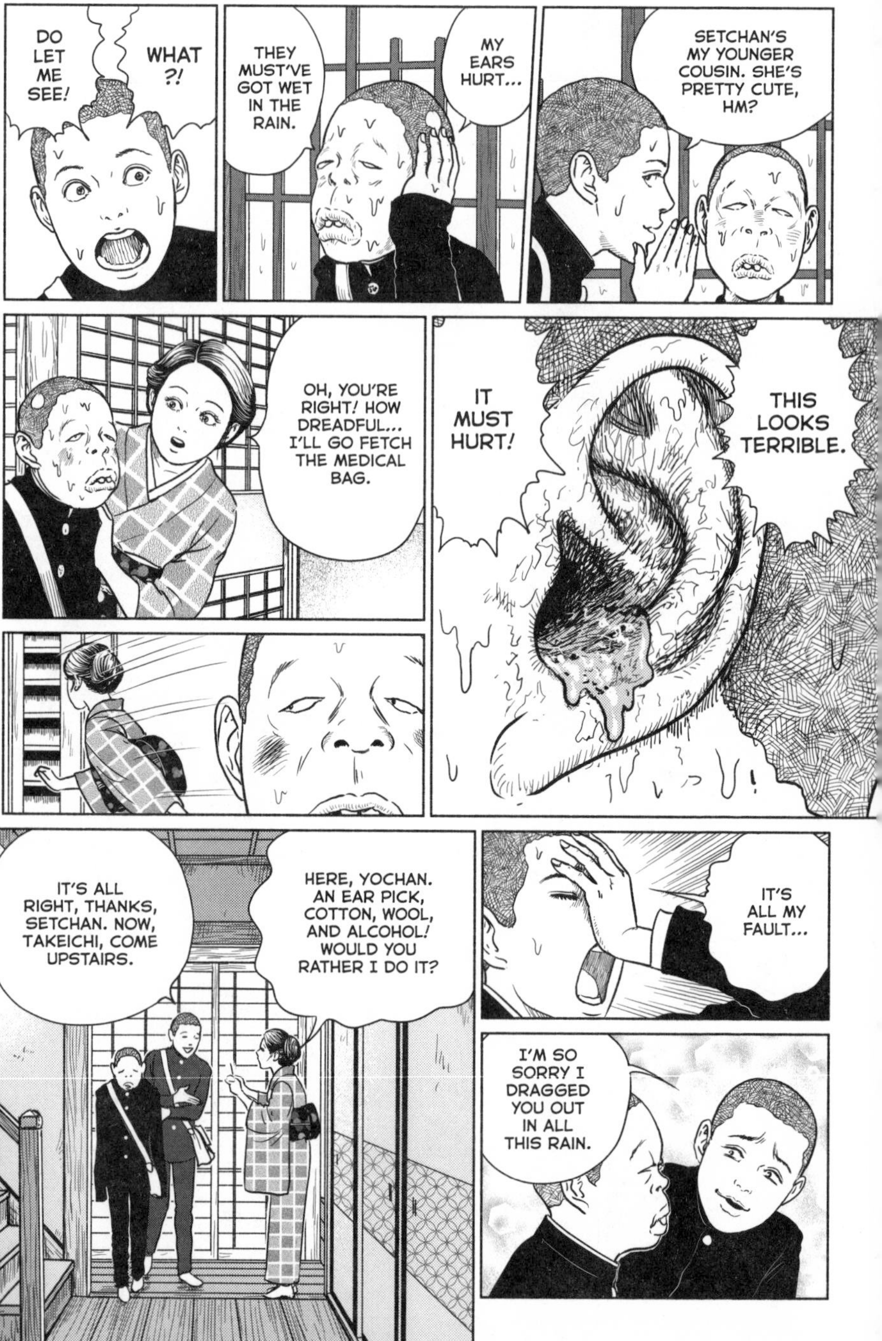
SETCHAN'S MY YOUNGER COUSIN. SHE'S PRETTY CUTE, HM?
MY EARS HURT...
THEY MUST'VE GOT WET IN THE RAIN.
WHAT ?!
DO LET ME SEE!
THIS LOOKS TERRIBLE.
IT MUST HURT!
OH, YOU'RE RIGHT! HOW DREADFUL... I'LL GO FETCH THE MEDICAL BAG.
IT'S ALL MY FAULT...
I'M SO SORRY I DRAGGED YOU OUT IN ALL THIS RAIN.
HERE, YOCHAN. AN EAR PICK, COTTON, WOOL, AND ALCOHOL! WOULD YOU RATHER I DO IT?
IT'S ALL RIGHT, THANKS, SETCHAN. NOW, TAKEICHI, COME UPSTAIRS.

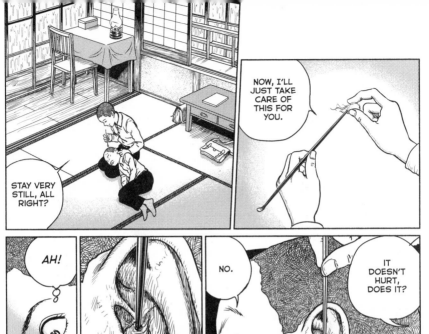

NOW, I'LL JUST TAKE CARE OF THIS FOR YOU.
STAY VERY STILL, ALL RIGHT?
IT DOESN'T HURT, DOES IT?
NO.
AH!
Then a fearsome thought rose up in the back of my mind.
If I were to simply take this metal ear pick and...

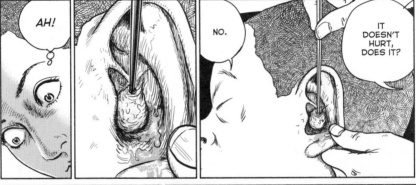

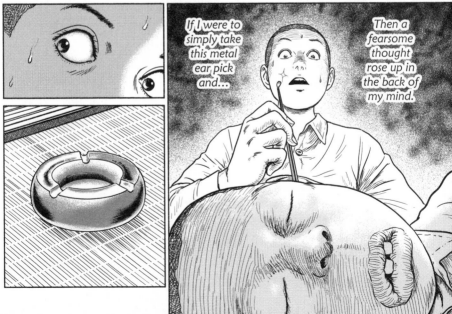

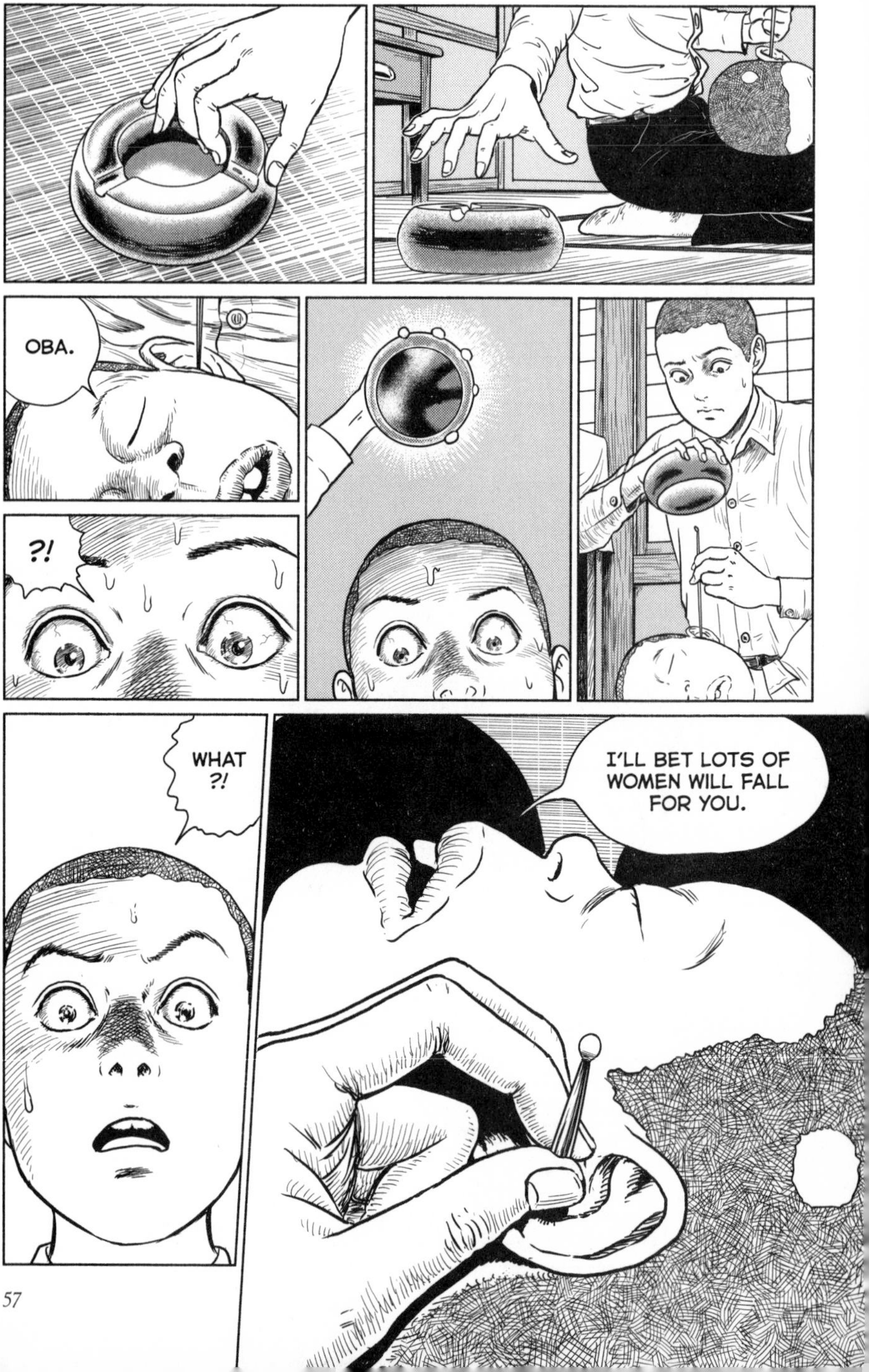
OBA.
?!
I'LL BET LOTS OF WOMEN WILL FALL FOR YOU.
WHAT ?!

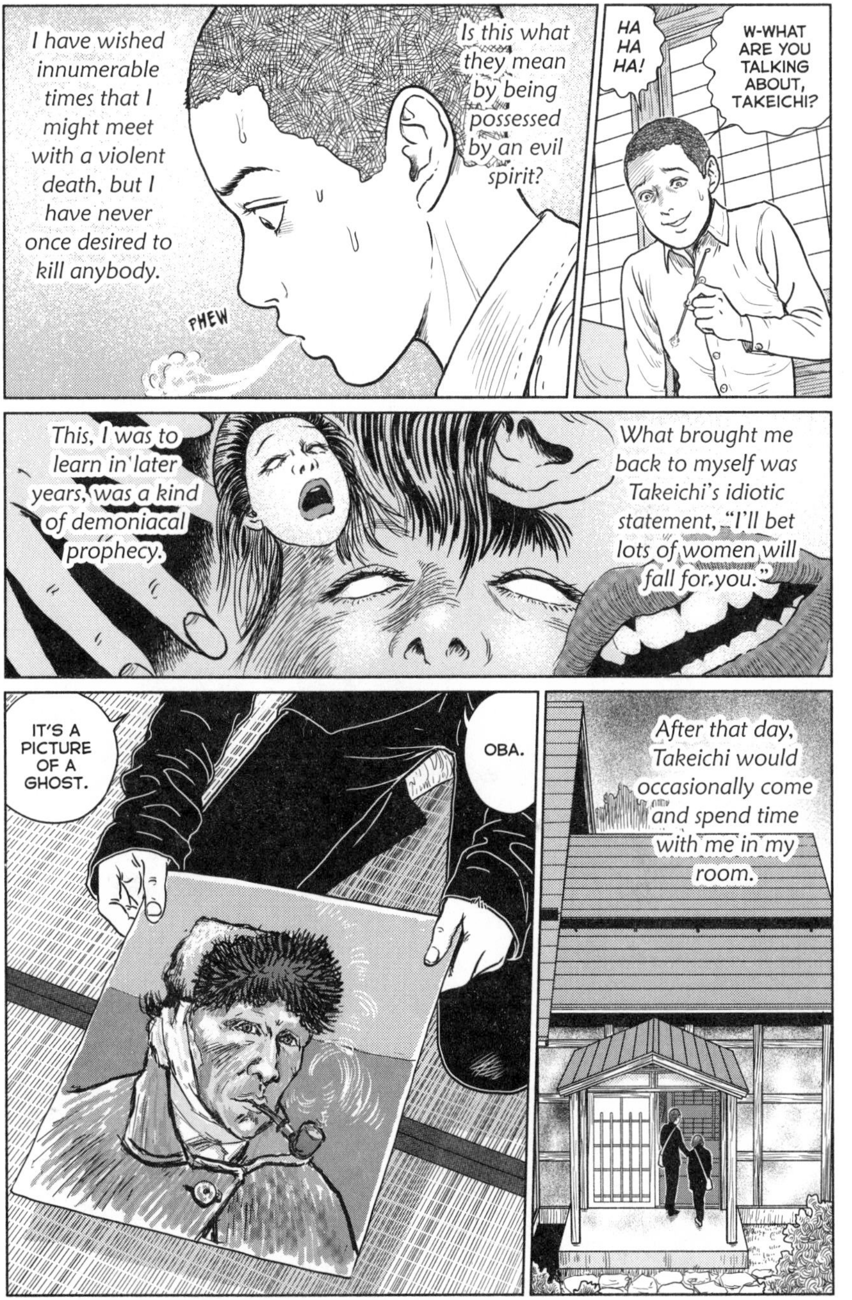
W-WHAT ARE YOU TALKING ABOUT, TAKEICHI?
HA HA HA!
Is this what they mean by being possessed by an evil spirit?
I have wished innumerable times that I might meet with a violent death, but I have never once desired to kill anybody.
PHEW
What brought me back to myself was Takeichi's idiotic statement, "I'll bet lots of women will fall for you."
This, I was to learn in later years, was a kind of demoniacal prophecy.
After that day, Takeichi would occasionally come and spend time with me in my room.
OBA.
IT'S A PICTURE OF A GHOST.

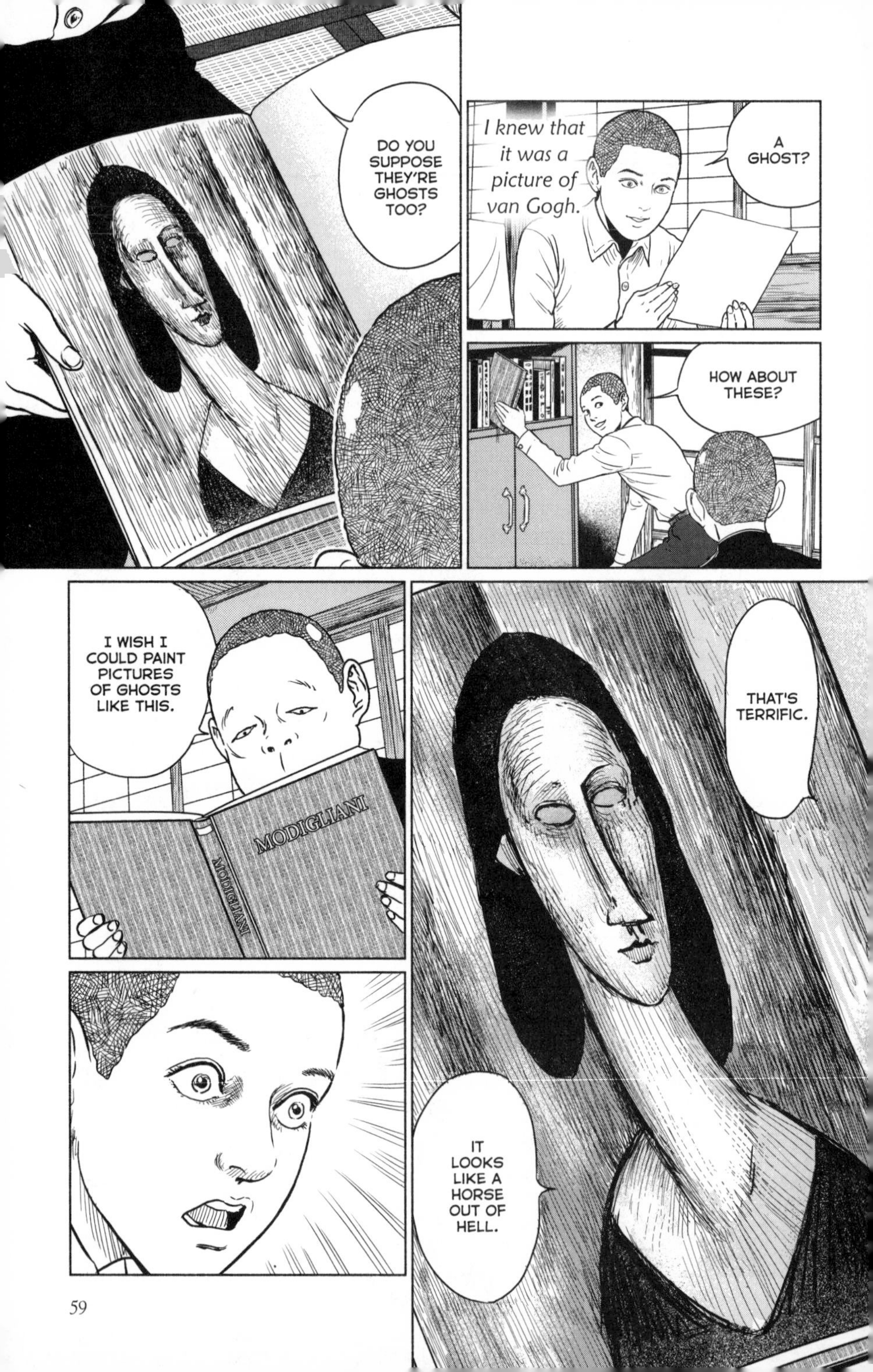
A GHOST?
I knew that it was a picture of van Gogh.
HOW ABOUT THESE?
DO YOU SUPPOSE THEY'RE GHOSTS TOO?
THAT'S TERRIFIC.
IT LOOKS LIKE A HORSE OUT OF HELL.
I WISH I COULD PAINT PICTURES OF GHOSTS LIKE THIS.
MODIGLIANI
MODIGLIANI

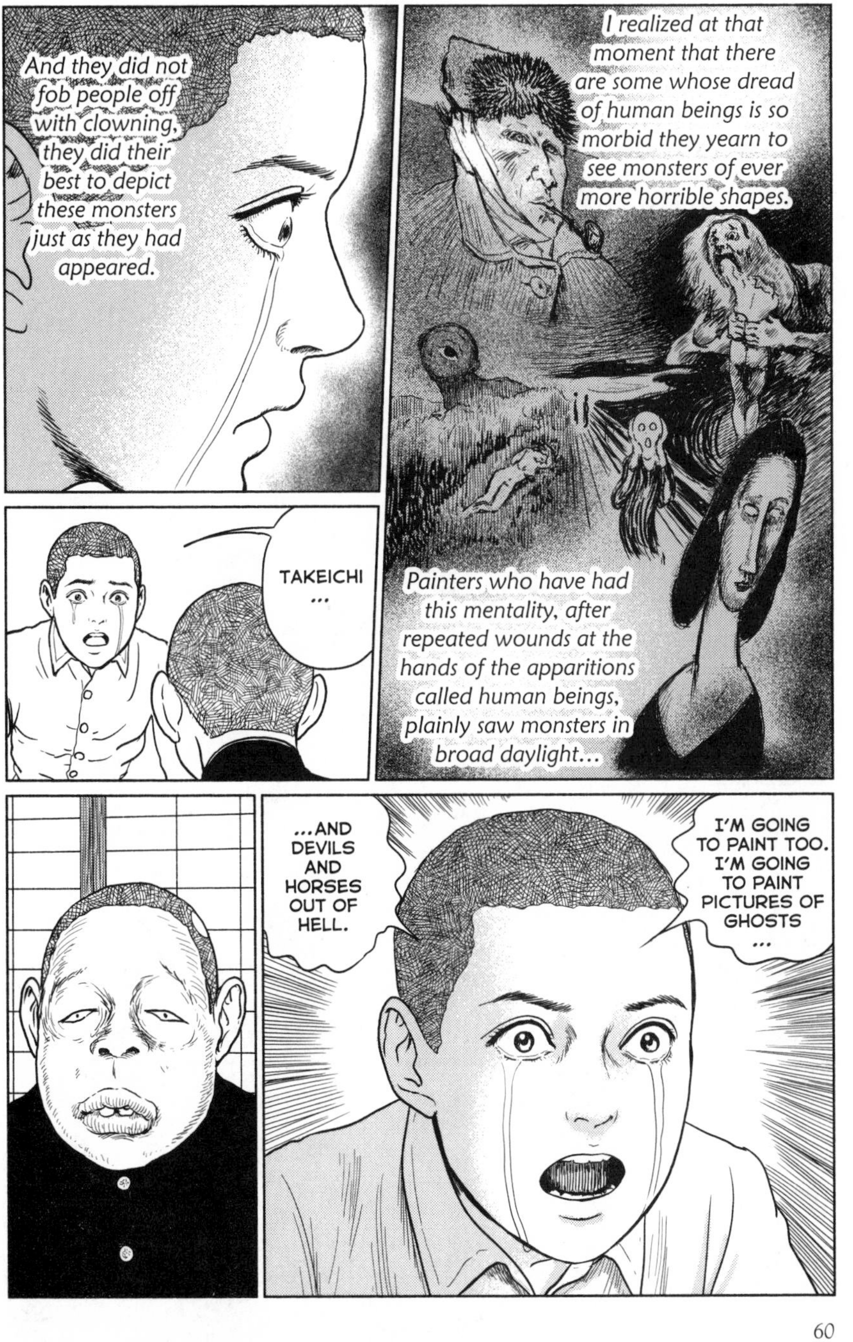
I realized at that moment that there are some whose dread of human beings is so morbid they yearn to see monsters of ever more horrible shapes.
Painters who have had this mentality, after repeated wounds at the hands of the apparitions called human beings, plainly saw monsters in broad daylight...
And they did not fob people off with clowning, they did their best to depict these monsters just as they had appeared.
TAKEICHI ...
I'M GOING TO PAINT TOO. I'M GOING TO PAINT PICTURES OF GHOSTS ...
...AND DEVILS AND HORSES OUT OF HELL.

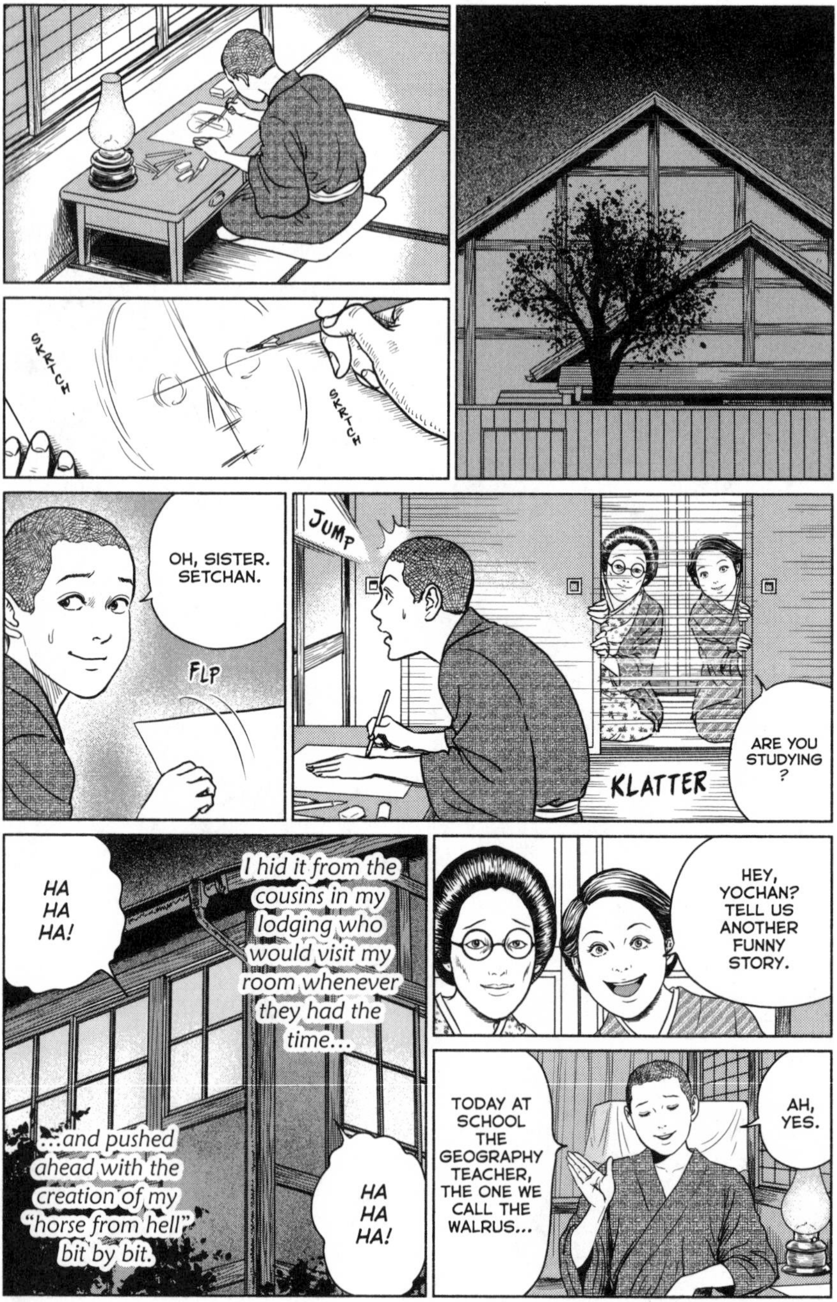
SKRTCH
SKRTCH
ARE YOU STUDYING ?
KLATTER
JUMP
OH, SISTER. SETCHAN.
FLP
HEY, YOCHAN? TELL US ANOTHER FUNNY STORY.
AH, YES.
TODAY AT SCHOOL THE GEOGRAPHY TEACHER, THE ONE WE CALL THE WALRUS...
I hid it from the cousins in my lodging who would visit my room whenever they had the time...
HA HA HA!
HA HA HA!
...and pushed ahead with the creation of my "horse from hell" bit by bit.

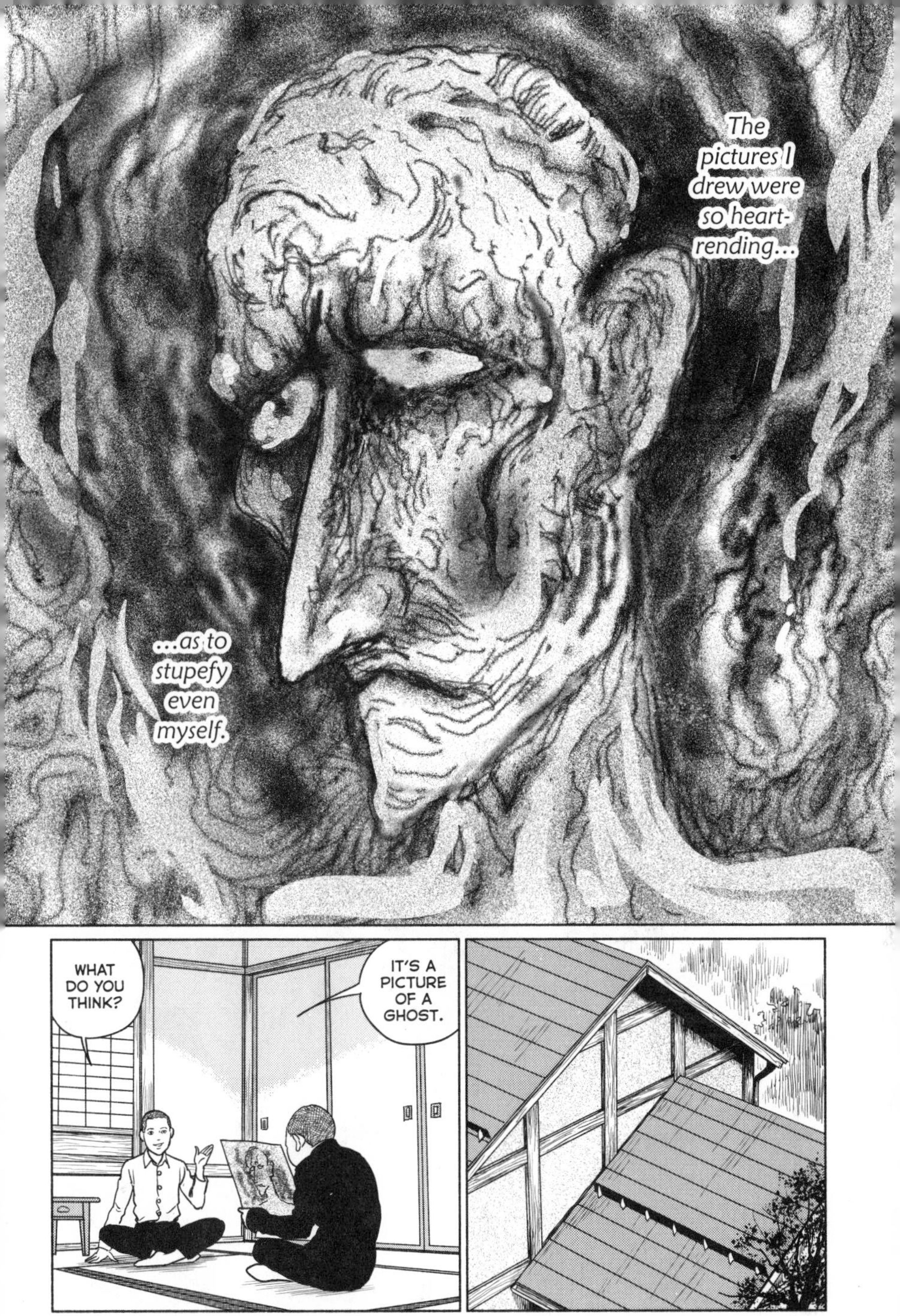
The pictures I drew were so heart-rending...
...as to stupefy even myself.
IT'S A PICTURE OF A GHOST.
WHAT DO YOU THINK?

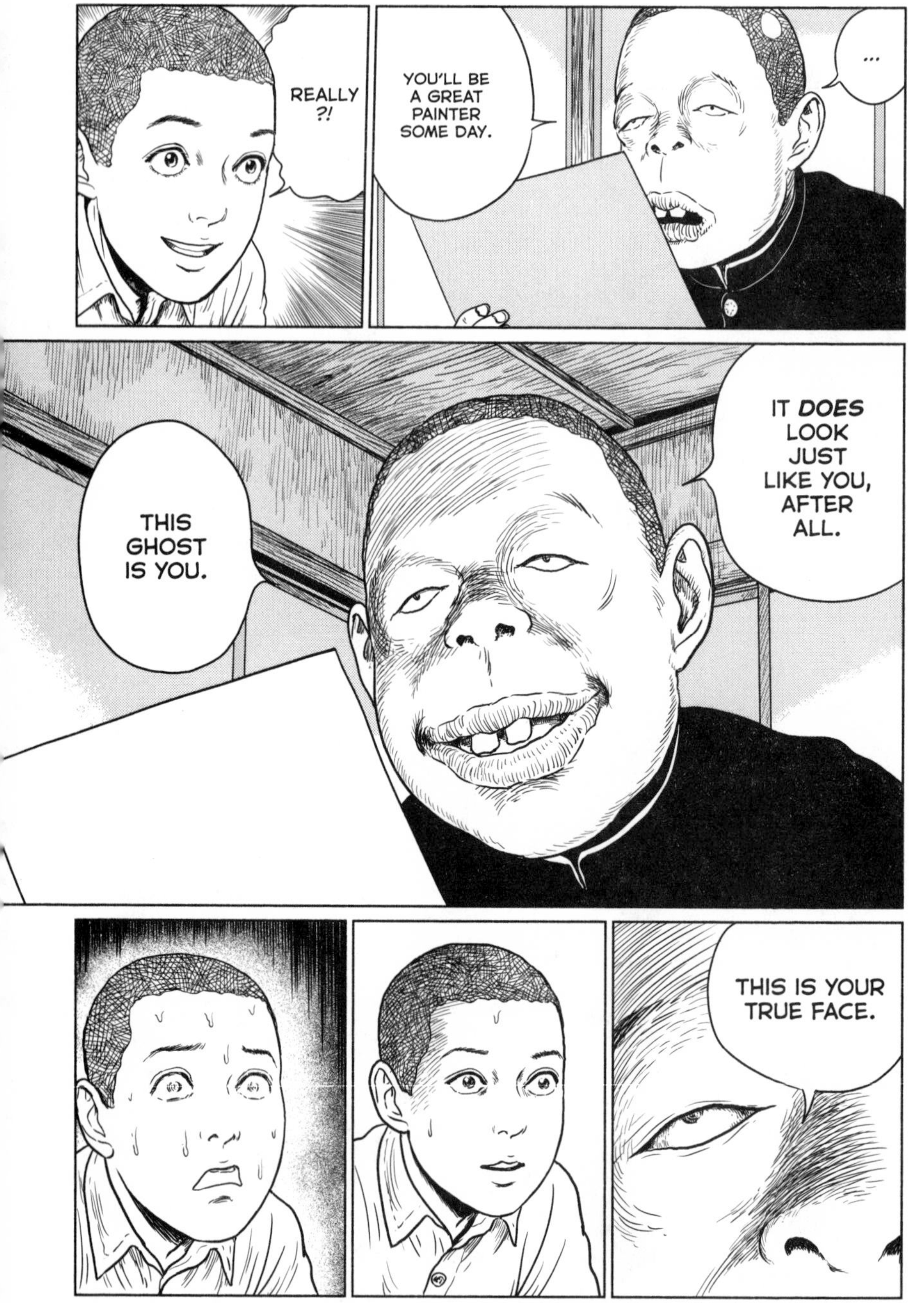
...
YOU'LL BE A GREAT PAINTER SOME DAY.
REALLY ?!
IT *DOES* LOOK JUST LIKE YOU, AFTER ALL.
THIS GHOST IS YOU.
THIS IS YOUR TRUE FACE.

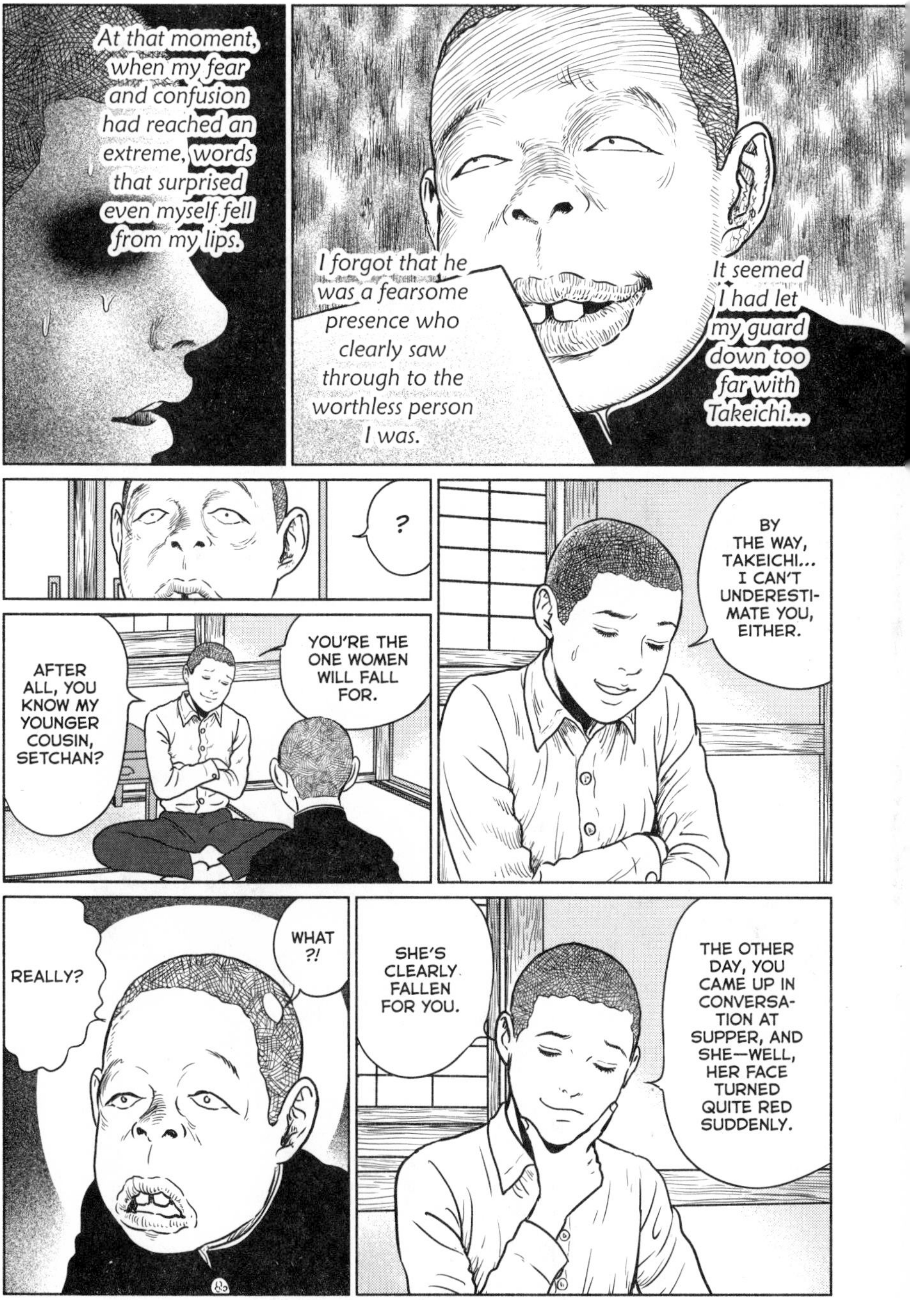
It seemed I had let my guard down too far with Takeichi...
I forgot that he was a fearsome presence who clearly saw through to the worthless person I was.
At that moment, when my fear and confusion had reached an extreme, words that surprised even myself fell from my lips.
BY THE WAY, TAKEICHI... I CAN'T UNDERESTIMATE YOU, EITHER.
?
YOU'RE THE ONE WOMEN WILL FALL FOR.
AFTER ALL, YOU KNOW MY YOUNGER COUSIN, SETCHAN?
THE OTHER DAY, YOU CAME UP IN CONVERSA-TION AT SUPPER, AND SHE—WELL, HER FACE TURNED QUITE RED SUDDENLY.
SHE'S CLEARLY FALLEN FOR YOU.
WHAT ?!
REALLY?

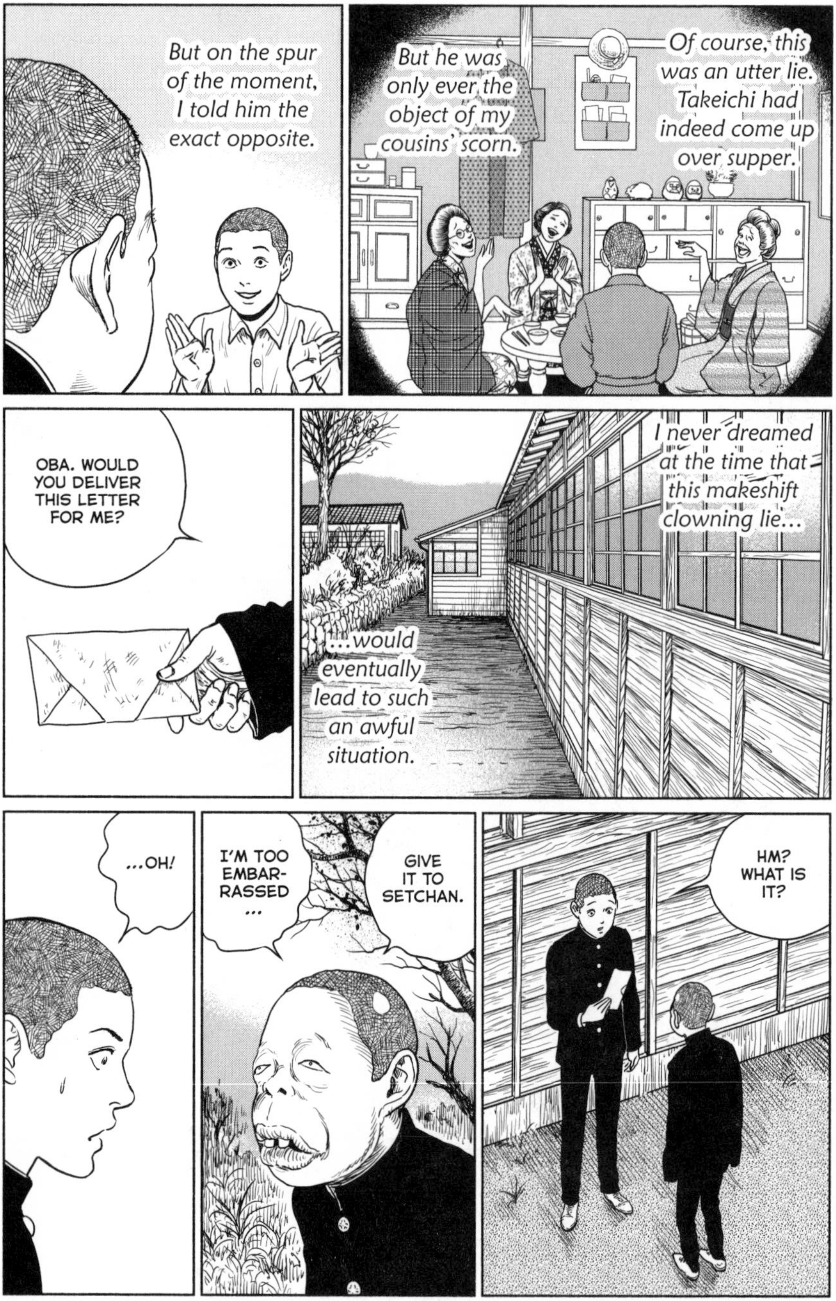
Of course, this was an utter lie. Takeichi had indeed come up over supper.
But he was only ever the object of my cousins' scorn.
But on the spur of the moment, I told him the exact opposite.
I never dreamed at the time that this makeshift clowning lie...
...would eventually lead to such an awful situation.
OBA. WOULD YOU DELIVER THIS LETTER FOR ME?
HM? WHAT IS IT?
GIVE IT TO SETCHAN.
I'M TOO EMBARRASSED...
...OH!

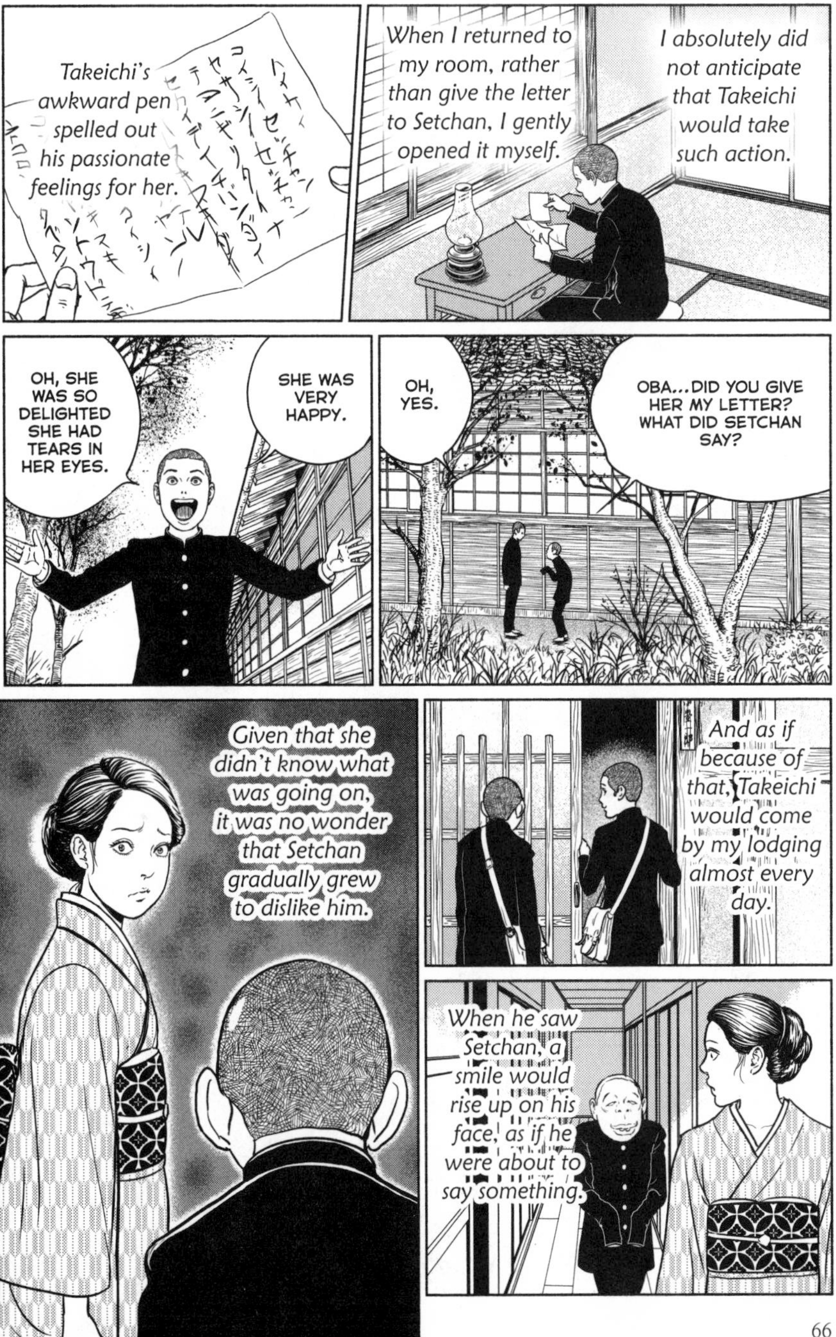
I absolutely did not anticipate that Takeichi would take such action.
When I returned to my room, rather than give the letter to Setchan, I gently opened it myself.
Takeichi's awkward pen spelled out his passionate feelings for her.
OBA...DID YOU GIVE HER MY LETTER? WHAT DID SETCHAN SAY?
OH, YES.
SHE WAS VERY HAPPY.
OH, SHE WAS SO DELIGHTED SHE HAD TEARS IN HER EYES.
And as if because of that, Takeichi would come by my lodging almost every day.
When he saw Setchan, a smile would rise up on his face, as if he were about to say something.
Given that she didn't know what was going on, it was no wonder that Setchan gradually grew to dislike him.

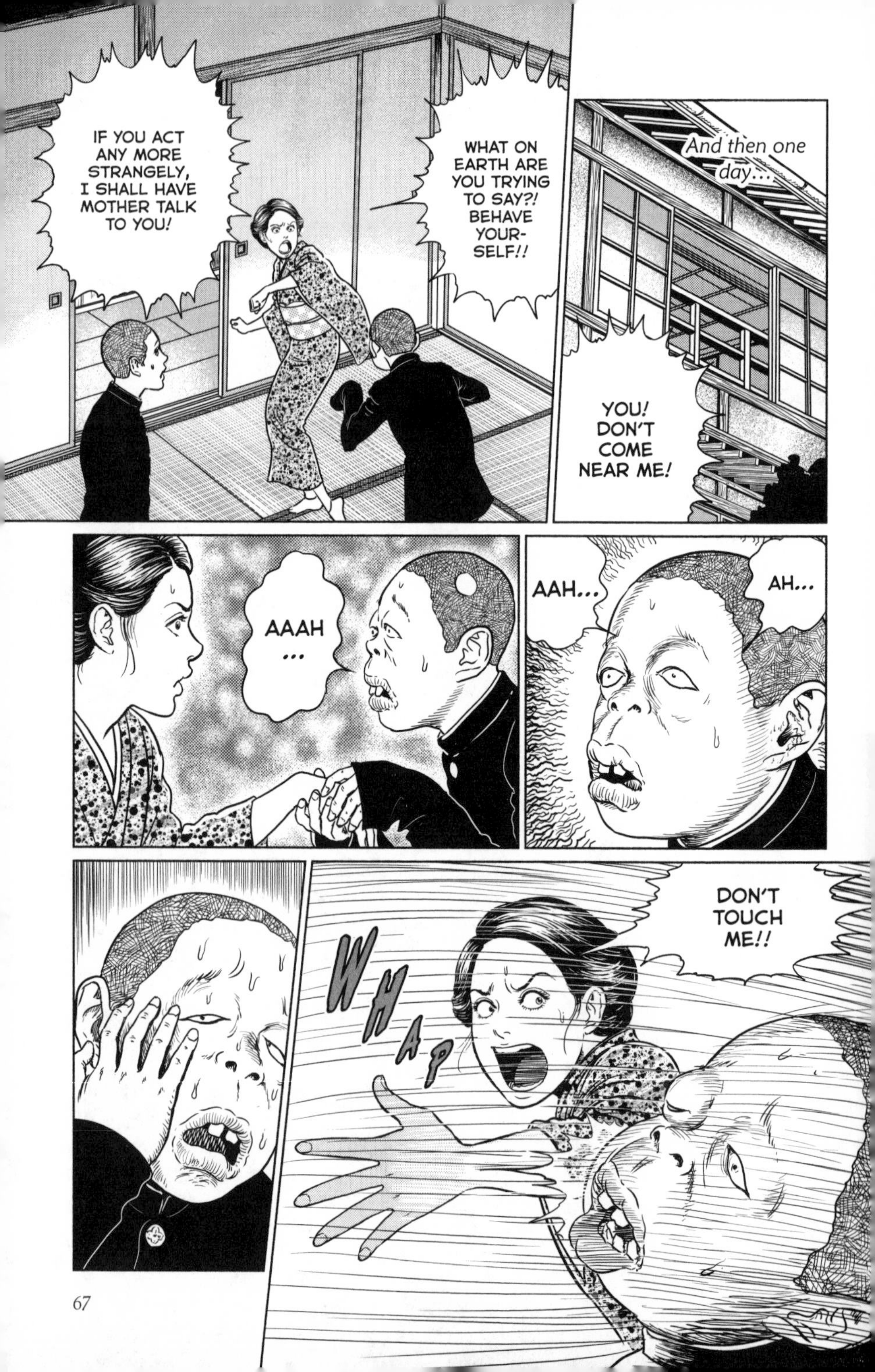
And then one day...
YOU! DON'T COME NEAR ME!
WHAT ON EARTH ARE YOU TRYING TO SAY?! BEHAVE YOURSELF!!
IF YOU ACT ANY MORE STRANGELY, I SHALL HAVE MOTHER TALK TO YOU!
AH...
AAH...
AAAH ...
DON'T TOUCH ME!!
WHAP

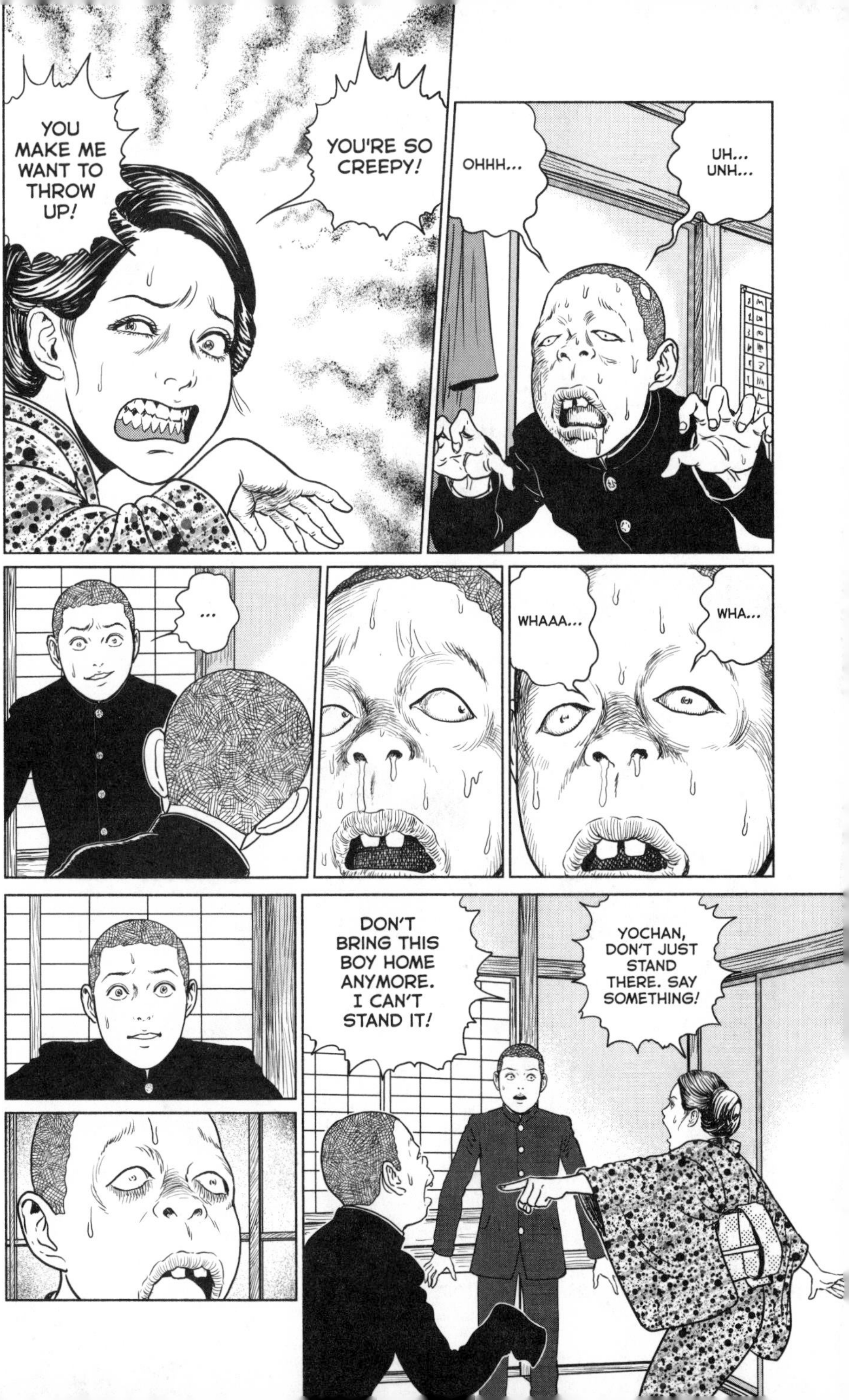
UH... UNH...
OHHH...
YOU'RE SO CREEPY!
YOU MAKE ME WANT TO THROW UP!
WHA...
WHAAA...
...
YOCHAN, DON'T JUST STAND THERE. SAY SOMETHING!
DON'T BRING THIS BOY HOME ANYMORE. I CAN'T STAND IT!

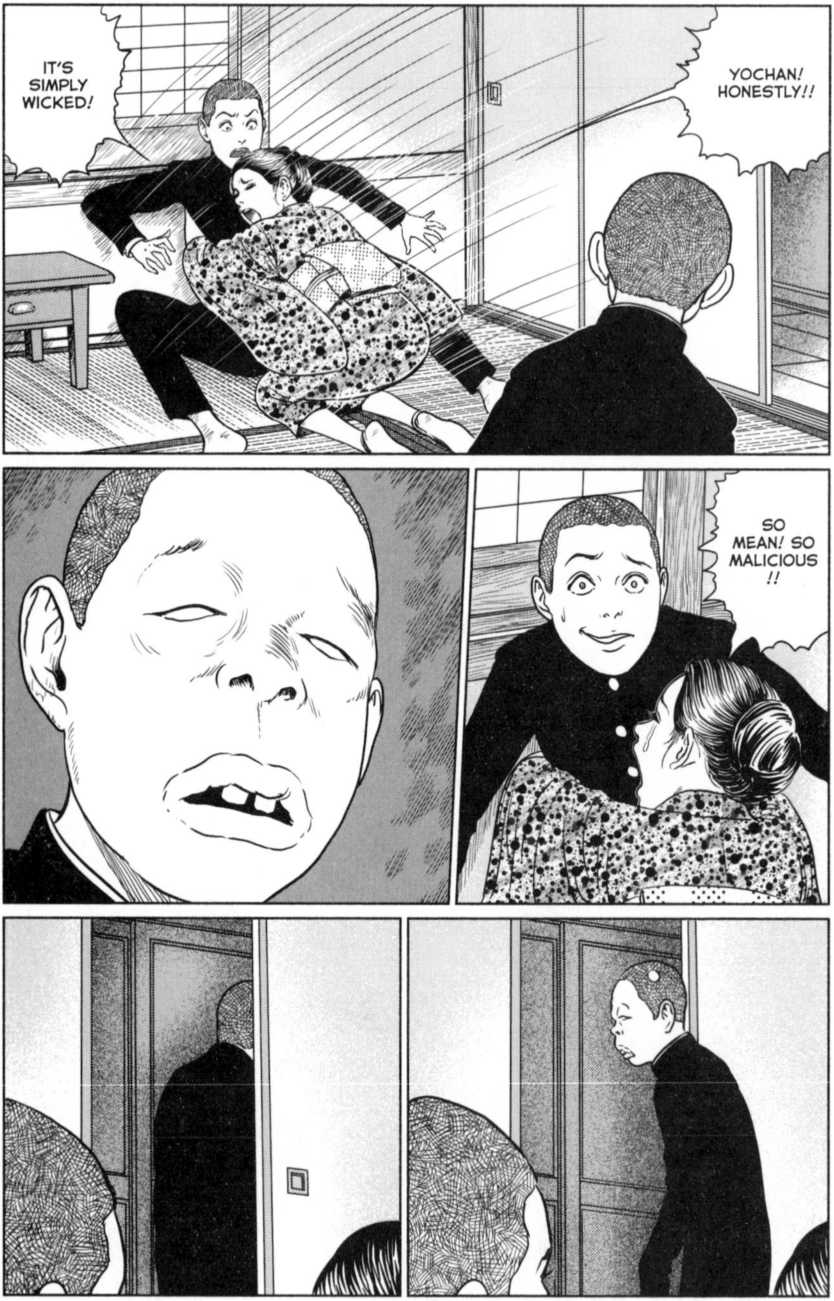
YOCHAN! HONESTLY!!
IT'S SIMPLY WICKED!
SO MEAN! SO MALICIOUS !!

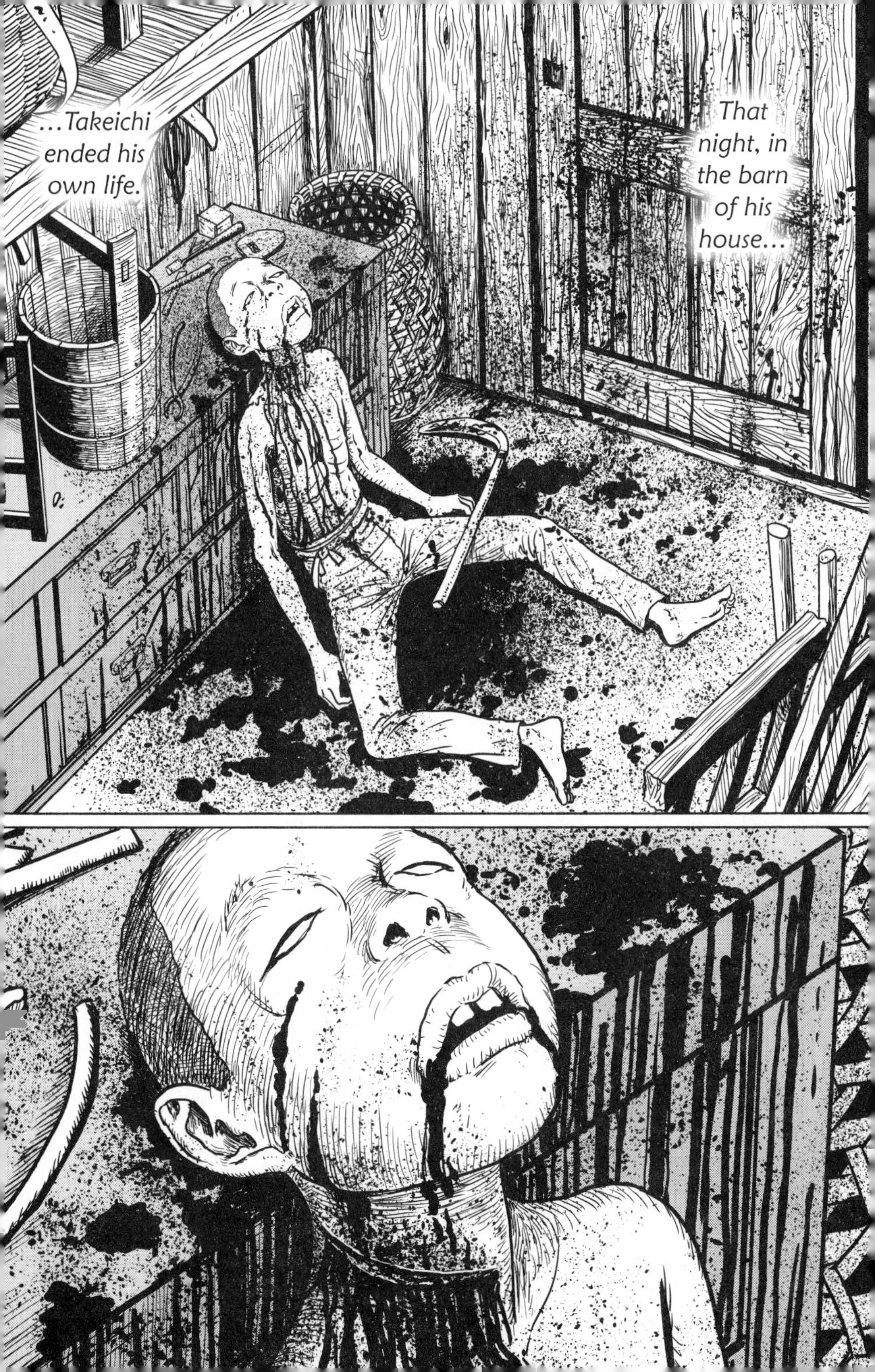
That night, in the barn of his house...
...Takeichi ended his own life.

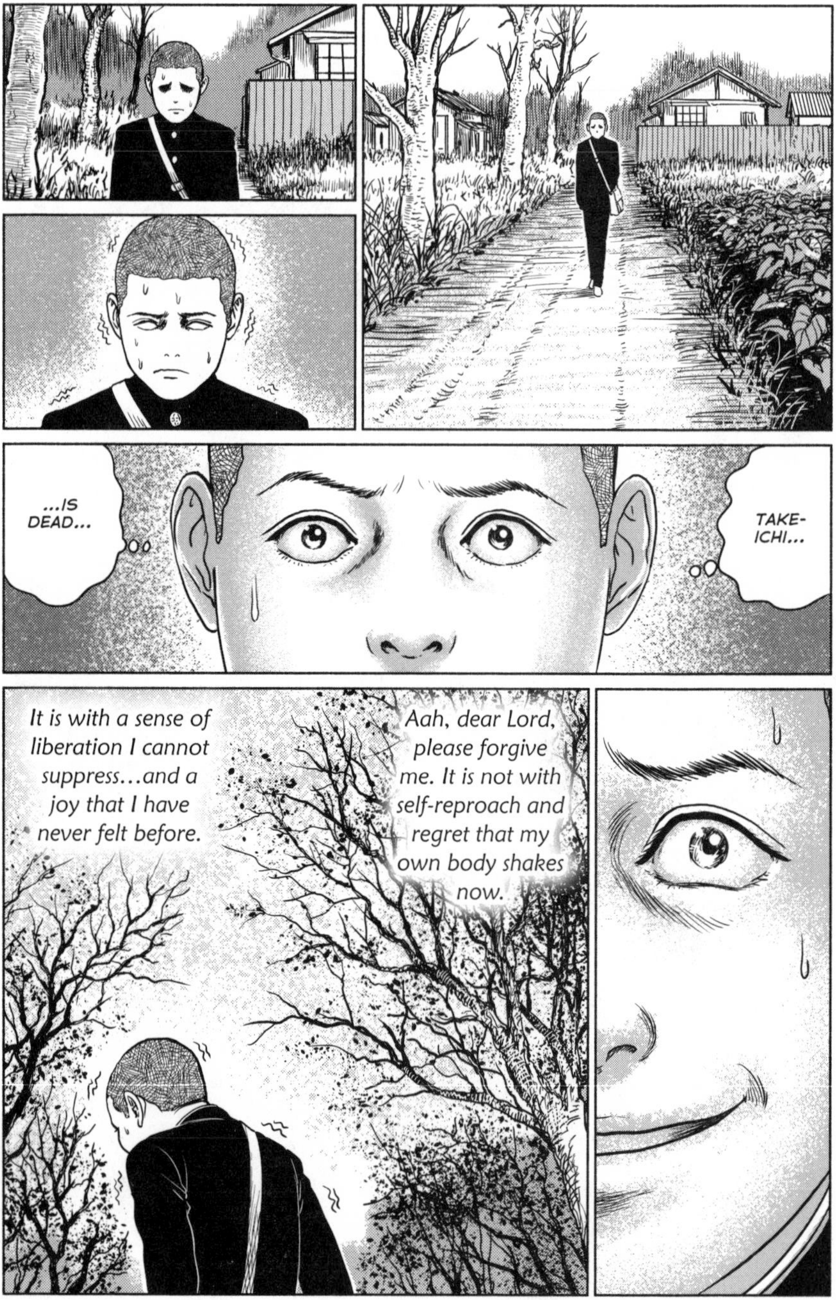
TAKE-ICHI...
...IS DEAD...
Aah, dear Lord, please forgive me. It is not with self-reproach and regret that my own body shakes now.
It is with a sense of liberation I cannot suppress...and a joy that I have never felt before.

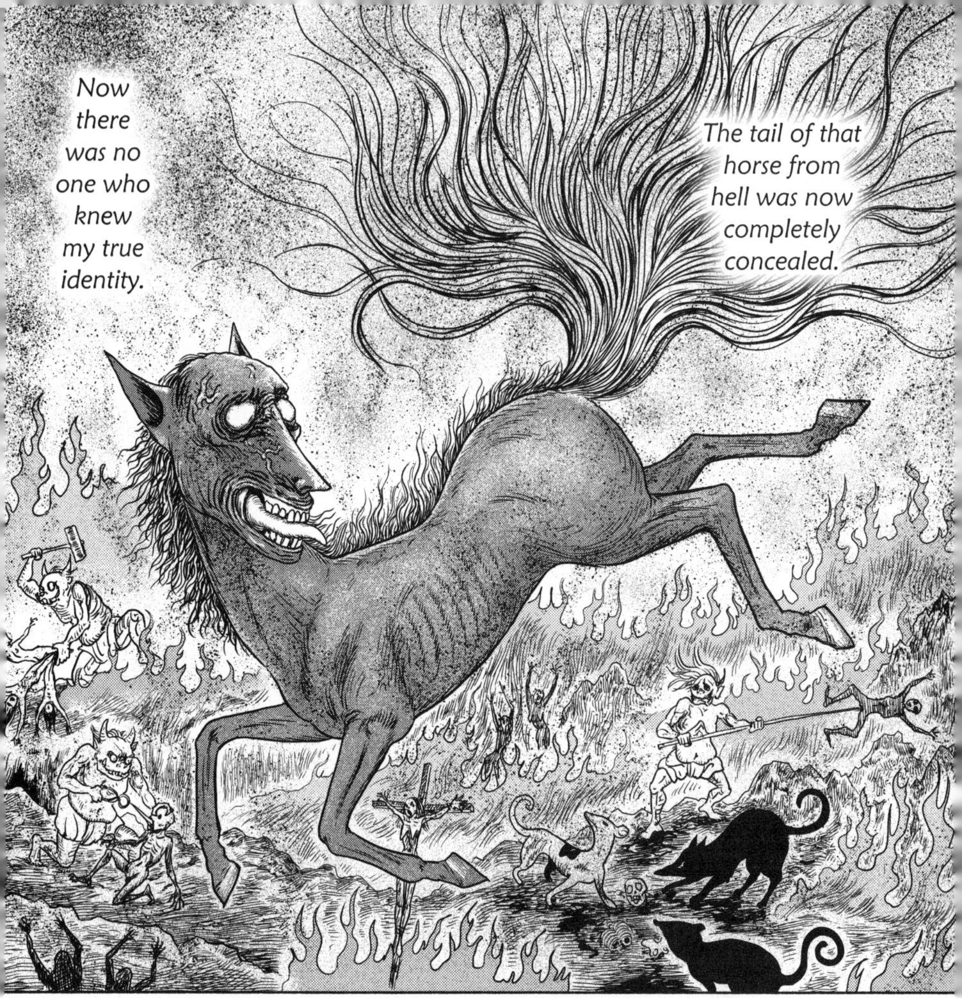
The tail of that horse from hell was now completely concealed.
Now there was no one who knew my true identity.

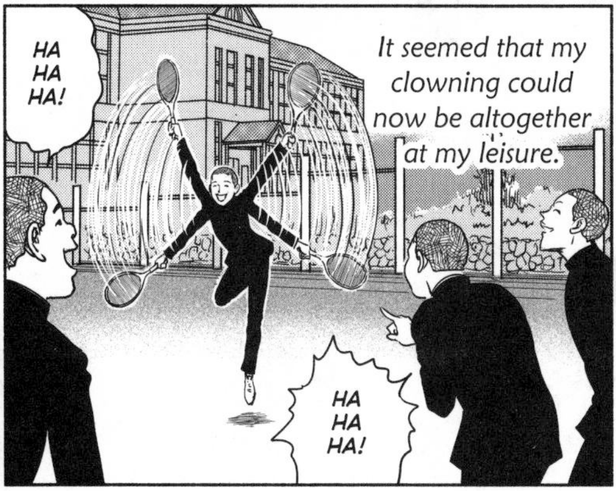
It seemed that my clowning could now be altogether at my leisure.
HA HA HA!
HA HA HA!

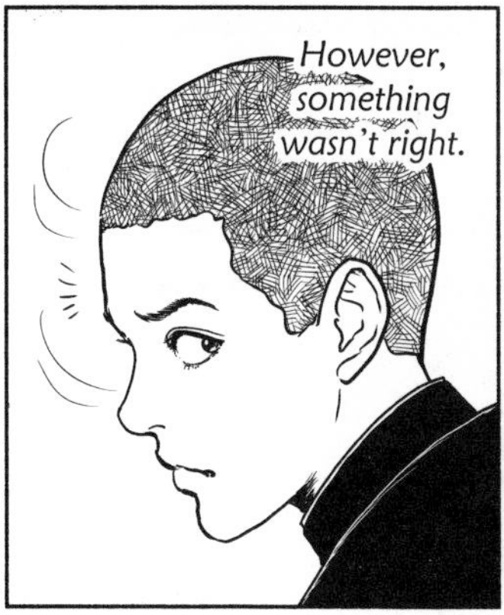
However, something wasn't right.

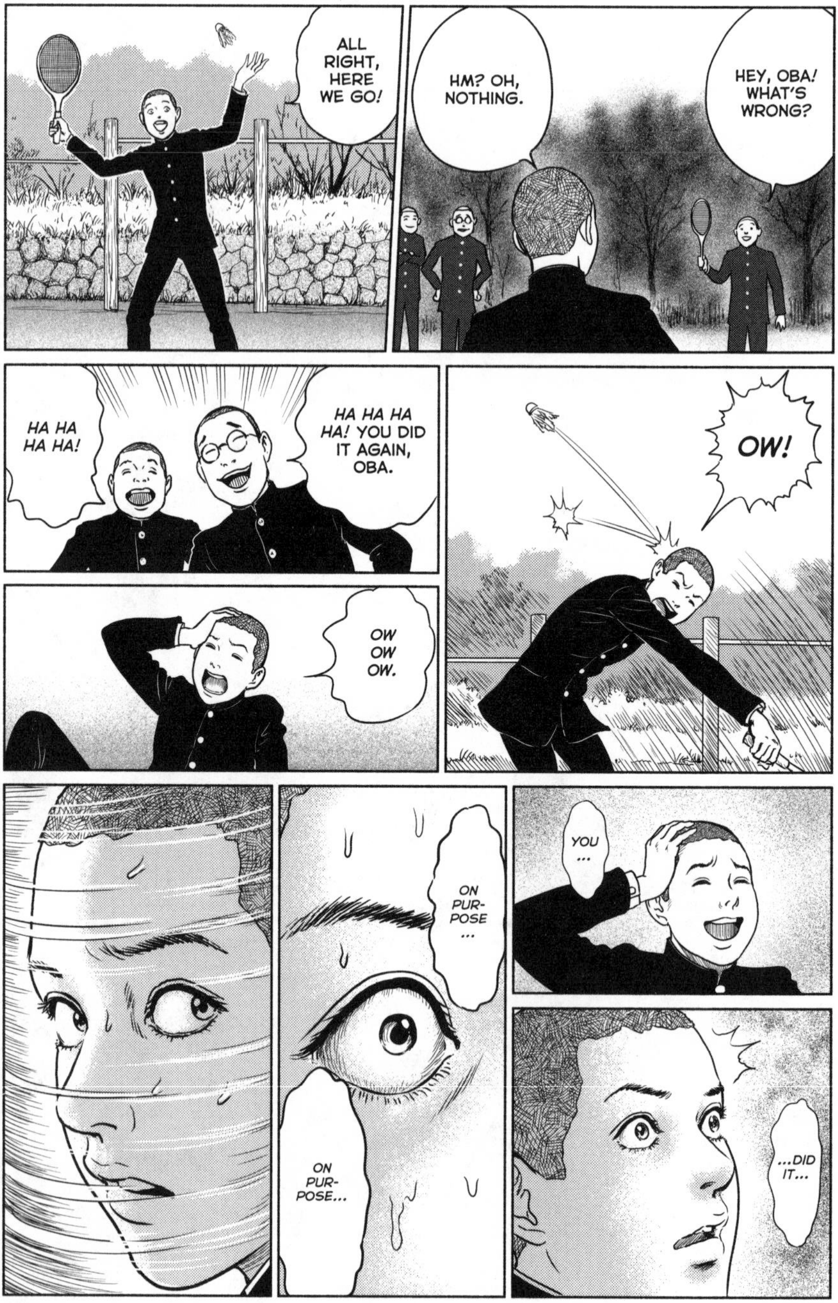
HEY, OBA! WHAT'S WRONG?
HM? OH, NOTHING.
ALL RIGHT, HERE WE GO!
OW!
HA HA HA HA! YOU DID IT AGAIN, OBA.
HA HA HA HA!
OW OW OW.
YOU ...
...DID IT...
ON PUR-POSE ...
ON PUR-POSE...

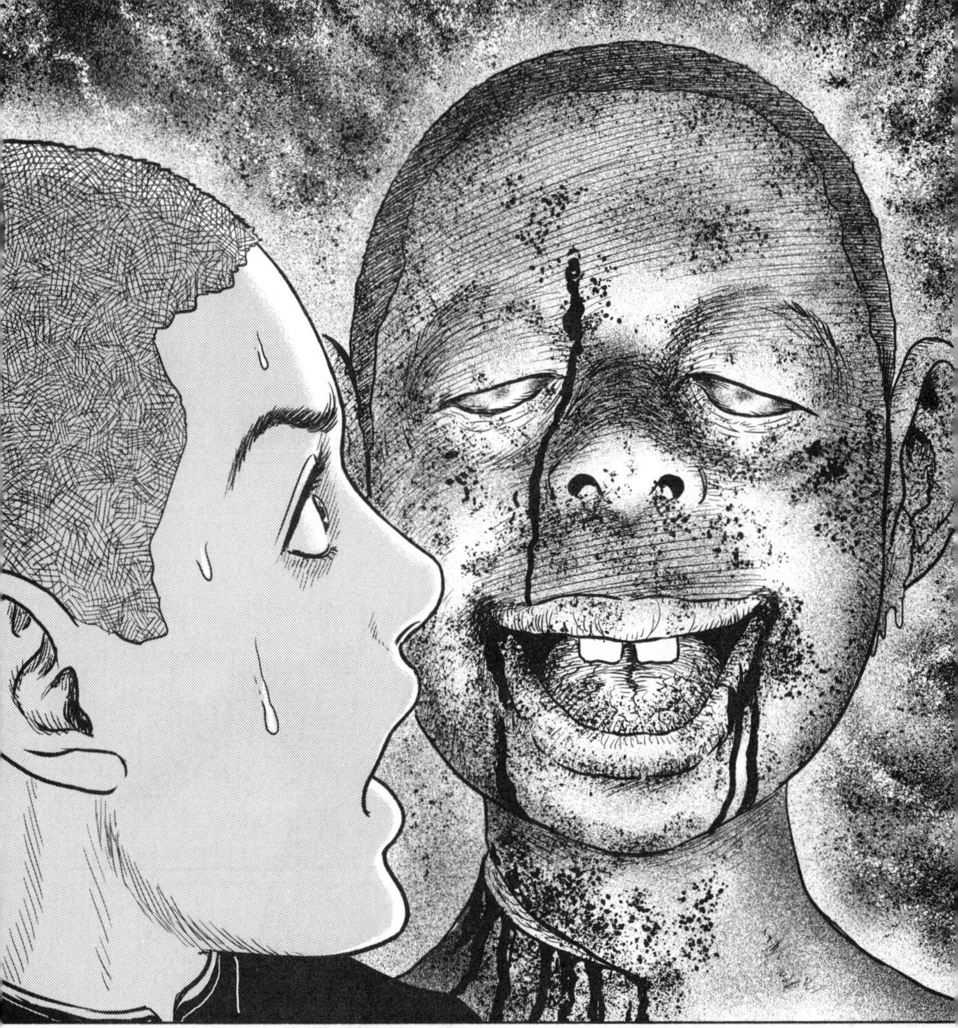

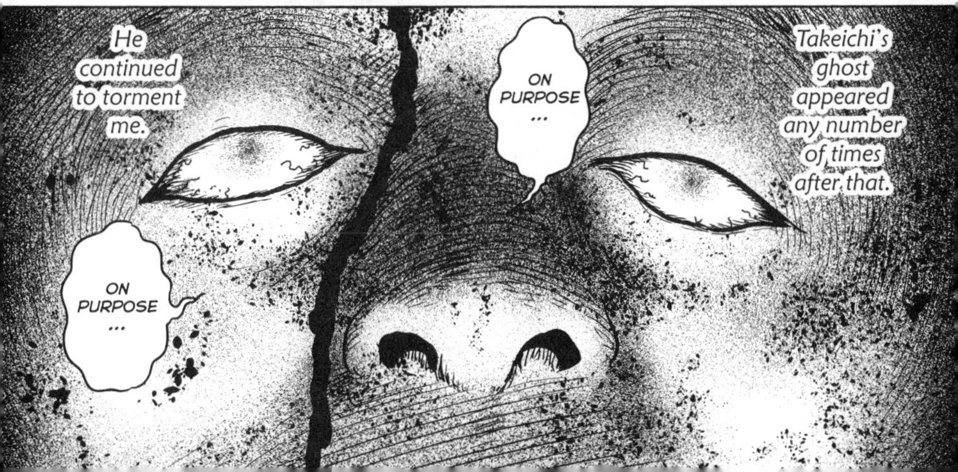
Takeichi's ghost appeared any number of times after that.
ON PURPOSE ...
He continued to torment me.
ON PURPOSE ...

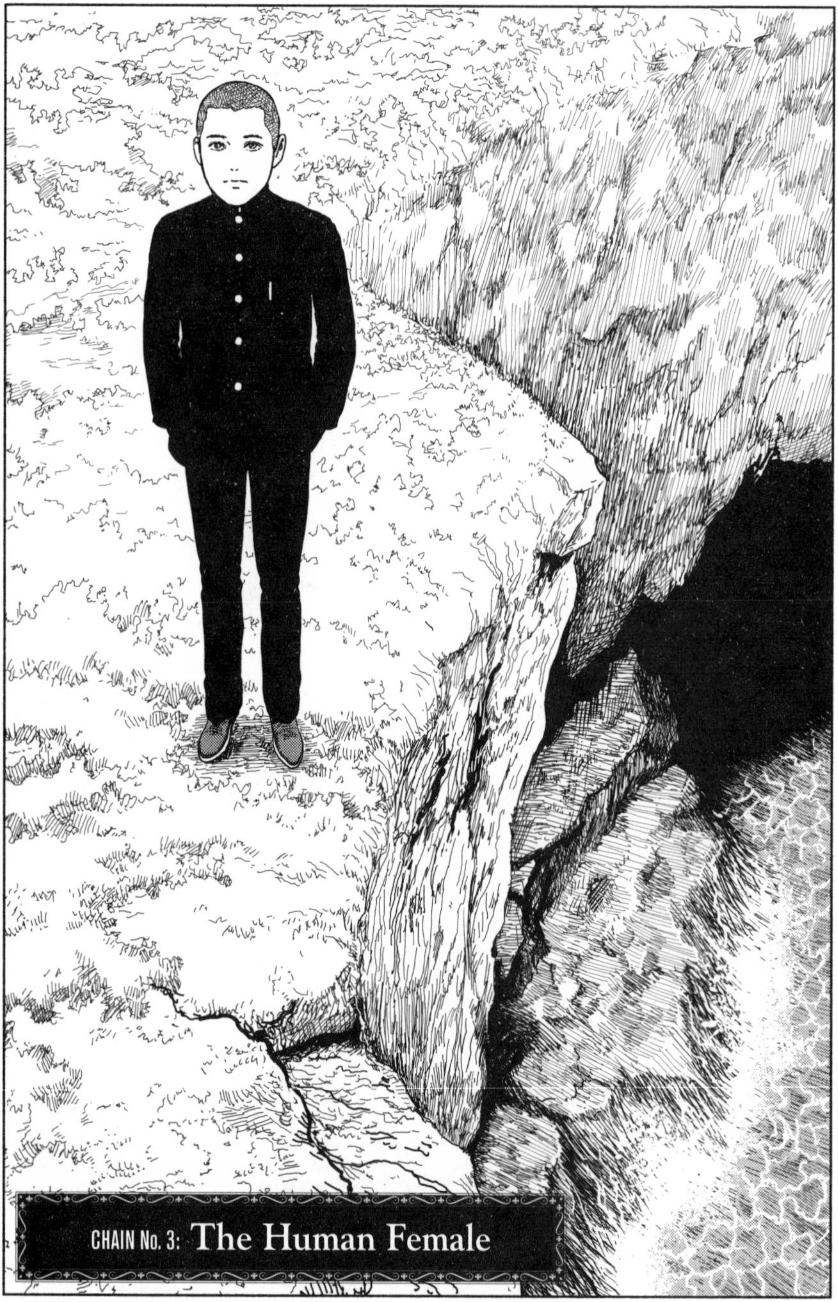
CHAIN No. 3: The Human Female

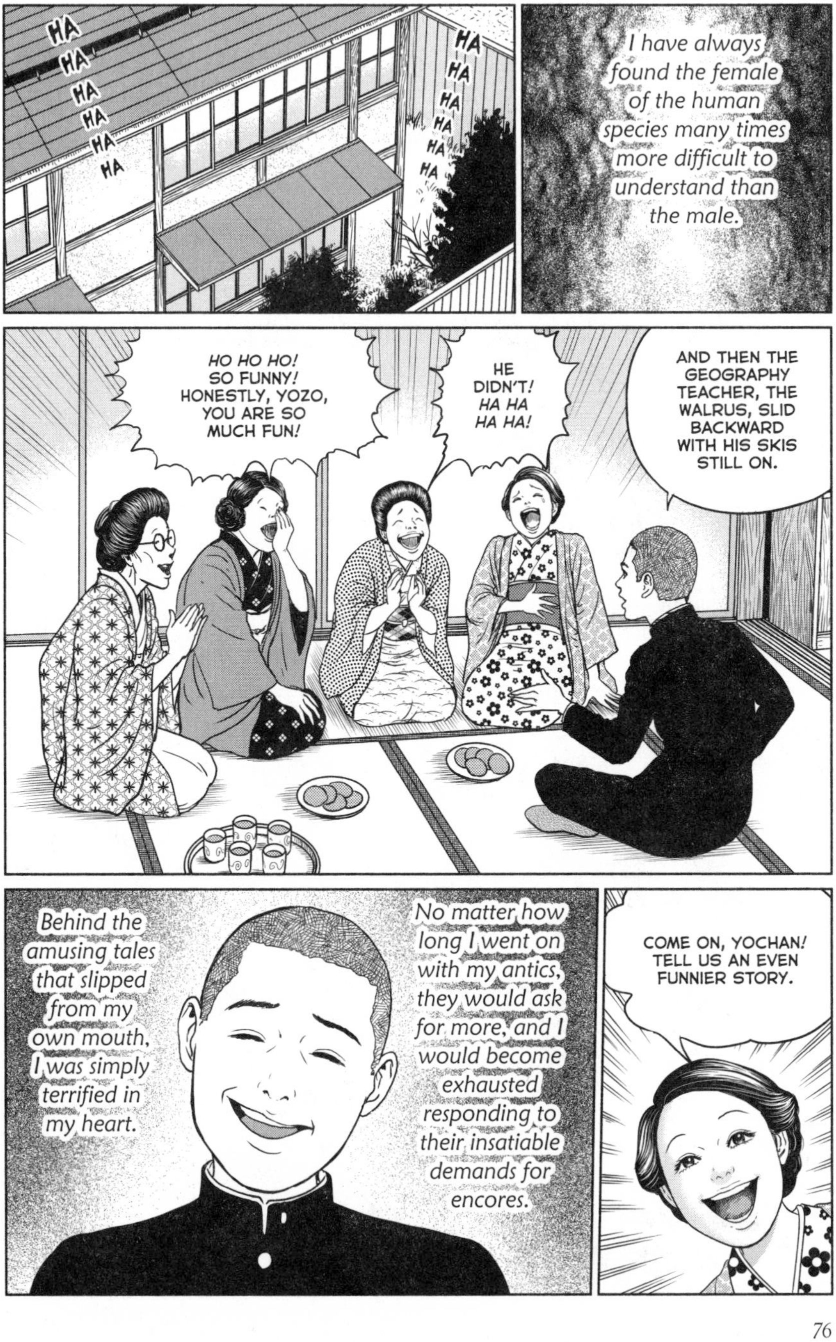
I have always found the female of the human species many times more difficult to understand than the male.
HA HA HA HA HA HA
HA HA HA HA HA HA
AND THEN THE GEOGRAPHY TEACHER, THE WALRUS, SLID BACKWARD WITH HIS SKIS STILL ON.
HE DIDN'T! HA HA HA HA!
HO HO HO! SO FUNNY! HONESTLY, YOZO, YOU ARE SO MUCH FUN!
COME ON, YOCHAN! TELL US AN EVEN FUNNIER STORY.
No matter how long I went on with my antics, they would ask for more, and I would become exhausted responding to their insatiable demands for encores.
Behind the amusing tales that slipped from my own mouth, I was simply terrified in my heart.

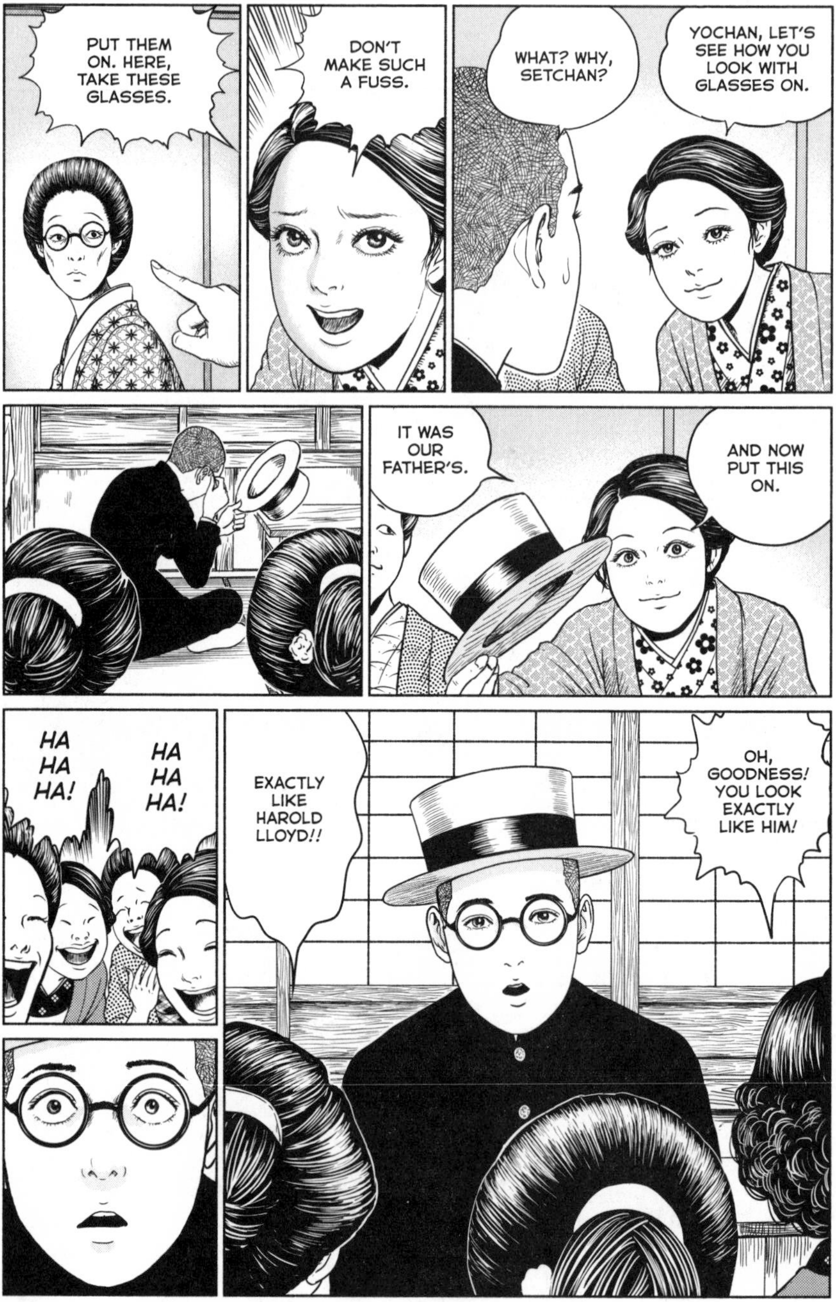
YOCHAN, LET'S SEE HOW YOU LOOK WITH GLASSES ON.
WHAT? WHY, SETCHAN?
DON'T MAKE SUCH A FUSS.
PUT THEM ON. HERE, TAKE THESE GLASSES.
AND NOW PUT THIS ON.
IT WAS OUR FATHER'S.
OH, GOODNESS! YOU LOOK EXACTLY LIKE HIM!
EXACTLY LIKE HAROLD LLOYD!!
HA HA HA!
HA HA HA!

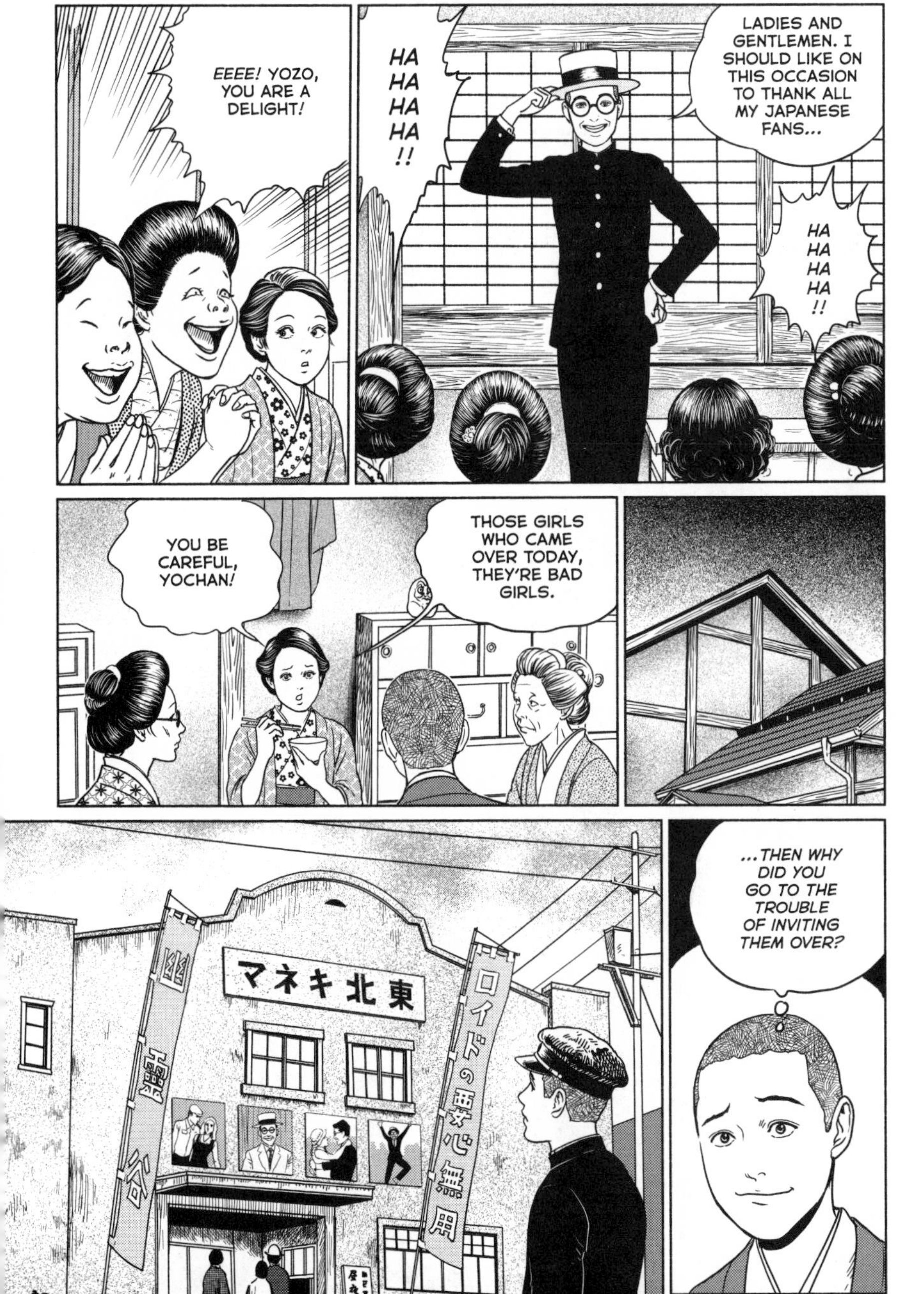
LADIES AND GENTLEMEN. I SHOULD LIKE ON THIS OCCASION TO THANK ALL MY JAPANESE FANS...
HA HA HA HA !!
HA HA HA HA !!
EEEE! YOZO, YOU ARE A DELIGHT!
THOSE GIRLS WHO CAME OVER TODAY, THEY'RE BAD GIRLS.
YOU BE CAREFUL, YOCHAN!
...THEN WHY DID YOU GO TO THE TROUBLE OF INVITING THEM OVER?
東北キネマ
ロイドの要心無用
幽霊谷

*Sign: Tohoku Cinema
Banners: *Harold Lloyd in Safety Last!*, *Haunted Valley*

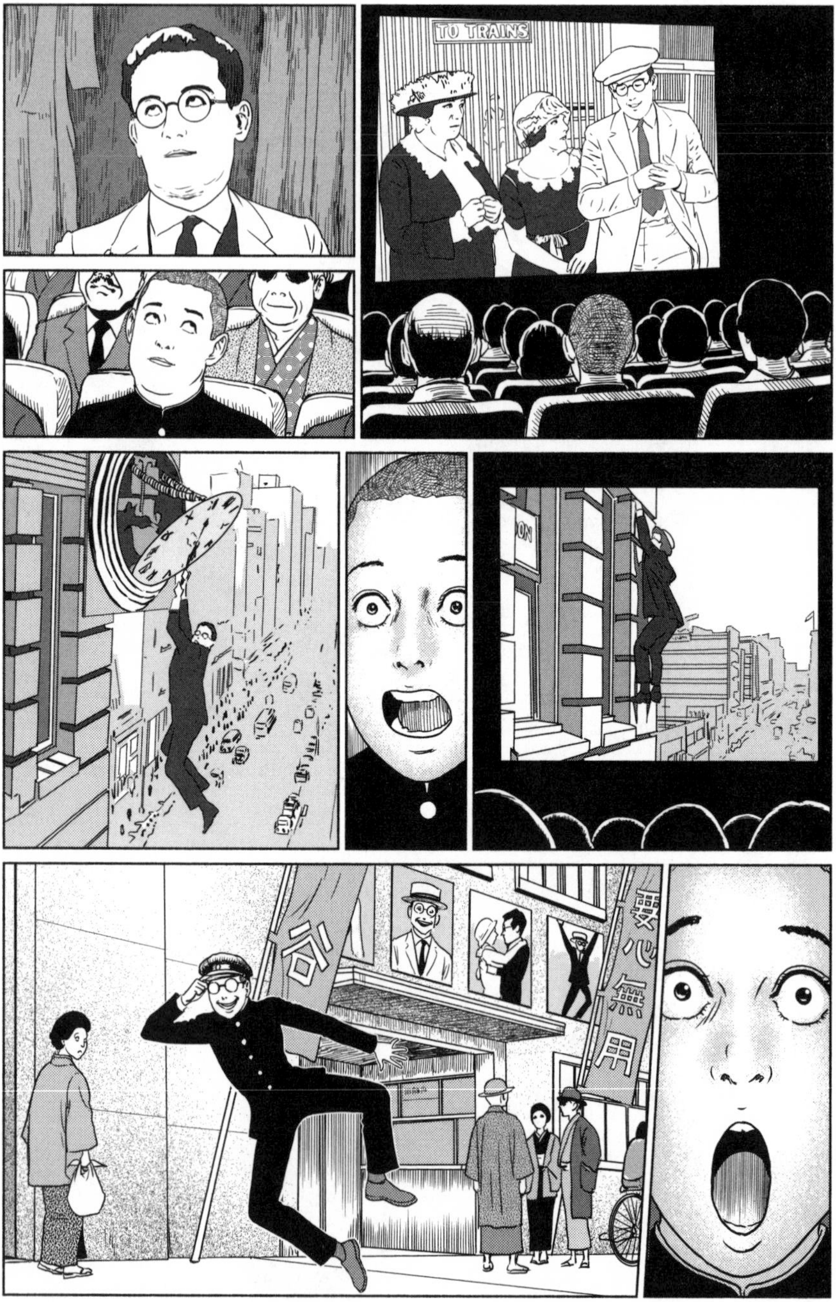
TO TRAINS
ON
要心無用
谷

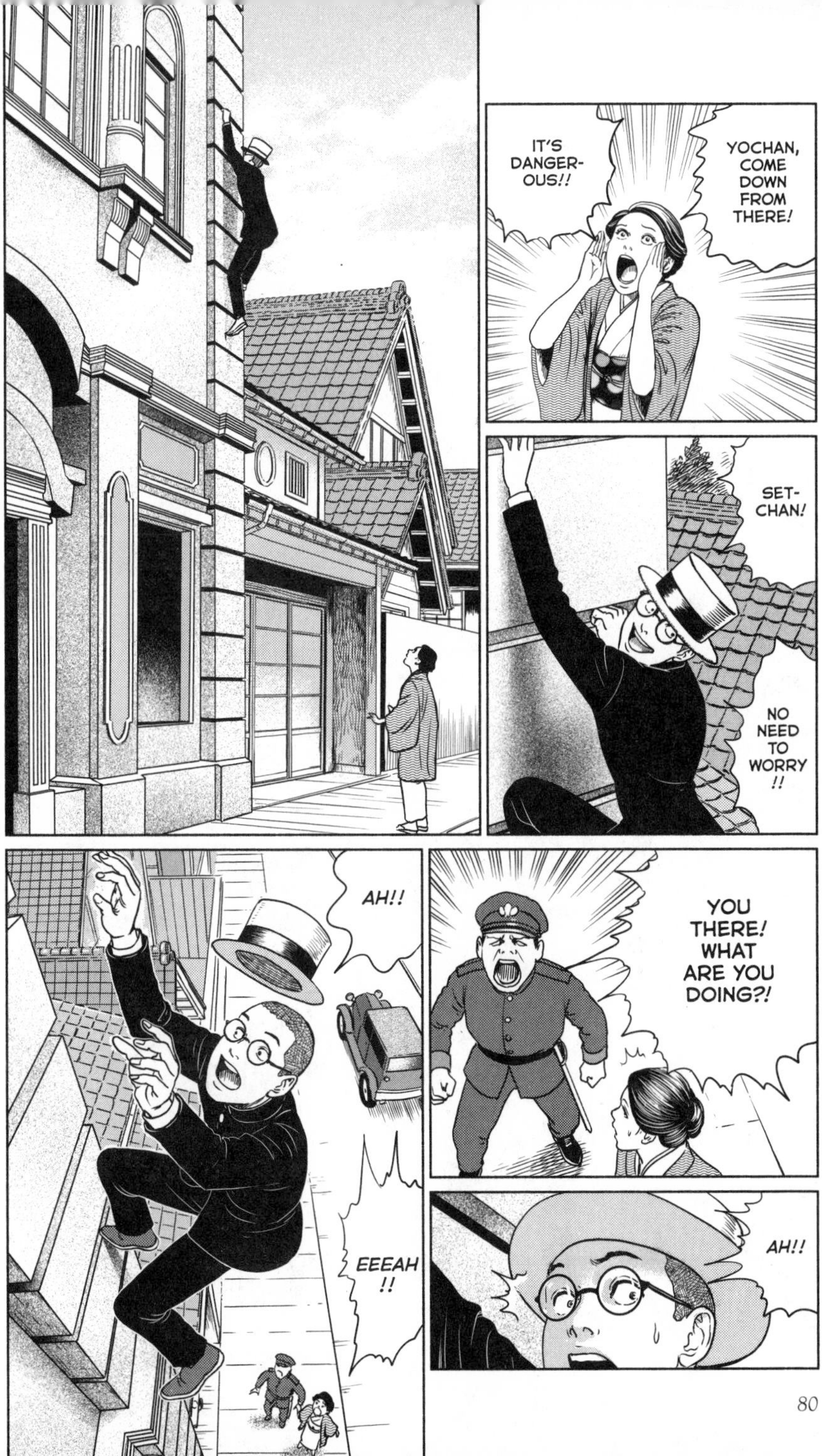
YOCHAN, COME DOWN FROM THERE!
IT'S DANGER-OUS!!
SET-CHAN!
NO NEED TO WORRY!!
YOU THERE! WHAT ARE YOU DOING?!
AH!!
AH!!
EEEAH!!

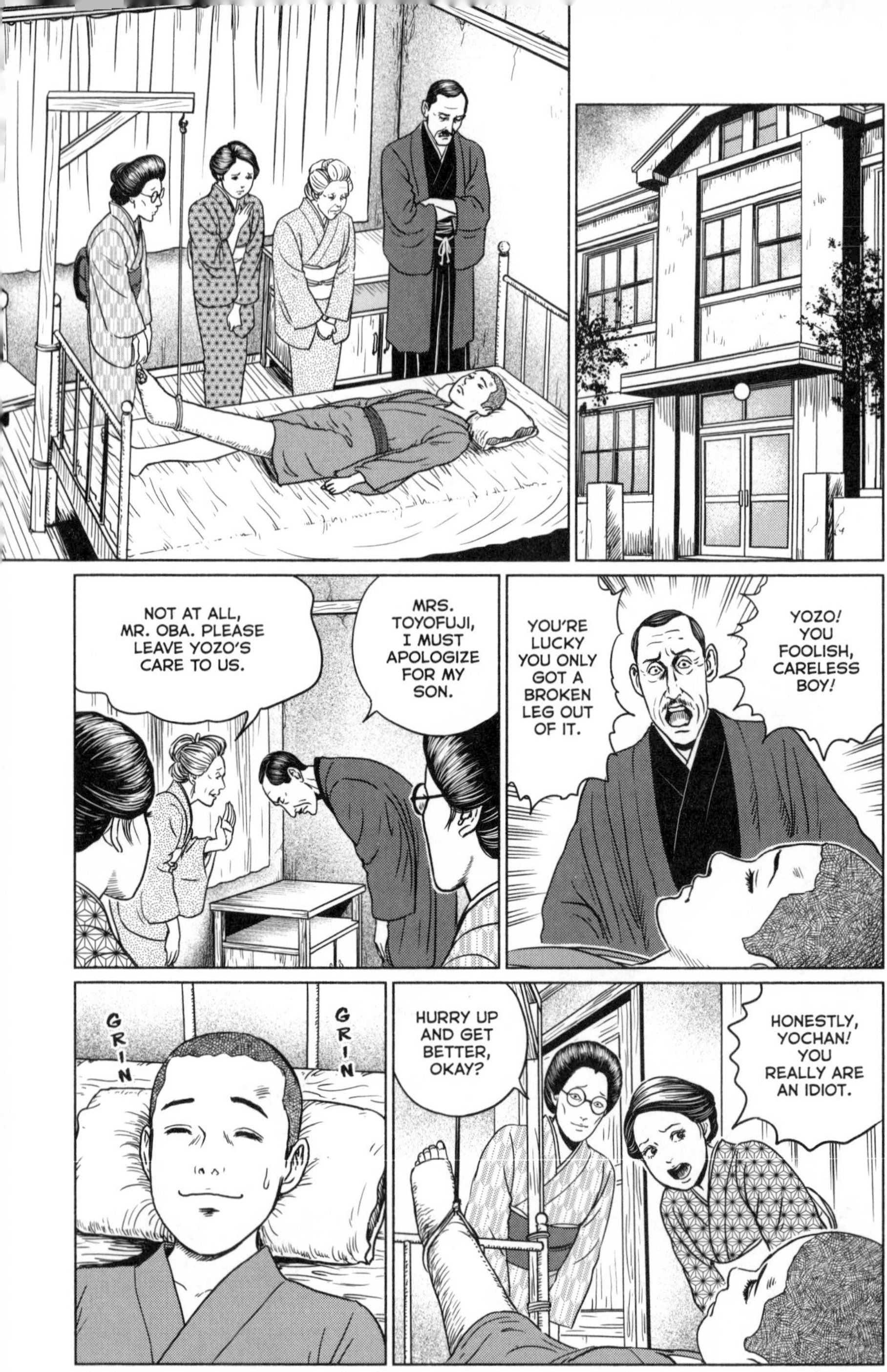
YOZO! YOU FOOLISH, CARELESS BOY!
YOU'RE LUCKY YOU ONLY GOT A BROKEN LEG OUT OF IT.
MRS. TOYOFUJI, I MUST APOLOGIZE FOR MY SON.
NOT AT ALL, MR. OBA. PLEASE LEAVE YOZO'S CARE TO US.
HONESTLY, YOCHAN! YOU REALLY ARE AN IDIOT.
HURRY UP AND GET BETTER, OKAY?
GRIN
GRIN

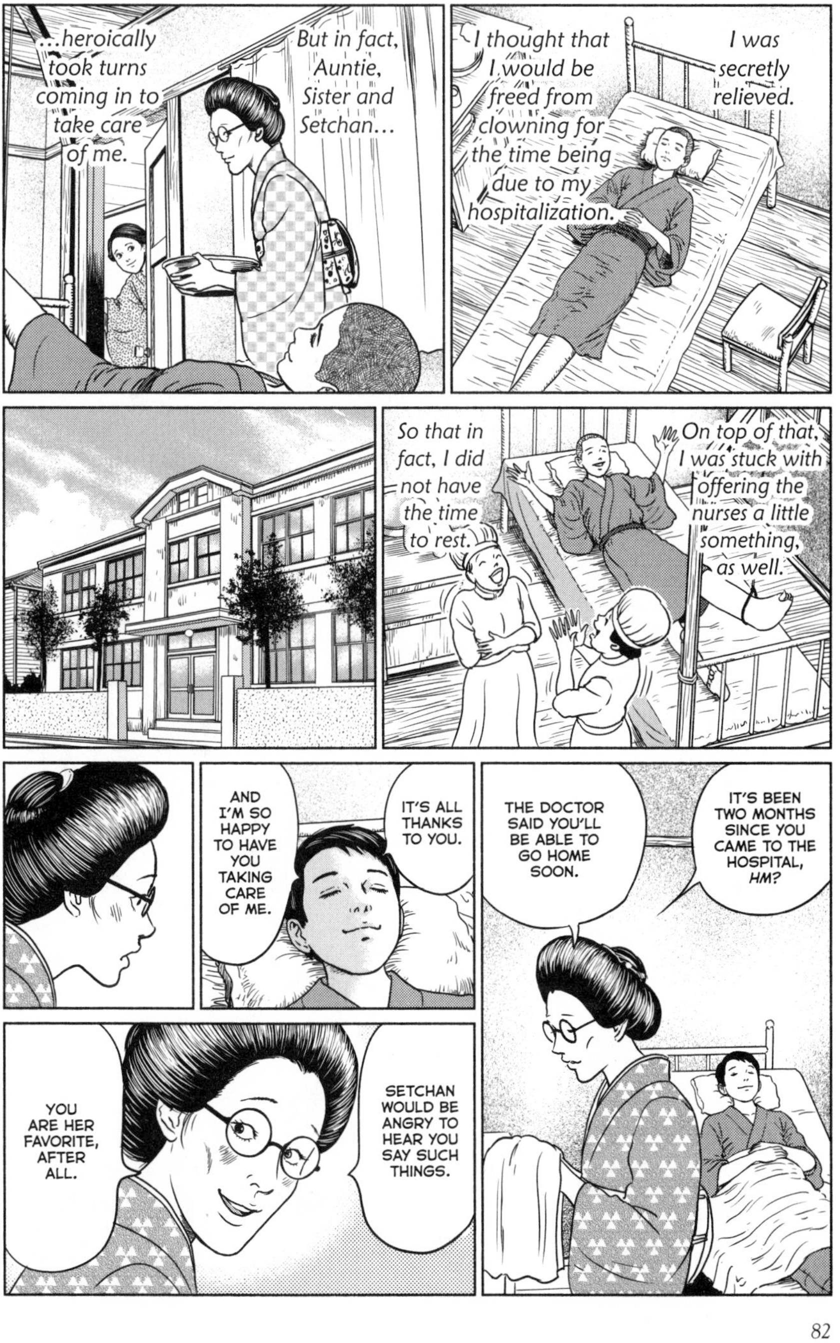
I was secretly relieved.
I thought that I would be freed from clowning for the time being due to my hospitalization.
But in fact, Auntie, Sister and Setchan…
…heroically took turns coming in to take care of me.
On top of that, I was stuck with offering the nurses a little something, as well.
So that in fact, I did not have the time to rest.
IT'S BEEN TWO MONTHS SINCE YOU CAME TO THE HOSPITAL, *HM?*
THE DOCTOR SAID YOU'LL BE ABLE TO GO HOME SOON.
IT'S ALL THANKS TO YOU.
AND I'M SO HAPPY TO HAVE YOU TAKING CARE OF ME.
SETCHAN WOULD BE ANGRY TO HEAR YOU SAY SUCH THINGS.
YOU ARE HER FAVORITE, AFTER ALL.

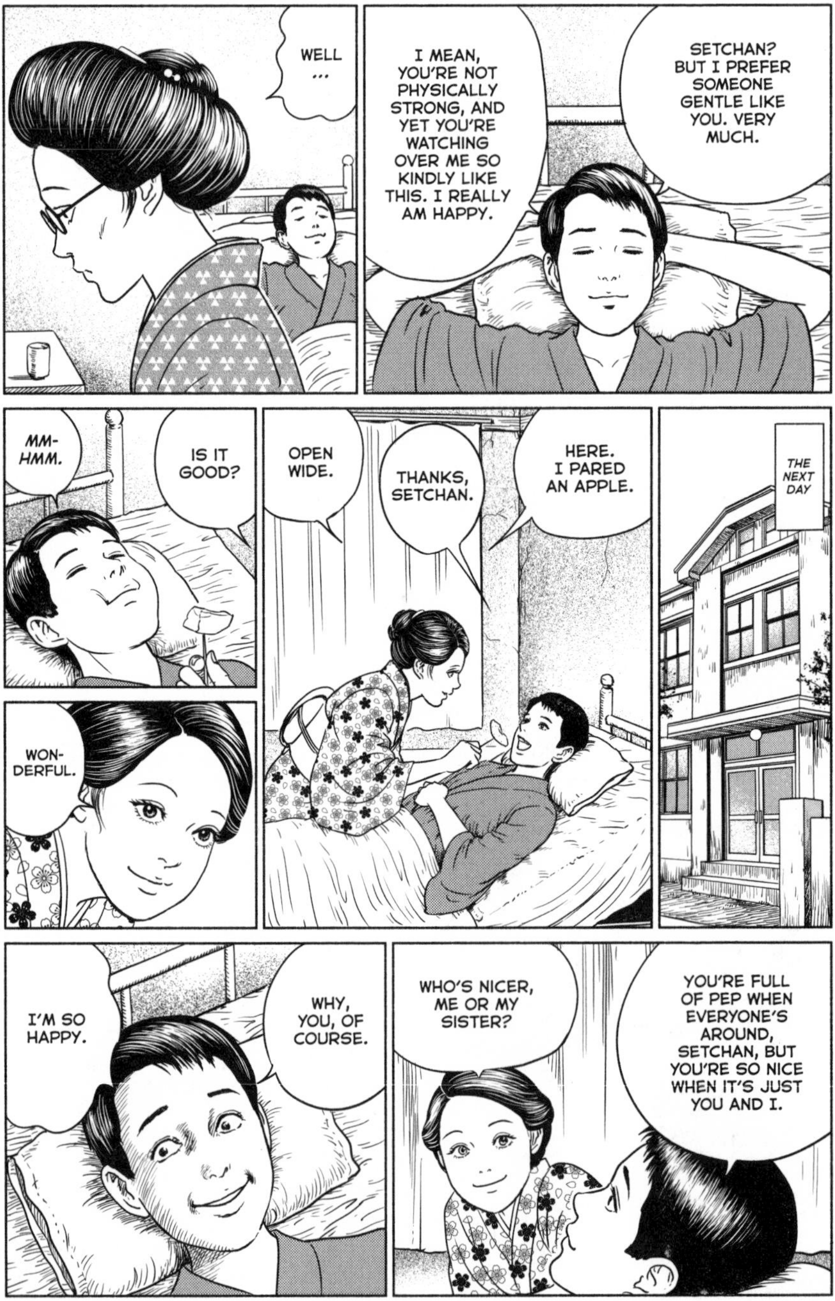
SETCHAN? BUT I PREFER SOMEONE GENTLE LIKE YOU. VERY MUCH.
I MEAN, YOU'RE NOT PHYSICALLY STRONG, AND YET YOU'RE WATCHING OVER ME SO KINDLY LIKE THIS. I REALLY AM HAPPY.
WELL ...
THE NEXT DAY
HERE. I PARED AN APPLE.
THANKS, SETCHAN.
OPEN WIDE.
IS IT GOOD?
MM-HMM.
WON-DERFUL.
YOU'RE FULL OF PEP WHEN EVERYONE'S AROUND, SETCHAN, BUT YOU'RE SO NICE WHEN IT'S JUST YOU AND I.
WHO'S NICER, ME OR MY SISTER?
WHY, YOU, OF COURSE.
I'M SO HAPPY.

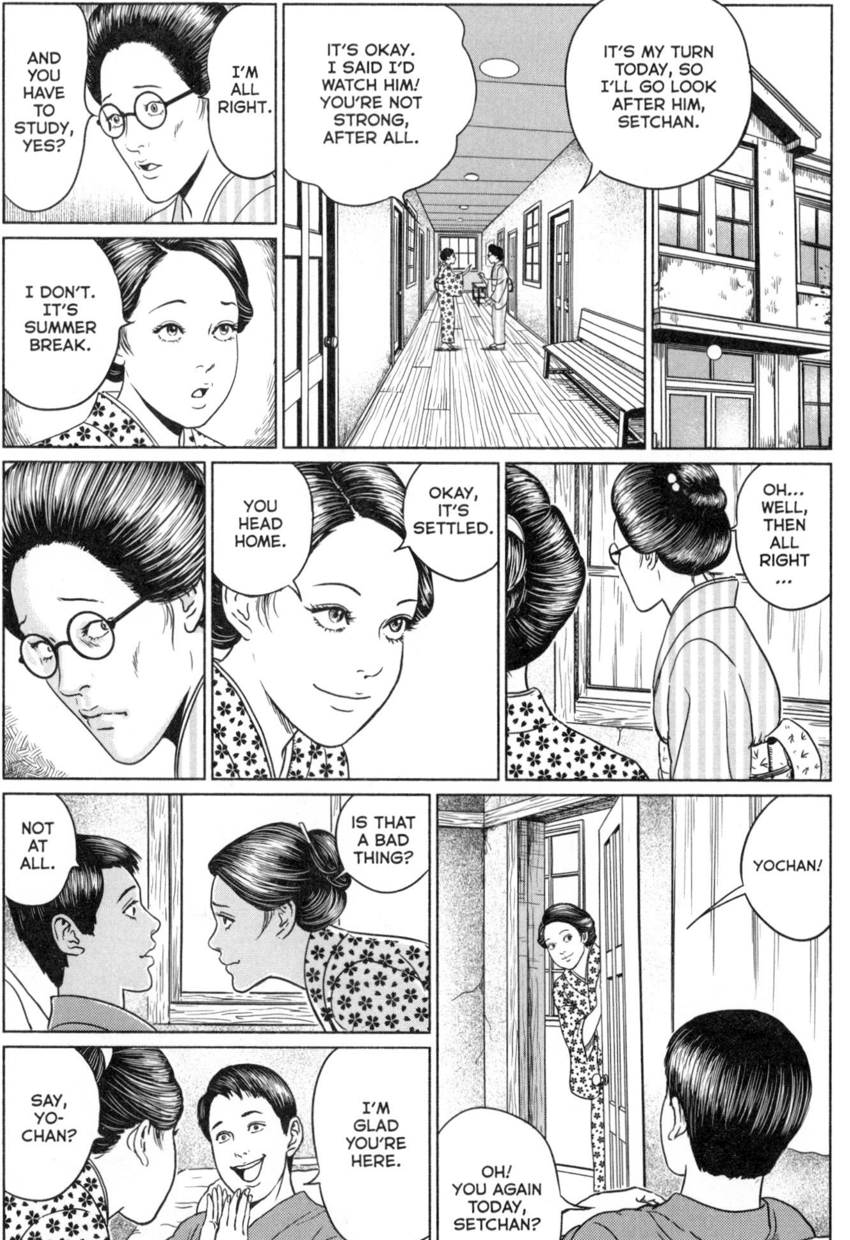
IT'S MY TURN TODAY, SO I'LL GO LOOK AFTER HIM, SETCHAN.
IT'S OKAY. I SAID I'D WATCH HIM! YOU'RE NOT STRONG, AFTER ALL.
I'M ALL RIGHT.
AND YOU HAVE TO STUDY, YES?
I DON'T. IT'S SUMMER BREAK.
OH... WELL, THEN ALL RIGHT ...
OKAY, IT'S SETTLED.
YOU HEAD HOME.
YOCHAN!
OH! YOU AGAIN TODAY, SETCHAN?
IS THAT A BAD THING?
NOT AT ALL.
I'M GLAD YOU'RE HERE.
SAY, YO-CHAN?

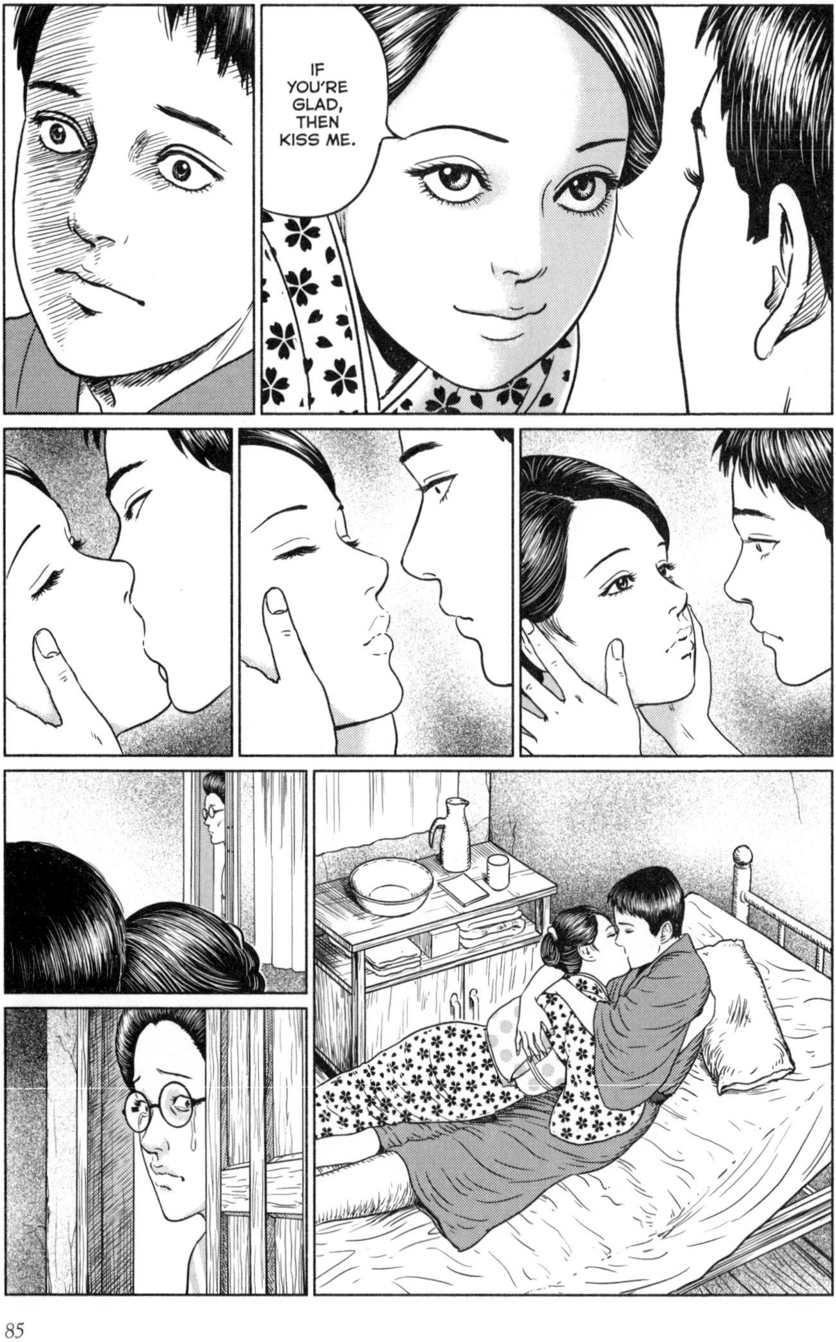
IF YOU'RE GLAD, THEN KISS ME.

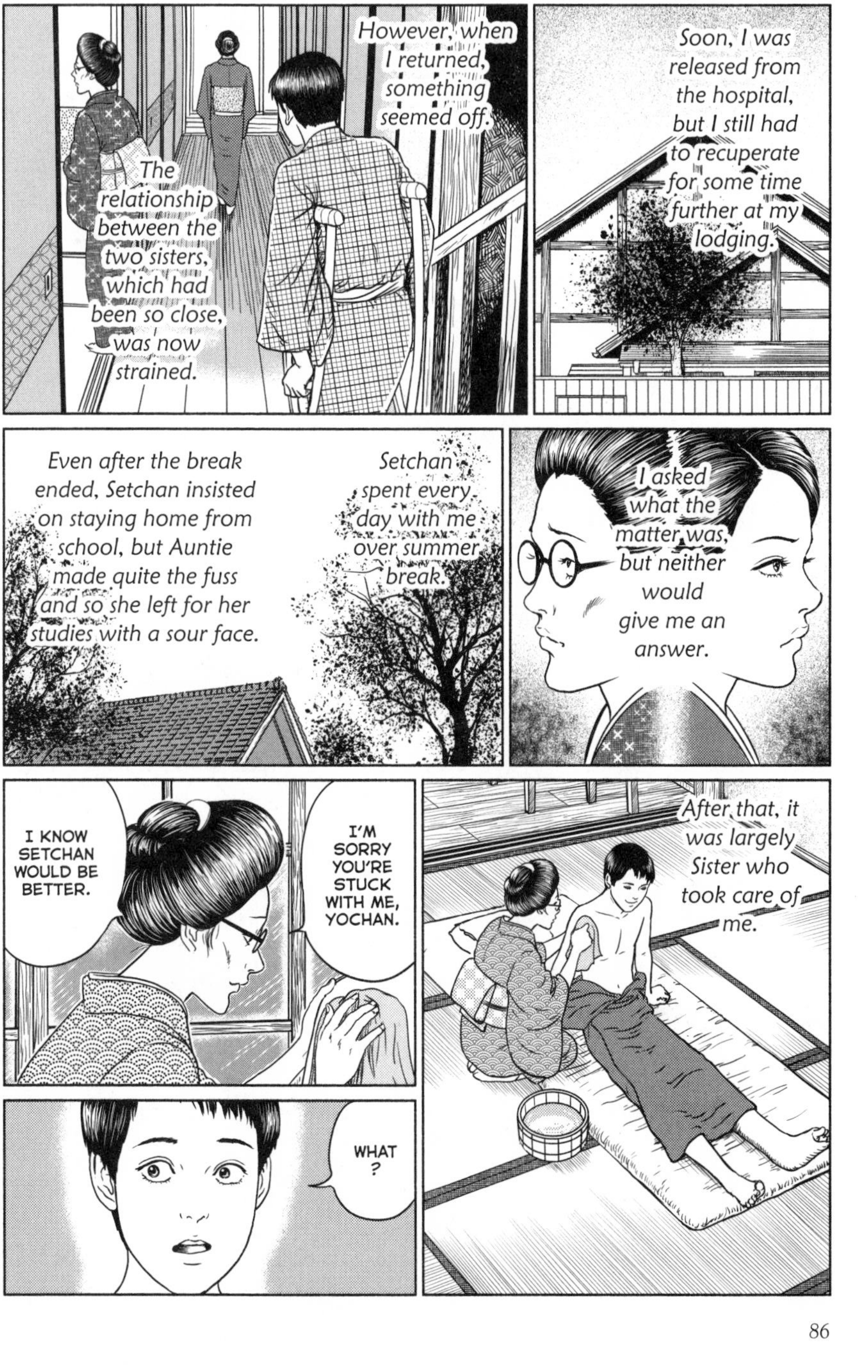
Soon, I was released from the hospital, but I still had to recuperate for some time further at my lodging.
However, when I returned, something seemed off.
The relationship between the two sisters, which had been so close, was now strained.
I asked what the matter was, but neither would give me an answer.
Setchan spent every day with me over summer break.
Even after the break ended, Setchan insisted on staying home from school, but Auntie made quite the fuss and so she left for her studies with a sour face.
After that, it was largely Sister who took care of me.
I'M SORRY YOU'RE STUCK WITH ME, YOCHAN.
I KNOW SETCHAN WOULD BE BETTER.
WHAT?

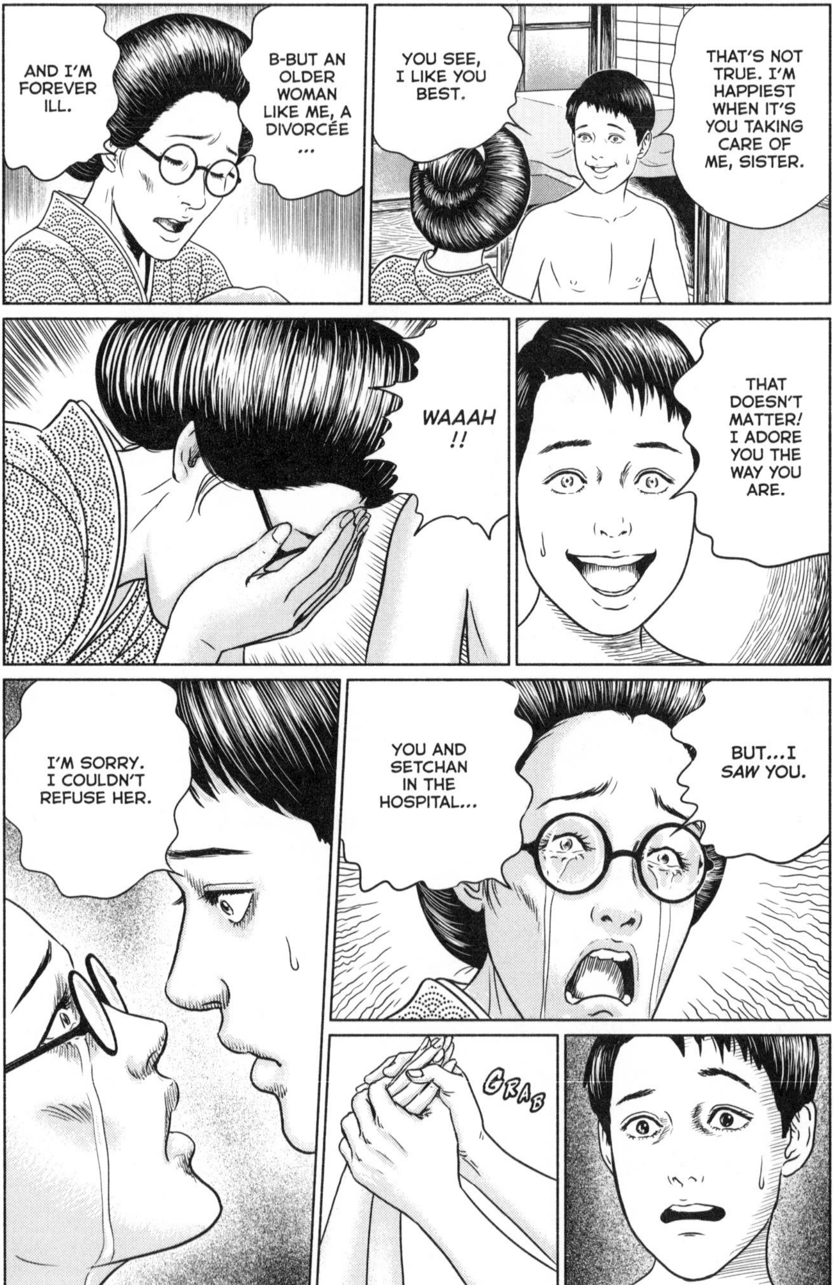
THAT'S NOT TRUE. I'M HAPPIEST WHEN IT'S YOU TAKING CARE OF ME, SISTER.
YOU SEE, I LIKE YOU BEST.
B-BUT AN OLDER WOMAN LIKE ME, A DIVORCÉE ...
AND I'M FOREVER ILL.
THAT DOESN'T MATTER! I ADORE YOU THE WAY YOU ARE.
WAAAH !!
BUT...I *SAW* YOU.
YOU AND SETCHAN IN THE HOSPITAL...
GRAB
I'M SORRY. I COULDN'T REFUSE HER.

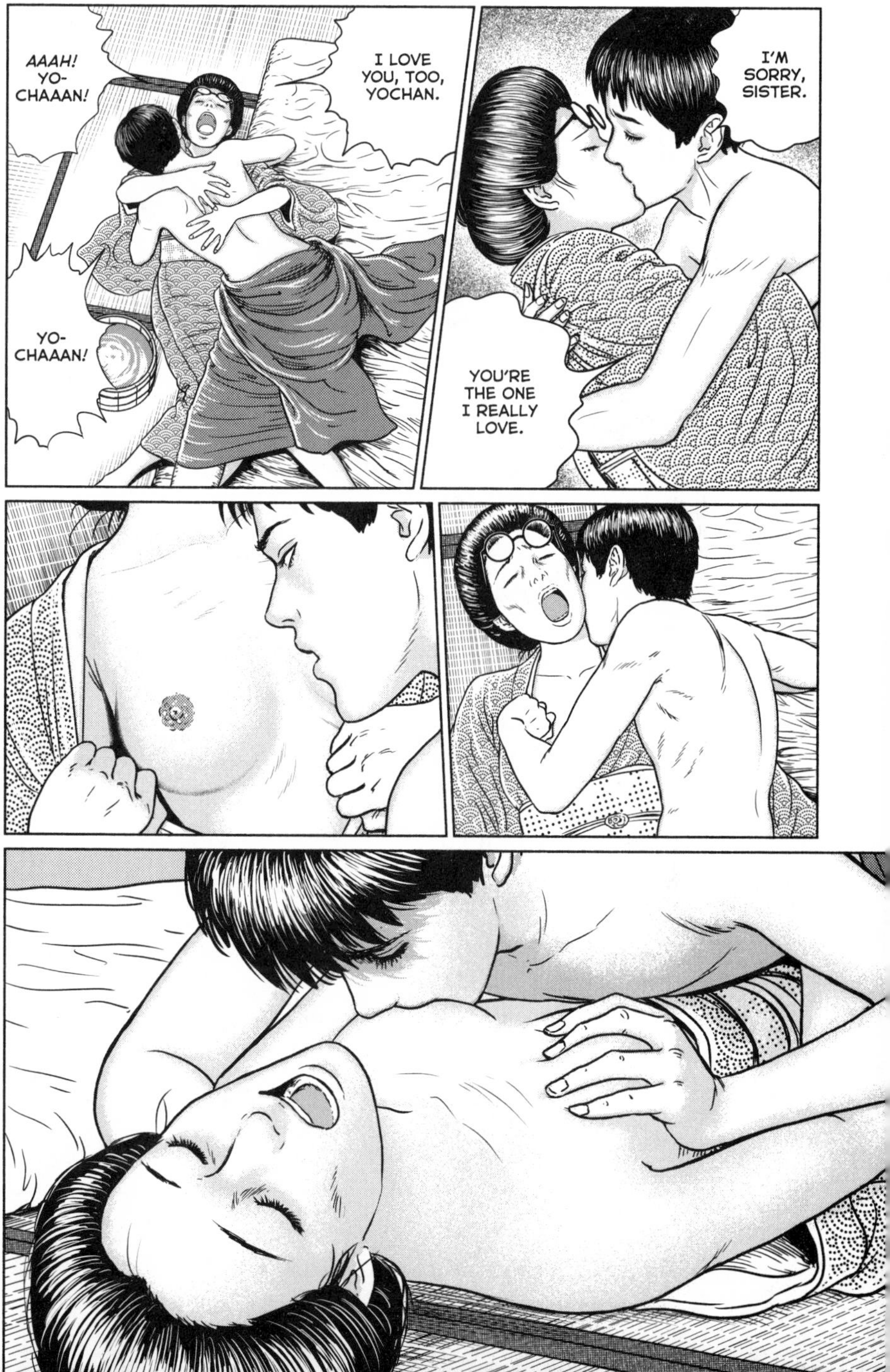
I'M SORRY, SISTER.
YOU'RE THE ONE I REALLY LOVE.
I LOVE YOU, TOO, YOCHAN.
AAAH! YO-CHAAAN!
YO-CHAAAN!

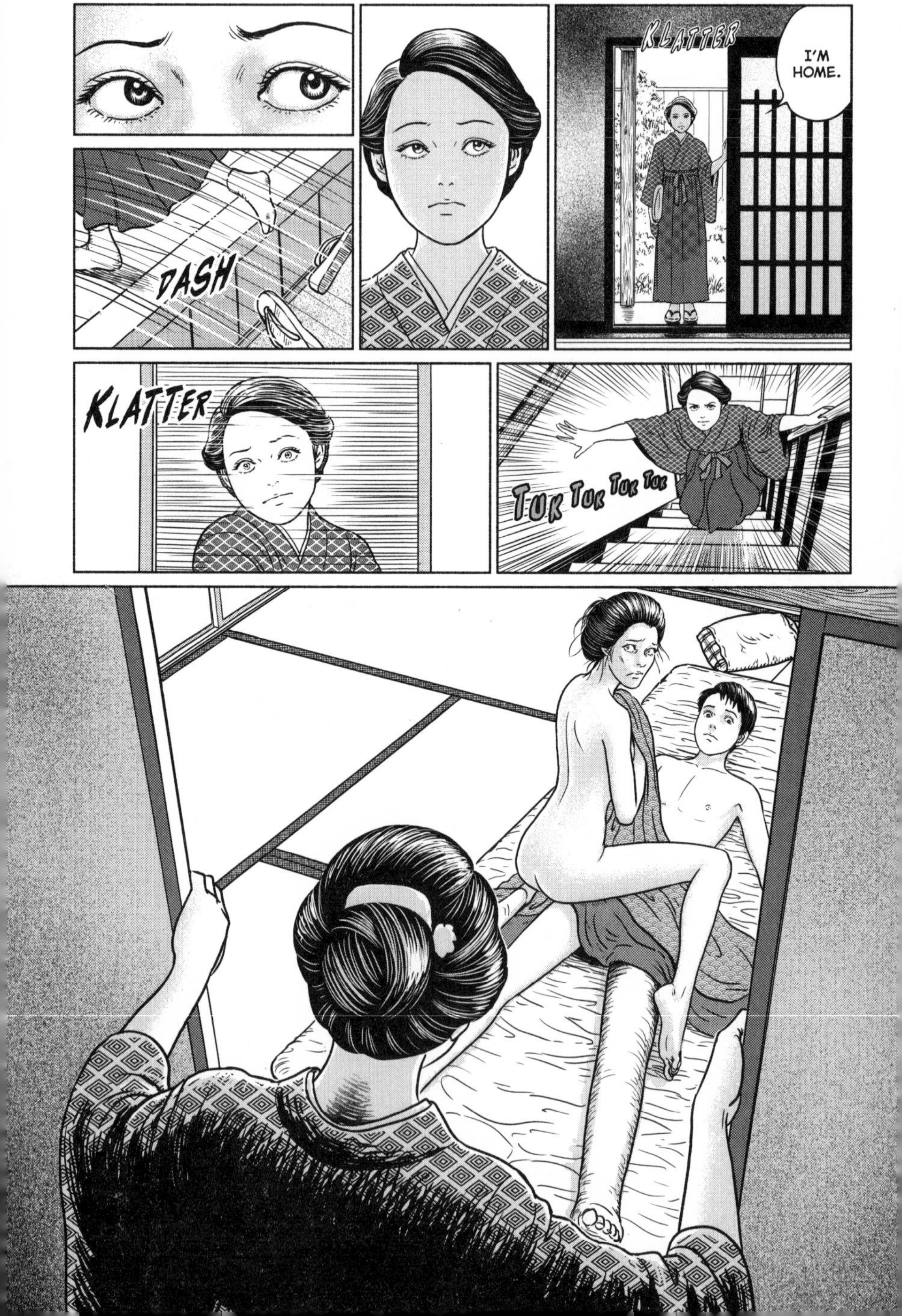
KLATTER
I'M HOME.
DASH
TUK TUK TUK TUK
KLATTER

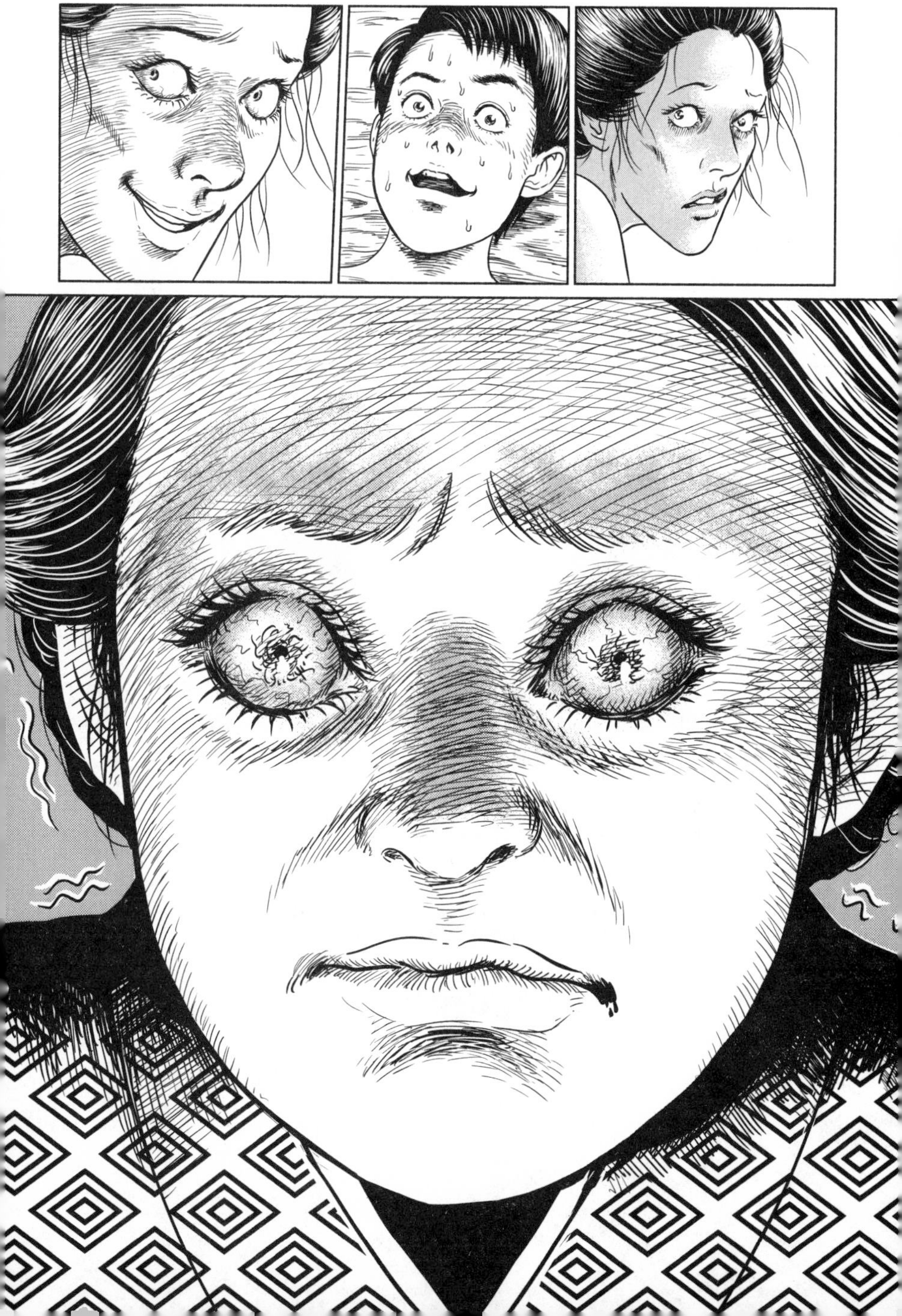

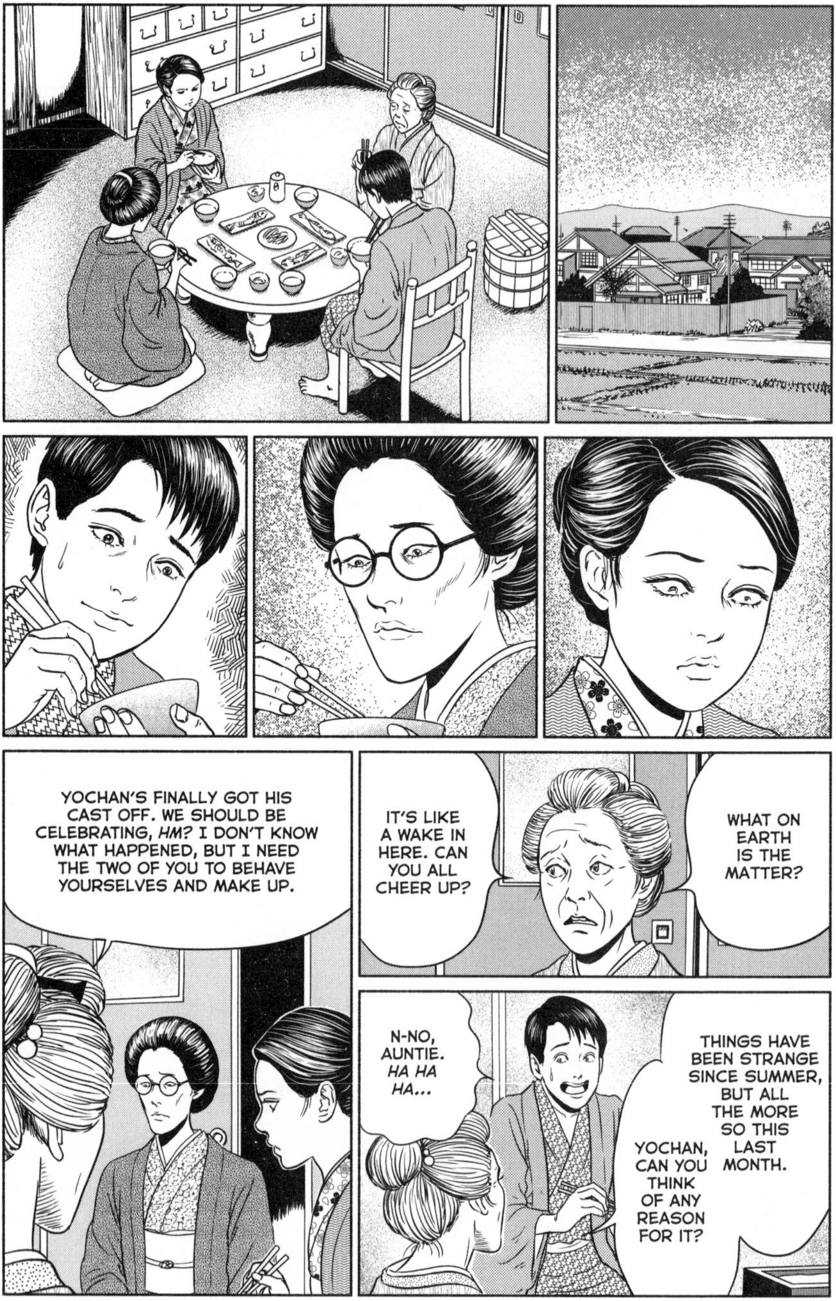
WHAT ON EARTH IS THE MATTER?
IT'S LIKE A WAKE IN HERE. CAN YOU ALL CHEER UP?
THINGS HAVE BEEN STRANGE SINCE SUMMER, BUT ALL THE MORE SO THIS LAST MONTH.
YOCHAN, CAN YOU THINK OF ANY REASON FOR IT?
N-NO, AUNTIE. *HA HA HA...*
YOCHAN'S FINALLY GOT HIS CAST OFF. WE SHOULD BE CELEBRATING, *HM?* I DON'T KNOW WHAT HAPPENED, BUT I NEED THE TWO OF YOU TO BEHAVE YOURSELVES AND MAKE UP.

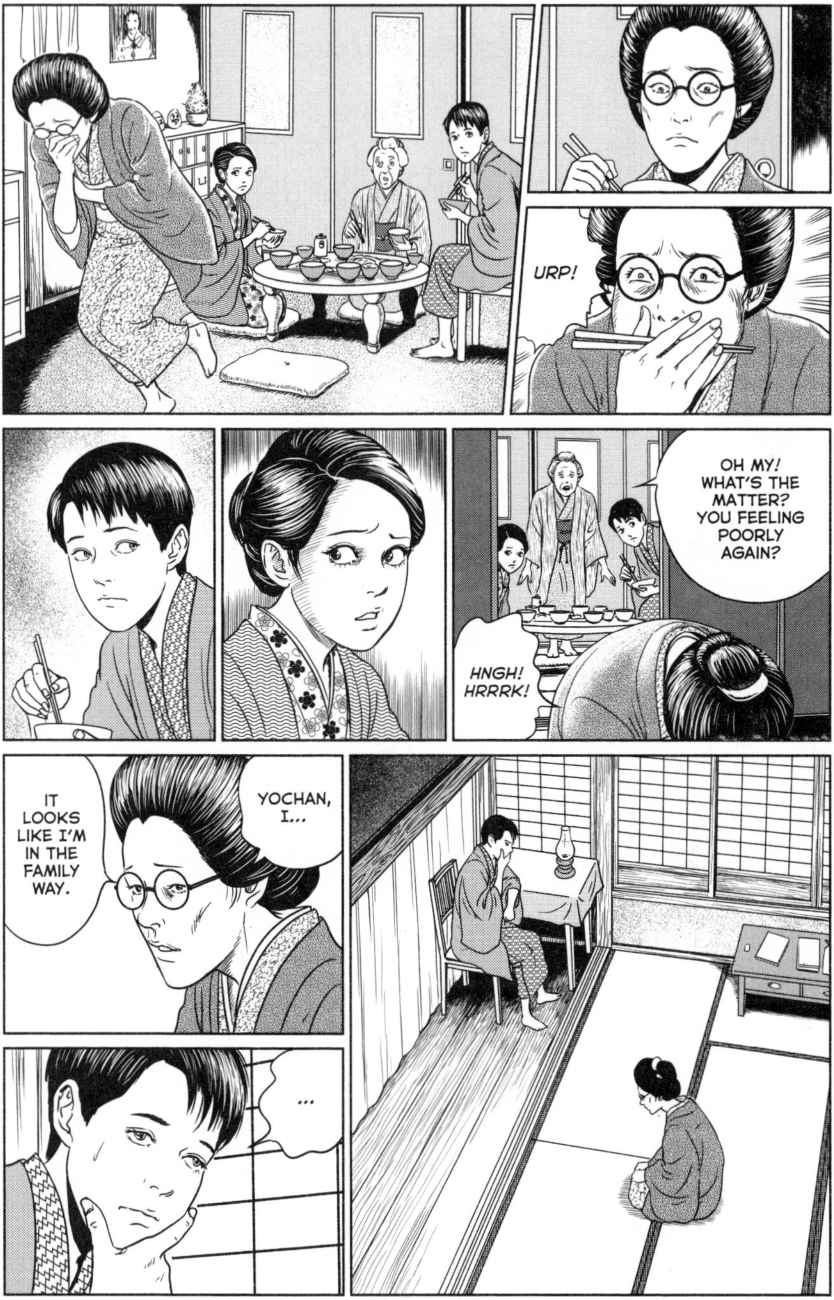
URP!
OH MY! WHAT'S THE MATTER? YOU FEELING POORLY AGAIN?
HNGH! HRRRK!
YOCHAN, I...
IT LOOKS LIKE I'M IN THE FAMILY WAY.
...

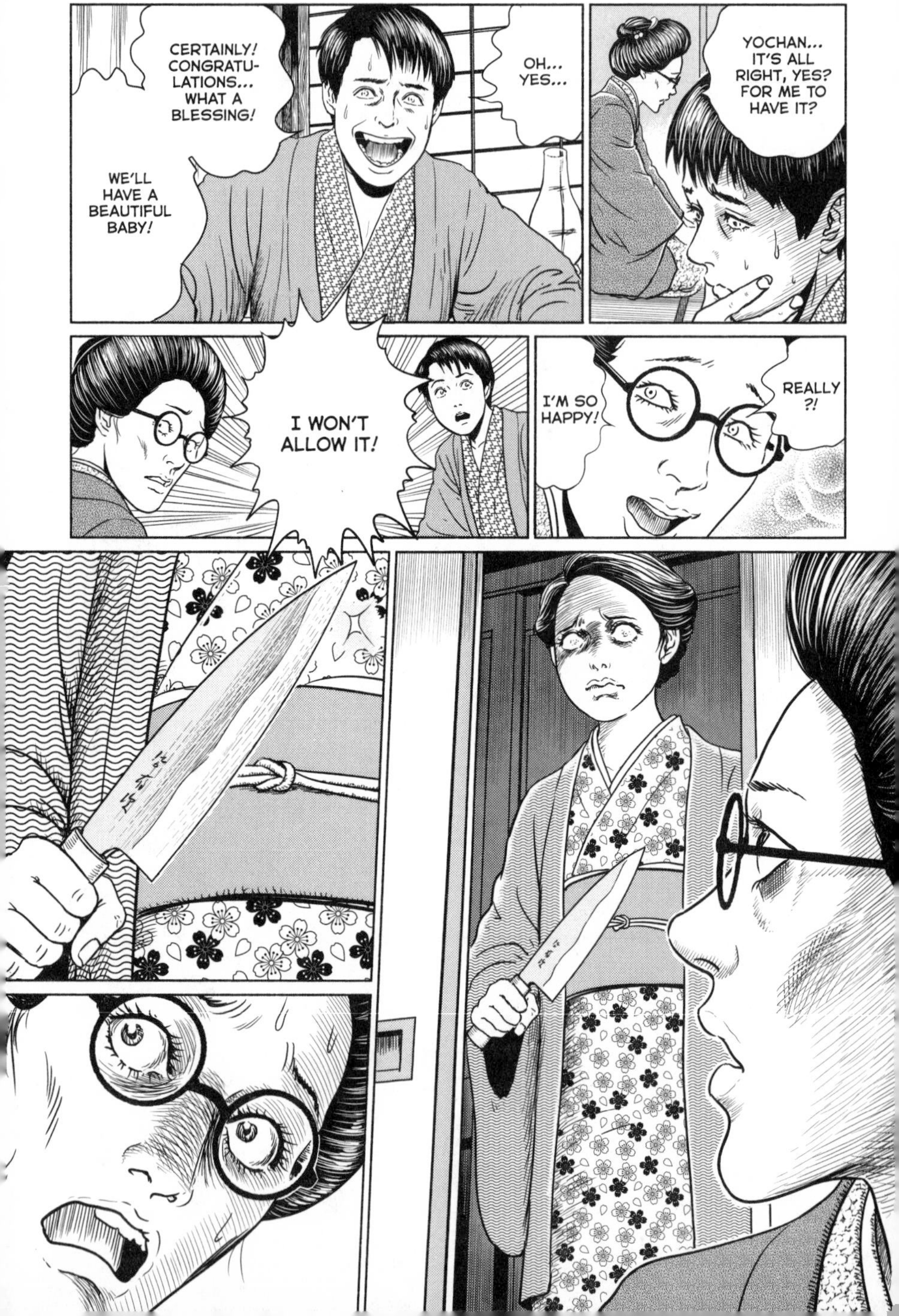
YOCHAN... IT'S ALL RIGHT, YES? FOR ME TO HAVE IT?
OH... YES...
CERTAINLY! CONGRATULATIONS... WHAT A BLESSING!
WE'LL HAVE A BEAUTIFUL BABY!
REALLY ?!
I'M SO HAPPY!
I WON'T ALLOW IT!

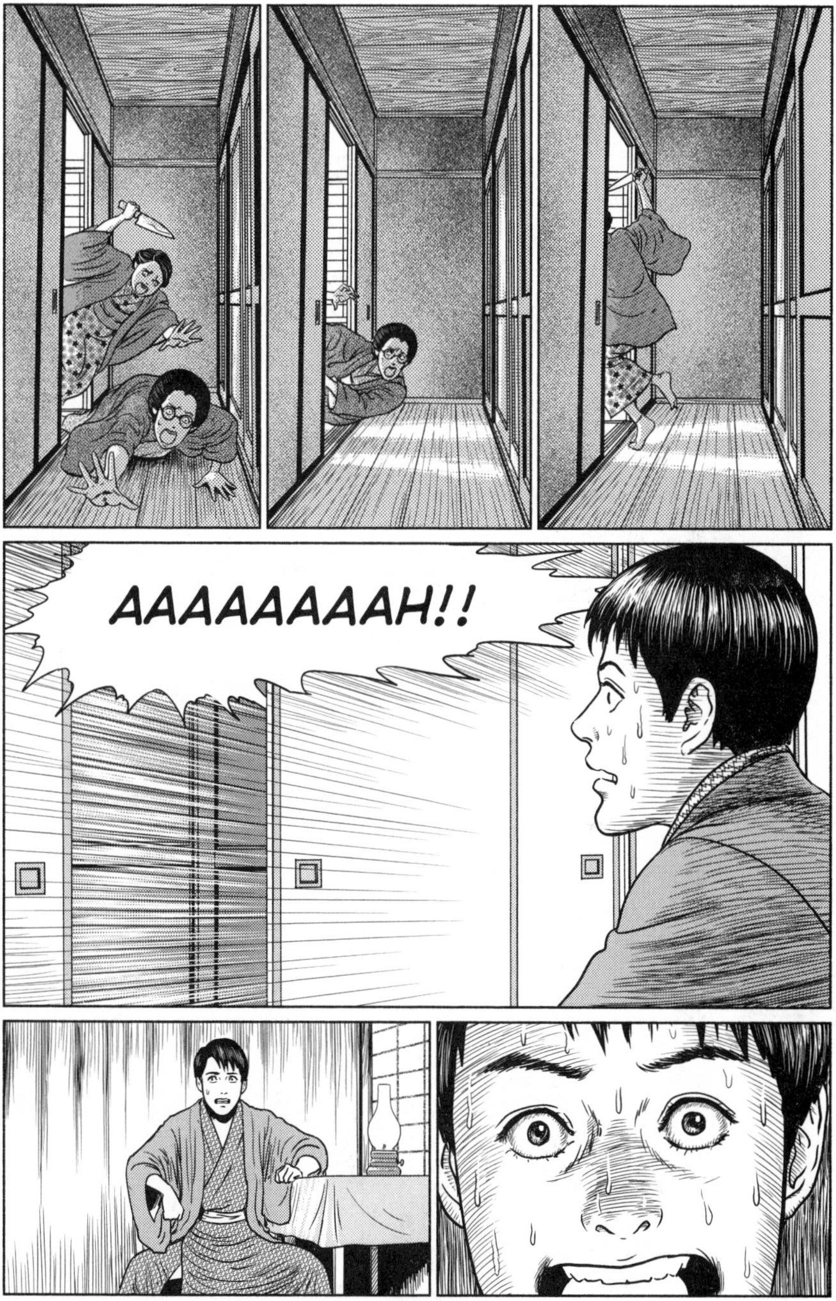
AAAAAAAAH!!

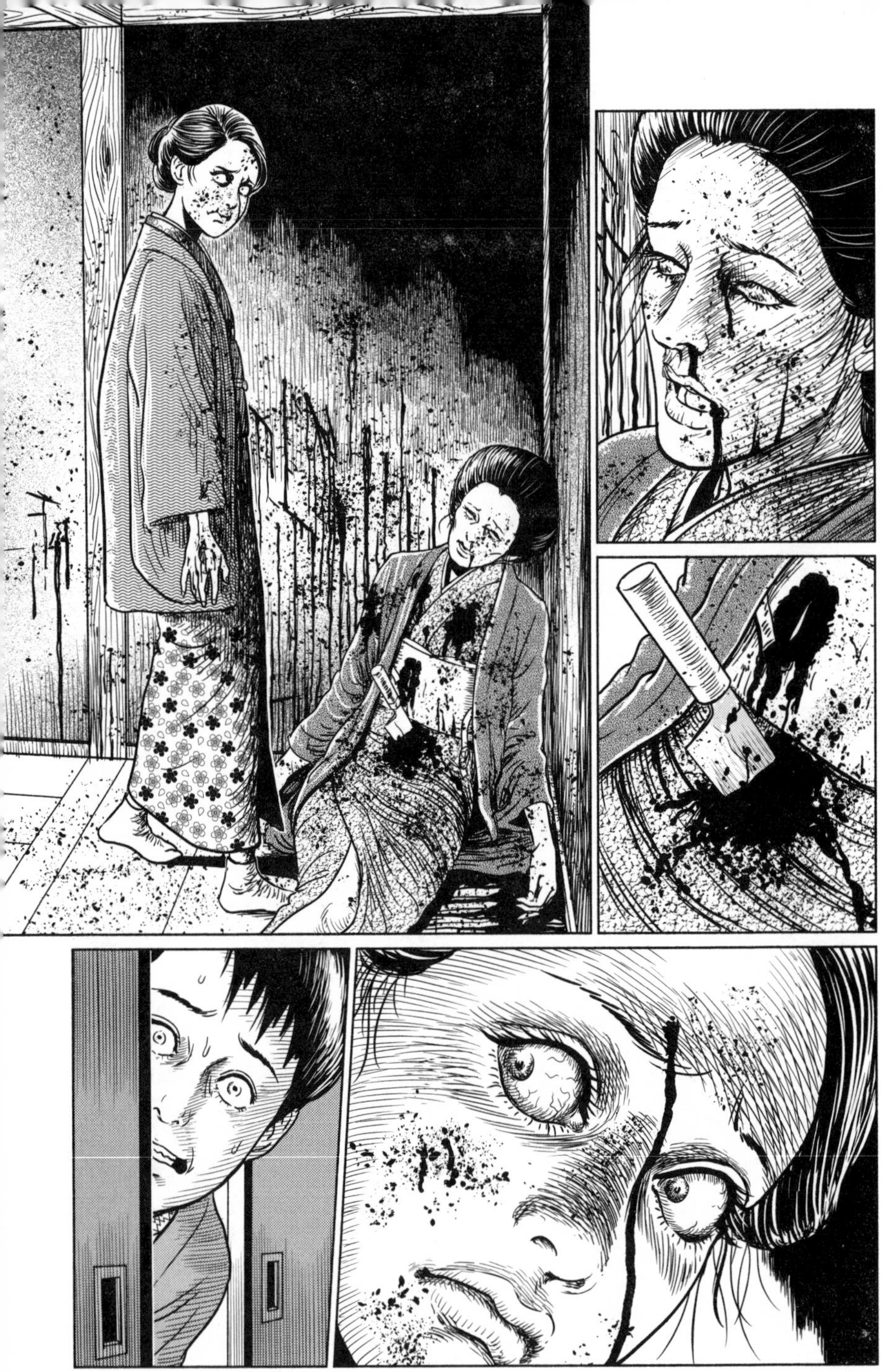

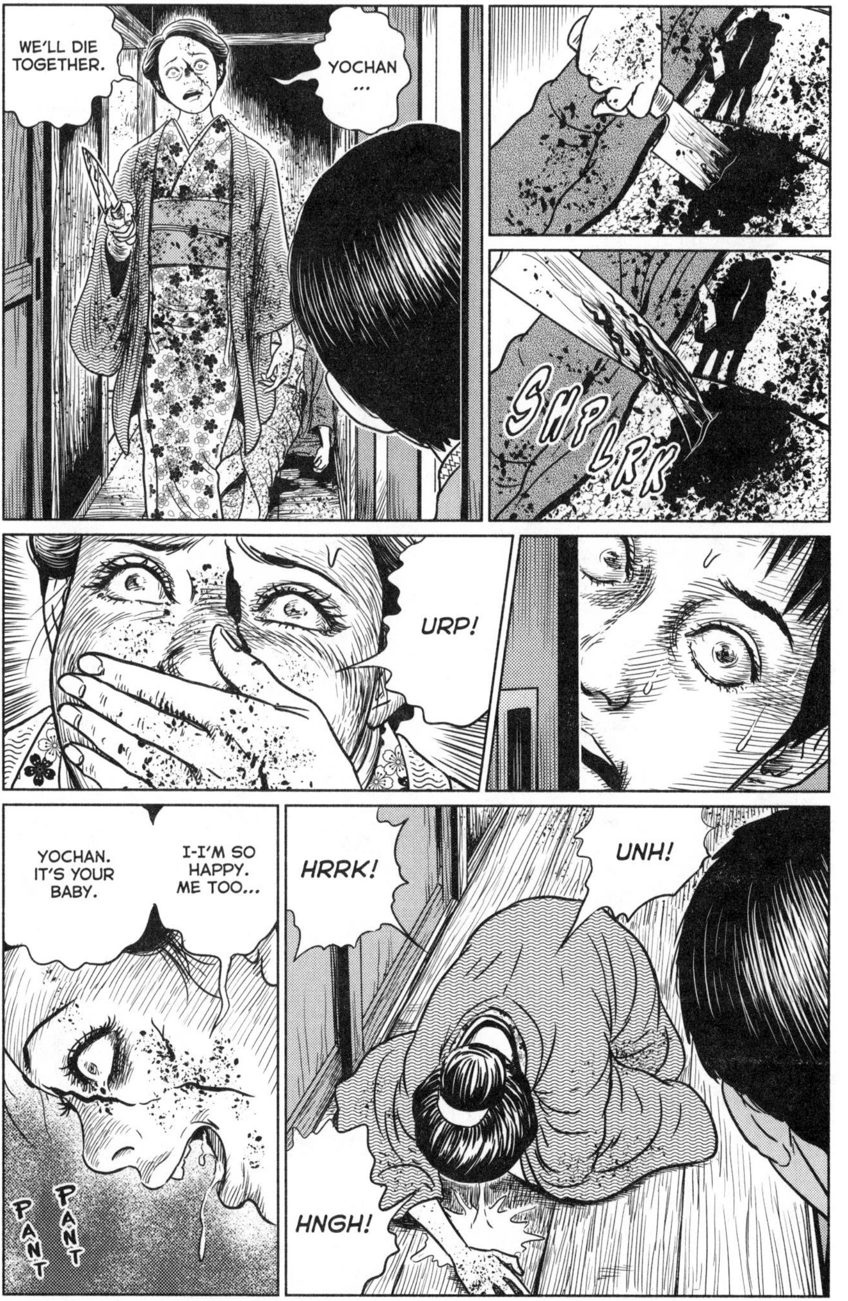
SHPLRK
YOCHAN ...
WE'LL DIE TOGETHER.
URP!
UNH!
HRRK!
HNGH!
I-I'M SO HAPPY. ME TOO...
YOCHAN. IT'S YOUR BABY.
PANT PANT

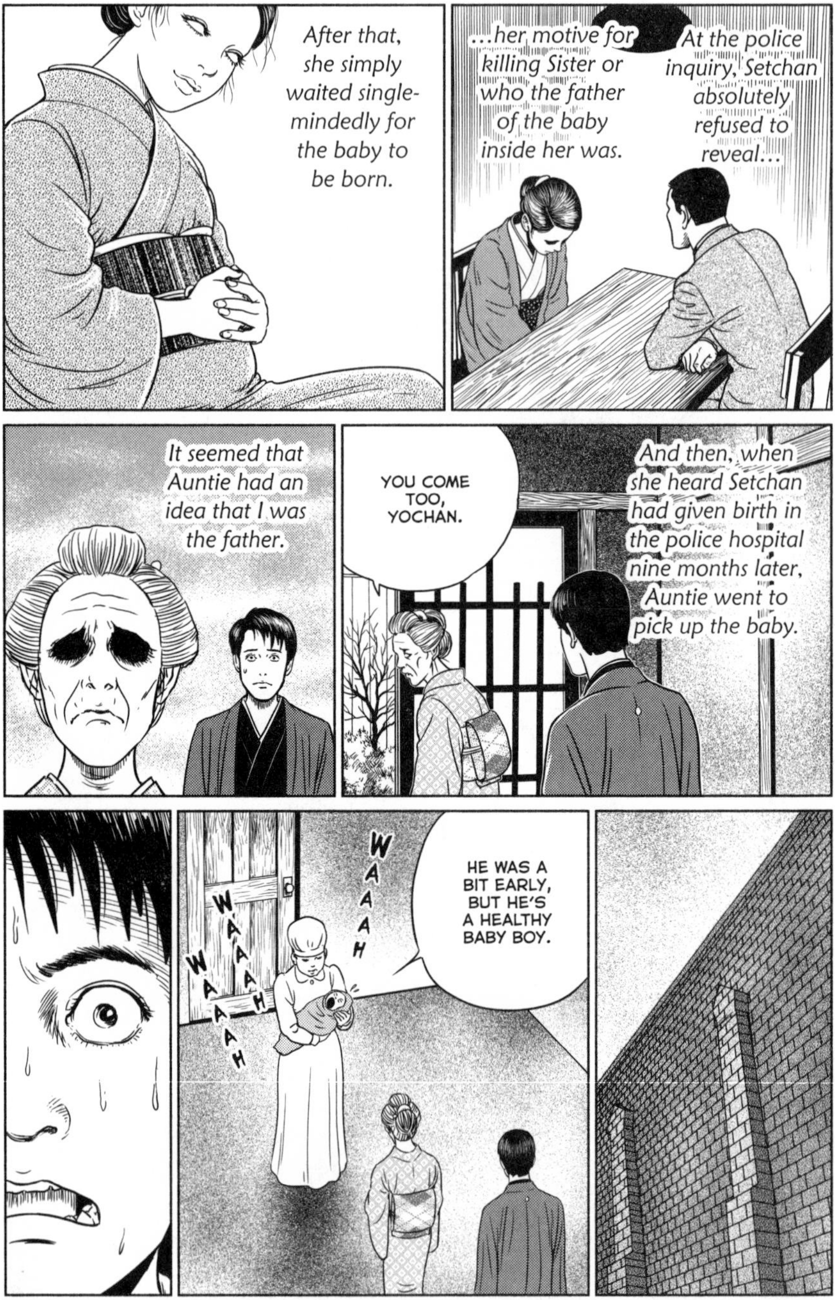
At the police inquiry, Setchan absolutely refused to reveal…
…her motive for killing Sister or who the father of the baby inside her was.
After that, she simply waited single-mindedly for the baby to be born.
And then, when she heard Setchan had given birth in the police hospital nine months later, Auntie went to pick up the baby.
YOU COME TOO, YOCHAN.
It seemed that Auntie had an idea that I was the father.
HE WAS A BIT EARLY, BUT HE'S A HEALTHY BABY BOY.
WAAAAH
WAAAAH
WAAAAH

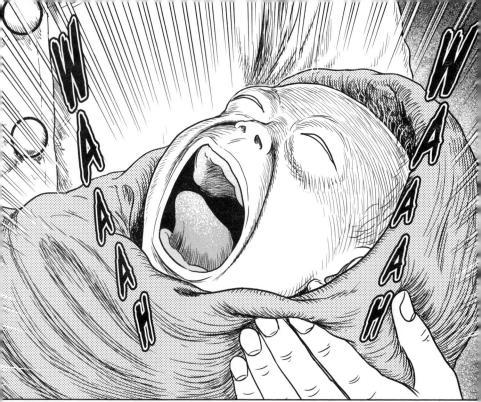

WAAAAH
WAAAH
WHAT A HOMELY FACE...
WHO ON EARTH IS THE FATHER OF THIS CHILD?
I trembled. The baby was a perfect copy of Takeichi.
But there was no way it could have been his child. He had killed himself over a year earlier...

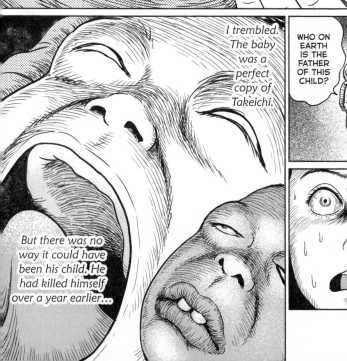

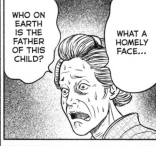

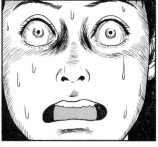

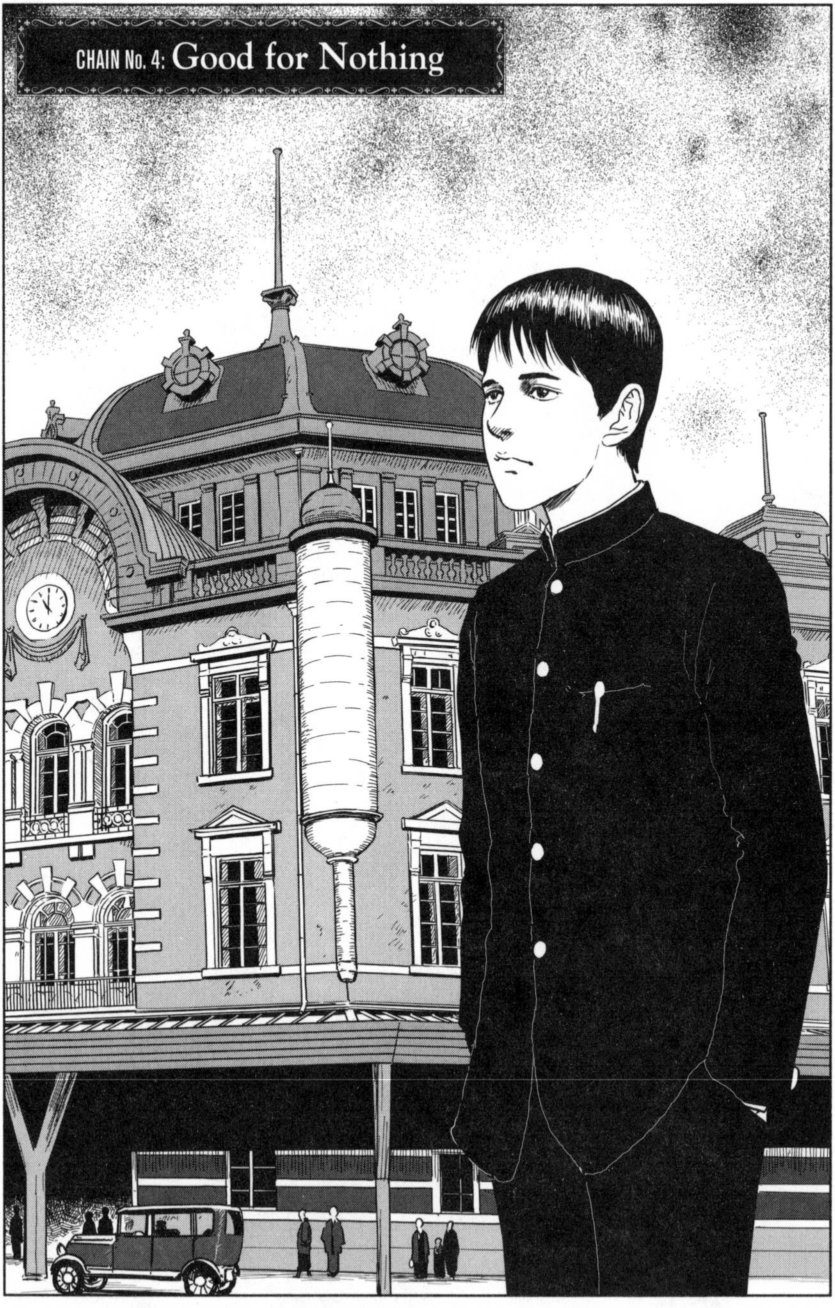
CHAIN No. 4: Good for Nothing

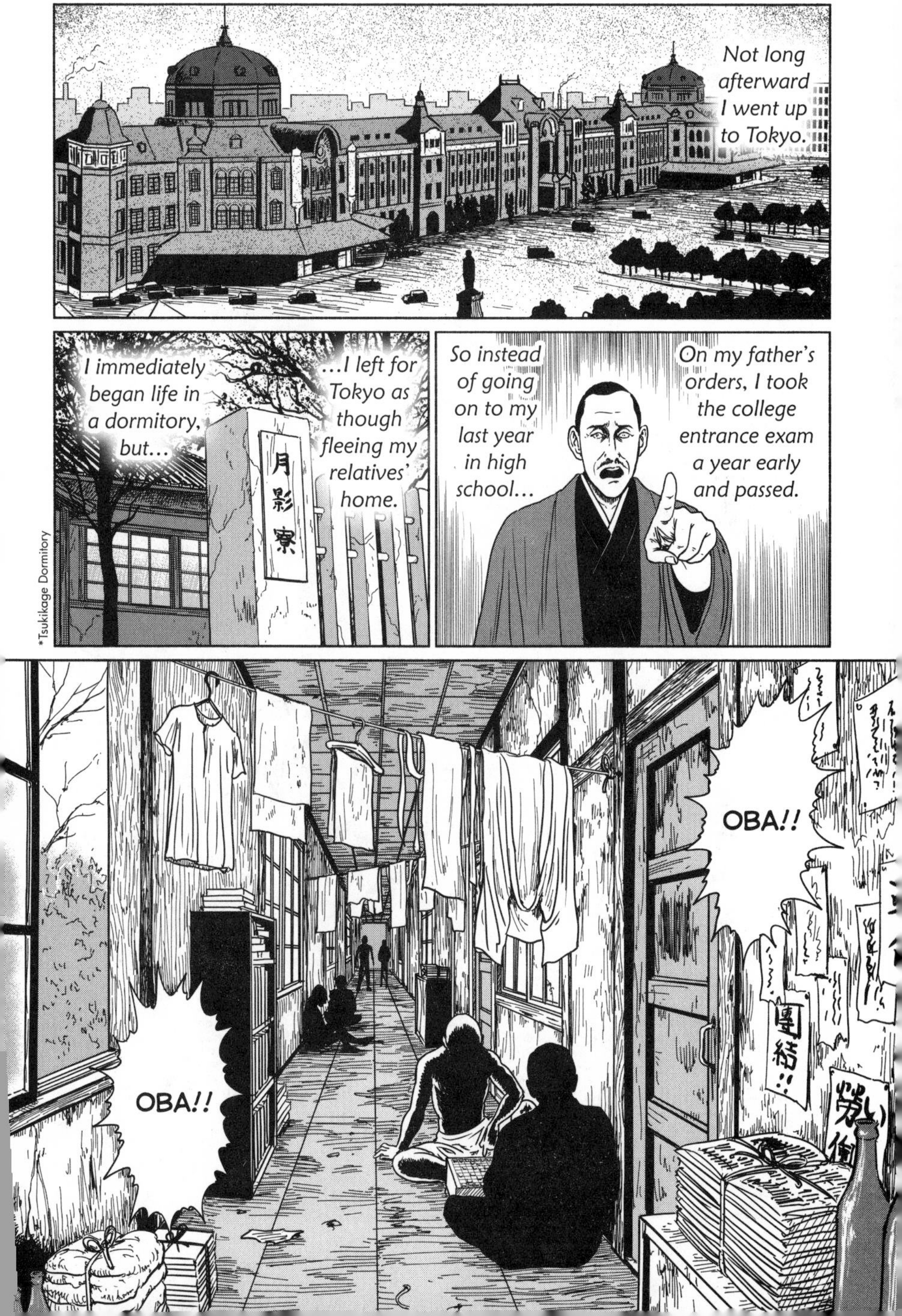
Not long afterward I went up to Tokyo.
On my father's orders, I took the college entrance exam a year early and passed.
So instead of going on to my last year in high school…
…I left for Tokyo as though fleeing my relatives' home.
I immediately began life in a dormitory, but…
月影寮
*Tsukikage Dormitory
OBA!!
團結!!
OBA!!

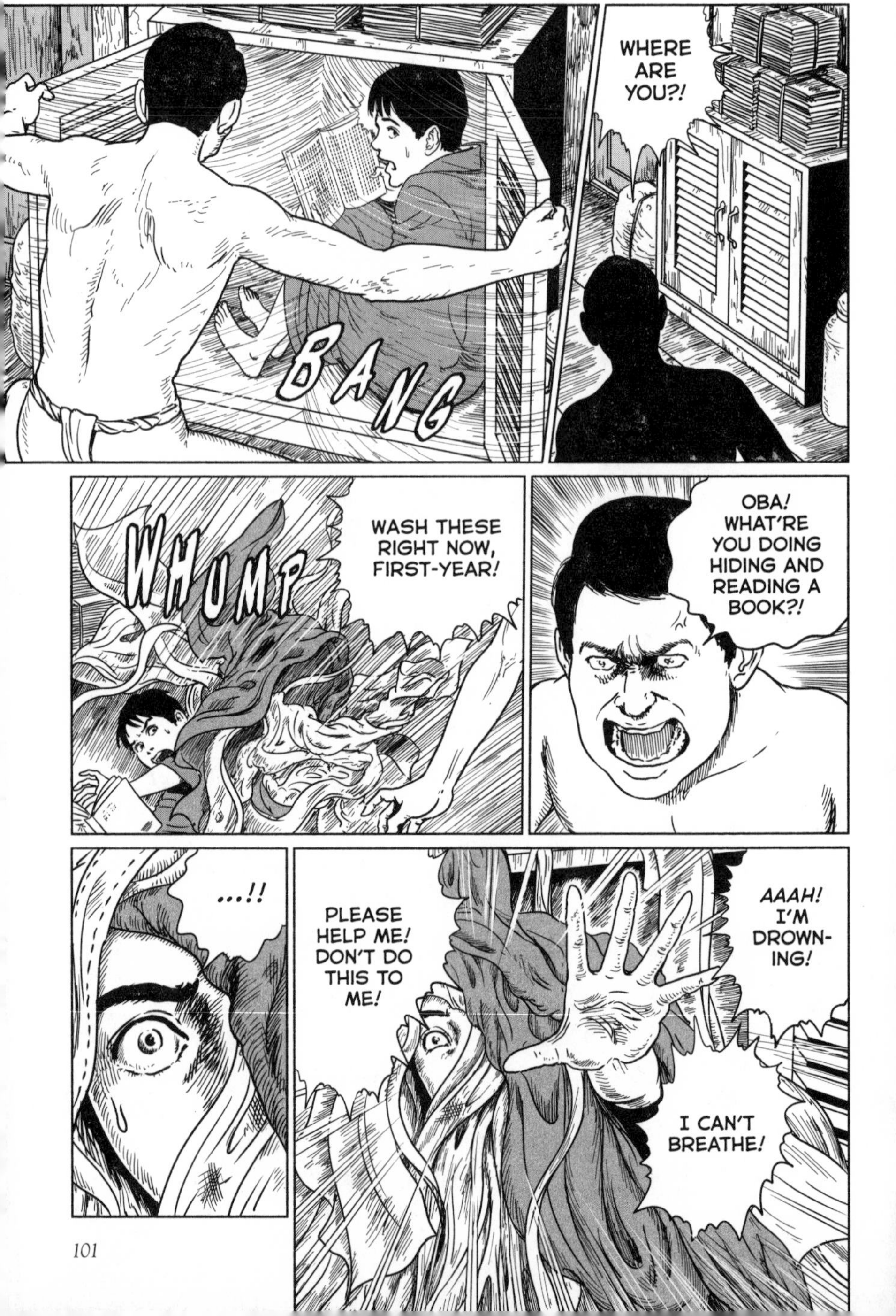
WHERE ARE YOU?!
BANG
OBA! WHAT'RE YOU DOING HIDING AND READING A BOOK?!
WASH THESE RIGHT NOW, FIRST-YEAR!
WHUMP
AAAH! I'M DROWN- ING!
PLEASE HELP ME! DON'T DO THIS TO ME!
I CAN'T BREATHE!
...!!

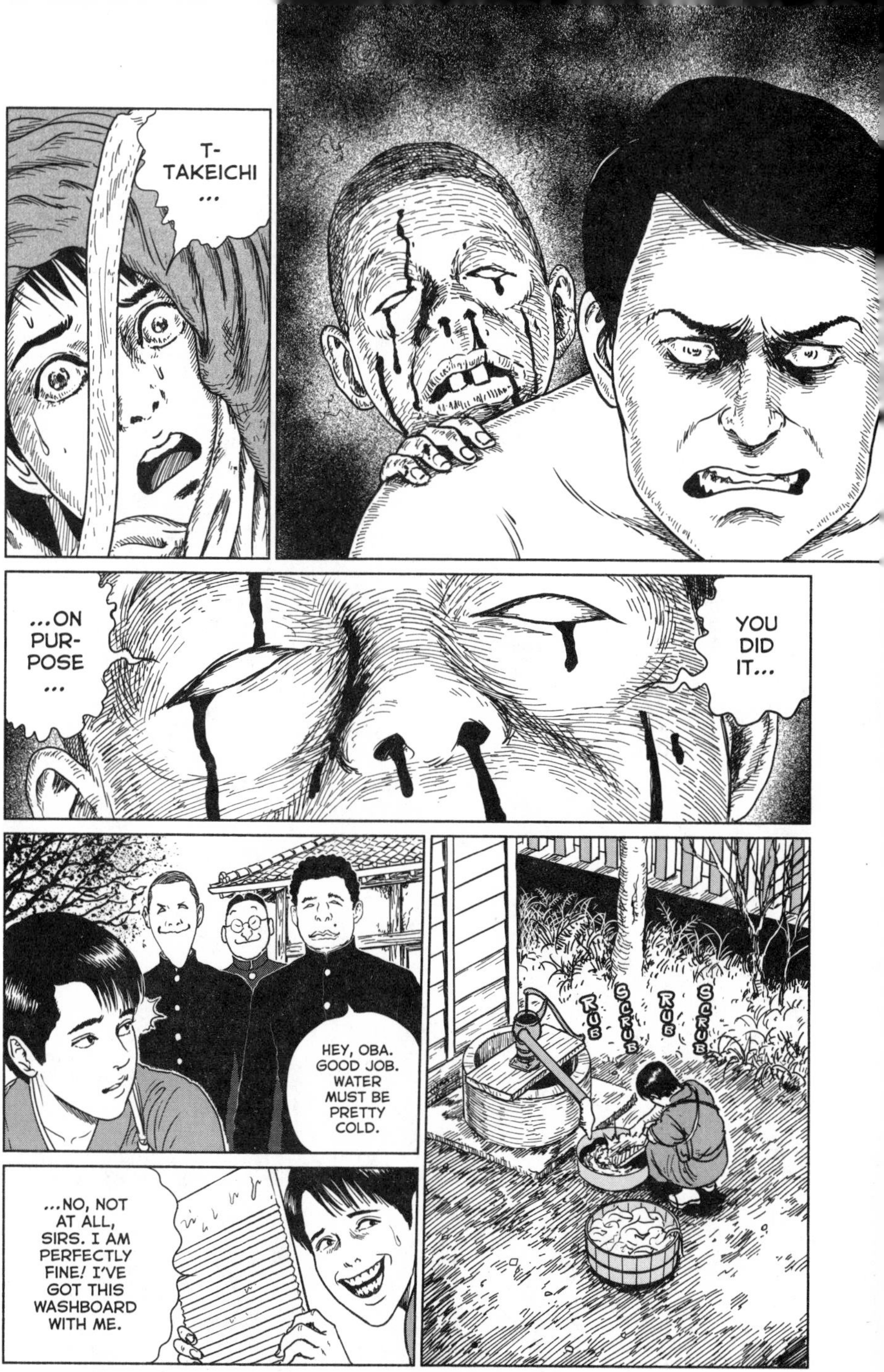
T-TAKEICHI ...
YOU DID IT...
...ON PURPOSE ...
SCRUB
RUB
SCRUB
RUB
HEY, OBA. GOOD JOB. WATER MUST BE PRETTY COLD.
...NO, NOT AT ALL, SIRS. I AM PERFECTLY FINE! I'VE GOT THIS WASHBOARD WITH ME.

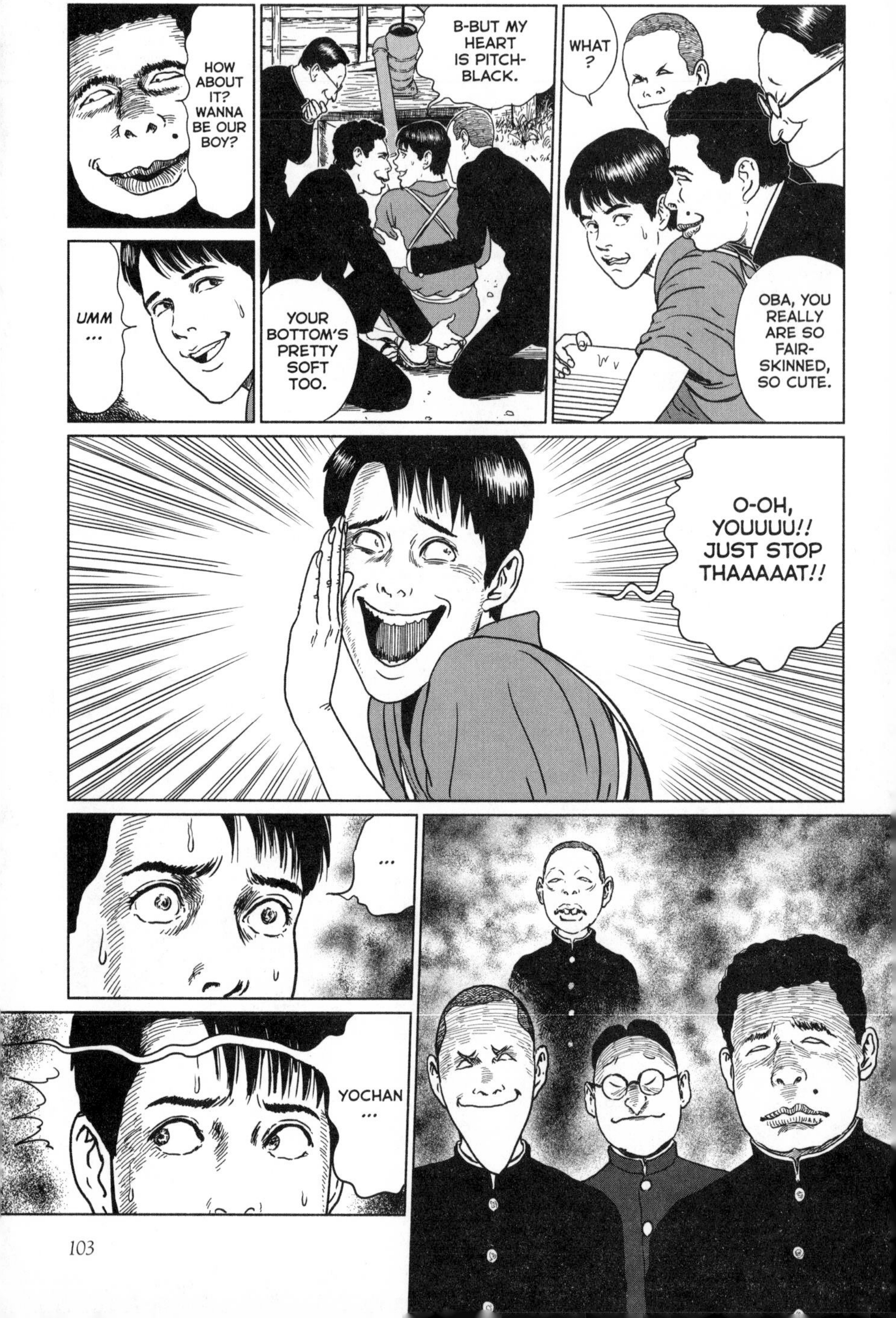
WHAT?
OBA, YOU REALLY ARE SO FAIR-SKINNED, SO CUTE.
B-BUT MY HEART IS PITCH-BLACK.
YOUR BOTTOM'S PRETTY SOFT TOO.
HOW ABOUT IT? WANNA BE OUR BOY?
UMM ...
O-OH, YOUUUU!! JUST STOP THAAAAAT!!
...
YOCHAN ...

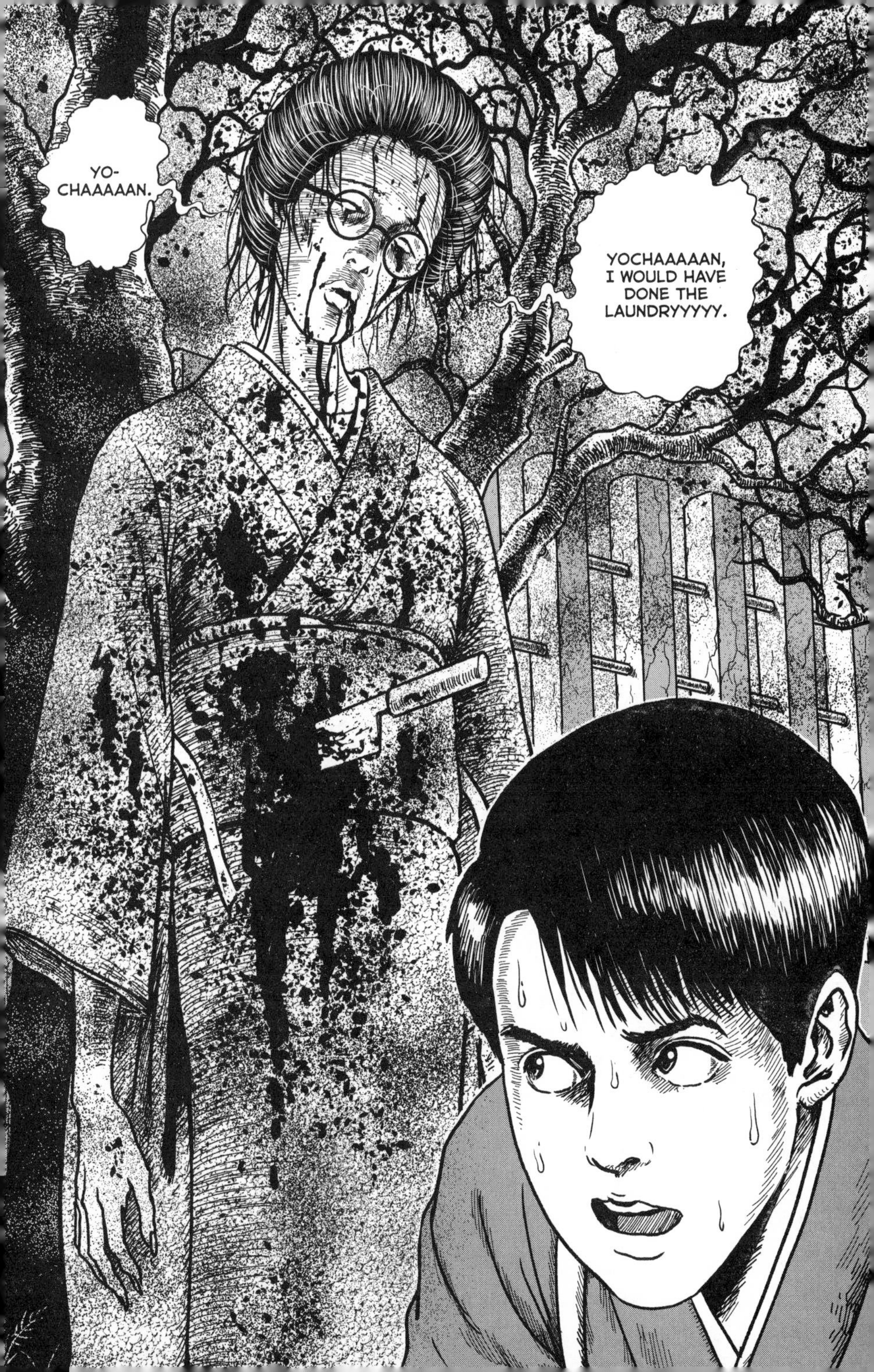
YOCHAAAAAN, I WOULD HAVE DONE THE LAUNDRYYYYY.
YO-CHAAAAAN.

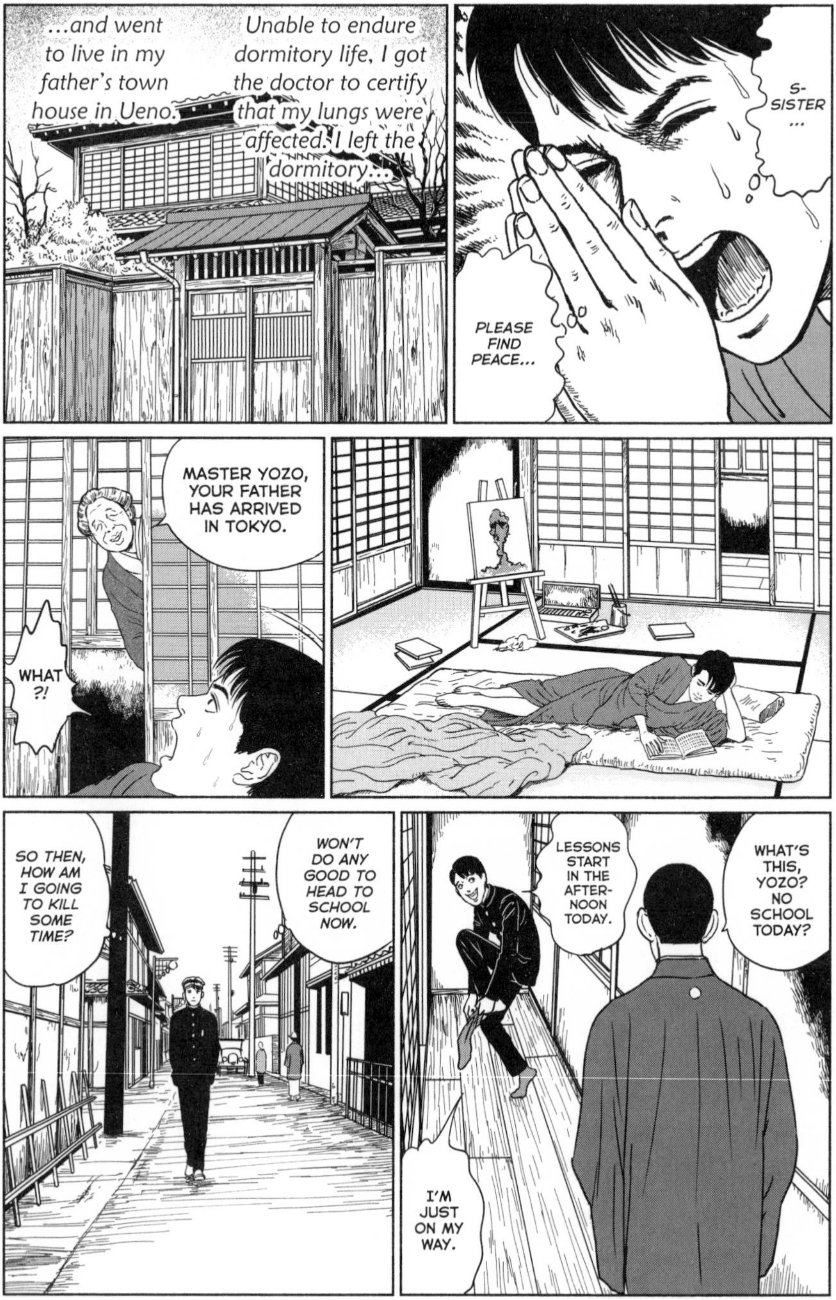
S-SISTER...
PLEASE FIND PEACE...
Unable to endure dormitory life, I got the doctor to certify that my lungs were affected. I left the dormitory...
...and went to live in my father's town house in Ueno.
MASTER YOZO, YOUR FATHER HAS ARRIVED IN TOKYO.
WHAT?!
WHAT'S THIS, YOZO? NO SCHOOL TODAY?
LESSONS START IN THE AFTERNOON TODAY.
I'M JUST ON MY WAY.
WON'T DO ANY GOOD TO HEAD TO SCHOOL NOW.
SO THEN, HOW AM I GOING TO KILL SOME TIME?

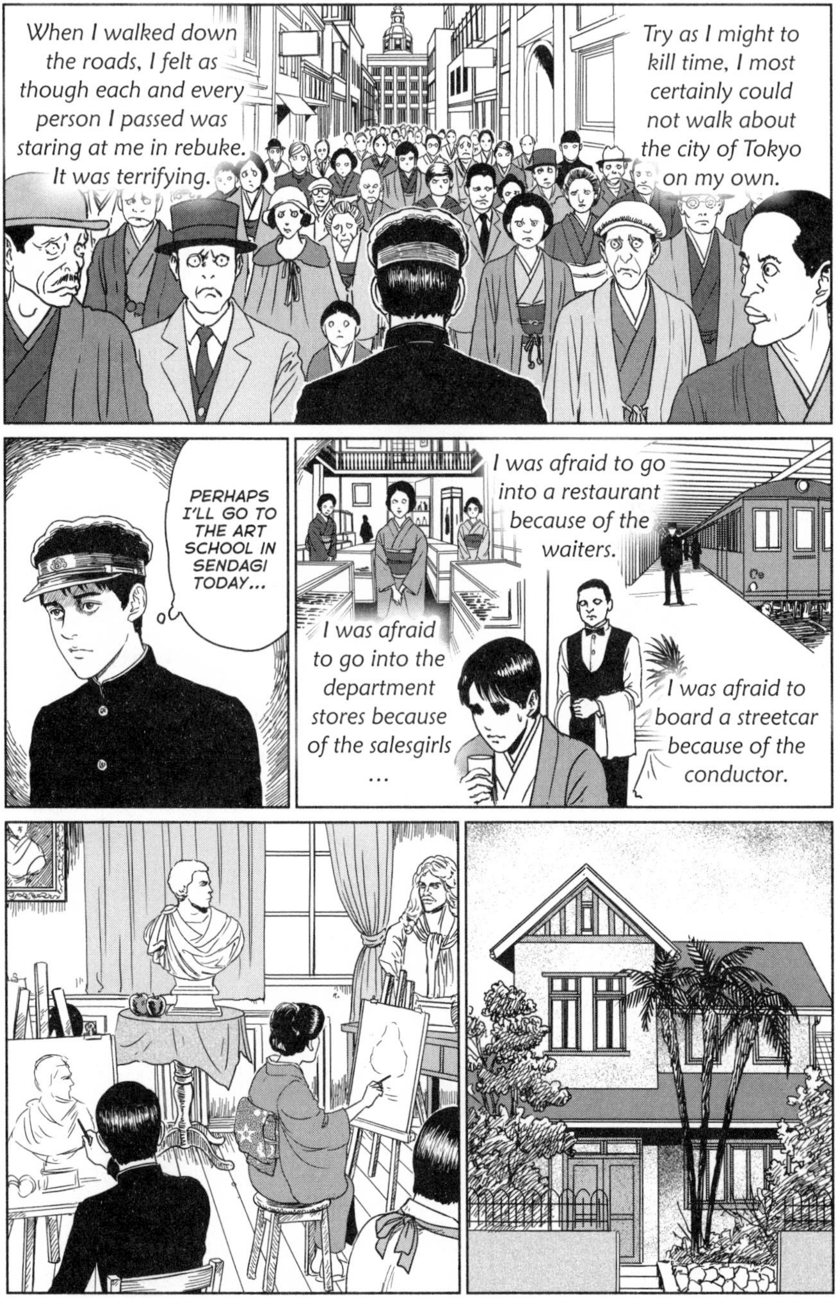
Try as I might to kill time, I most certainly could not walk about the city of Tokyo on my own.
When I walked down the roads, I felt as though each and every person I passed was staring at me in rebuke. It was terrifying.
I was afraid to go into a restaurant because of the waiters.
I was afraid to board a streetcar because of the conductor.
I was afraid to go into the department stores because of the salesgirls …
PERHAPS I'LL GO TO THE ART SCHOOL IN SENDAGI TODAY...

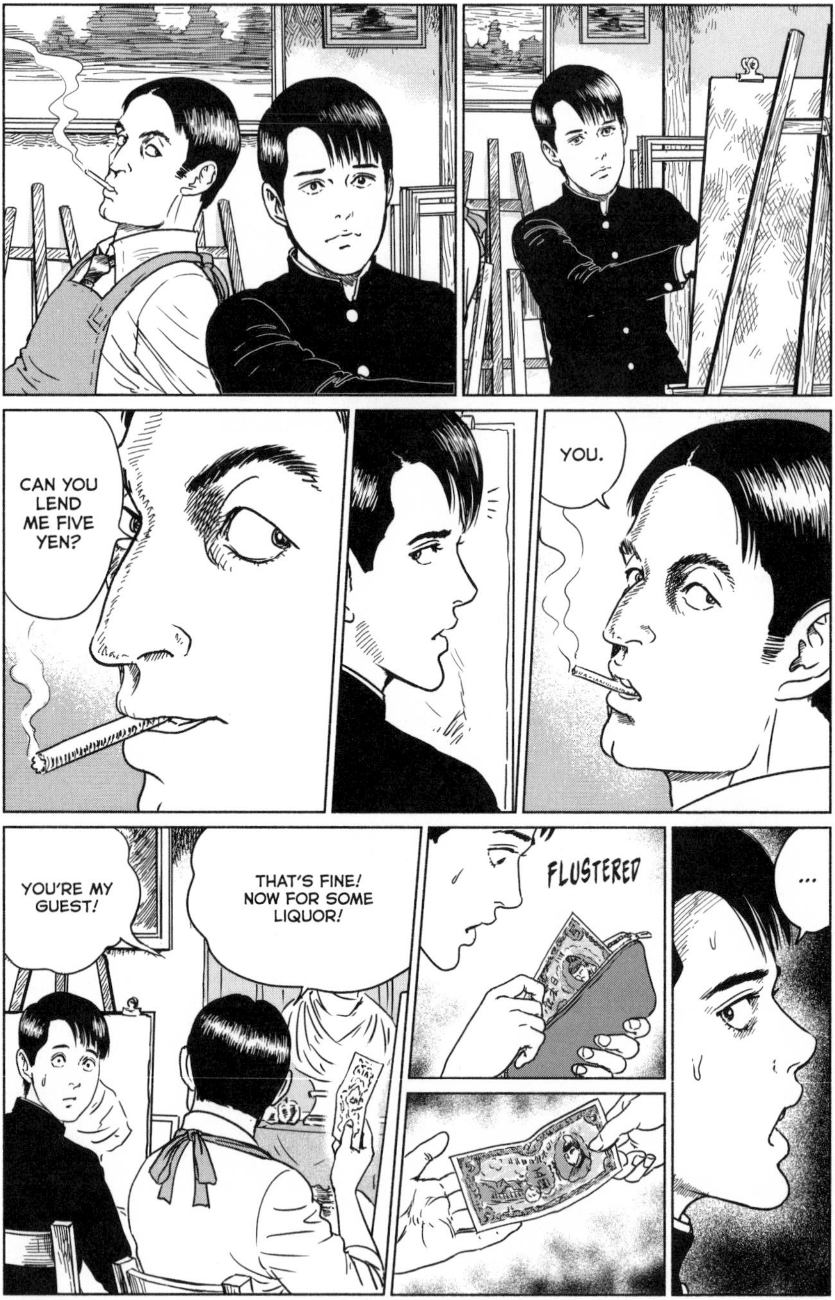
YOU.
CAN YOU LEND ME FIVE YEN?
...
FLUSTERED
THAT'S FINE! NOW FOR SOME LIQUOR!
YOU'RE MY GUEST!

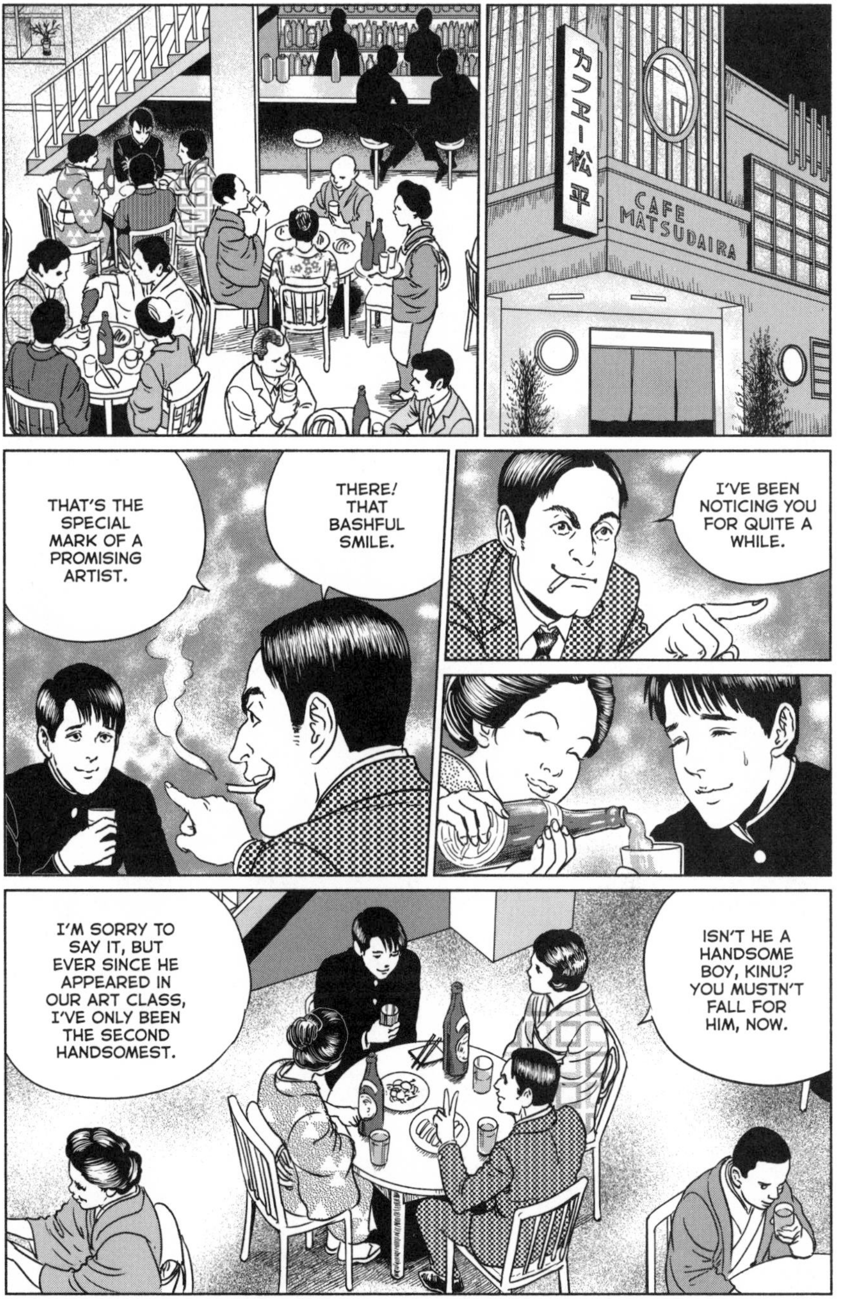
カフェー松平
CAFE MATSUDAIRA
I'VE BEEN NOTICING YOU FOR QUITE A WHILE.
THERE! THAT BASHFUL SMILE.
THAT'S THE SPECIAL MARK OF A PROMISING ARTIST.
ISN'T HE A HANDSOME BOY, KINU? YOU MUSTN'T FALL FOR HIM, NOW.
I'M SORRY TO SAY IT, BUT EVER SINCE HE APPEARED IN OUR ART CLASS, I'VE ONLY BEEN THE SECOND HANDSOMEST.

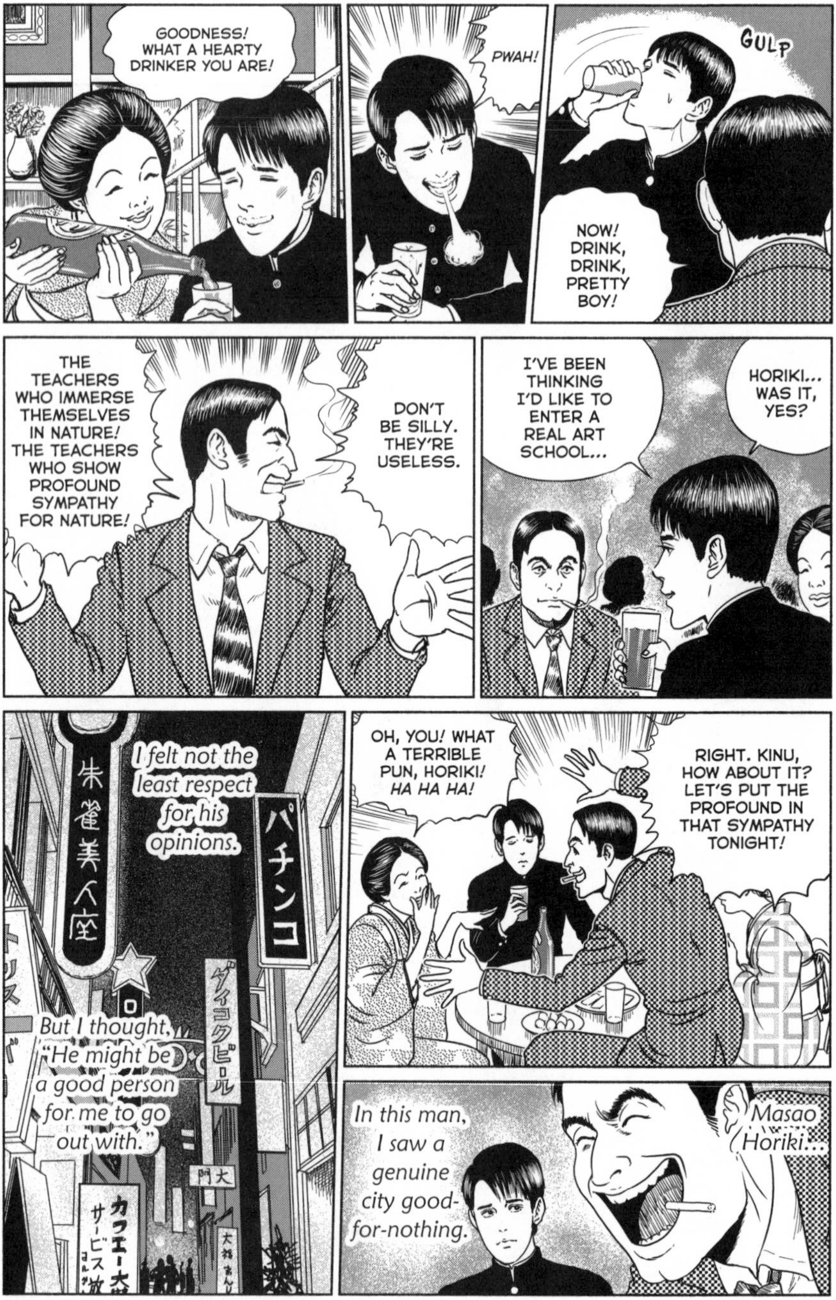
GULP
NOW! DRINK, DRINK, PRETTY BOY!
PWAH!
GOODNESS! WHAT A HEARTY DRINKER YOU ARE!
HORIKI... WAS IT, YES?
I'VE BEEN THINKING I'D LIKE TO ENTER A REAL ART SCHOOL...
DON'T BE SILLY. THEY'RE USELESS.
THE TEACHERS WHO IMMERSE THEMSELVES IN NATURE! THE TEACHERS WHO SHOW PROFOUND SYMPATHY FOR NATURE!
RIGHT. KINU, HOW ABOUT IT? LET'S PUT THE PROFOUND IN THAT SYMPATHY TONIGHT!
OH, YOU! WHAT A TERRIBLE PUN, HORIKI! *HA HA HA!*
Masao Horiki...
In this man, I saw a genuine city good-for-nothing.
パチンコ
朱雀美人座
I felt not the least respect for his opinions.
ダイコクビル
But I thought, "He might be a good person for me to go out with."

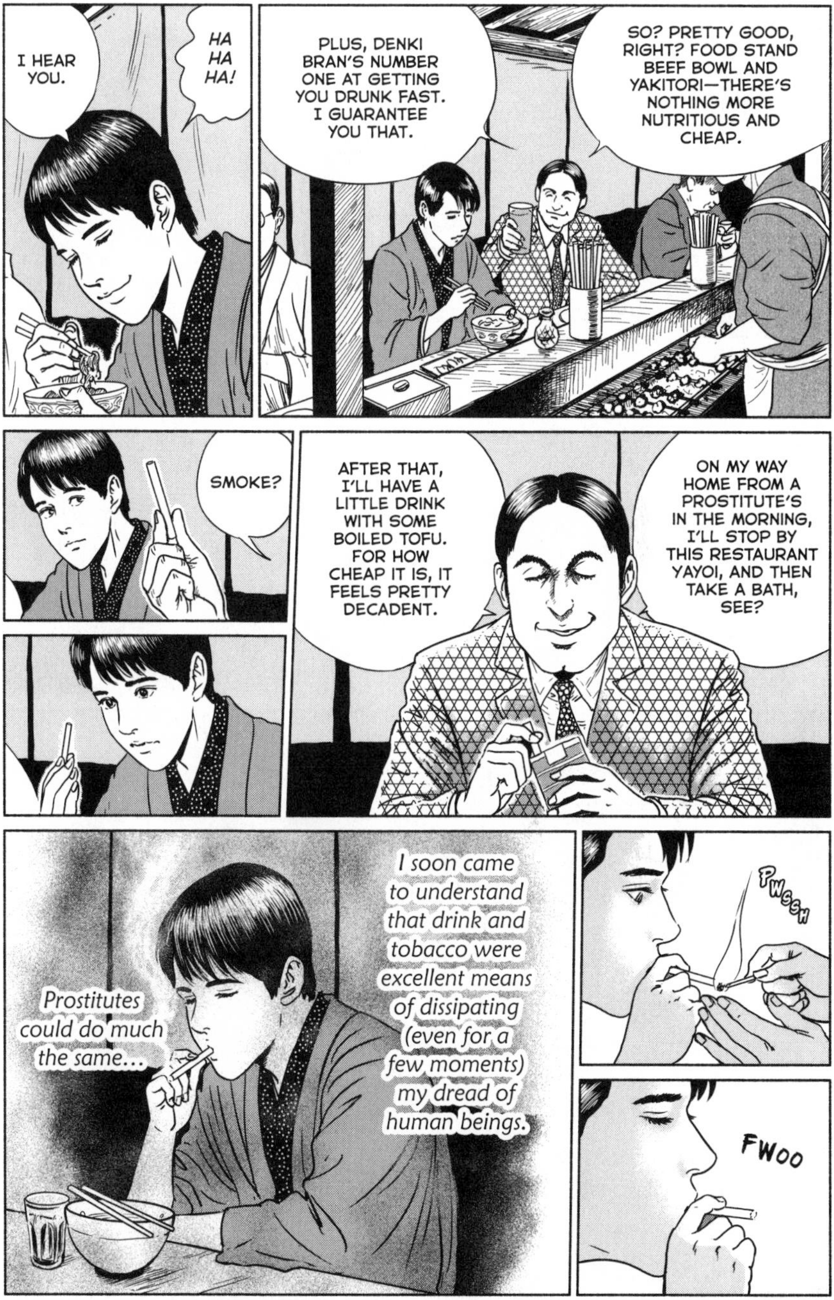
SO? PRETTY GOOD, RIGHT? FOOD STAND BEEF BOWL AND YAKITORI—THERE'S NOTHING MORE NUTRITIOUS AND CHEAP.
PLUS, DENKI BRAN'S NUMBER ONE AT GETTING YOU DRUNK FAST. I GUARANTEE YOU THAT.
HA HA HA!
I HEAR YOU.
ON MY WAY HOME FROM A PROSTITUTE'S IN THE MORNING, I'LL STOP BY THIS RESTAURANT YAYOI, AND THEN TAKE A BATH, SEE?
AFTER THAT, I'LL HAVE A LITTLE DRINK WITH SOME BOILED TOFU. FOR HOW CHEAP IT IS, IT FEELS PRETTY DECADENT.
SMOKE?
PWSSH
FWOO
I soon came to understand that drink and tobacco were excellent means of dissipating (even for a few moments) my dread of human beings.
Prostitutes could do much the same...

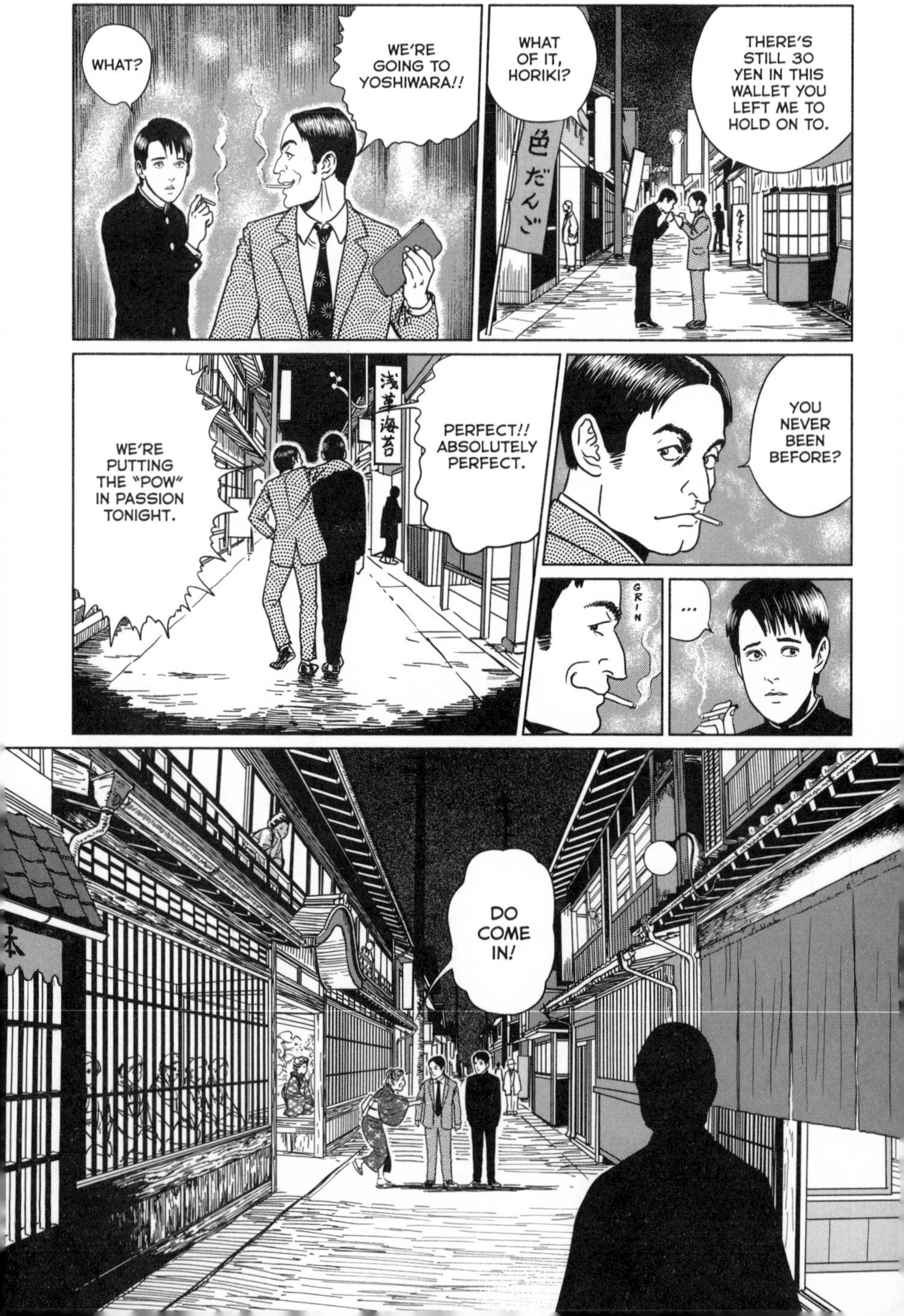
THERE'S STILL 30 YEN IN THIS WALLET YOU LEFT ME TO HOLD ON TO.
WHAT OF IT, HORIKI?
色だんご
WE'RE GOING TO YOSHIWARA!!
WHAT?
YOU NEVER BEEN BEFORE?
...
GRIN
浅草海苔
PERFECT!! ABSOLUTELY PERFECT.
WE'RE PUTTING THE "POW" IN PASSION TONIGHT.
DO COME IN!

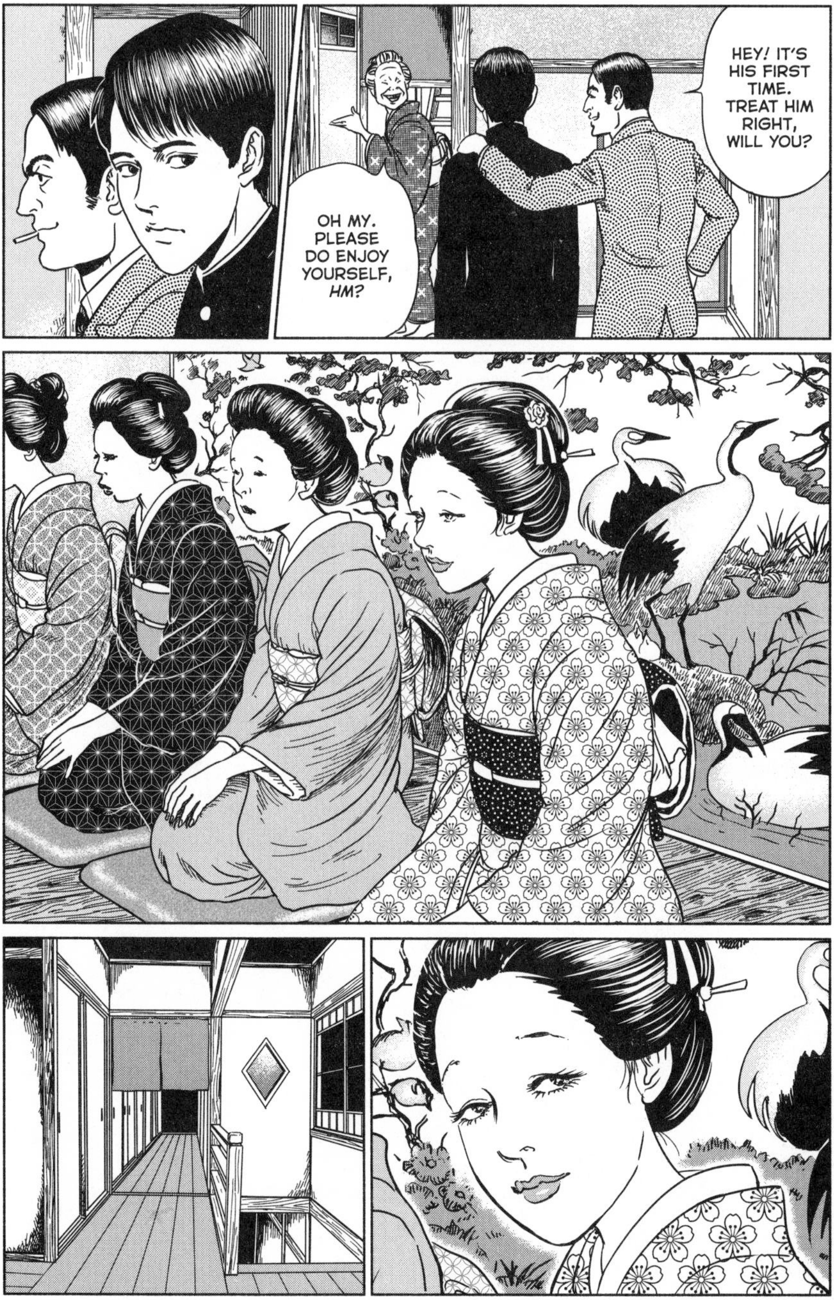
HEY! IT'S HIS FIRST TIME. TREAT HIM RIGHT, WILL YOU?
OH MY. PLEASE DO ENJOY YOURSELF, *HM?*

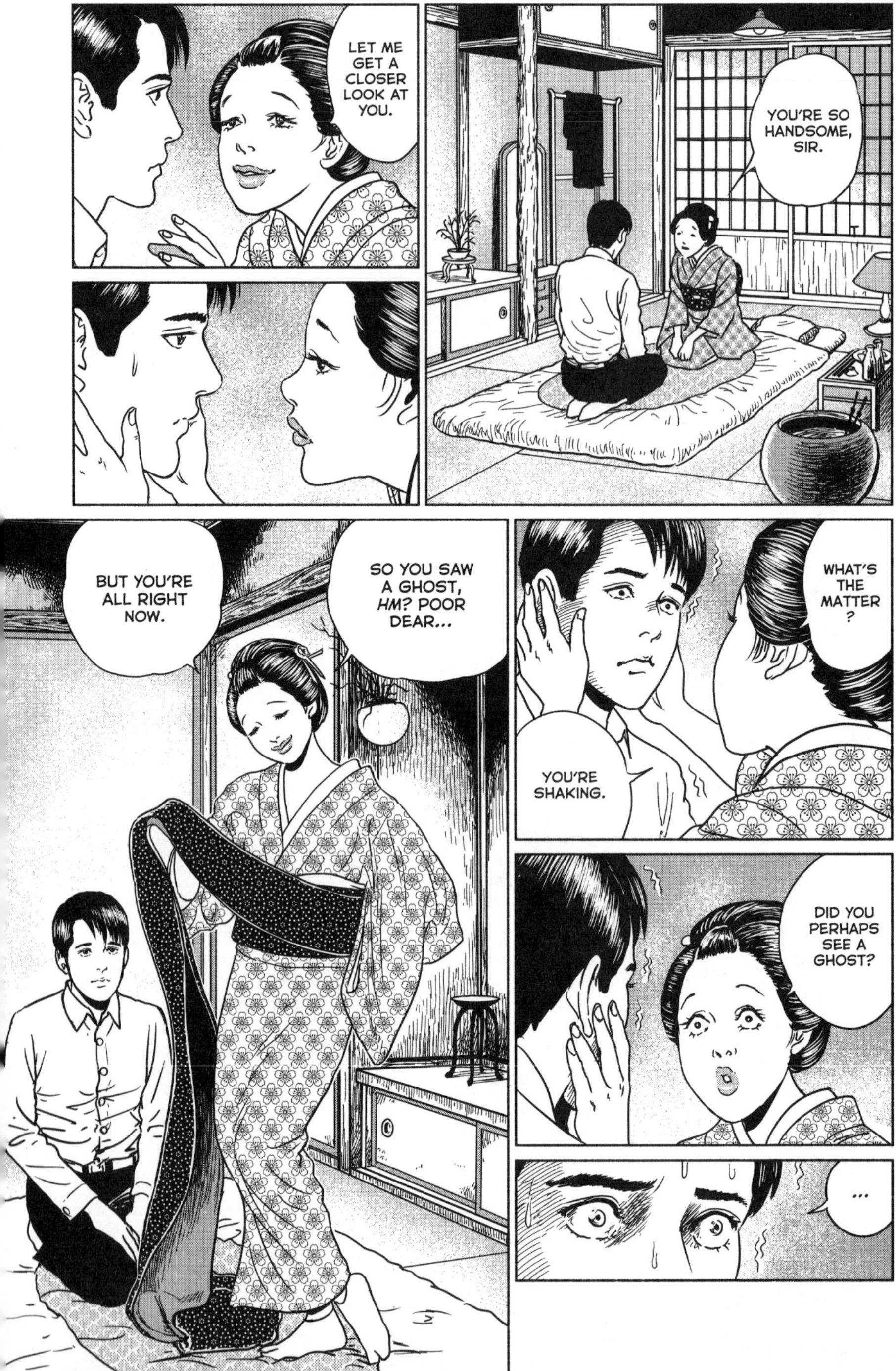
YOU'RE SO HANDSOME, SIR.
LET ME GET A CLOSER LOOK AT YOU.
WHAT'S THE MATTER?
YOU'RE SHAKING.
DID YOU PERHAPS SEE A GHOST?
...
SO YOU SAW A GHOST, *HM?* POOR DEAR...
BUT YOU'RE ALL RIGHT NOW.

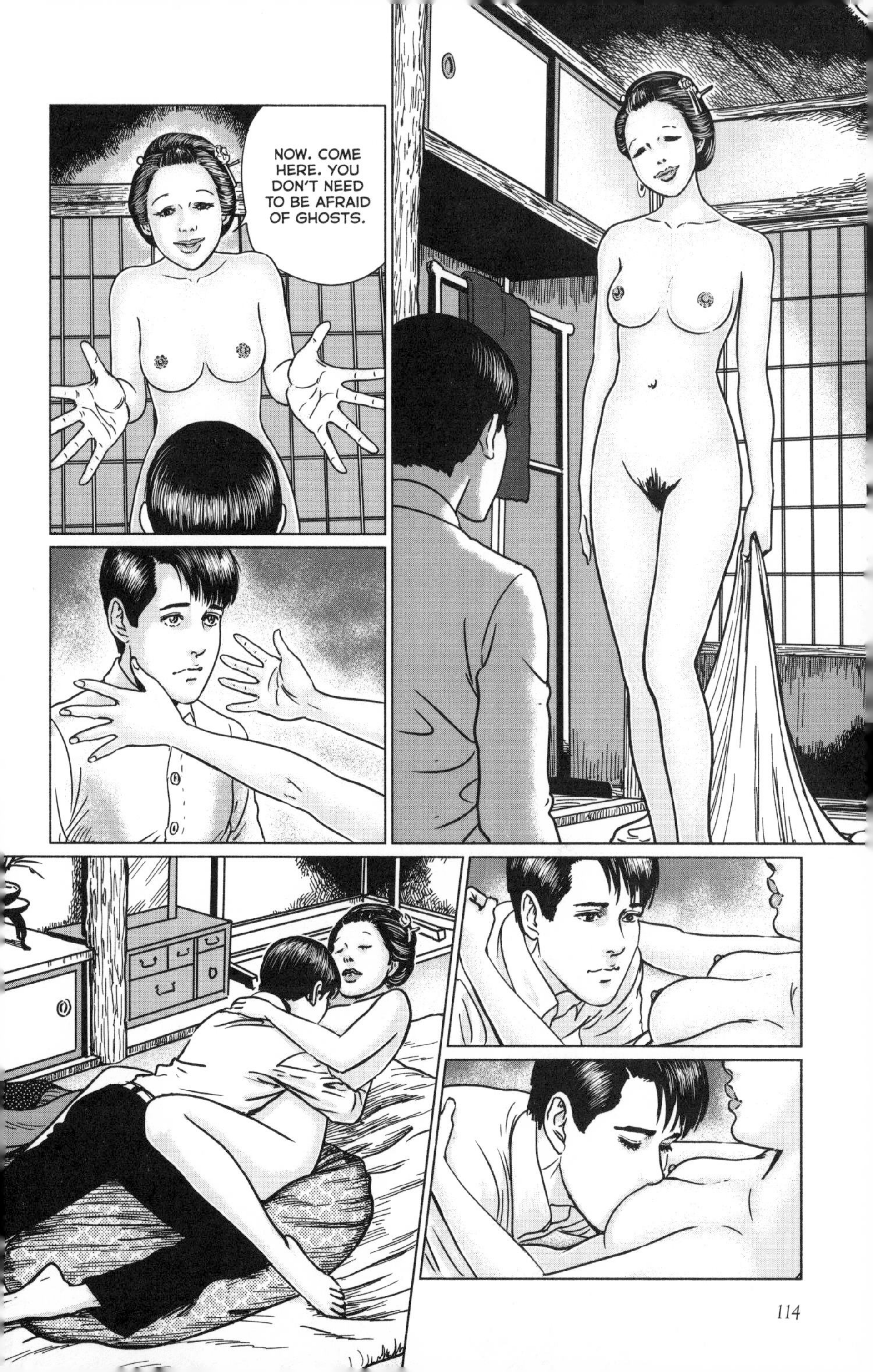
NOW. COME HERE. YOU DON'T NEED TO BE AFRAID OF GHOSTS.

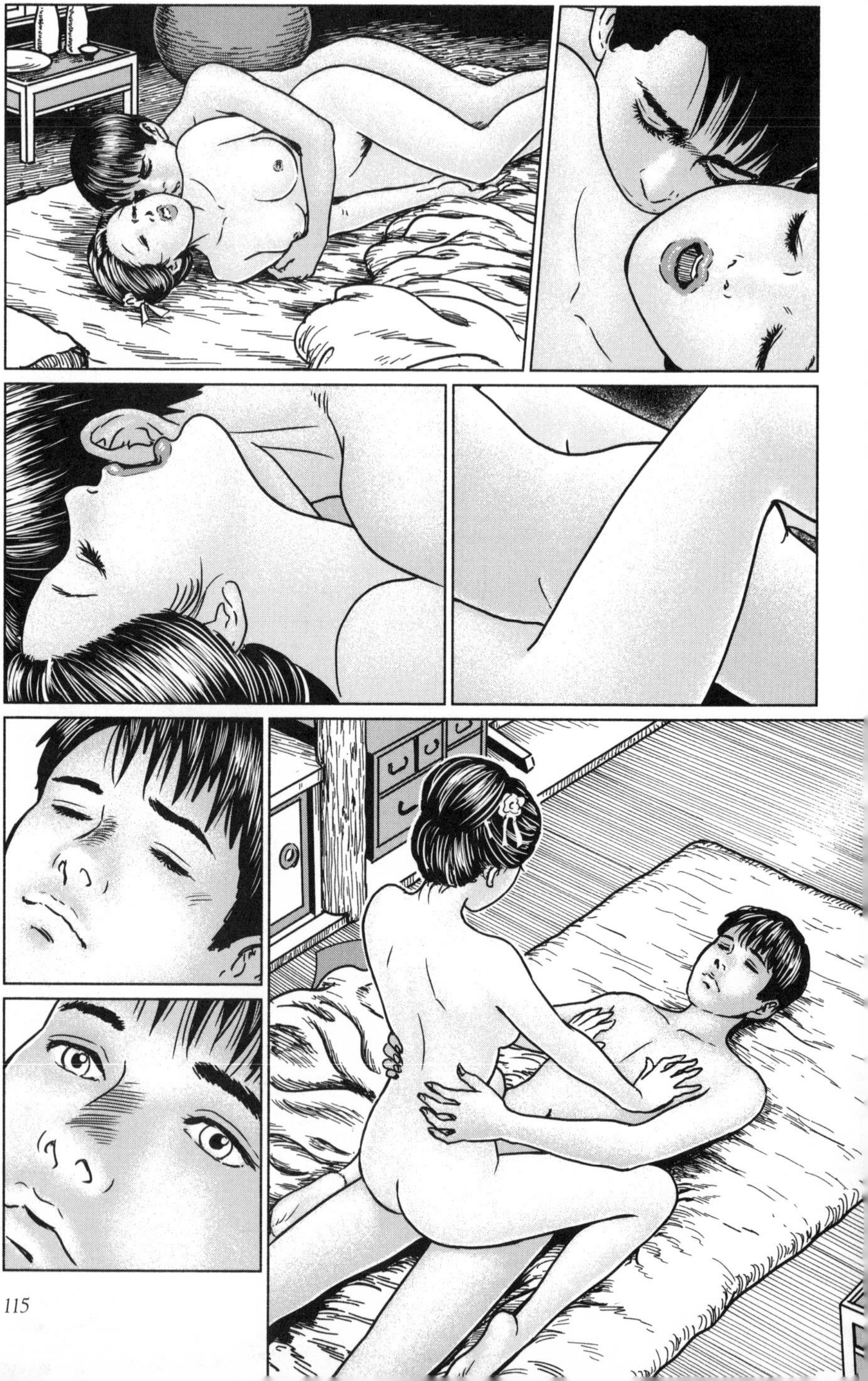

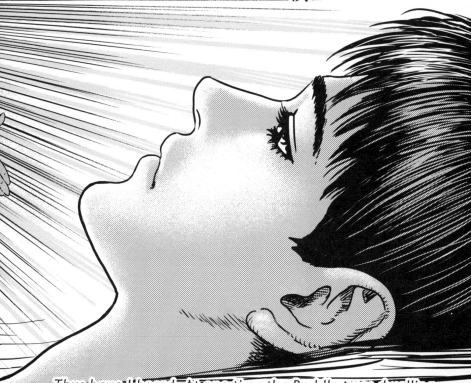

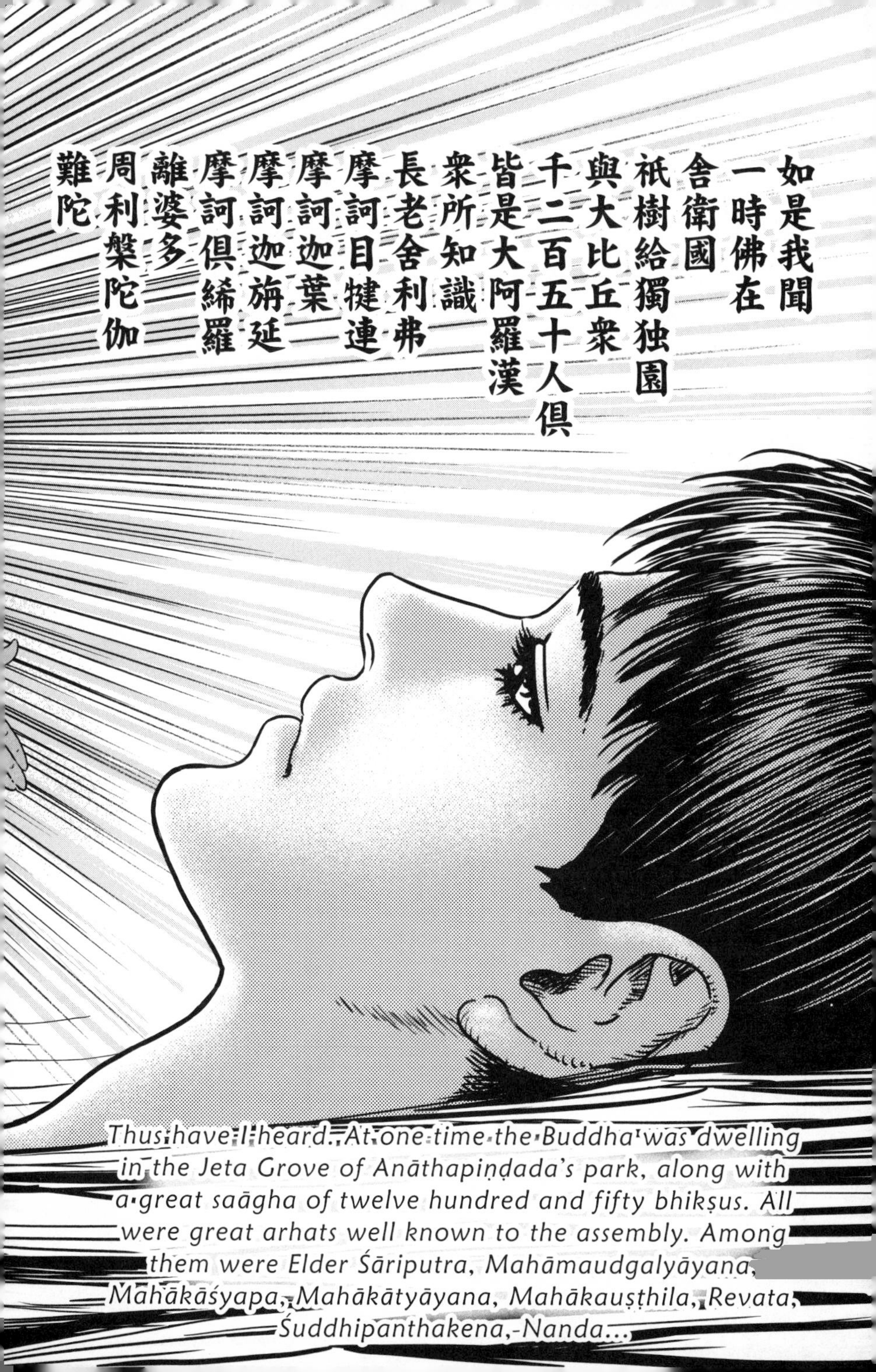

如是我聞
一時佛在
舍衛國
祇樹給獨園
與大比丘衆
千二百五十人俱
皆是大阿羅漢
衆所知識
長老舍利弗
摩訶目犍連
摩訶迦葉
摩訶迦旃延
摩訶俱絺羅
離婆多
周利槃陀伽
難陀

Thus have I heard. At one time the Buddha was dwelling in the Jeta Grove of Anāthapiṇḍada's park, along with a great saāgha of twelve hundred and fifty bhikṣus. All were great arhats well known to the assembly. Among them were Elder Śāriputra, Mahāmaudgalyāyana, Mahākāśyapa, Mahākātyāyana, Mahākauṣṭhila, Revata, Śuddhipanthakena, Nanda...

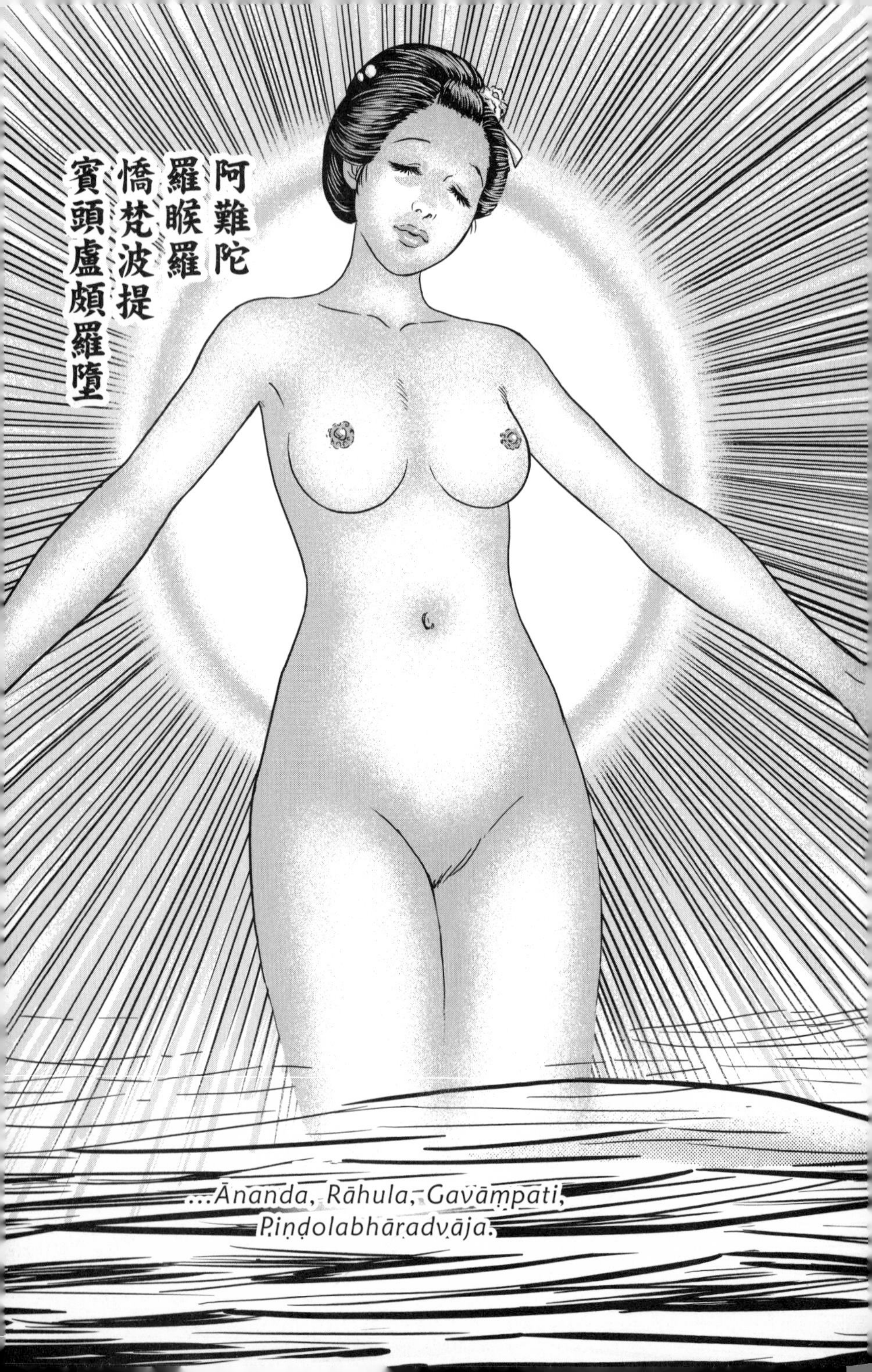
阿難陀
羅睺羅
憍梵波提
賓頭盧頗羅墮
...Ānanda, Rāhula, Gavāṃpati,
Piṇḍolabhāradvāja.

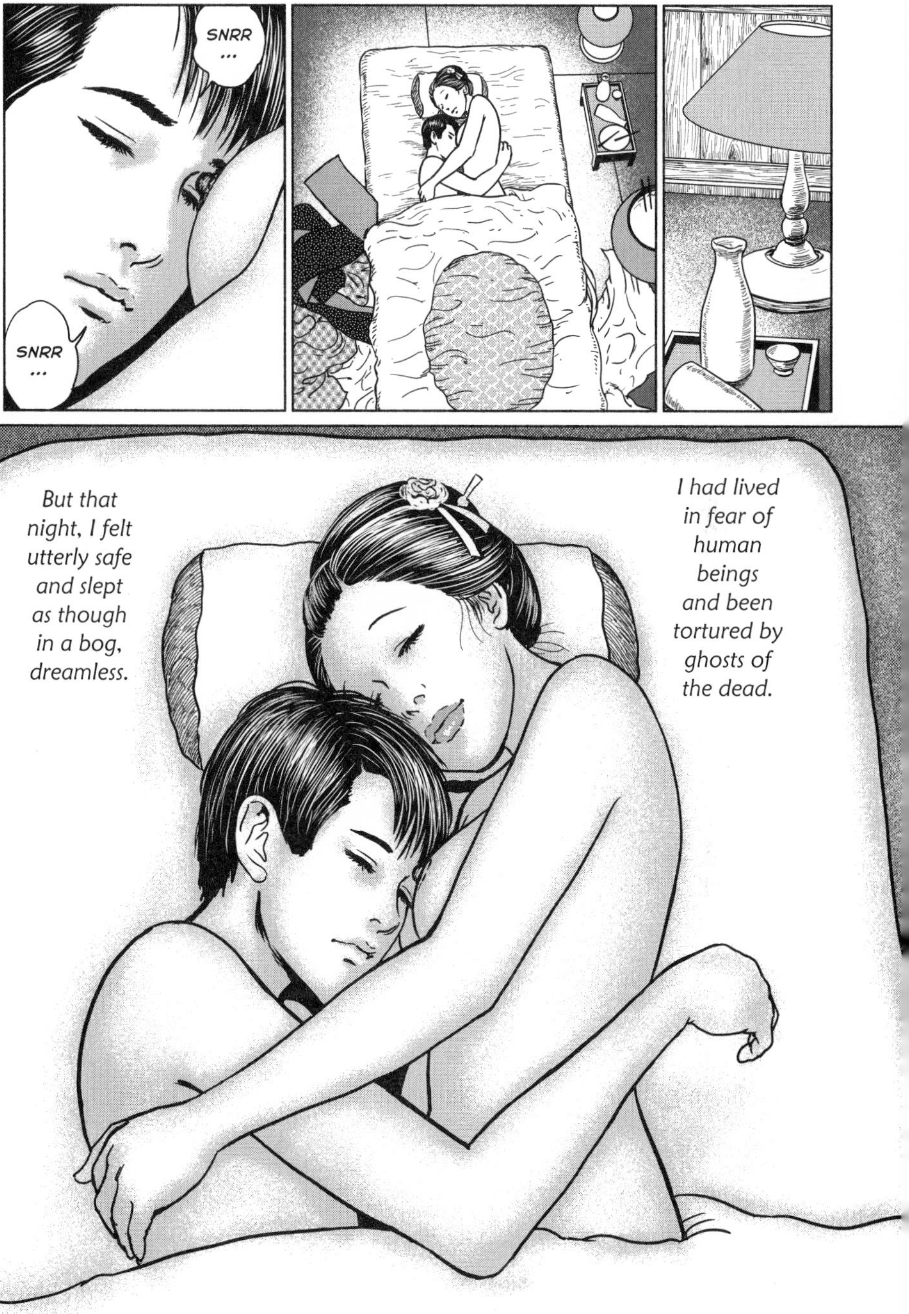
SNRR ...
SNRR ...
I had lived in fear of human beings and been tortured by ghosts of the dead.
But that night, I felt utterly safe and slept as though in a bog, dreamless.

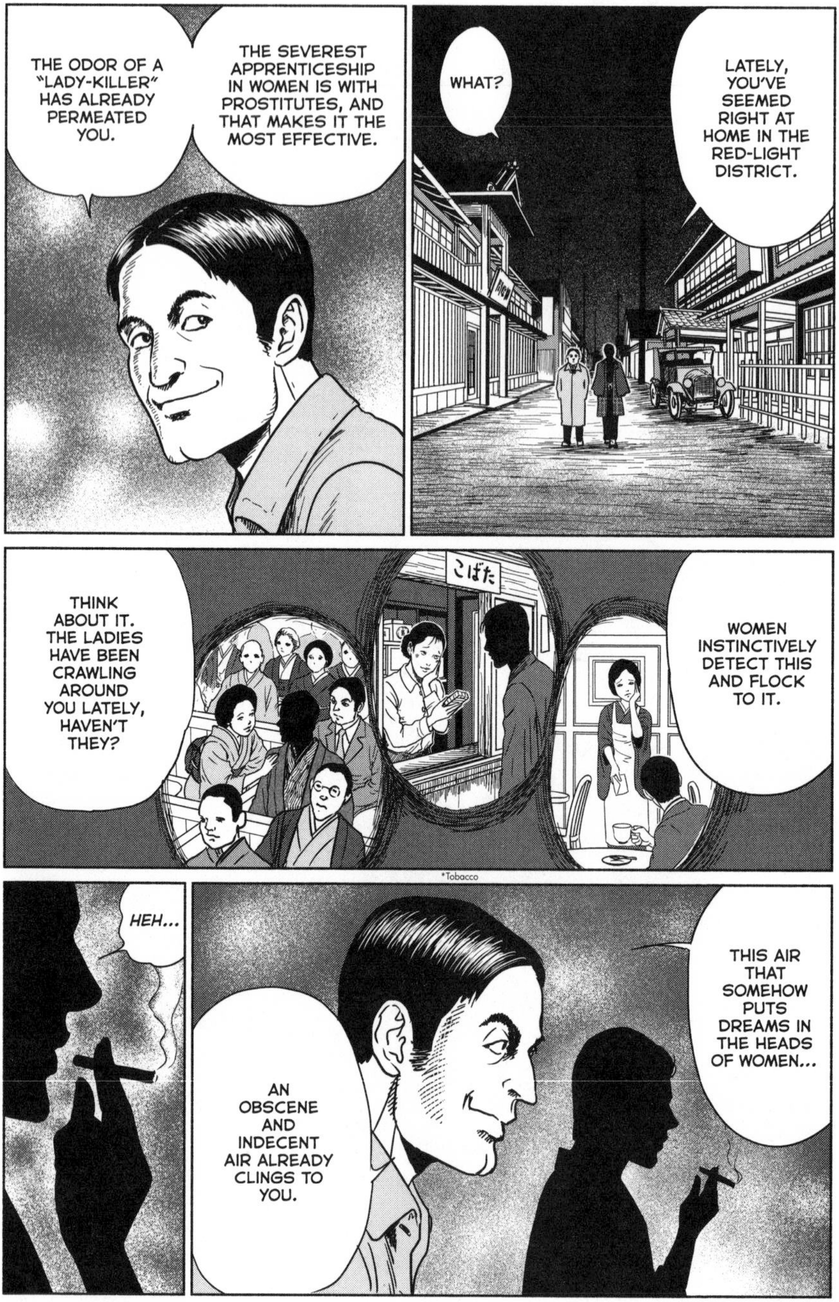
LATELY, YOU'VE SEEMED RIGHT AT HOME IN THE RED-LIGHT DISTRICT.
WHAT?
THE SEVEREST APPRENTICESHIP IN WOMEN IS WITH PROSTITUTES, AND THAT MAKES IT THE MOST EFFECTIVE.
THE ODOR OF A "LADY-KILLER" HAS ALREADY PERMEATED YOU.
WOMEN INSTINCTIVELY DETECT THIS AND FLOCK TO IT.
こばた
THINK ABOUT IT. THE LADIES HAVE BEEN CRAWLING AROUND YOU LATELY, HAVEN'T THEY?
*Tobacco
THIS AIR THAT SOMEHOW PUTS DREAMS IN THE HEADS OF WOMEN...
AN OBSCENE AND INDECENT AIR ALREADY CLINGS TO YOU.
HEH...

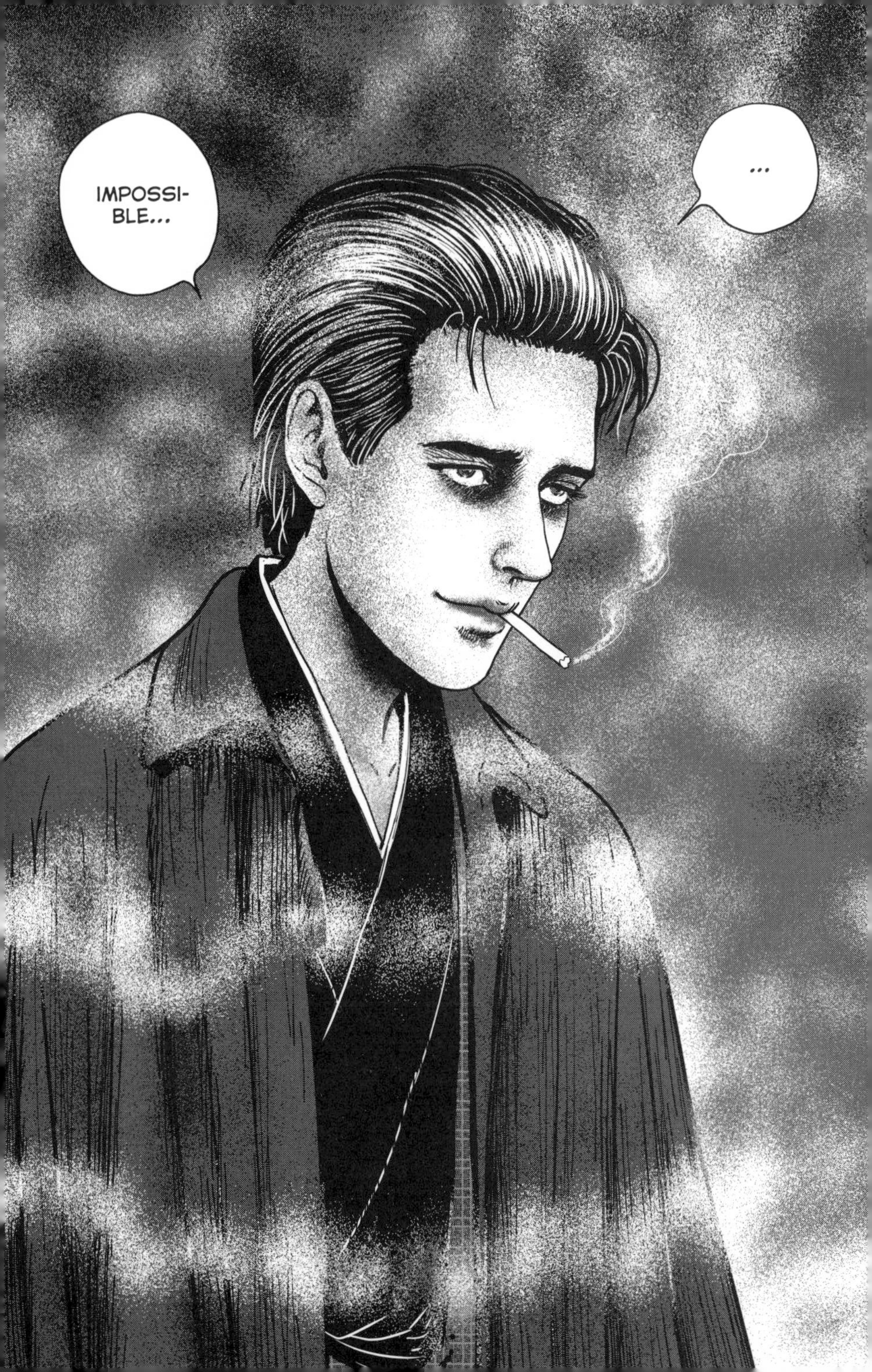
...
IMPOSSI-
BLE...

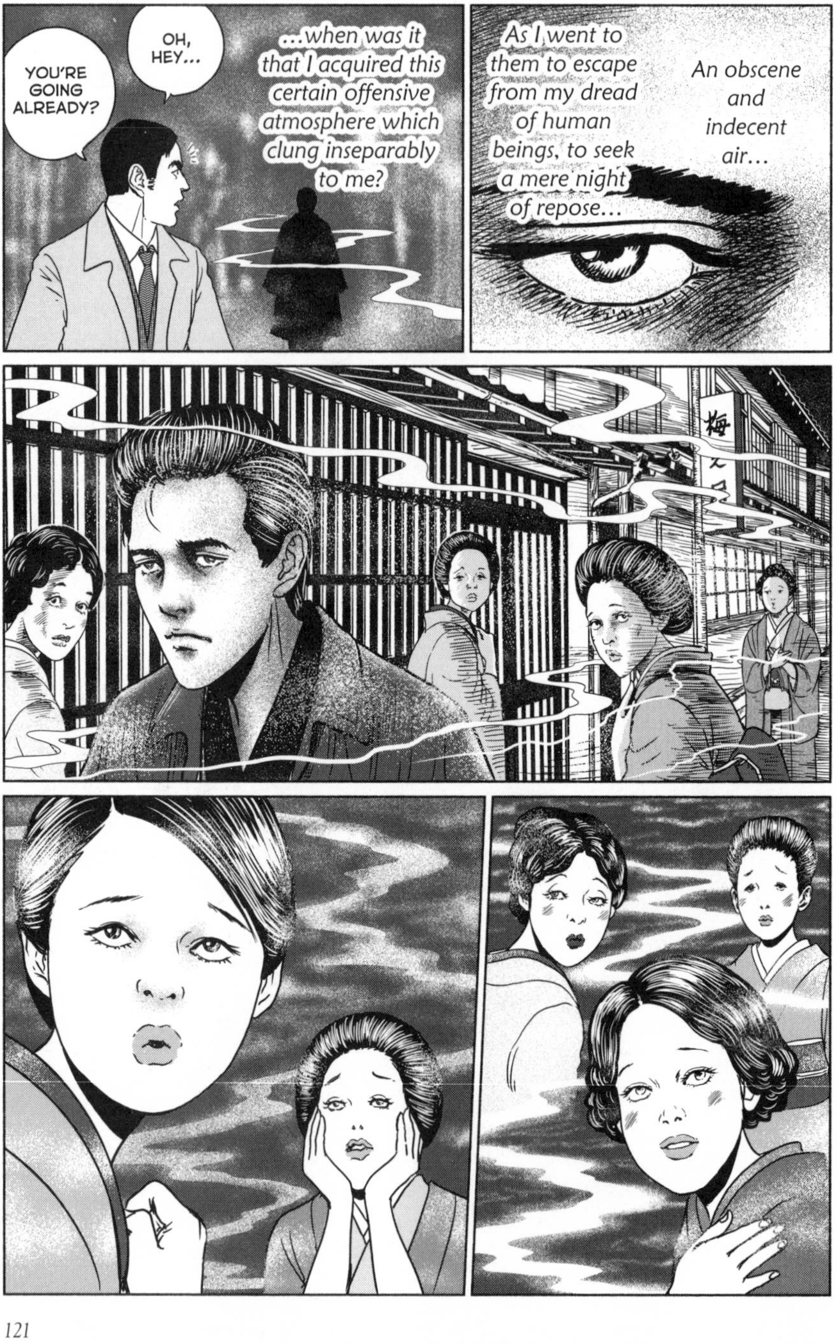
An obscene and indecent air…
As I went to them to escape from my dread of human beings, to seek a mere night of repose…
…when was it that I acquired this certain offensive atmosphere which clung inseparably to me?
OH, HEY…
YOU'RE GOING ALREADY?

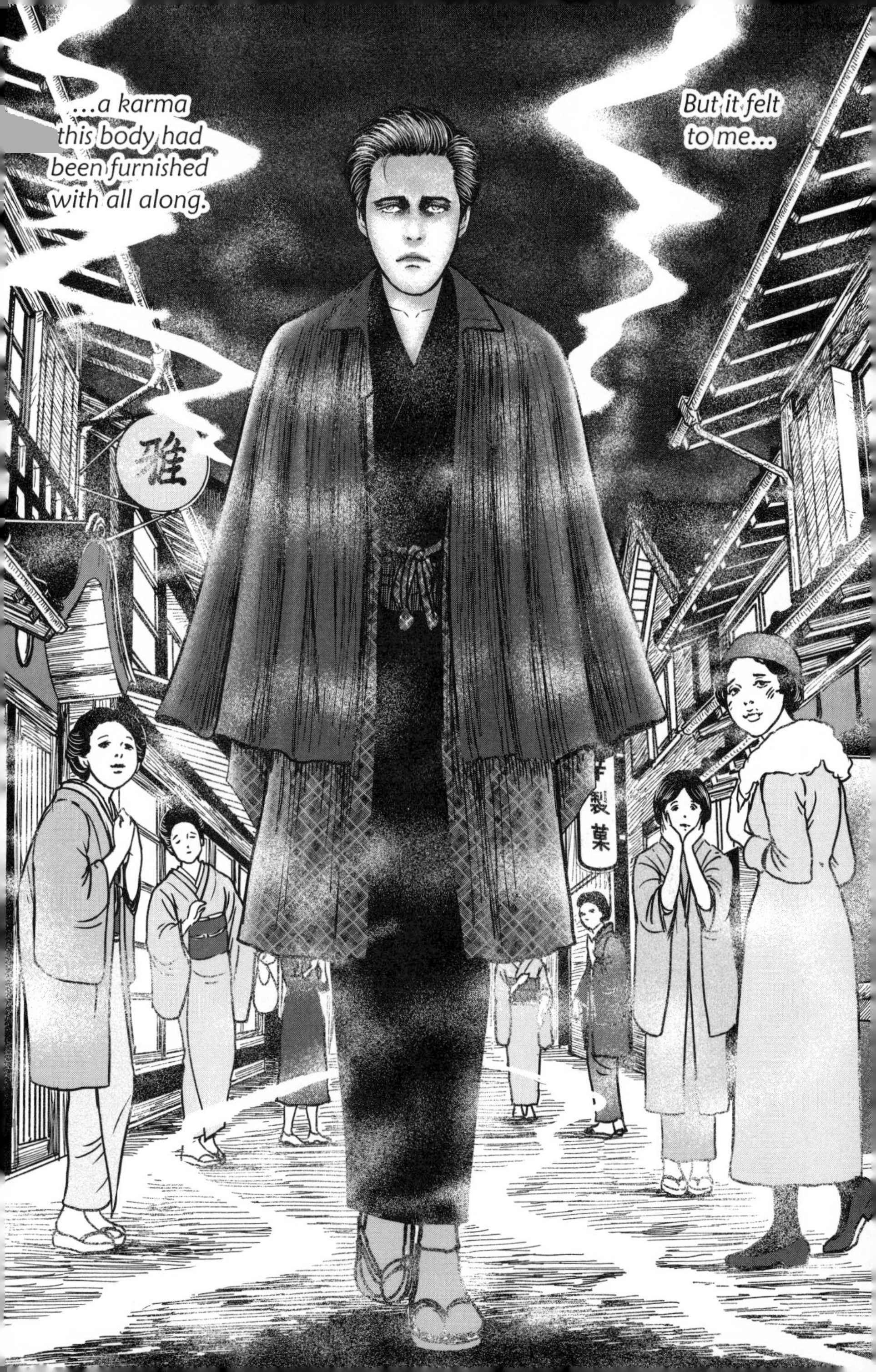
But it felt to me...
...a karma this body had been furnished with all along.
雅
製菓

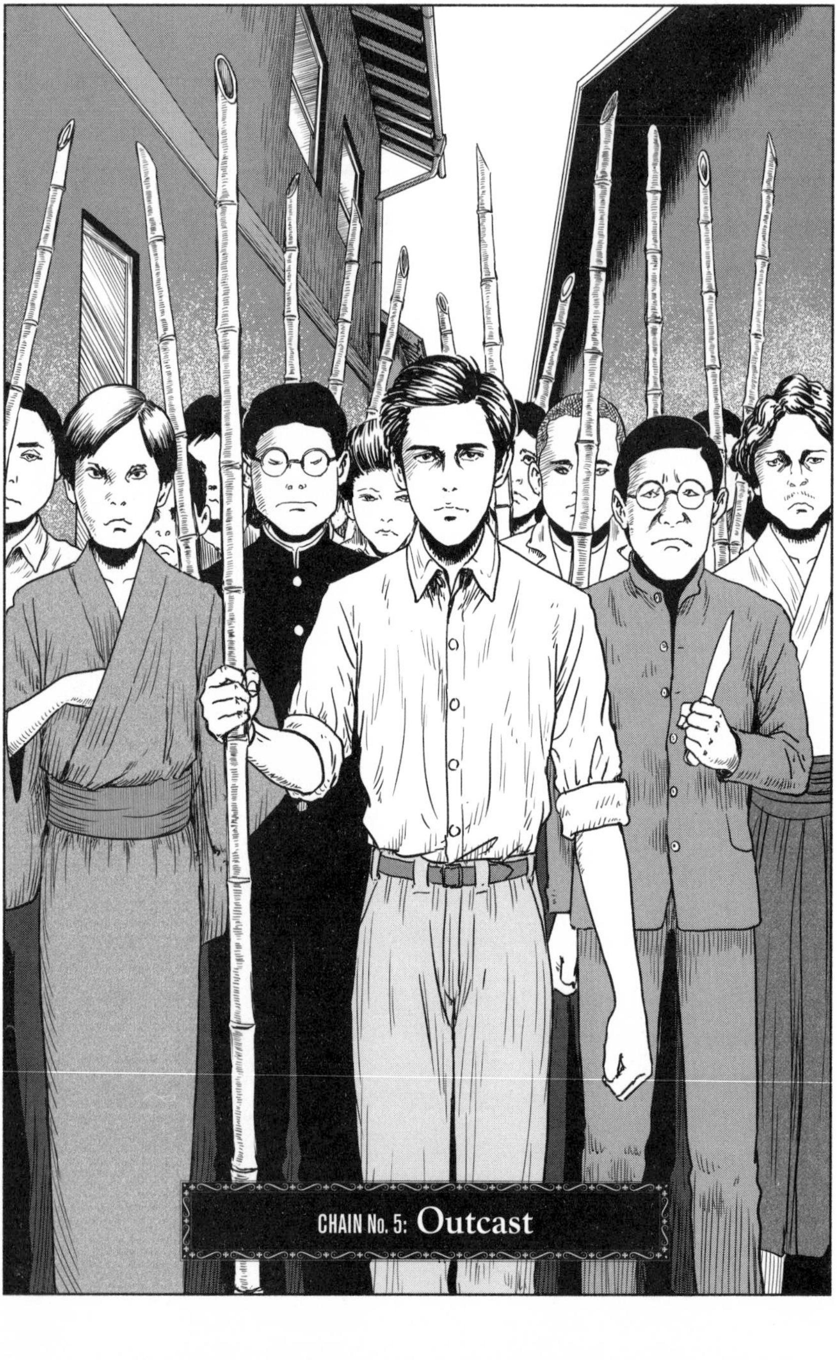
CHAIN No. 5: Outcast

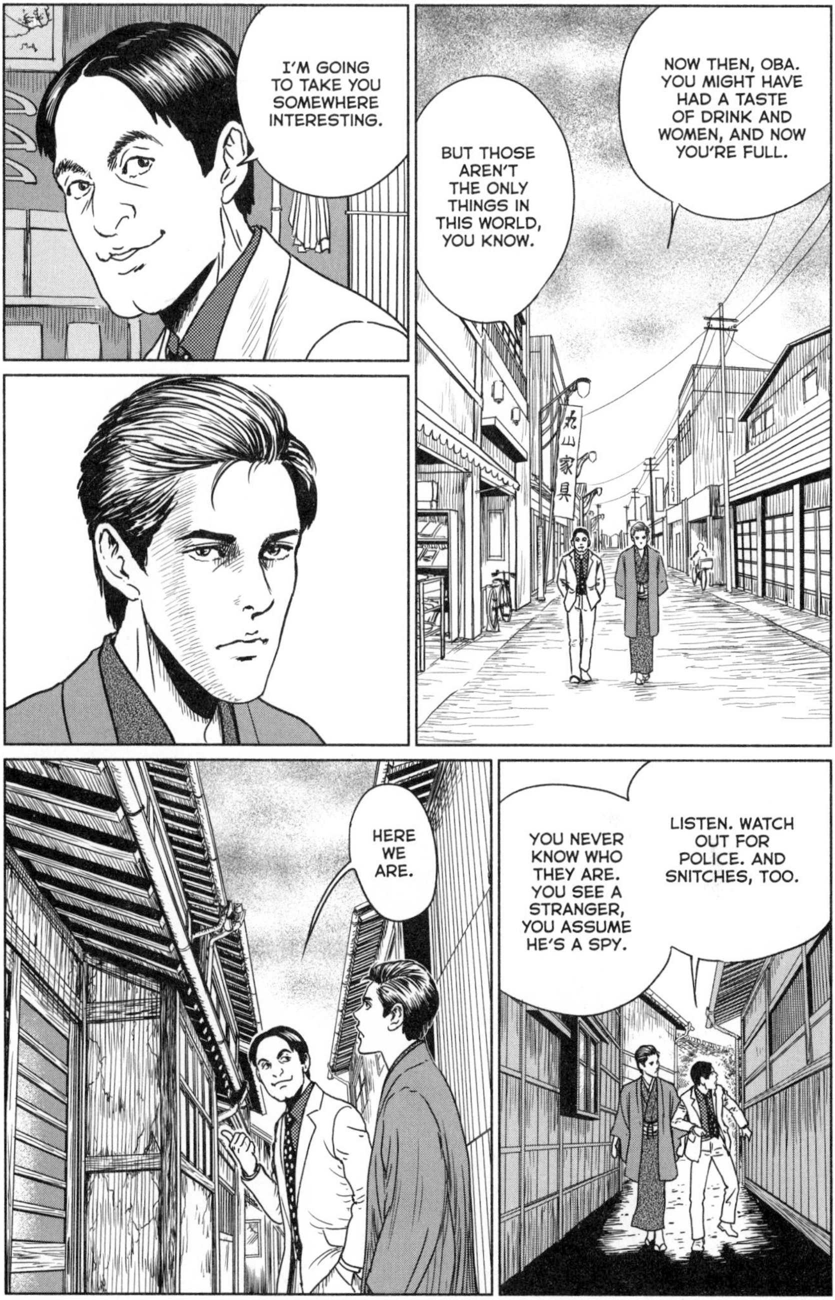
NOW THEN, OBA. YOU MIGHT HAVE HAD A TASTE OF DRINK AND WOMEN, AND NOW YOU'RE FULL.
BUT THOSE AREN'T THE ONLY THINGS IN THIS WORLD, YOU KNOW.
丸山家具
I'M GOING TO TAKE YOU SOMEWHERE INTERESTING.
LISTEN. WATCH OUT FOR POLICE. AND SNITCHES, TOO.
YOU NEVER KNOW WHO THEY ARE. YOU SEE A STRANGER, YOU ASSUME HE'S A SPY.
HERE WE ARE.

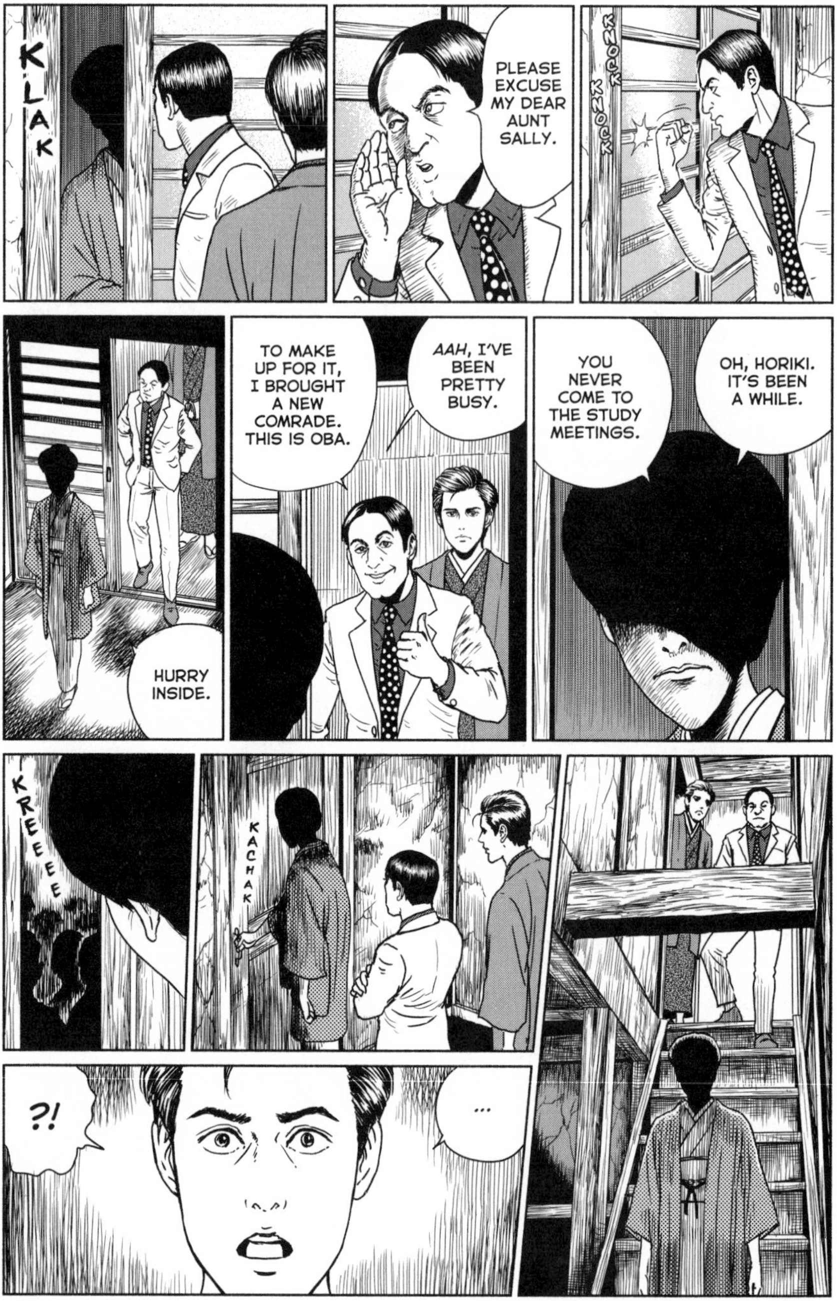
KNOCK KNOCK
PLEASE EXCUSE MY DEAR AUNT SALLY.
KLAK
OH, HORIKI. IT'S BEEN A WHILE.
YOU NEVER COME TO THE STUDY MEETINGS.
AAH, I'VE BEEN PRETTY BUSY.
TO MAKE UP FOR IT, I BROUGHT A NEW COMRADE. THIS IS OBA.
HURRY INSIDE.
KACHAK
KREEEEE
...
?!

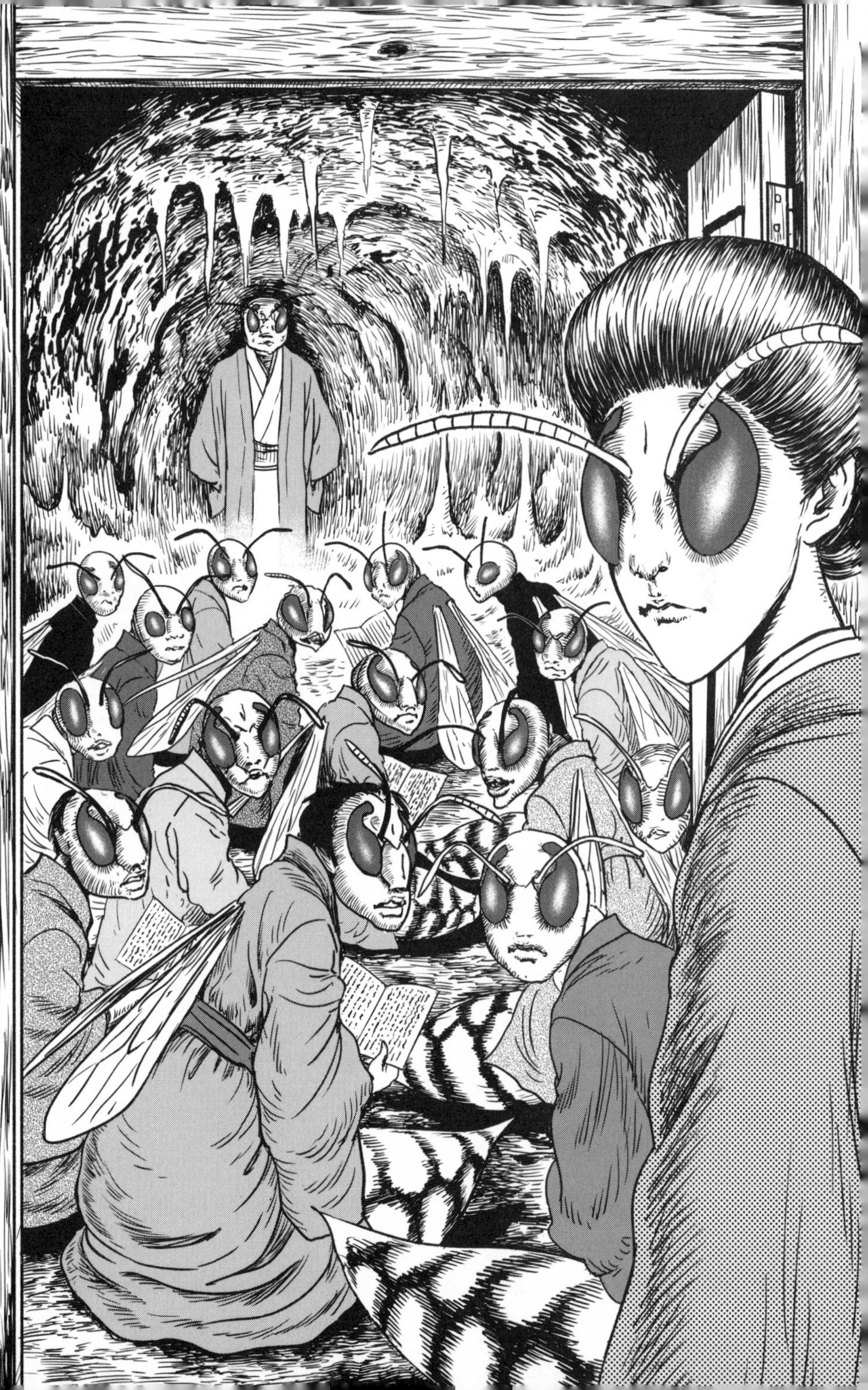

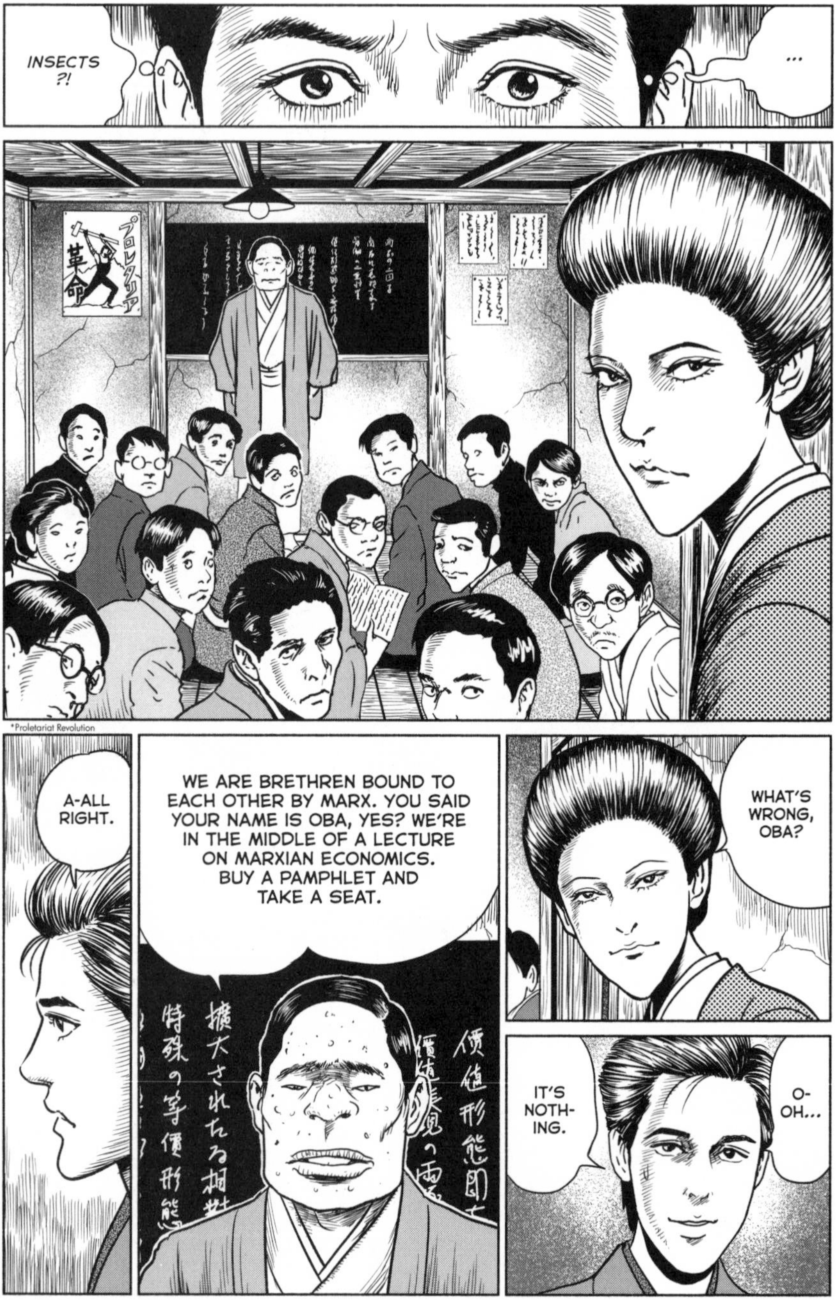
...
INSECTS ?!
プロレタリア革命
WHAT'S WRONG, OBA?
O-OH...
IT'S NOTHING.
WE ARE BRETHREN BOUND TO EACH OTHER BY MARX. YOU SAID YOUR NAME IS OBA, YES? WE'RE IN THE MIDDLE OF A LECTURE ON MARXIAN ECONOMICS. BUY A PAMPHLET AND TAKE A SEAT.
A-ALL RIGHT.

*Proletariat Revolution

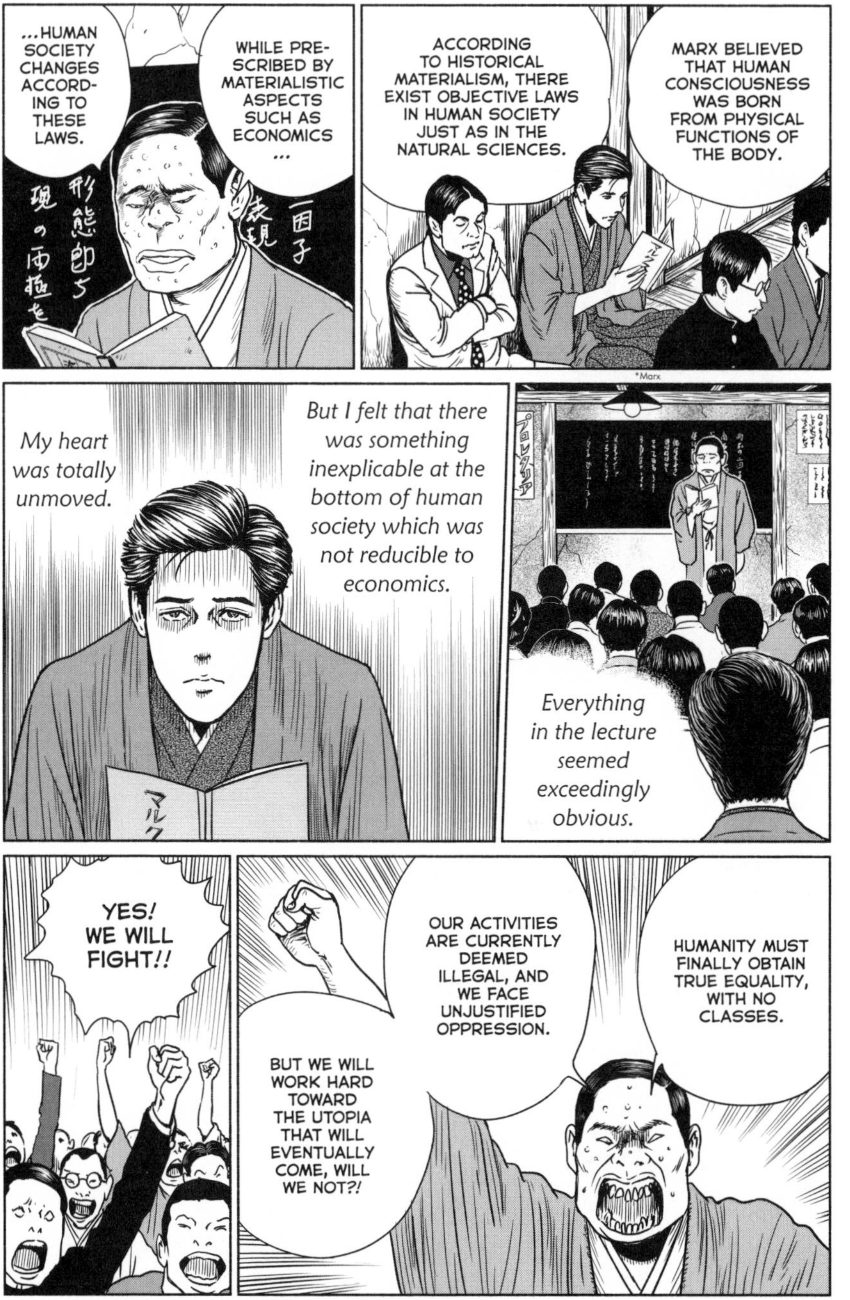
MARX BELIEVED THAT HUMAN CONSCIOUSNESS WAS BORN FROM PHYSICAL FUNCTIONS OF THE BODY.
ACCORDING TO HISTORICAL MATERIALISM, THERE EXIST OBJECTIVE LAWS IN HUMAN SOCIETY JUST AS IN THE NATURAL SCIENCES.
WHILE PRE-SCRIBED BY MATERIALISTIC ASPECTS SUCH AS ECONOMICS ...
...HUMAN SOCIETY CHANGES ACCORD-ING TO THESE LAWS.
*Marx
Everything in the lecture seemed exceedingly obvious.
But I felt that there was something inexplicable at the bottom of human society which was not reducible to economics.
My heart was totally unmoved.
HUMANITY MUST FINALLY OBTAIN TRUE EQUALITY, WITH NO CLASSES.
OUR ACTIVITIES ARE CURRENTLY DEEMED ILLEGAL, AND WE FACE UNJUSTIFIED OPPRESSION.
BUT WE WILL WORK HARD TOWARD THE UTOPIA THAT WILL EVENTUALLY COME, WILL WE NOT?!
YES! WE WILL FIGHT!!

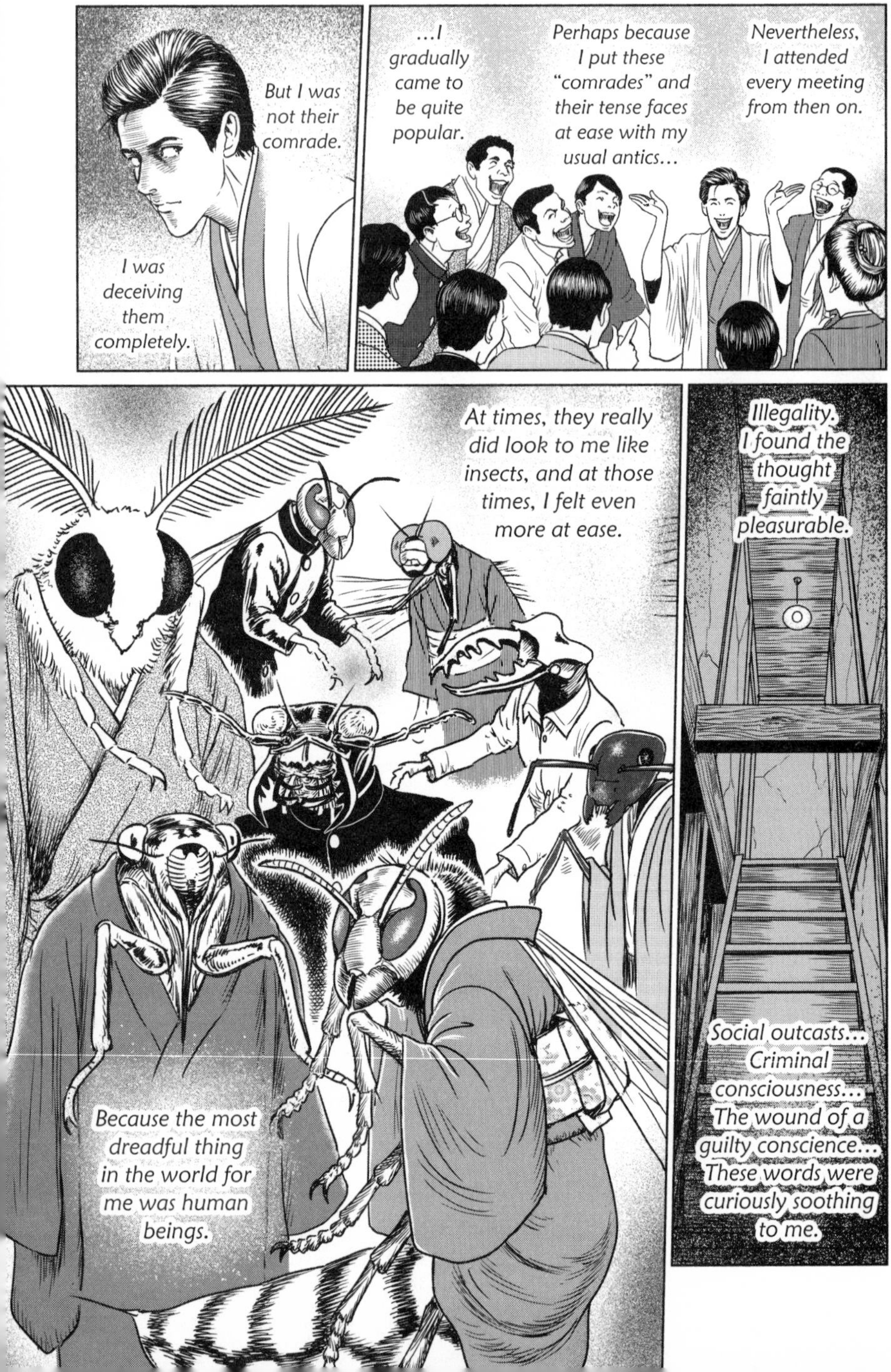
Nevertheless, I attended every meeting from then on.
Perhaps because I put these "comrades" and their tense faces at ease with my usual antics…
…I gradually came to be quite popular.
But I was not their comrade.
I was deceiving them completely.
Illegality. I found the thought faintly pleasurable.
Social outcasts… Criminal consciousness… The wound of a guilty conscience… These words were curiously soothing to me.
At times, they really did look to me like insects, and at those times, I felt even more at ease.
Because the most dreadful thing in the world for me was human beings.

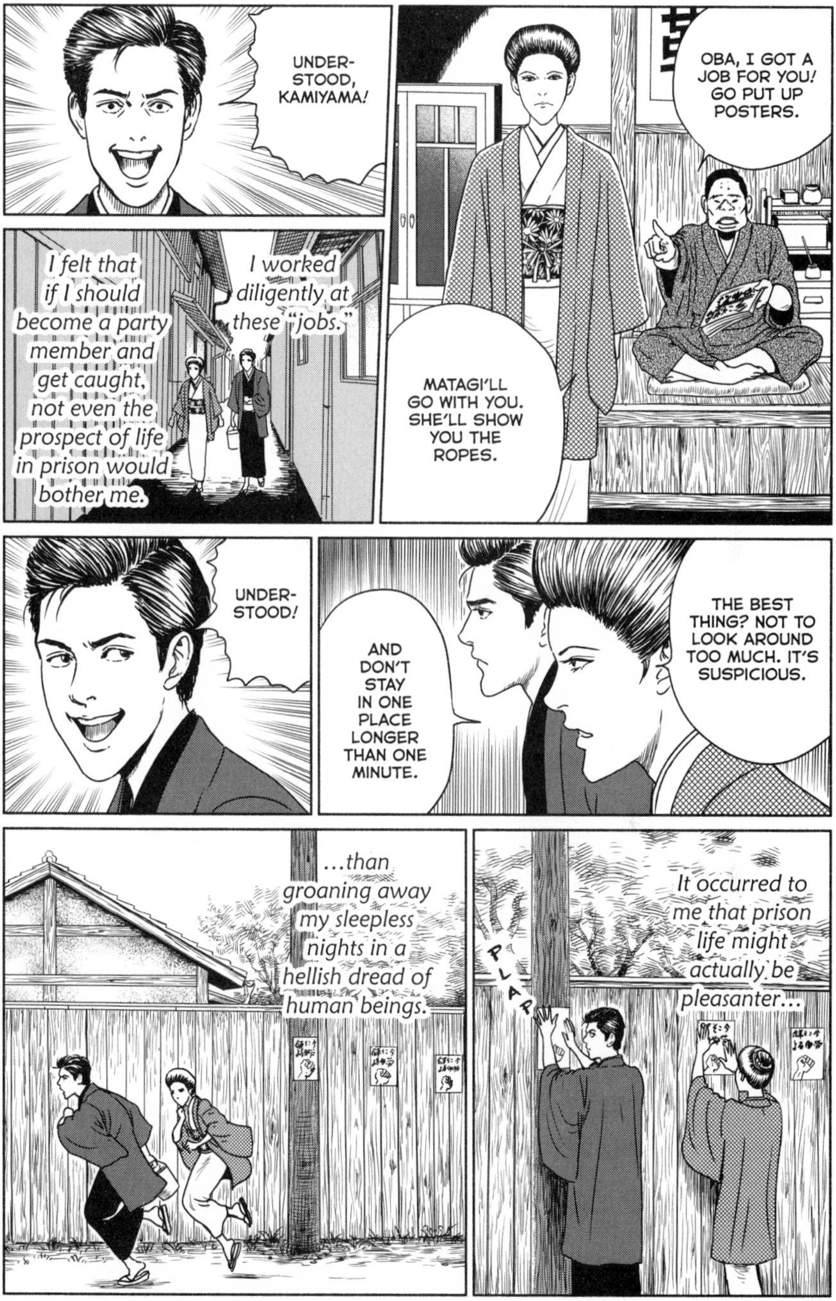
OBA, I GOT A JOB FOR YOU! GO PUT UP POSTERS.
MATAGI'LL GO WITH YOU. SHE'LL SHOW YOU THE ROPES.
UNDER-STOOD, KAMIYAMA!
I worked diligently at these "jobs."
I felt that if I should become a party member and get caught, not even the prospect of life in prison would bother me.
THE BEST THING? NOT TO LOOK AROUND TOO MUCH. IT'S SUSPICIOUS.
AND DON'T STAY IN ONE PLACE LONGER THAN ONE MINUTE.
UNDER-STOOD!
It occurred to me that prison life might actually be pleasanter...
PLAP
...than groaning away my sleepless nights in a hellish dread of human beings.

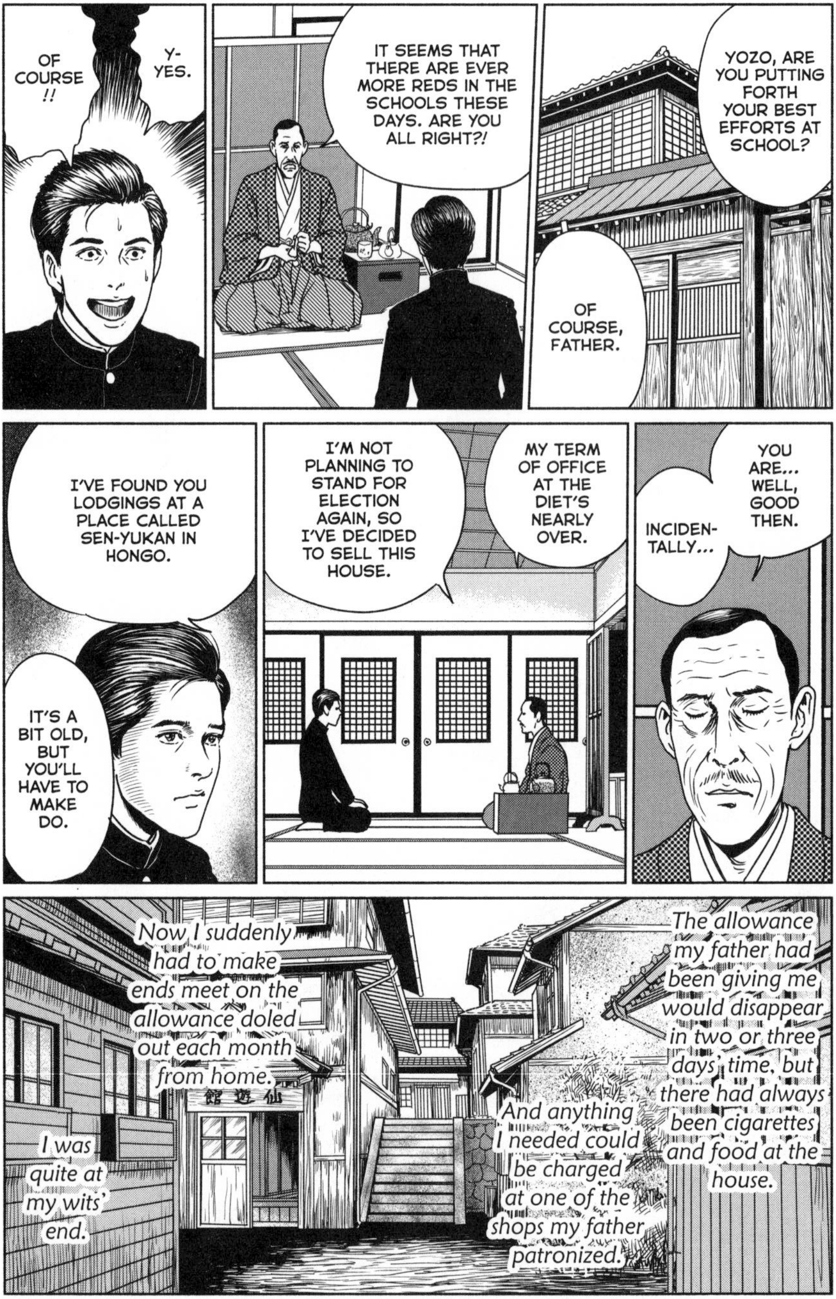
YOZO, ARE YOU PUTTING FORTH YOUR BEST EFFORTS AT SCHOOL?
OF COURSE, FATHER.
IT SEEMS THAT THERE ARE EVER MORE REDS IN THE SCHOOLS THESE DAYS. ARE YOU ALL RIGHT?!
Y-YES.
OF COURSE!!
YOU ARE... WELL, GOOD THEN.
INCIDENTALLY...
MY TERM OF OFFICE AT THE DIET'S NEARLY OVER.
I'M NOT PLANNING TO STAND FOR ELECTION AGAIN, SO I'VE DECIDED TO SELL THIS HOUSE.
I'VE FOUND YOU LODGINGS AT A PLACE CALLED SEN-YUKAN IN HONGO.
IT'S A BIT OLD, BUT YOU'LL HAVE TO MAKE DO.
The allowance my father had been giving me would disappear in two or three days' time, but there had always been cigarettes and food at the house.
And anything I needed could be charged at one of the shops my father patronized.
Now I suddenly had to make ends meet on the allowance doled out each month from home.
仙遊館
I was quite at my wits' end.

*Sen-yukan

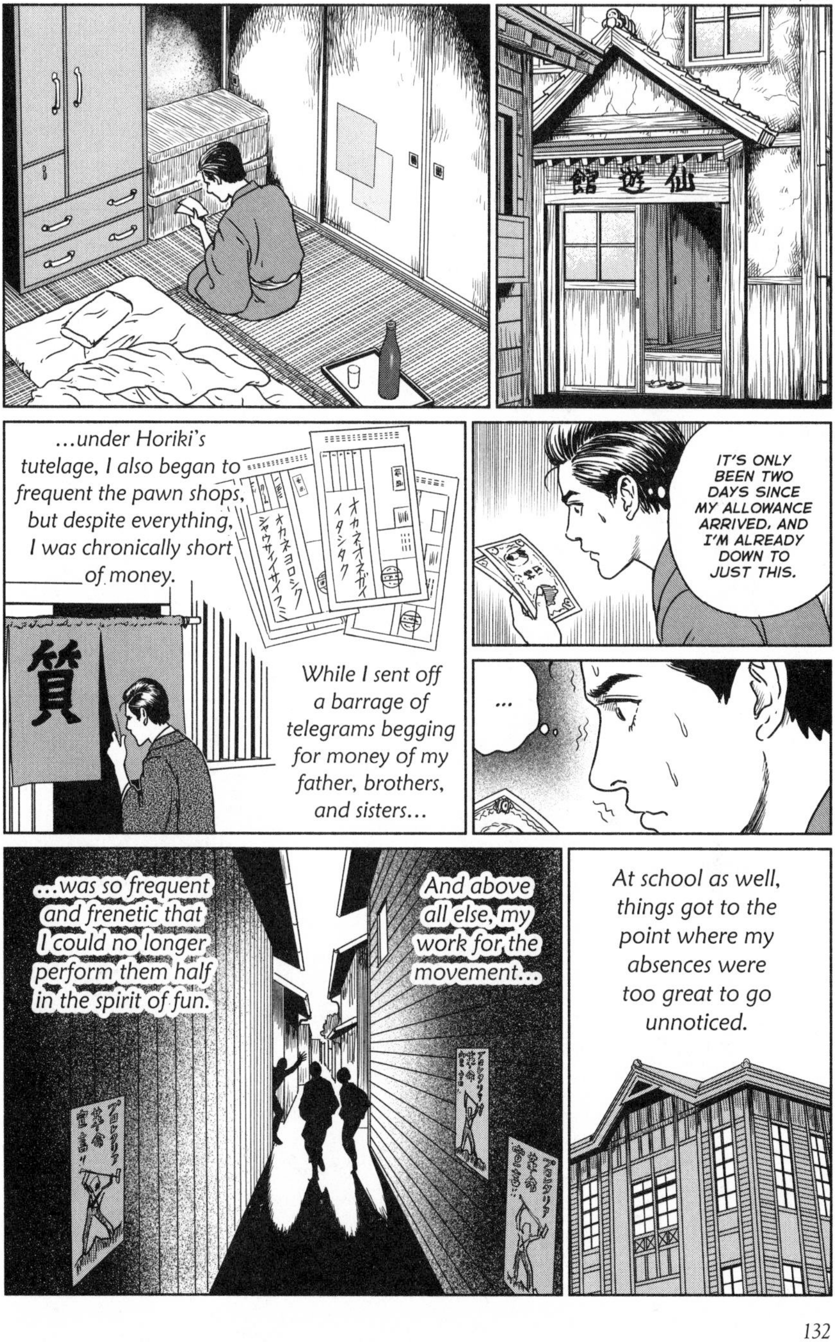
仙遊館
...under Horiki's tutelage, I also began to frequent the pawn shops, but despite everything, I was chronically short of money.
オカネオネガイイタシタク
オカネヨロシクシャウサイサイフミ
質
While I sent off a barrage of telegrams begging for money of my father, brothers, and sisters...
IT'S ONLY BEEN TWO DAYS SINCE MY ALLOWANCE ARRIVED, AND I'M ALREADY DOWN TO JUST THIS.
...
At school as well, things got to the point where my absences were too great to go unnoticed.
And above all else, my work for the movement...
...was so frequent and frenetic that I could no longer perform them half in the spirit of fun.

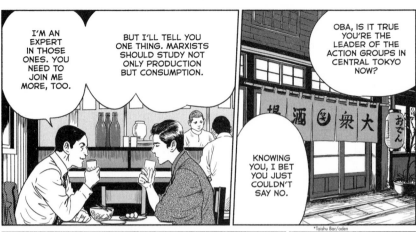

OBA, IS IT TRUE YOU'RE THE LEADER OF THE ACTION GROUPS IN CENTRAL TOKYO NOW?
大衆酒場
おでん
KNOWING YOU, I BET YOU JUST COULDN'T SAY NO.
BUT I'LL TELL YOU ONE THING. MARXISTS SHOULD STUDY NOT ONLY PRODUCTION BUT CONSUMPTION.
I'M AN EXPERT IN THOSE ONES. YOU NEED TO JOIN ME MORE, TOO.
HAVING FUN, *HM?*
HORIKI, YOU'RE NEVER AT THE MEETINGS.
KAMIYAMA'S LOST ALL HOPE IN YOU.
H-HOW SURPRISING, NAEKO MATAGI. I AM FIGHTING THE CLASS WAR IN MY OWN WAY.
TO WIT, I AM GIVING THIS DRINK ITS TRANSACTIONAL VALUE OF 50 SEN.
ENOUGH SMALL TALK.
OBA... I HAVE SOMETHING IMPORTANT TO DISCUSS.
*Taishu Bar/oden

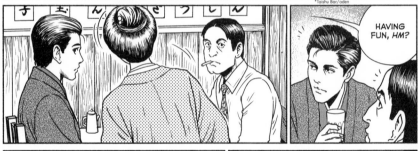

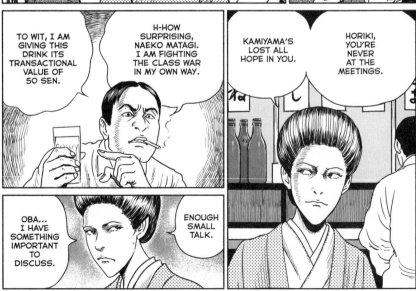

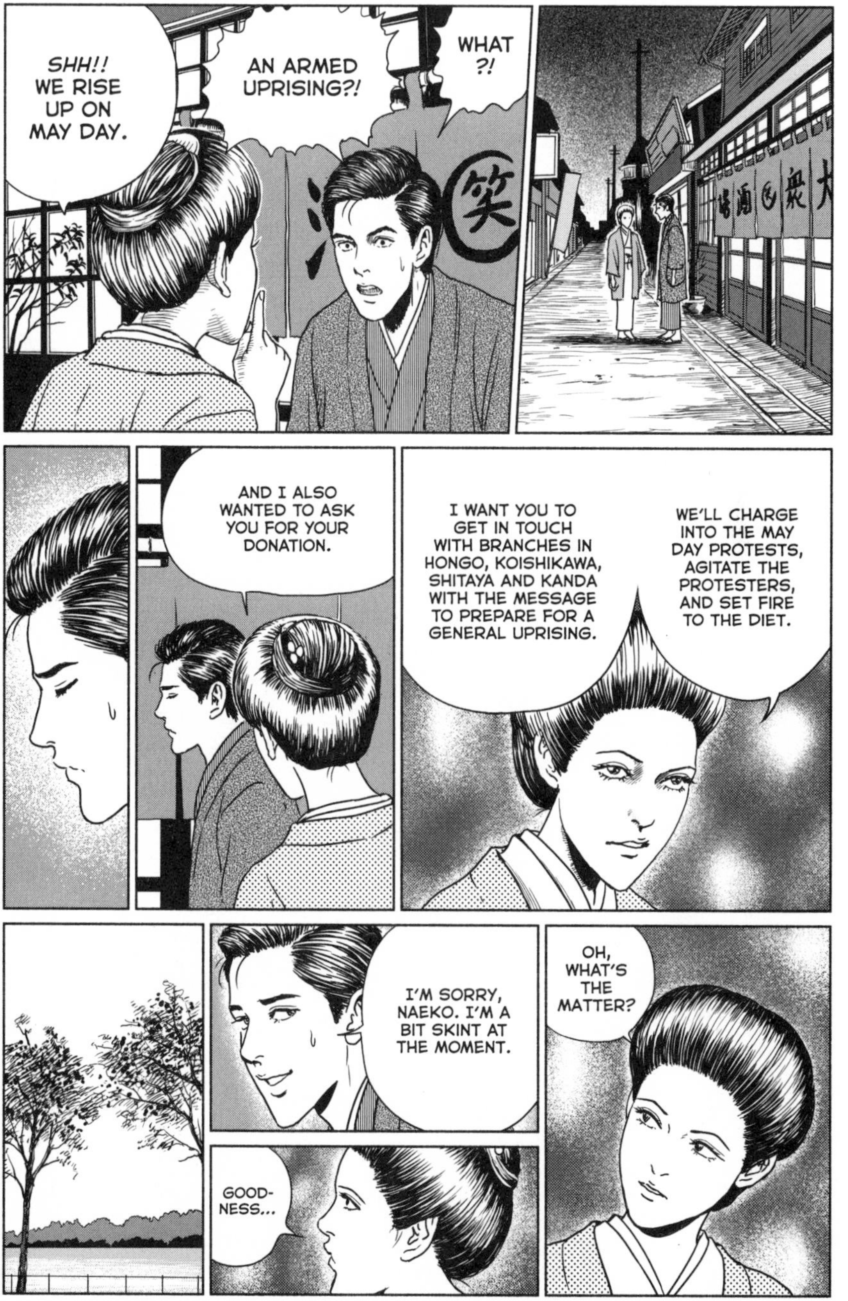
WHAT ?!
AN ARMED UPRISING?!
SHH!! WE RISE UP ON MAY DAY.
WE'LL CHARGE INTO THE MAY DAY PROTESTS, AGITATE THE PROTESTERS, AND SET FIRE TO THE DIET.
I WANT YOU TO GET IN TOUCH WITH BRANCHES IN HONGO, KOISHIKAWA, SHITAYA AND KANDA WITH THE MESSAGE TO PREPARE FOR A GENERAL UPRISING.
AND I ALSO WANTED TO ASK YOU FOR YOUR DONATION.
OH, WHAT'S THE MATTER?
I'M SORRY, NAEKO. I'M A BIT SKINT AT THE MOMENT.
GOOD-NESS...

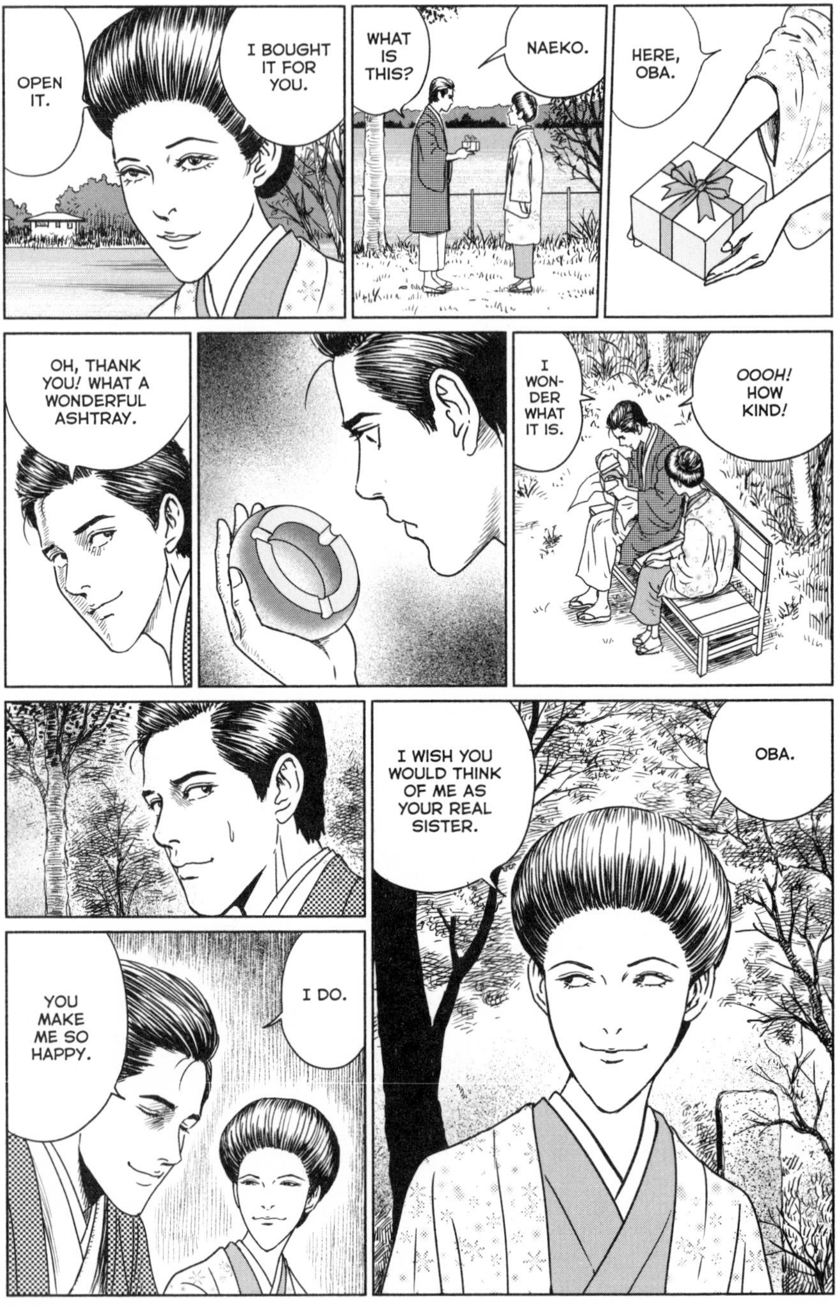
HERE, OBA.
NAEKO.
WHAT IS THIS?
I BOUGHT IT FOR YOU.
OPEN IT.
OOOH! HOW KIND!
I WONDER WHAT IT IS.
OH, THANK YOU! WHAT A WONDERFUL ASHTRAY.
OBA.
I WISH YOU WOULD THINK OF ME AS YOUR REAL SISTER.
I DO.
YOU MAKE ME SO HAPPY.

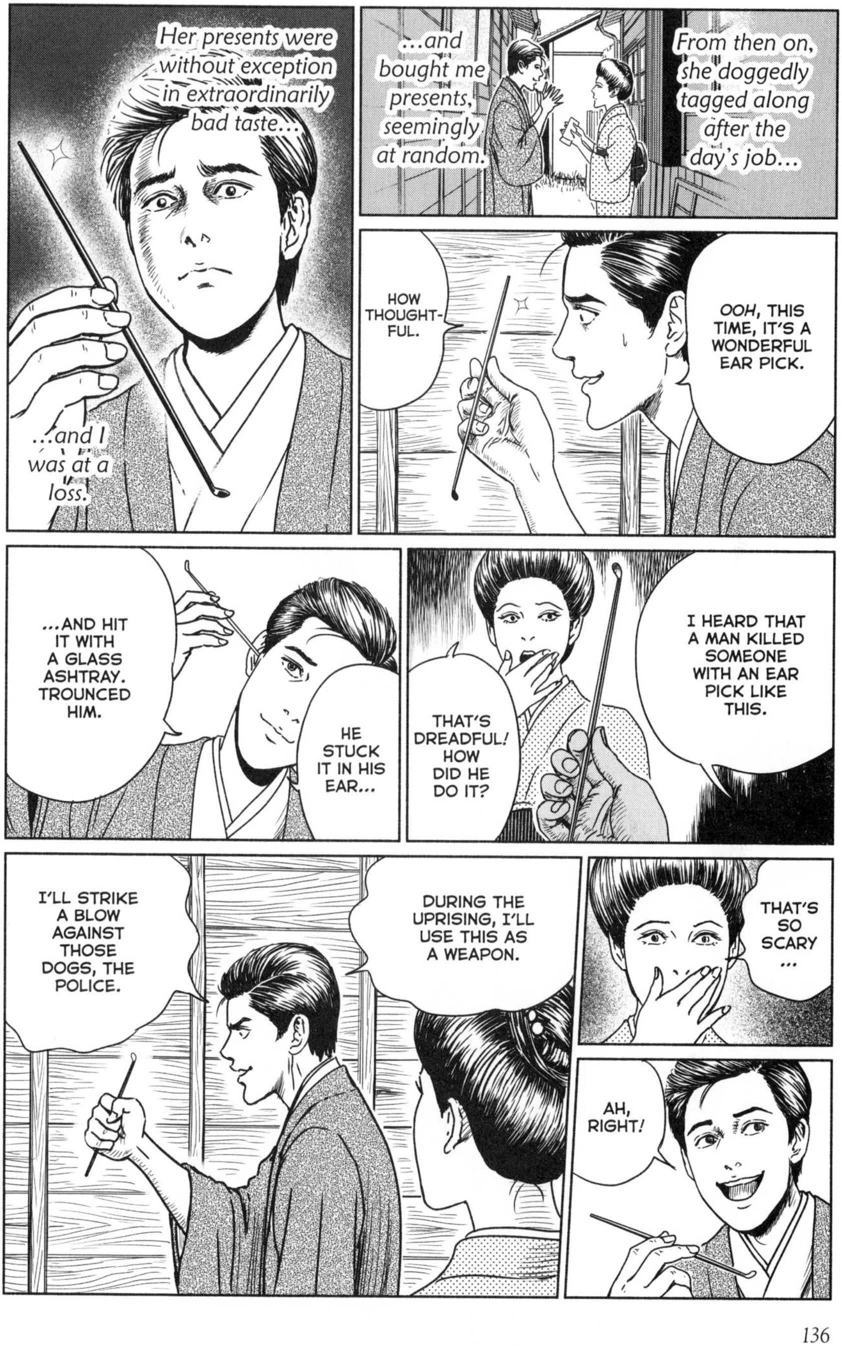
From then on, she doggedly tagged along after the day's job...
...and bought me presents, seemingly at random.
OOH, THIS TIME, IT'S A WONDERFUL EAR PICK.
HOW THOUGHTFUL.
Her presents were without exception in extraordinarily bad taste...
...and I was at a loss.
I HEARD THAT A MAN KILLED SOMEONE WITH AN EAR PICK LIKE THIS.
THAT'S DREADFUL! HOW DID HE DO IT?
HE STUCK IT IN HIS EAR...
...AND HIT IT WITH A GLASS ASHTRAY. TROUNCED HIM.
THAT'S SO SCARY...
AH, RIGHT!
DURING THE UPRISING, I'LL USE THIS AS A WEAPON.
I'LL STRIKE A BLOW AGAINST THOSE DOGS, THE POLICE.

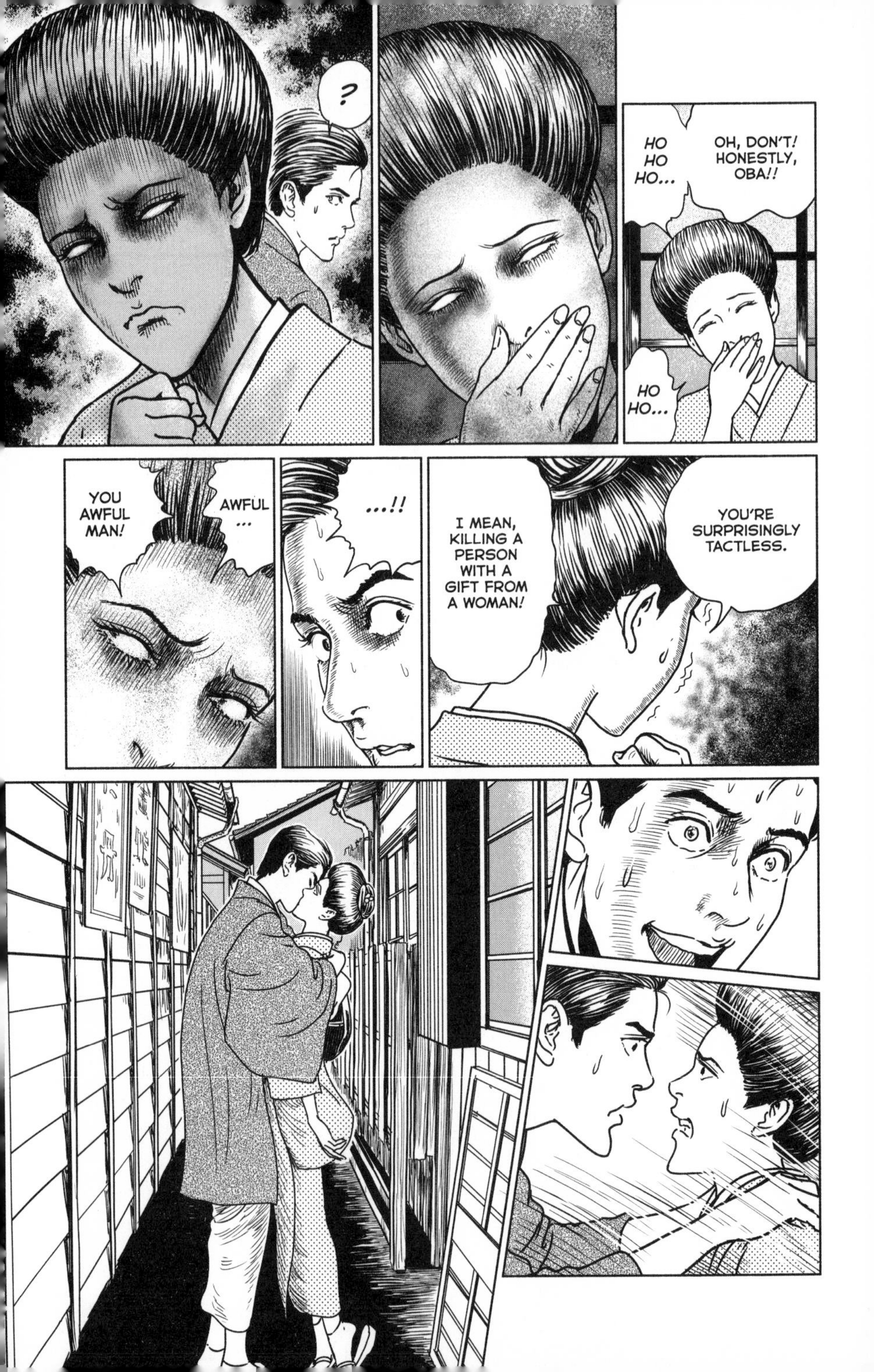
OH, DON'T! HONESTLY, OBA!!
HO HO HO...
HO HO...
?
YOU'RE SURPRISINGLY TACTLESS.
I MEAN, KILLING A PERSON WITH A GIFT FROM A WOMAN!
...!!
AWFUL ...
YOU AWFUL MAN!

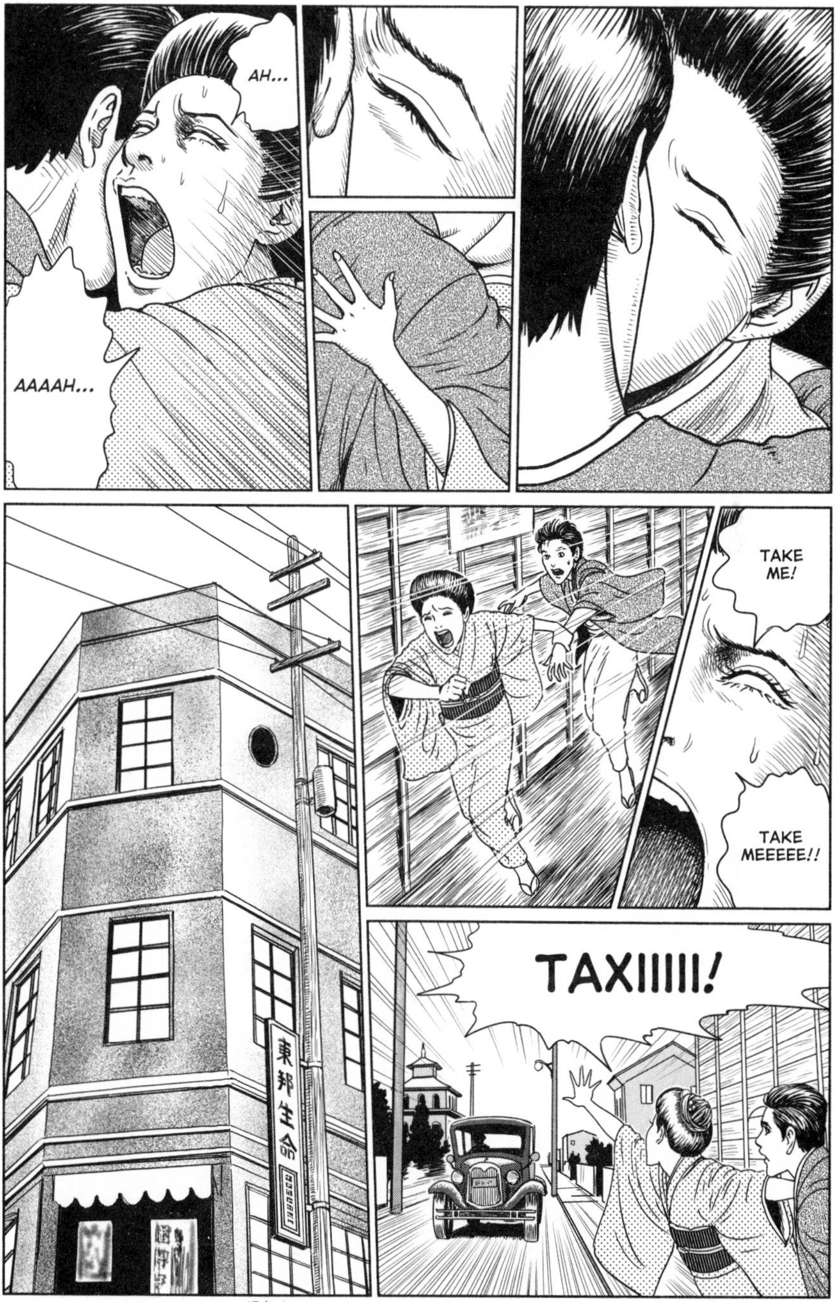
AH...
AAAAH...
TAKE ME!
TAKE MEEEEE!!
TAXIIIII!
東邦生命

*Toho Insurance

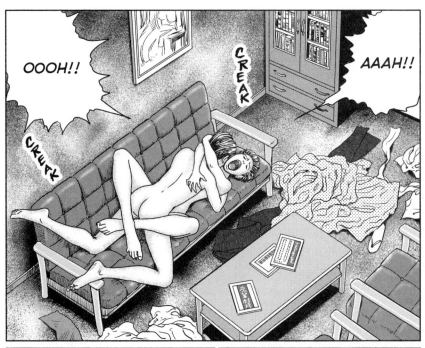

OOOH!!

CREAK

AAAH!!

CRWTK

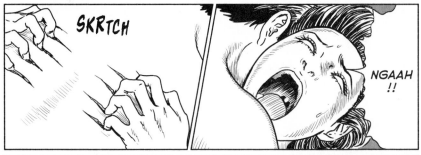

SKRTCH

NGAAH!!

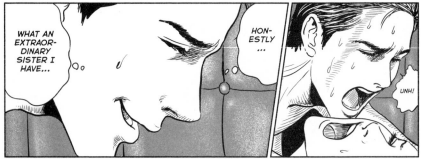

WHAT AN EXTRAORDINARY SISTER I HAVE...

HONESTLY...

UNH!

*Flags: Prevent unemployment
No pay cuts! No dismissals!
Welfare for the unemployed
An eight-hour workday
Minimum wage laws

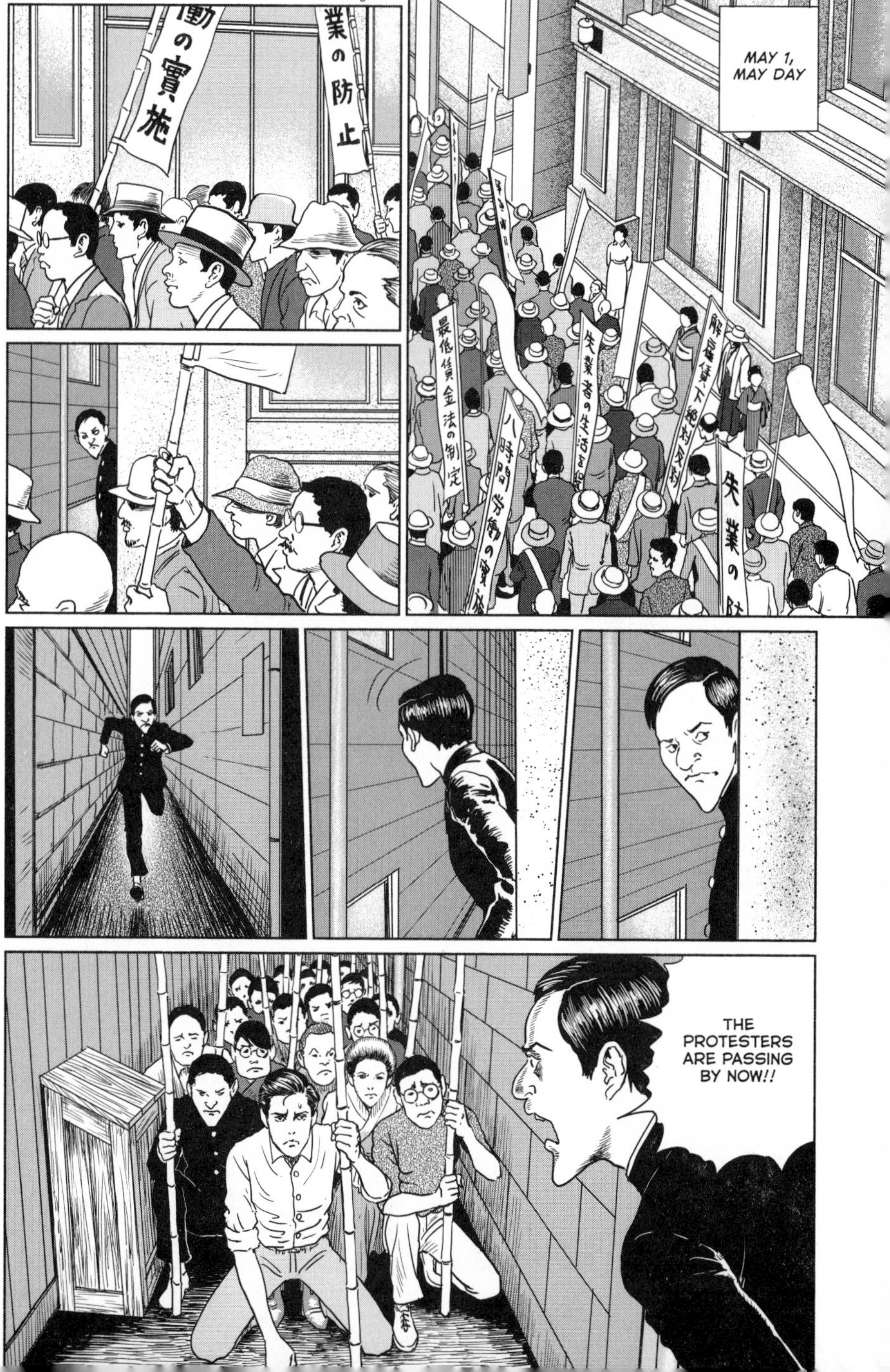
MAY 1, MAY DAY
解雇賃下絶対反対
最低賃金法の制定
THE PROTESTERS ARE PASSING BY NOW!!

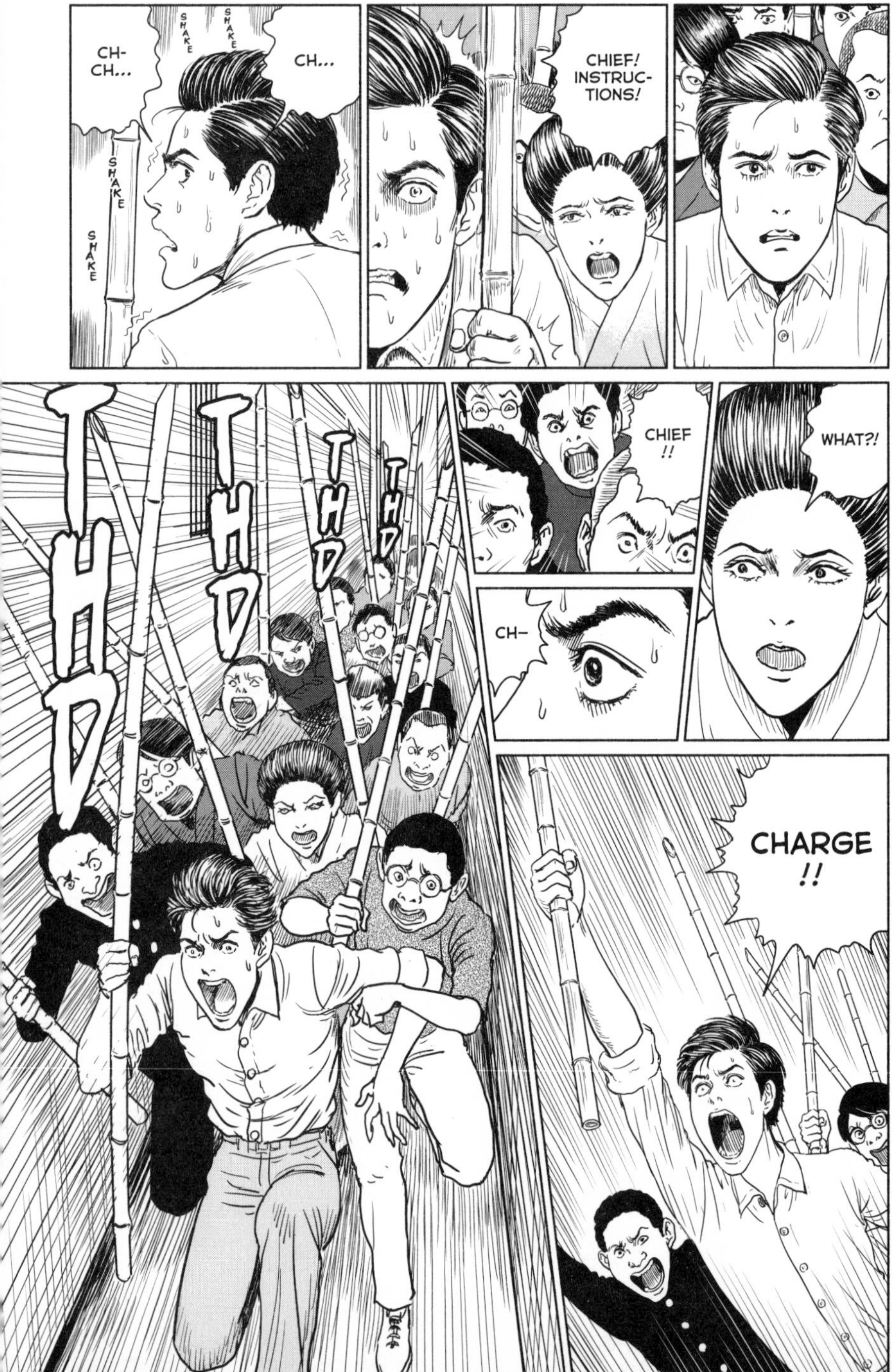
CHIEF! INSTRUCTIONS!
SHAKE
SHAKE
CH...
CH- CH...
SHAKE
SHAKE
WHAT?!
CHIEF!!
CH–
CHARGE!!
THD
THD
THD
THD

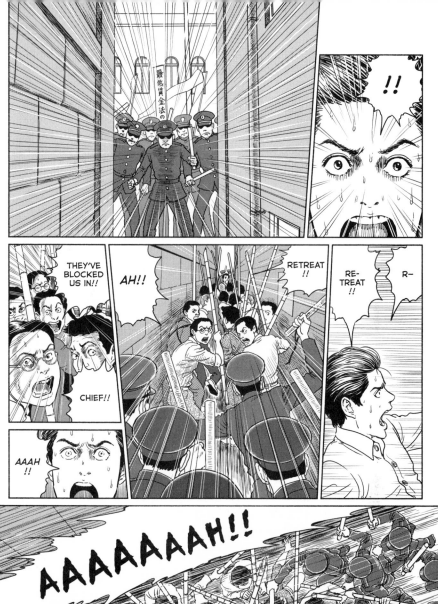

!!

THEY'VE BLOCKED US IN!!

AH!!

RETREAT !!

RE-TREAT !!

R–

CHIEF!!

AAAH !!

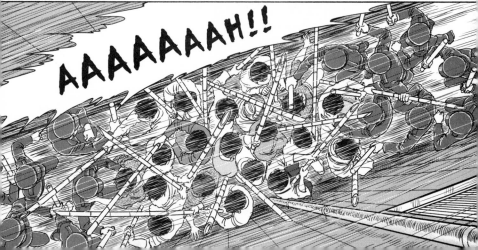

AAAAAAAH!!

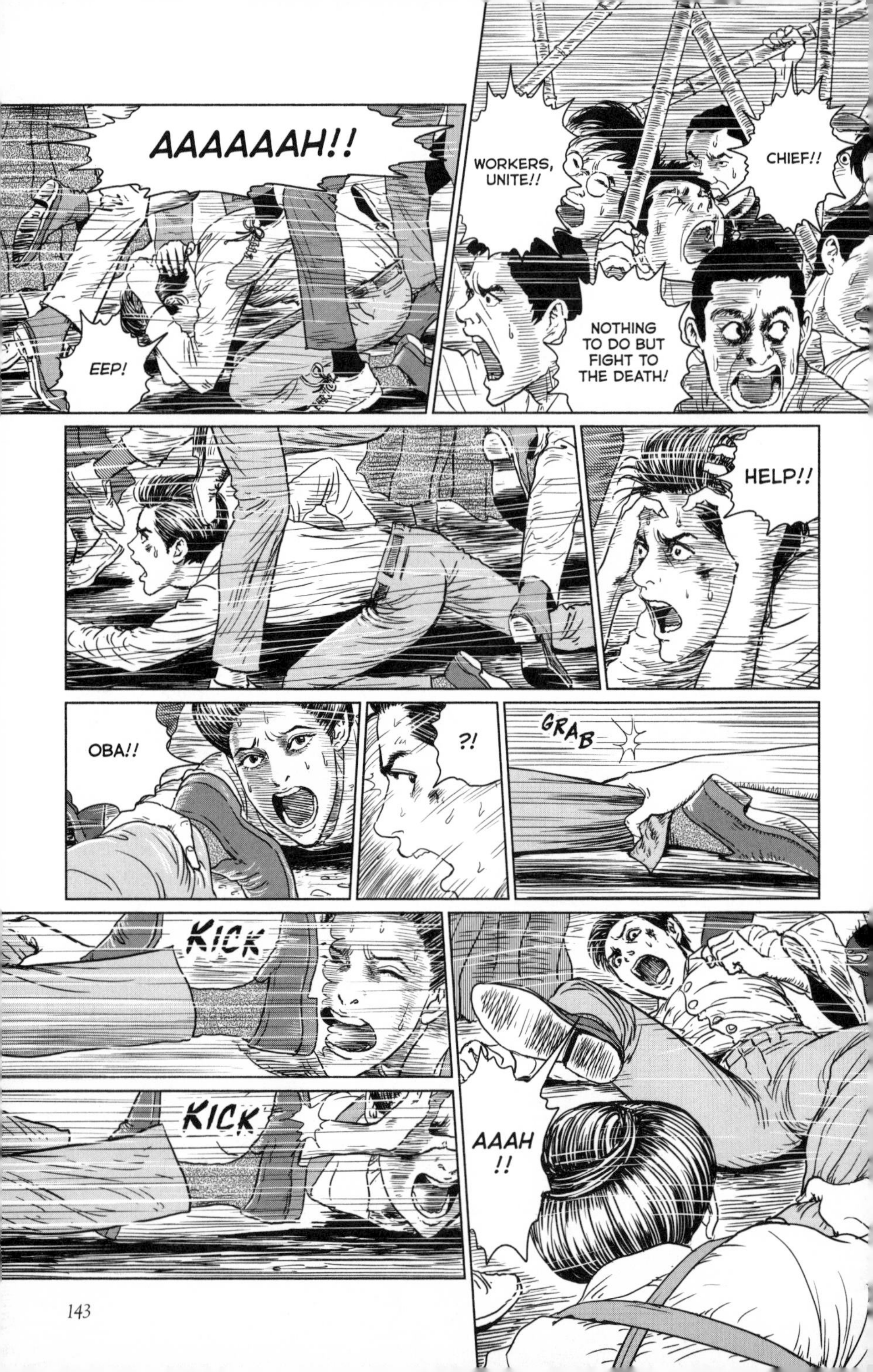
CHIEF!!
WORKERS, UNITE!!
NOTHING TO DO BUT FIGHT TO THE DEATH!
AAAAAAH!!
EEP!
HELP!!
GRAB
?!
OBA!!
AAAH !!
KICK
KICK

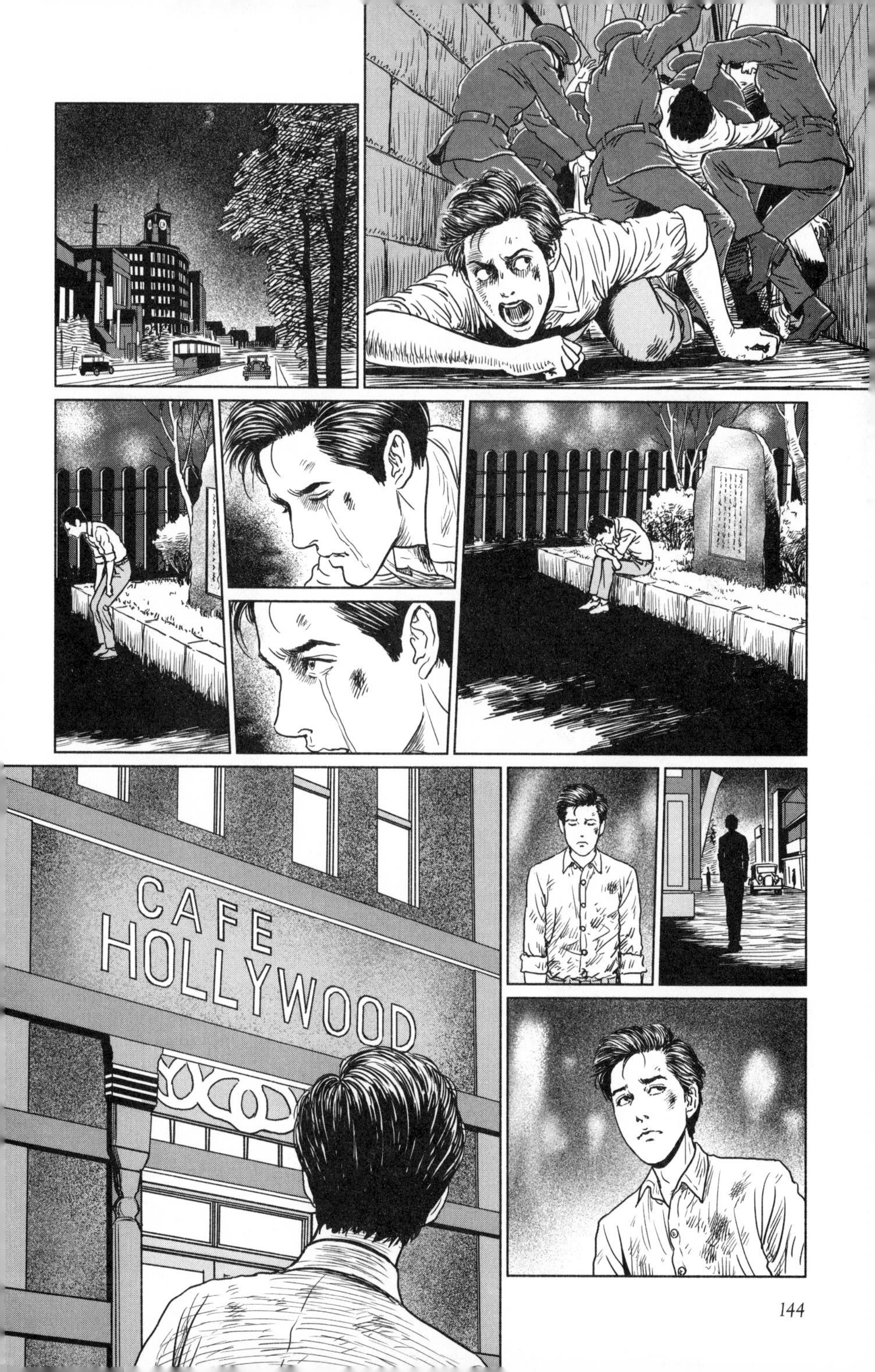
CAFE
HOLLYWOOD

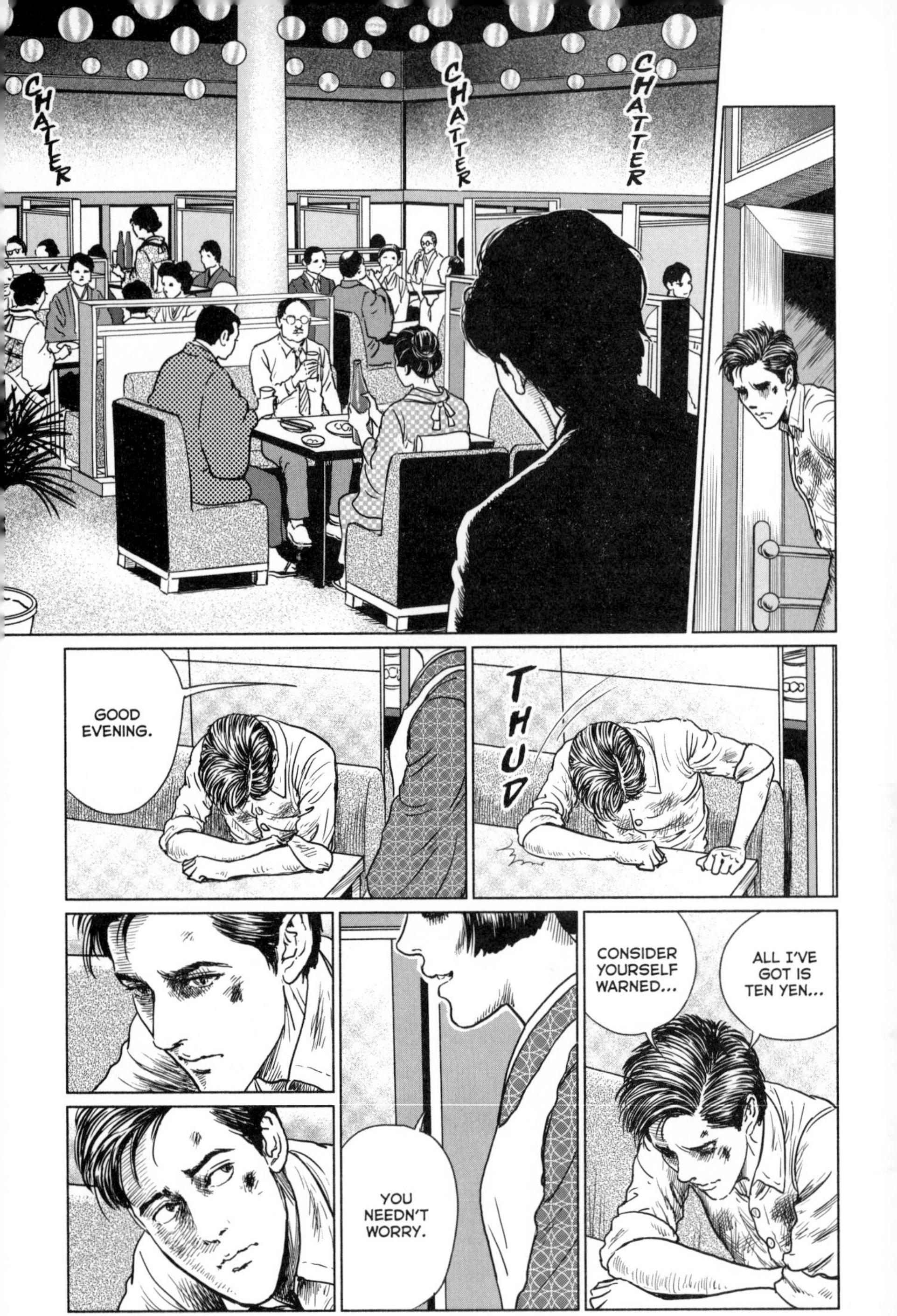
CHATTER
CHATTER
CHATTER
THUD
GOOD EVENING.
ALL I'VE GOT IS TEN YEN...
CONSIDER YOURSELF WARNED...
YOU NEEDN'T WORRY.

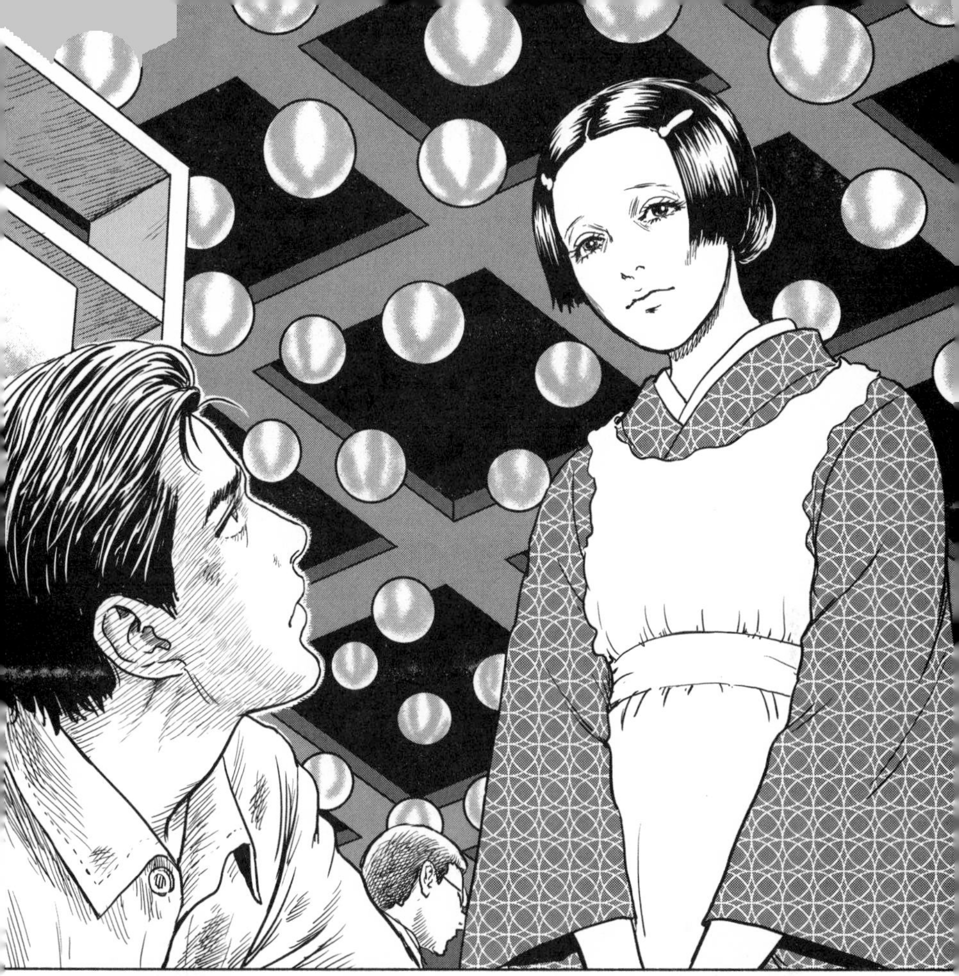

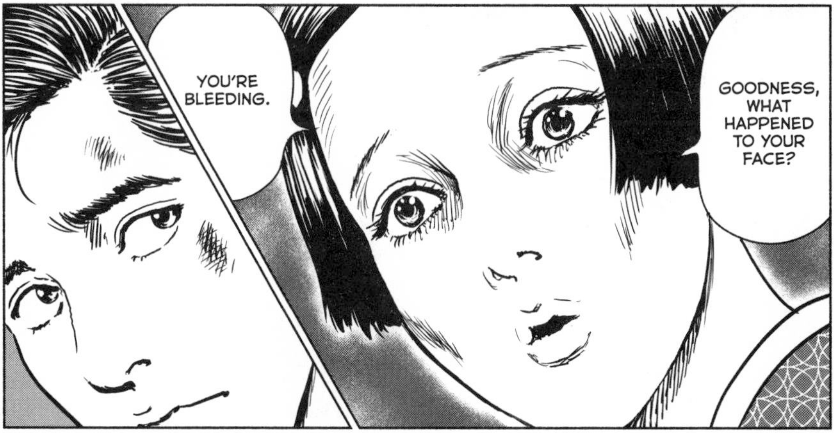
GOODNESS, WHAT HAPPENED TO YOUR FACE?
YOU'RE BLEEDING.

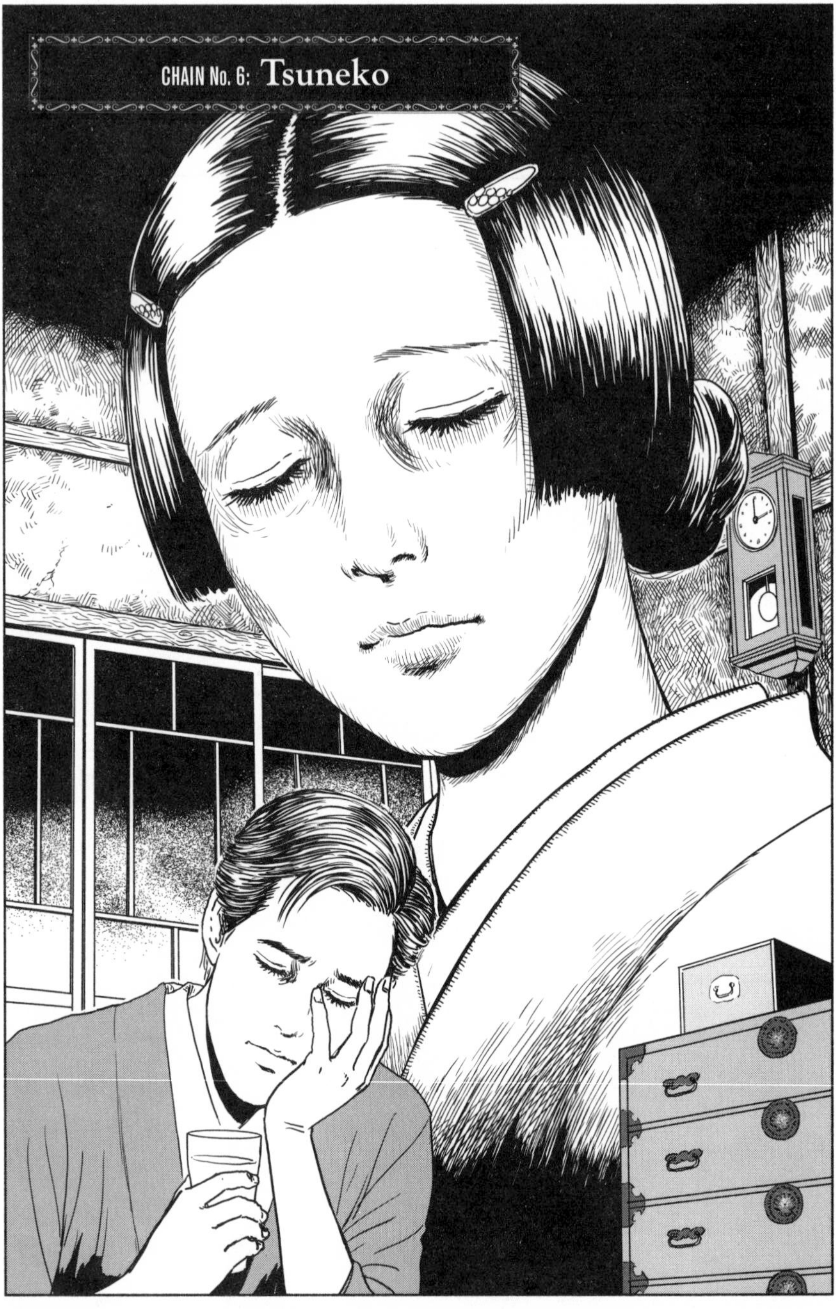
CHAIN No. 6: Tsuneko

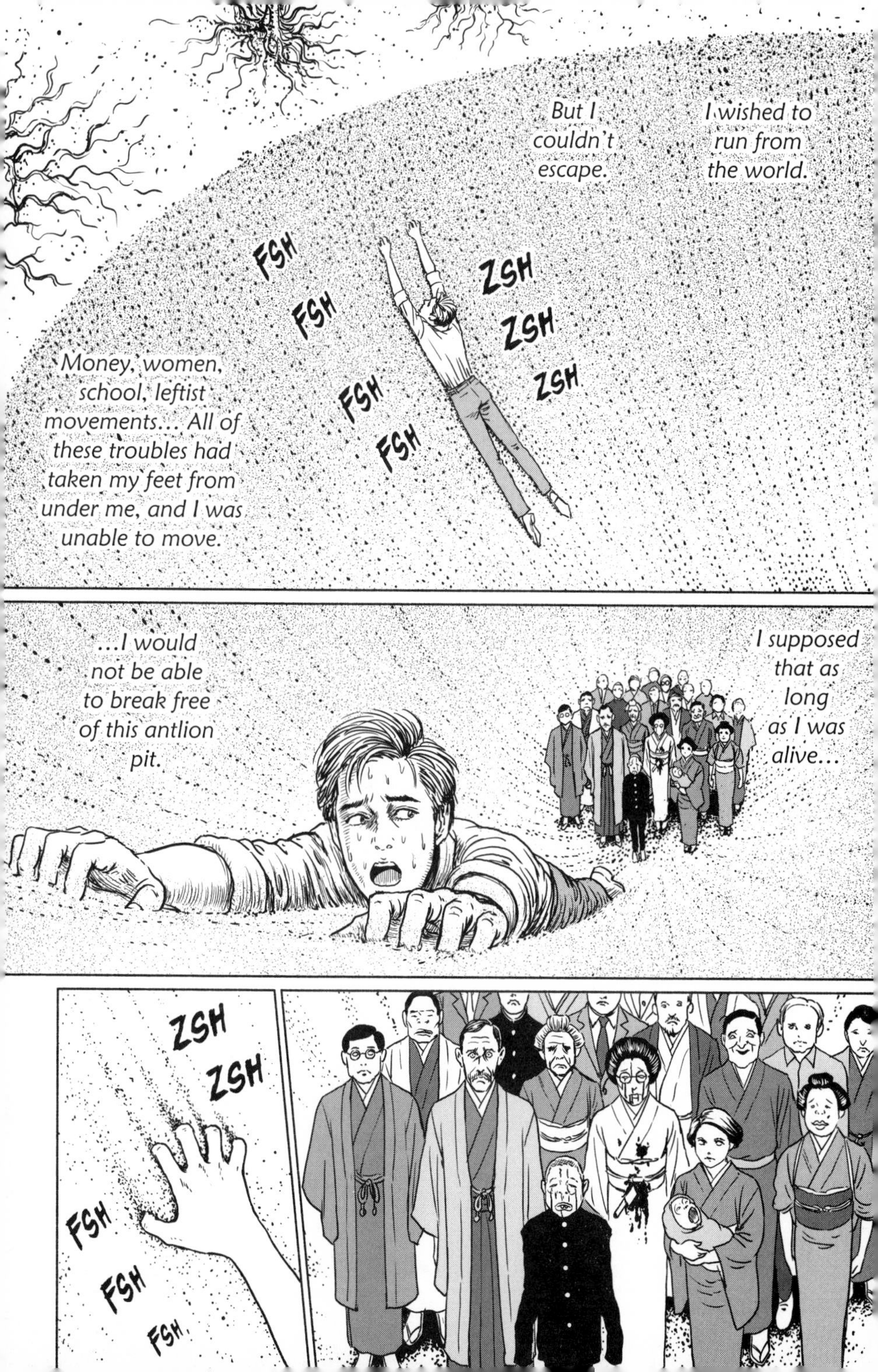
I wished to run from the world.
But I couldn't escape.
ZSH
ZSH
ZSH
FSH
FSH
FSH
FSH
Money, women, school, leftist movements… All of these troubles had taken my feet from under me, and I was unable to move.
I supposed that as long as I was alive…
…I would not be able to break free of this antlion pit.
ZSH
ZSH
FSH
FSH
FSH

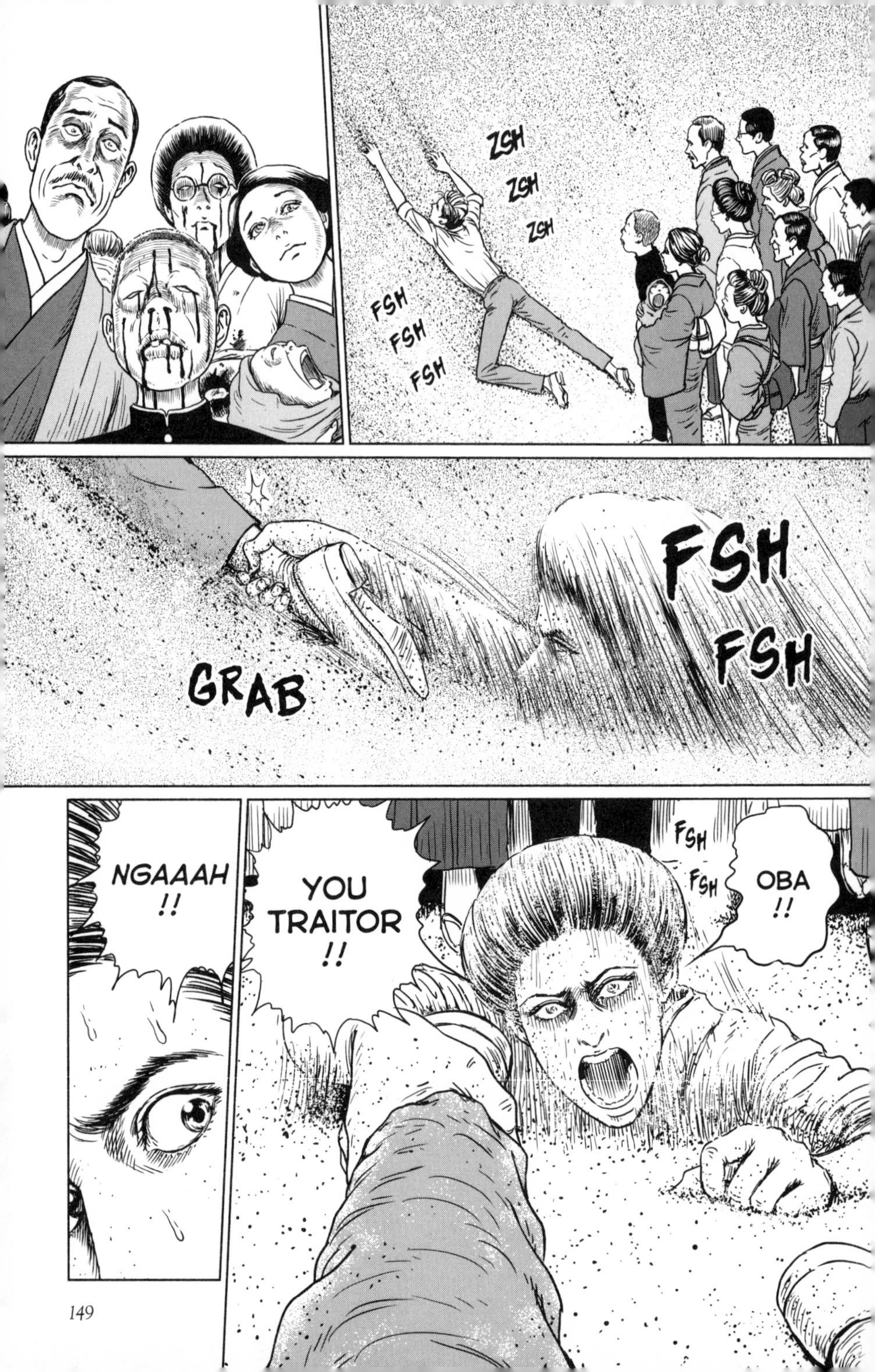
ZSH
ZSH
ZSH
FSH
FSH
FSH
FSH
FSH
GRAB
OBA !!
FSH
FSH
YOU TRAITOR !!
NGAAAH !!

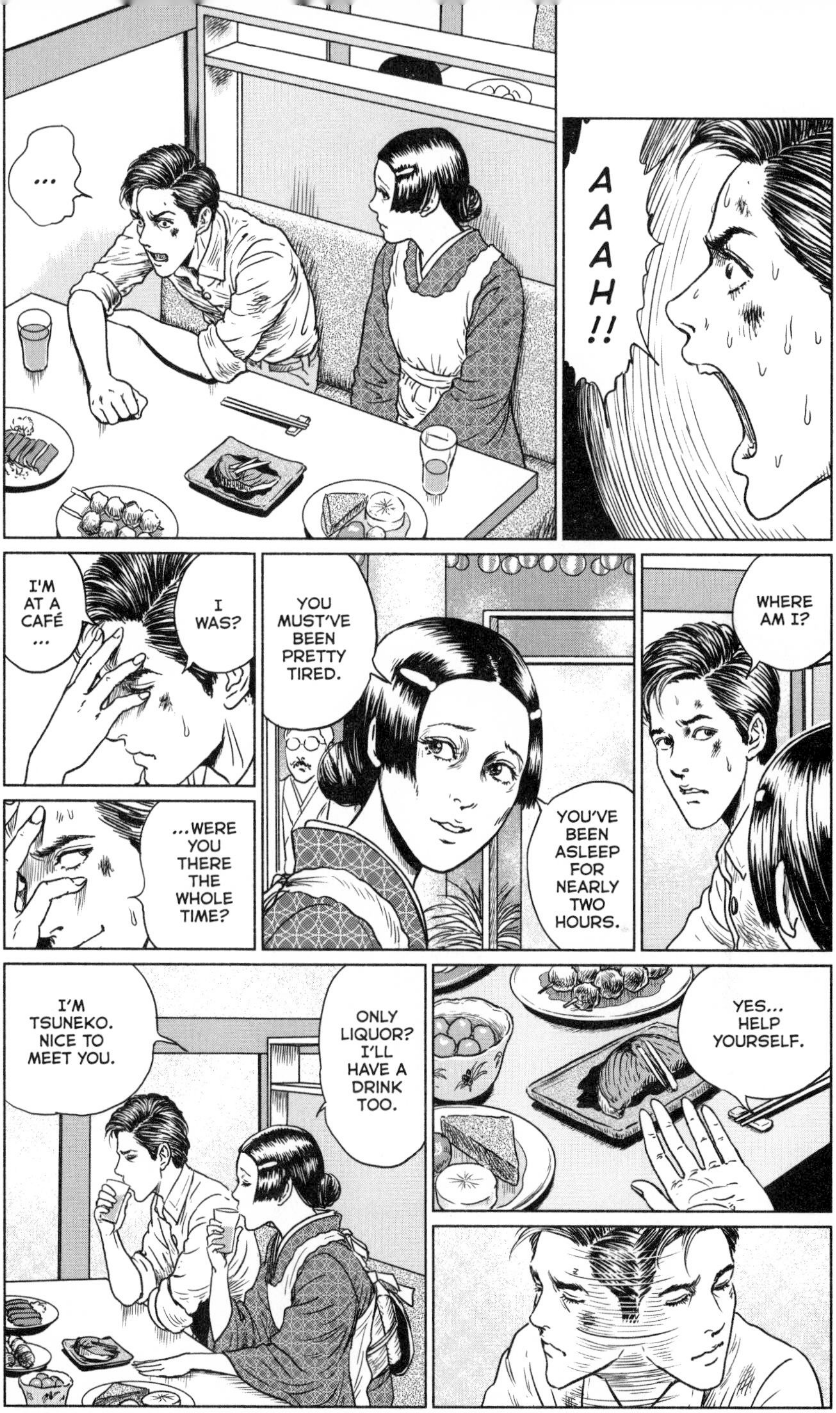
AAAAH!!
...
WHERE AM I?
YOU'VE BEEN ASLEEP FOR NEARLY TWO HOURS.
YOU MUST'VE BEEN PRETTY TIRED.
I WAS?
I'M AT A CAFÉ ...
...WERE YOU THERE THE WHOLE TIME?
YES... HELP YOURSELF.
ONLY LIQUOR? I'LL HAVE A DRINK TOO.
I'M TSUNEKO. NICE TO MEET YOU.

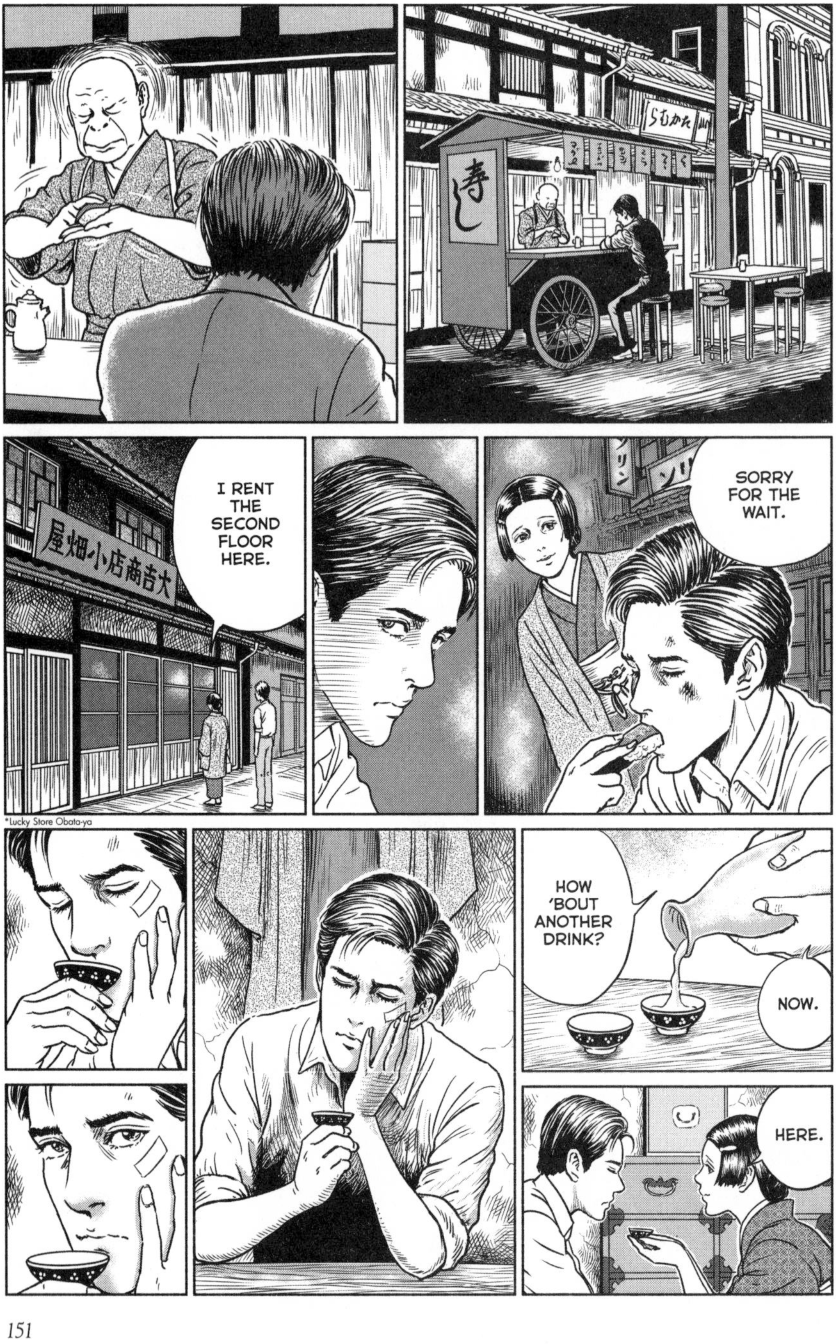
寿し
SORRY FOR THE WAIT.
I RENT THE SECOND FLOOR HERE.
大吉商店小畑屋
HOW 'BOUT ANOTHER DRINK?
NOW.
HERE.
*Lucky Store Obata-ya

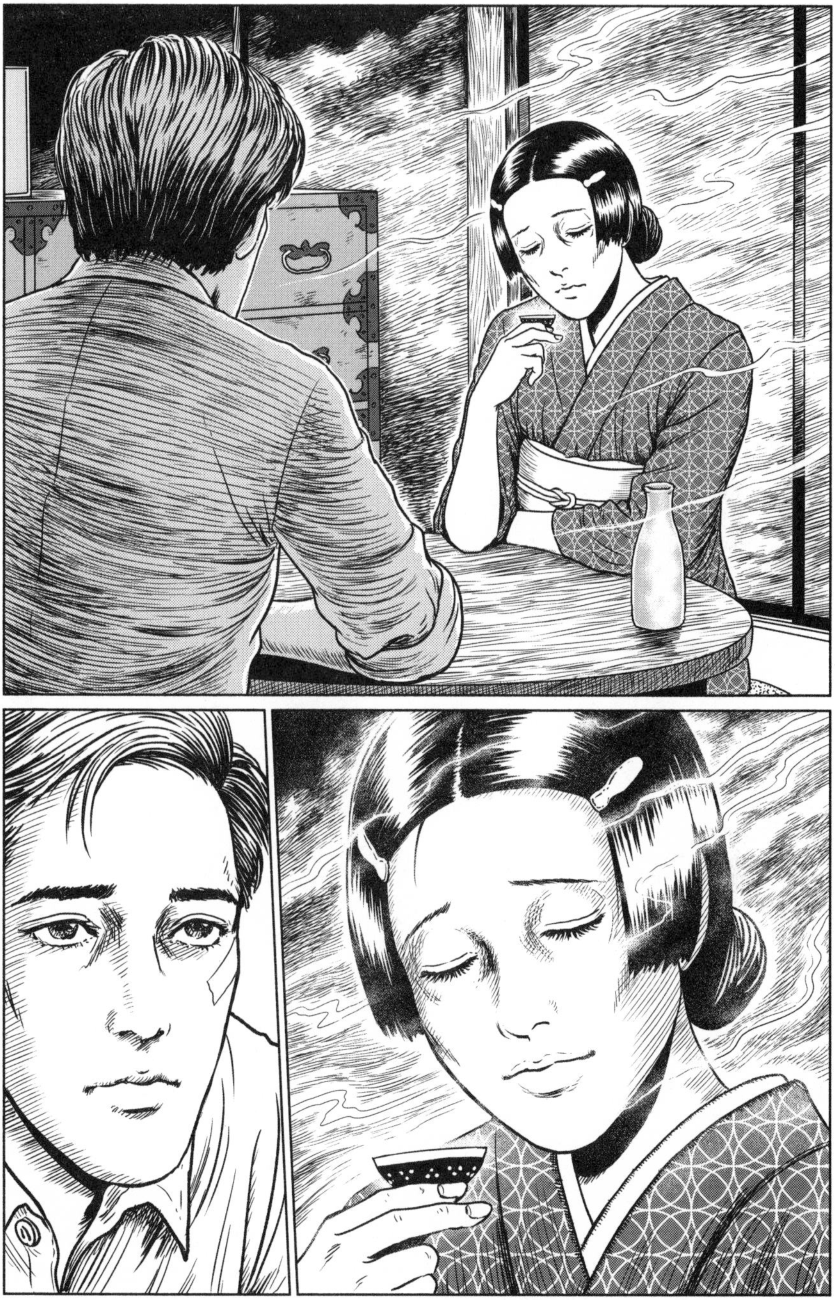

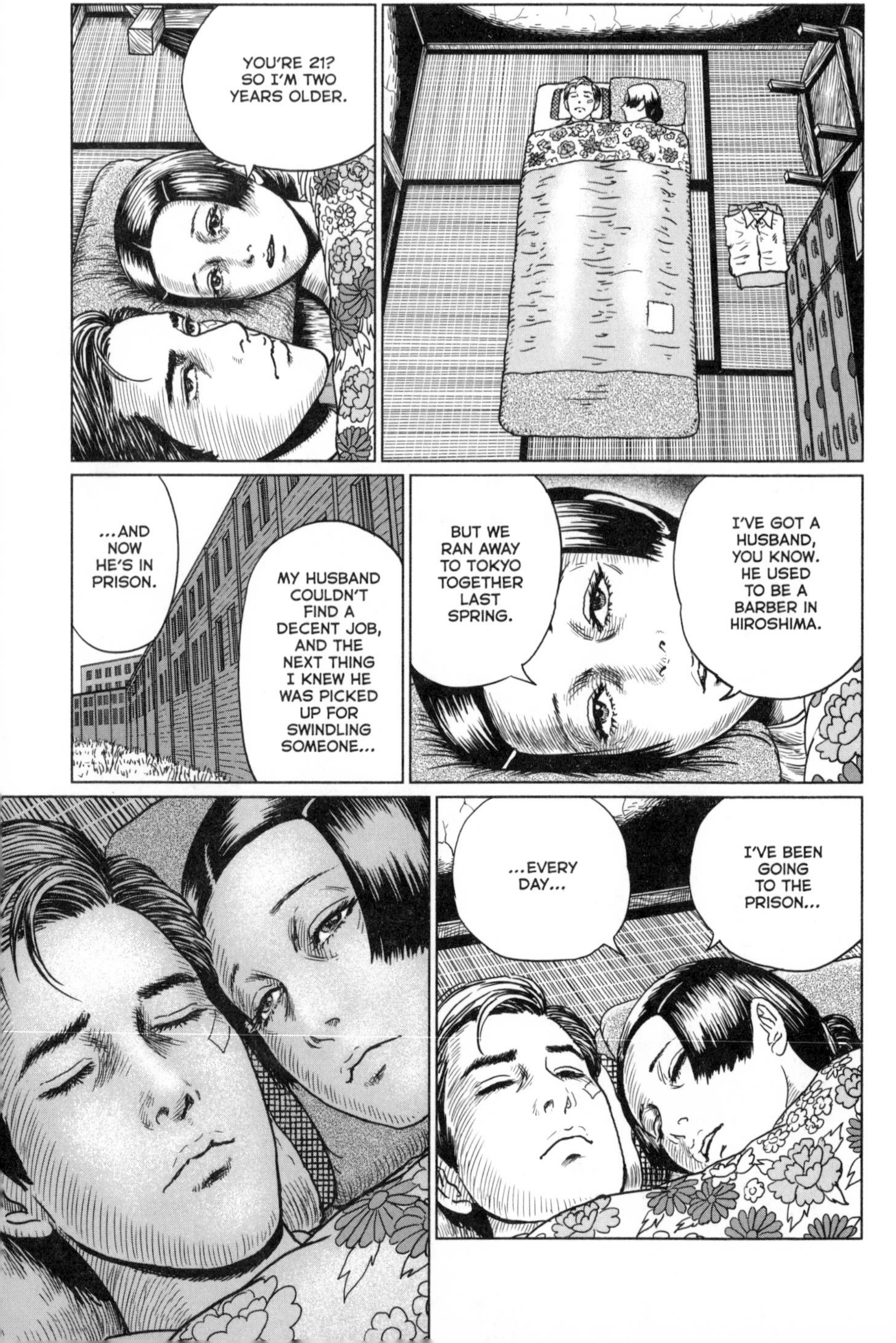
YOU'RE 21? SO I'M TWO YEARS OLDER.
I'VE GOT A HUSBAND, YOU KNOW. HE USED TO BE A BARBER IN HIROSHIMA.
BUT WE RAN AWAY TO TOKYO TOGETHER LAST SPRING.
MY HUSBAND COULDN'T FIND A DECENT JOB, AND THE NEXT THING I KNEW HE WAS PICKED UP FOR SWINDLING SOMEONE...
...AND NOW HE'S IN PRISON.
I'VE BEEN GOING TO THE PRISON...
...EVERY DAY...

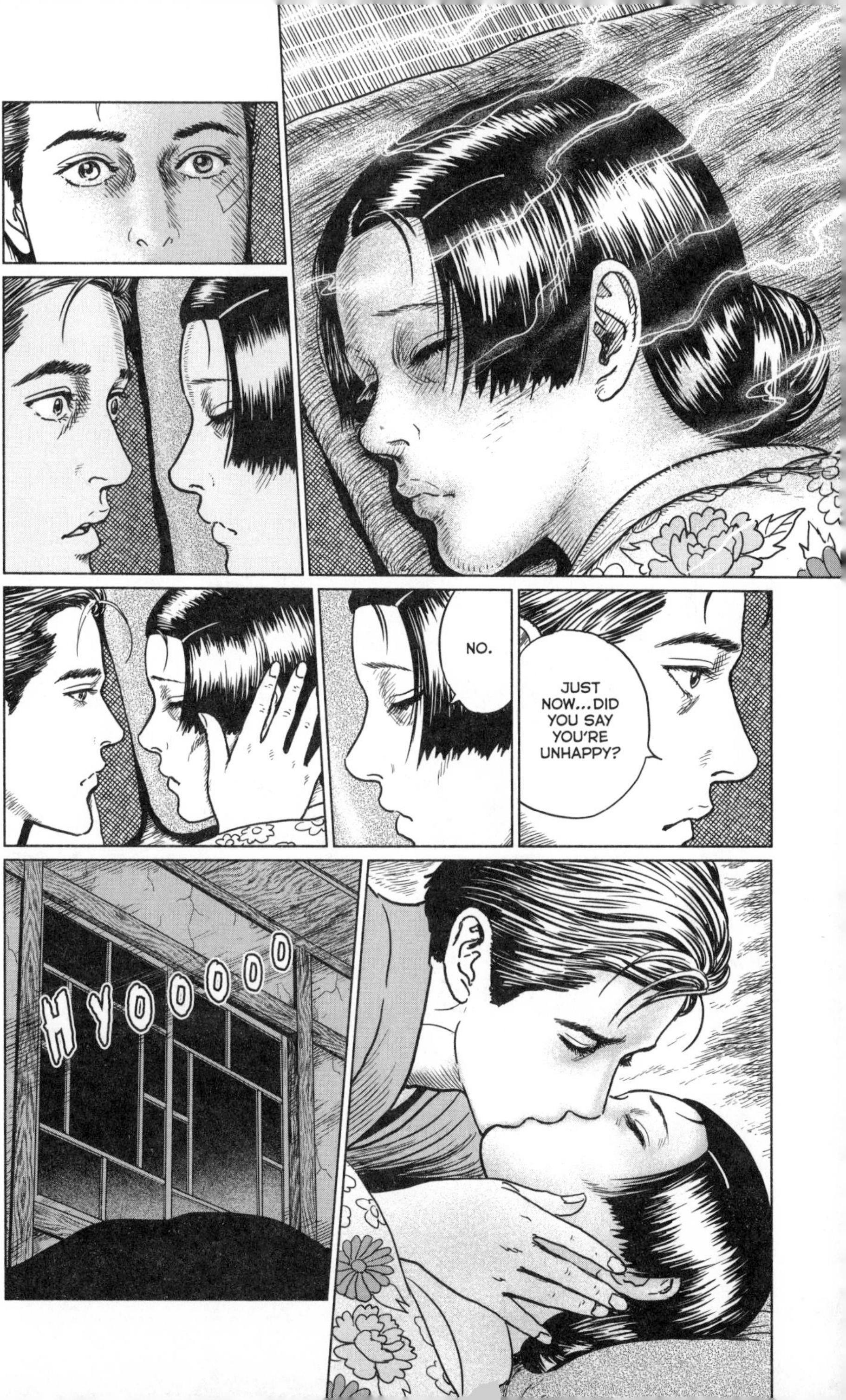
JUST NOW...DID YOU SAY YOU'RE UNHAPPY?
NO.
HYOOOOOO

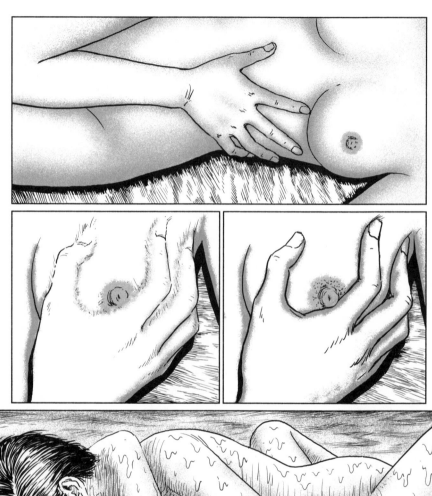

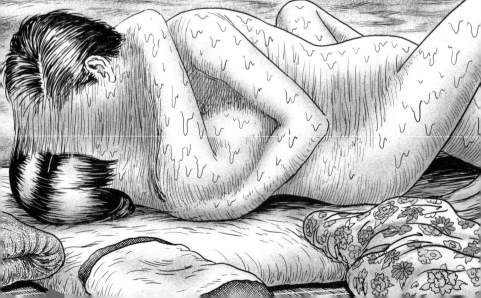

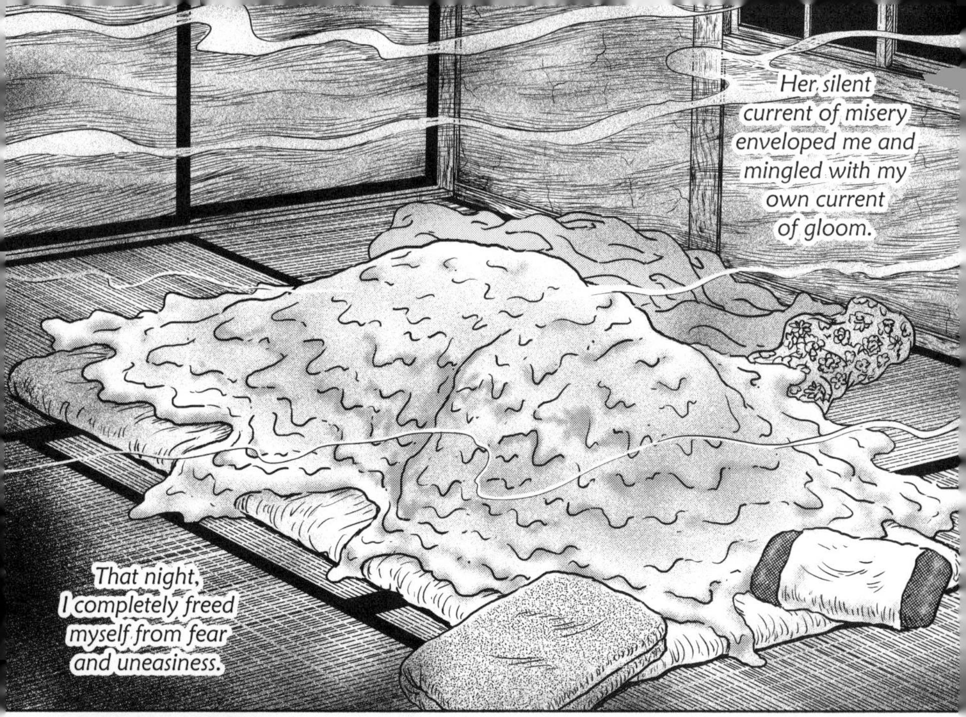
Her silent current of misery enveloped me and mingled with my own current of gloom.
That night, I completely freed myself from fear and uneasiness.

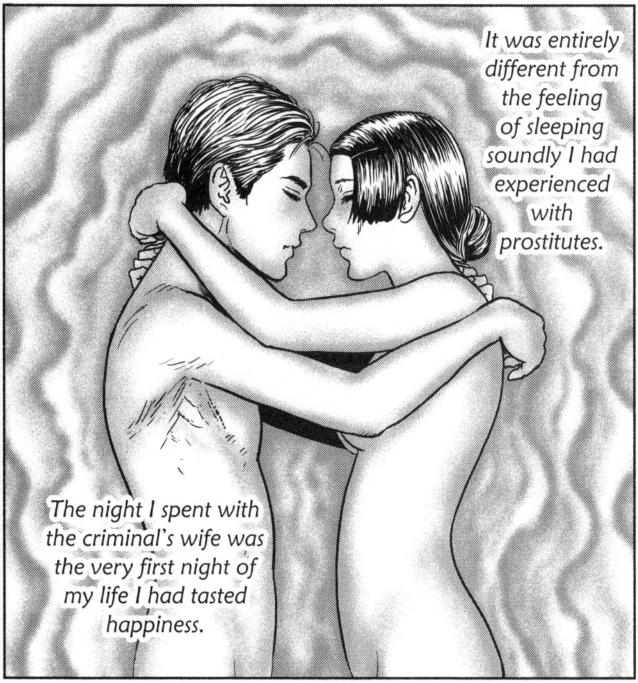
It was entirely different from the feeling of sleeping soundly I had experienced with prostitutes.
The night I spent with the criminal's wife was the very first night of my life I had tasted happiness.

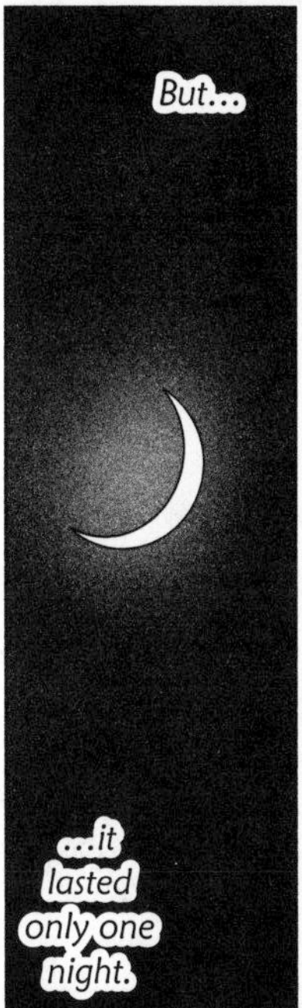
But...
...it lasted only one night.

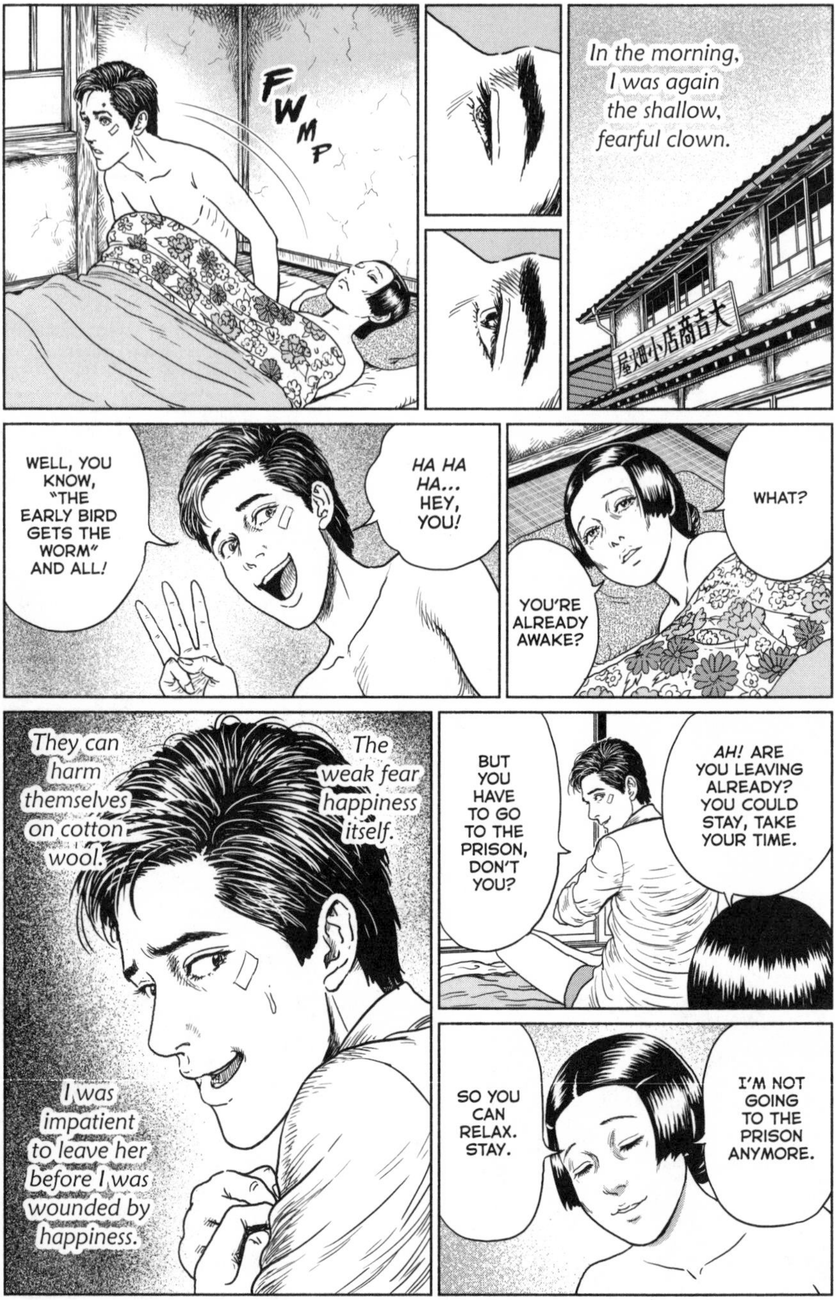
In the morning, I was again the shallow, fearful clown.
大吉商店小畑屋
FWMP
WHAT?
YOU'RE ALREADY AWAKE?
HA HA HA... HEY, YOU!
WELL, YOU KNOW, "THE EARLY BIRD GETS THE WORM" AND ALL!
AH! ARE YOU LEAVING ALREADY? YOU COULD STAY, TAKE YOUR TIME.
BUT YOU HAVE TO GO TO THE PRISON, DON'T YOU?
I'M NOT GOING TO THE PRISON ANYMORE.
SO YOU CAN RELAX. STAY.
The weak fear happiness itself.
They can harm themselves on cotton wool.
I was impatient to leave her before I was wounded by happiness.

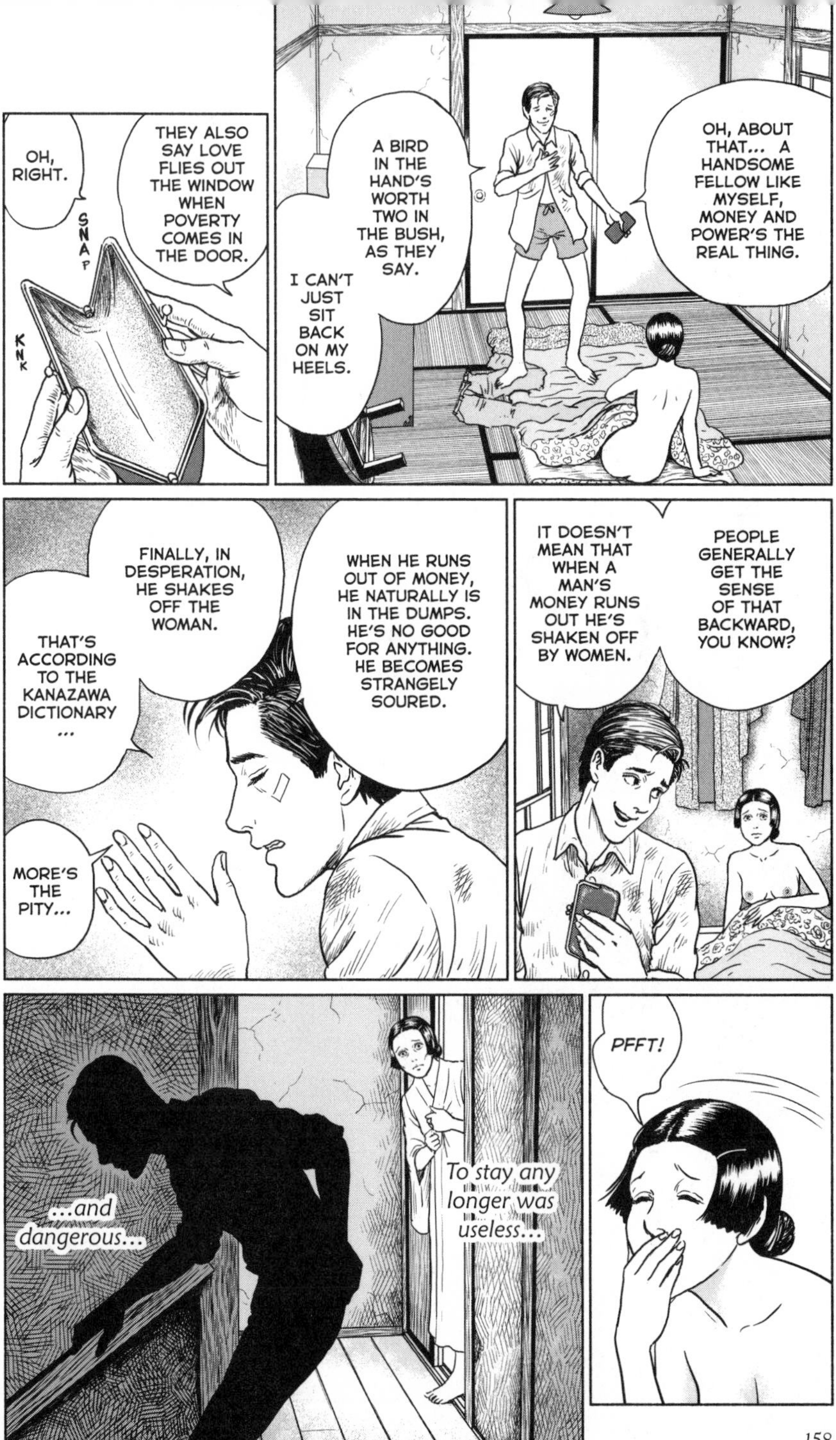
OH, ABOUT THAT... A HANDSOME FELLOW LIKE MYSELF, MONEY AND POWER'S THE REAL THING.
A BIRD IN THE HAND'S WORTH TWO IN THE BUSH, AS THEY SAY.
I CAN'T JUST SIT BACK ON MY HEELS.
THEY ALSO SAY LOVE FLIES OUT THE WINDOW WHEN POVERTY COMES IN THE DOOR.
OH, RIGHT.
SNAP
KNK
PEOPLE GENERALLY GET THE SENSE OF THAT BACKWARD, YOU KNOW?
IT DOESN'T MEAN THAT WHEN A MAN'S MONEY RUNS OUT HE'S SHAKEN OFF BY WOMEN.
WHEN HE RUNS OUT OF MONEY, HE NATURALLY IS IN THE DUMPS. HE'S NO GOOD FOR ANYTHING. HE BECOMES STRANGELY SOURED.
FINALLY, IN DESPERATION, HE SHAKES OFF THE WOMAN.
THAT'S ACCORDING TO THE KANAZAWA DICTIONARY...
MORE'S THE PITY...
PFFT!
To stay any longer was useless...
...and dangerous...

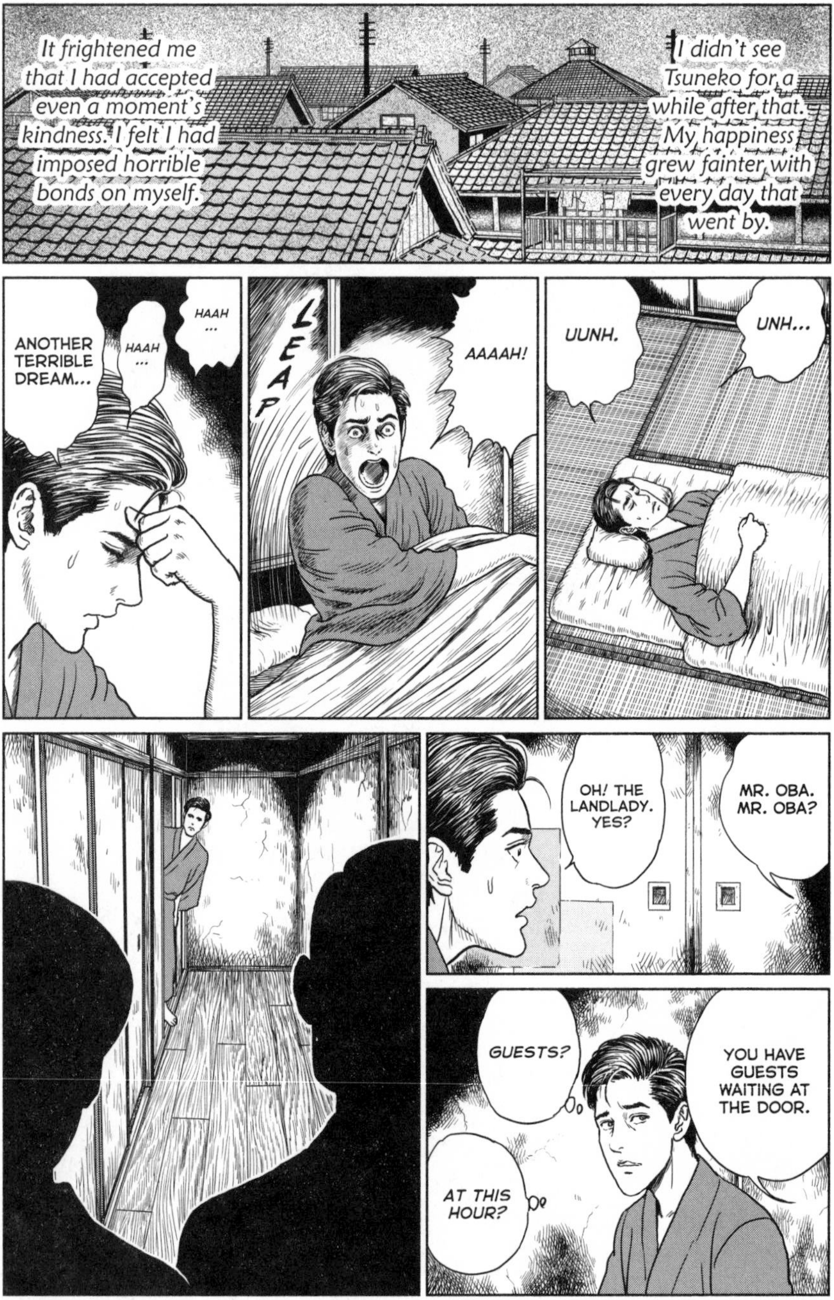
I didn't see Tsuneko for a while after that. My happiness grew fainter with every day that went by.
It frightened me that I had accepted even a moment's kindness. I felt I had imposed horrible bonds on myself.
UNH...
UUNH.
AAAAH!
LEAP
HAAH ...
HAAH ...
ANOTHER TERRIBLE DREAM...
MR. OBA. MR. OBA?
OH! THE LANDLADY. YES?
YOU HAVE GUESTS WAITING AT THE DOOR.
GUESTS?
AT THIS HOUR?

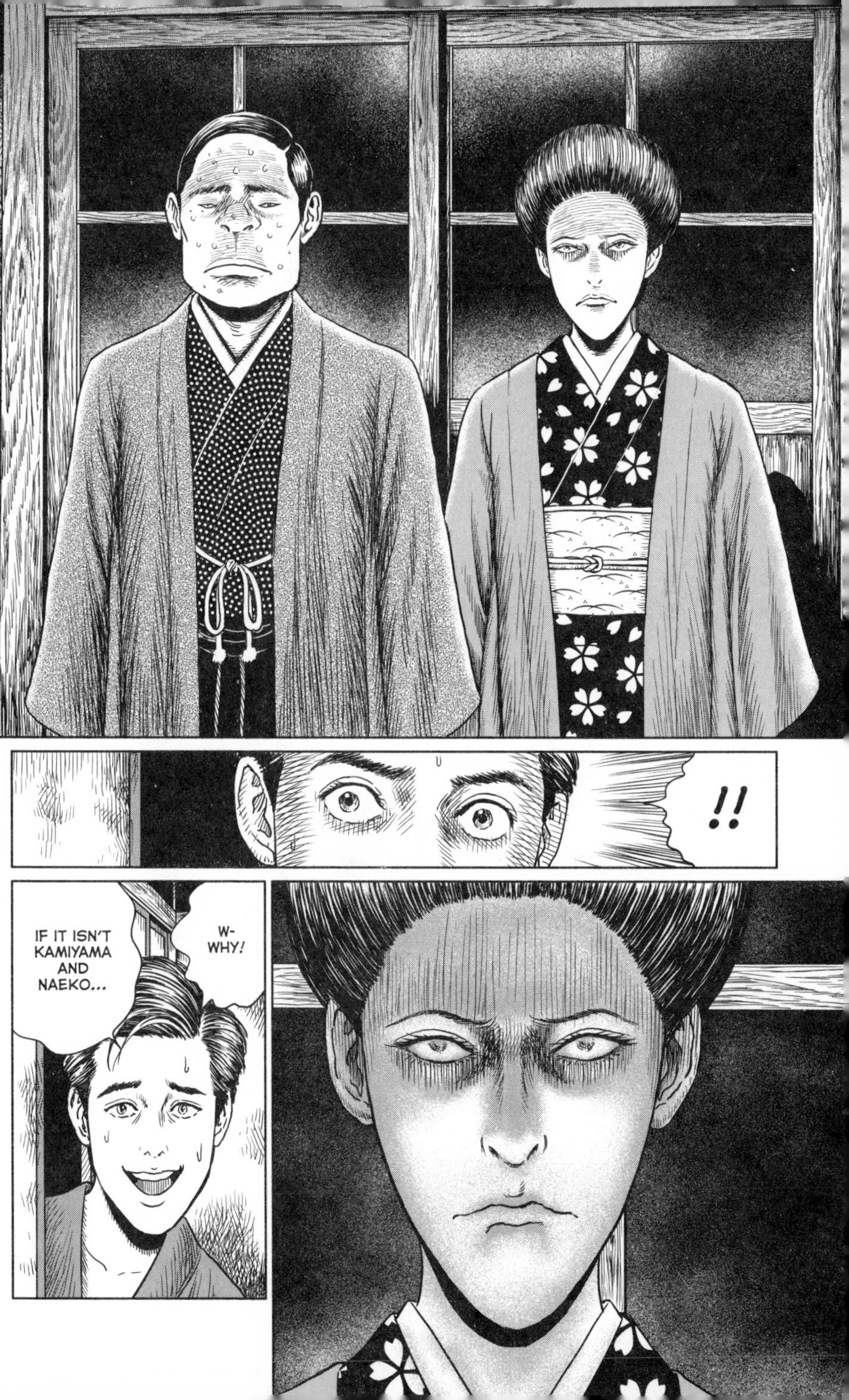
!!
W-WHY!
IF IT ISN'T KAMIYAMA AND NAEKO...

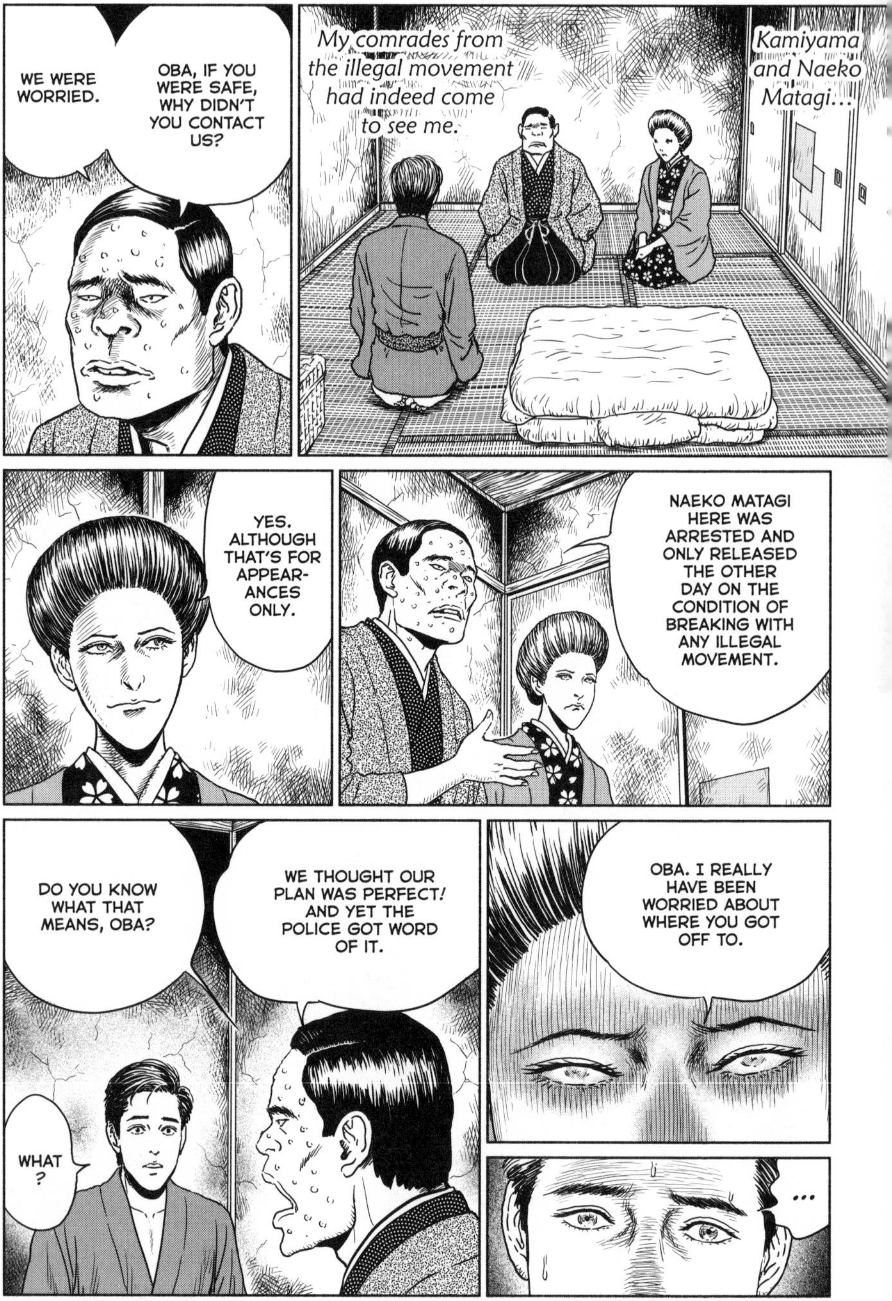

My comrades from the illegal movement had indeed come to see me.
Kamiyama and Naeko Matagi…
OBA, IF YOU WERE SAFE, WHY DIDN'T YOU CONTACT US?
WE WERE WORRIED.
NAEKO MATAGI HERE WAS ARRESTED AND ONLY RELEASED THE OTHER DAY ON THE CONDITION OF BREAKING WITH ANY ILLEGAL MOVEMENT.
YES. ALTHOUGH THAT'S FOR APPEARANCES ONLY.
OBA. I REALLY HAVE BEEN WORRIED ABOUT WHERE YOU GOT OFF TO.
...
WE THOUGHT OUR PLAN WAS PERFECT! AND YET THE POLICE GOT WORD OF IT.
DO YOU KNOW WHAT THAT MEANS, OBA?
WHAT?

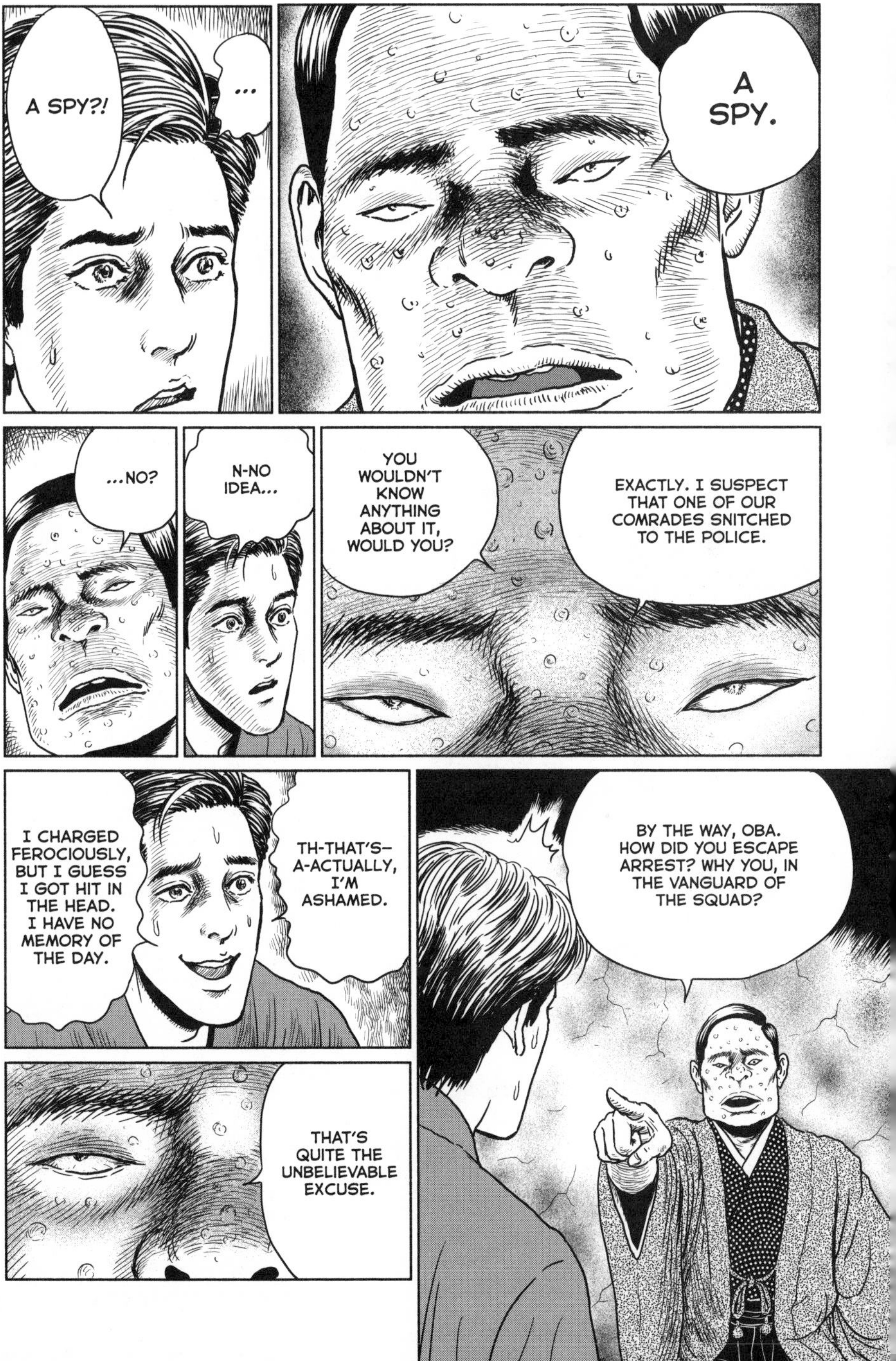
A SPY.
...
A SPY?!
EXACTLY. I SUSPECT THAT ONE OF OUR COMRADES SNITCHED TO THE POLICE.
YOU WOULDN'T KNOW ANYTHING ABOUT IT, WOULD YOU?
N-NO IDEA...
...NO?
BY THE WAY, OBA. HOW DID YOU ESCAPE ARREST? WHY YOU, IN THE VANGUARD OF THE SQUAD?
TH-THAT'S— A-ACTUALLY, I'M ASHAMED.
I CHARGED FEROCIOUSLY, BUT I GUESS I GOT HIT IN THE HEAD. I HAVE NO MEMORY OF THE DAY.
THAT'S QUITE THE UNBELIEVABLE EXCUSE.

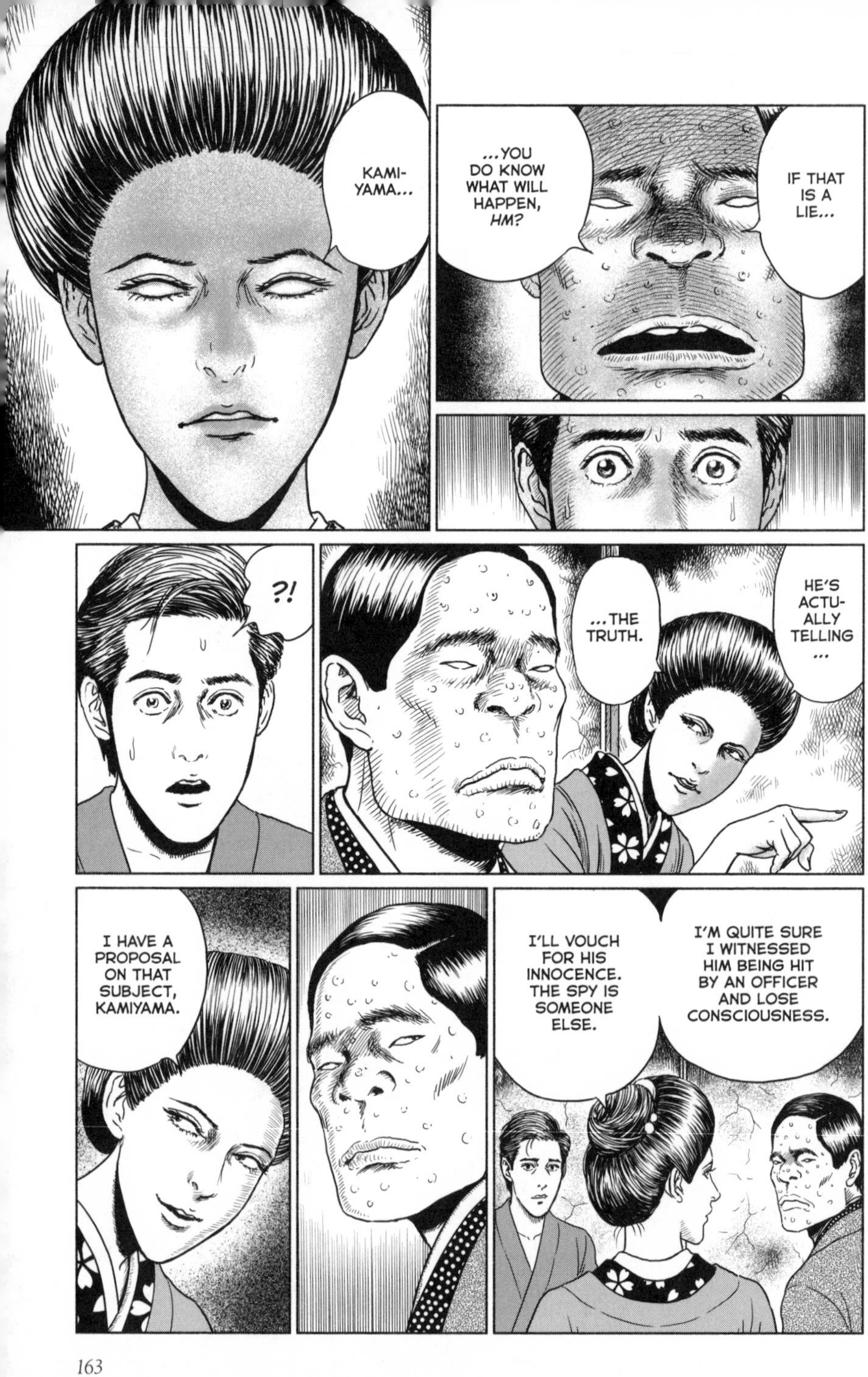
IF THAT IS A LIE...
...YOU DO KNOW WHAT WILL HAPPEN, *HM?*
KAMI-YAMA...
HE'S ACTU-ALLY TELLING...
...THE TRUTH.
?!
I'M QUITE SURE I WITNESSED HIM BEING HIT BY AN OFFICER AND LOSE CONSCIOUSNESS.
I'LL VOUCH FOR HIS INNOCENCE. THE SPY IS SOMEONE ELSE.
I HAVE A PROPOSAL ON THAT SUBJECT, KAMIYAMA.

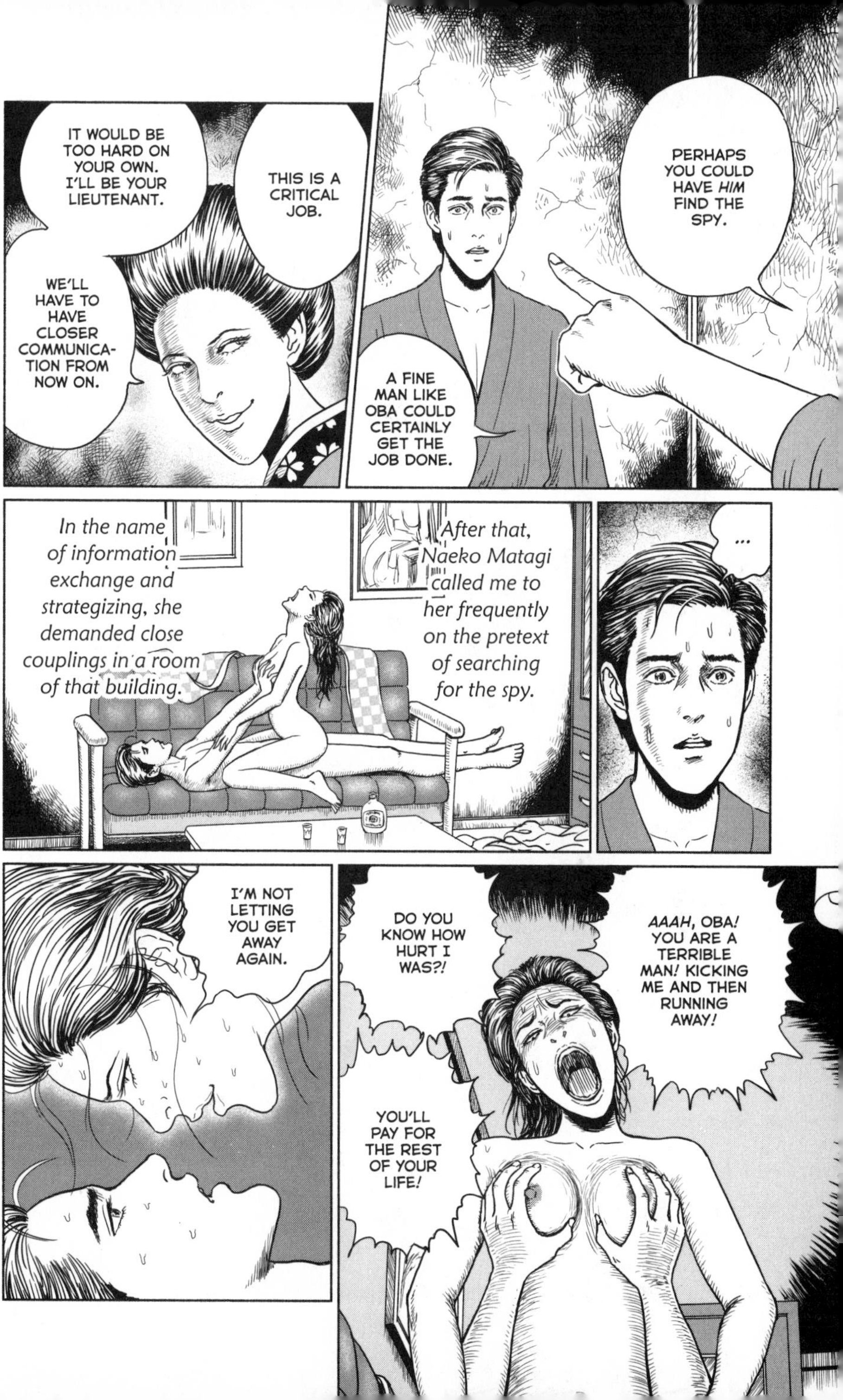
PERHAPS YOU COULD HAVE *HIM* FIND THE SPY.
A FINE MAN LIKE OBA COULD CERTAINLY GET THE JOB DONE.
THIS IS A CRITICAL JOB.
IT WOULD BE TOO HARD ON YOUR OWN. I'LL BE YOUR LIEUTENANT.
WE'LL HAVE TO HAVE CLOSER COMMUNICA-TION FROM NOW ON.
...
After that, Naeko Matagi called me to her frequently on the pretext of searching for the spy.
In the name of information exchange and strategizing, she demanded close couplings in a room of that building.
AAAH, OBA! YOU ARE A TERRIBLE MAN! KICKING ME AND THEN RUNNING AWAY!
DO YOU KNOW HOW HURT I WAS?!
YOU'LL PAY FOR THE REST OF YOUR LIFE!
I'M NOT LETTING YOU GET AWAY AGAIN.

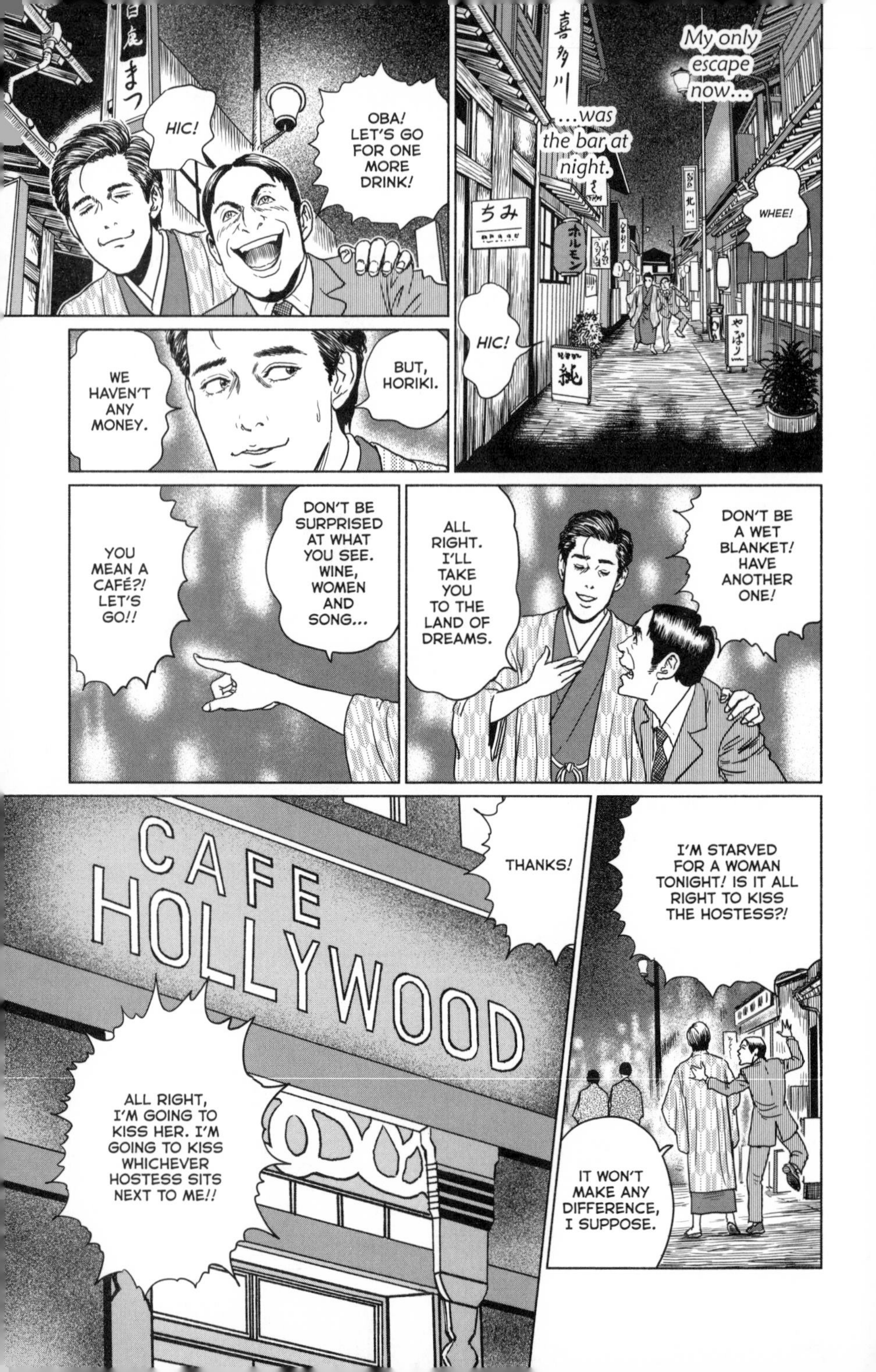
My only escape now...
...was the bar at night.
喜多川
ちみ
ホルモン
WHEE!
HIC!
OBA! LET'S GO FOR ONE MORE DRINK!
HIC!
BUT, HORIKI.
WE HAVEN'T ANY MONEY.
DON'T BE A WET BLANKET! HAVE ANOTHER ONE!
ALL RIGHT. I'LL TAKE YOU TO THE LAND OF DREAMS.
DON'T BE SURPRISED AT WHAT YOU SEE. WINE, WOMEN AND SONG...
YOU MEAN A CAFÉ?! LET'S GO!!
I'M STARVED FOR A WOMAN TONIGHT! IS IT ALL RIGHT TO KISS THE HOSTESS?!
IT WON'T MAKE ANY DIFFERENCE, I SUPPOSE.
THANKS!
CAFE HOLLYWOOD
ALL RIGHT, I'M GOING TO KISS HER. I'M GOING TO KISS WHICHEVER HOSTESS SITS NEXT TO ME!!

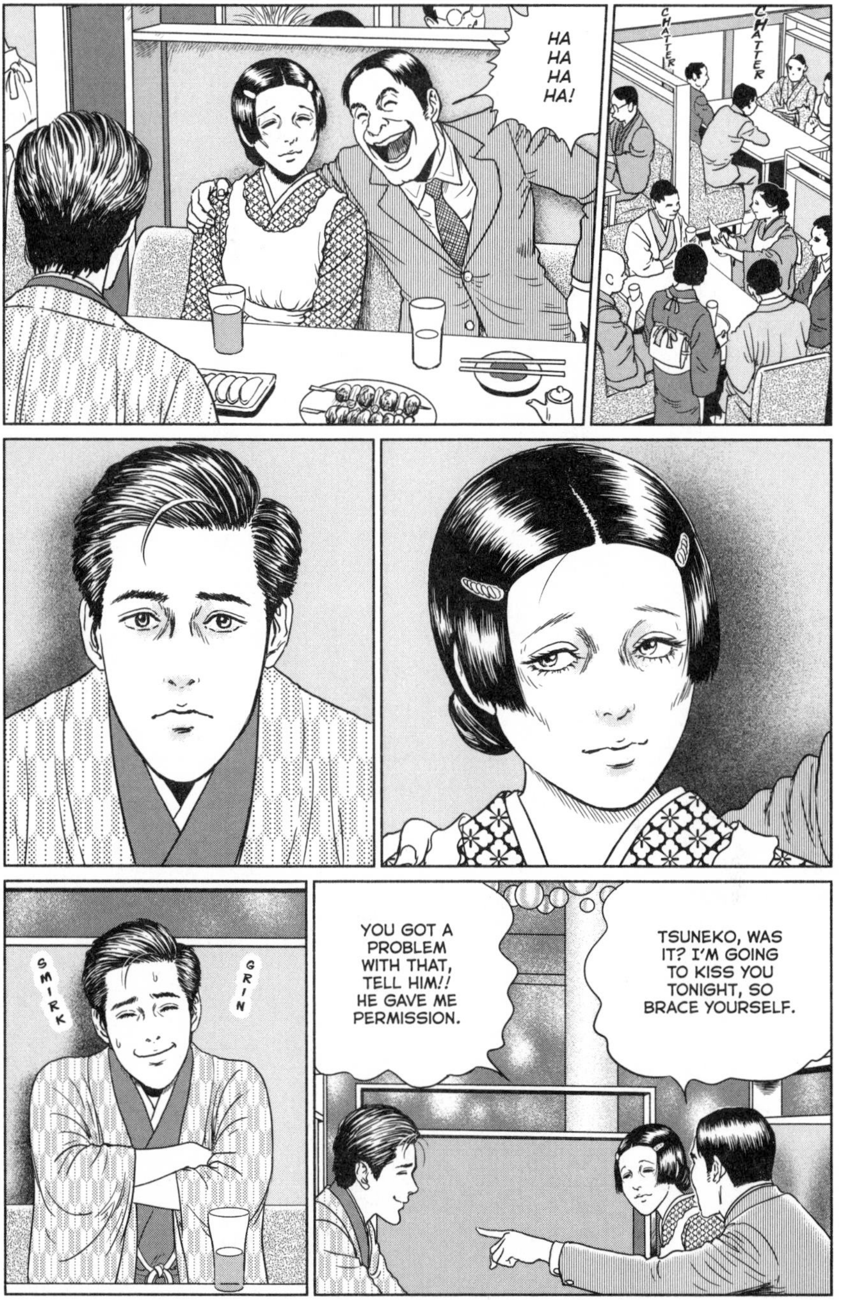
CHATTER
CHATTER
HA HA HA HA!
TSUNEKO, WAS IT? I'M GOING TO KISS YOU TONIGHT, SO BRACE YOURSELF.
YOU GOT A PROBLEM WITH THAT, TELL HIM!! HE GAVE ME PERMISSION.
GRIN
SMIRK

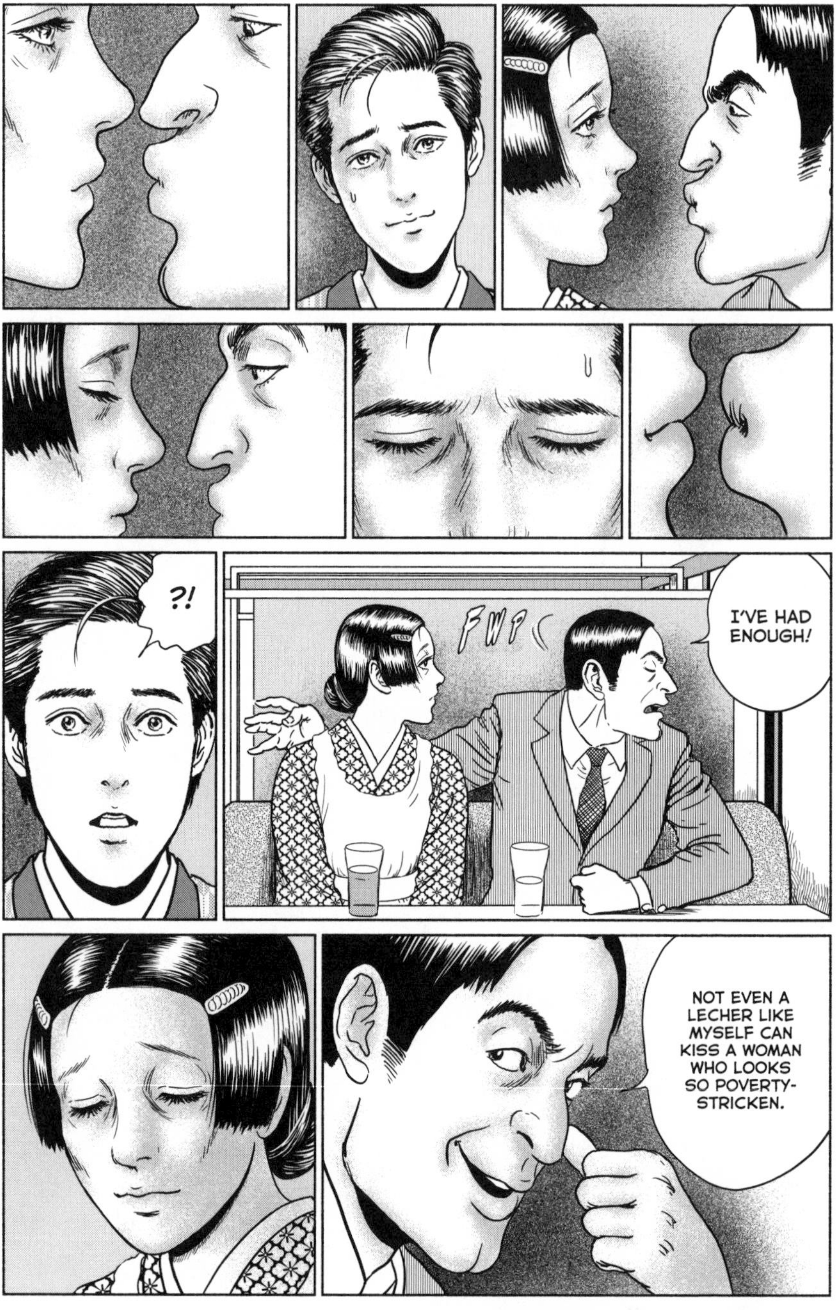
FWP
I'VE HAD ENOUGH!
?!
NOT EVEN A LECHER LIKE MYSELF CAN KISS A WOMAN WHO LOOKS SO POVERTY-STRICKEN.

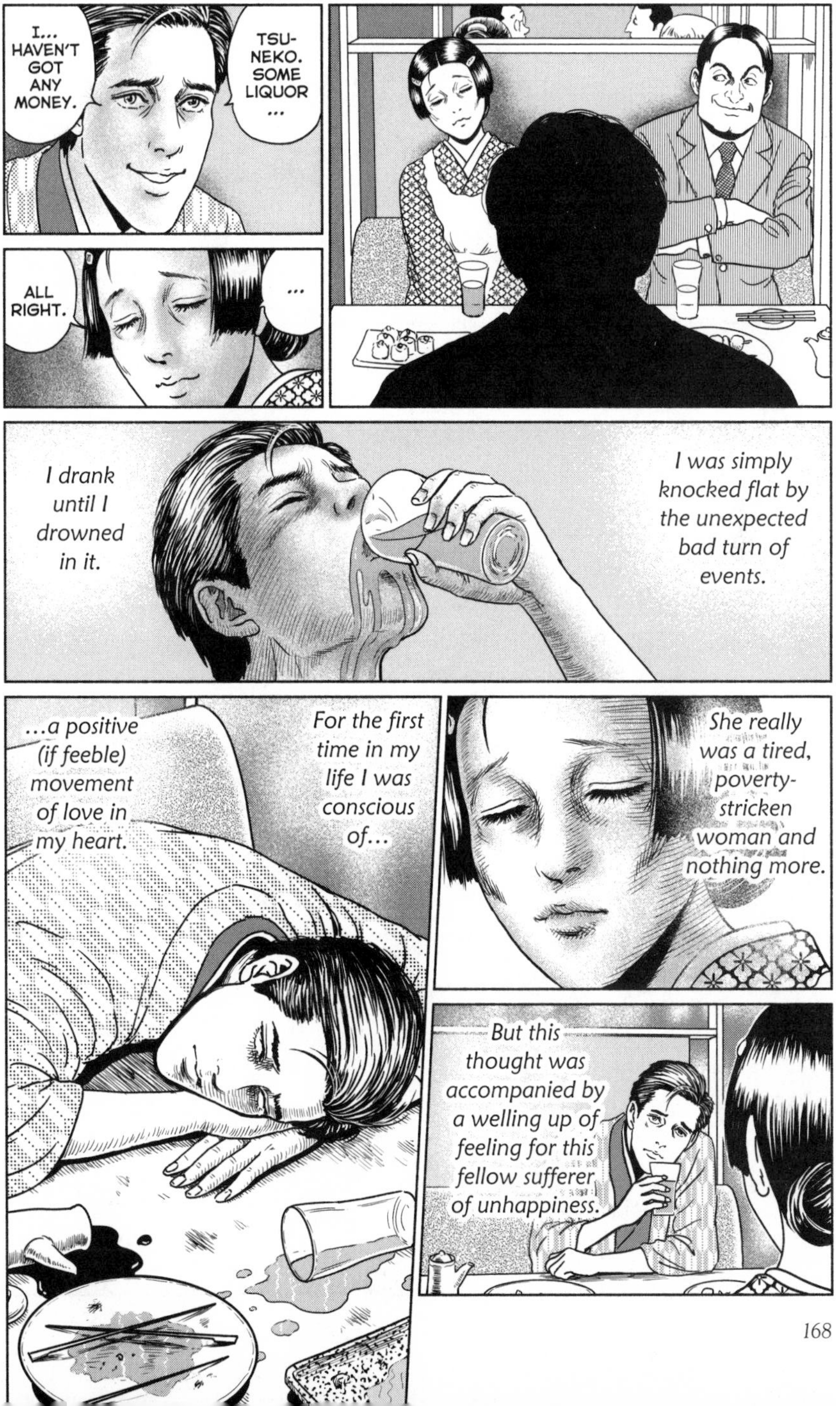
TSU-NEKO. SOME LIQUOR ...
I... HAVEN'T GOT ANY MONEY.
...
ALL RIGHT.
I was simply knocked flat by the unexpected bad turn of events.
I drank until I drowned in it.
She really was a tired, poverty-stricken woman and nothing more.
But this thought was accompanied by a welling up of feeling for this fellow sufferer of unhappiness.
For the first time in my life I was conscious of...
...a positive (if feeble) movement of love in my heart.

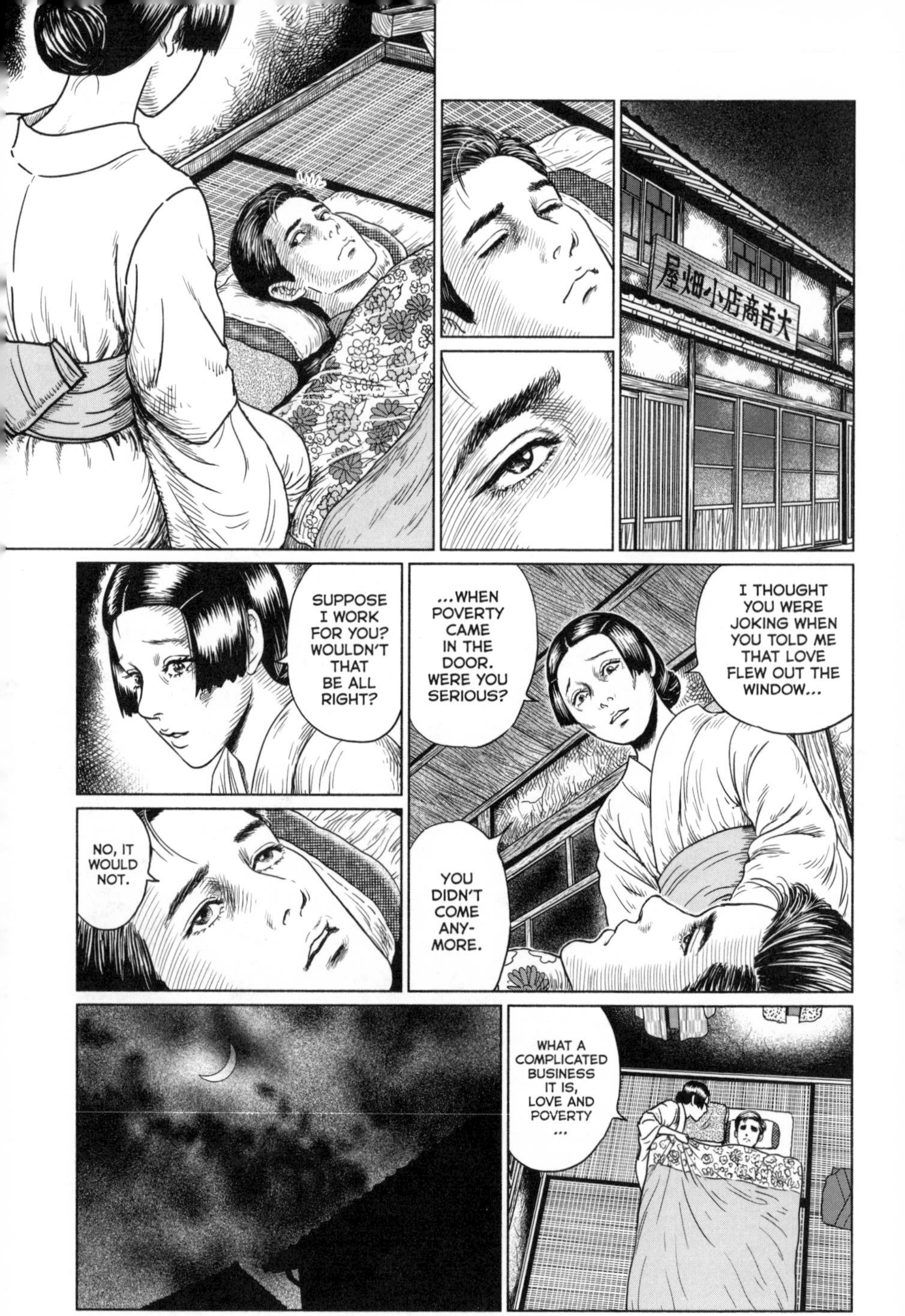

大吉商店小畑屋
I THOUGHT YOU WERE JOKING WHEN YOU TOLD ME THAT LOVE FLEW OUT THE WINDOW...
...WHEN POVERTY CAME IN THE DOOR. WERE YOU SERIOUS?
YOU DIDN'T COME ANYMORE.
SUPPOSE I WORK FOR YOU? WOULDN'T THAT BE ALL RIGHT?
NO, IT WOULD NOT.
WHAT A COMPLICATED BUSINESS IT IS, LOVE AND POVERTY ...

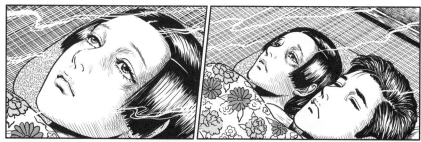

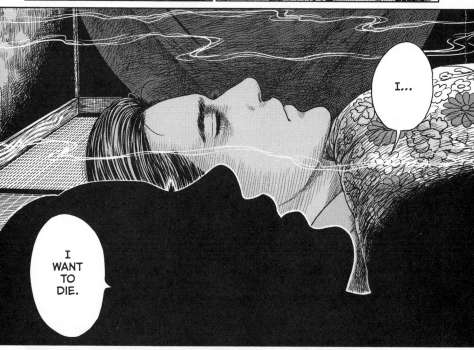

I...

I
WANT
TO
DIE.

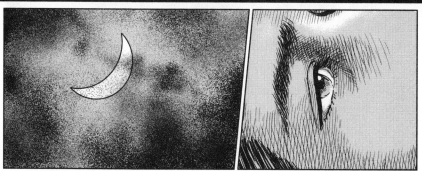

CHAIN No. 7: Paradise

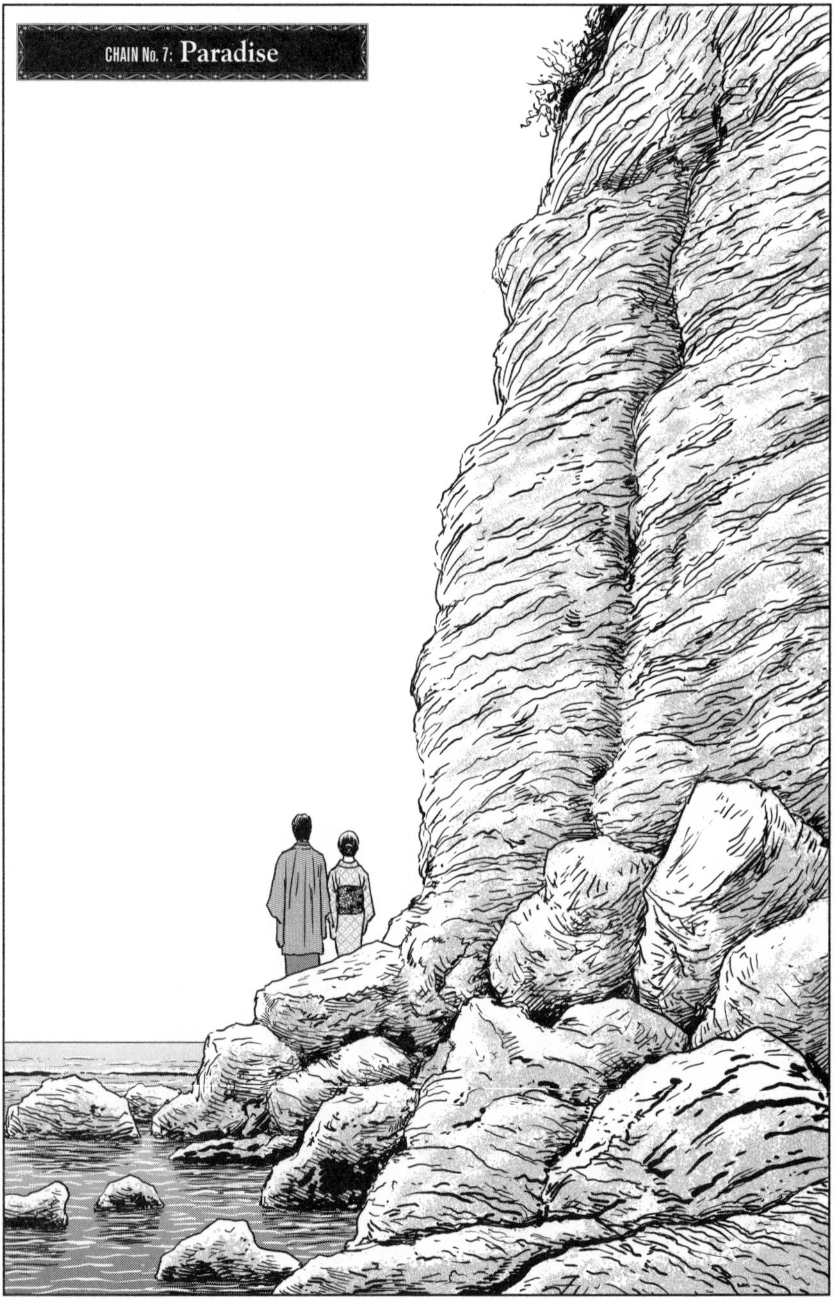

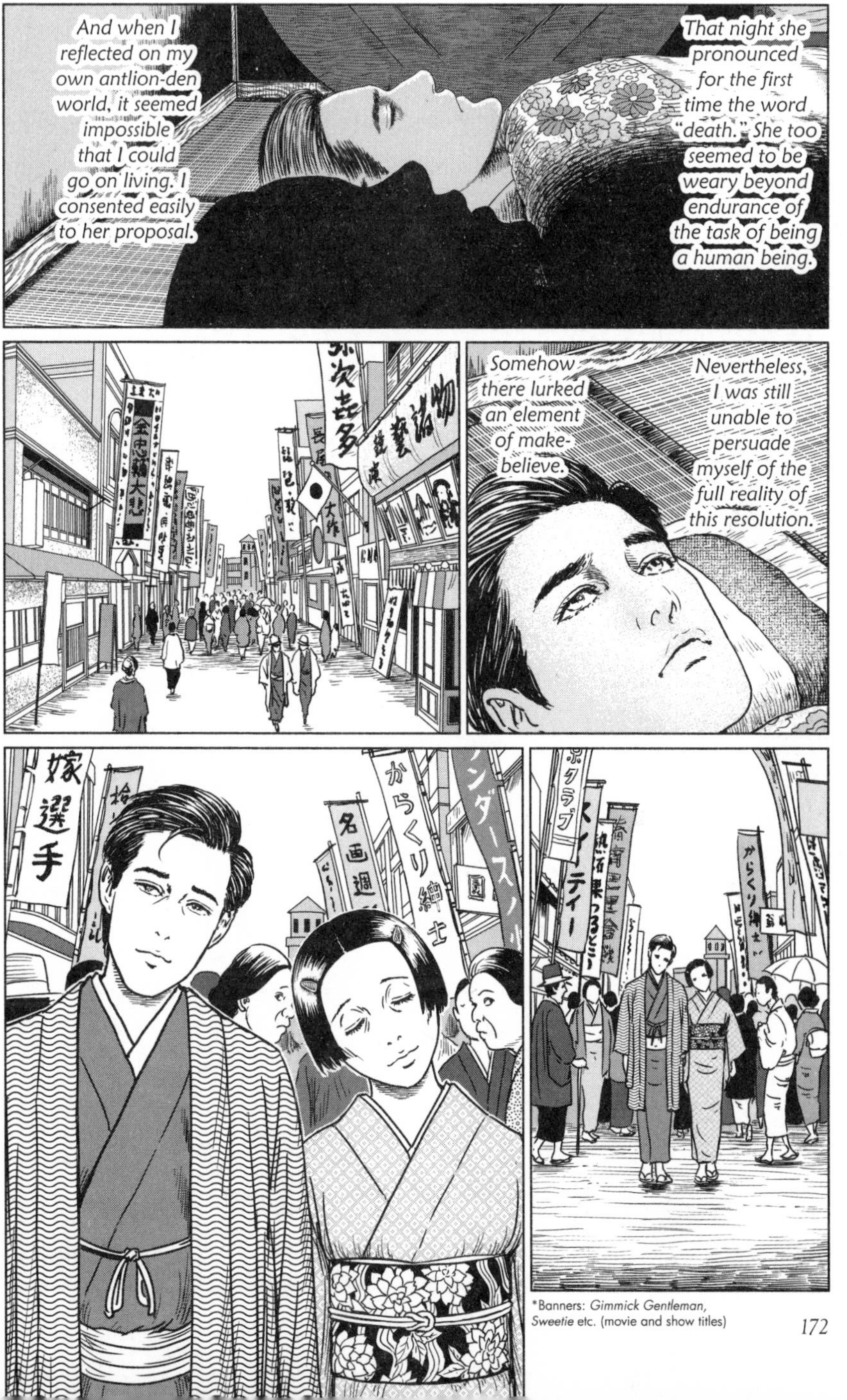
That night she pronounced for the first time the word "death." She too seemed to be weary beyond endurance of the task of being a human being.
And when I reflected on my own antlion-den world, it seemed impossible that I could go on living. I consented easily to her proposal.
Nevertheless, I was still unable to persuade myself of the full reality of this resolution.
Somehow there lurked an element of make-believe.
からくり紳士
嫁選手
からくり紳士
名画週

*Banners: *Gimmick Gentleman*, *Sweetie* etc. (movie and show titles)

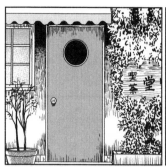

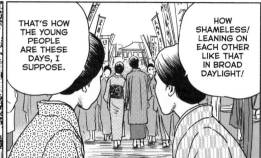

HOW SHAMELESS! LEANING ON EACH OTHER LIKE THAT IN BROAD DAYLIGHT!
THAT'S HOW THE YOUNG PEOPLE ARE THESE DAYS, I SUPPOSE.
Had I ever before looked someone in the eyes like this?
I felt a love for her from the bottom of my heart, a fondness.
When I considered that this peace would soon be eternal, I felt strangely buoyant.
SHALL WE DROWN OURSELVES THEN?
I SUPPOSE... LET'S DO IT IN KAMAKURA.

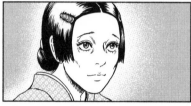

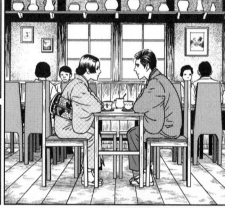

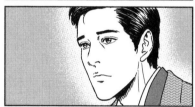

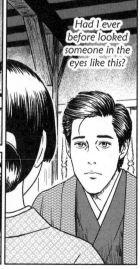

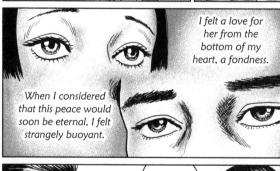

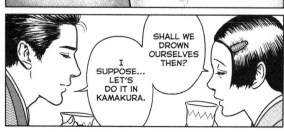

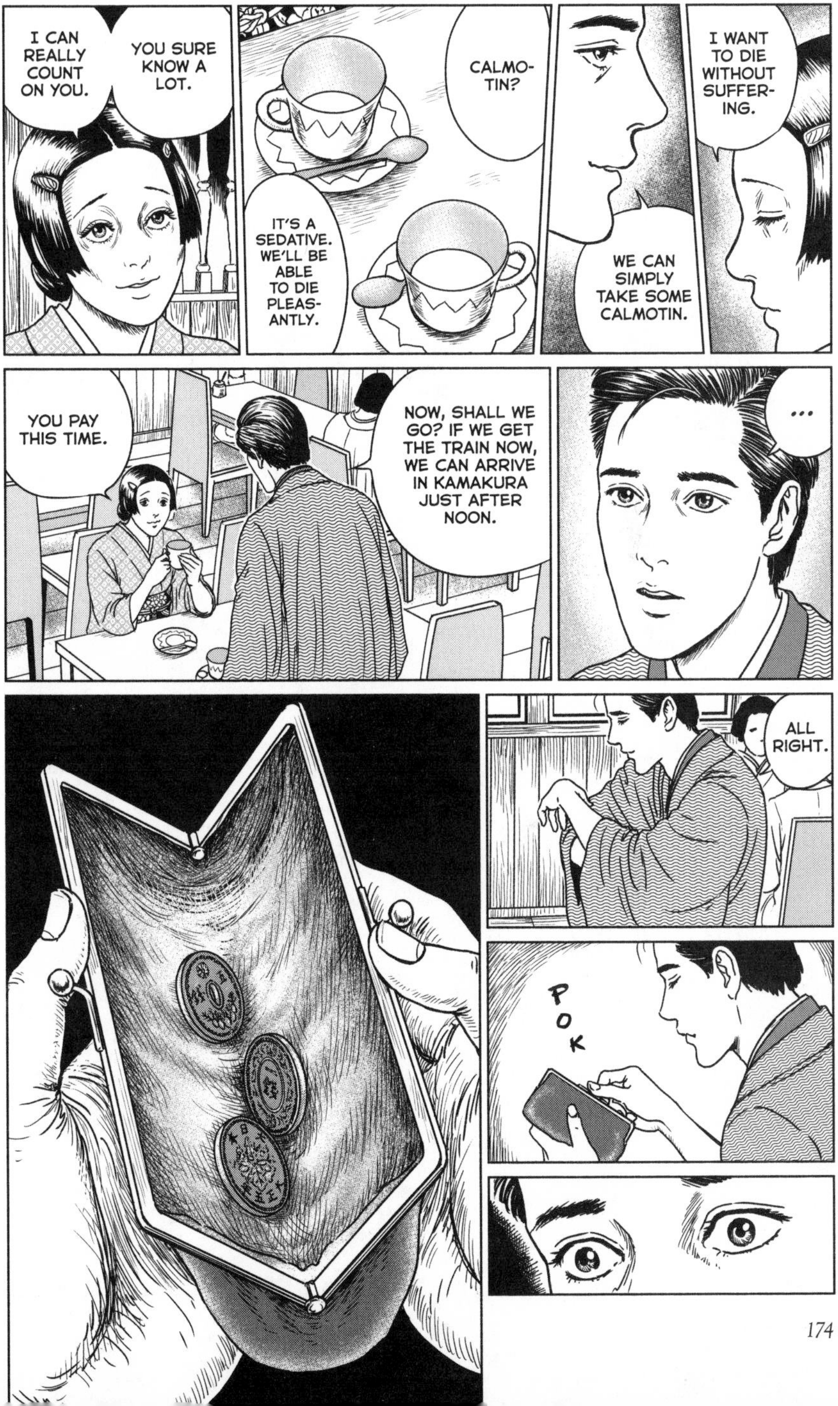
I WANT TO DIE WITHOUT SUFFERING.
WE CAN SIMPLY TAKE SOME CALMOTIN.
CALMOTIN?
IT'S A SEDATIVE. WE'LL BE ABLE TO DIE PLEASANTLY.
YOU SURE KNOW A LOT.
I CAN REALLY COUNT ON YOU.
...
NOW, SHALL WE GO? IF WE GET THE TRAIN NOW, WE CAN ARRIVE IN KAMAKURA JUST AFTER NOON.
YOU PAY THIS TIME.
ALL RIGHT.
POK

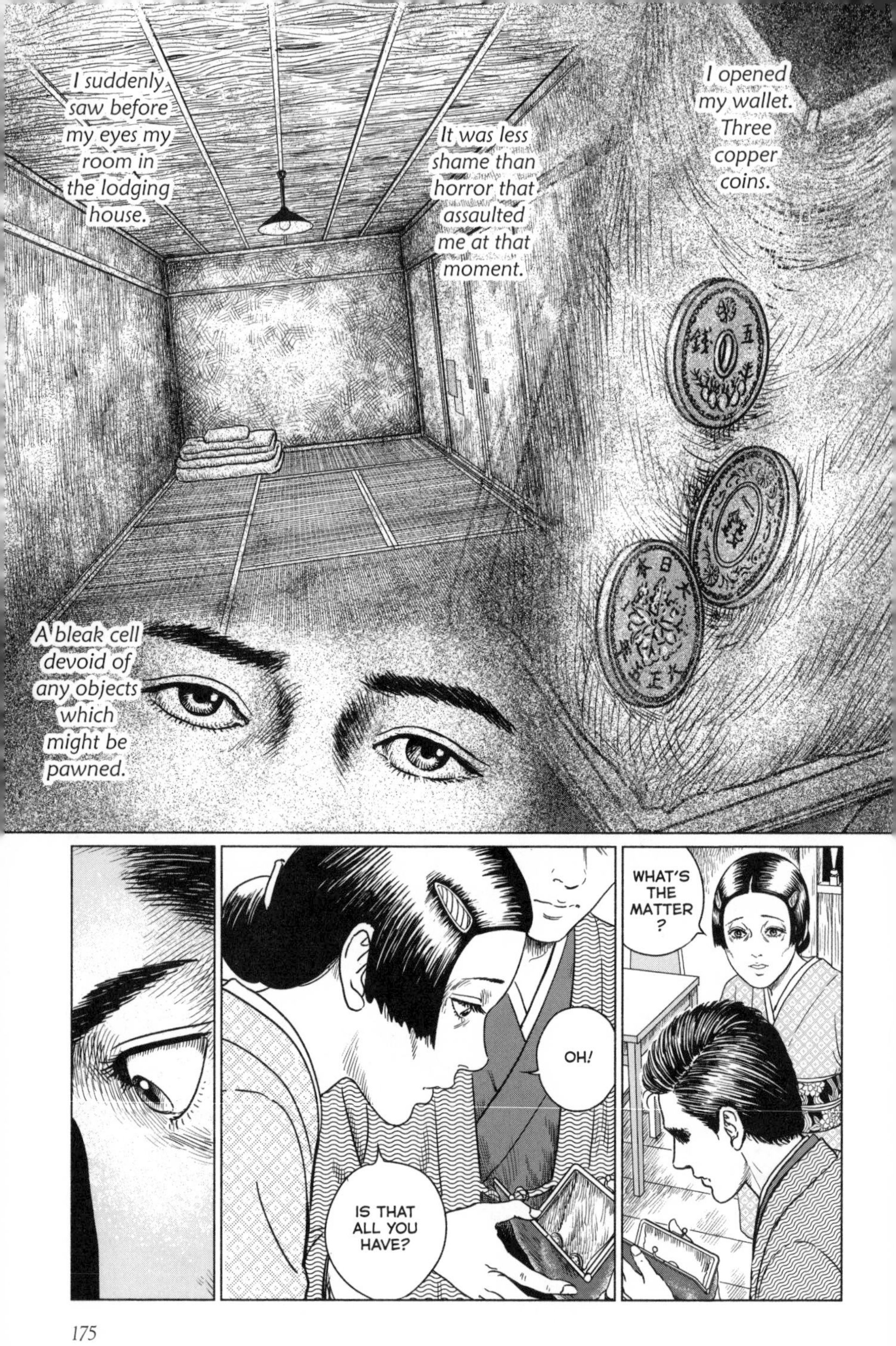
I opened my wallet. Three copper coins.
It was less shame than horror that assaulted me at that moment.
I suddenly saw before my eyes my room in the lodging house.
A bleak cell devoid of any objects which might be pawned.
WHAT'S THE MATTER?
OH!
IS THAT ALL YOU HAVE?

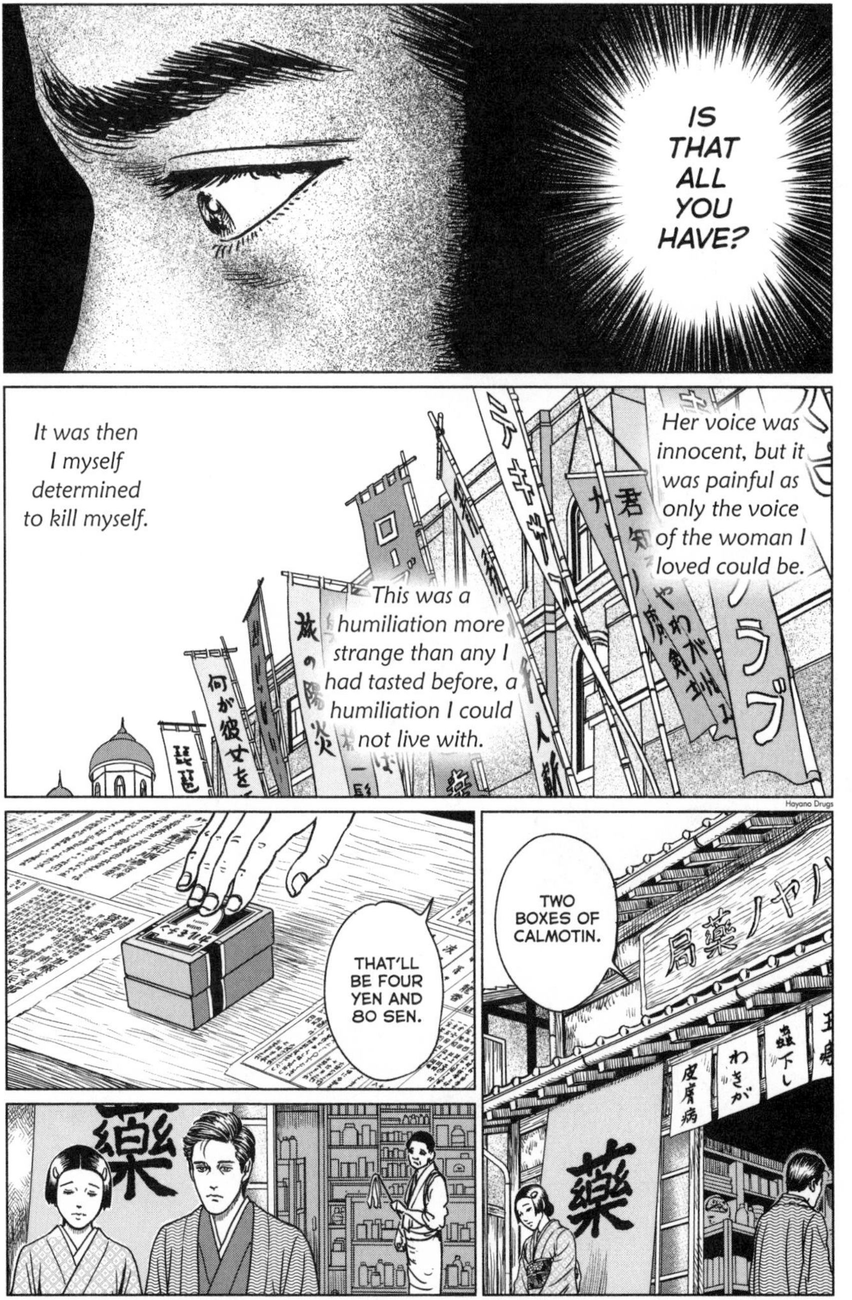

IS THAT ALL YOU HAVE?
Her voice was innocent, but it was painful as only the voice of the woman I loved could be.
This was a humiliation more strange than any I had tasted before, a humiliation I could not live with.
It was then I myself determined to kill myself.
Hayano Drugs
TWO BOXES OF CALMOTIN.
THAT'LL BE FOUR YEN AND 80 SEN.

*Hayano Drugstore

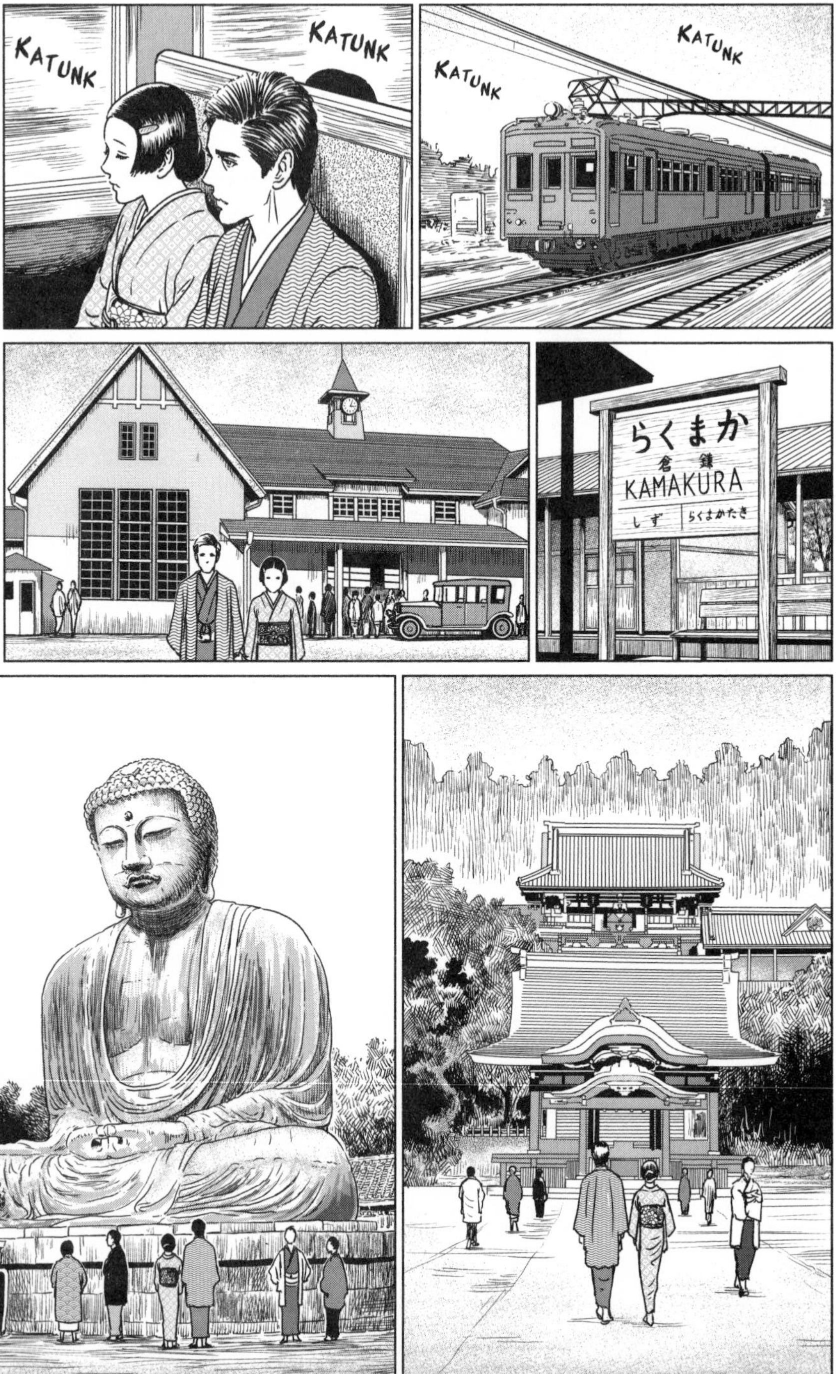
KATUNK
KATUNK
KATUNK
KATUNK
らくまか
倉鎌
KAMAKURA
しず
らくまかたき

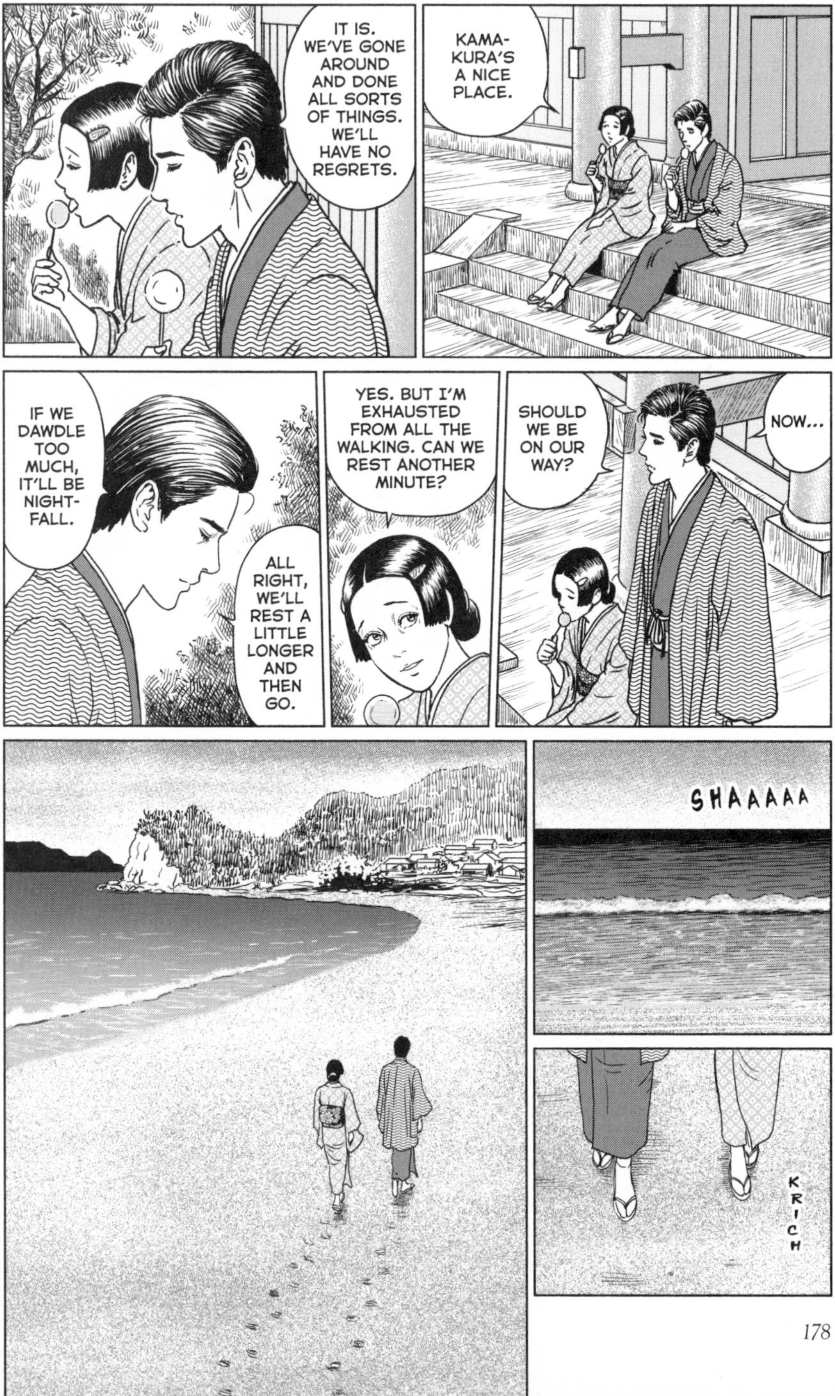
KAMA-KURA'S A NICE PLACE.
IT IS. WE'VE GONE AROUND AND DONE ALL SORTS OF THINGS. WE'LL HAVE NO REGRETS.
NOW...
SHOULD WE BE ON OUR WAY?
YES. BUT I'M EXHAUSTED FROM ALL THE WALKING. CAN WE REST ANOTHER MINUTE?
IF WE DAWDLE TOO MUCH, IT'LL BE NIGHT-FALL.
ALL RIGHT, WE'LL REST A LITTLE LONGER AND THEN GO.
SHAAAAA
KRICH

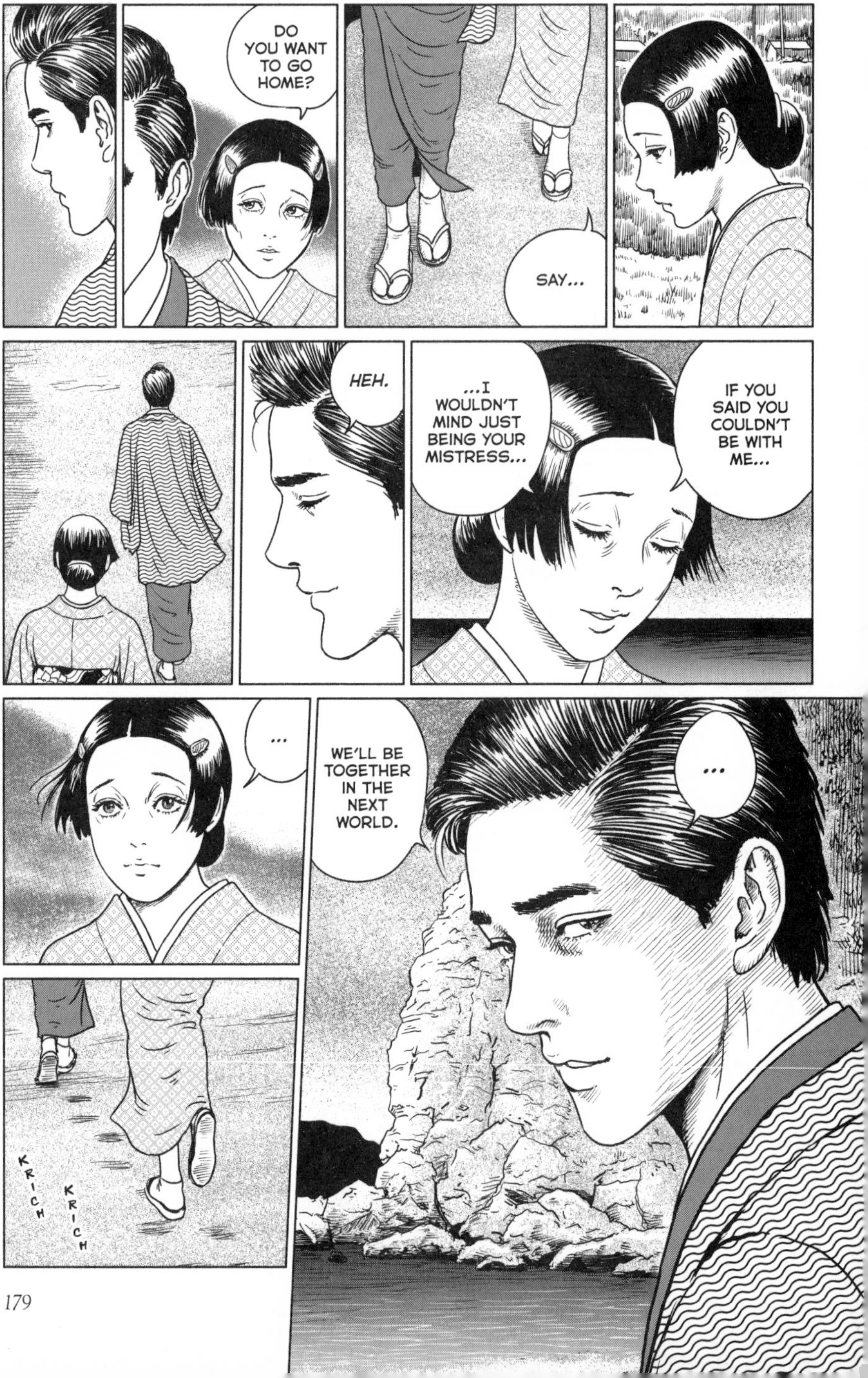
SAY...
DO YOU WANT TO GO HOME?
IF YOU SAID YOU COULDN'T BE WITH ME...
...I WOULDN'T MIND JUST BEING YOUR MISTRESS...
HEH.
...
WE'LL BE TOGETHER IN THE NEXT WORLD.
...
KRICH
KRICH

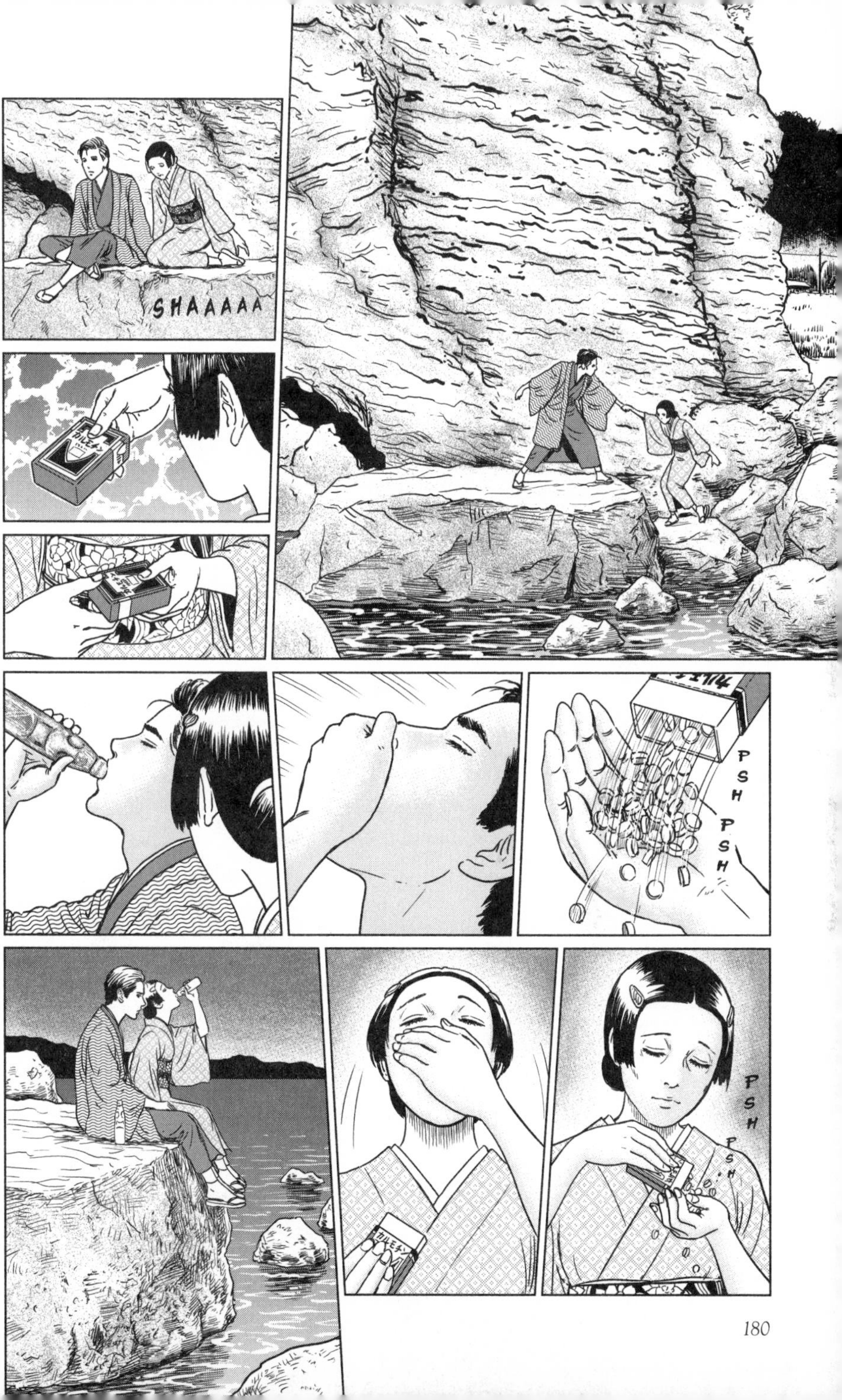
SHAAAAA
PSH PSH
PSH PSH

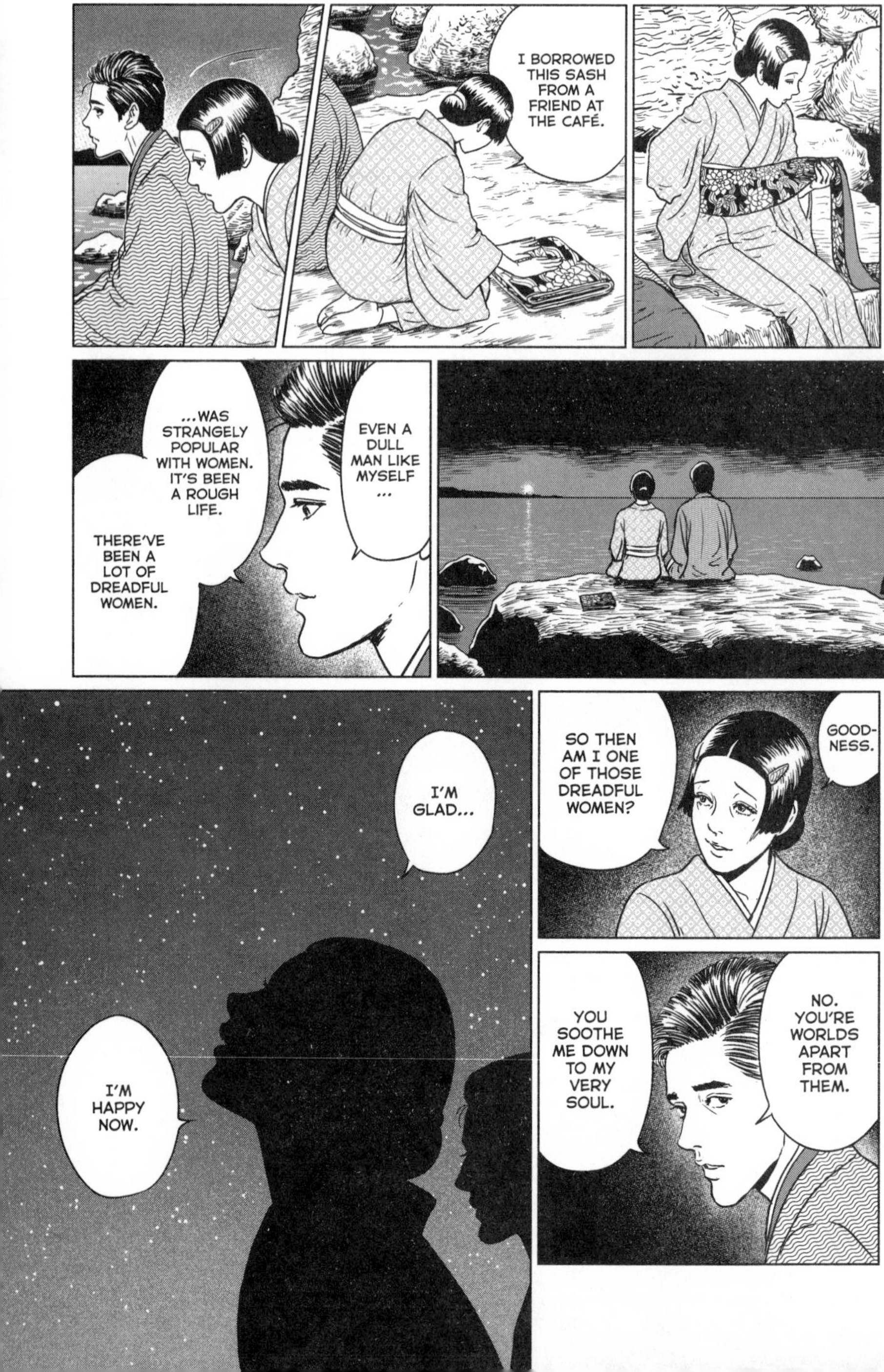
I BORROWED THIS SASH FROM A FRIEND AT THE CAFÉ.
EVEN A DULL MAN LIKE MYSELF ...
...WAS STRANGELY POPULAR WITH WOMEN. IT'S BEEN A ROUGH LIFE.
THERE'VE BEEN A LOT OF DREADFUL WOMEN.
GOOD-NESS.
SO THEN AM I ONE OF THOSE DREADFUL WOMEN?
NO. YOU'RE WORLDS APART FROM THEM.
YOU SOOTHE ME DOWN TO MY VERY SOUL.
I'M GLAD...
I'M HAPPY NOW.

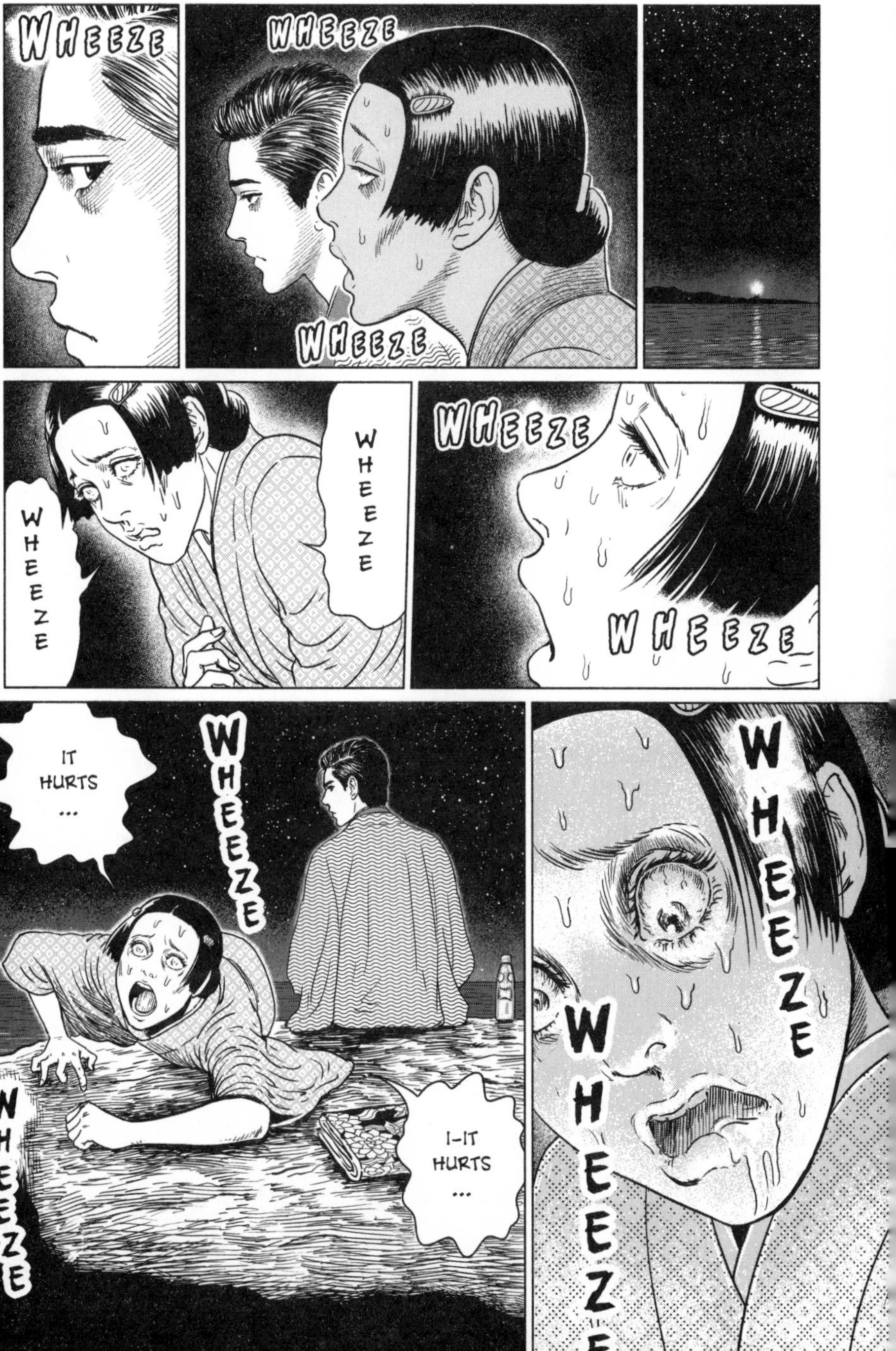
WHEEZE
WHEEZE
WHEEZE
WHEEZE
WHEEZE
WHEEZE
WHEEZE
WHEEZE
WHEEZE
IT HURTS ...
WHEEZE
I-IT HURTS ...
WHEEZE

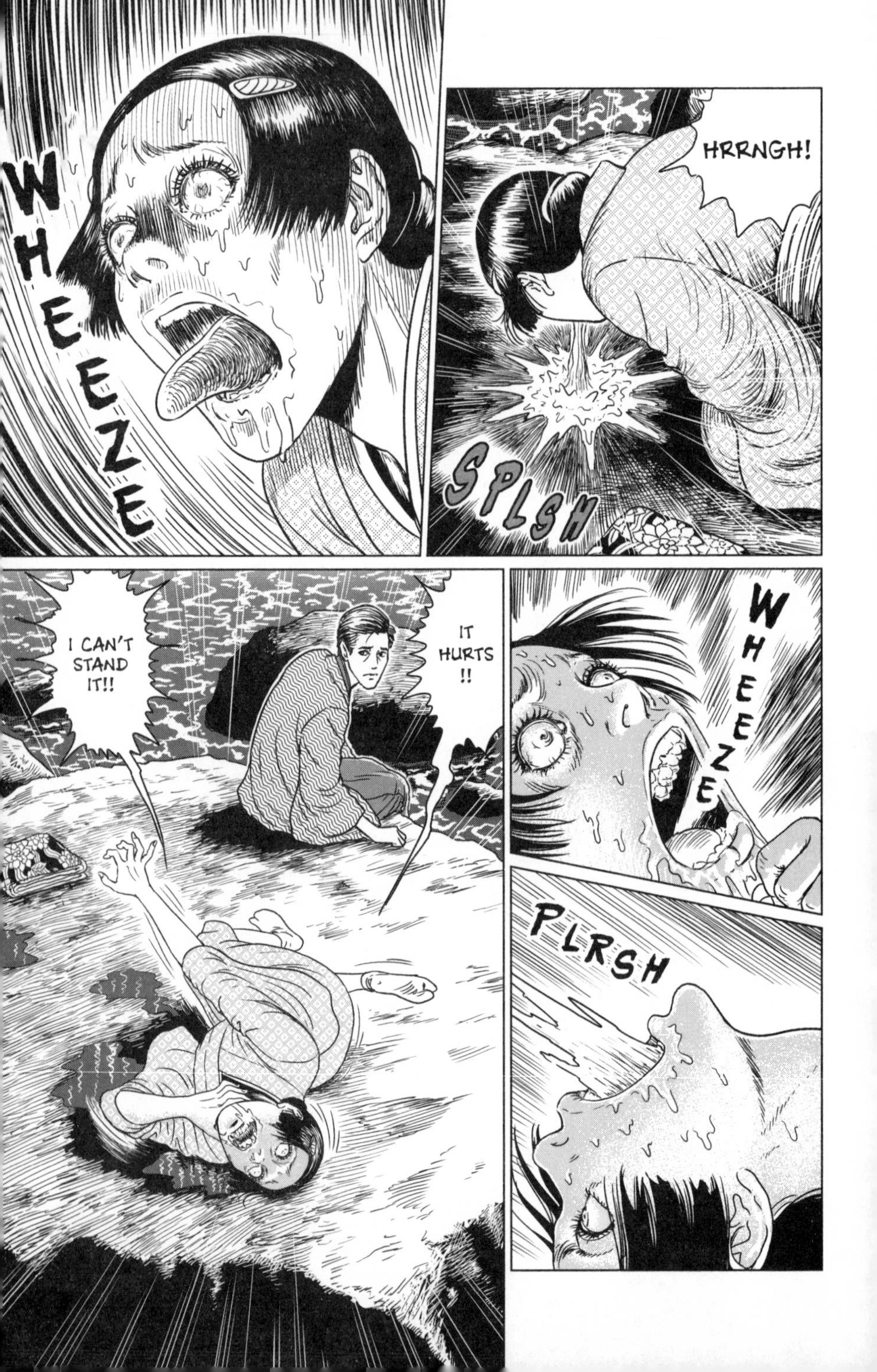
HRRNGH!
SPLSH
WHEEZE
WHEEZE
PLRSH
IT HURTS !!
I CAN'T STAND IT!!

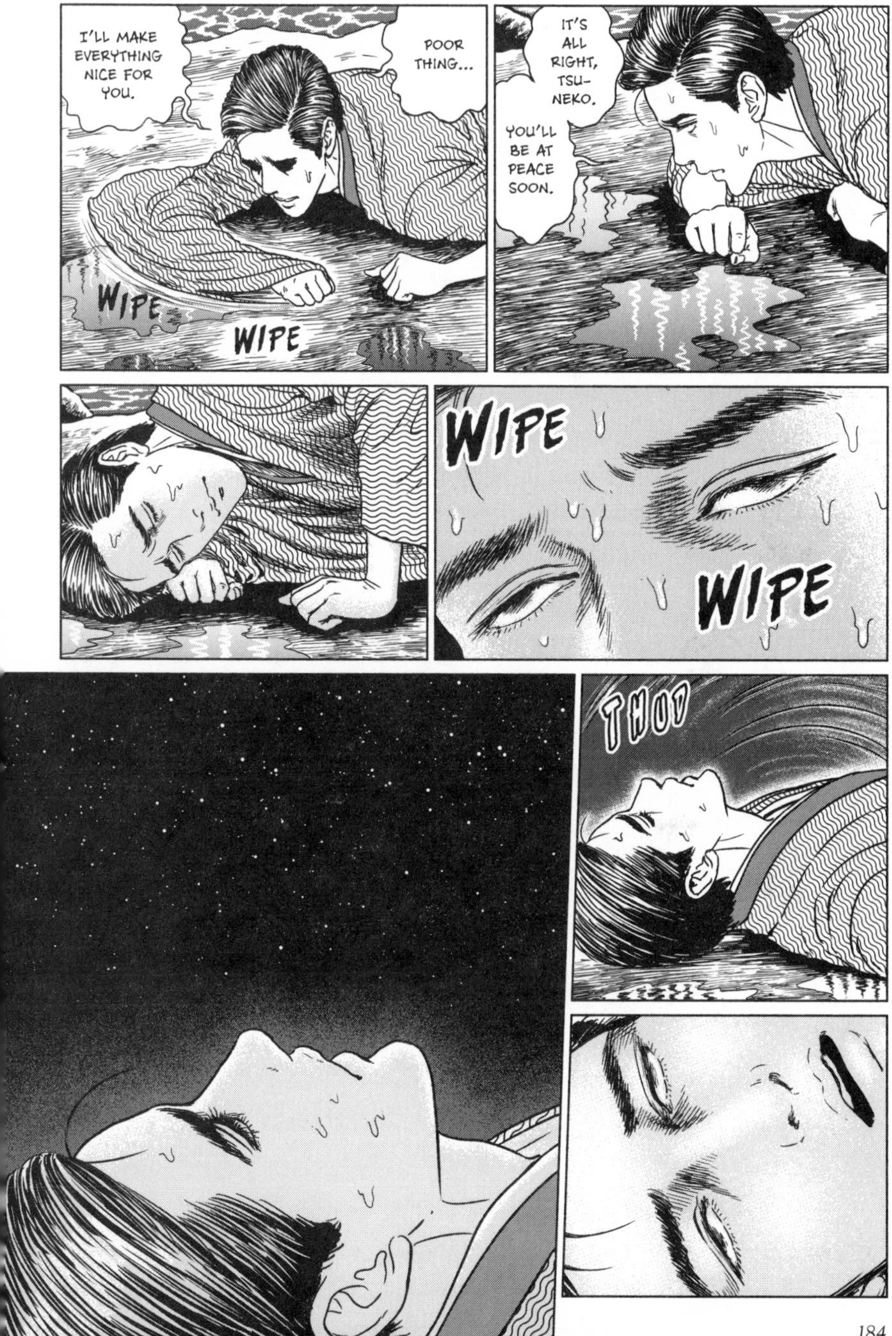
IT'S ALL RIGHT, TSUNEKO.
YOU'LL BE AT PEACE SOON.
POOR THING...
I'LL MAKE EVERYTHING NICE FOR YOU.
WIPE
WIPE
WIPE
WIPE
THUD

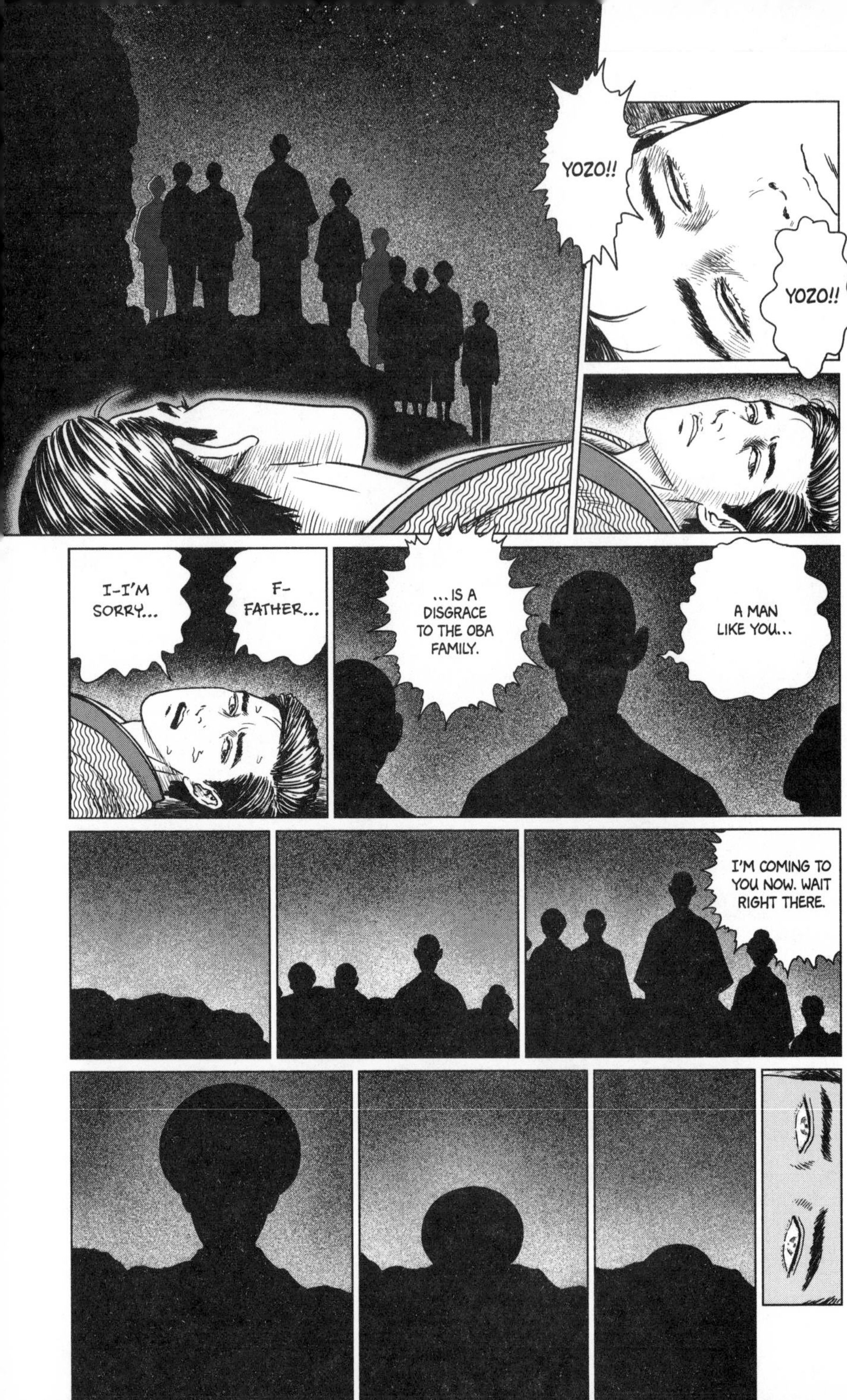
YOZO!!
YOZO!!
A MAN LIKE YOU...
...IS A DISGRACE TO THE OBA FAMILY.
F-FATHER...
I-I'M SORRY...
I'M COMING TO YOU NOW. WAIT RIGHT THERE.

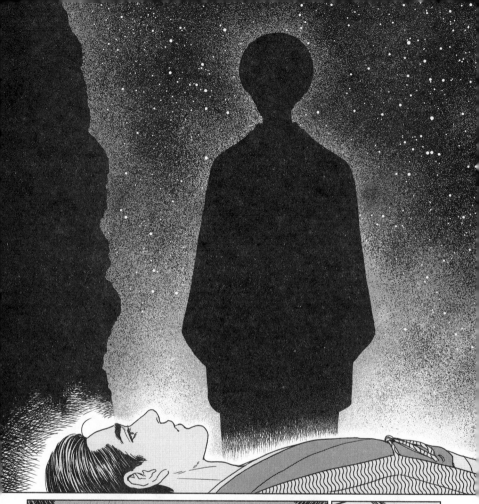
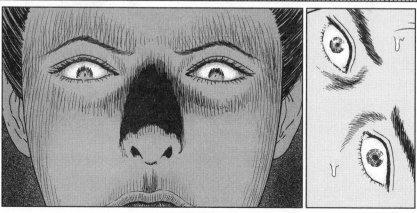

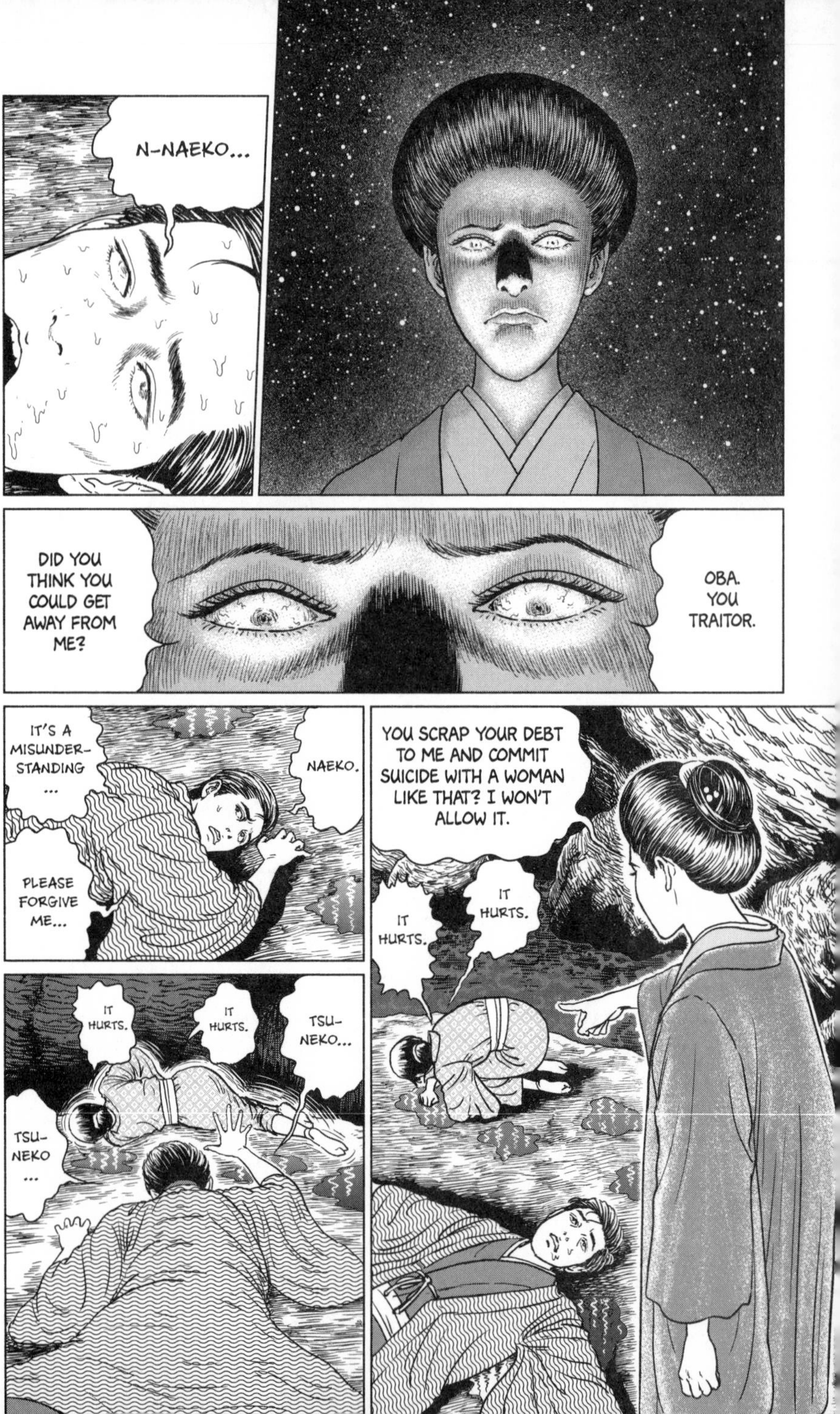
N-NAEKO...
OBA. YOU TRAITOR.
DID YOU THINK YOU COULD GET AWAY FROM ME?
YOU SCRAP YOUR DEBT TO ME AND COMMIT SUICIDE WITH A WOMAN LIKE THAT? I WON'T ALLOW IT.
IT HURTS.
IT HURTS.
NAEKO.
IT'S A MISUNDER-STANDING ...
PLEASE FORGIVE ME...
TSU-NEKO...
IT HURTS.
IT HURTS.
TSU-NEKO ...

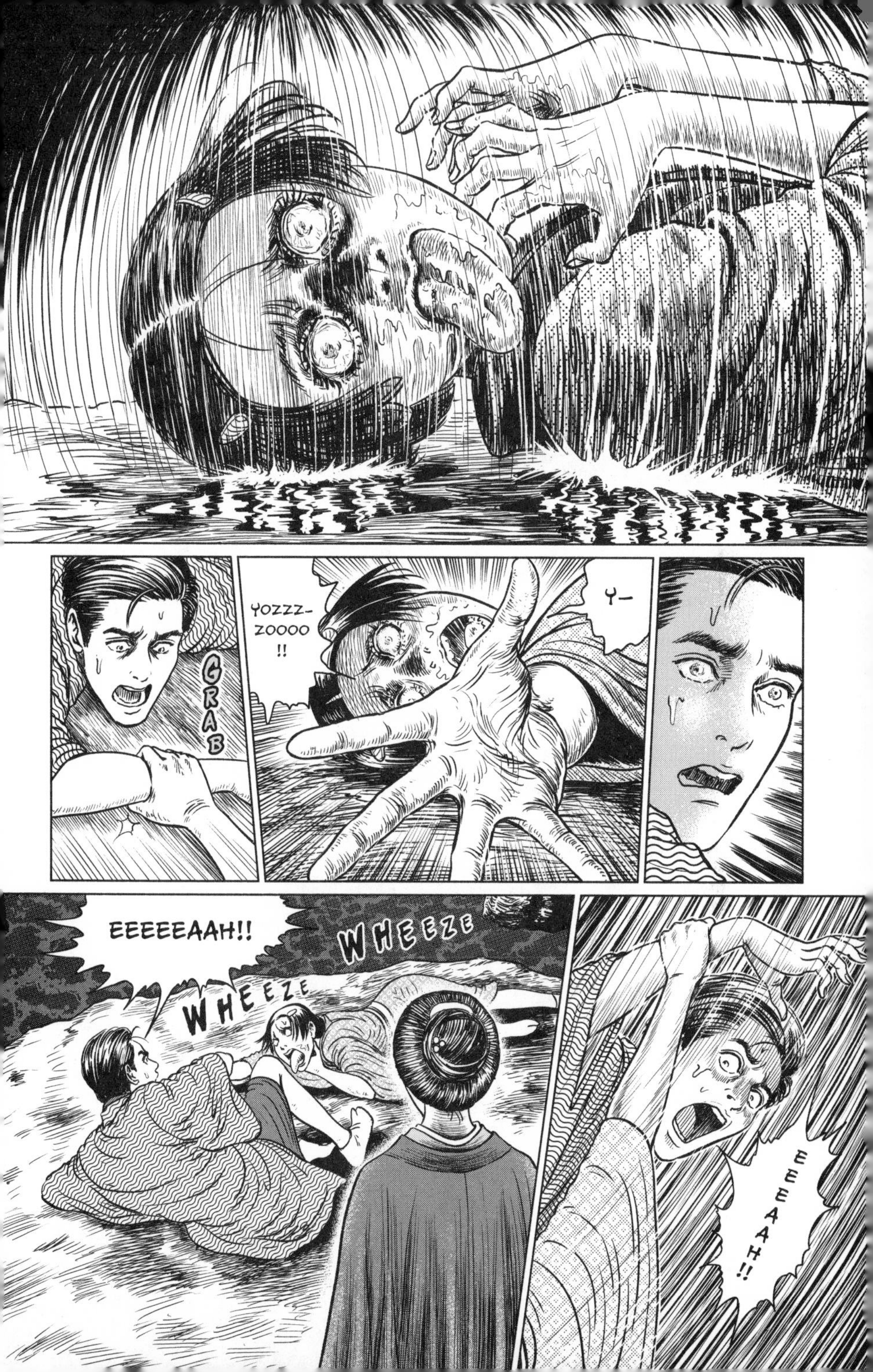
Y—
YOZZZ-ZOOOO !!
GRAB
EEEEAAH!!
EEEEEAAH!!
WHEEZE
WHEEZE

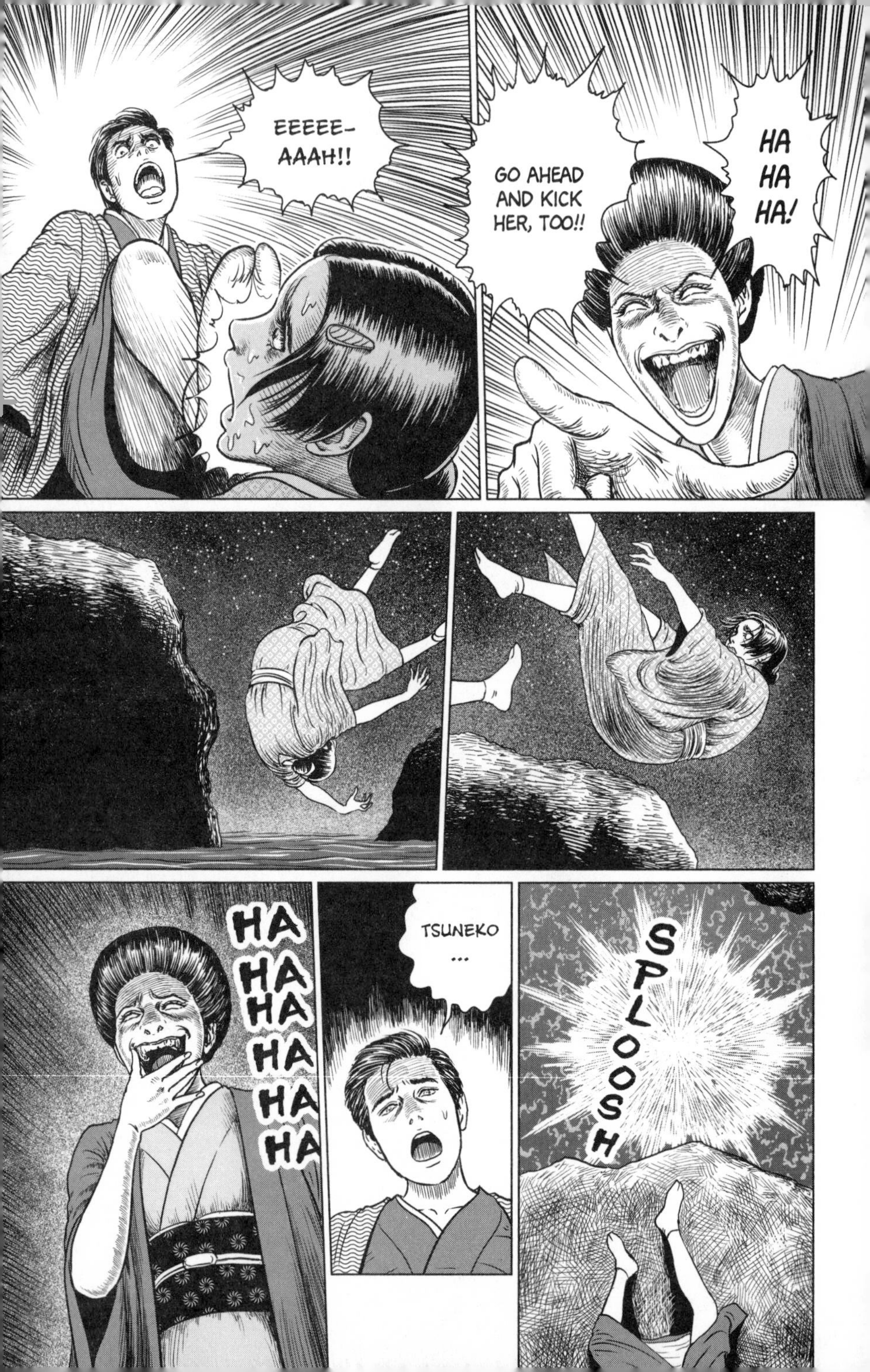
HA HA HA!
GO AHEAD AND KICK HER, TOO!!
EEEEE-AAAH!!
SPLOOSH
TSUNEKO ...
HA HA HA HA HA HA

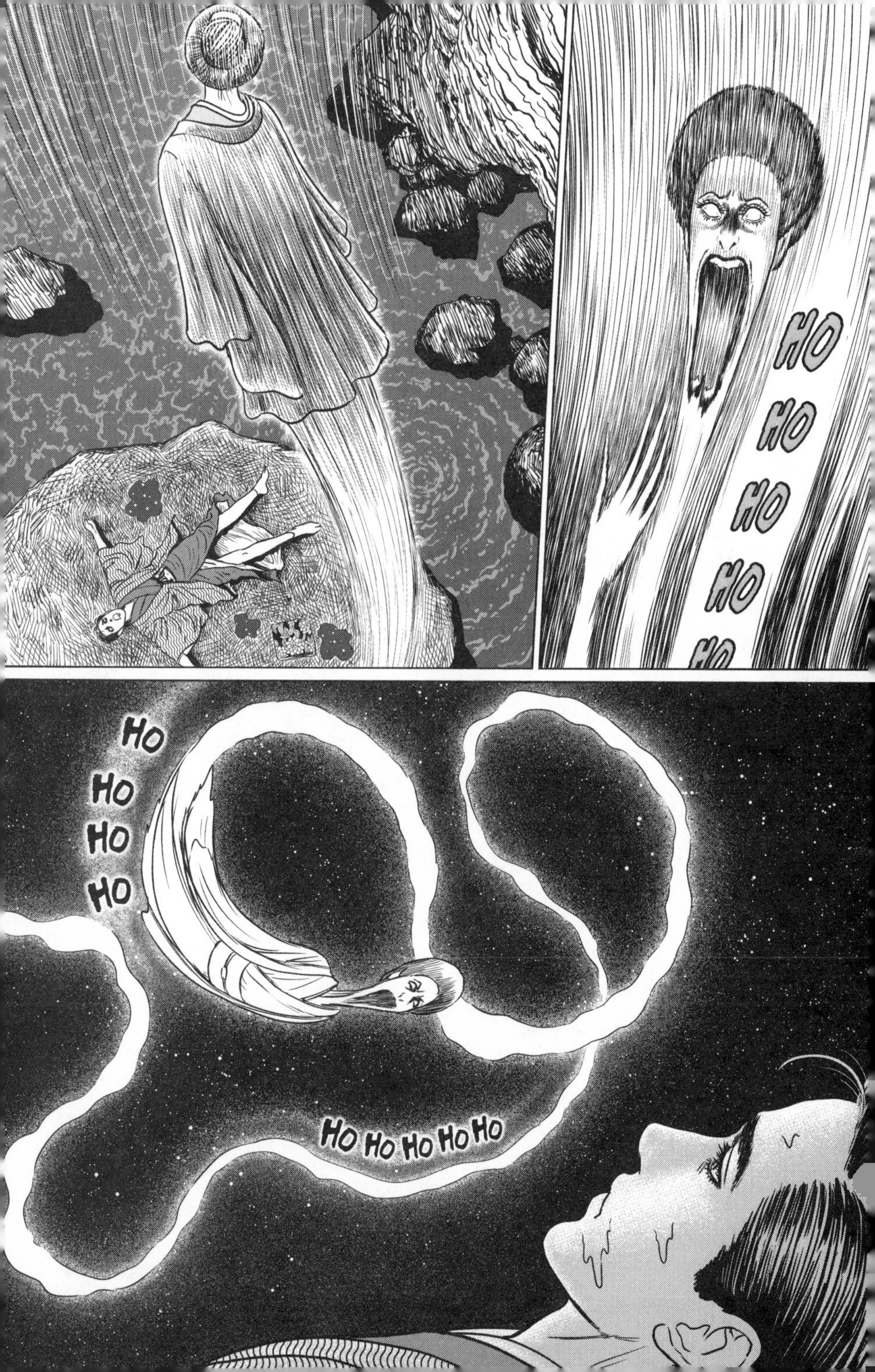
HO
HO
HO
HO
HO
HO
HO
HO
HO
HO HO HO HO HO

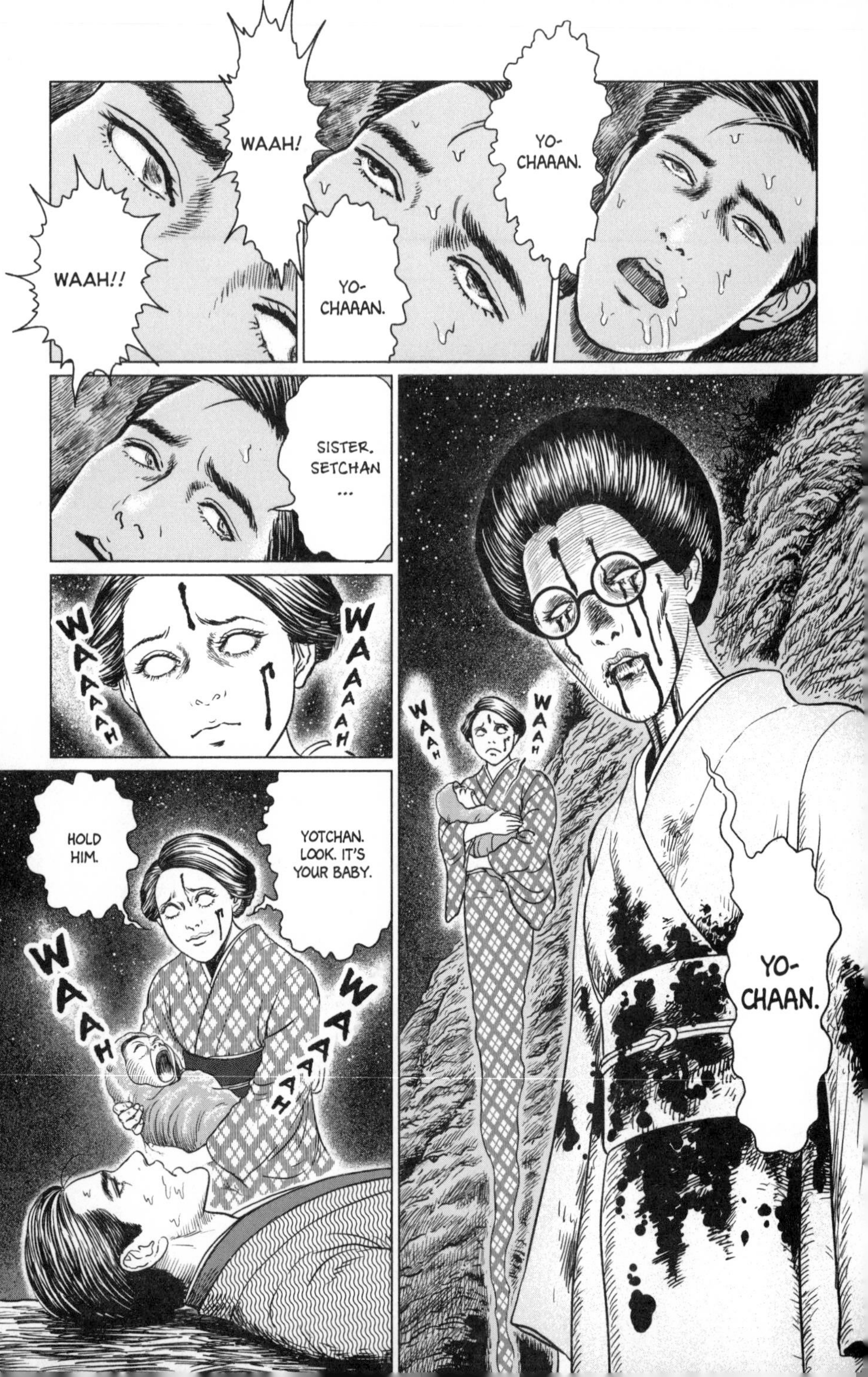
YO-
CHAAAN.
YO-
CHAAAN.
WAAH!
WAAH!!
WAAH
WAAH
YO-
CHAAN.
SISTER. SETCHAN ...
WAAAAH
WAAAAH
YOTCHAN. LOOK. IT'S YOUR BABY.
HOLD HIM.
WAAAAH
WAAH

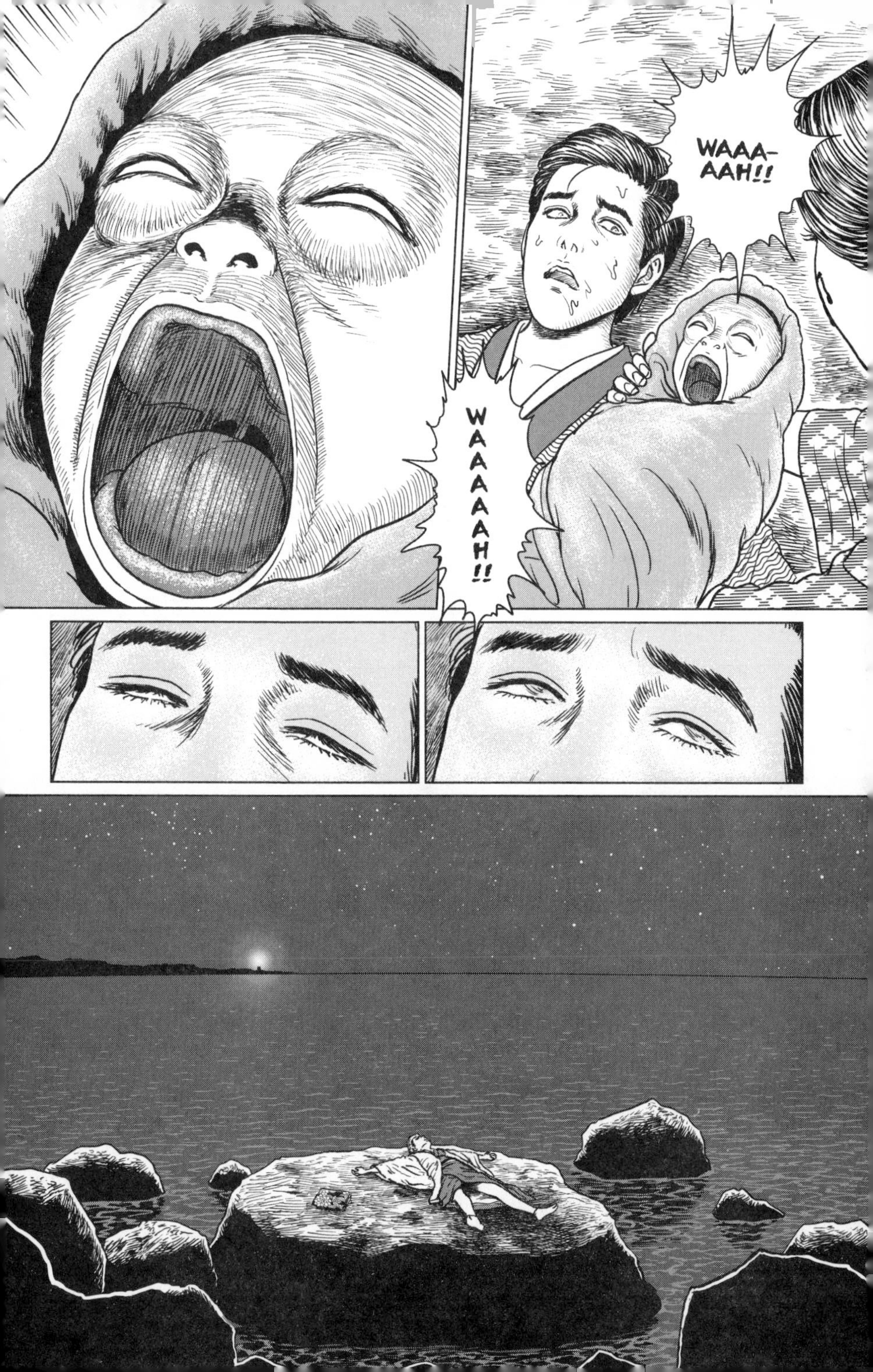
WAAA-
AAH!!
WAAAAAH!!

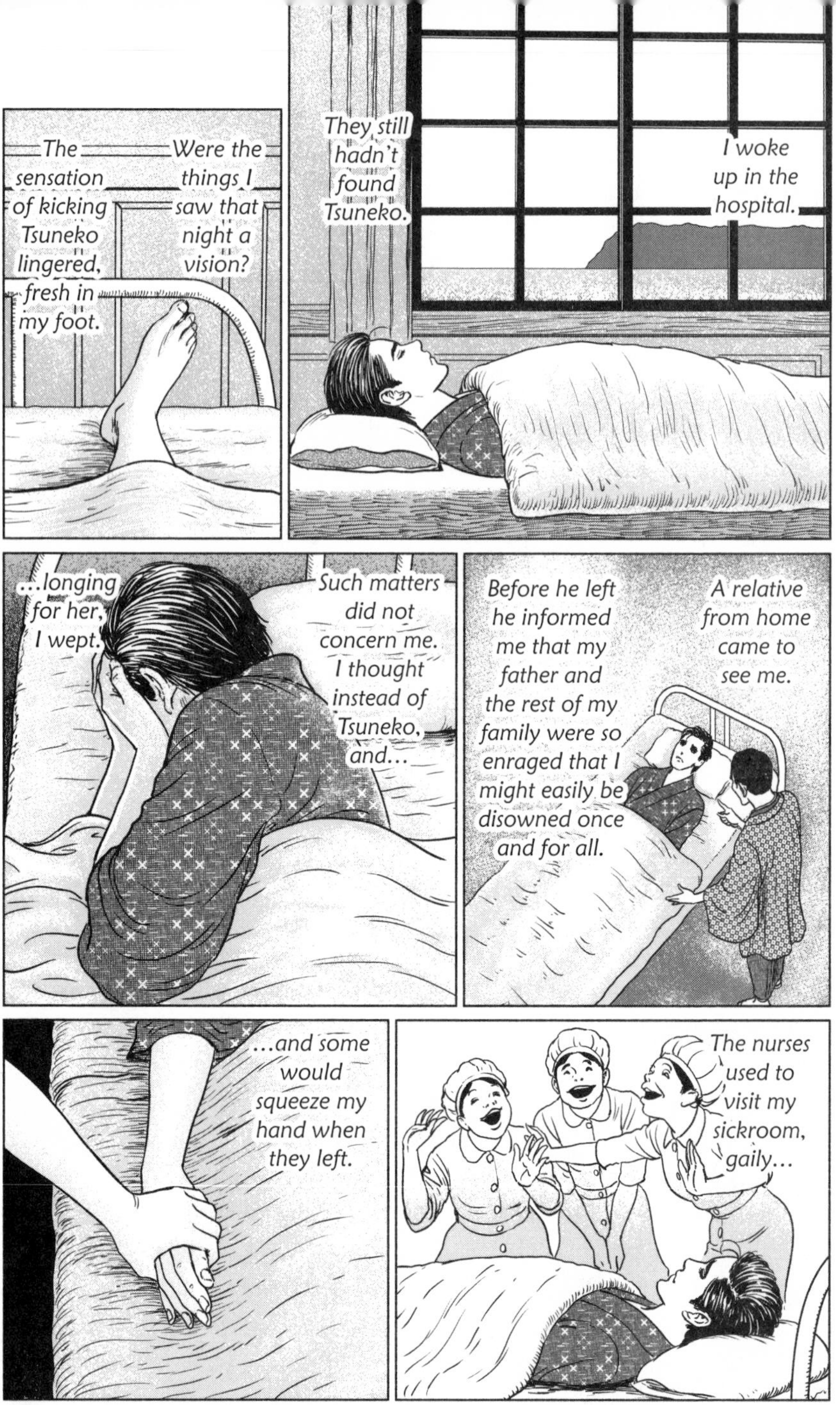
I woke up in the hospital.
They still hadn't found Tsuneko.
Were the things I saw that night a vision?
The sensation of kicking Tsuneko lingered, fresh in my foot.
A relative from home came to see me.
Before he left he informed me that my father and the rest of my family were so enraged that I might easily be disowned once and for all.
Such matters did not concern me. I thought instead of Tsuneko, and…
…longing for her, I wept.
The nurses used to visit my sickroom, gaily…
…and some would squeeze my hand when they left.

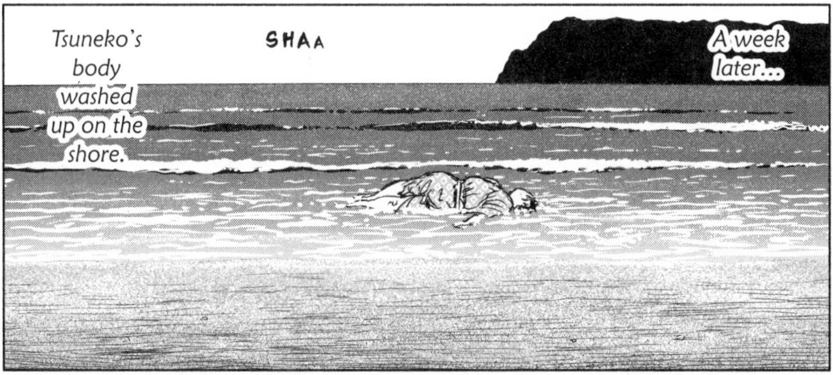
A week later…
SHAA
Tsuneko's body washed up on the shore.
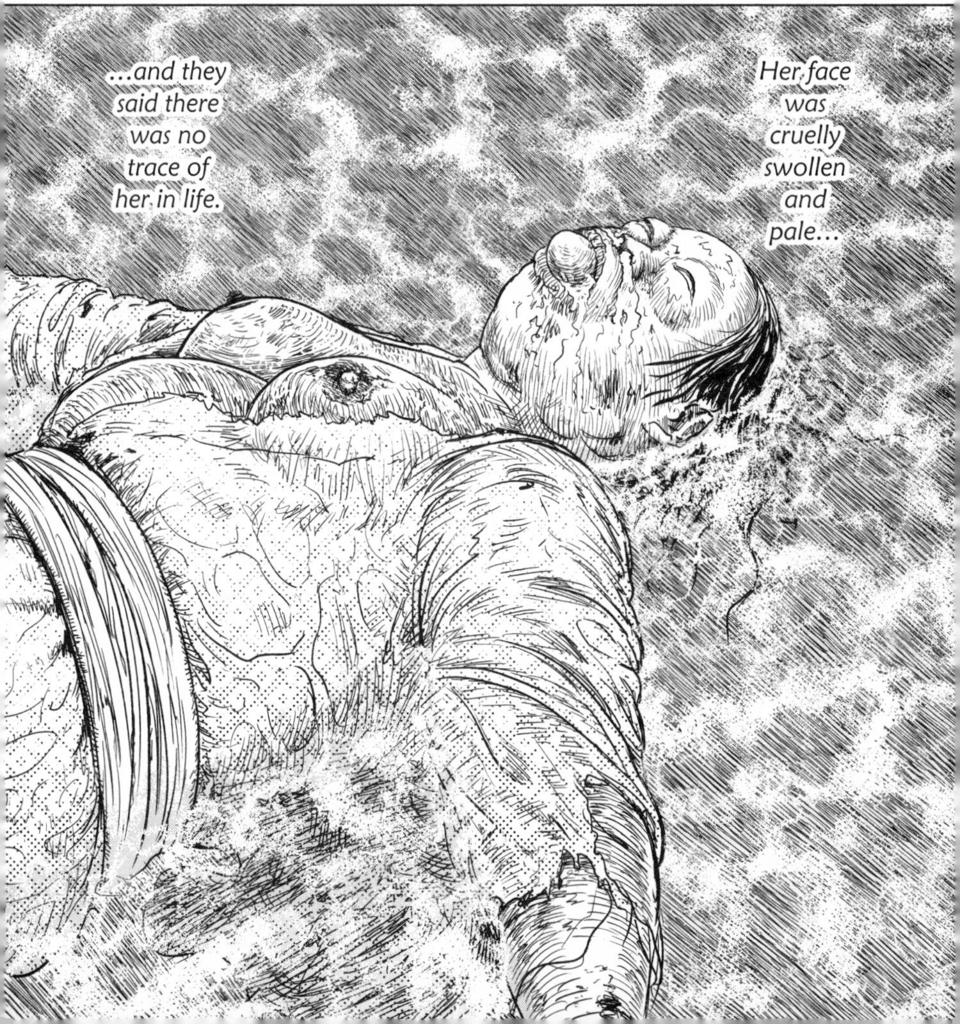
Her face was cruelly swollen and pale…
…and they said there was no trace of her in life.

CHAIN No. 8: Cold Sweat

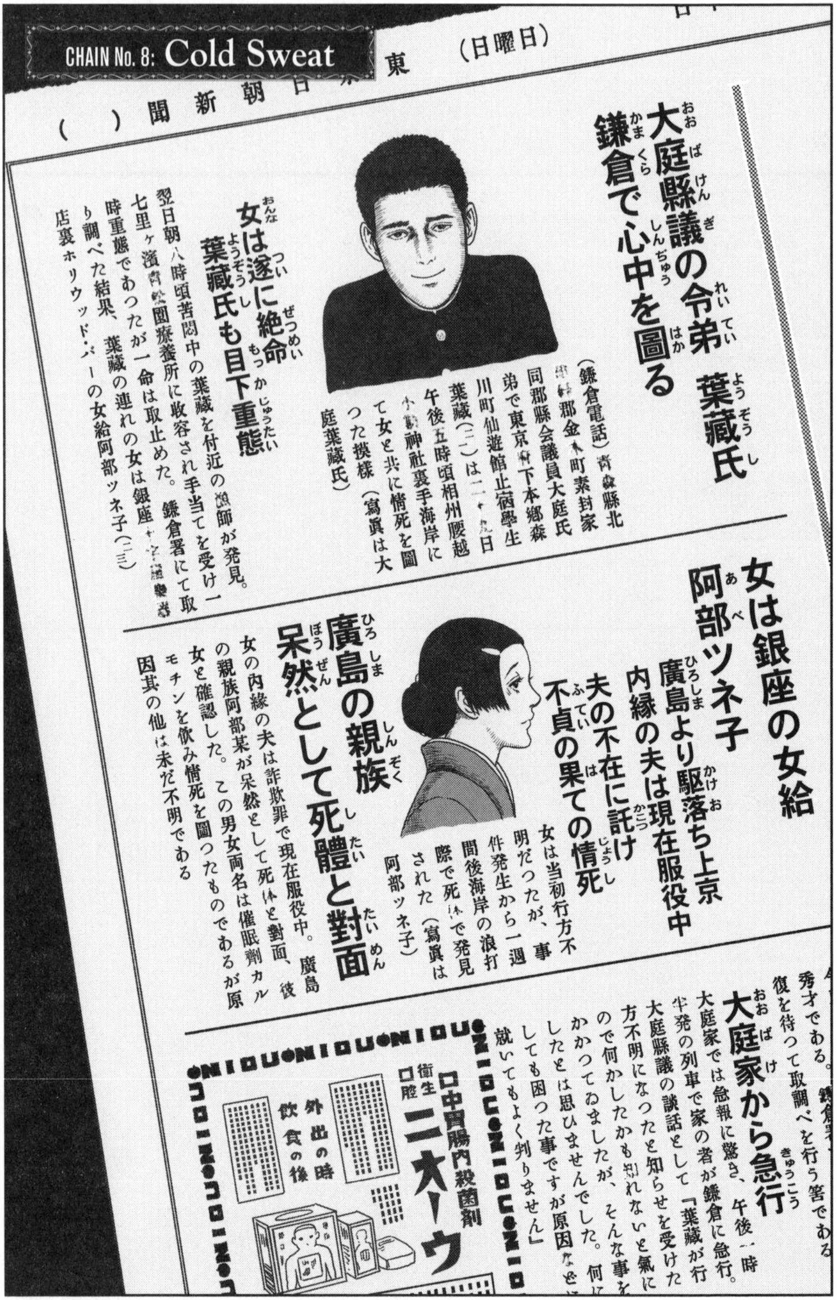

東京日朝新聞
(日曜日)
大庭縣議の令弟 葉蔵氏
鎌倉で心中を圖る
(鎌倉電話)青森縣北津軽郡金木町素封家同郡縣会議員大庭氏弟で東京府下本郷森川町仙遊館止宿學生葉蔵(二一)は二十九日午後五時頃相州腰越小動神社裏手海岸にて女と共に情死を圖つた摸様(寫眞は大庭葉蔵氏)
女は遂に絶命
葉蔵氏も目下重態
翌日朝八時頃苦悶中の葉蔵を付近の漁師が発見。七里ヶ濱恵風園療養所に收容され手当てを受け一時重態であつたが一命は取止めた。鎌倉署にて取り調べた結果、葉蔵の連れの女は銀座十字屋喫茶店裏ホリウッド・バーの女給阿部ツネ子(二三)
女は銀座の女給
阿部ツネ子
廣島より駆落ち上京
内縁の夫は現在服役中
夫の不在に託け
不貞の果ての情死
女は当初行方不明だつたが、事件発生から一週間後海岸の浪打際で死体で発見された(寫眞は阿部ツネ子)
廣島の親族
呆然として死體と對面
女の内縁の夫は詐欺罪で現在服役中。廣島の親族阿部某が呆然として死体と對面、彼女と確認した。この男女両名は催眠剤カルモチンを飲み情死を圖つたものであるが原因其の他は未だ不明である
秀才である。
復を待つて取調べを行う筈である。
大庭家から急行
大庭家では急報に驚き、午後一時半発の列車で家の者が鎌倉に急行。大庭縣議の談話として『葉蔵が行方不明になつたと知らせを受けたので何かしたかも知れないと氣にかかつてゐましたが、そんな事をしたとは思ひませんでした。何にしても困つた事ですが原因などに就いてもよく判りません』
口中胃腸内殺菌剤
衛生 口腔
二大ーウ
外出の時
飲食の後

Headline: Assemblyman Oba's brother attempts a lovers' suicide
*see page 614 for full translation.

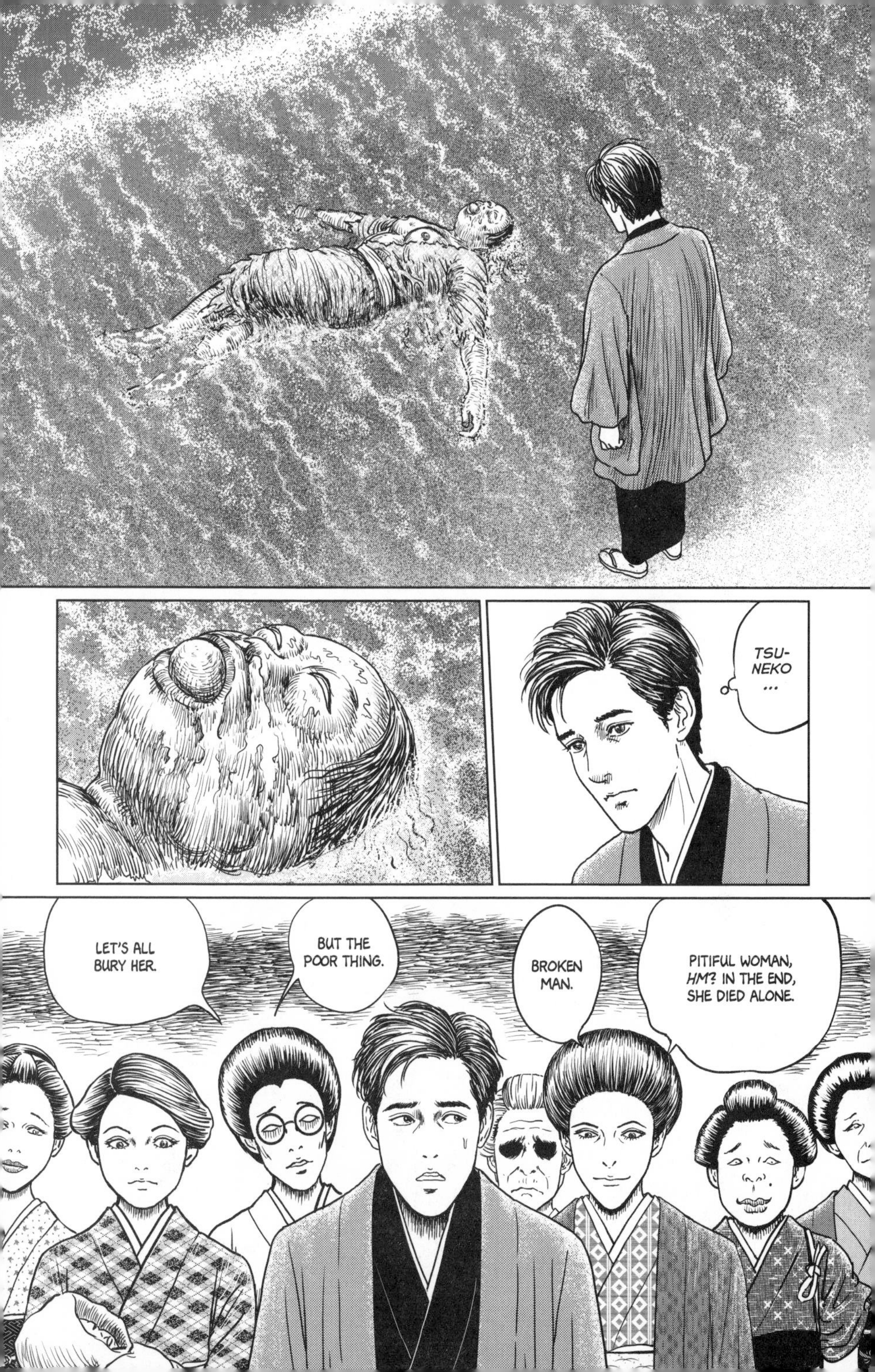
TSU-NEKO...
PITIFUL WOMAN, *HM?* IN THE END, SHE DIED ALONE.
BROKEN MAN.
BUT THE POOR THING.
LET'S ALL BURY HER.

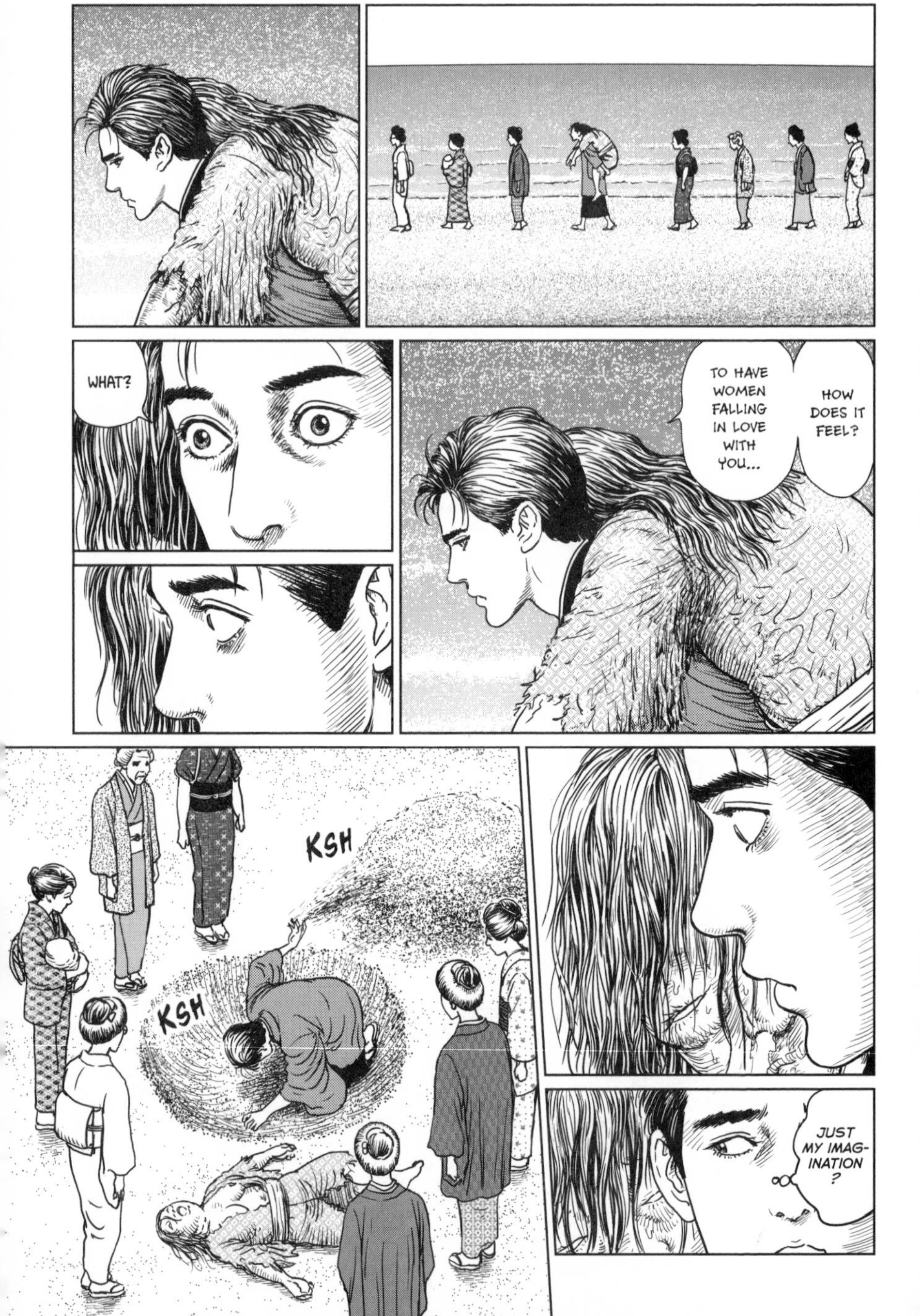
HOW DOES IT FEEL?
TO HAVE WOMEN FALLING IN LOVE WITH YOU...
WHAT?
JUST MY IMAG-INATION?
KSH
KSH

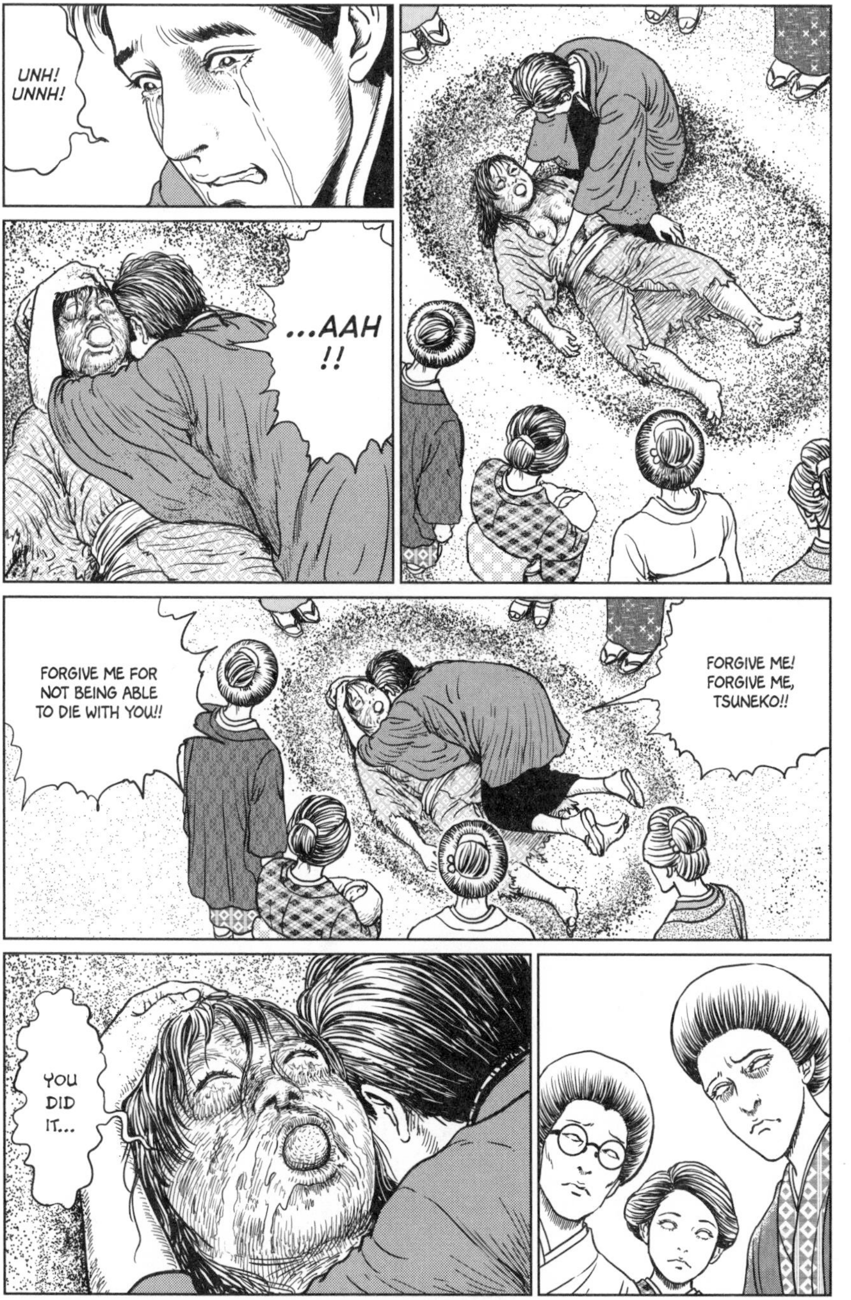
UNH! UNNH!
...AAH !!
FORGIVE ME! FORGIVE ME, TSUNEKO!!
FORGIVE ME FOR NOT BEING ABLE TO DIE WITH YOU!!
YOU DID IT...

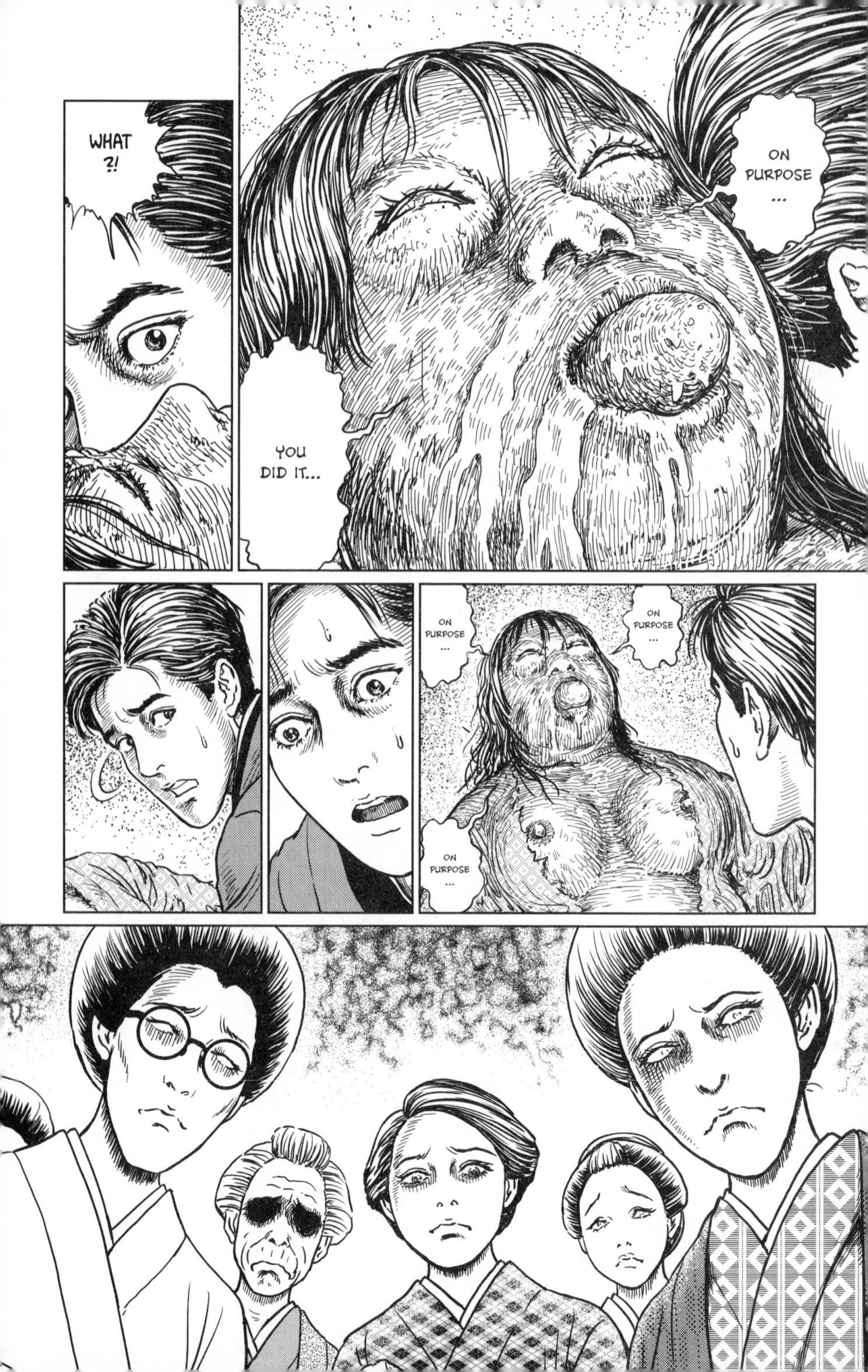
ON PURPOSE ...
YOU DID IT...
WHAT ?!
ON PURPOSE ...
ON PURPOSE ...
ON PURPOSE ...

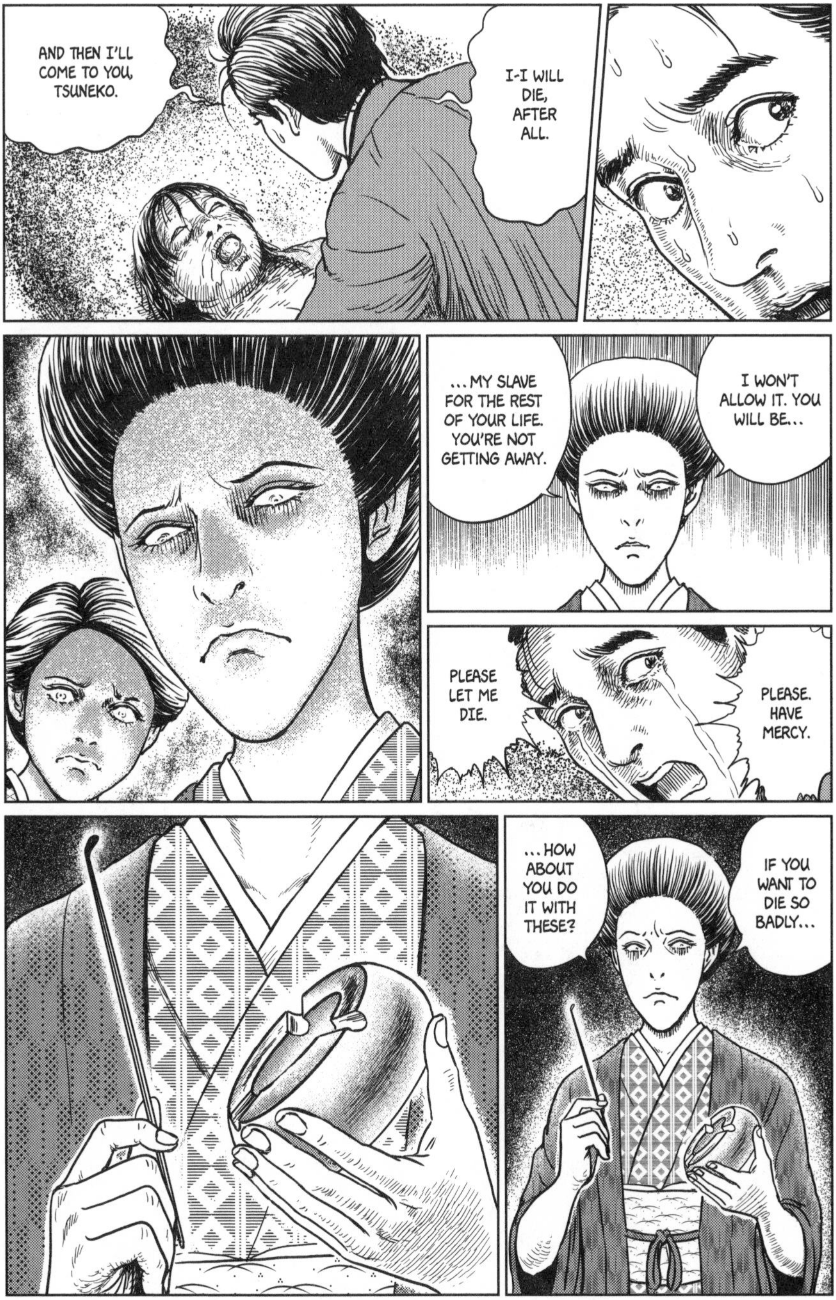
I-I WILL DIE, AFTER ALL.
AND THEN I'LL COME TO YOU, TSUNEKO.
I WON'T ALLOW IT. YOU WILL BE...
...MY SLAVE FOR THE REST OF YOUR LIFE. YOU'RE NOT GETTING AWAY.
PLEASE. HAVE MERCY.
PLEASE LET ME DIE.
IF YOU WANT TO DIE SO BADLY...
...HOW ABOUT YOU DO IT WITH THESE?

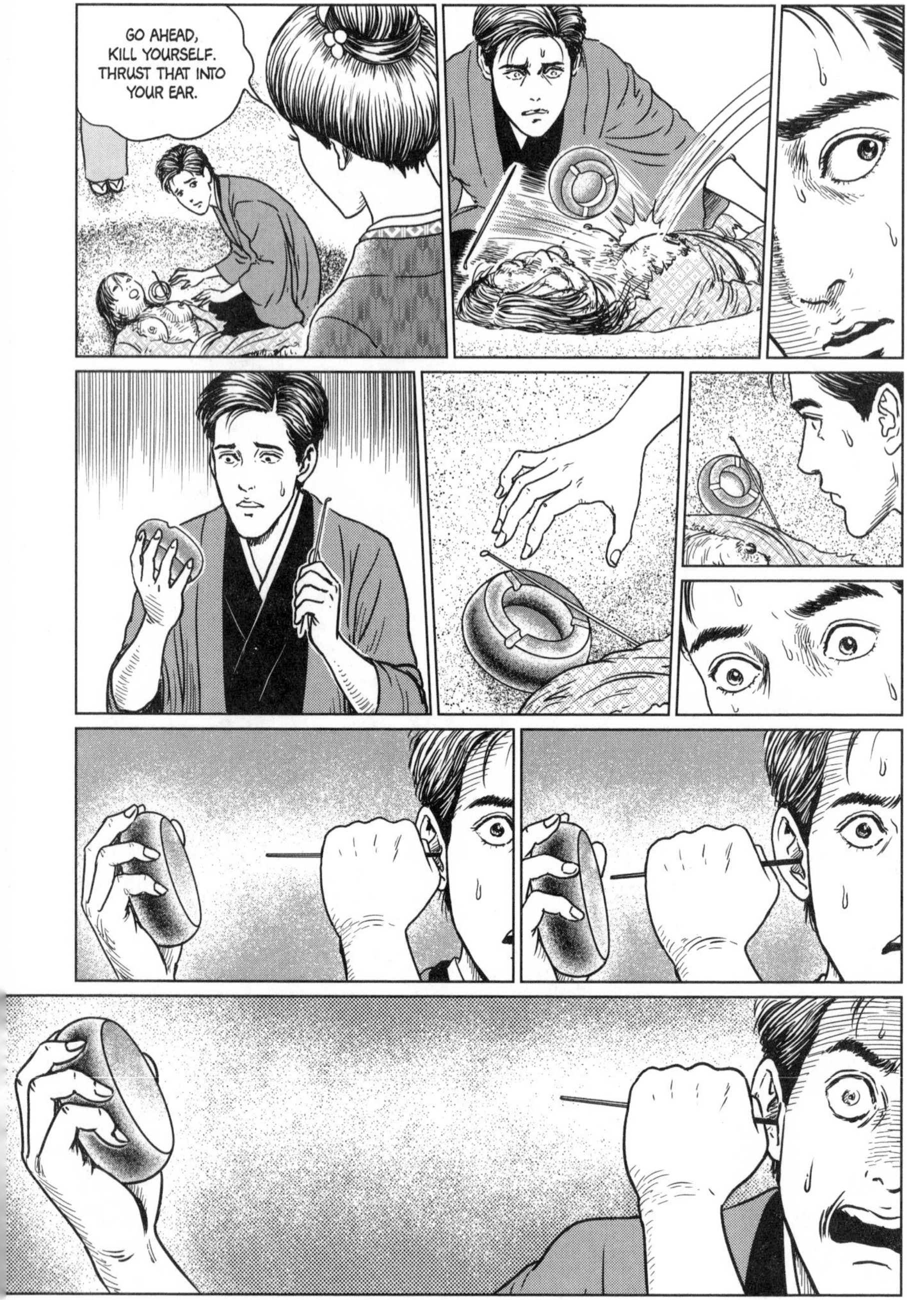
GO AHEAD, KILL YOURSELF. THRUST THAT INTO YOUR EAR.

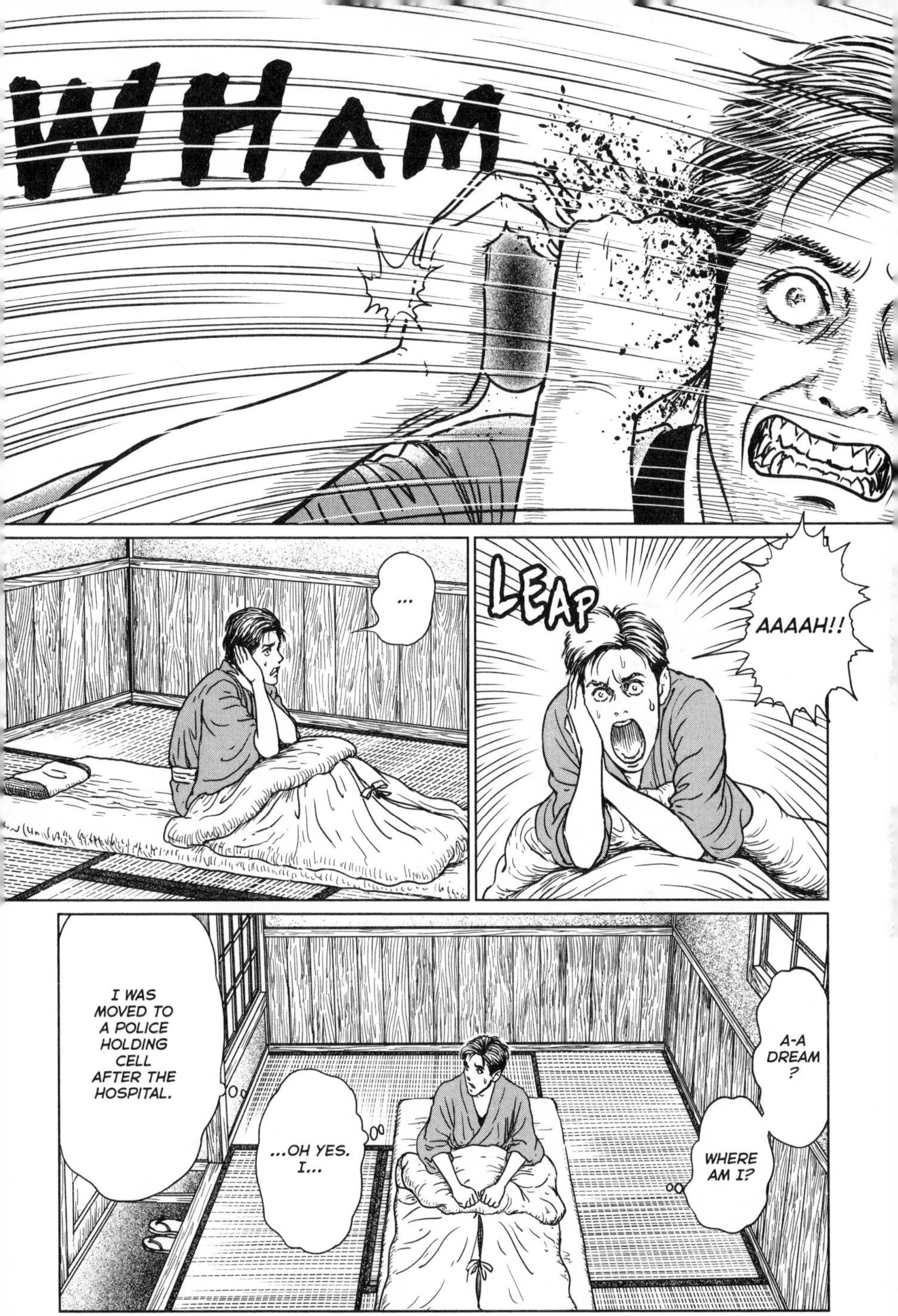
WHAM
LEAP
AAAAH!!
...
A-A DREAM?
WHERE AM I?
...OH YES. I...
I WAS MOVED TO A POLICE HOLDING CELL AFTER THE HOSPITAL.

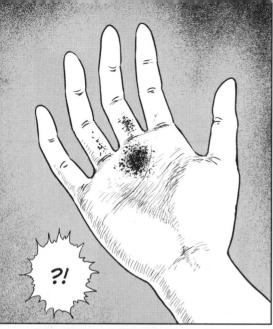

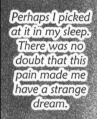

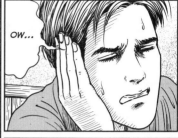

OW...
?!
This was blood from the pimple that had appeared under my ear a few days earlier.
Perhaps I picked at it in my sleep. There was no doubt that this pain made me have a strange dream.
YOZO OBA.
QUES-TIONING.

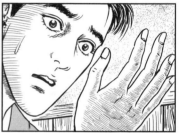

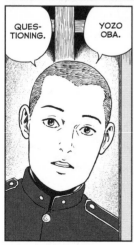

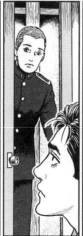

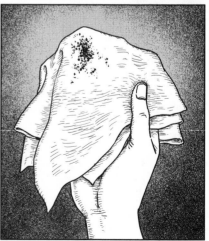

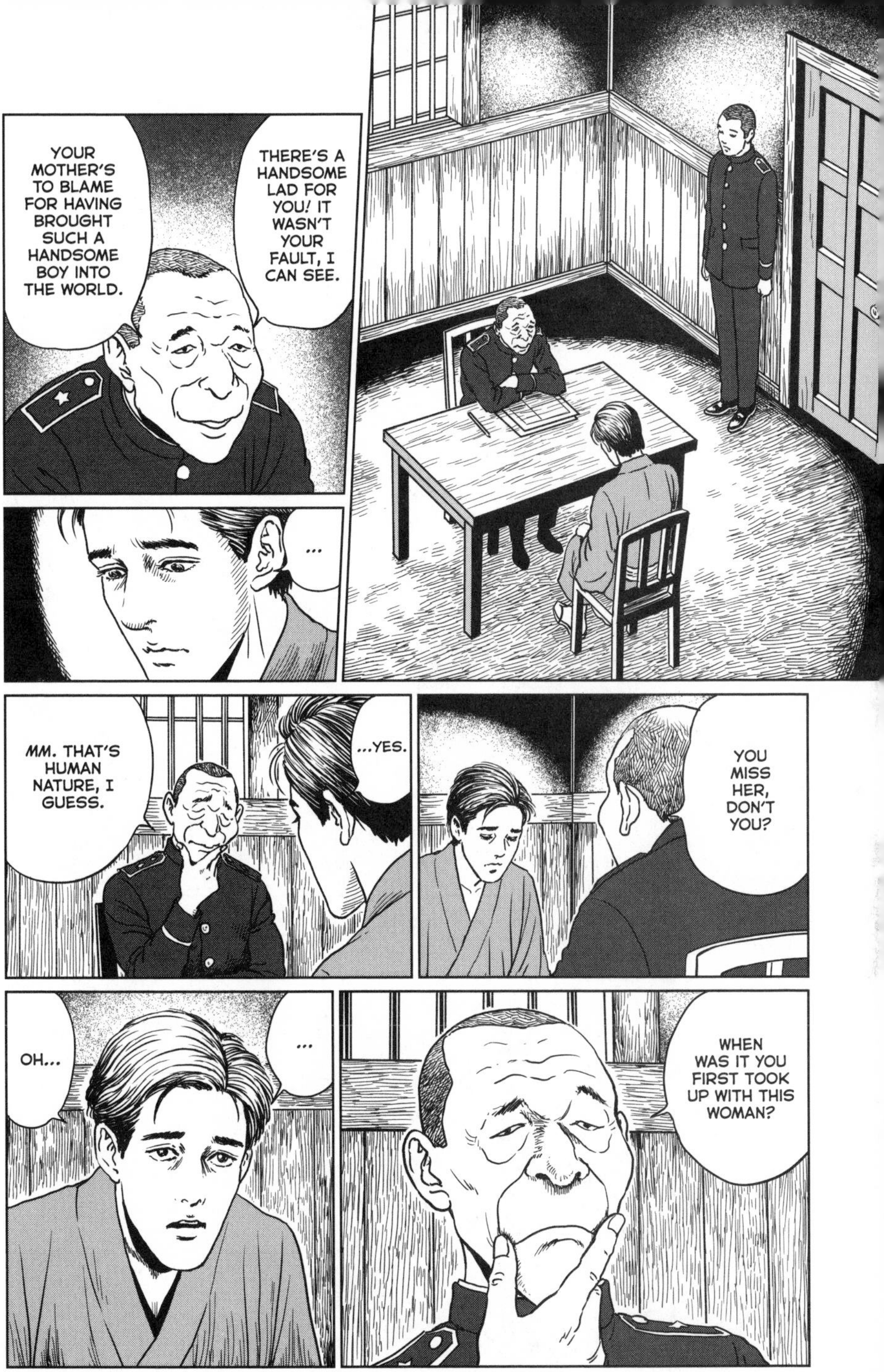
THERE'S A HANDSOME LAD FOR YOU! IT WASN'T YOUR FAULT, I CAN SEE.
YOUR MOTHER'S TO BLAME FOR HAVING BROUGHT SUCH A HANDSOME BOY INTO THE WORLD.
...
YOU MISS HER, DON'T YOU?
...YES.
MM. THAT'S HUMAN NATURE, I GUESS.
WHEN WAS IT YOU FIRST TOOK UP WITH THIS WOMAN?
...
OH...

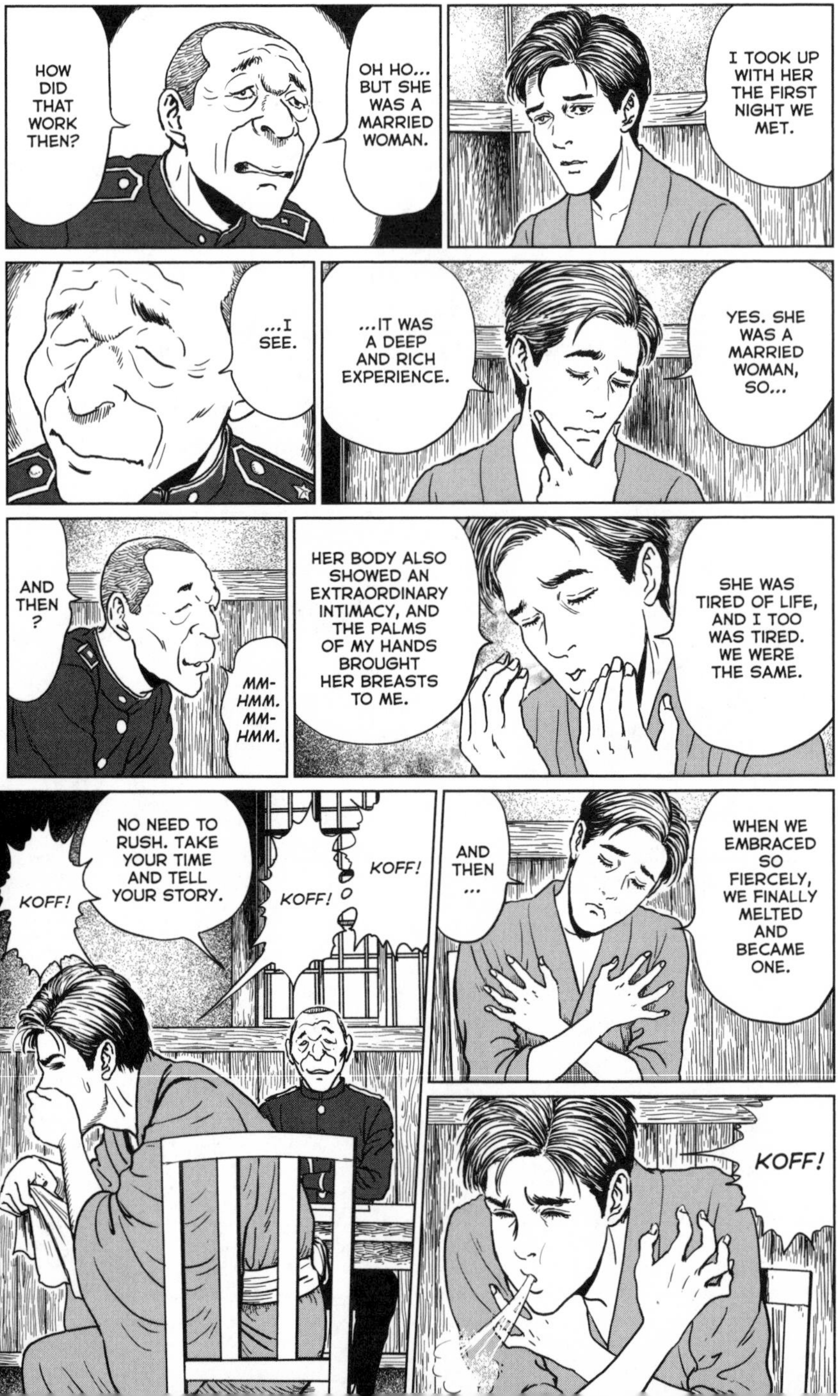
I TOOK UP WITH HER THE FIRST NIGHT WE MET.
OH HO... BUT SHE WAS A MARRIED WOMAN.
HOW DID THAT WORK THEN?
YES. SHE WAS A MARRIED WOMAN, SO...
...IT WAS A DEEP AND RICH EXPERIENCE.
...I SEE.
SHE WAS TIRED OF LIFE, AND I TOO WAS TIRED. WE WERE THE SAME.
HER BODY ALSO SHOWED AN EXTRAORDINARY INTIMACY, AND THE PALMS OF MY HANDS BROUGHT HER BREASTS TO ME.
MM-HMM. MM-HMM.
AND THEN?
WHEN WE EMBRACED SO FIERCELY, WE FINALLY MELTED AND BECAME ONE.
AND THEN...
KOFF!
KOFF!
KOFF!
NO NEED TO RUSH. TAKE YOUR TIME AND TELL YOUR STORY.
KOFF!

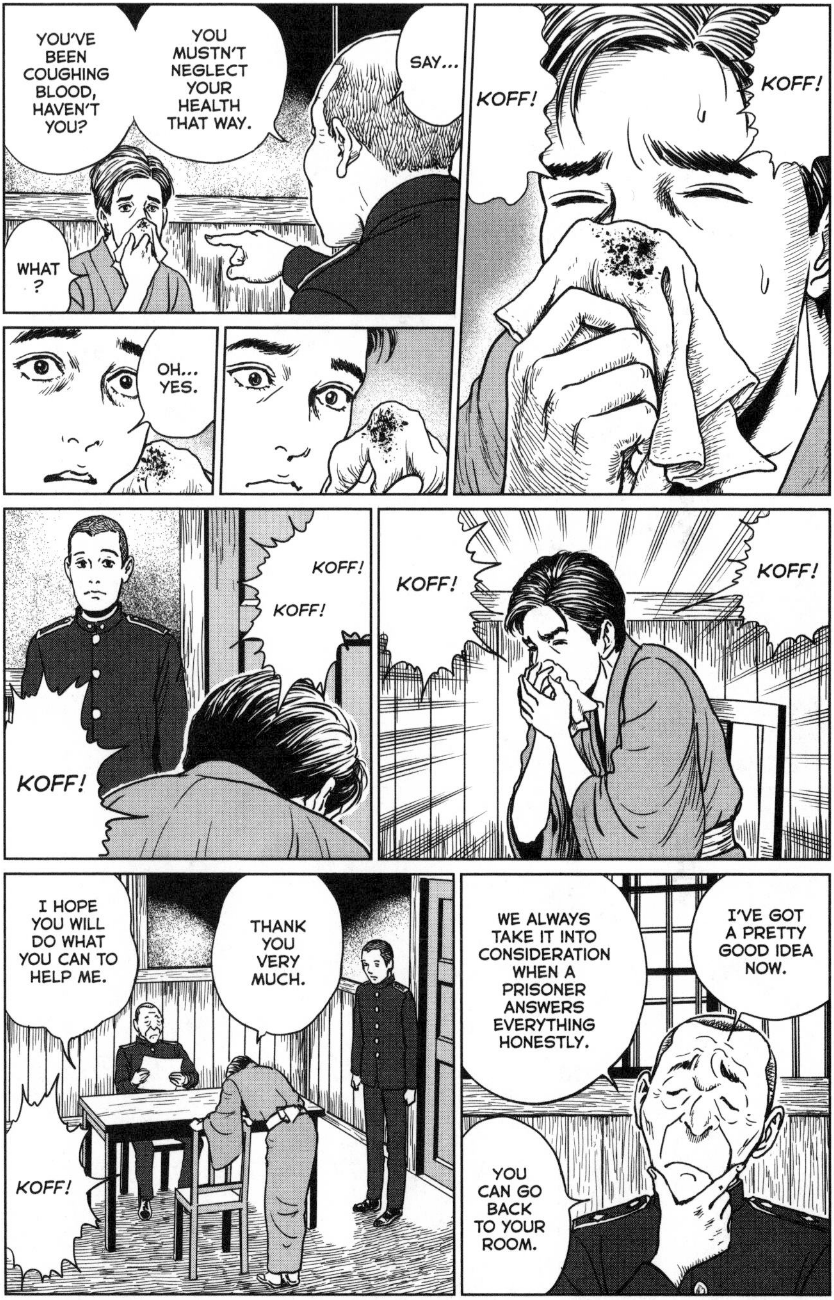
KOFF!
KOFF!
SAY...
YOU MUSTN'T NEGLECT YOUR HEALTH THAT WAY.
YOU'VE BEEN COUGHING BLOOD, HAVEN'T YOU?
WHAT?
OH... YES.
KOFF!
KOFF!
KOFF!
KOFF!
KOFF!
KOFF!
I'VE GOT A PRETTY GOOD IDEA NOW.
WE ALWAYS TAKE IT INTO CONSIDERATION WHEN A PRISONER ANSWERS EVERYTHING HONESTLY.
YOU CAN GO BACK TO YOUR ROOM.
THANK YOU VERY MUCH.
I HOPE YOU WILL DO WHAT YOU CAN TO HELP ME.
KOFF!

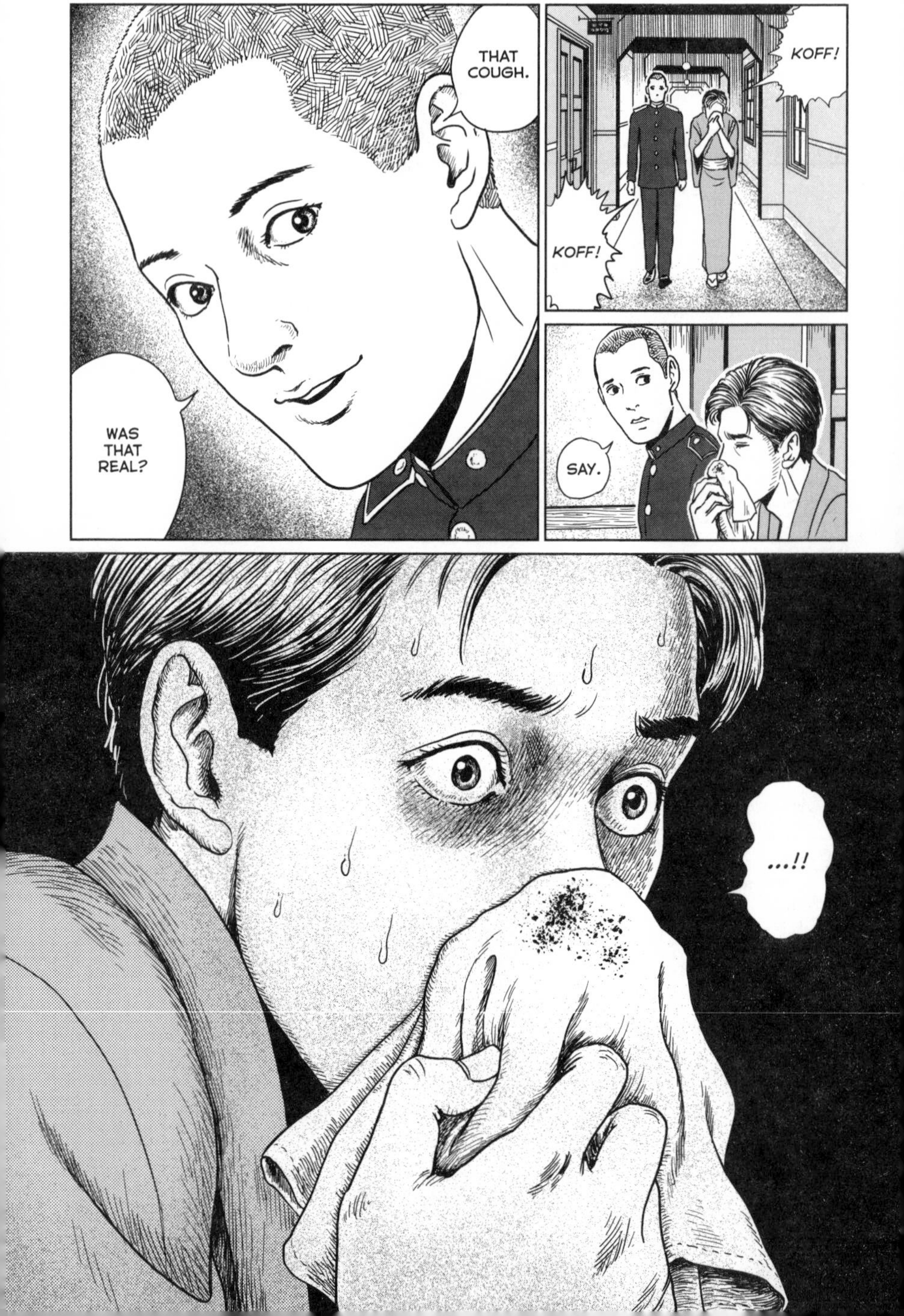
KOFF!
KOFF!
SAY.
THAT COUGH.
WAS THAT REAL?
...!!

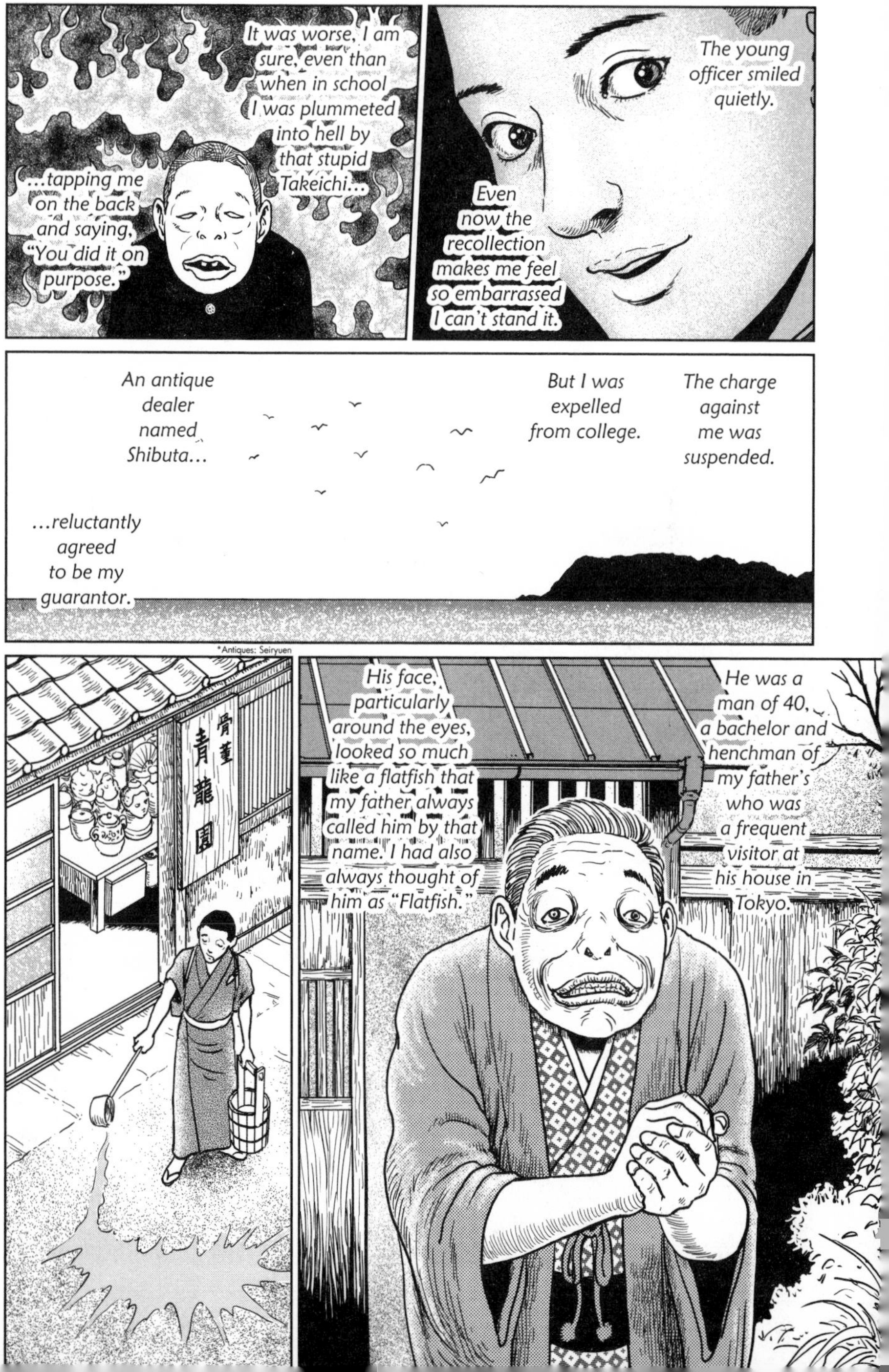
The young officer smiled quietly.
Even now the recollection makes me feel so embarrassed I can't stand it.
It was worse, I am sure, even than when in school I was plummeted into hell by that stupid Takeichi...
...tapping me on the back and saying, "You did it on purpose."
The charge against me was suspended.
But I was expelled from college.
An antique dealer named Shibuta...
...reluctantly agreed to be my guarantor.
He was a man of 40, a bachelor and henchman of my father's who was a frequent visitor at his house in Tokyo.
His face, particularly around the eyes, looked so much like a flatfish that my father always called him by that name. I had also always thought of him as "Flatfish."
*Antiques: Seiryuen
骨董
青龍園

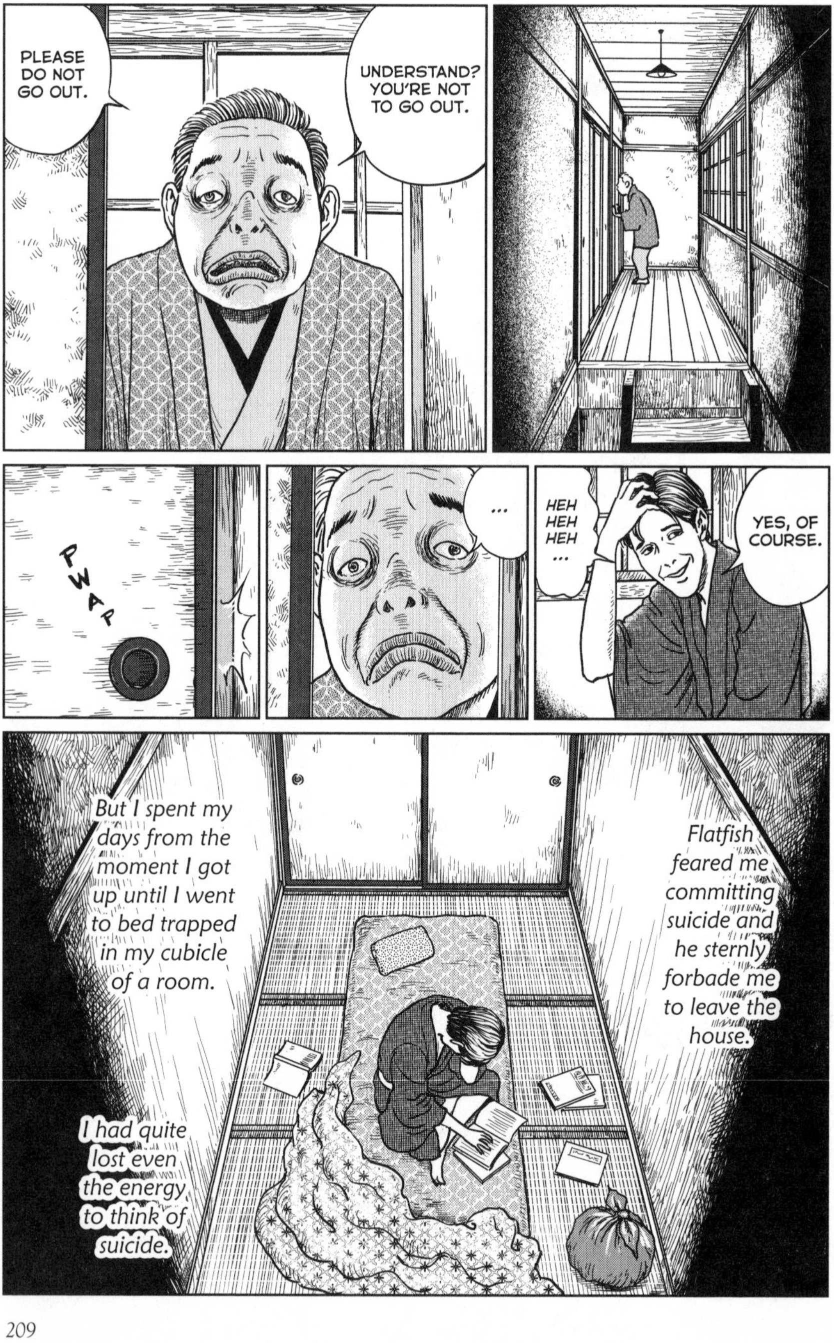
UNDERSTAND? YOU'RE NOT TO GO OUT.
PLEASE DO NOT GO OUT.
YES, OF COURSE.
HEH HEH HEH ...
...
PWAP
Flatfish feared me committing suicide and he sternly forbade me to leave the house.
But I spent my days from the moment I got up until I went to bed trapped in my cubicle of a room.
I had quite lost even the energy to think of suicide.

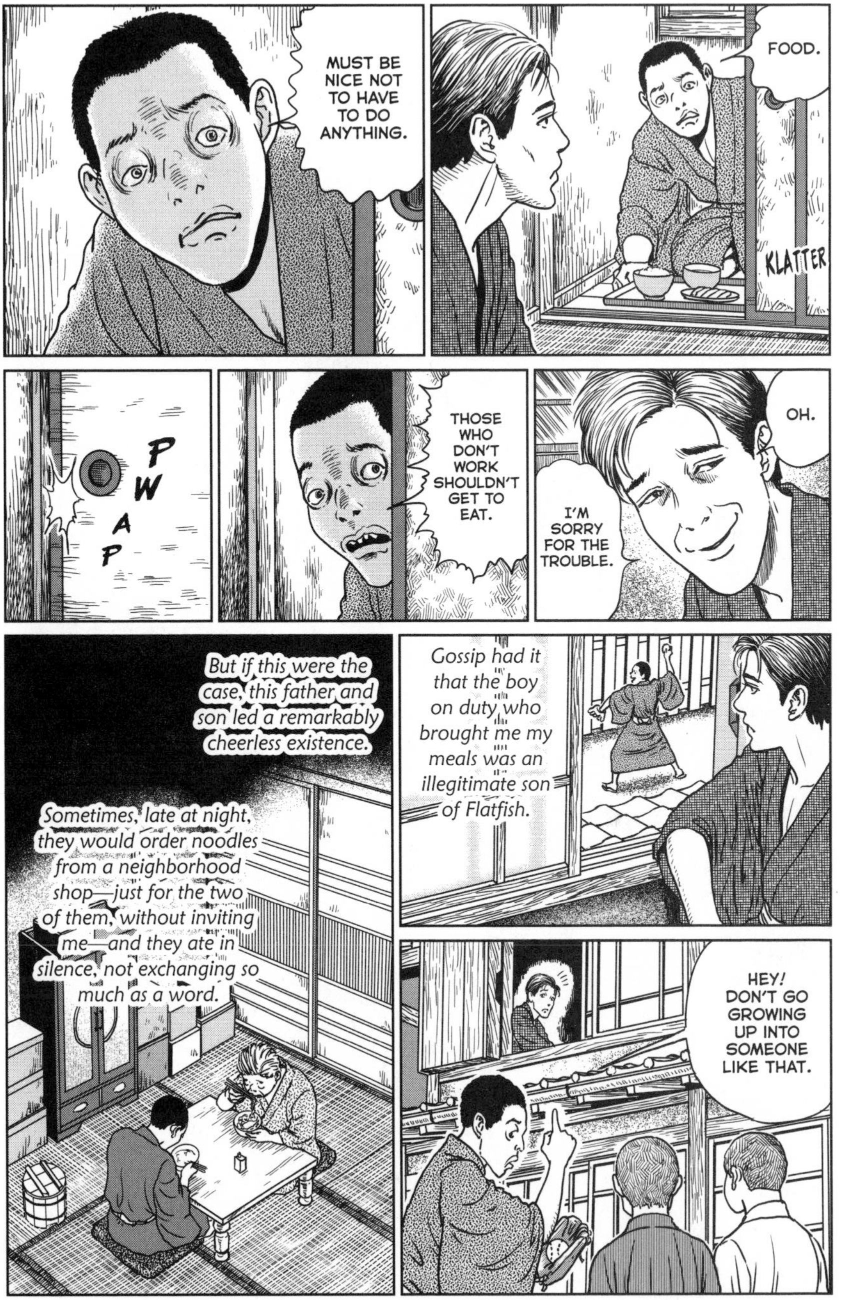
FOOD.
KLATTER
MUST BE NICE NOT TO HAVE TO DO ANYTHING.
OH.
I'M SORRY FOR THE TROUBLE.
THOSE WHO DON'T WORK SHOULDN'T GET TO EAT.
PWAP
Gossip had it that the boy on duty who brought me my meals was an illegitimate son of Flatfish.
HEY! DON'T GO GROWING UP INTO SOMEONE LIKE THAT.
But if this were the case, this father and son led a remarkably cheerless existence.
Sometimes, late at night, they would order noodles from a neighborhood shop—just for the two of them, without inviting me—and they ate in silence, not exchanging so much as a word.

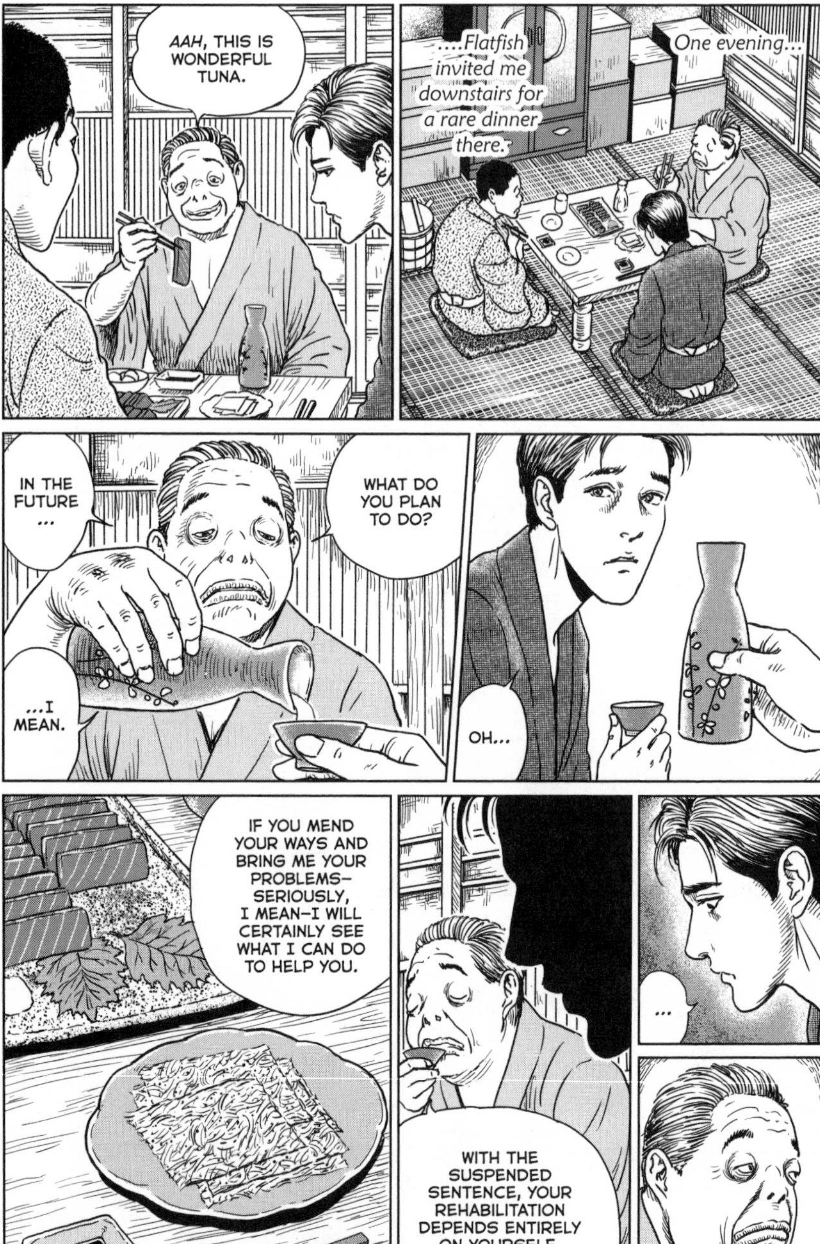
One evening...
....Flatfish invited me downstairs for a rare dinner there.
AAH, THIS IS WONDERFUL TUNA.
OH...
WHAT DO YOU PLAN TO DO?
IN THE FUTURE ...
...I MEAN.
...
WITH THE SUSPENDED SENTENCE, YOUR REHABILITATION DEPENDS ENTIRELY ON YOURSELF.
IF YOU MEND YOUR WAYS AND BRING ME YOUR PROBLEMS—SERIOUSLY, I MEAN—I WILL CERTAINLY SEE WHAT I CAN DO TO HELP YOU.

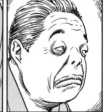

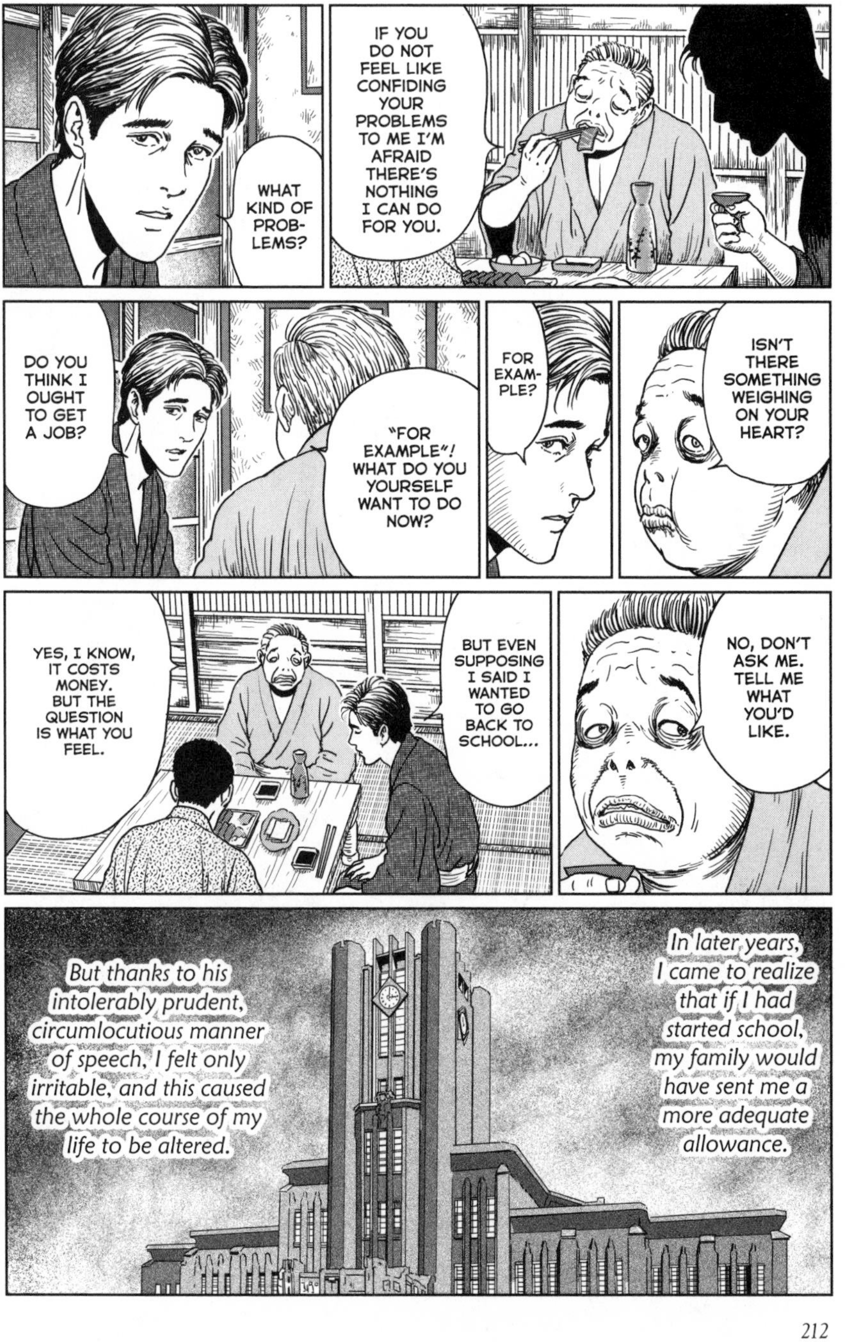

IF YOU DO NOT FEEL LIKE CONFIDING YOUR PROBLEMS TO ME I'M AFRAID THERE'S NOTHING I CAN DO FOR YOU.
WHAT KIND OF PROB-LEMS?
ISN'T THERE SOMETHING WEIGHING ON YOUR HEART?
FOR EXAM-PLE?
"FOR EXAMPLE"! WHAT DO YOU YOURSELF WANT TO DO NOW?
DO YOU THINK I OUGHT TO GET A JOB?
NO, DON'T ASK ME. TELL ME WHAT YOU'D LIKE.
BUT EVEN SUPPOSING I SAID I WANTED TO GO BACK TO SCHOOL...
YES, I KNOW, IT COSTS MONEY. BUT THE QUESTION IS WHAT YOU FEEL.
In later years, I came to realize that if I had started school, my family would have sent me a more adequate allowance.
But thanks to his intolerably prudent, circumlocutious manner of speech, I felt only irritable, and this caused the whole course of my life to be altered.

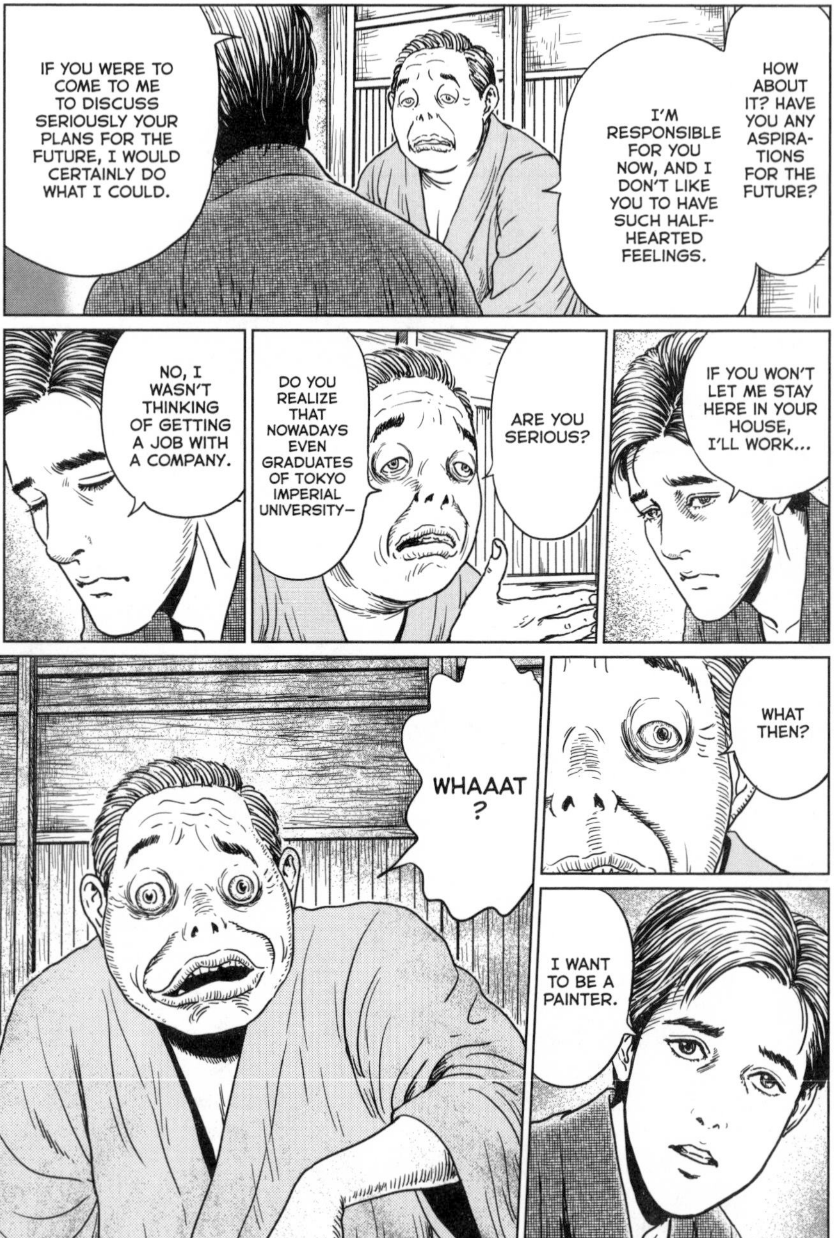
HOW ABOUT IT? HAVE YOU ANY ASPIRATIONS FOR THE FUTURE?
I'M RESPONSIBLE FOR YOU NOW, AND I DON'T LIKE YOU TO HAVE SUCH HALF-HEARTED FEELINGS.
IF YOU WERE TO COME TO ME TO DISCUSS SERIOUSLY YOUR PLANS FOR THE FUTURE, I WOULD CERTAINLY DO WHAT I COULD.
IF YOU WON'T LET ME STAY HERE IN YOUR HOUSE, I'LL WORK...
ARE YOU SERIOUS?
DO YOU REALIZE THAT NOWADAYS EVEN GRADUATES OF TOKYO IMPERIAL UNIVERSITY—
NO, I WASN'T THINKING OF GETTING A JOB WITH A COMPANY.
WHAT THEN?
I WANT TO BE A PAINTER.
WHAAAT?

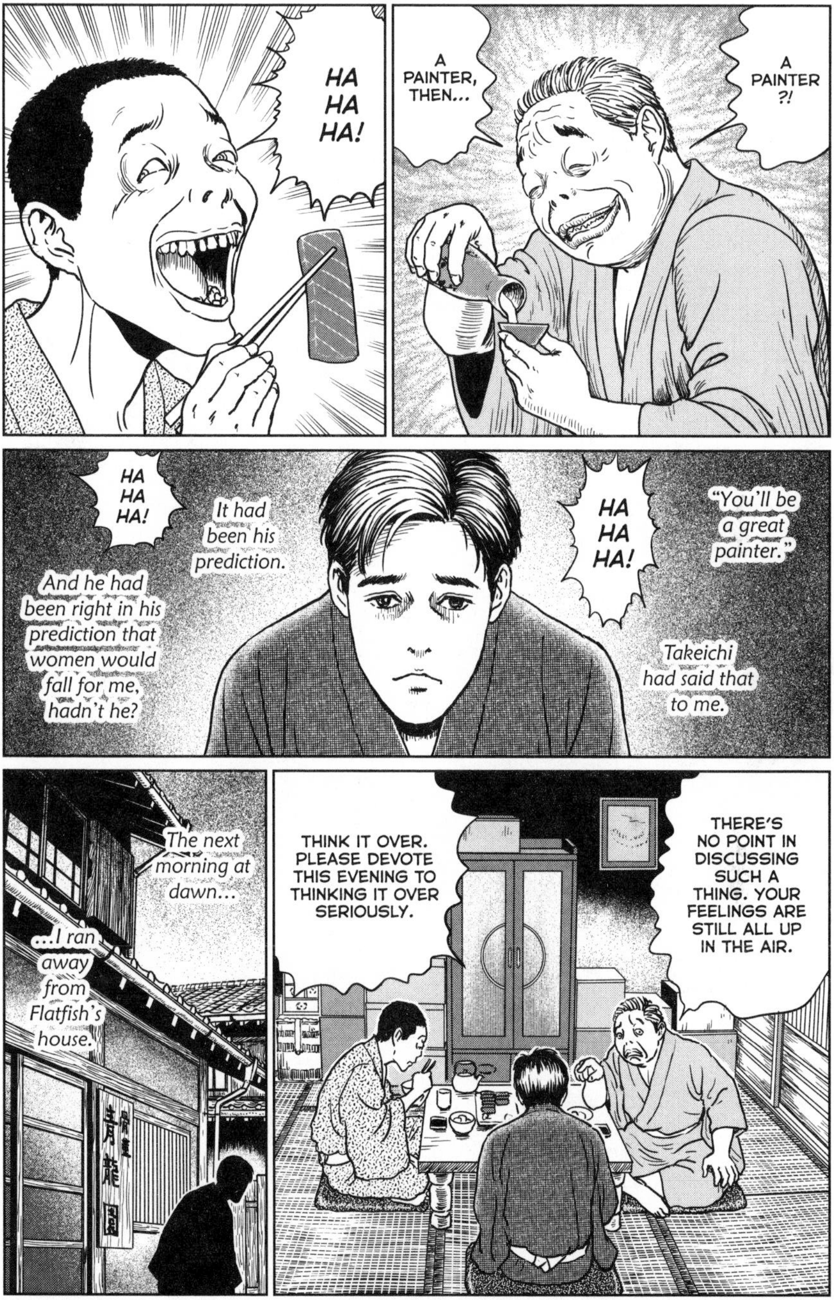
A PAINTER ?!
A PAINTER, THEN...
HA HA HA!
"You'll be a great painter."
Takeichi had said that to me.
HA HA HA!
It had been his prediction.
HA HA HA!
And he had been right in his prediction that women would fall for me, hadn't he?
THERE'S NO POINT IN DISCUSSING SUCH A THING. YOUR FEELINGS ARE STILL ALL UP IN THE AIR.
THINK IT OVER. PLEASE DEVOTE THIS EVENING TO THINKING IT OVER SERIOUSLY.
The next morning at dawn...
...I ran away from Flatfish's house.
青龍園

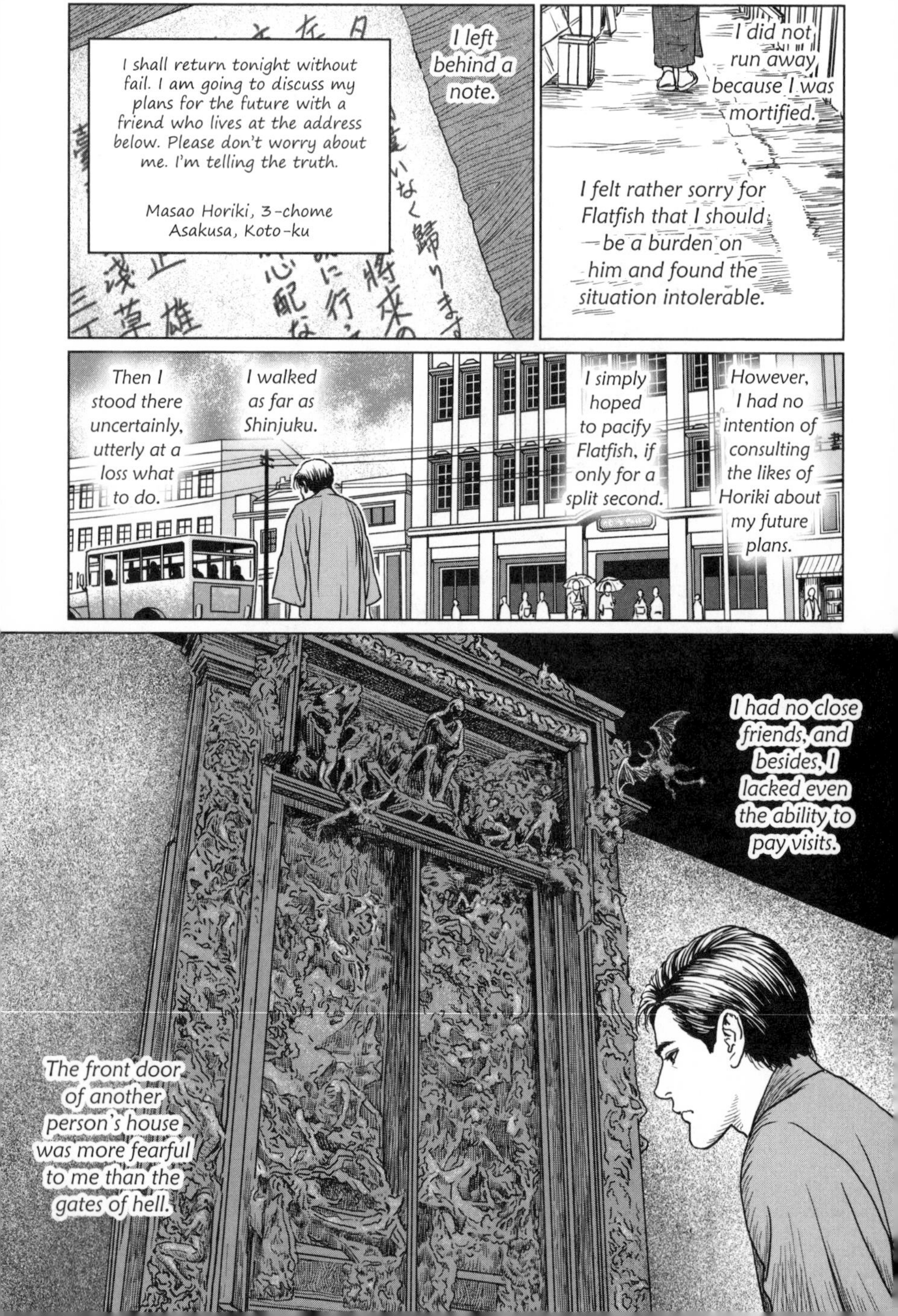
I did not run away because I was mortified.
I felt rather sorry for Flatfish that I should be a burden on him and found the situation intolerable.
I left behind a note.
I shall return tonight without fail. I am going to discuss my plans for the future with a friend who lives at the address below. Please don't worry about me. I'm telling the truth.
Masao Horiki, 3-chome Asakusa, Koto-ku
However, I had no intention of consulting the likes of Horiki about my future plans.
I simply hoped to pacify Flatfish, if only for a split second.
I walked as far as Shinjuku.
Then I stood there uncertainly, utterly at a loss what to do.
I had no close friends, and besides, I lacked even the ability to pay visits.
The front door of another person's house was more fearful to me than the gates of hell.

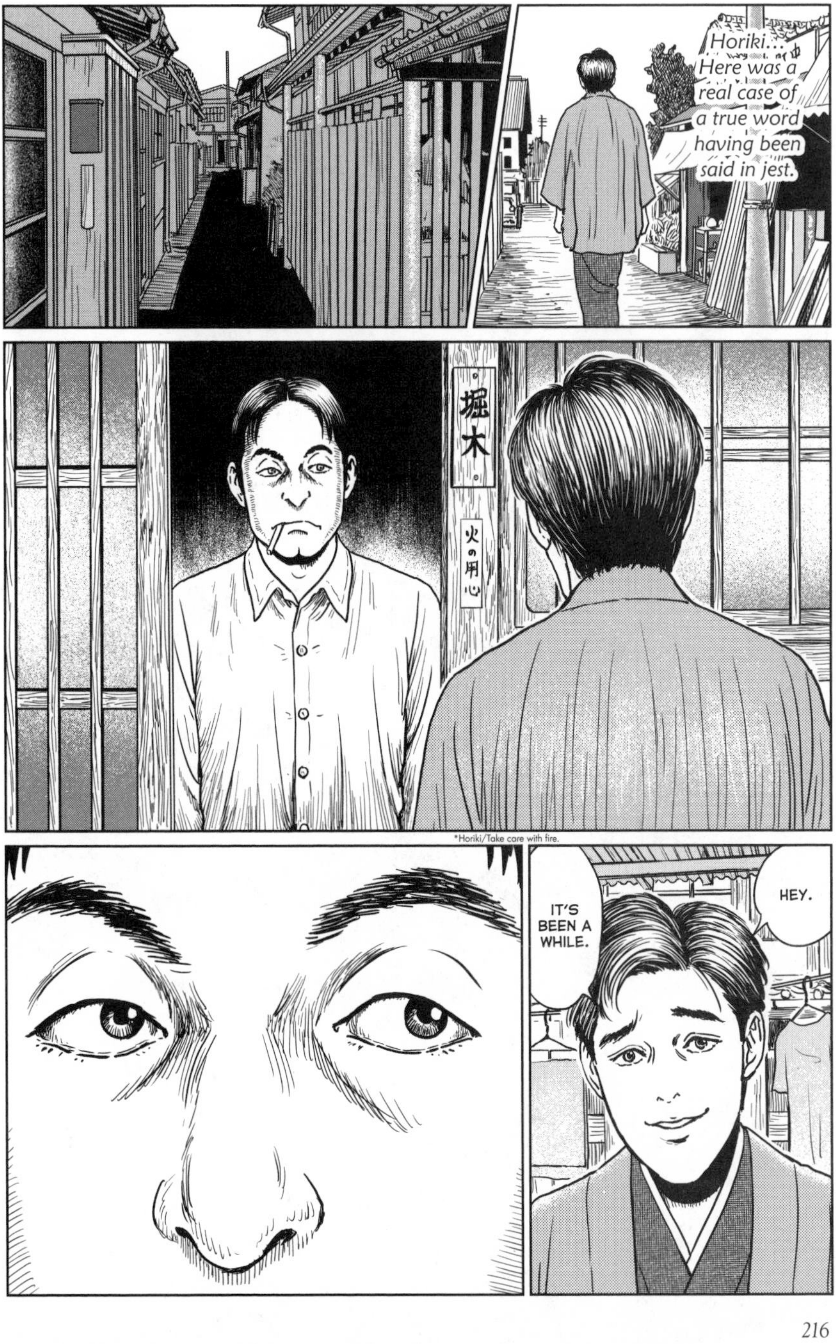
Horiki... Here was a real case of a true word having been said in jest.
堀木
火の用心
HEY.
IT'S BEEN A WHILE.
*Horiki/Take care with fire.

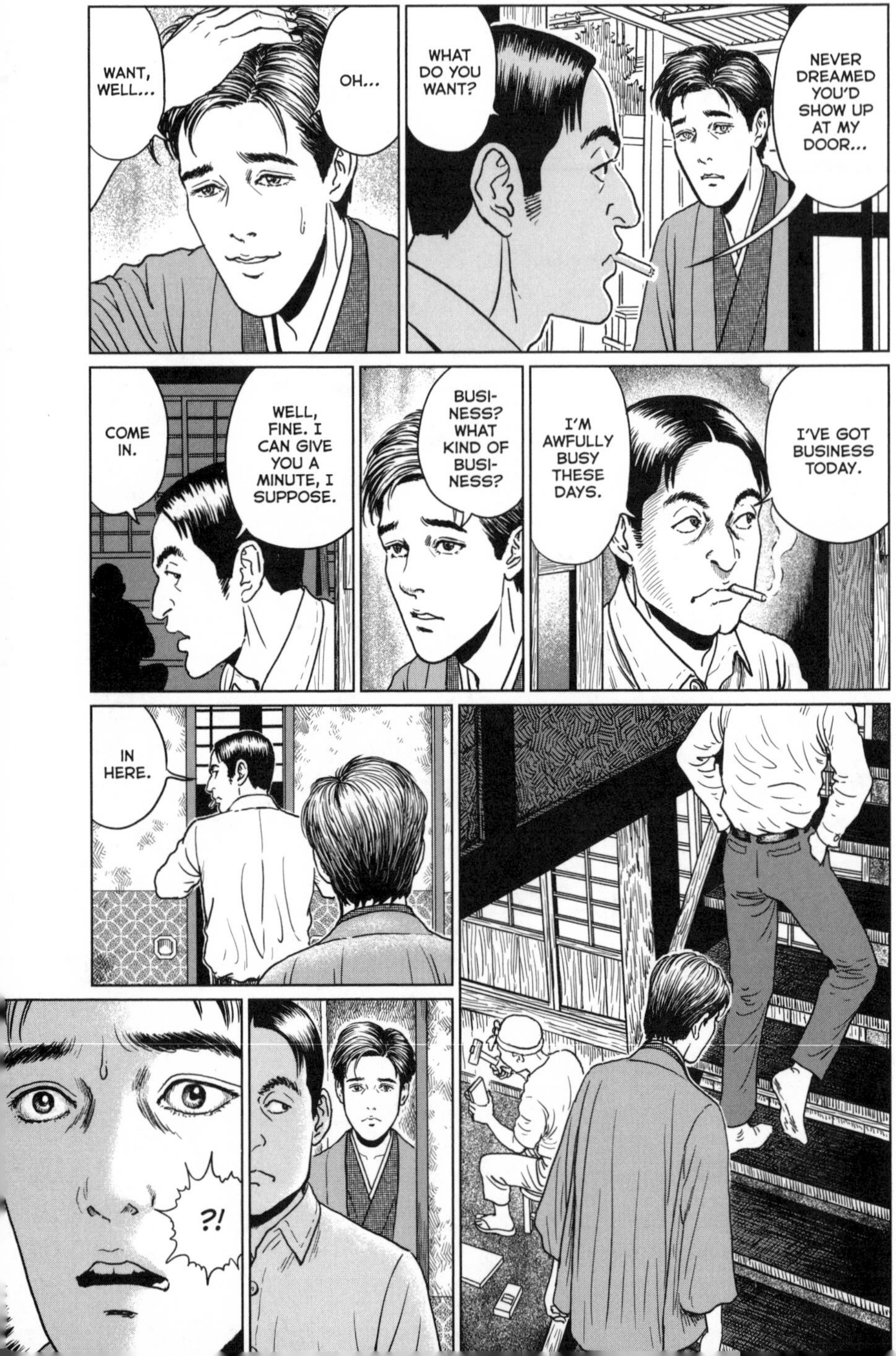
NEVER DREAMED YOU'D SHOW UP AT MY DOOR...
WHAT DO YOU WANT?
OH...
WANT, WELL...
I'VE GOT BUSINESS TODAY.
I'M AWFULLY BUSY THESE DAYS.
BUSI-NESS? WHAT KIND OF BUSI-NESS?
WELL, FINE. I CAN GIVE YOU A MINUTE, I SUPPOSE.
COME IN.
IN HERE.
?!

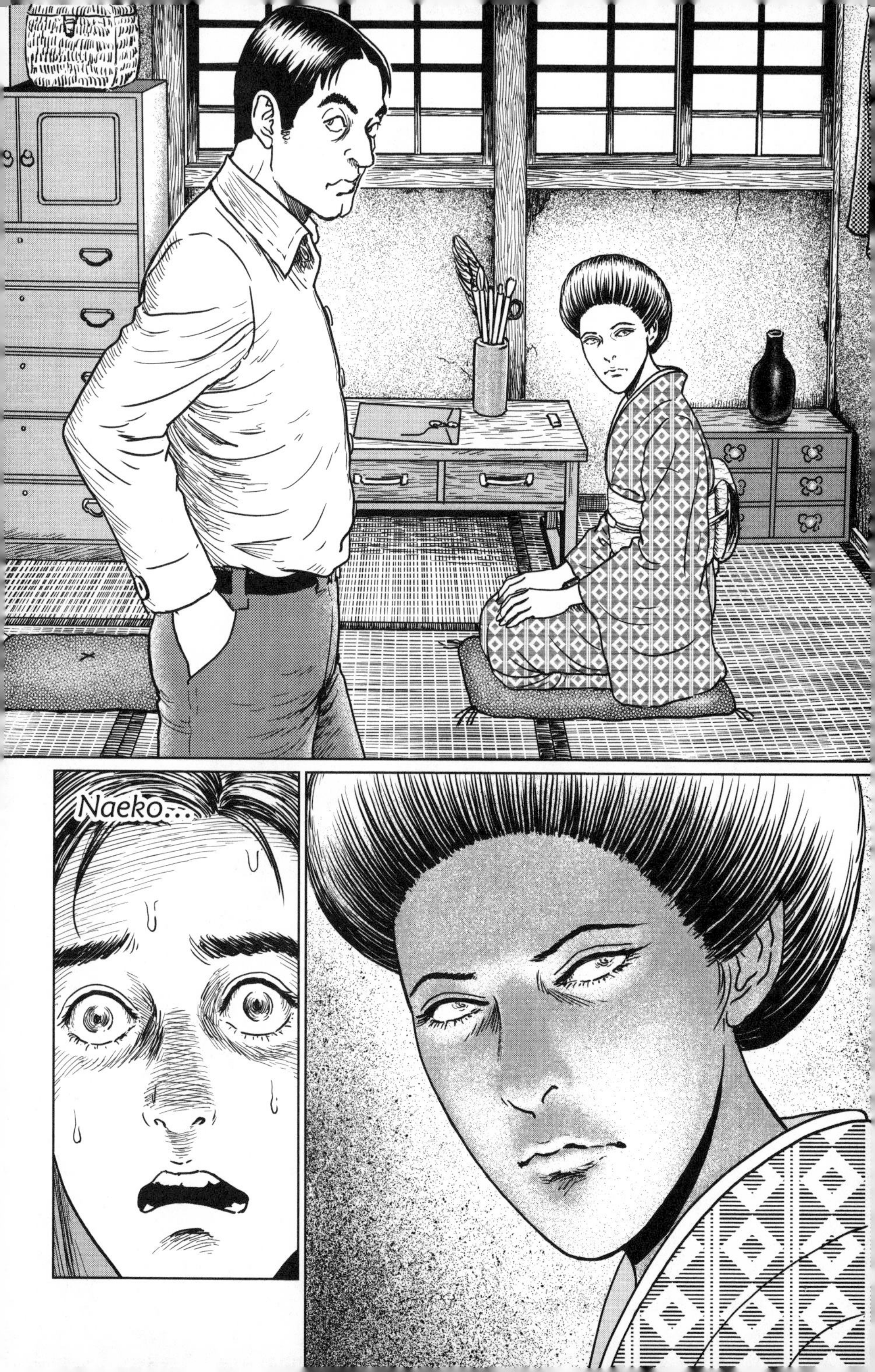
Naeko...

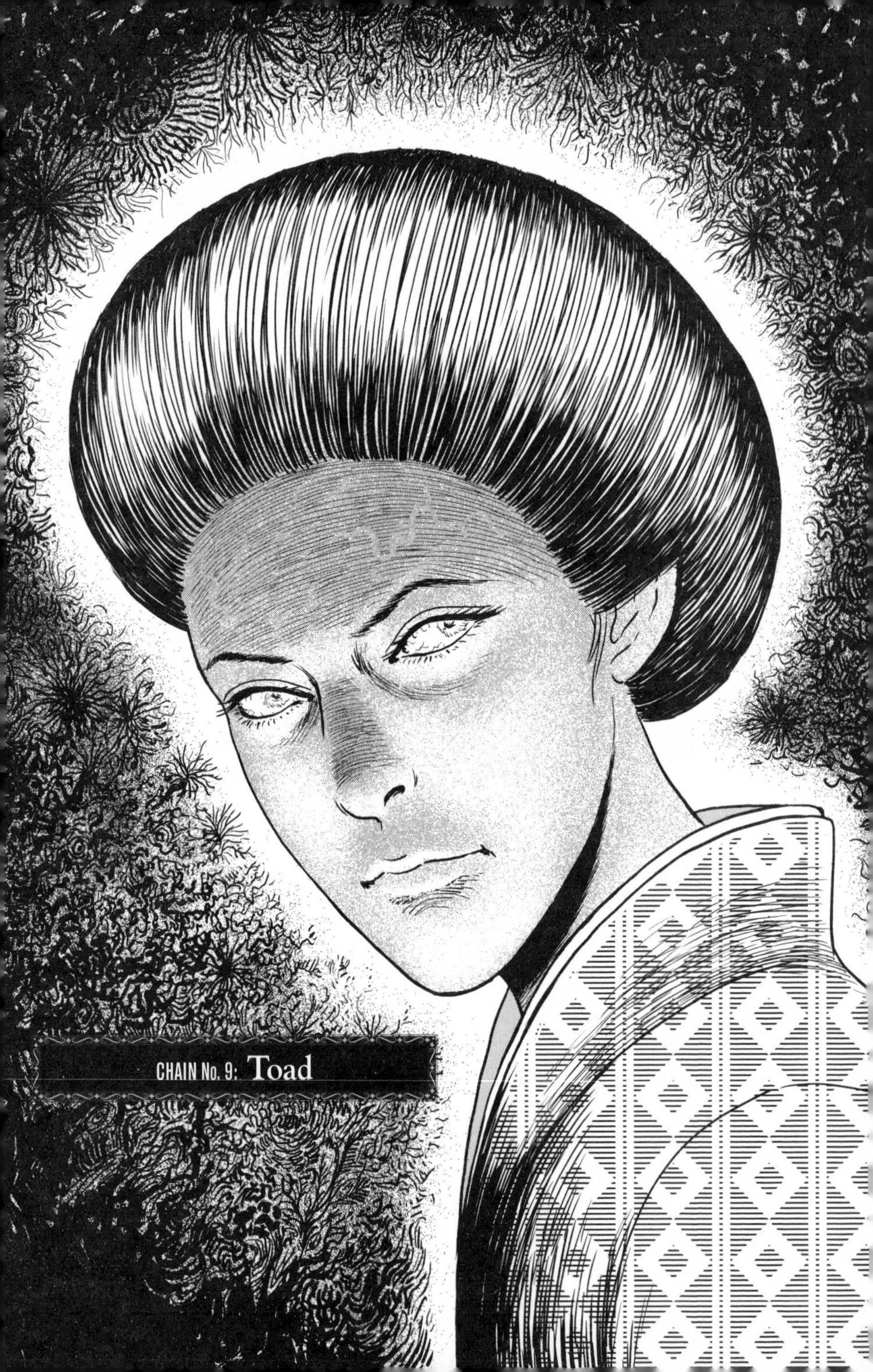
CHAIN No. 9: Toad

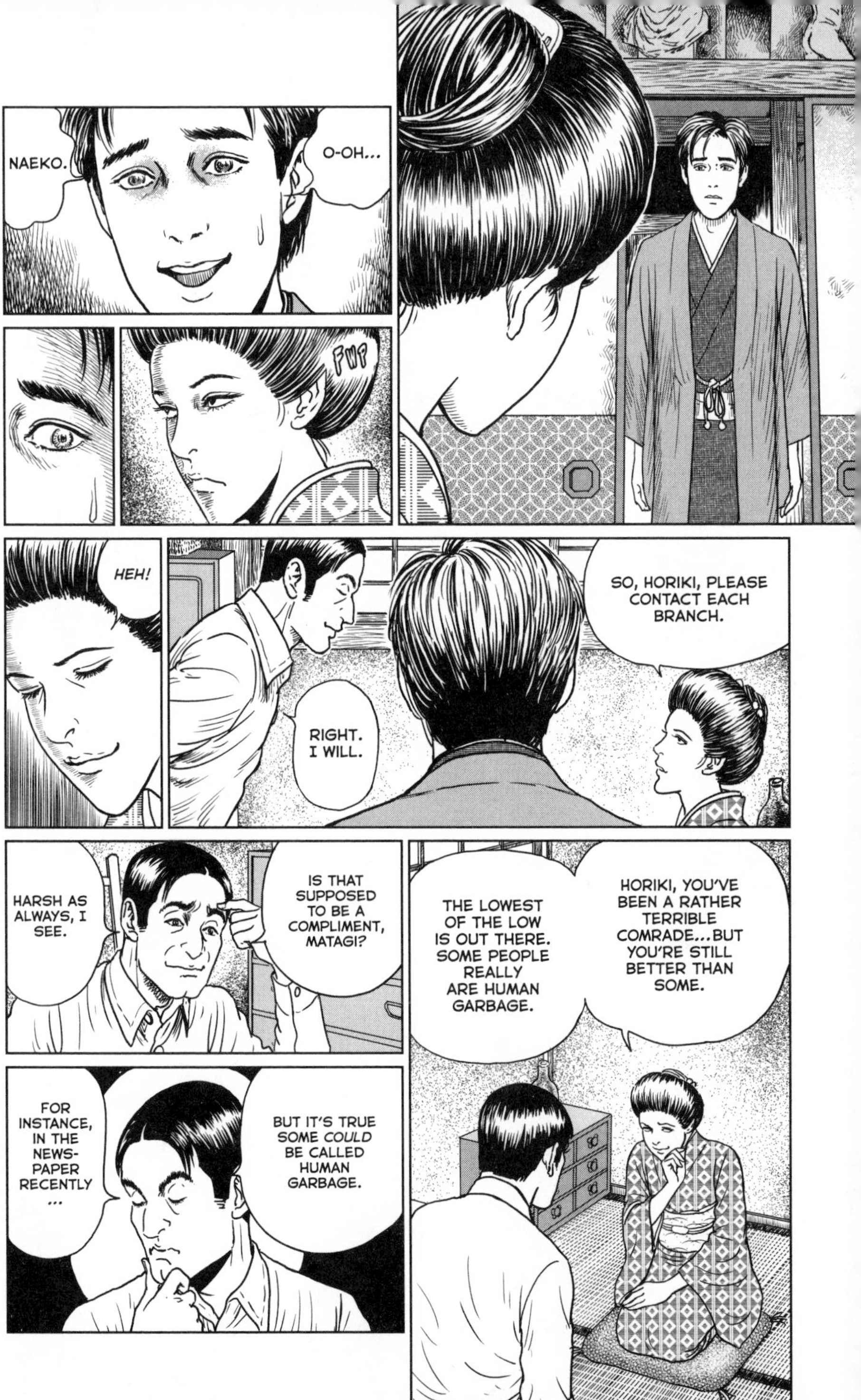
O-OH...
NAEKO.
FWP
SO, HORIKI, PLEASE CONTACT EACH BRANCH.
RIGHT. I WILL.
HEH!
HORIKI, YOU'VE BEEN A RATHER TERRIBLE COMRADE...BUT YOU'RE STILL BETTER THAN SOME.
THE LOWEST OF THE LOW IS OUT THERE. SOME PEOPLE REALLY ARE HUMAN GARBAGE.
IS THAT SUPPOSED TO BE A COMPLIMENT, MATAGI?
HARSH AS ALWAYS, I SEE.
BUT IT'S TRUE SOME *COULD* BE CALLED HUMAN GARBAGE.
FOR INSTANCE, IN THE NEWS-PAPER RECENTLY...

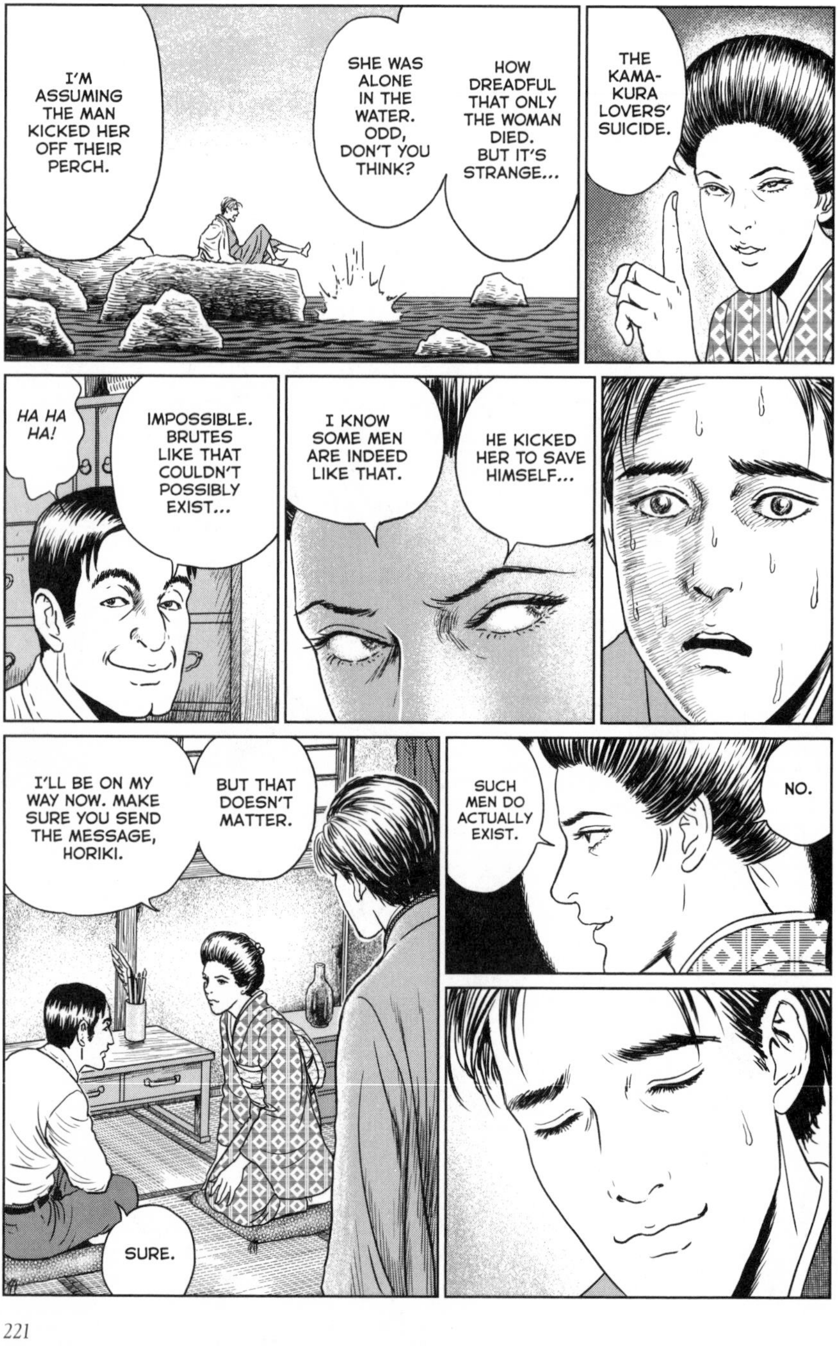
THE KAMA-KURA LOVERS' SUICIDE.
HOW DREADFUL THAT ONLY THE WOMAN DIED. BUT IT'S STRANGE...
SHE WAS ALONE IN THE WATER. ODD, DON'T YOU THINK?
I'M ASSUMING THE MAN KICKED HER OFF THEIR PERCH.
HE KICKED HER TO SAVE HIMSELF...
I KNOW SOME MEN ARE INDEED LIKE THAT.
IMPOSSIBLE. BRUTES LIKE THAT COULDN'T POSSIBLY EXIST...
HA HA HA!
NO.
SUCH MEN DO ACTUALLY EXIST.
BUT THAT DOESN'T MATTER.
I'LL BE ON MY WAY NOW. MAKE SURE YOU SEND THE MESSAGE, HORIKI.
SURE.

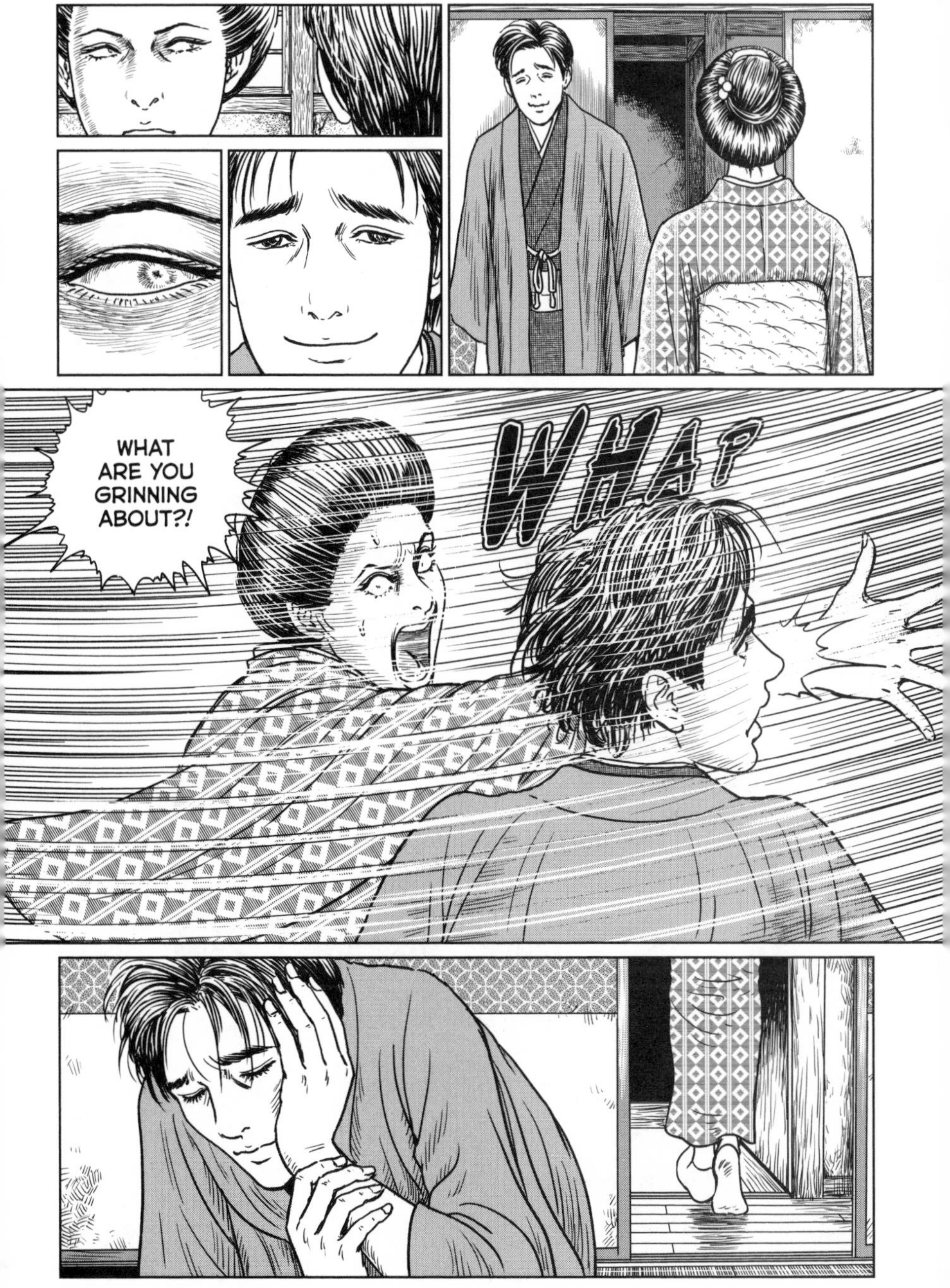
WHAT ARE YOU GRINNING ABOUT?!
WHAP

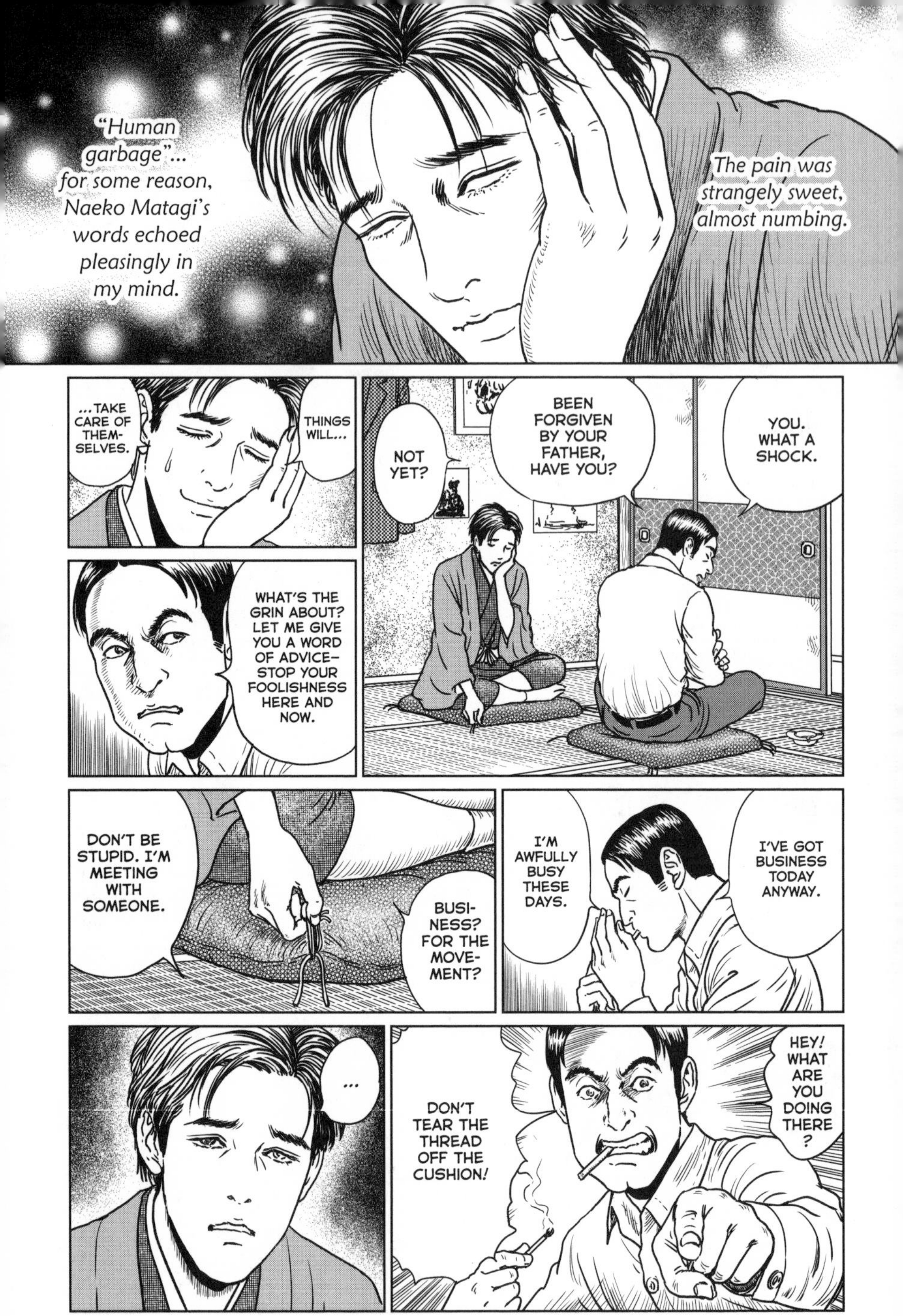
The pain was strangely sweet, almost numbing.
"Human garbage"... for some reason, Naeko Matagi's words echoed pleasingly in my mind.
YOU. WHAT A SHOCK.
BEEN FORGIVEN BY YOUR FATHER, HAVE YOU?
NOT YET?
THINGS WILL...
...TAKE CARE OF THEM-SELVES.
WHAT'S THE GRIN ABOUT? LET ME GIVE YOU A WORD OF ADVICE–STOP YOUR FOOLISHNESS HERE AND NOW.
I'VE GOT BUSINESS TODAY ANYWAY.
I'M AWFULLY BUSY THESE DAYS.
BUSI-NESS? FOR THE MOVE-MENT?
DON'T BE STUPID. I'M MEETING WITH SOMEONE.
HEY! WHAT ARE YOU DOING THERE?
DON'T TEAR THE THREAD OFF THE CUSHION!
...

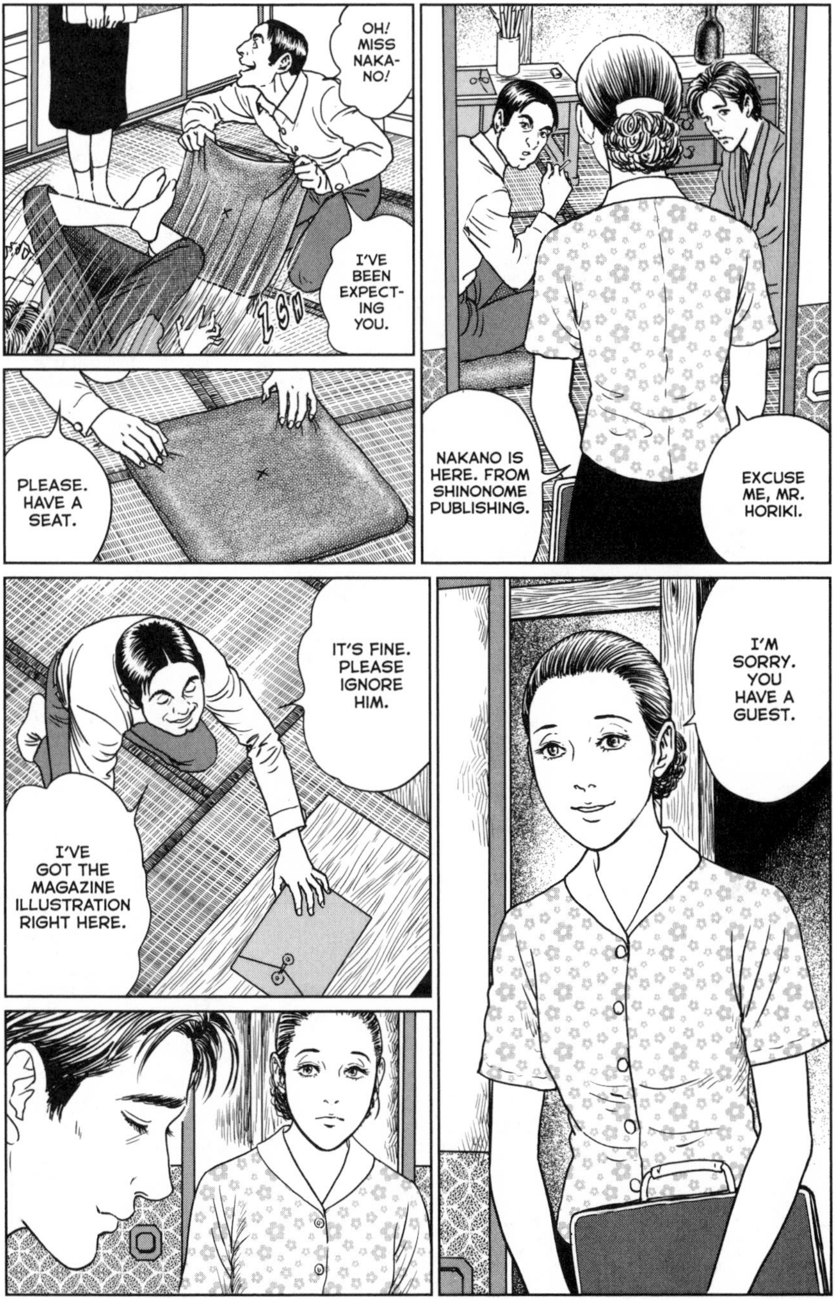
EXCUSE ME, MR. HORIKI.
NAKANO IS HERE. FROM SHINONOME PUBLISHING.
OH! MISS NAKANO!
I'VE BEEN EXPECTING YOU.
ZOSH
PLEASE. HAVE A SEAT.
I'M SORRY. YOU HAVE A GUEST.
IT'S FINE. PLEASE IGNORE HIM.
I'VE GOT THE MAGAZINE ILLUSTRATION RIGHT HERE.

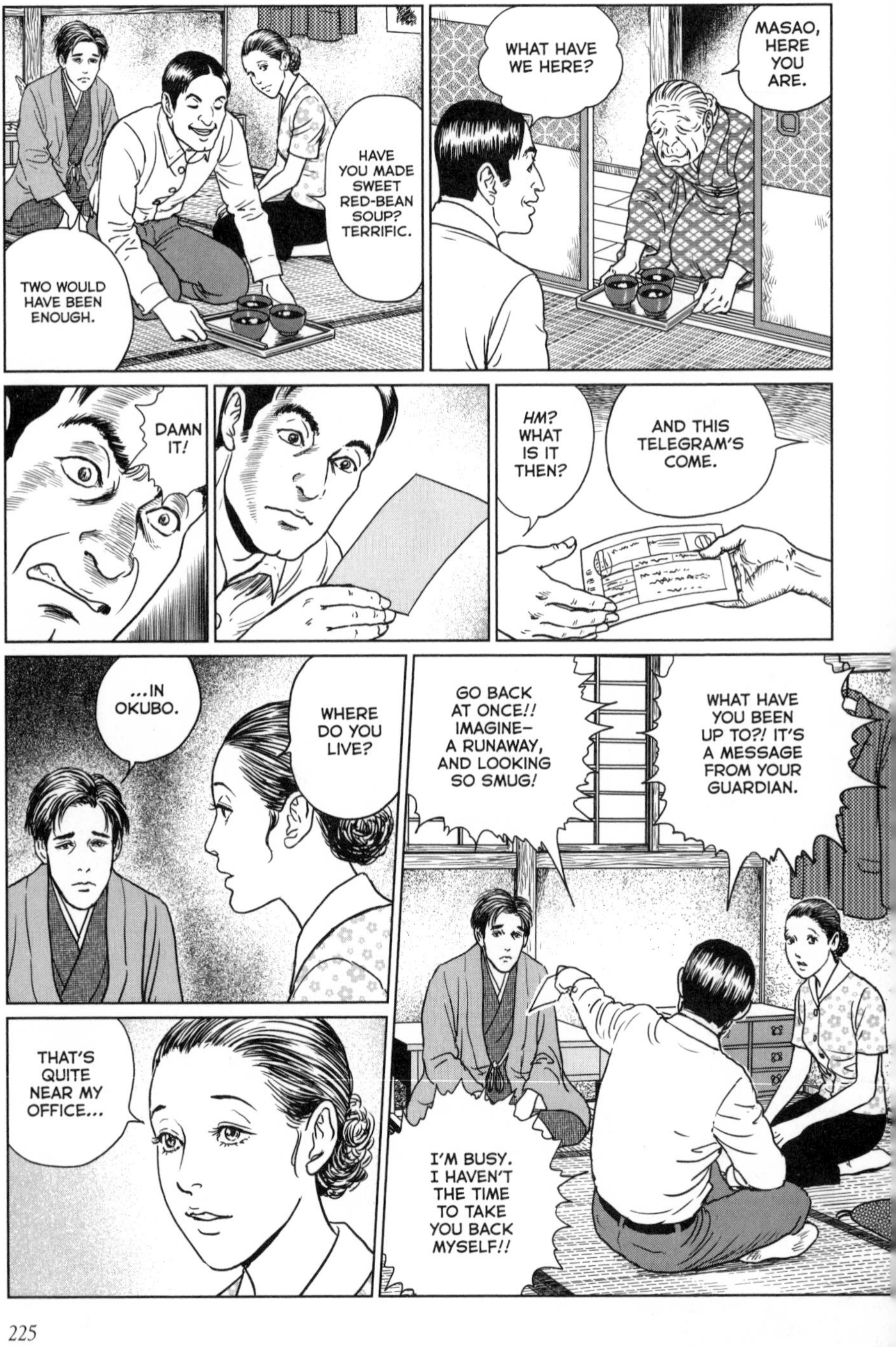
MASAO, HERE YOU ARE.
WHAT HAVE WE HERE?
HAVE YOU MADE SWEET RED-BEAN SOUP? TERRIFIC.
TWO WOULD HAVE BEEN ENOUGH.
AND THIS TELEGRAM'S COME.
HM? WHAT IS IT THEN?
DAMN IT!
WHAT HAVE YOU BEEN UP TO?! IT'S A MESSAGE FROM YOUR GUARDIAN.
GO BACK AT ONCE!! IMAGINE— A RUNAWAY, AND LOOKING SO SMUG!
I'M BUSY. I HAVEN'T THE TIME TO TAKE YOU BACK MYSELF!!
WHERE DO YOU LIVE?
...IN OKUBO.
THAT'S QUITE NEAR MY OFFICE...

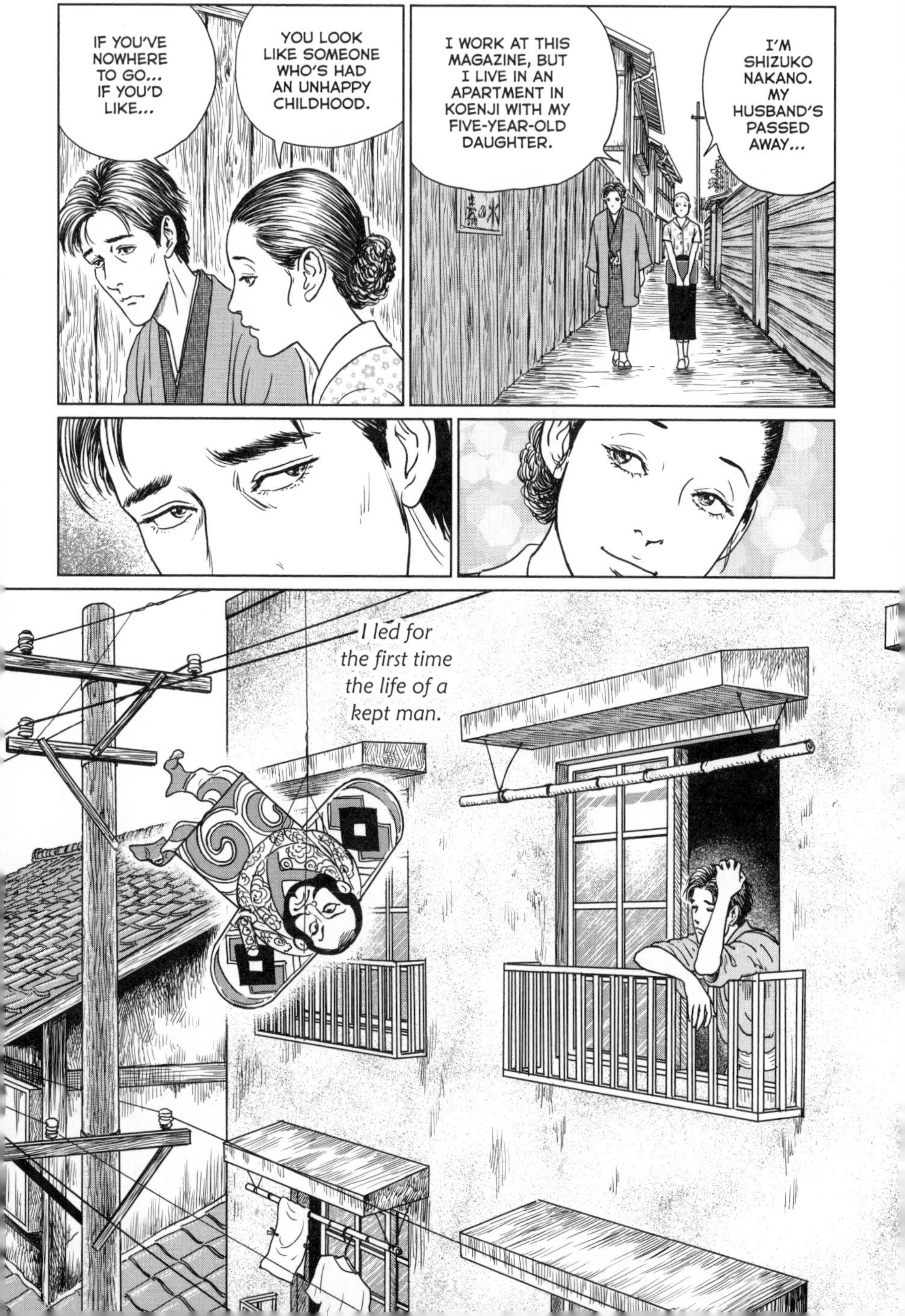
I'M SHIZUKO NAKANO. MY HUSBAND'S PASSED AWAY...
I WORK AT THIS MAGAZINE, BUT I LIVE IN AN APARTMENT IN KOENJI WITH MY FIVE-YEAR-OLD DAUGHTER.
YOU LOOK LIKE SOMEONE WHO'S HAD AN UNHAPPY CHILDHOOD.
IF YOU'VE NOWHERE TO GO... IF YOU'D LIKE...
I led for the first time the life of a kept man.

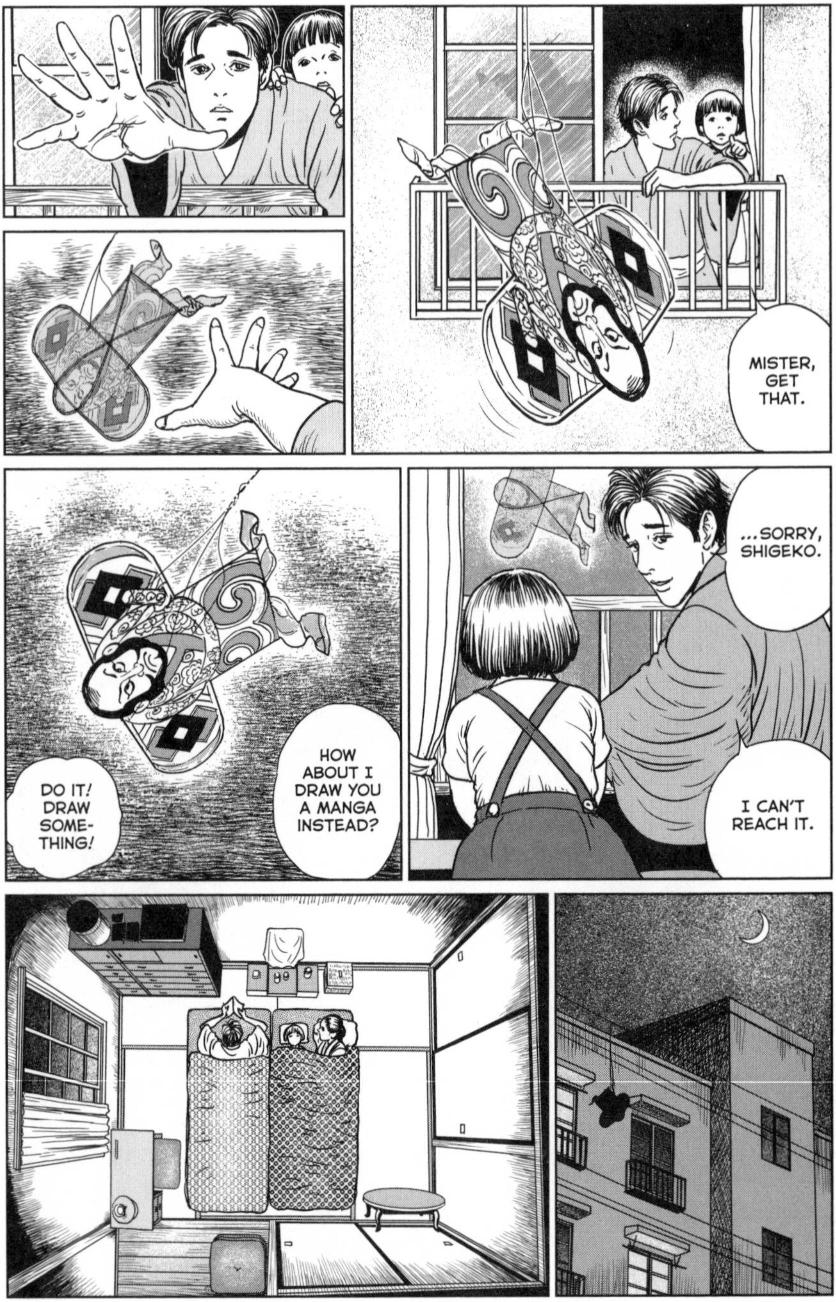
MISTER, GET THAT.
...SORRY, SHIGEKO.
I CAN'T REACH IT.
HOW ABOUT I DRAW YOU A MANGA INSTEAD?
DO IT! DRAW SOME-THING!

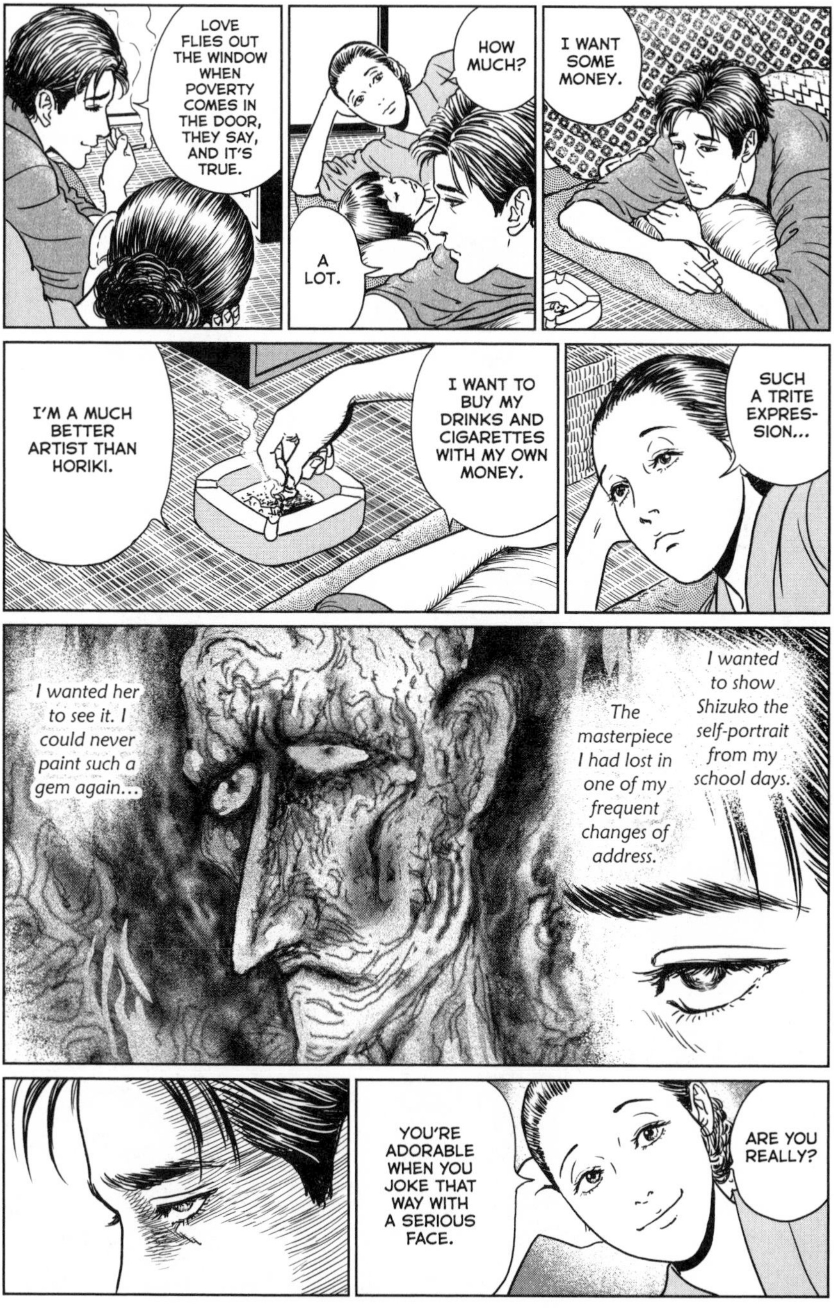
I WANT SOME MONEY.
HOW MUCH?
A LOT.
LOVE FLIES OUT THE WINDOW WHEN POVERTY COMES IN THE DOOR, THEY SAY, AND IT'S TRUE.
SUCH A TRITE EXPRES-SION...
I WANT TO BUY MY DRINKS AND CIGARETTES WITH MY OWN MONEY.
I'M A MUCH BETTER ARTIST THAN HORIKI.
I wanted to show Shizuko the self-portrait from my school days.
The masterpiece I had lost in one of my frequent changes of address.
I wanted her to see it. I could never paint such a gem again...
ARE YOU REALLY?
YOU'RE ADORABLE WHEN YOU JOKE THAT WAY WITH A SERIOUS FACE.

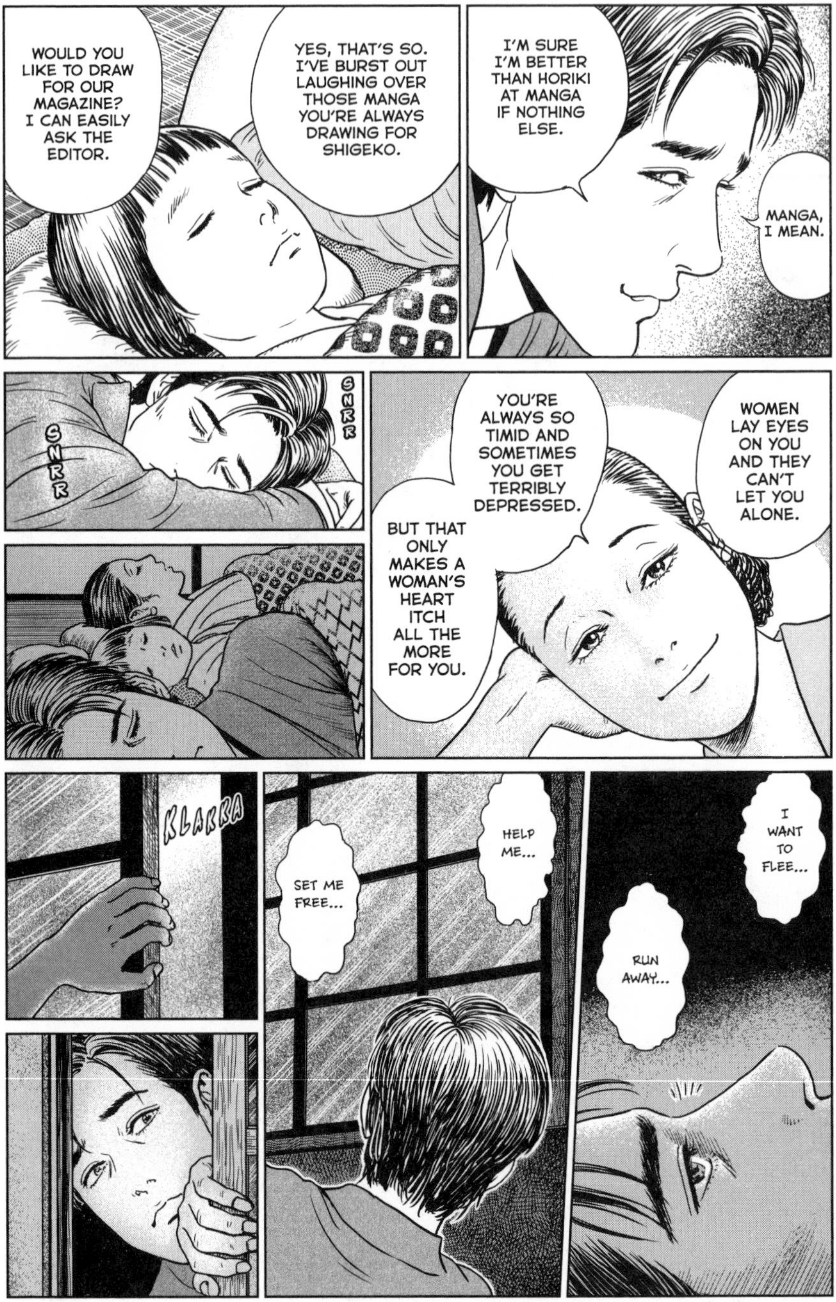

I'M SURE I'M BETTER THAN HORIKI AT MANGA IF NOTHING ELSE.
MANGA, I MEAN.
YES, THAT'S SO. I'VE BURST OUT LAUGHING OVER THOSE MANGA YOU'RE ALWAYS DRAWING FOR SHIGEKO.
WOULD YOU LIKE TO DRAW FOR OUR MAGAZINE? I CAN EASILY ASK THE EDITOR.
WOMEN LAY EYES ON YOU AND THEY CAN'T LET YOU ALONE.
YOU'RE ALWAYS SO TIMID AND SOMETIMES YOU GET TERRIBLY DEPRESSED.
BUT THAT ONLY MAKES A WOMAN'S HEART ITCH ALL THE MORE FOR YOU.
SNRR
SNRR
I WANT TO FLEE...
RUN AWAY...
HELP ME...
SET ME FREE...
KLAKRA

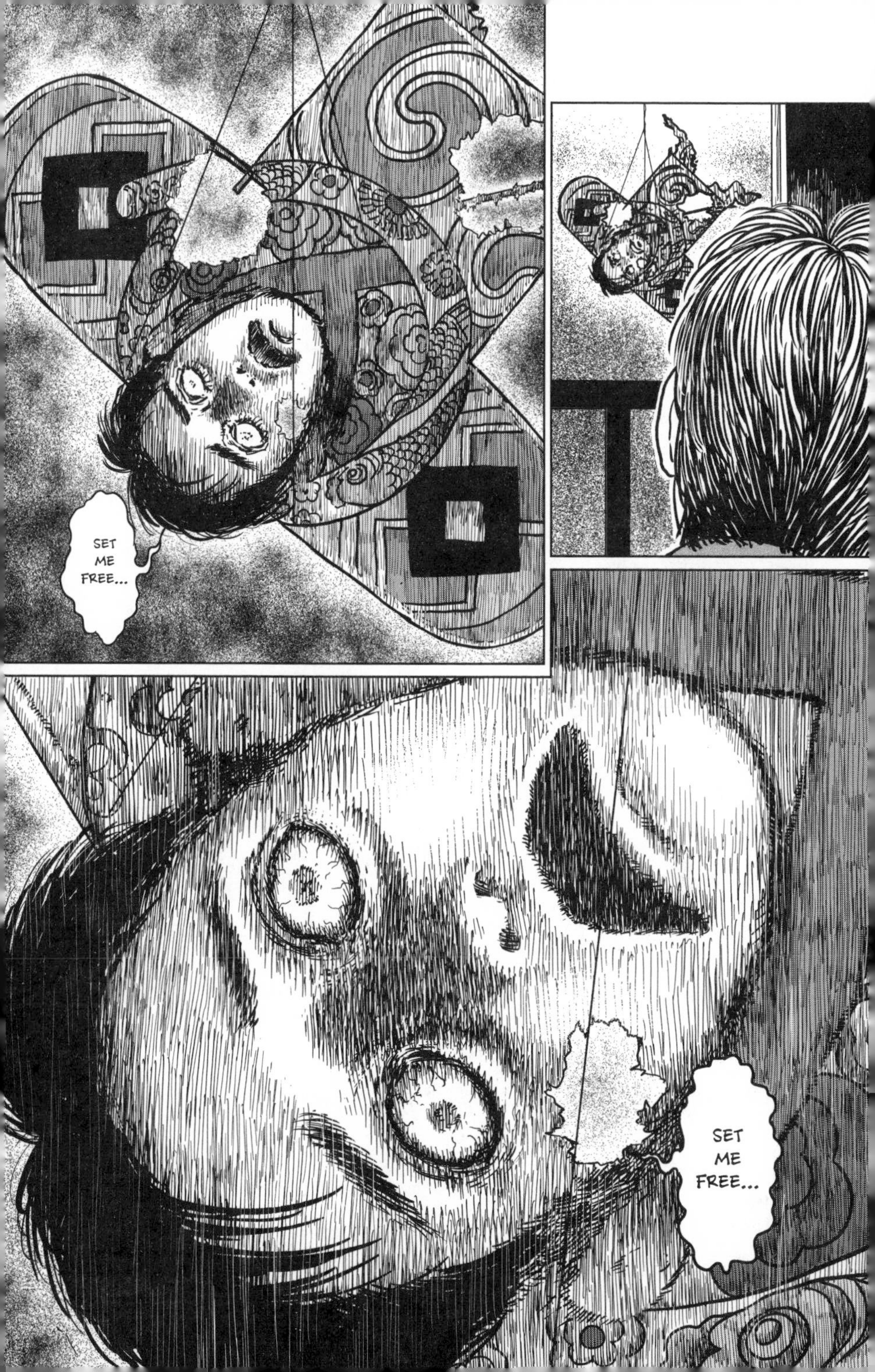
SET ME FREE...
SET ME FREE...

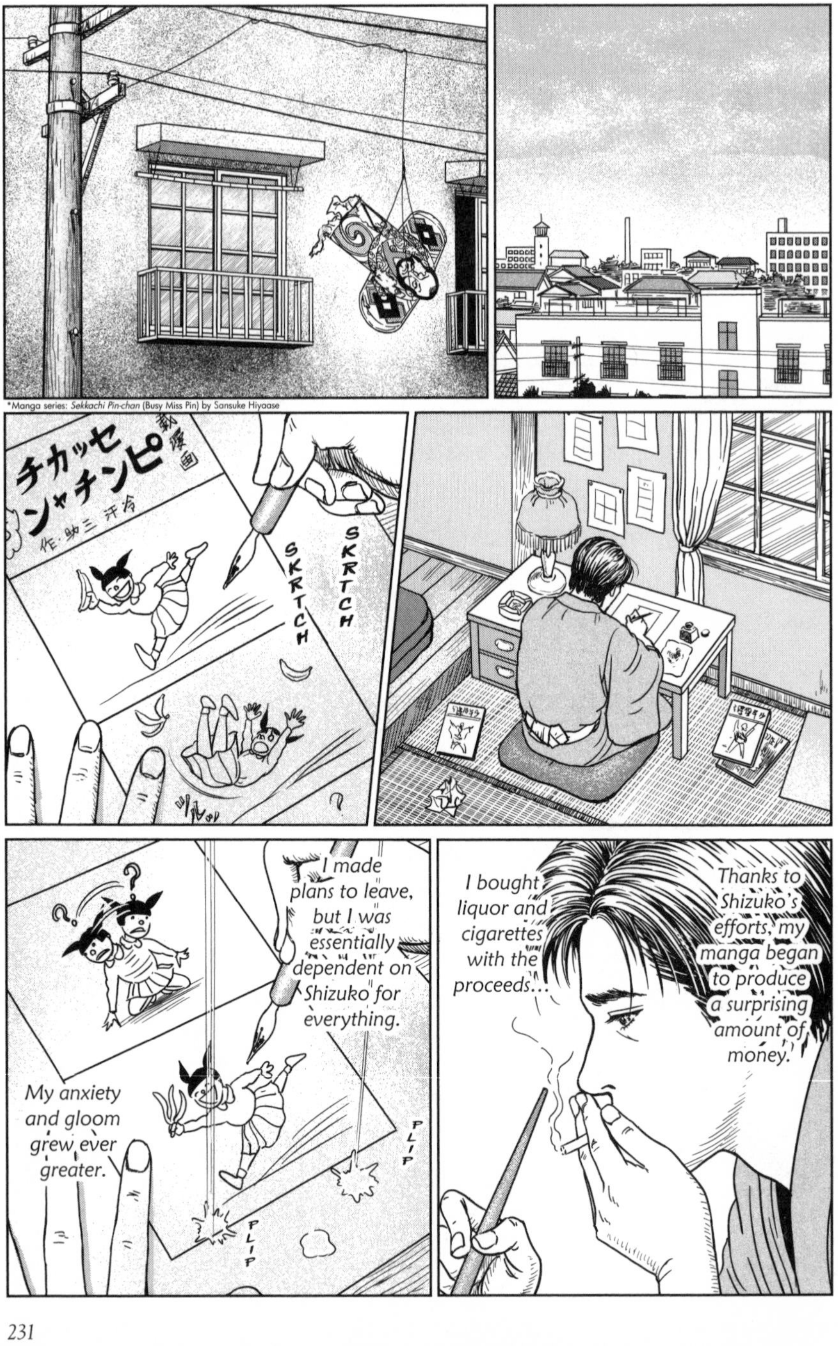
SKRTCH
SKRTCH
セッカチピンチャン
漫画
作・冷汗三助
Thanks to Shizuko's efforts, my manga began to produce a surprising amount of money.
I bought liquor and cigarettes with the proceeds...
I made plans to leave, but I was essentially dependent on Shizuko for everything.
My anxiety and gloom grew ever greater.
PLIP
PLIP
*Manga series: *Sekkachi Pin-chan* (Busy Miss Pin) by Sansuke Hiyaase

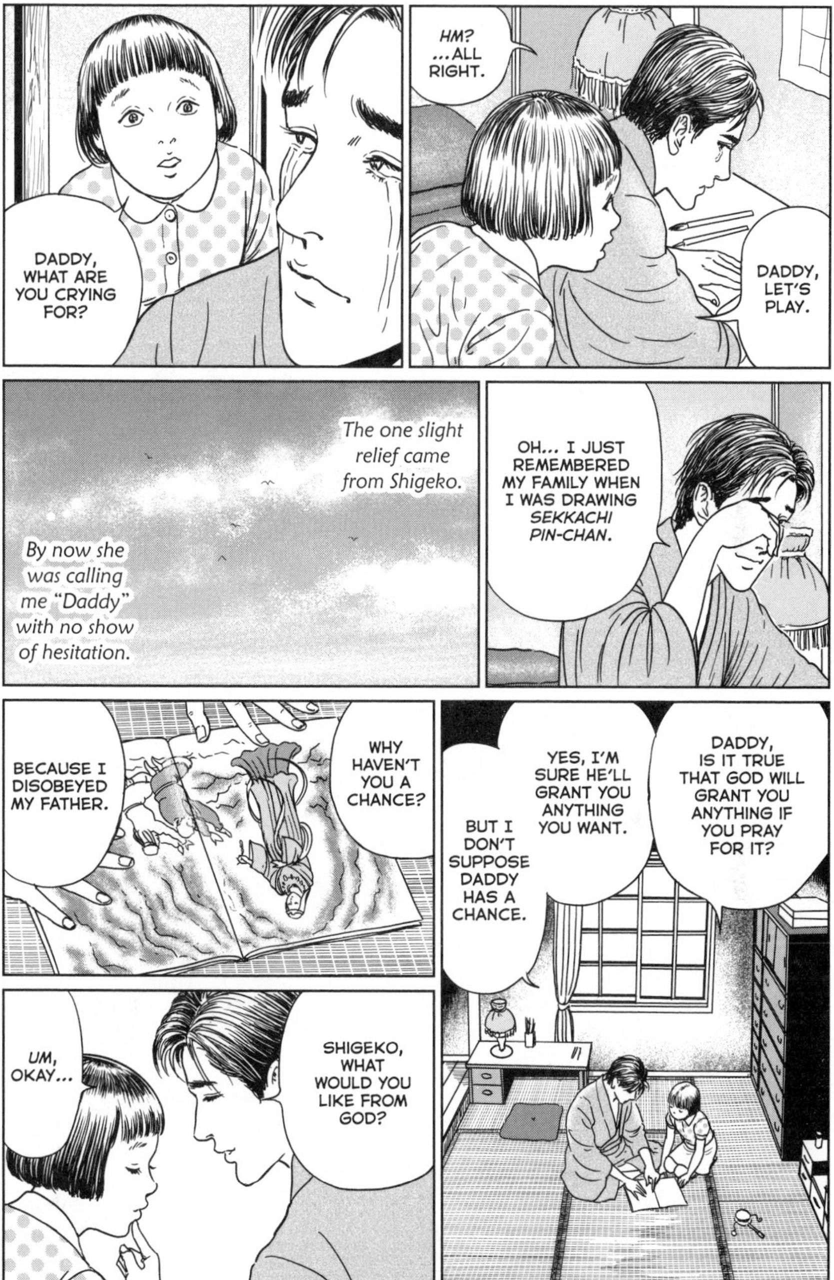
DADDY, LET'S PLAY.
HM? ...ALL RIGHT.
DADDY, WHAT ARE YOU CRYING FOR?
OH... I JUST REMEMBERED MY FAMILY WHEN I WAS DRAWING *SEKKACHI PIN-CHAN*.
The one slight relief came from Shigeko.
By now she was calling me "Daddy" with no show of hesitation.
DADDY, IS IT TRUE THAT GOD WILL GRANT YOU ANYTHING IF YOU PRAY FOR IT?
YES, I'M SURE HE'LL GRANT YOU ANYTHING YOU WANT.
BUT I DON'T SUPPOSE DADDY HAS A CHANCE.
WHY HAVEN'T YOU A CHANCE?
BECAUSE I DISOBEYED MY FATHER.
SHIGEKO, WHAT WOULD YOU LIKE FROM GOD?
UM, OKAY...

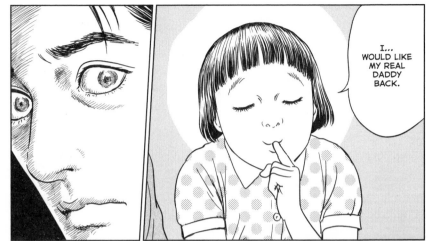

I...
WOULD LIKE
MY REAL
DADDY
BACK.

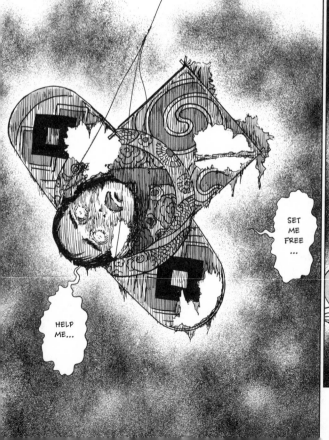

SET
ME
FREE
...

HELP
ME...

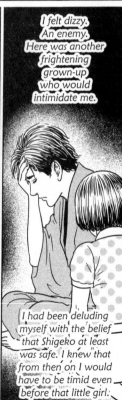

I felt dizzy.
An enemy.
Here was another
frightening
grown-up
who would
intimidate me.

I had been deluding
myself with the belief
that Shigeko at least
was safe. I knew that
from then on I would
have to be timid even
before that little girl.

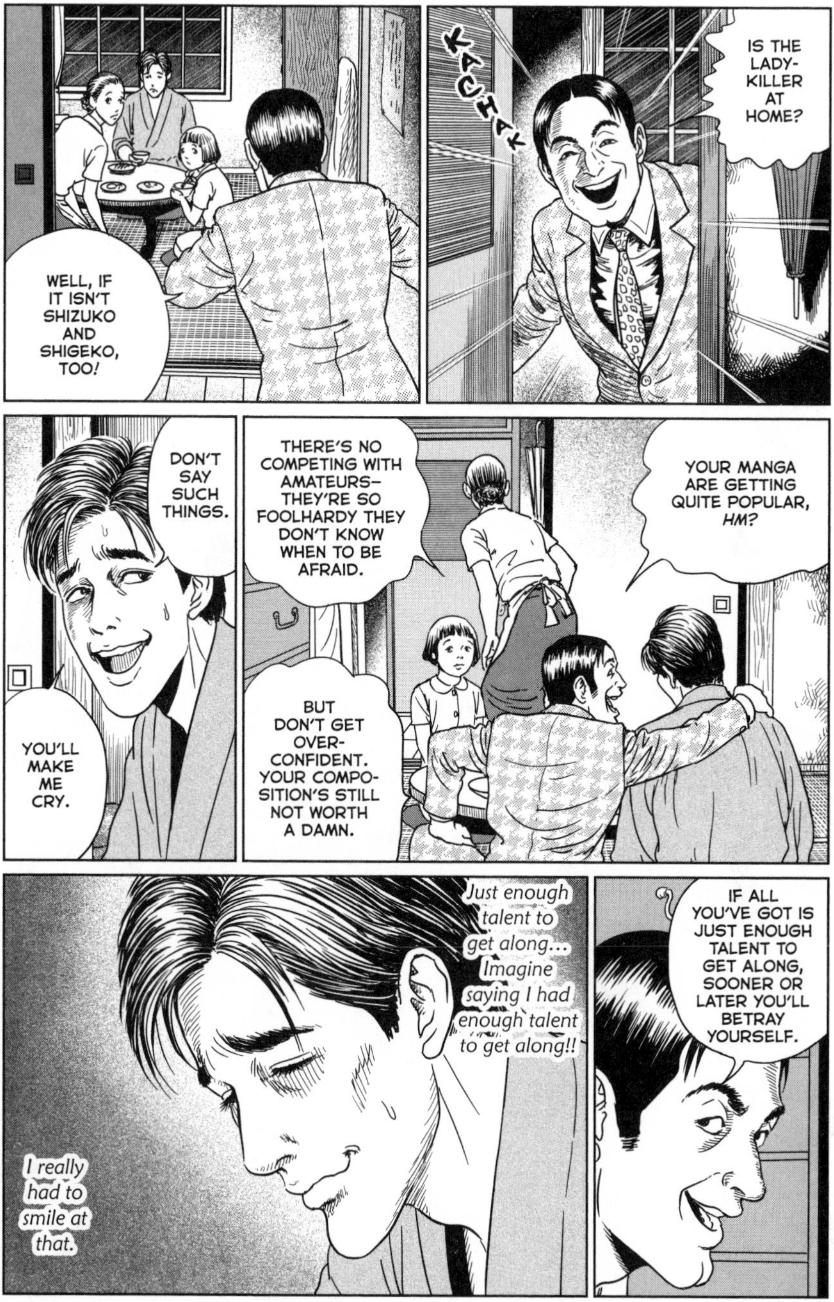
KACHAK
IS THE LADY-KILLER AT HOME?
WELL, IF IT ISN'T SHIZUKO AND SHIGEKO, TOO!
YOUR MANGA ARE GETTING QUITE POPULAR, *HM?*
THERE'S NO COMPETING WITH AMATEURS—THEY'RE SO FOOLHARDY THEY DON'T KNOW WHEN TO BE AFRAID.
BUT DON'T GET OVER-CONFIDENT. YOUR COMPOSITION'S STILL NOT WORTH A DAMN.
DON'T SAY SUCH THINGS.
YOU'LL MAKE ME CRY.
IF ALL YOU'VE GOT IS JUST ENOUGH TALENT TO GET ALONG, SOONER OR LATER YOU'LL BETRAY YOURSELF.
Just enough talent to get along… Imagine saying I had enough talent to get along!!
I really had to smile at that.

*Oden

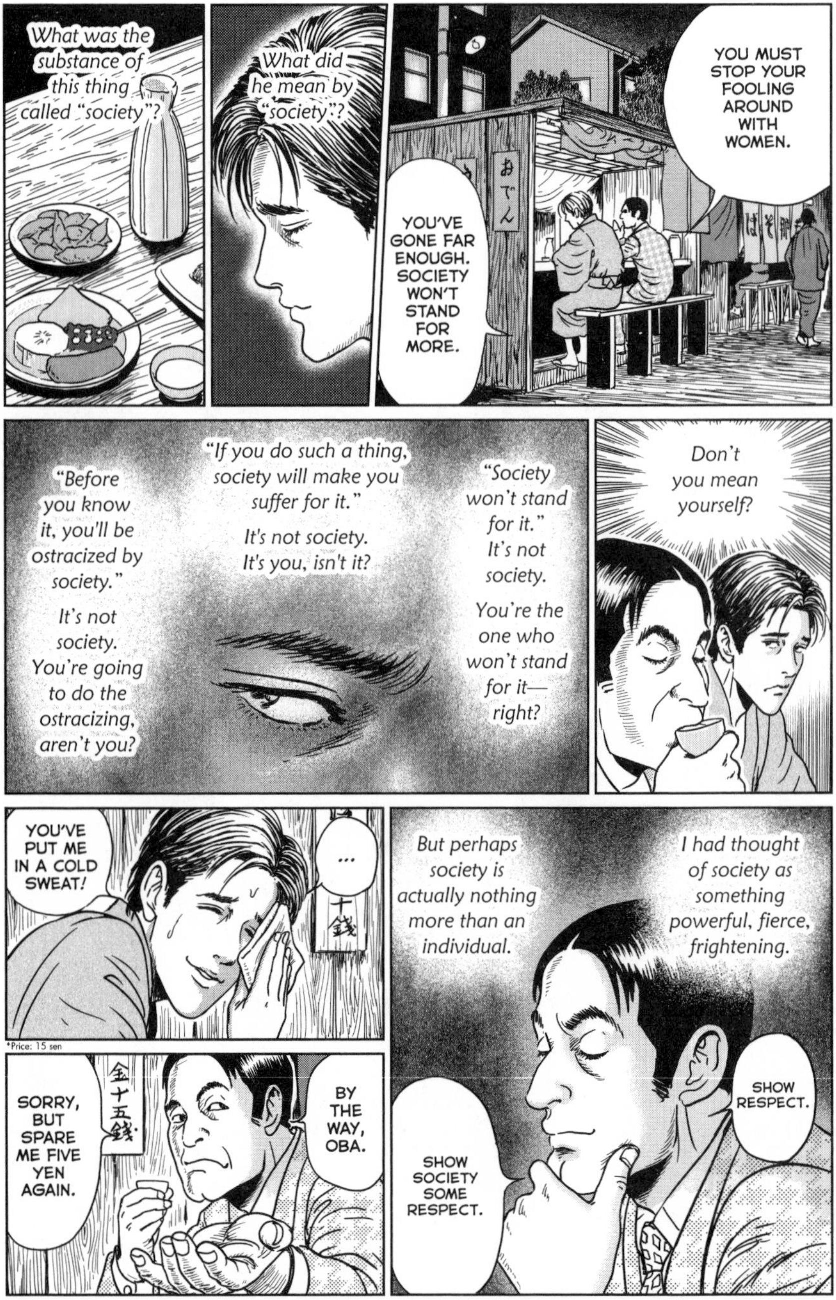
YOU MUST STOP YOUR FOOLING AROUND WITH WOMEN.
おでん
YOU'VE GONE FAR ENOUGH. SOCIETY WON'T STAND FOR MORE.
What did he mean by "society"?
What was the substance of this thing called "society"?
Don't you mean yourself?
"Society won't stand for it." It's not society. You're the one who won't stand for it—right?
"If you do such a thing, society will make you suffer for it." It's not society. It's you, isn't it?
"Before you know it, you'll be ostracized by society." It's not society. You're going to do the ostracizing, aren't you?
I had thought of society as something powerful, fierce, frightening.
But perhaps society is actually nothing more than an individual.
SHOW RESPECT.
SHOW SOCIETY SOME RESPECT.
...
YOU'VE PUT ME IN A COLD SWEAT!
BY THE WAY, OBA.
金十五銭
SORRY, BUT SPARE ME FIVE YEN AGAIN.

*Price: 15 sen

*Manga series: *Sekkachi Pin-chan* (Busy Miss Pin)
Manga series: *Nonki Osho* (The Happy-Go-Lucky Priest) by Sansuke Hiyaase, No. 27

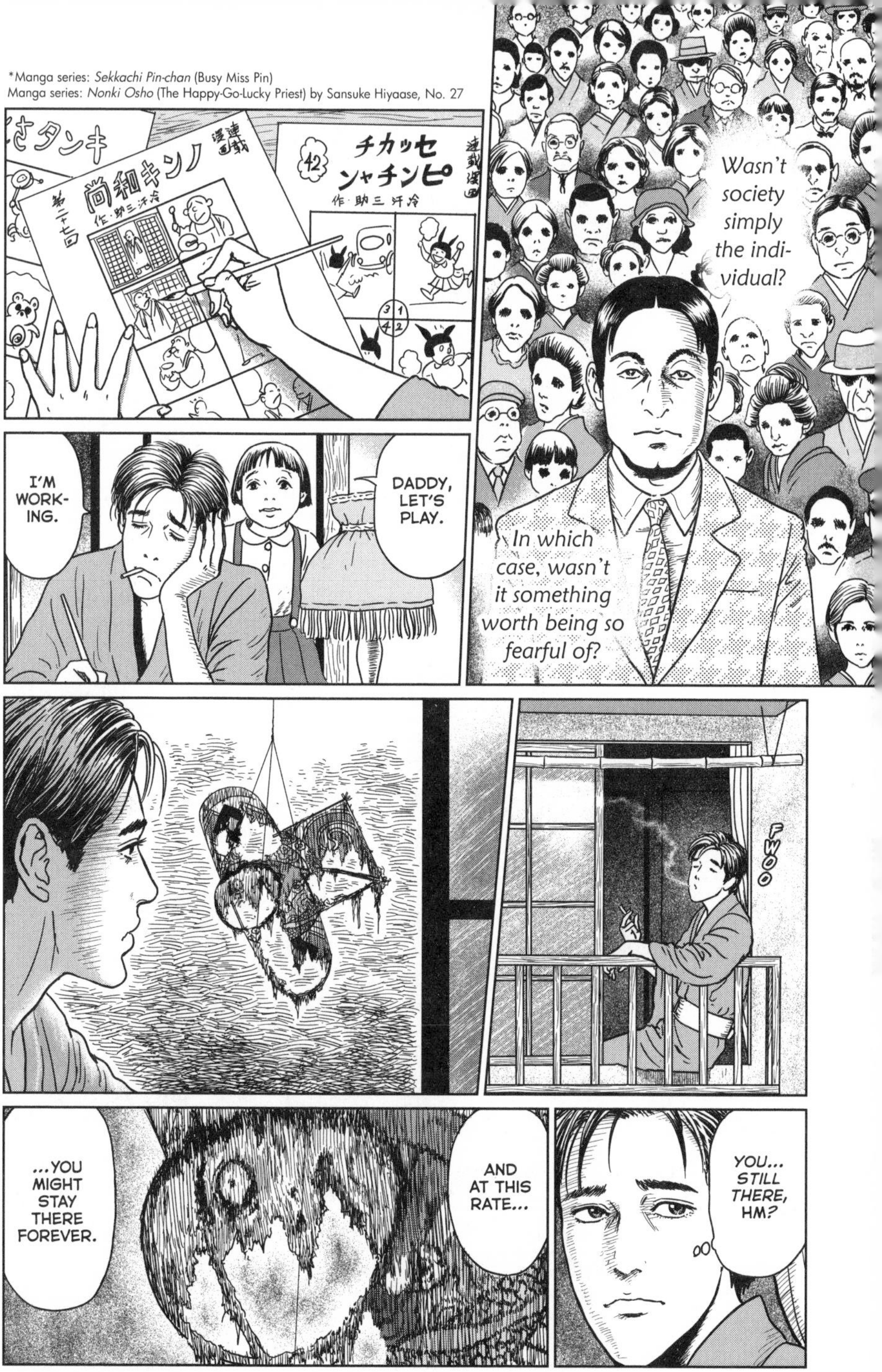
Wasn't society simply the individual?
In which case, wasn't it something worth being so fearful of?
連載漫画
セッカチ ピンチャン
作・冷汗三助
連載漫画
ノンキ和尚
第二十七回
作・冷汗三助
DADDY, LET'S PLAY.
I'M WORKING.
FWOO
YOU... STILL THERE, HM?
AND AT THIS RATE...
...YOU MIGHT STAY THERE FOREVER.

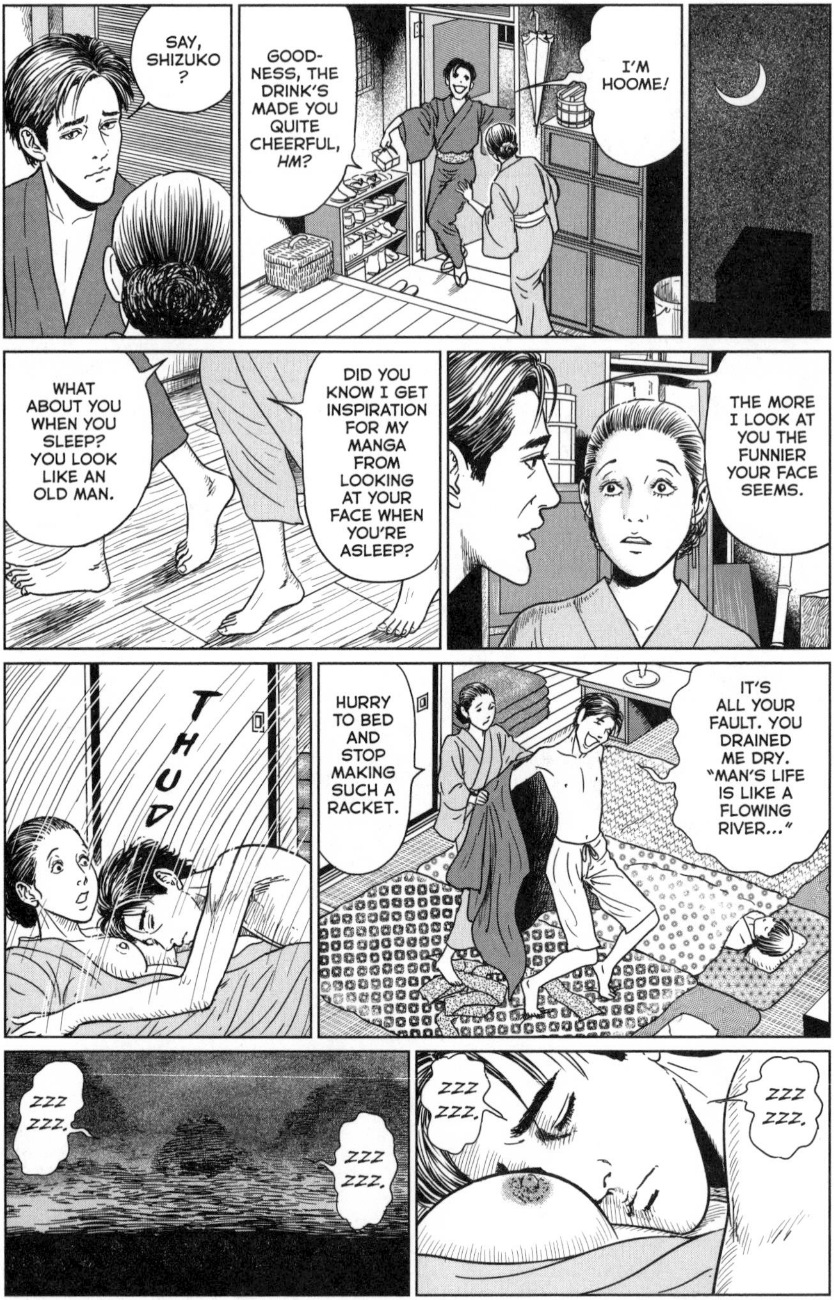
I'M HOOME!
GOOD-NESS, THE DRINK'S MADE YOU QUITE CHEERFUL, HM?
SAY, SHIZUKO?
THE MORE I LOOK AT YOU THE FUNNIER YOUR FACE SEEMS.
DID YOU KNOW I GET INSPIRATION FOR MY MANGA FROM LOOKING AT YOUR FACE WHEN YOU'RE ASLEEP?
WHAT ABOUT YOU WHEN YOU SLEEP? YOU LOOK LIKE AN OLD MAN.
IT'S ALL YOUR FAULT. YOU DRAINED ME DRY. "MAN'S LIFE IS LIKE A FLOWING RIVER..."
HURRY TO BED AND STOP MAKING SUCH A RACKET.
THUD
ZZZ ZZZ.
ZZZ ZZZ.
ZZZ ZZZ.
ZZZ ZZZ.

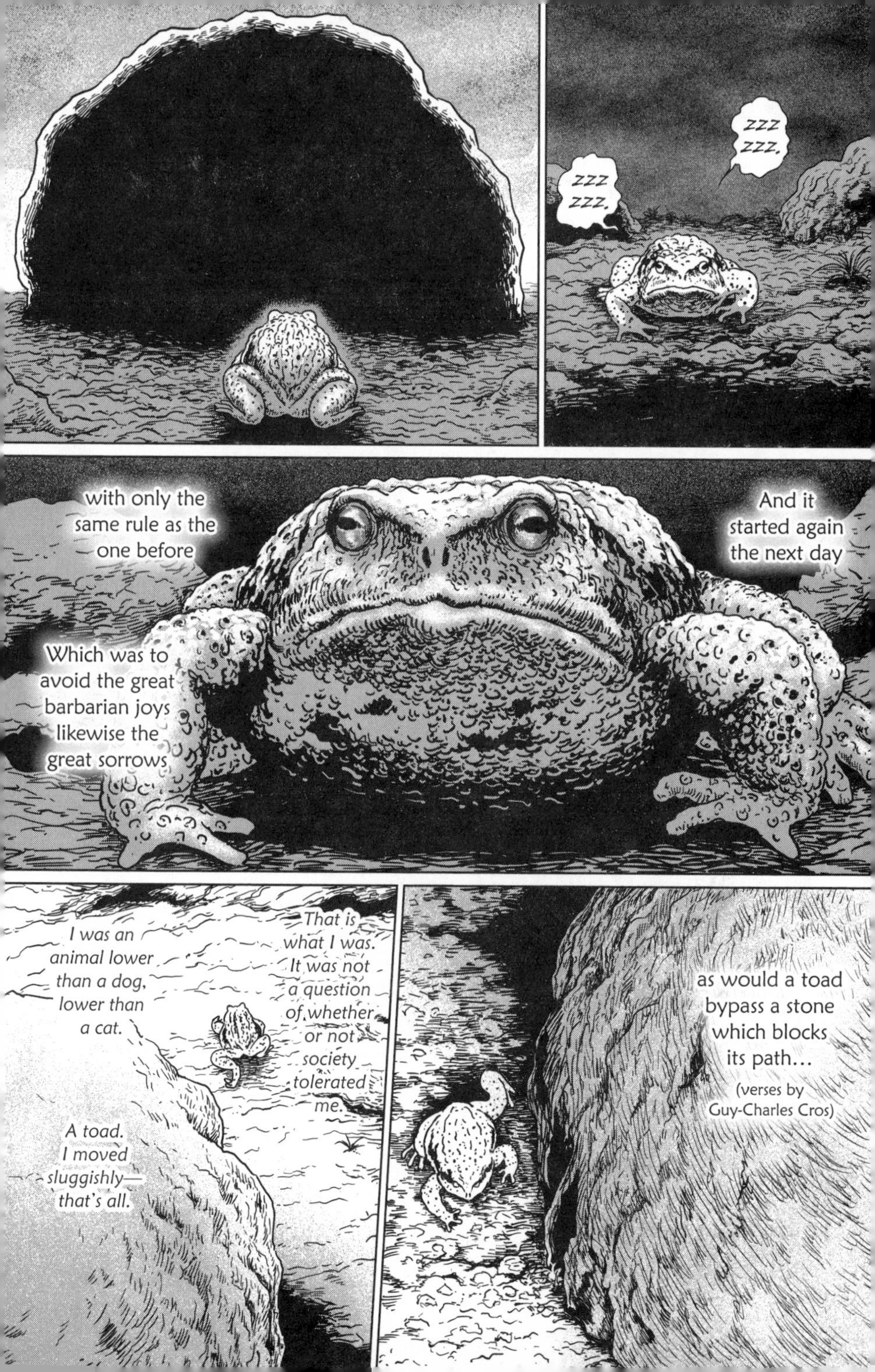
ZZZ ZZZ.
ZZZ ZZZ.
And it started again the next day
with only the same rule as the one before
Which was to avoid the great barbarian joys likewise the great sorrows
as would a toad bypass a stone which blocks its path…
(verses by Guy-Charles Cros)
That is what I was. It was not a question of whether or not society tolerated me.
I was an animal lower than a dog, lower than a cat.
A toad. I moved sluggishly— that's all.

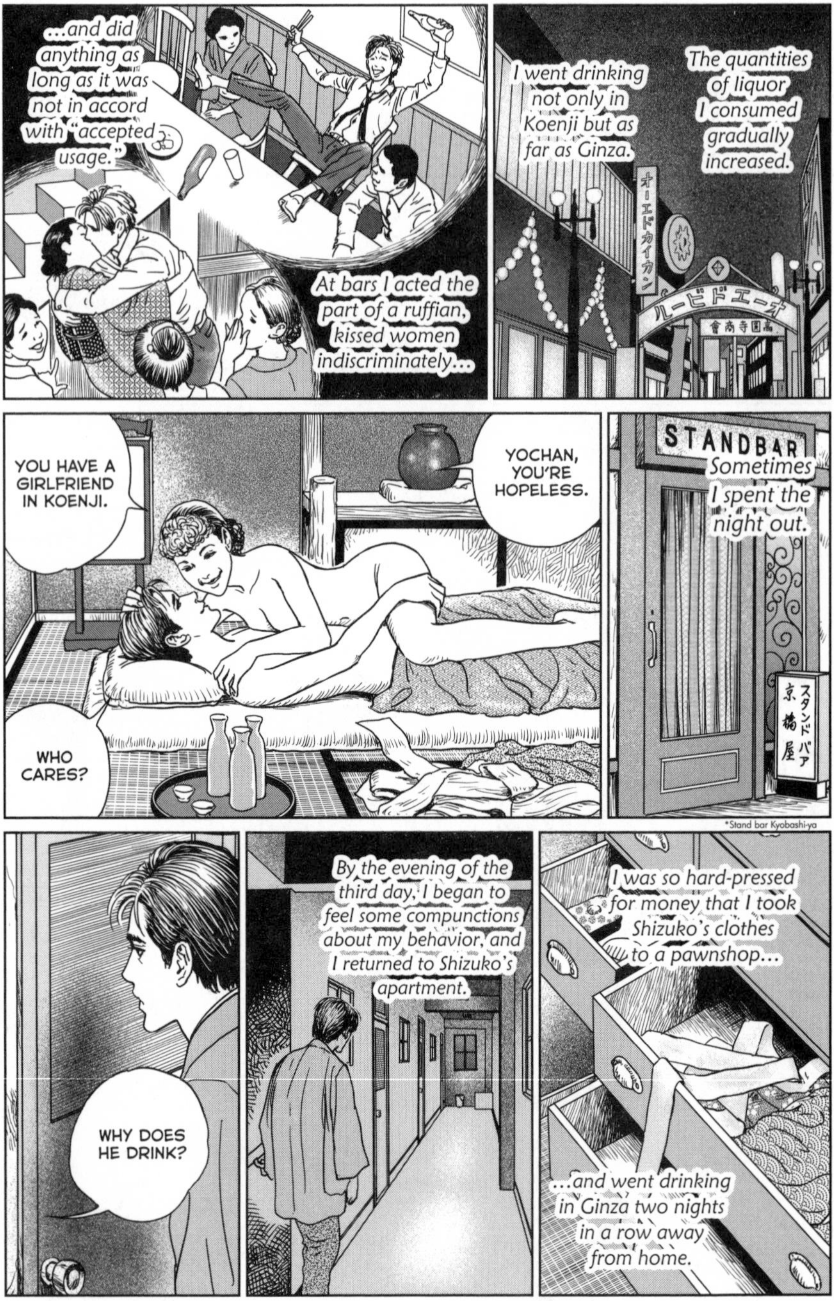
The quantities of liquor I consumed gradually increased.
I went drinking not only in Koenji but as far as Ginza.
オーエドカイカン
At bars I acted the part of a ruffian, kissed women indiscriminately...
...and did anything as long as it was not in accord with "accepted usage."
STANDBAR
Sometimes I spent the night out.
スタンドバア
京橋屋
YOCHAN, YOU'RE HOPELESS.
YOU HAVE A GIRLFRIEND IN KOENJI.
WHO CARES?
I was so hard-pressed for money that I took Shizuko's clothes to a pawnshop...
...and went drinking in Ginza two nights in a row away from home.
By the evening of the third day, I began to feel some compunctions about my behavior, and I returned to Shizuko's apartment.
WHY DOES HE DRINK?
*Stand bar Kyobashi-ya

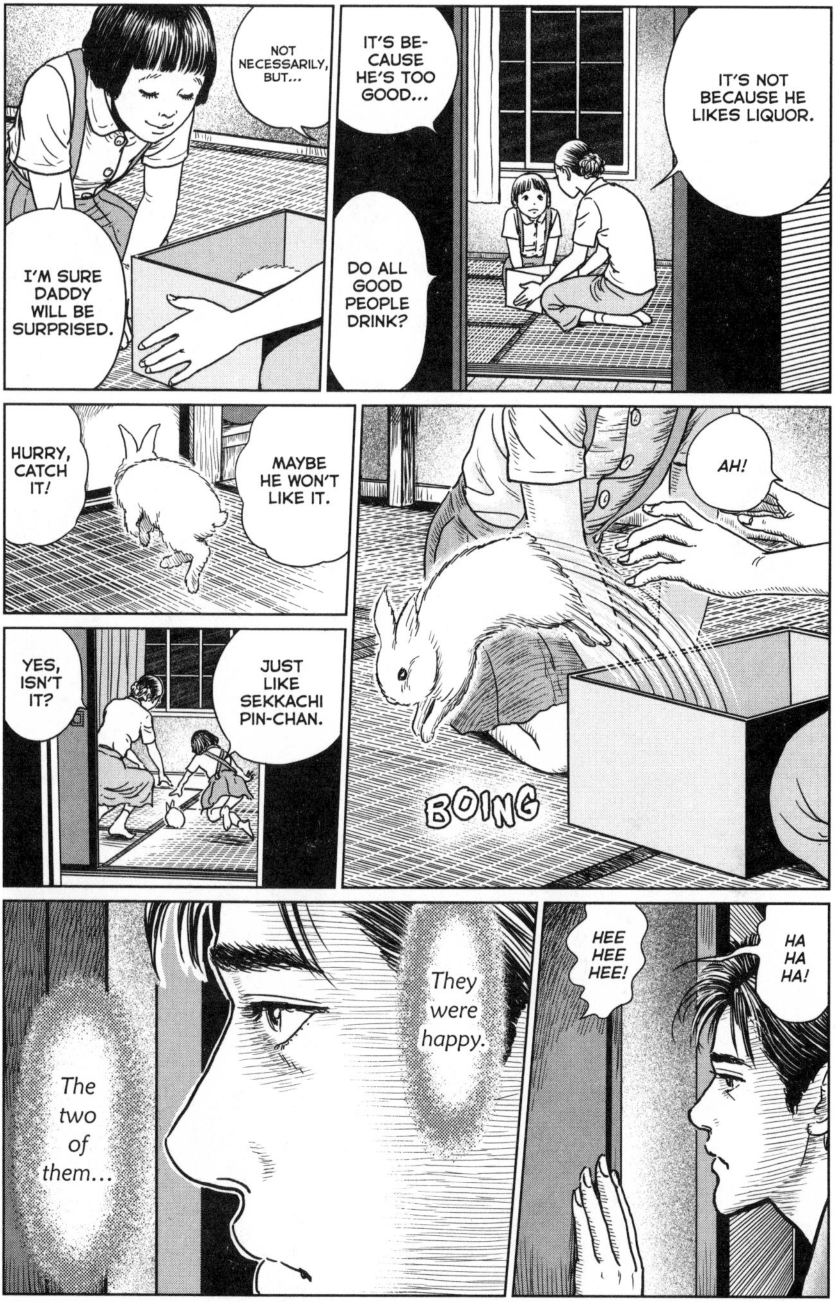
IT'S NOT BECAUSE HE LIKES LIQUOR.
IT'S BE-CAUSE HE'S TOO GOOD...
DO ALL GOOD PEOPLE DRINK?
NOT NECESSARILY, BUT...
I'M SURE DADDY WILL BE SURPRISED.
AH!
BOING
MAYBE HE WON'T LIKE IT.
HURRY, CATCH IT!
JUST LIKE SEKKACHI PIN-CHAN.
YES, ISN'T IT?
HA HA HA!
HEE HEE HEE!
They were happy.
The two of them...

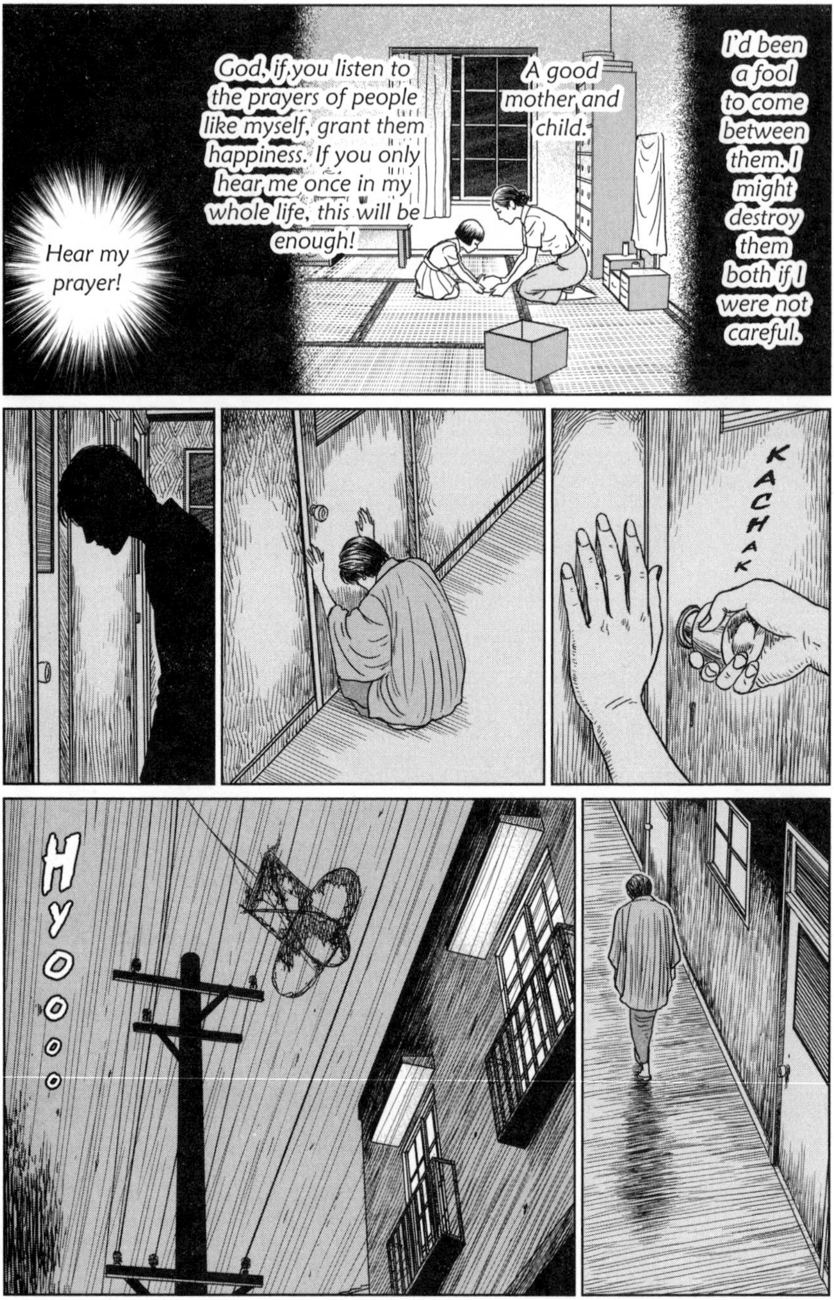
I'd been a fool to come between them. I might destroy them both if I were not careful.
A good mother and child.
God, if you listen to the prayers of people like myself, grant them happiness. If you only hear me once in my whole life, this will be enough!
Hear my prayer!
KACHAK
HYOOOOO

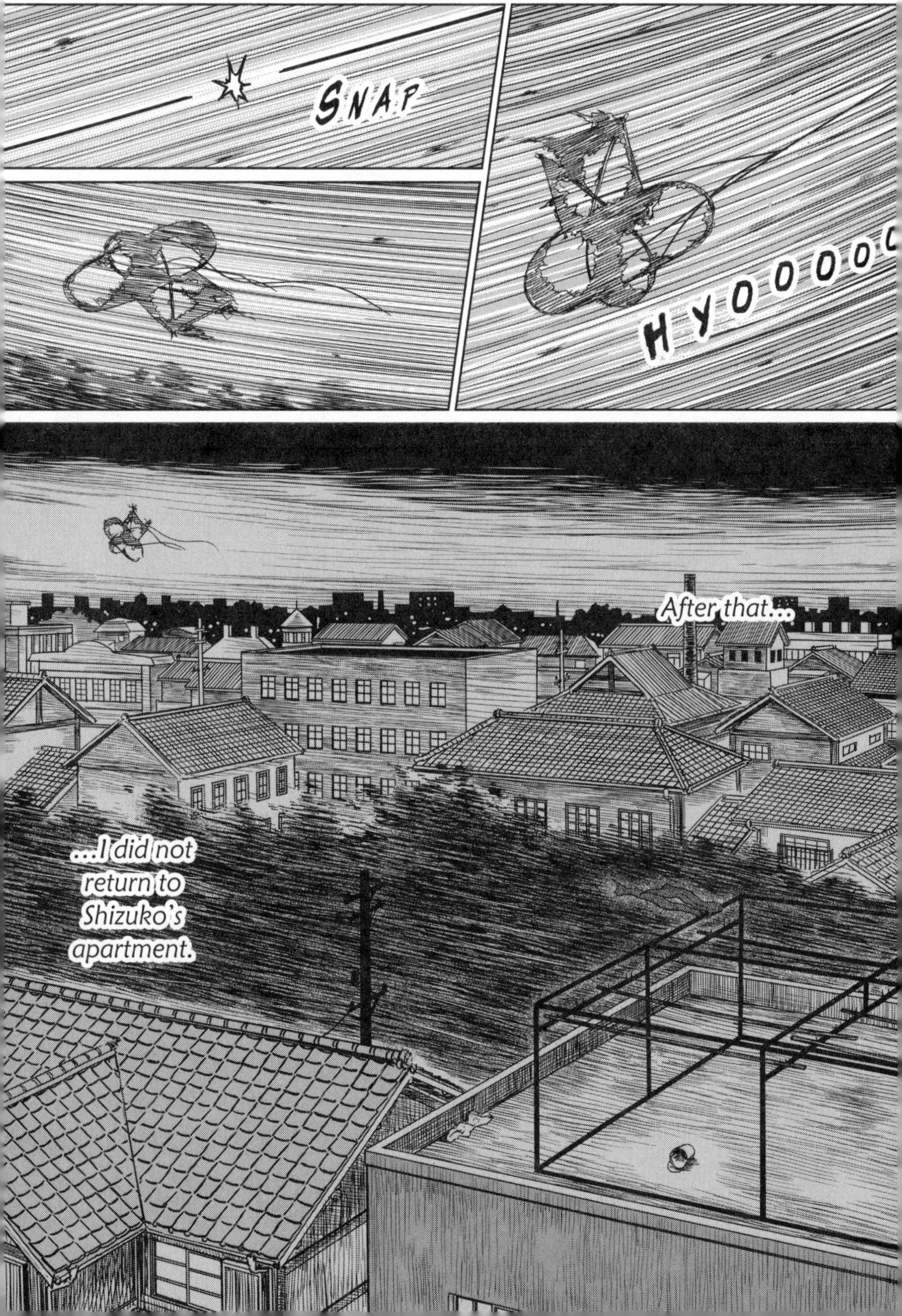
HYOOOOO
SNAP
After that...
...I did not return to Shizuko's apartment.

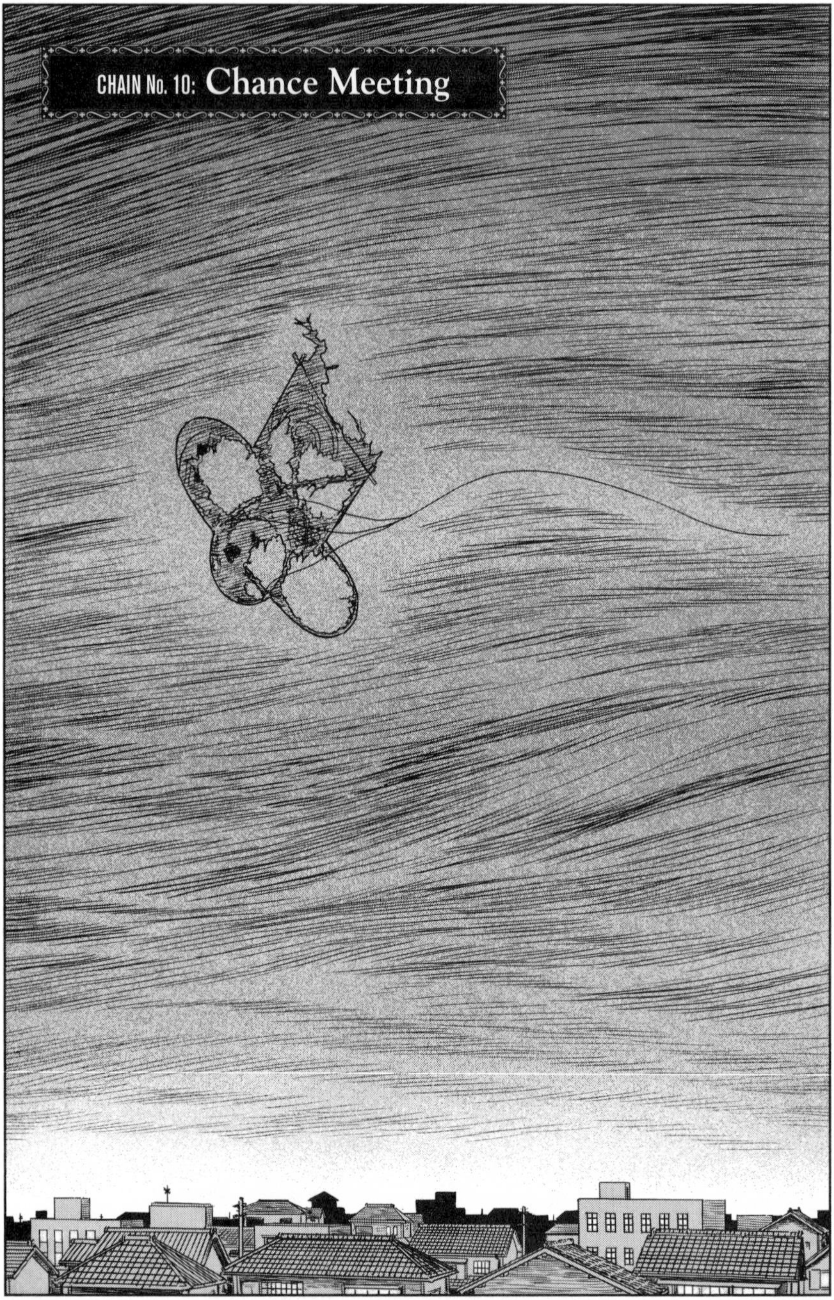
CHAIN No. 10: Chance Meeting

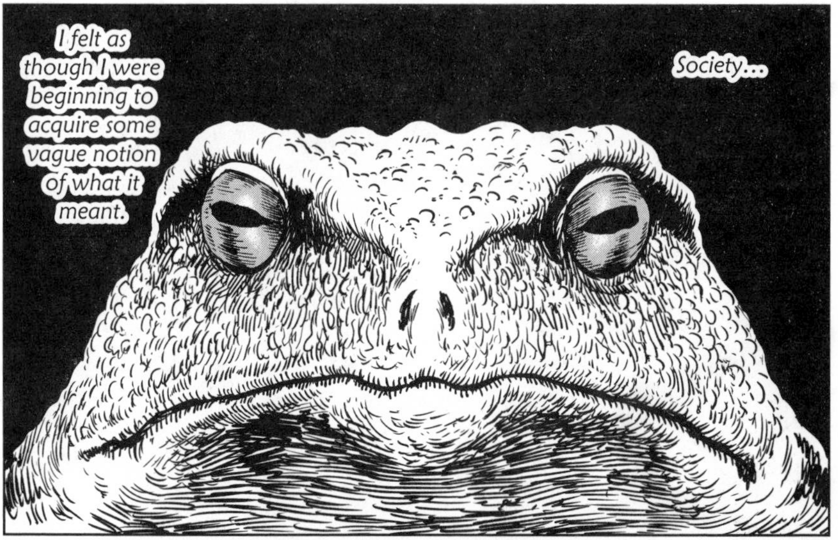
Society...
I felt as though I were beginning to acquire some vague notion of what it meant.

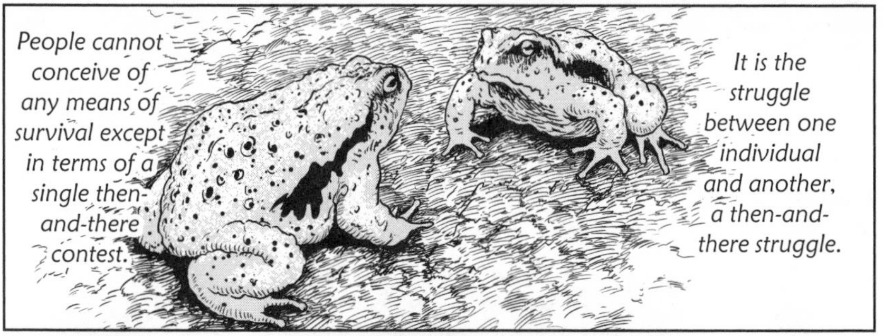
It is the struggle between one individual and another, a then-and-there struggle.
People cannot conceive of any means of survival except in terms of a single then-and-there contest.

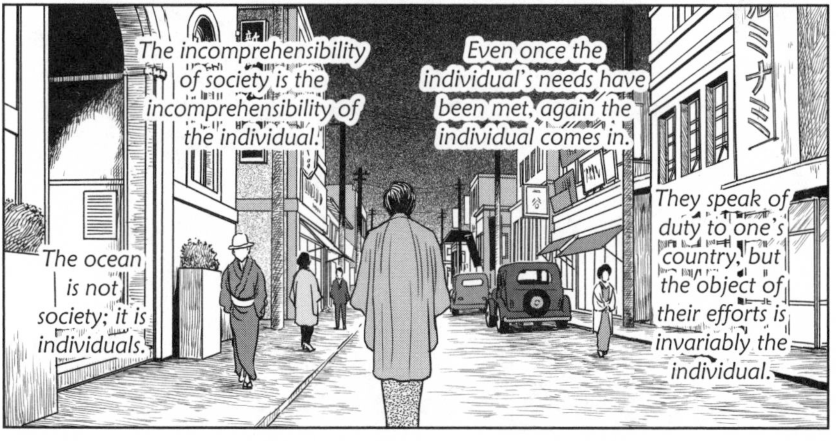
Even once the individual's needs have been met, again the individual comes in.
The incomprehensibility of society is the incomprehensibility of the individual.
They speak of duty to one's country, but the object of their efforts is invariably the individual.
The ocean is not society; it is individuals.

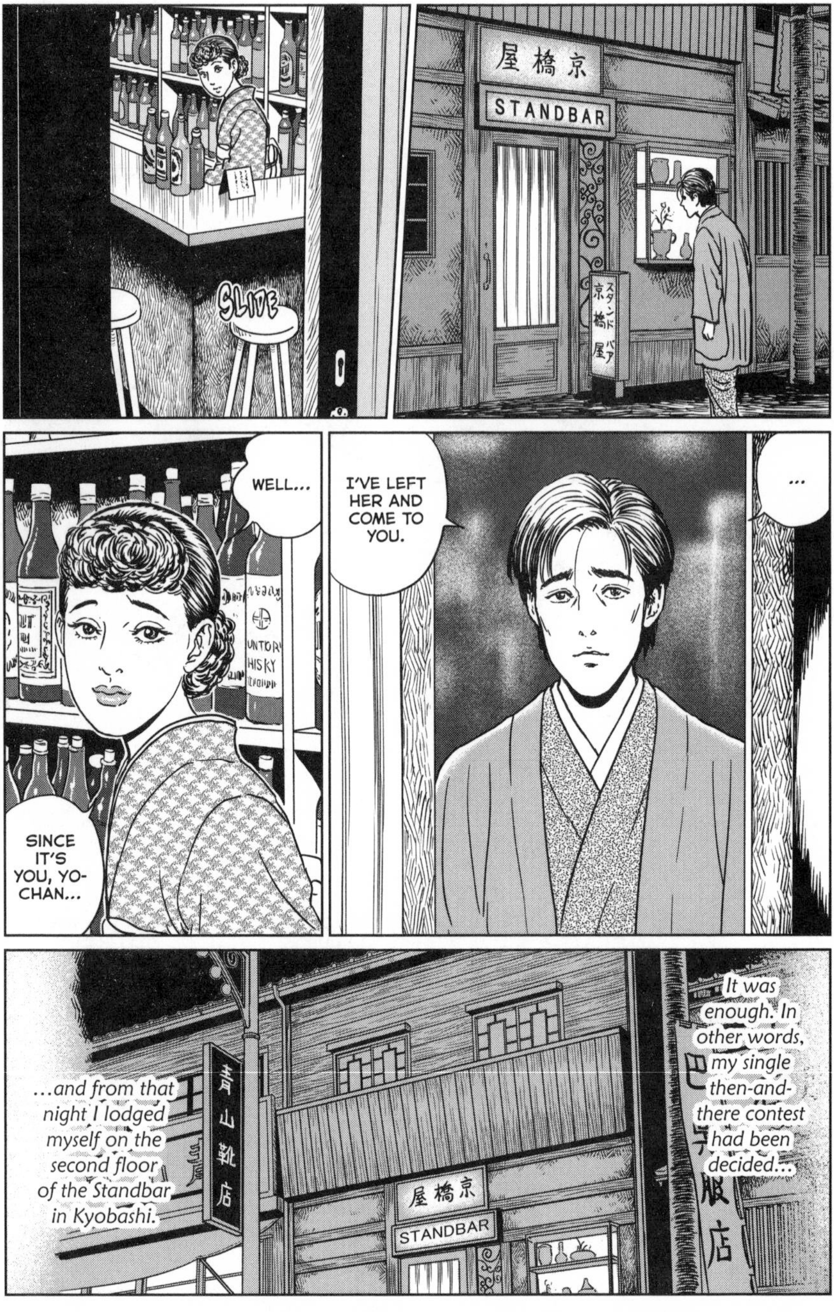
京橋屋
STANDBAR
スタンドバア
京橋屋
SLIDE
...
I'VE LEFT HER AND COME TO YOU.
WELL...
SINCE IT'S YOU, YO-CHAN...
It was enough. In other words, my single then-and-there contest had been decided...
...and from that night I lodged myself on the second floor of the Standbar in Kyobashi.
青山靴店
京橋屋
STANDBAR

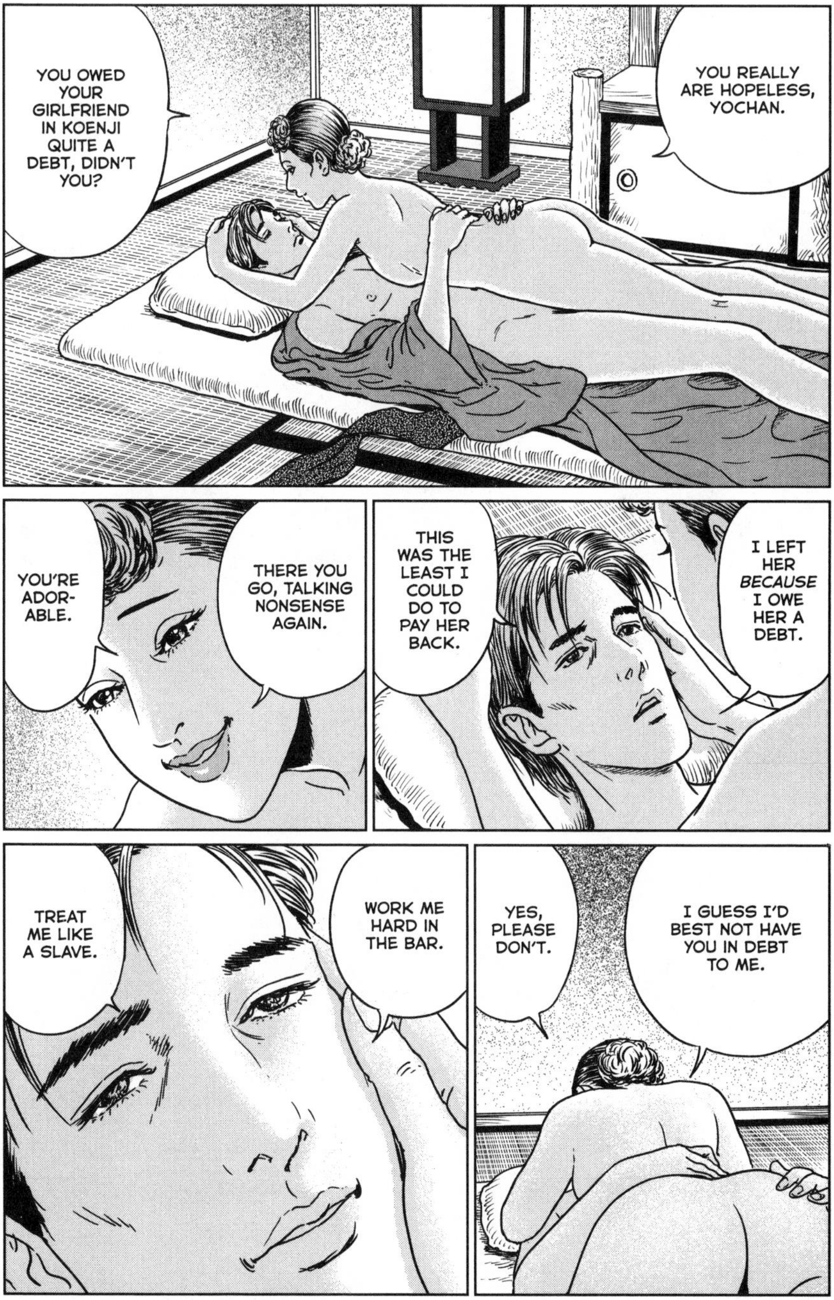
YOU REALLY ARE HOPELESS, YOCHAN.
YOU OWED YOUR GIRLFRIEND IN KOENJI QUITE A DEBT, DIDN'T YOU?
I LEFT HER *BECAUSE* I OWE HER A DEBT.
THIS WAS THE LEAST I COULD DO TO PAY HER BACK.
THERE YOU GO, TALKING NONSENSE AGAIN.
YOU'RE ADOR-ABLE.
I GUESS I'D BEST NOT HAVE YOU IN DEBT TO ME.
YES, PLEASE DON'T.
WORK ME HARD IN THE BAR.
TREAT ME LIKE A SLAVE.

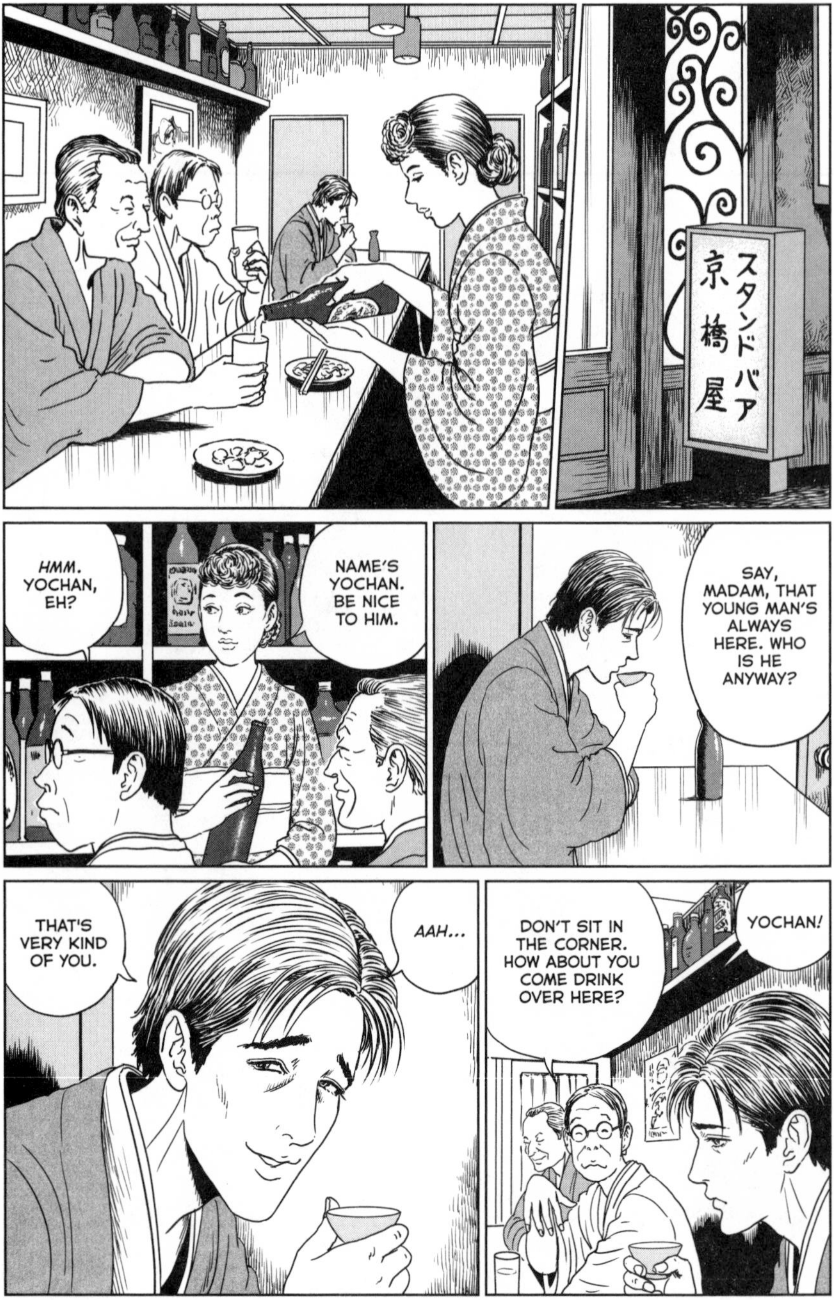
スタンドバア
京橋屋
SAY, MADAM, THAT YOUNG MAN'S ALWAYS HERE. WHO IS HE ANYWAY?
NAME'S YOCHAN. BE NICE TO HIM.
HMM. YOCHAN, EH?
YOCHAN!
DON'T SIT IN THE CORNER. HOW ABOUT YOU COME DRINK OVER HERE?
AAH...
THAT'S VERY KIND OF YOU.

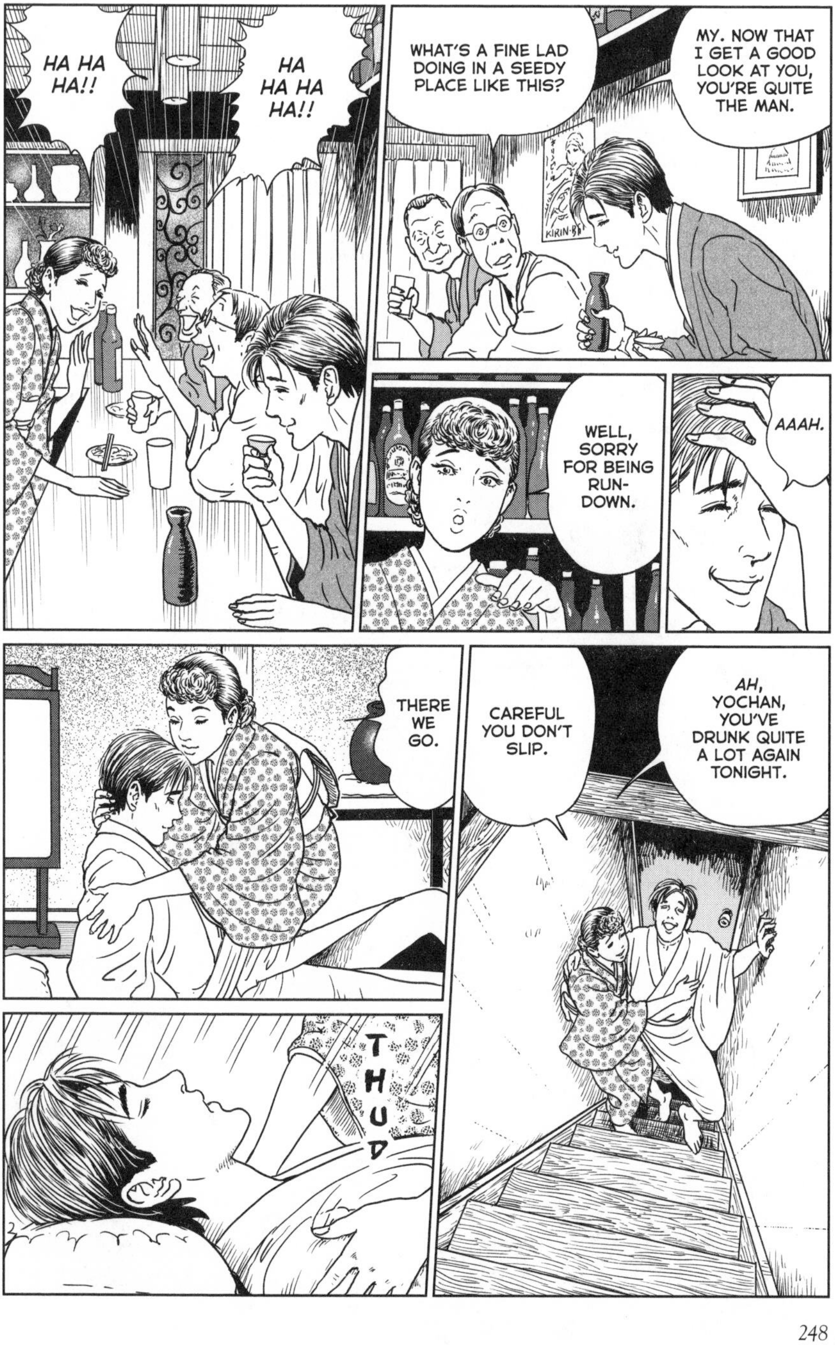
MY. NOW THAT I GET A GOOD LOOK AT YOU, YOU'RE QUITE THE MAN.
WHAT'S A FINE LAD DOING IN A SEEDY PLACE LIKE THIS?
AAAH.
WELL, SORRY FOR BEING RUN-DOWN.
HA HA HA HA!!
HA HA HA!!
AH, YOCHAN, YOU'VE DRUNK QUITE A LOT AGAIN TONIGHT.
CAREFUL YOU DON'T SLIP.
THERE WE GO.
THUD

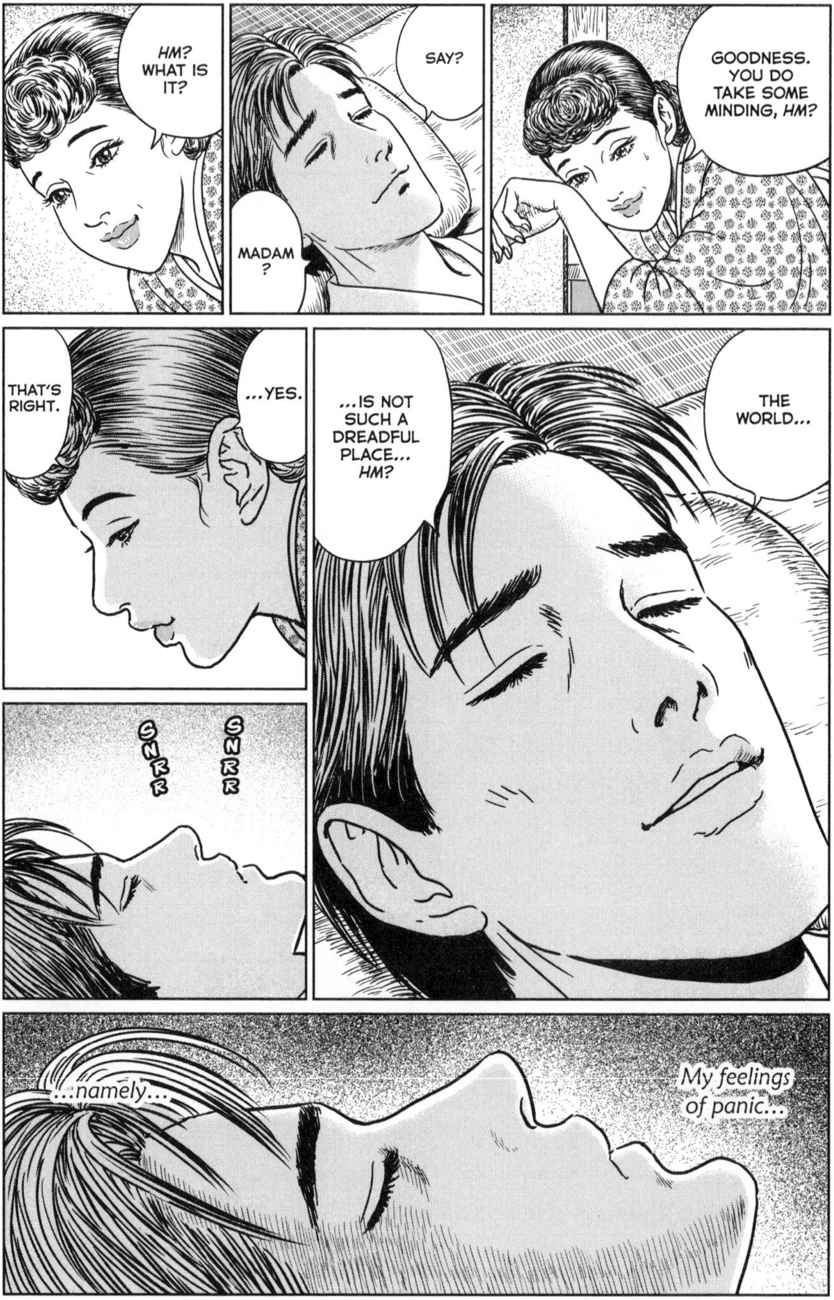
GOODNESS. YOU DO TAKE SOME MINDING, *HM?*
SAY?
MADAM ?
HM? WHAT IS IT?
THE WORLD...
...IS NOT SUCH A DREADFUL PLACE... *HM?*
...YES.
THAT'S RIGHT.
SNRR
SNRR
My feelings of panic...
...namely...

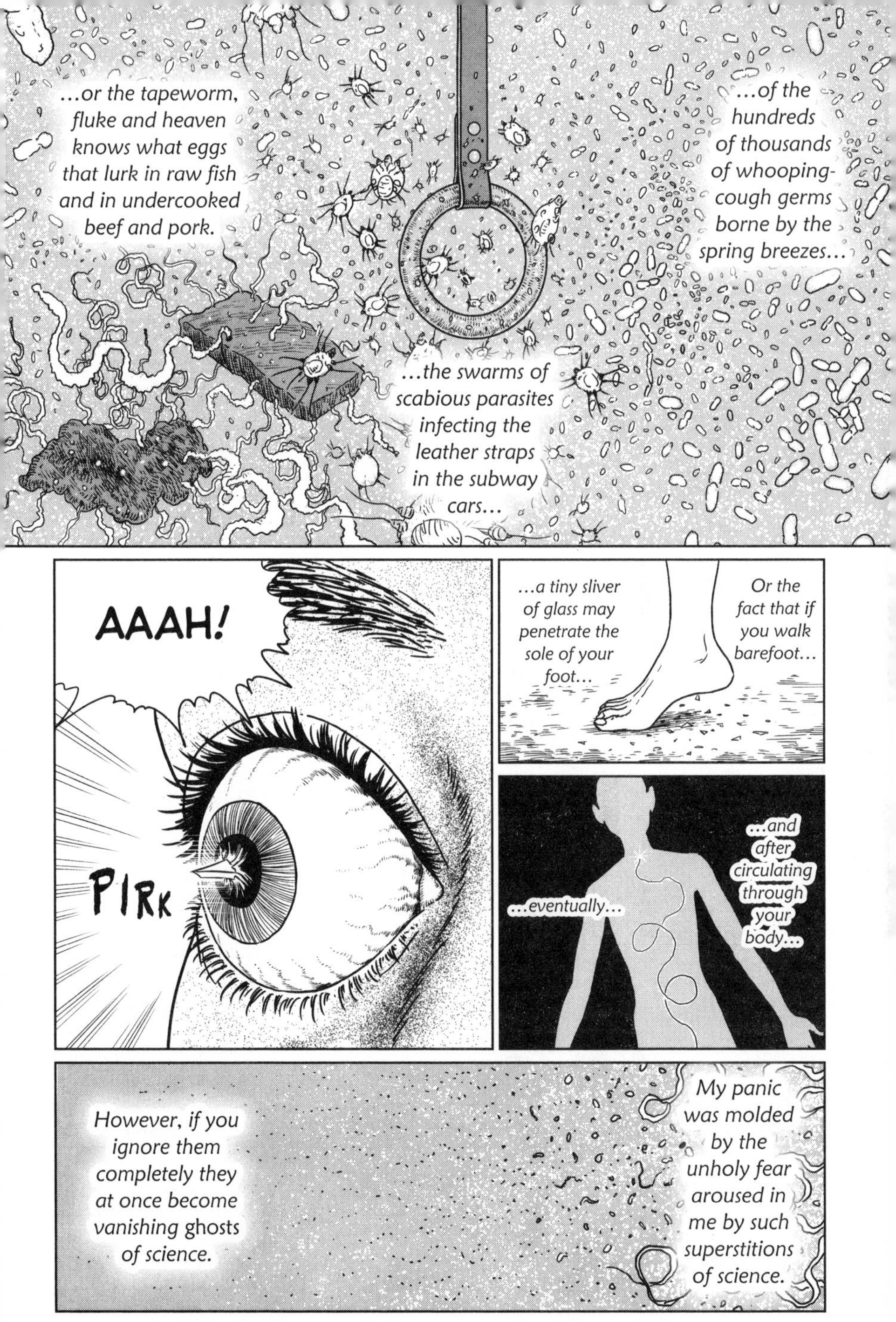
...of the hundreds of thousands of whooping-cough germs borne by the spring breezes...
...the swarms of scabious parasites infecting the leather straps in the subway cars...
...or the tapeworm, fluke and heaven knows what eggs that lurk in raw fish and in undercooked beef and pork.
Or the fact that if you walk barefoot...
...a tiny sliver of glass may penetrate the sole of your foot...
...and after circulating through your body...
...eventually...
AAAH!
PIRK
My panic was molded by the unholy fear aroused in me by such superstitions of science.
However, if you ignore them completely they at once become vanishing ghosts of science.

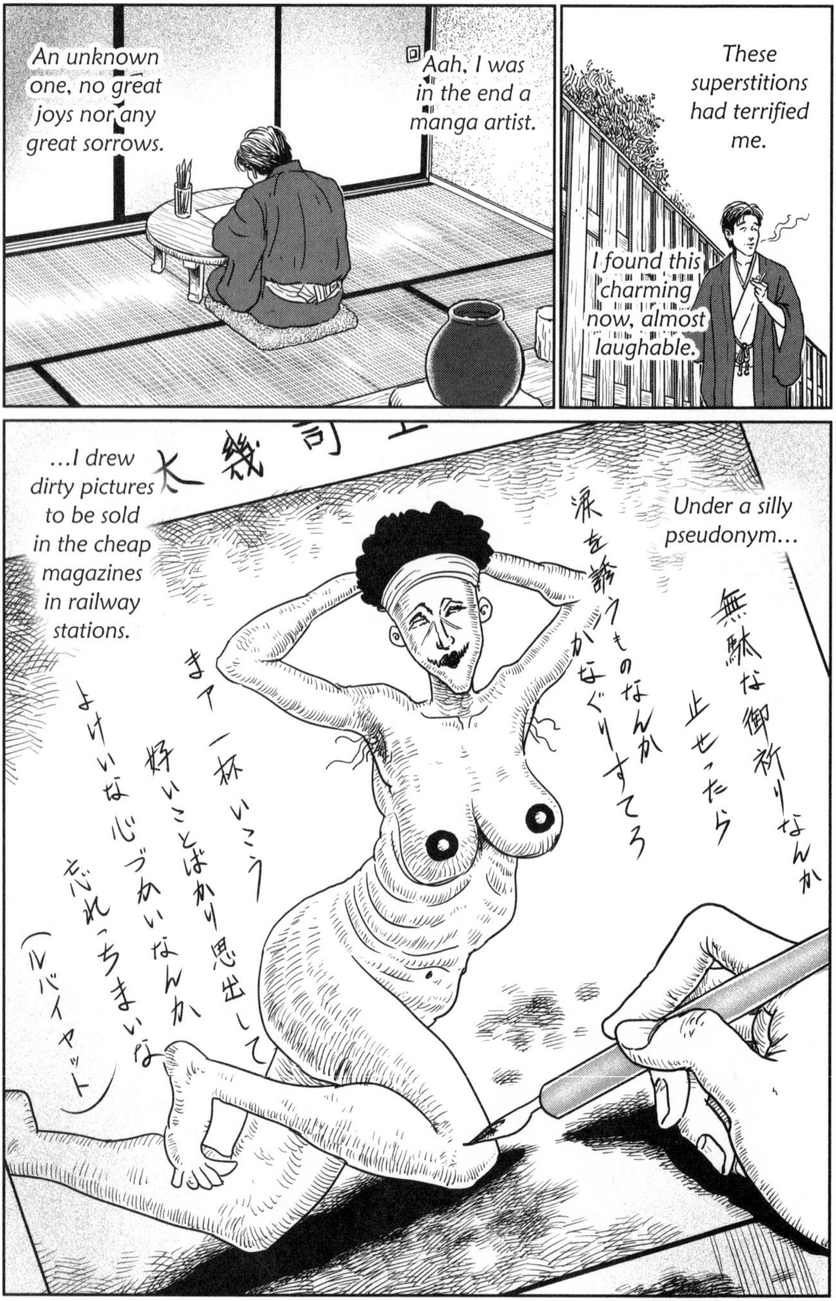
These superstitions had terrified me.
I found this charming now, almost laughable.
An unknown one, no great joys nor any great sorrows.
Aah, I was in the end a manga artist.
Under a silly pseudonym…
…I drew dirty pictures to be sold in the cheap magazines in railway stations.
無駄な御祈りなんか
止せったら
涙を誘うものなんか
かなぐりすてろ
まァ一杯いこう
好いことばかり思出して
よけいな心づかいなんか
忘れっちまいな
(ルバイヤット)

Waste not your Hour, nor in the vain pursuit
Of This and That endeavor and dispute
Better be merry with the fruitful Grape
Than sadden after none, or bitter Fruit
(Rubaiyat)

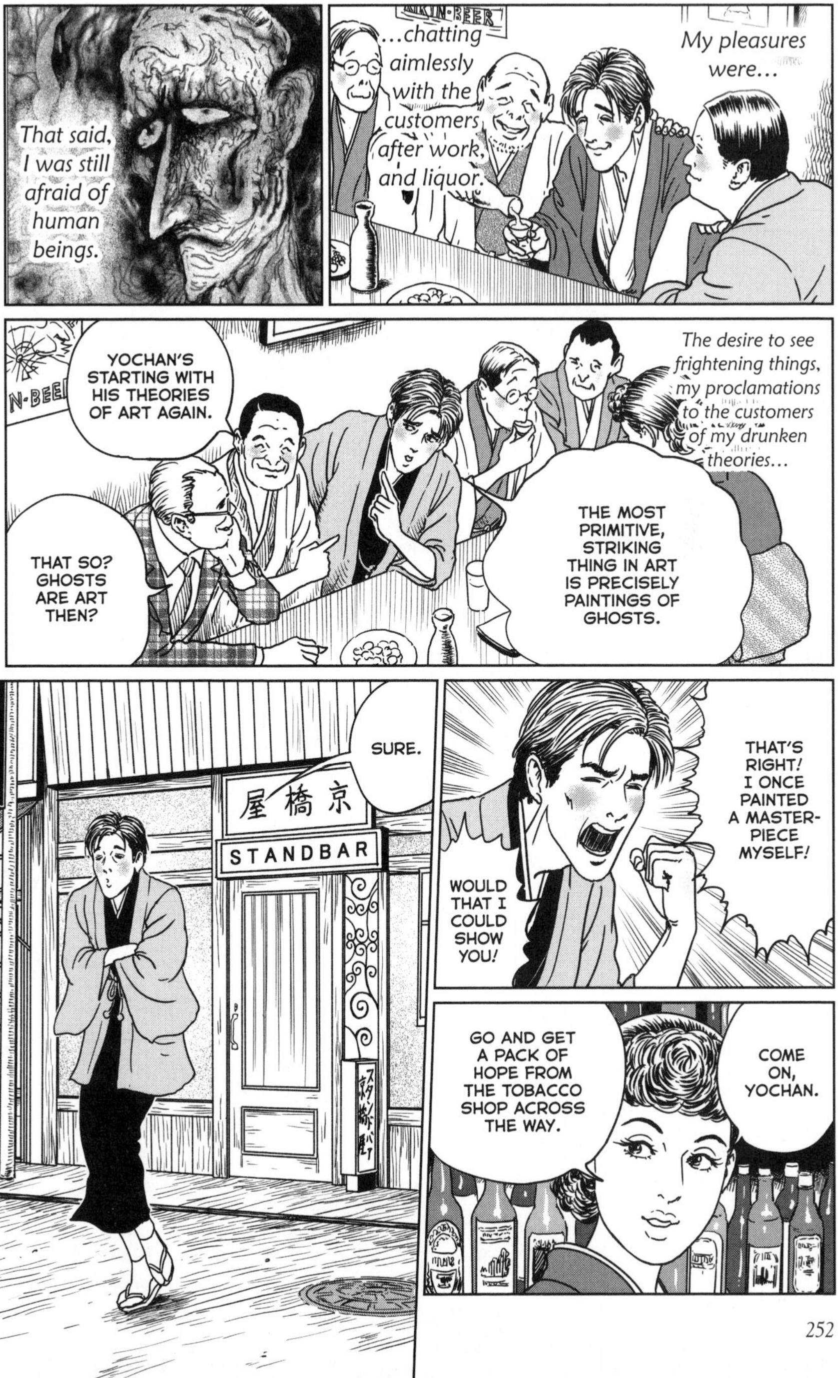
My pleasures were…
…chatting aimlessly with the customers after work, and liquor.
That said, I was still afraid of human beings.
The desire to see frightening things, my proclamations to the customers of my drunken theories…
THE MOST PRIMITIVE, STRIKING THING IN ART IS PRECISELY PAINTINGS OF GHOSTS.
YOCHAN'S STARTING WITH HIS THEORIES OF ART AGAIN.
THAT SO? GHOSTS ARE ART THEN?
THAT'S RIGHT! I ONCE PAINTED A MASTERPIECE MYSELF!
WOULD THAT I COULD SHOW YOU!
COME ON, YOCHAN.
GO AND GET A PACK OF HOPE FROM THE TOBACCO SHOP ACROSS THE WAY.
SURE.
京橋屋
STANDBAR

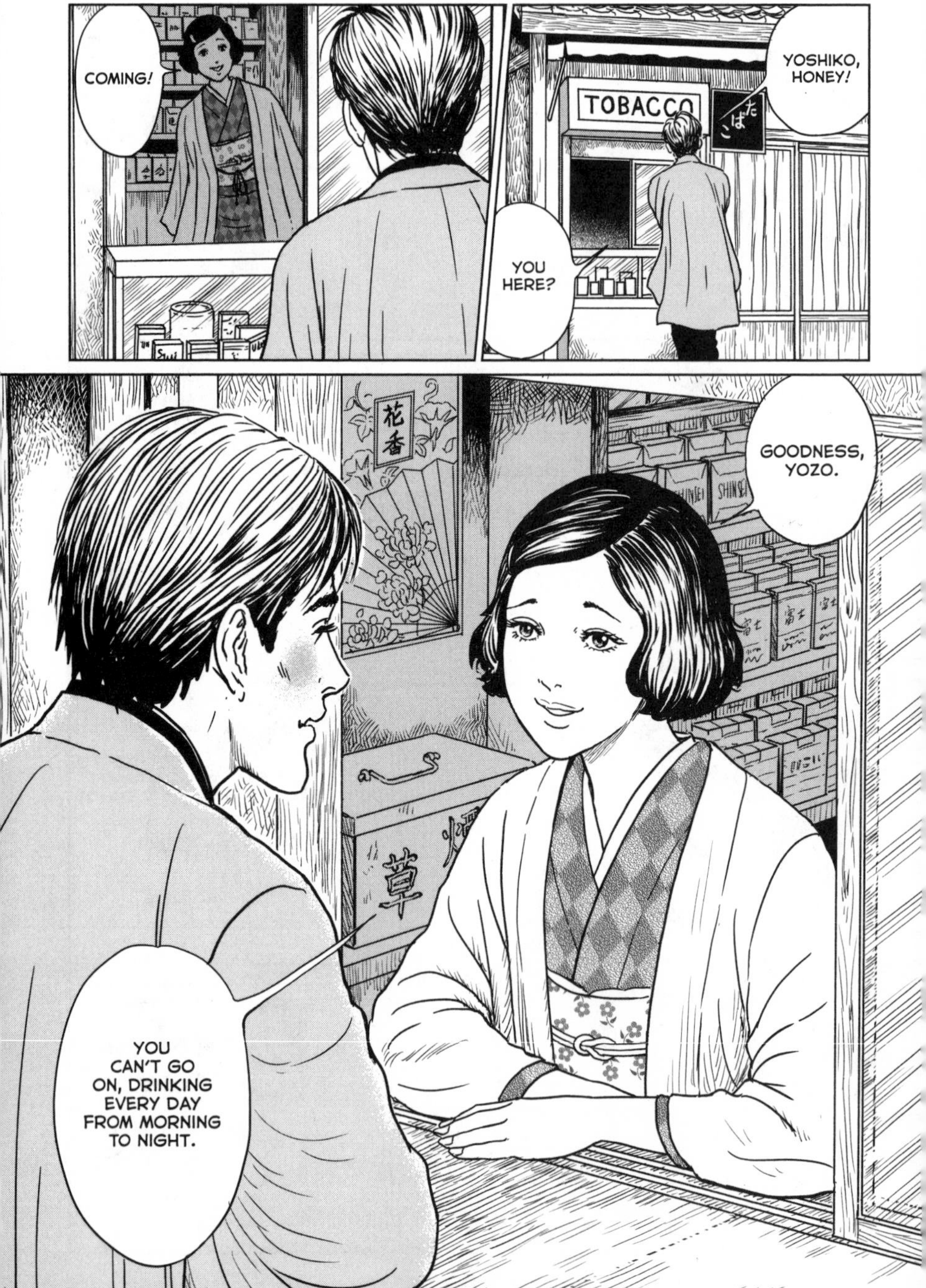
YOSHIKO, HONEY!
TOBACCO
たばこ
YOU HERE?
COMING!
花香
GOODNESS, YOZO.
YOU CAN'T GO ON, DRINKING EVERY DAY FROM MORNING TO NIGHT.

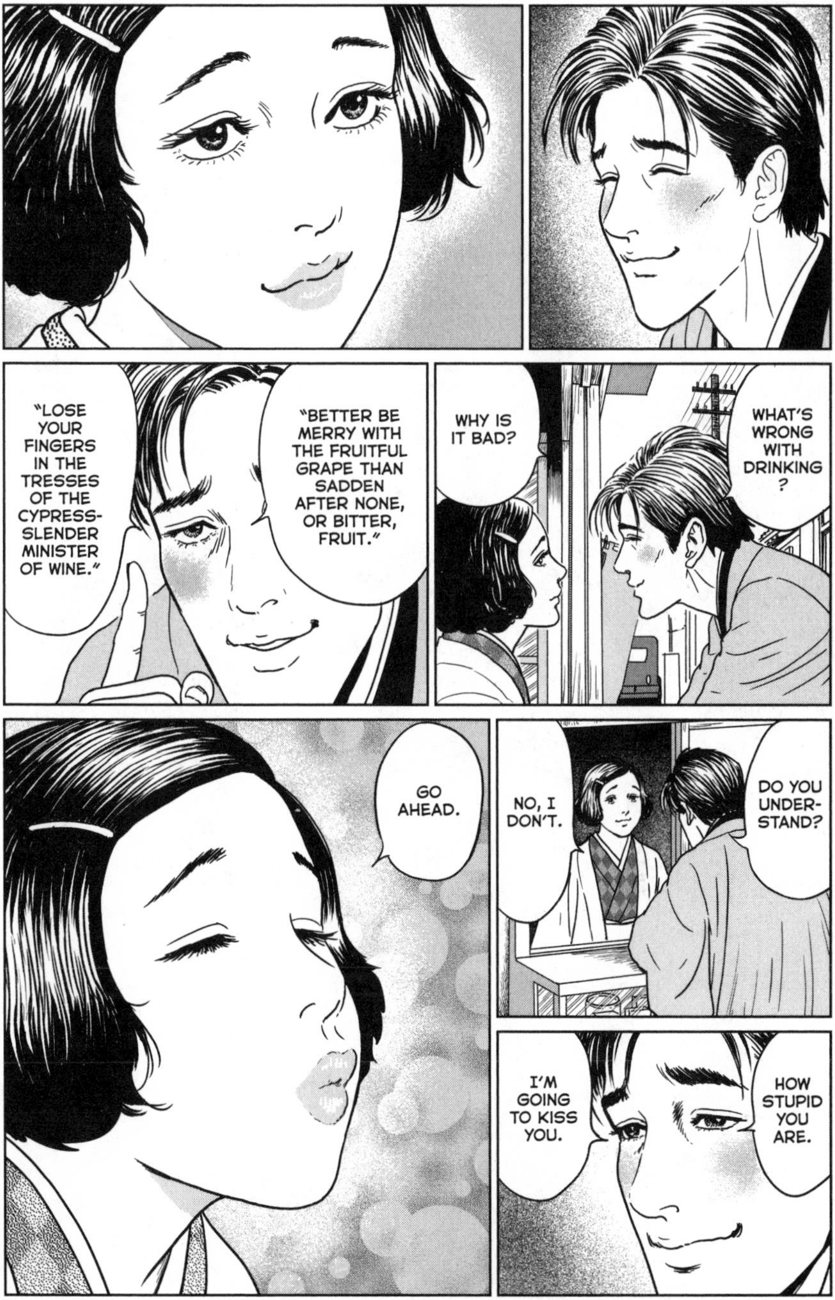
WHAT'S WRONG WITH DRINKING?
WHY IS IT BAD?
"BETTER BE MERRY WITH THE FRUITFUL GRAPE THAN SADDEN AFTER NONE, OR BITTER, FRUIT."
"LOSE YOUR FINGERS IN THE TRESSES OF THE CYPRESS-SLENDER MINISTER OF WINE."
DO YOU UNDERSTAND?
NO, I DON'T.
HOW STUPID YOU ARE.
I'M GOING TO KISS YOU.
GO AHEAD.

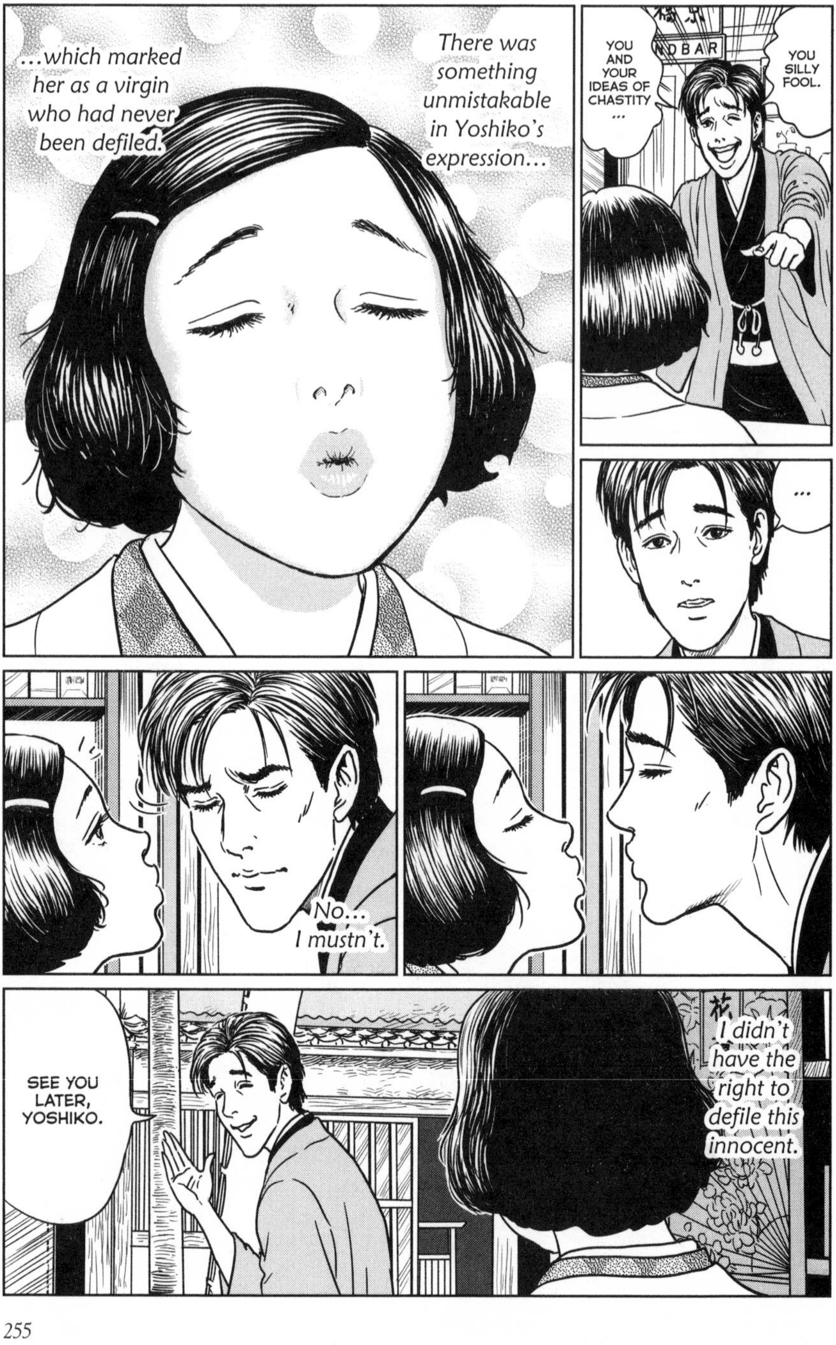
YOU SILLY FOOL.
YOU AND YOUR IDEAS OF CHASTITY ...
...
There was something unmistakable in Yoshiko's expression...
...which marked her as a virgin who had never been defiled.
No... I mustn't.
I didn't have the right to defile this innocent.
SEE YOU LATER, YOSHIKO.

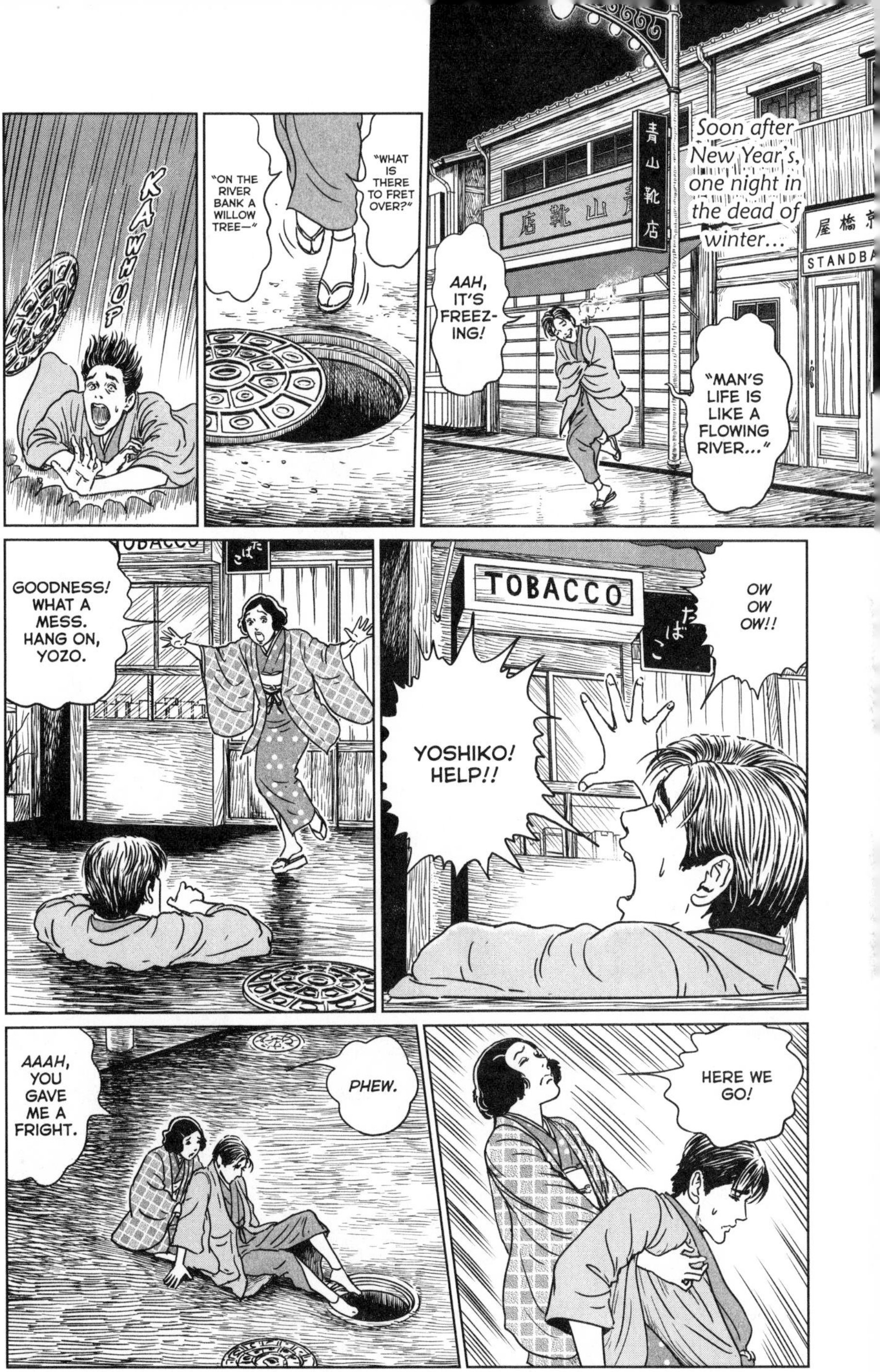

Soon after New Year's, one night in the dead of winter…
青山靴店
京橋屋
STANDBA
AAH, IT'S FREEZING!
"MAN'S LIFE IS LIKE A FLOWING RIVER…"
"WHAT IS THERE TO FRET OVER?"
"ON THE RIVER BANK A WILLOW TREE—"
KAWHUP
TOBACCO
たばこ
OW OW OW!!
YOSHIKO! HELP!!
GOODNESS! WHAT A MESS. HANG ON, YOZO.
HERE WE GO!
PHEW.
AAAH, YOU GAVE ME A FRIGHT.

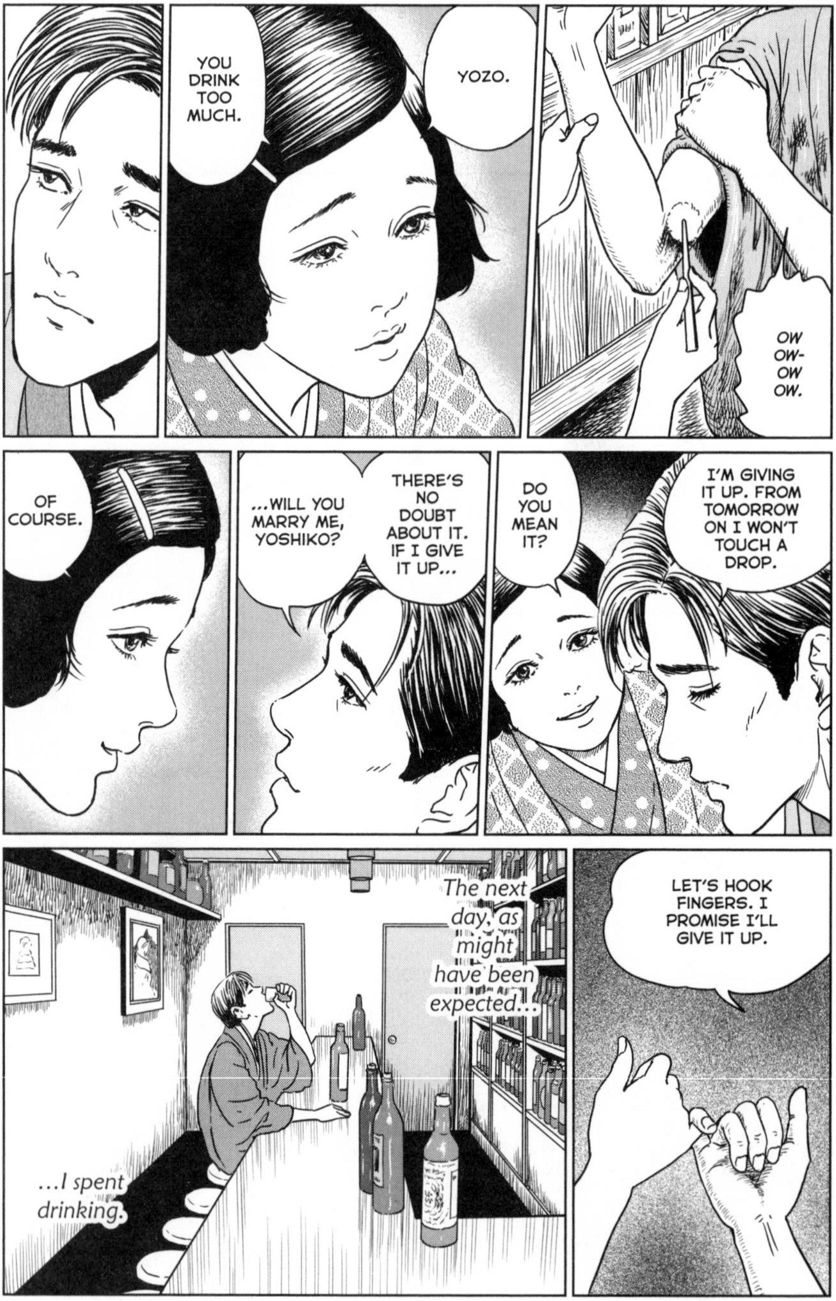
OW OW- OW OW.
YOZO.
YOU DRINK TOO MUCH.
I'M GIVING IT UP. FROM TOMORROW ON I WON'T TOUCH A DROP.
DO YOU MEAN IT?
THERE'S NO DOUBT ABOUT IT. IF I GIVE IT UP...
...WILL YOU MARRY ME, YOSHIKO?
OF COURSE.
LET'S HOOK FINGERS. I PROMISE I'LL GIVE IT UP.
The next day, as might have been expected...
...I spent drinking.

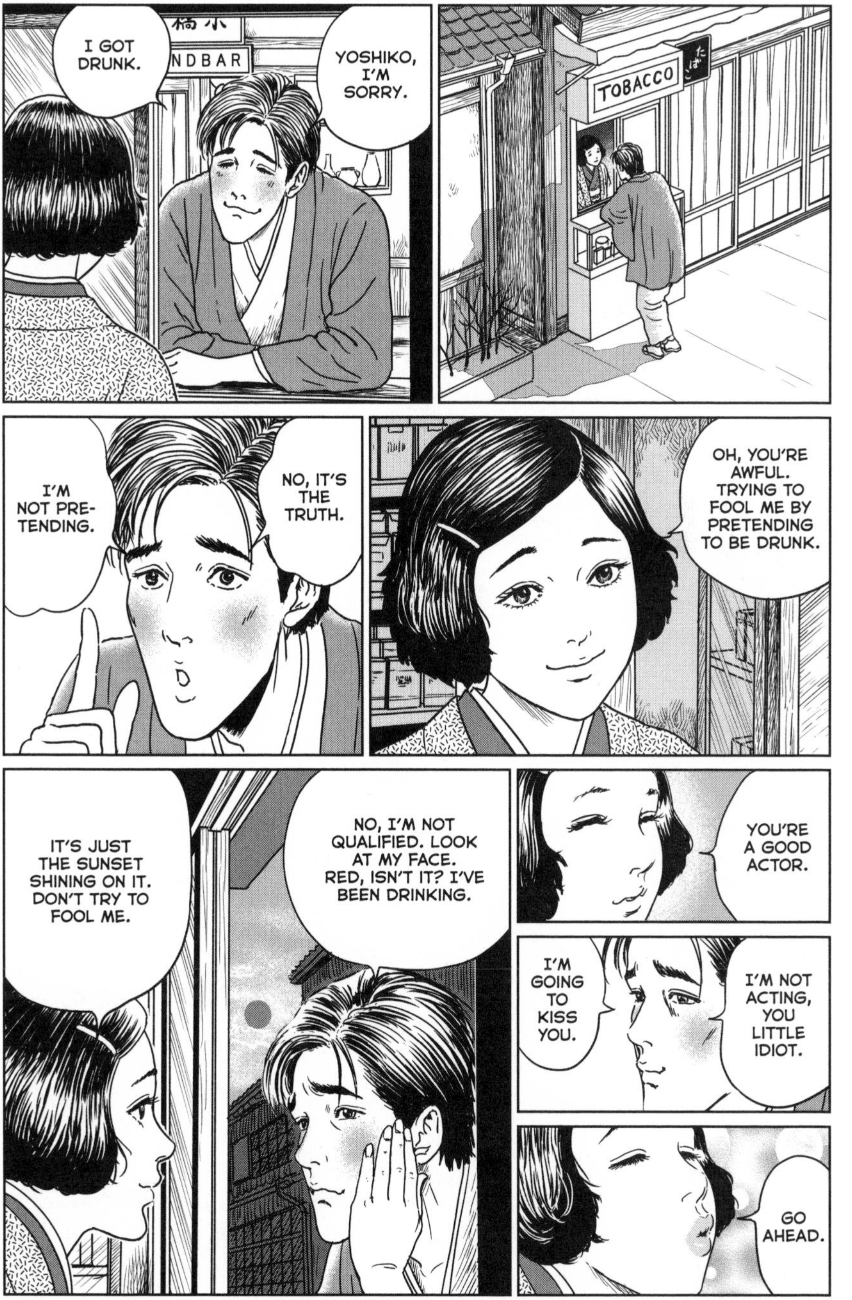
TOBACCO
YOSHIKO, I'M SORRY.
I GOT DRUNK.
NDBAR
OH, YOU'RE AWFUL. TRYING TO FOOL ME BY PRETENDING TO BE DRUNK.
NO, IT'S THE TRUTH.
I'M NOT PRE-TENDING.
YOU'RE A GOOD ACTOR.
I'M NOT ACTING, YOU LITTLE IDIOT.
I'M GOING TO KISS YOU.
GO AHEAD.
NO, I'M NOT QUALIFIED. LOOK AT MY FACE. RED, ISN'T IT? I'VE BEEN DRINKING.
IT'S JUST THE SUNSET SHINING ON IT. DON'T TRY TO FOOL ME.

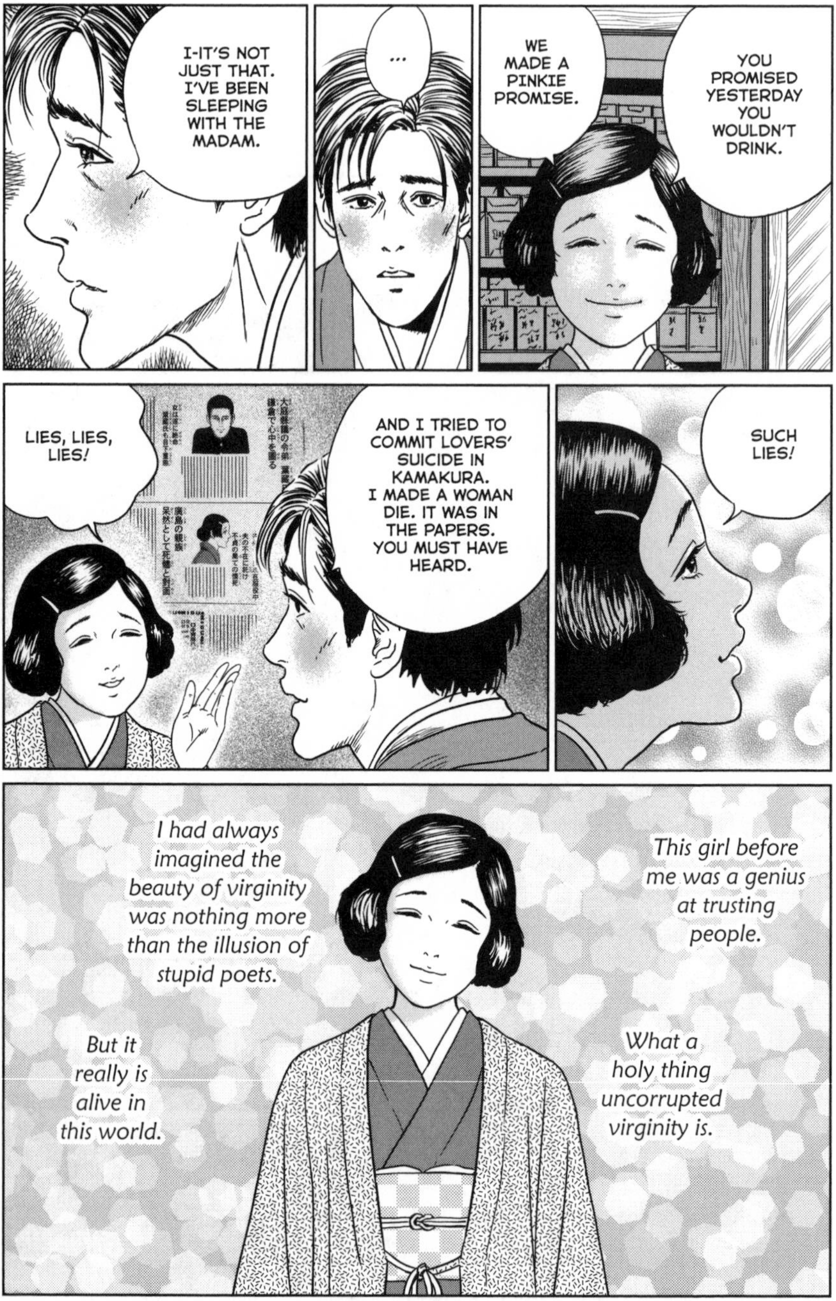
YOU PROMISED YESTERDAY YOU WOULDN'T DRINK.
WE MADE A PINKIE PROMISE.
...
I-IT'S NOT JUST THAT. I'VE BEEN SLEEPING WITH THE MADAM.
SUCH LIES!
AND I TRIED TO COMMIT LOVERS' SUICIDE IN KAMAKURA. I MADE A WOMAN DIE. IT WAS IN THE PAPERS. YOU MUST HAVE HEARD.
LIES, LIES, LIES!
This girl before me was a genius at trusting people.
What a holy thing uncorrupted virginity is.
I had always imagined the beauty of virginity was nothing more than the illusion of stupid poets.
But it really is alive in this world.

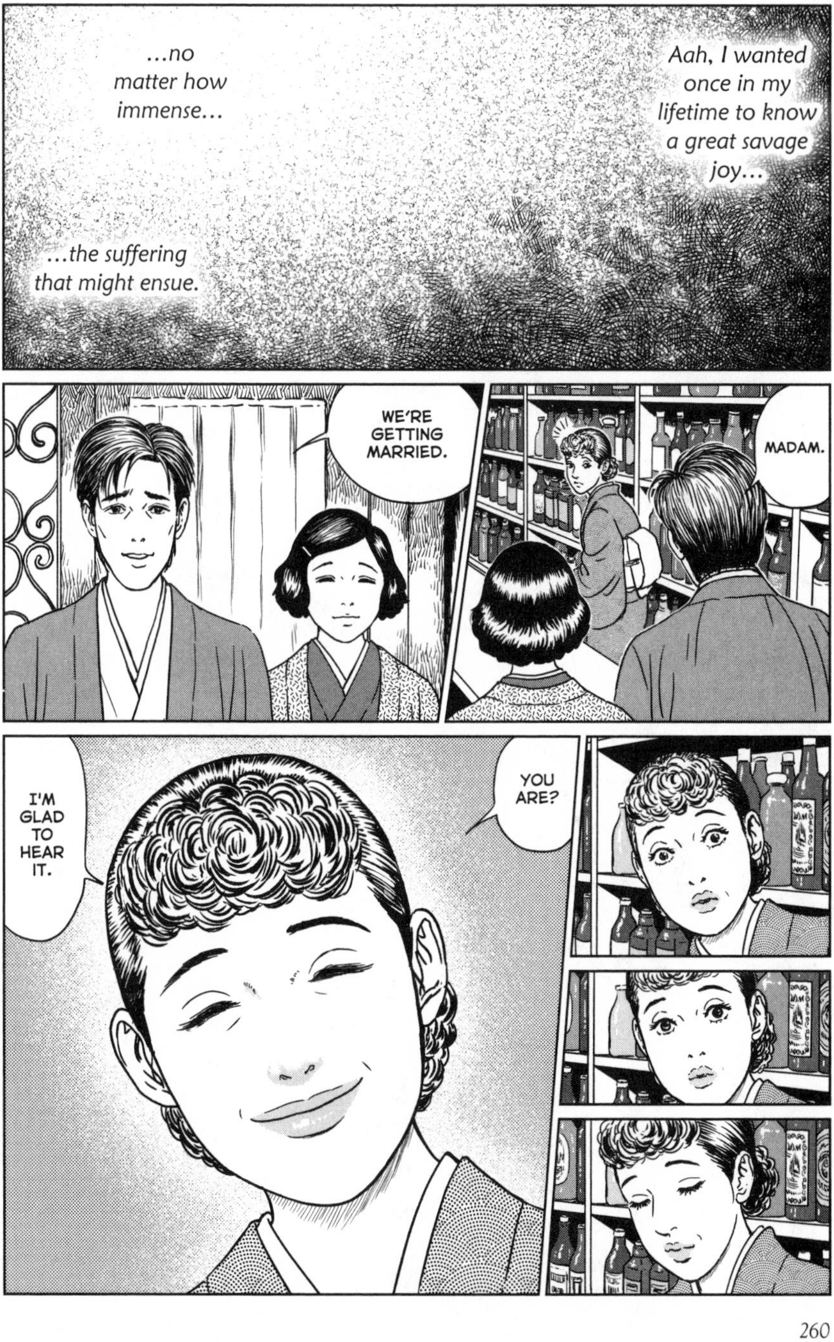
Aah, I wanted once in my lifetime to know a great savage joy…
…no matter how immense…
…the suffering that might ensue.
MADAM.
WE'RE GETTING MARRIED.
YOU ARE?
I'M GLAD TO HEAR IT.

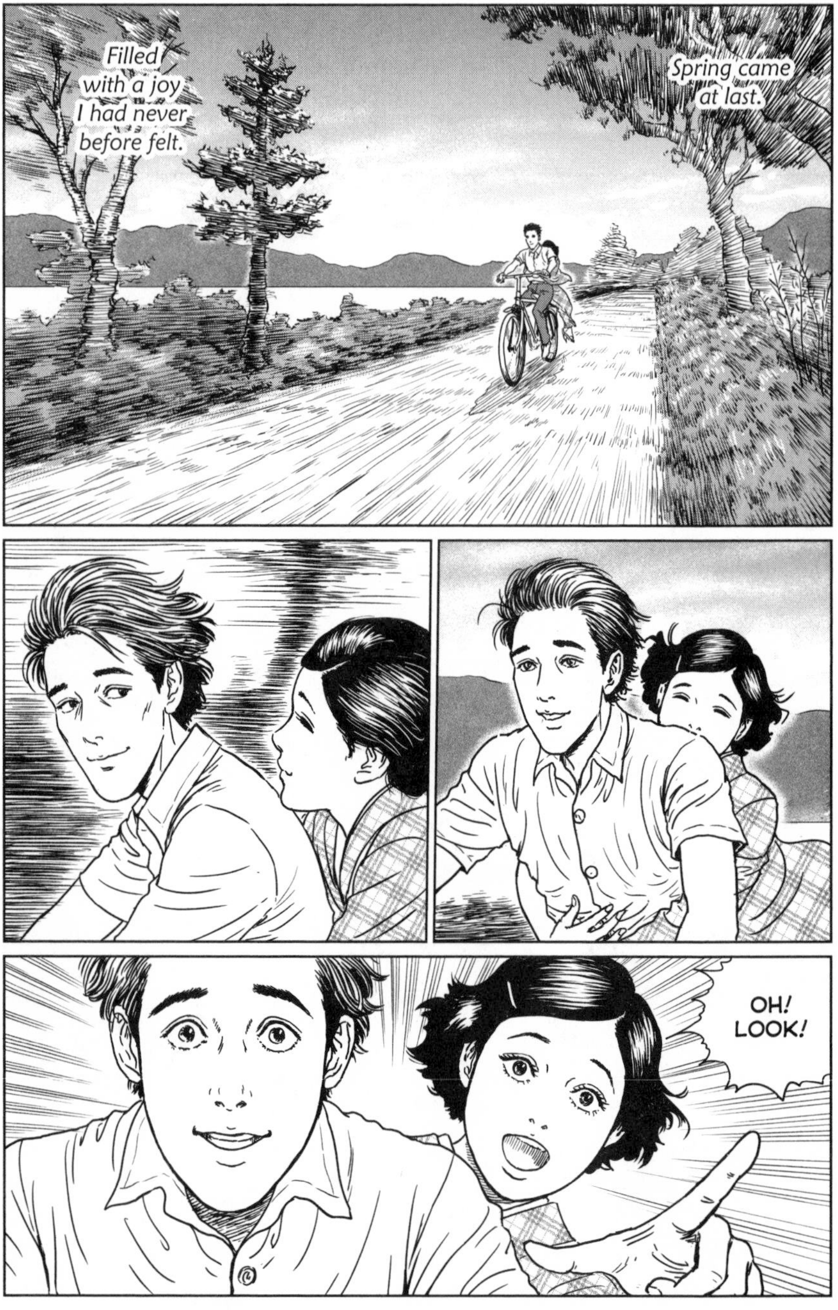
Spring came at last.
Filled with a joy I had never before felt.
OH! LOOK!

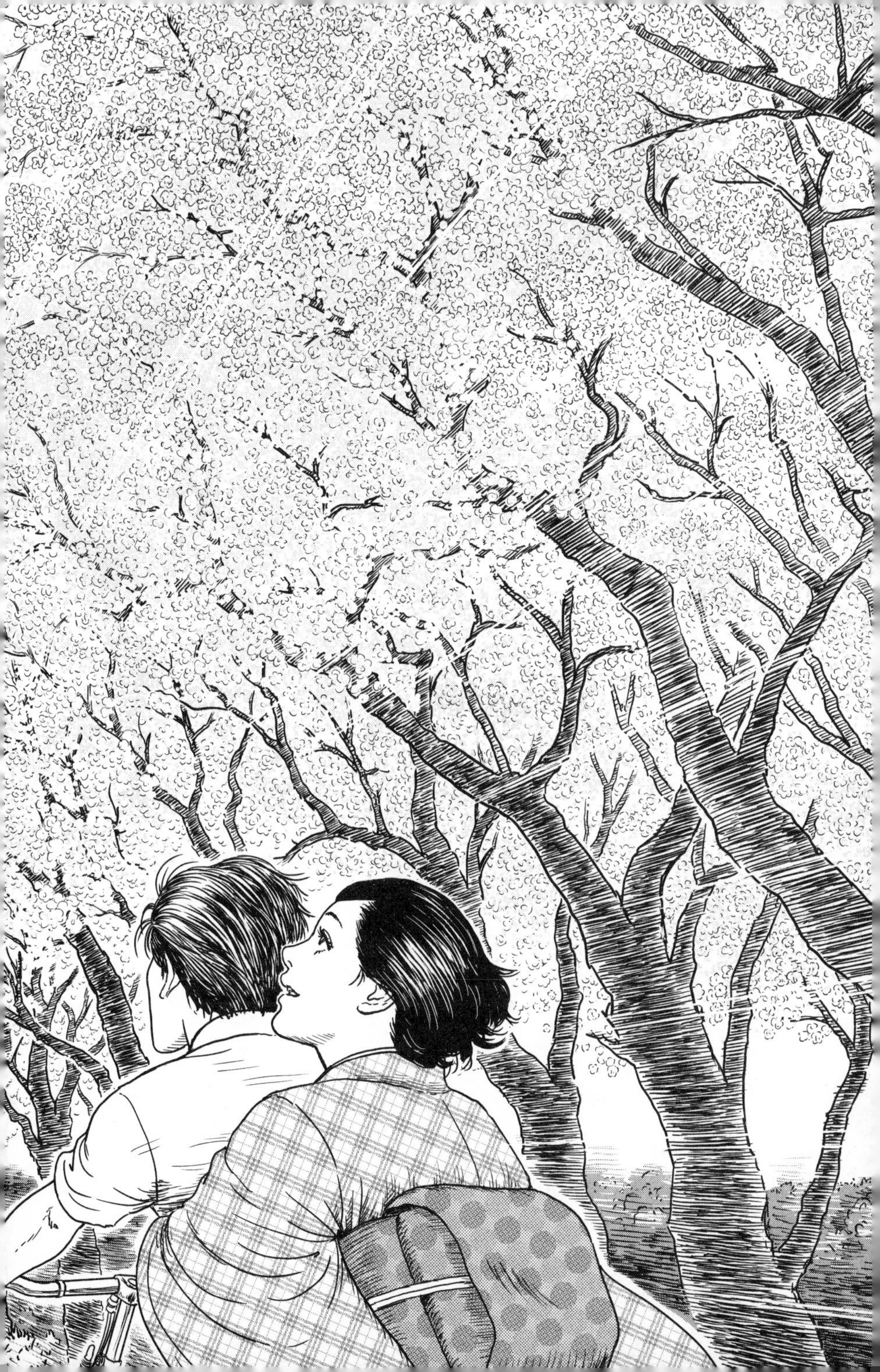

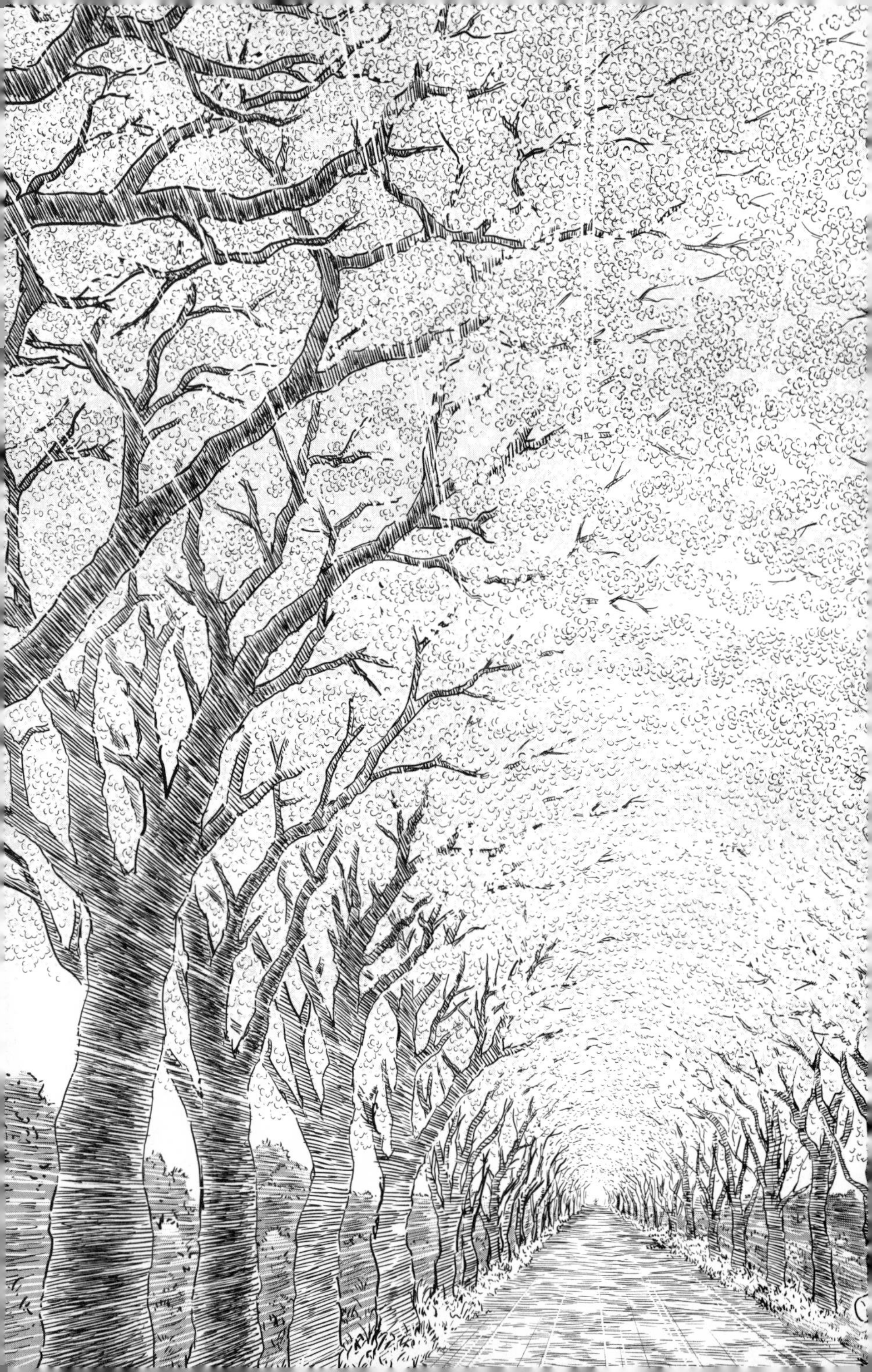

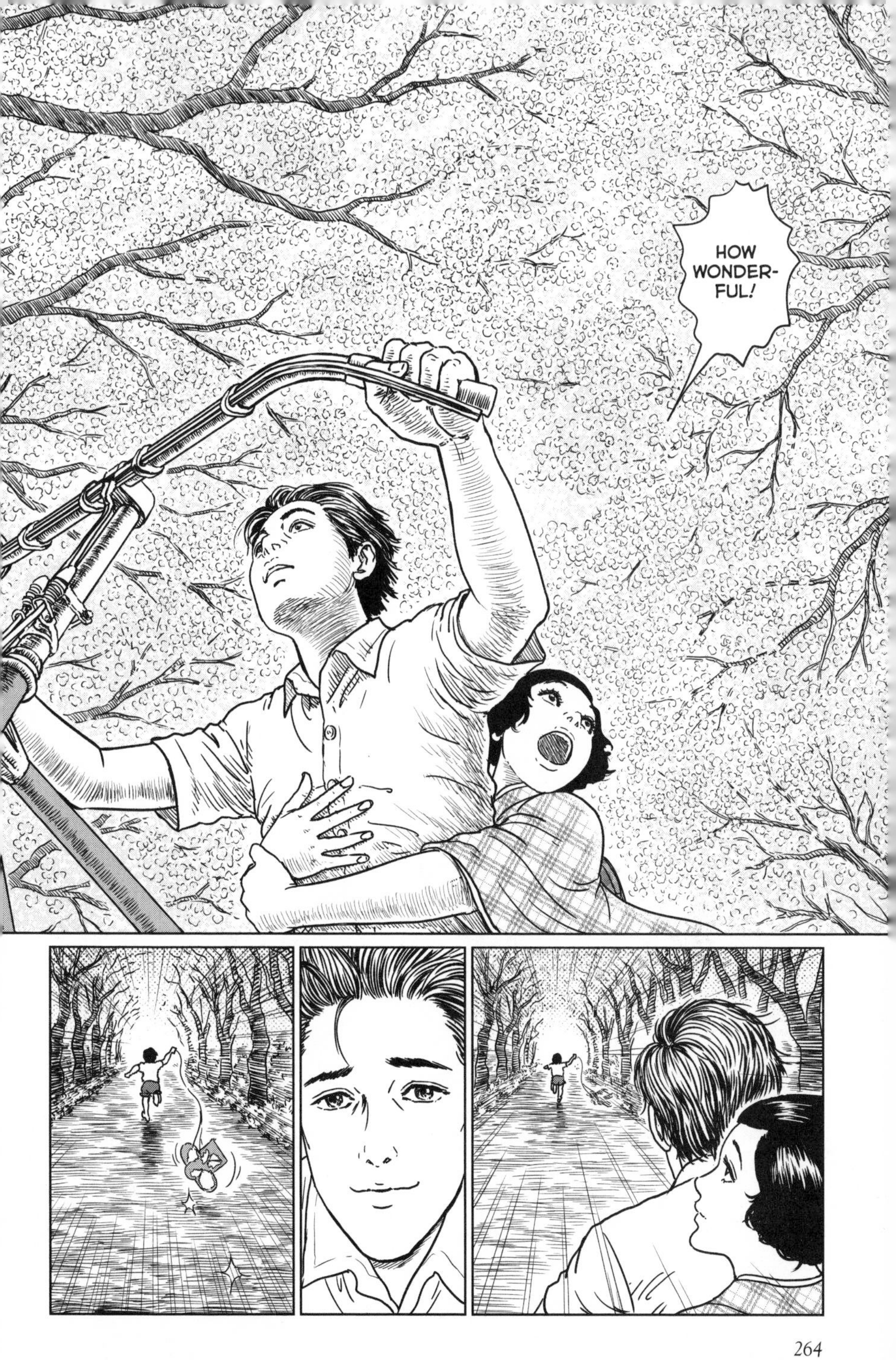
HOW WONDER-FUL!

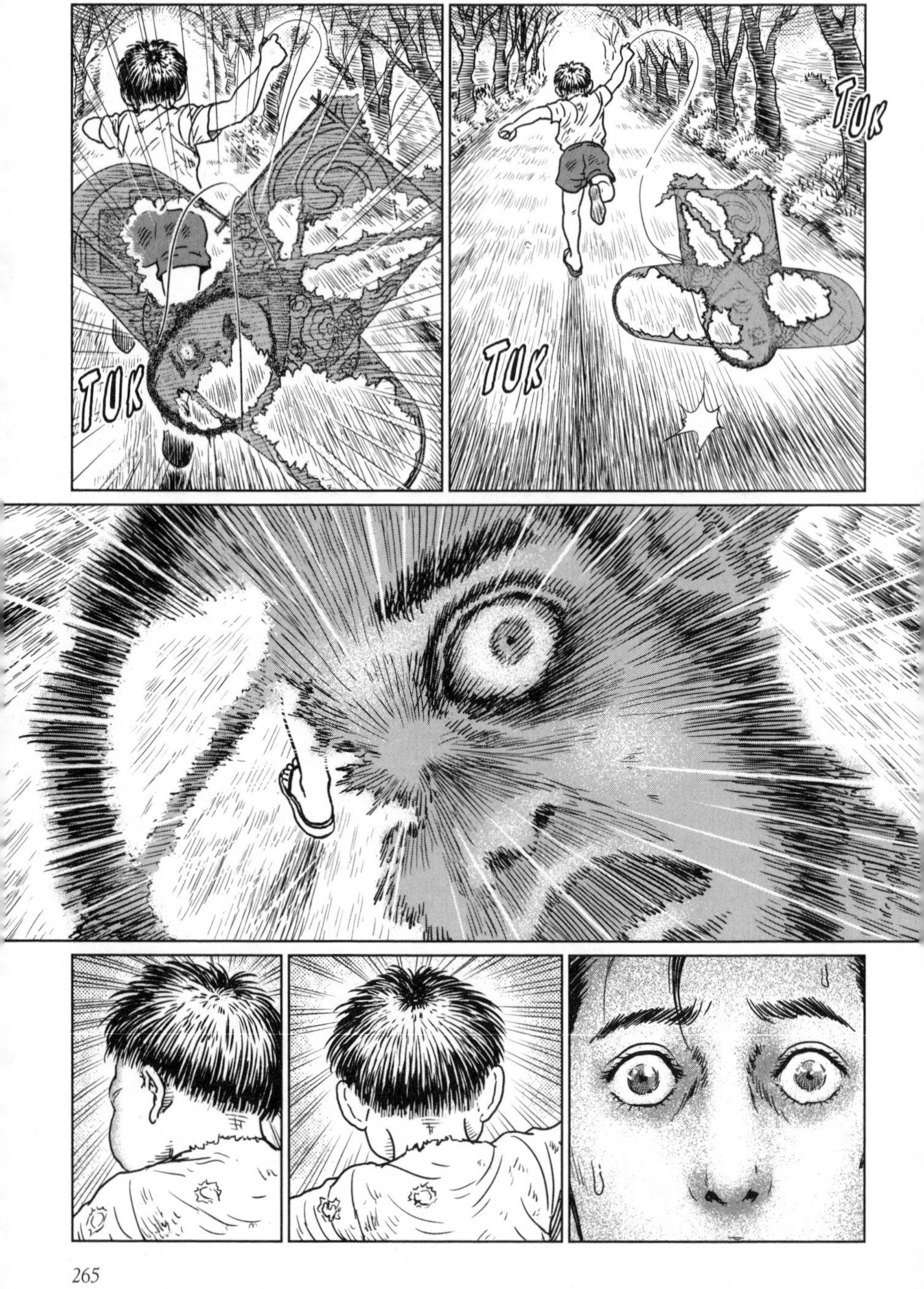
TUK
TUK
TUK

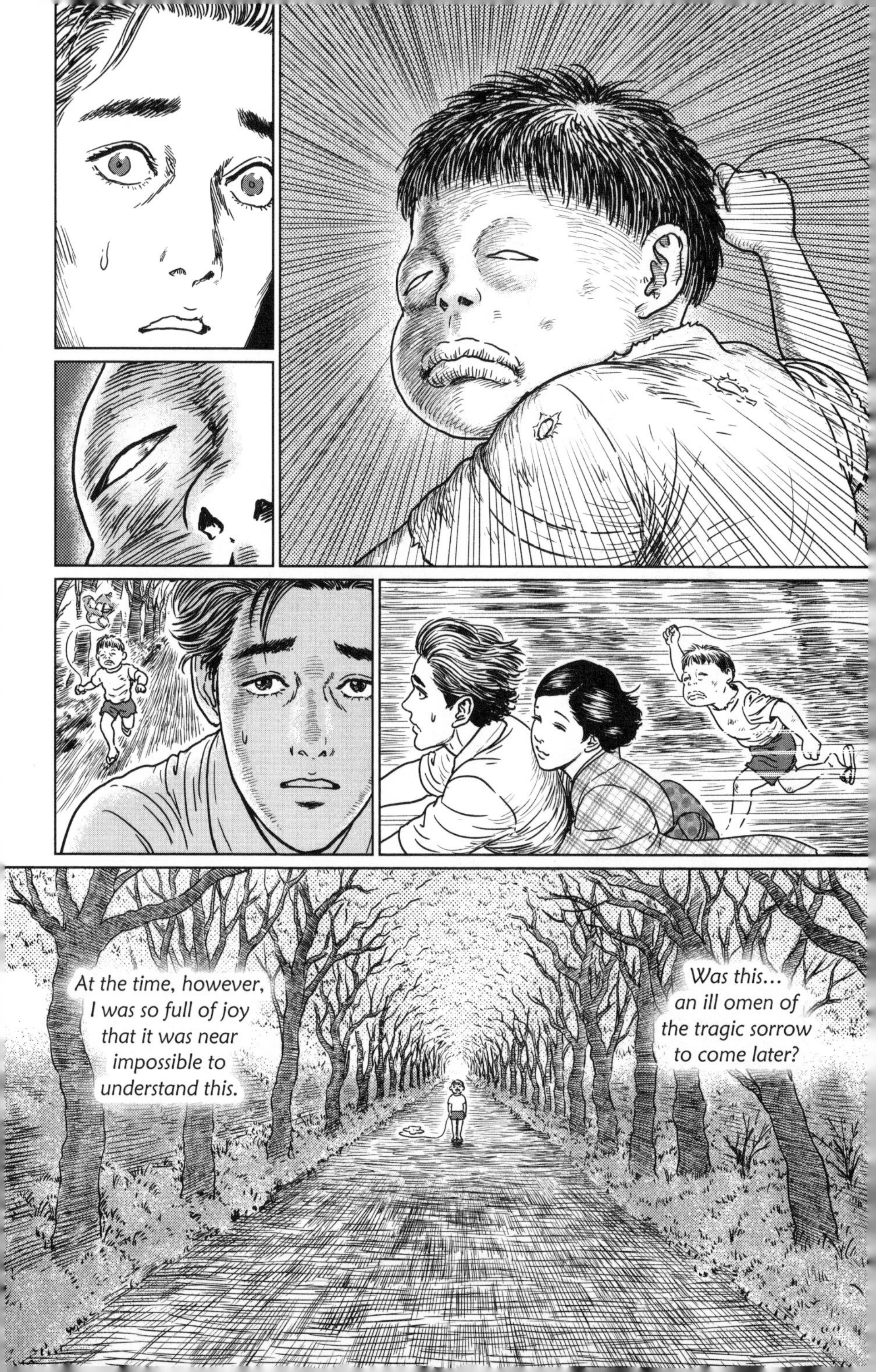
Was this… an ill omen of the tragic sorrow to come later?
At the time, however, I was so full of joy that it was near impossible to understand this.

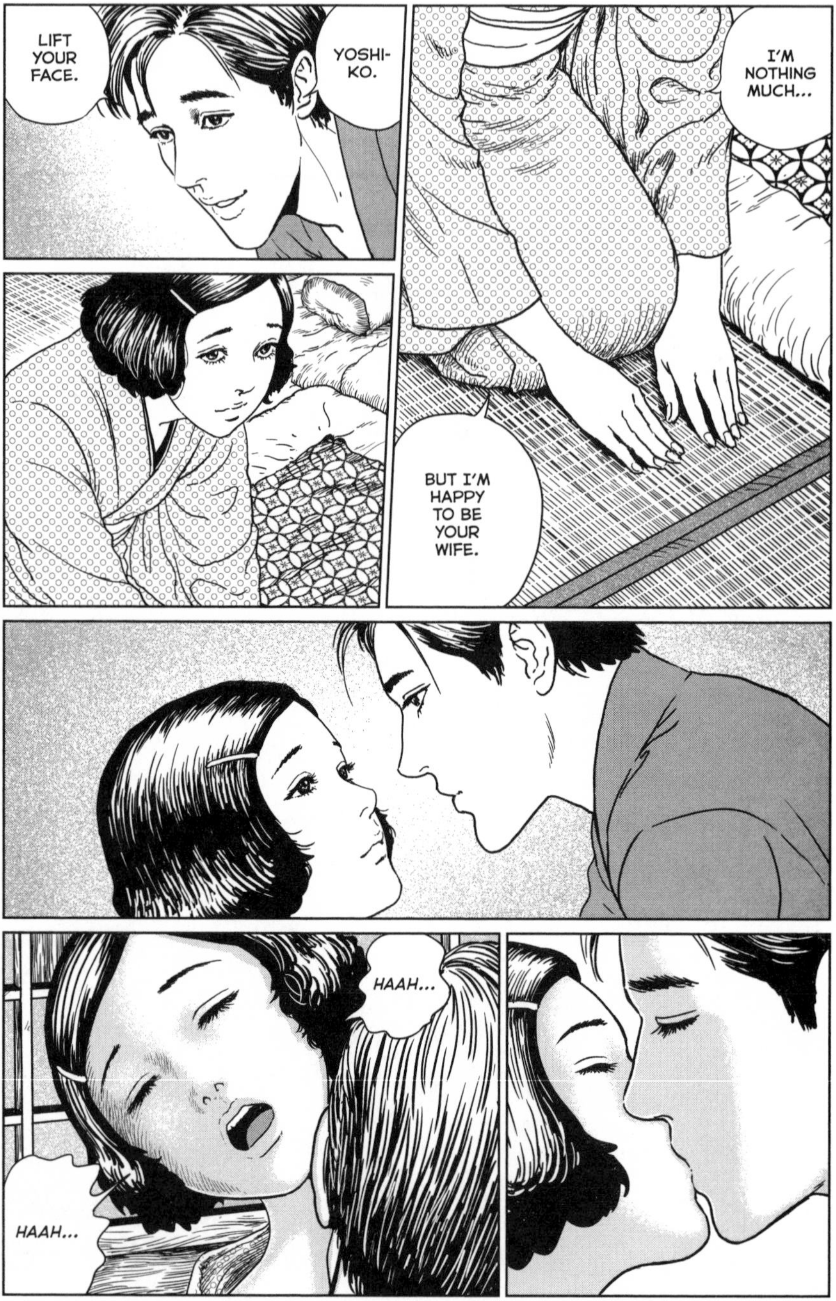
I'M NOTHING MUCH...
BUT I'M HAPPY TO BE YOUR WIFE.
YOSHI-KO.
LIFT YOUR FACE.
HAAH...
HAAH...

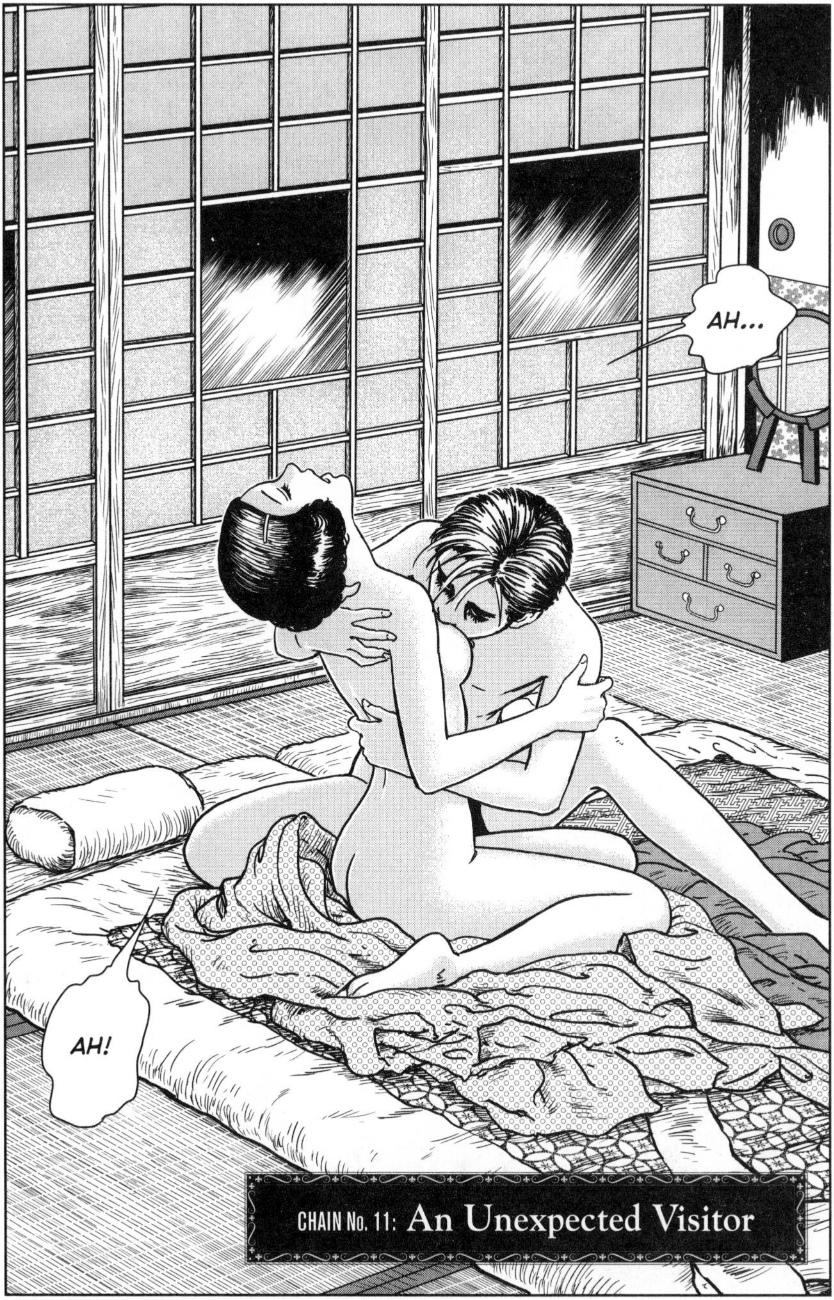
AH...
AH!
CHAIN No. 11: An Unexpected Visitor

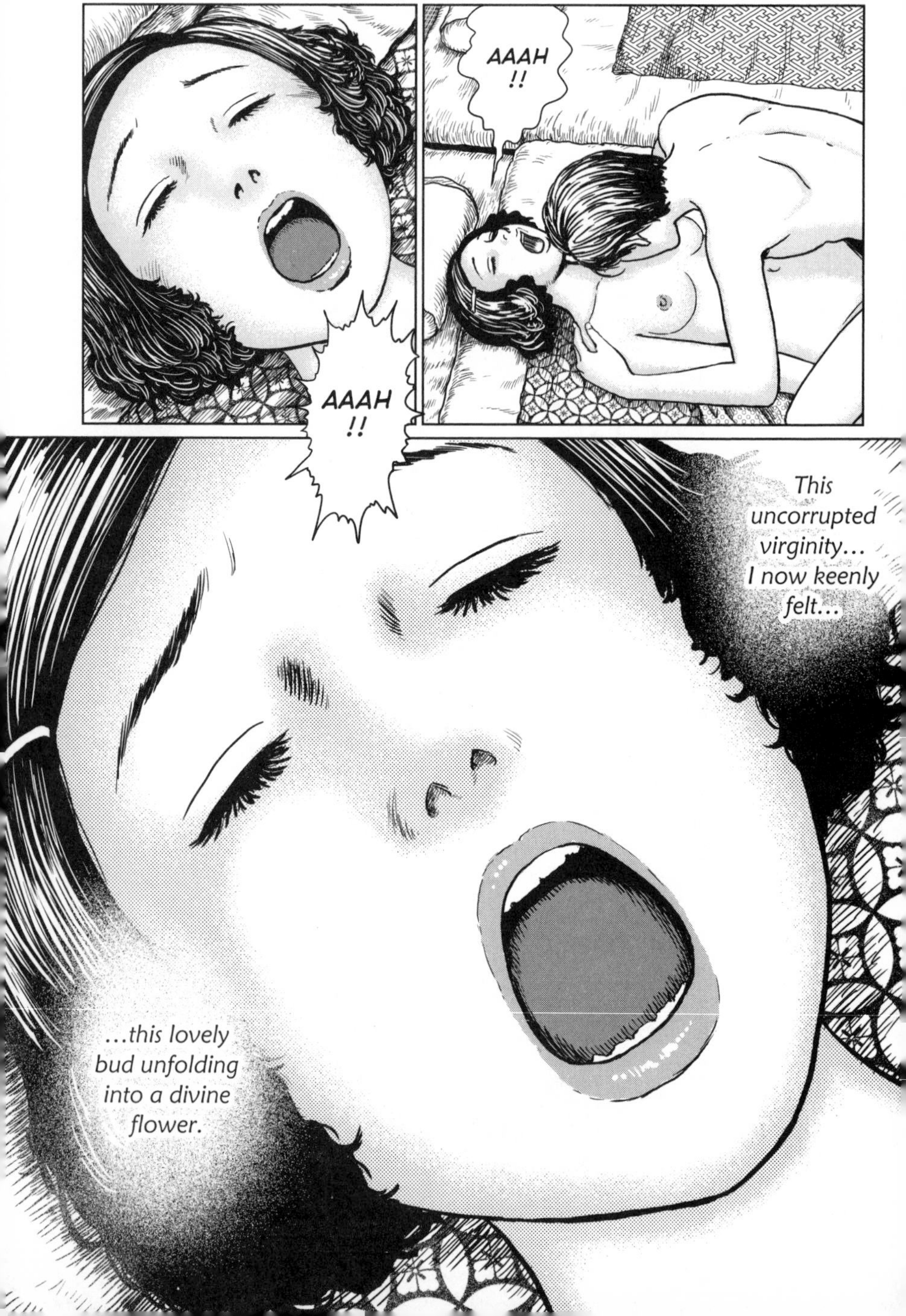
AAAH !!
AAAH !!
This uncorrupted virginity… I now keenly felt…
…this lovely bud unfolding into a divine flower.

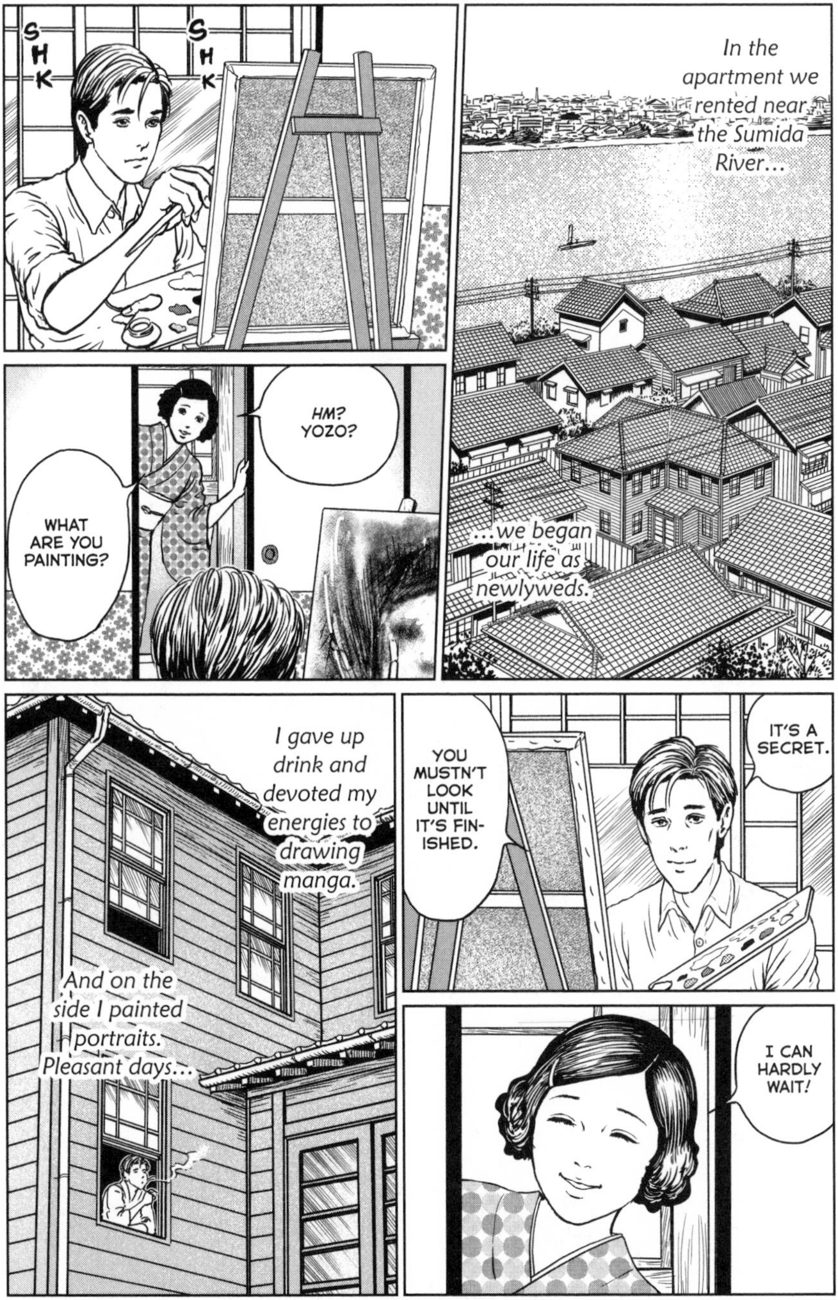
In the apartment we rented near the Sumida River...
...we began our life as newlyweds.
SHK
SHK
HM? YOZO?
WHAT ARE YOU PAINTING?
IT'S A SECRET.
YOU MUSTN'T LOOK UNTIL IT'S FIN-ISHED.
I CAN HARDLY WAIT!
I gave up drink and devoted my energies to drawing manga.
And on the side I painted portraits. Pleasant days...

Gidayu Nitohei (Puppet Theater Private) by Ikita Joshi

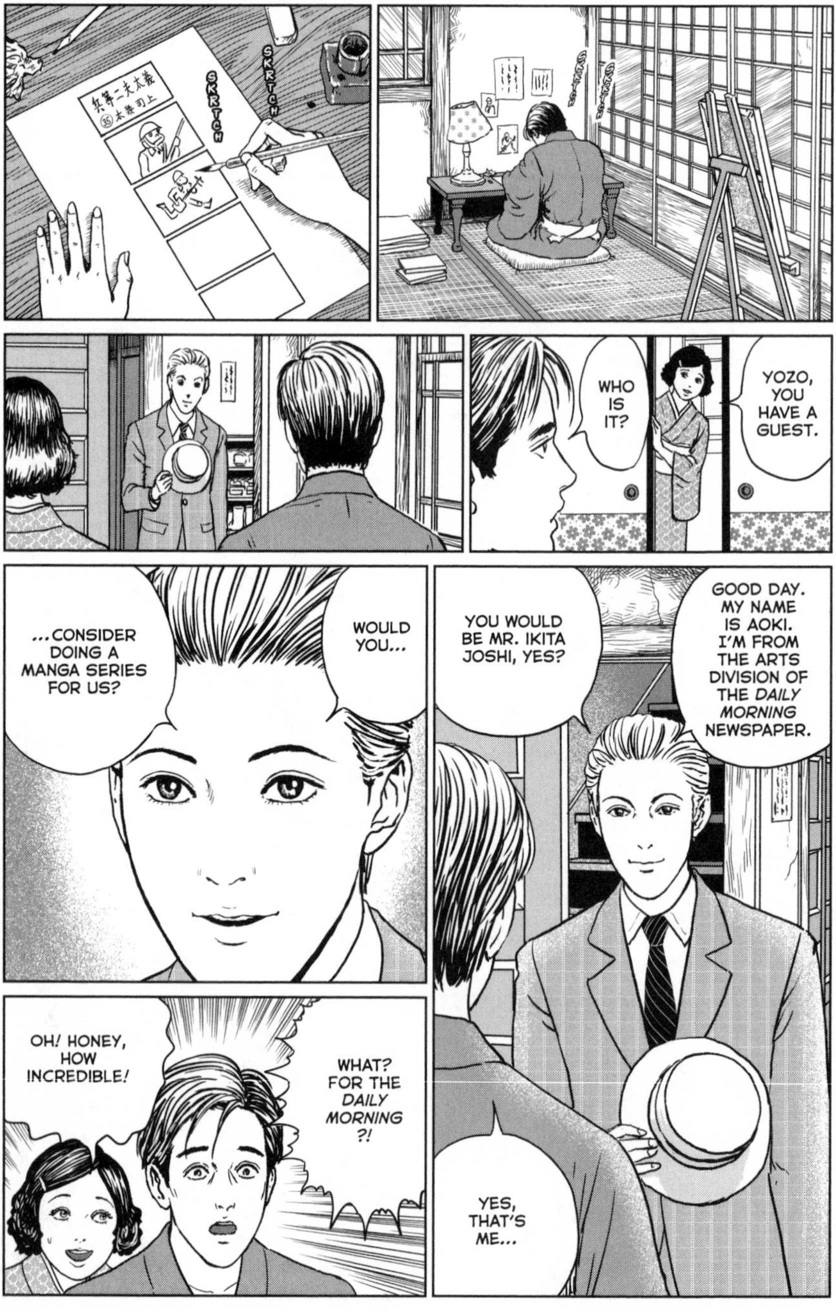
SKRTCH
SKRTCH
SKRTCH
SKRTCH
YOZO, YOU HAVE A GUEST.
WHO IS IT?
GOOD DAY. MY NAME IS AOKI. I'M FROM THE ARTS DIVISION OF THE *DAILY MORNING* NEWSPAPER.
YOU WOULD BE MR. IKITA JOSHI, YES?
YES, THAT'S ME...
WOULD YOU...
...CONSIDER DOING A MANGA SERIES FOR US?
WHAT? FOR THE *DAILY MORNING* ?!
OH! HONEY, HOW INCREDIBLE!

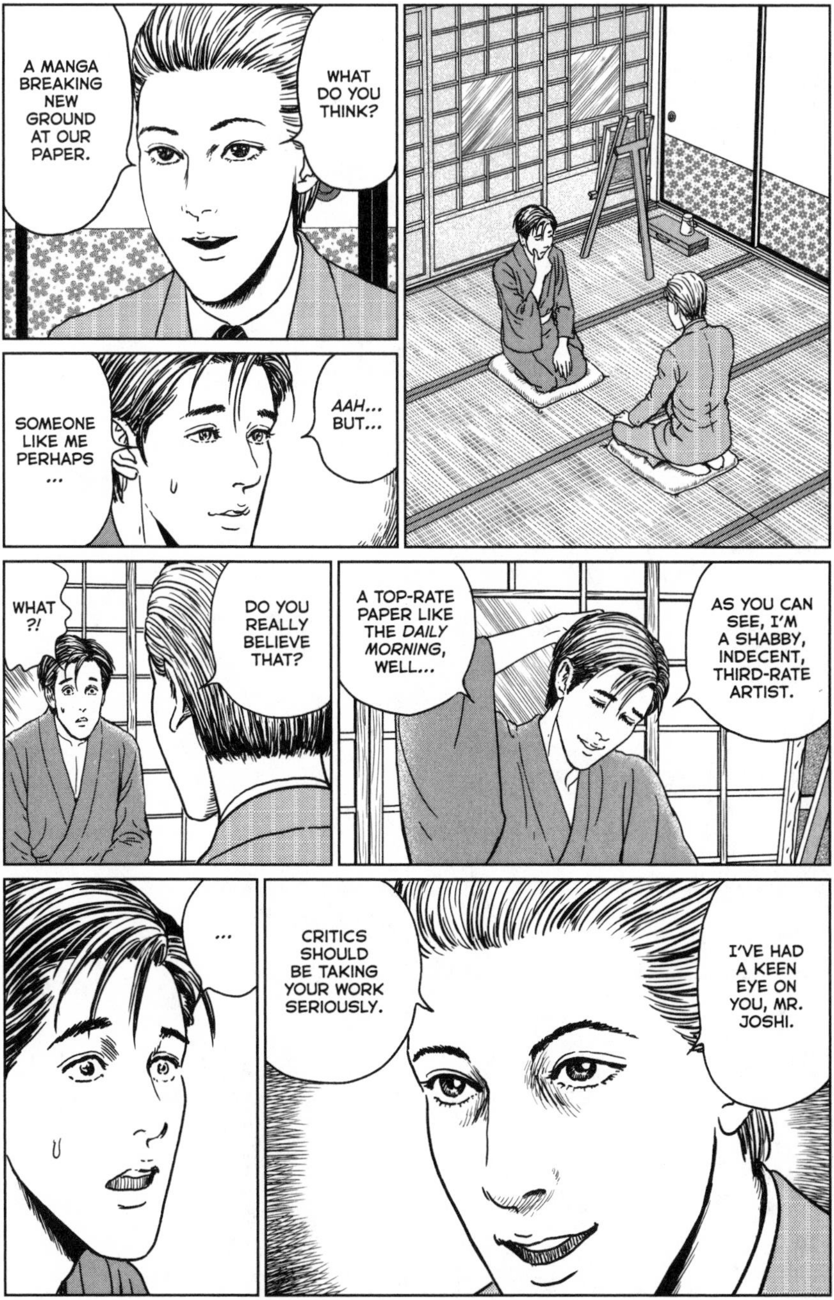
WHAT DO YOU THINK?
A MANGA BREAKING NEW GROUND AT OUR PAPER.
AAH... BUT...
SOMEONE LIKE ME PERHAPS ...
AS YOU CAN SEE, I'M A SHABBY, INDECENT, THIRD-RATE ARTIST.
A TOP-RATE PAPER LIKE THE *DAILY MORNING*, WELL...
DO YOU REALLY BELIEVE THAT?
WHAT ?!
I'VE HAD A KEEN EYE ON YOU, MR. JOSHI.
CRITICS SHOULD BE TAKING YOUR WORK SERIOUSLY.
...

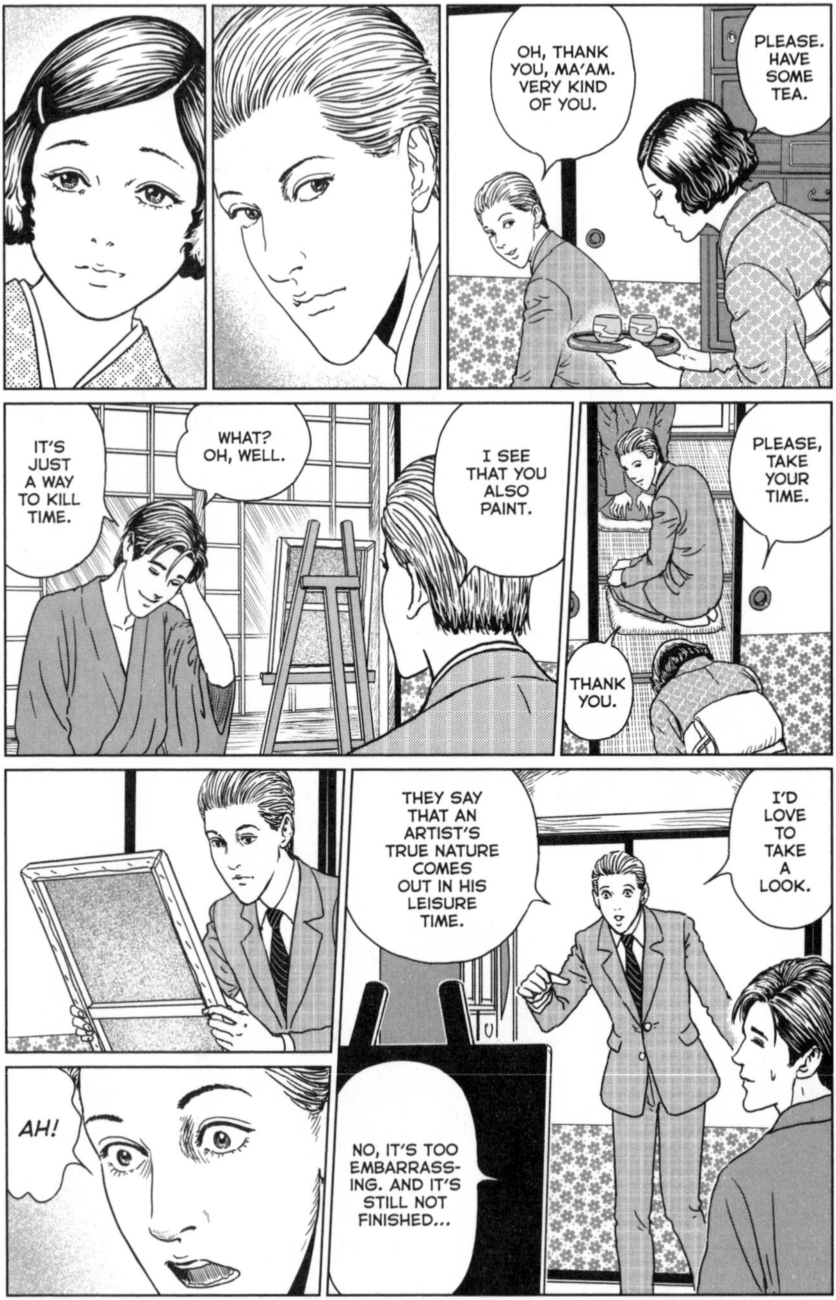
PLEASE. HAVE SOME TEA.
OH, THANK YOU, MA'AM. VERY KIND OF YOU.
PLEASE, TAKE YOUR TIME.
THANK YOU.
I SEE THAT YOU ALSO PAINT.
WHAT? OH, WELL.
IT'S JUST A WAY TO KILL TIME.
I'D LOVE TO TAKE A LOOK.
THEY SAY THAT AN ARTIST'S TRUE NATURE COMES OUT IN HIS LEISURE TIME.
NO, IT'S TOO EMBARRASSING. AND IT'S STILL NOT FINISHED...
AH!

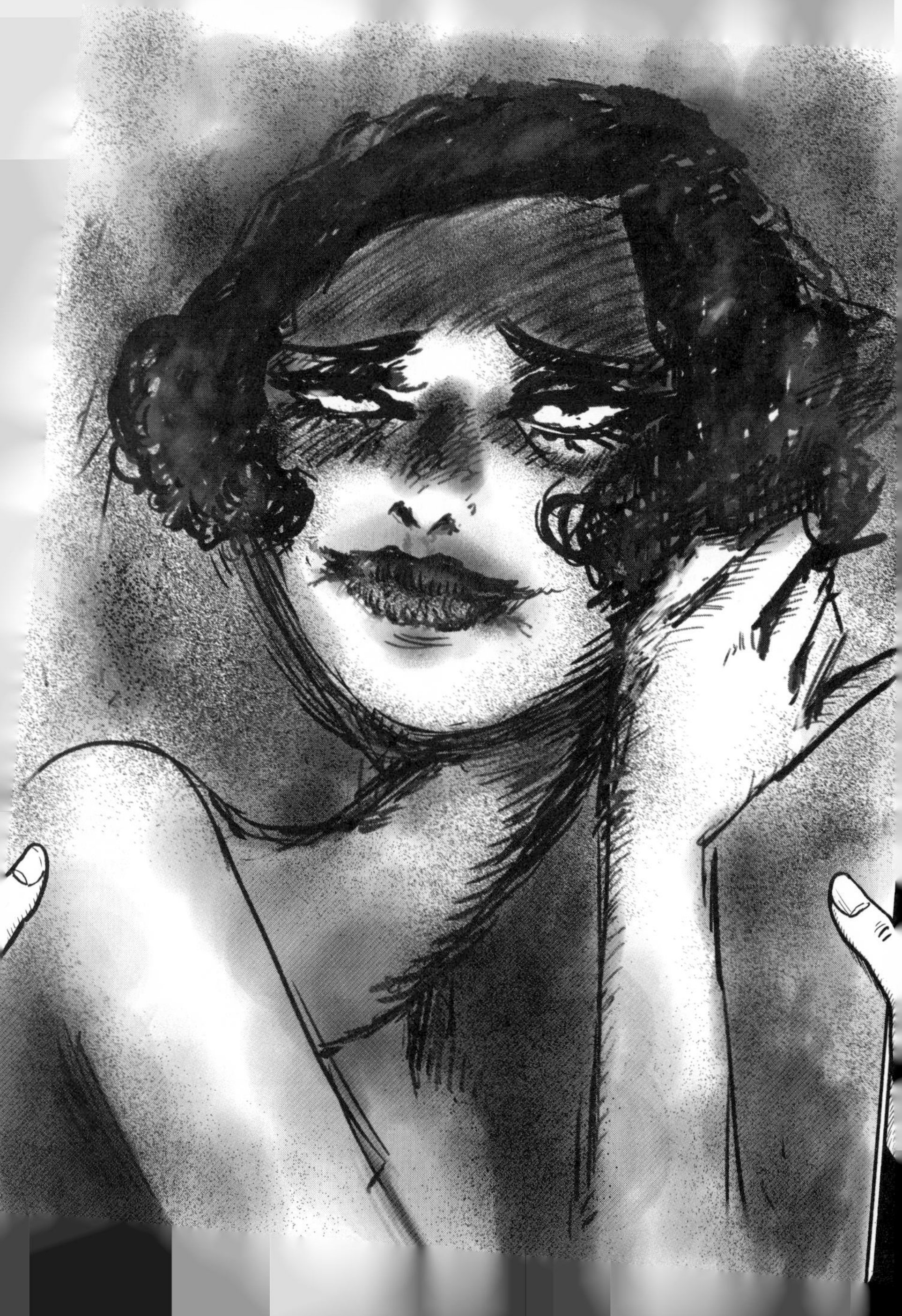

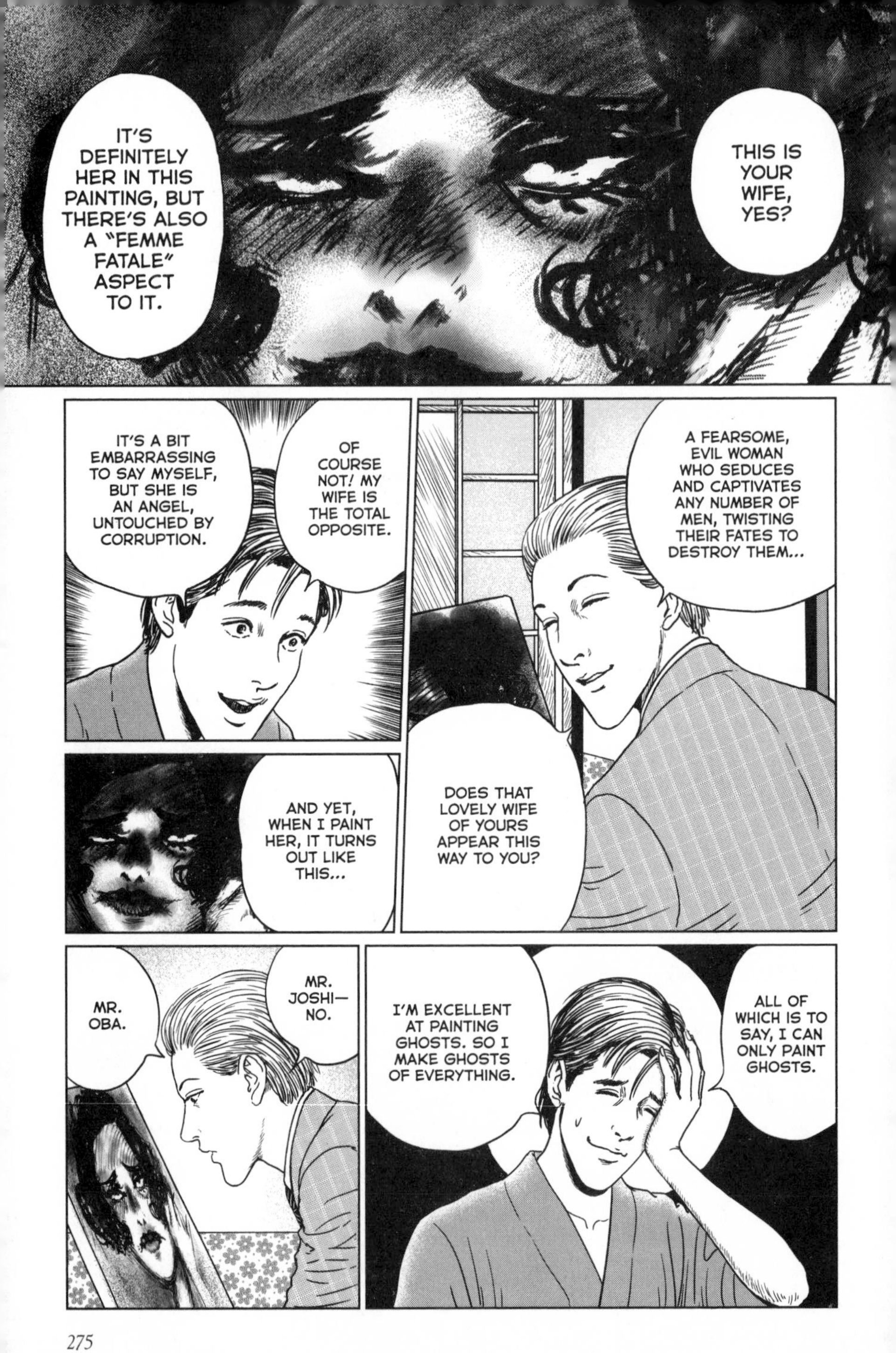
THIS IS YOUR WIFE, YES?
IT'S DEFINITELY HER IN THIS PAINTING, BUT THERE'S ALSO A "FEMME FATALE" ASPECT TO IT.
A FEARSOME, EVIL WOMAN WHO SEDUCES AND CAPTIVATES ANY NUMBER OF MEN, TWISTING THEIR FATES TO DESTROY THEM...
DOES THAT LOVELY WIFE OF YOURS APPEAR THIS WAY TO YOU?
OF COURSE NOT! MY WIFE IS THE TOTAL OPPOSITE.
IT'S A BIT EMBARRASSING TO SAY MYSELF, BUT SHE IS AN ANGEL, UNTOUCHED BY CORRUPTION.
AND YET, WHEN I PAINT HER, IT TURNS OUT LIKE THIS...
I'M EXCELLENT AT PAINTING GHOSTS. SO I MAKE GHOSTS OF EVERYTHING.
ALL OF WHICH IS TO SAY, I CAN ONLY PAINT GHOSTS.
MR. JOSHI-NO.
MR. OBA.

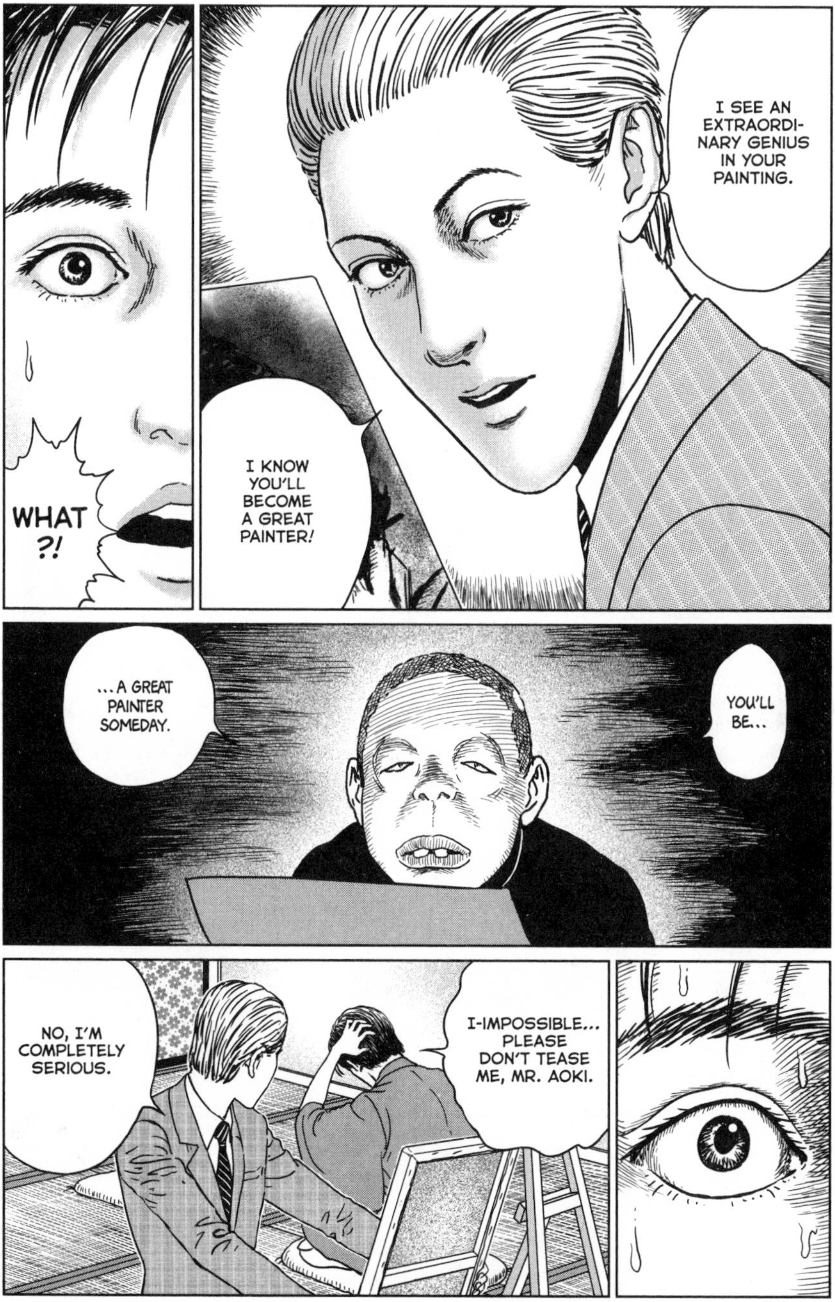
I SEE AN EXTRAORDINARY GENIUS IN YOUR PAINTING.
I KNOW YOU'LL BECOME A GREAT PAINTER!
WHAT ?!
YOU'LL BE...
...A GREAT PAINTER SOMEDAY.
I-IMPOSSIBLE... PLEASE DON'T TEASE ME, MR. AOKI.
NO, I'M COMPLETELY SERIOUS.

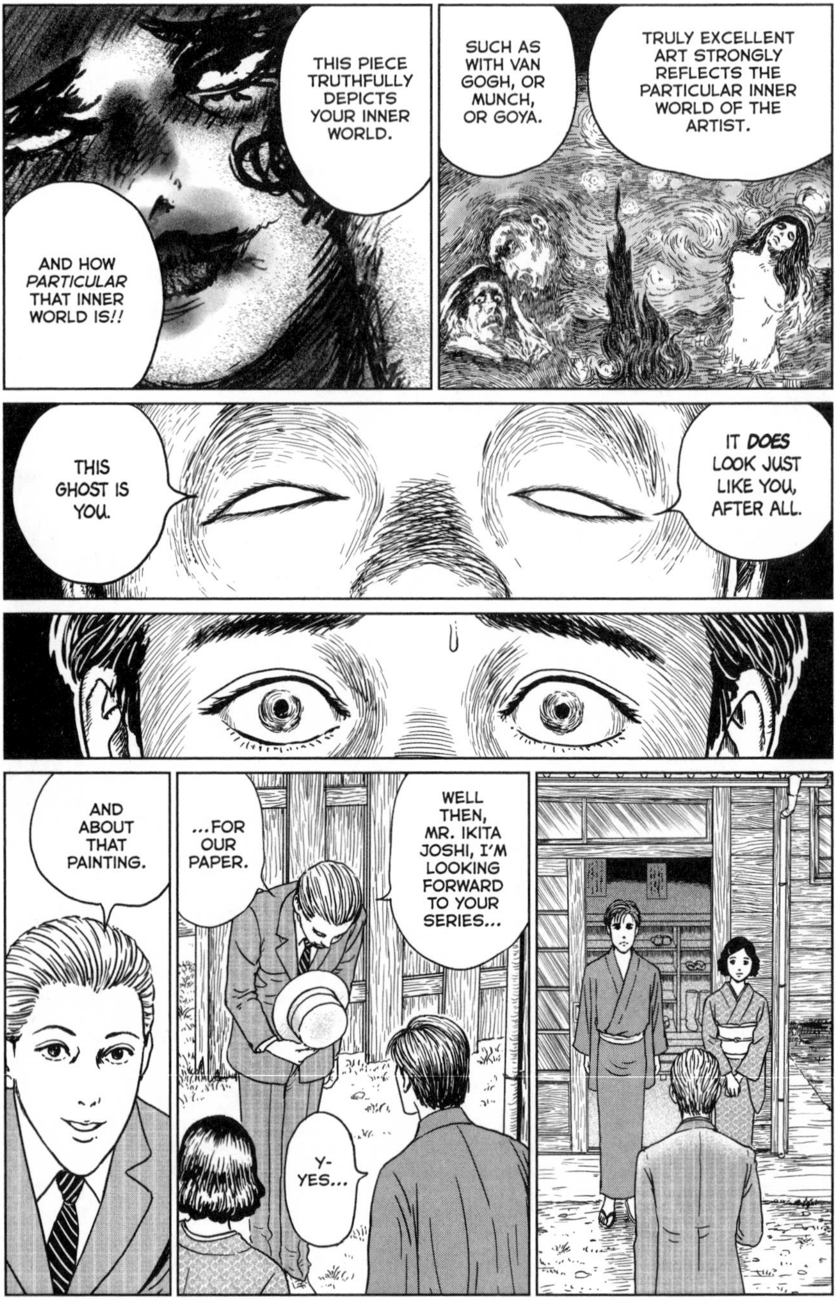
TRULY EXCELLENT ART STRONGLY REFLECTS THE PARTICULAR INNER WORLD OF THE ARTIST.
SUCH AS WITH VAN GOGH, OR MUNCH, OR GOYA.
THIS PIECE TRUTHFULLY DEPICTS YOUR INNER WORLD.
AND HOW *PARTICULAR* THAT INNER WORLD IS!!
IT **DOES** LOOK JUST LIKE YOU, AFTER ALL.
THIS GHOST IS YOU.
WELL THEN, MR. IKITA JOSHI, I'M LOOKING FORWARD TO YOUR SERIES...
...FOR OUR PAPER.
Y-YES...
AND ABOUT THAT PAINTING.

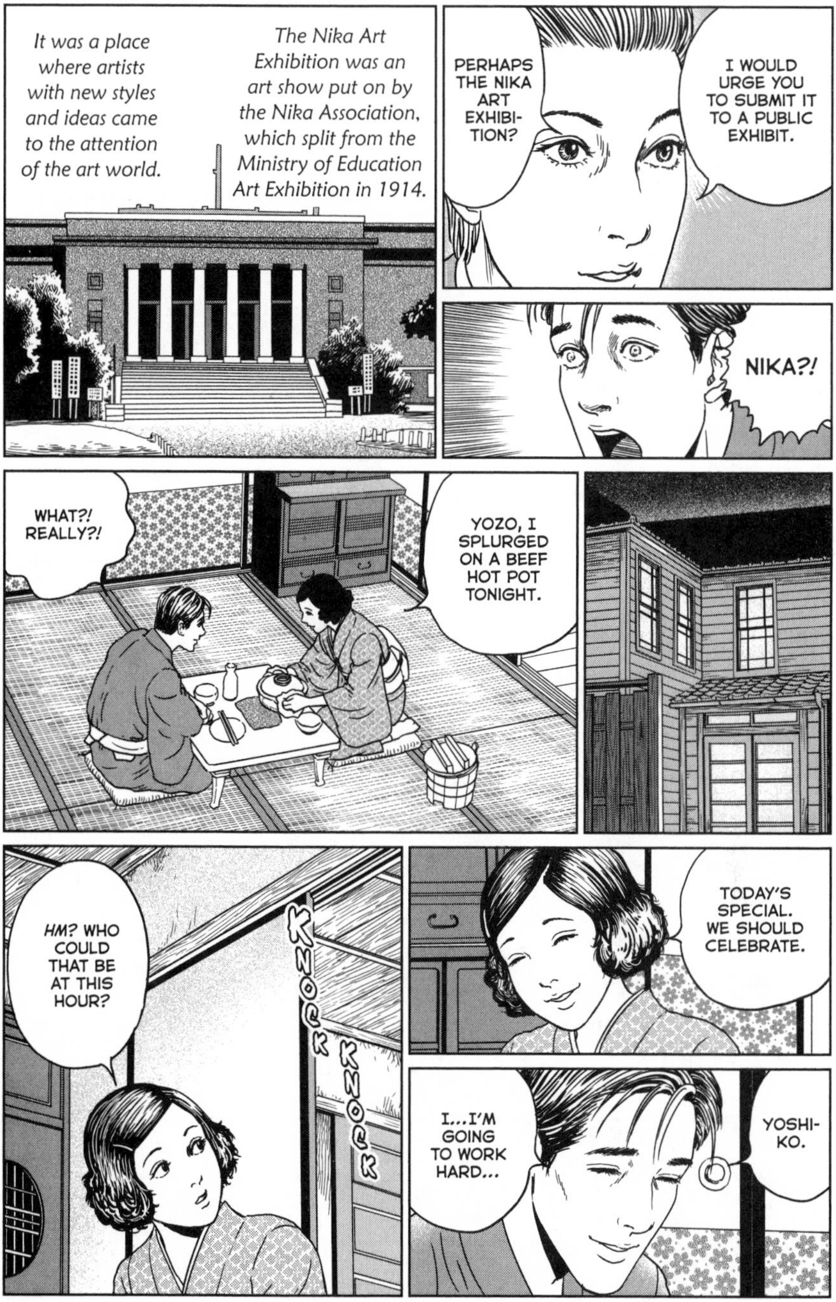
I WOULD URGE YOU TO SUBMIT IT TO A PUBLIC EXHIBIT.
PERHAPS THE NIKA ART EXHIBITION?
NIKA?!
The Nika Art Exhibition was an art show put on by the Nika Association, which split from the Ministry of Education Art Exhibition in 1914.
It was a place where artists with new styles and ideas came to the attention of the art world.
YOZO, I SPLURGED ON A BEEF HOT POT TONIGHT.
WHAT?! REALLY?!
TODAY'S SPECIAL. WE SHOULD CELEBRATE.
YOSHIKO.
I...I'M GOING TO WORK HARD...
KNOCK KNOCK
HM? WHO COULD THAT BE AT THIS HOUR?

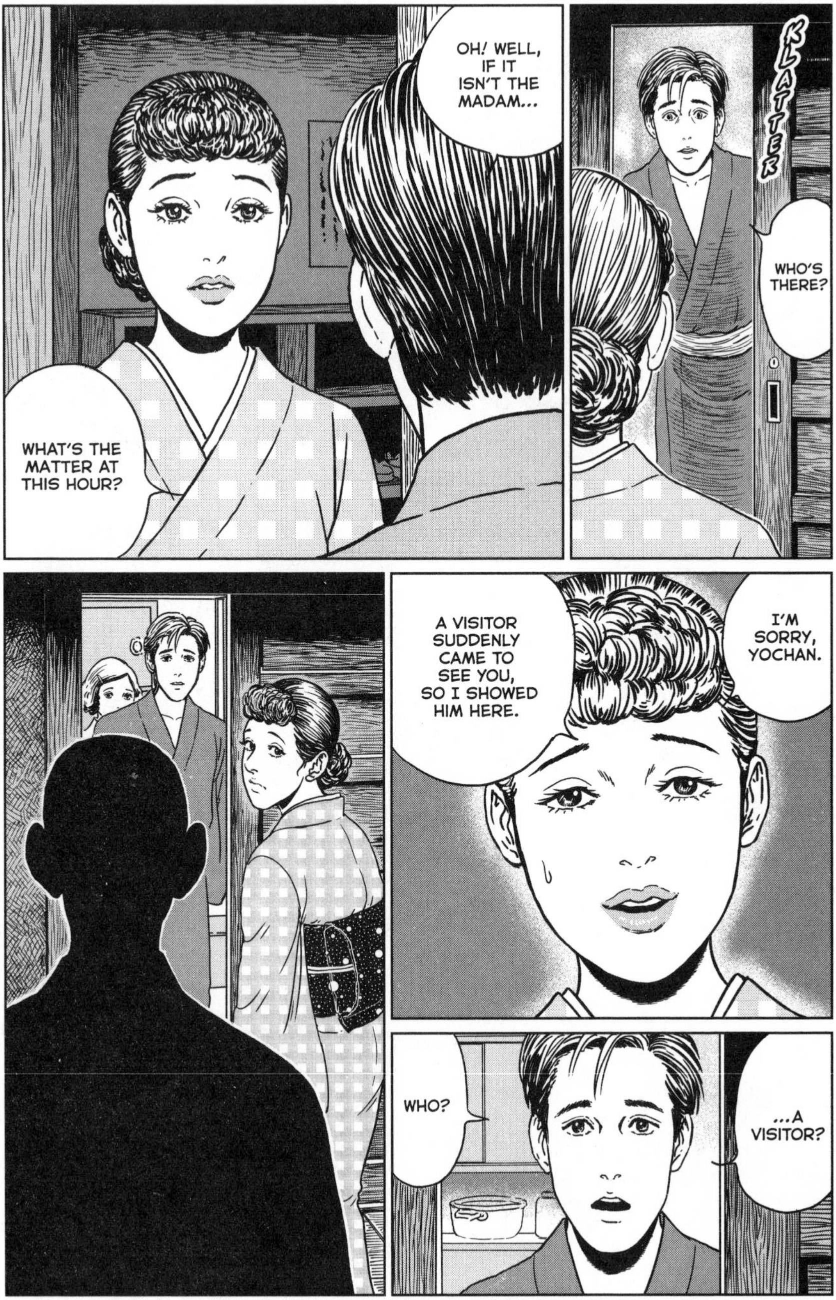
KLATTER
WHO'S THERE?
OH! WELL, IF IT ISN'T THE MADAM...
WHAT'S THE MATTER AT THIS HOUR?
I'M SORRY, YOCHAN.
A VISITOR SUDDENLY CAME TO SEE YOU, SO I SHOWED HIM HERE.
...A VISITOR?
WHO?

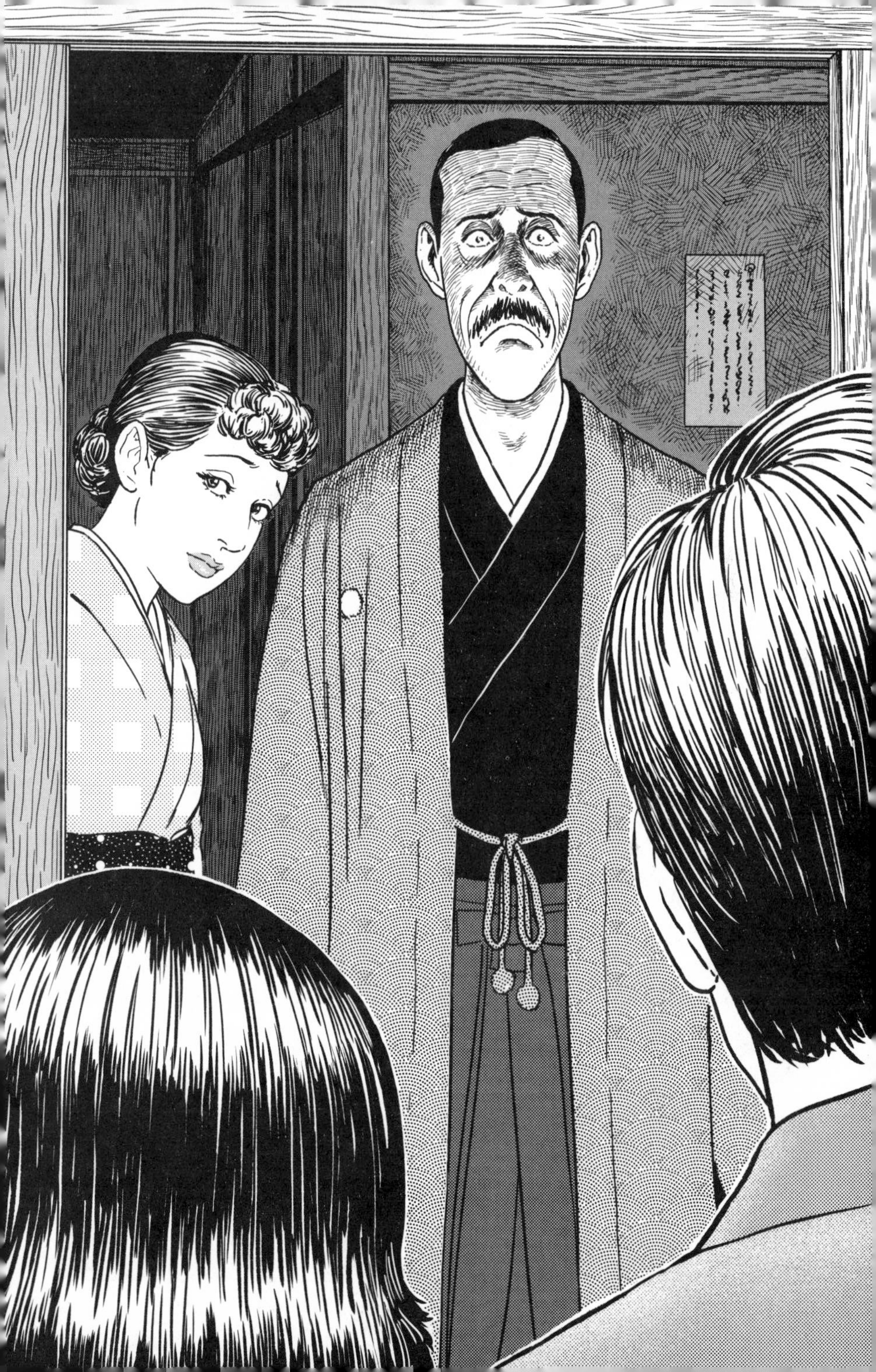

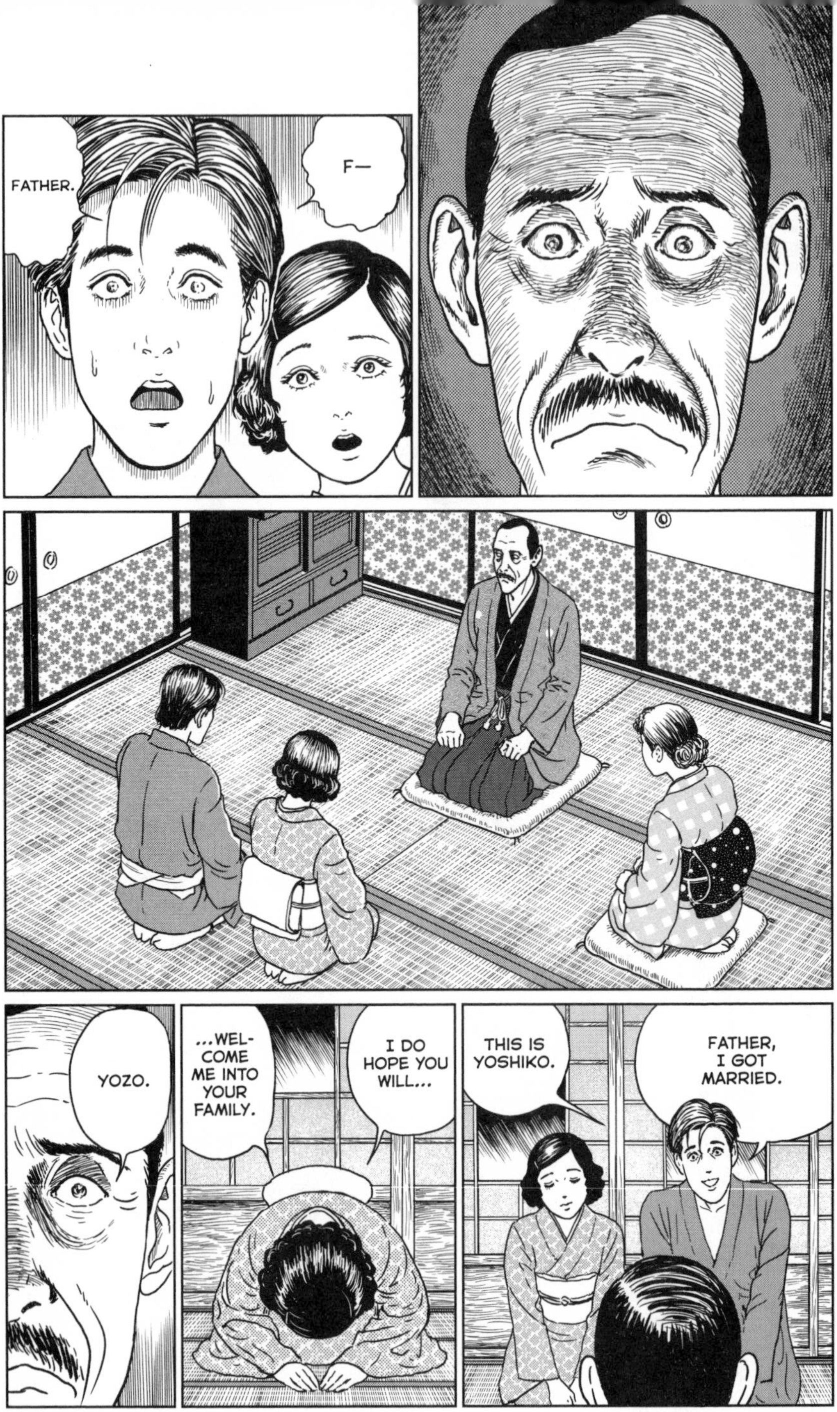
F—
FATHER.
FATHER, I GOT MARRIED.
THIS IS YOSHIKO.
I DO HOPE YOU WILL...
...WEL-COME ME INTO YOUR FAMILY.
YOZO.

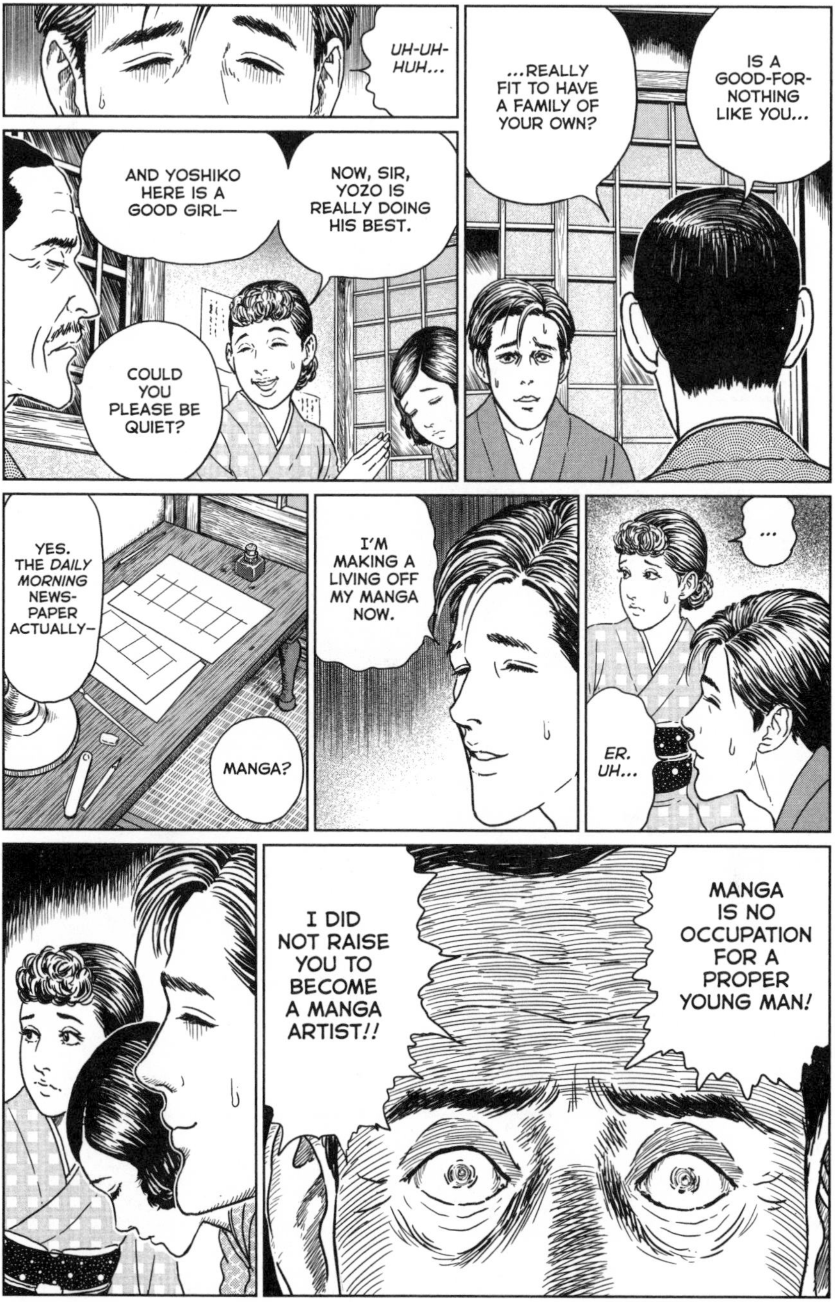
IS A GOOD-FOR-NOTHING LIKE YOU...
...REALLY FIT TO HAVE A FAMILY OF YOUR OWN?
UH-UH-HUH...
NOW, SIR, YOZO IS REALLY DOING HIS BEST.
AND YOSHIKO HERE IS A GOOD GIRL—
COULD YOU PLEASE BE QUIET?
...
ER. UH...
I'M MAKING A LIVING OFF MY MANGA NOW.
MANGA?
YES. THE *DAILY MORNING* NEWSPAPER ACTUALLY—
MANGA IS NO OCCUPATION FOR A PROPER YOUNG MAN!
I DID NOT RAISE YOU TO BECOME A MANGA ARTIST!!

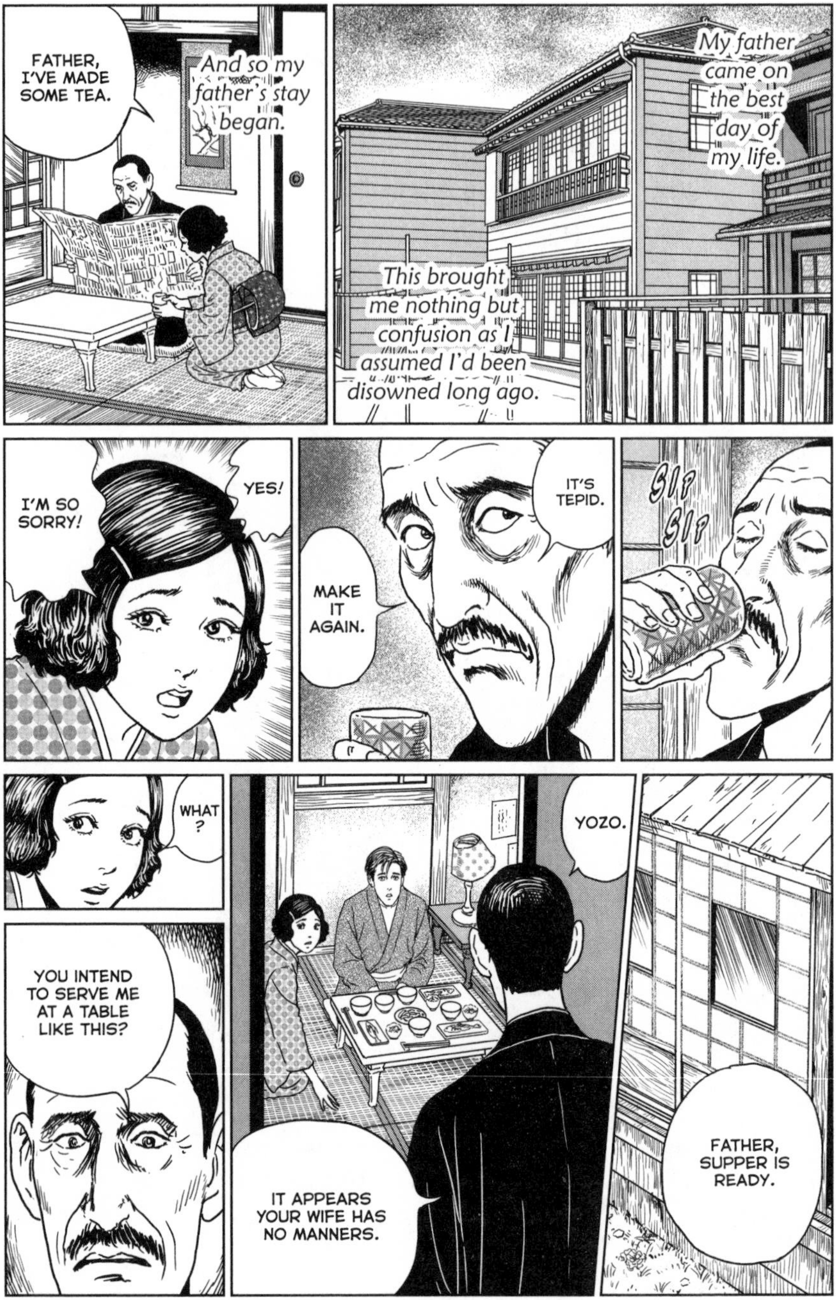
My father came on the best day of my life.
This brought me nothing but confusion as I assumed I'd been disowned long ago.
And so my father's stay began.
FATHER, I'VE MADE SOME TEA.
SIP SIP
IT'S TEPID.
MAKE IT AGAIN.
YES!
I'M SO SORRY!
FATHER, SUPPER IS READY.
YOZO.
IT APPEARS YOUR WIFE HAS NO MANNERS.
WHAT?
YOU INTEND TO SERVE ME AT A TABLE LIKE THIS?

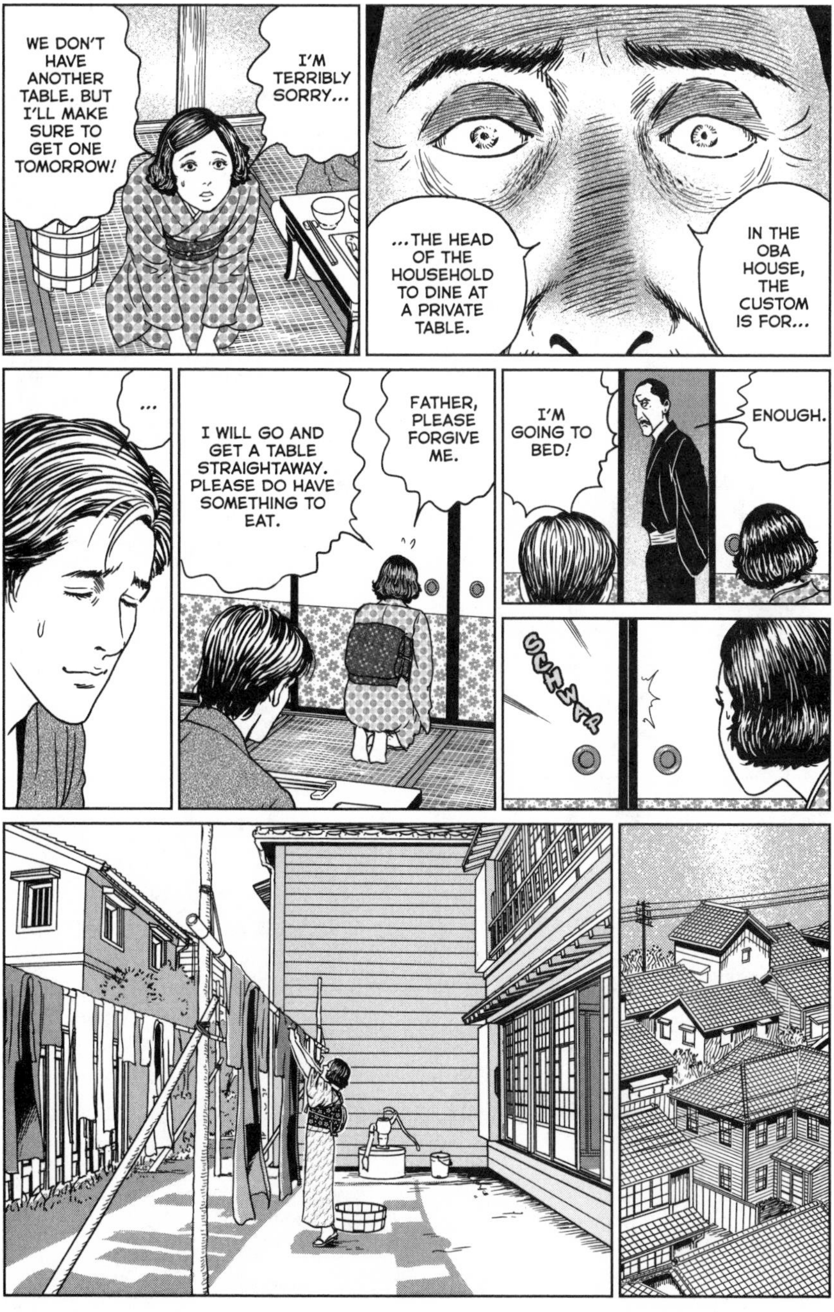

IN THE OBA HOUSE, THE CUSTOM IS FOR...
...THE HEAD OF THE HOUSEHOLD TO DINE AT A PRIVATE TABLE.
I'M TERRIBLY SORRY...
WE DON'T HAVE ANOTHER TABLE. BUT I'LL MAKE SURE TO GET ONE TOMORROW!
ENOUGH.
I'M GOING TO BED!
SCHWAA
FATHER, PLEASE FORGIVE ME.
I WILL GO AND GET A TABLE STRAIGHTAWAY. PLEASE DO HAVE SOMETHING TO EAT.
...

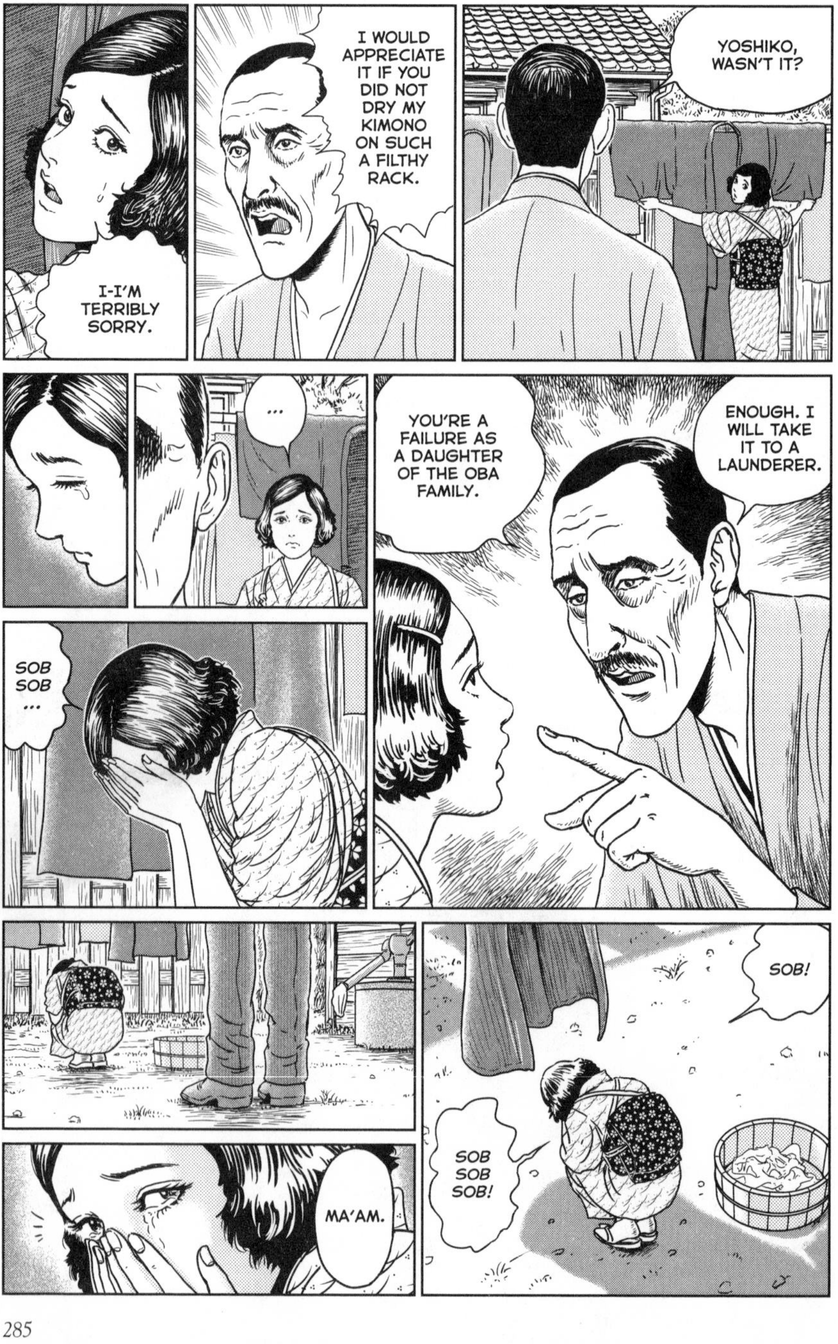
YOSHIKO, WASN'T IT?
I WOULD APPRECIATE IT IF YOU DID NOT DRY MY KIMONO ON SUCH A FILTHY RACK.
I-I'M TERRIBLY SORRY.
ENOUGH. I WILL TAKE IT TO A LAUNDERER.
YOU'RE A FAILURE AS A DAUGHTER OF THE OBA FAMILY.
...
SOB SOB ...
SOB!
SOB SOB SOB!
MA'AM.

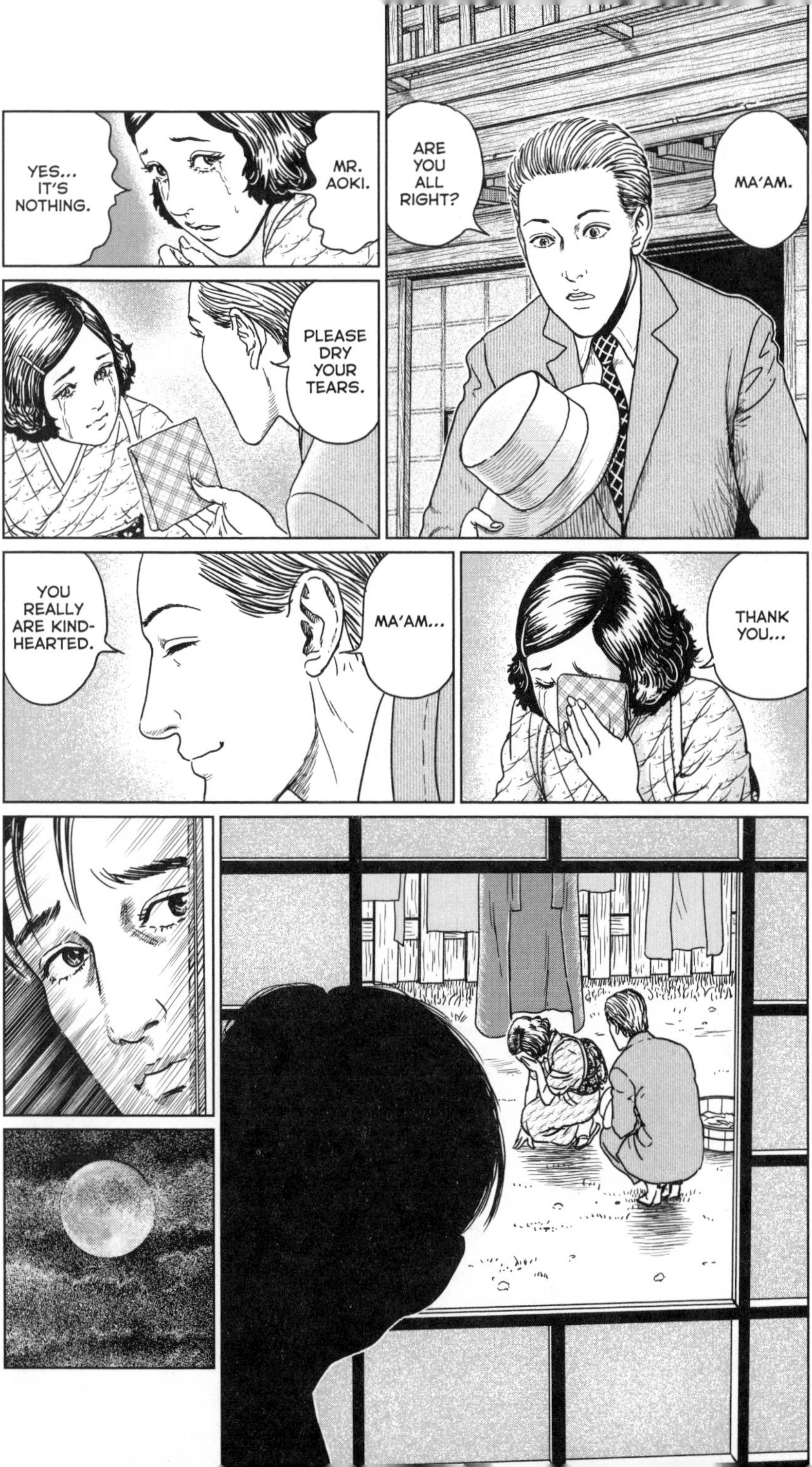
MA'AM.
ARE YOU ALL RIGHT?
MR. AOKI.
YES... IT'S NOTHING.
PLEASE DRY YOUR TEARS.
THANK YOU...
MA'AM...
YOU REALLY ARE KIND-HEARTED.

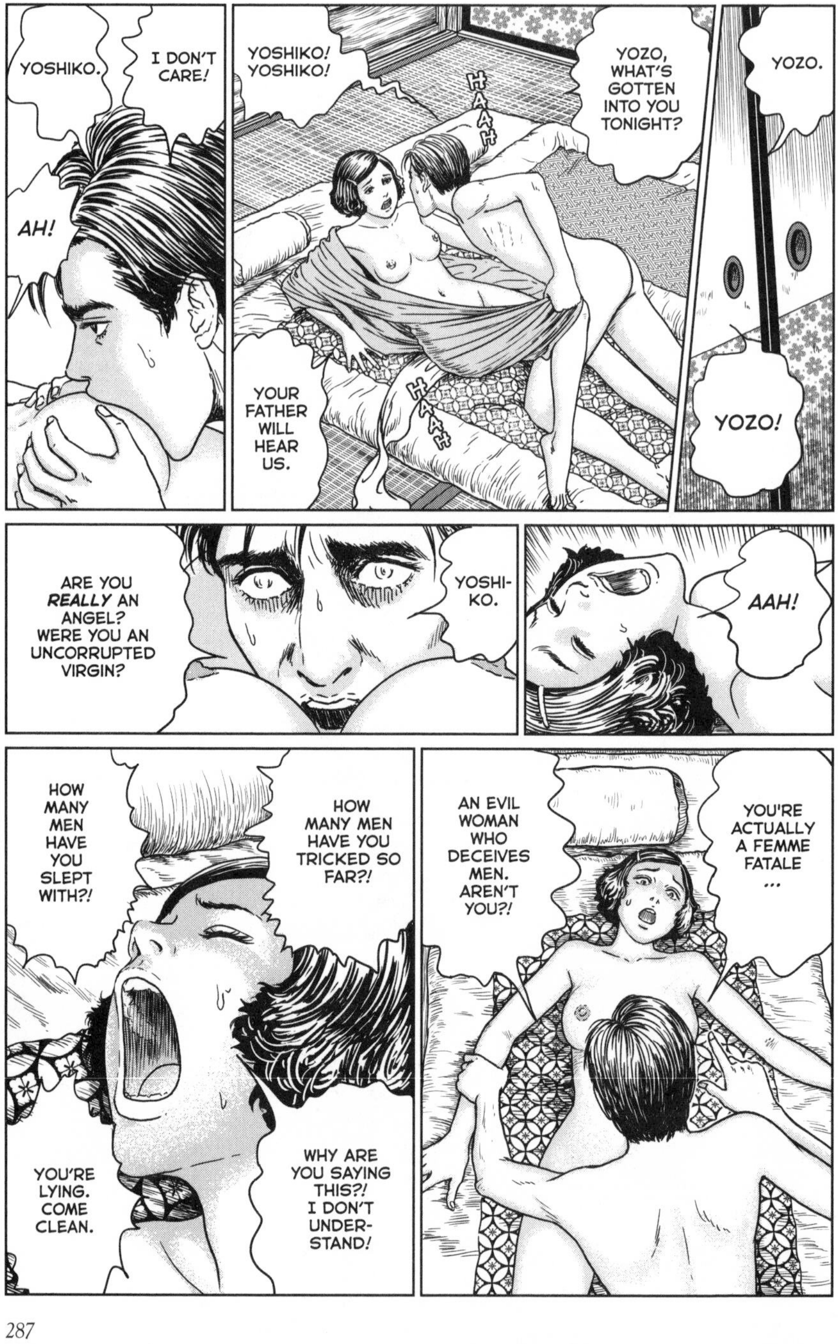
YOZO.
YOZO!
YOZO, WHAT'S GOTTEN INTO YOU TONIGHT?
YOSHIKO! YOSHIKO!
HAAH
YOUR FATHER WILL HEAR US.
HAAH
I DON'T CARE!
YOSHIKO.
AH!
AAH!
YOSHI-KO.
ARE YOU REALLY AN ANGEL? WERE YOU AN UNCORRUPTED VIRGIN?
YOU'RE ACTUALLY A FEMME FATALE ...
AN EVIL WOMAN WHO DECEIVES MEN. AREN'T YOU?!
HOW MANY MEN HAVE YOU TRICKED SO FAR?!
HOW MANY MEN HAVE YOU SLEPT WITH?!
WHY ARE YOU SAYING THIS?! I DON'T UNDER-STAND!
YOU'RE LYING. COME CLEAN.

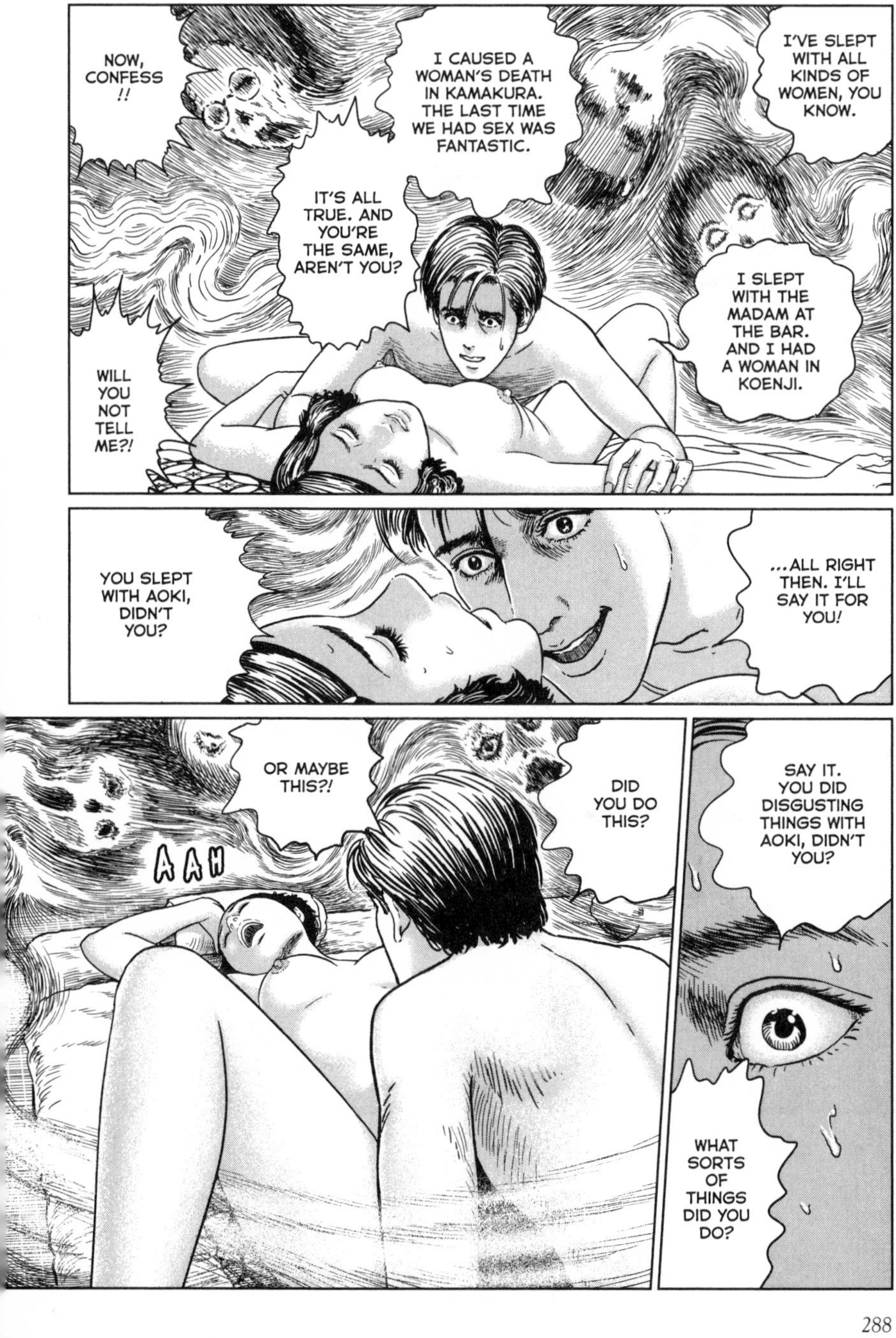
I'VE SLEPT WITH ALL KINDS OF WOMEN, YOU KNOW.
I CAUSED A WOMAN'S DEATH IN KAMAKURA. THE LAST TIME WE HAD SEX WAS FANTASTIC.
NOW, CONFESS!!
I SLEPT WITH THE MADAM AT THE BAR. AND I HAD A WOMAN IN KOENJI.
IT'S ALL TRUE. AND YOU'RE THE SAME, AREN'T YOU?
WILL YOU NOT TELL ME?!
...ALL RIGHT THEN. I'LL SAY IT FOR YOU!
YOU SLEPT WITH AOKI, DIDN'T YOU?
SAY IT. YOU DID DISGUSTING THINGS WITH AOKI, DIDN'T YOU?
WHAT SORTS OF THINGS DID YOU DO?
DID YOU DO THIS?
OR MAYBE THIS?!
AAH

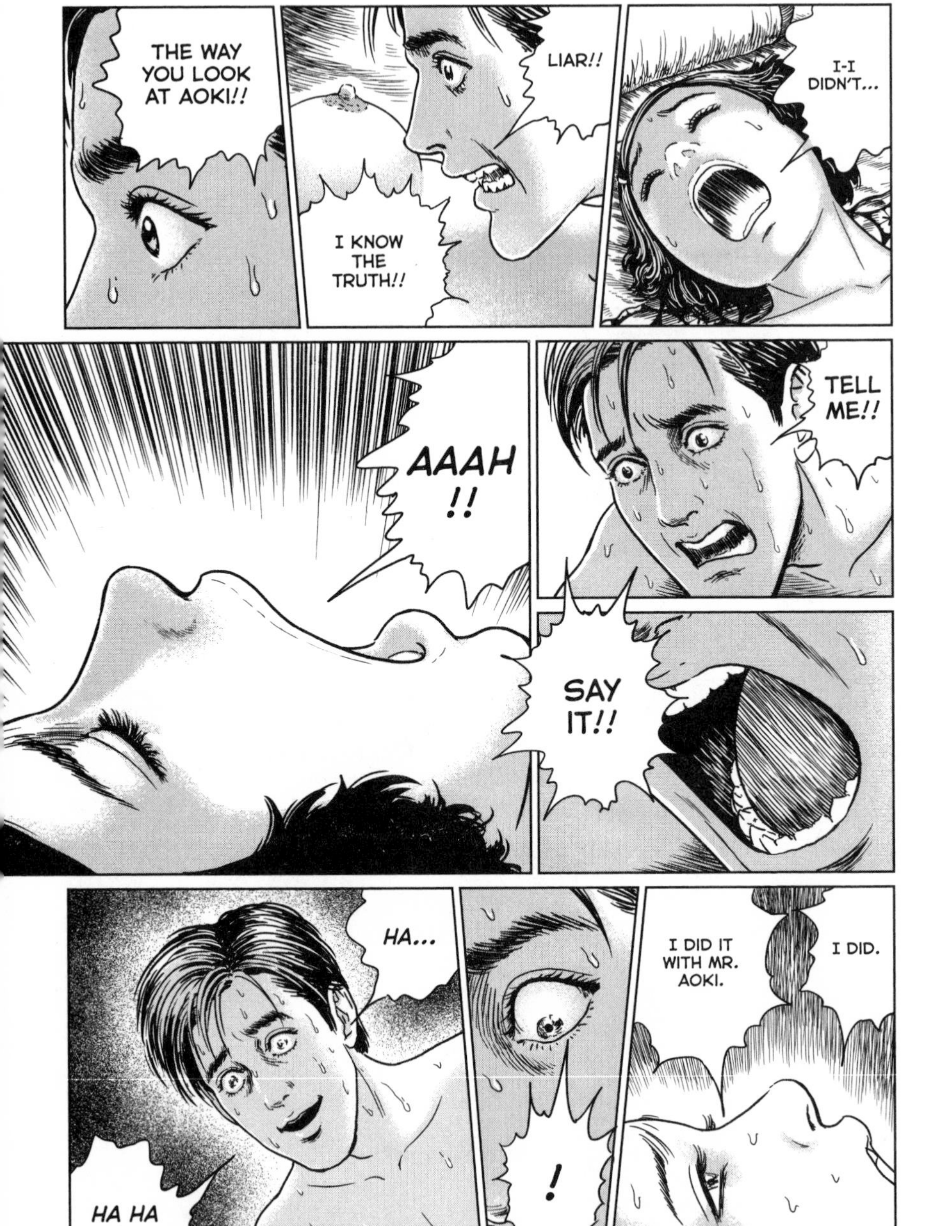
I-I DIDN'T...
LIAR!!
I KNOW THE TRUTH!!
THE WAY YOU LOOK AT AOKI!!
TELL ME!!
SAY IT!!
AAAH!!
I DID.
I DID IT WITH MR. AOKI.
!
HA...
HA HA HA...

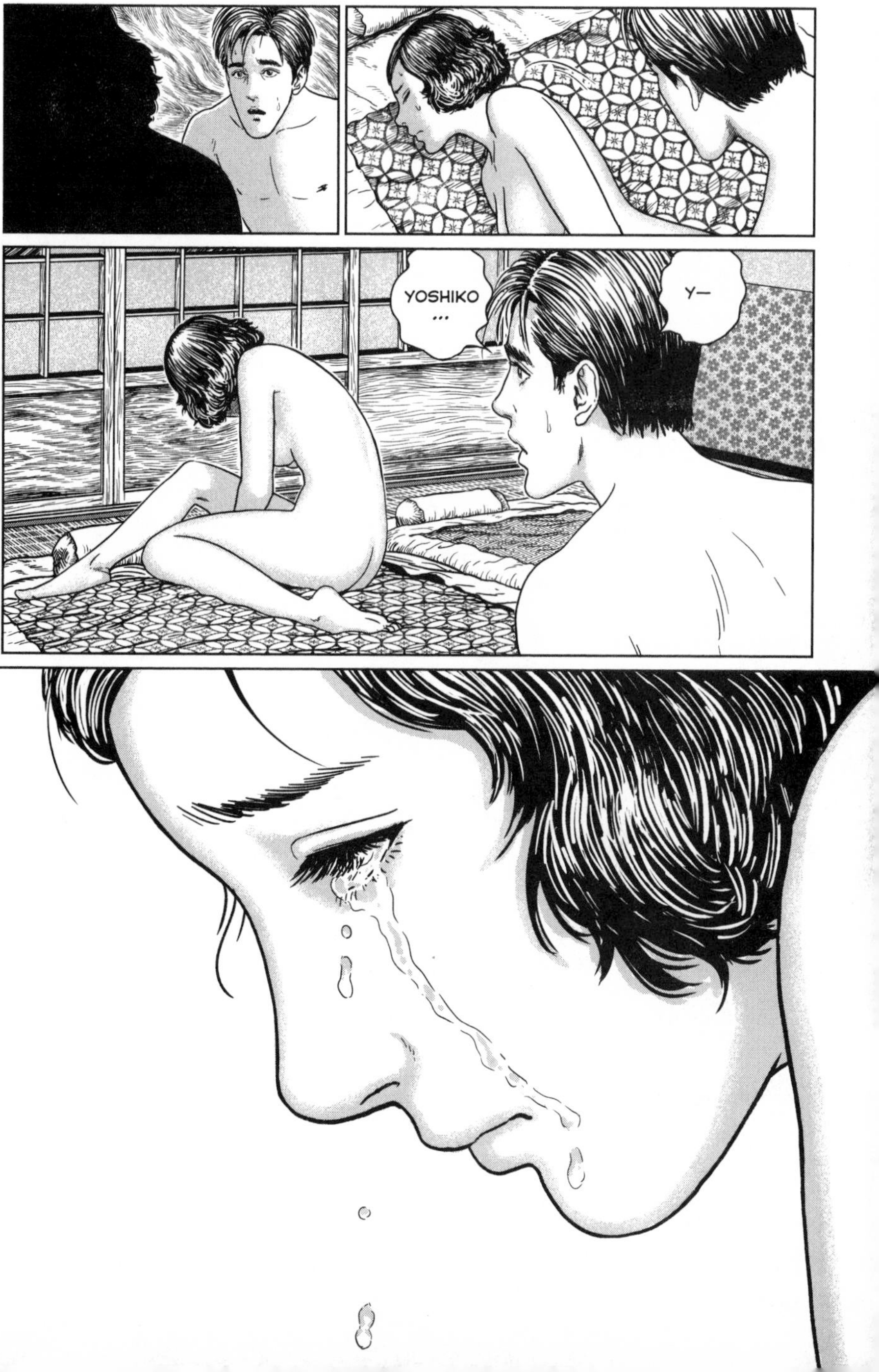
Y—
YOSHIKO ...

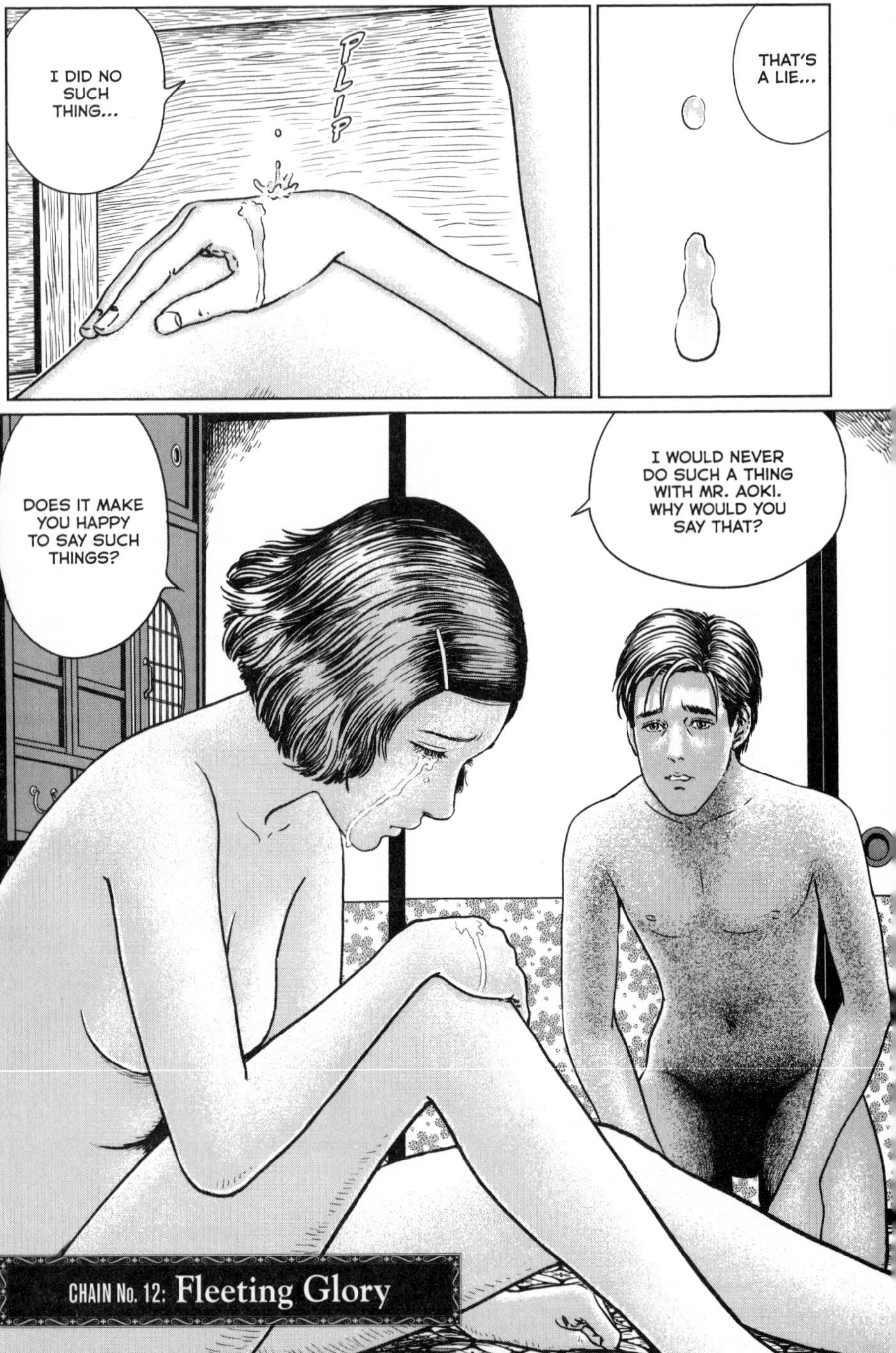
THAT'S A LIE...
I DID NO SUCH THING...
PLIP
I WOULD NEVER DO SUCH A THING WITH MR. AOKI. WHY WOULD YOU SAY THAT?
DOES IT MAKE YOU HAPPY TO SAY SUCH THINGS?
CHAIN No. 12: Fleeting Glory

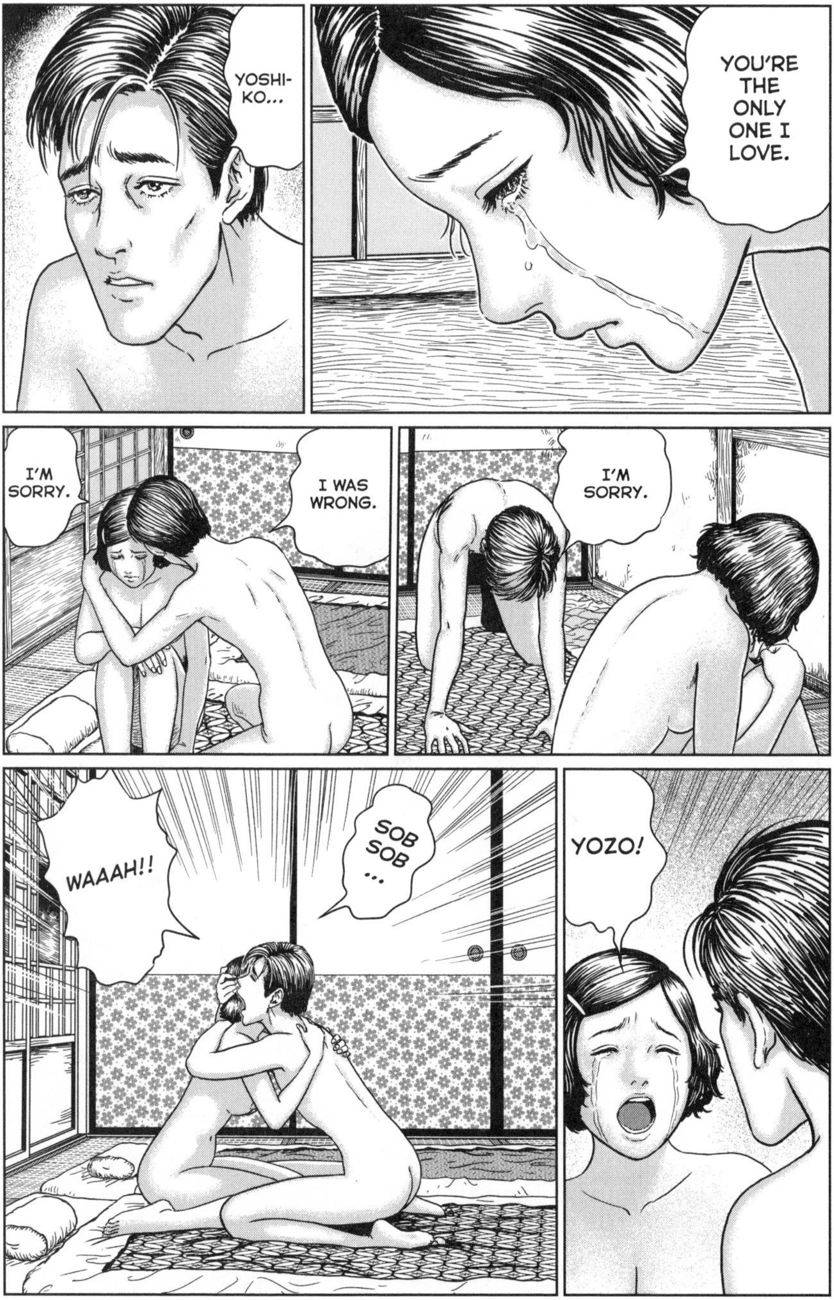
YOU'RE THE ONLY ONE I LOVE.
YOSHI-KO...
I'M SORRY.
I WAS WRONG.
I'M SORRY.
YOZO!
SOB SOB ...
WAAAH!!

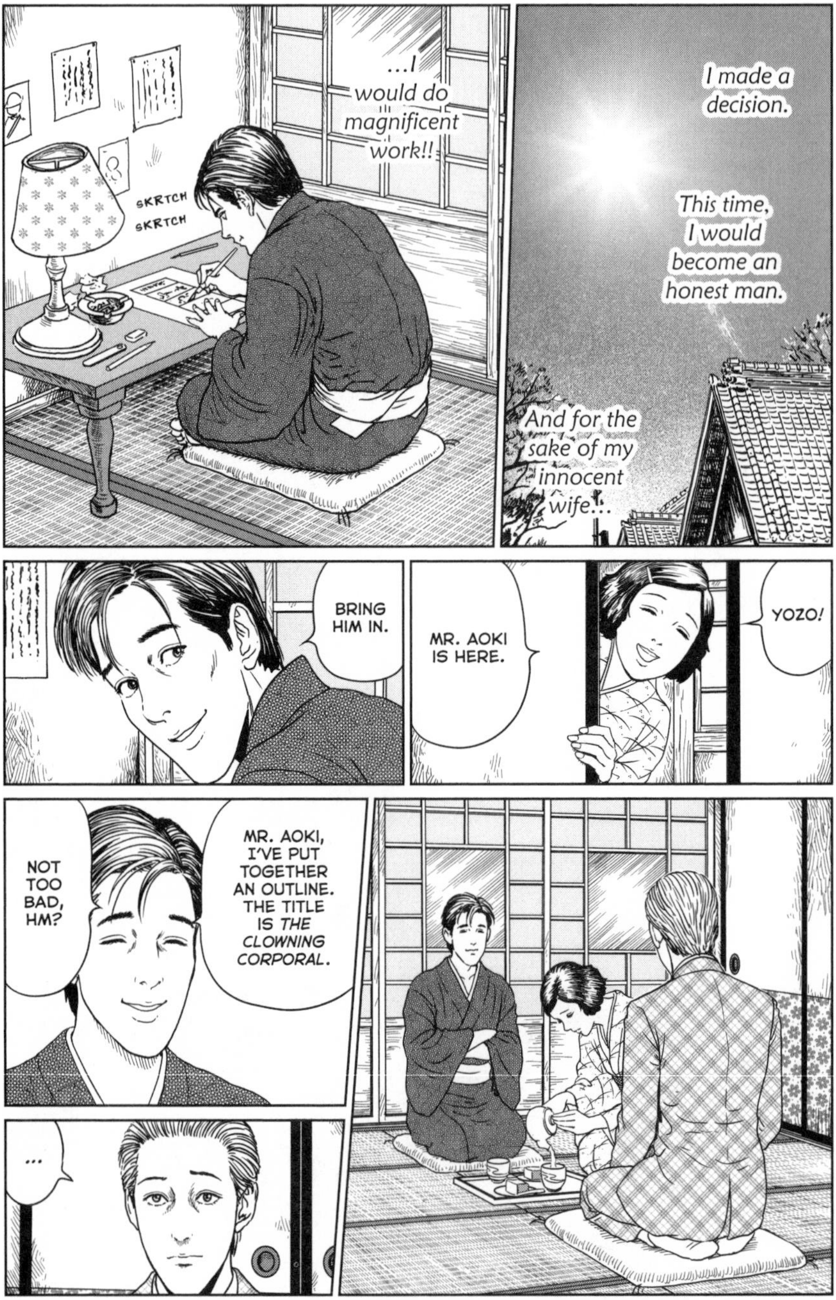
I made a decision.
This time, I would become an honest man.
And for the sake of my innocent wife...
...I would do magnificent work!!
SKRTCH
SKRTCH
YOZO!
MR. AOKI IS HERE.
BRING HIM IN.
MR. AOKI, I'VE PUT TOGETHER AN OUTLINE. THE TITLE IS *THE CLOWNING CORPORAL*.
NOT TOO BAD, HM?
...

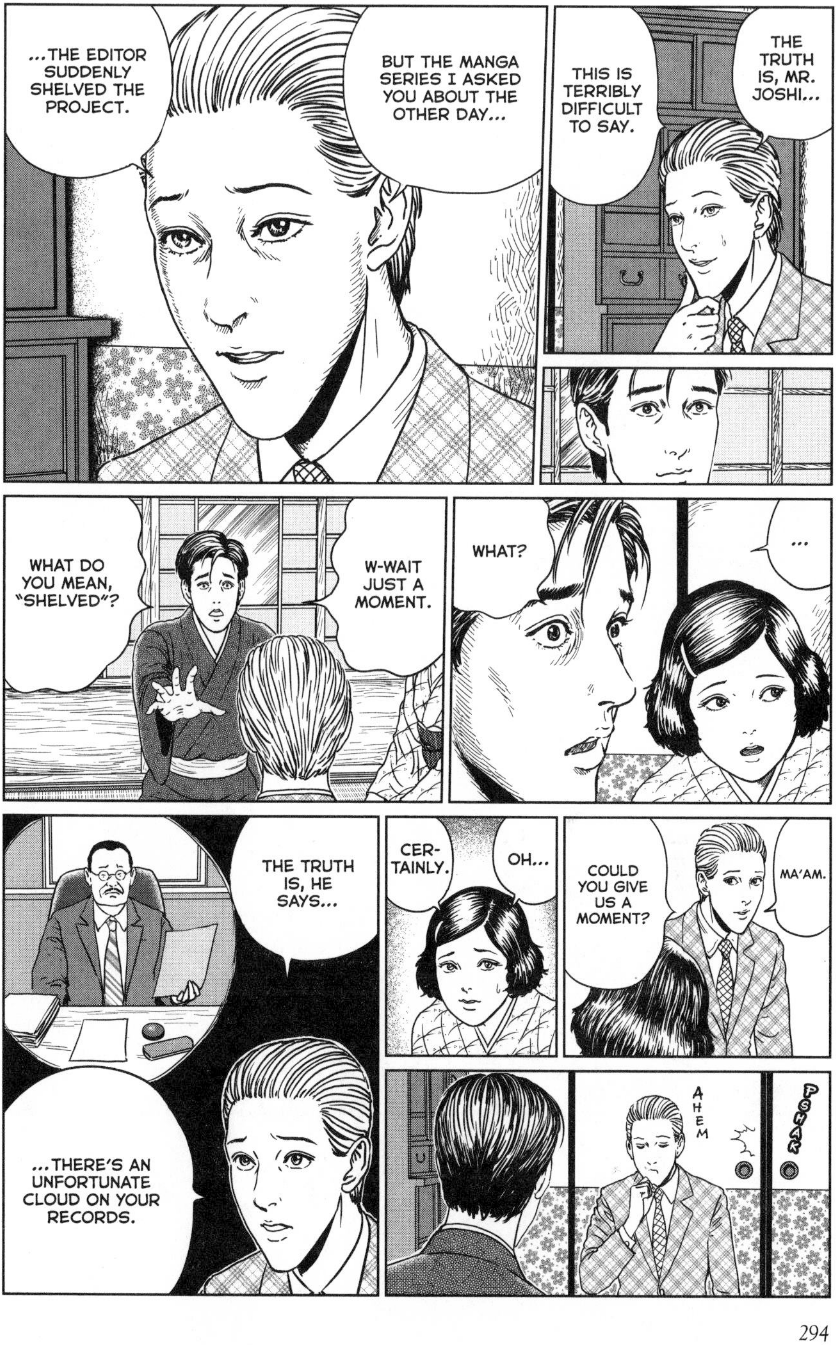
THE TRUTH IS, MR. JOSHI...
THIS IS TERRIBLY DIFFICULT TO SAY.
BUT THE MANGA SERIES I ASKED YOU ABOUT THE OTHER DAY...
...THE EDITOR SUDDENLY SHELVED THE PROJECT.
...
WHAT?
W-WAIT JUST A MOMENT.
WHAT DO YOU MEAN, "SHELVED"?
MA'AM.
COULD YOU GIVE US A MOMENT?
OH...
CER-TAINLY.
PSHAK
AHEM
THE TRUTH IS, HE SAYS...
...THERE'S AN UNFORTUNATE CLOUD ON YOUR RECORDS.

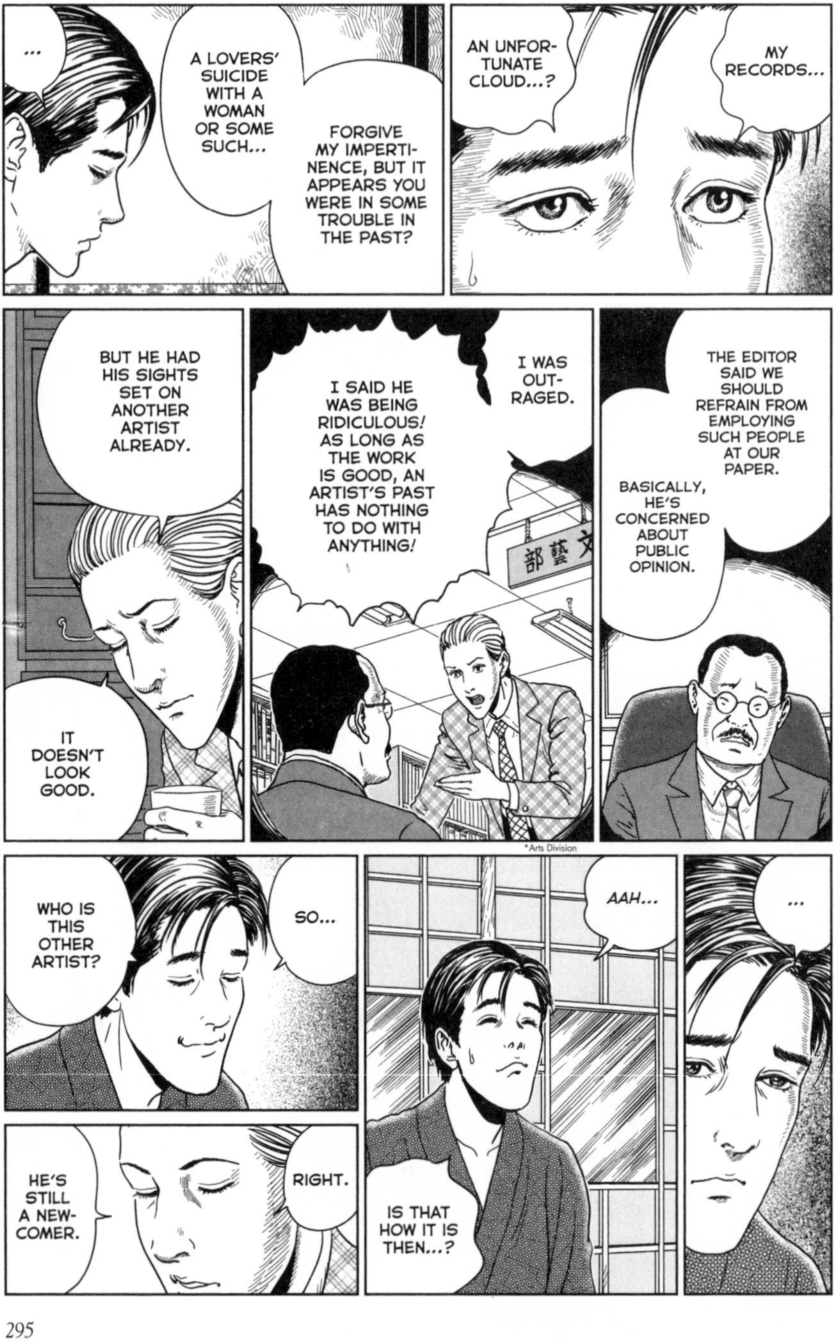
MY RECORDS...
AN UNFORTUNATE CLOUD...?
A LOVERS' SUICIDE WITH A WOMAN OR SOME SUCH...
FORGIVE MY IMPERTINENCE, BUT IT APPEARS YOU WERE IN SOME TROUBLE IN THE PAST?
...
THE EDITOR SAID WE SHOULD REFRAIN FROM EMPLOYING SUCH PEOPLE AT OUR PAPER.
BASICALLY, HE'S CONCERNED ABOUT PUBLIC OPINION.
I WAS OUTRAGED.
I SAID HE WAS BEING RIDICULOUS! AS LONG AS THE WORK IS GOOD, AN ARTIST'S PAST HAS NOTHING TO DO WITH ANYTHING!
文藝部
BUT HE HAD HIS SIGHTS SET ON ANOTHER ARTIST ALREADY.
IT DOESN'T LOOK GOOD.
*Arts Division
...
AAH...
IS THAT HOW IT IS THEN...?
SO...
WHO IS THIS OTHER ARTIST?
RIGHT.
HE'S STILL A NEWCOMER.

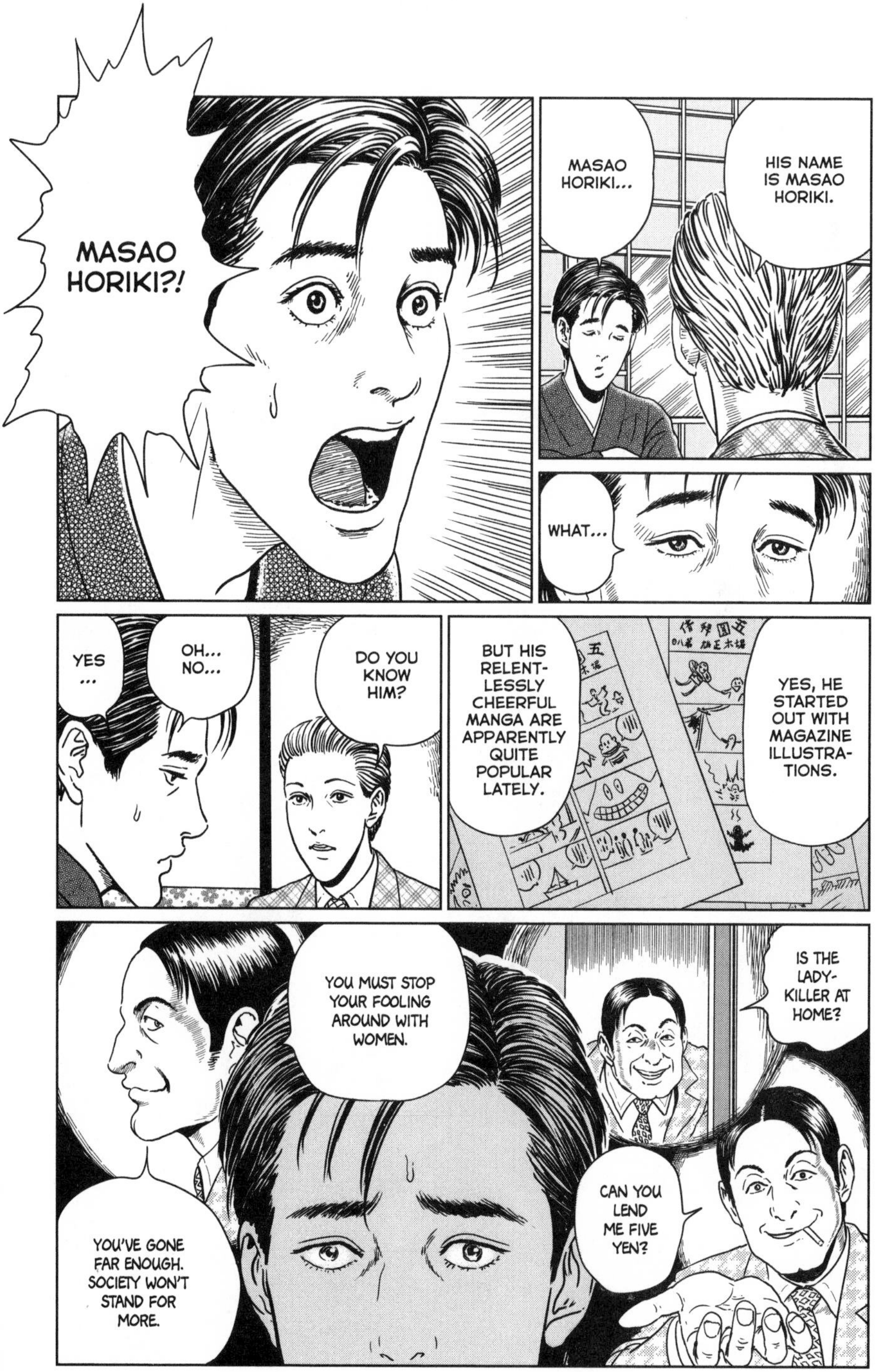
HIS NAME IS MASAO HORIKI.
MASAO HORIKI...
WHAT...
MASAO HORIKI?!
YES, HE STARTED OUT WITH MAGAZINE ILLUSTRATIONS.
BUT HIS RELENTLESSLY CHEERFUL MANGA ARE APPARENTLY QUITE POPULAR LATELY.
DO YOU KNOW HIM?
OH... NO...
YES ...
IS THE LADY-KILLER AT HOME?
CAN YOU LEND ME FIVE YEN?
YOU MUST STOP YOUR FOOLING AROUND WITH WOMEN.
YOU'VE GONE FAR ENOUGH. SOCIETY WON'T STAND FOR MORE.

*Bookstore
Banner: *Modern Economics* complete set
Sign: Collection of long fiction

**Lend Me Five Yen* No.12 by Masao Horiki

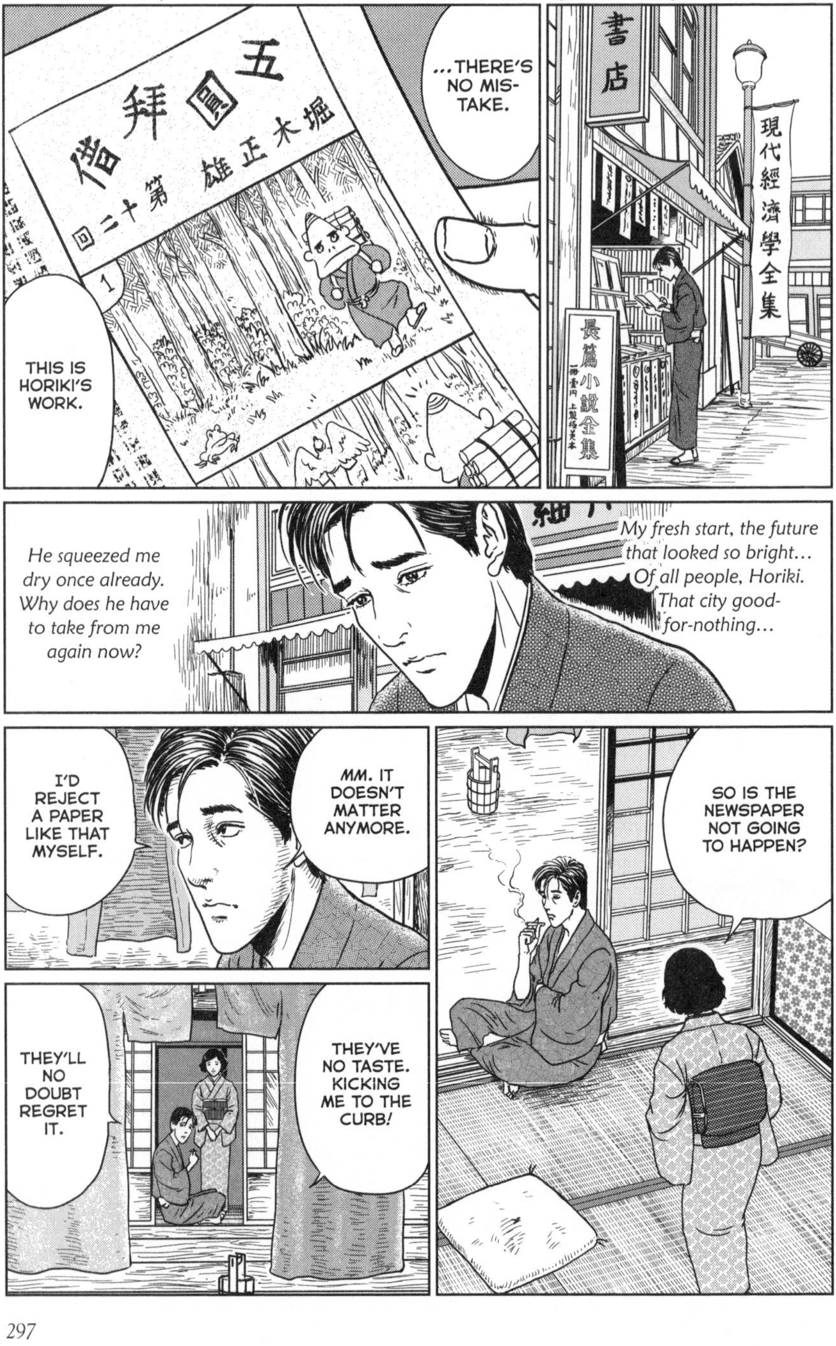
書店
現代經濟學全集
長篇小説全集
一冊壹円 上製特美本
五圓拜借
堀木正雄
第十二回
...THERE'S NO MISTAKE.
THIS IS HORIKI'S WORK.
My fresh start, the future that looked so bright... Of all people, Horiki. That city good-for-nothing...
He squeezed me dry once already. Why does he have to take from me again now?
SO IS THE NEWSPAPER NOT GOING TO HAPPEN?
MM. IT DOESN'T MATTER ANYMORE.
I'D REJECT A PAPER LIKE THAT MYSELF.
THEY'VE NO TASTE. KICKING ME TO THE CURB!
THEY'LL NO DOUBT REGRET IT.

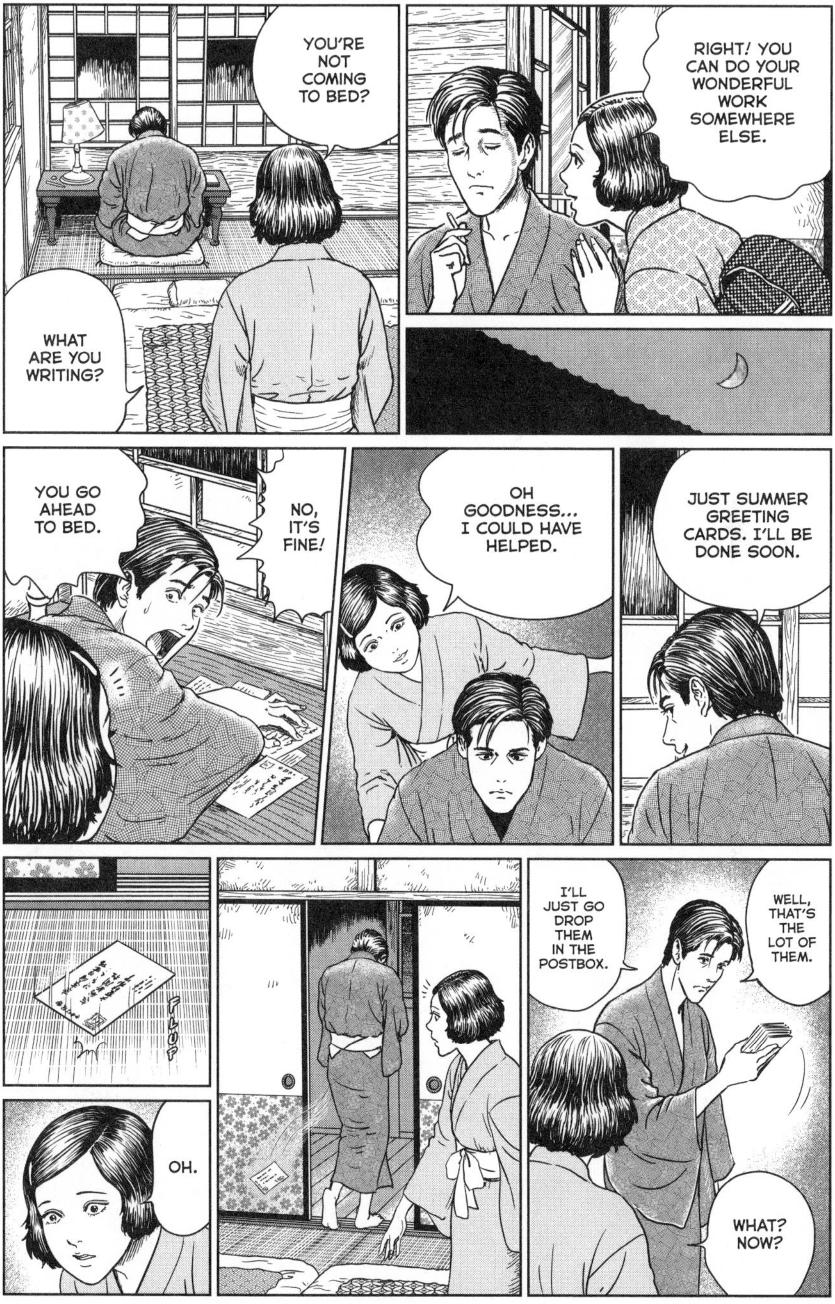
RIGHT! YOU CAN DO YOUR WONDERFUL WORK SOMEWHERE ELSE.
YOU'RE NOT COMING TO BED?
WHAT ARE YOU WRITING?
JUST SUMMER GREETING CARDS. I'LL BE DONE SOON.
OH GOODNESS... I COULD HAVE HELPED.
NO, IT'S FINE!
YOU GO AHEAD TO BED.
WELL, THAT'S THE LOT OF THEM.
I'LL JUST GO DROP THEM IN THE POSTBOX.
WHAT? NOW?
FLUP
OH.

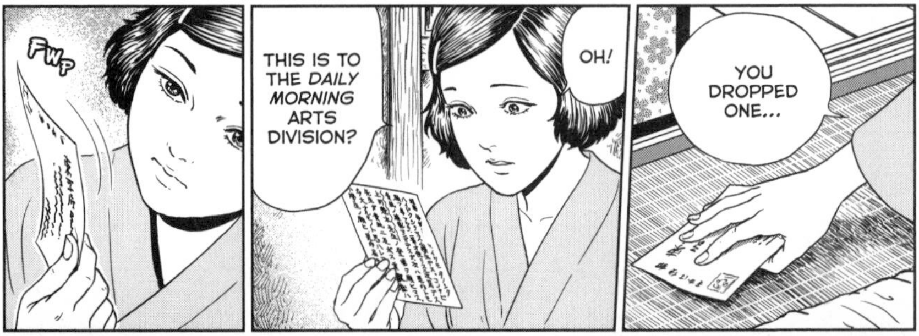
YOU DROPPED ONE...
OH!
THIS IS TO THE *DAILY MORNING* ARTS DIVISION?
FWP

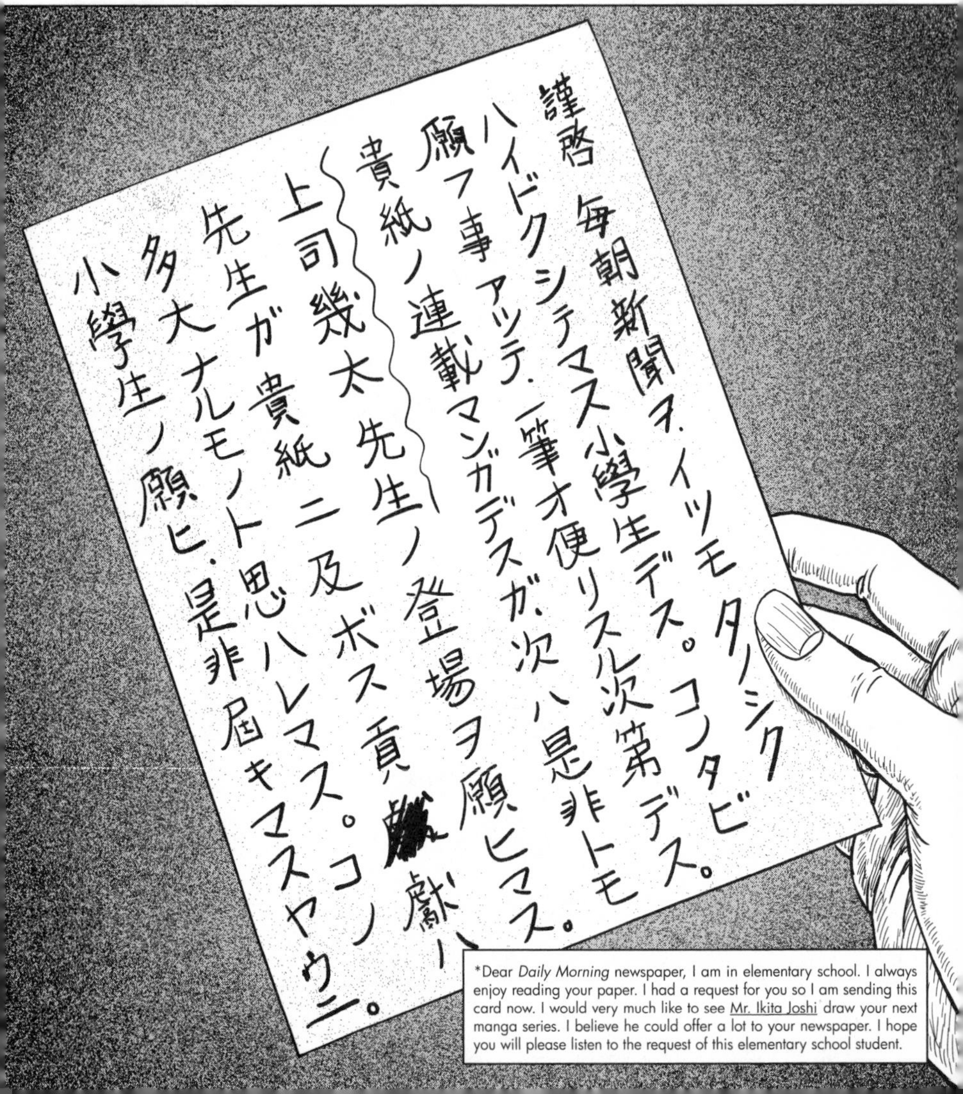
謹啓 毎朝新聞ヲ、イツモタノシク
ハイドクシテマス小學生デス。コンタビ
願フ事アッテ、一筆オ便リスル次第デス。
貴紙ノ連載マンガデスガ、次ハ是非トモ
上司幾太 先生ノ登場ヲ願ヒマス。
先生ガ貴紙ニ及ボス貢獻ハ
多大ナルモノト思ハレマス。コノ
小學生ノ願ヒ、是非届キマスヤウニ。
*Dear *Daily Morning* newspaper, I am in elementary school. I always enjoy reading your paper. I had a request for you so I am sending this card now. I would very much like to see Mr. Ikita Joshi draw your next manga series. I believe he could offer a lot to your newspaper. I hope you will please listen to the request of this elementary school student.

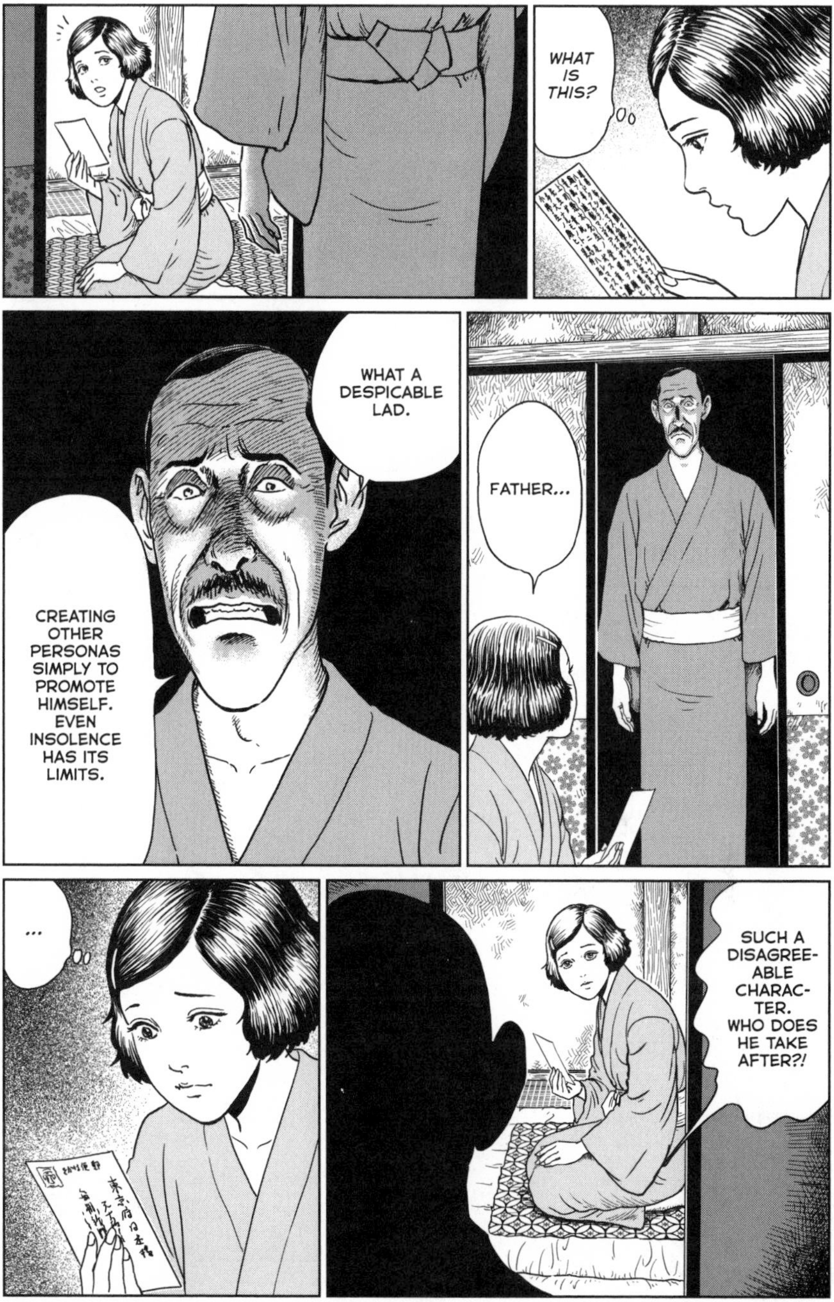
WHAT IS THIS?
FATHER...
WHAT A DESPICABLE LAD.
CREATING OTHER PERSONAS SIMPLY TO PROMOTE HIMSELF. EVEN INSOLENCE HAS ITS LIMITS.
SUCH A DISAGREE-ABLE CHARAC-TER. WHO DOES HE TAKE AFTER?!
...

*Tokyo Daily Morning Newspaper

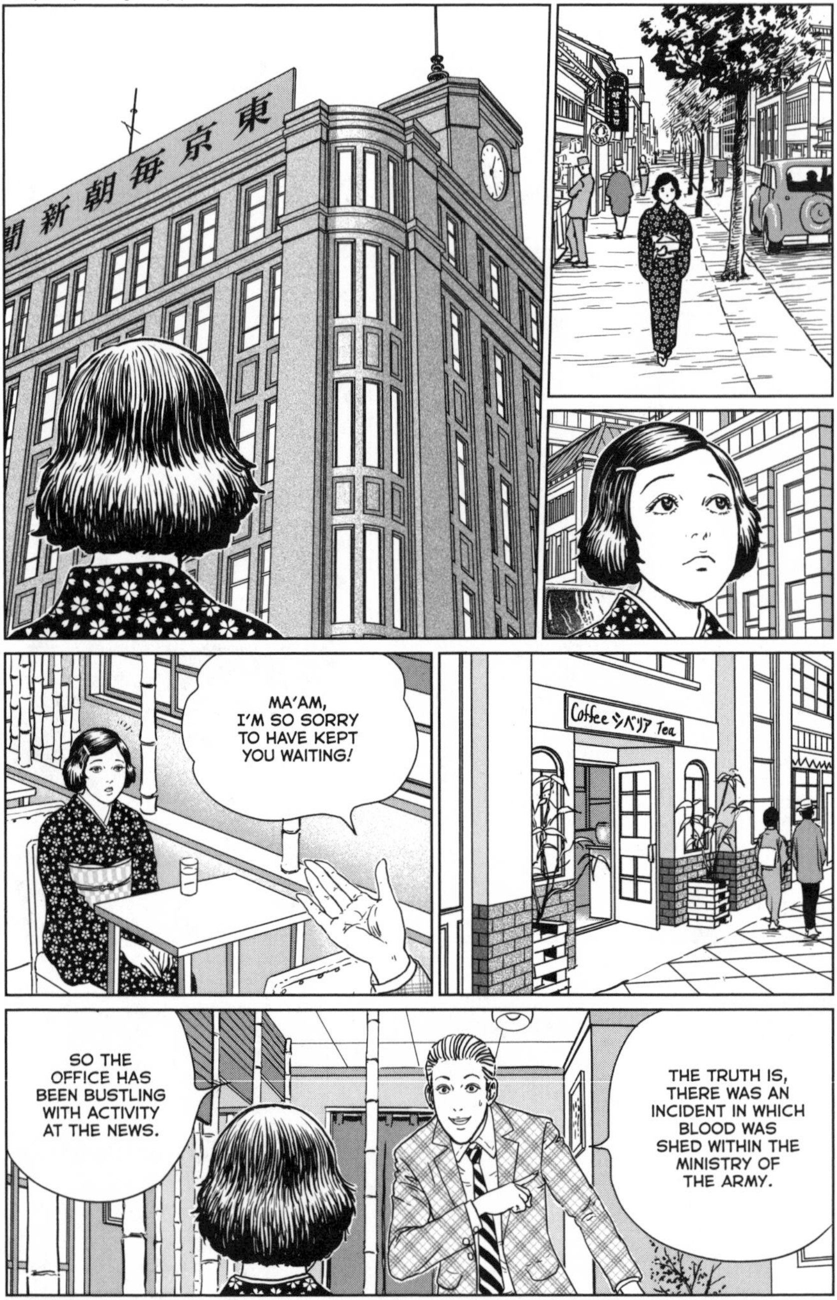
東京毎朝新聞
Coffee シベリア Tea
MA'AM, I'M SO SORRY TO HAVE KEPT YOU WAITING!
THE TRUTH IS, THERE WAS AN INCIDENT IN WHICH BLOOD WAS SHED WITHIN THE MINISTRY OF THE ARMY.
SO THE OFFICE HAS BEEN BUSTLING WITH ACTIVITY AT THE NEWS.

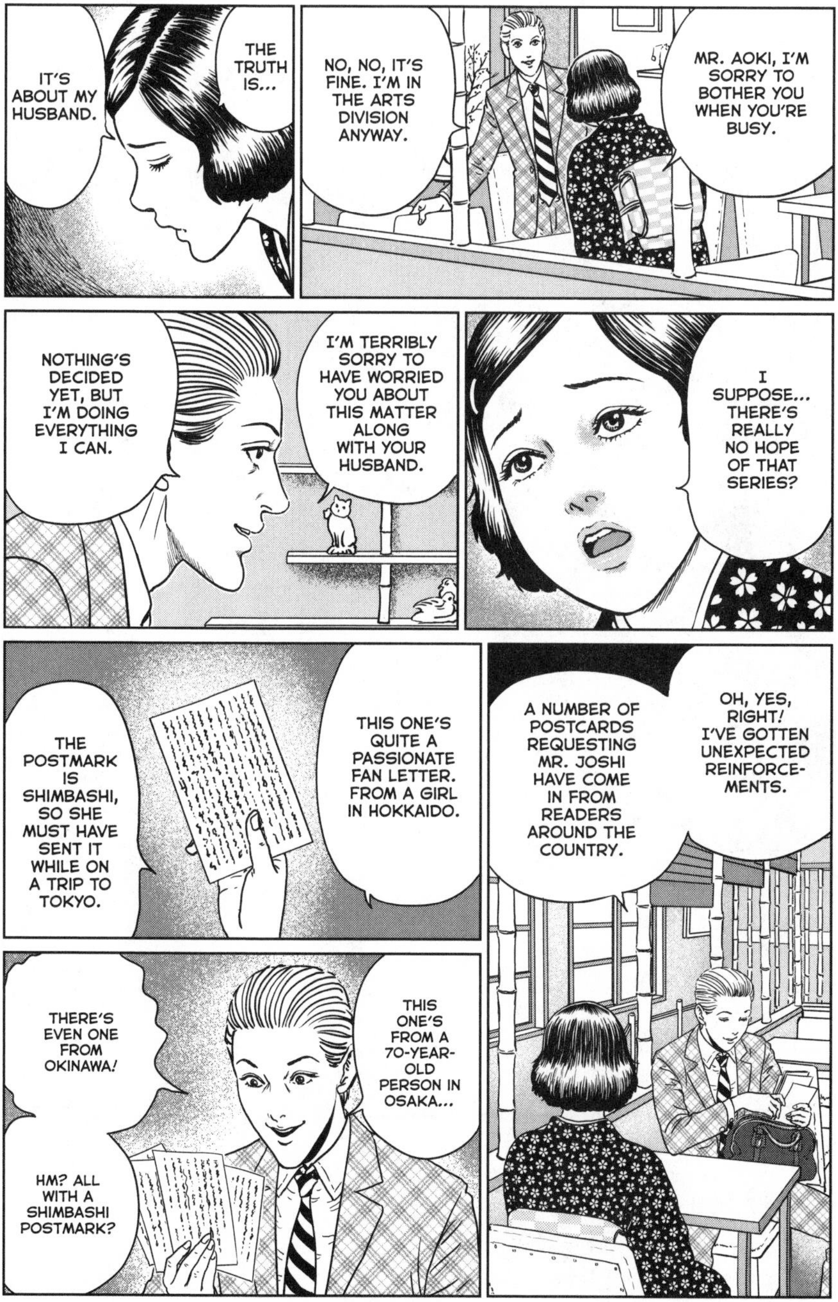
MR. AOKI, I'M SORRY TO BOTHER YOU WHEN YOU'RE BUSY.
NO, NO, IT'S FINE. I'M IN THE ARTS DIVISION ANYWAY.
THE TRUTH IS...
IT'S ABOUT MY HUSBAND.
I SUPPOSE... THERE'S REALLY NO HOPE OF THAT SERIES?
I'M TERRIBLY SORRY TO HAVE WORRIED YOU ABOUT THIS MATTER ALONG WITH YOUR HUSBAND.
NOTHING'S DECIDED YET, BUT I'M DOING EVERYTHING I CAN.
OH, YES, RIGHT! I'VE GOTTEN UNEXPECTED REINFORCE-MENTS.
A NUMBER OF POSTCARDS REQUESTING MR. JOSHI HAVE COME IN FROM READERS AROUND THE COUNTRY.
THIS ONE'S QUITE A PASSIONATE FAN LETTER. FROM A GIRL IN HOKKAIDO.
THE POSTMARK IS SHIMBASHI, SO SHE MUST HAVE SENT IT WHILE ON A TRIP TO TOKYO.
THIS ONE'S FROM A 70-YEAR-OLD PERSON IN OSAKA...
THERE'S EVEN ONE FROM OKINAWA!
HM? ALL WITH A SHIMBASHI POSTMARK?

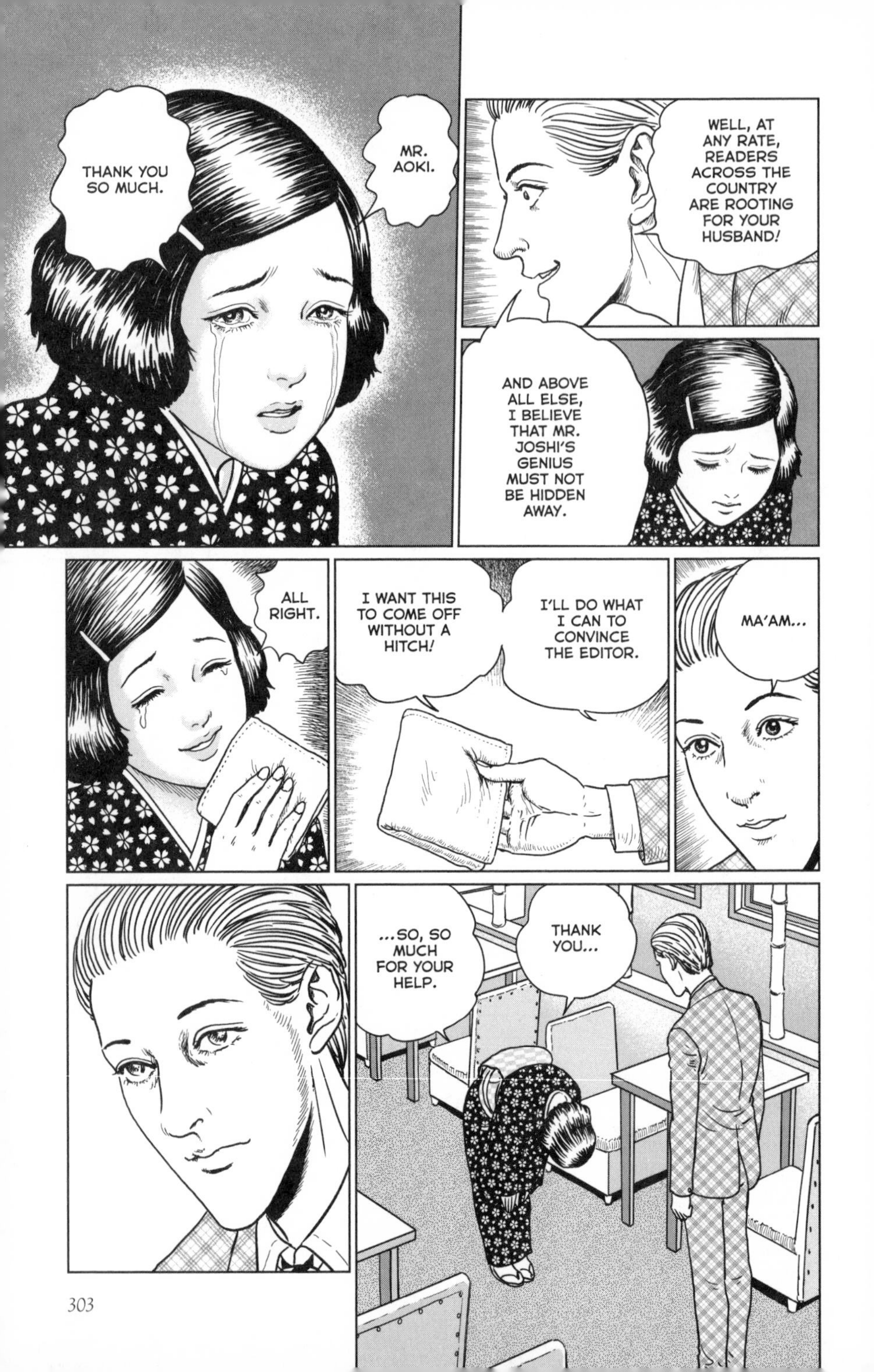
WELL, AT ANY RATE, READERS ACROSS THE COUNTRY ARE ROOTING FOR YOUR HUSBAND!
AND ABOVE ALL ELSE, I BELIEVE THAT MR. JOSHI'S GENIUS MUST NOT BE HIDDEN AWAY.
MR. AOKI.
THANK YOU SO MUCH.
MA'AM...
I'LL DO WHAT I CAN TO CONVINCE THE EDITOR.
I WANT THIS TO COME OFF WITHOUT A HITCH!
ALL RIGHT.
THANK YOU...
...SO, SO MUCH FOR YOUR HELP.

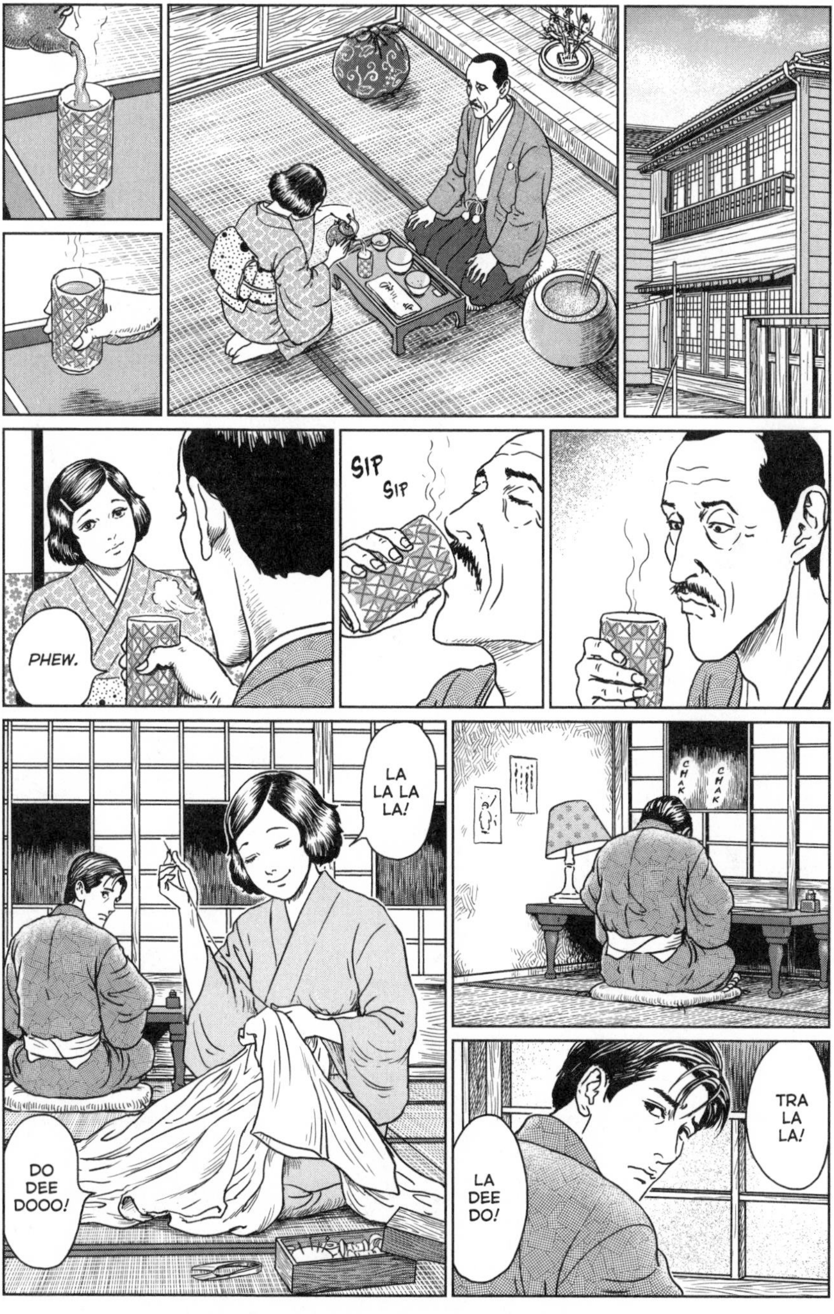
SIP
SIP
PHEW.
CHAK CHAK
TRA LA LA!
LA DEE DO!
LA LA LA LA!
DO DEE DOOO!

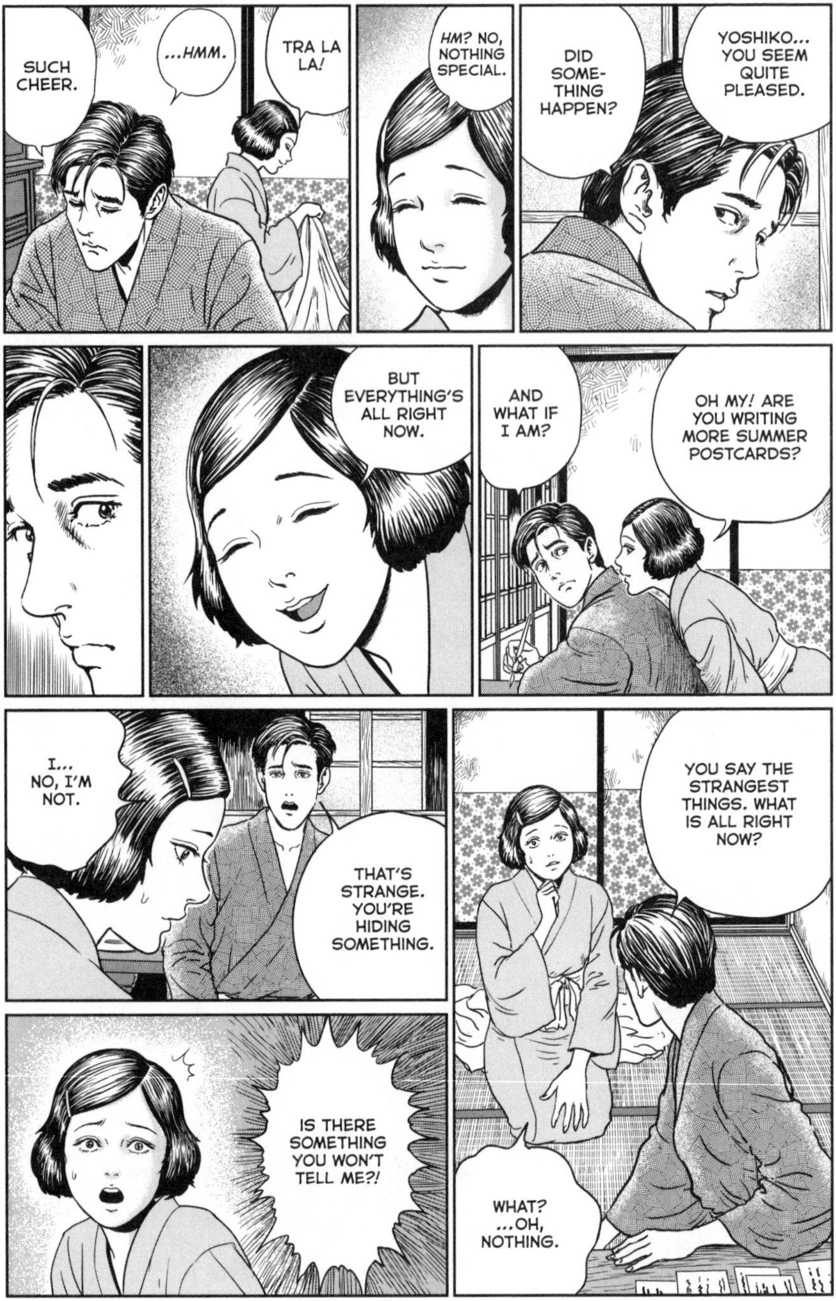
YOSHIKO... YOU SEEM QUITE PLEASED.
DID SOMETHING HAPPEN?
HM? NO, NOTHING SPECIAL.
TRA LA LA!
...HMM.
SUCH CHEER.
OH MY! ARE YOU WRITING MORE SUMMER POSTCARDS?
AND WHAT IF I AM?
BUT EVERYTHING'S ALL RIGHT NOW.
YOU SAY THE STRANGEST THINGS. WHAT IS ALL RIGHT NOW?
WHAT? ...OH, NOTHING.
THAT'S STRANGE. YOU'RE HIDING SOMETHING.
I... NO, I'M NOT.
IS THERE SOMETHING YOU WON'T TELL ME?!

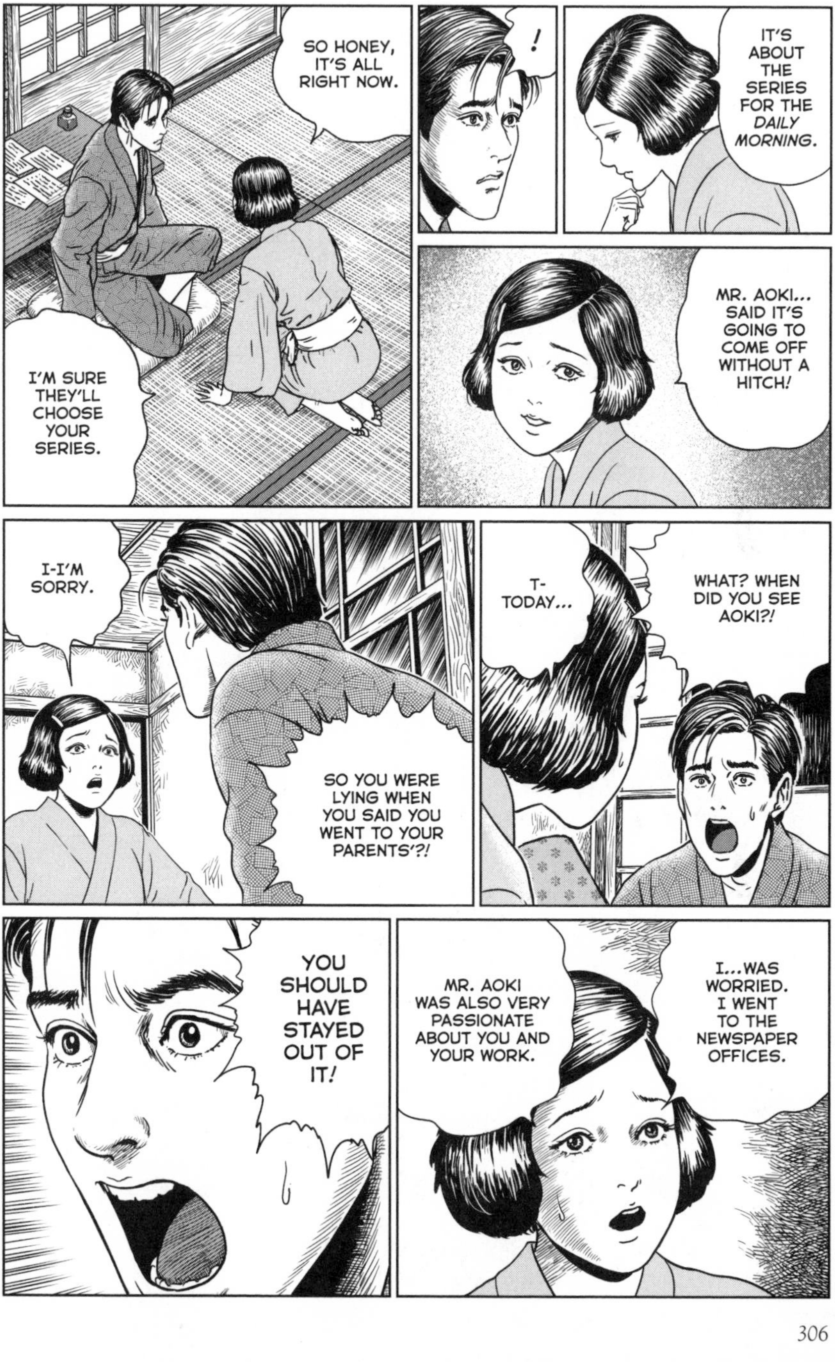
IT'S ABOUT THE SERIES FOR THE *DAILY MORNING*.
!
MR. AOKI... SAID IT'S GOING TO COME OFF WITHOUT A HITCH!
SO HONEY, IT'S ALL RIGHT NOW.
I'M SURE THEY'LL CHOOSE YOUR SERIES.
WHAT? WHEN DID YOU SEE AOKI?!
T- TODAY...
SO YOU WERE LYING WHEN YOU SAID YOU WENT TO YOUR PARENTS'?!
I-I'M SORRY.
I...WAS WORRIED. I WENT TO THE NEWSPAPER OFFICES.
MR. AOKI WAS ALSO VERY PASSIONATE ABOUT YOU AND YOUR WORK.
YOU SHOULD HAVE STAYED OUT OF IT!

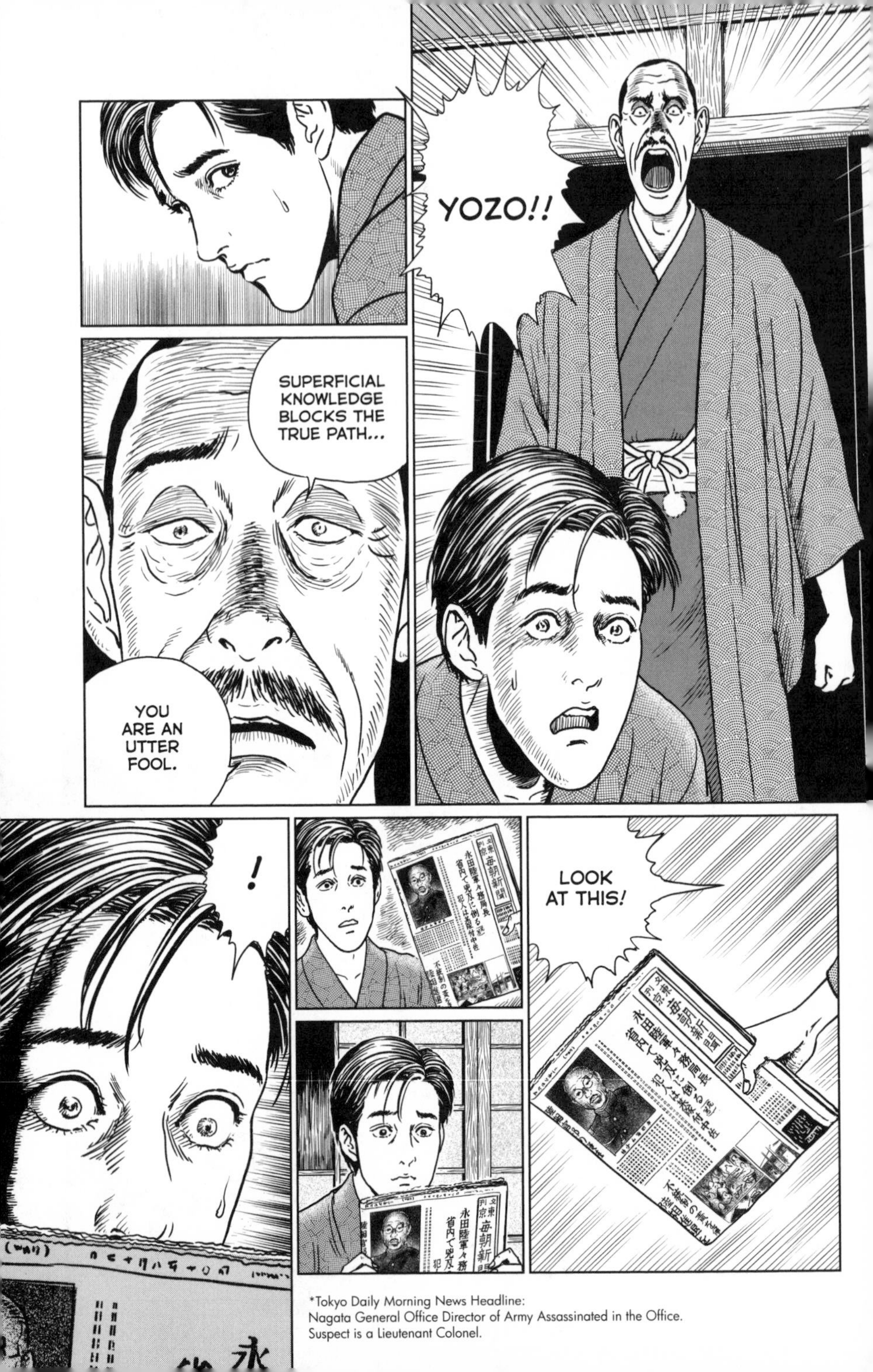
YOZO!!
SUPERFICIAL KNOWLEDGE BLOCKS THE TRUE PATH...
YOU ARE AN UTTER FOOL.
LOOK AT THIS!
!

*Tokyo Daily Morning News Headline:
Nagata General Office Director of Army Assassinated in the Office.
Suspect is a Lieutenant Colonel.

*Notice
Beginning on September 1, the morning edition will begin a new manga series *Mr. Pathos* drawn by promising young artist Mr. Masao Horiki.

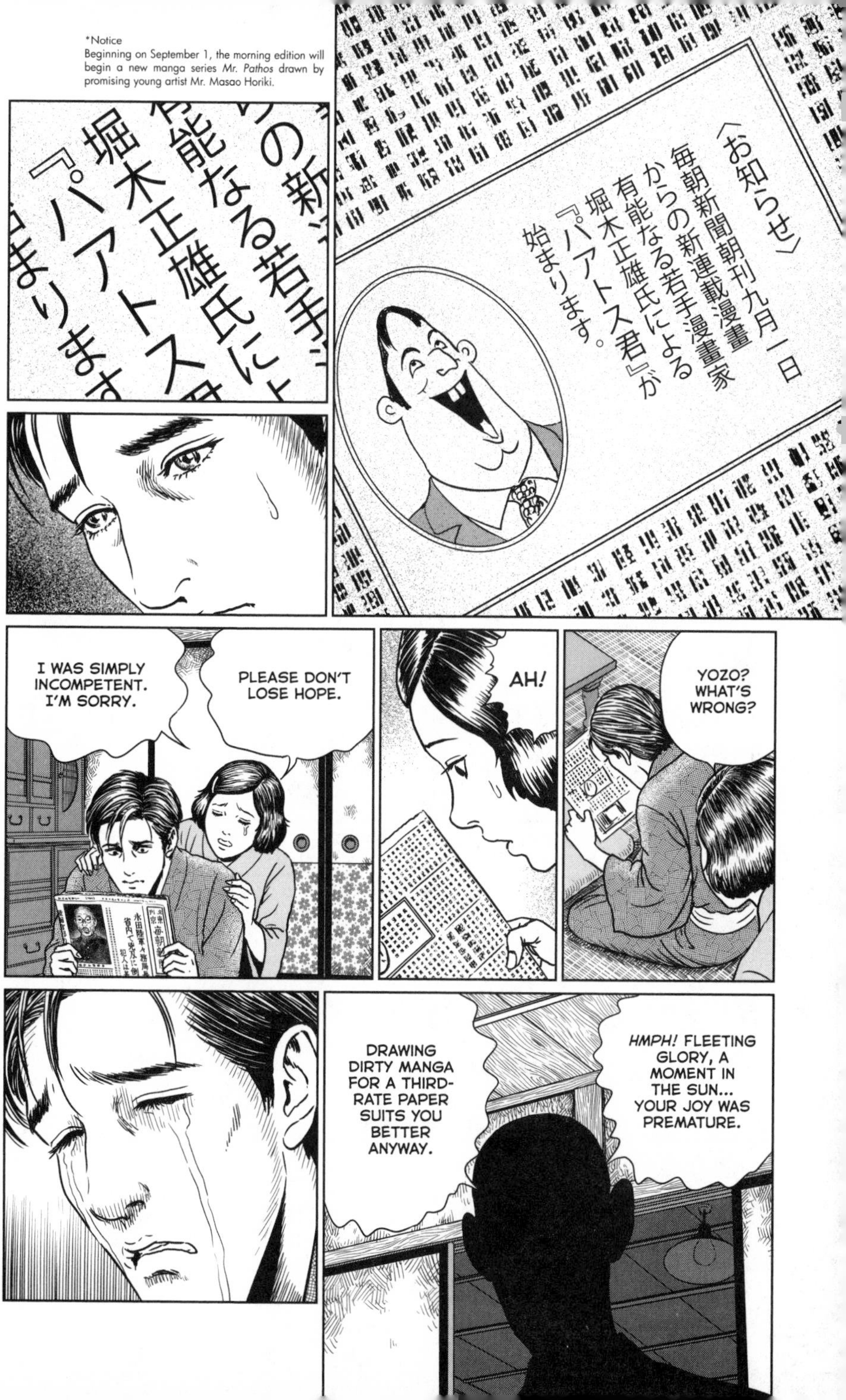
〈お知らせ〉
毎朝新聞朝刊九月一日
からの新連載漫畫
有能なる若手漫畫家
堀木正雄氏による
『パアトス君』が
始まります。
YOZO? WHAT'S WRONG?
AH!
I WAS SIMPLY INCOMPETENT. I'M SORRY.
PLEASE DON'T LOSE HOPE.
HMPH! FLEETING GLORY, A MOMENT IN THE SUN... YOUR JOY WAS PREMATURE.
DRAWING DIRTY MANGA FOR A THIRD-RATE PAPER SUITS YOU BETTER ANYWAY.

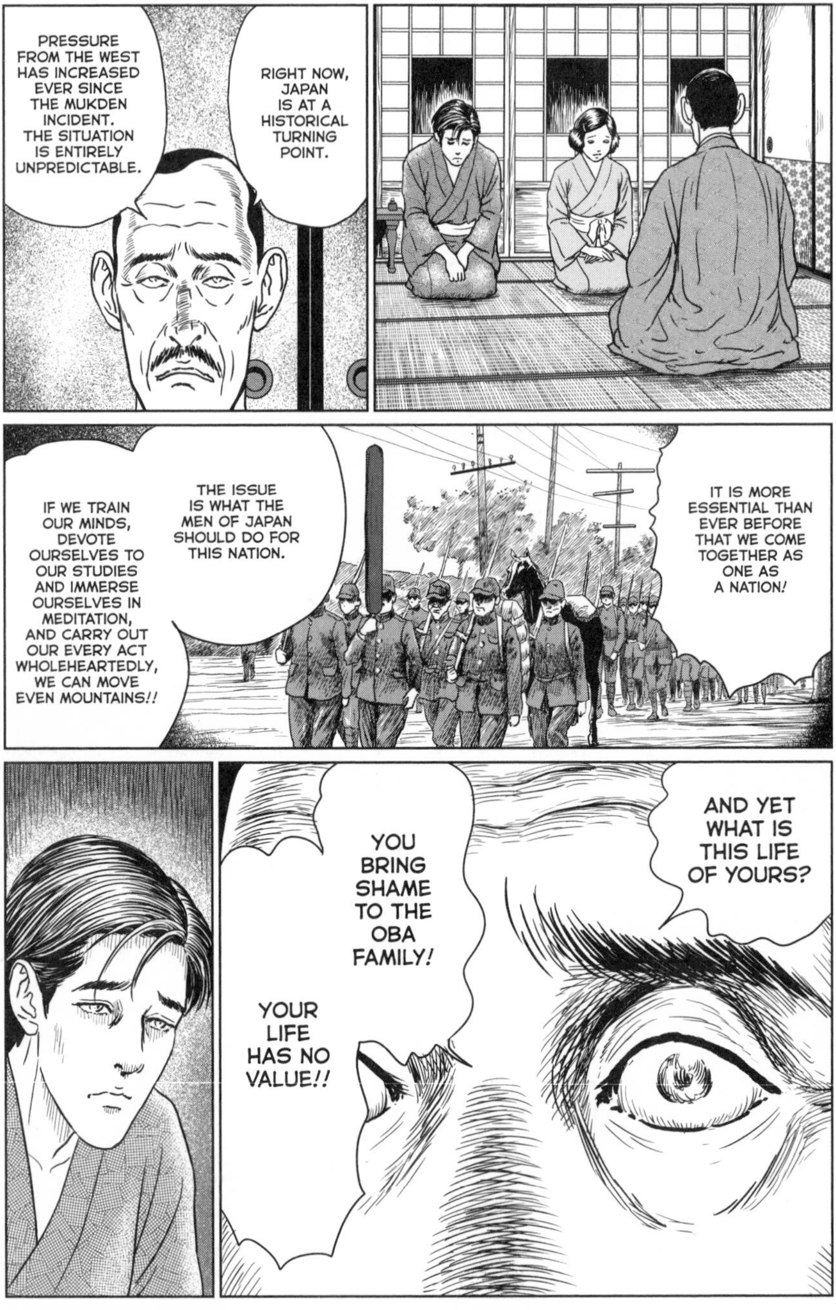
RIGHT NOW, JAPAN IS AT A HISTORICAL TURNING POINT.
PRESSURE FROM THE WEST HAS INCREASED EVER SINCE THE MUKDEN INCIDENT. THE SITUATION IS ENTIRELY UNPREDICTABLE.
IT IS MORE ESSENTIAL THAN EVER BEFORE THAT WE COME TOGETHER AS ONE AS A NATION!
THE ISSUE IS WHAT THE MEN OF JAPAN SHOULD DO FOR THIS NATION.
IF WE TRAIN OUR MINDS, DEVOTE OURSELVES TO OUR STUDIES AND IMMERSE OURSELVES IN MEDITATION, AND CARRY OUT OUR EVERY ACT WHOLEHEARTEDLY, WE CAN MOVE EVEN MOUNTAINS!!
AND YET WHAT IS THIS LIFE OF YOURS?
YOU BRING SHAME TO THE OBA FAMILY!
YOUR LIFE HAS NO VALUE!!

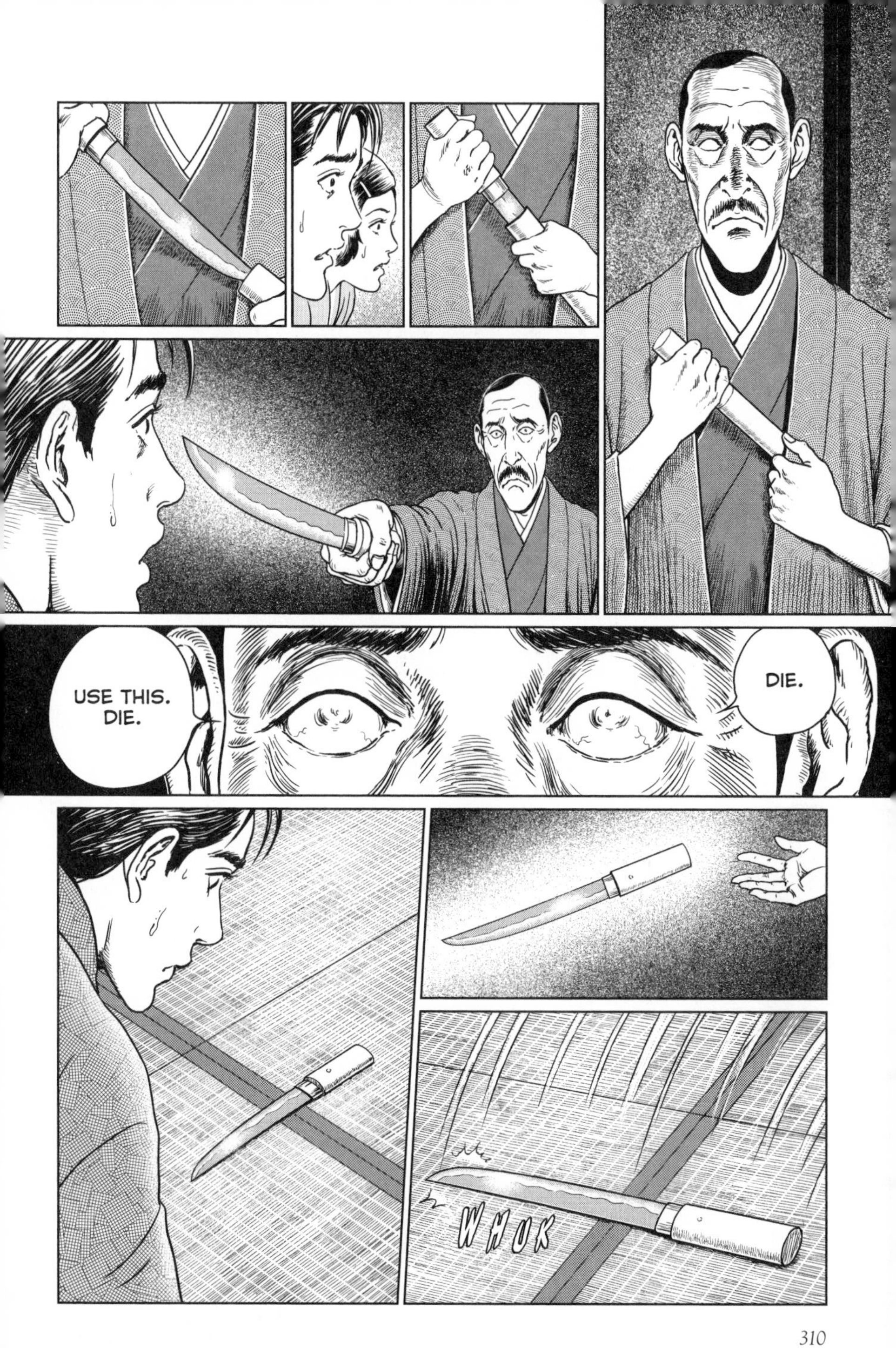
DIE.
USE THIS.
DIE.
WHUK

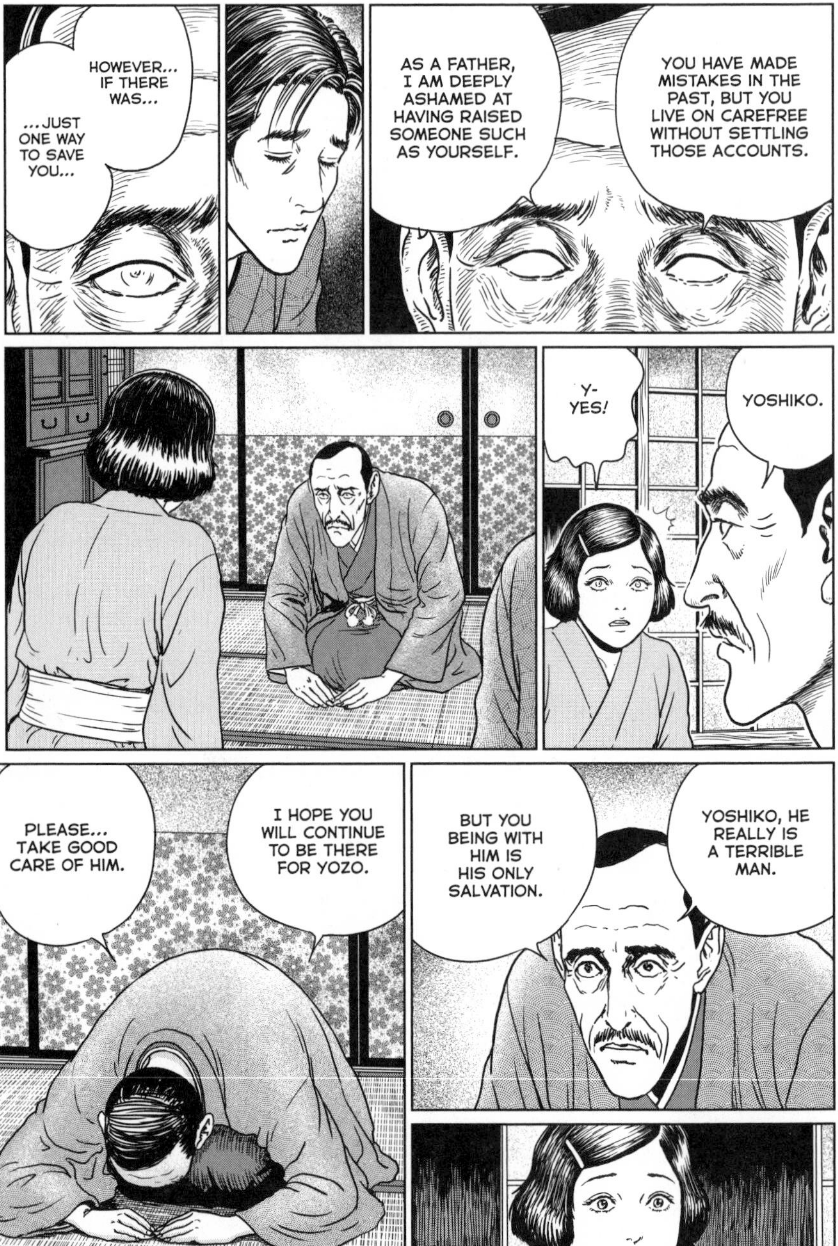
YOU HAVE MADE MISTAKES IN THE PAST, BUT YOU LIVE ON CAREFREE WITHOUT SETTLING THOSE ACCOUNTS.
AS A FATHER, I AM DEEPLY ASHAMED AT HAVING RAISED SOMEONE SUCH AS YOURSELF.
HOWEVER... IF THERE WAS...
...JUST ONE WAY TO SAVE YOU...
YOSHIKO.
Y- YES!
YOSHIKO, HE REALLY IS A TERRIBLE MAN.
BUT YOU BEING WITH HIM IS HIS ONLY SALVATION.
I HOPE YOU WILL CONTINUE TO BE THERE FOR YOZO.
PLEASE... TAKE GOOD CARE OF HIM.

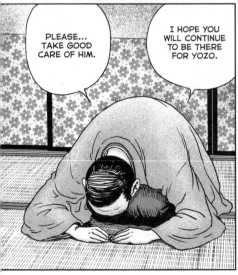

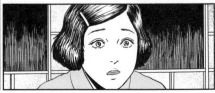

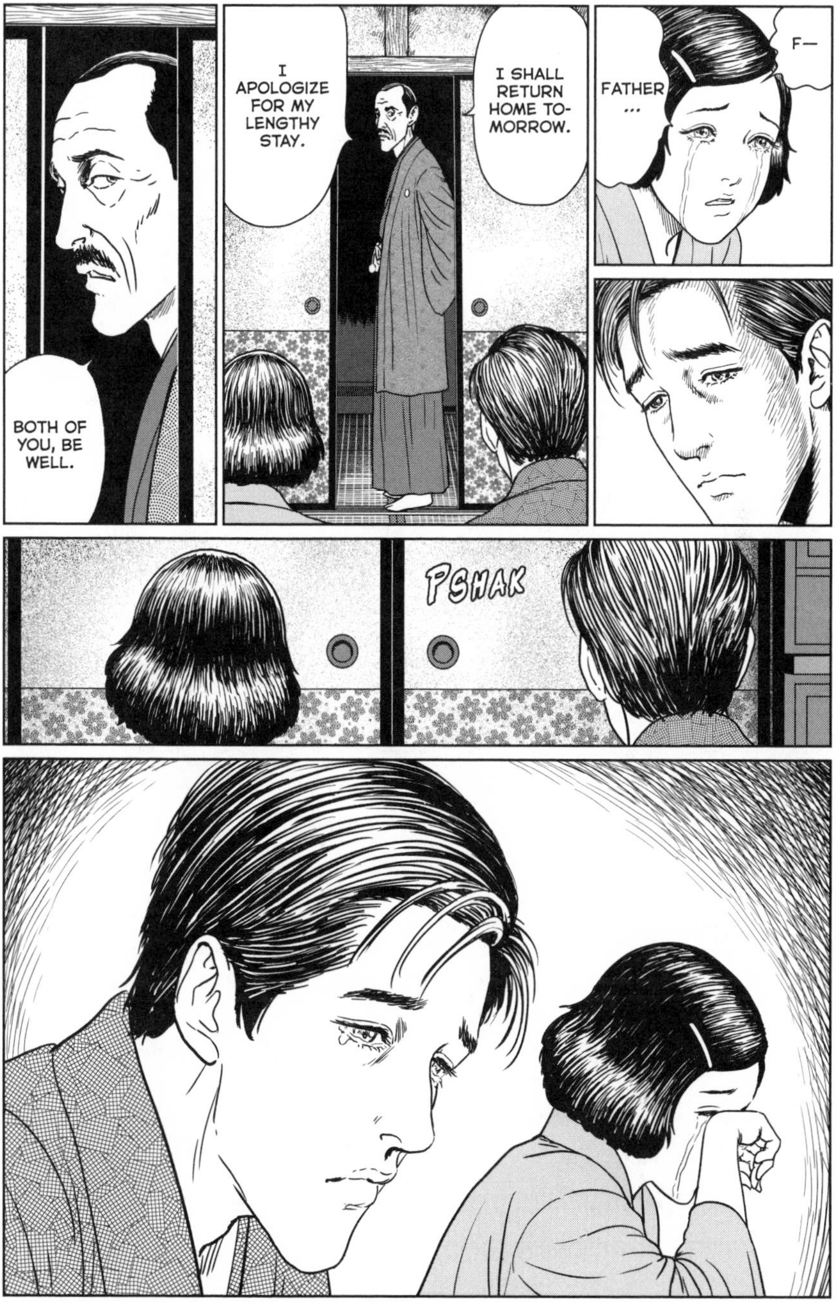
F—
FATHER ...
I SHALL RETURN HOME TO-MORROW.
I APOLOGIZE FOR MY LENGTHY STAY.
BOTH OF YOU, BE WELL.
PSHAK

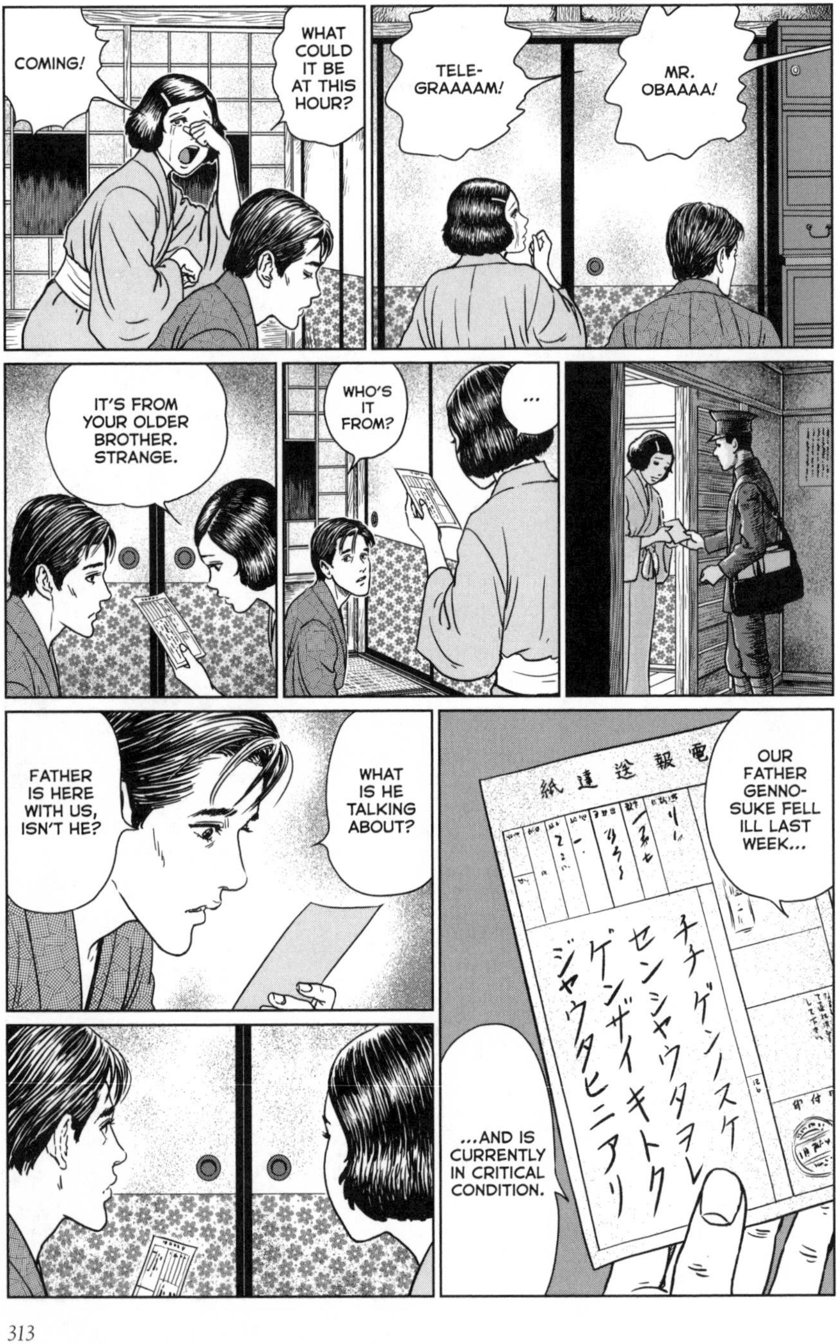
MR. OBAAAA!
TELE-GRAAAAM!
WHAT COULD IT BE AT THIS HOUR?
COMING!
...
WHO'S IT FROM?
IT'S FROM YOUR OLDER BROTHER. STRANGE.
OUR FATHER GENNO-SUKE FELL ILL LAST WEEK...
電報送達紙
チチゲンノスケ
センシャウタヲレ
ゲンザイキトク
ジャウタヒニアリ
...AND IS CURRENTLY IN CRITICAL CONDITION.
WHAT IS HE TALKING ABOUT?
FATHER IS HERE WITH US, ISN'T HE?

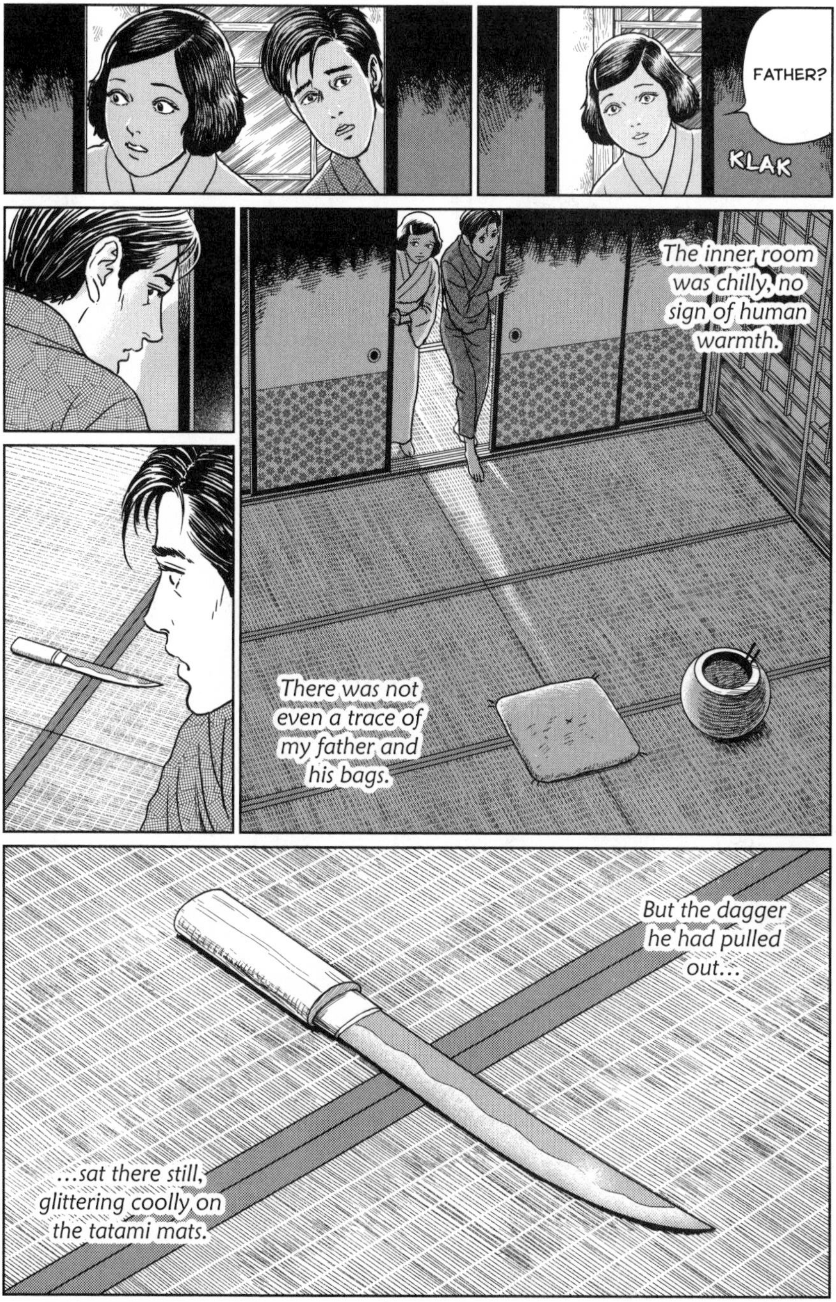
FATHER?
KLAK
The inner room was chilly, no sign of human warmth.
There was not even a trace of my father and his bags.
But the dagger he had pulled out...
...sat there still, glittering coolly on the tatami mats.

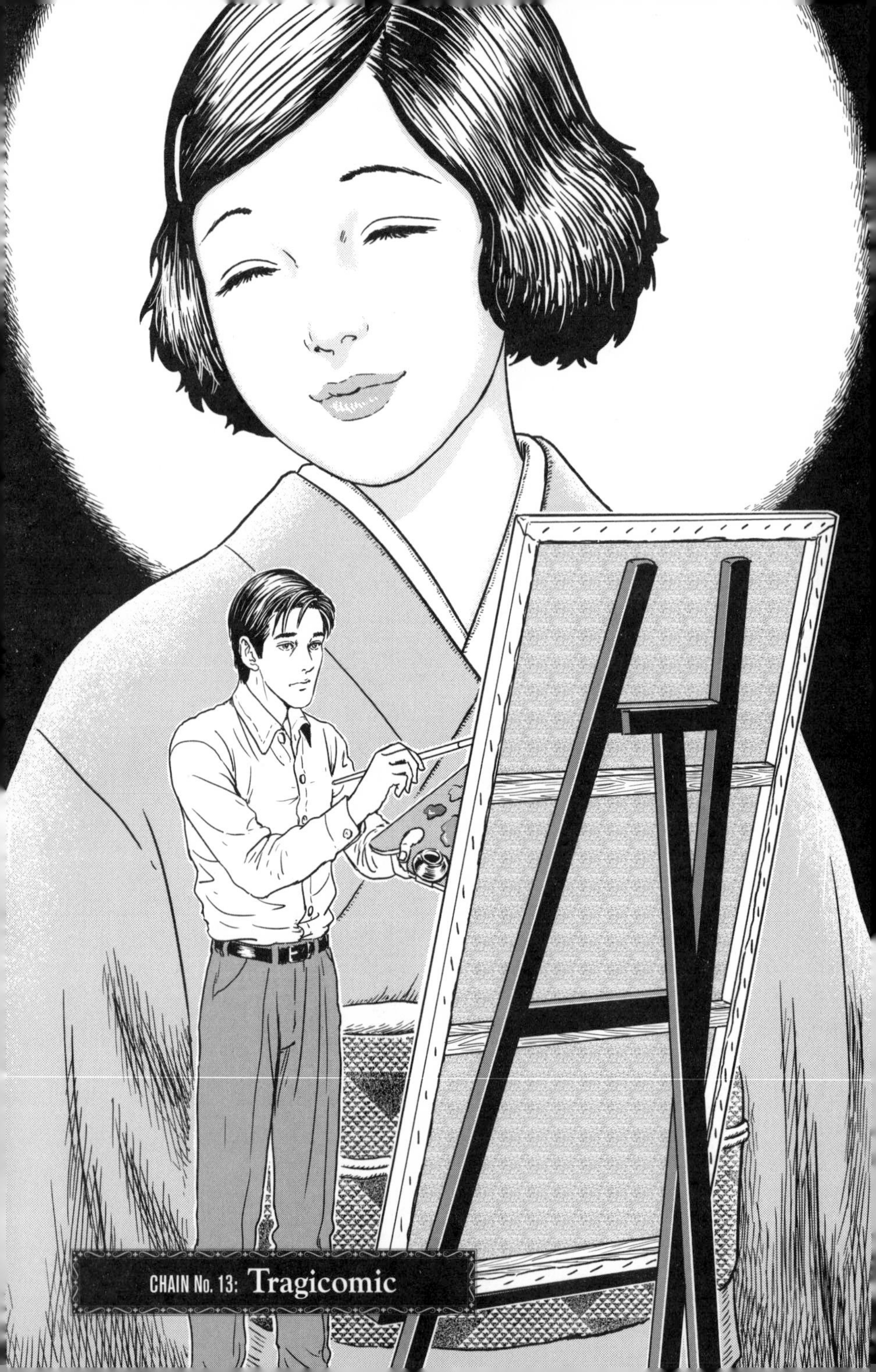

CHAIN No. 13: Tragicomic

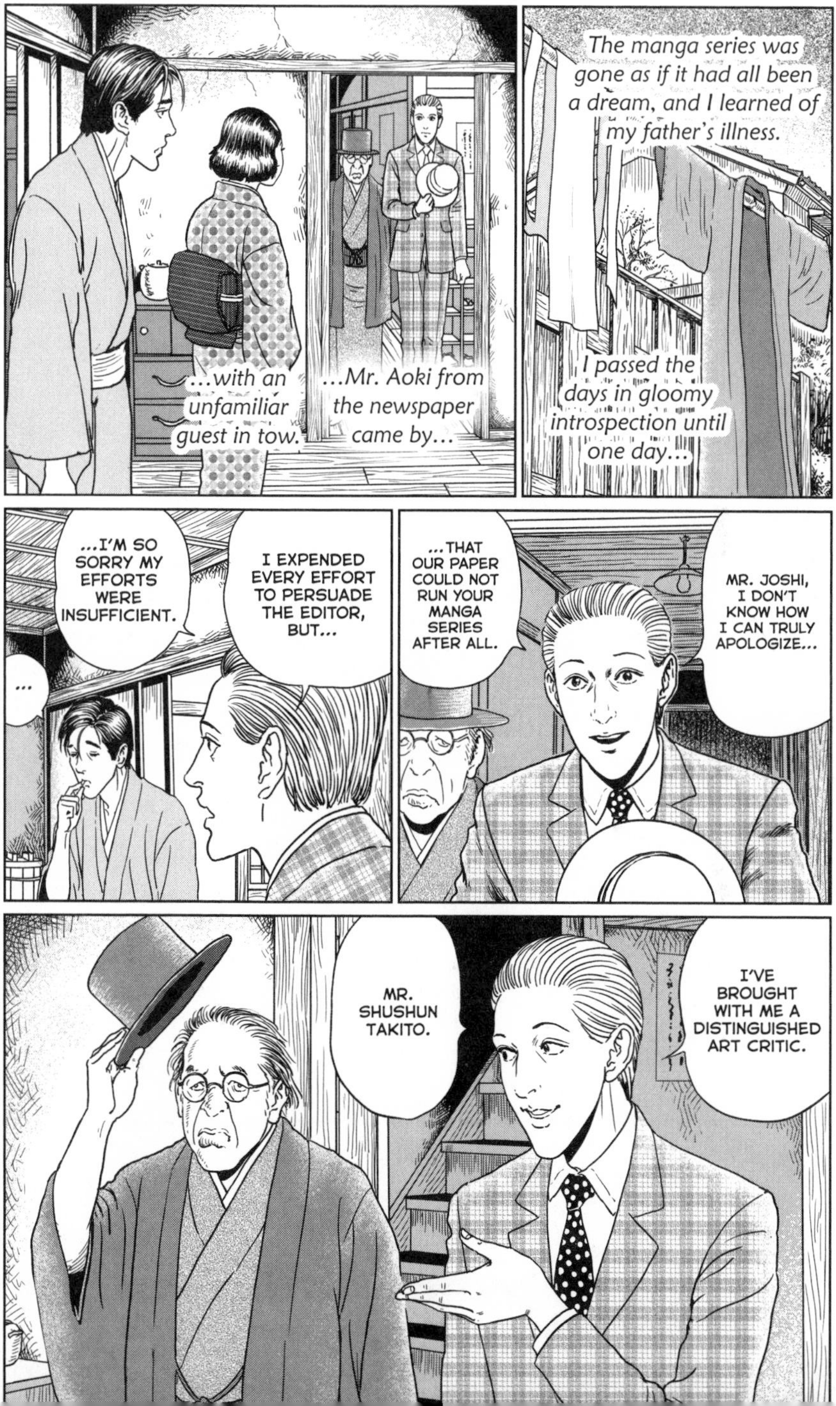
The manga series was gone as if it had all been a dream, and I learned of my father's illness.
I passed the days in gloomy introspection until one day...
...Mr. Aoki from the newspaper came by...
...with an unfamiliar guest in tow.
MR. JOSHI, I DON'T KNOW HOW I CAN TRULY APOLOGIZE...
...THAT OUR PAPER COULD NOT RUN YOUR MANGA SERIES AFTER ALL.
I EXPENDED EVERY EFFORT TO PERSUADE THE EDITOR, BUT...
...I'M SO SORRY MY EFFORTS WERE INSUFFICIENT.
...
I'VE BROUGHT WITH ME A DISTINGUISHED ART CRITIC.
MR. SHUSHUN TAKITO.

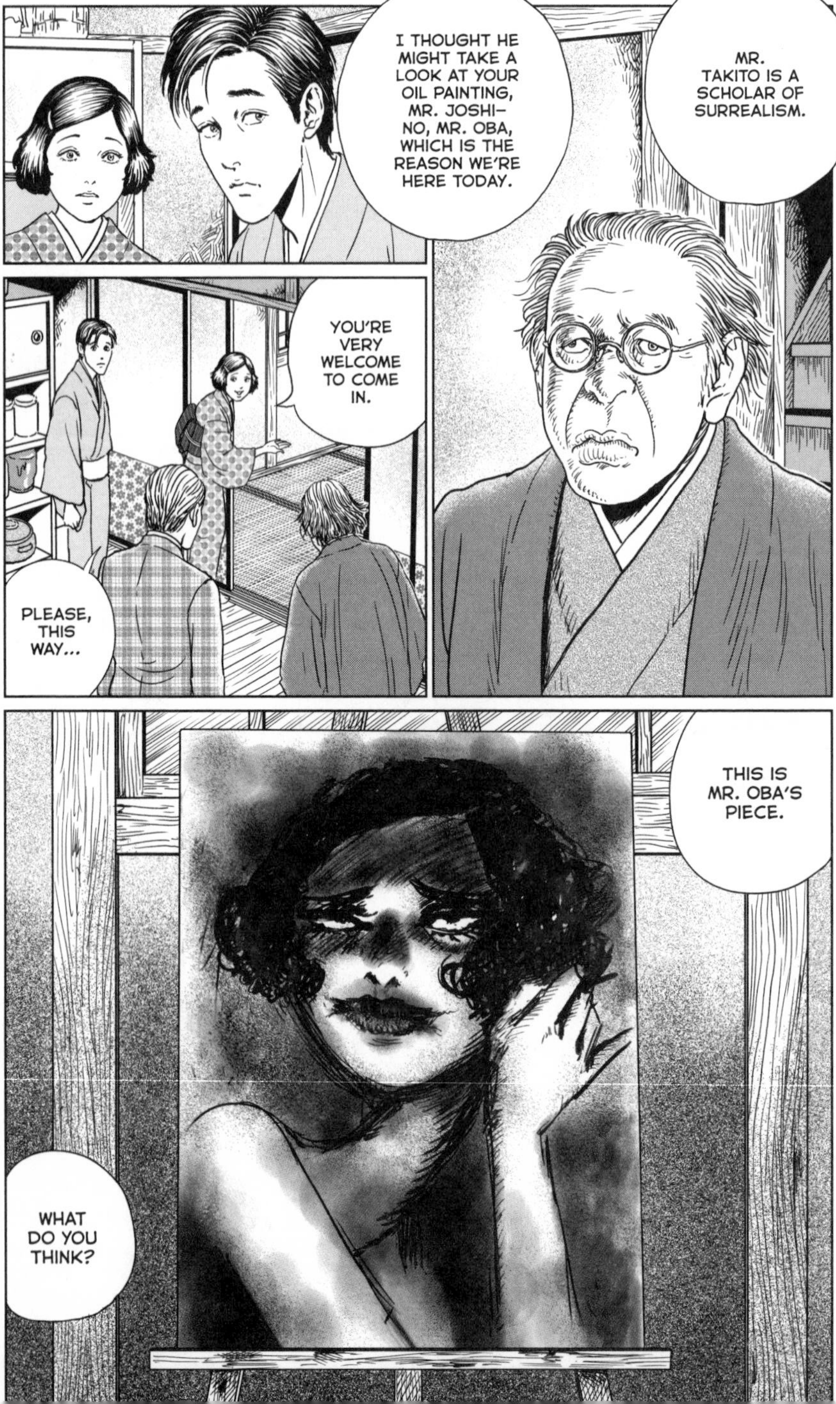
MR. TAKITO IS A SCHOLAR OF SURREALISM.
I THOUGHT HE MIGHT TAKE A LOOK AT YOUR OIL PAINTING, MR. JOSHI-NO, MR. OBA, WHICH IS THE REASON WE'RE HERE TODAY.
YOU'RE VERY WELCOME TO COME IN.
PLEASE, THIS WAY...
THIS IS MR. OBA'S PIECE.
WHAT DO YOU THINK?

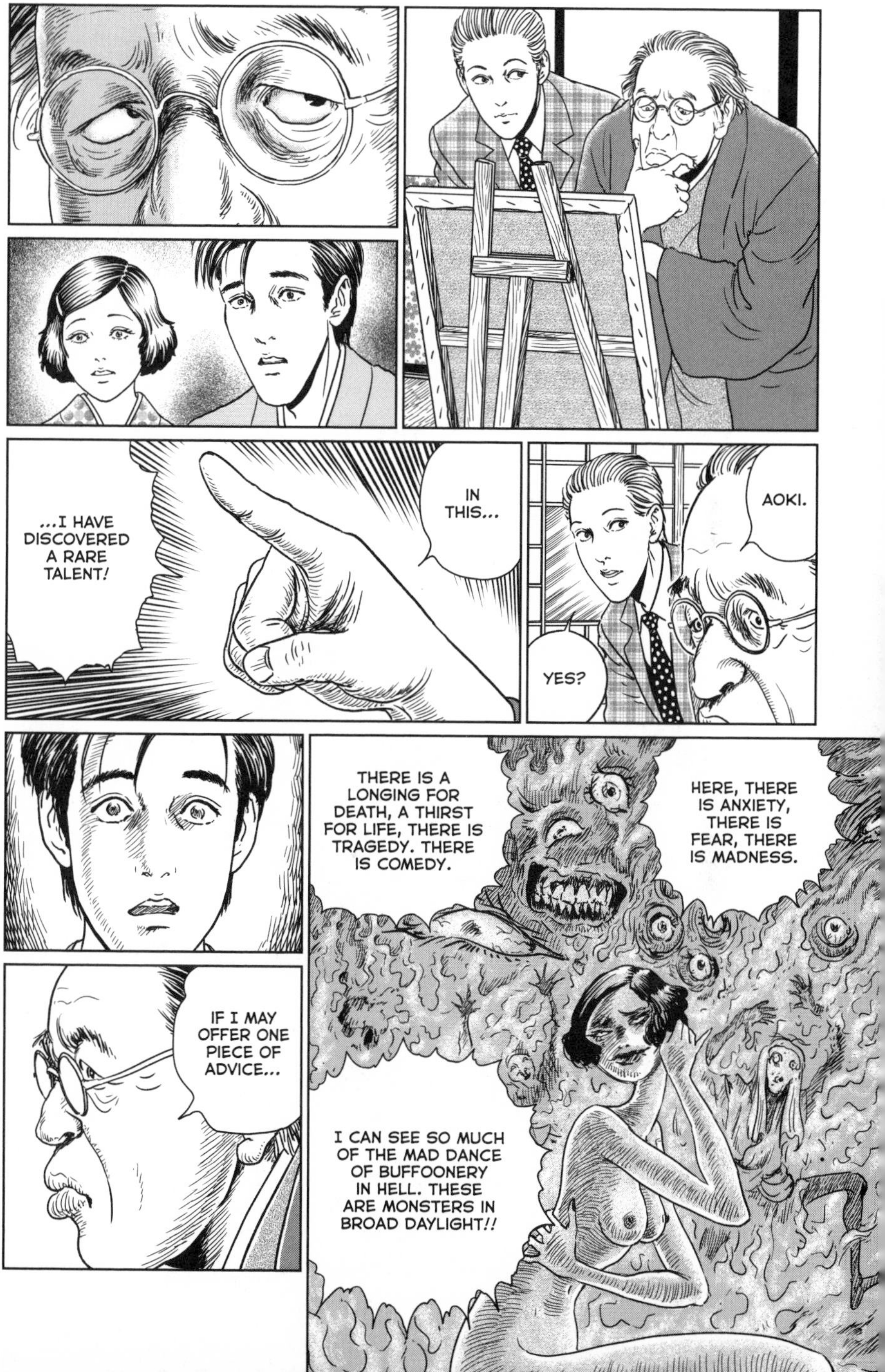
AOKI.
YES?
IN THIS...
...I HAVE DISCOVERED A RARE TALENT!
HERE, THERE IS ANXIETY, THERE IS FEAR, THERE IS MADNESS.
THERE IS A LONGING FOR DEATH, A THIRST FOR LIFE, THERE IS TRAGEDY. THERE IS COMEDY.
I CAN SEE SO MUCH OF THE MAD DANCE OF BUFFOONERY IN HELL. THESE ARE MONSTERS IN BROAD DAYLIGHT!!
IF I MAY OFFER ONE PIECE OF ADVICE...

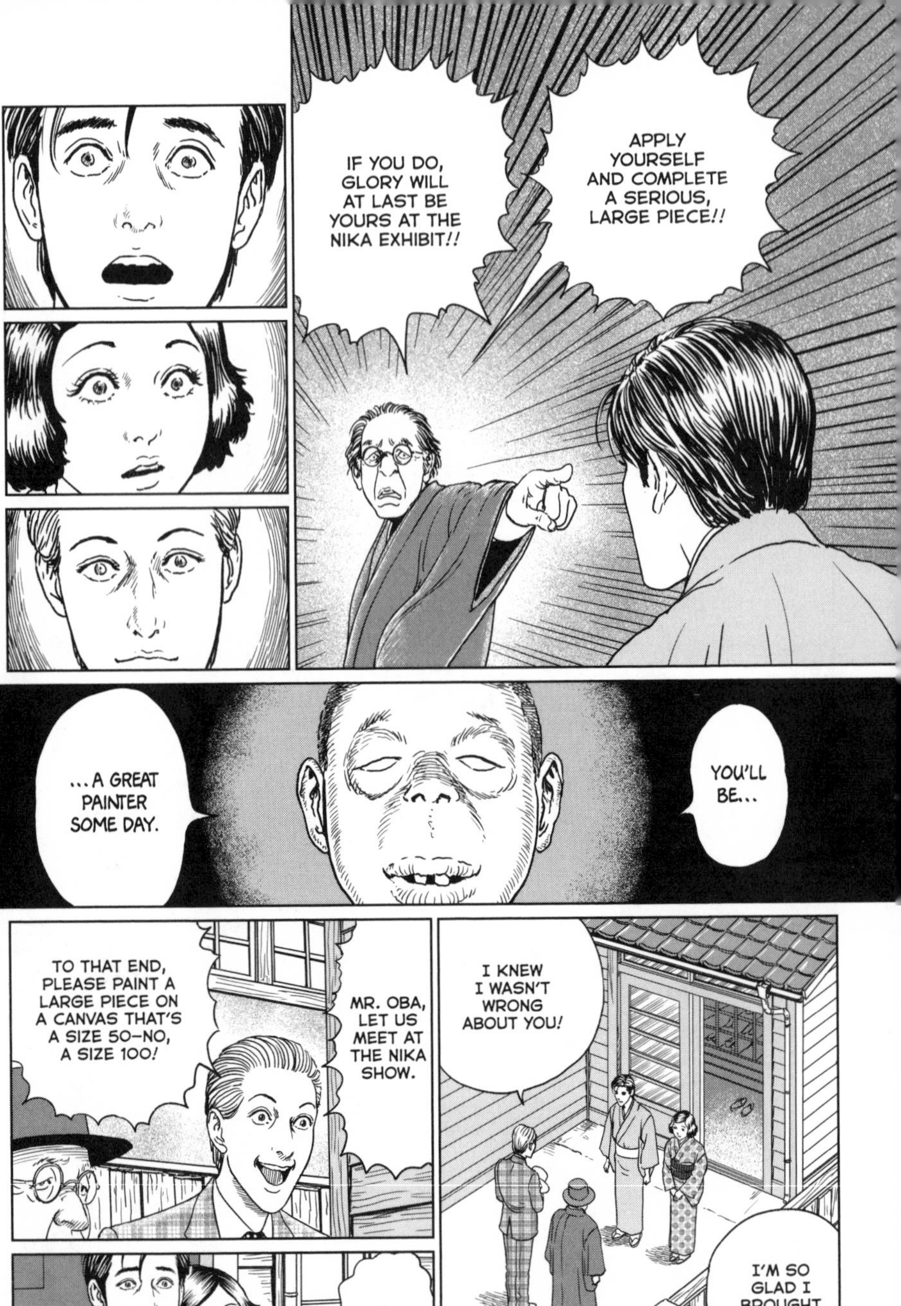
APPLY YOURSELF AND COMPLETE A SERIOUS, LARGE PIECE!!
IF YOU DO, GLORY WILL AT LAST BE YOURS AT THE NIKA EXHIBIT!!
YOU'LL BE...
...A GREAT PAINTER SOME DAY.
I KNEW I WASN'T WRONG ABOUT YOU!
I'M SO GLAD I BROUGHT MR. TAKITO.
MR. OBA, LET US MEET AT THE NIKA SHOW.
TO THAT END, PLEASE PAINT A LARGE PIECE ON A CANVAS THAT'S A SIZE 50–NO, A SIZE 100!
H-HONEY...

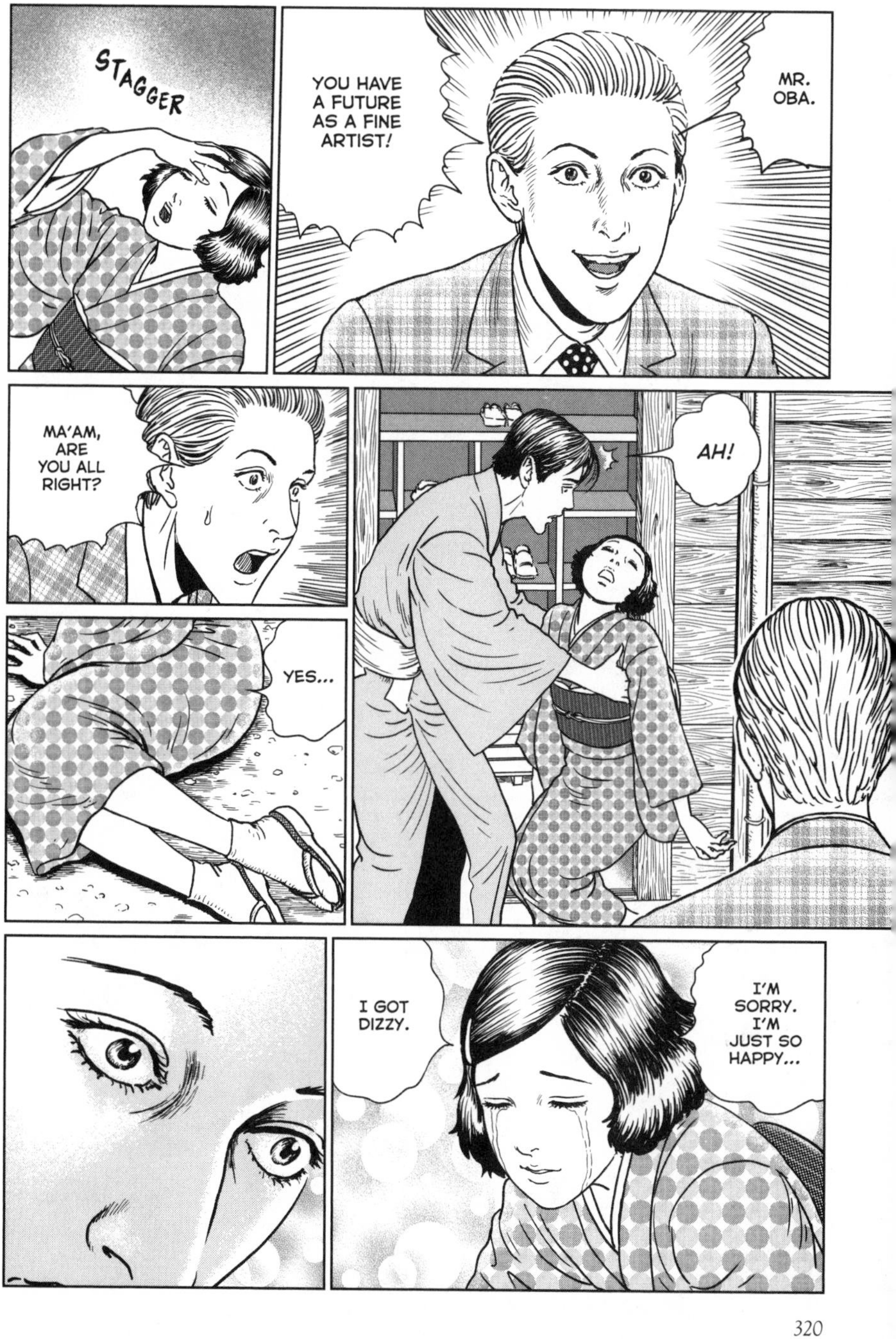
MR. OBA.
YOU HAVE A FUTURE AS A FINE ARTIST!
STAGGER
AH!
MA'AM, ARE YOU ALL RIGHT?
YES...
I'M SORRY. I'M JUST SO HAPPY...
I GOT DIZZY.

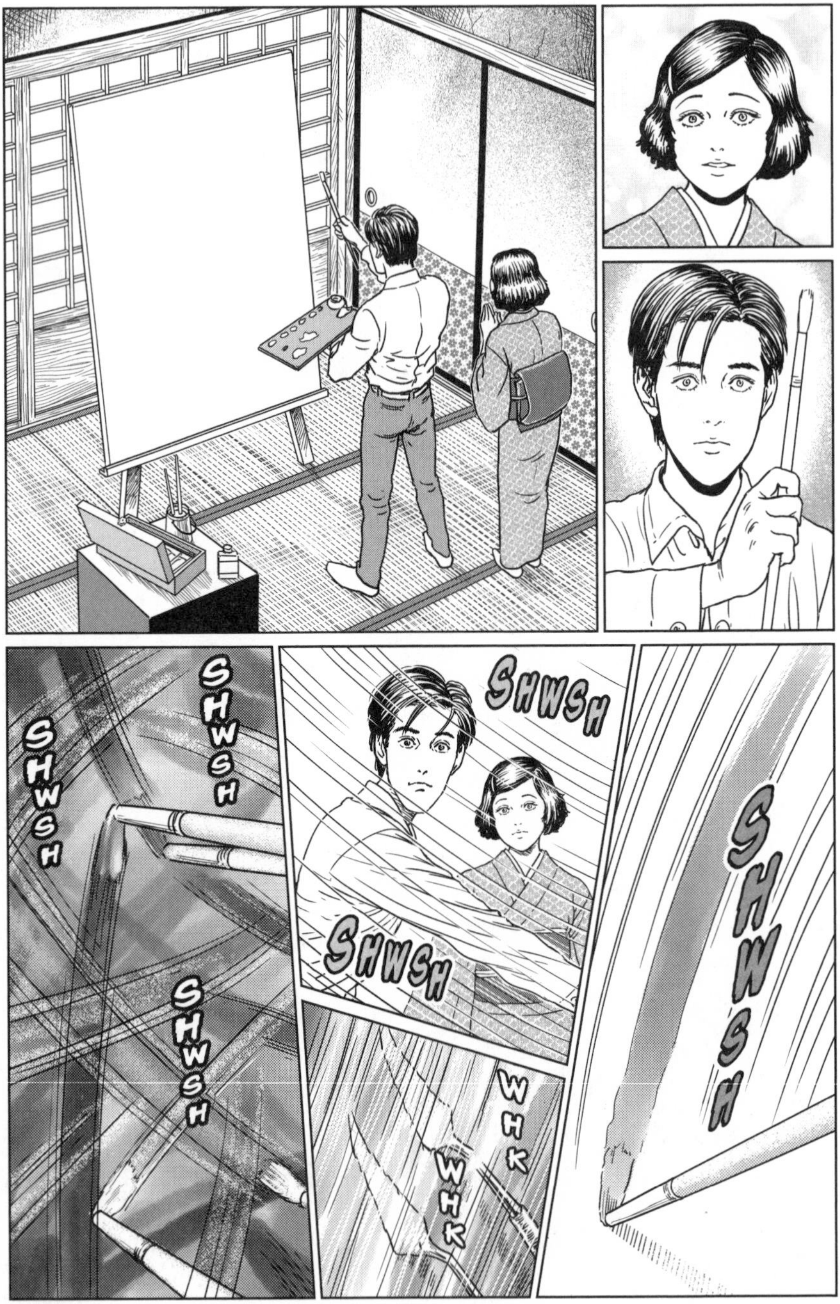
SHWSH
SHWSH
SHWSH
WHK
WHK
SHWSH
SHWSH
SHWSH

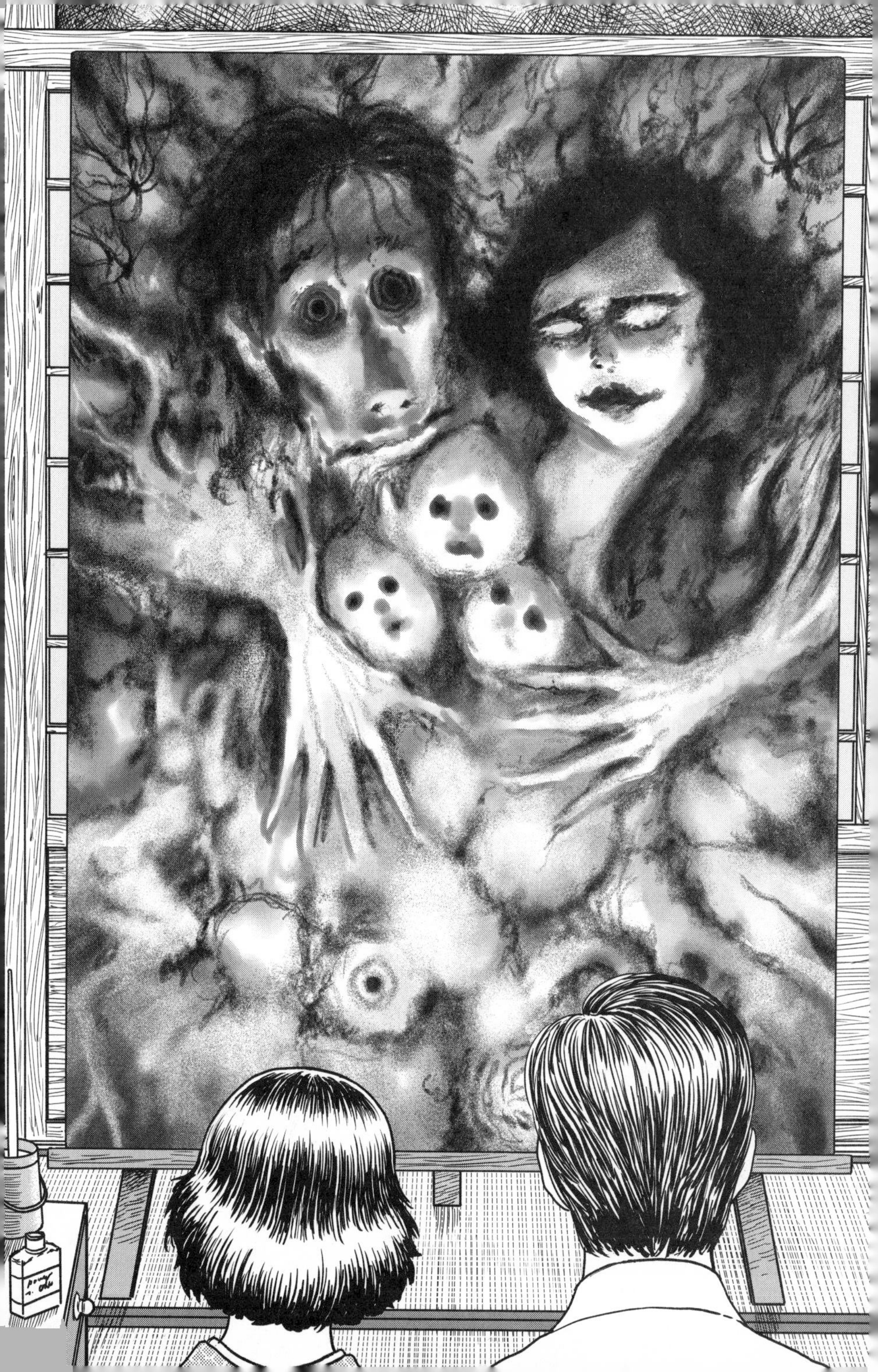

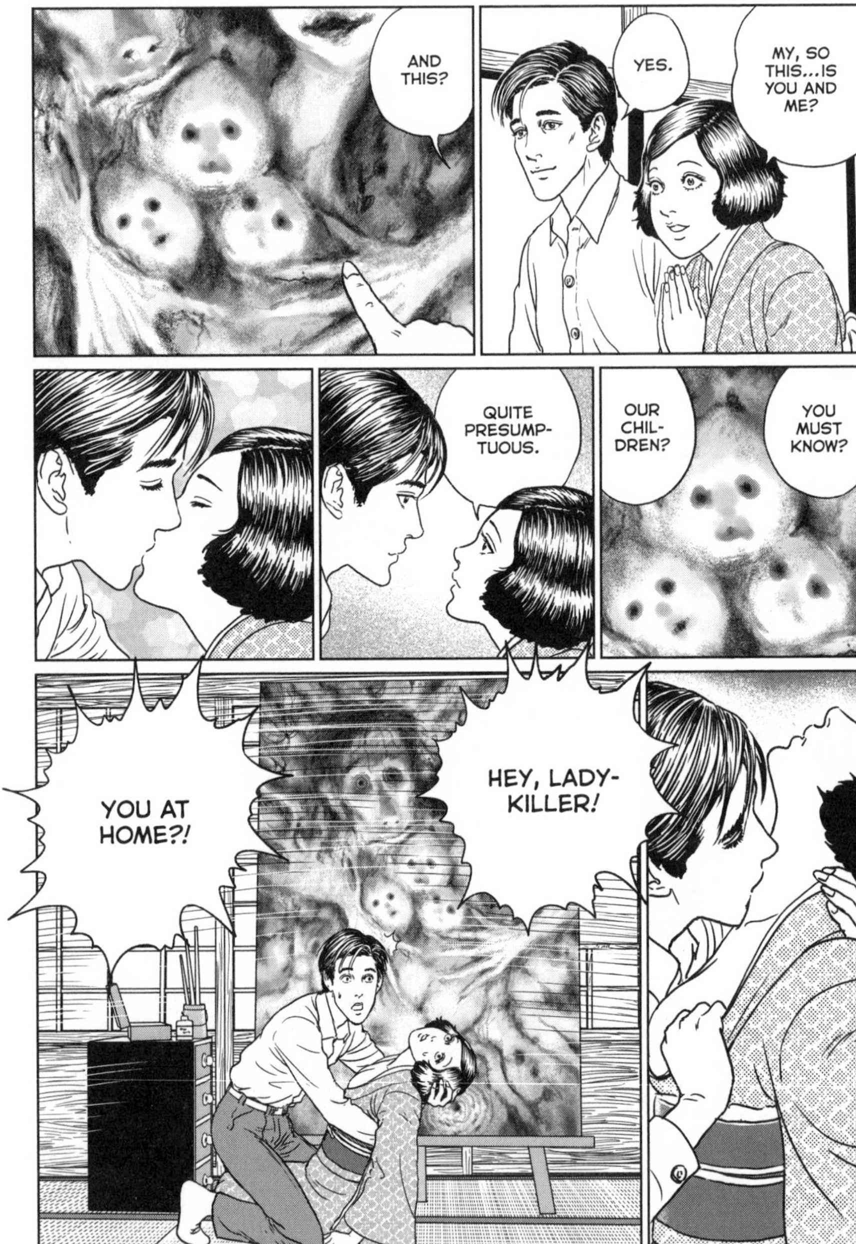
MY, SO THIS...IS YOU AND ME?
YES.
AND THIS?
YOU MUST KNOW?
OUR CHIL-DREN?
QUITE PRESUMP-TUOUS.
HEY, LADY-KILLER!
YOU AT HOME?!

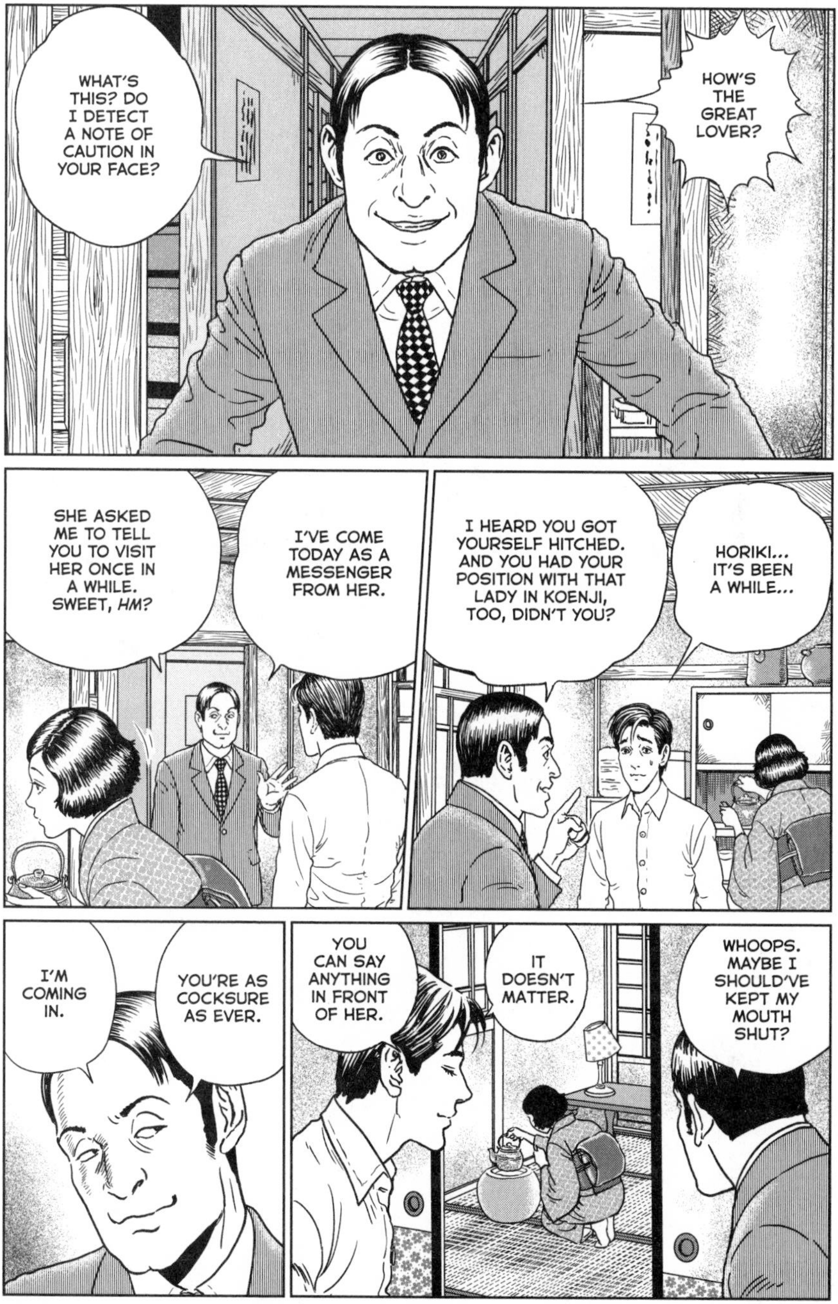
HOW'S THE GREAT LOVER?
WHAT'S THIS? DO I DETECT A NOTE OF CAUTION IN YOUR FACE?
HORIKI... IT'S BEEN A WHILE...
I HEARD YOU GOT YOURSELF HITCHED. AND YOU HAD YOUR POSITION WITH THAT LADY IN KOENJI, TOO, DIDN'T YOU?
I'VE COME TODAY AS A MESSENGER FROM HER.
SHE ASKED ME TO TELL YOU TO VISIT HER ONCE IN A WHILE. SWEET, *HM*?
WHOOPS. MAYBE I SHOULD'VE KEPT MY MOUTH SHUT?
IT DOESN'T MATTER.
YOU CAN SAY ANYTHING IN FRONT OF HER.
YOU'RE AS COCKSURE AS EVER.
I'M COMING IN.

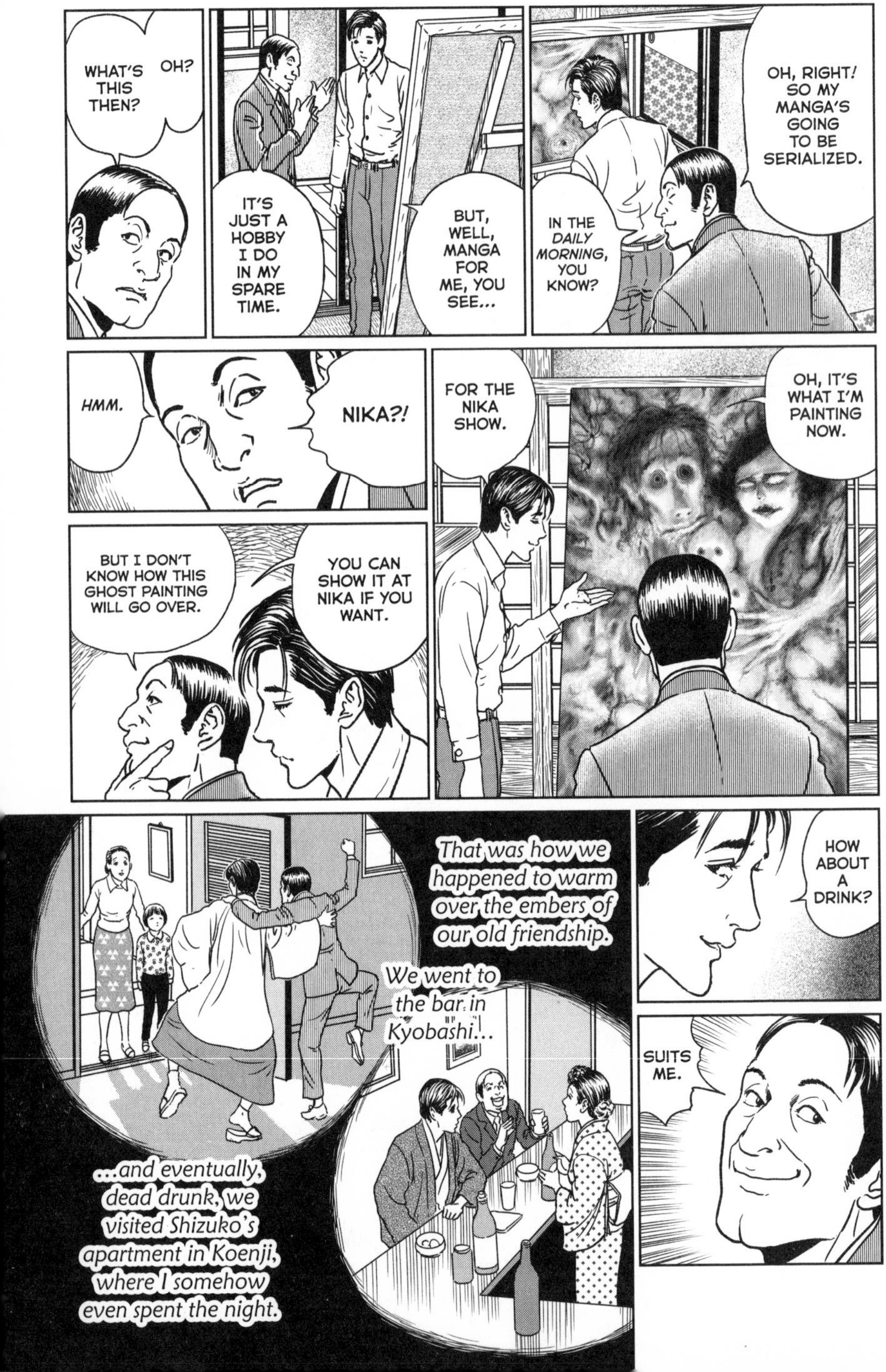
OH, RIGHT! SO MY MANGA'S GOING TO BE SERIALIZED.
IN THE *DAILY MORNING*, YOU KNOW?
BUT, WELL, MANGA FOR ME, YOU SEE...
IT'S JUST A HOBBY I DO IN MY SPARE TIME.
OH?
WHAT'S THIS THEN?
OH, IT'S WHAT I'M PAINTING NOW.
FOR THE NIKA SHOW.
NIKA?!
HMM.
YOU CAN SHOW IT AT NIKA IF YOU WANT.
BUT I DON'T KNOW HOW THIS GHOST PAINTING WILL GO OVER.
HOW ABOUT A DRINK?
SUITS ME.
That was how we happened to warm over the embers of our old friendship.
We went to the bar in Kyobashi...
...and eventually, dead drunk, we visited Shizuko's apartment in Koenji, where I somehow even spent the night.

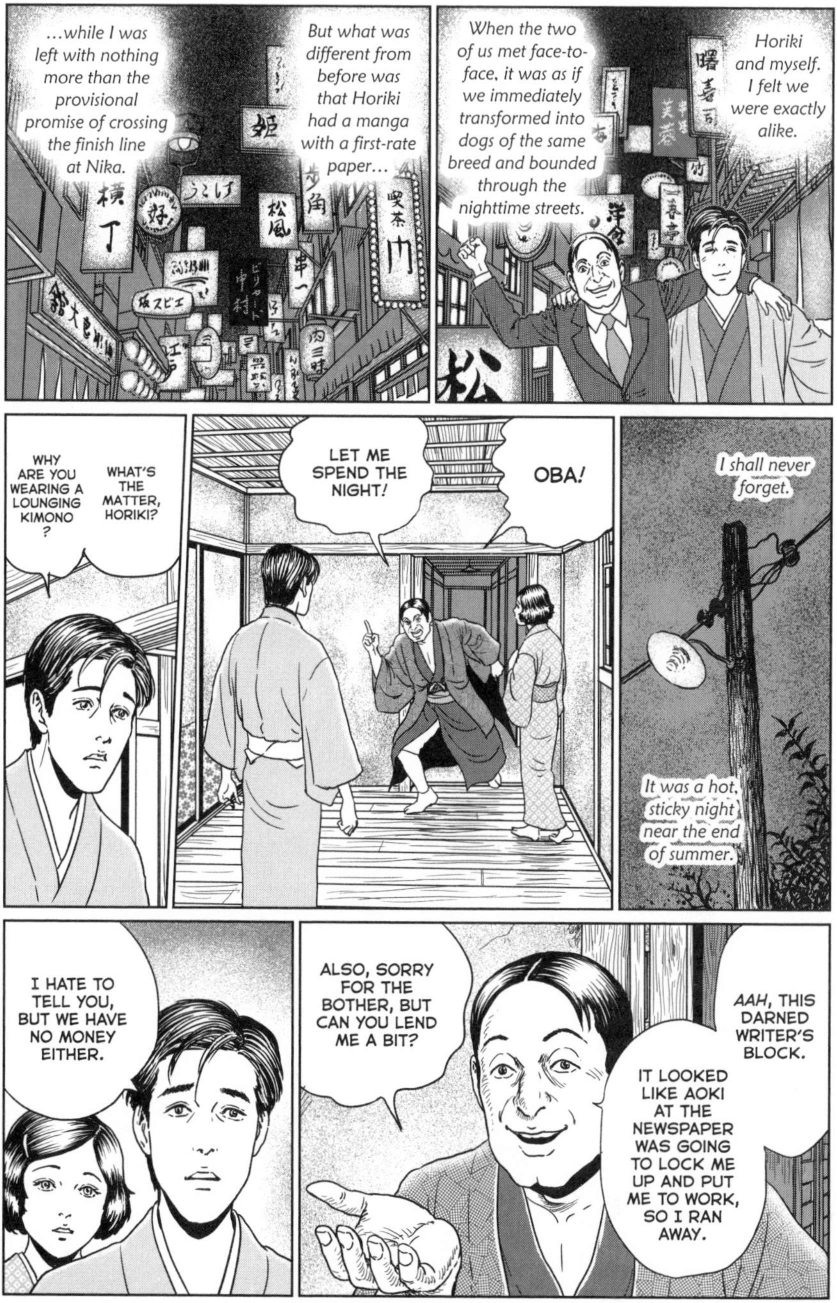
Horiki and myself. I felt we were exactly alike.
When the two of us met face-to-face, it was as if we immediately transformed into dogs of the same breed and bounded through the nighttime streets.
But what was different from before was that Horiki had a manga with a first-rate paper…
…while I was left with nothing more than the provisional promise of crossing the finish line at Nika.
I shall never forget.
It was a hot, sticky night near the end of summer.
OBA!
LET ME SPEND THE NIGHT!
WHAT'S THE MATTER, HORIKI?
WHY ARE YOU WEARING A LOUNGING KIMONO?
AAH, THIS DARNED WRITER'S BLOCK.
IT LOOKED LIKE AOKI AT THE NEWSPAPER WAS GOING TO LOCK ME UP AND PUT ME TO WORK, SO I RAN AWAY.
ALSO, SORRY FOR THE BOTHER, BUT CAN YOU LEND ME A BIT?
I HATE TO TELL YOU, BUT WE HAVE NO MONEY EITHER.

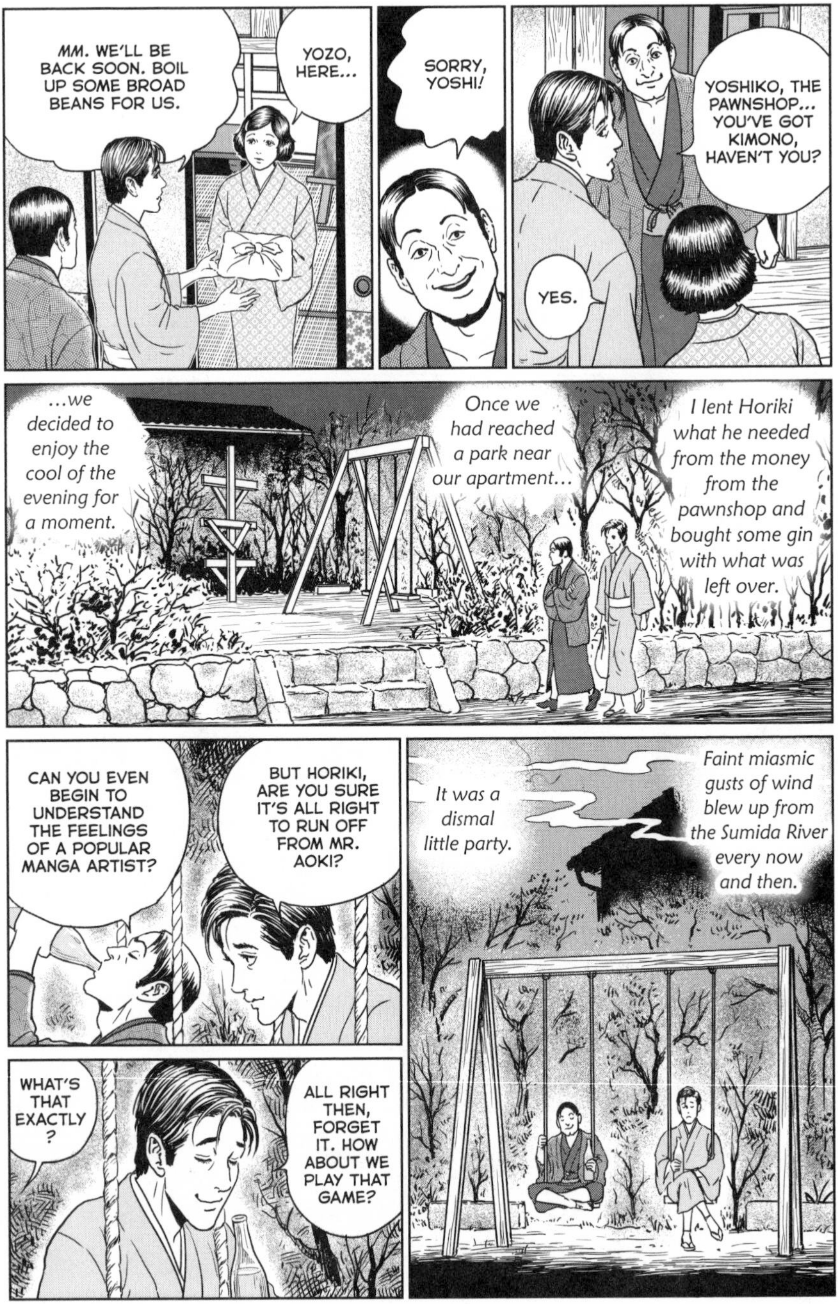
YOSHIKO, THE PAWNSHOP... YOU'VE GOT KIMONO, HAVEN'T YOU?
YES.
SORRY, YOSHI!
YOZO, HERE...
MM. WE'LL BE BACK SOON. BOIL UP SOME BROAD BEANS FOR US.
I lent Horiki what he needed from the money from the pawnshop and bought some gin with what was left over.
Once we had reached a park near our apartment...
...we decided to enjoy the cool of the evening for a moment.
Faint miasmic gusts of wind blew up from the Sumida River every now and then.
It was a dismal little party.
BUT HORIKI, ARE YOU SURE IT'S ALL RIGHT TO RUN OFF FROM MR. AOKI?
CAN YOU EVEN BEGIN TO UNDERSTAND THE FEELINGS OF A POPULAR MANGA ARTIST?
ALL RIGHT THEN, FORGET IT. HOW ABOUT WE PLAY THAT GAME?
WHAT'S THAT EXACTLY?

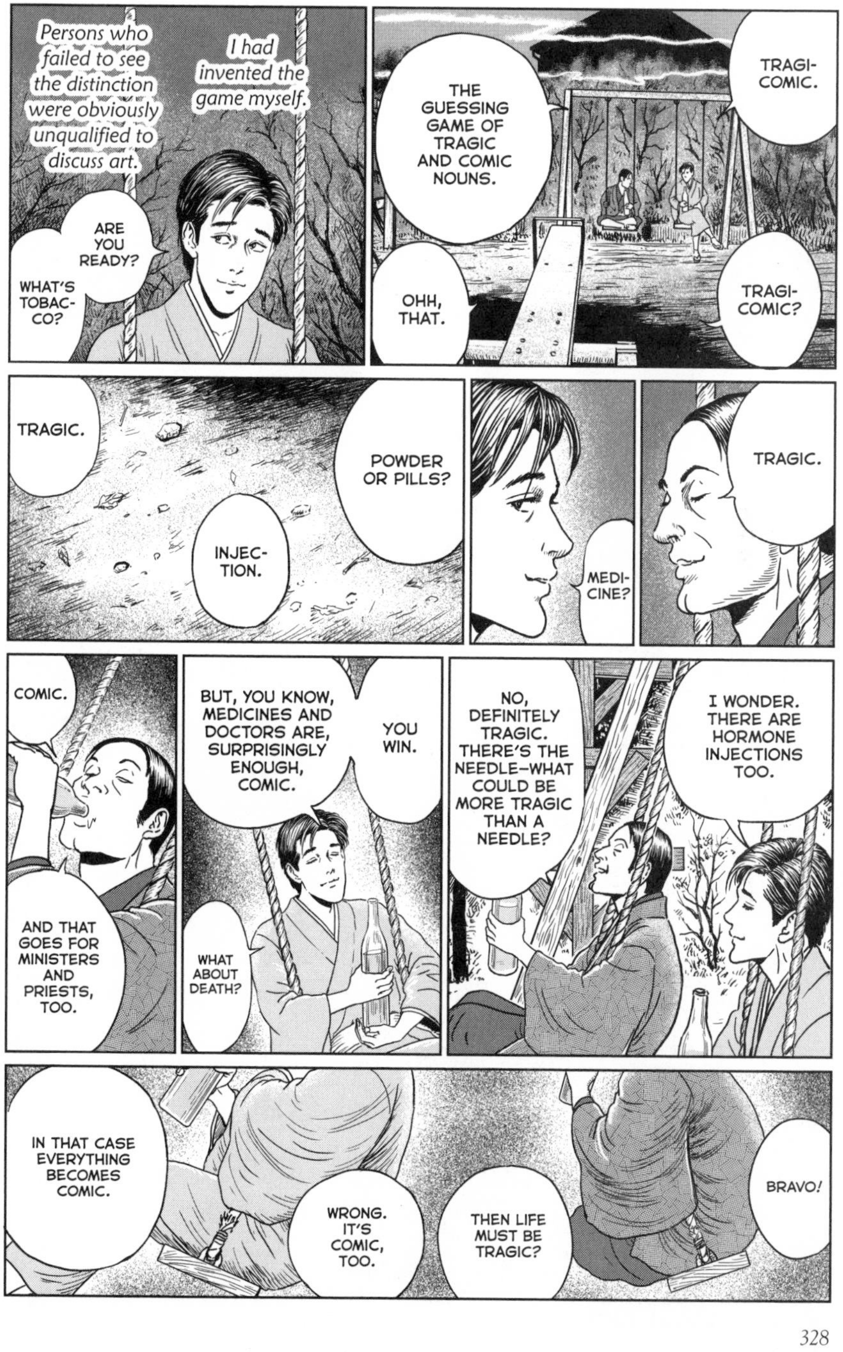
TRAGI-COMIC.
THE GUESSING GAME OF TRAGIC AND COMIC NOUNS.
TRAGI-COMIC?
OHH, THAT.
I had invented the game myself.
Persons who failed to see the distinction were obviously unqualified to discuss art.
ARE YOU READY?
WHAT'S TOBACCO?
TRAGIC.
MEDI-CINE?
POWDER OR PILLS?
TRAGIC.
INJEC-TION.
I WONDER. THERE ARE HORMONE INJECTIONS TOO.
NO, DEFINITELY TRAGIC. THERE'S THE NEEDLE—WHAT COULD BE MORE TRAGIC THAN A NEEDLE?
YOU WIN.
BUT, YOU KNOW, MEDICINES AND DOCTORS ARE, SURPRISINGLY ENOUGH, COMIC.
WHAT ABOUT DEATH?
COMIC.
AND THAT GOES FOR MINISTERS AND PRIESTS, TOO.
BRAVO!
THEN LIFE MUST BE TRAGIC?
WRONG. IT'S COMIC, TOO.
IN THAT CASE EVERYTHING BECOMES COMIC.

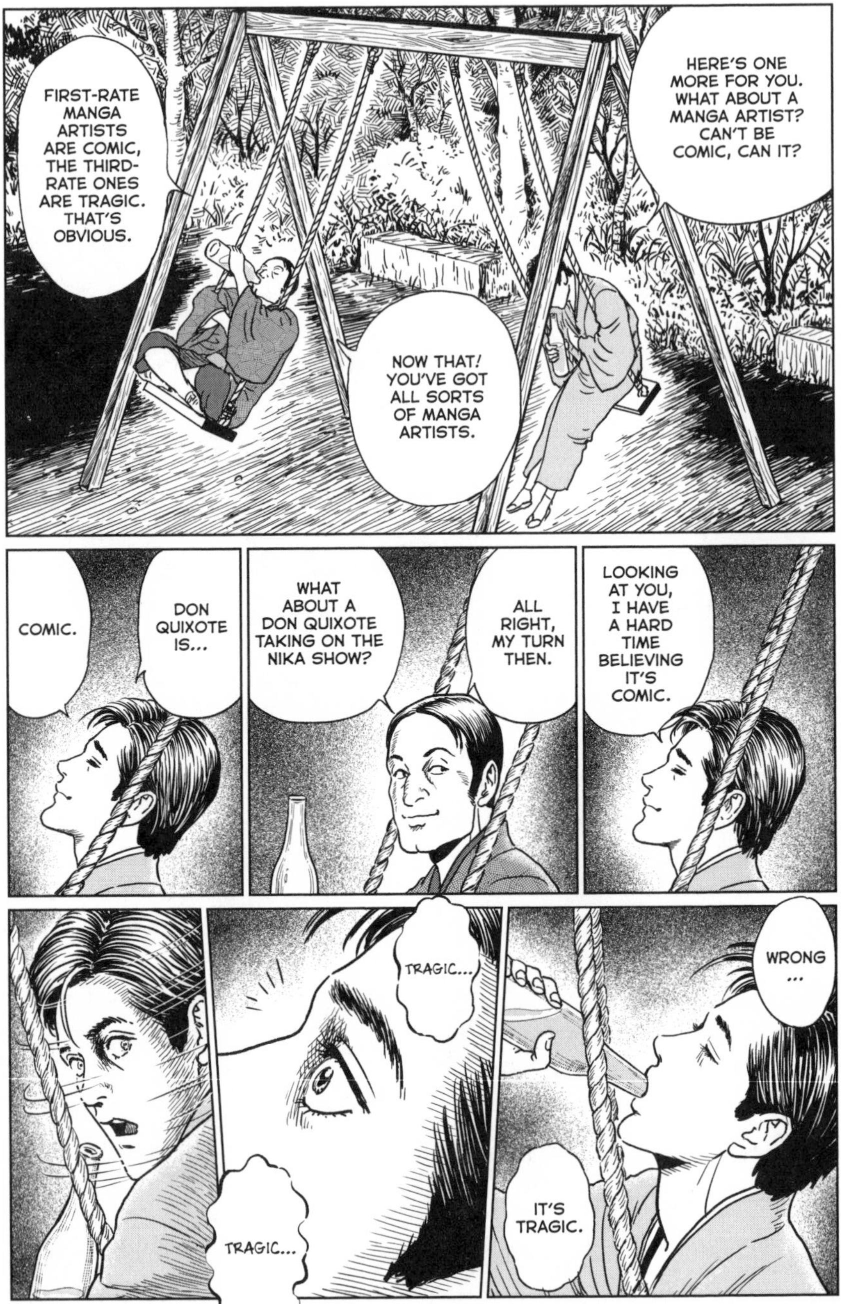
HERE'S ONE MORE FOR YOU. WHAT ABOUT A MANGA ARTIST? CAN'T BE COMIC, CAN IT?
NOW THAT! YOU'VE GOT ALL SORTS OF MANGA ARTISTS.
FIRST-RATE MANGA ARTISTS ARE COMIC, THE THIRD-RATE ONES ARE TRAGIC. THAT'S OBVIOUS.
LOOKING AT YOU, I HAVE A HARD TIME BELIEVING IT'S COMIC.
ALL RIGHT, MY TURN THEN.
WHAT ABOUT A DON QUIXOTE TAKING ON THE NIKA SHOW?
DON QUIXOTE IS...
COMIC.
WRONG...
IT'S TRAGIC.
TRAGIC...
TRAGIC...

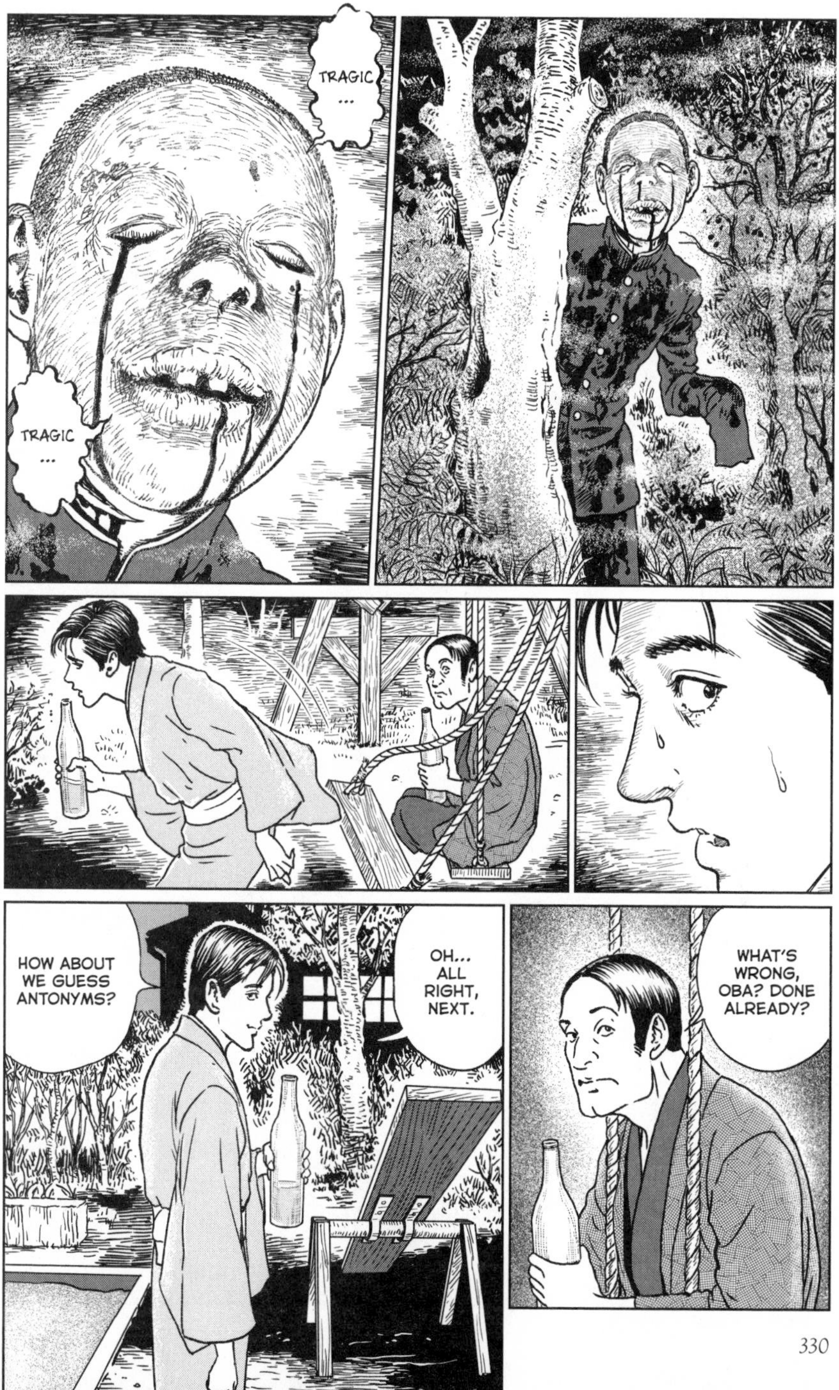
TRAGIC ...
TRAGIC ...
WHAT'S WRONG, OBA? DONE ALREADY?
OH... ALL RIGHT, NEXT.
HOW ABOUT WE GUESS ANTONYMS?

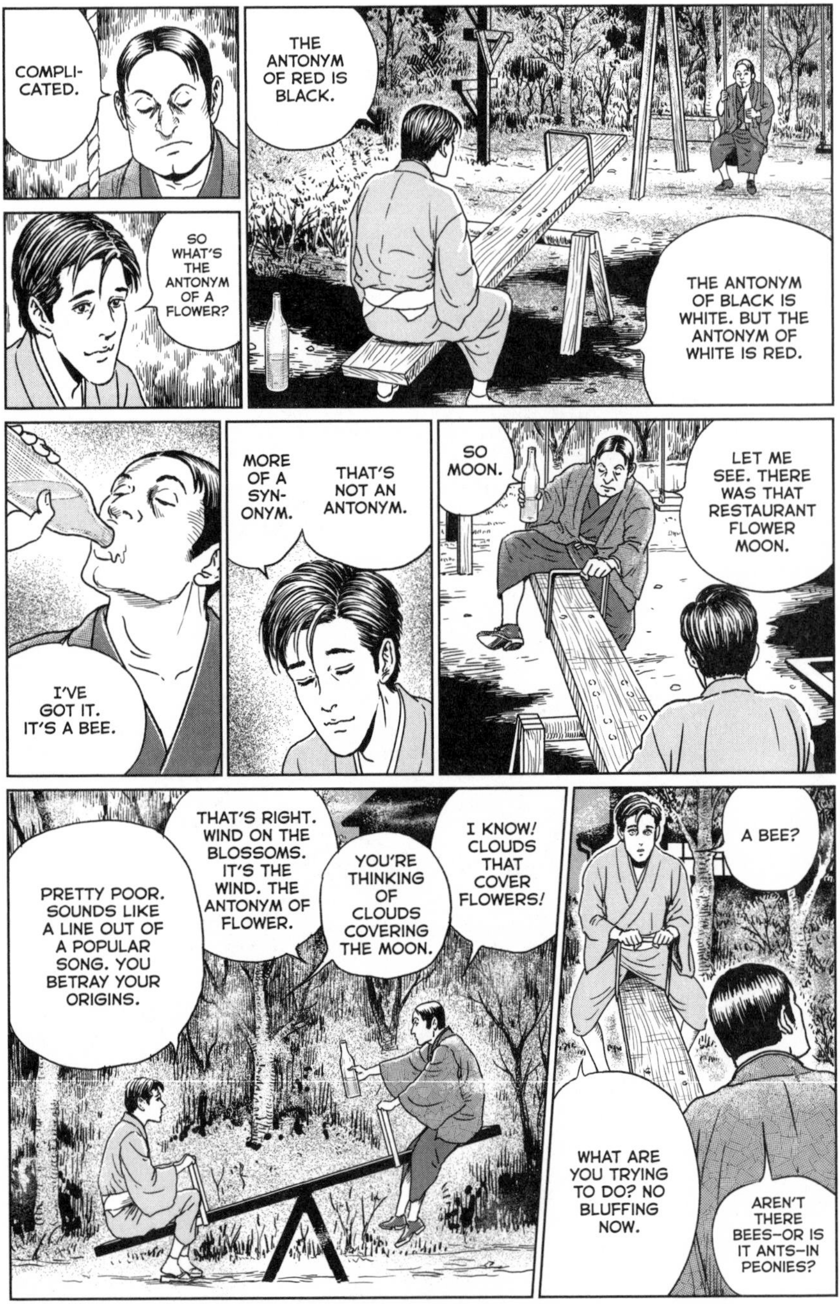
THE ANTONYM OF RED IS BLACK.
THE ANTONYM OF BLACK IS WHITE. BUT THE ANTONYM OF WHITE IS RED.
COMPLI-CATED.
SO WHAT'S THE ANTONYM OF A FLOWER?
LET ME SEE. THERE WAS THAT RESTAURANT FLOWER MOON.
SO MOON.
THAT'S NOT AN ANTONYM.
MORE OF A SYN-ONYM.
I'VE GOT IT. IT'S A BEE.
A BEE?
AREN'T THERE BEES—OR IS IT ANTS—IN PEONIES?
WHAT ARE YOU TRYING TO DO? NO BLUFFING NOW.
I KNOW! CLOUDS THAT COVER FLOWERS!
YOU'RE THINKING OF CLOUDS COVERING THE MOON.
THAT'S RIGHT. WIND ON THE BLOSSOMS. IT'S THE WIND. THE ANTONYM OF FLOWER.
PRETTY POOR. SOUNDS LIKE A LINE OUT OF A POPULAR SONG. YOU BETRAY YOUR ORIGINS.

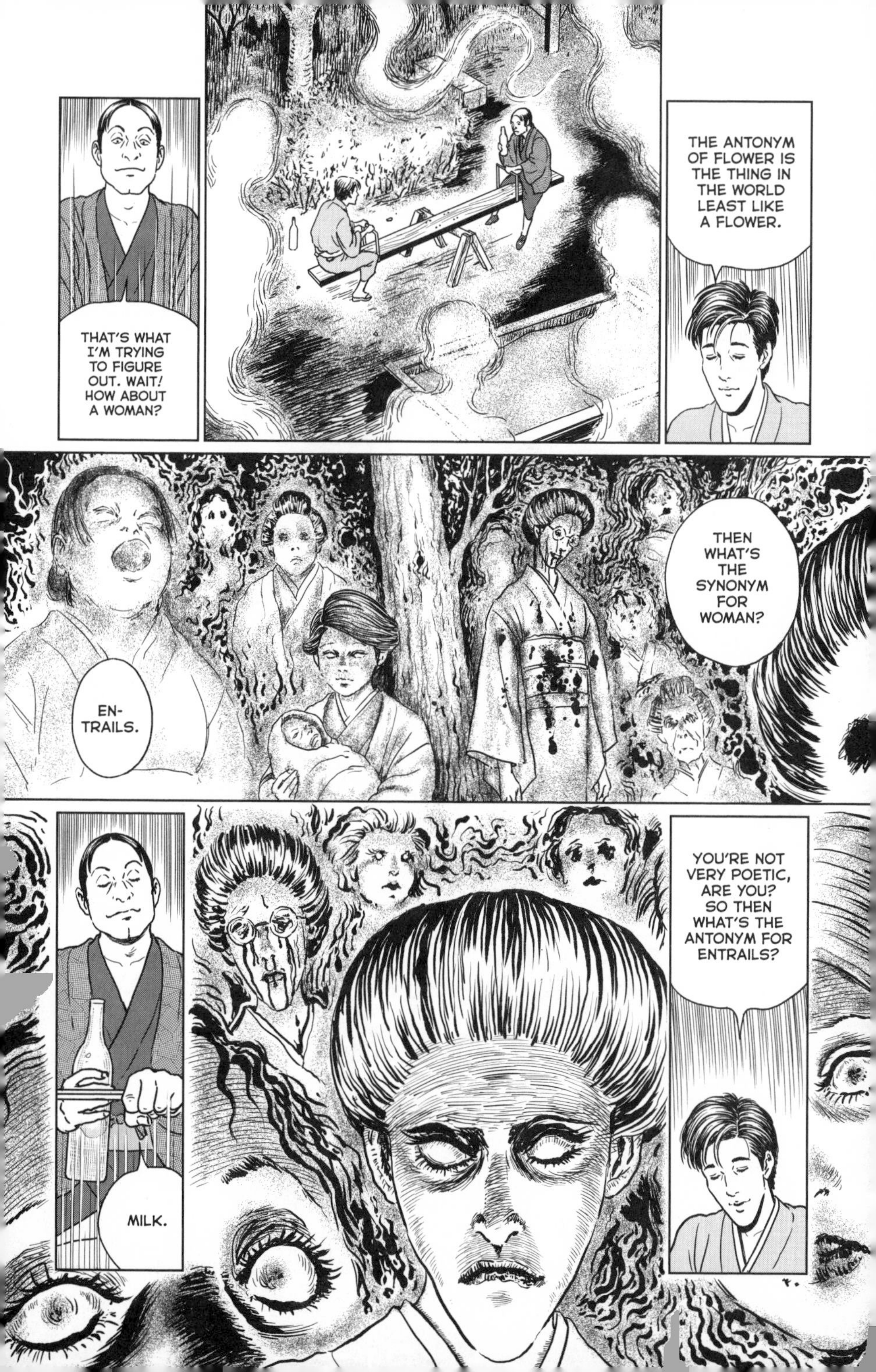
THE ANTONYM OF FLOWER IS THE THING IN THE WORLD LEAST LIKE A FLOWER.
THAT'S WHAT I'M TRYING TO FIGURE OUT. WAIT! HOW ABOUT A WOMAN?
THEN WHAT'S THE SYNONYM FOR WOMAN?
EN-TRAILS.
YOU'RE NOT VERY POETIC, ARE YOU? SO THEN WHAT'S THE ANTONYM FOR ENTRAILS?
MILK.

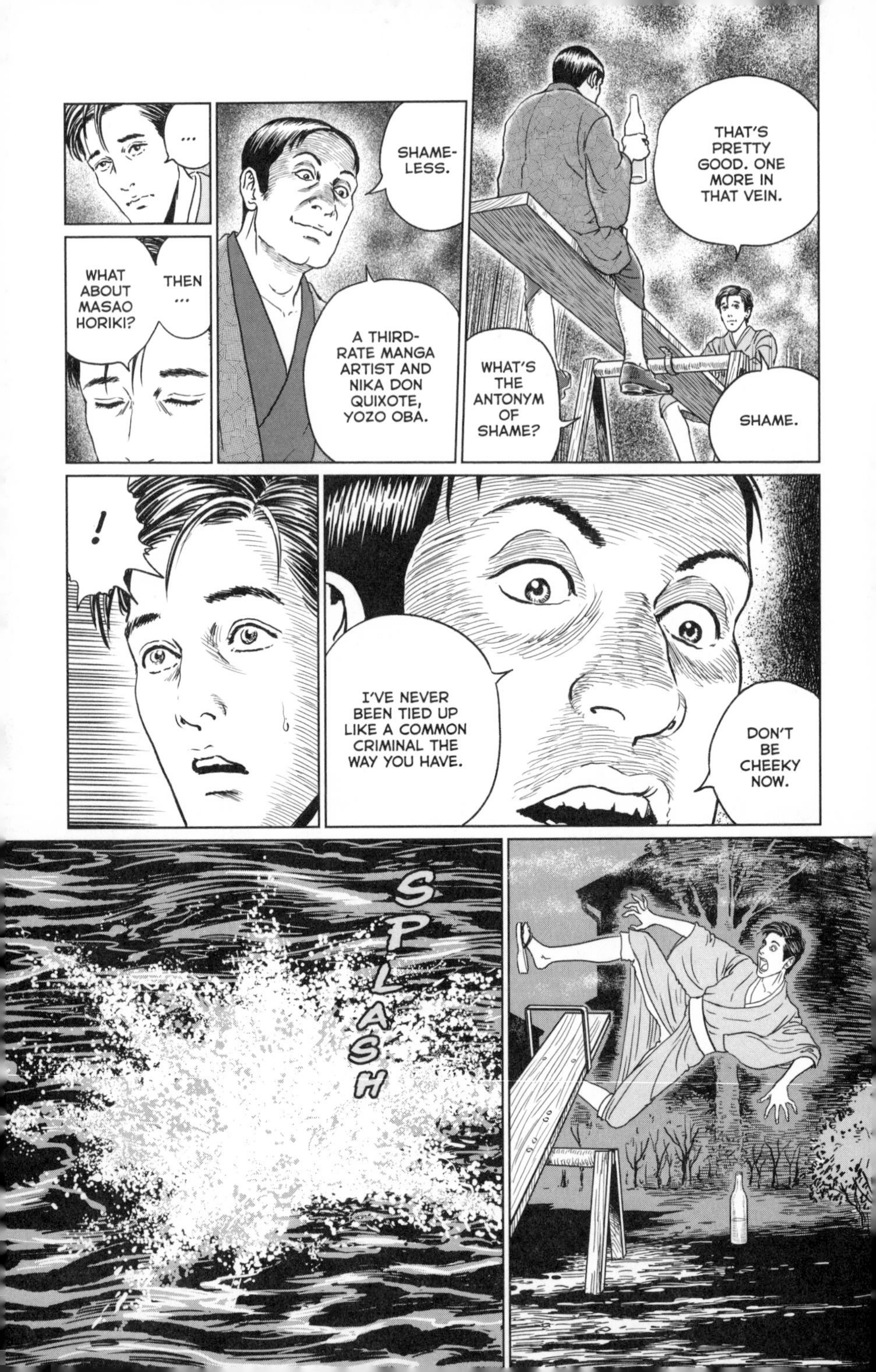
THAT'S PRETTY GOOD. ONE MORE IN THAT VEIN.
WHAT'S THE ANTONYM OF SHAME?
SHAME.
SHAME-LESS.
A THIRD-RATE MANGA ARTIST AND NIKA DON QUIXOTE, YOZO OBA.
...
THEN ...
WHAT ABOUT MASAO HORIKI?
DON'T BE CHEEKY NOW.
I'VE NEVER BEEN TIED UP LIKE A COMMON CRIMINAL THE WAY YOU HAVE.
!
SPLASH

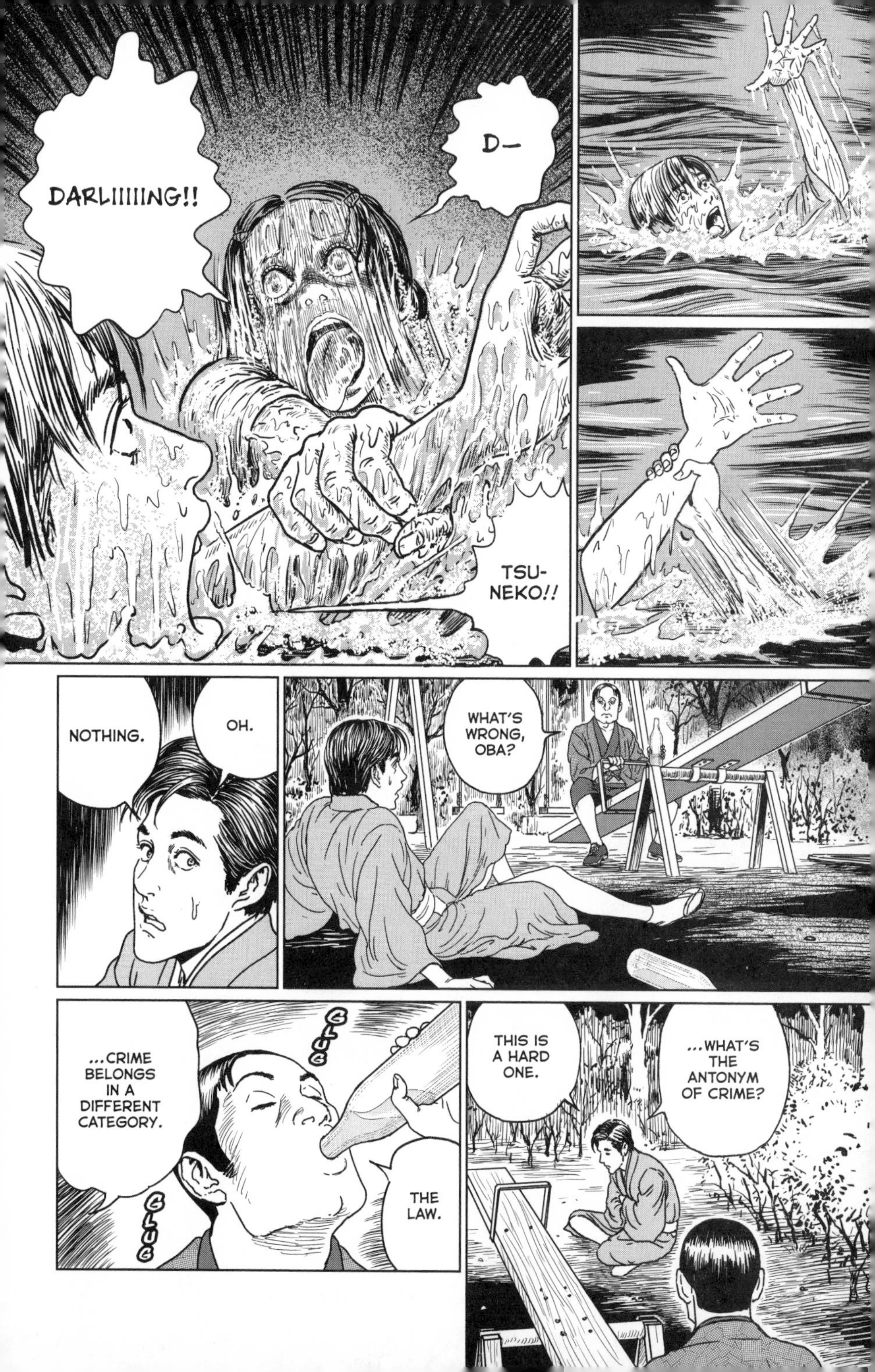
D–
DARLIIIIING!!
TSU-NEKO!!
WHAT'S WRONG, OBA?
OH.
NOTHING.
...WHAT'S THE ANTONYM OF CRIME?
THIS IS A HARD ONE.
GLUG
...CRIME BELONGS IN A DIFFERENT CATEGORY.
THE LAW.
GLUG

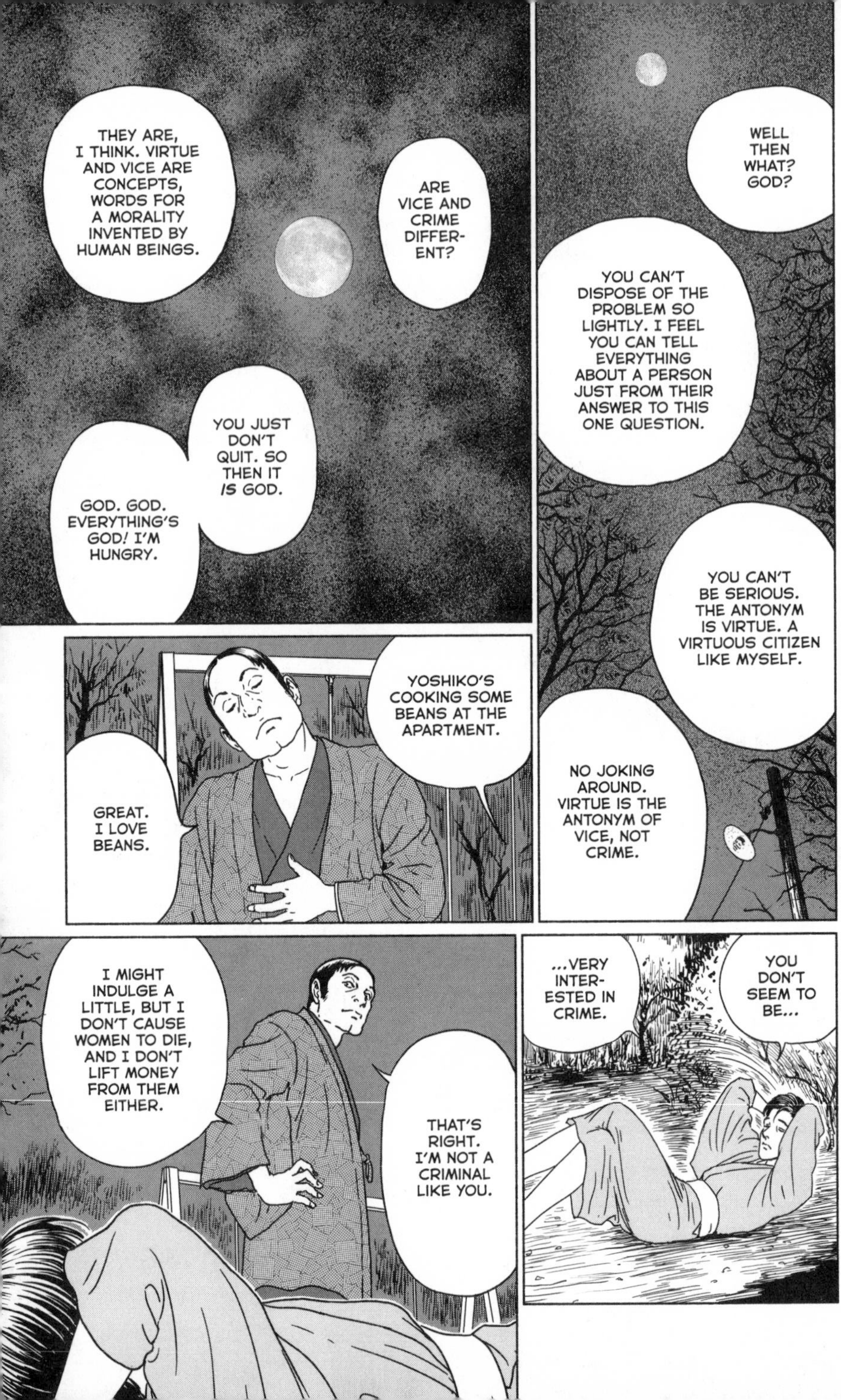
WELL THEN WHAT? GOD?
YOU CAN'T DISPOSE OF THE PROBLEM SO LIGHTLY. I FEEL YOU CAN TELL EVERYTHING ABOUT A PERSON JUST FROM THEIR ANSWER TO THIS ONE QUESTION.
YOU CAN'T BE SERIOUS. THE ANTONYM IS VIRTUE. A VIRTUOUS CITIZEN LIKE MYSELF.
NO JOKING AROUND. VIRTUE IS THE ANTONYM OF VICE, NOT CRIME.
ARE VICE AND CRIME DIFFER-ENT?
THEY ARE, I THINK. VIRTUE AND VICE ARE CONCEPTS, WORDS FOR A MORALITY INVENTED BY HUMAN BEINGS.
YOU JUST DON'T QUIT. SO THEN IT *IS* GOD.
GOD. GOD. EVERYTHING'S GOD! I'M HUNGRY.
YOSHIKO'S COOKING SOME BEANS AT THE APARTMENT.
GREAT. I LOVE BEANS.
YOU DON'T SEEM TO BE...
...VERY INTER-ESTED IN CRIME.
THAT'S RIGHT. I'M NOT A CRIMINAL LIKE YOU.
I MIGHT INDULGE A LITTLE, BUT I DON'T CAUSE WOMEN TO DIE, AND I DON'T LIFT MONEY FROM THEM EITHER.

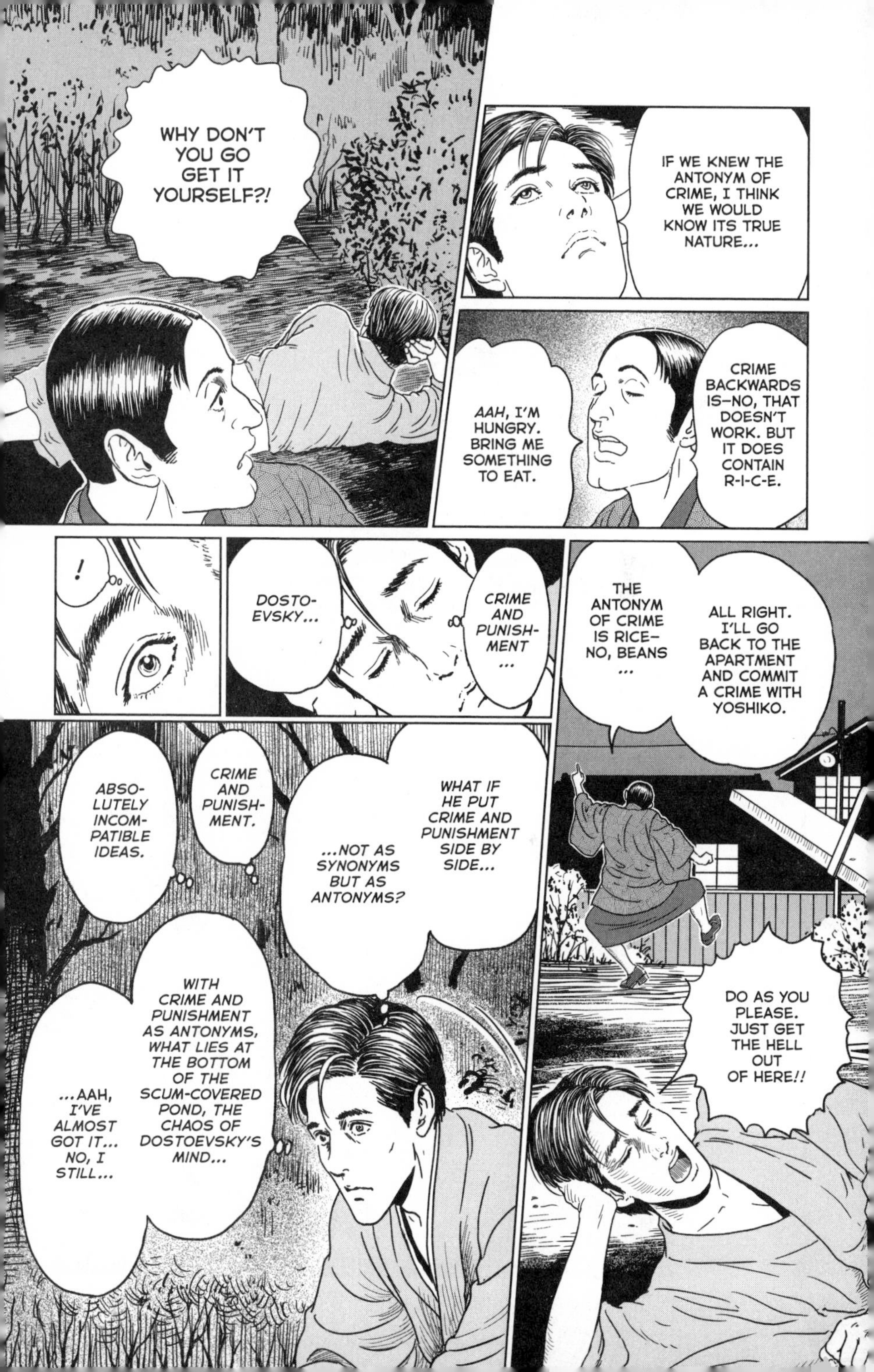
IF WE KNEW THE ANTONYM OF CRIME, I THINK WE WOULD KNOW ITS TRUE NATURE...
CRIME BACKWARDS IS—NO, THAT DOESN'T WORK. BUT IT DOES CONTAIN R-I-C-E.
AAH, I'M HUNGRY. BRING ME SOMETHING TO EAT.
WHY DON'T YOU GO GET IT YOURSELF?!
ALL RIGHT. I'LL GO BACK TO THE APARTMENT AND COMMIT A CRIME WITH YOSHIKO.
THE ANTONYM OF CRIME IS RICE— NO, BEANS ...
DO AS YOU PLEASE. JUST GET THE HELL OUT OF HERE!!
CRIME AND PUNISHMENT ...
DOSTOEVSKY...
!
WHAT IF HE PUT CRIME AND PUNISHMENT SIDE BY SIDE...
...NOT AS SYNONYMS BUT AS ANTONYMS?
CRIME AND PUNISHMENT.
ABSOLUTELY INCOMPATIBLE IDEAS.
WITH CRIME AND PUNISHMENT AS ANTONYMS, WHAT LIES AT THE BOTTOM OF THE SCUM-COVERED POND, THE CHAOS OF DOSTOEVSKY'S MIND...
...AAH, I'VE ALMOST GOT IT... NO, I STILL...

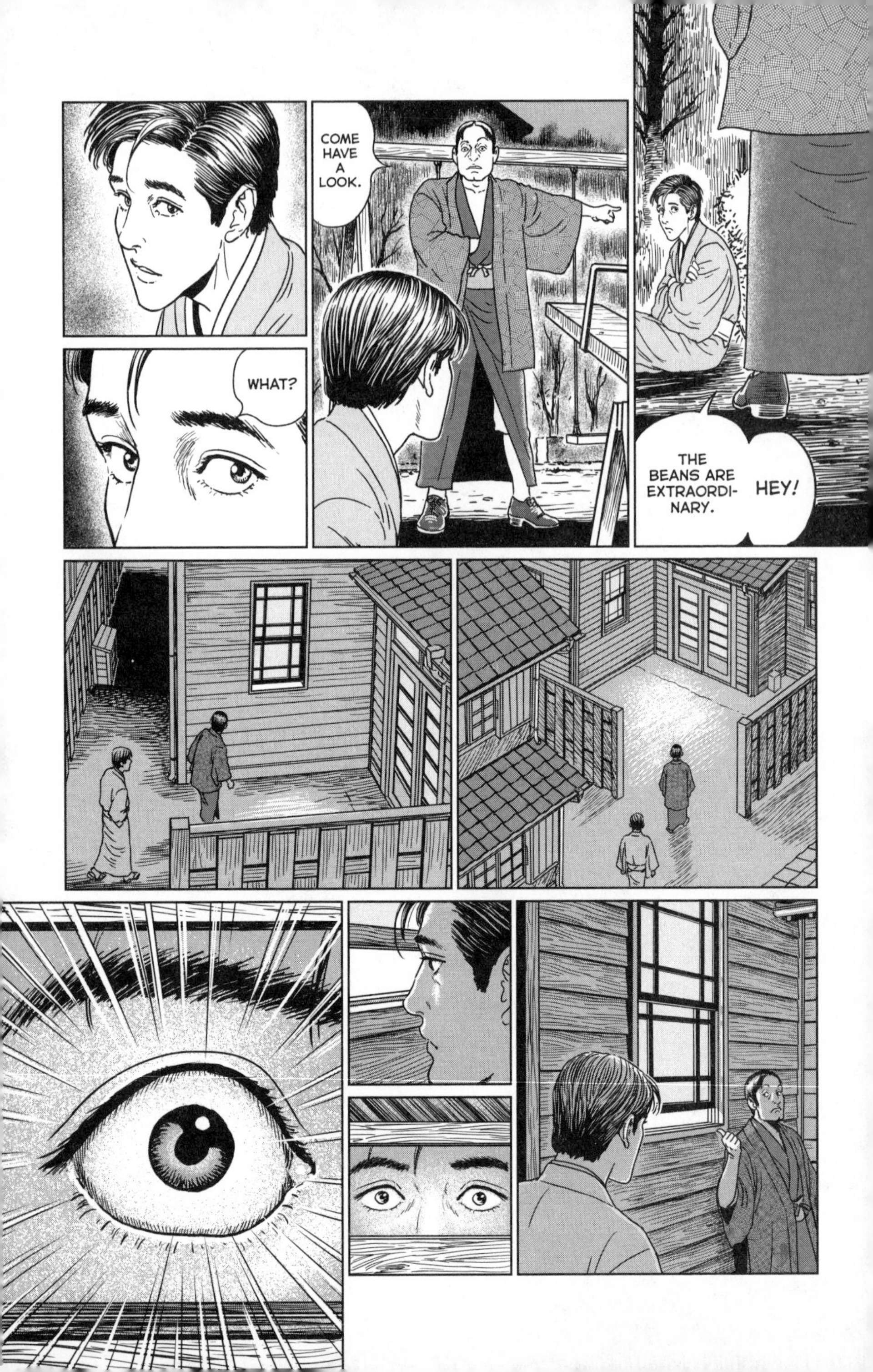
HEY!
THE BEANS ARE EXTRAORDINARY.
COME HAVE A LOOK.
WHAT?

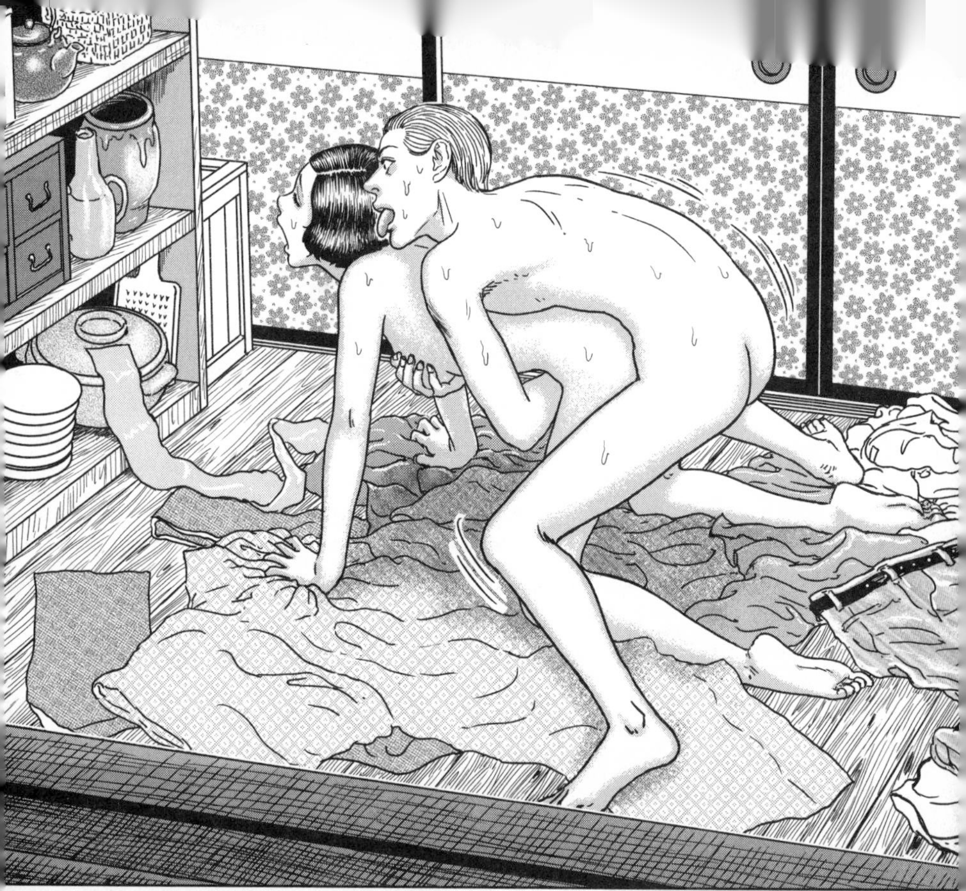

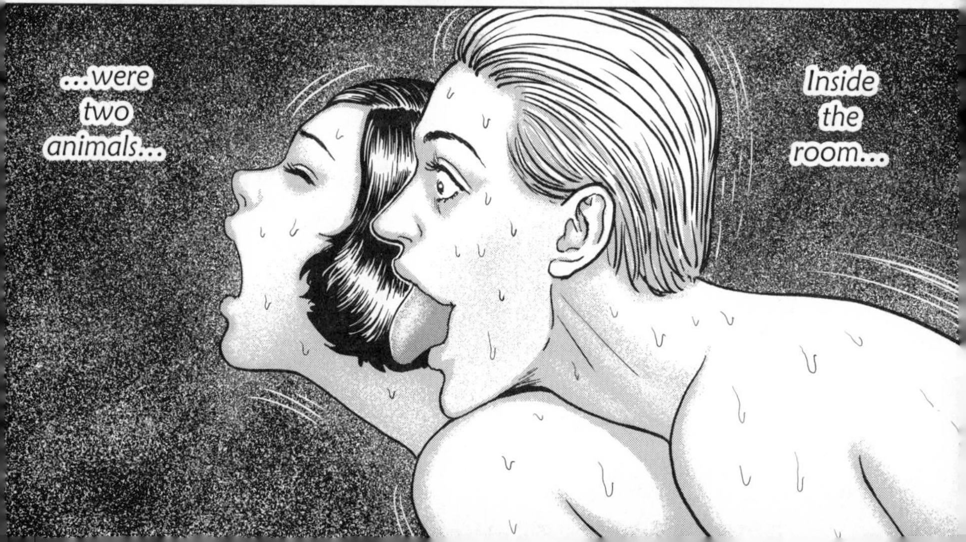
Inside the room...
...were two animals...

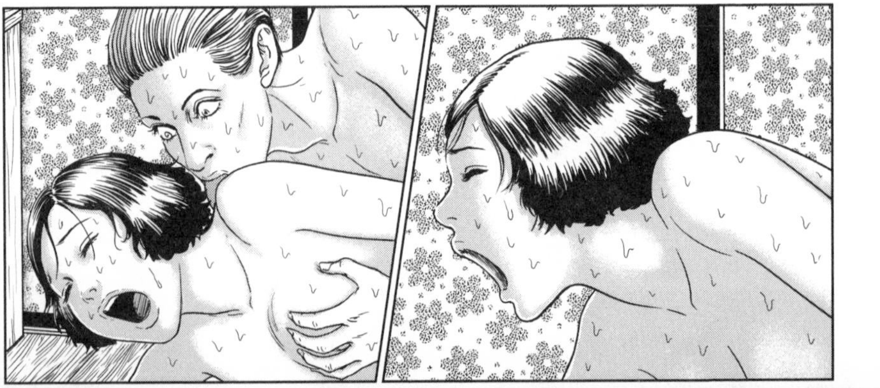

CHAIN No. 14: Aspects of Human Behavior

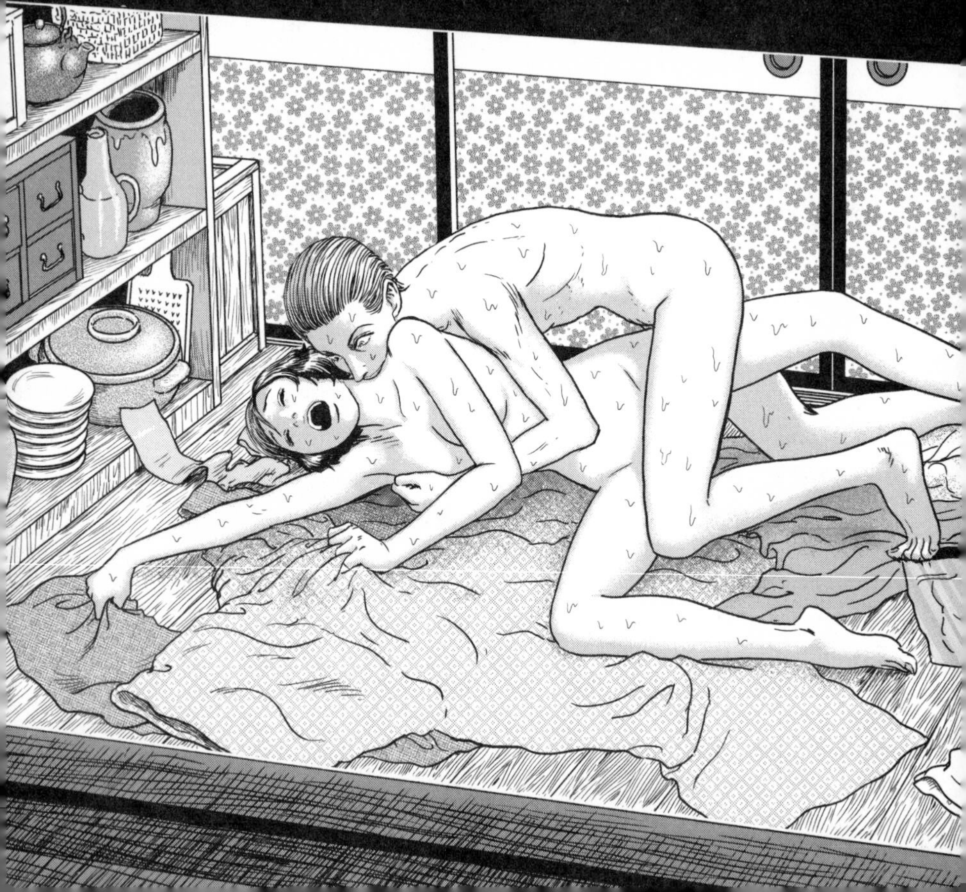

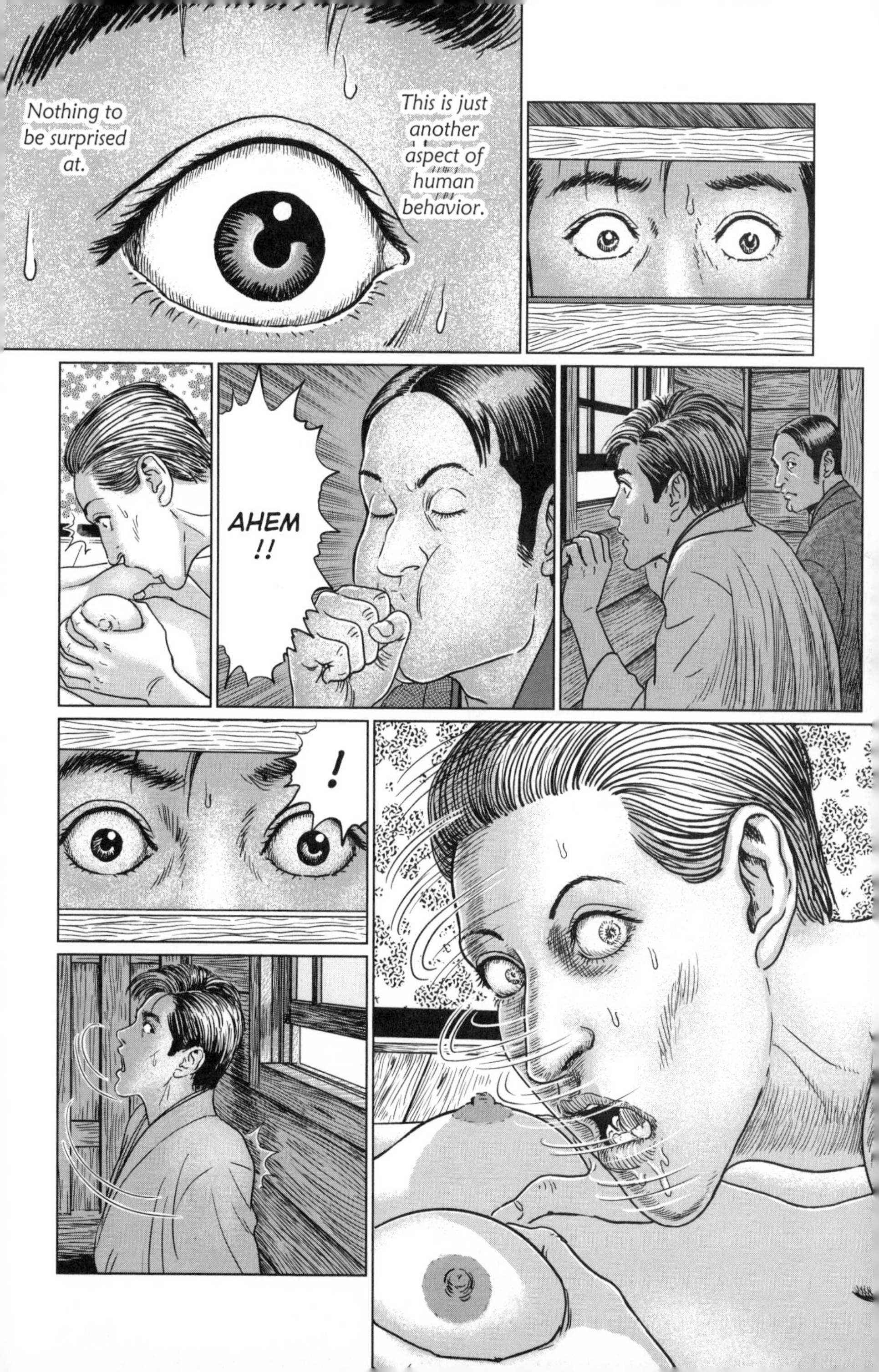
This is just another aspect of human behavior.
Nothing to be surprised at.
AHEM !!
!

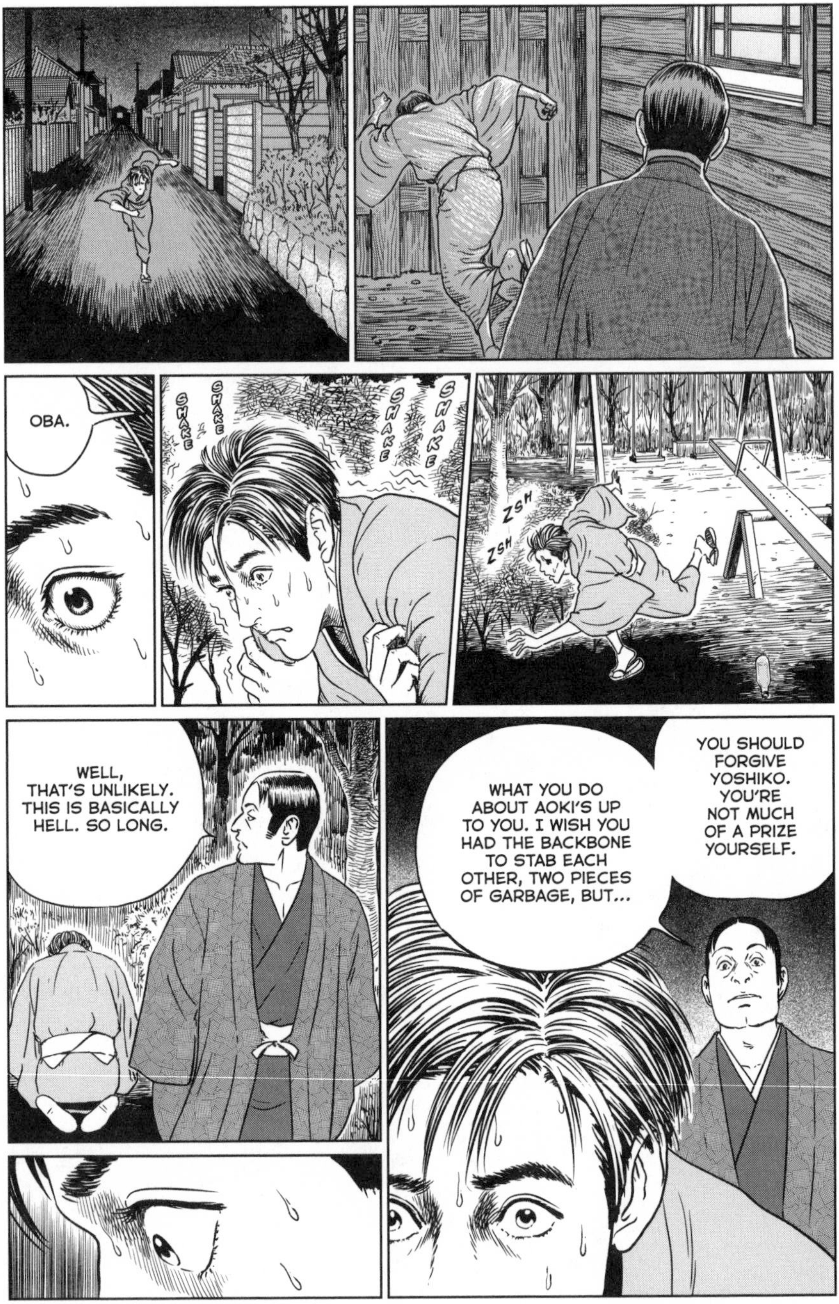
ZSH
ZSH
SHAKE
SHAKE
SHAKE
SHAKE
OBA.
YOU SHOULD FORGIVE YOSHIKO. YOU'RE NOT MUCH OF A PRIZE YOURSELF.
WHAT YOU DO ABOUT AOKI'S UP TO YOU. I WISH YOU HAD THE BACKBONE TO STAB EACH OTHER, TWO PIECES OF GARBAGE, BUT...
WELL, THAT'S UNLIKELY. THIS IS BASICALLY HELL. SO LONG.

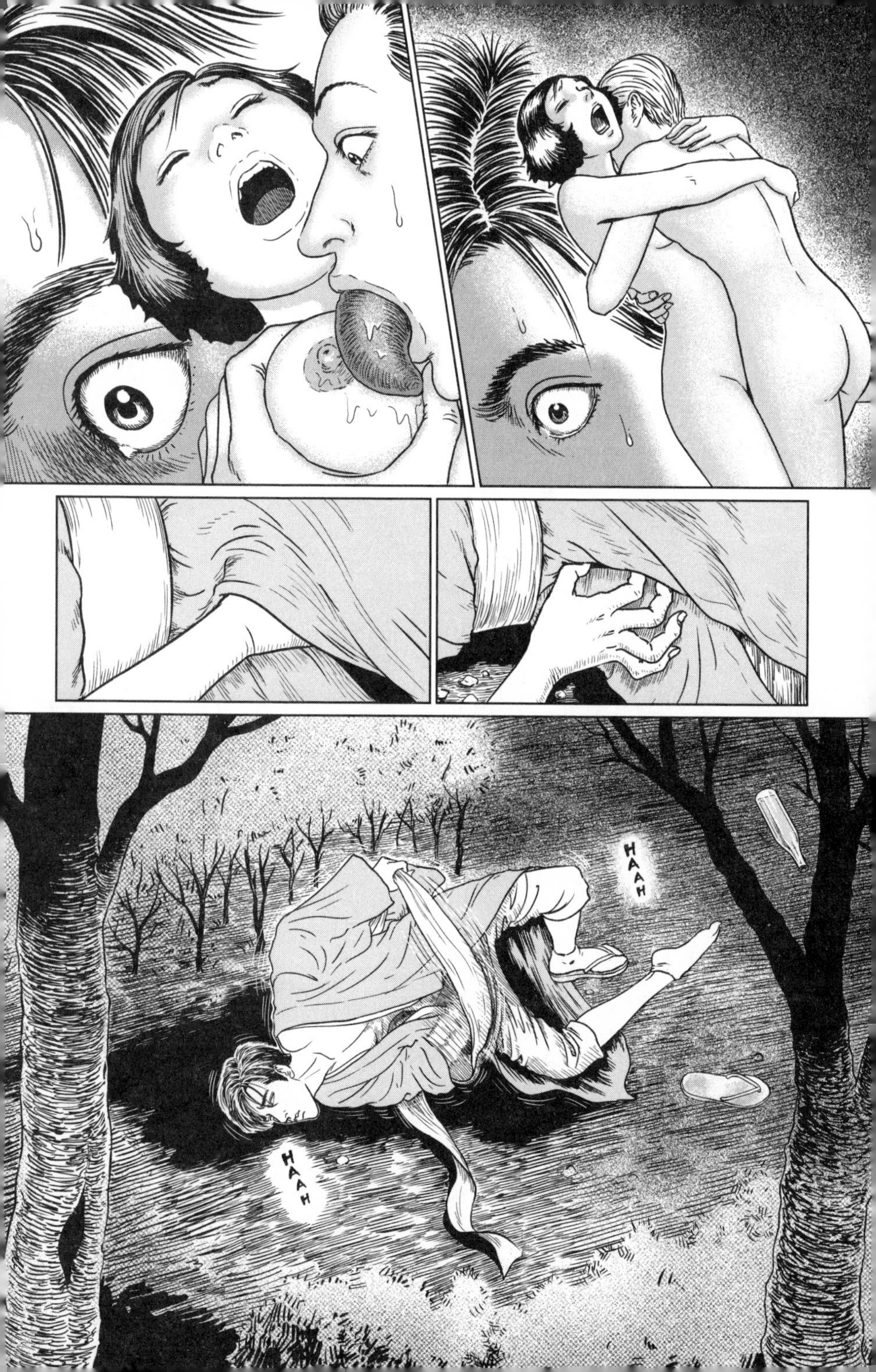
HAAH
HAAH

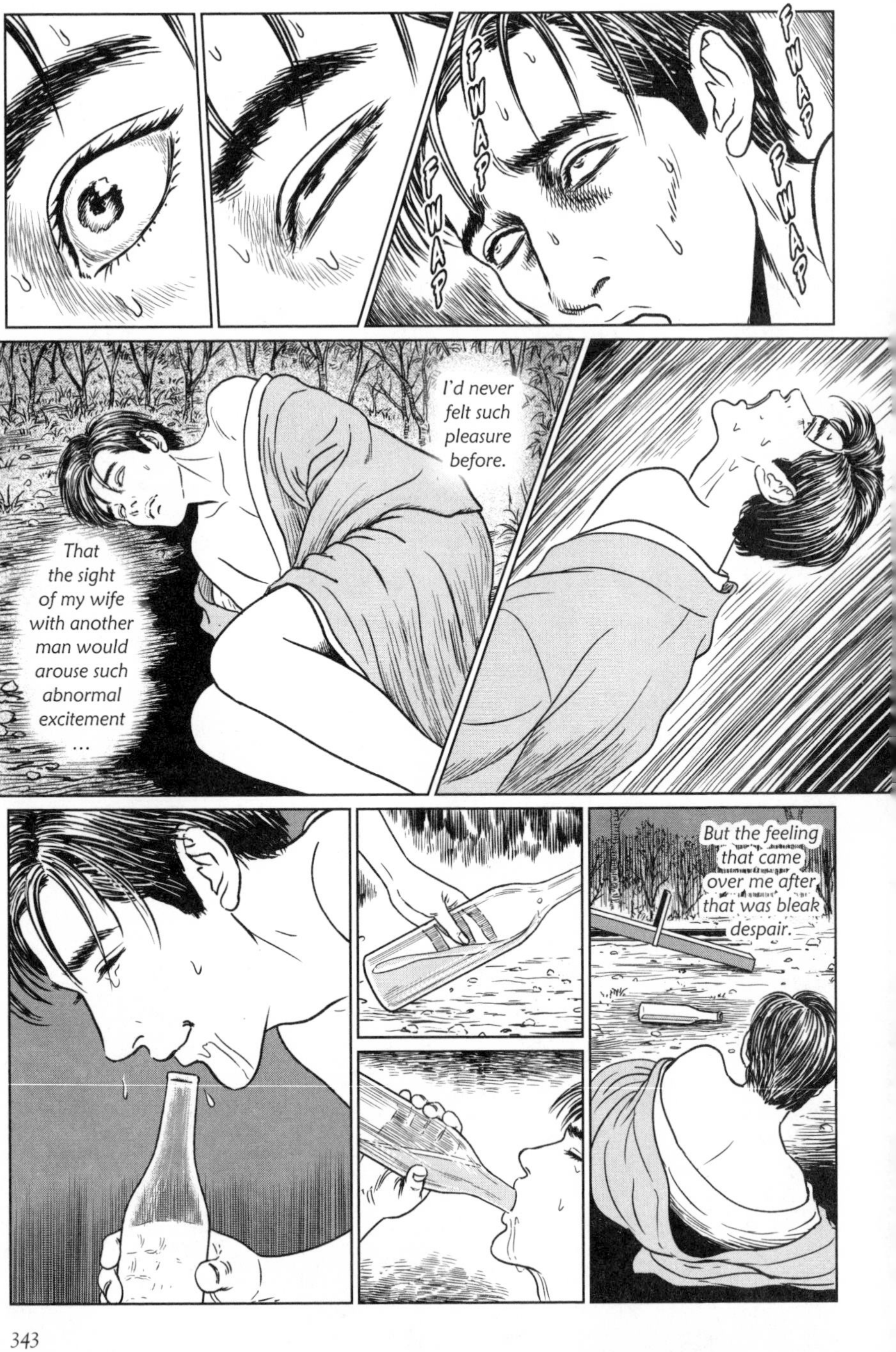
FWAP
FWAP
FWAP
FWAP
FWAP
I'd never felt such pleasure before.
That the sight of my wife with another man would arouse such abnormal excitement …
But the feeling that came over me after that was bleak despair.

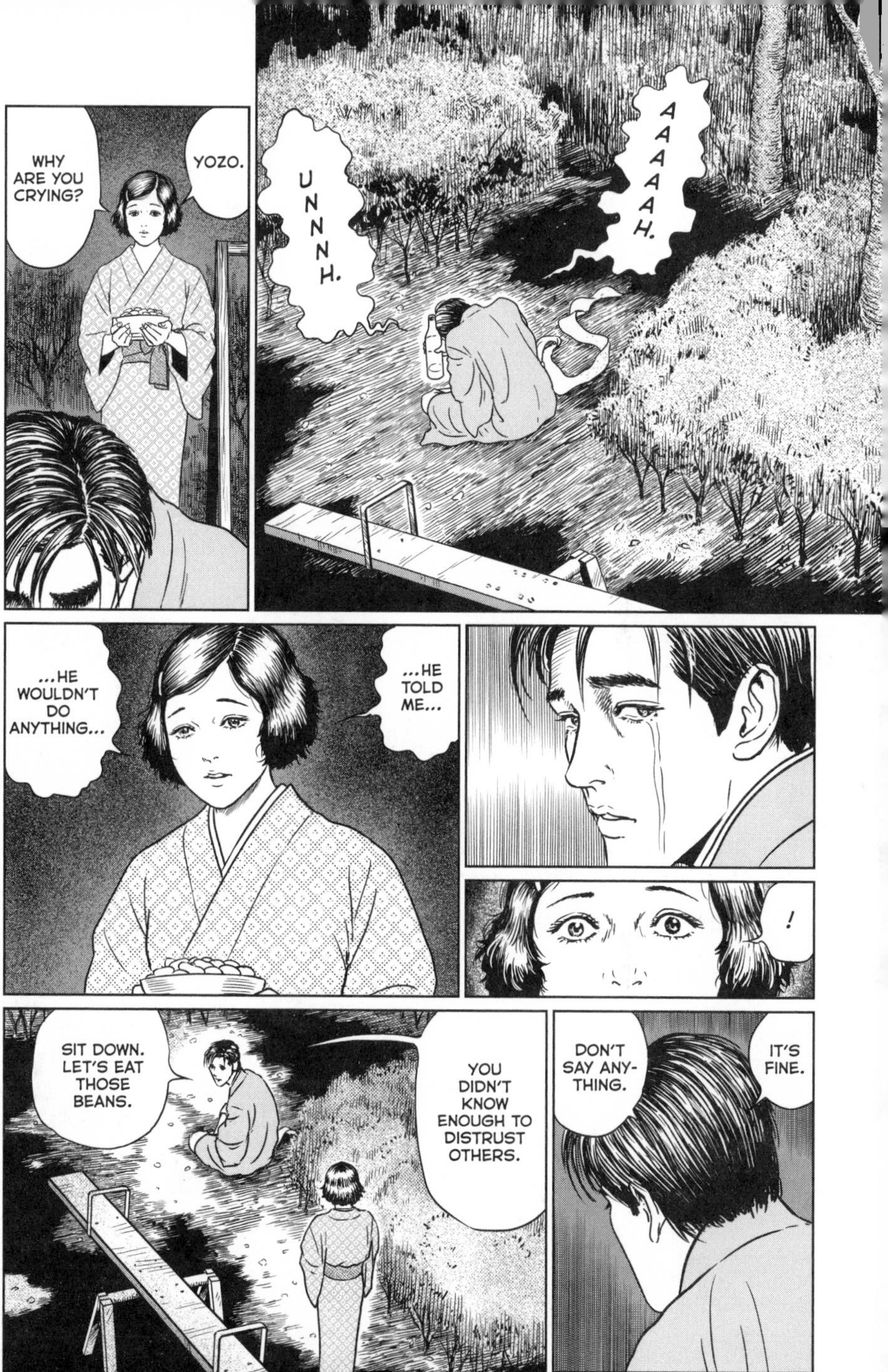
AAAAAH.
UNNNH.
YOZO.
WHY ARE YOU CRYING?
!
...HE TOLD ME...
...HE WOULDN'T DO ANYTHING...
IT'S FINE.
DON'T SAY ANYTHING.
YOU DIDN'T KNOW ENOUGH TO DISTRUST OTHERS.
SIT DOWN. LET'S EAT THOSE BEANS.

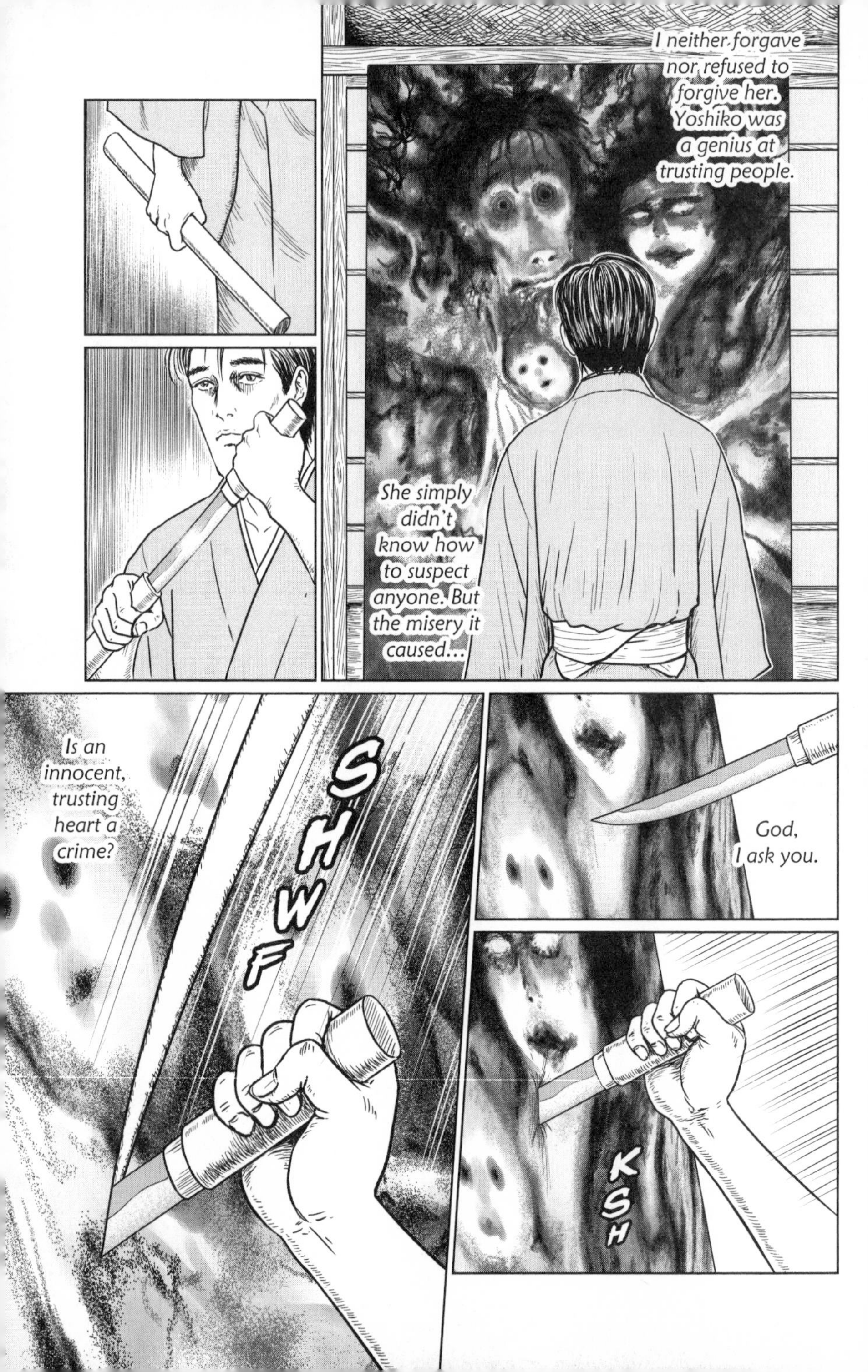
I neither forgave nor refused to forgive her. Yoshiko was a genius at trusting people.
She simply didn't know how to suspect anyone. But the misery it caused...
God, I ask you.
KSH
Is an innocent, trusting heart a crime?
SHWF

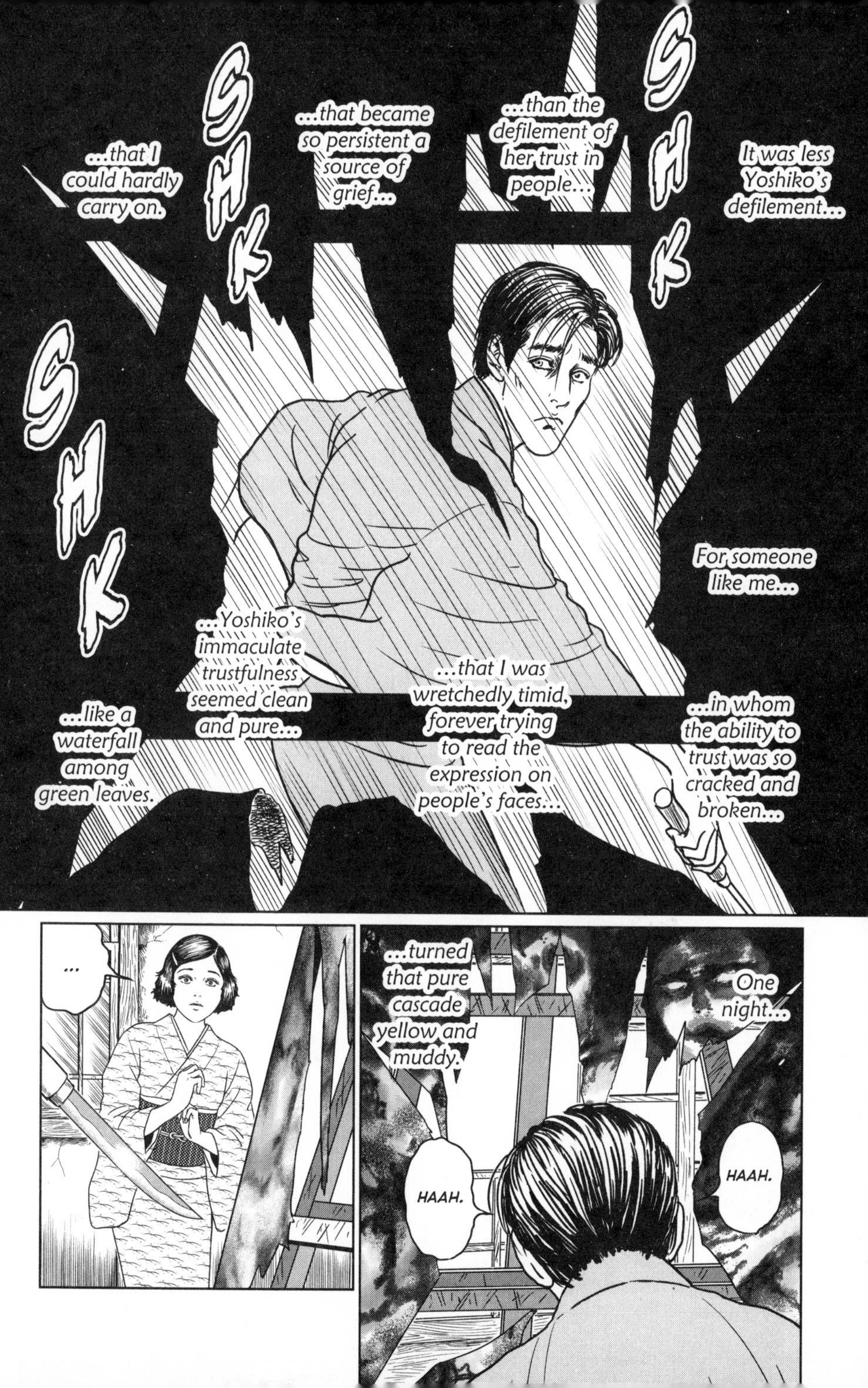
It was less Yoshiko's defilement...
...than the defilement of her trust in people...
SHK
...that became so persistent a source of grief...
SHK
...that I could hardly carry on.
SHK
For someone like me...
...in whom the ability to trust was so cracked and broken...
...that I was wretchedly timid, forever trying to read the expression on people's faces...
...Yoshiko's immaculate trustfulness seemed clean and pure...
...like a waterfall among green leaves.
One night...
...turned that pure cascade yellow and muddy.
HAAH.
HAAH.
...

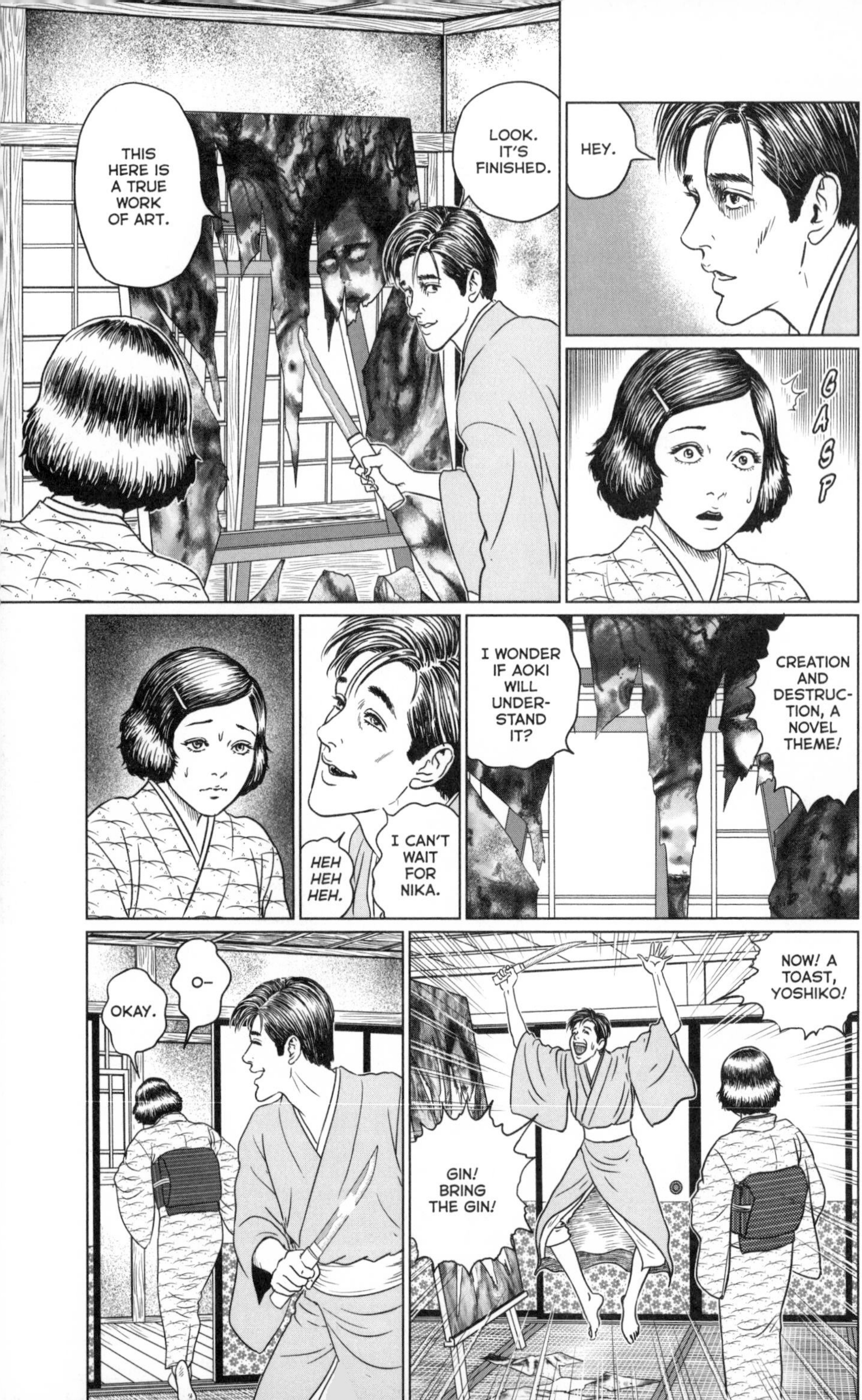
HEY.
GASP
LOOK. IT'S FINISHED.
THIS HERE IS A TRUE WORK OF ART.
CREATION AND DESTRUCTION, A NOVEL THEME!
I WONDER IF AOKI WILL UNDERSTAND IT?
I CAN'T WAIT FOR NIKA.
HEH HEH HEH.
NOW! A TOAST, YOSHIKO!
GIN! BRING THE GIN!
O–
OKAY.

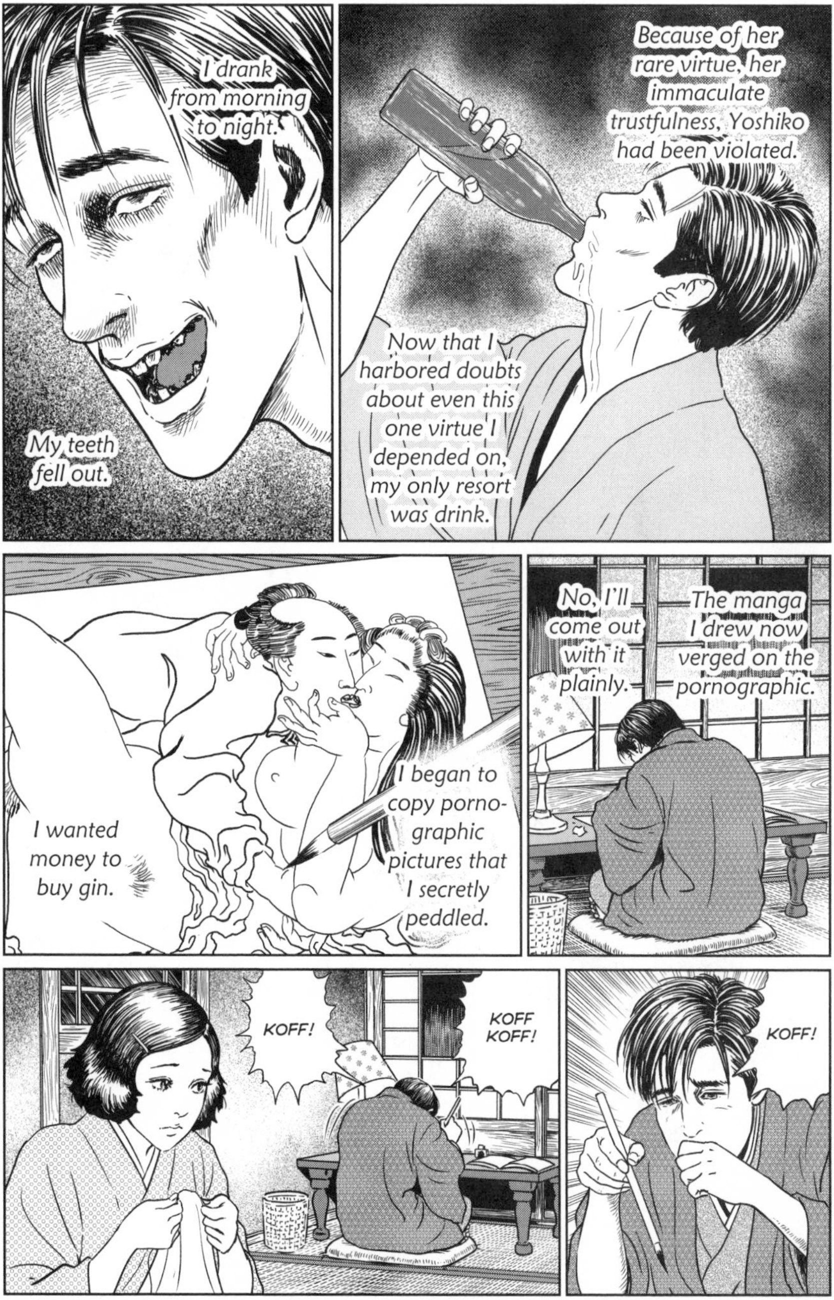
Because of her rare virtue, her immaculate trustfulness, Yoshiko had been violated.
Now that I harbored doubts about even this one virtue I depended on, my only resort was drink.
I drank from morning to night.
My teeth fell out.
The manga I drew now verged on the pornographic.
No, I'll come out with it plainly.
I began to copy porno-graphic pictures that I secretly peddled.
I wanted money to buy gin.
KOFF!
KOFF KOFF!
KOFF!

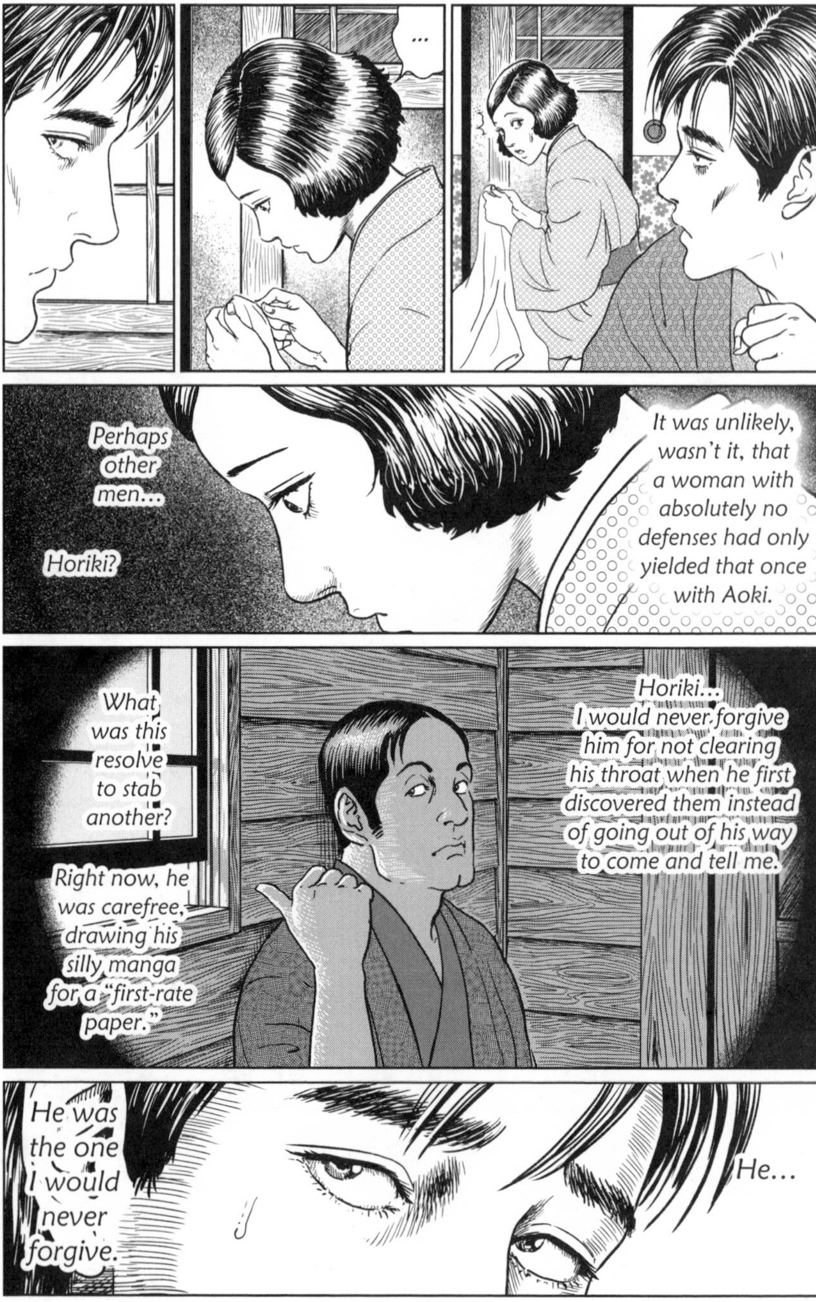
...
It was unlikely, wasn't it, that a woman with absolutely no defenses had only yielded that once with Aoki.
Perhaps other men...
Horiki?
Horiki... I would never forgive him for not clearing his throat when he first discovered them instead of going out of his way to come and tell me.
What was this resolve to stab another?
Right now, he was carefree, drawing his silly manga for a "first-rate paper."
He...
He was the one I would never forgive.

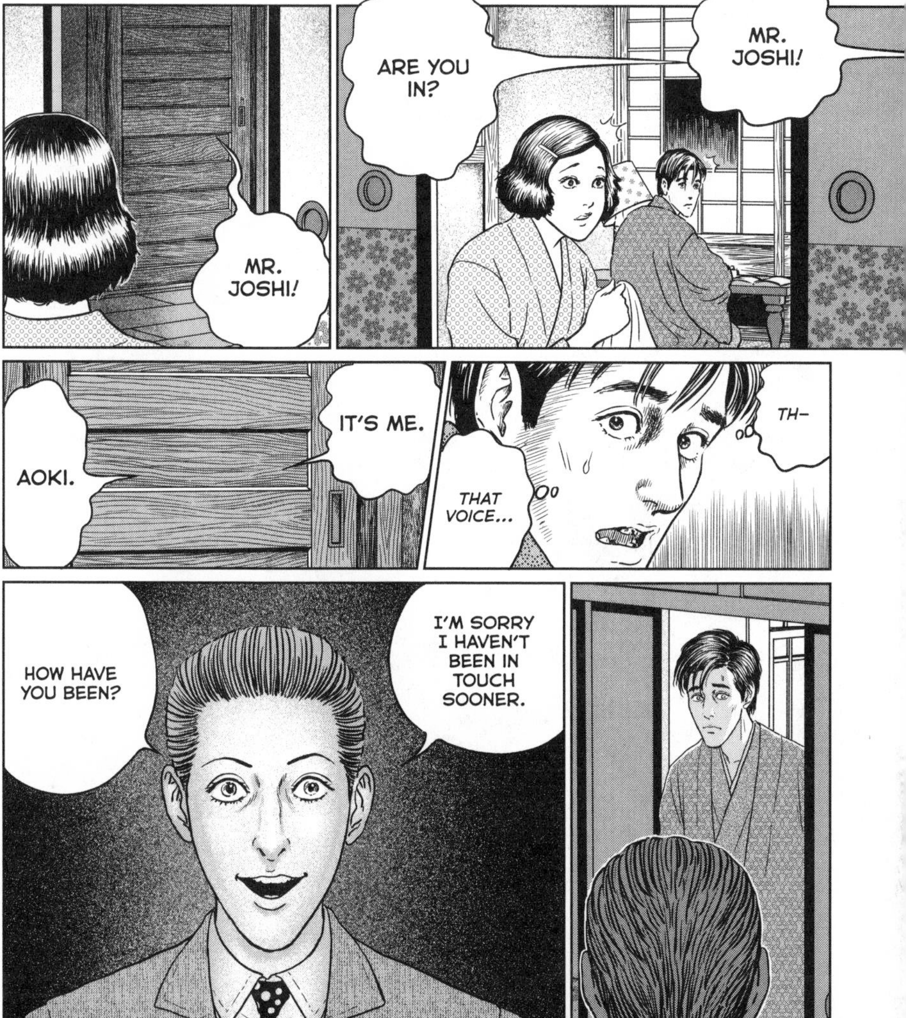

MR. JOSHI!
ARE YOU IN?
MR. JOSHI!
TH-
THAT VOICE...
IT'S ME.
AOKI.
I'M SORRY I HAVEN'T BEEN IN TOUCH SOONER.
HOW HAVE YOU BEEN?

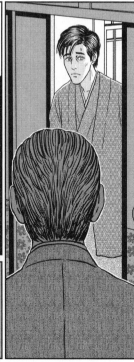

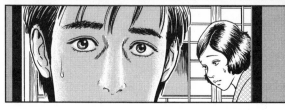

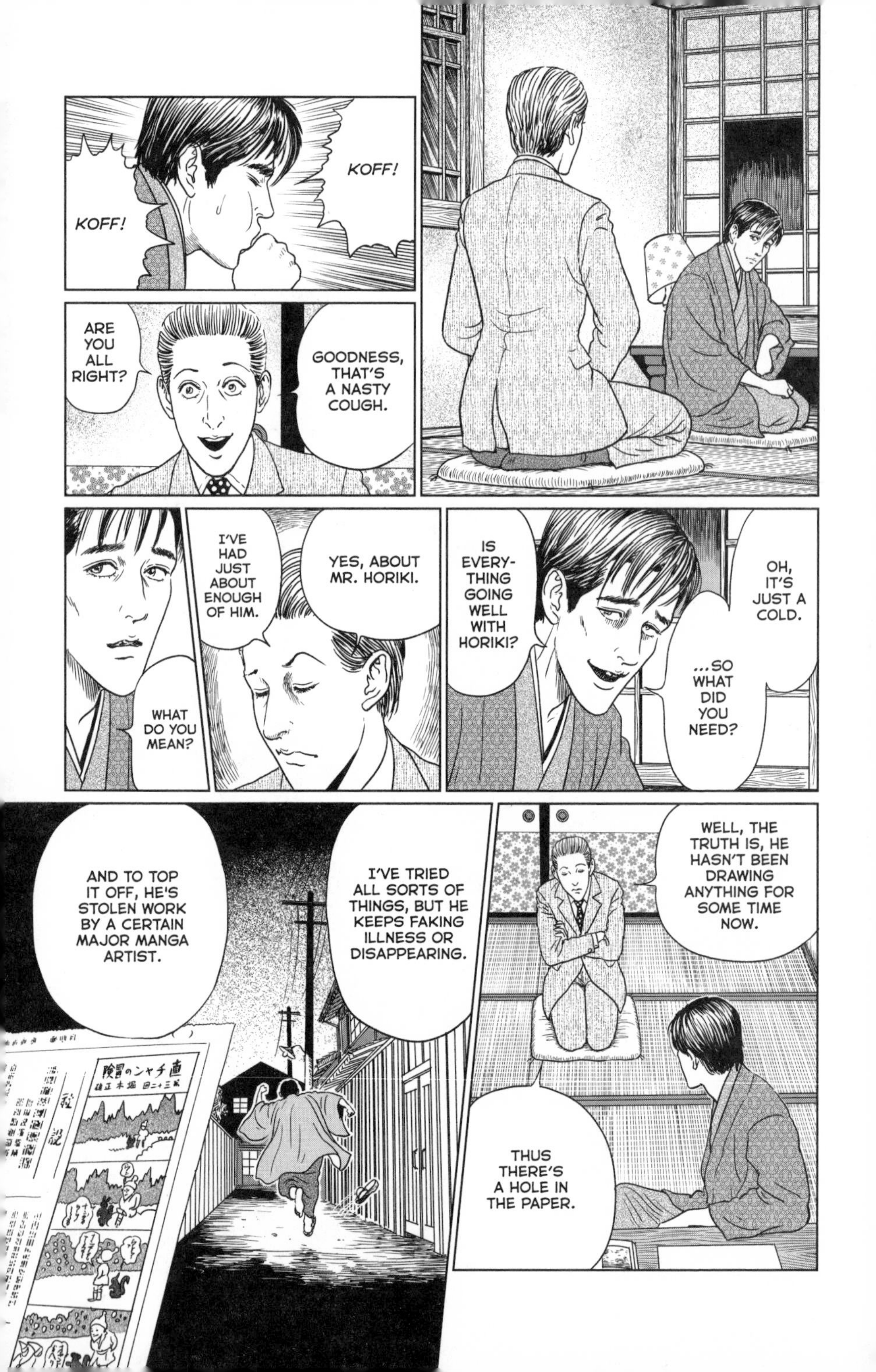
KOFF!
KOFF!
ARE YOU ALL RIGHT?
GOODNESS, THAT'S A NASTY COUGH.
OH, IT'S JUST A COLD.
...SO WHAT DID YOU NEED?
IS EVERYTHING GOING WELL WITH HORIKI?
YES, ABOUT MR. HORIKI.
I'VE HAD JUST ABOUT ENOUGH OF HIM.
WHAT DO YOU MEAN?
WELL, THE TRUTH IS, HE HASN'T BEEN DRAWING ANYTHING FOR SOME TIME NOW.
THUS THERE'S A HOLE IN THE PAPER.
I'VE TRIED ALL SORTS OF THINGS, BUT HE KEEPS FAKING ILLNESS OR DISAPPEARING.
AND TO TOP IT OFF, HE'S STOLEN WORK BY A CERTAIN MAJOR MANGA ARTIST.

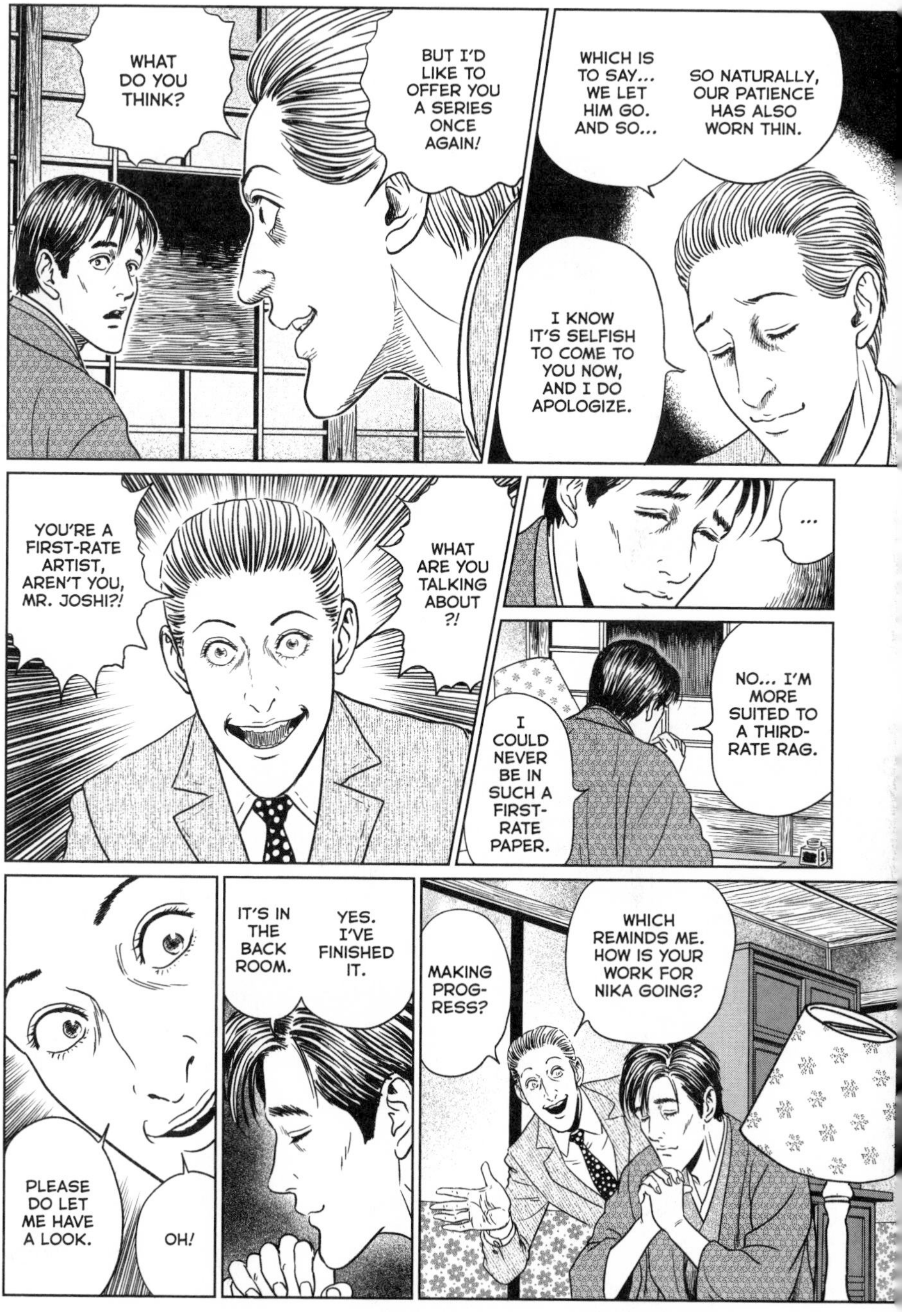
SO NATURALLY, OUR PATIENCE HAS ALSO WORN THIN.
WHICH IS TO SAY... WE LET HIM GO. AND SO...
I KNOW IT'S SELFISH TO COME TO YOU NOW, AND I DO APOLOGIZE.
BUT I'D LIKE TO OFFER YOU A SERIES ONCE AGAIN!
WHAT DO YOU THINK?
...
NO... I'M MORE SUITED TO A THIRD-RATE RAG.
I COULD NEVER BE IN SUCH A FIRST-RATE PAPER.
WHAT ARE YOU TALKING ABOUT?!
YOU'RE A FIRST-RATE ARTIST, AREN'T YOU, MR. JOSHI?!
WHICH REMINDS ME. HOW IS YOUR WORK FOR NIKA GOING?
MAKING PROGRESS?
YES. I'VE FINISHED IT.
IT'S IN THE BACK ROOM.
OH!
PLEASE DO LET ME HAVE A LOOK.

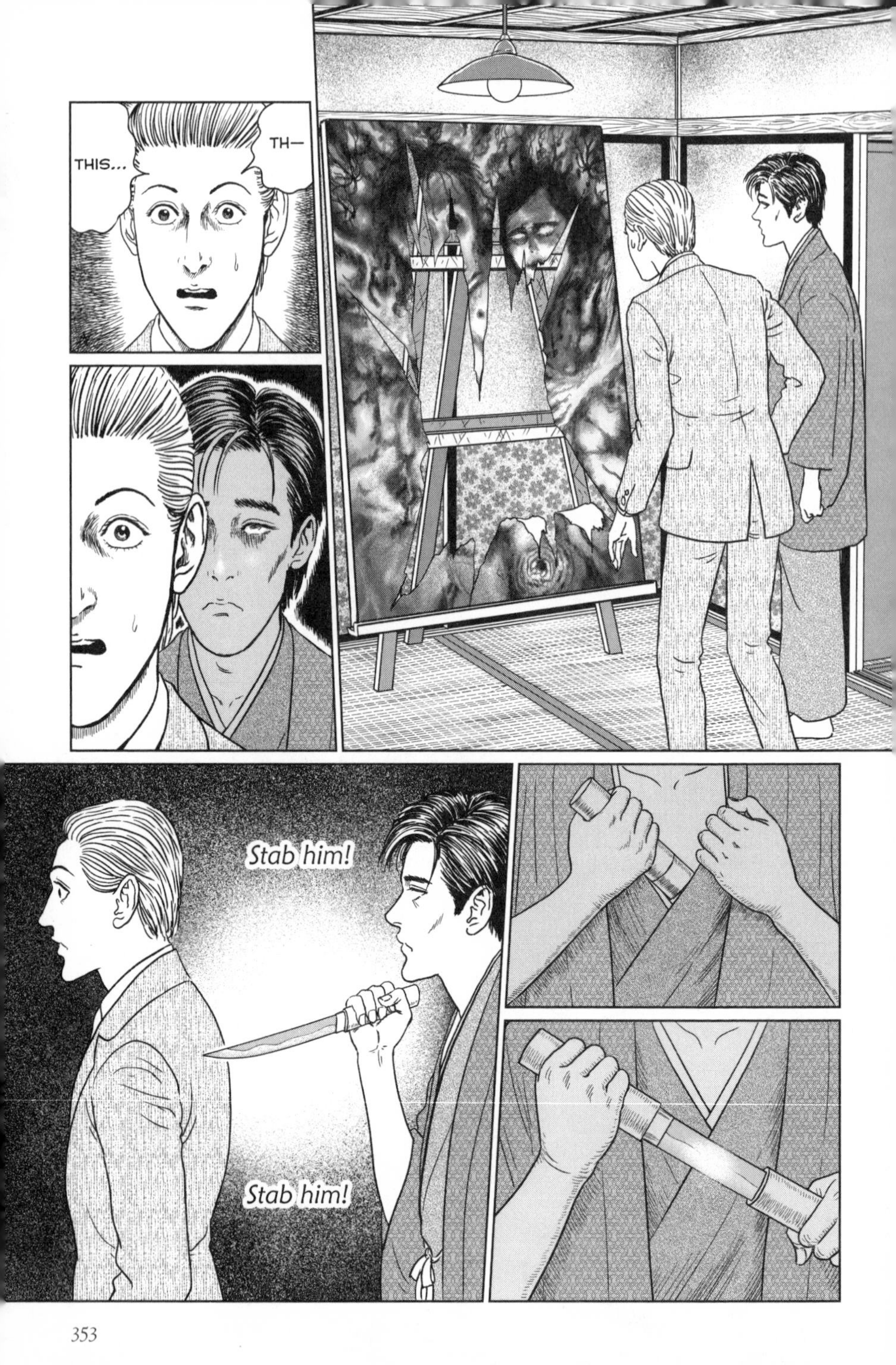
TH—
THIS...
Stab him!
Stab him!

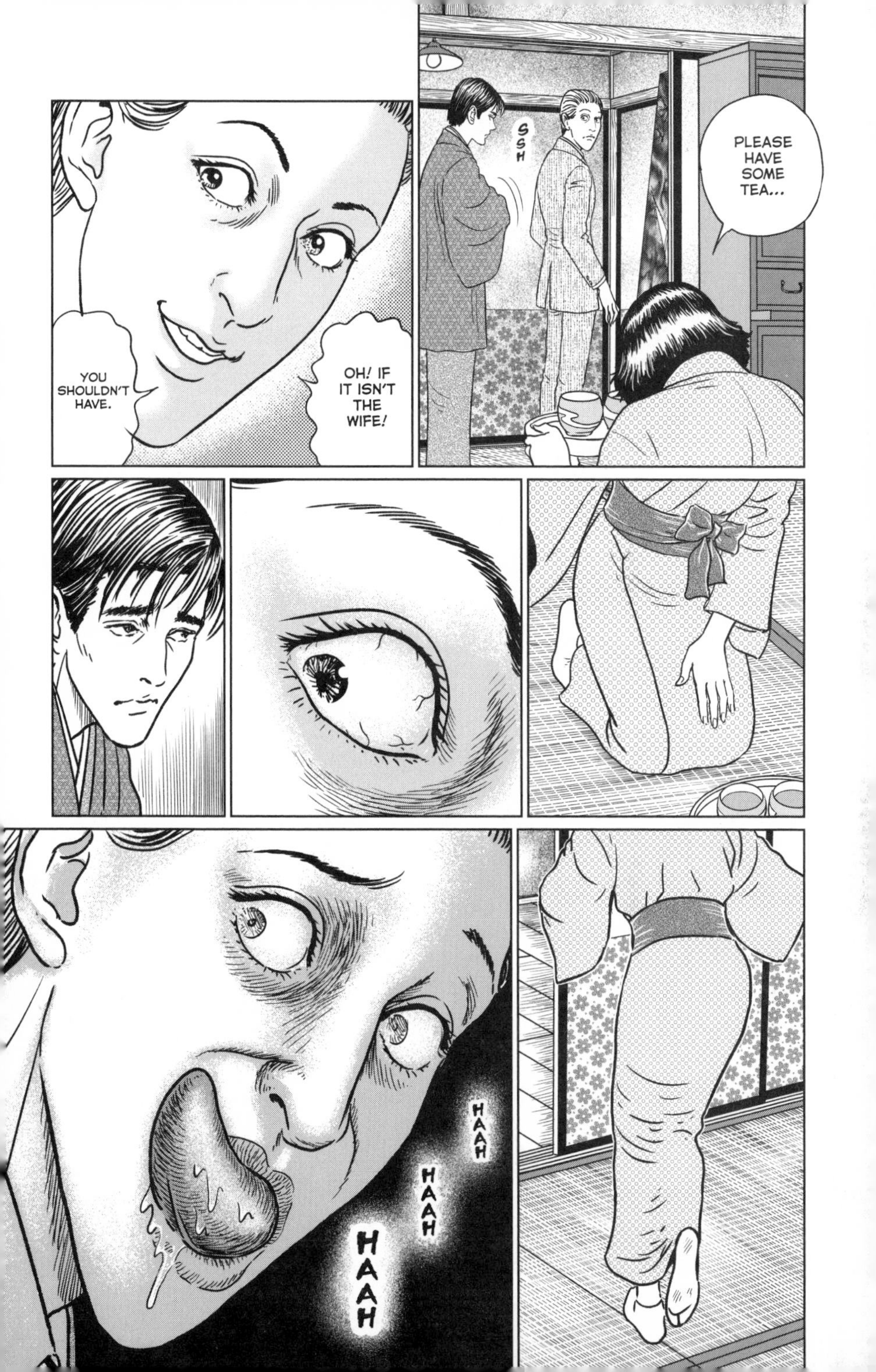
PLEASE HAVE SOME TEA...
SSH
OH! IF IT ISN'T THE WIFE!
YOU SHOULDN'T HAVE.
HAAH
HAAH
HAAH

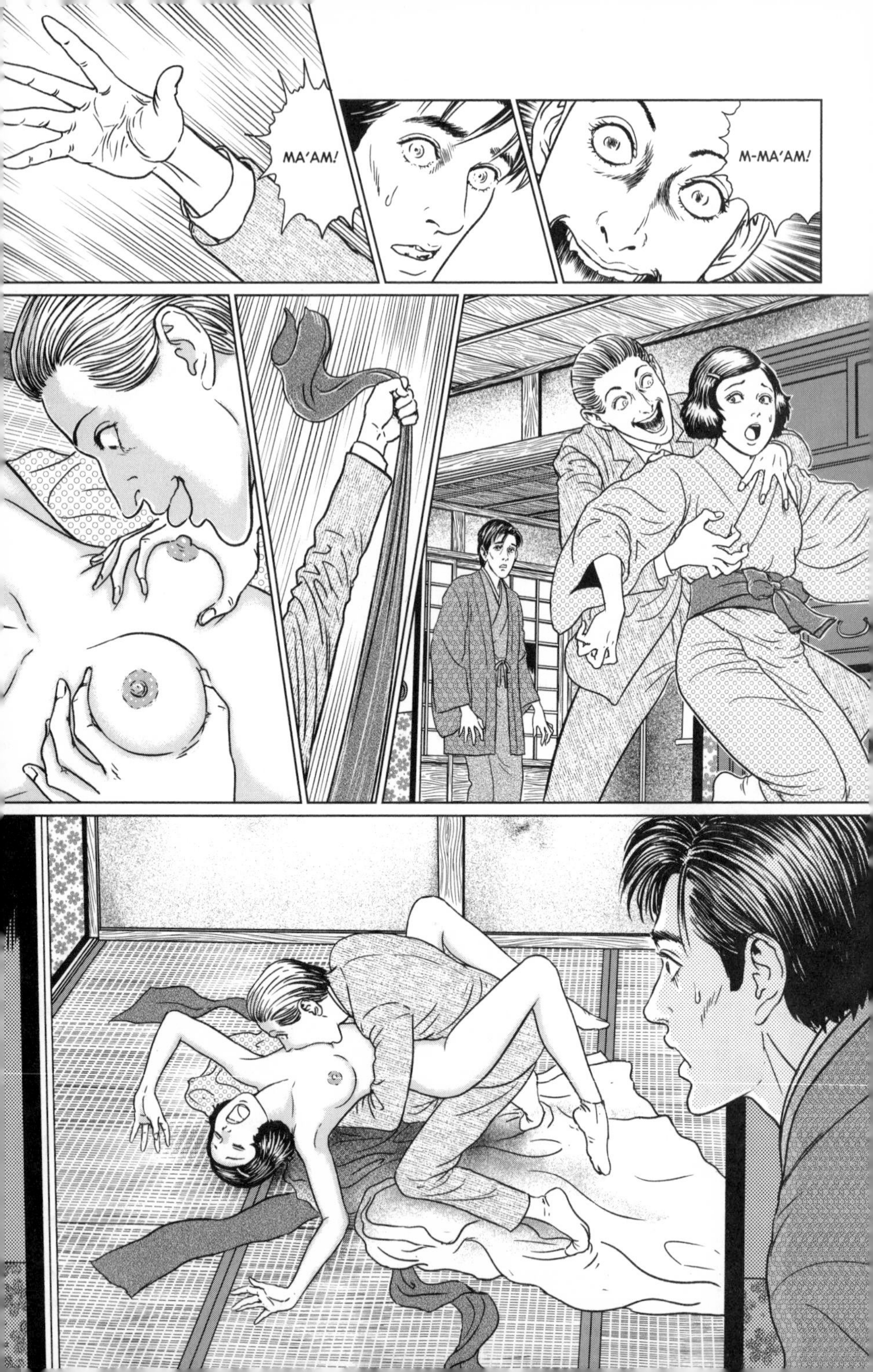
M-MA'AM!
MA'AM!

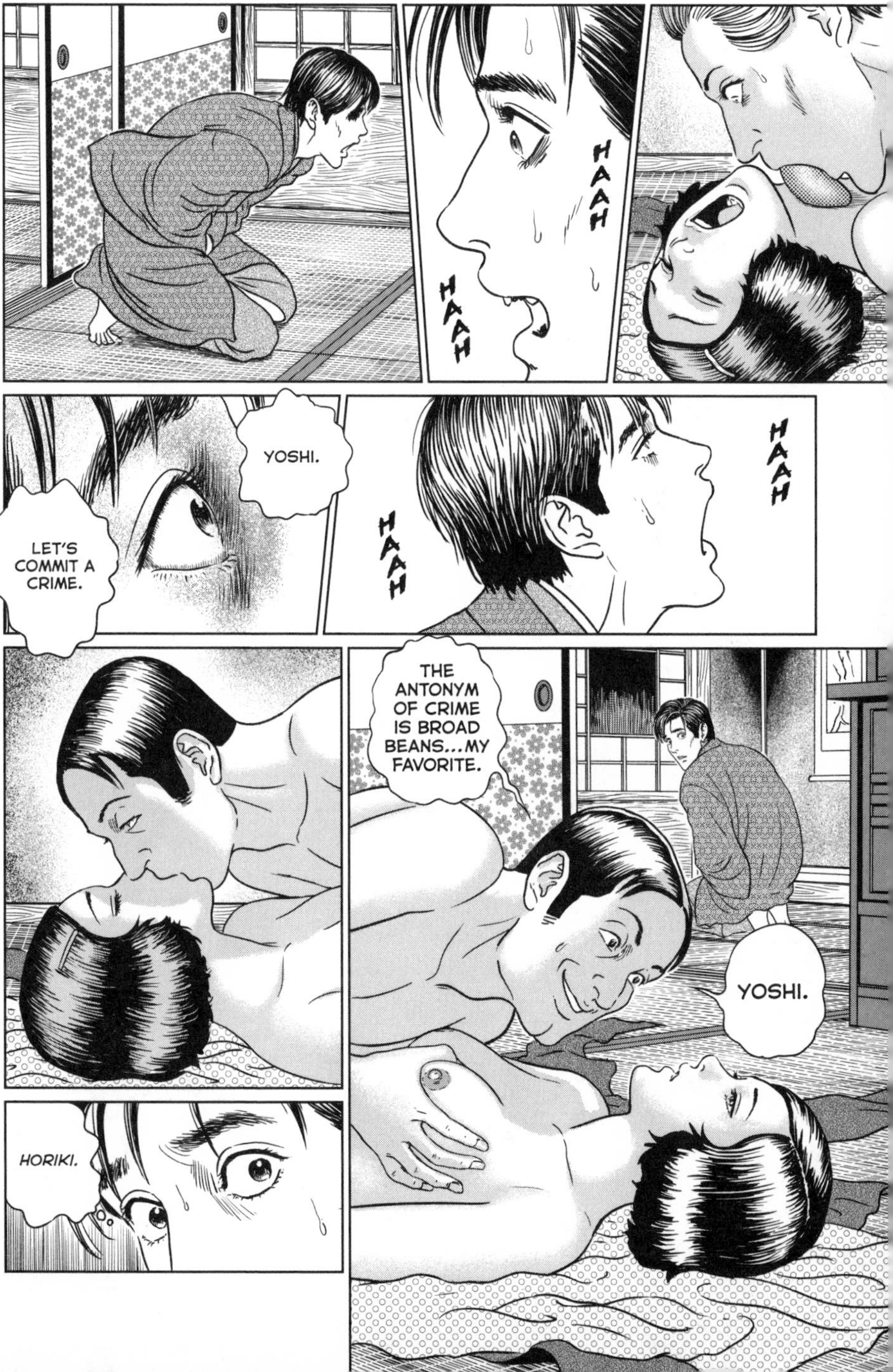
HAAH
HAAH
HAAH
HAAH
YOSHI.
LET'S COMMIT A CRIME.
THE ANTONYM OF CRIME IS BROAD BEANS...MY FAVORITE.
YOSHI.
HORIKI.

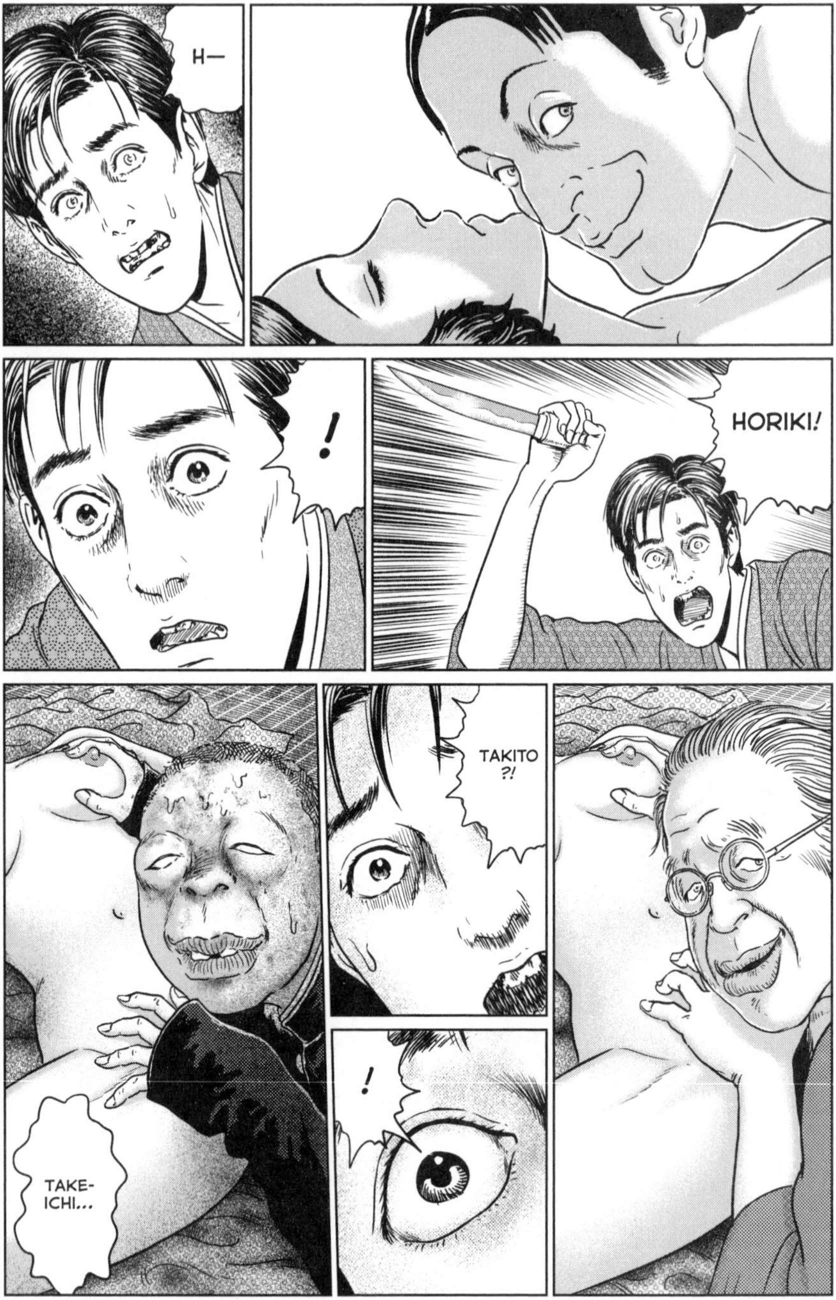
H—
HORIKI!
!
TAKITO ?!
!
TAKE-ICHI...

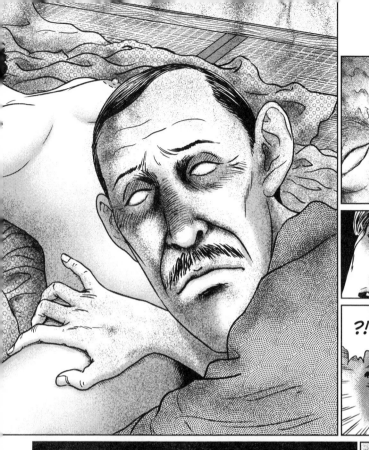

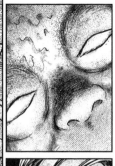

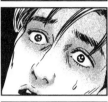

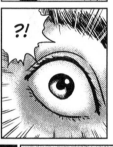

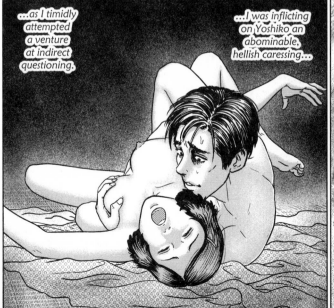

?!
How much was truth?
How much was illusion?
Before I knew it…
…I was inflicting on Yoshiko an abominable, hellish caressing…
…as I timidly attempted a venture at indirect questioning.

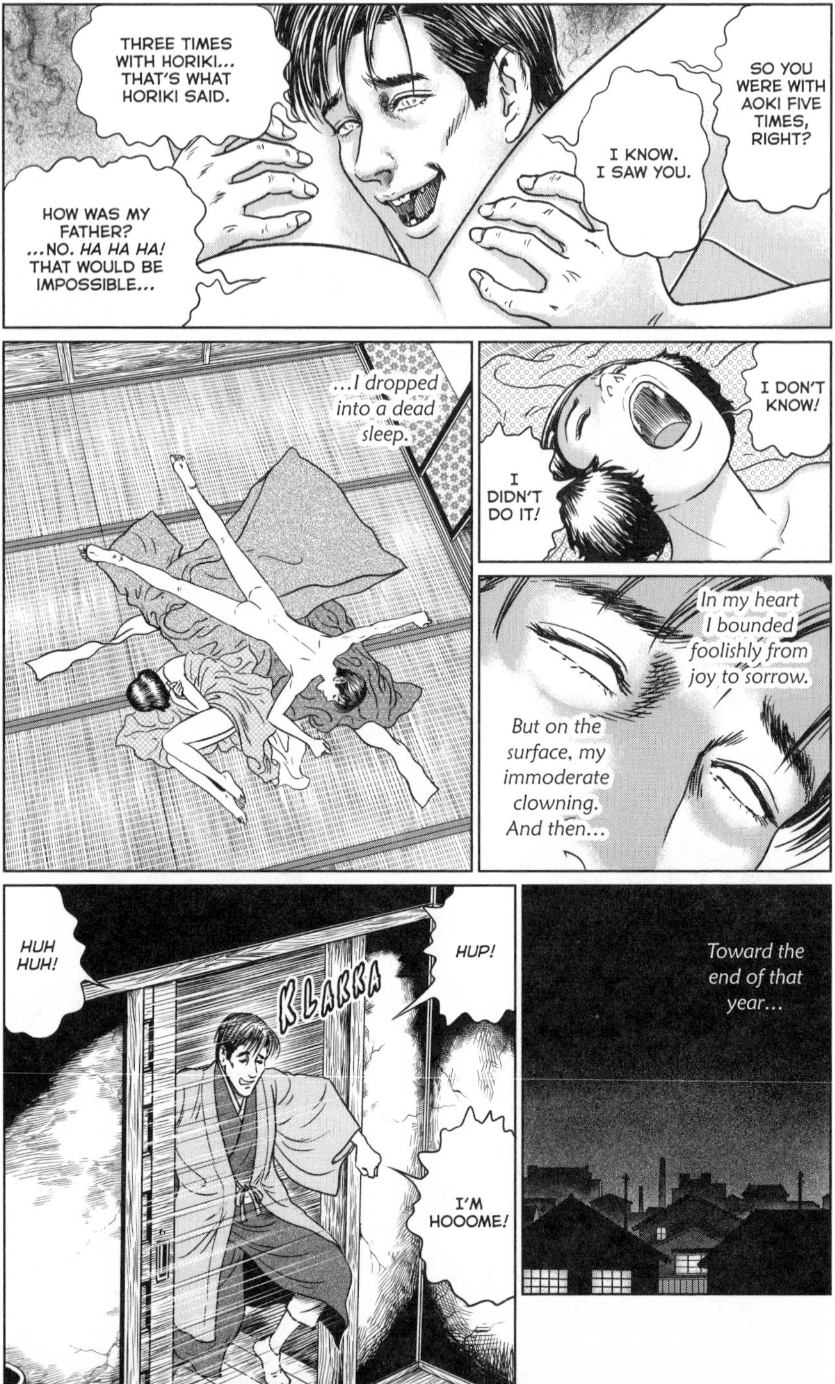
SO YOU WERE WITH AOKI FIVE TIMES, RIGHT?
I KNOW. I SAW YOU.
THREE TIMES WITH HORIKI... THAT'S WHAT HORIKI SAID.
HOW WAS MY FATHER? ...NO. *HA HA HA!* THAT WOULD BE IMPOSSIBLE...
I DON'T KNOW!
I DIDN'T DO IT!
In my heart I bounded foolishly from joy to sorrow.
But on the surface, my immoderate clowning. And then...
...I dropped into a dead sleep.
Toward the end of that year...
HUP!
HUH HUH!
KLAKKA
I'M HOOOME!

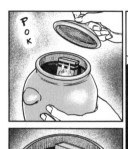

SUGAR-WATER, SUGAR-WATER...
KOFF! KOFF!
POK
DIAL
DIAL...
DIAL
...
The writing had been scratched off, but the part in Western letters remained intact.
Yoshiko couldn't read Western letters, so she must have thought this would be enough.
DIAL
The contents of this box of sleeping pills was more than enough to cause death.
The poor girl likely hid it here for when she felt like I would need it.
DIAL

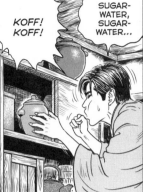

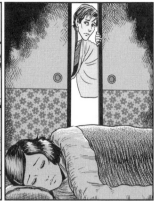

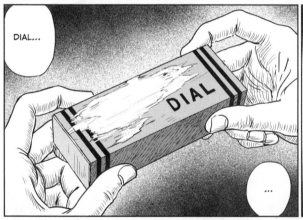

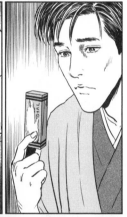

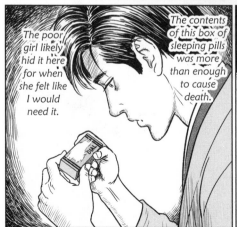

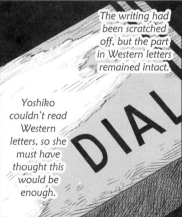

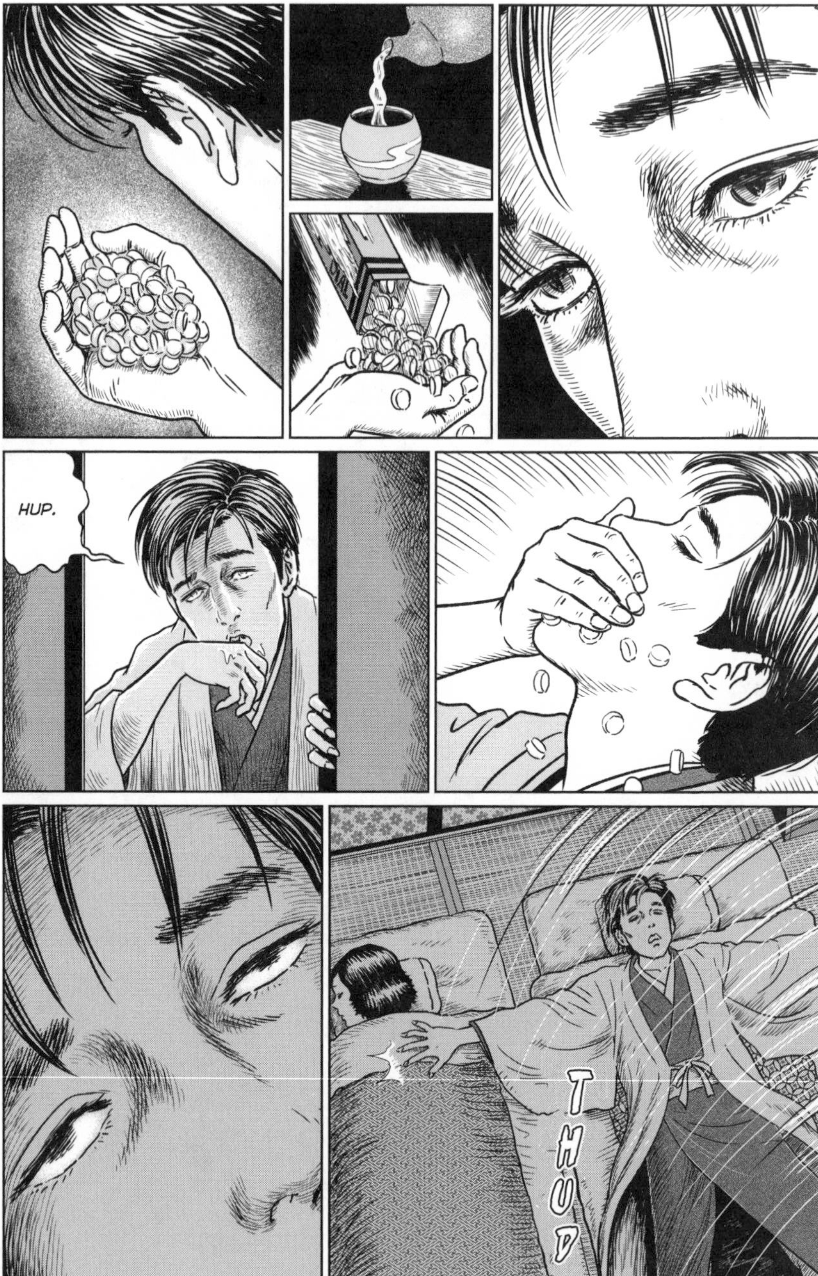
HUP.
THUD

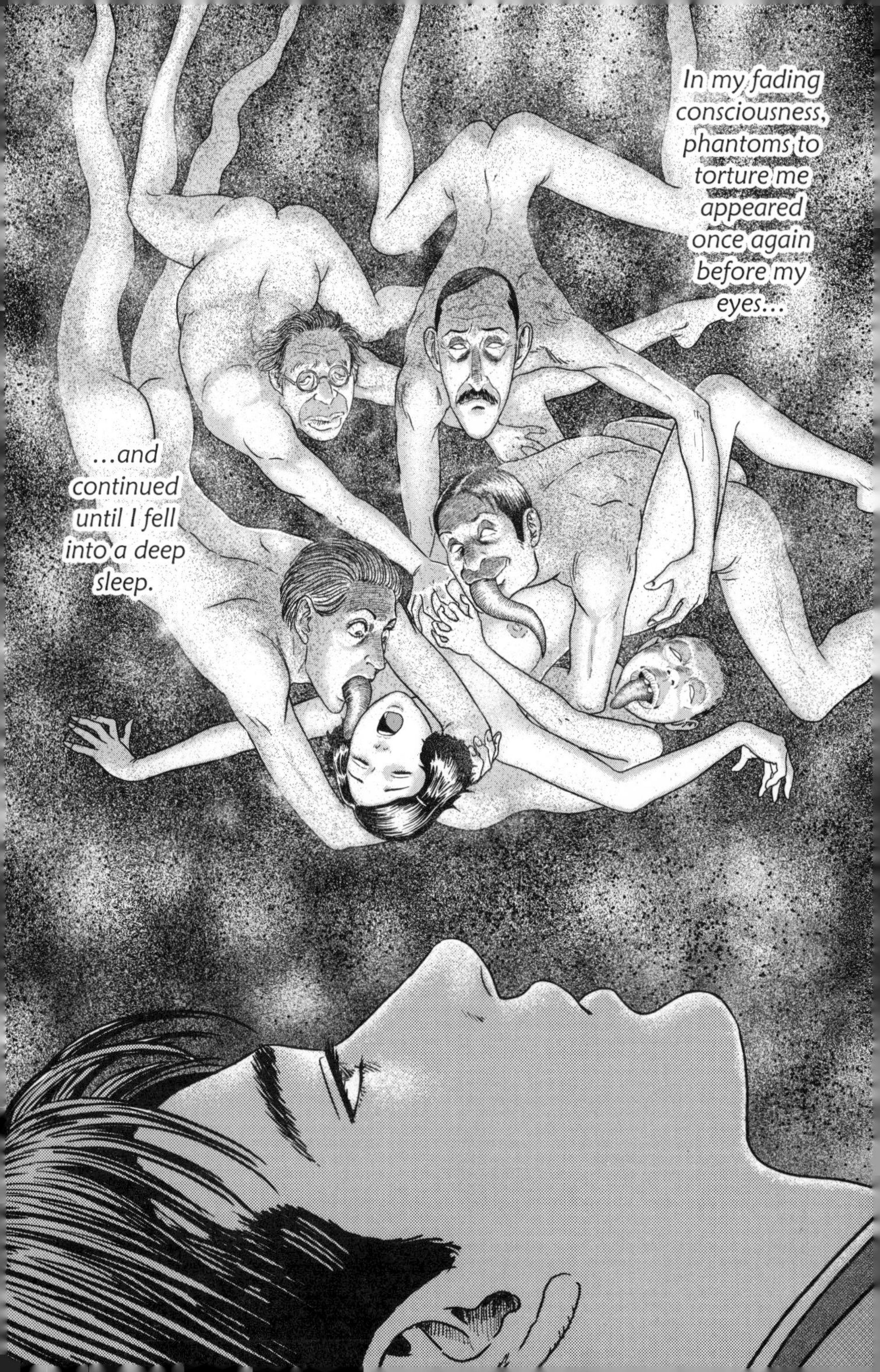
In my fading consciousness, phantoms to torture me appeared once again before my eyes...
...and continued until I fell into a deep sleep.

CHAIN No. 15: The Deepest Hell

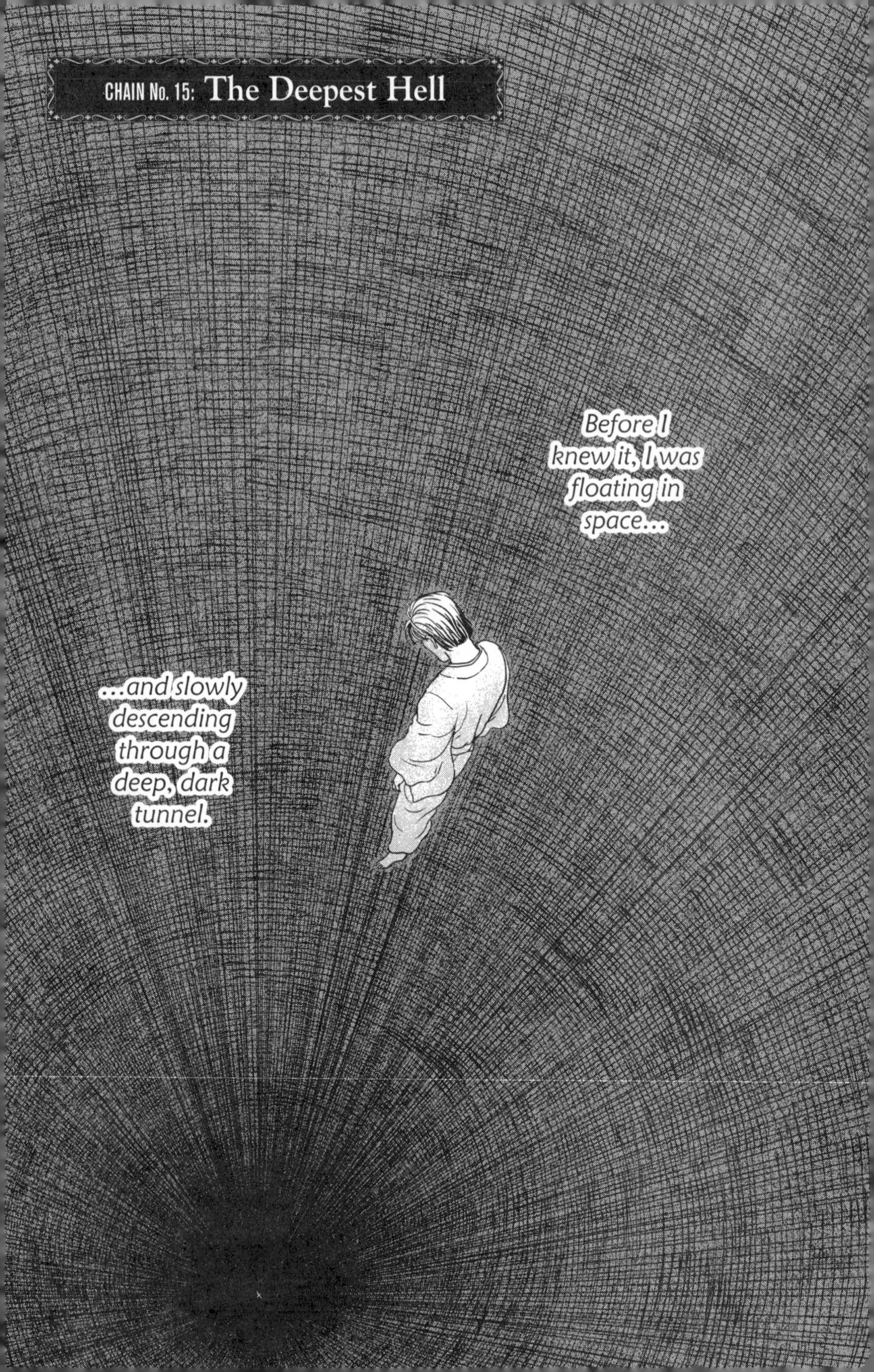
Before I knew it, I was floating in space...
...and slowly descending through a deep, dark tunnel.

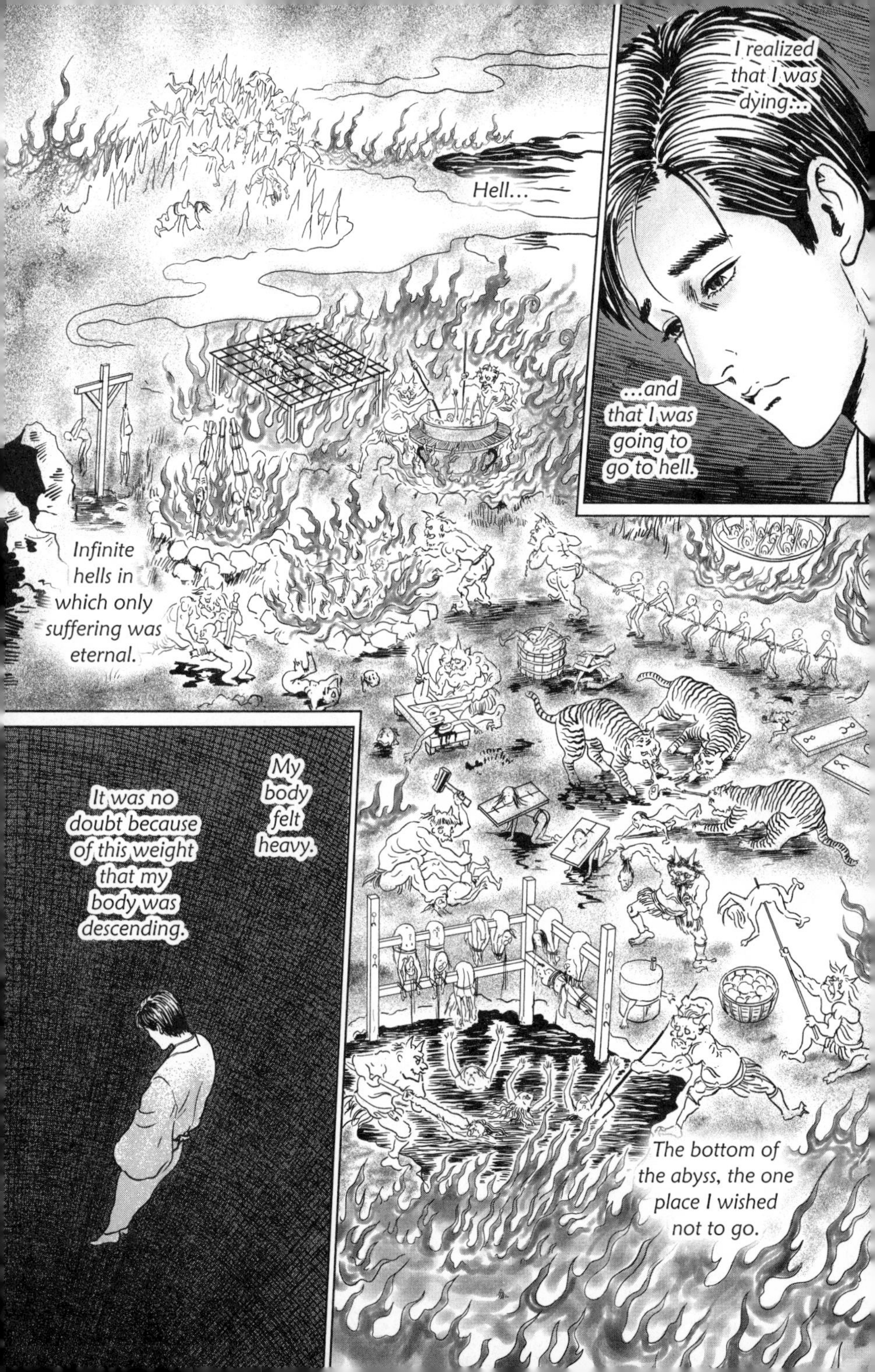
I realized that I was dying…
…and that I was going to go to hell.
Hell…
Infinite hells in which only suffering was eternal.
The bottom of the abyss, the one place I wished not to go.
My body felt heavy.
It was no doubt because of this weight that my body was descending.

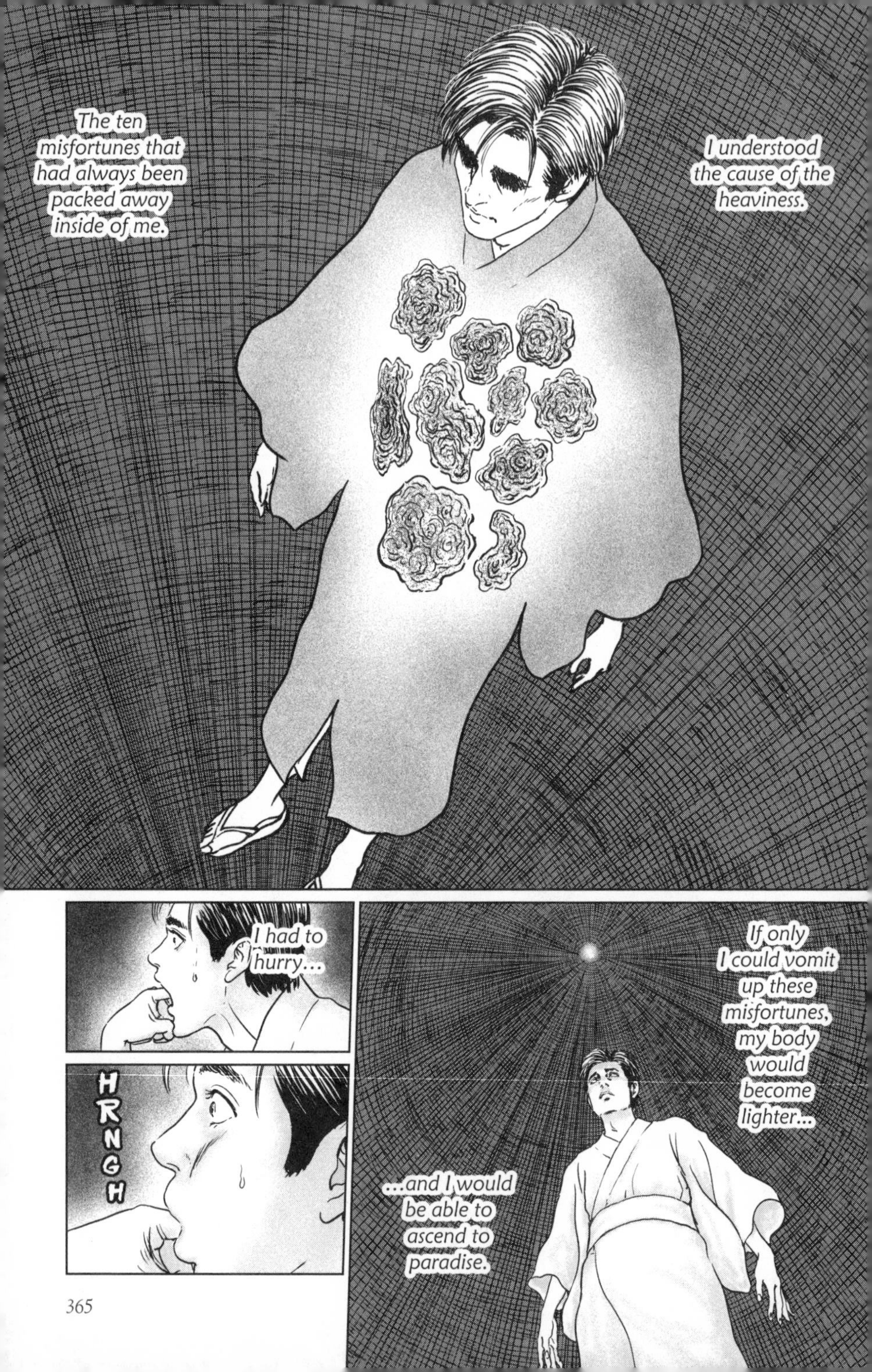
I understood the cause of the heaviness.
The ten misfortunes that had always been packed away inside of me.
If only I could vomit up these misfortunes, my body would become lighter...
...and I would be able to ascend to paradise.
I had to hurry...
HRNGH

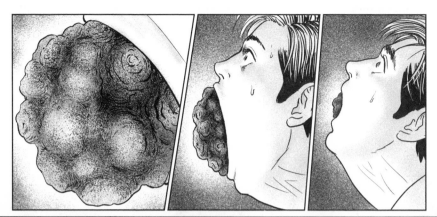

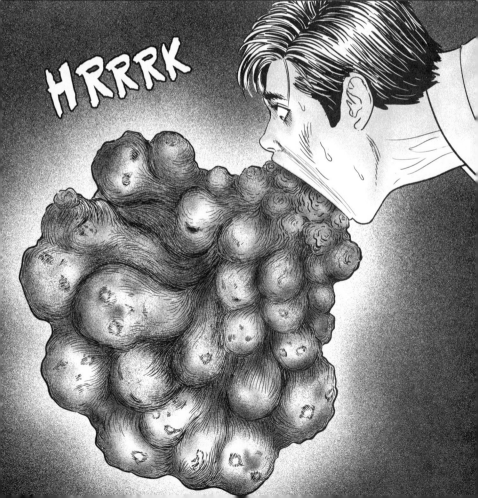

HRRRK

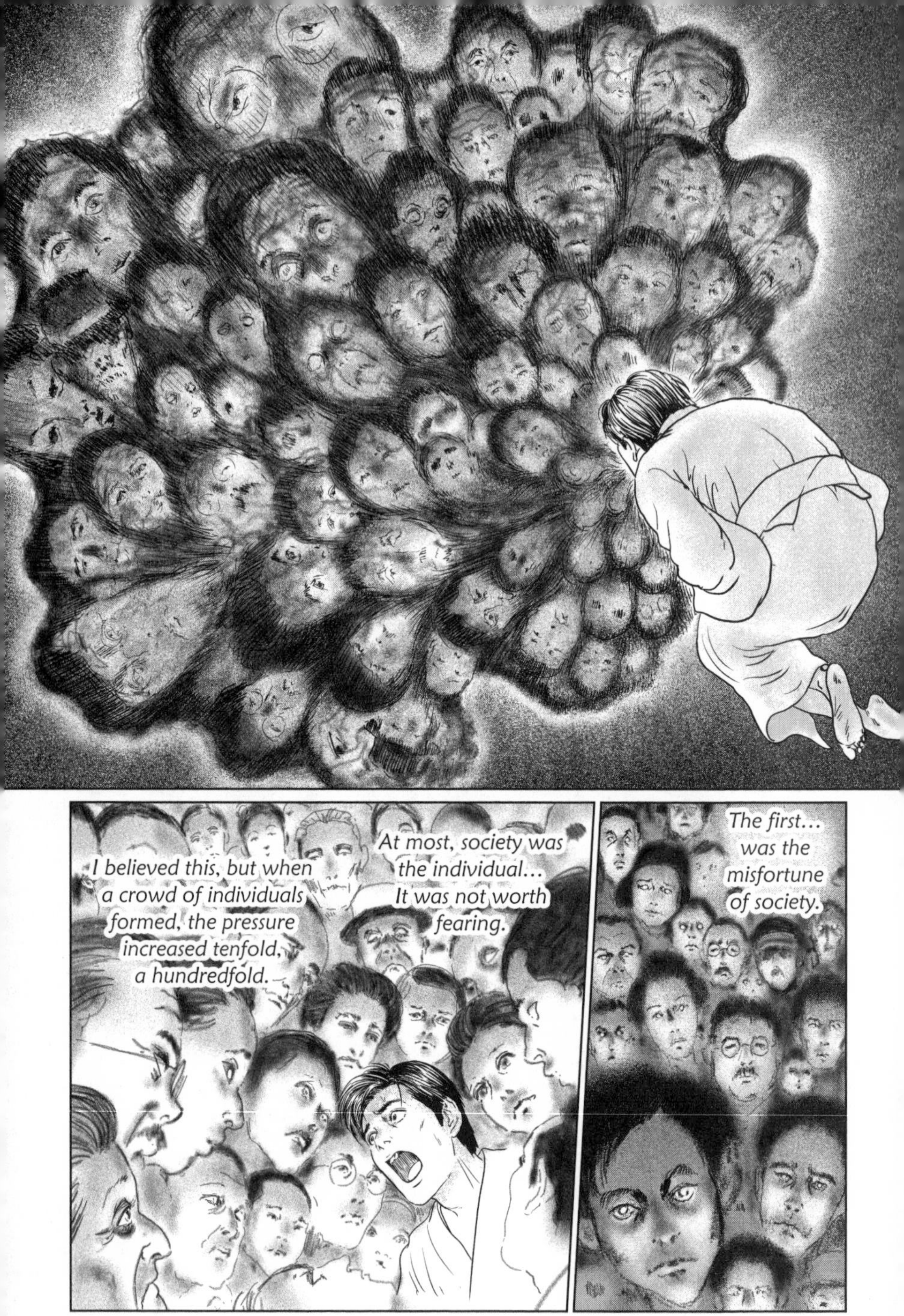
The first… was the misfortune of society.
At most, society was the individual… It was not worth fearing.
I believed this, but when a crowd of individuals formed, the pressure increased tenfold, a hundredfold.

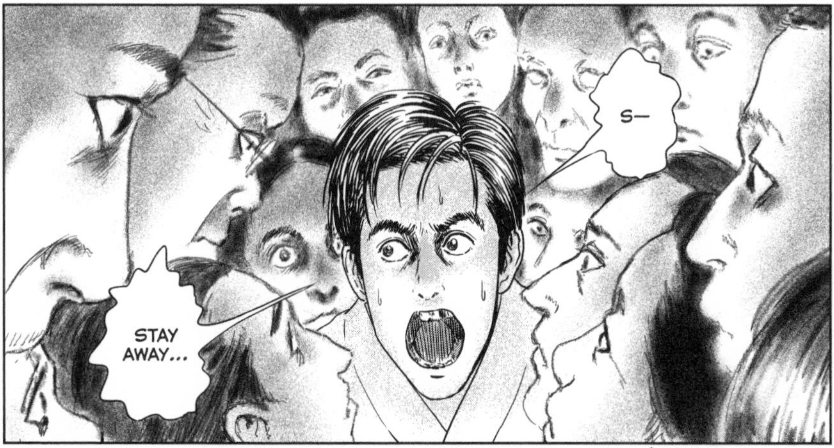
S—
STAY AWAY...

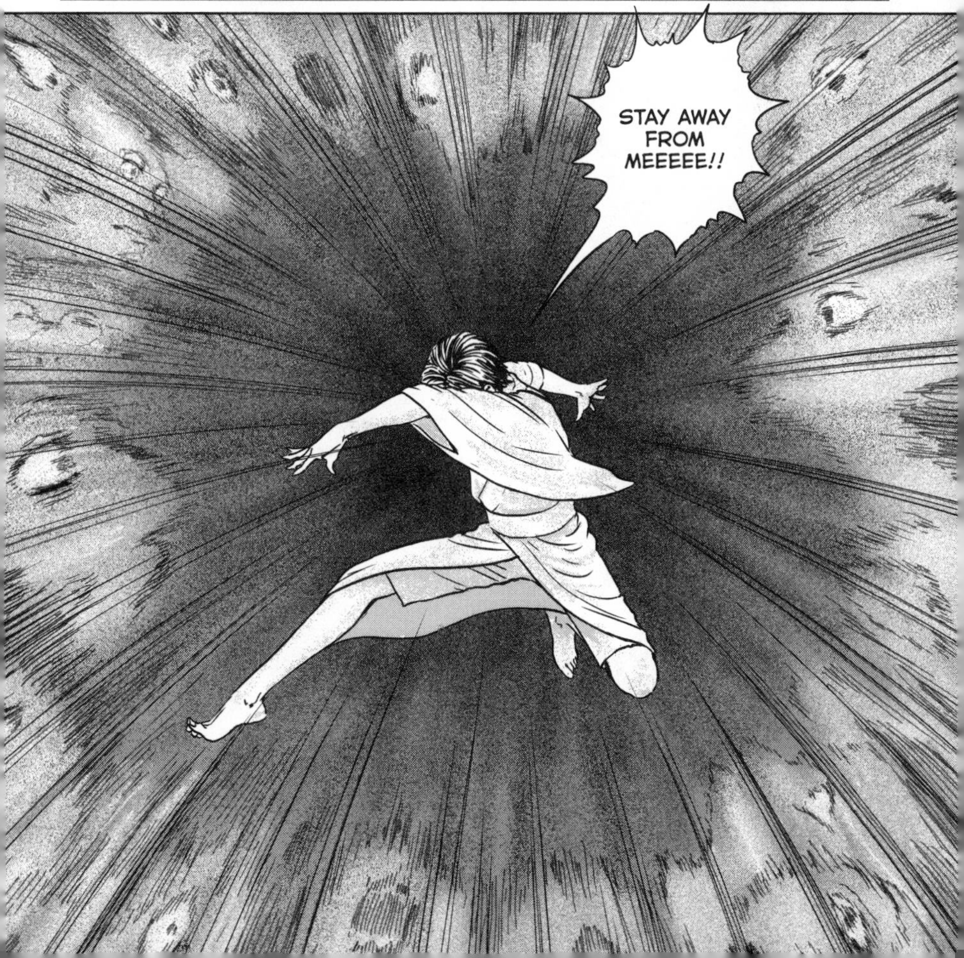
STAY AWAY FROM MEEEEE!!

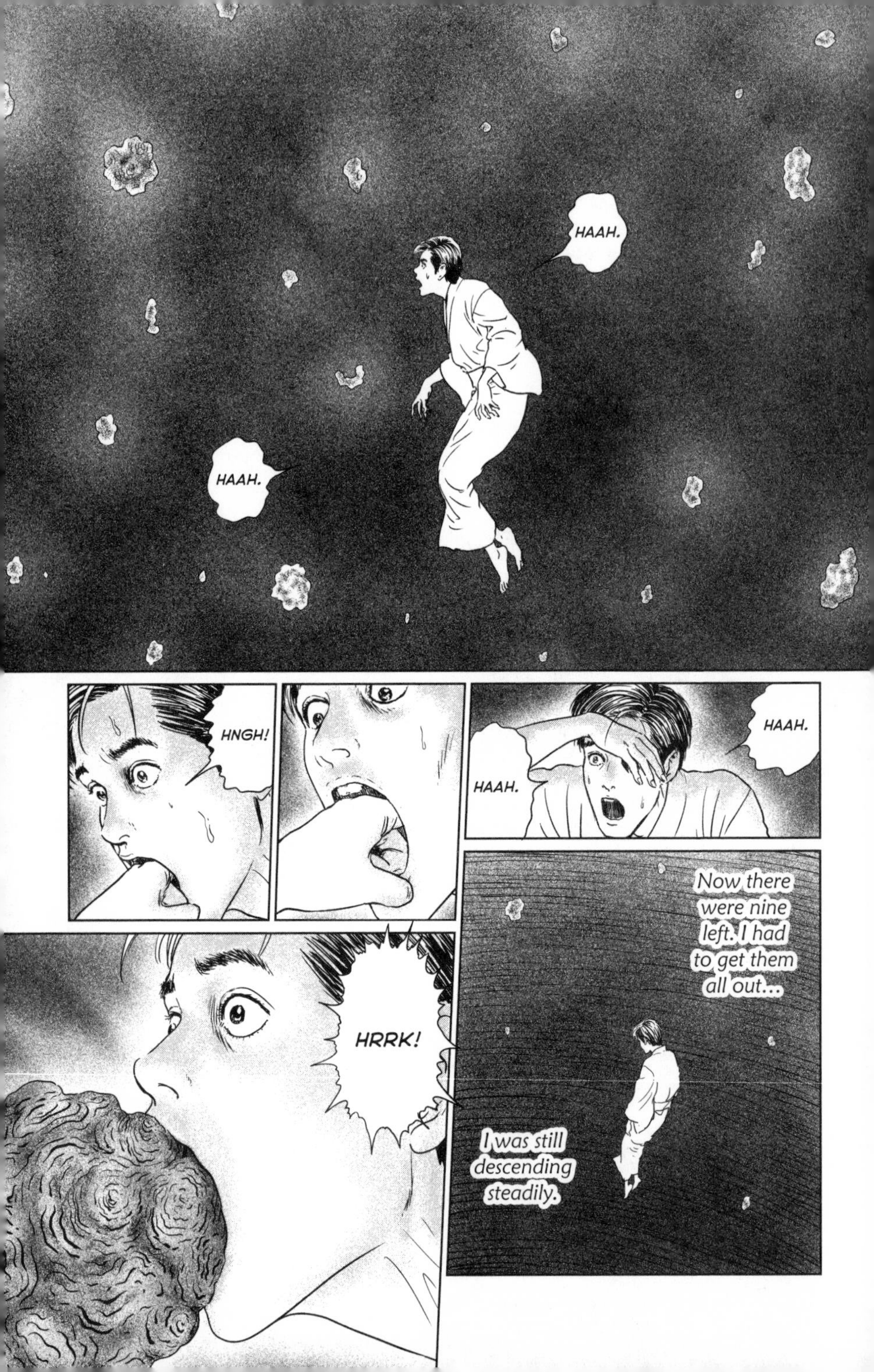
HAAH.
HAAH.
HAAH.
HAAH.
HNGH!
Now there were nine left. I had to get them all out...
I was still descending steadily.
HRRK!

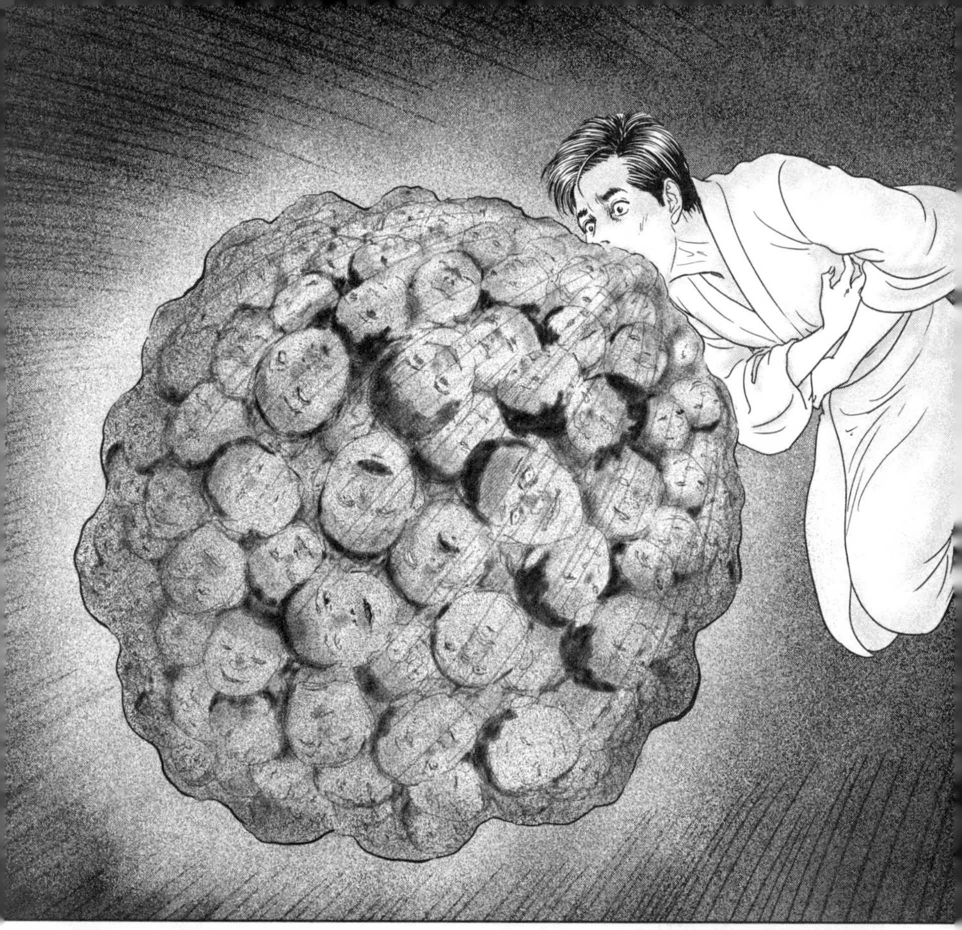

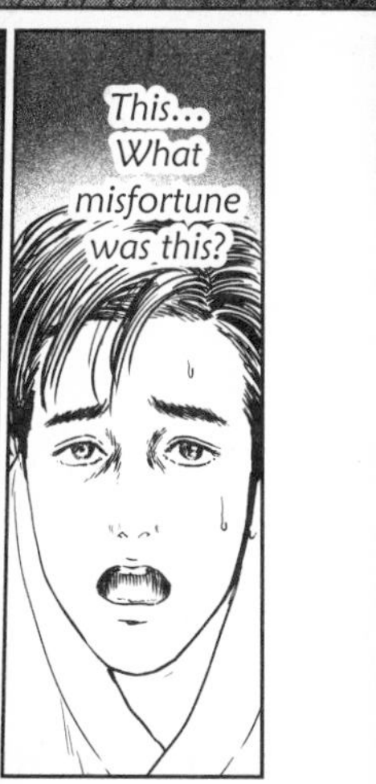
This... What misfortune was this?

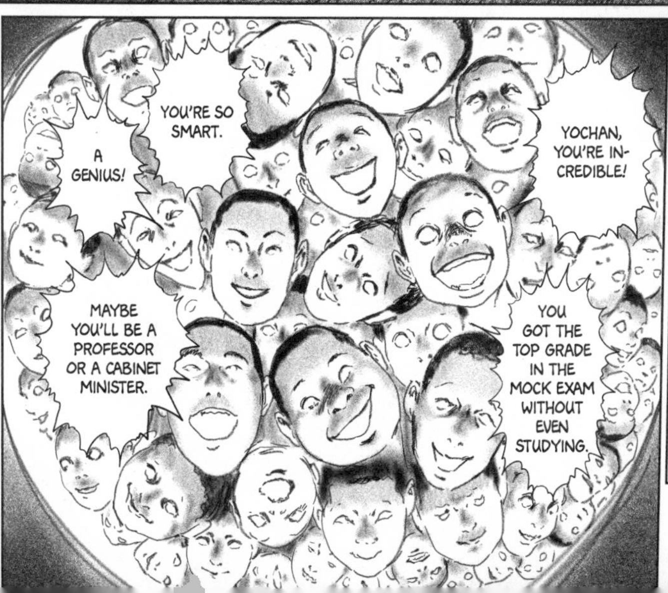
YOCHAN, YOU'RE IN-CREDIBLE!
YOU'RE SO SMART.
A GENIUS!
YOU GOT THE TOP GRADE IN THE MOCK EXAM WITHOUT EVEN STUDYING.
MAYBE YOU'LL BE A PROFESSOR OR A CABINET MINISTER.

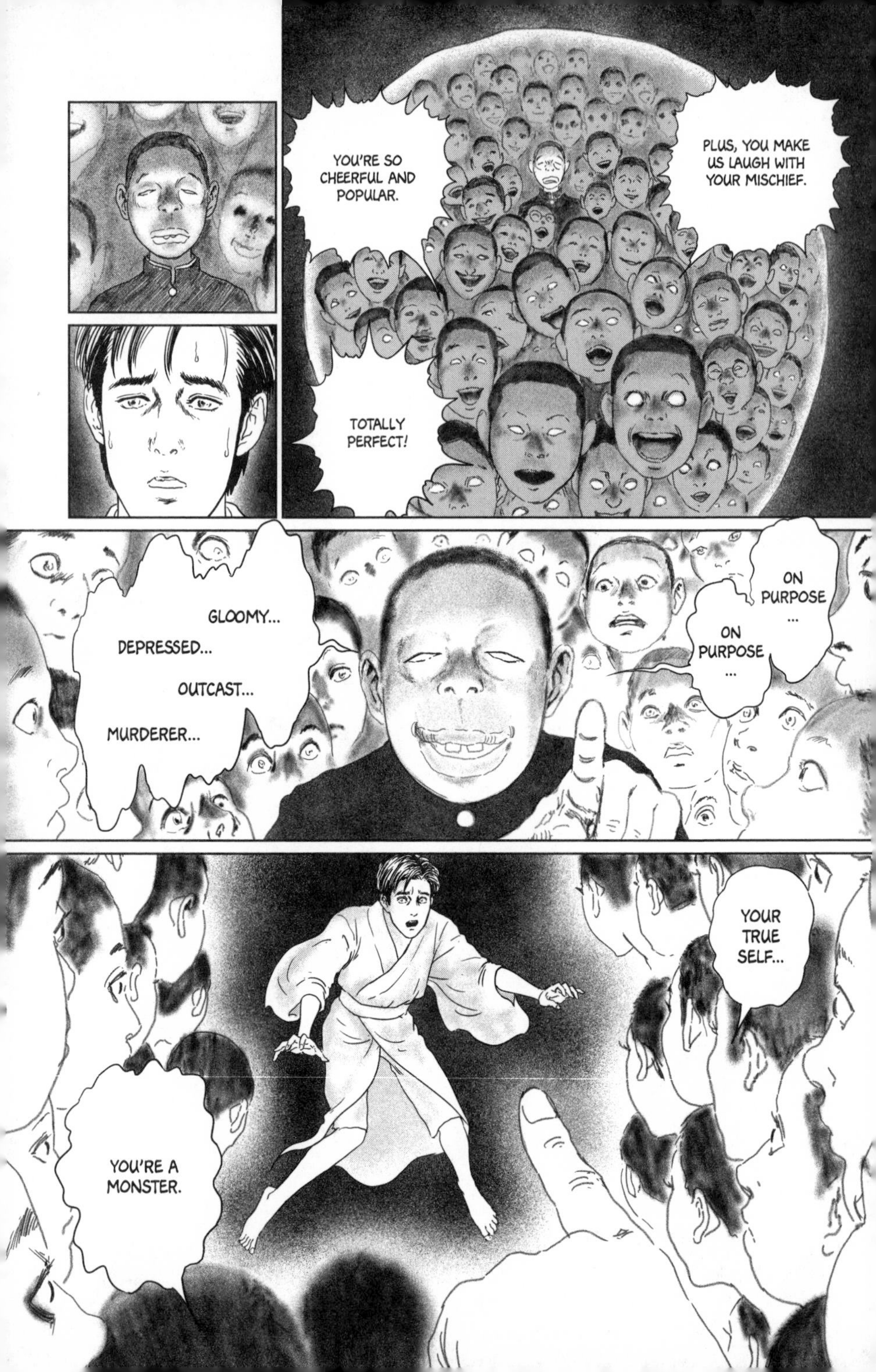

PLUS, YOU MAKE US LAUGH WITH YOUR MISCHIEF.
YOU'RE SO CHEERFUL AND POPULAR.
TOTALLY PERFECT!
ON PURPOSE ...
ON PURPOSE ...
GLOOMY... DEPRESSED... OUTCAST... MURDERER...
YOUR TRUE SELF...
YOU'RE A MONSTER.

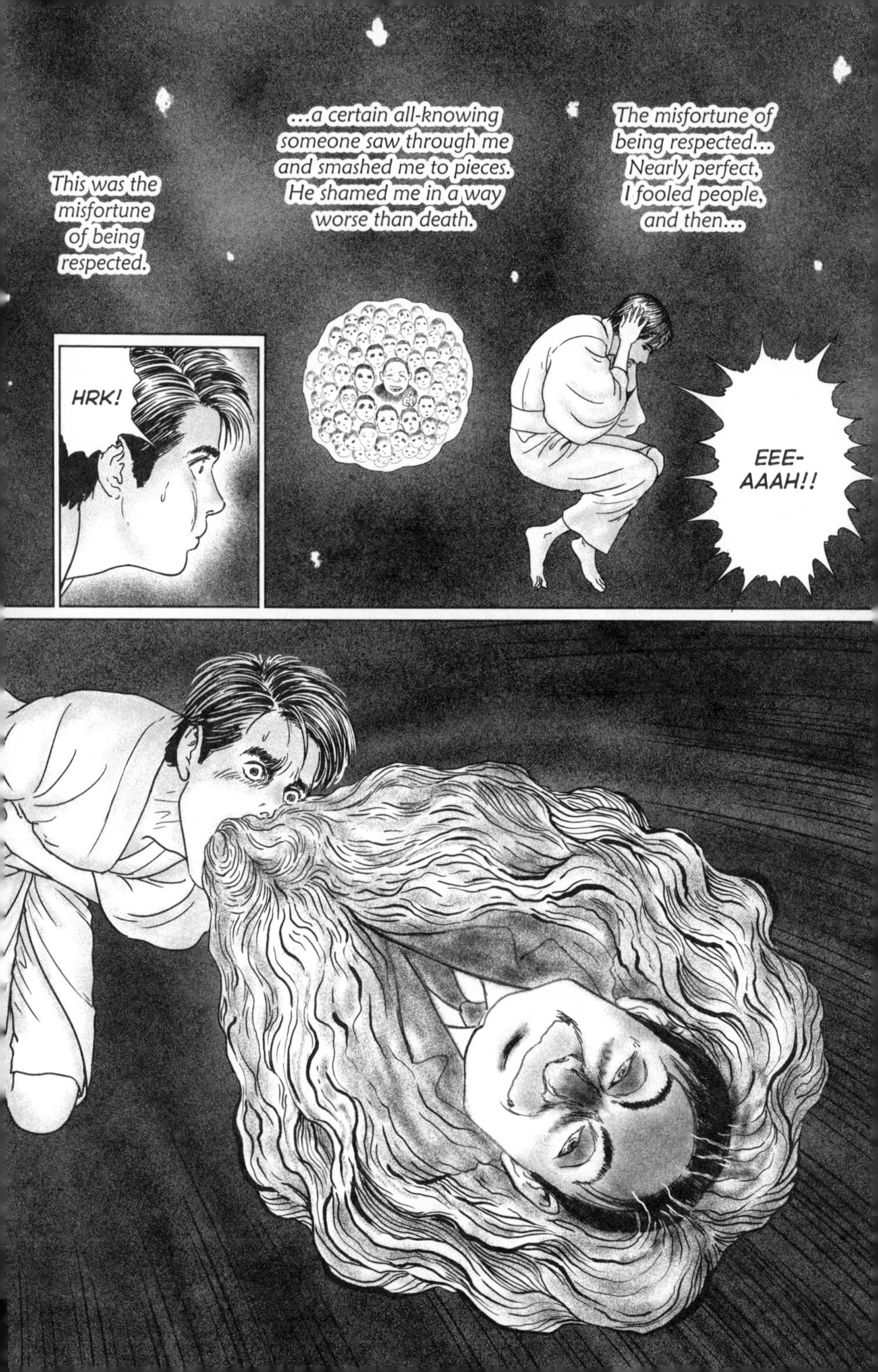
The misfortune of being respected... Nearly perfect, I fooled people, and then...
...a certain all-knowing someone saw through me and smashed me to pieces. He shamed me in a way worse than death.
This was the misfortune of being respected.
EEE-AAAH!!
HRK!

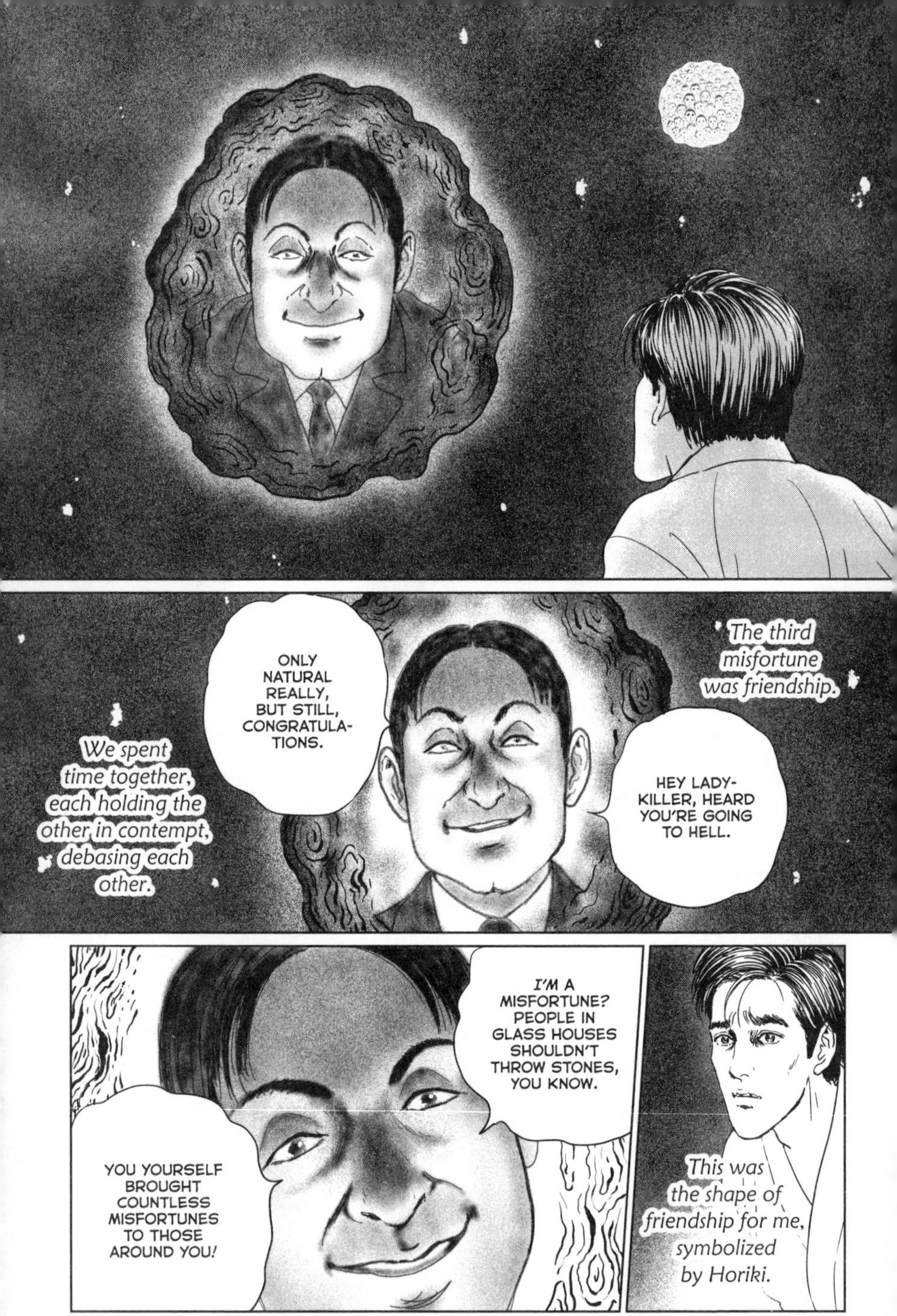
The third misfortune was friendship.
HEY LADY-KILLER, HEARD YOU'RE GOING TO HELL.
ONLY NATURAL REALLY, BUT STILL, CONGRATULATIONS.
We spent time together, each holding the other in contempt, debasing each other.
This was the shape of friendship for me, symbolized by Horiki.
I'M A MISFORTUNE? PEOPLE IN GLASS HOUSES SHOULDN'T THROW STONES, YOU KNOW.
YOU YOURSELF BROUGHT COUNTLESS MISFORTUNES TO THOSE AROUND YOU!

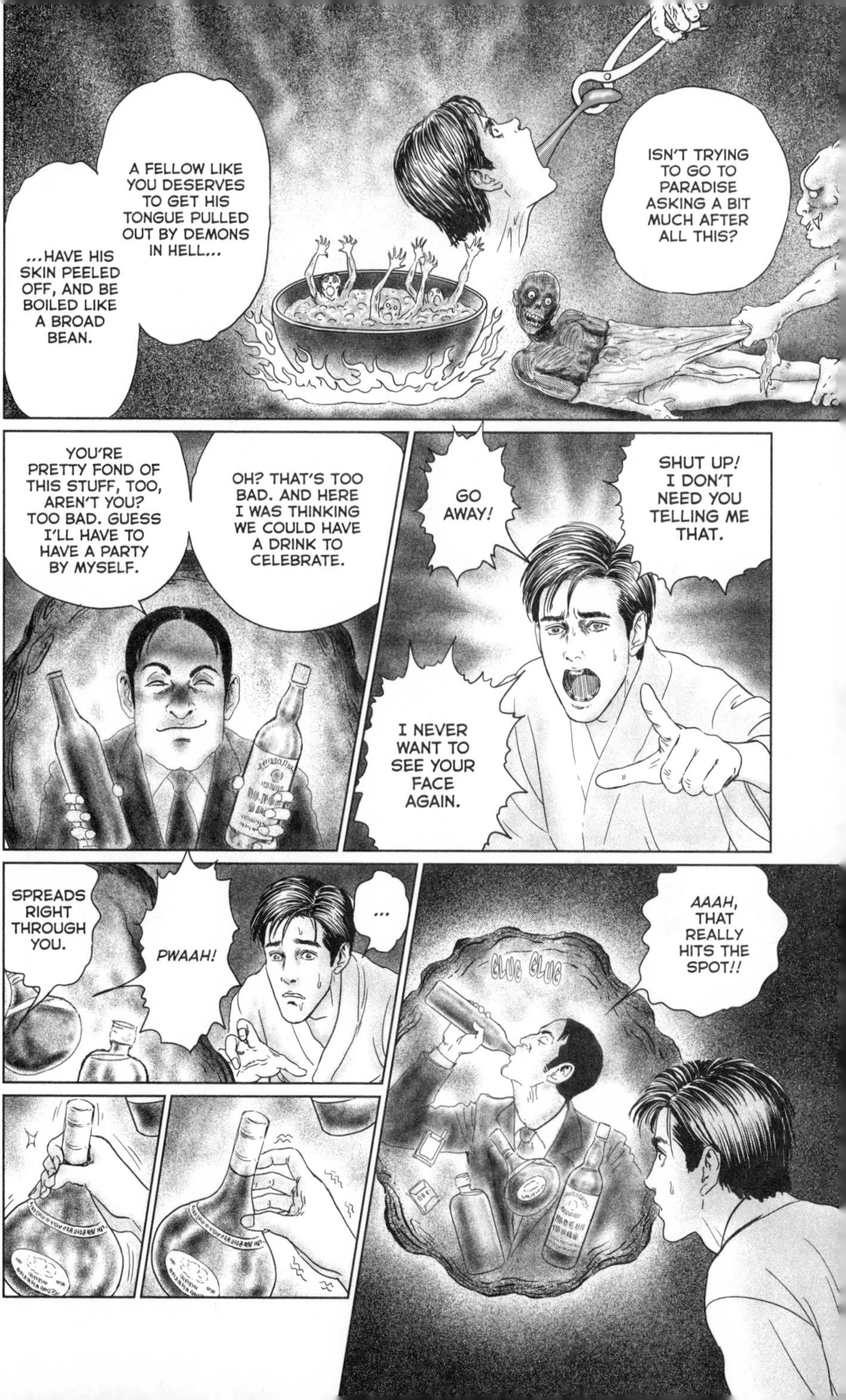
ISN'T TRYING TO GO TO PARADISE ASKING A BIT MUCH AFTER ALL THIS?
A FELLOW LIKE YOU DESERVES TO GET HIS TONGUE PULLED OUT BY DEMONS IN HELL...
...HAVE HIS SKIN PEELED OFF, AND BE BOILED LIKE A BROAD BEAN.
SHUT UP! I DON'T NEED YOU TELLING ME THAT.
GO AWAY!
I NEVER WANT TO SEE YOUR FACE AGAIN.
OH? THAT'S TOO BAD. AND HERE I WAS THINKING WE COULD HAVE A DRINK TO CELEBRATE.
YOU'RE PRETTY FOND OF THIS STUFF, TOO, AREN'T YOU? TOO BAD. GUESS I'LL HAVE TO HAVE A PARTY BY MYSELF.
AAAH, THAT REALLY HITS THE SPOT!!
GLUG GLUG
...
PWAAH!
SPREADS RIGHT THROUGH YOU.

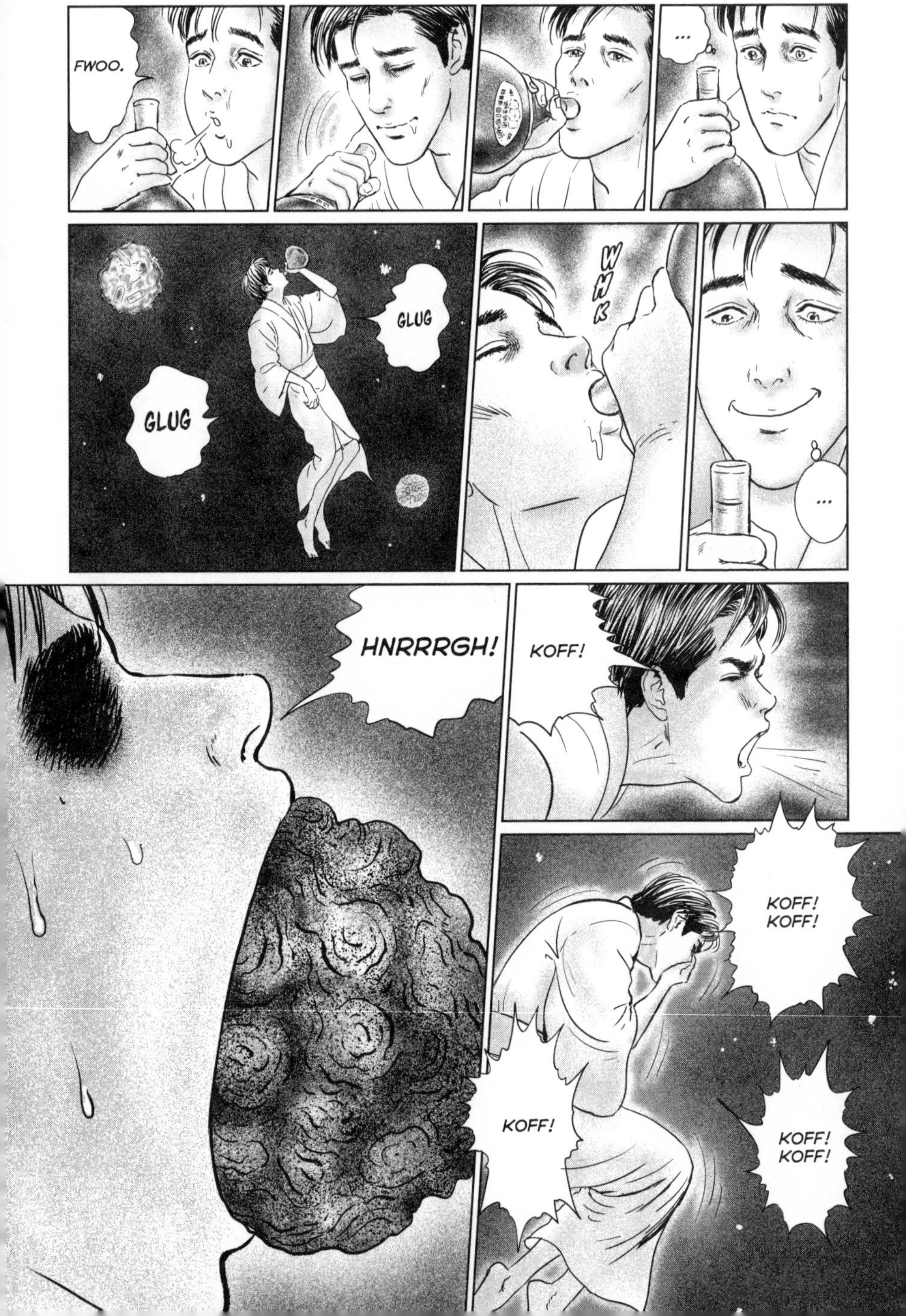
...
FWOO.
...
WHK
GLUG
GLUG
KOFF!
KOFF! KOFF!
KOFF! KOFF!
KOFF!
HNRRRGH!

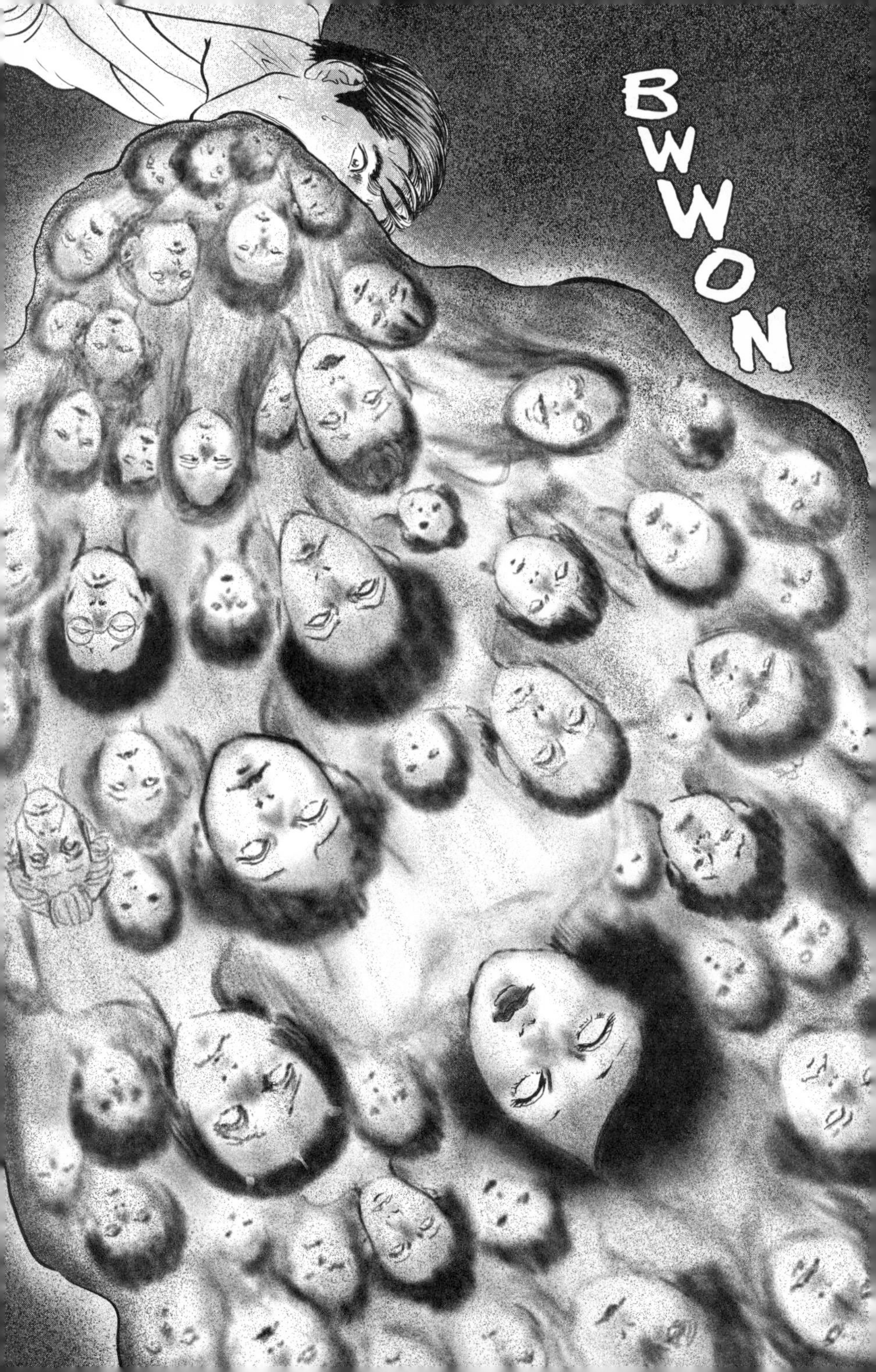
BWWON

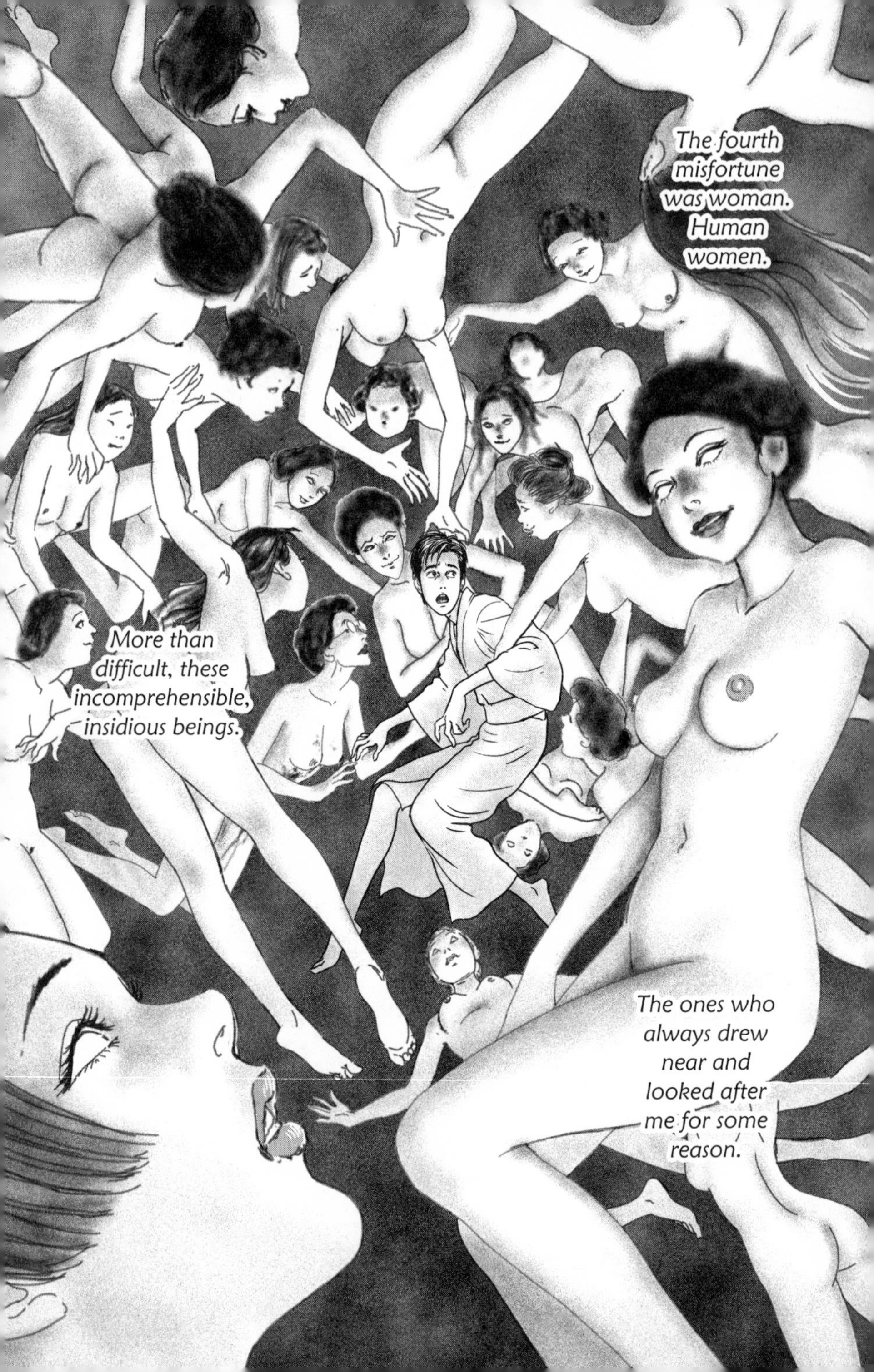
The fourth misfortune was woman. Human women.
More than difficult, these incomprehensible, insidious beings.
The ones who always drew near and looked after me for some reason.

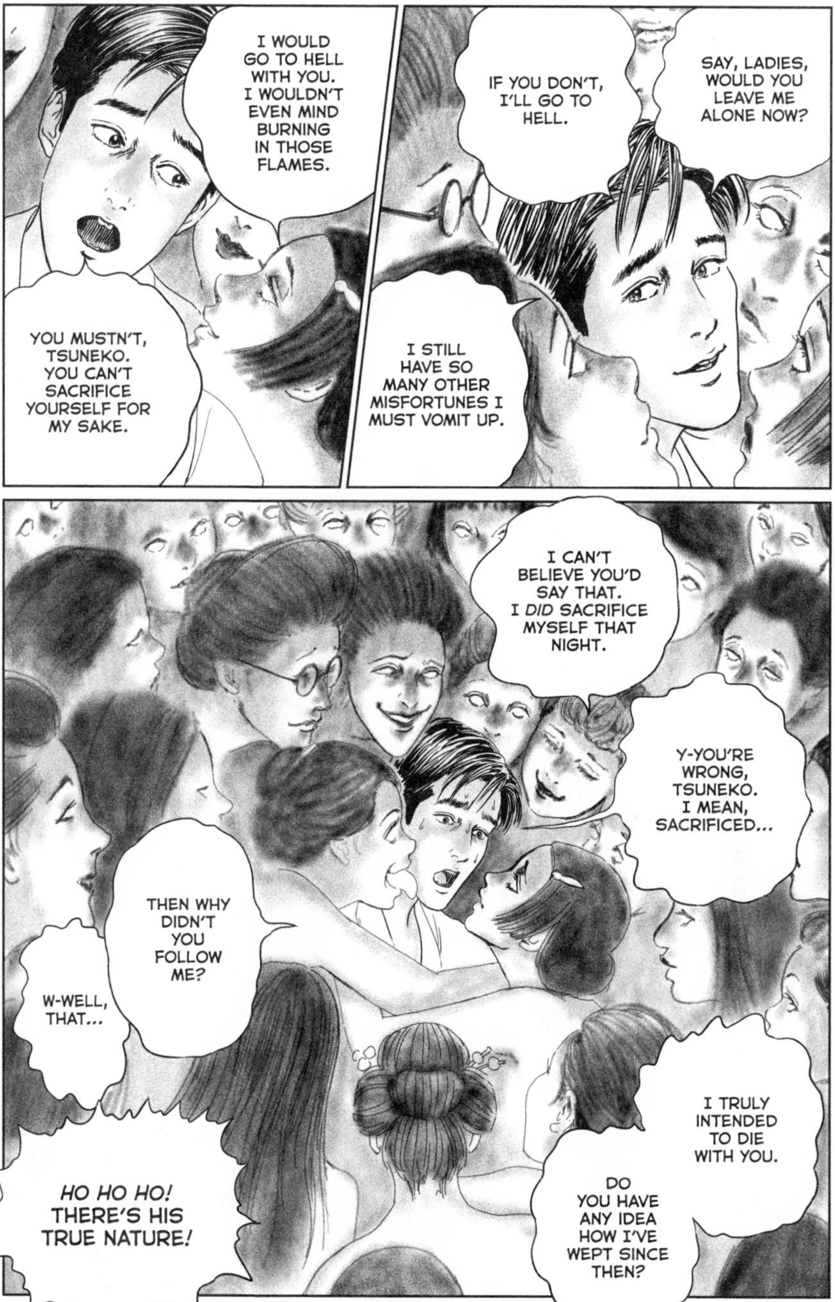
SAY, LADIES, WOULD YOU LEAVE ME ALONE NOW?
IF YOU DON'T, I'LL GO TO HELL.
I STILL HAVE SO MANY OTHER MISFORTUNES I MUST VOMIT UP.
I WOULD GO TO HELL WITH YOU. I WOULDN'T EVEN MIND BURNING IN THOSE FLAMES.
YOU MUSTN'T, TSUNEKO. YOU CAN'T SACRIFICE YOURSELF FOR MY SAKE.
I CAN'T BELIEVE YOU'D SAY THAT. I *DID* SACRIFICE MYSELF THAT NIGHT.
Y-YOU'RE WRONG, TSUNEKO. I MEAN, SACRIFICED...
THEN WHY DIDN'T YOU FOLLOW ME?
W-WELL, THAT...
I TRULY INTENDED TO DIE WITH YOU.
DO YOU HAVE ANY IDEA HOW I'VE WEPT SINCE THEN?
HO HO HO! THERE'S HIS TRUE NATURE*!*

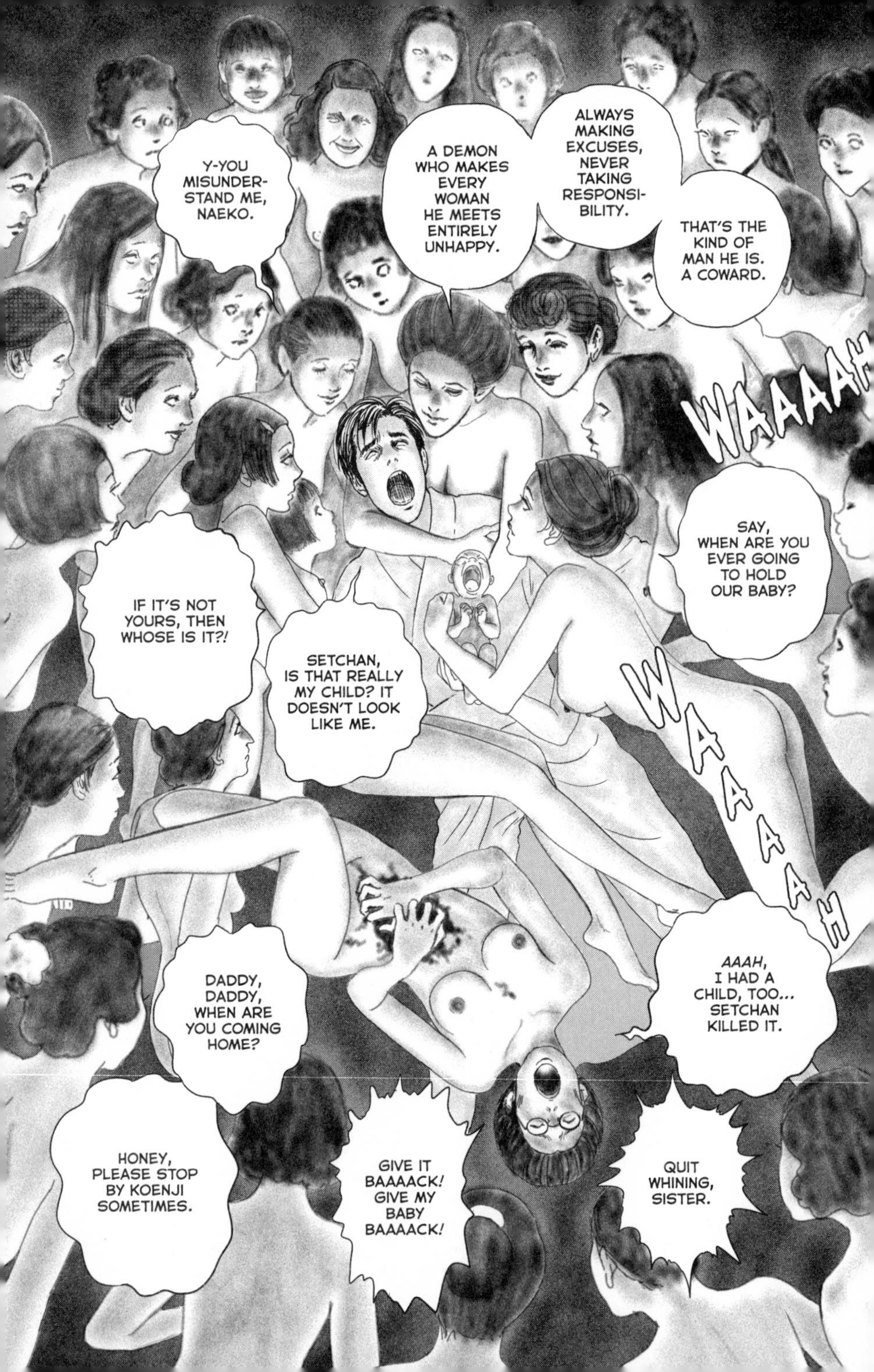
A DEMON WHO MAKES EVERY WOMAN HE MEETS ENTIRELY UNHAPPY.
ALWAYS MAKING EXCUSES, NEVER TAKING RESPONSI-BILITY.
THAT'S THE KIND OF MAN HE IS. A COWARD.
Y-YOU MISUNDER-STAND ME, NAEKO.
WAAAAH
SAY, WHEN ARE YOU EVER GOING TO HOLD OUR BABY?
WAAAAAAH
SETCHAN, IS THAT REALLY MY CHILD? IT DOESN'T LOOK LIKE ME.
IF IT'S NOT YOURS, THEN WHOSE IS IT?!
AAAH, I HAD A CHILD, TOO... SETCHAN KILLED IT.
DADDY, DADDY, WHEN ARE YOU COMING HOME?
QUIT WHINING, SISTER.
GIVE IT BAAAACK! GIVE MY BABY BAAAACK!
HONEY, PLEASE STOP BY KOENJI SOMETIMES.

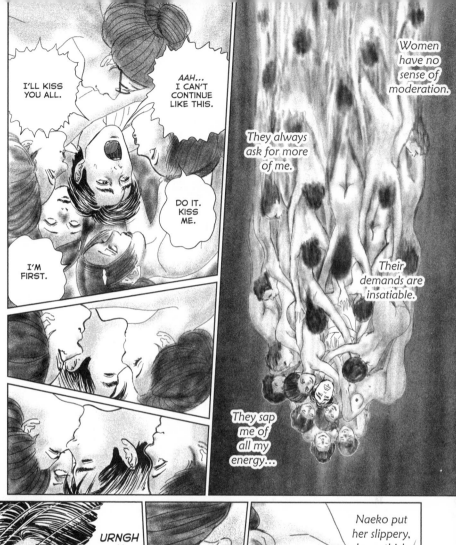

I'LL KISS YOU ALL.

AAH... I CAN'T CONTINUE LIKE THIS.

DO IT. KISS ME.

I'M FIRST.

Women have no sense of moderation.

They always ask for more of me.

Their demands are insatiable.

They sap me of all my energy...

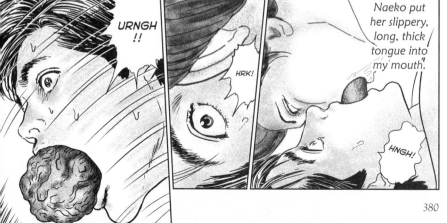

URNGH!!

HRK!

Naeko put her slippery, long, thick tongue into my mouth.

HNGH!

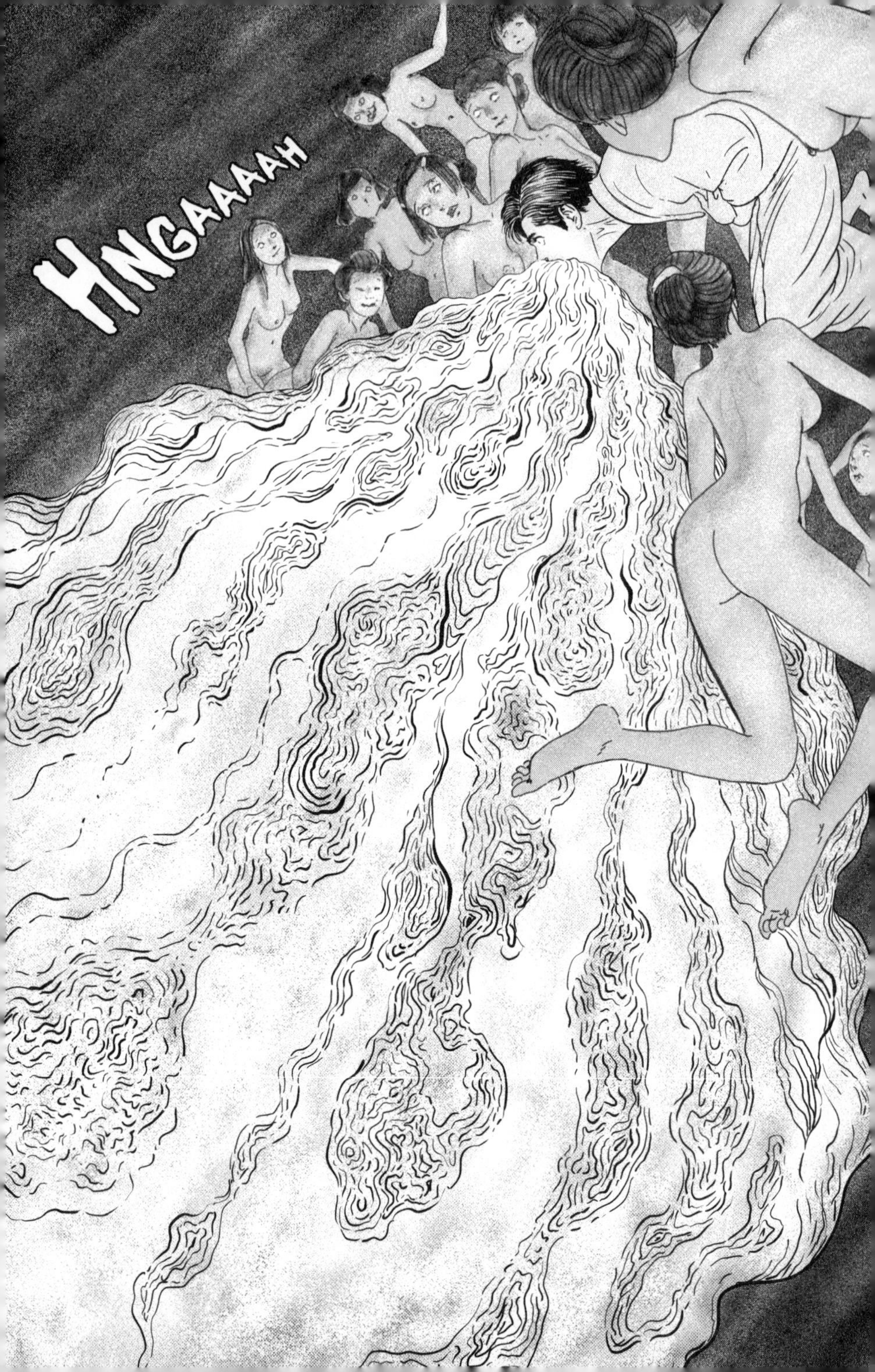
HNGAAAAH

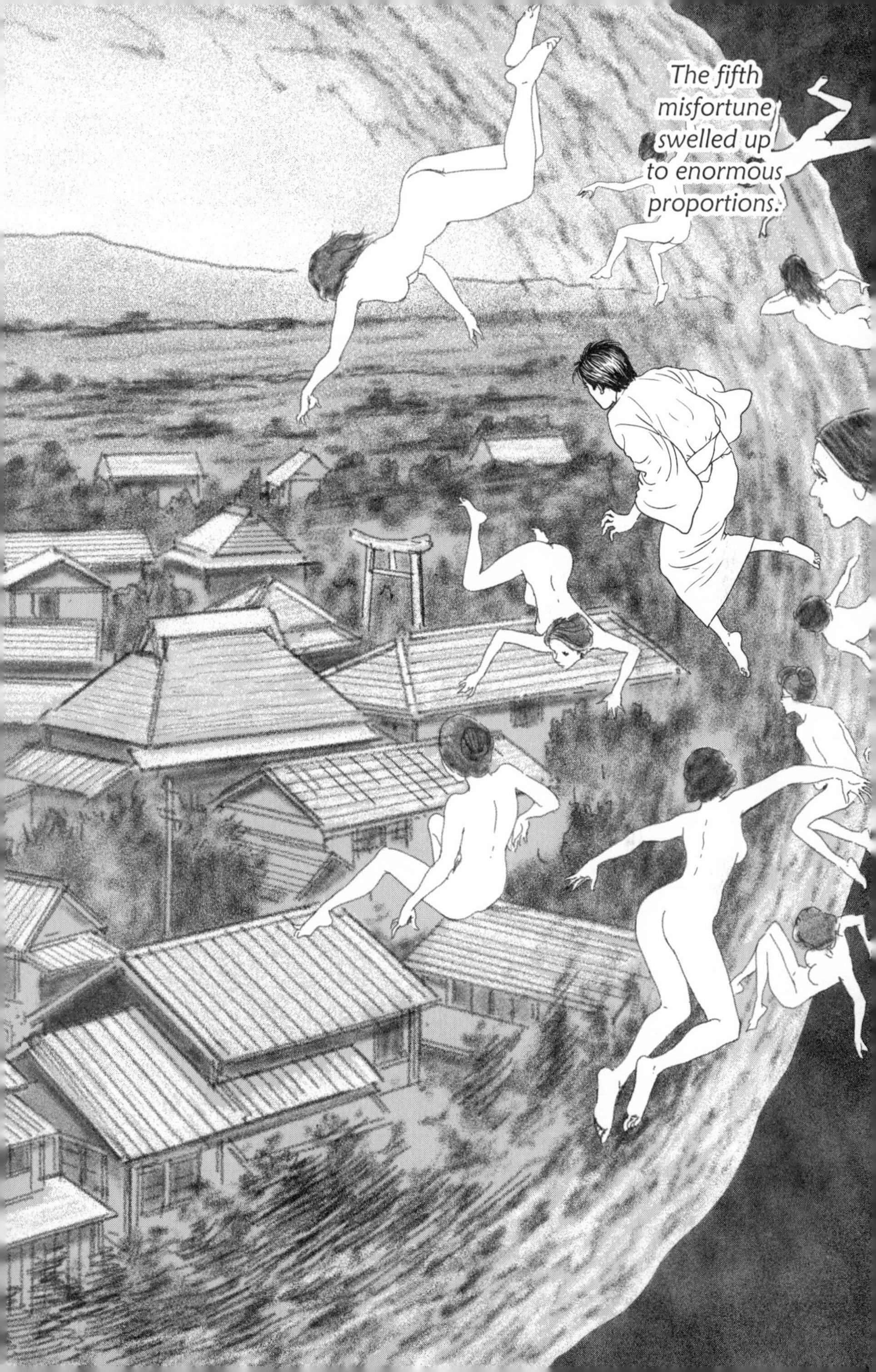
The fifth misfortune swelled up to enormous proportions.

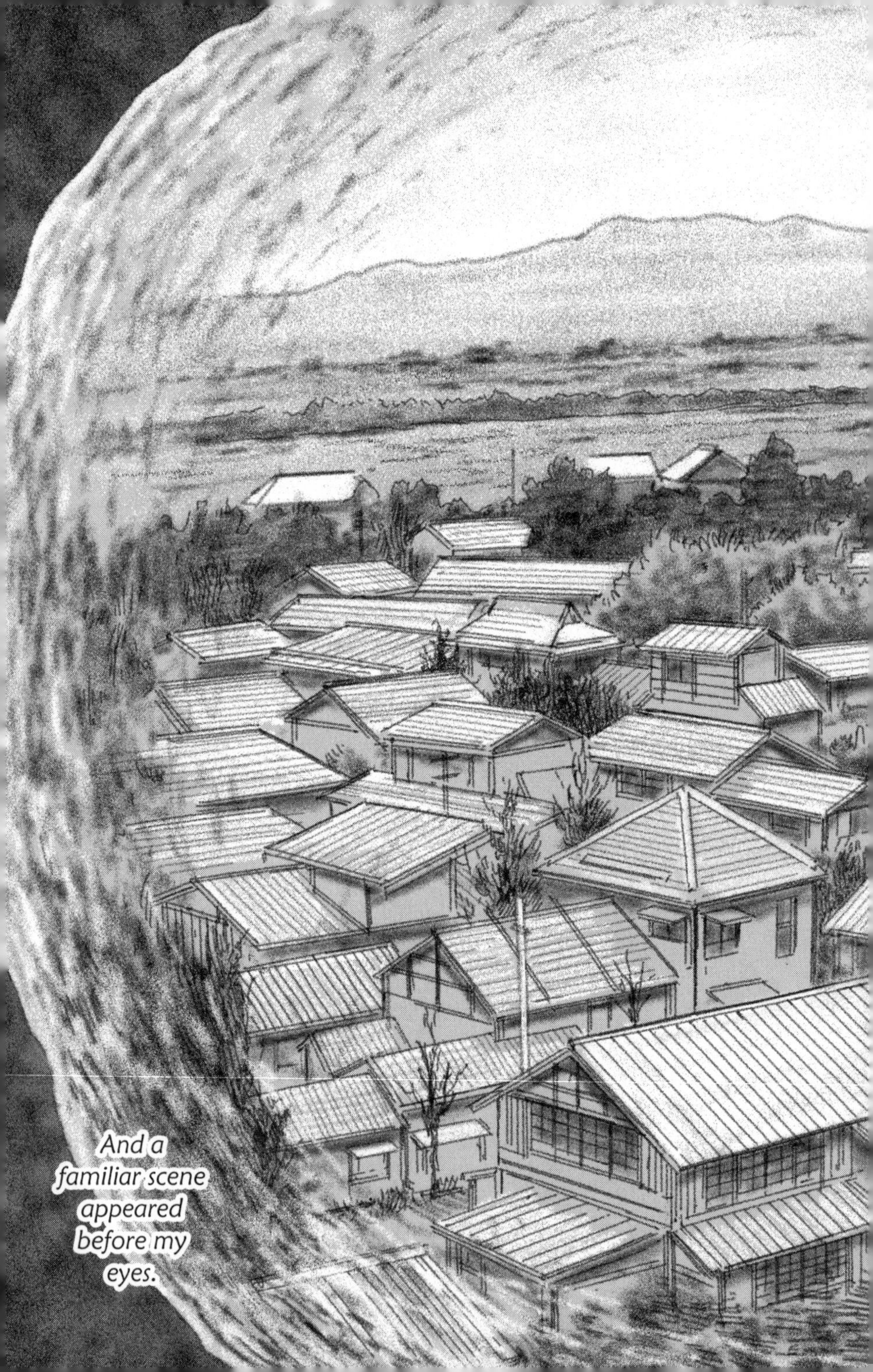
And a familiar scene appeared before my eyes.

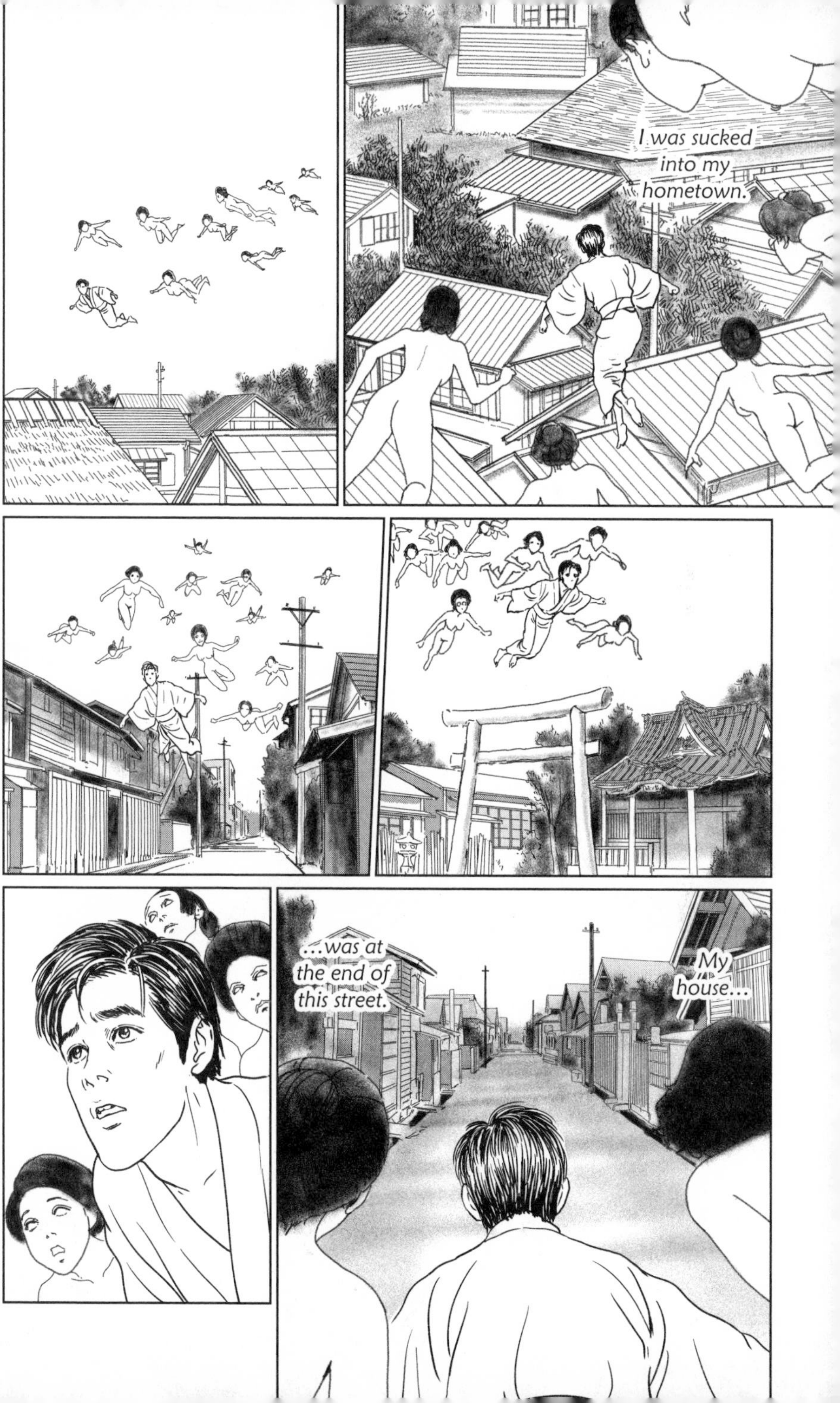
I was sucked into my hometown.
My house…
…was at the end of this street.

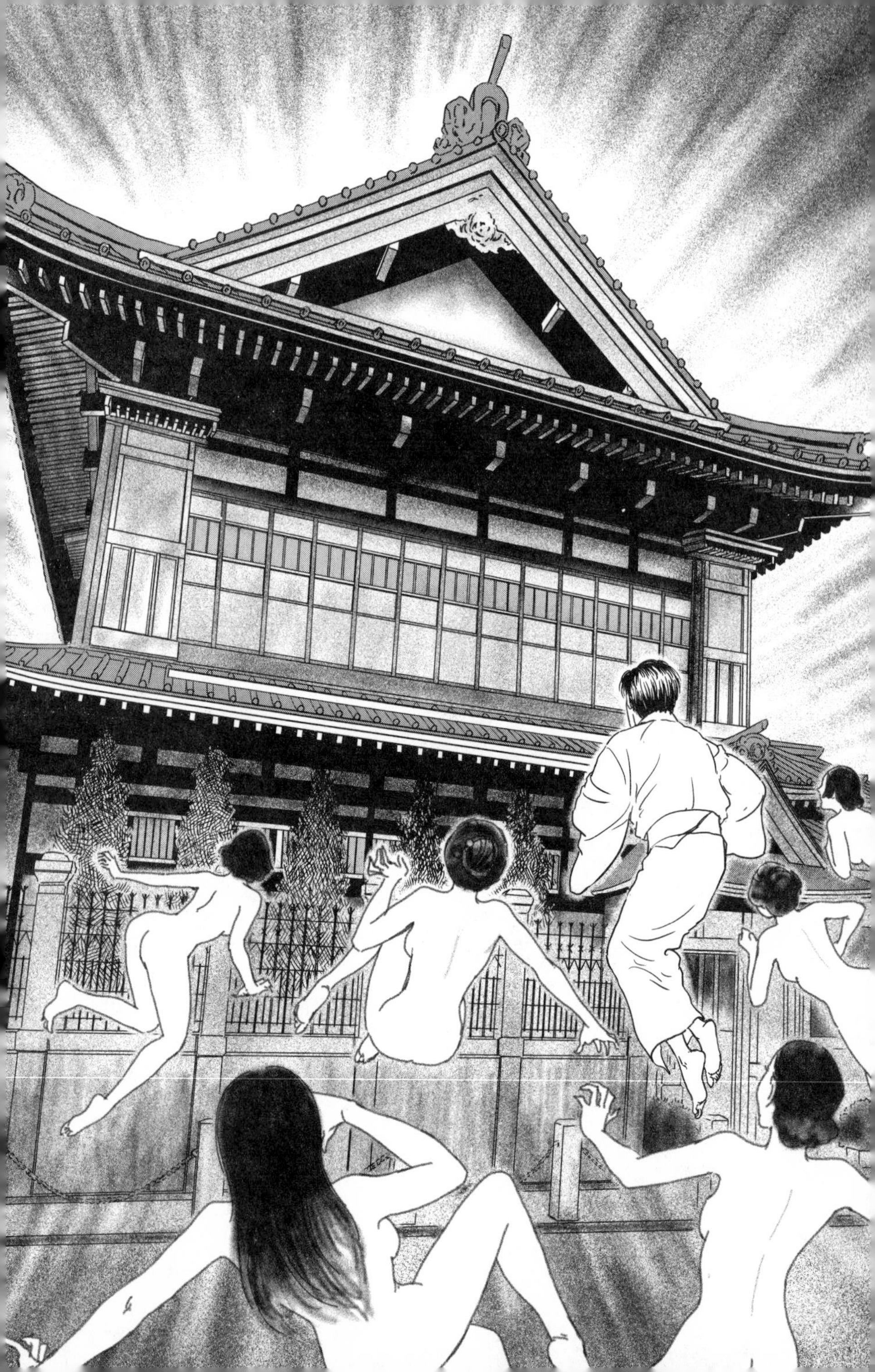

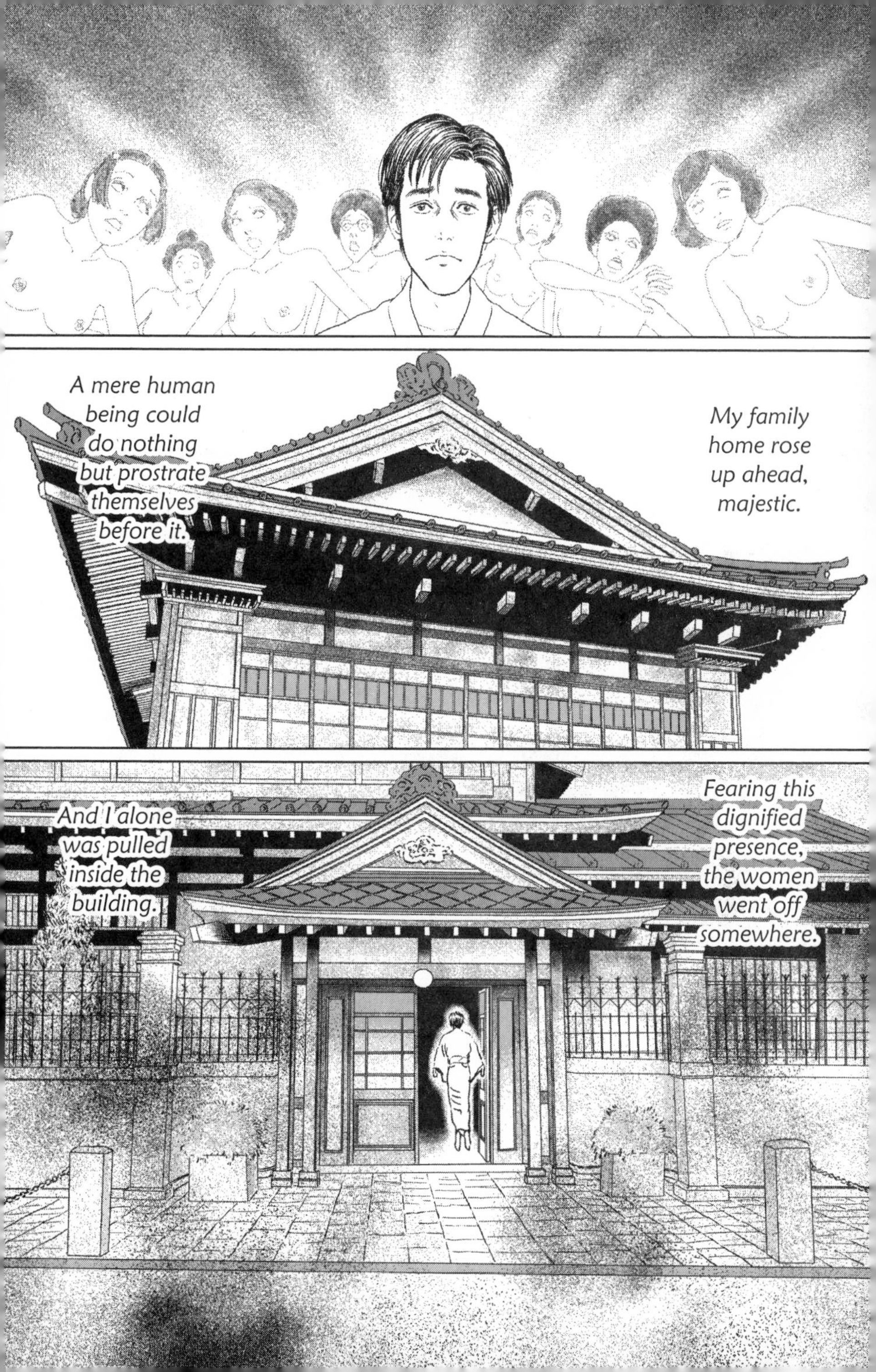
My family home rose up ahead, majestic.
A mere human being could do nothing but prostrate themselves before it.
Fearing this dignified presence, the women went off somewhere.
And I alone was pulled inside the building.

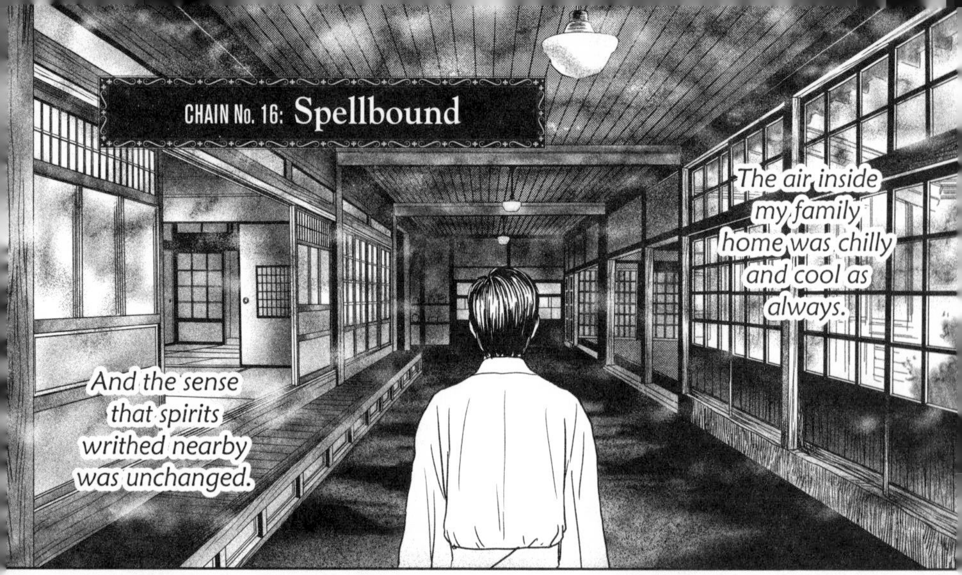
CHAIN No. 16: Spellbound
The air inside my family home was chilly and cool as always.
And the sense that spirits writhed nearby was unchanged.
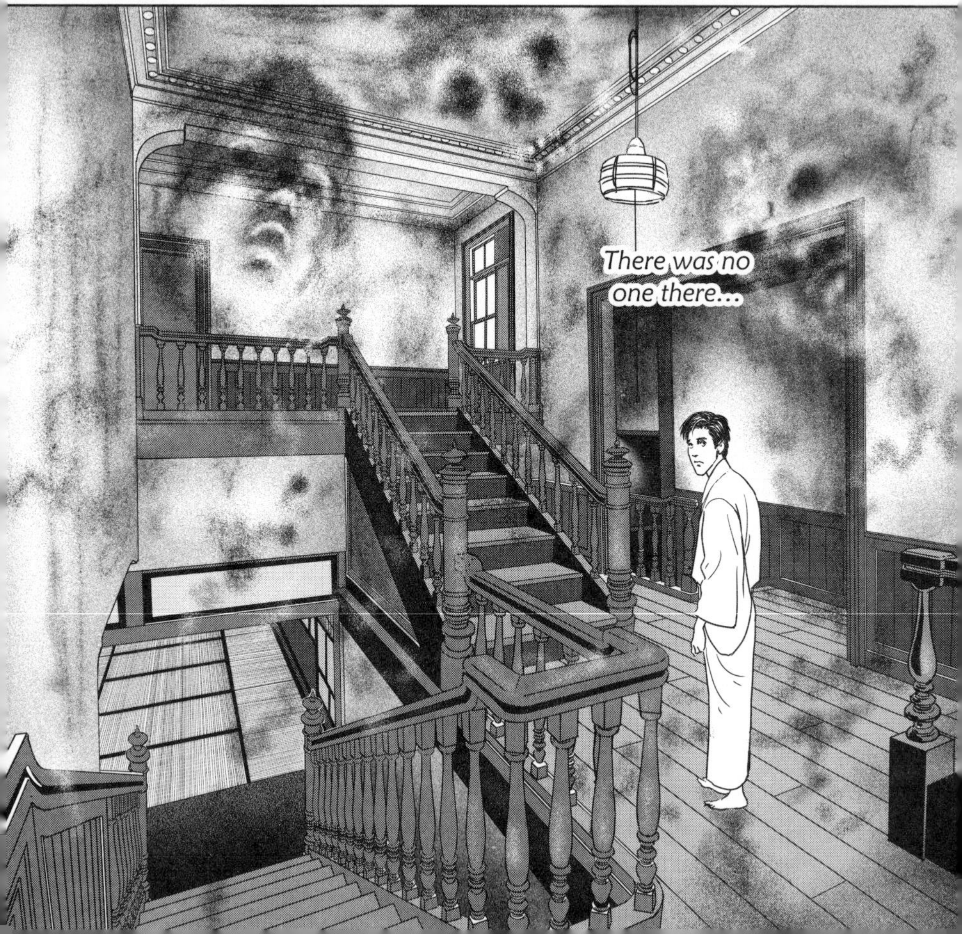
There was no one there...

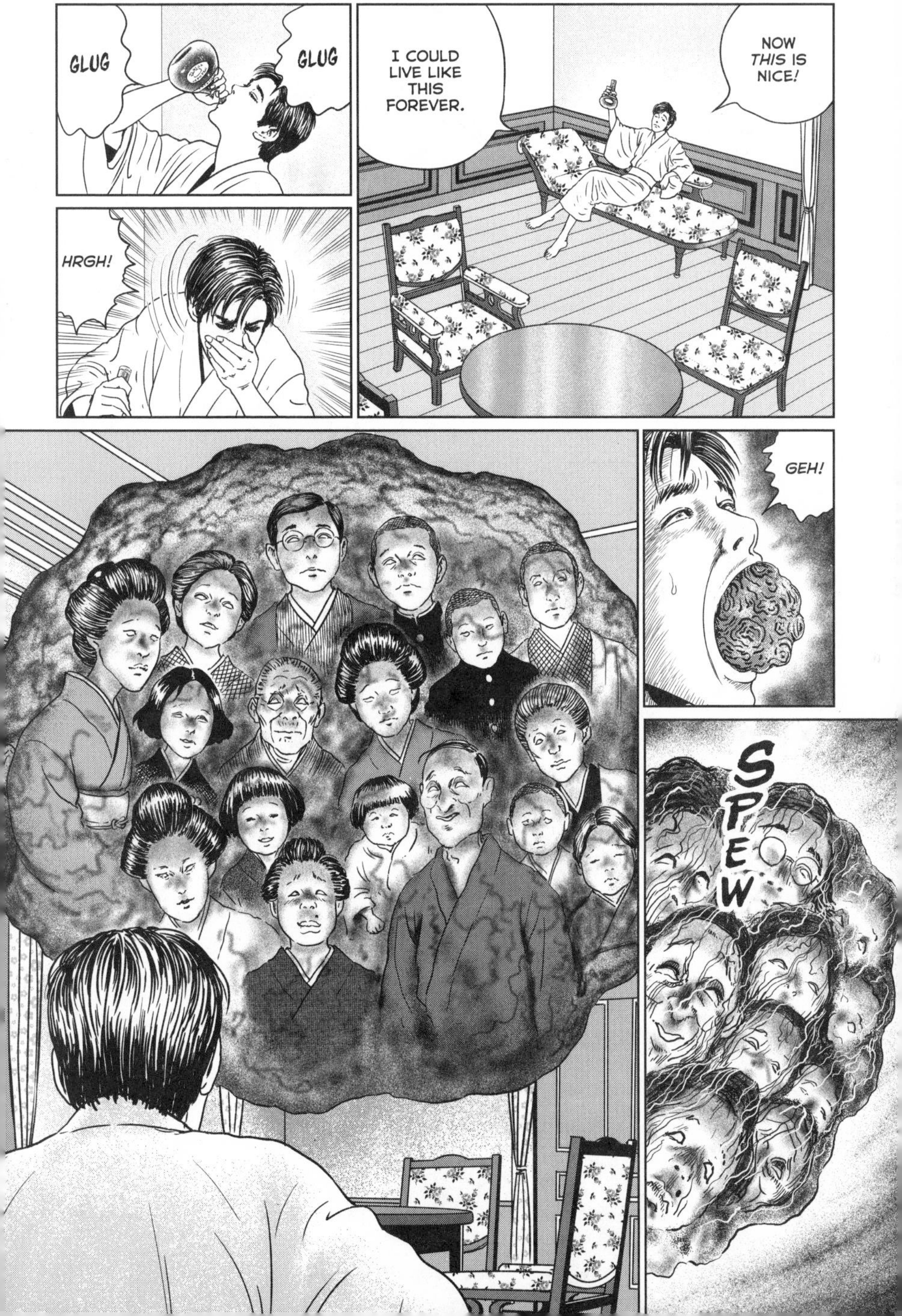
NOW THIS IS NICE!
I COULD LIVE LIKE THIS FOREVER.
GLUG
GLUG
HRGH!
GEH!
SPEW

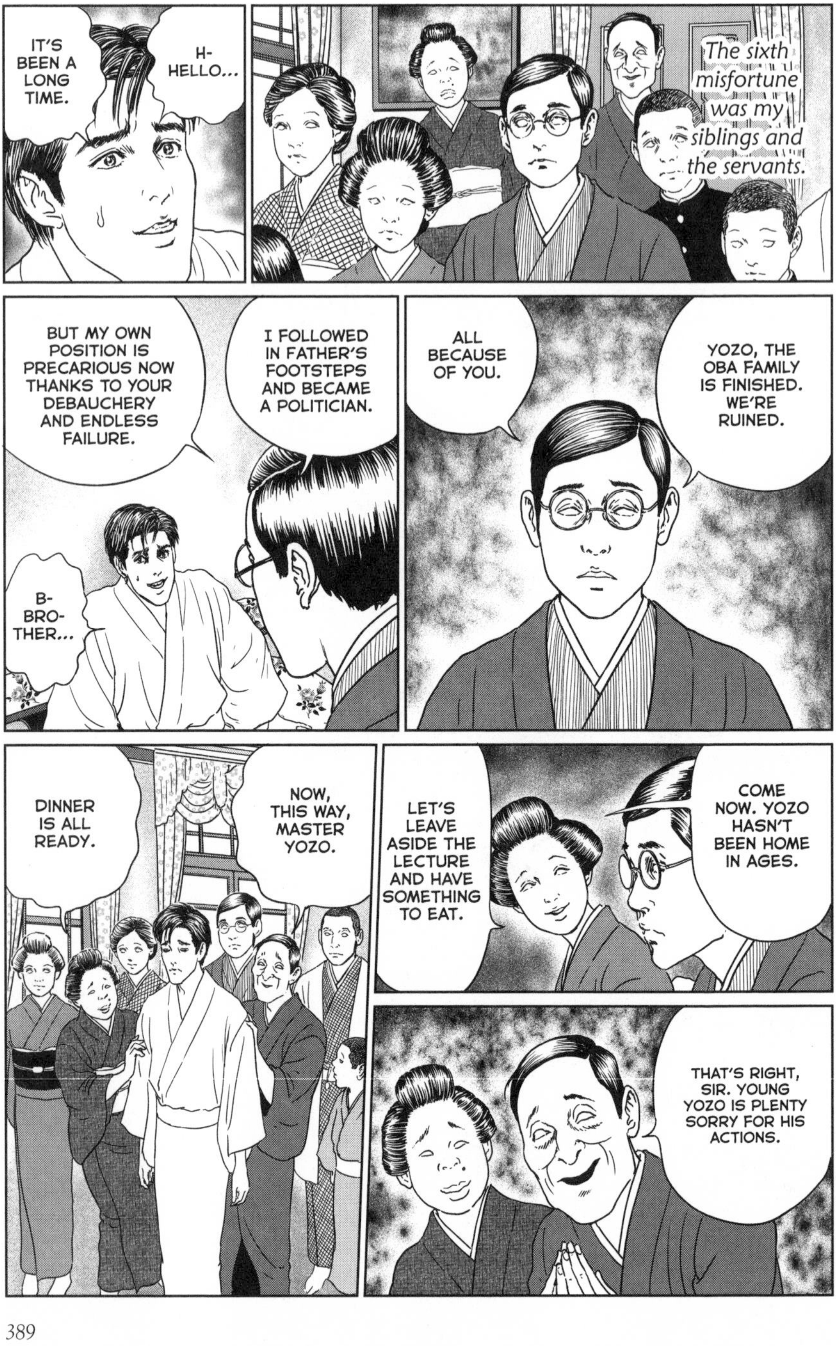
The sixth misfortune was my siblings and the servants.
H-HELLO...
IT'S BEEN A LONG TIME.
YOZO, THE OBA FAMILY IS FINISHED. WE'RE RUINED.
ALL BECAUSE OF YOU.
I FOLLOWED IN FATHER'S FOOTSTEPS AND BECAME A POLITICIAN.
BUT MY OWN POSITION IS PRECARIOUS NOW THANKS TO YOUR DEBAUCHERY AND ENDLESS FAILURE.
B-BRO-THER...
COME NOW. YOZO HASN'T BEEN HOME IN AGES.
LET'S LEAVE ASIDE THE LECTURE AND HAVE SOMETHING TO EAT.
THAT'S RIGHT, SIR. YOUNG YOZO IS PLENTY SORRY FOR HIS ACTIONS.
NOW, THIS WAY, MASTER YOZO.
DINNER IS ALL READY.

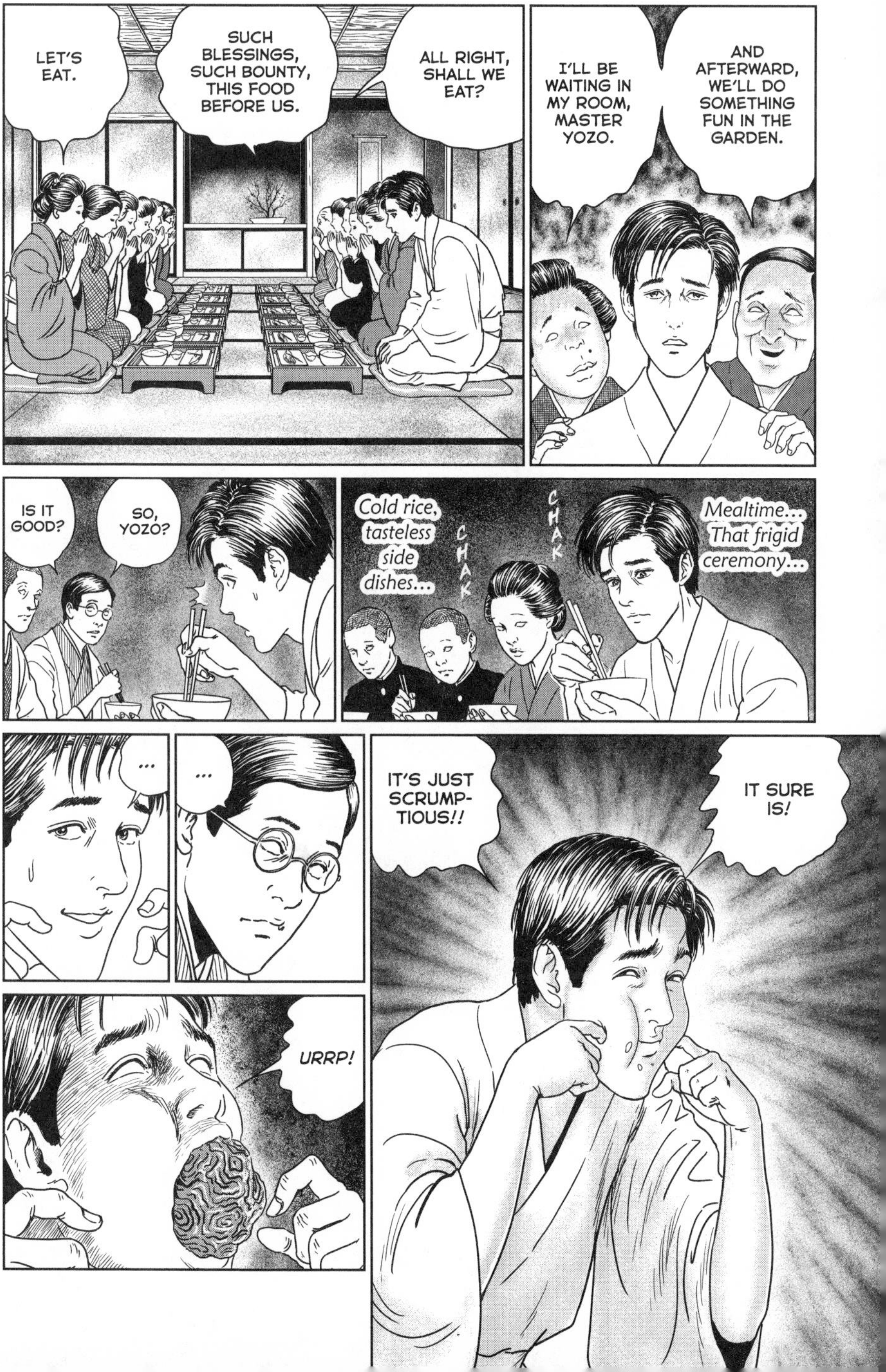
AND AFTERWARD, WE'LL DO SOMETHING FUN IN THE GARDEN.
I'LL BE WAITING IN MY ROOM, MASTER YOZO.
ALL RIGHT, SHALL WE EAT?
SUCH BLESSINGS, SUCH BOUNTY, THIS FOOD BEFORE US.
LET'S EAT.
Mealtime... That frigid ceremony...
CHAK
CHAK
Cold rice, tasteless side dishes...
SO, YOZO?
IS IT GOOD?
IT SURE IS!
IT'S JUST SCRUMP-TIOUS!!
...
...
URRP!

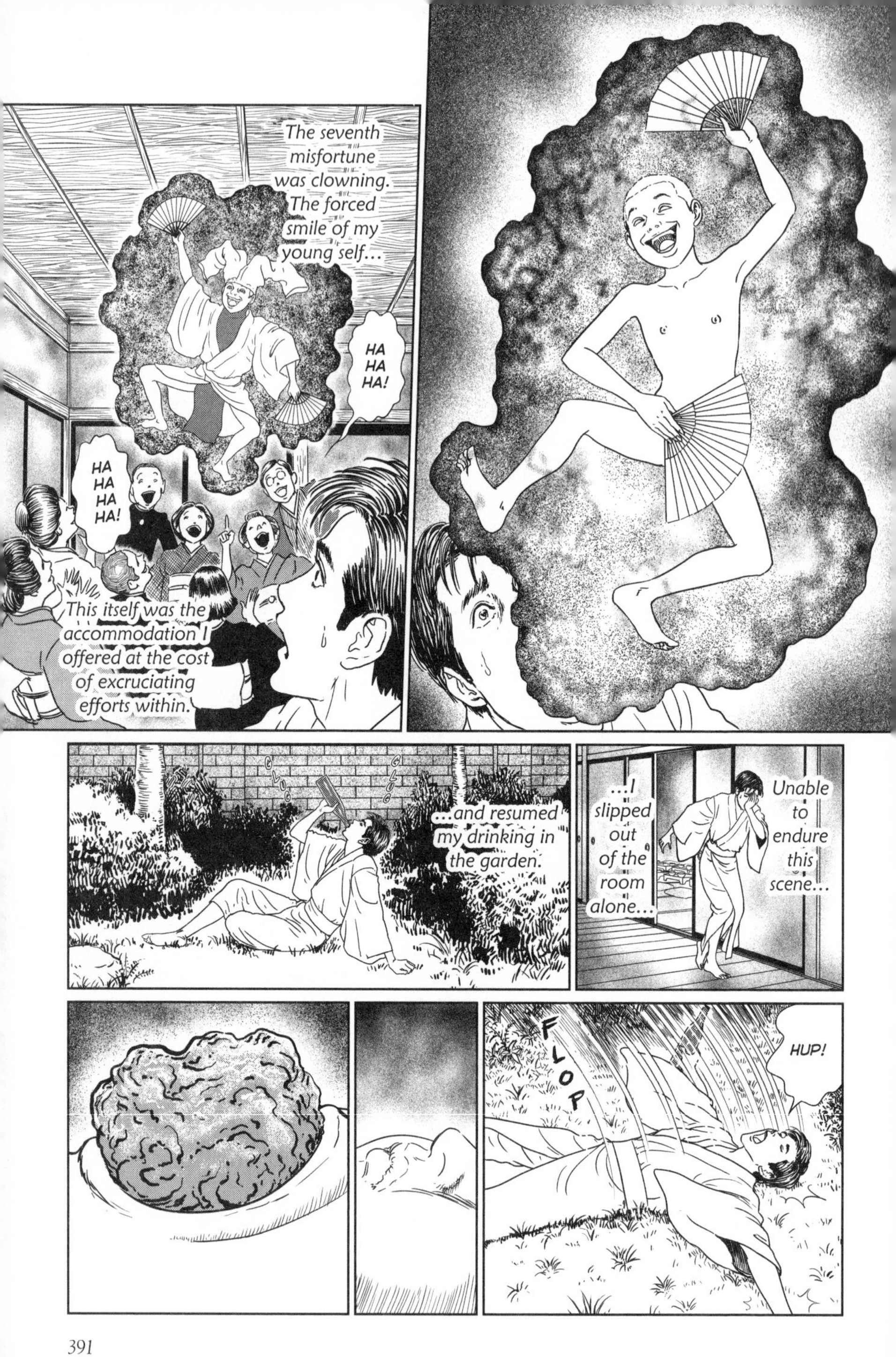
The seventh misfortune was clowning. The forced smile of my young self…
HA HA HA!
HA HA HA HA!
This itself was the accommodation I offered at the cost of excruciating efforts within.
Unable to endure this scene…
…I slipped out of the room alone…
GLUG
GLUG
…and resumed my drinking in the garden.
HUP!
FLOP

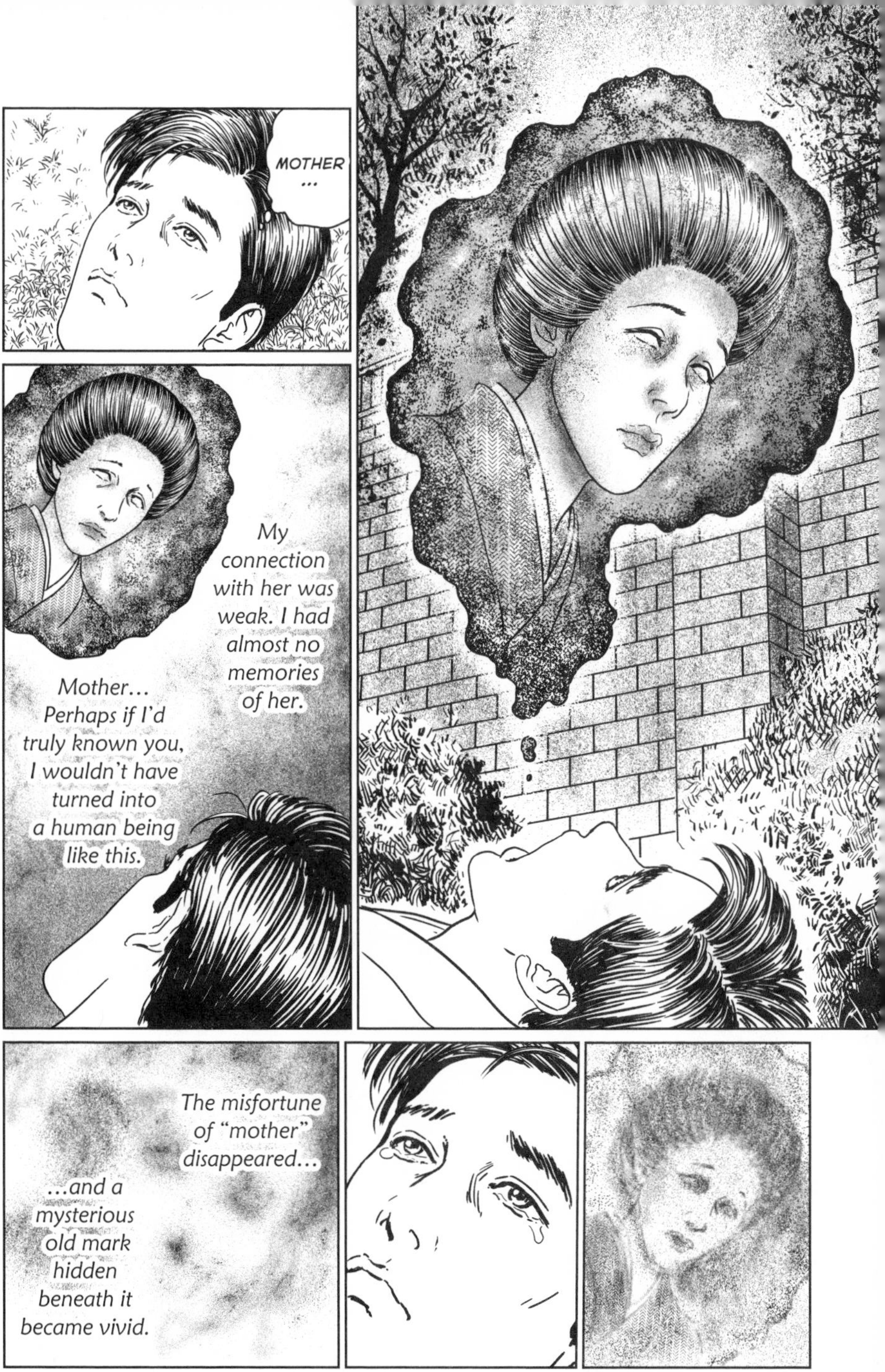
MOTHER ...
My connection with her was weak. I had almost no memories of her.
Mother... Perhaps if I'd truly known you, I wouldn't have turned into a human being like this.
The misfortune of "mother" disappeared...
...and a mysterious old mark hidden beneath it became vivid.

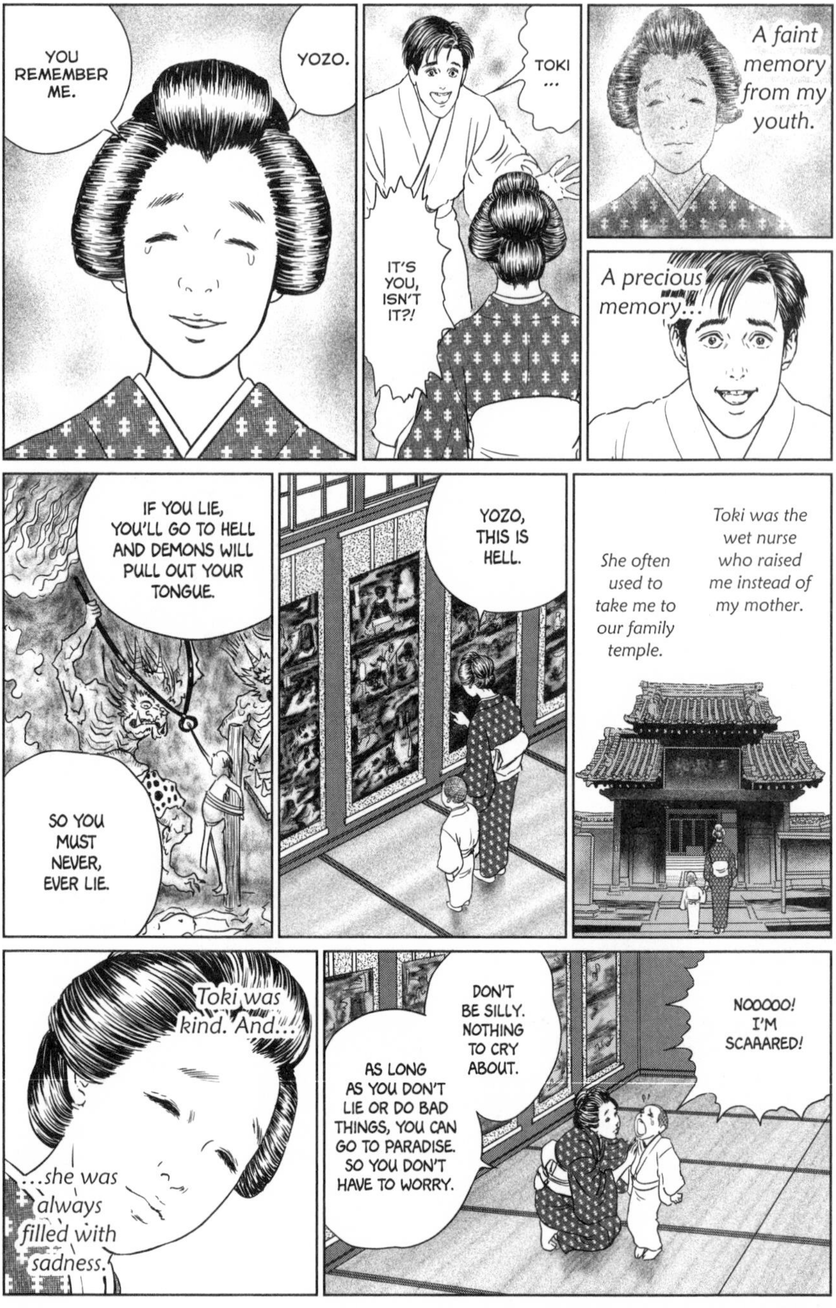
A faint memory from my youth.
A precious memory...
TOKI ...
IT'S YOU, ISN'T IT?!
YOZO.
YOU REMEMBER ME.
Toki was the wet nurse who raised me instead of my mother.
She often used to take me to our family temple.
YOZO, THIS IS HELL.
IF YOU LIE, YOU'LL GO TO HELL AND DEMONS WILL PULL OUT YOUR TONGUE.
SO YOU MUST NEVER, EVER LIE.
NOOOOO! I'M SCAAARED!
DON'T BE SILLY. NOTHING TO CRY ABOUT.
AS LONG AS YOU DON'T LIE OR DO BAD THINGS, YOU CAN GO TO PARADISE. SO YOU DON'T HAVE TO WORRY.
Toki was kind. And...
...she was always filled with sadness.

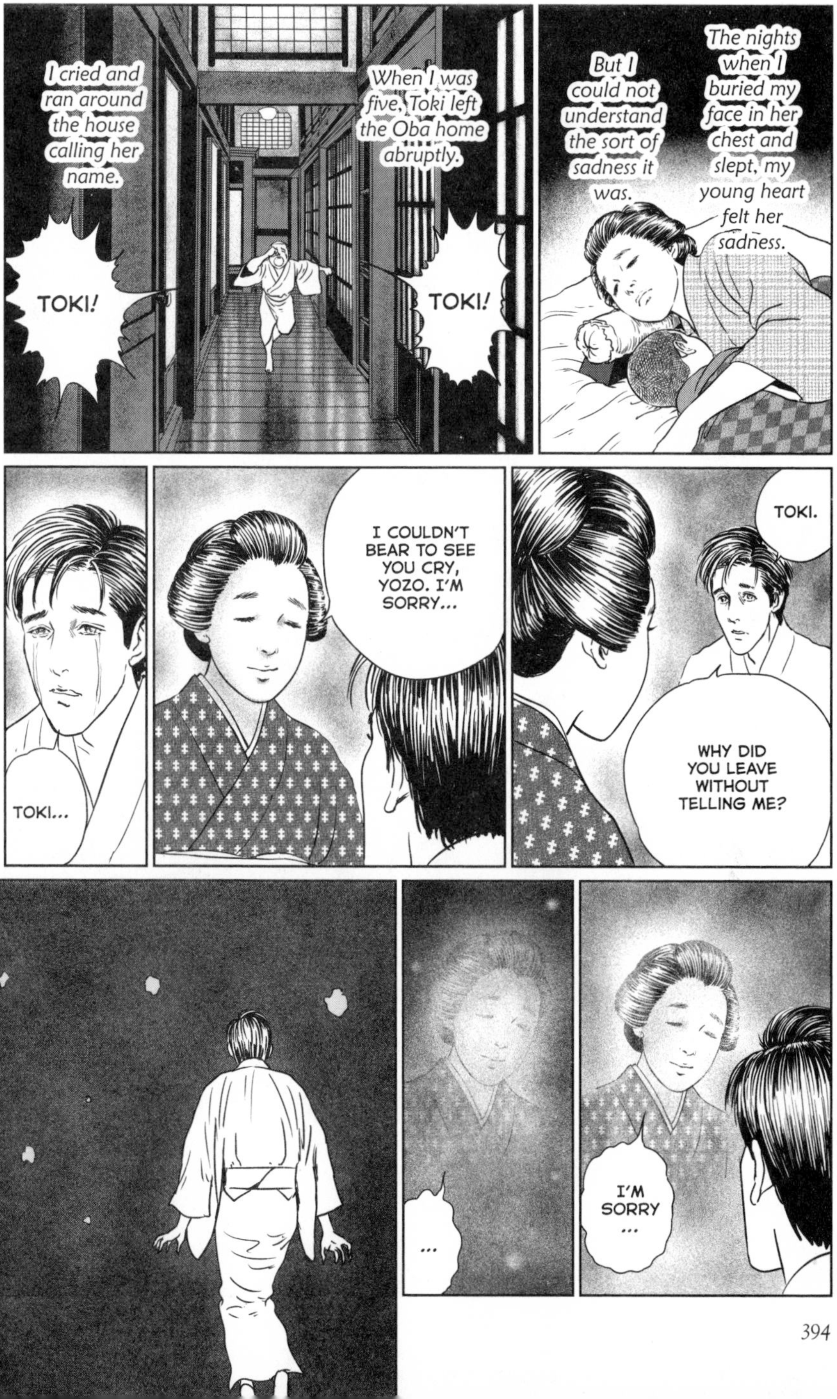
The nights when I buried my face in her chest and slept, my young heart felt her sadness.
But I could not understand the sort of sadness it was.
When I was five, Toki left the Oba home abruptly.
I cried and ran around the house calling her name.
TOKI!
TOKI!
TOKI.
WHY DID YOU LEAVE WITHOUT TELLING ME?
I COULDN'T BEAR TO SEE YOU CRY, YOZO. I'M SORRY...
TOKI...
I'M SORRY ...
...

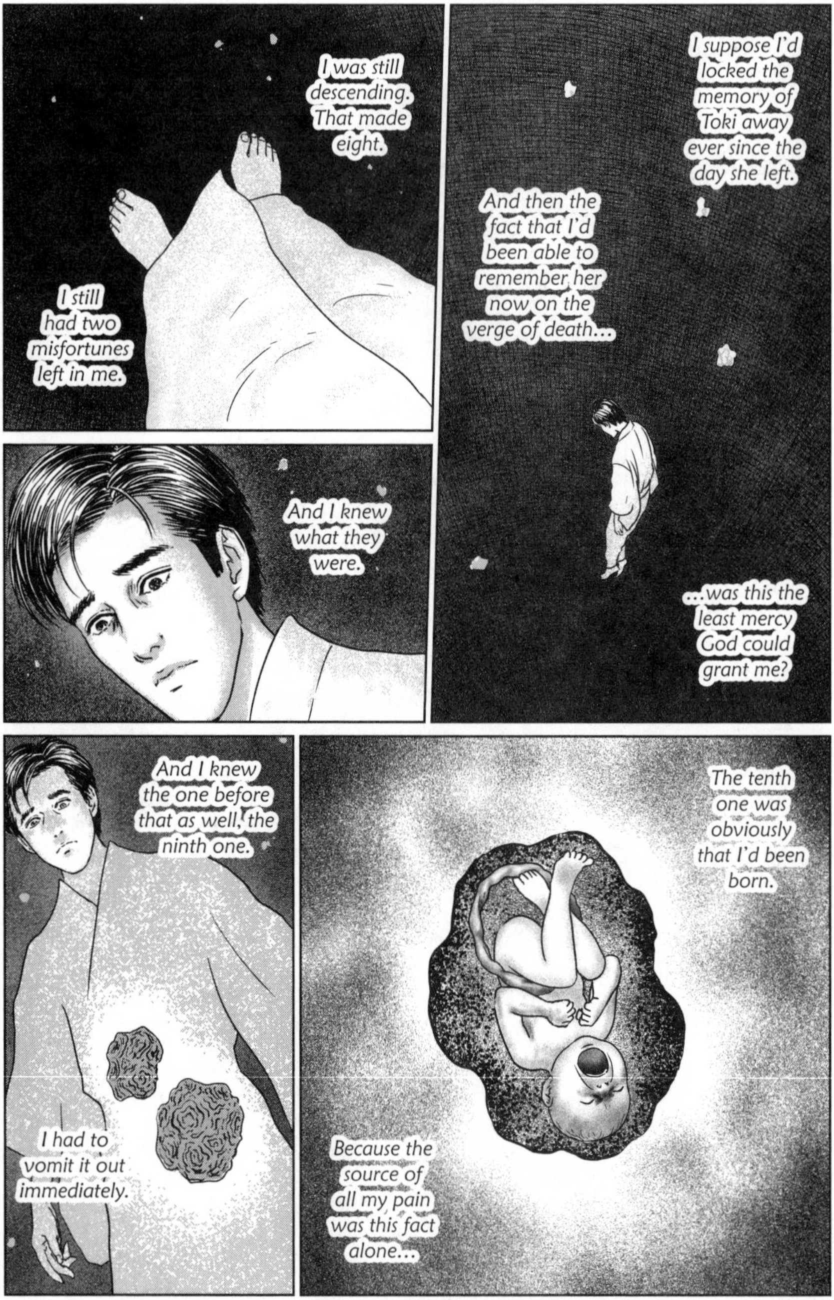
I suppose I'd locked the memory of Toki away ever since the day she left.
And then the fact that I'd been able to remember her now on the verge of death...
...was this the least mercy God could grant me?
I was still descending. That made eight.
I still had two misfortunes left in me.
And I knew what they were.
The tenth one was obviously that I'd been born.
Because the source of all my pain was this fact alone...
And I knew the one before that as well, the ninth one.
I had to vomit it out immediately.

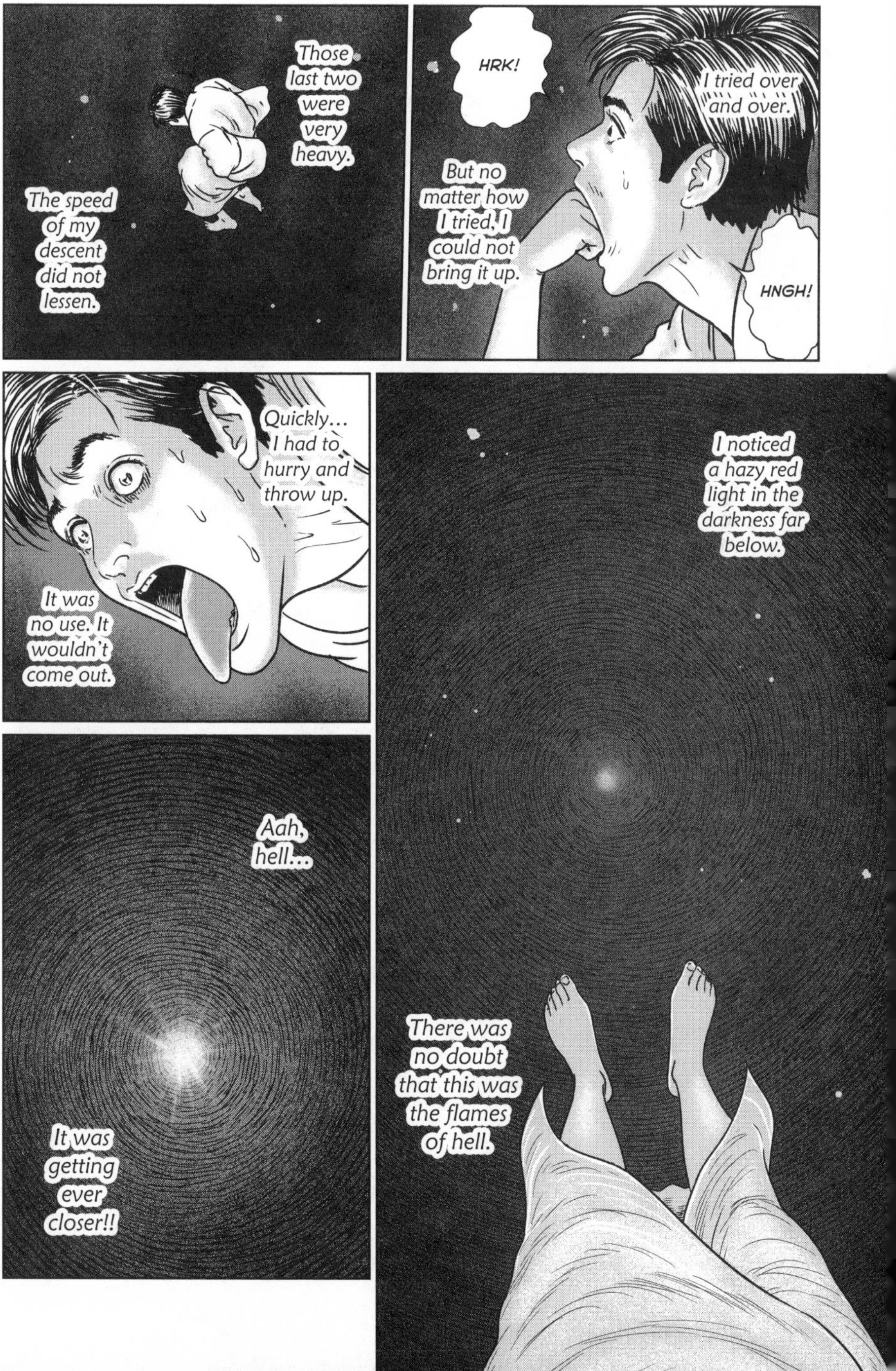
I tried over and over.
HRK!
But no matter how I tried, I could not bring it up.
HNGH!
Those last two were very heavy.
The speed of my descent did not lessen.
I noticed a hazy red light in the darkness far below.
There was no doubt that this was the flames of hell.
Quickly... I had to hurry and throw up.
It was no use. It wouldn't come out.
Aah, hell...
It was getting ever closer!!

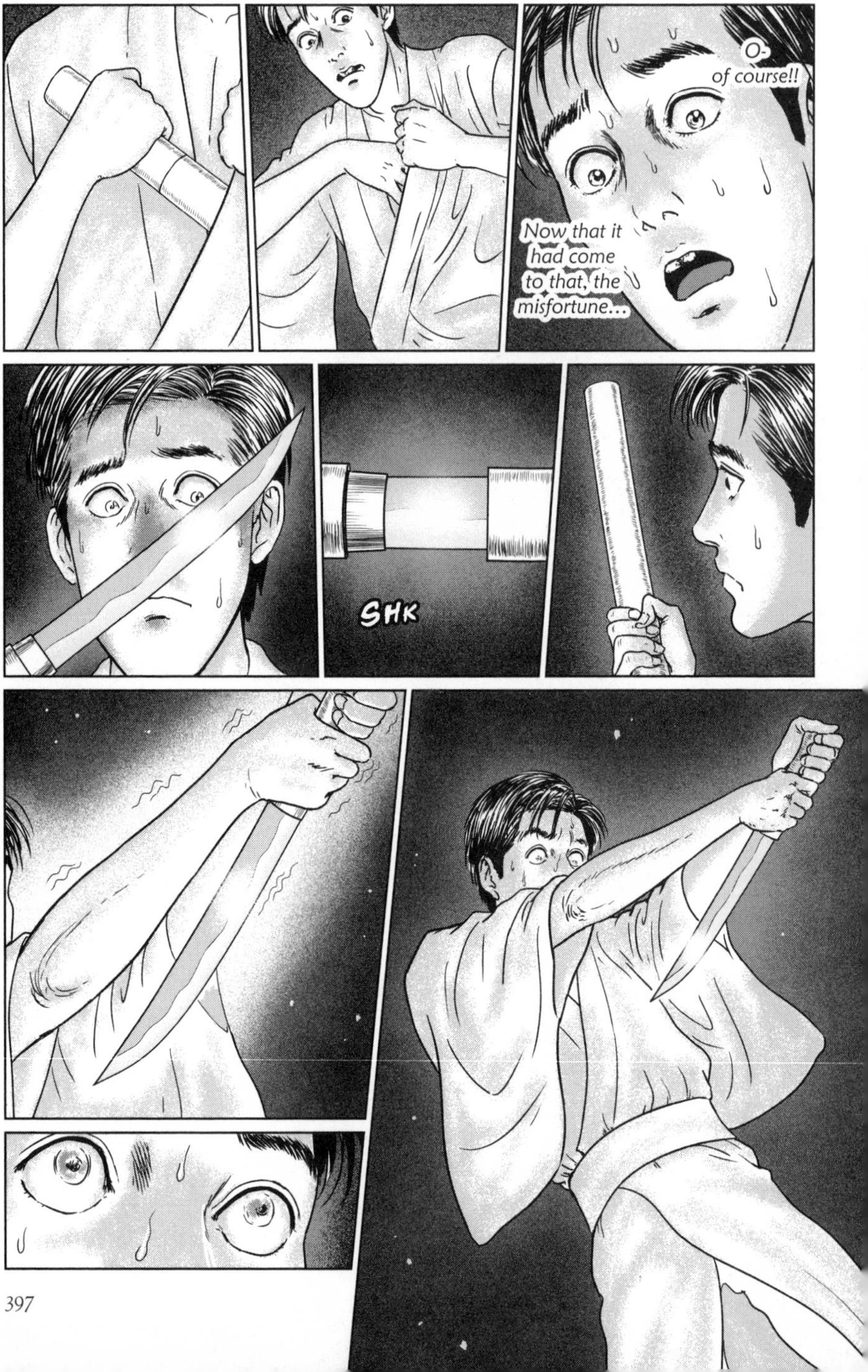
O-
of course!!
Now that it had come to that, the misfortune…
SHK

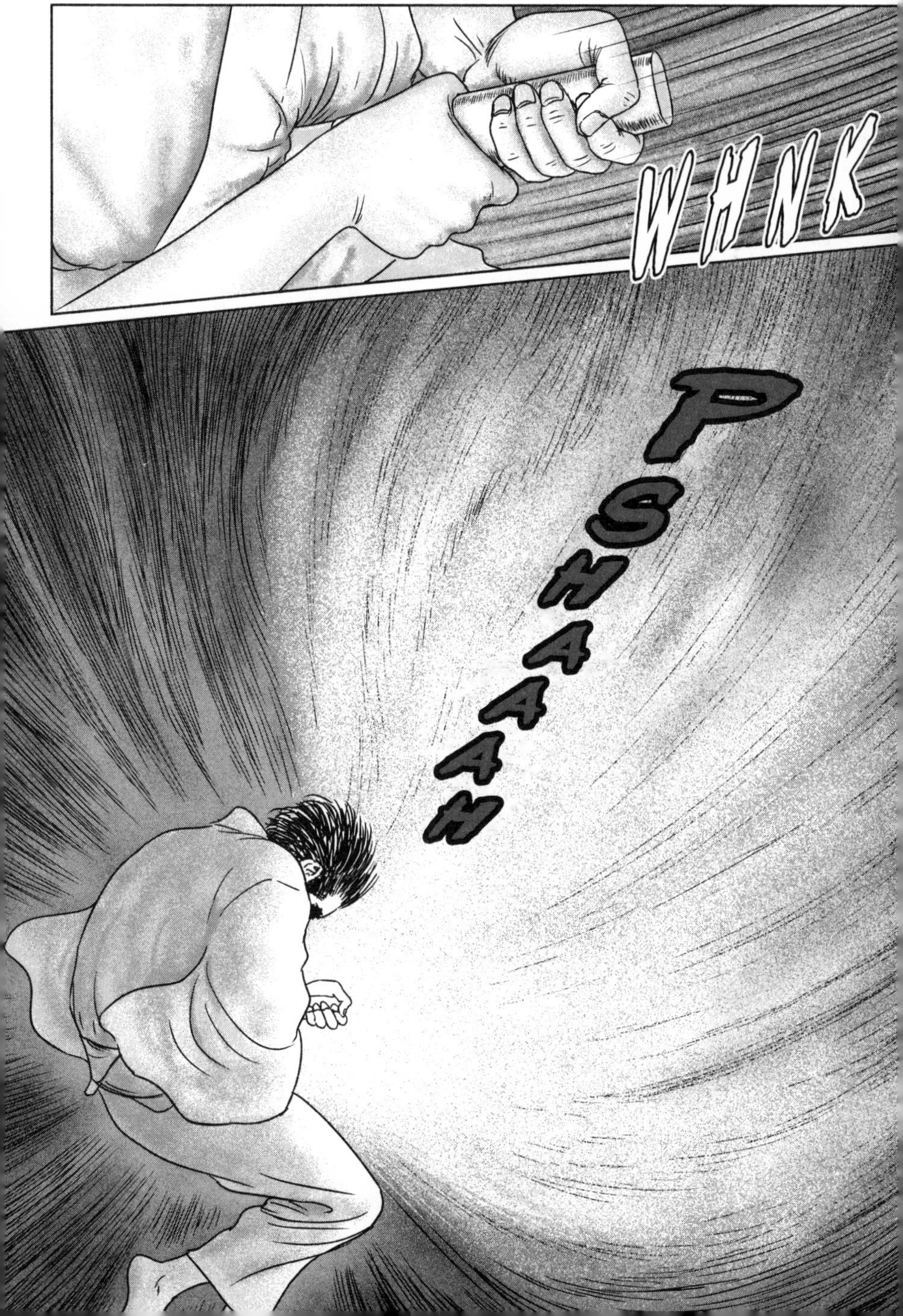
WHNK
PSHAAAAH

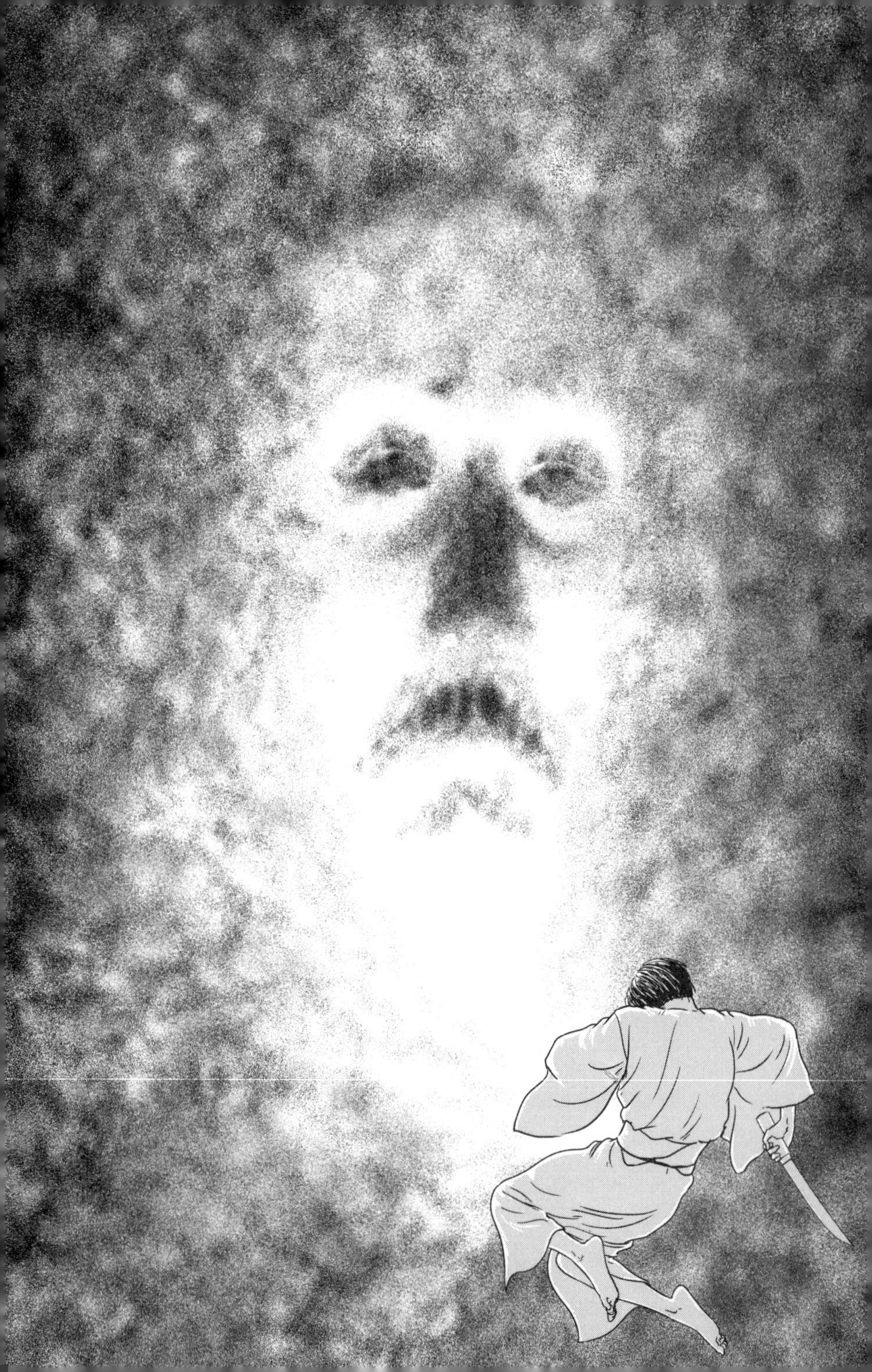

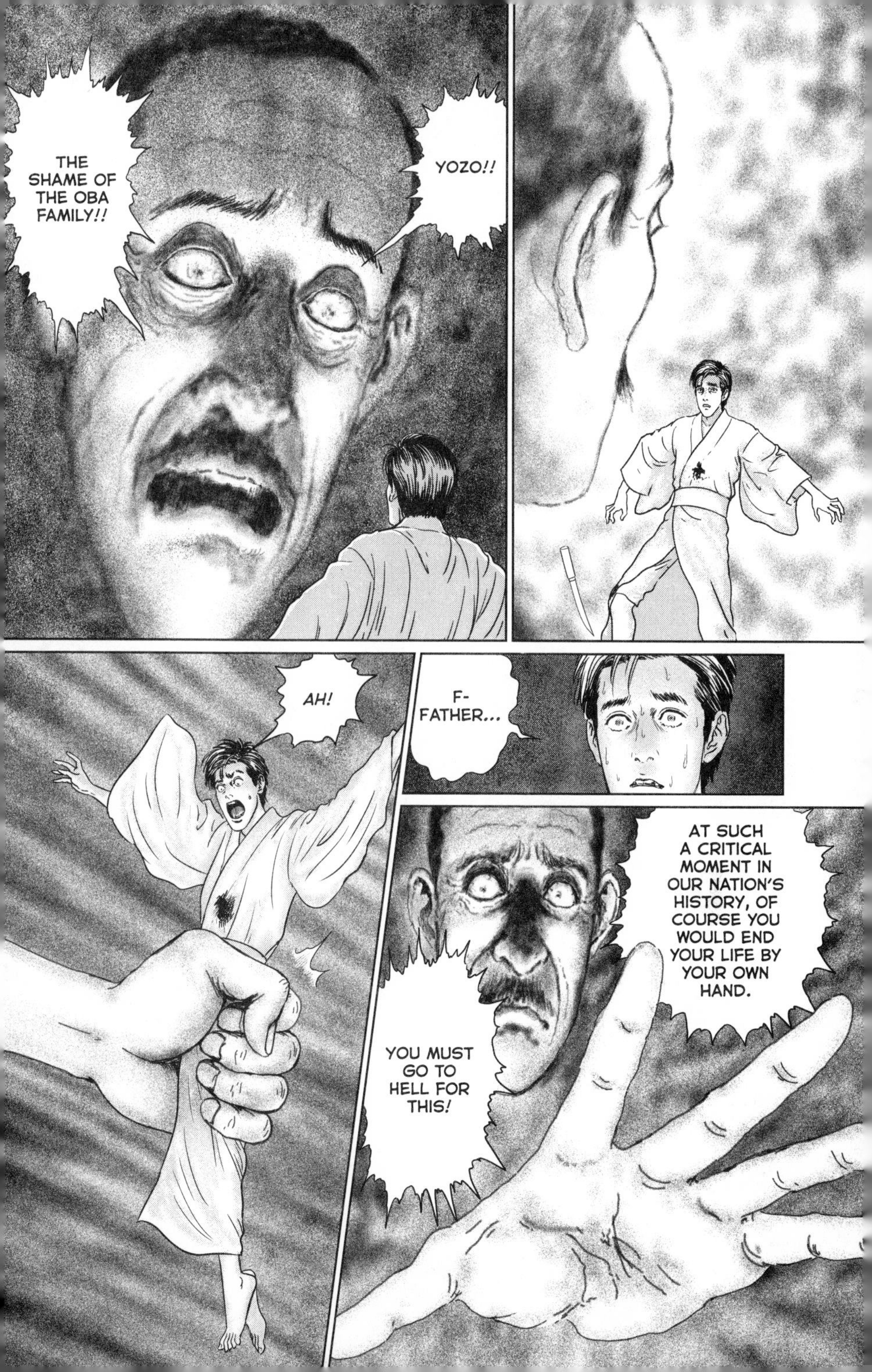
YOZO!!
THE SHAME OF THE OBA FAMILY!!
F- FATHER...
AT SUCH A CRITICAL MOMENT IN OUR NATION'S HISTORY, OF COURSE YOU WOULD END YOUR LIFE BY YOUR OWN HAND.
YOU MUST GO TO HELL FOR THIS!
AH!

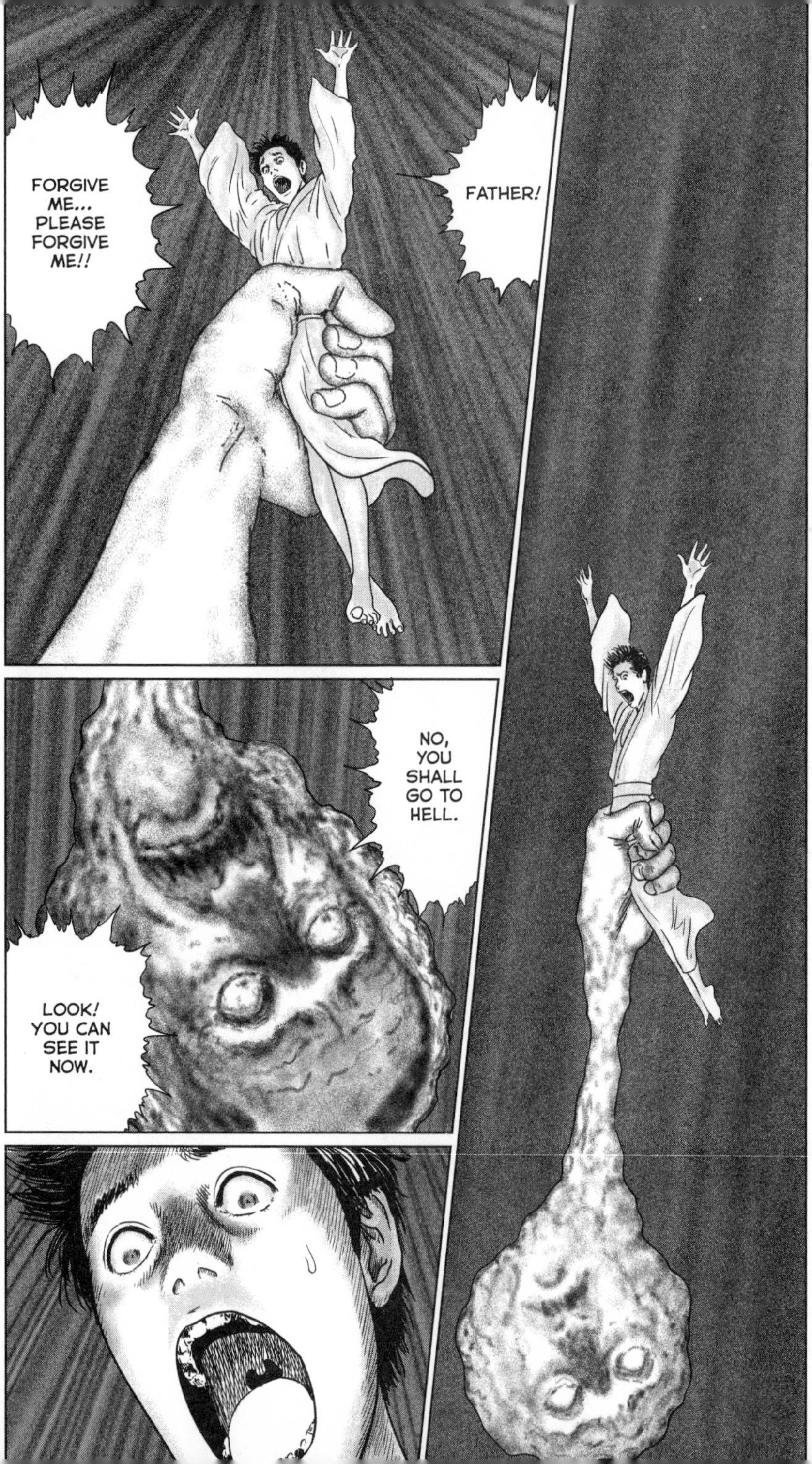
FATHER!
FORGIVE ME... PLEASE FORGIVE ME!!
NO, YOU SHALL GO TO HELL.
LOOK! YOU CAN SEE IT NOW.

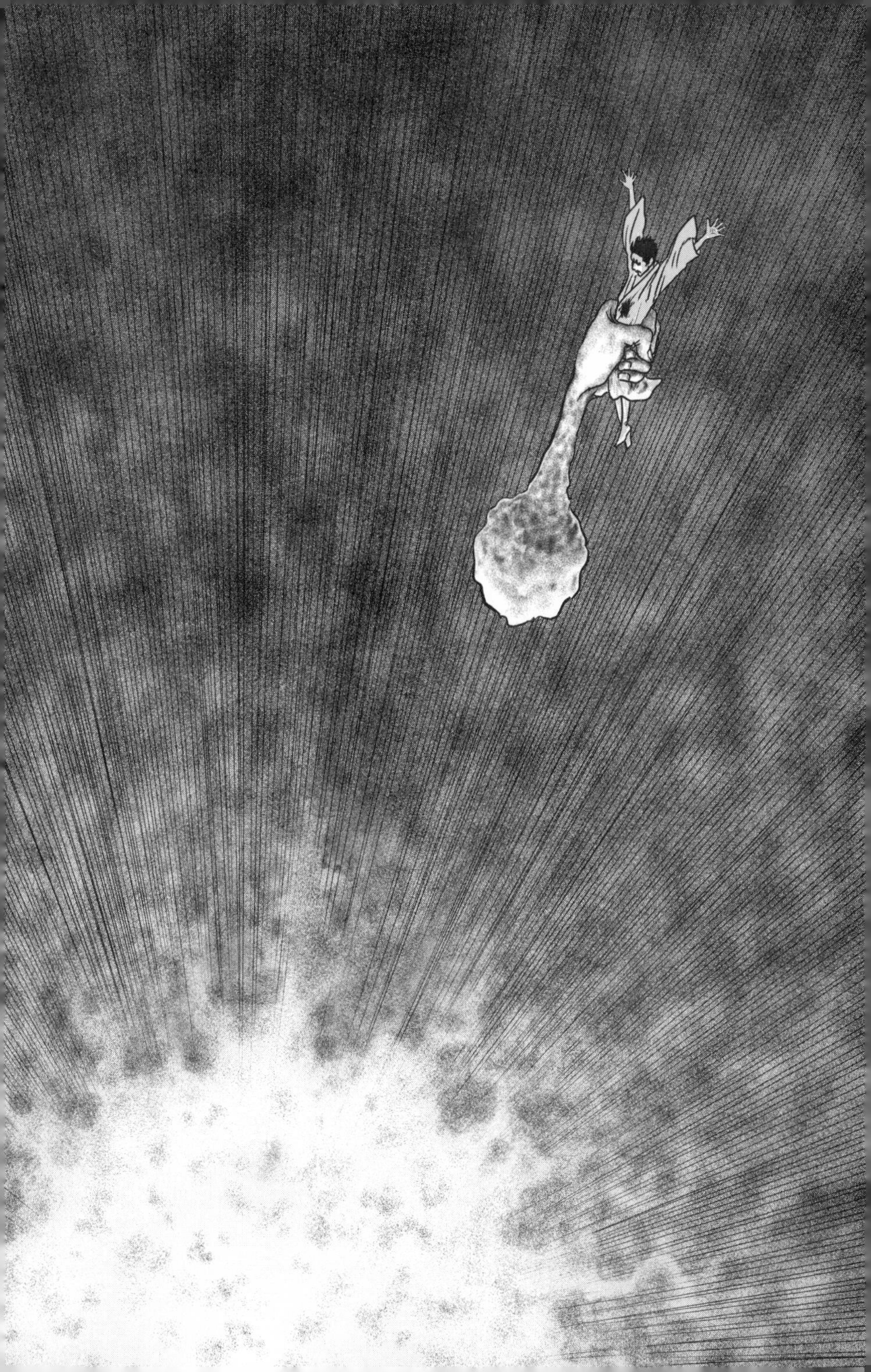

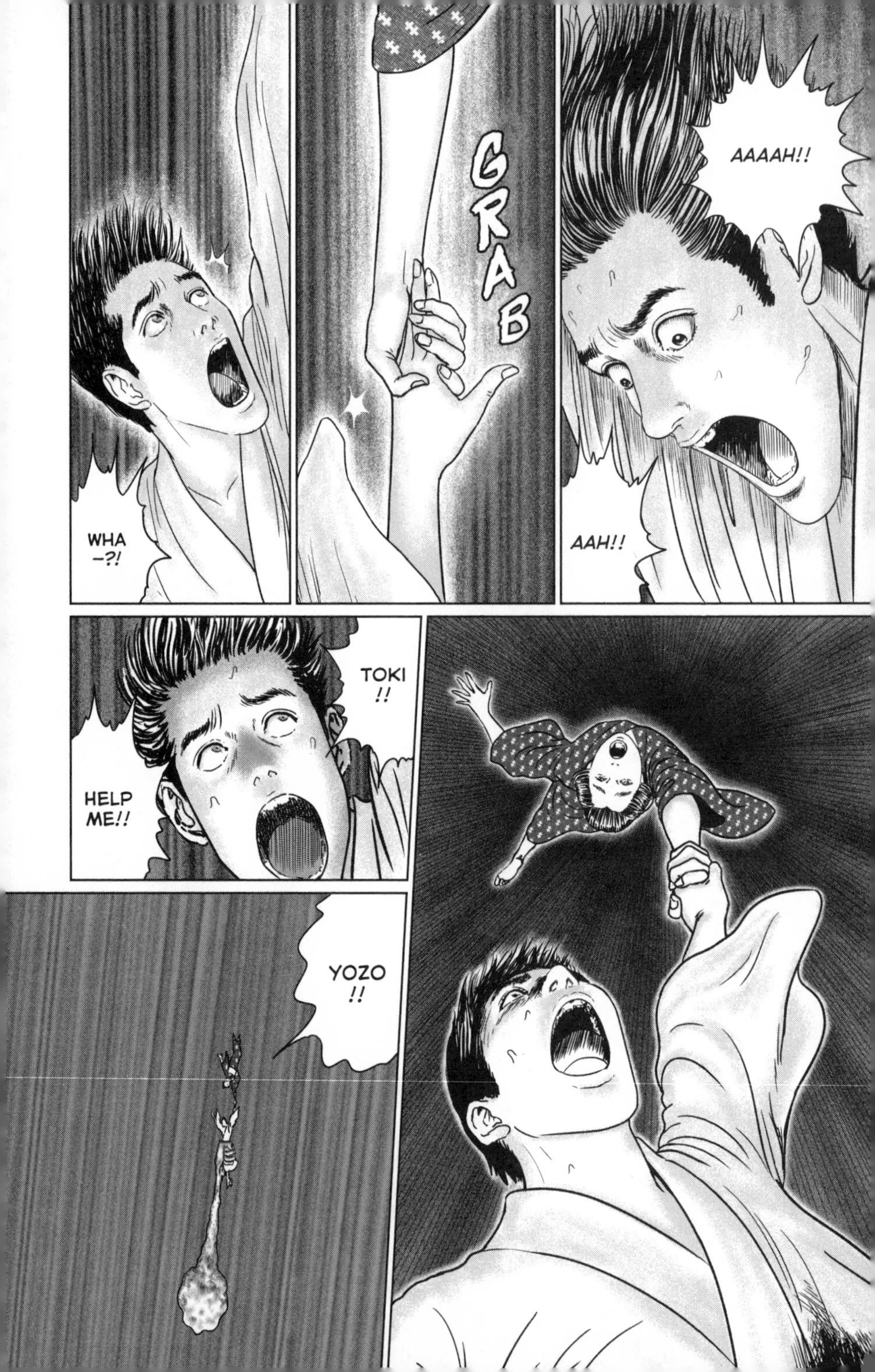
AAAAH!!
AAH!!
GRAB
WHA –?!
TOKI !!
HELP ME!!
YOZO !!

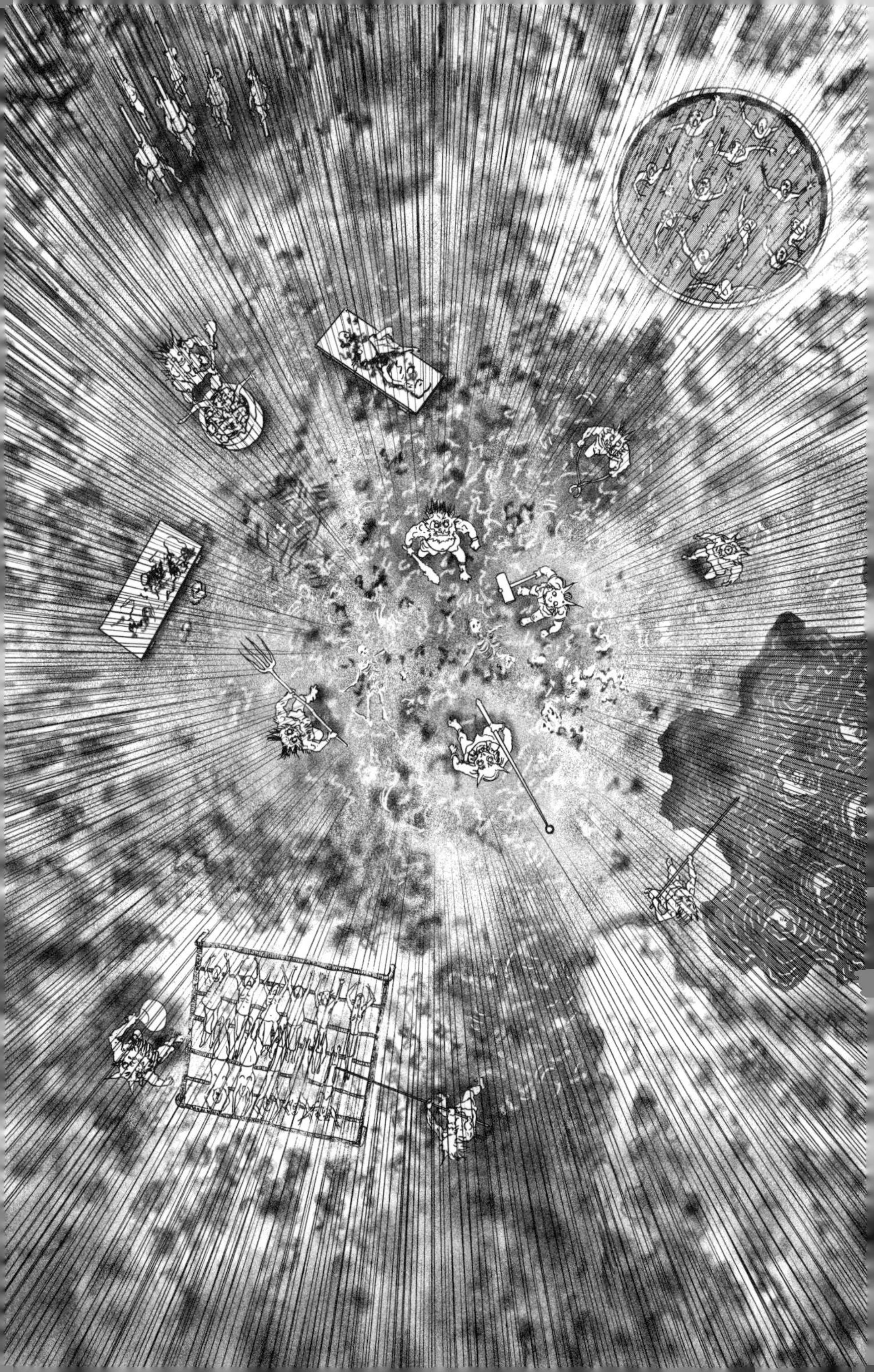

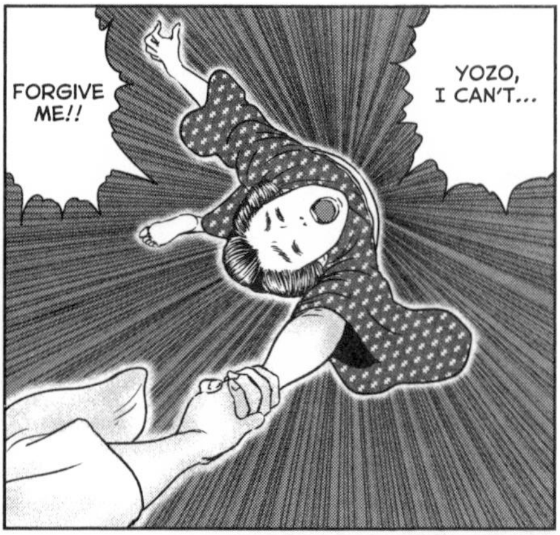
YOZO, I CAN'T...
FORGIVE ME!!
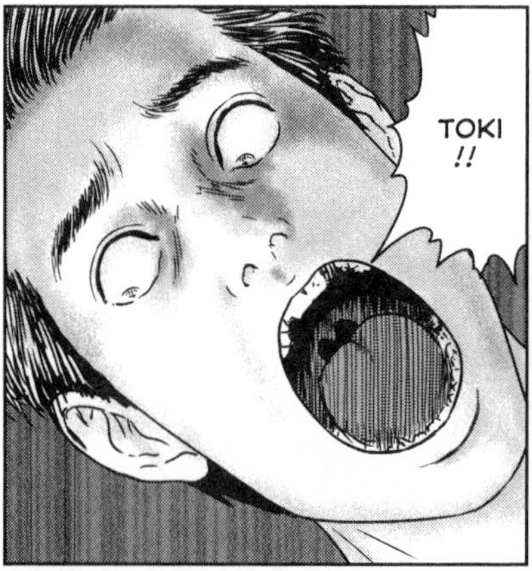
TOKI !!
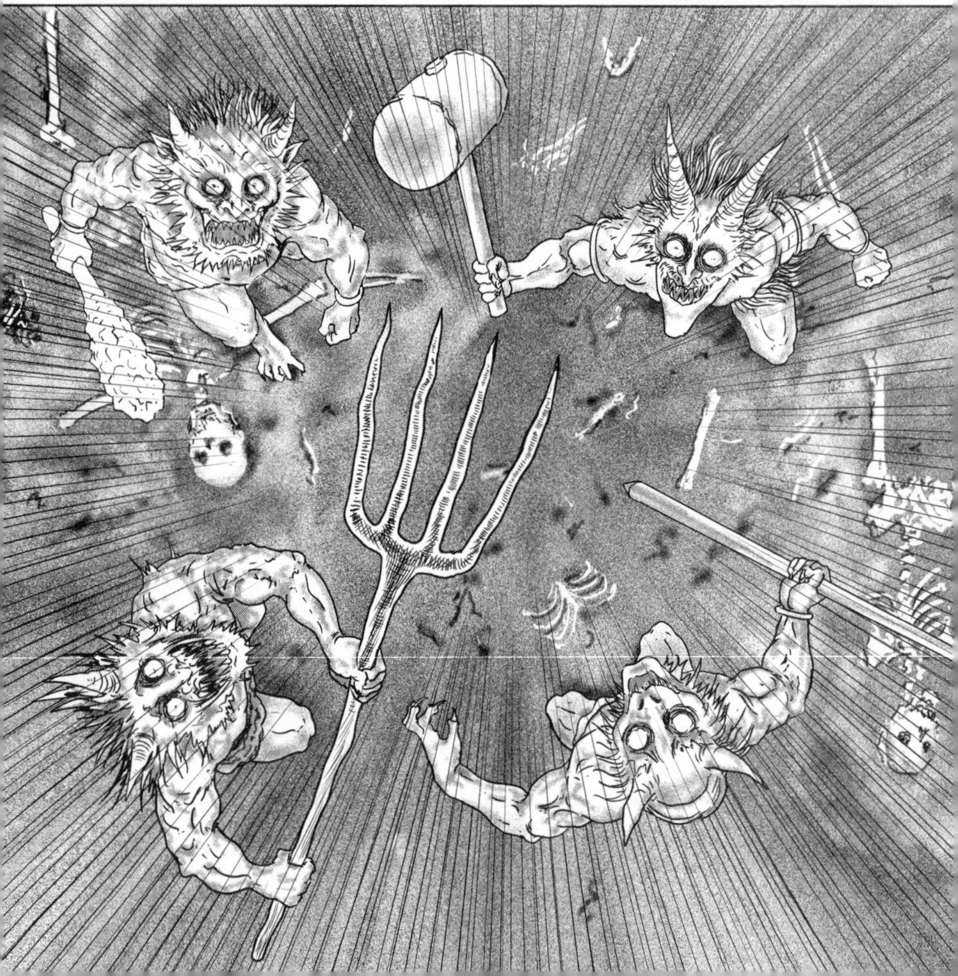

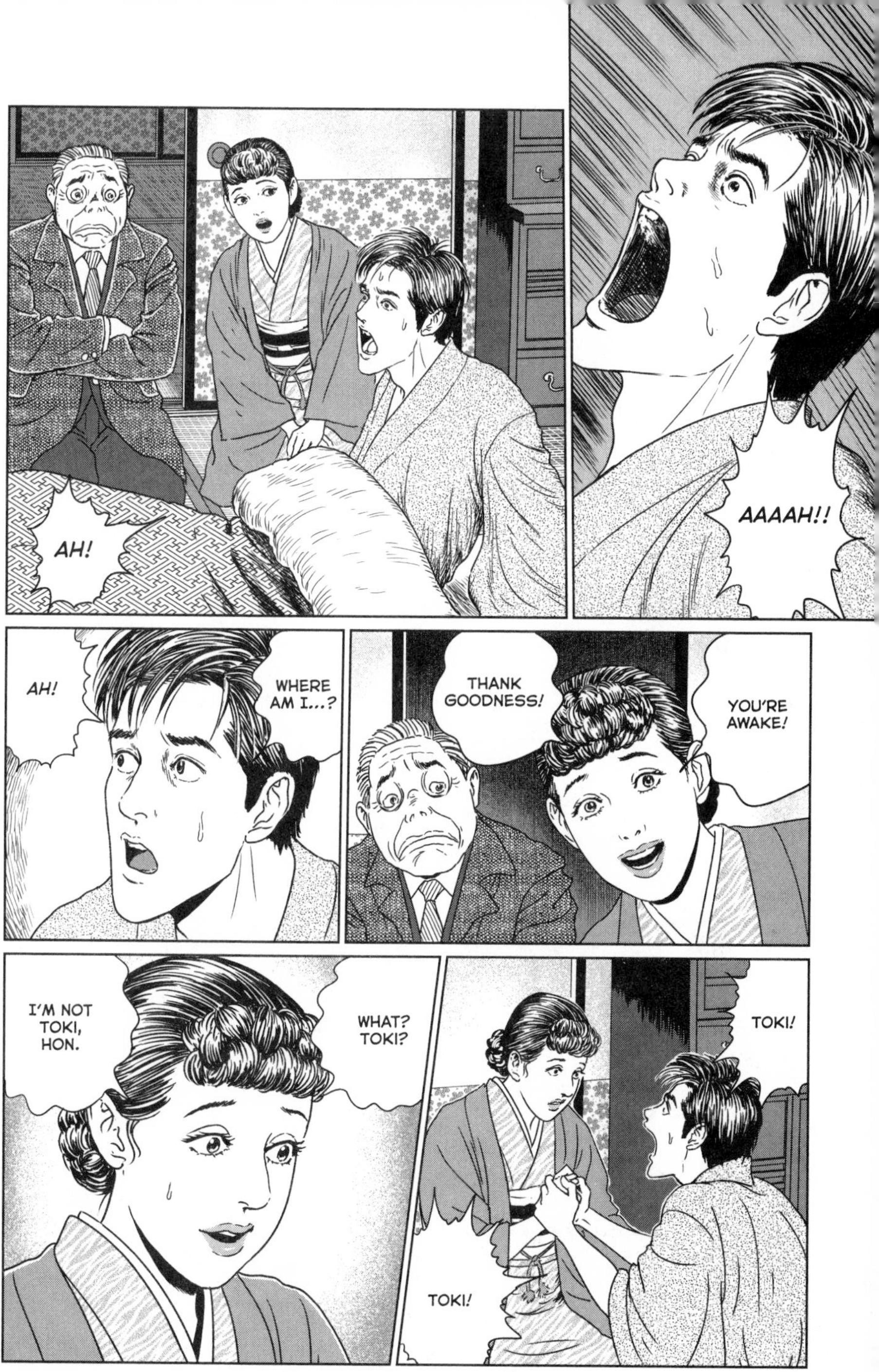
AAAAH!!
AH!
YOU'RE AWAKE!
THANK GOODNESS!
WHERE AM I...?
AH!
TOKI!
TOKI!
WHAT? TOKI?
I'M NOT TOKI, HON.

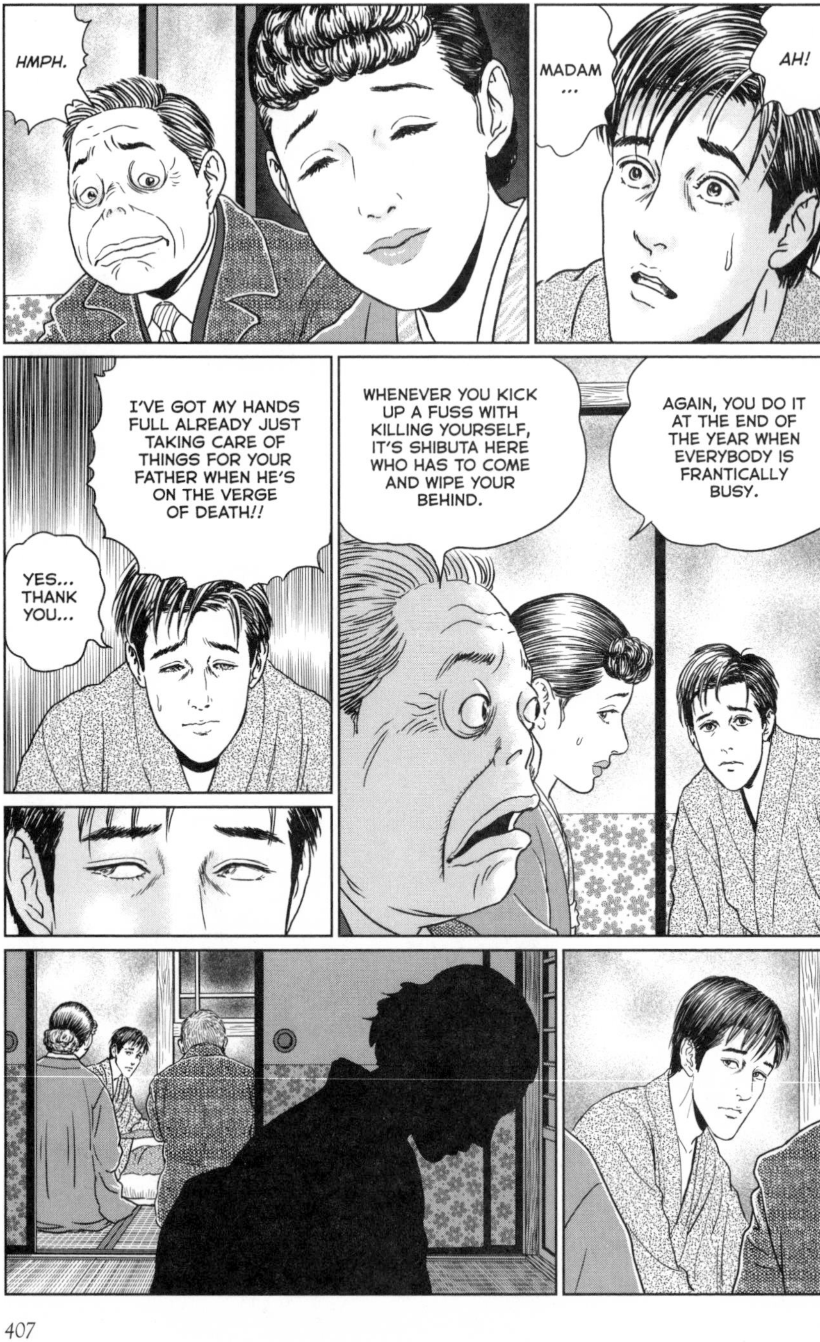
AH!
MADAM ...
HMPH.
AGAIN, YOU DO IT AT THE END OF THE YEAR WHEN EVERYBODY IS FRANTICALLY BUSY.
WHENEVER YOU KICK UP A FUSS WITH KILLING YOURSELF, IT'S SHIBUTA HERE WHO HAS TO COME AND WIPE YOUR BEHIND.
I'VE GOT MY HANDS FULL ALREADY JUST TAKING CARE OF THINGS FOR YOUR FATHER WHEN HE'S ON THE VERGE OF DEATH!!
YES... THANK YOU...

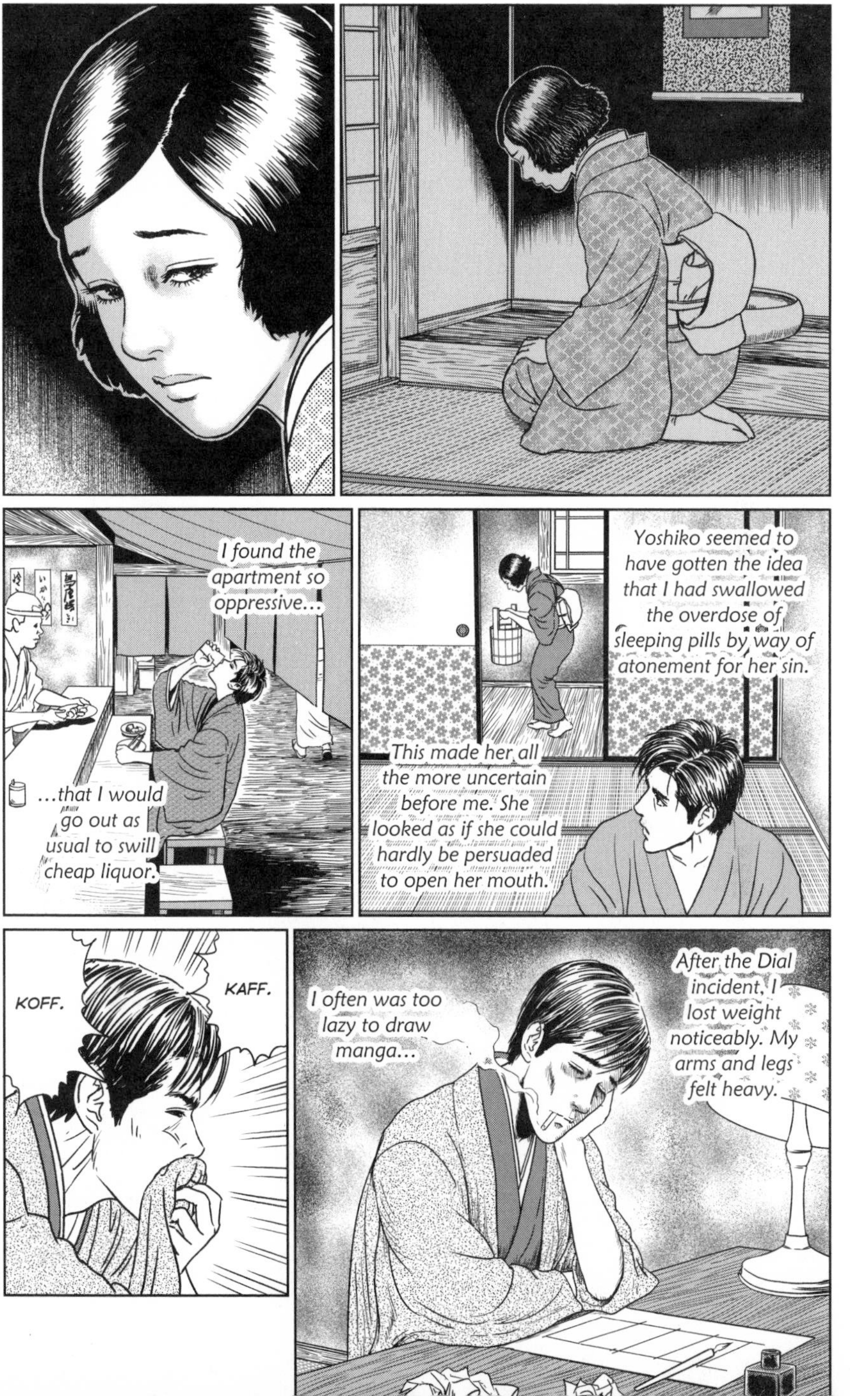
Yoshiko seemed to have gotten the idea that I had swallowed the overdose of sleeping pills by way of atonement for her sin.
This made her all the more uncertain before me. She looked as if she could hardly be persuaded to open her mouth.
I found the apartment so oppressive…
…that I would go out as usual to swill cheap liquor.
After the Dial incident, I lost weight noticeably. My arms and legs felt heavy.
I often was too lazy to draw manga…
KAFF.
KOFF.

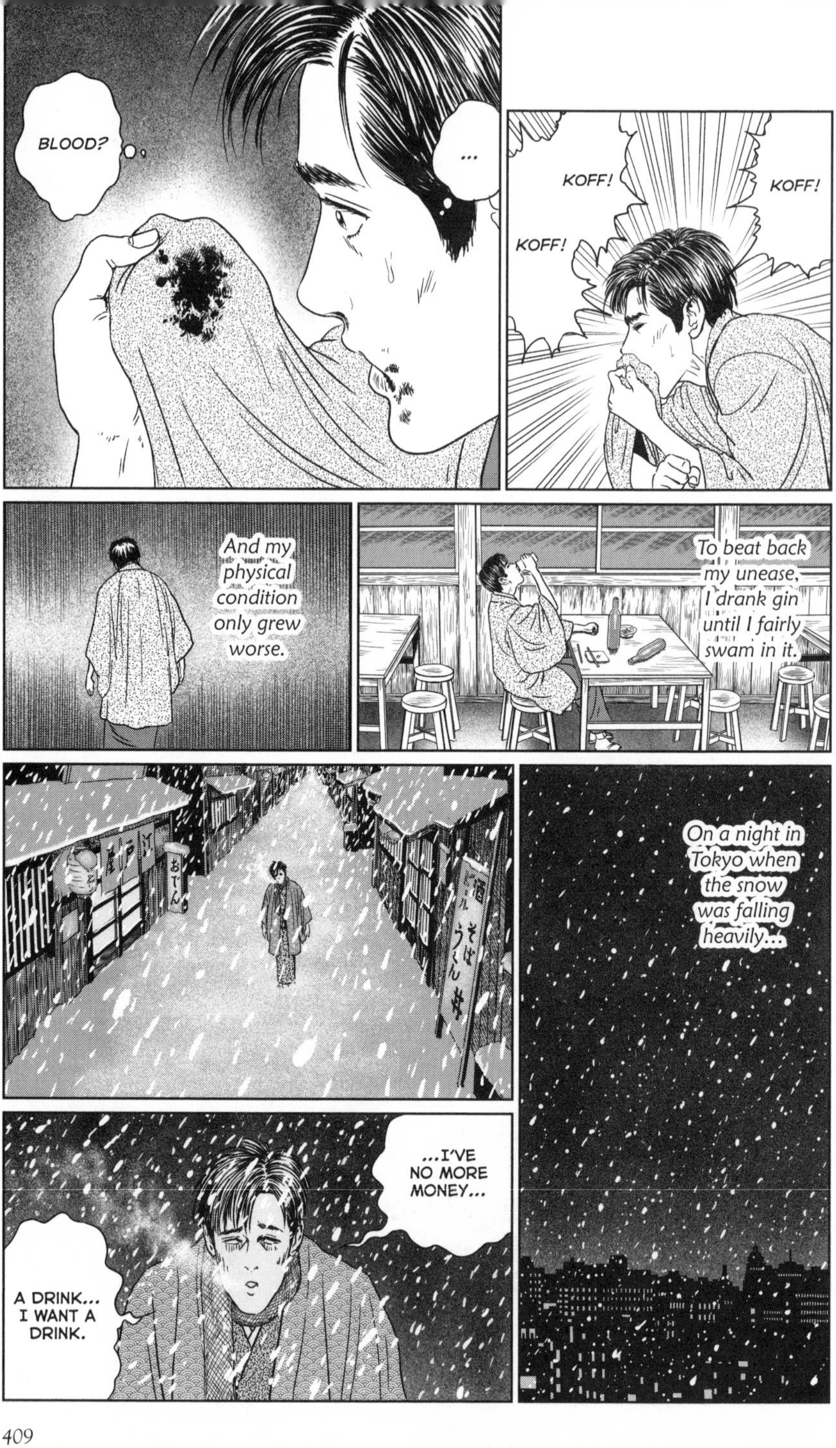
KOFF!
KOFF!
KOFF!
...
BLOOD?
To beat back my unease, I drank gin until I fairly swam in it.
And my physical condition only grew worse.
On a night in Tokyo when the snow was falling heavily...
...I'VE NO MORE MONEY...
A DRINK... I WANT A DRINK.

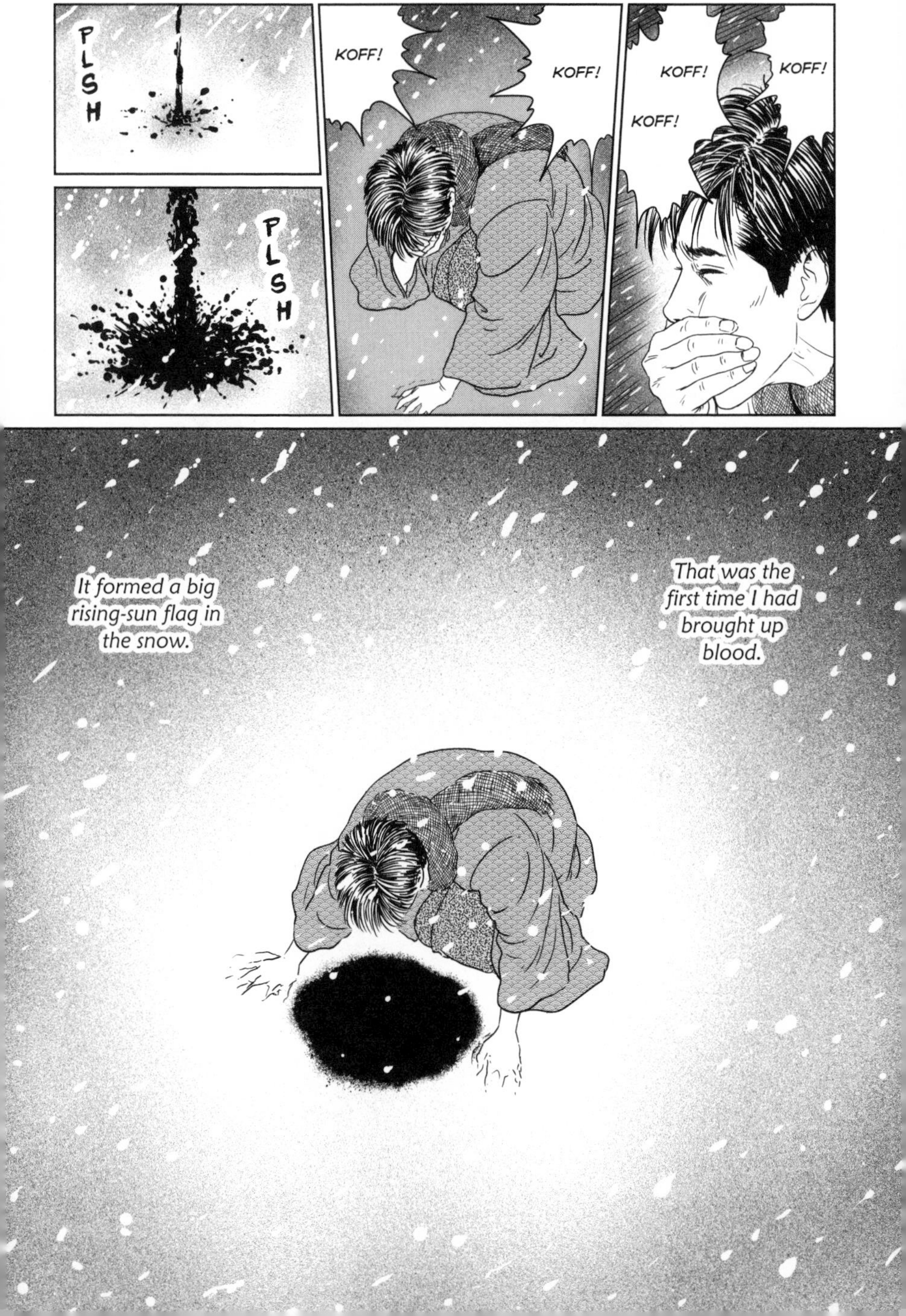
KOFF!
KOFF!
KOFF!
KOFF!
KOFF!
PLSH
PLSH
That was the first time I had brought up blood.
It formed a big rising-sun flag in the snow.

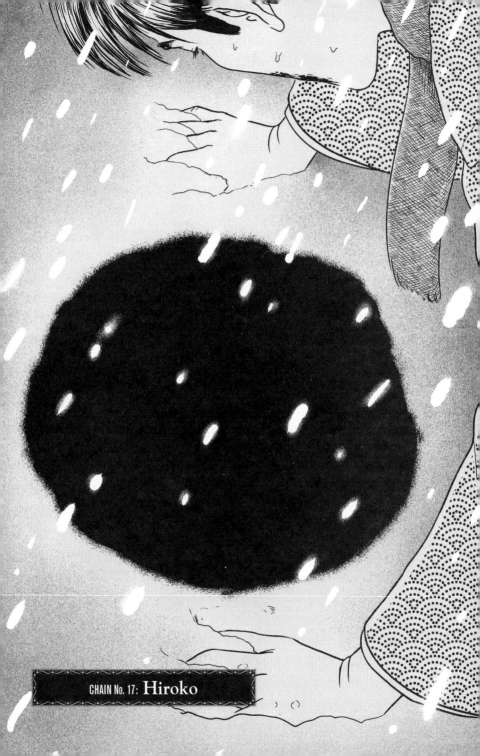

CHAIN No. 17: Hiroko

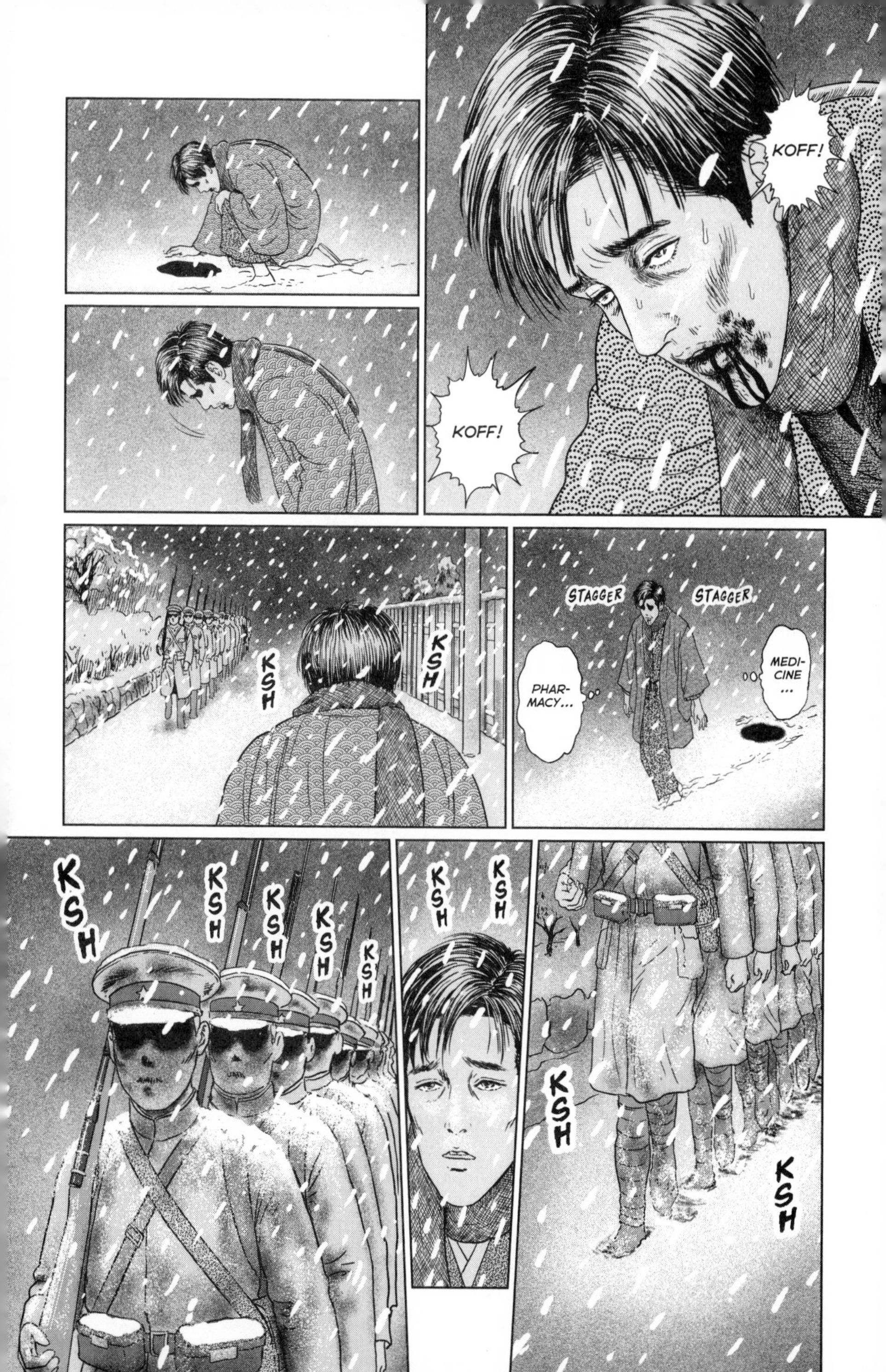
KOFF!
KOFF!
STAGGER
STAGGER
MEDICINE...
PHARMACY...
KSH
KSH
KSH
KSH
KSH
KSH
KSH
KSH
KSH
KSH
KSH

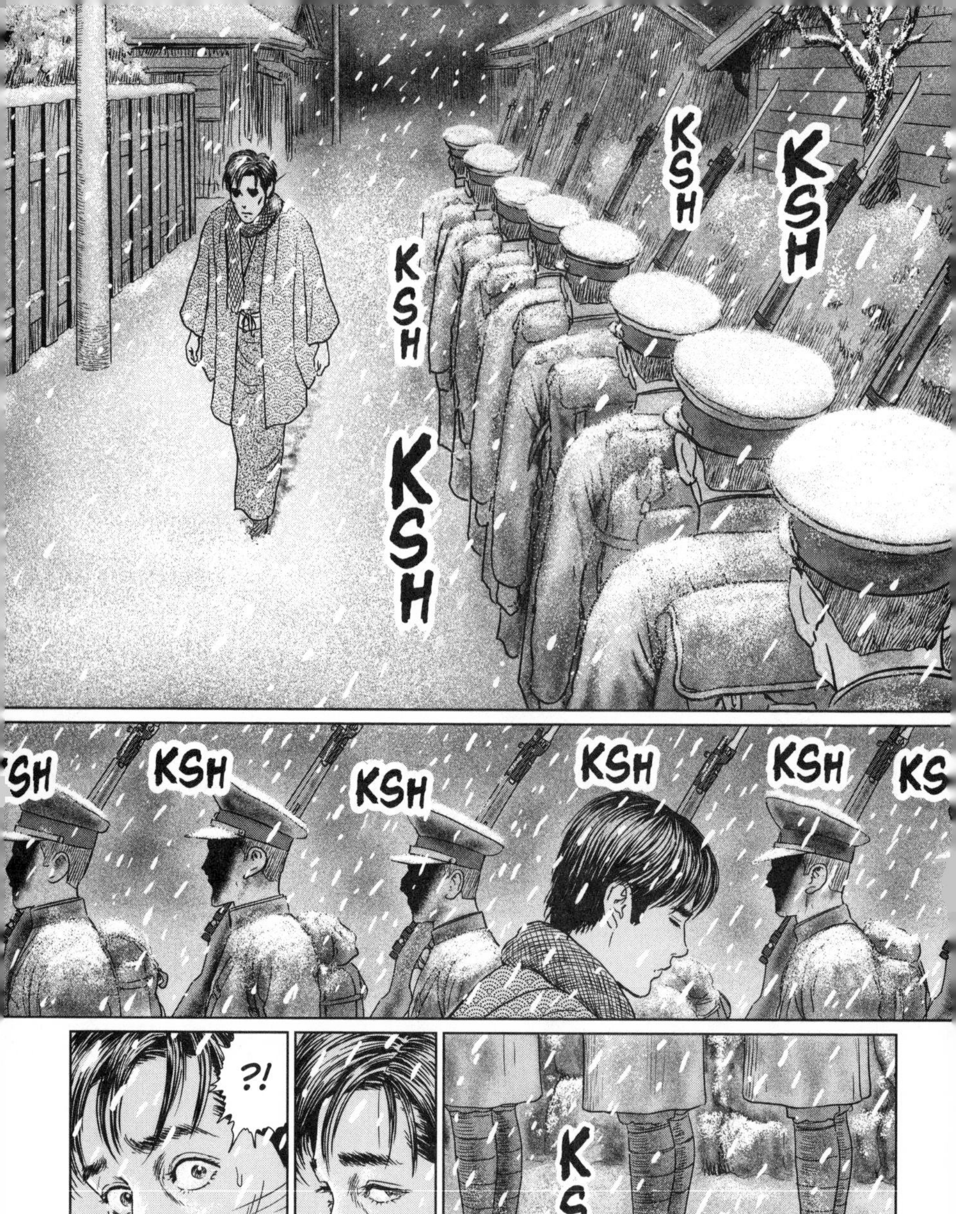
KSH
KSH
KSH
KSH
KS
KSH
KSH
KSH
KSH
SH
KSH
?!

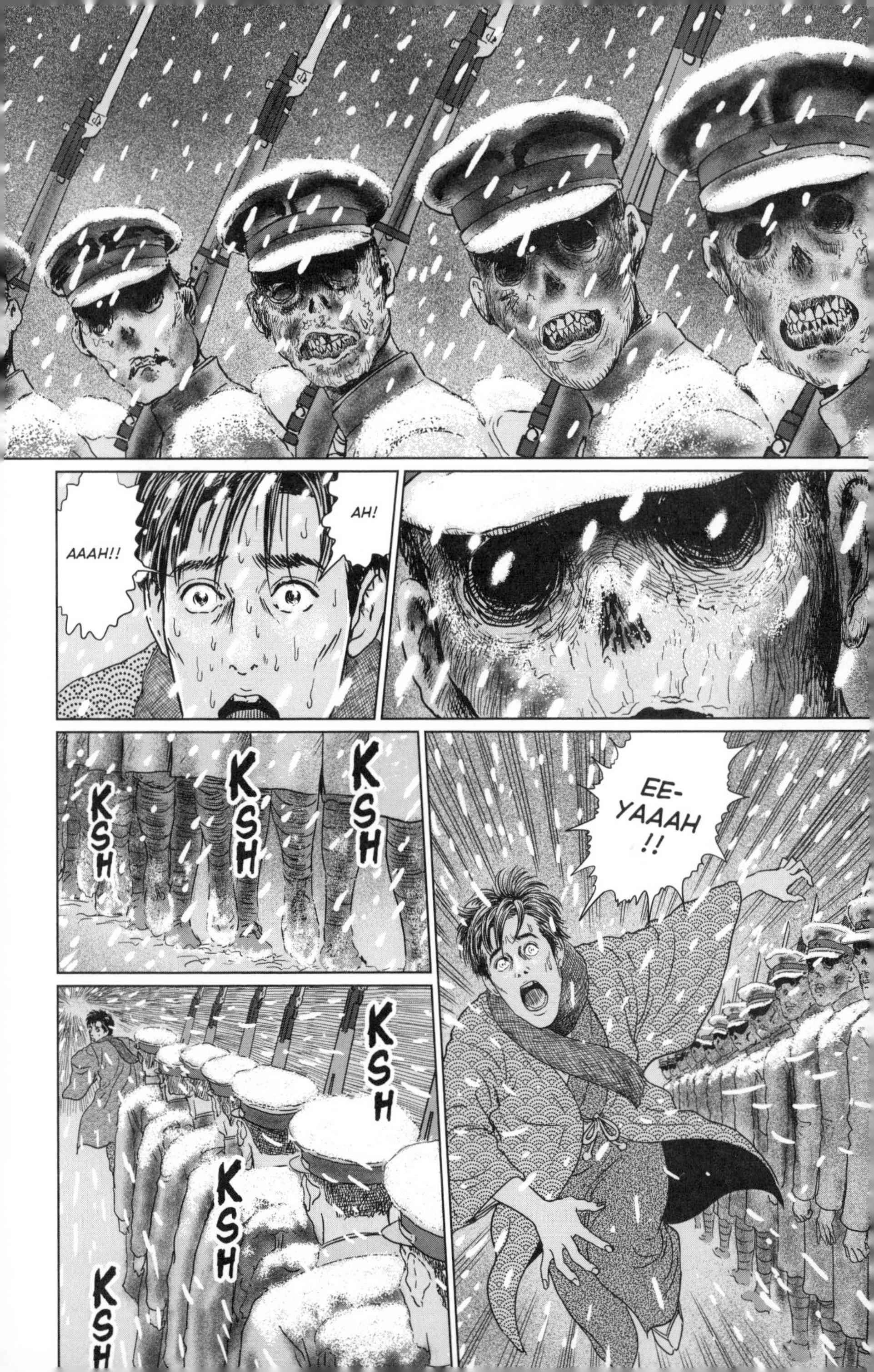
AH!
AAAH!!
EE-YAAAH!!
KSH
KSH
KSH
KSH
KSH
KSH

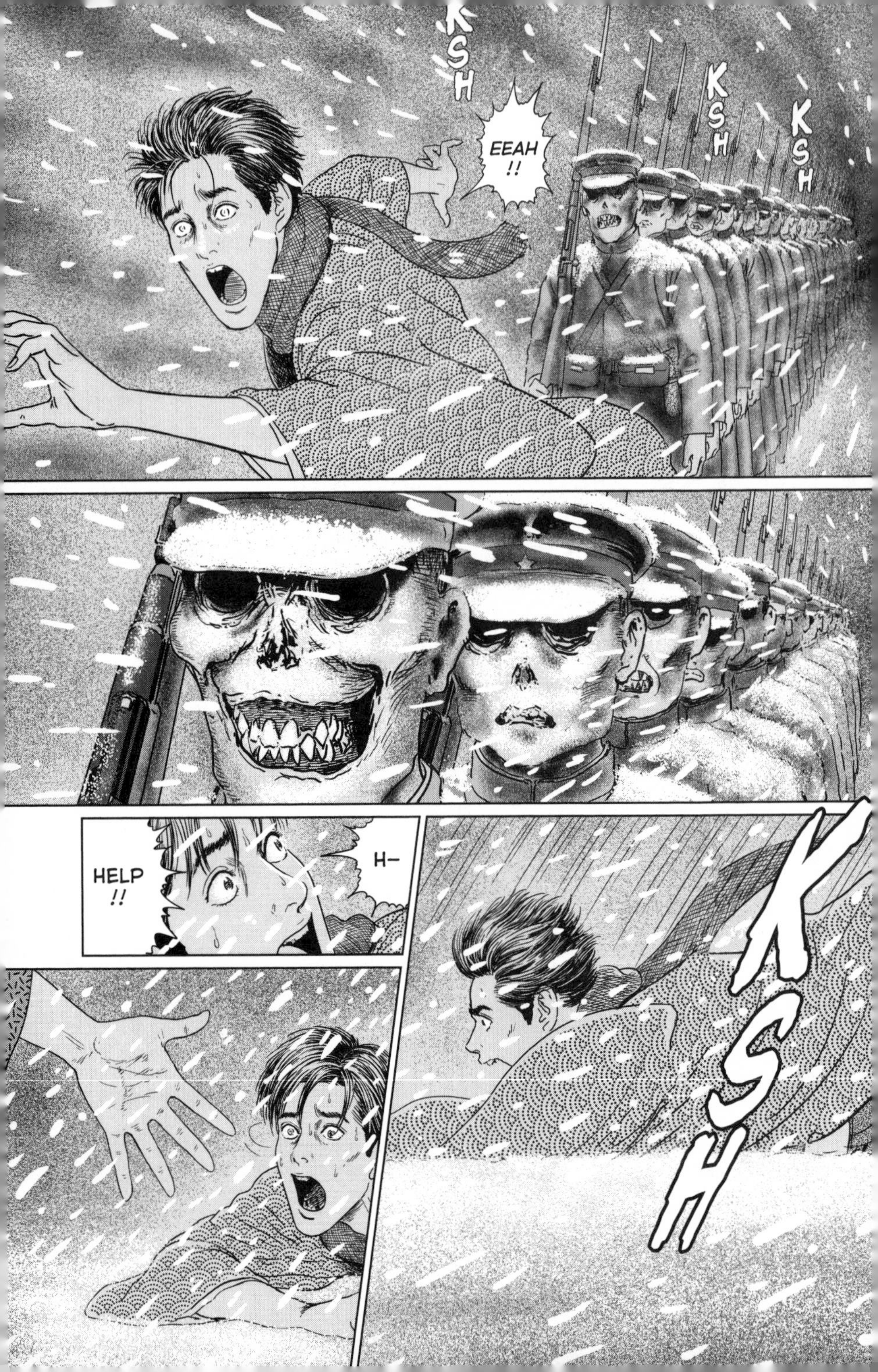
KSH
KSH
KSH
EEAH !!
KSH
H–
HELP !!

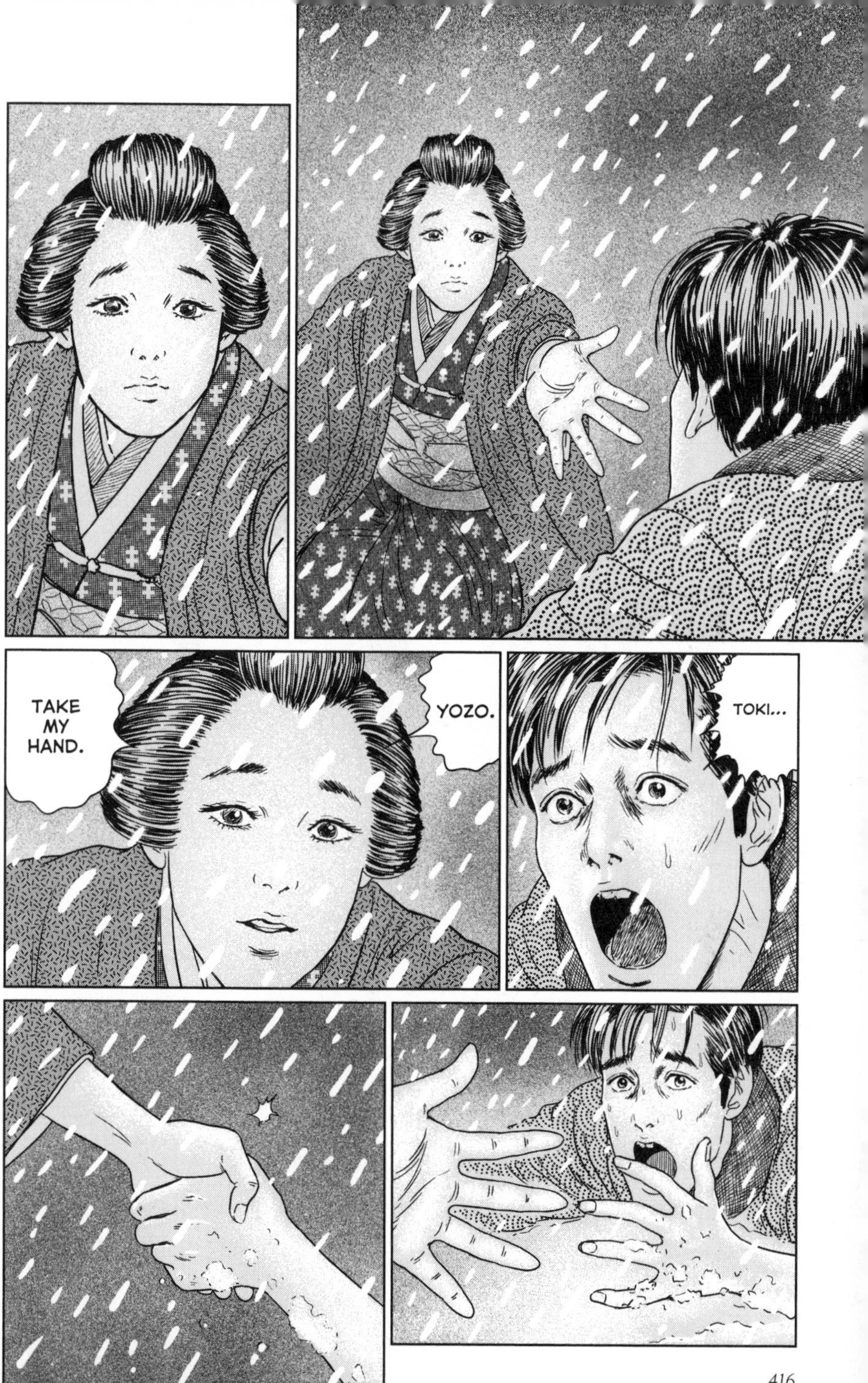
TOKI...
YOZO.
TAKE MY HAND.

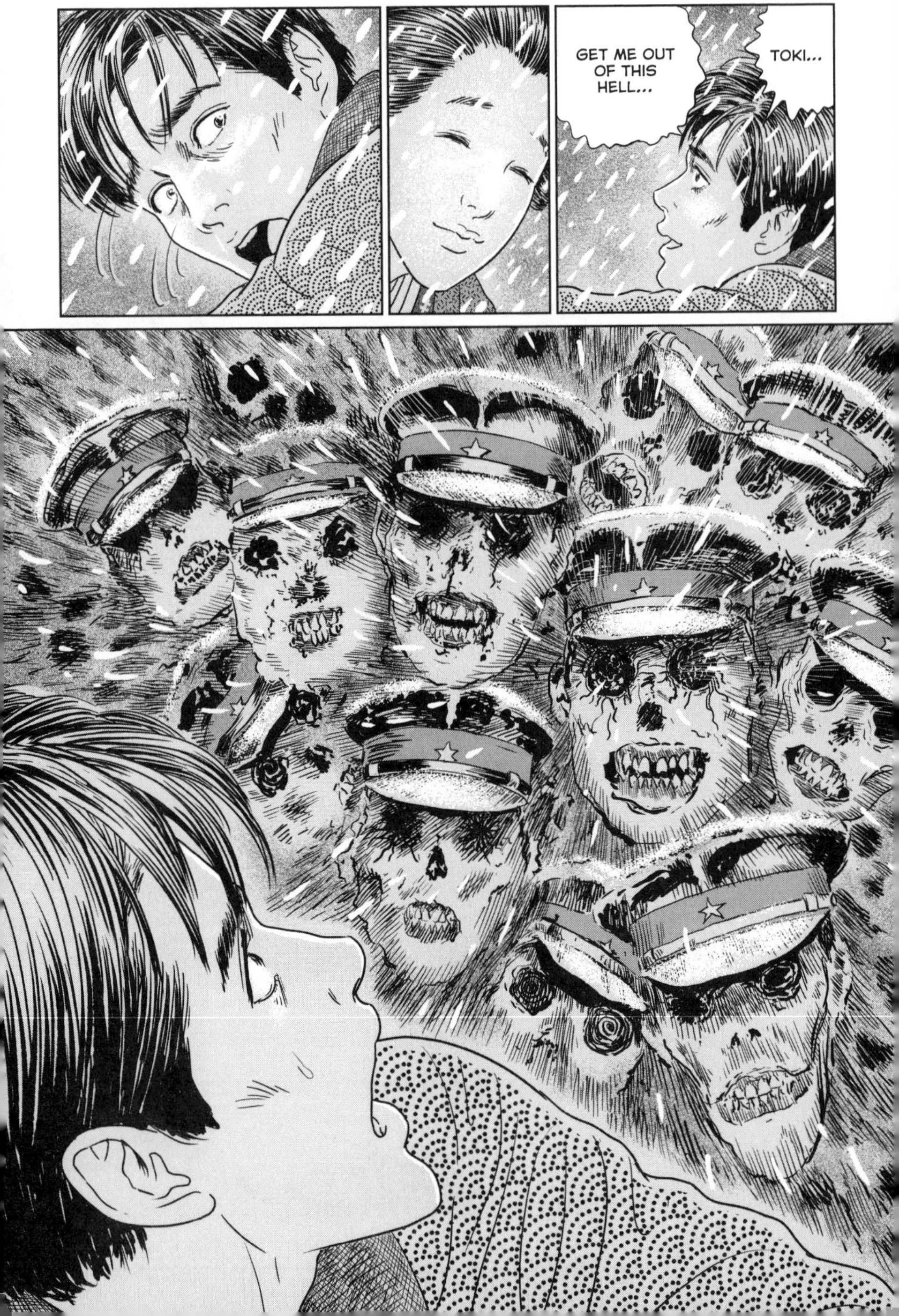
TOKI...
GET ME OUT OF THIS HELL...

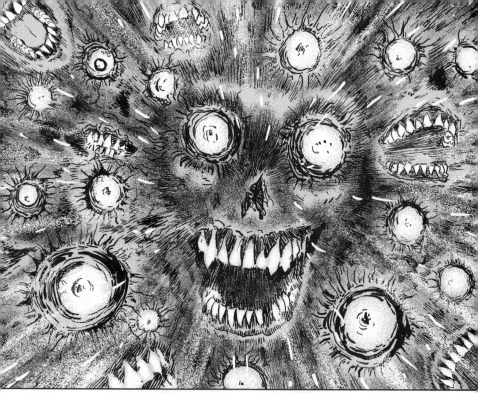

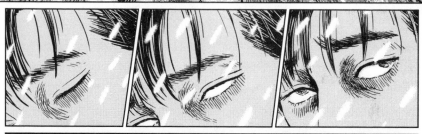

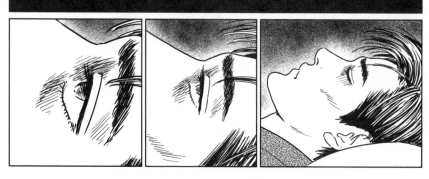

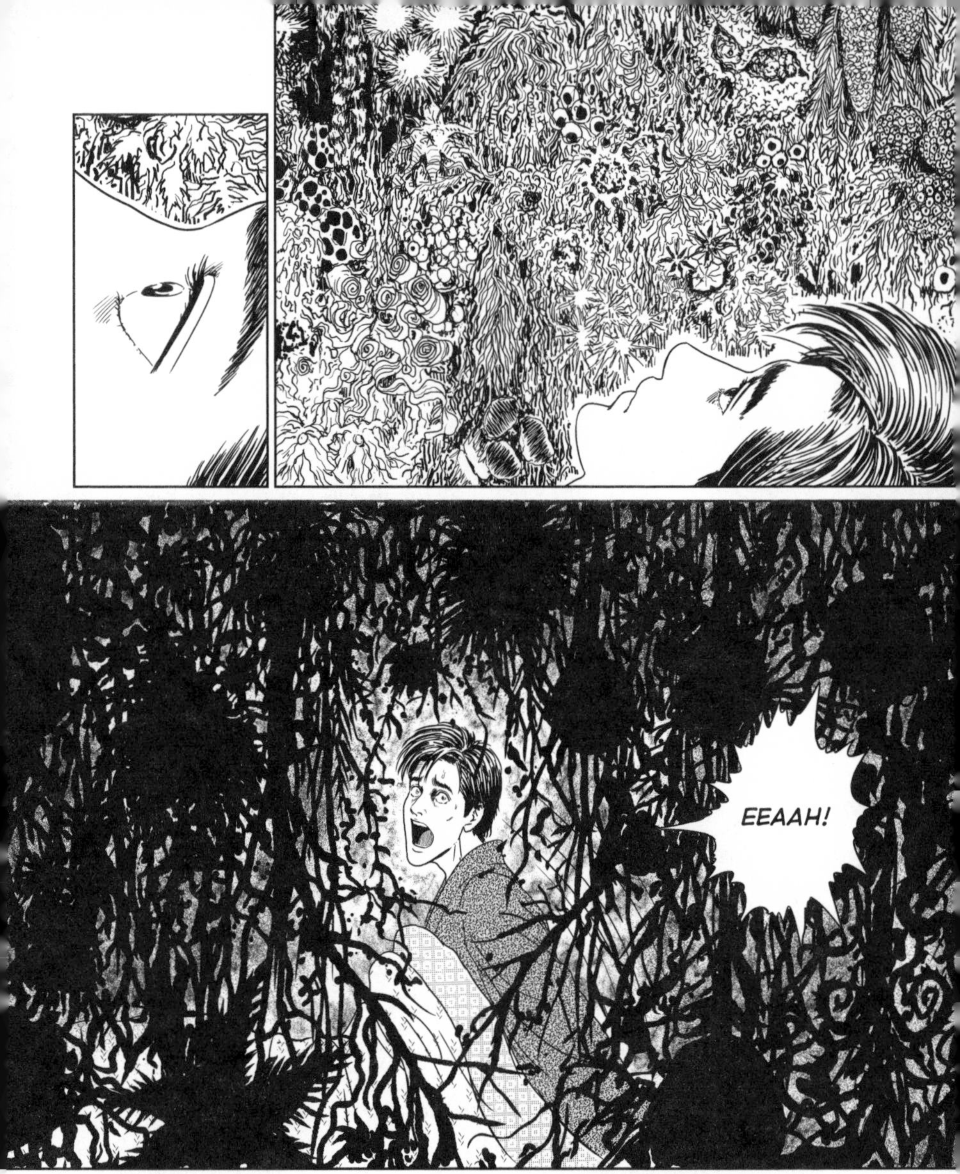
EEAAH!
HELL?! IS THIS HELL?!
TOKI... TOKI!!
!

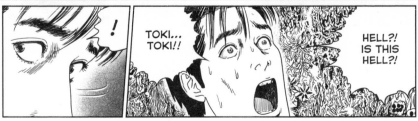

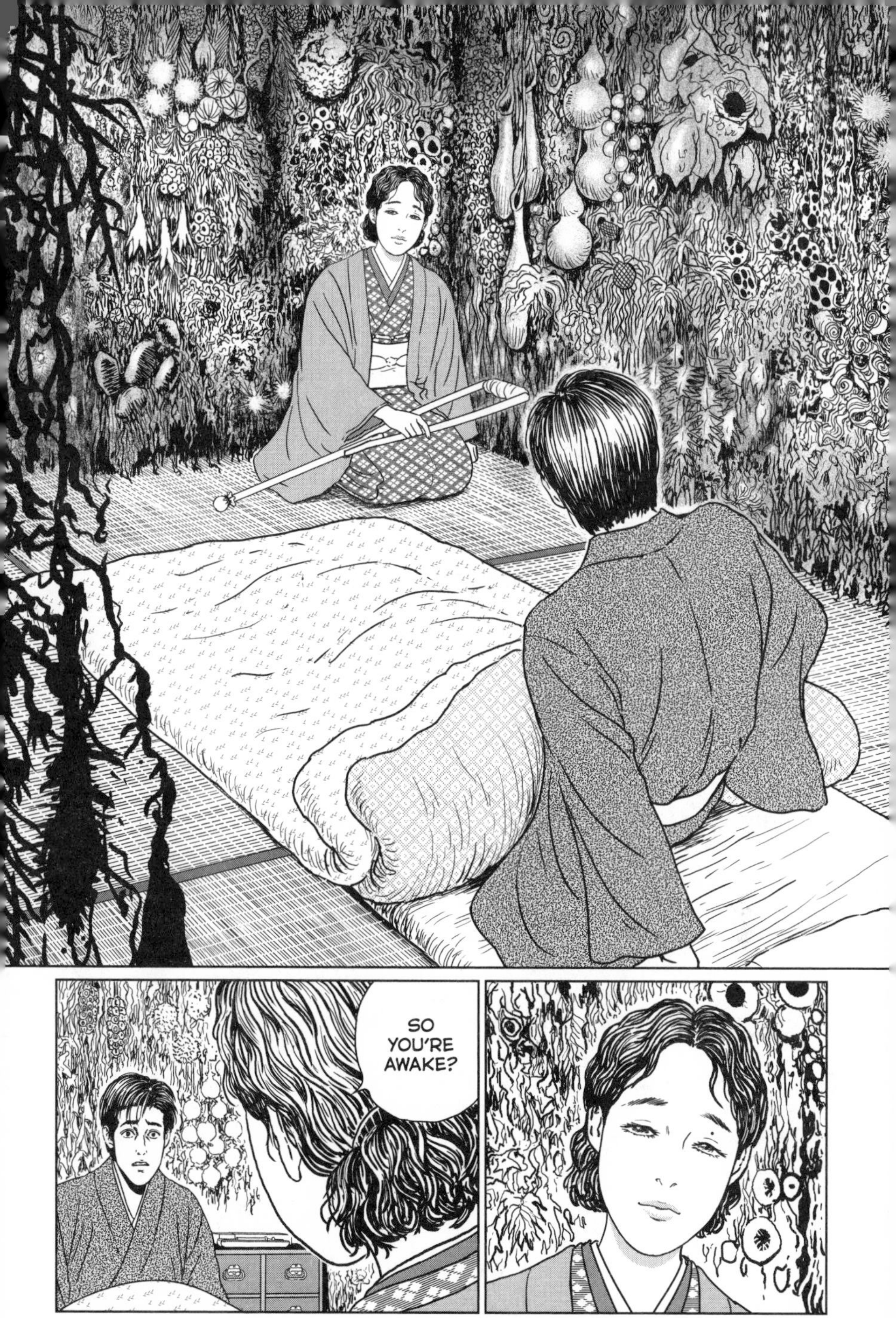
SO YOU'RE AWAKE?

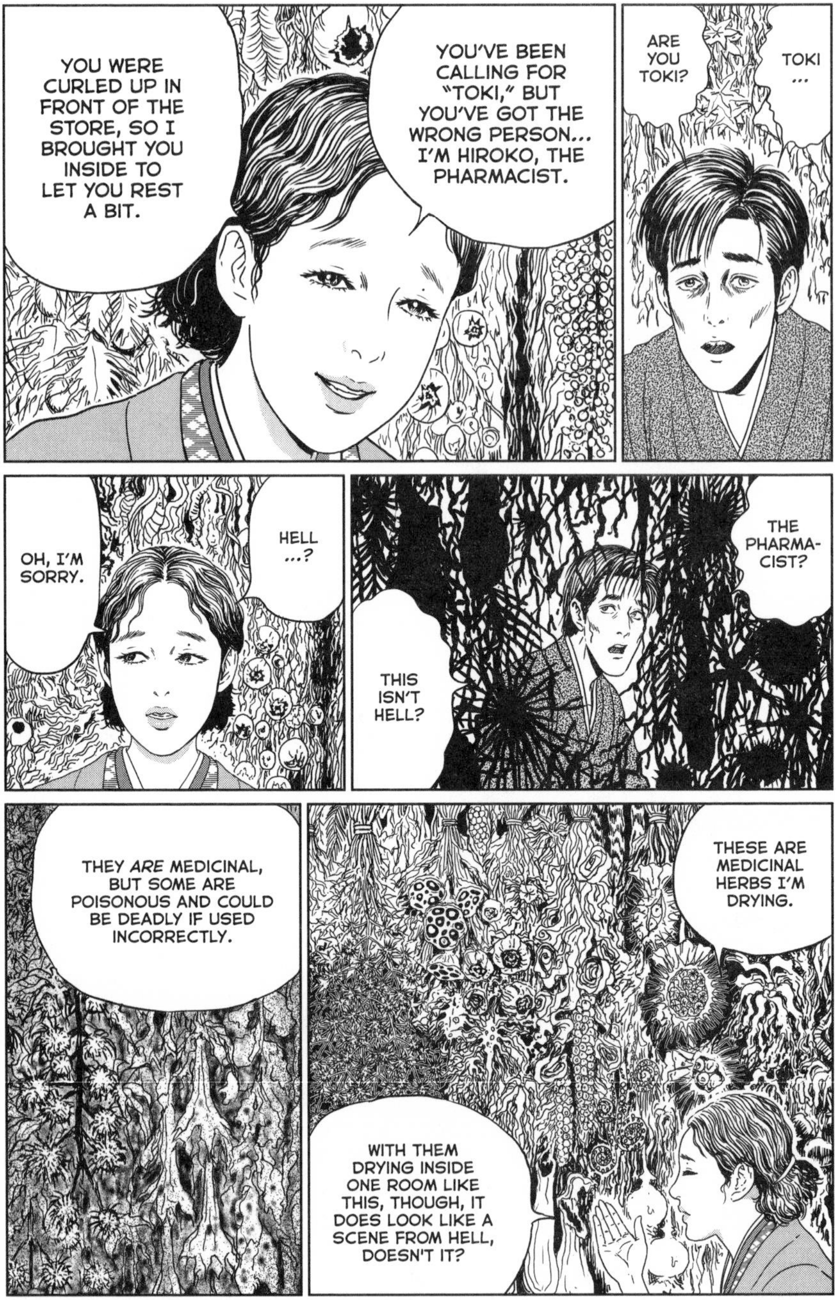
TOKI ...
ARE YOU TOKI?
YOU'VE BEEN CALLING FOR "TOKI," BUT YOU'VE GOT THE WRONG PERSON... I'M HIROKO, THE PHARMACIST.
YOU WERE CURLED UP IN FRONT OF THE STORE, SO I BROUGHT YOU INSIDE TO LET YOU REST A BIT.
THE PHARMACIST?
THIS ISN'T HELL?
HELL ...?
OH, I'M SORRY.
THESE ARE MEDICINAL HERBS I'M DRYING.
WITH THEM DRYING INSIDE ONE ROOM LIKE THIS, THOUGH, IT DOES LOOK LIKE A SCENE FROM HELL, DOESN'T IT?
THEY *ARE* MEDICINAL, BUT SOME ARE POISONOUS AND COULD BE DEADLY IF USED INCORRECTLY.

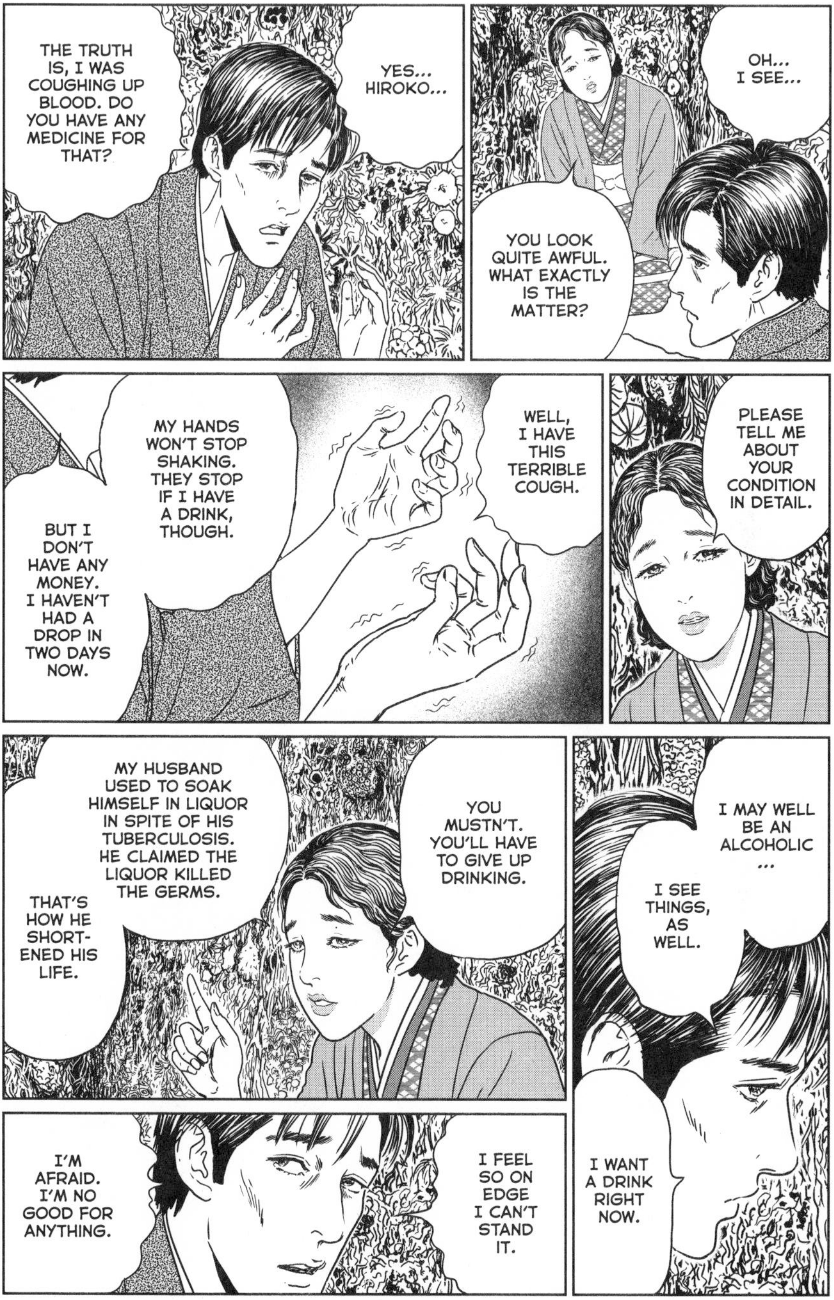
OH... I SEE...
YOU LOOK QUITE AWFUL. WHAT EXACTLY IS THE MATTER?
YES... HIROKO...
THE TRUTH IS, I WAS COUGHING UP BLOOD. DO YOU HAVE ANY MEDICINE FOR THAT?
PLEASE TELL ME ABOUT YOUR CONDITION IN DETAIL.
WELL, I HAVE THIS TERRIBLE COUGH.
MY HANDS WON'T STOP SHAKING. THEY STOP IF I HAVE A DRINK, THOUGH.
BUT I DON'T HAVE ANY MONEY. I HAVEN'T HAD A DROP IN TWO DAYS NOW.
I MAY WELL BE AN ALCOHOLIC ...
I SEE THINGS, AS WELL.
I WANT A DRINK RIGHT NOW.
YOU MUSTN'T. YOU'LL HAVE TO GIVE UP DRINKING.
MY HUSBAND USED TO SOAK HIMSELF IN LIQUOR IN SPITE OF HIS TUBERCULOSIS. HE CLAIMED THE LIQUOR KILLED THE GERMS.
THAT'S HOW HE SHORT-ENED HIS LIFE.
I FEEL SO ON EDGE I CAN'T STAND IT.
I'M AFRAID. I'M NO GOOD FOR ANYTHING.

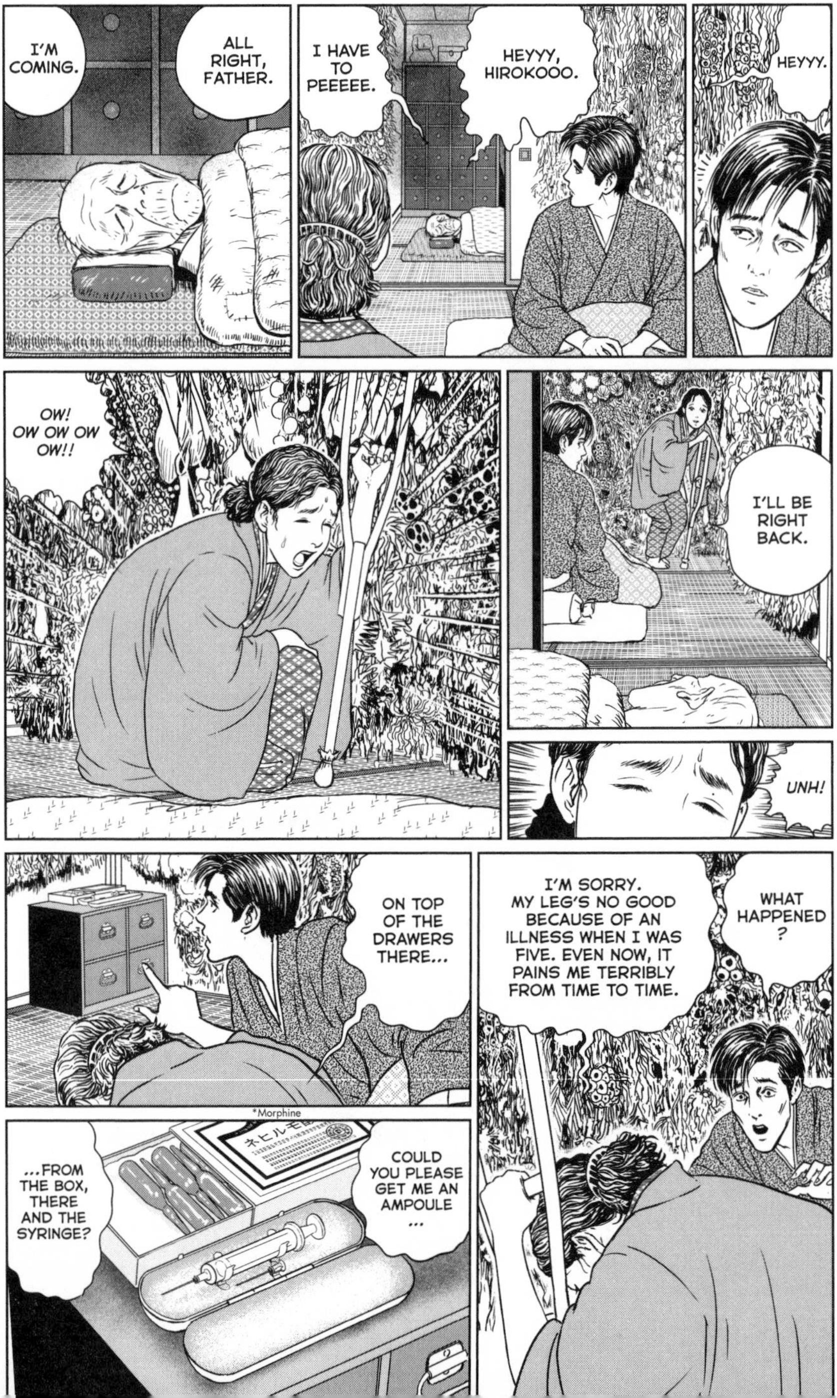
HEYYY.
HEYYY, HIROKOOO.
I HAVE TO PEEEEE.
ALL RIGHT, FATHER.
I'M COMING.
I'LL BE RIGHT BACK.
UNH!
OW! OW OW OW OW!!
WHAT HAPPENED?
I'M SORRY. MY LEG'S NO GOOD BECAUSE OF AN ILLNESS WHEN I WAS FIVE. EVEN NOW, IT PAINS ME TERRIBLY FROM TIME TO TIME.
ON TOP OF THE DRAWERS THERE...
COULD YOU PLEASE GET ME AN AMPOULE ...
...FROM THE BOX, THERE AND THE SYRINGE?

*Morphine

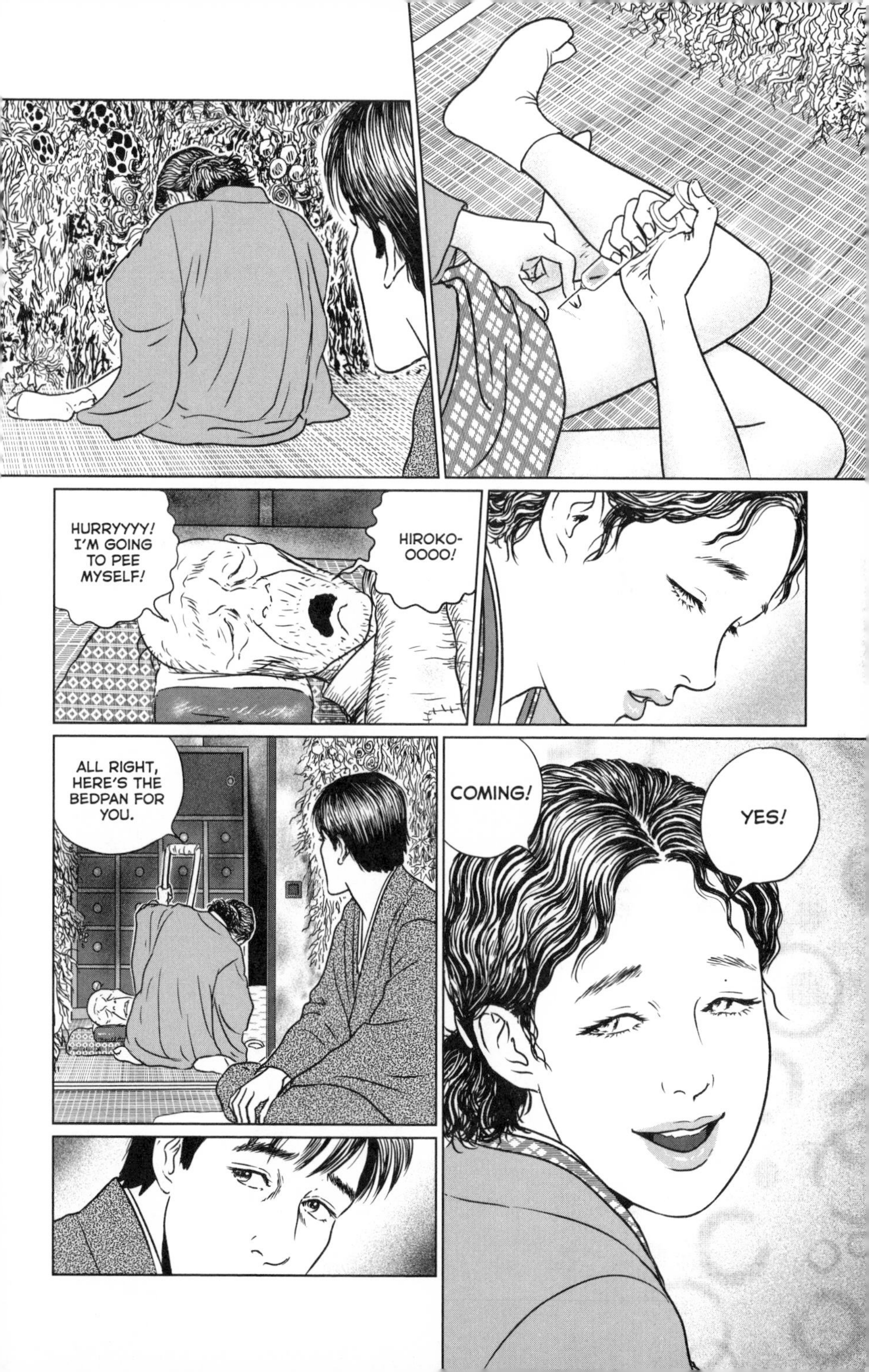
HIROKO-OOOO!
HURRYYYY! I'M GOING TO PEE MYSELF!
YES!
COMING!
ALL RIGHT, HERE'S THE BEDPAN FOR YOU.

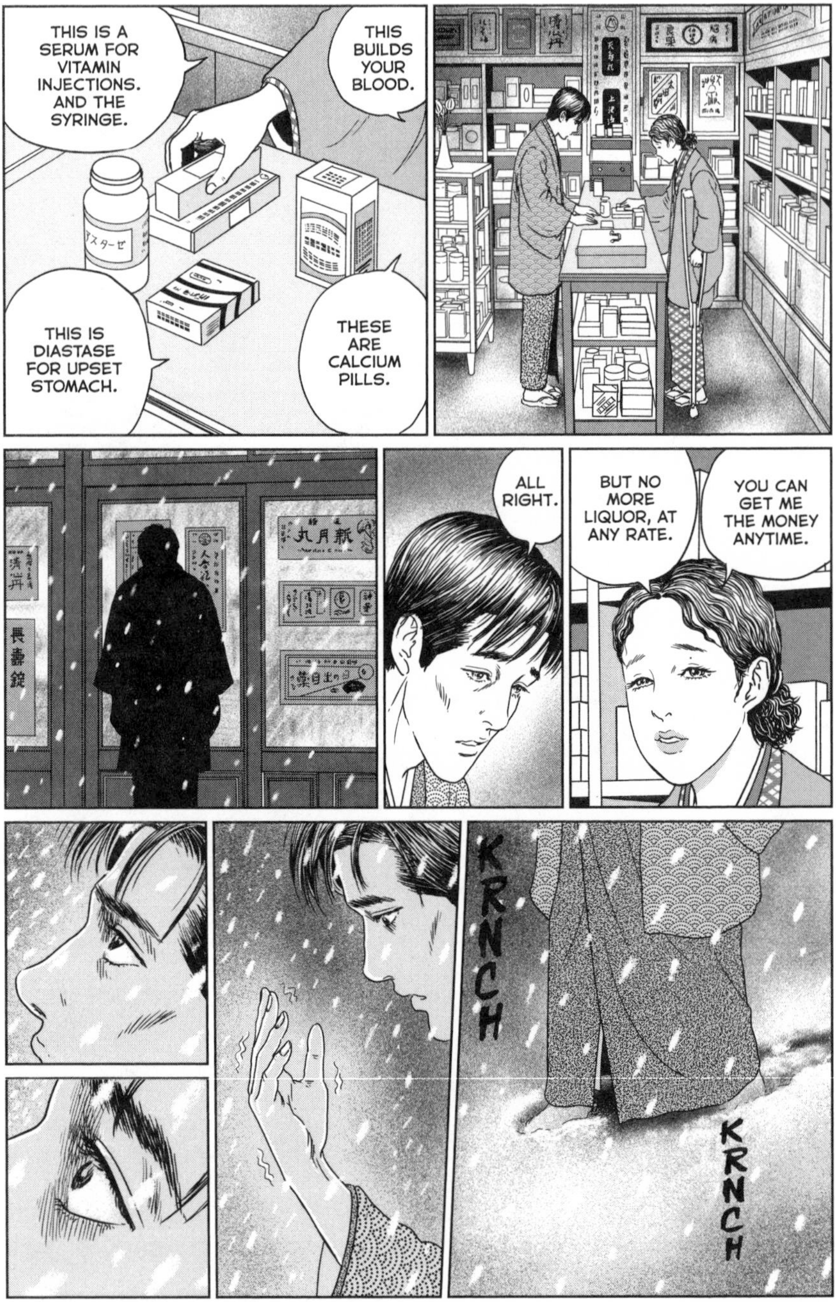
THIS BUILDS YOUR BLOOD.
THIS IS A SERUM FOR VITAMIN INJECTIONS. AND THE SYRINGE.
アスターゼ
THESE ARE CALCIUM PILLS.
THIS IS DIASTASE FOR UPSET STOMACH.
YOU CAN GET ME THE MONEY ANYTIME.
BUT NO MORE LIQUOR, AT ANY RATE.
ALL RIGHT.
KRNCH
KRNCH

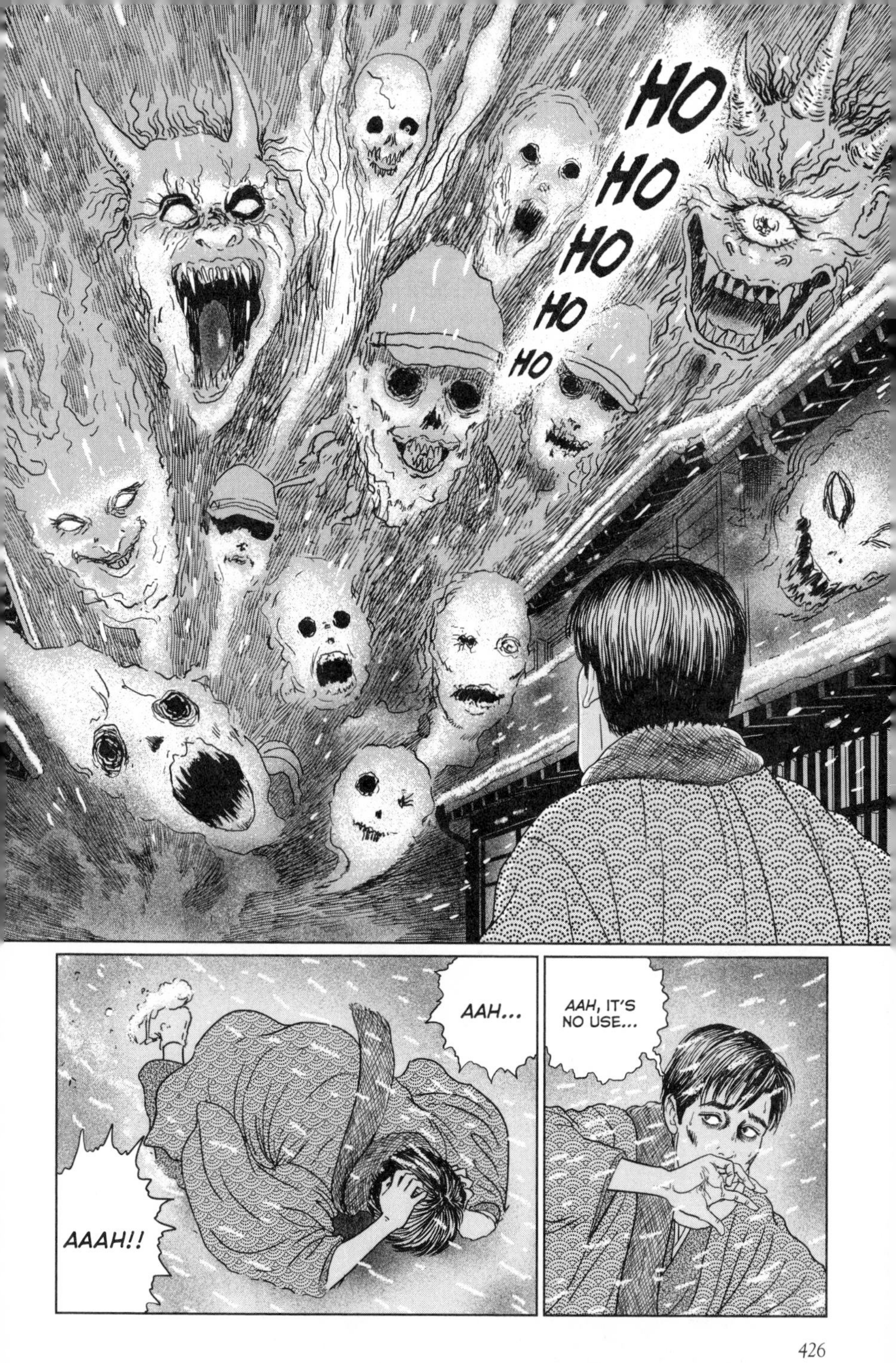
HO
HO
HO
HO
HO
AAH, IT'S NO USE...
AAH...
AAAH!!

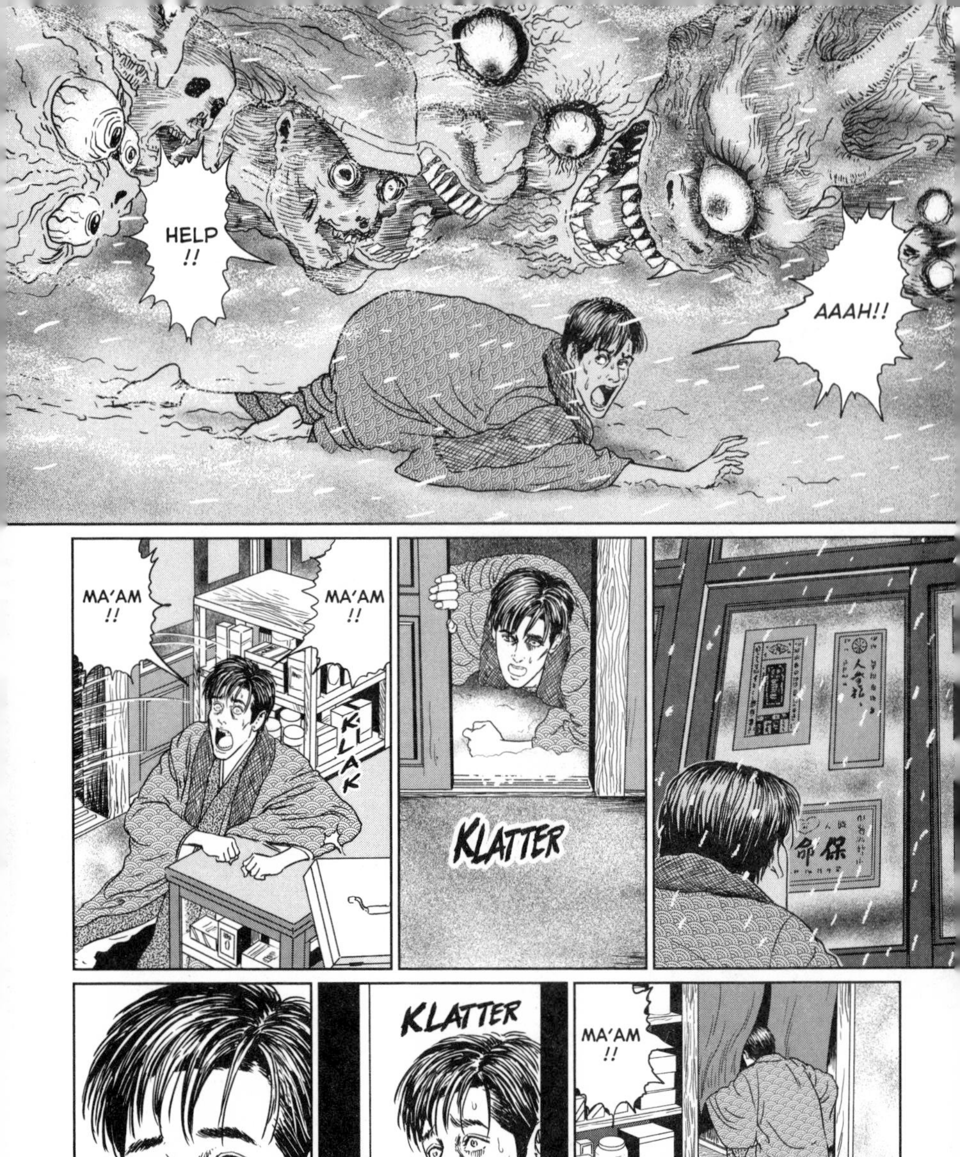
AAAH!!
HELP!!
KLATTER
MA'AM!!
MA'AM!!
KLAK
MA'AM!!
KLATTER
MA'AM!!

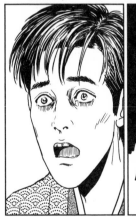

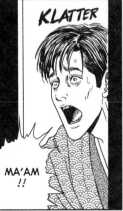

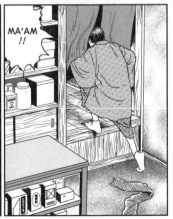

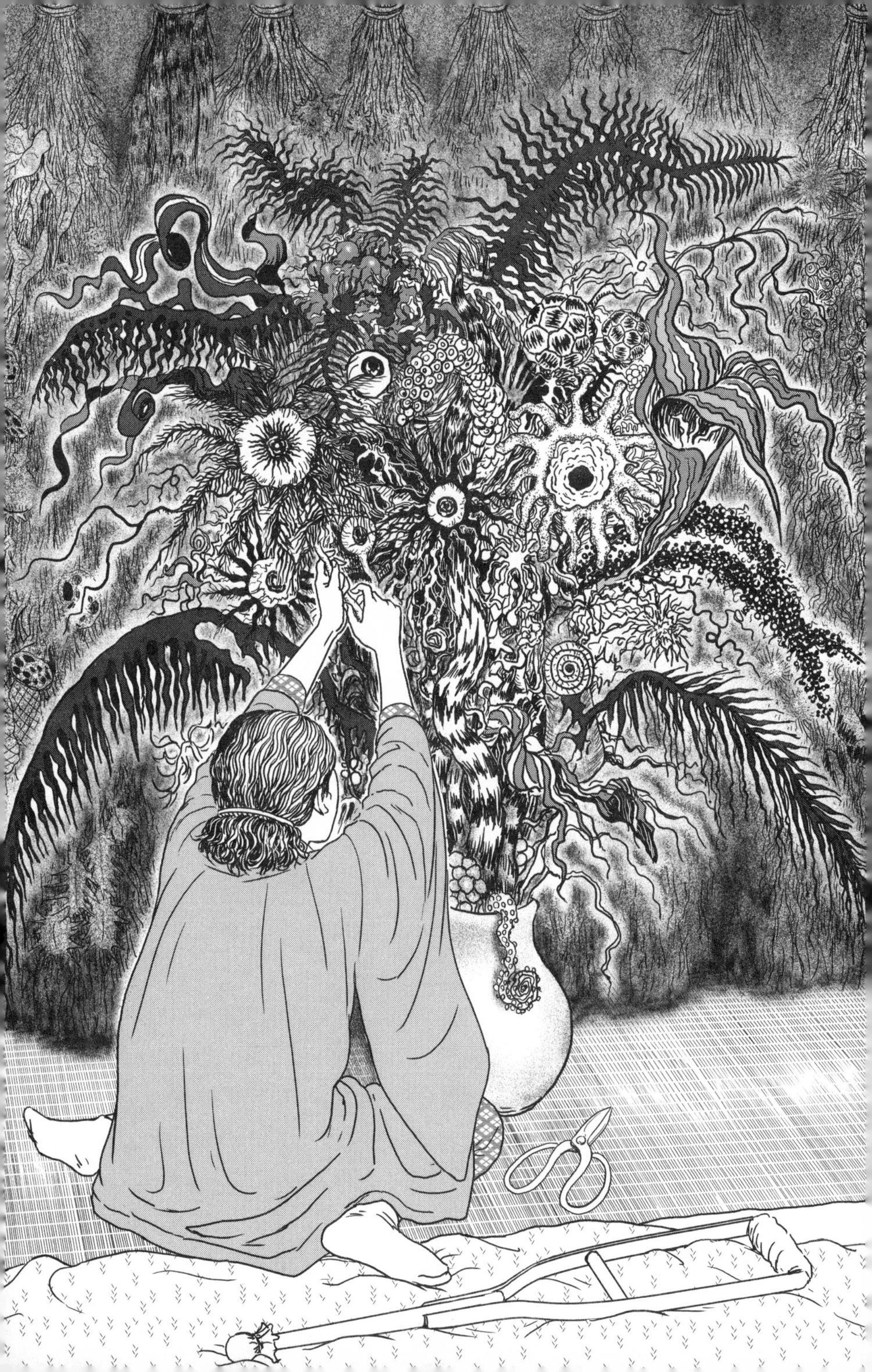

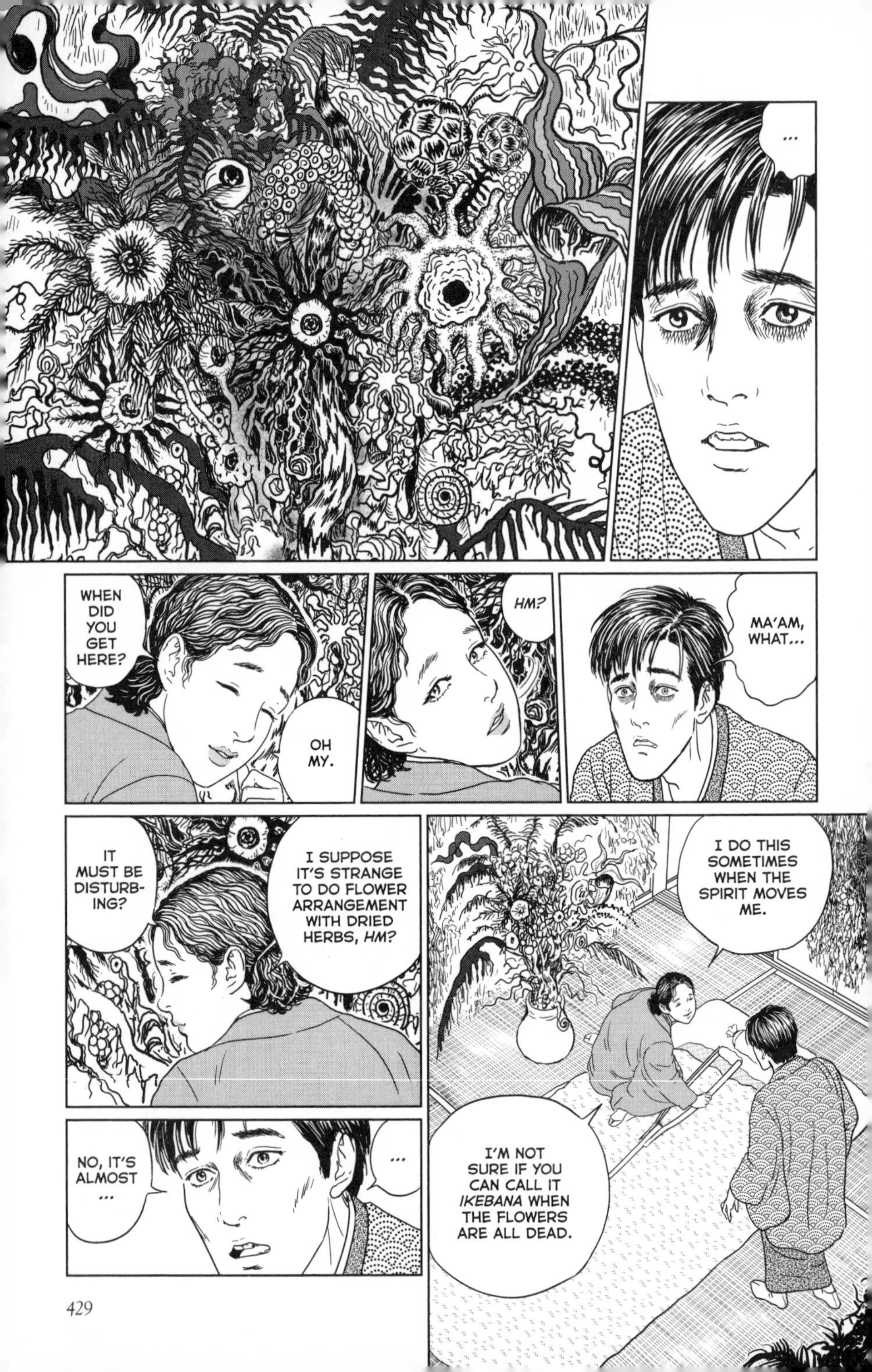

...
MA'AM, WHAT...
HM?
OH MY.
WHEN DID YOU GET HERE?
I DO THIS SOMETIMES WHEN THE SPIRIT MOVES ME.
I'M NOT SURE IF YOU CAN CALL IT *IKEBANA* WHEN THE FLOWERS ARE ALL DEAD.
I SUPPOSE IT'S STRANGE TO DO FLOWER ARRANGEMENT WITH DRIED HERBS, *HM?*
IT MUST BE DISTURBING?
...
NO, IT'S ALMOST ...

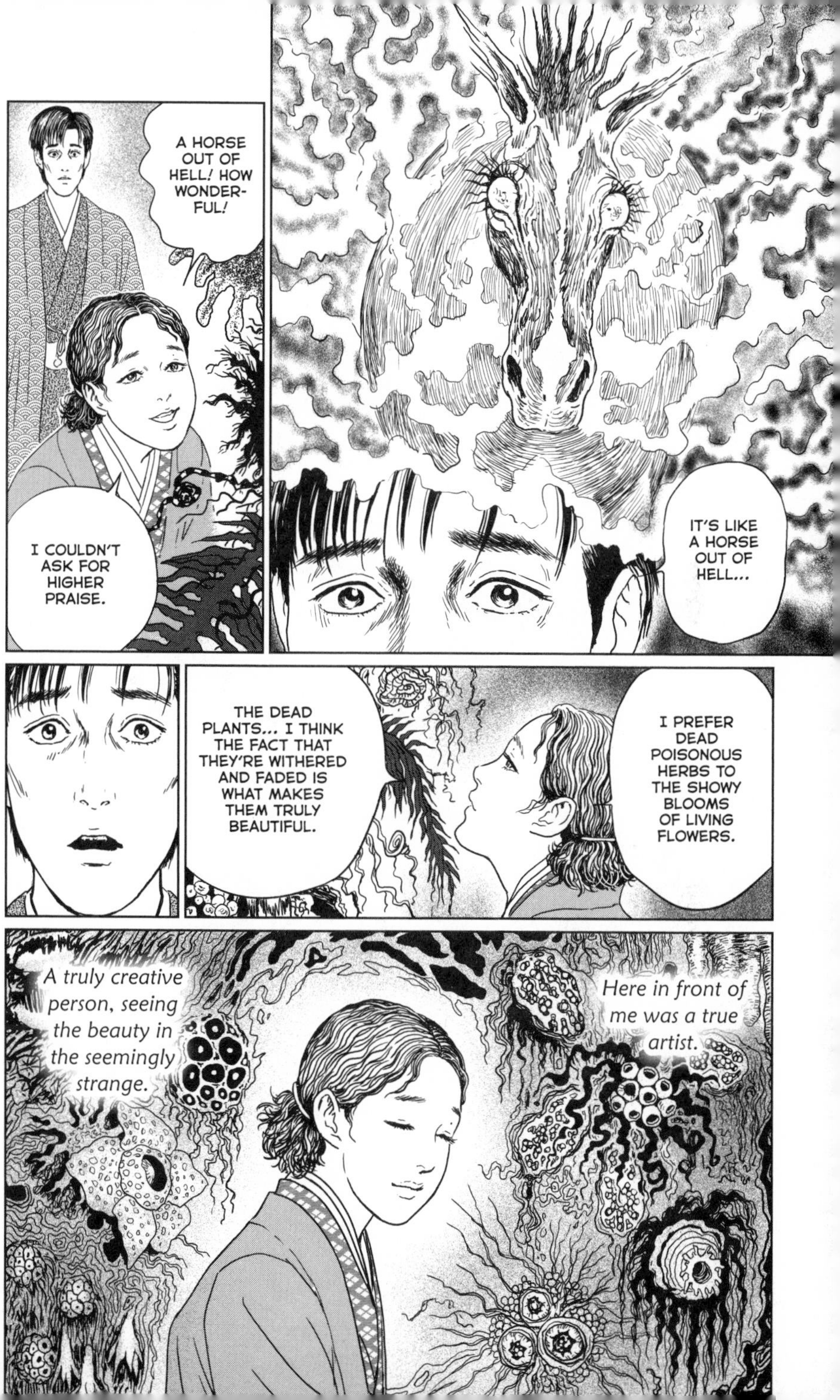
IT'S LIKE A HORSE OUT OF HELL...
A HORSE OUT OF HELL! HOW WONDERFUL!
I COULDN'T ASK FOR HIGHER PRAISE.
I PREFER DEAD POISONOUS HERBS TO THE SHOWY BLOOMS OF LIVING FLOWERS.
THE DEAD PLANTS... I THINK THE FACT THAT THEY'RE WITHERED AND FADED IS WHAT MAKES THEM TRULY BEAUTIFUL.
Here in front of me was a true artist.
A truly creative person, seeing the beauty in the seemingly strange.

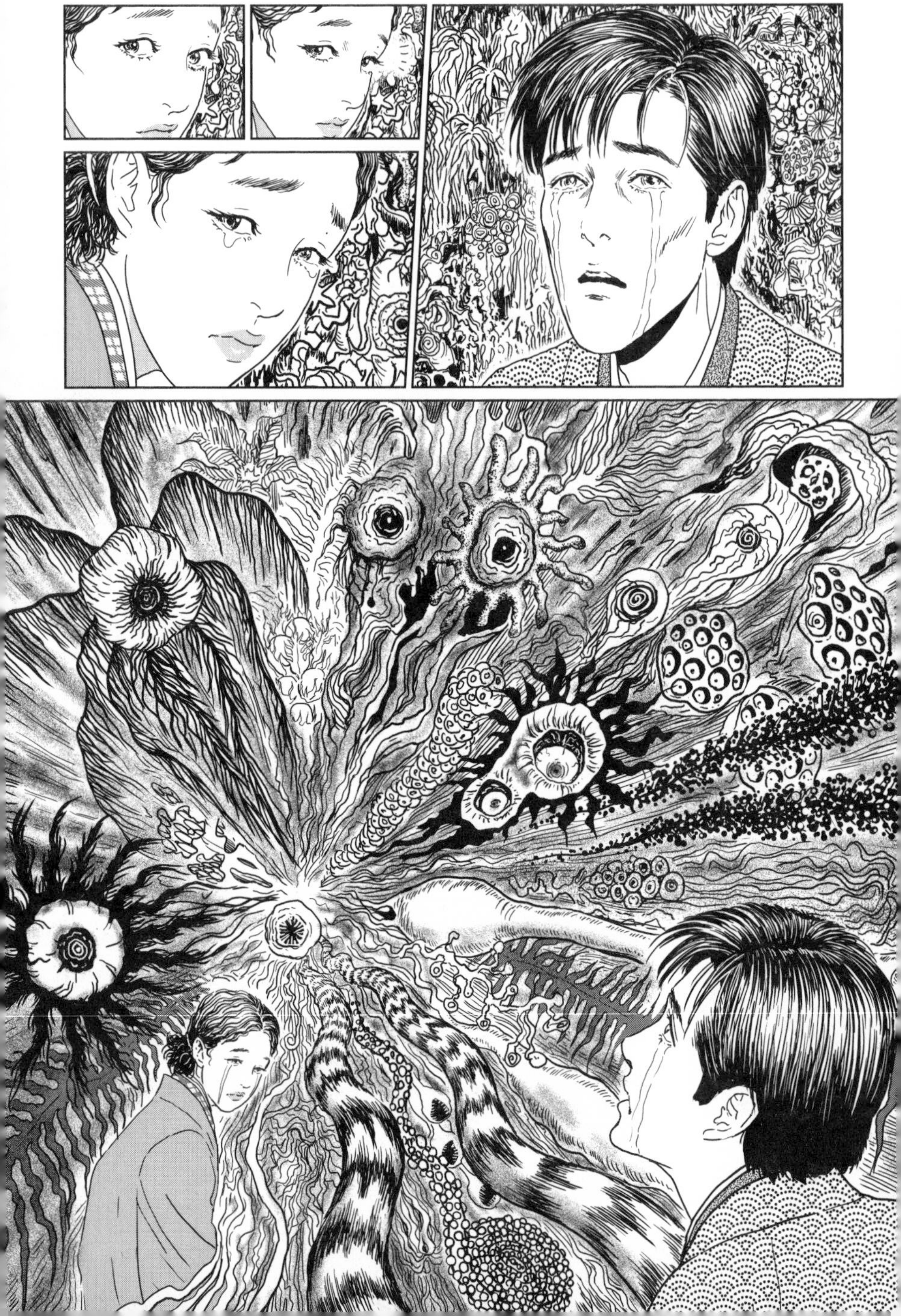

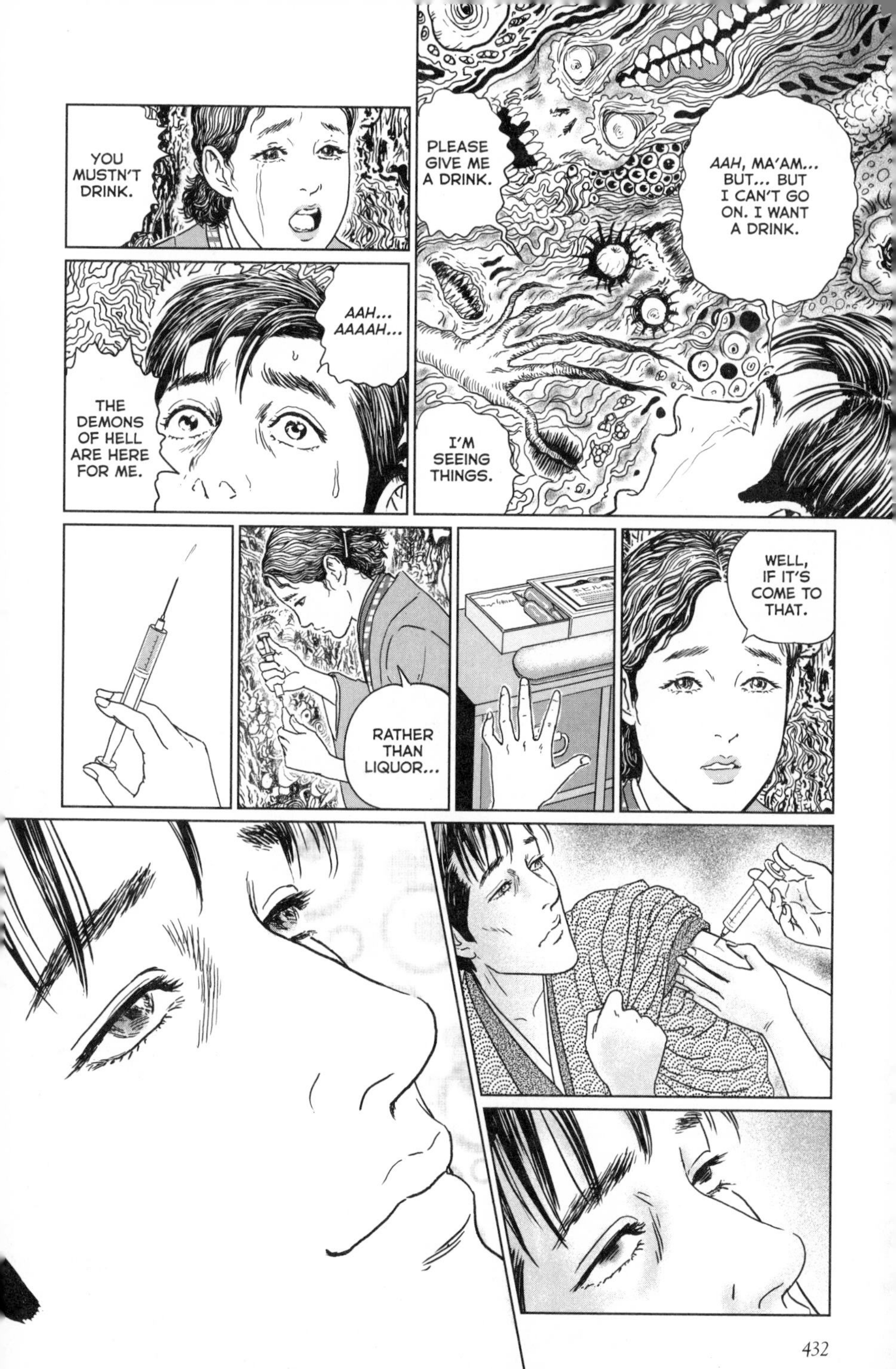
AAH, MA'AM... BUT... BUT I CAN'T GO ON. I WANT A DRINK.
PLEASE GIVE ME A DRINK.
I'M SEEING THINGS.
YOU MUSTN'T DRINK.
AAH... AAAAH...
THE DEMONS OF HELL ARE HERE FOR ME.
WELL, IF IT'S COME TO THAT.
RATHER THAN LIQUOR...

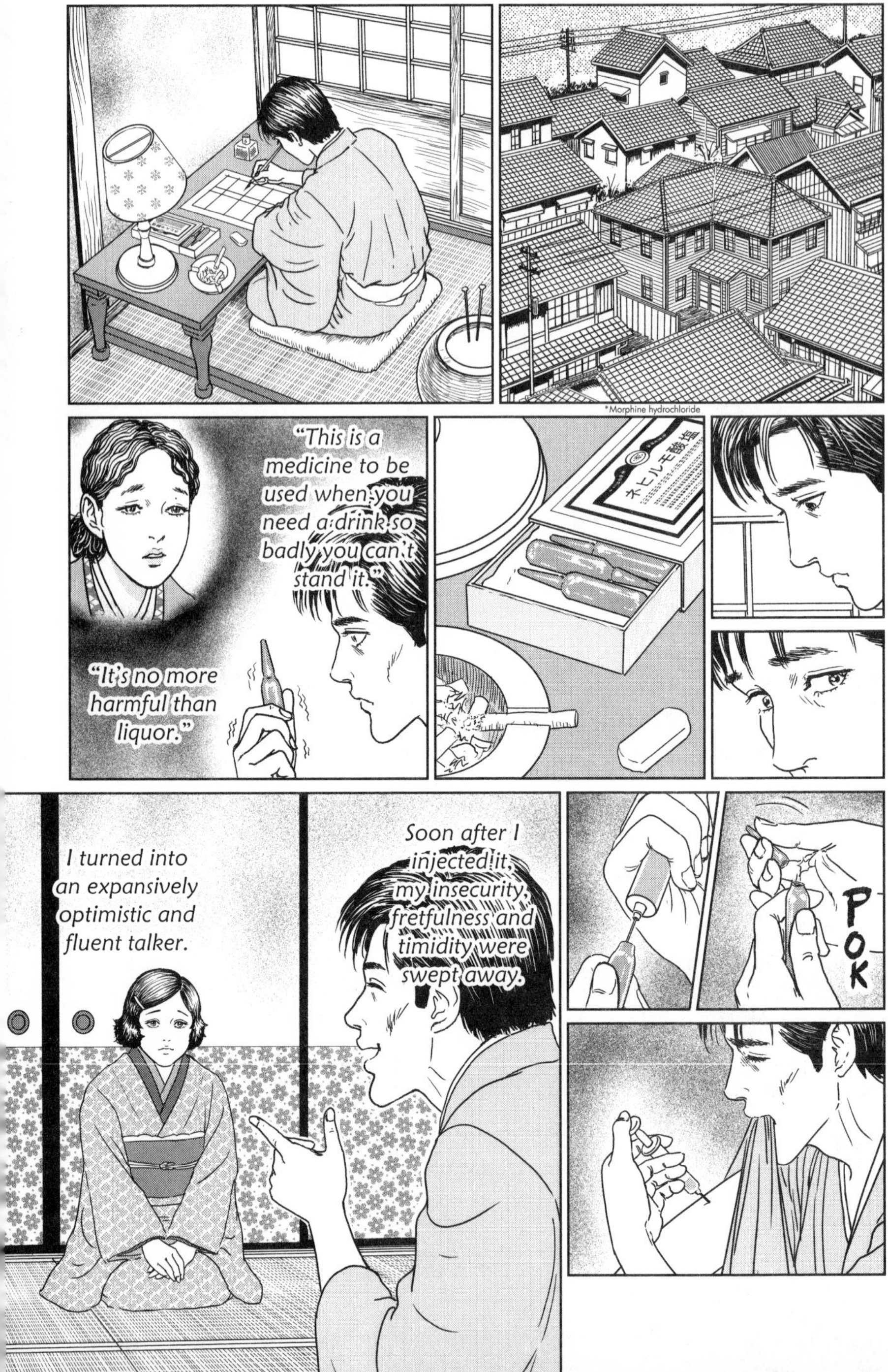
*Morphine hydrochloride
塩酸モルヒネ
"This is a medicine to be used when you need a drink so badly you can't stand it."
"It's no more harmful than liquor."
POK
Soon after I injected it, my insecurity, fretfulness and timidity were swept away.
I turned into an expansively optimistic and fluent talker.

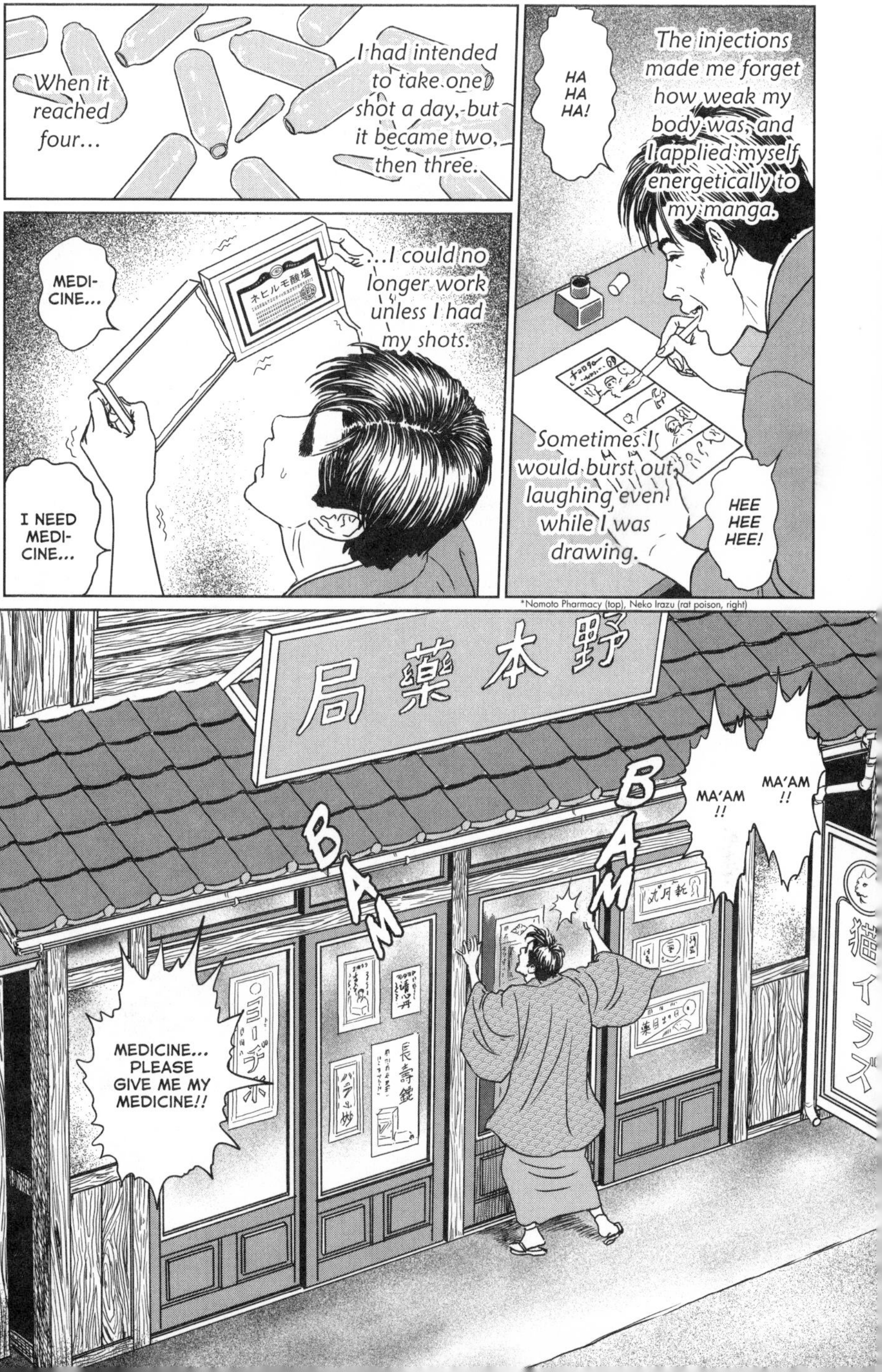
The injections made me forget how weak my body was, and I applied myself energetically to my manga.
HA HA HA!
Sometimes I would burst out laughing even while I was drawing.
HEE HEE HEE!
I had intended to take one shot a day, but it became two, then three.
When it reached four…
…I could no longer work unless I had my shots.
ネヒルモ酸塩
MEDI-CINE…
I NEED MEDI-CINE…
野本薬局
MA'AM!!
MA'AM!!
BAM
BAM
猫イラズ
MEDICINE… PLEASE GIVE ME MY MEDICINE!!

*Nomoto Pharmacy (top), Neko Irazu (rat poison, right)

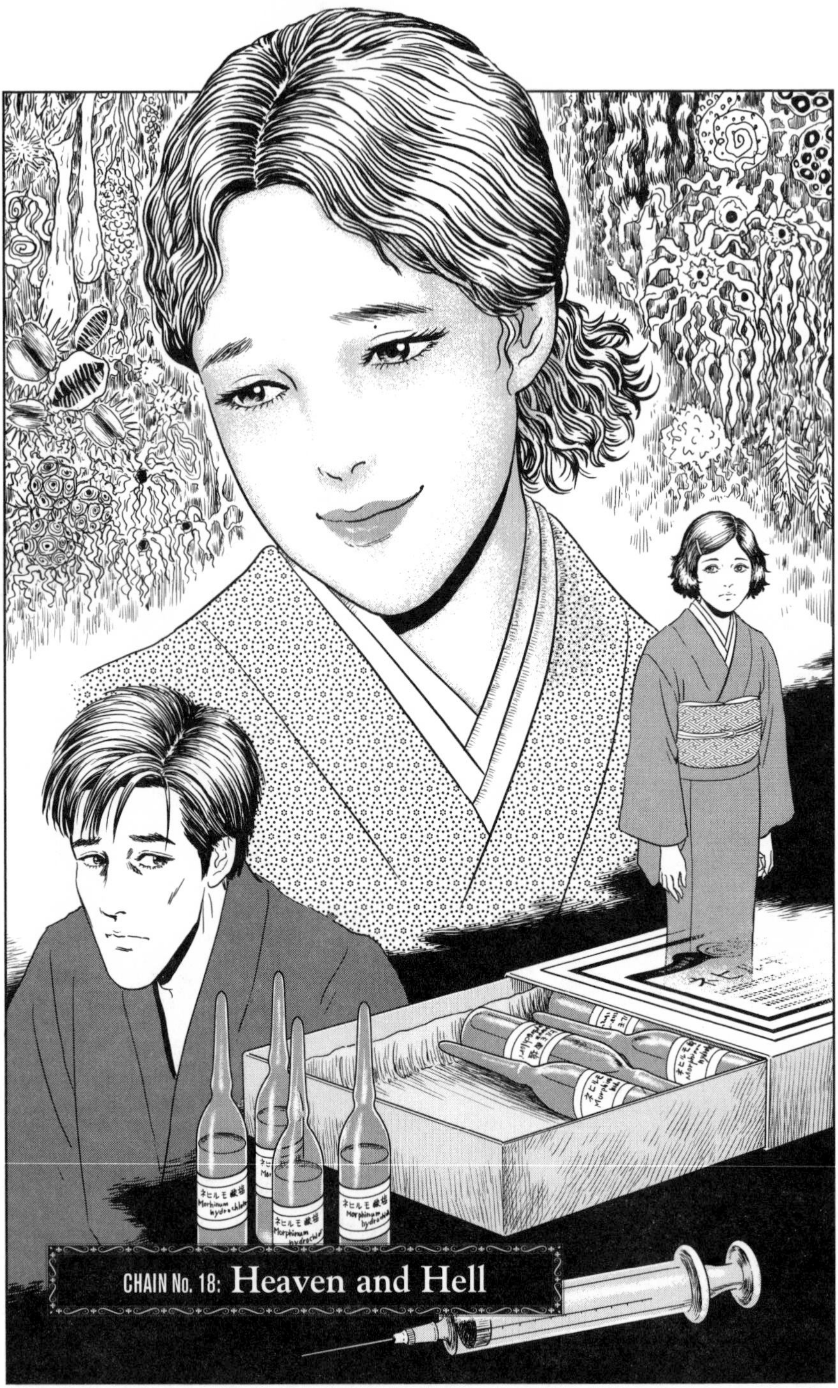

CHAIN No. 18: Heaven and Hell

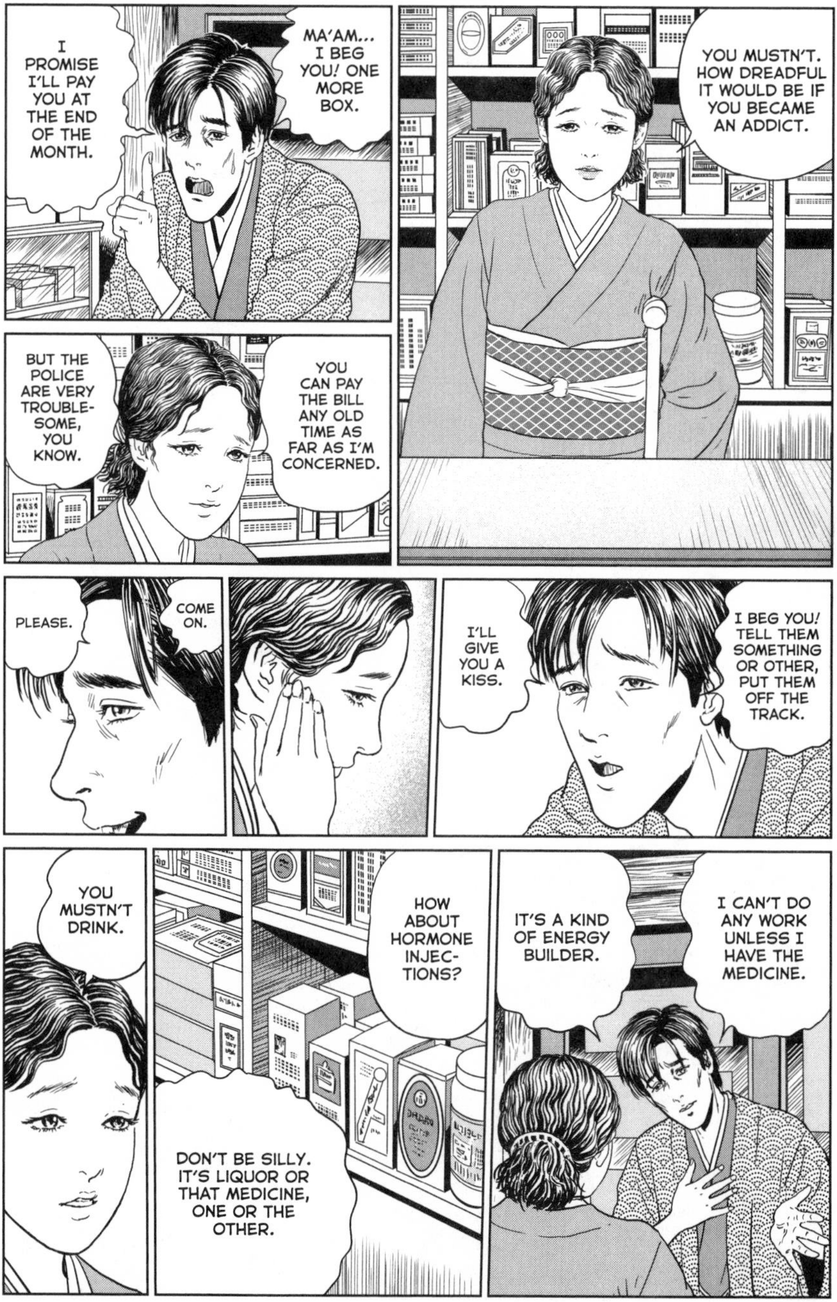
YOU MUSTN'T. HOW DREADFUL IT WOULD BE IF YOU BECAME AN ADDICT.
MA'AM... I BEG YOU! ONE MORE BOX.
I PROMISE I'LL PAY YOU AT THE END OF THE MONTH.
YOU CAN PAY THE BILL ANY OLD TIME AS FAR AS I'M CONCERNED.
BUT THE POLICE ARE VERY TROUBLE-SOME, YOU KNOW.
I BEG YOU! TELL THEM SOMETHING OR OTHER, PUT THEM OFF THE TRACK.
I'LL GIVE YOU A KISS.
COME ON.
PLEASE.
I CAN'T DO ANY WORK UNLESS I HAVE THE MEDICINE.
IT'S A KIND OF ENERGY BUILDER.
HOW ABOUT HORMONE INJEC-TIONS?
DON'T BE SILLY. IT'S LIQUOR OR THAT MEDICINE, ONE OR THE OTHER.
YOU MUSTN'T DRINK.

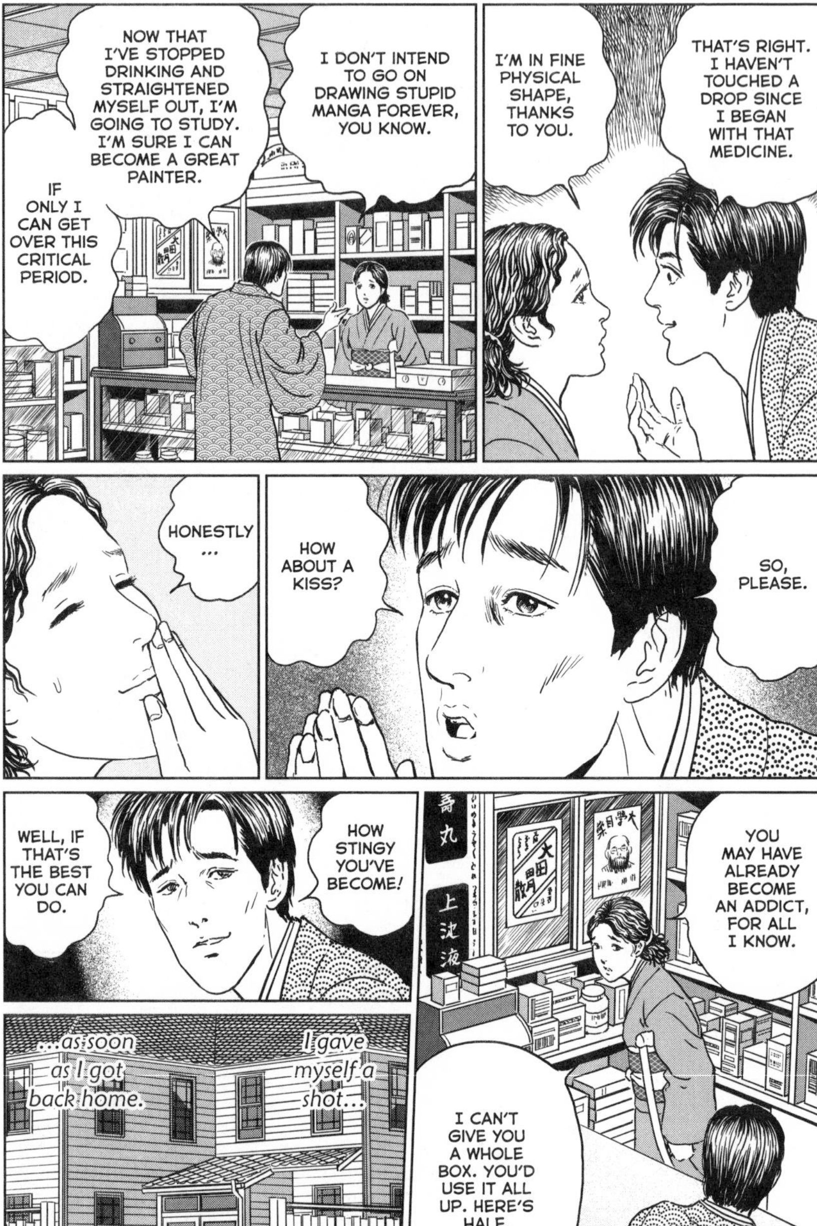
THAT'S RIGHT. I HAVEN'T TOUCHED A DROP SINCE I BEGAN WITH THAT MEDICINE.
I'M IN FINE PHYSICAL SHAPE, THANKS TO YOU.
I DON'T INTEND TO GO ON DRAWING STUPID MANGA FOREVER, YOU KNOW.
NOW THAT I'VE STOPPED DRINKING AND STRAIGHTENED MYSELF OUT, I'M GOING TO STUDY. I'M SURE I CAN BECOME A GREAT PAINTER.
IF ONLY I CAN GET OVER THIS CRITICAL PERIOD.
SO, PLEASE.
HOW ABOUT A KISS?
HONESTLY ...
YOU MAY HAVE ALREADY BECOME AN ADDICT, FOR ALL I KNOW.
I CAN'T GIVE YOU A WHOLE BOX. YOU'D USE IT ALL UP. HERE'S HALF.
HOW STINGY YOU'VE BECOME!
WELL, IF THAT'S THE BEST YOU CAN DO.
I gave myself a shot...
...as soon as I got back home.

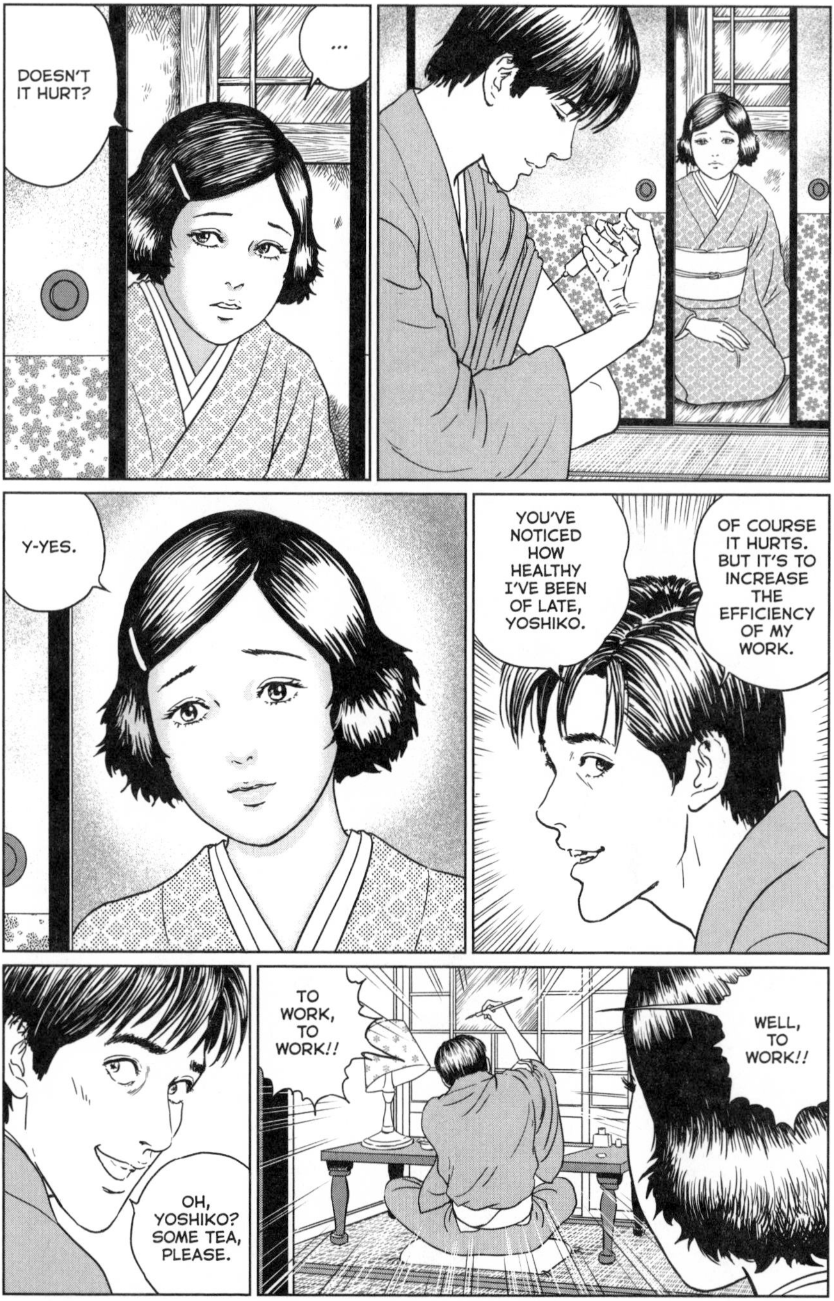
...
DOESN'T IT HURT?
OF COURSE IT HURTS. BUT IT'S TO INCREASE THE EFFICIENCY OF MY WORK.
YOU'VE NOTICED HOW HEALTHY I'VE BEEN OF LATE, YOSHIKO.
Y-YES.
WELL, TO WORK!!
TO WORK, TO WORK!!
OH, YOSHIKO? SOME TEA, PLEASE.

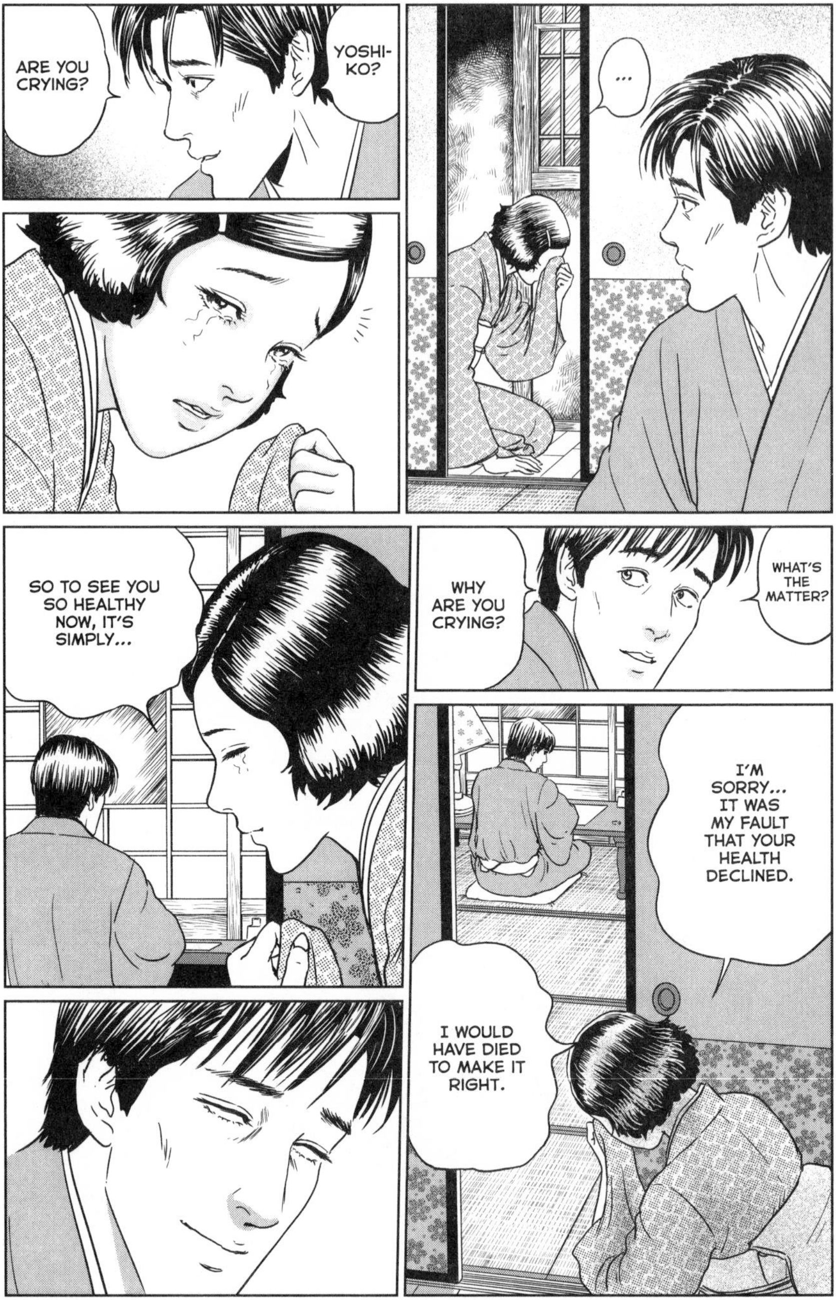
...
YOSHI-KO?
ARE YOU CRYING?
WHAT'S THE MATTER?
WHY ARE YOU CRYING?
I'M SORRY... IT WAS MY FAULT THAT YOUR HEALTH DECLINED.
I WOULD HAVE DIED TO MAKE IT RIGHT.
SO TO SEE YOU SO HEALTHY NOW, IT'S SIMPLY...

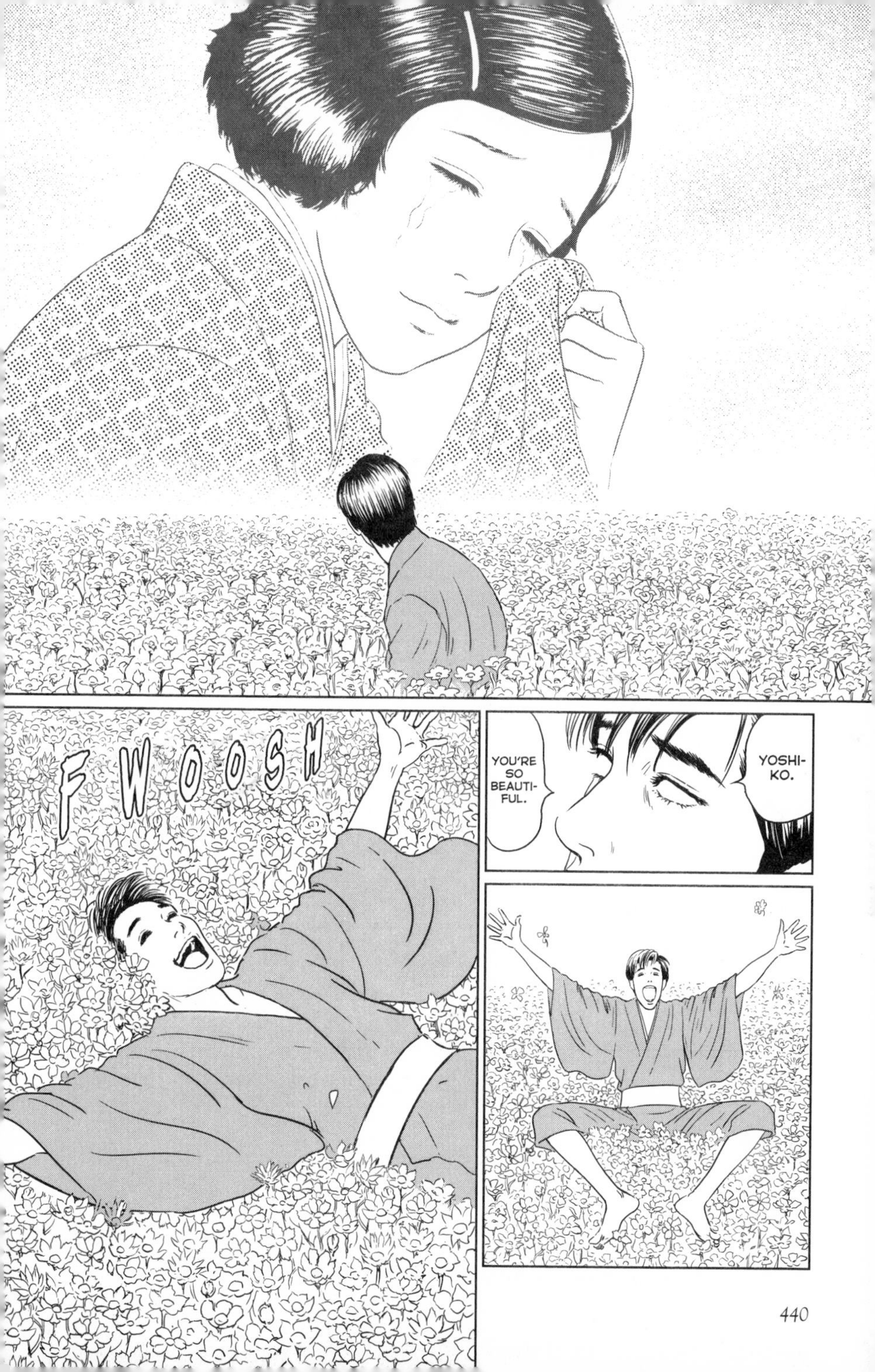
YOSHI-
KO.
YOU'RE
SO
BEAUTI-
FUL.
FWOOSH

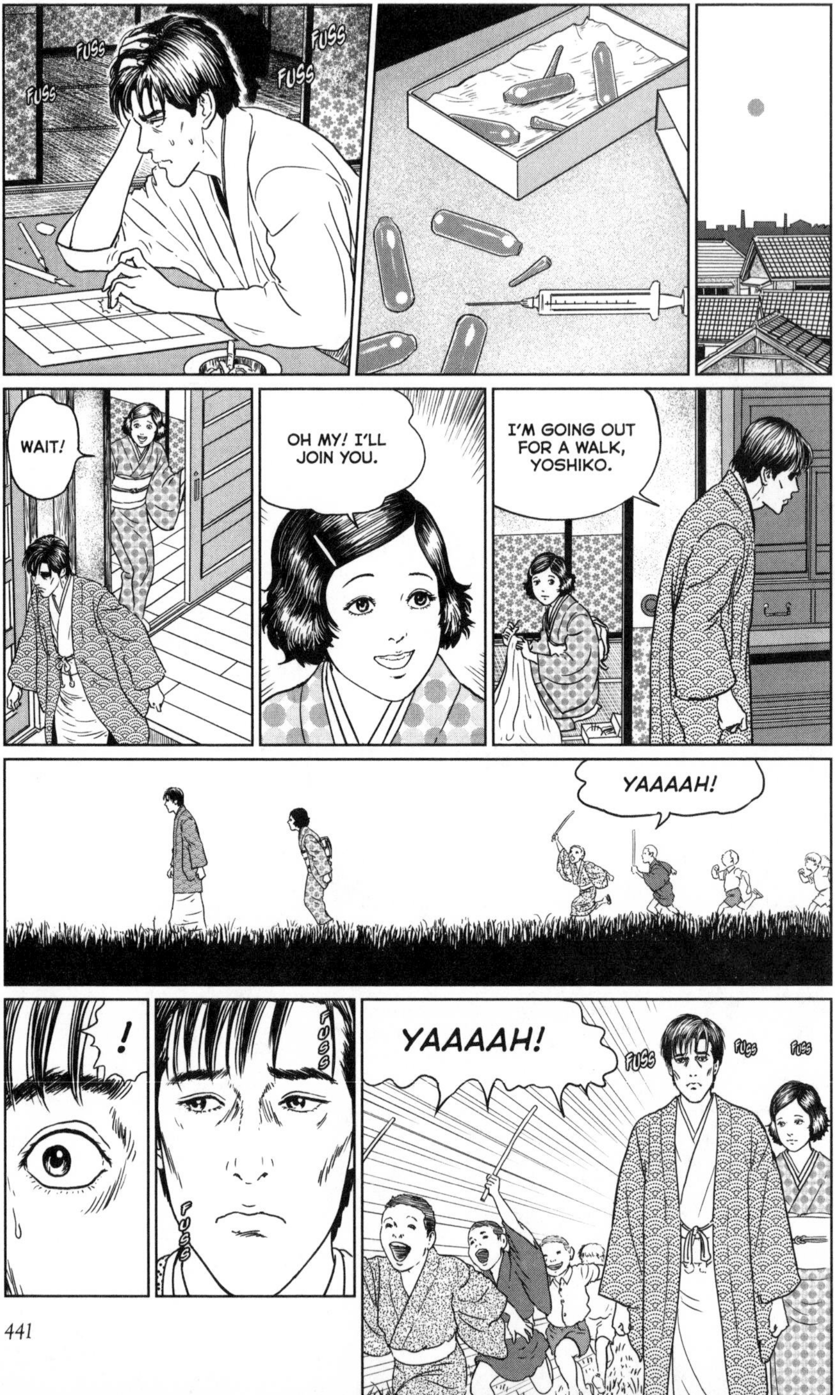
FUSS
FUSS
FUSS
FUSS
I'M GOING OUT FOR A WALK, YOSHIKO.
OH MY! I'LL JOIN YOU.
WAIT!
YAAAAH!
YAAAAH!
FUSS
FUSS
FUSS
FUSS
FUSS
!

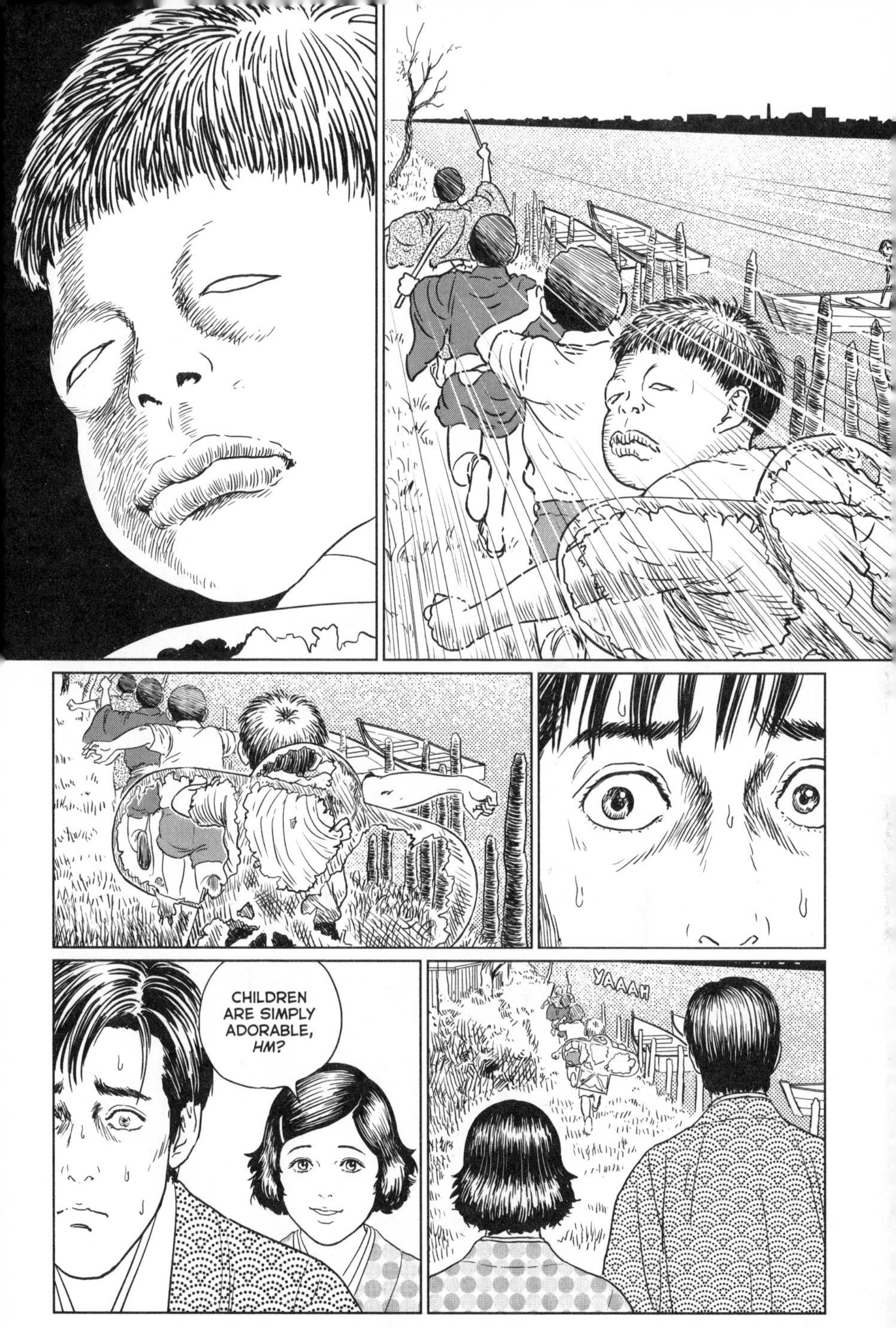
YAAAH
CHILDREN ARE SIMPLY ADORABLE, HM?

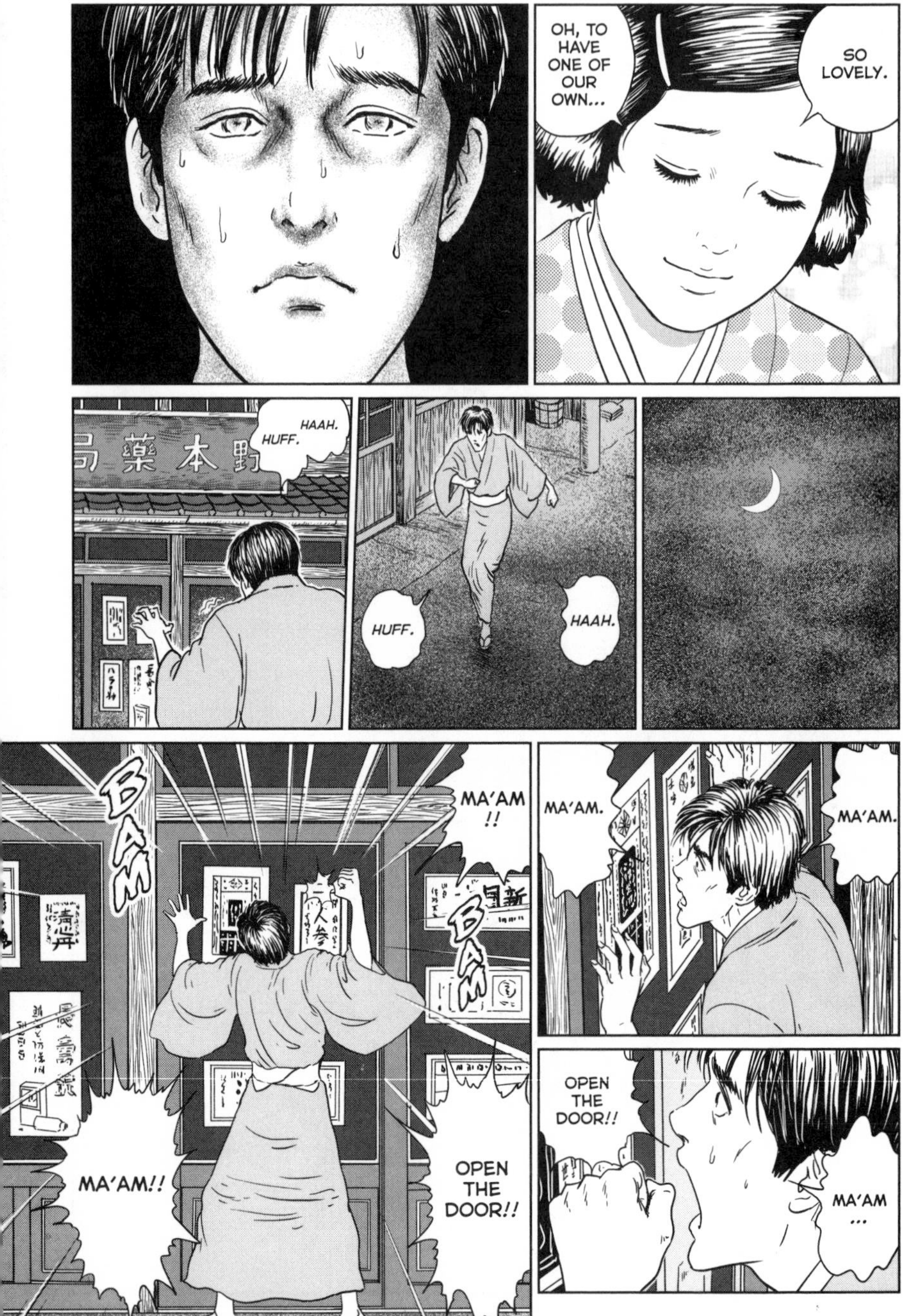
SO LOVELY.
OH, TO HAVE ONE OF OUR OWN...
HAAH.
HUFF.
HAAH.
HUFF.
野本薬局
MA'AM.
MA'AM.
MA'AM ...
OPEN THE DOOR!!
MA'AM !!
BAM
BAM
OPEN THE DOOR!!
MA'AM!!
清心丹
人参

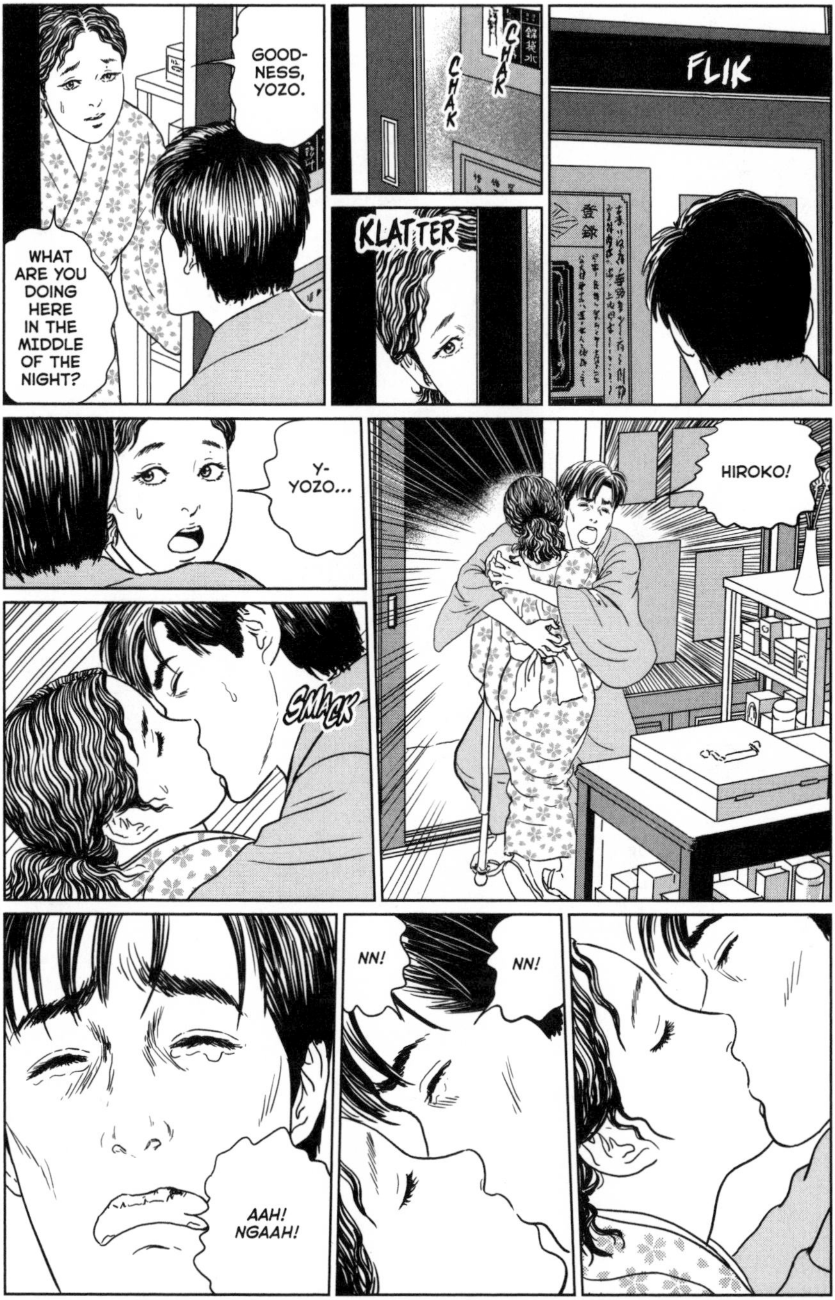
FLIK
CHAK
CHAK
KLATTER
GOODNESS, YOZO.
WHAT ARE YOU DOING HERE IN THE MIDDLE OF THE NIGHT?
HIROKO!
Y-YOZO...
SMACK
NN!
NN!
AAH! NGAAH!

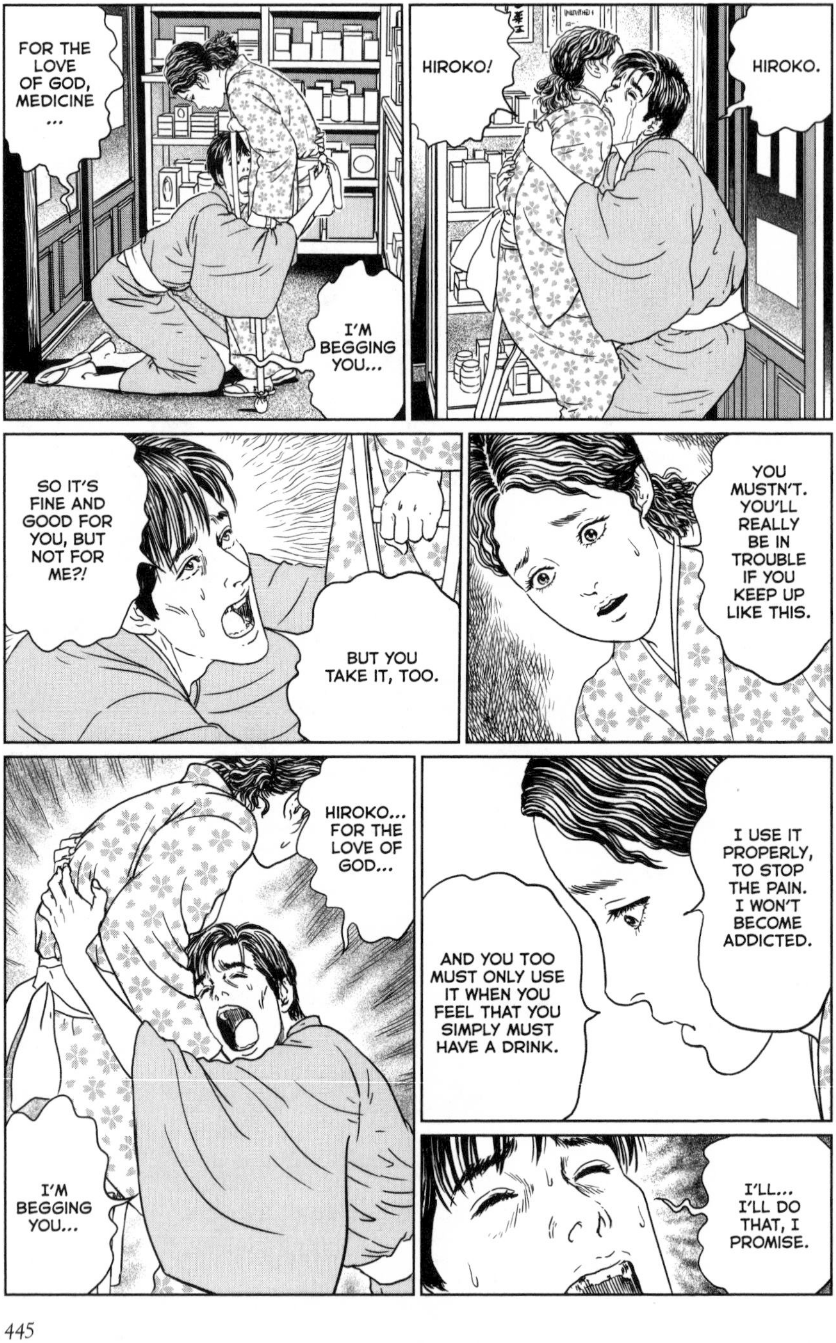
HIROKO.
HIROKO!
FOR THE LOVE OF GOD, MEDICINE ...
I'M BEGGING YOU...
YOU MUSTN'T. YOU'LL REALLY BE IN TROUBLE IF YOU KEEP UP LIKE THIS.
BUT YOU TAKE IT, TOO.
SO IT'S FINE AND GOOD FOR YOU, BUT NOT FOR ME?!
I USE IT PROPERLY, TO STOP THE PAIN. I WON'T BECOME ADDICTED.
AND YOU TOO MUST ONLY USE IT WHEN YOU FEEL THAT YOU SIMPLY MUST HAVE A DRINK.
I'LL... I'LL DO THAT, I PROMISE.
HIROKO... FOR THE LOVE OF GOD...
I'M BEGGING YOU...

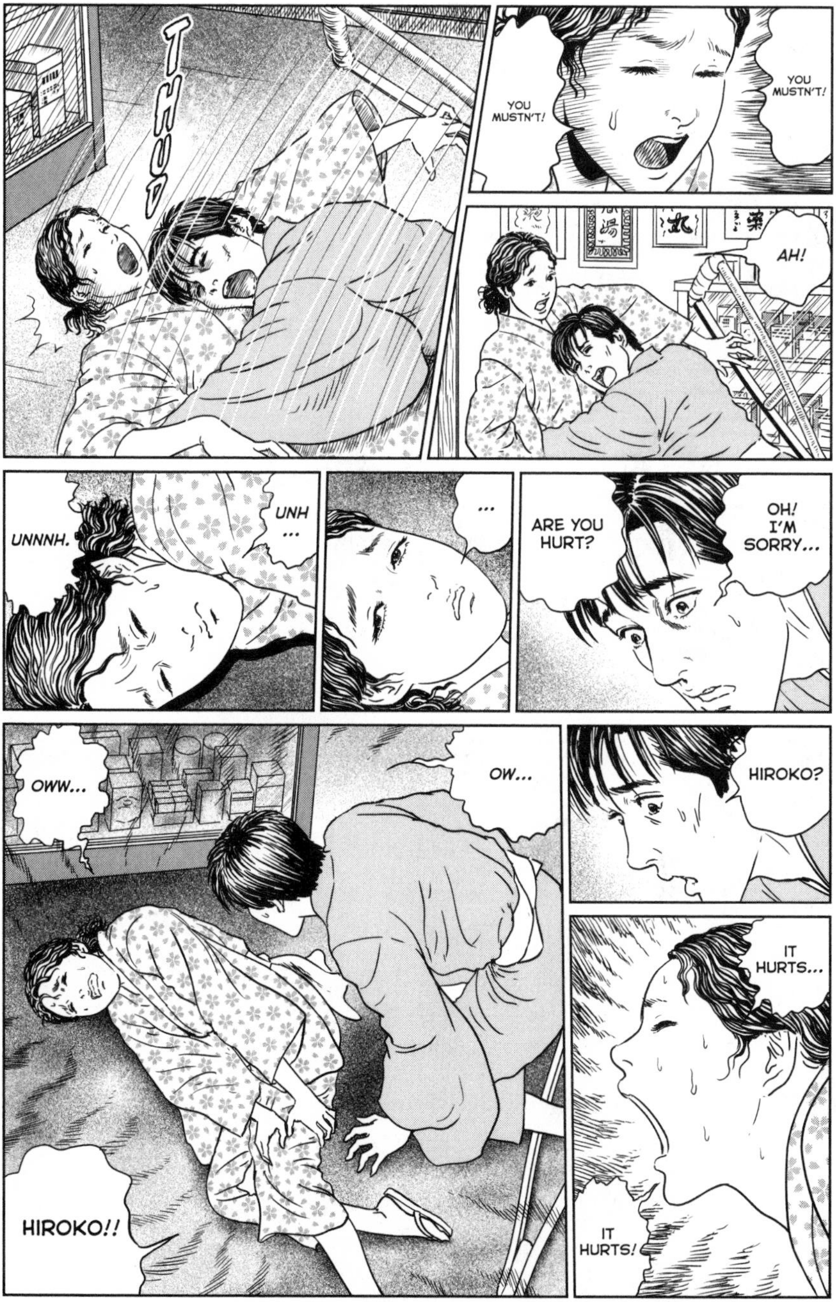
YOU MUSTN'T!
YOU MUSTN'T!
AH!
THUD
OH! I'M SORRY...
ARE YOU HURT?
...
UNH ...
UNNNH.
HIROKO?
IT HURTS...
IT HURTS!
OW...
OWW...
HIROKO!!

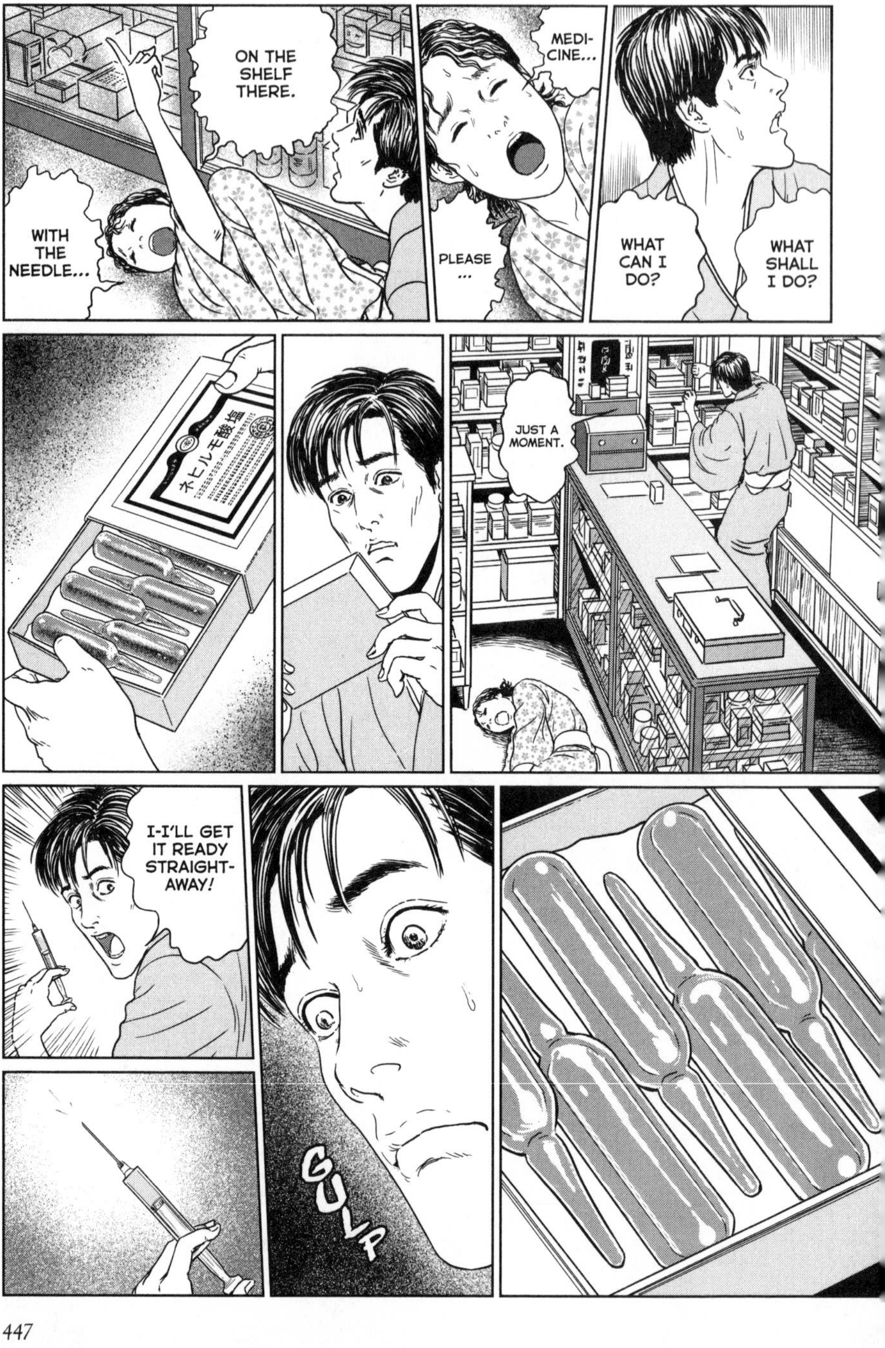
WHAT SHALL I DO?
WHAT CAN I DO?
MEDICINE...
PLEASE ...
ON THE SHELF THERE.
WITH THE NEEDLE...
JUST A MOMENT.
ネヒルモ酸塩
GULP
I-I'LL GET IT READY STRAIGHT-AWAY!

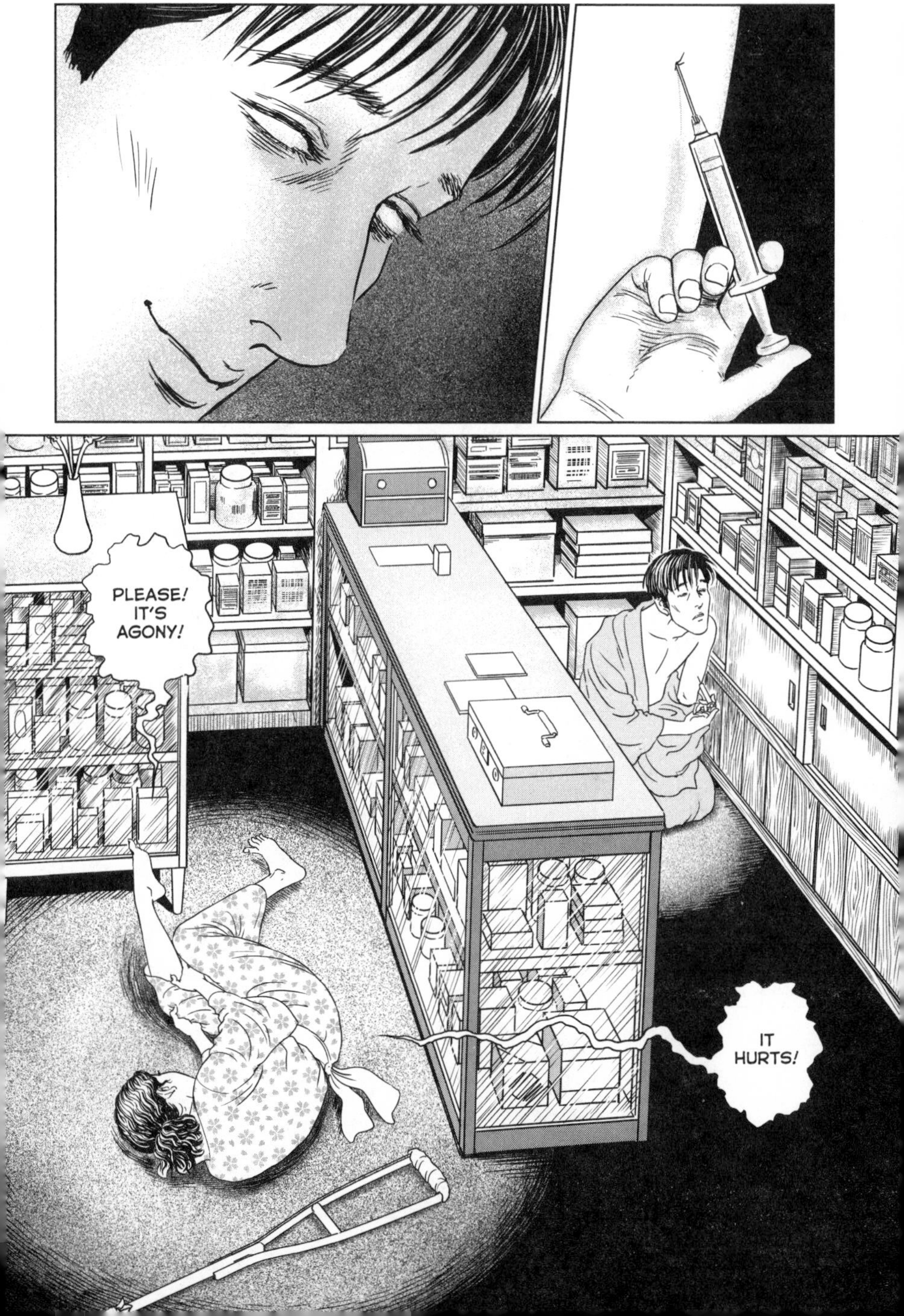
PLEASE! IT'S AGONY!
IT HURTS!

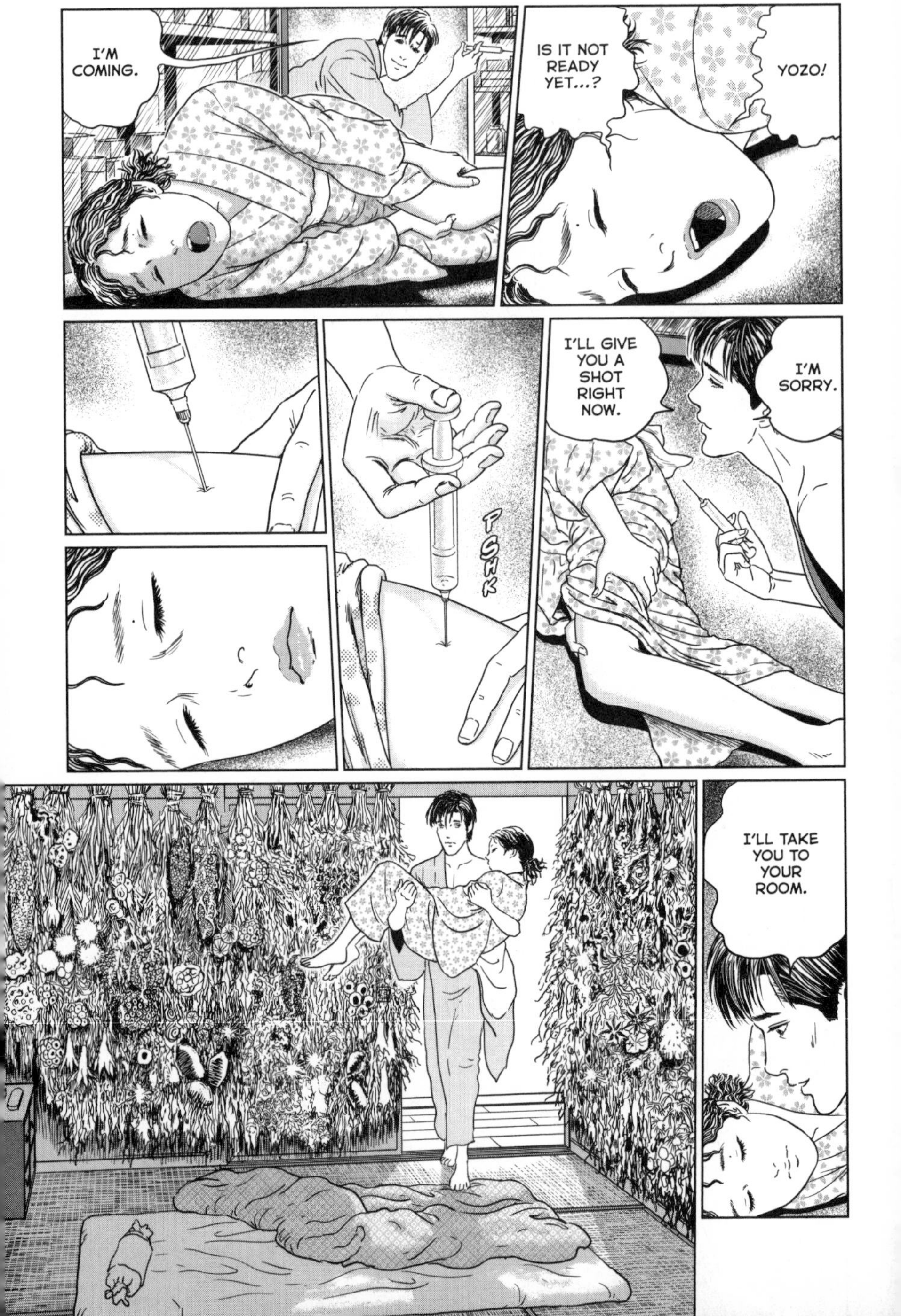
YOZO!
IS IT NOT READY YET...?
I'M COMING.
I'M SORRY.
I'LL GIVE YOU A SHOT RIGHT NOW.
PSHK
I'LL TAKE YOU TO YOUR ROOM.

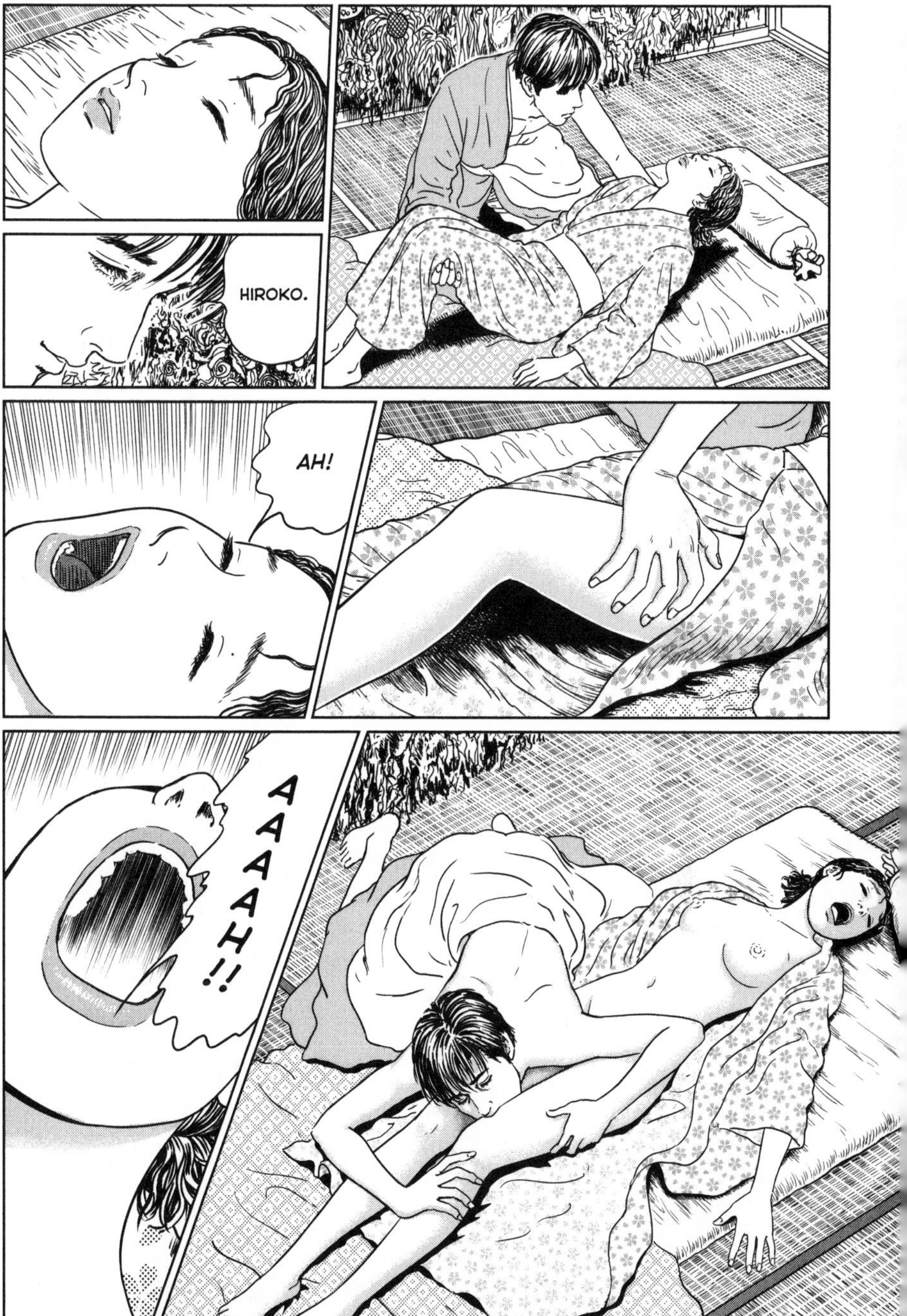
HIROKO.
AH!
AAAAAH!!

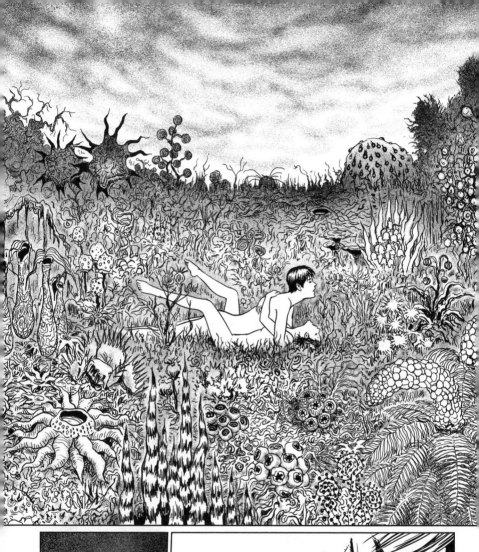

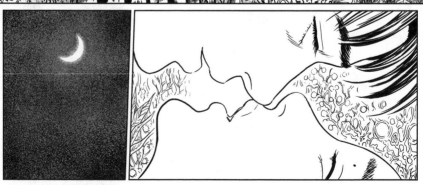

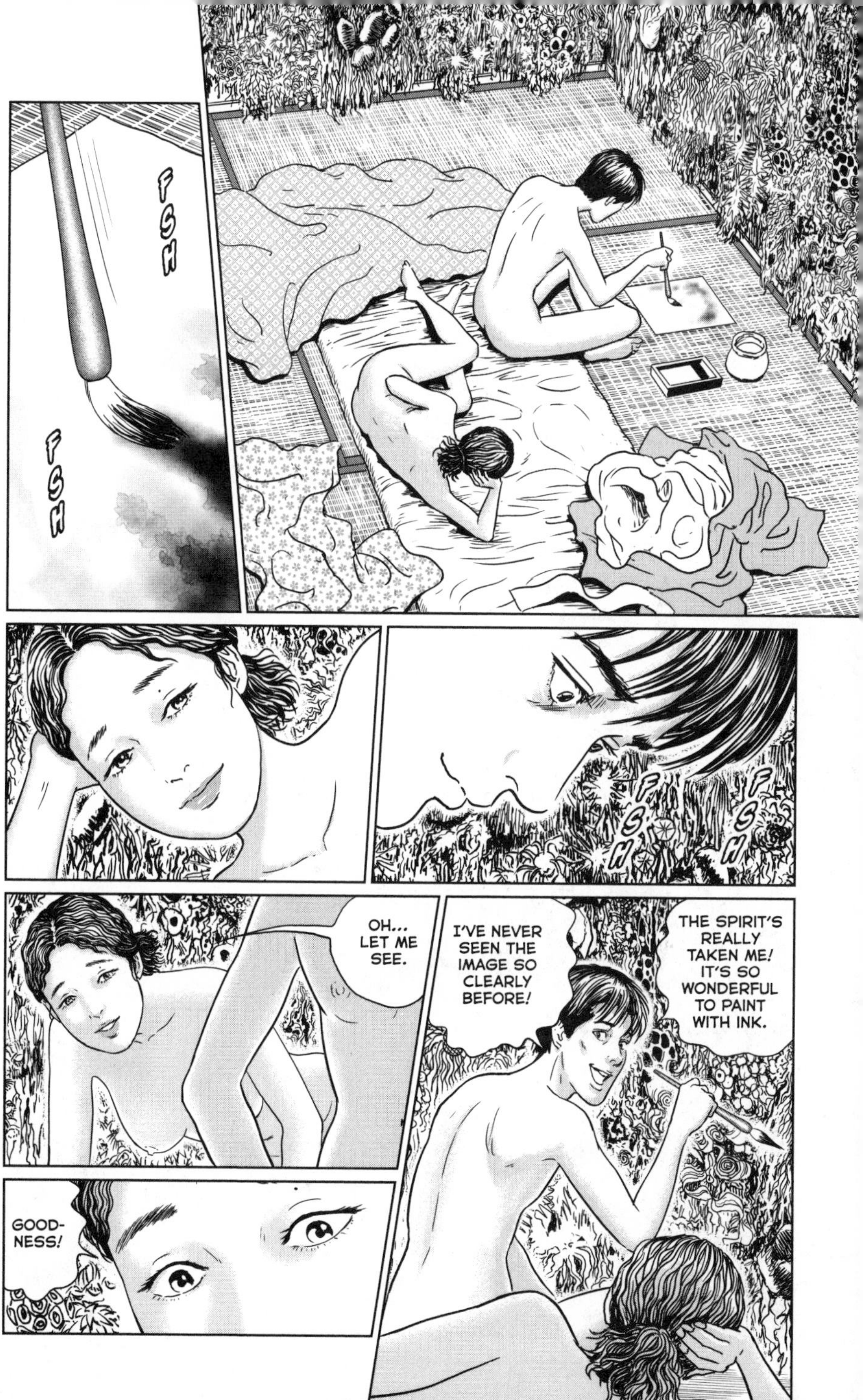
FSH
FSH
FSH
FSH
THE SPIRIT'S REALLY TAKEN ME! IT'S SO WONDERFUL TO PAINT WITH INK.
I'VE NEVER SEEN THE IMAGE SO CLEARLY BEFORE!
OH... LET ME SEE.
GOOD-NESS!

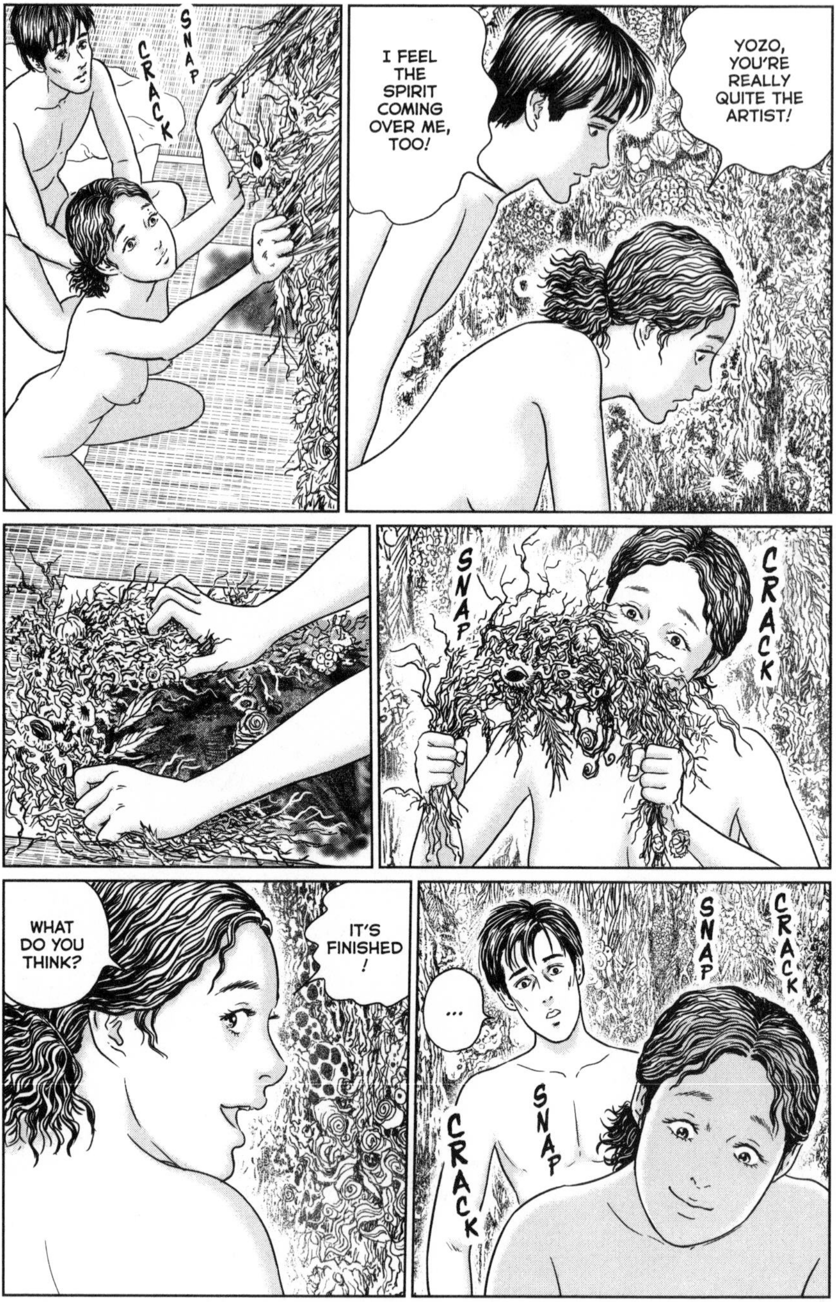
YOZO, YOU'RE REALLY QUITE THE ARTIST!
I FEEL THE SPIRIT COMING OVER ME, TOO!
SNAP
CRACK
CRACK
SNAP
CRACK
SNAP
...
SNAP
CRACK
IT'S FINISHED!
WHAT DO YOU THINK?

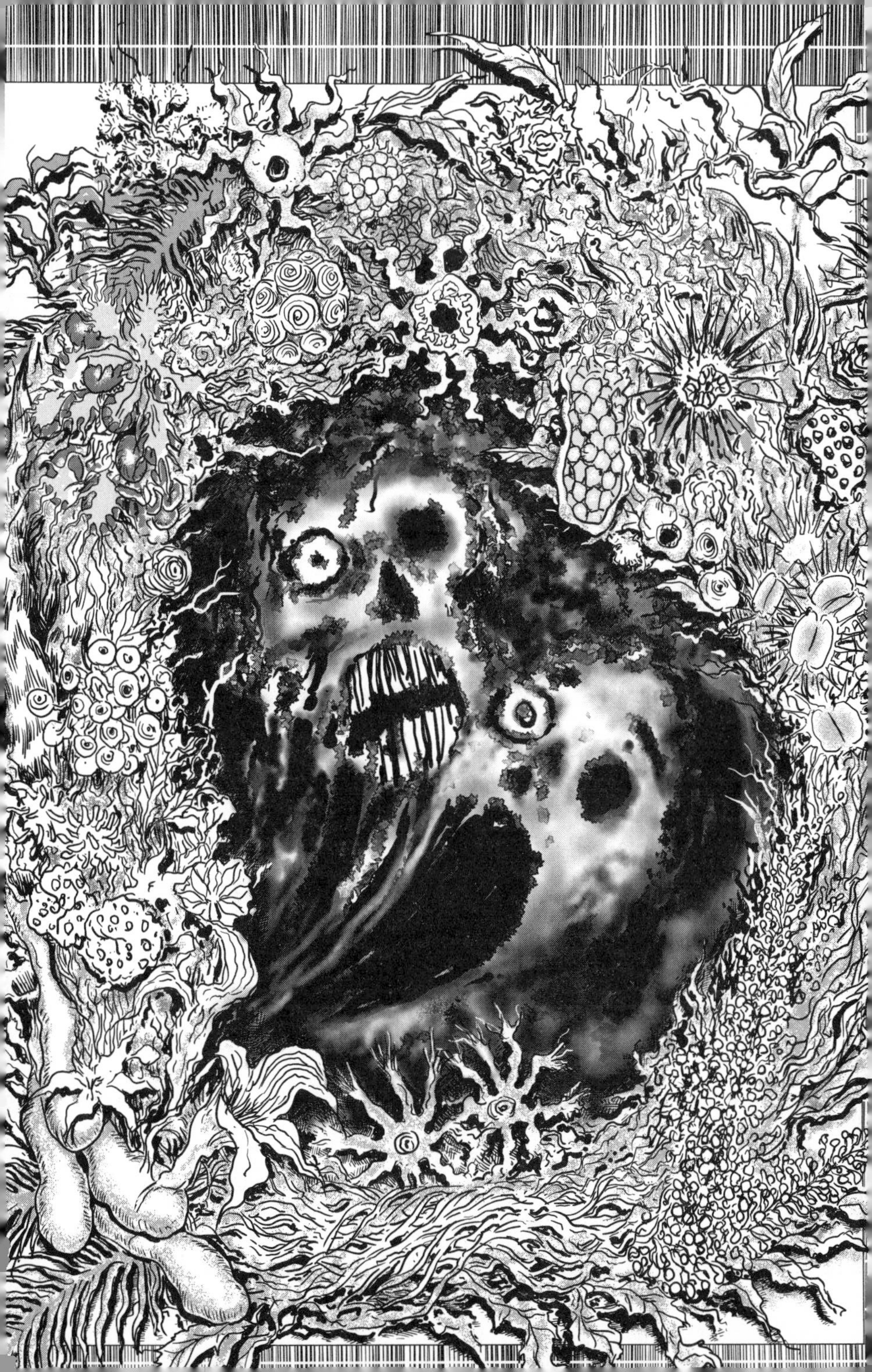

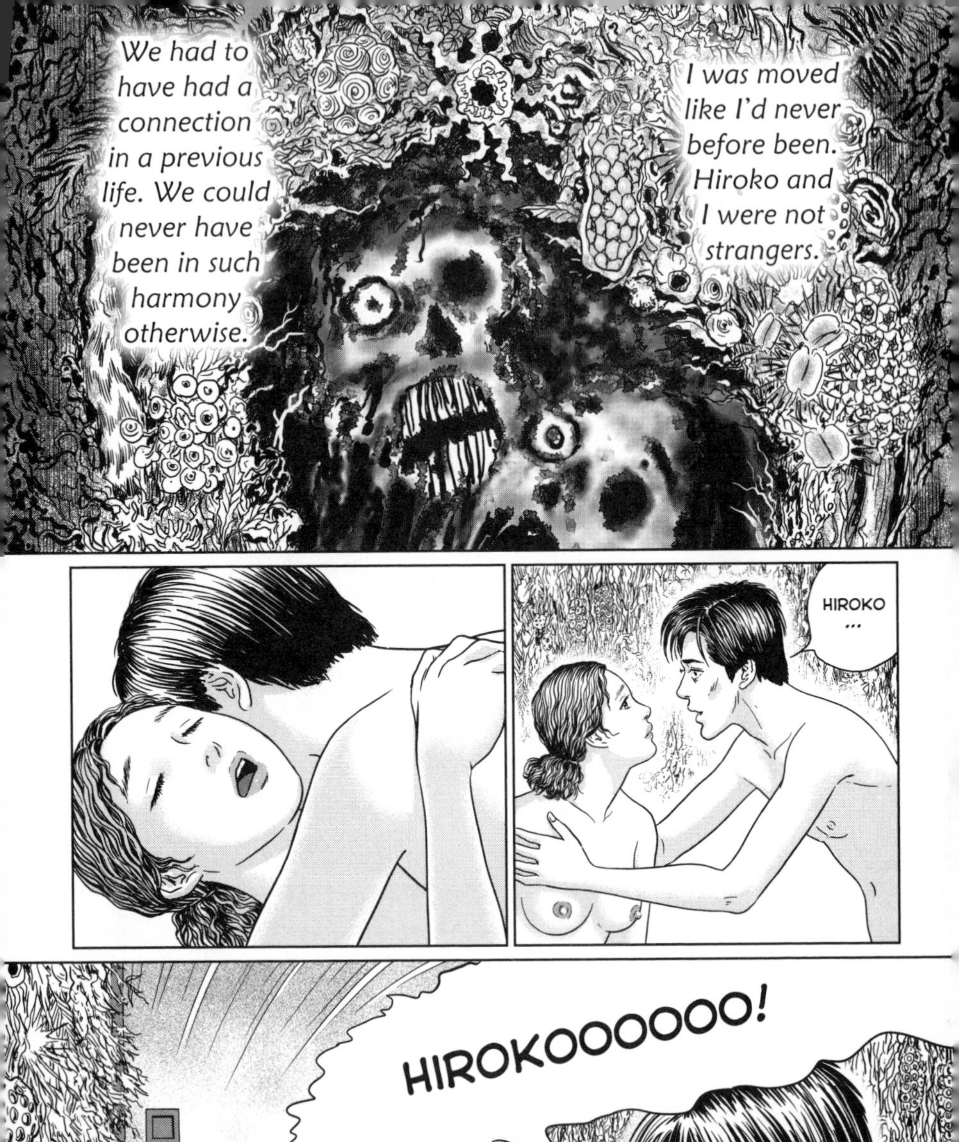
I was moved like I'd never before been. Hiroko and I were not strangers.
We had to have had a connection in a previous life. We could never have been in such harmony otherwise.
HIROKO ...
HIROKOOOOOOO!

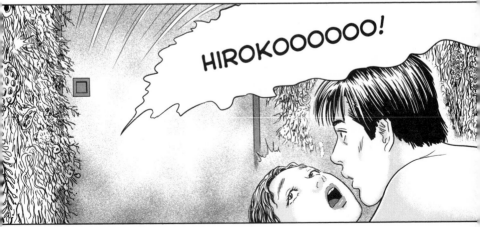

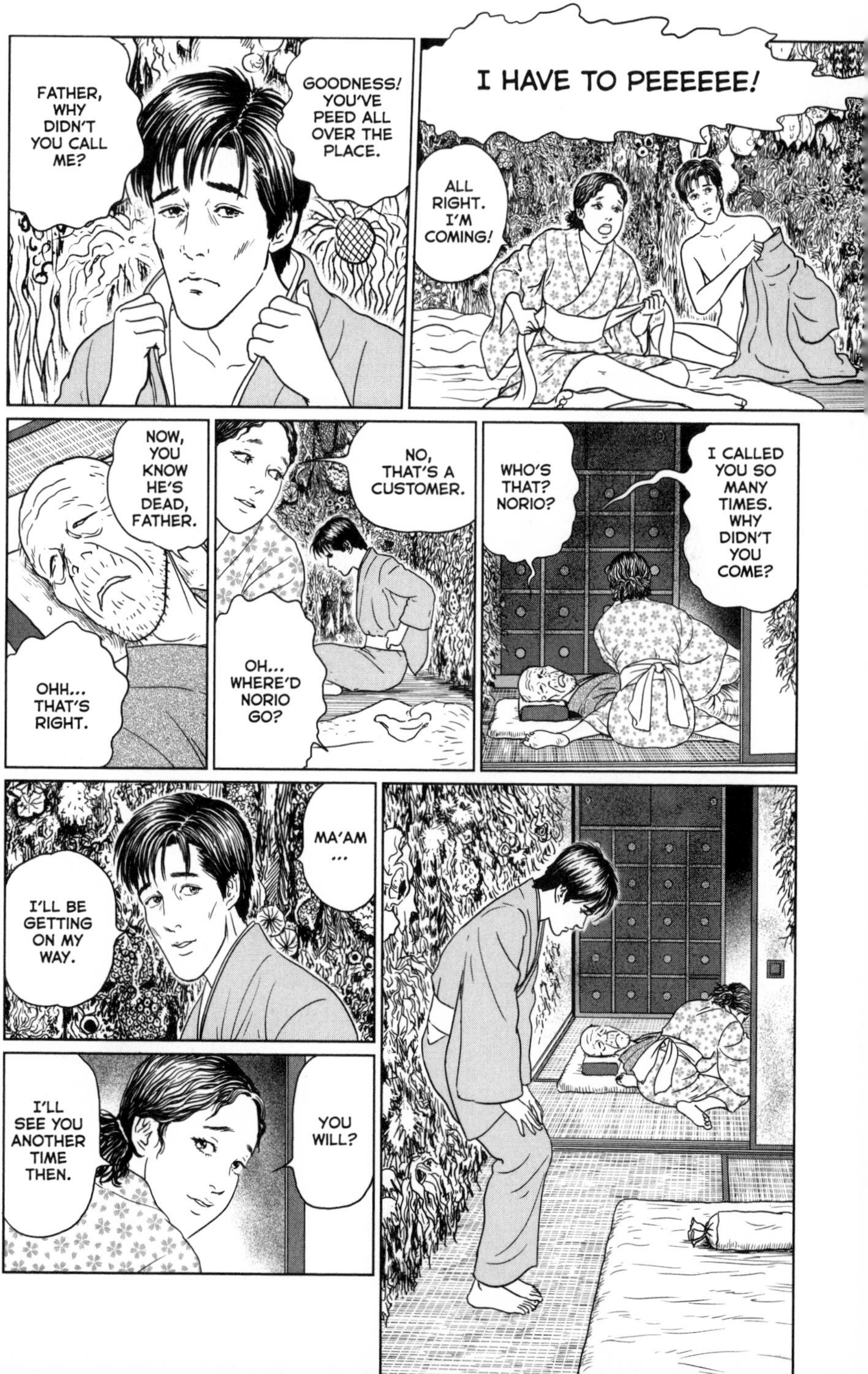
I HAVE TO PEEEEEE!
ALL RIGHT. I'M COMING!
GOODNESS! YOU'VE PEED ALL OVER THE PLACE.
FATHER, WHY DIDN'T YOU CALL ME?
I CALLED YOU SO MANY TIMES. WHY DIDN'T YOU COME?
WHO'S THAT? NORIO?
NO, THAT'S A CUSTOMER.
OH... WHERE'D NORIO GO?
NOW, YOU KNOW HE'S DEAD, FATHER.
OHH... THAT'S RIGHT.
MA'AM ...
I'LL BE GETTING ON MY WAY.
YOU WILL?
I'LL SEE YOU ANOTHER TIME THEN.

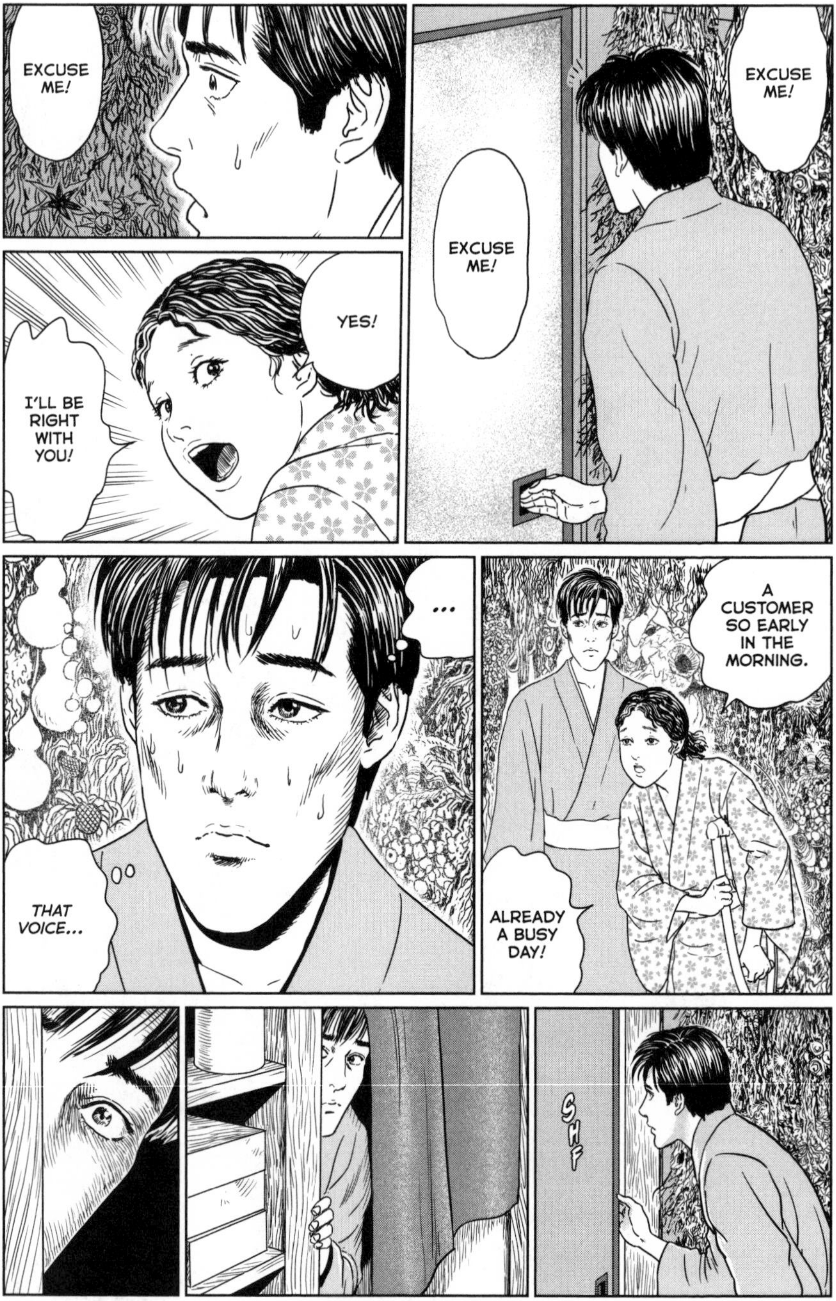
EXCUSE ME!
EXCUSE ME!
EXCUSE ME!
YES!
I'LL BE RIGHT WITH YOU!
A CUSTOMER SO EARLY IN THE MORNING.
ALREADY A BUSY DAY!
...
THAT VOICE...
SHF

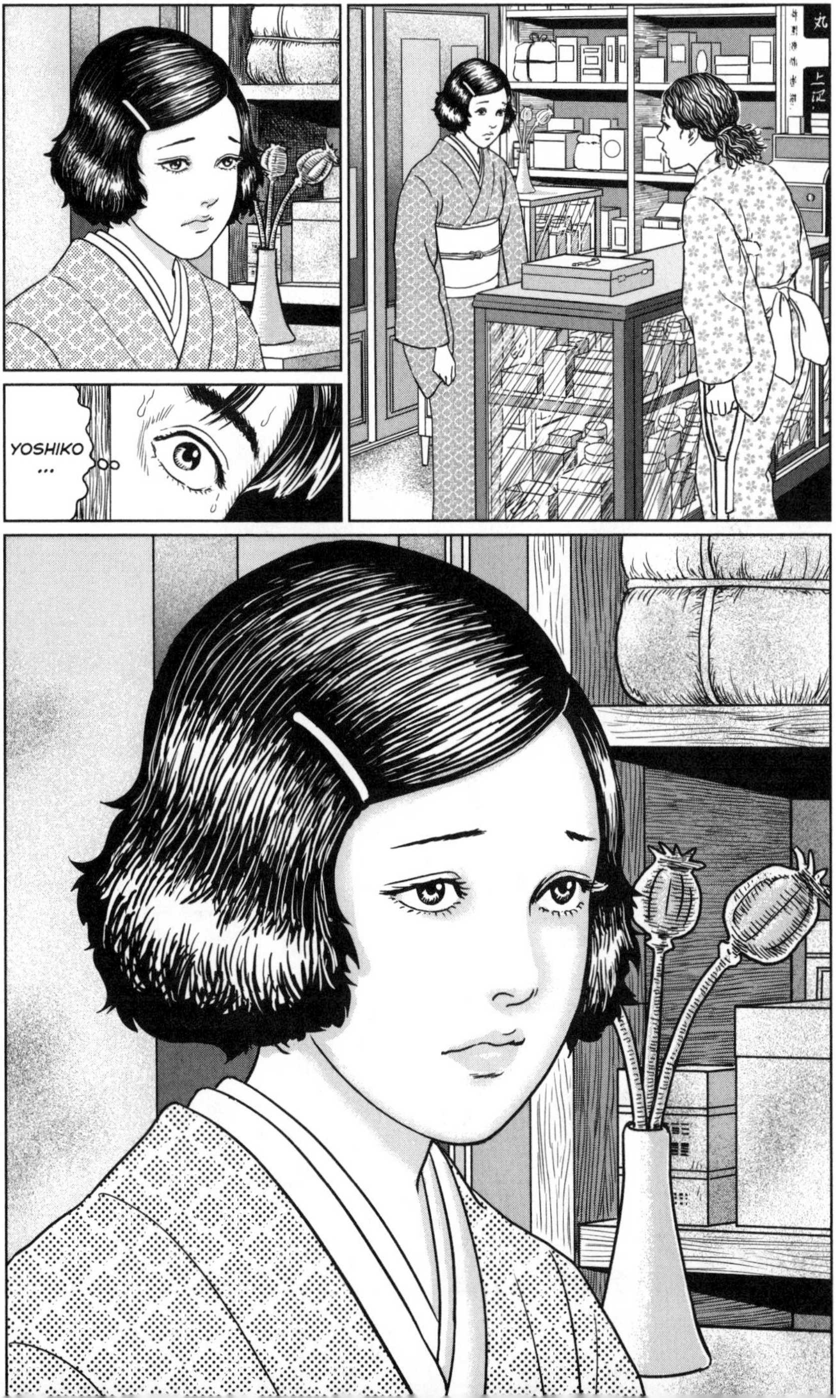
YOSHIKO ...

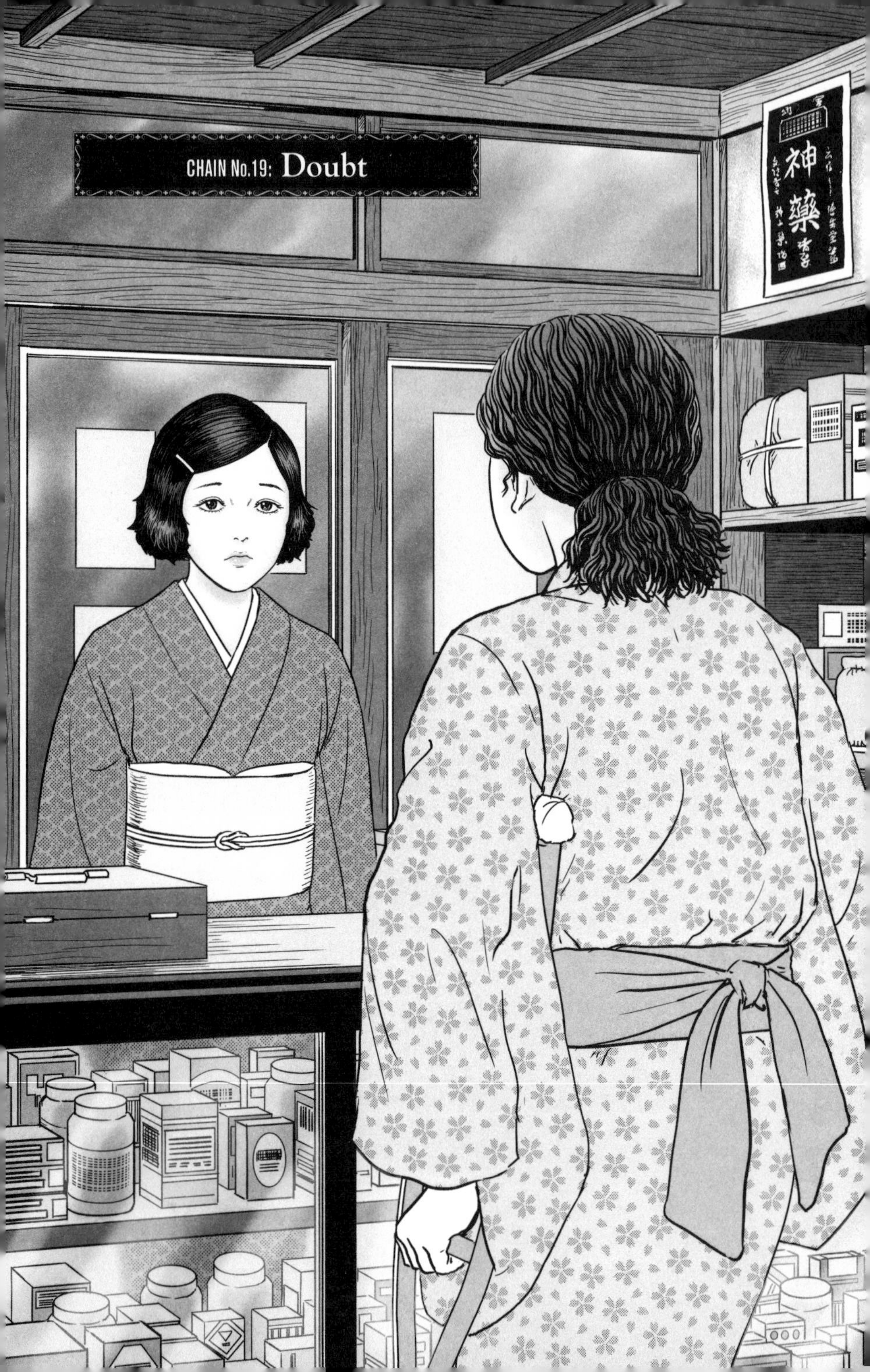
CHAIN No.19: Doubt
神藥

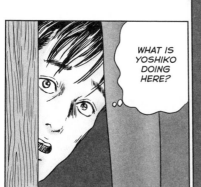

WHAT IS YOSHIKO DOING HERE?

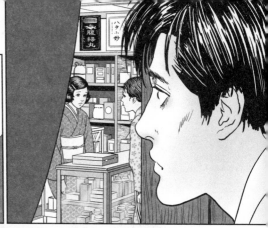

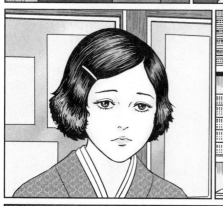

HOW CAN I HELP YOU, MA'AM?

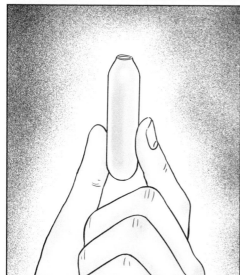

I'D LIKE TO BUY THIS MEDICINE.

UM...

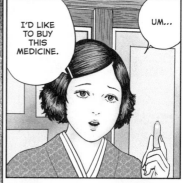

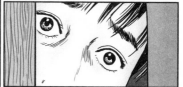

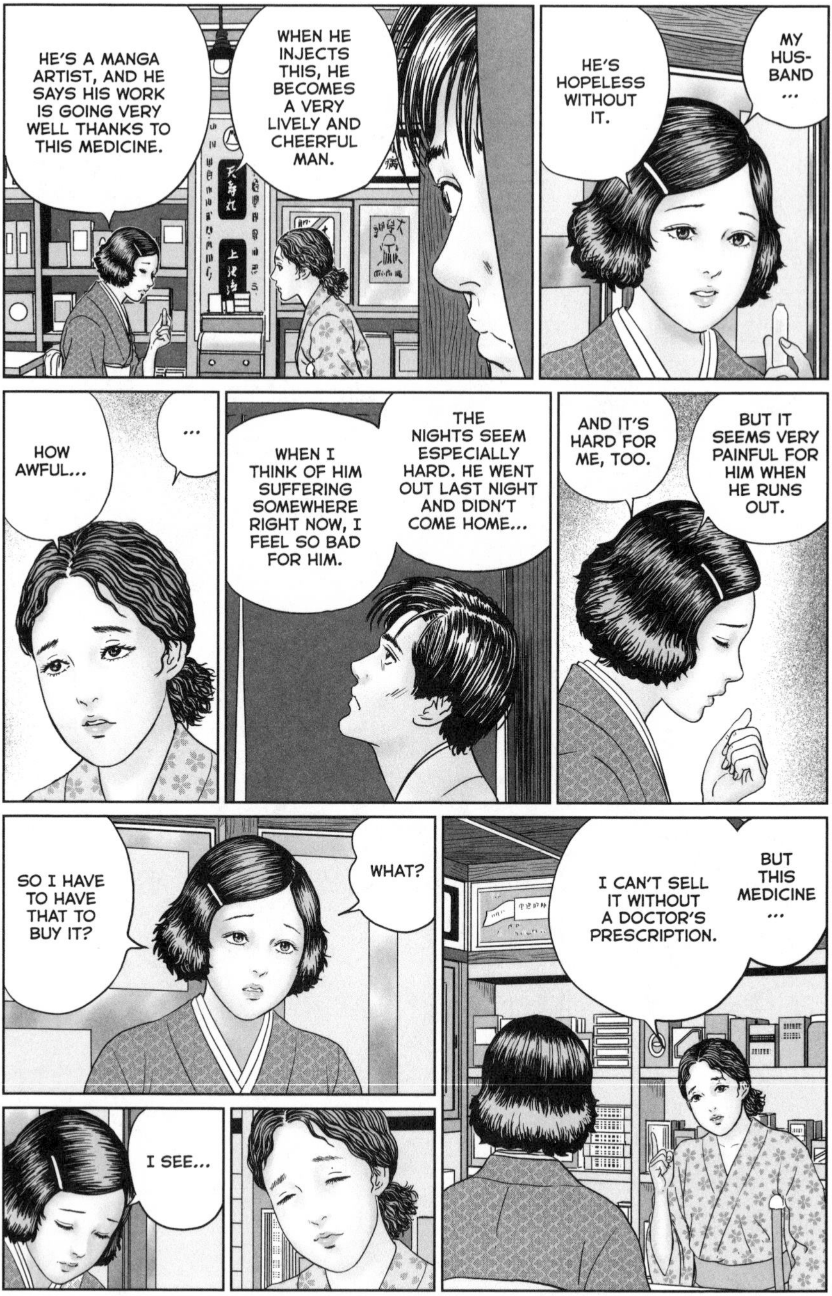
MY HUS-BAND ...
HE'S HOPELESS WITHOUT IT.
WHEN HE INJECTS THIS, HE BECOMES A VERY LIVELY AND CHEERFUL MAN.
HE'S A MANGA ARTIST, AND HE SAYS HIS WORK IS GOING VERY WELL THANKS TO THIS MEDICINE.
BUT IT SEEMS VERY PAINFUL FOR HIM WHEN HE RUNS OUT.
AND IT'S HARD FOR ME, TOO.
THE NIGHTS SEEM ESPECIALLY HARD. HE WENT OUT LAST NIGHT AND DIDN'T COME HOME...
WHEN I THINK OF HIM SUFFERING SOMEWHERE RIGHT NOW, I FEEL SO BAD FOR HIM.
...
HOW AWFUL...
BUT THIS MEDICINE ...
I CAN'T SELL IT WITHOUT A DOCTOR'S PRESCRIPTION.
WHAT?
SO I HAVE TO HAVE THAT TO BUY IT?
I SEE...

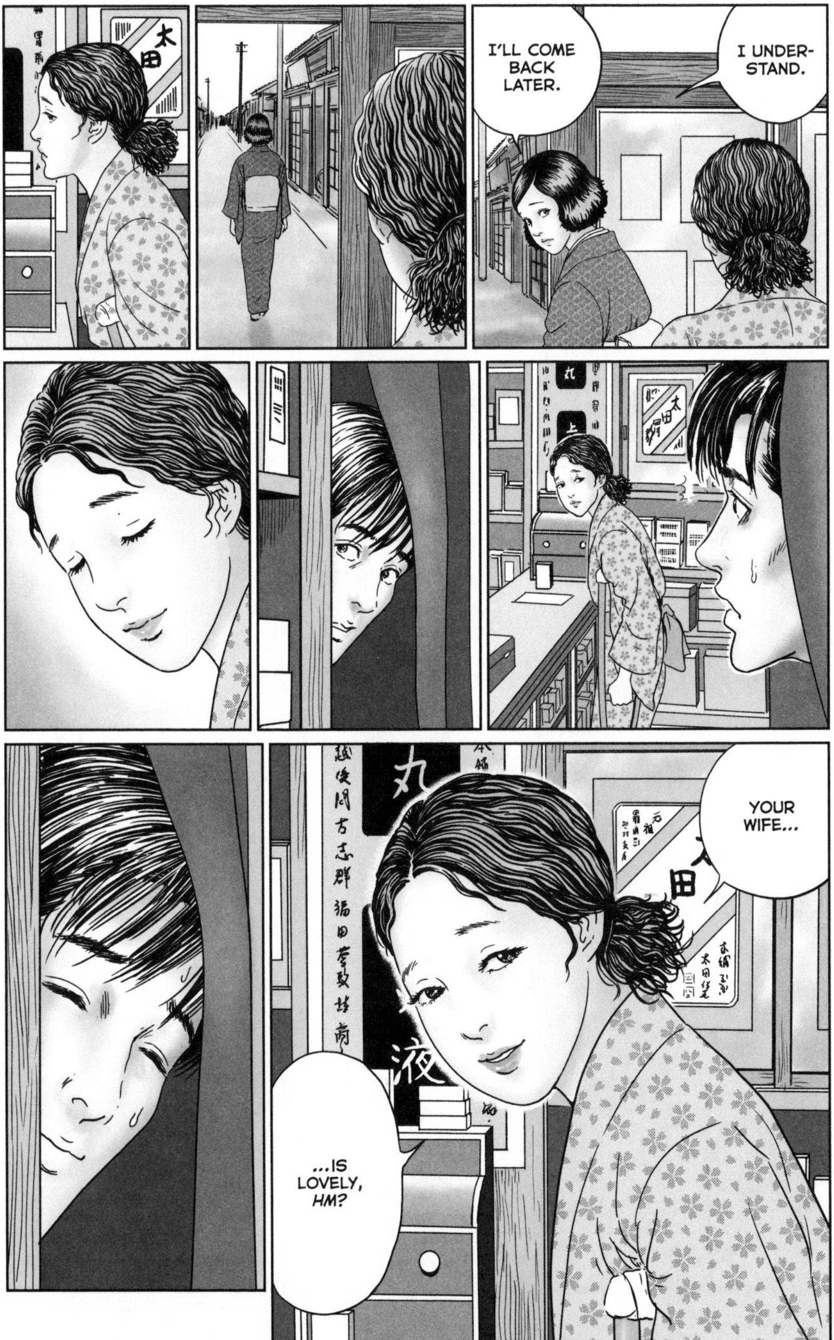
I UNDER-STAND.
I'LL COME BACK LATER.
YOUR WIFE...
...IS LOVELY, HM?

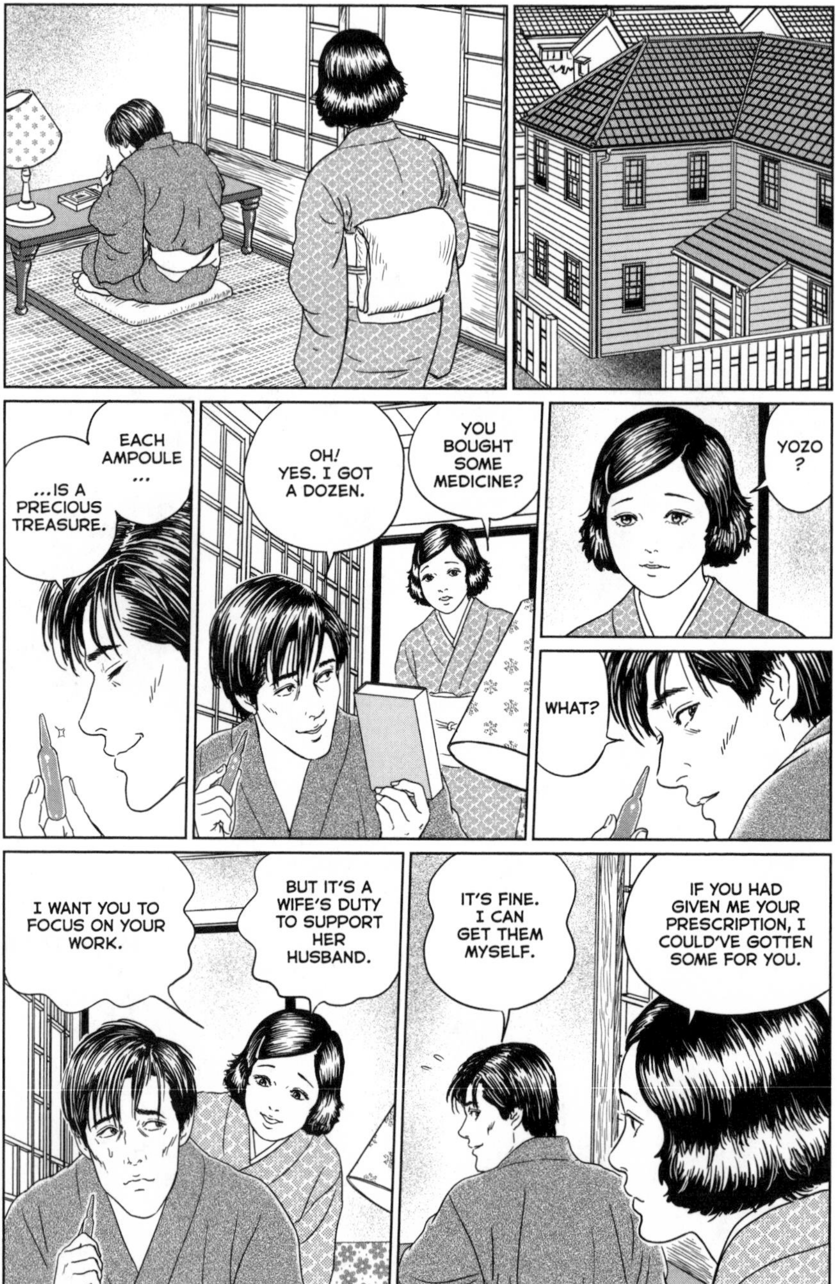
YOZO?
WHAT?
YOU BOUGHT SOME MEDICINE?
OH! YES. I GOT A DOZEN.
EACH AMPOULE ...
...IS A PRECIOUS TREASURE.
IF YOU HAD GIVEN ME YOUR PRESCRIPTION, I COULD'VE GOTTEN SOME FOR YOU.
IT'S FINE. I CAN GET THEM MYSELF.
BUT IT'S A WIFE'S DUTY TO SUPPORT HER HUSBAND.
I WANT YOU TO FOCUS ON YOUR WORK.

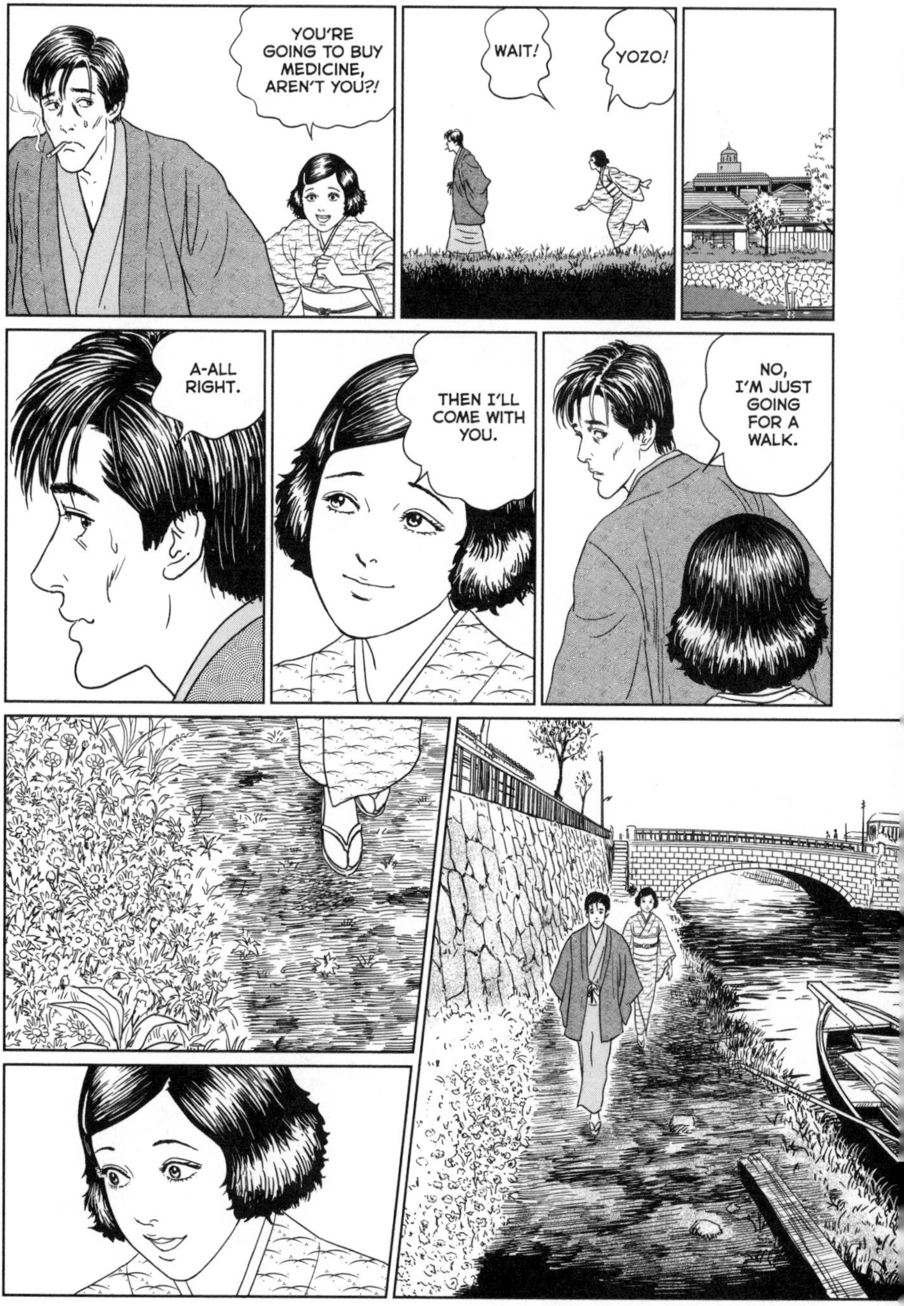
YOZO!
WAIT!
YOU'RE GOING TO BUY MEDICINE, AREN'T YOU?!
NO, I'M JUST GOING FOR A WALK.
THEN I'LL COME WITH YOU.
A-ALL RIGHT.

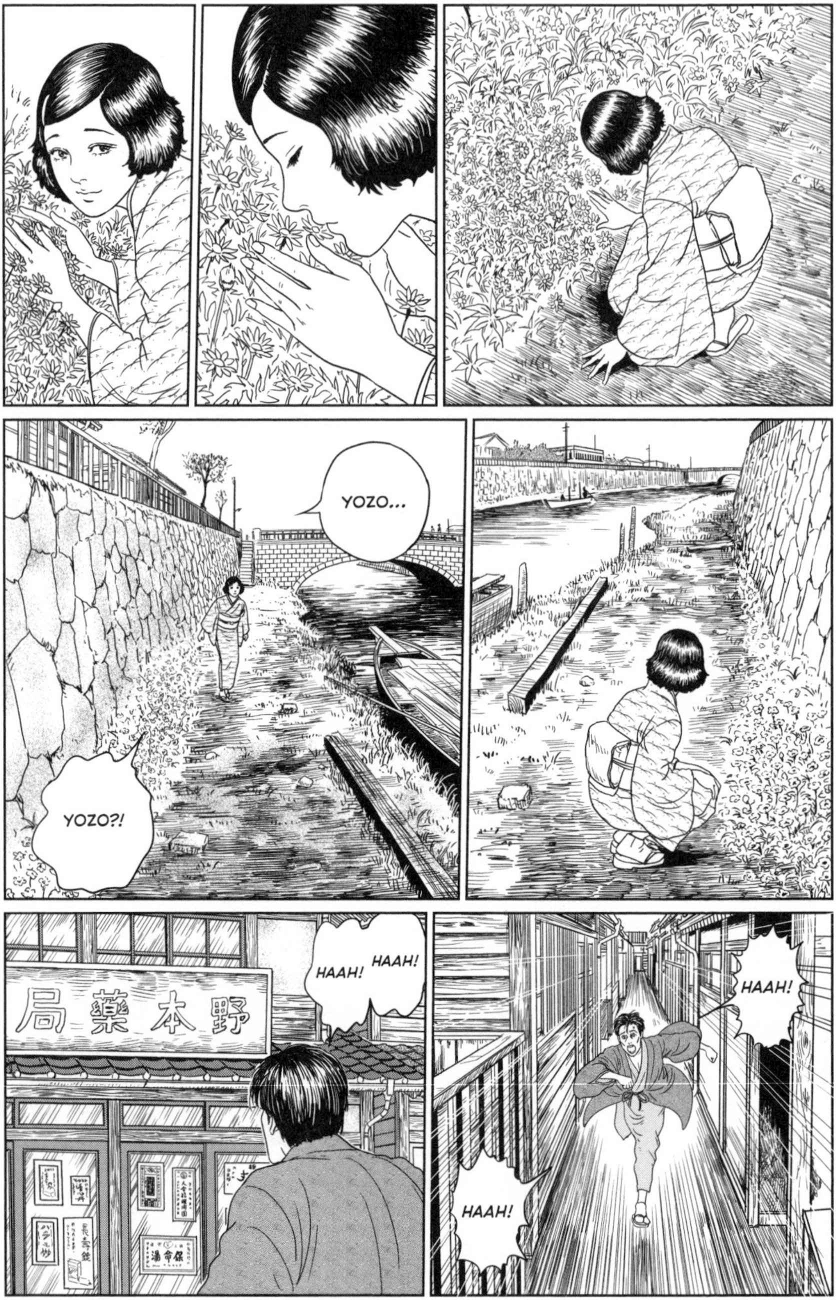
YOZO...
YOZO?!
HAAH!
HAAH!
野本薬局
HAAH!
HAAH!

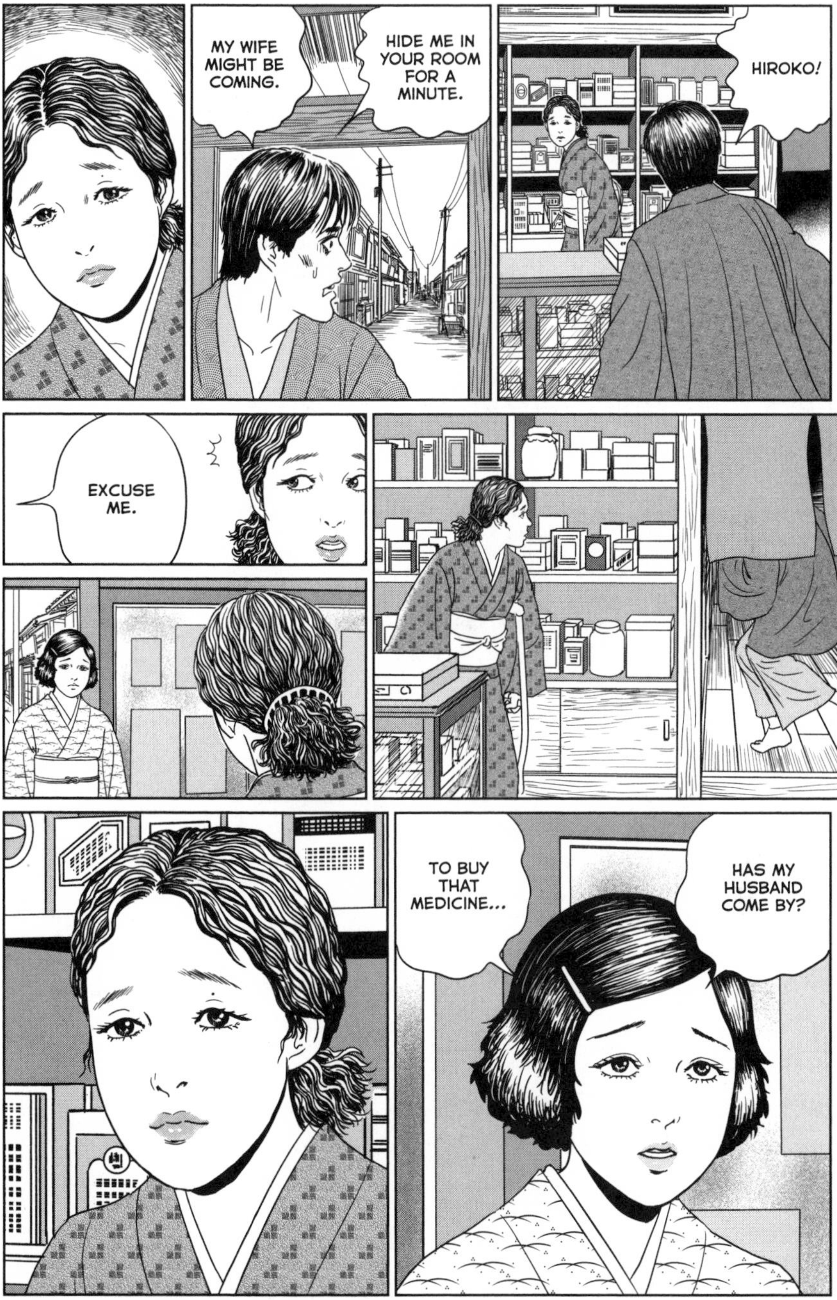
HIROKO!
HIDE ME IN YOUR ROOM FOR A MINUTE.
MY WIFE MIGHT BE COMING.
EXCUSE ME.
HAS MY HUSBAND COME BY?
TO BUY THAT MEDICINE...

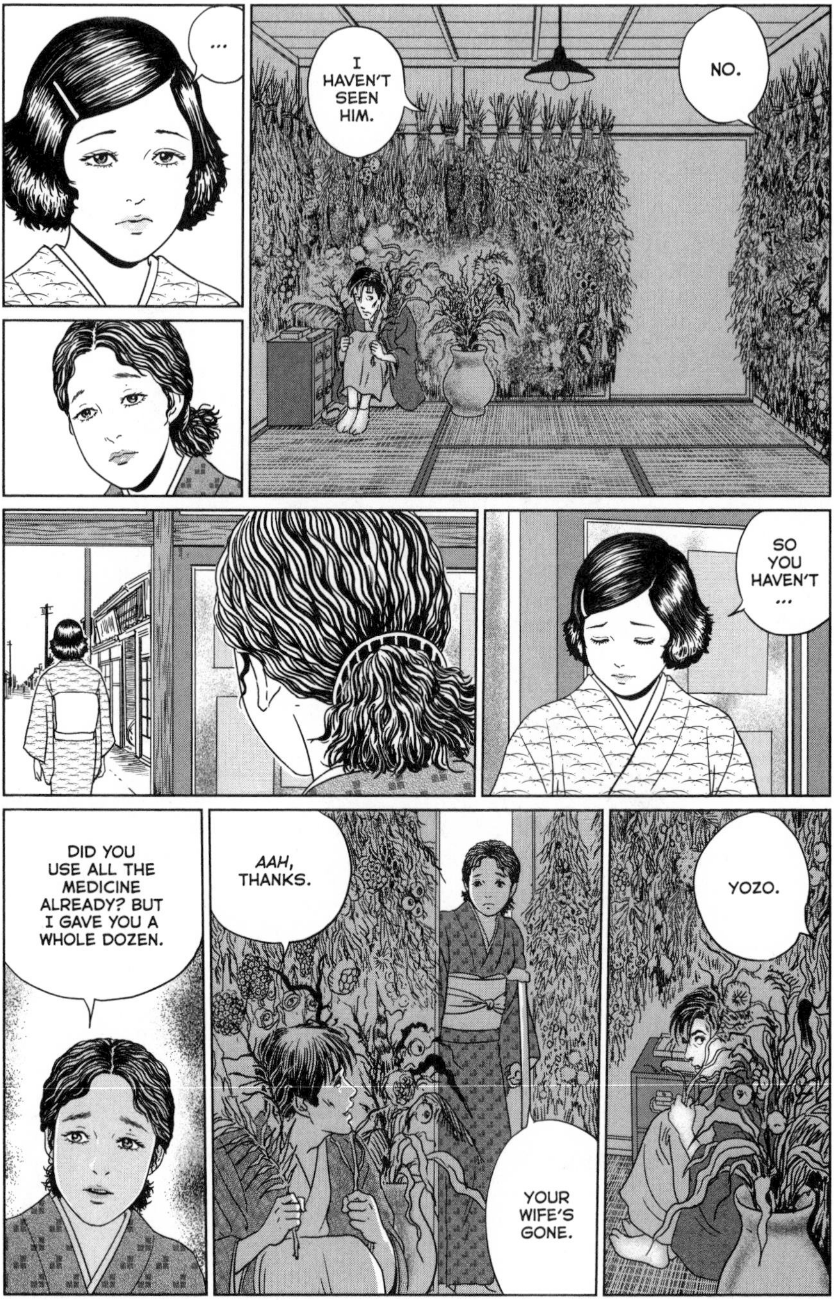
NO.
I HAVEN'T SEEN HIM.
...
SO YOU HAVEN'T ...
YOZO.
AAH, THANKS.
YOUR WIFE'S GONE.
DID YOU USE ALL THE MEDICINE ALREADY? BUT I GAVE YOU A WHOLE DOZEN.

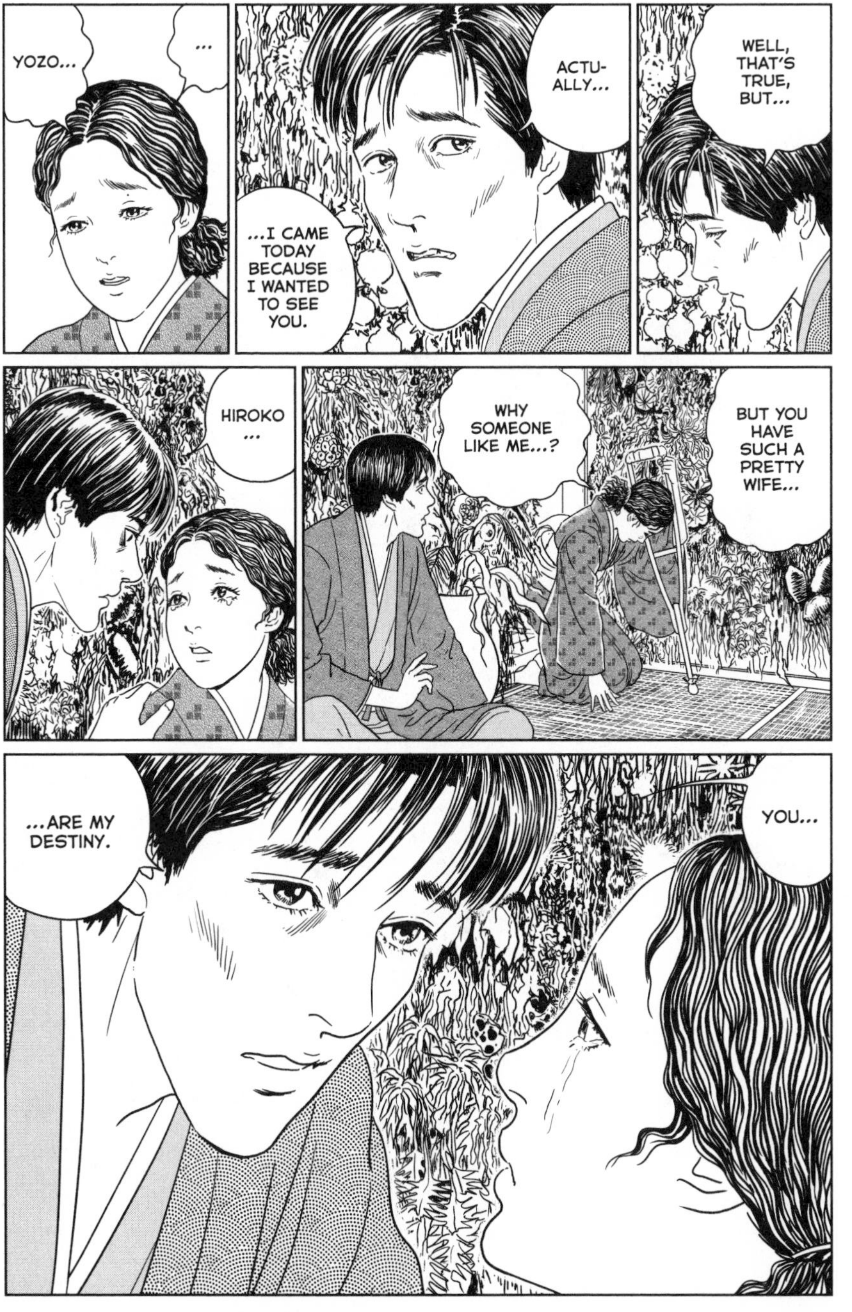
WELL, THAT'S TRUE, BUT...
ACTU-ALLY...
...I CAME TODAY BECAUSE I WANTED TO SEE YOU.
...
YOZO...
BUT YOU HAVE SUCH A PRETTY WIFE...
WHY SOMEONE LIKE ME...?
HIROKO ...
YOU...
...ARE MY DESTINY.

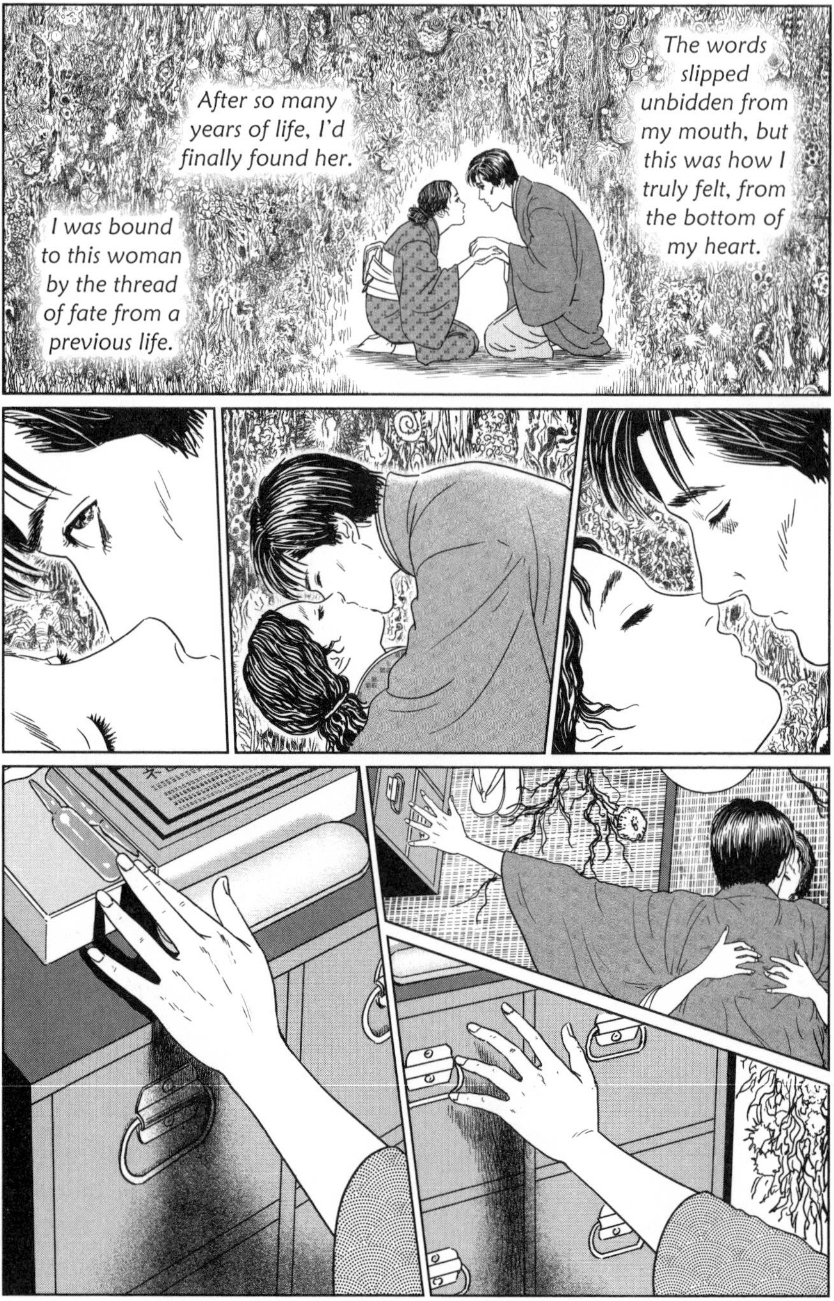
The words slipped unbidden from my mouth, but this was how I truly felt, from the bottom of my heart.
After so many years of life, I'd finally found her.
I was bound to this woman by the thread of fate from a previous life.

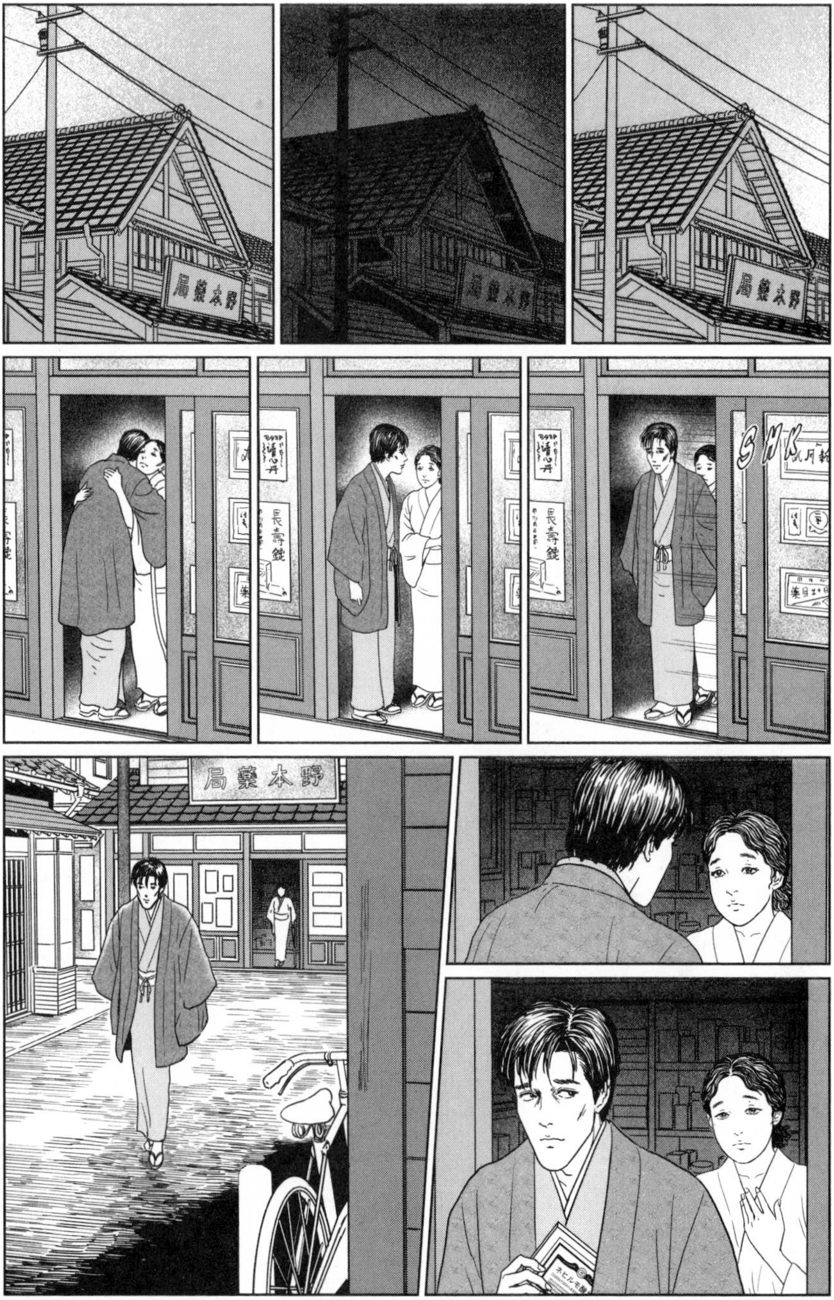
野本薬局
野本薬局
野本薬局
SHK
清心丹
長寿錠
清心丹
長寿錠
野本薬局

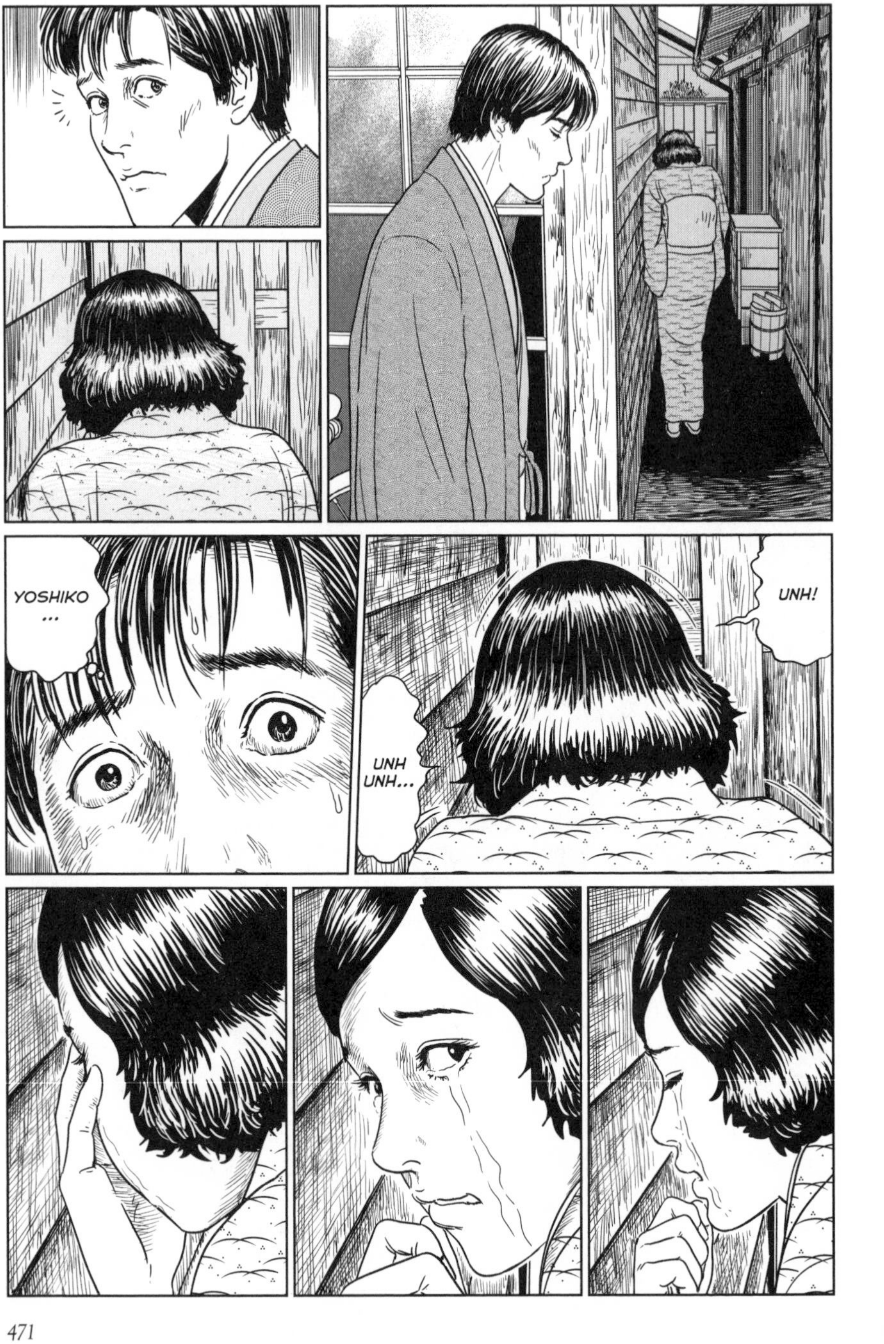
UNH!
UNH UNH...
YOSHIKO ...

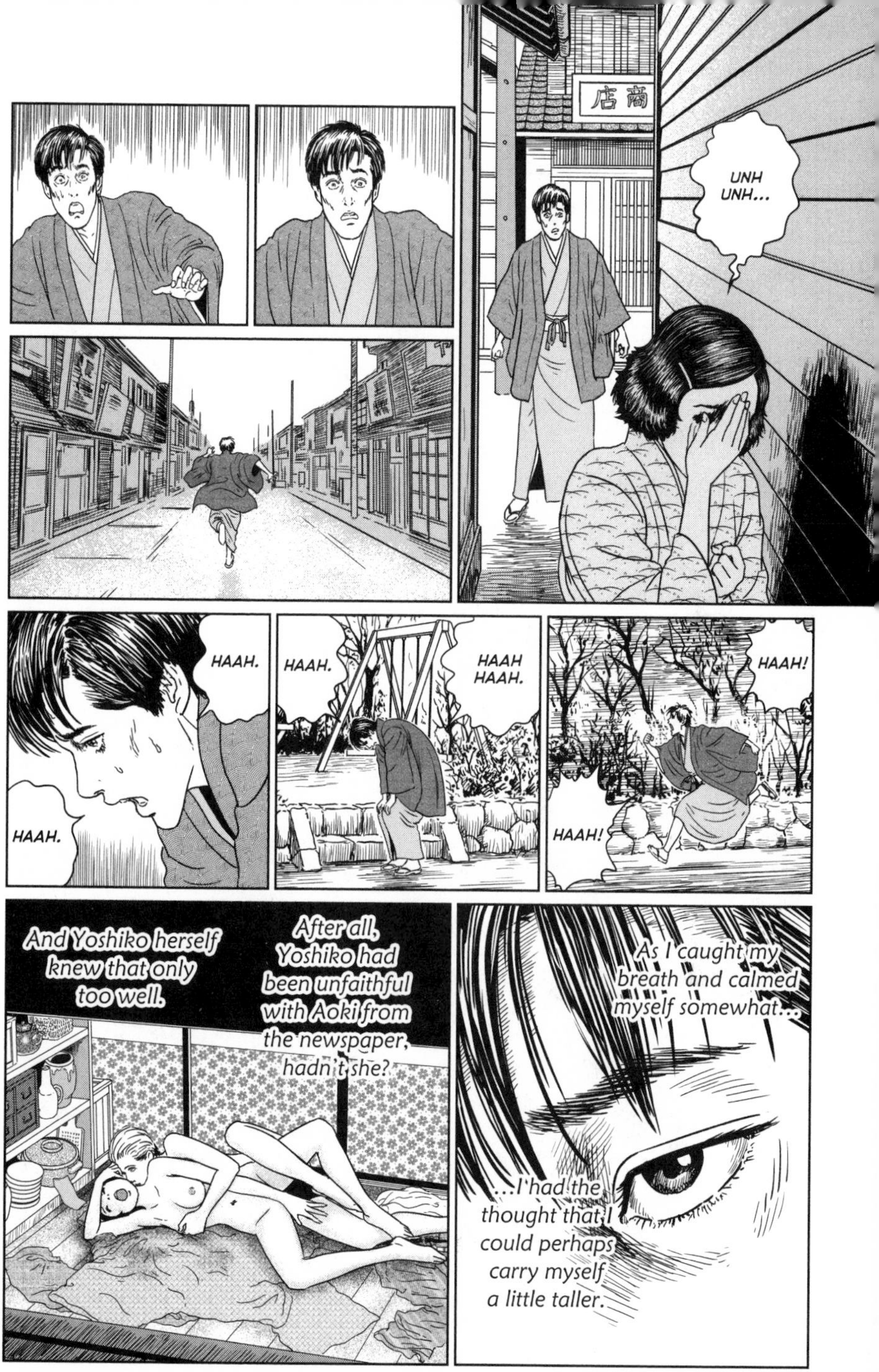
UNH UNH...
HAAH!
HAAH!
HAAH HAAH.
HAAH.
HAAH.
HAAH.
As I caught my breath and calmed myself somewhat...
...I had the thought that I could perhaps carry myself a little taller.
After all, Yoshiko had been unfaithful with Aoki from the newspaper, hadn't she?
And Yoshiko herself knew that only too well.

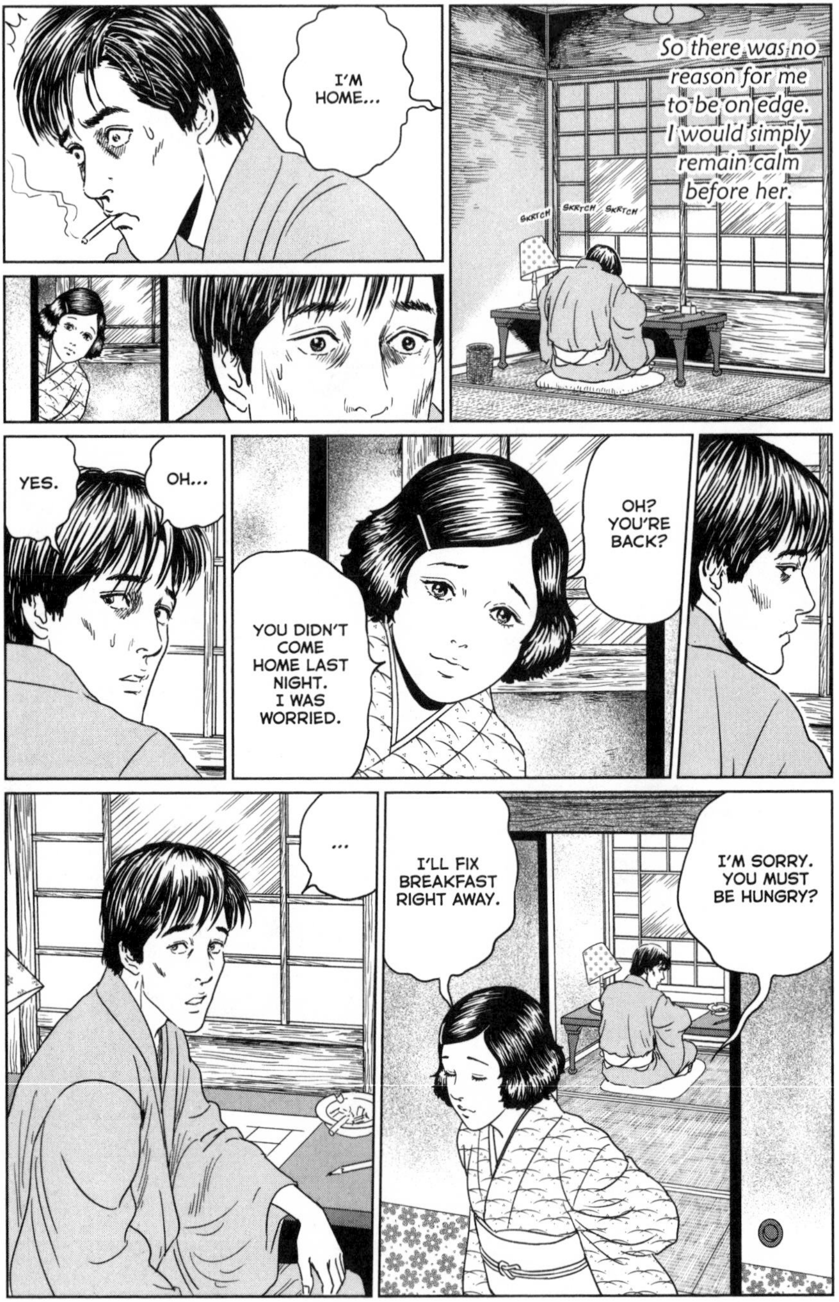
So there was no reason for me to be on edge. I would simply remain calm before her.
SKRTCH SKRTCH SKRTCH
I'M HOME...
OH? YOU'RE BACK?
YOU DIDN'T COME HOME LAST NIGHT. I WAS WORRIED.
OH...
YES.
I'M SORRY. YOU MUST BE HUNGRY?
I'LL FIX BREAKFAST RIGHT AWAY.
...

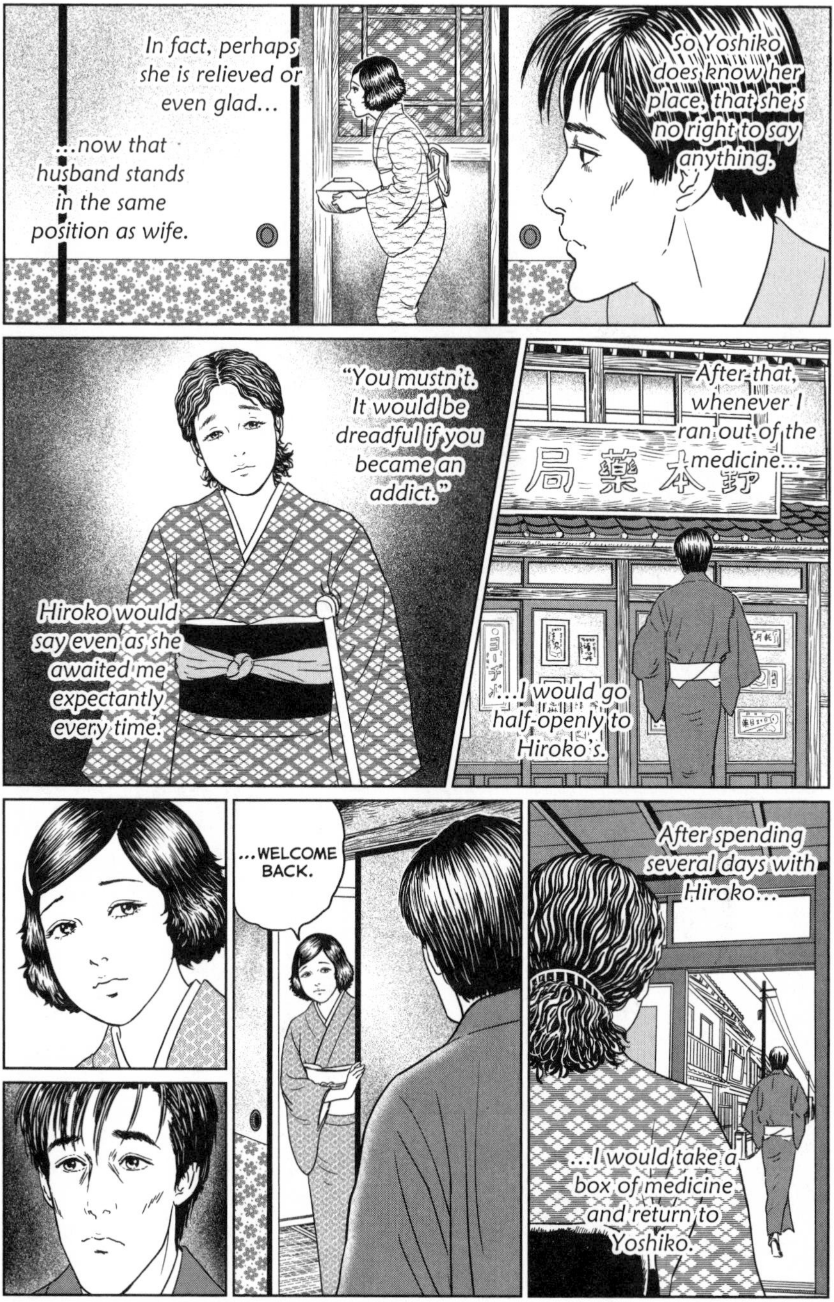
So Yoshiko does know her place, that she's no right to say anything.
In fact, perhaps she is relieved or even glad...
...now that husband stands in the same position as wife.
After that, whenever I ran out of the medicine...
...I would go half-openly to Hiroko's.
"You mustn't. It would be dreadful if you became an addict."
Hiroko would say even as she awaited me expectantly every time.
After spending several days with Hiroko...
...I would take a box of medicine and return to Yoshiko.
...WELCOME BACK.

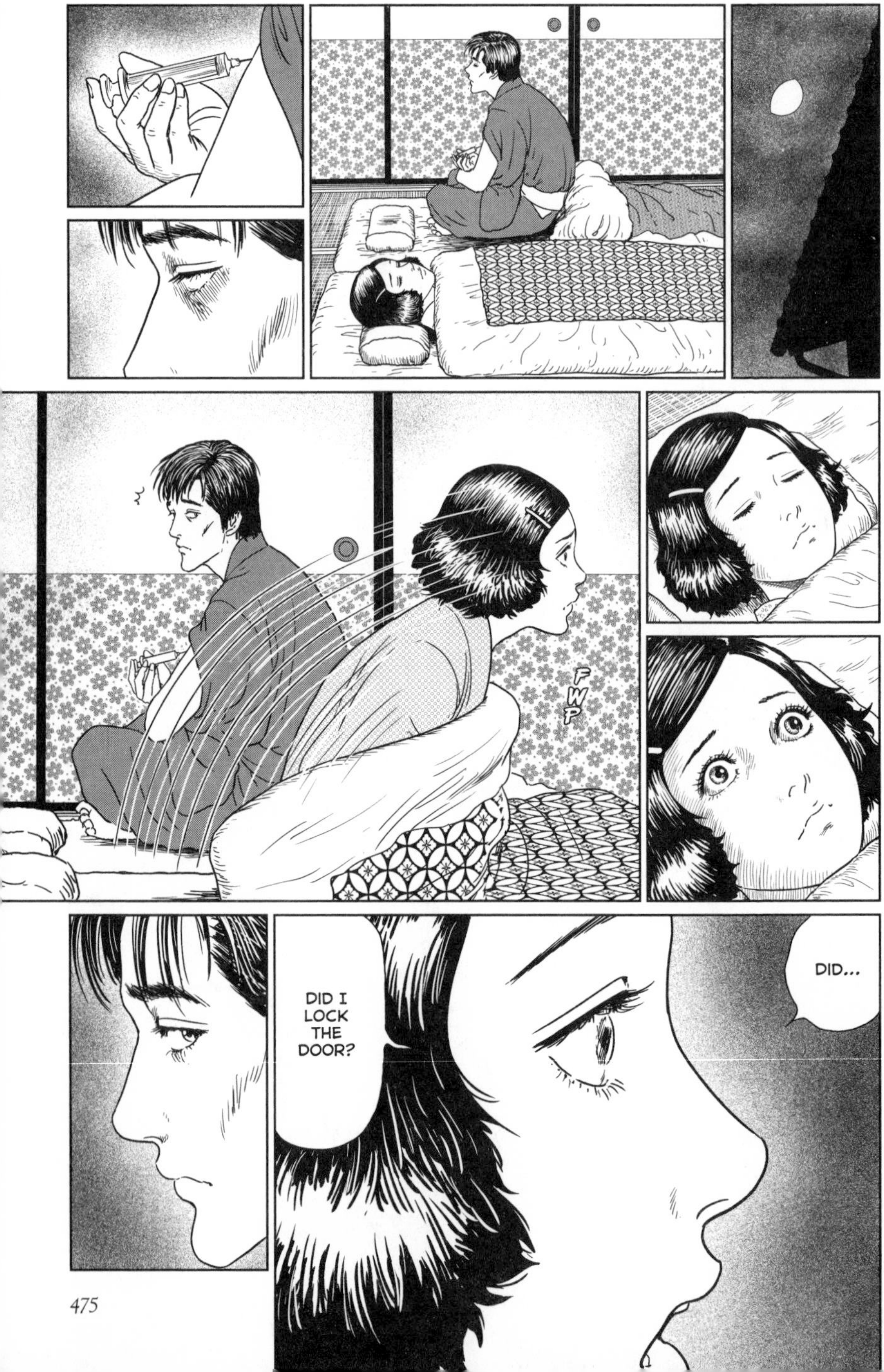
FWP
DID...
DID I LOCK THE DOOR?

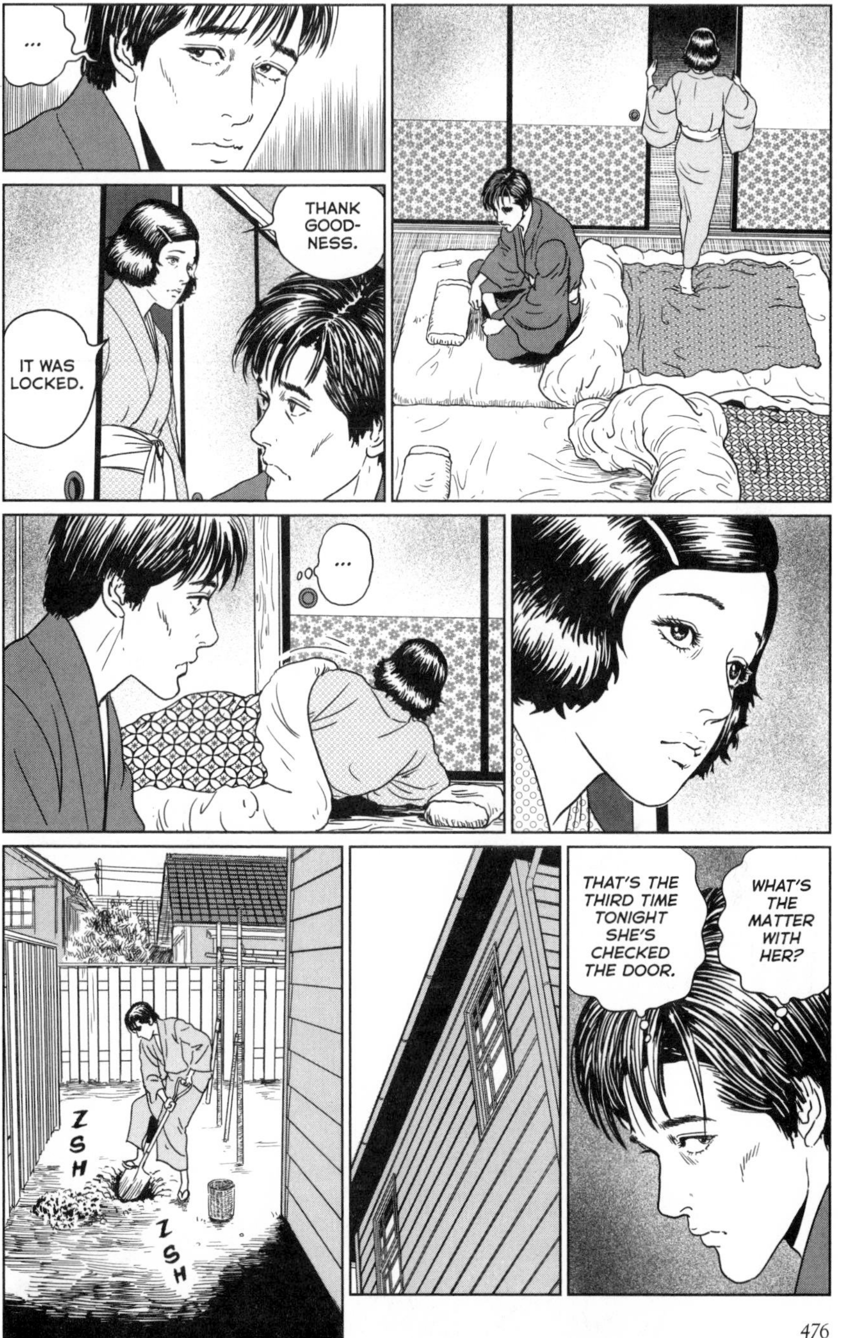
...
THANK GOOD-NESS.
IT WAS LOCKED.
...
WHAT'S THE MATTER WITH HER?
THAT'S THE THIRD TIME TONIGHT SHE'S CHECKED THE DOOR.
ZSH
ZSH

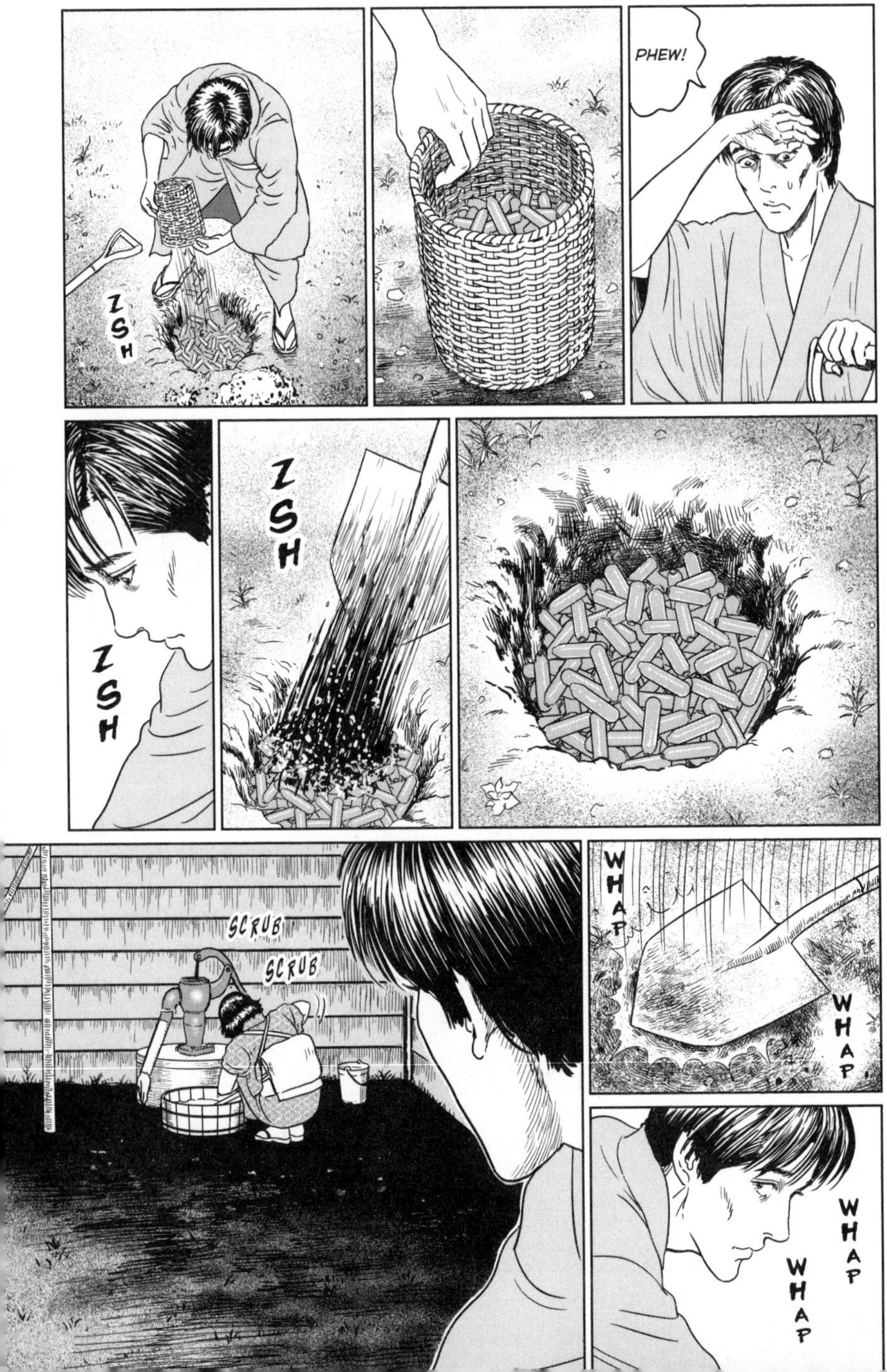
PHEW!
ZSH
ZSH
ZSH
WHAP
WHAP
WHAP
WHAP
WHAP
SCRUB
SCRUB

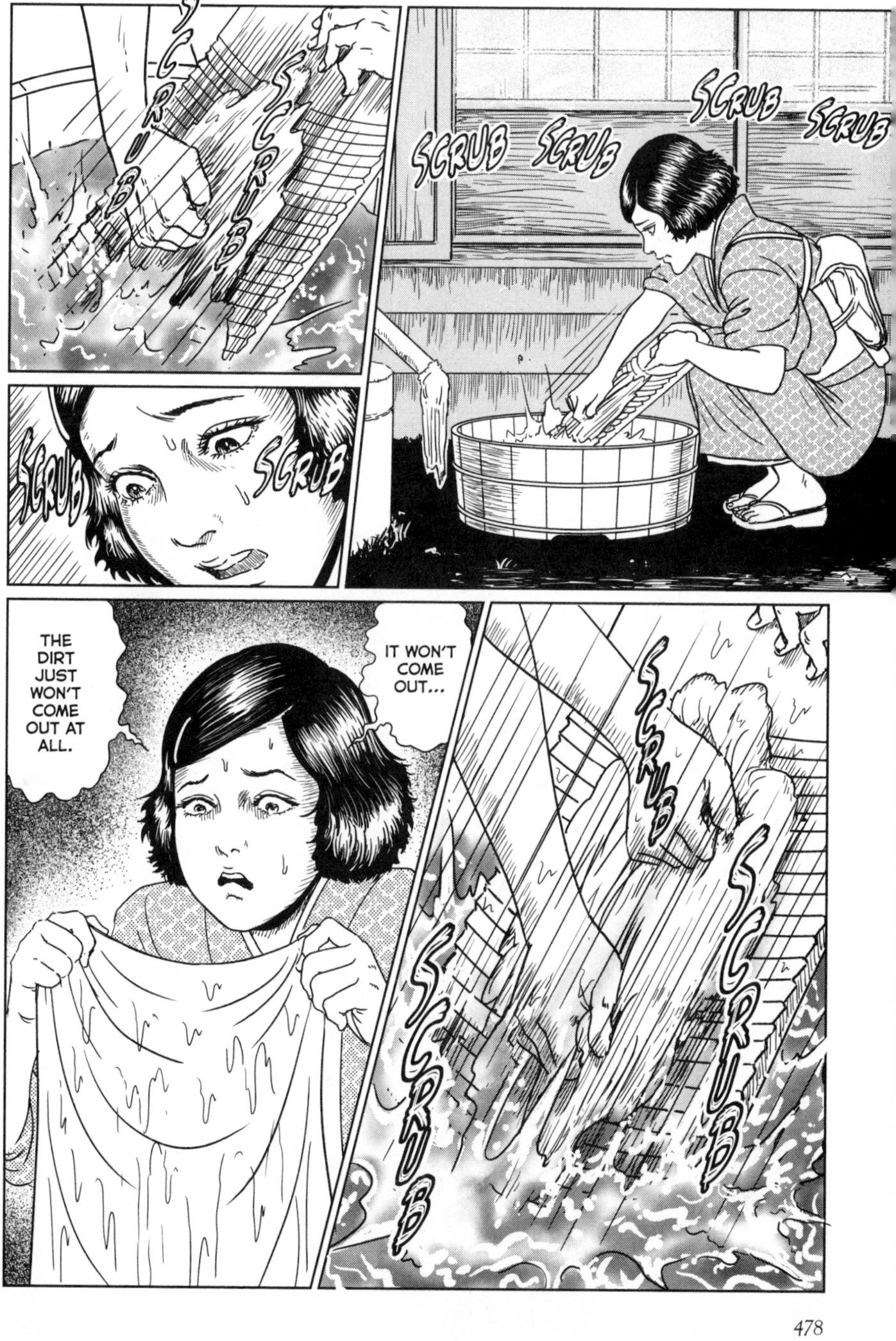
SCRUB
SCRUB
SCRUB
SCRUB
SCRUB
SCRUB
SCRUB
SCRUB
SCRUB
SCRUB
IT WON'T COME OUT...
THE DIRT JUST WON'T COME OUT AT ALL.

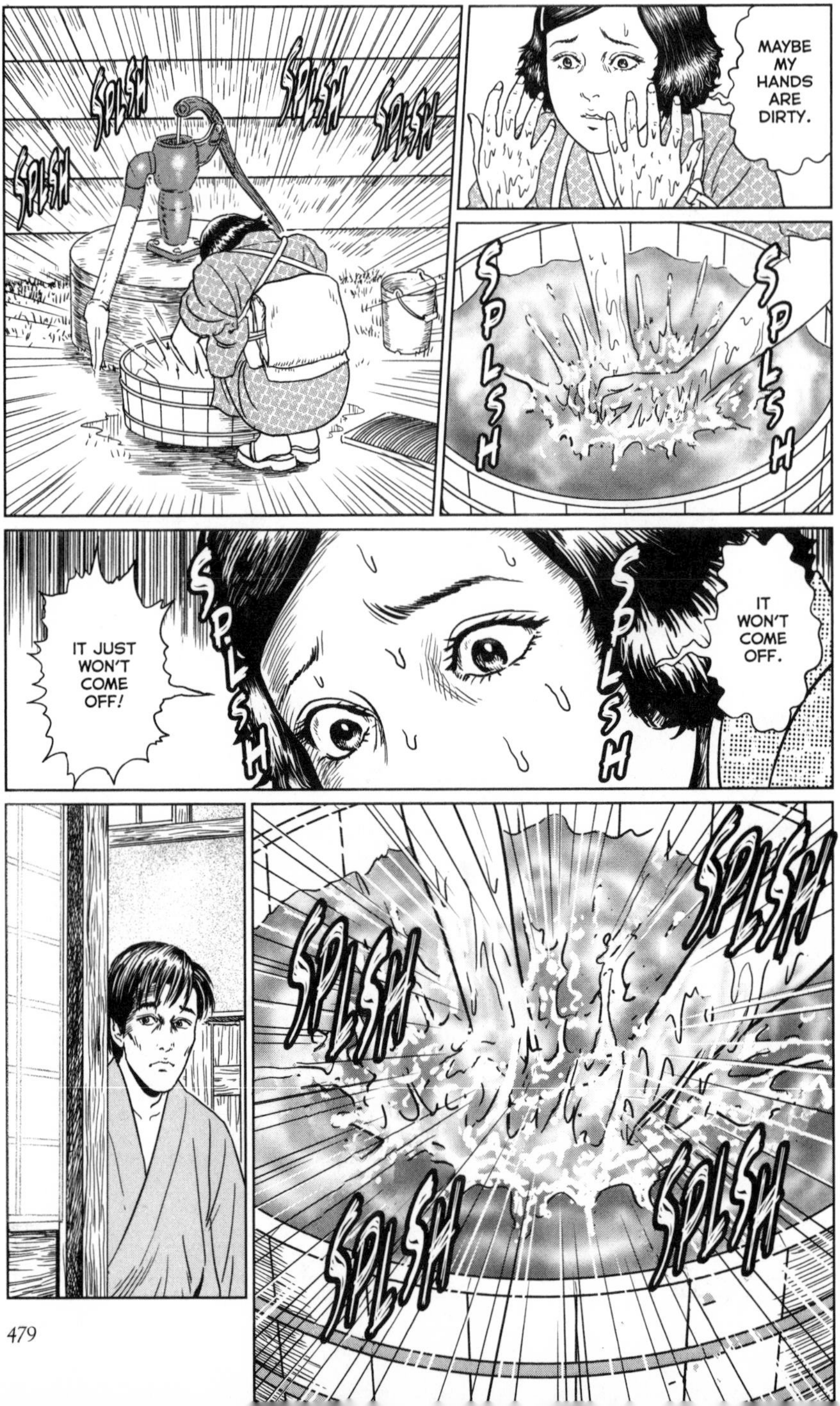
MAYBE MY HANDS ARE DIRTY.
SPLSH
SPLSH
SPLSH
SPLSH
SPLSH
SPLSH
IT WON'T COME OFF.
SPLSH
SPLSH
IT JUST WON'T COME OFF!
SPLSH
SPLSH
SPLSH
SPLSH

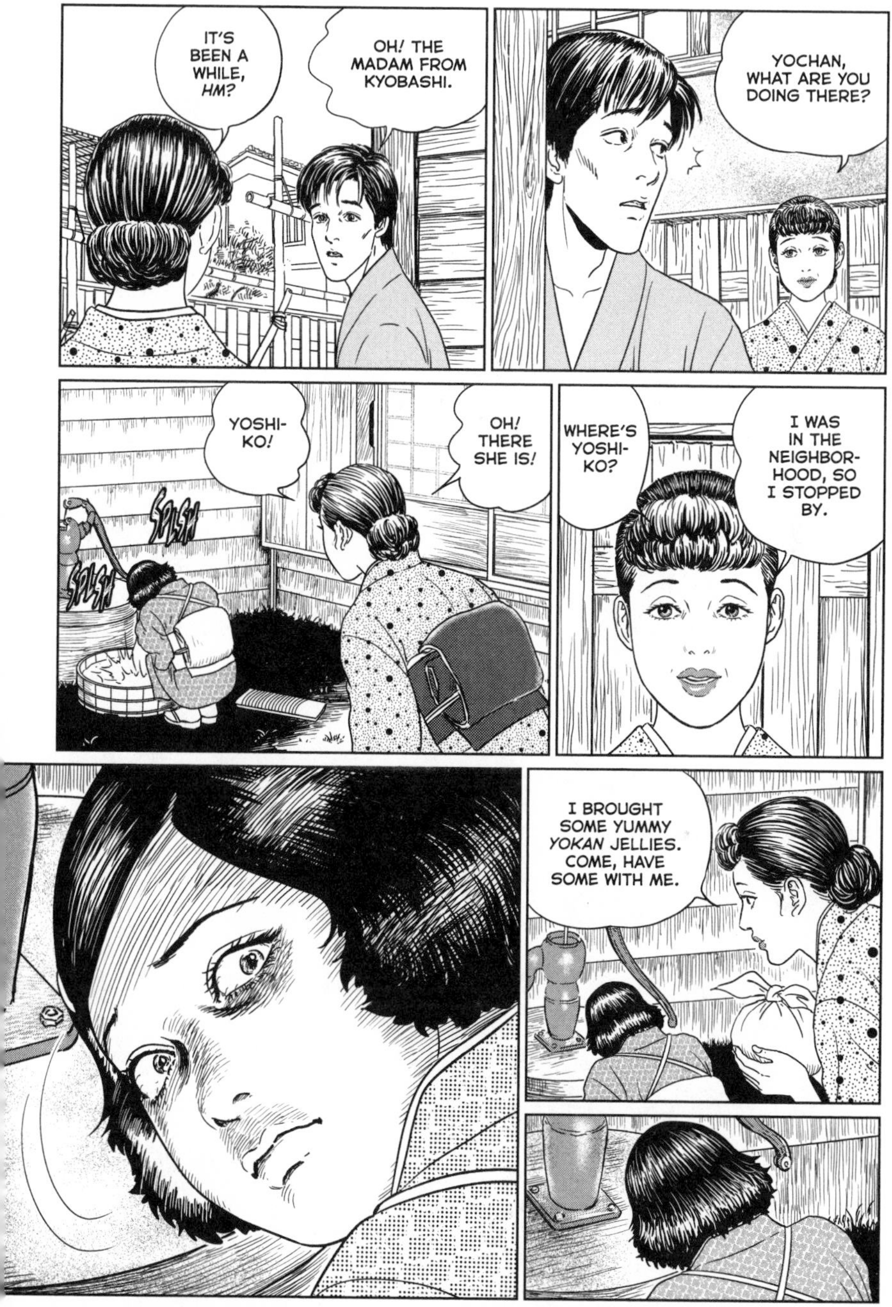
YOCHAN, WHAT ARE YOU DOING THERE?
OH! THE MADAM FROM KYOBASHI.
IT'S BEEN A WHILE, *HM?*
I WAS IN THE NEIGHBORHOOD, SO I STOPPED BY.
WHERE'S YOSHIKO?
OH! THERE SHE IS!
YOSHIKO!
SPLSH
SPLSH
I BROUGHT SOME YUMMY *YOKAN* JELLIES. COME, HAVE SOME WITH ME.

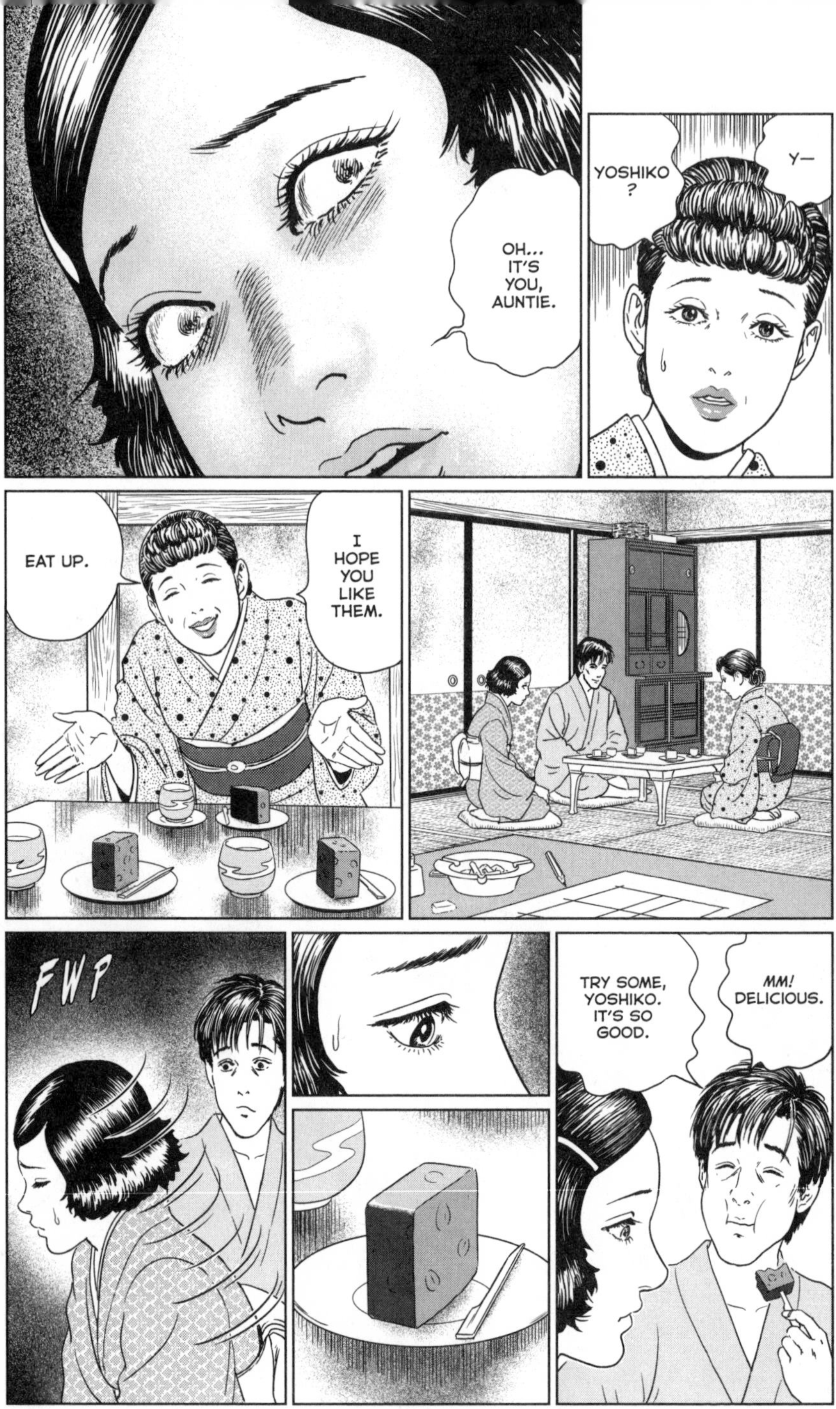
Y—
YOSHIKO?
OH... IT'S YOU, AUNTIE.
I HOPE YOU LIKE THEM.
EAT UP.
MM! DELICIOUS.
TRY SOME, YOSHIKO. IT'S SO GOOD.
FWP

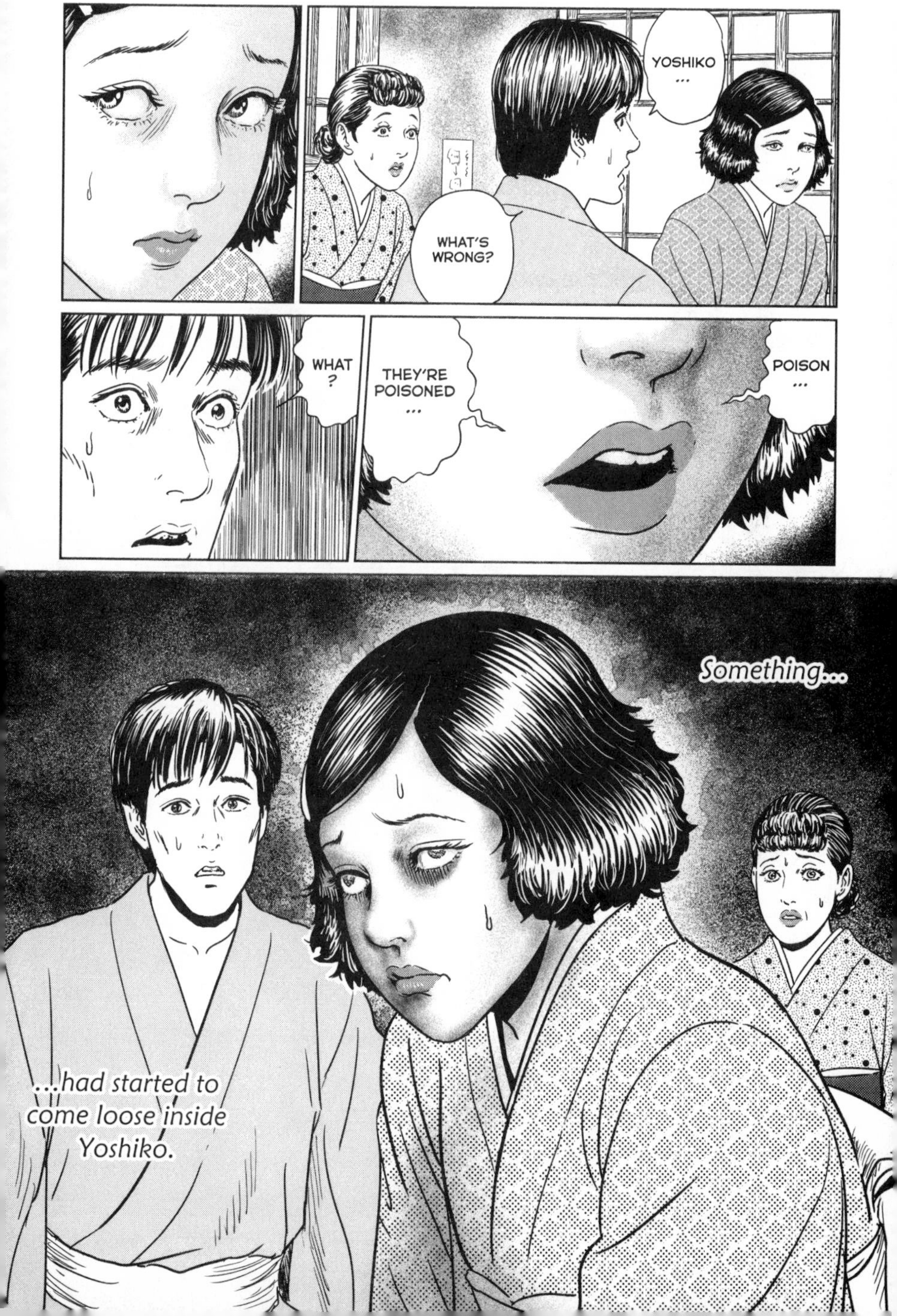
YOSHIKO ...
WHAT'S WRONG?
POISON ...
THEY'RE POISONED ...
WHAT ?
Something...
...had started to come loose inside Yoshiko.

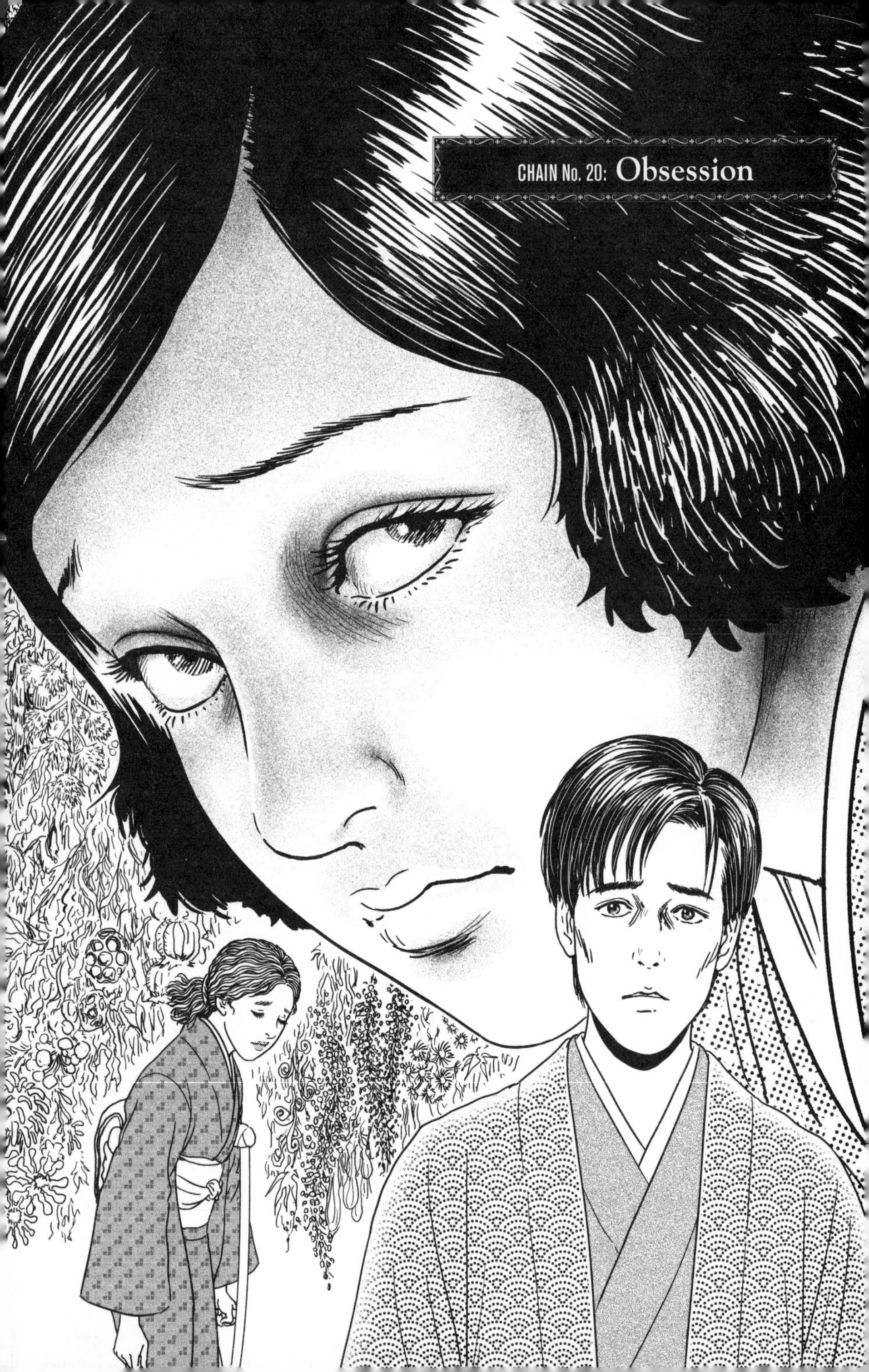
CHAIN No. 20: Obsession

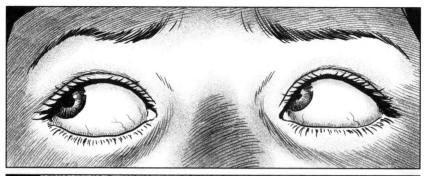

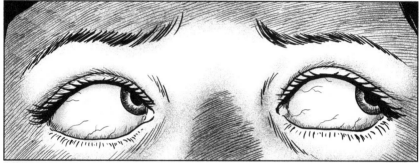

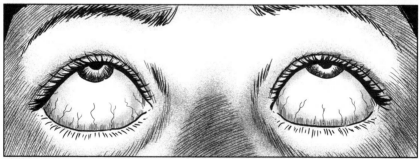

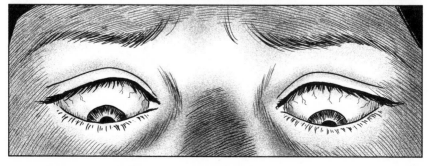

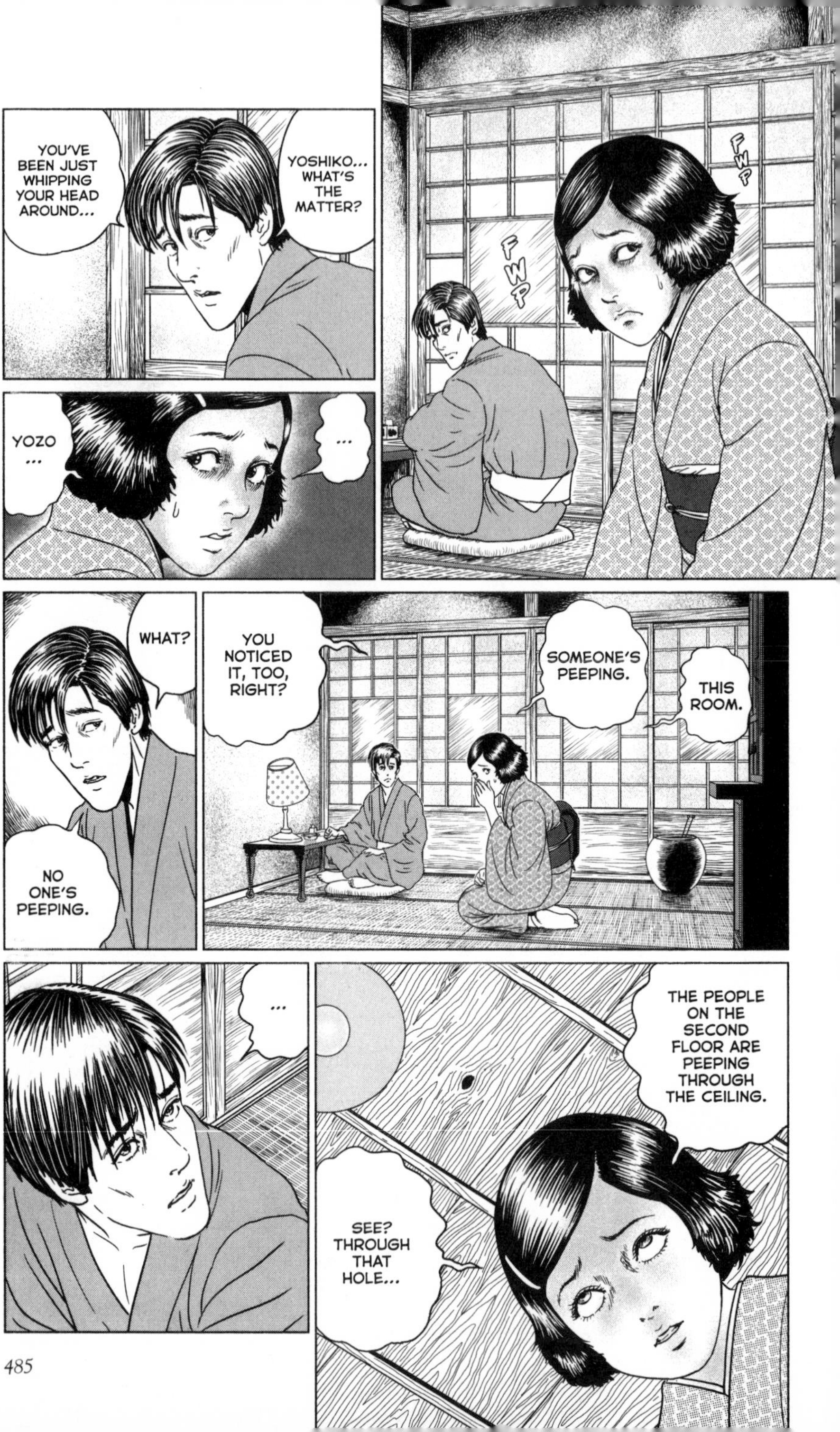
FWP
FWP
YOSHIKO... WHAT'S THE MATTER?
YOU'VE BEEN JUST WHIPPING YOUR HEAD AROUND...
...
YOZO ...
THIS ROOM.
SOMEONE'S PEEPING.
YOU NOTICED IT, TOO, RIGHT?
WHAT?
NO ONE'S PEEPING.
THE PEOPLE ON THE SECOND FLOOR ARE PEEPING THROUGH THE CEILING.
SEE? THROUGH THAT HOLE...
...

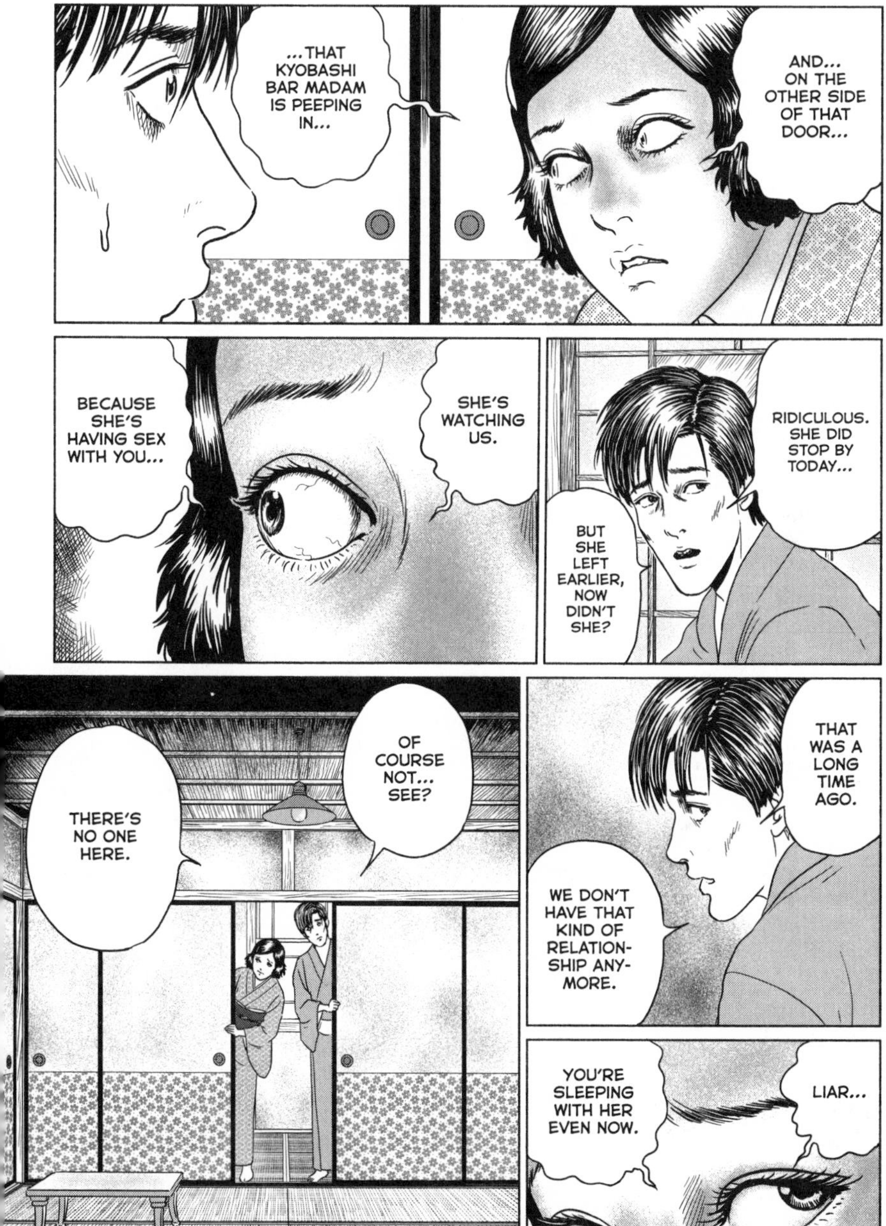
AND... ON THE OTHER SIDE OF THAT DOOR...
...THAT KYOBASHI BAR MADAM IS PEEPING IN...
RIDICULOUS. SHE DID STOP BY TODAY...
BUT SHE LEFT EARLIER, NOW DIDN'T SHE?
SHE'S WATCHING US.
BECAUSE SHE'S HAVING SEX WITH YOU...
THAT WAS A LONG TIME AGO.
WE DON'T HAVE THAT KIND OF RELATION-SHIP ANY-MORE.
LIAR...
YOU'RE SLEEPING WITH HER EVEN NOW.
OF COURSE NOT... SEE?
THERE'S NO ONE HERE.

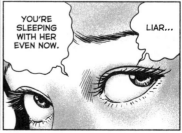

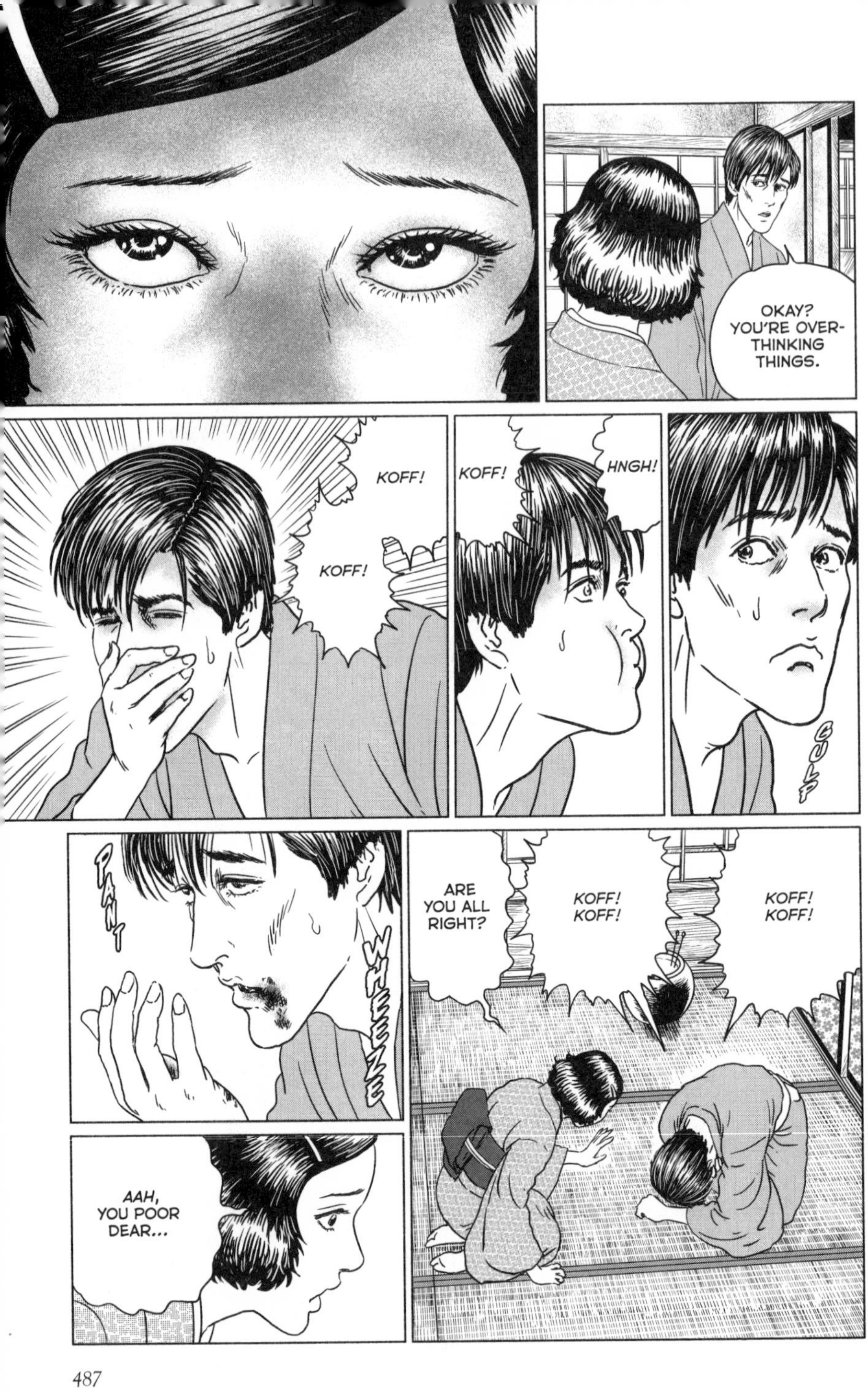
OKAY? YOU'RE OVER-THINKING THINGS.
GULP
HNGH!
KOFF!
KOFF!
KOFF!
KOFF! KOFF!
KOFF! KOFF!
ARE YOU ALL RIGHT?
WHEEZE
PANT
AAH, YOU POOR DEAR...

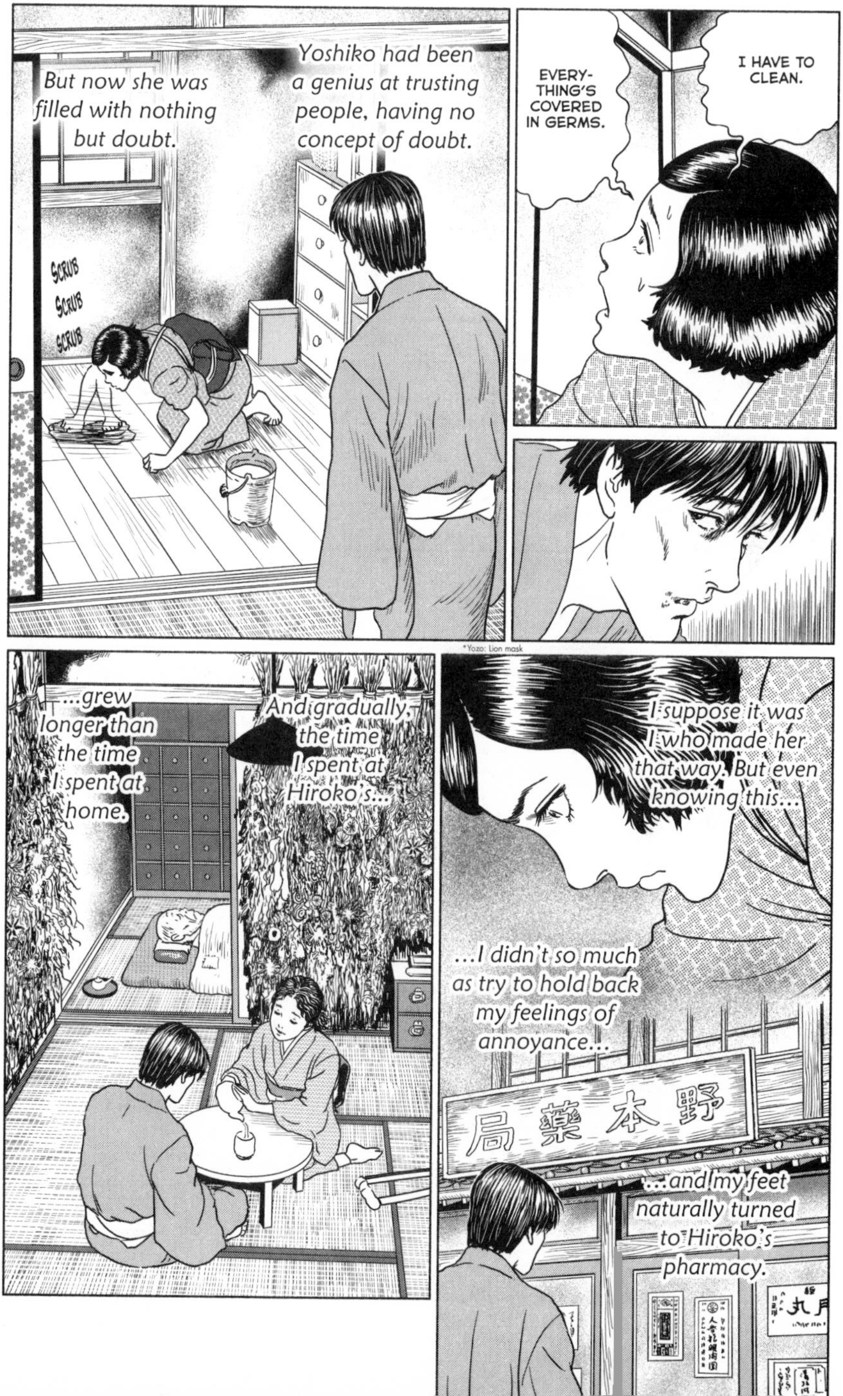
I HAVE TO CLEAN.
EVERYTHING'S COVERED IN GERMS.
Yoshiko had been a genius at trusting people, having no concept of doubt.
But now she was filled with nothing but doubt.
SCRUB SCRUB SCRUB
I suppose it was I who made her that way. But even knowing this...
...I didn't so much as try to hold back my feelings of annoyance...
野本薬局
...and my feet naturally turned to Hiroko's pharmacy.
And gradually, the time I spent at Hiroko's...
...grew longer than the time I spent at home.

*Yozo: Lion mask

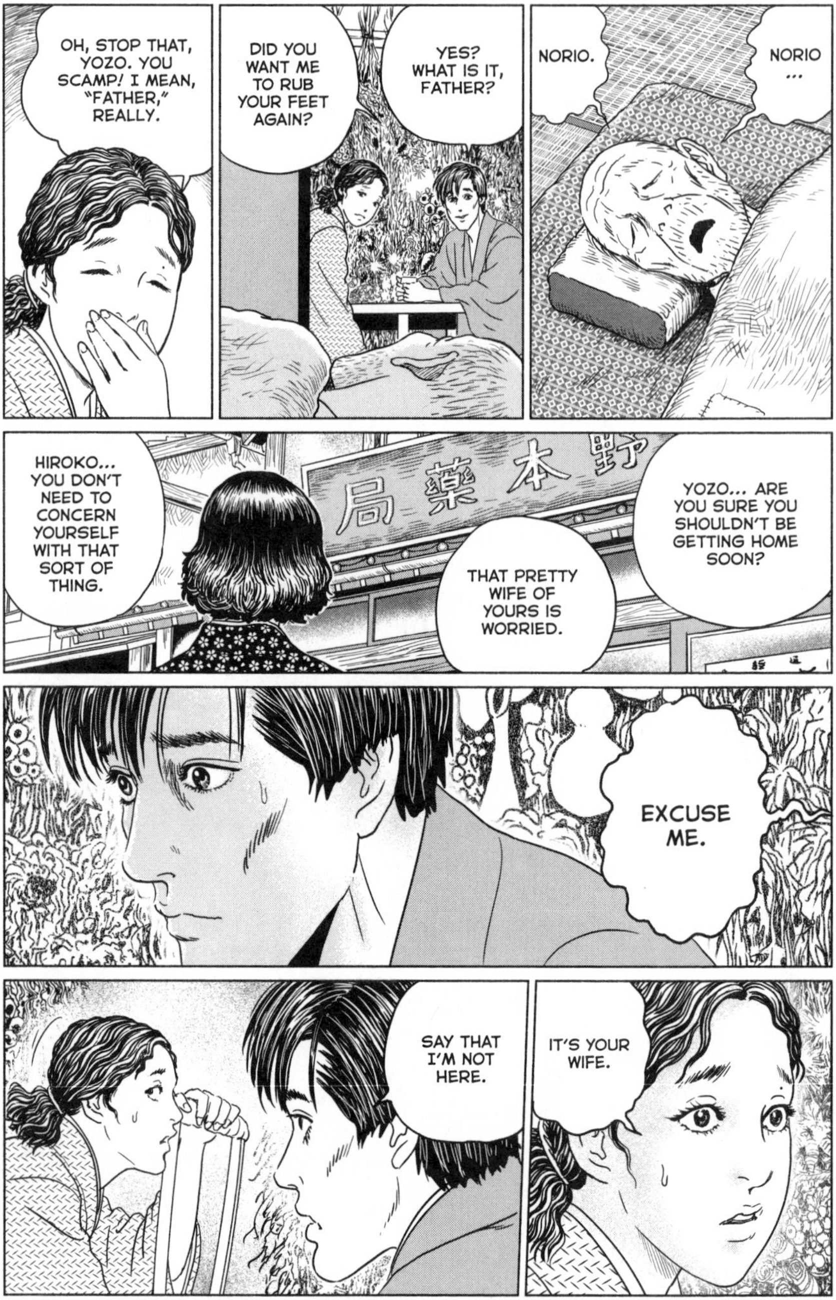
NORIO ...
NORIO.
YES? WHAT IS IT, FATHER?
DID YOU WANT ME TO RUB YOUR FEET AGAIN?
OH, STOP THAT, YOZO. YOU SCAMP! I MEAN, "FATHER," REALLY.
野本藥局
YOZO... ARE YOU SURE YOU SHOULDN'T BE GETTING HOME SOON?
THAT PRETTY WIFE OF YOURS IS WORRIED.
HIROKO... YOU DON'T NEED TO CONCERN YOURSELF WITH THAT SORT OF THING.
EXCUSE ME.
IT'S YOUR WIFE.
SAY THAT I'M NOT HERE.

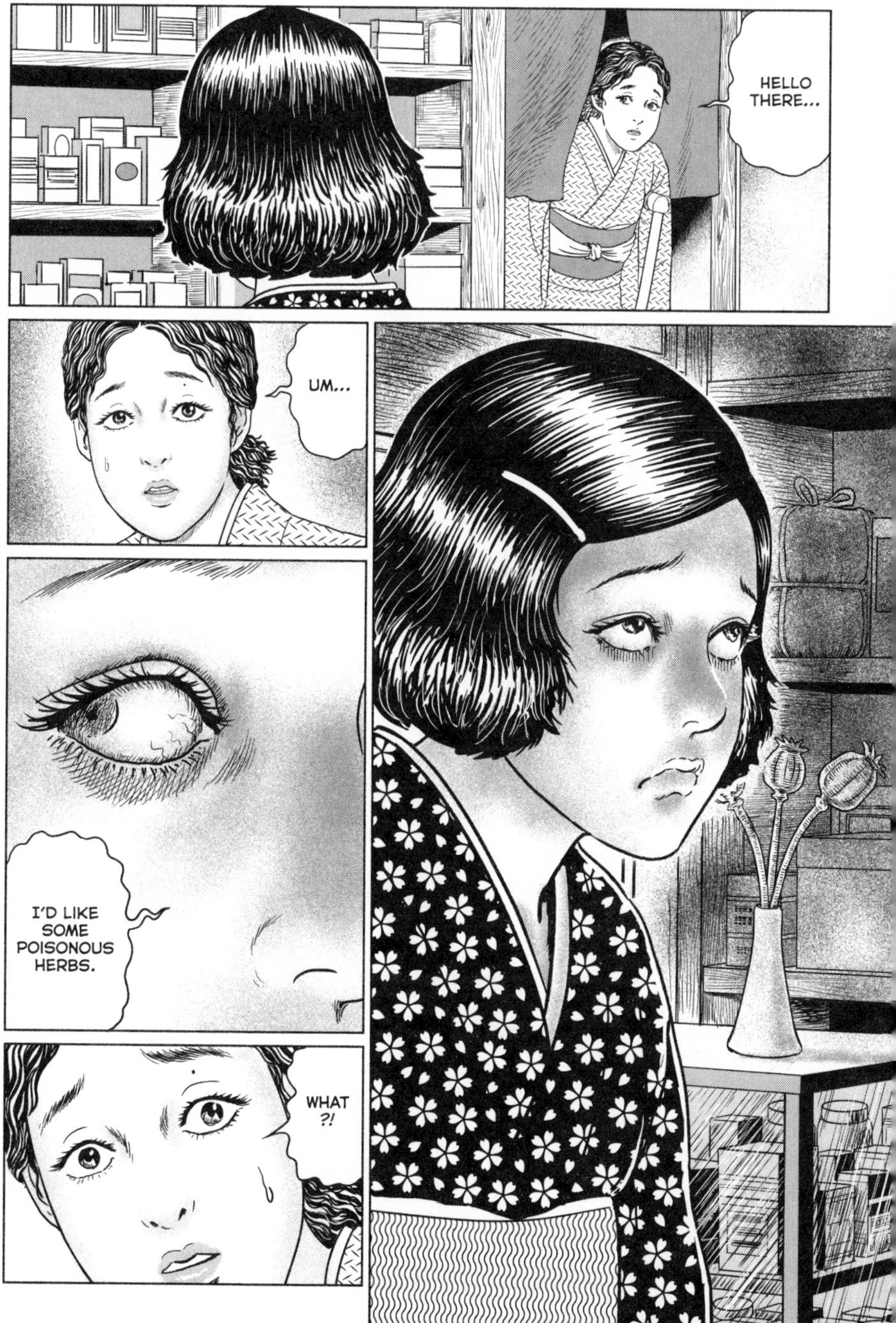
HELLO THERE...
UM...
I'D LIKE SOME POISONOUS HERBS.
WHAT ?!

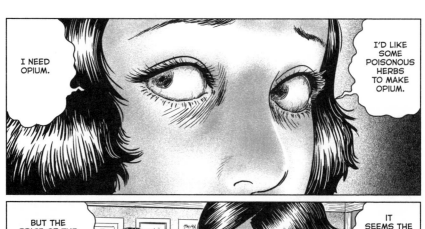

I'D LIKE SOME POISONOUS HERBS TO MAKE OPIUM.
I NEED OPIUM.
IT SEEMS THE MEDICINE MY HUSBAND USES IS OPIUM.
WHEN HE INJECTS THE OPIUM, HE BECOMES VERY LIVELY AND THE MOOD FOR WORK COMES OVER HIM.
BUT THE PRICE OF THE MEDICINE IS NOTHING TO SNEEZE AT. SO I THOUGHT IT BETTER TO CULTIVATE THE OPIUM...
FROM WHAT I HEAR, POPPIES TURN INTO OPIUM.
COULD YOU PLEASE SELL ME SOME POPPY SEEDS?
AAH... I'M SORRY TO SAY THAT WE DON'T CARRY POPPY SEEDS HERE.
WHAT? BUT...

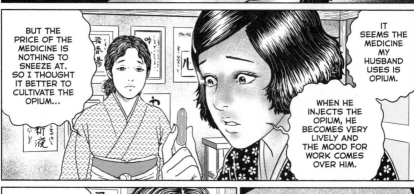

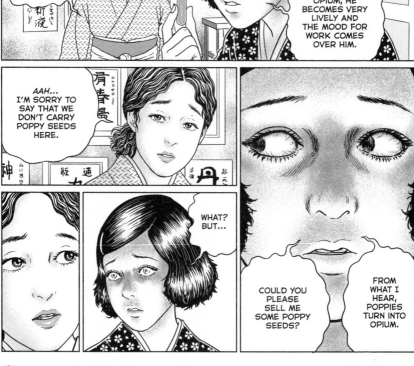

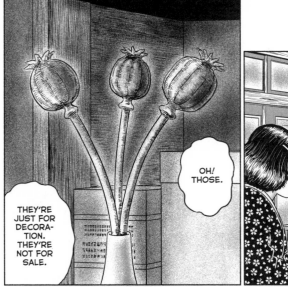

AREN'T THOSE POPPIES?

OH! THOSE.

THEY'RE JUST FOR DECORATION. THEY'RE NOT FOR SALE.

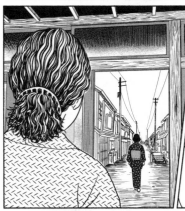

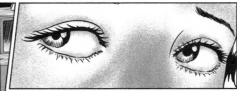

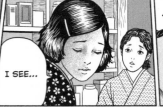

I SEE...

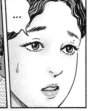

...

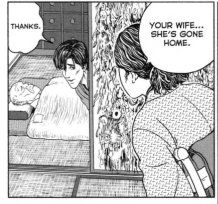

THANKS.

YOUR WIFE... SHE'S GONE HOME.

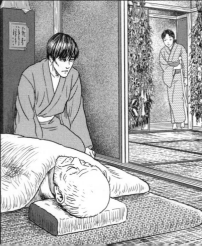

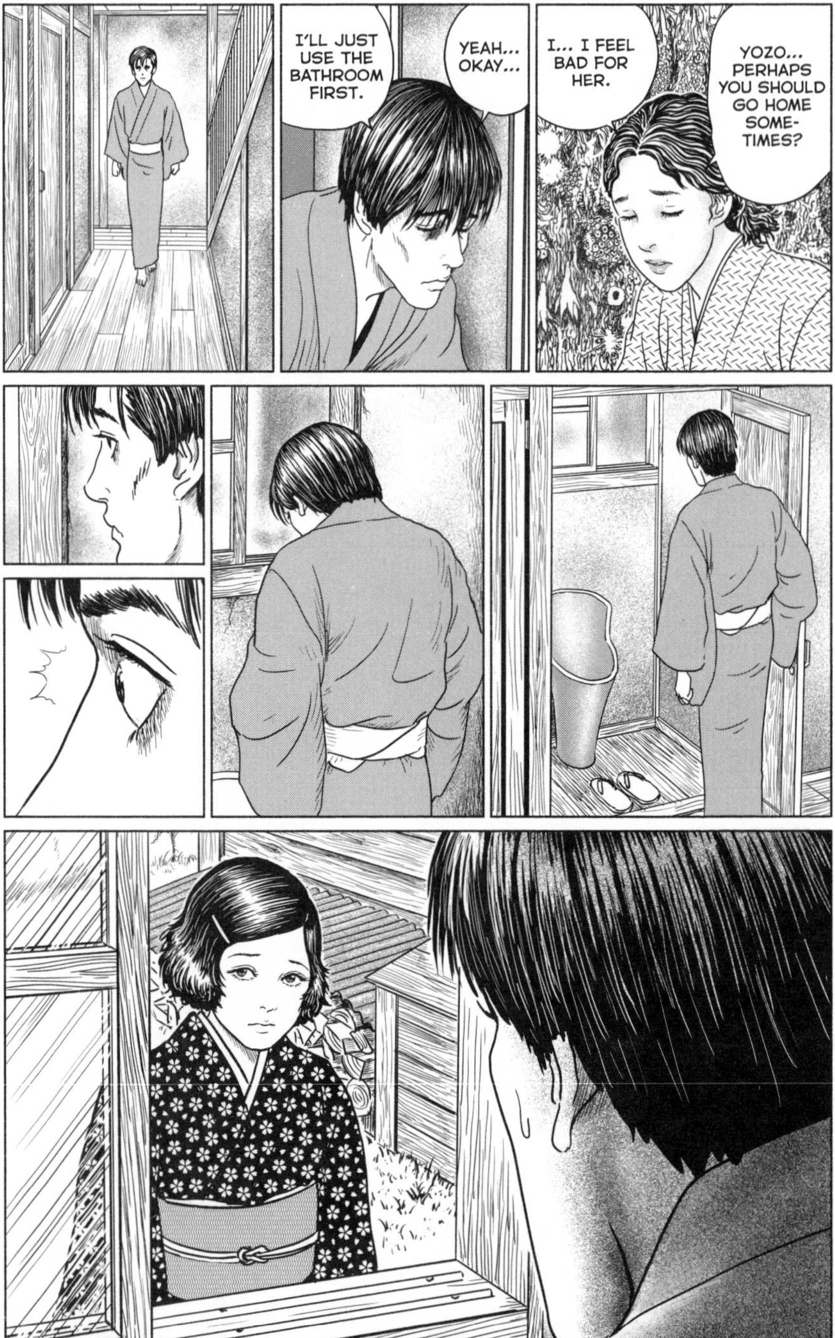
YOZO... PERHAPS YOU SHOULD GO HOME SOME-TIMES?
I... I FEEL BAD FOR HER.
YEAH... OKAY...
I'LL JUST USE THE BATHROOM FIRST.

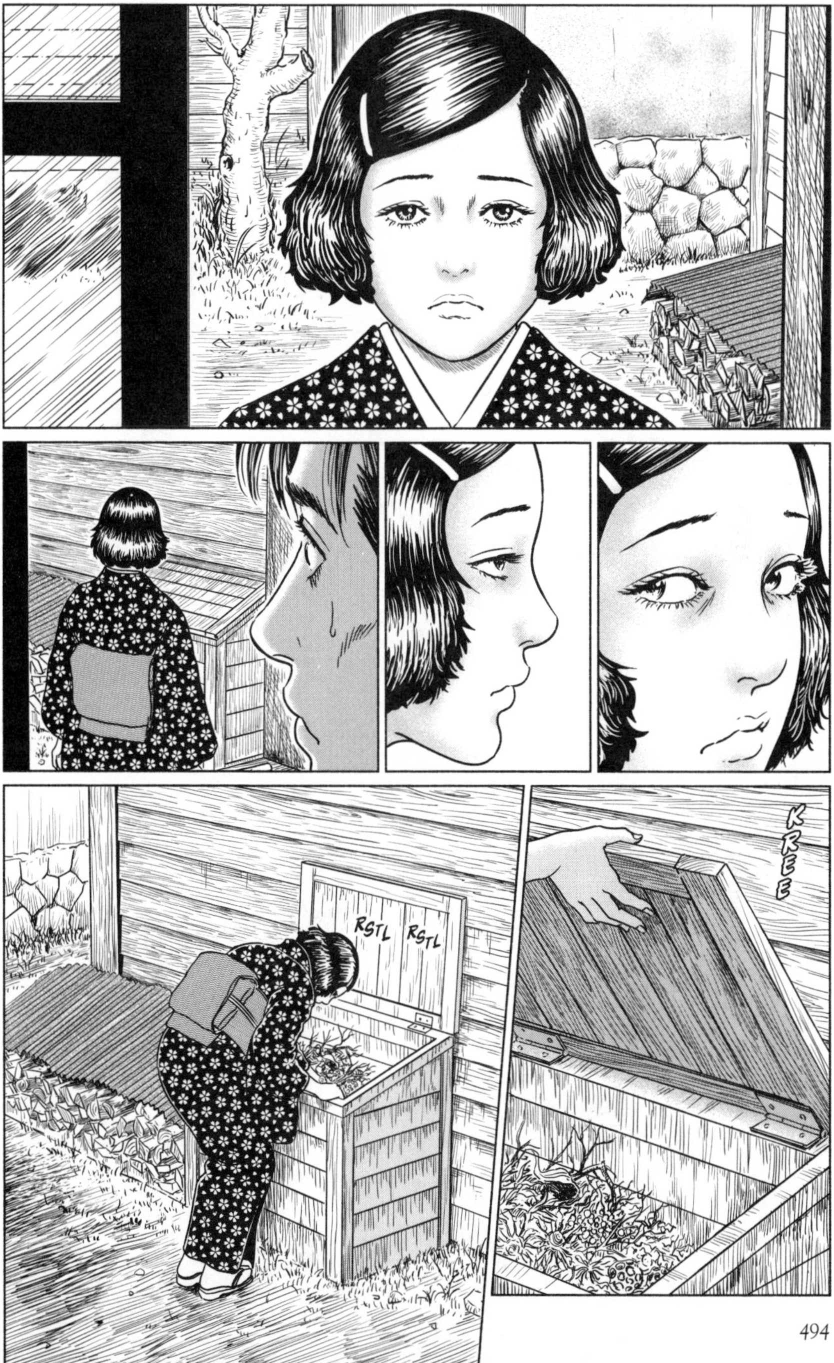
KREE
RSTL RSTL

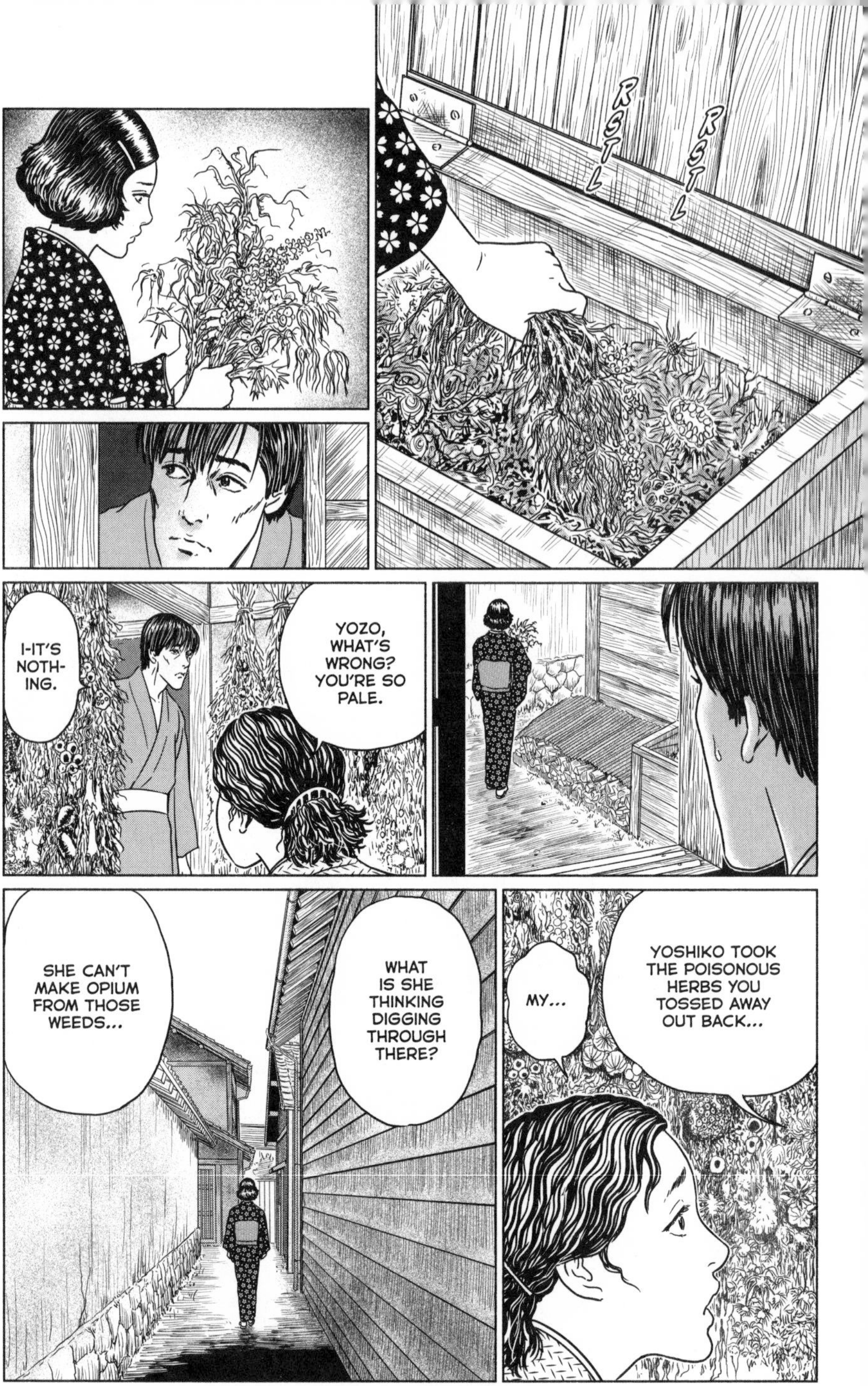
RSTL
RSTL
YOZO, WHAT'S WRONG? YOU'RE SO PALE.
I-IT'S NOTHING.
YOSHIKO TOOK THE POISONOUS HERBS YOU TOSSED AWAY OUT BACK...
MY...
WHAT IS SHE THINKING DIGGING THROUGH THERE?
SHE CAN'T MAKE OPIUM FROM THOSE WEEDS...

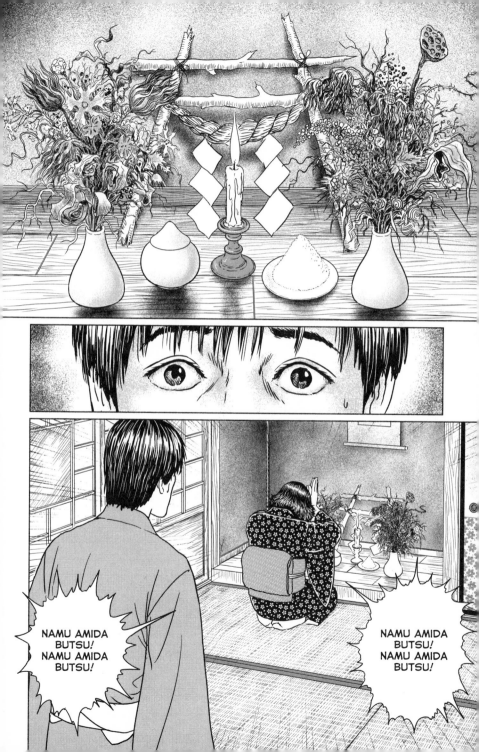

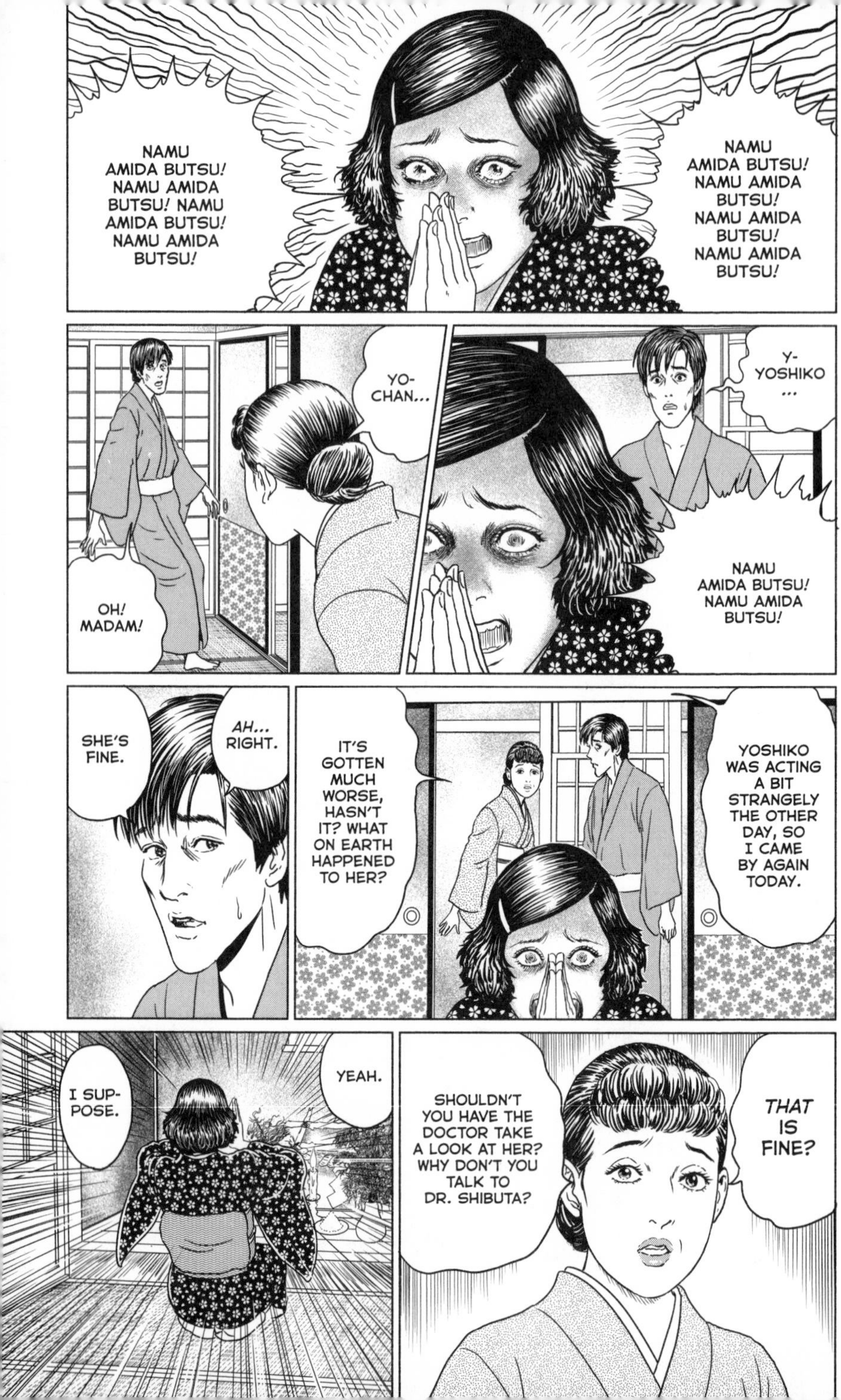
NAMU AMIDA BUTSU! NAMU AMIDA BUTSU! NAMU AMIDA BUTSU! NAMU AMIDA BUTSU!
NAMU AMIDA BUTSU! NAMU AMIDA BUTSU! NAMU AMIDA BUTSU! NAMU AMIDA BUTSU!
Y-YOSHIKO ...
NAMU AMIDA BUTSU! NAMU AMIDA BUTSU!
YO-CHAN...
OH! MADAM!
YOSHIKO WAS ACTING A BIT STRANGELY THE OTHER DAY, SO I CAME BY AGAIN TODAY.
IT'S GOTTEN MUCH WORSE, HASN'T IT? WHAT ON EARTH HAPPENED TO HER?
AH... RIGHT.
SHE'S FINE.
THAT IS FINE?
SHOULDN'T YOU HAVE THE DOCTOR TAKE A LOOK AT HER? WHY DON'T YOU TALK TO DR. SHIBUTA?
YEAH.
I SUPPOSE.

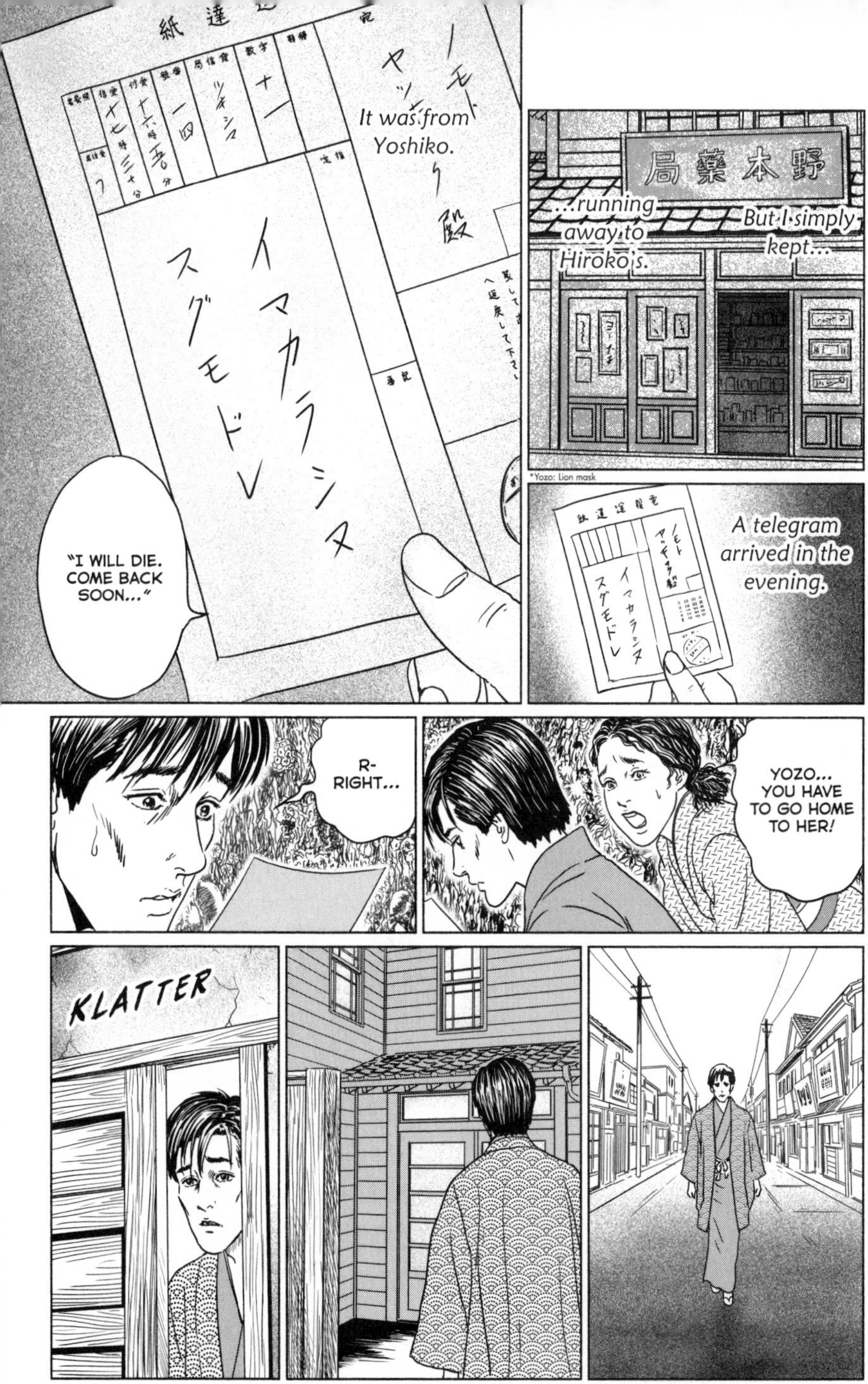
野本薬局
But I simply kept...
...running away to Hiroko's.
*Yozo: Lion mask
A telegram arrived in the evening.
It was from Yoshiko.
イマカラシヌ
スグモドレ
"I WILL DIE. COME BACK SOON..."
YOZO... YOU HAVE TO GO HOME TO HER!
R-RIGHT...
KLATTER

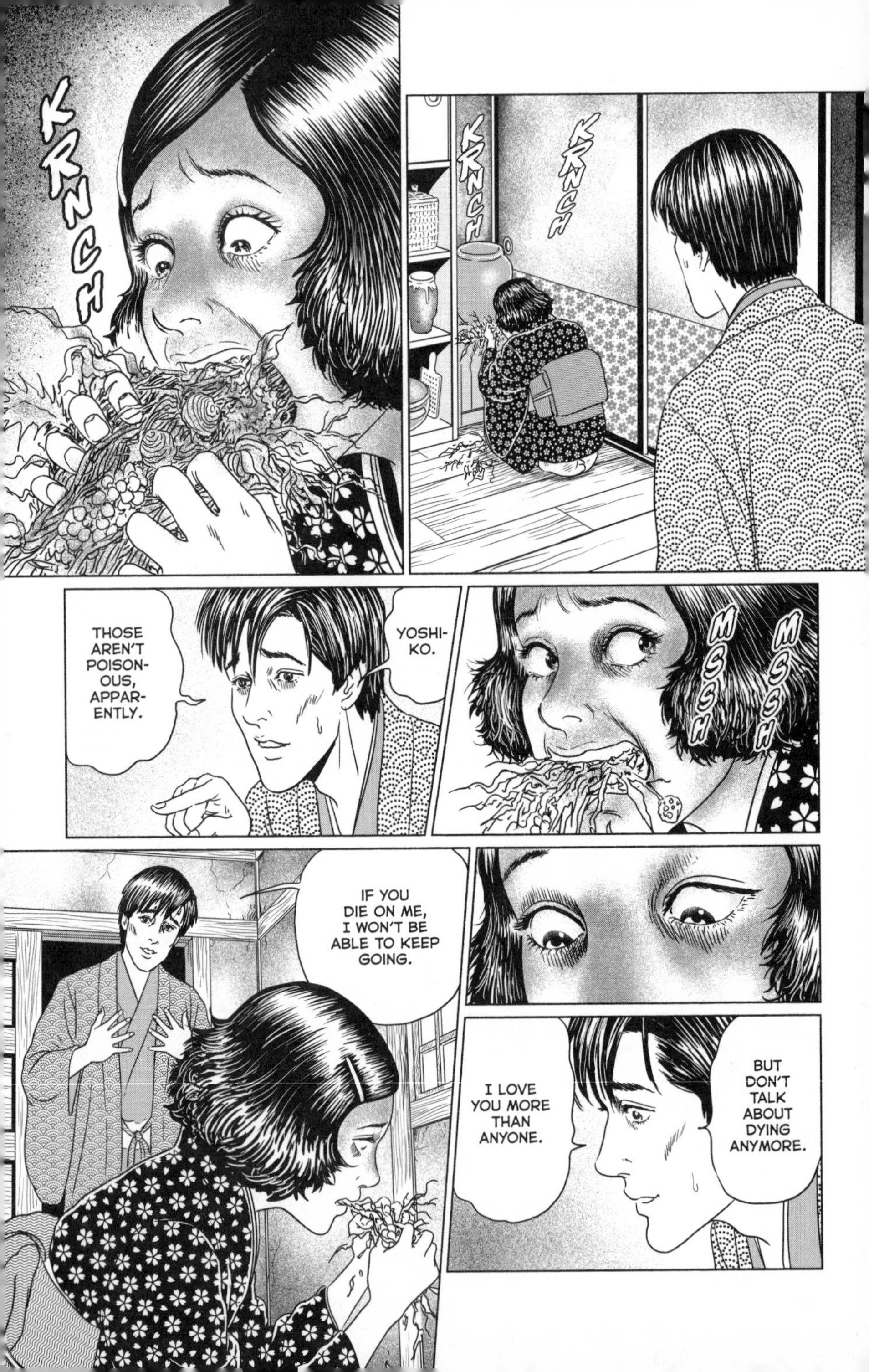
KRNCH
KRNCH
KRNCH
MSSH
MSSH
YOSHI-KO.
THOSE AREN'T POISONOUS, APPARENTLY.
BUT DON'T TALK ABOUT DYING ANYMORE.
I LOVE YOU MORE THAN ANYONE.
IF YOU DIE ON ME, I WON'T BE ABLE TO KEEP GOING.

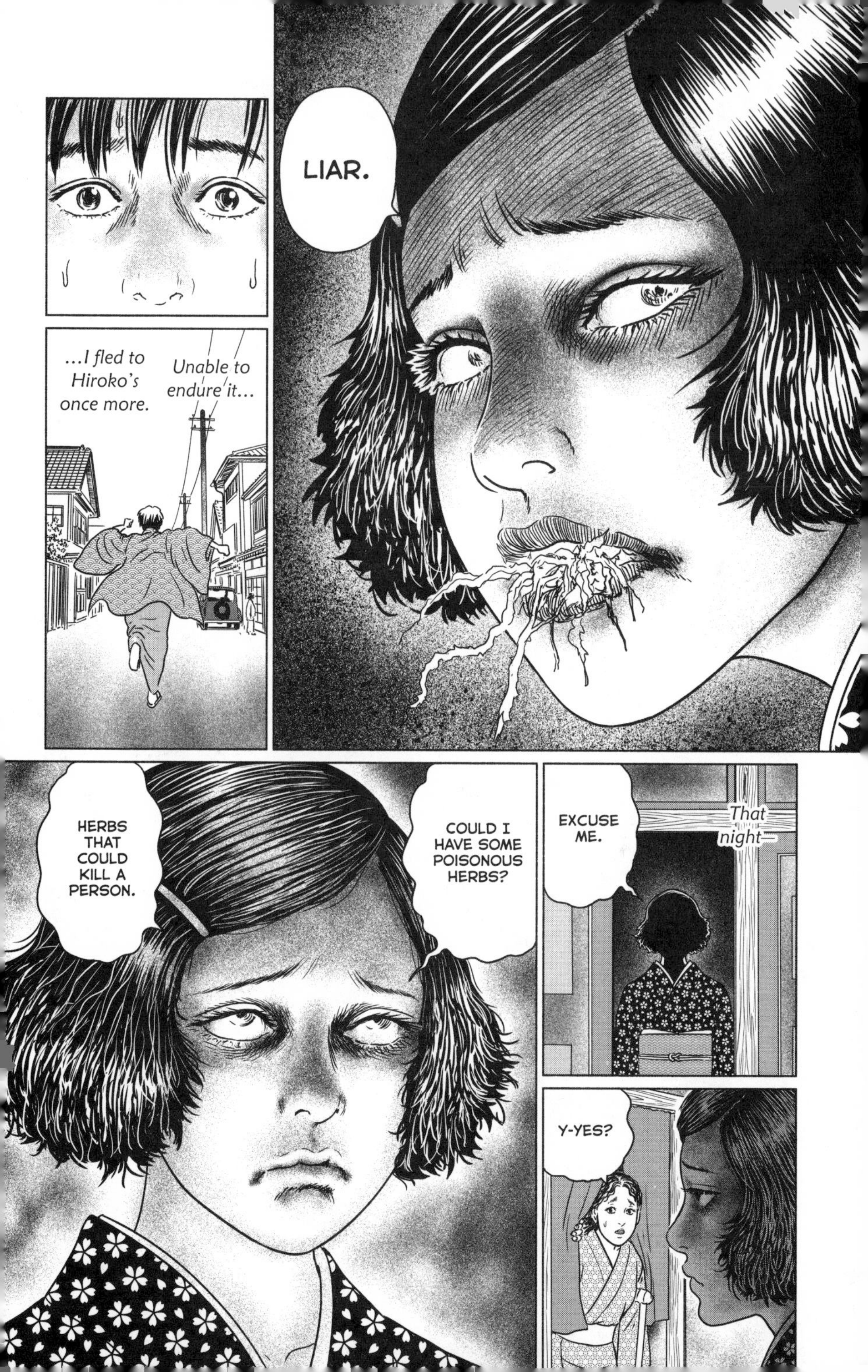
LIAR.
Unable to endure it…
…I fled to Hiroko's once more.
That night—
EXCUSE ME.
Y-YES?
COULD I HAVE SOME POISONOUS HERBS?
HERBS THAT COULD KILL A PERSON.

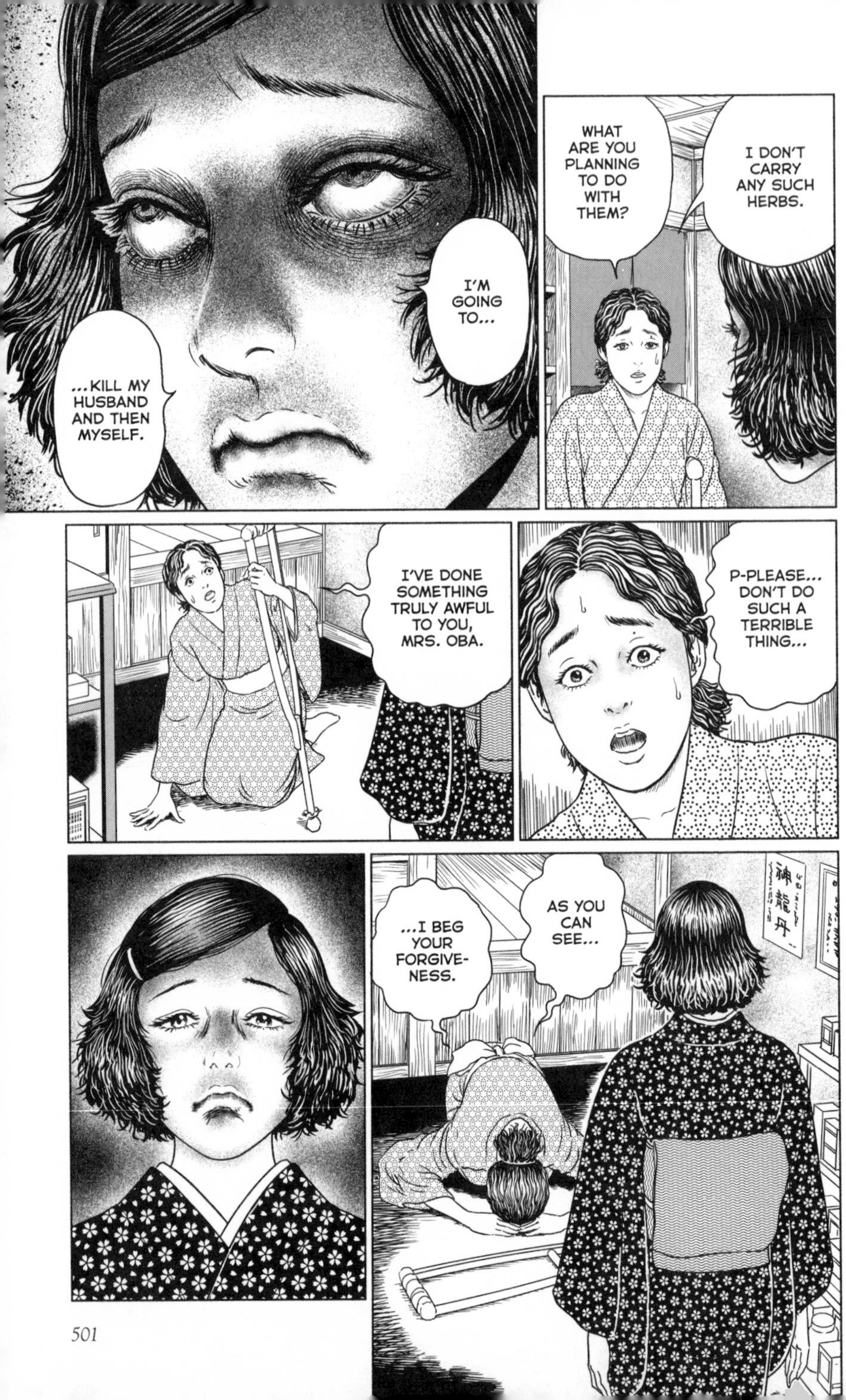

I DON'T CARRY ANY SUCH HERBS.
WHAT ARE YOU PLANNING TO DO WITH THEM?
I'M GOING TO...
...KILL MY HUSBAND AND THEN MYSELF.
P-PLEASE... DON'T DO SUCH A TERRIBLE THING...
I'VE DONE SOMETHING TRULY AWFUL TO YOU, MRS. OBA.
神龍丹
AS YOU CAN SEE...
...I BEG YOUR FORGIVENESS.

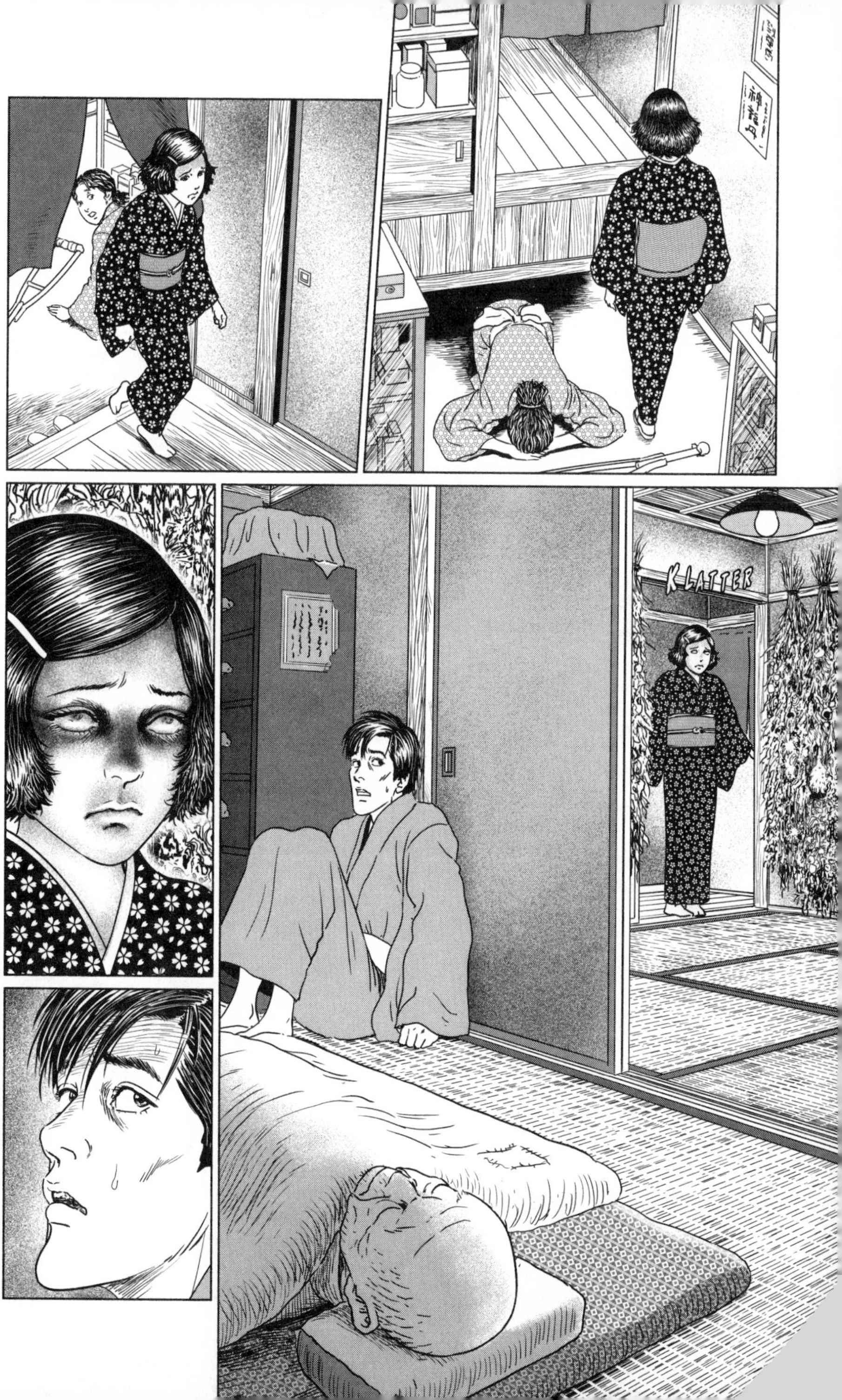
KLATTER

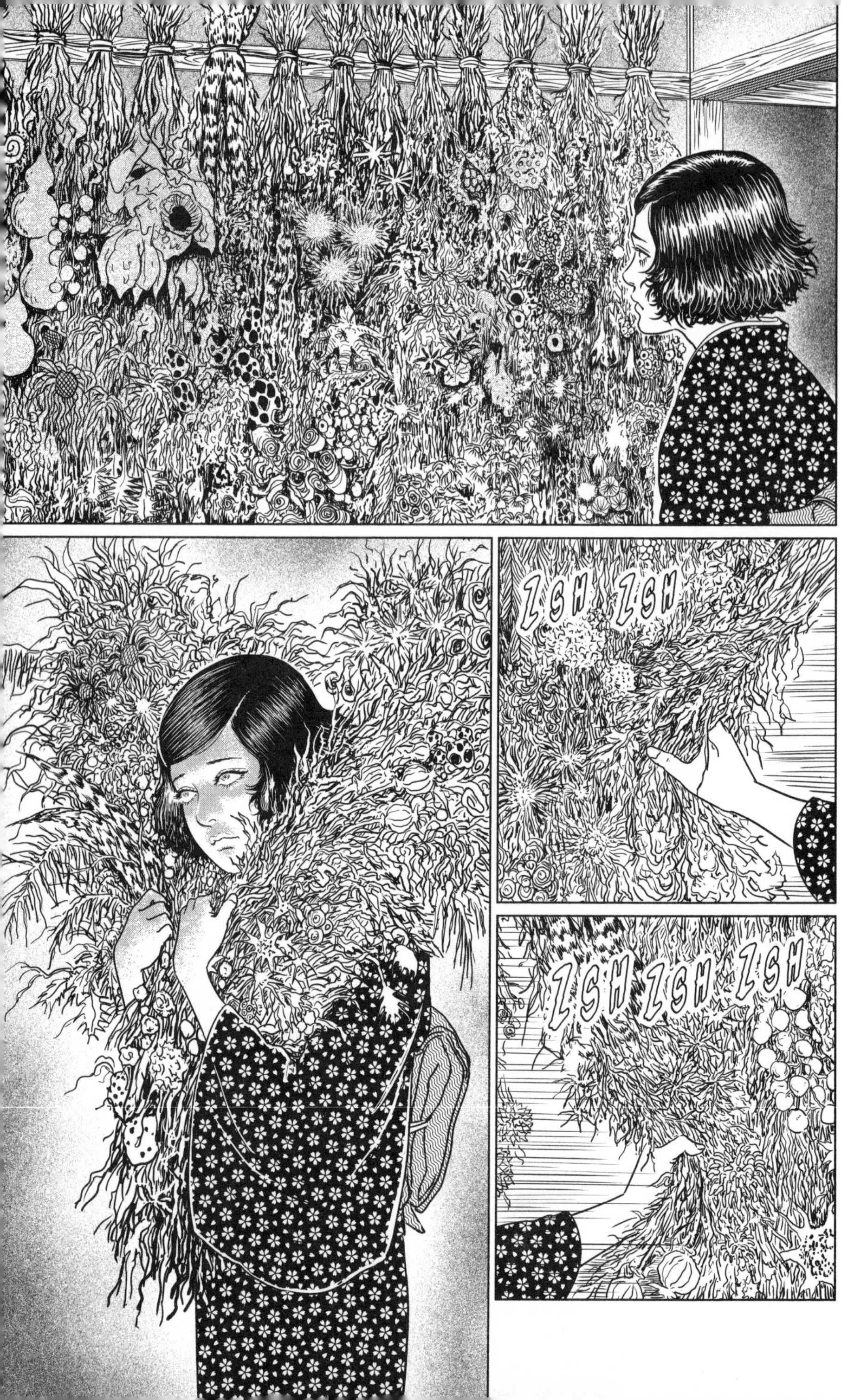
ZSH ZSH
ZSH ZSH ZSH

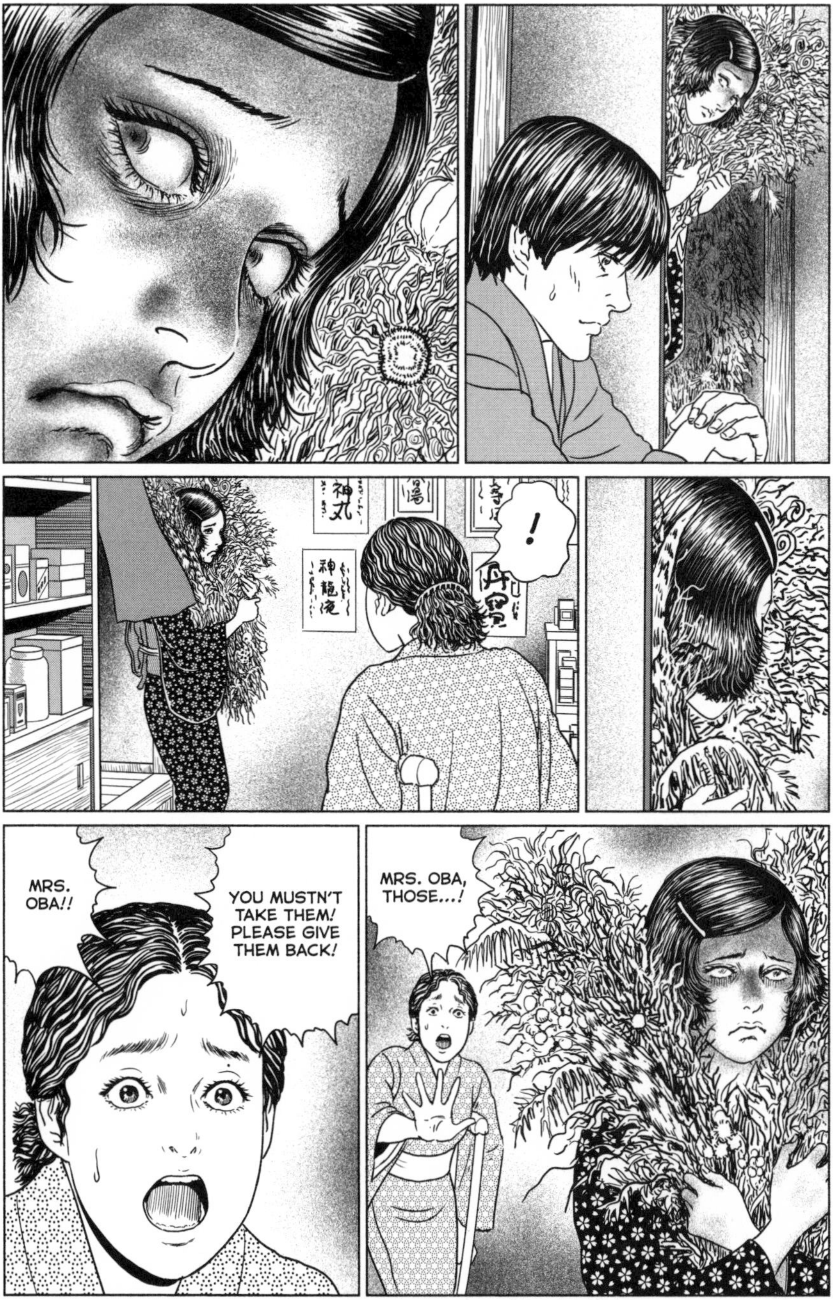
!
MRS. OBA, THOSE...!
YOU MUSTN'T TAKE THEM! PLEASE GIVE THEM BACK!
MRS. OBA!!

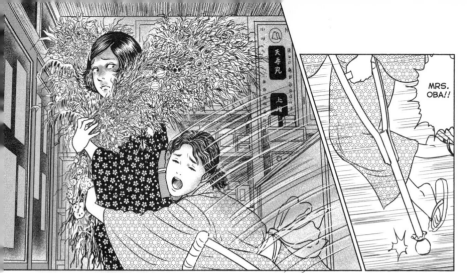

MRS. OBA!!

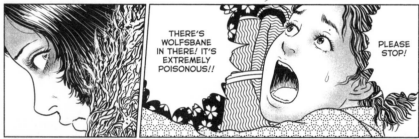

THERE'S WOLFSBANE IN THERE! IT'S EXTREMELY POISONOUS!!

PLEASE STOP!

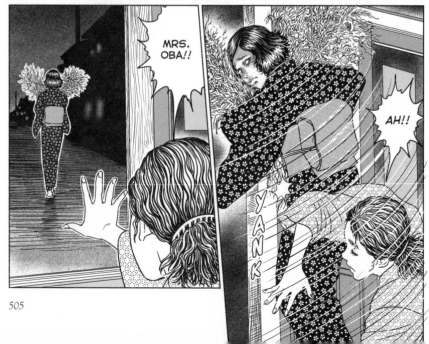

MRS. OBA!!

AH!!

YANK

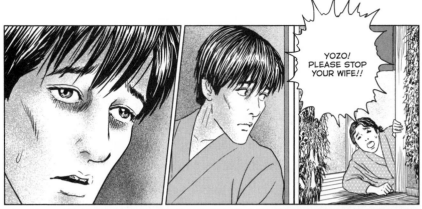

YOZO! PLEASE STOP YOUR WIFE!!
An hour later...
...another telegram came from Yoshiko.
"COME HOME NOW..."
"...OTHER-WISE, I WILL DIE ALONE."
YOZO!
PLEASE, YOU HAVE TO STOP YOUR WIFE.
IF YOU WON'T GO, I WILL!
PLEASE TELL ME YOUR ADDRESS!
IT'S ALL RIGHT...
IT'S ALL RIGHT...

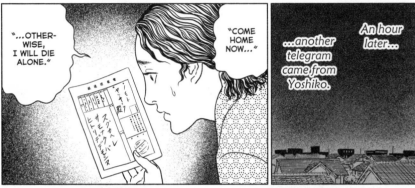

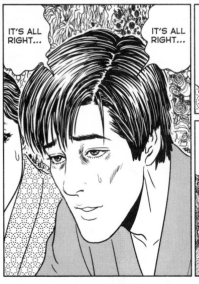

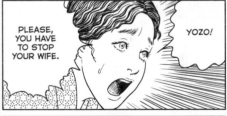

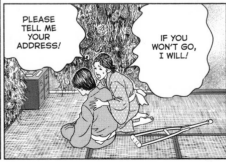

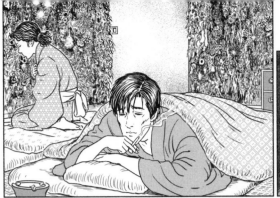

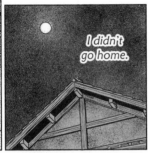

I didn't go home.

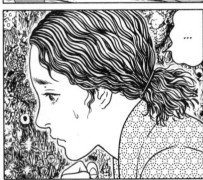

...

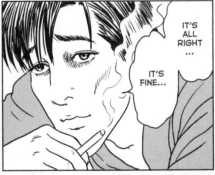

IT'S ALL RIGHT
...

IT'S FINE...

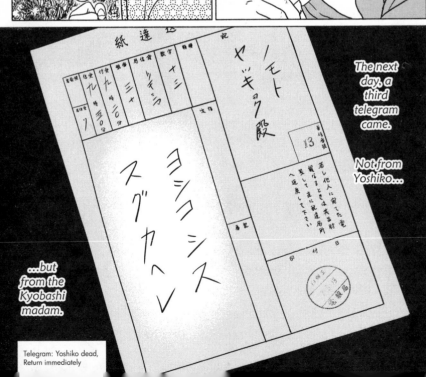

The next day, a third telegram came.

Not from Yoshiko...

...but from the Kyobashi madam.

Telegram: Yoshiko dead, Return immediately

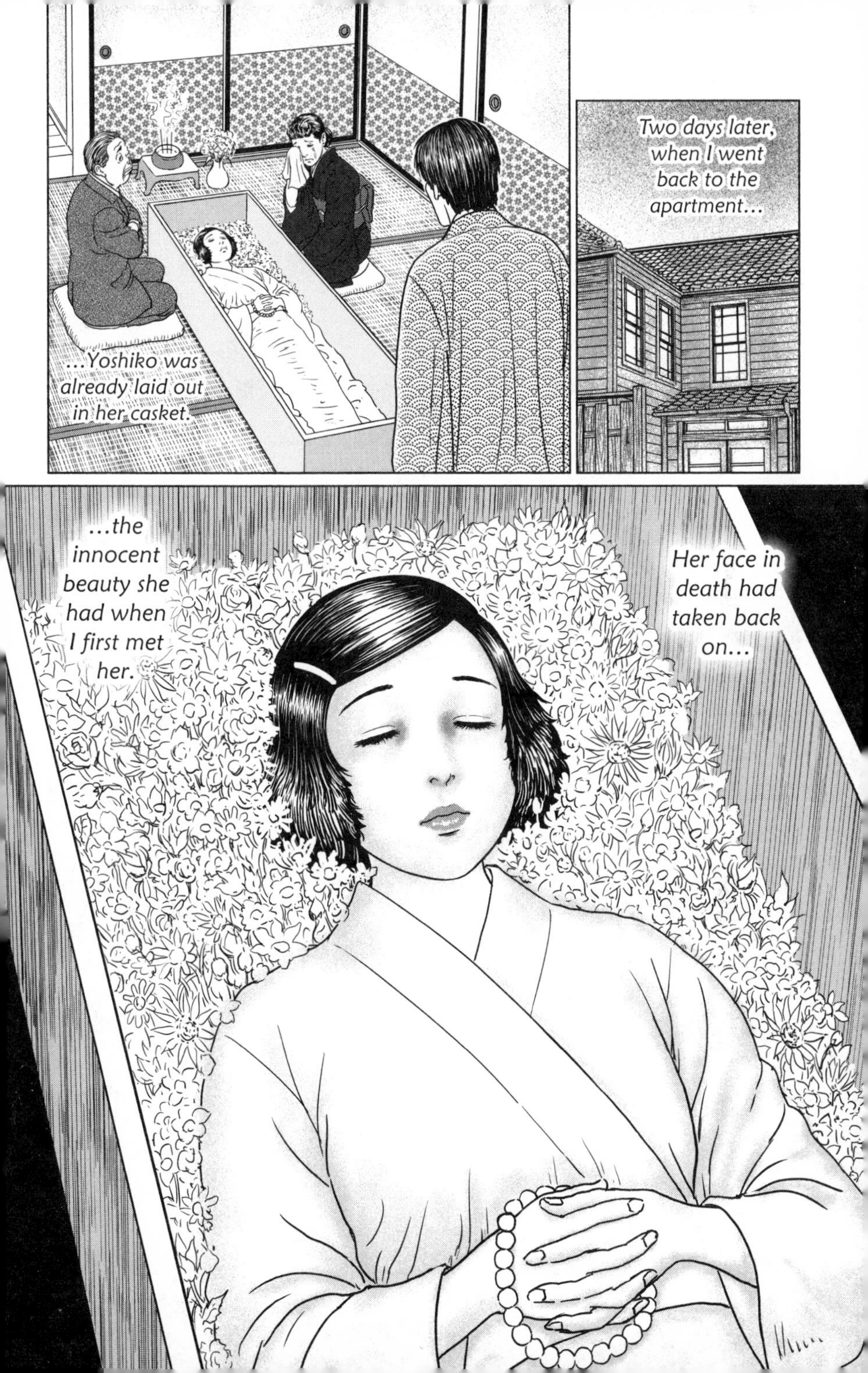
Two days later, when I went back to the apartment…
…Yoshiko was already laid out in her casket.
Her face in death had taken back on…
…the innocent beauty she had when I first met her.

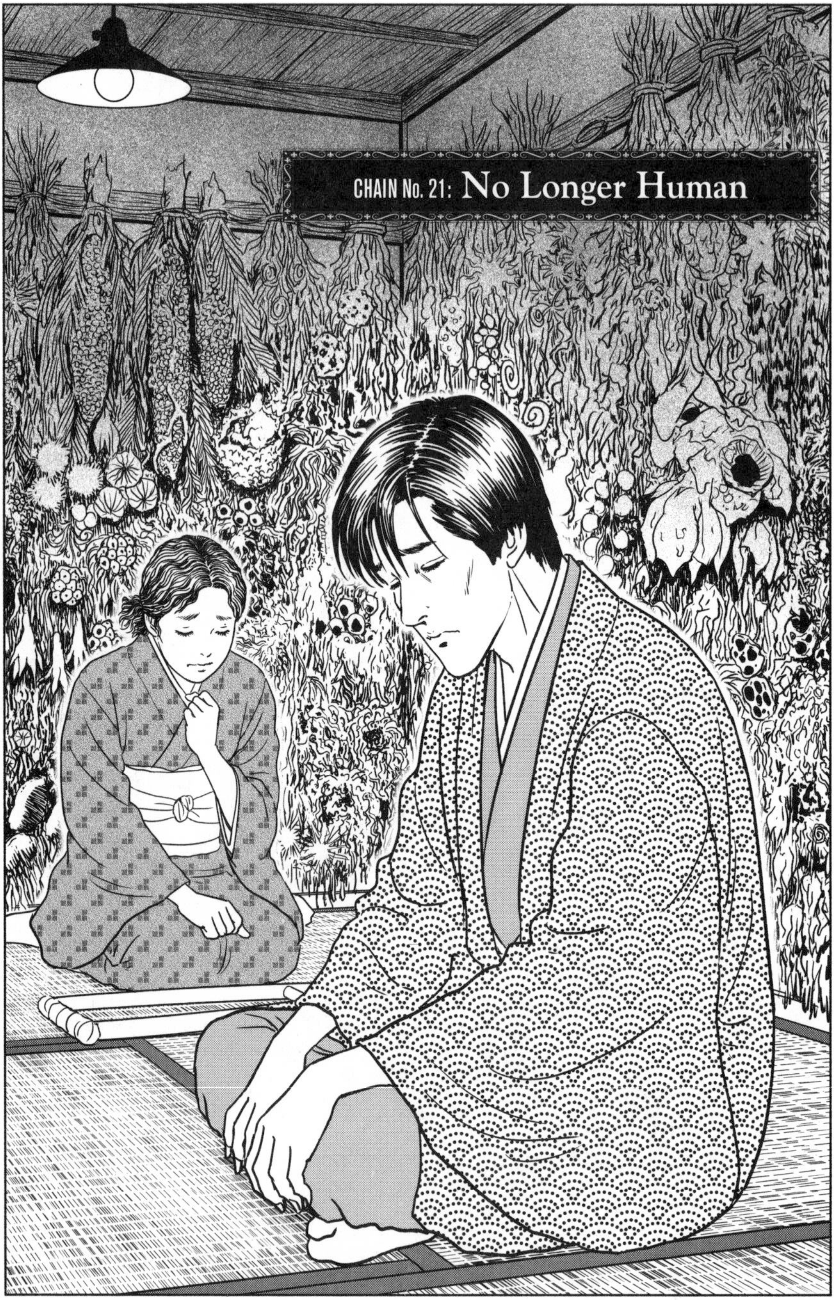
CHAIN No. 21: No Longer Human

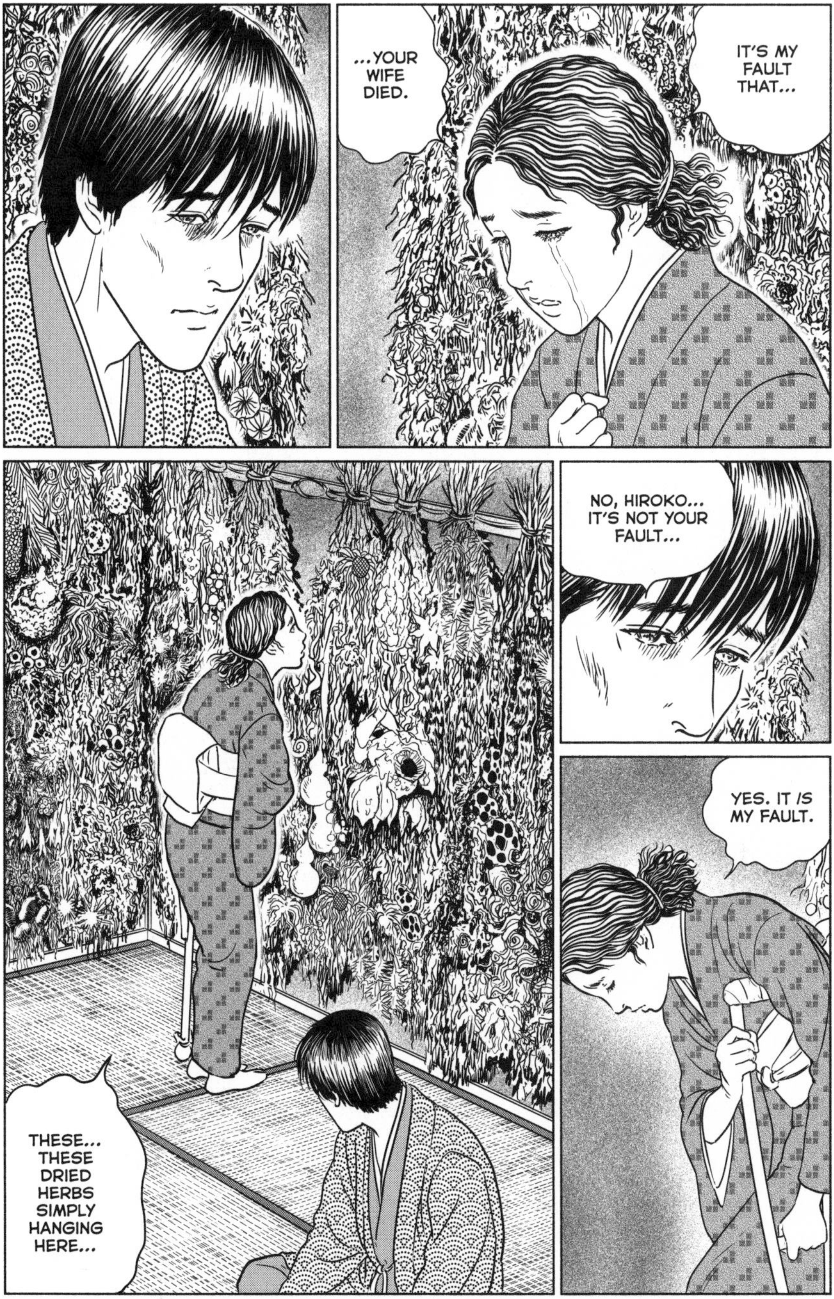
IT'S MY FAULT THAT...
...YOUR WIFE DIED.
NO, HIROKO... IT'S NOT YOUR FAULT...
YES. IT *IS* MY FAULT.
THESE... THESE DRIED HERBS SIMPLY HANGING HERE...

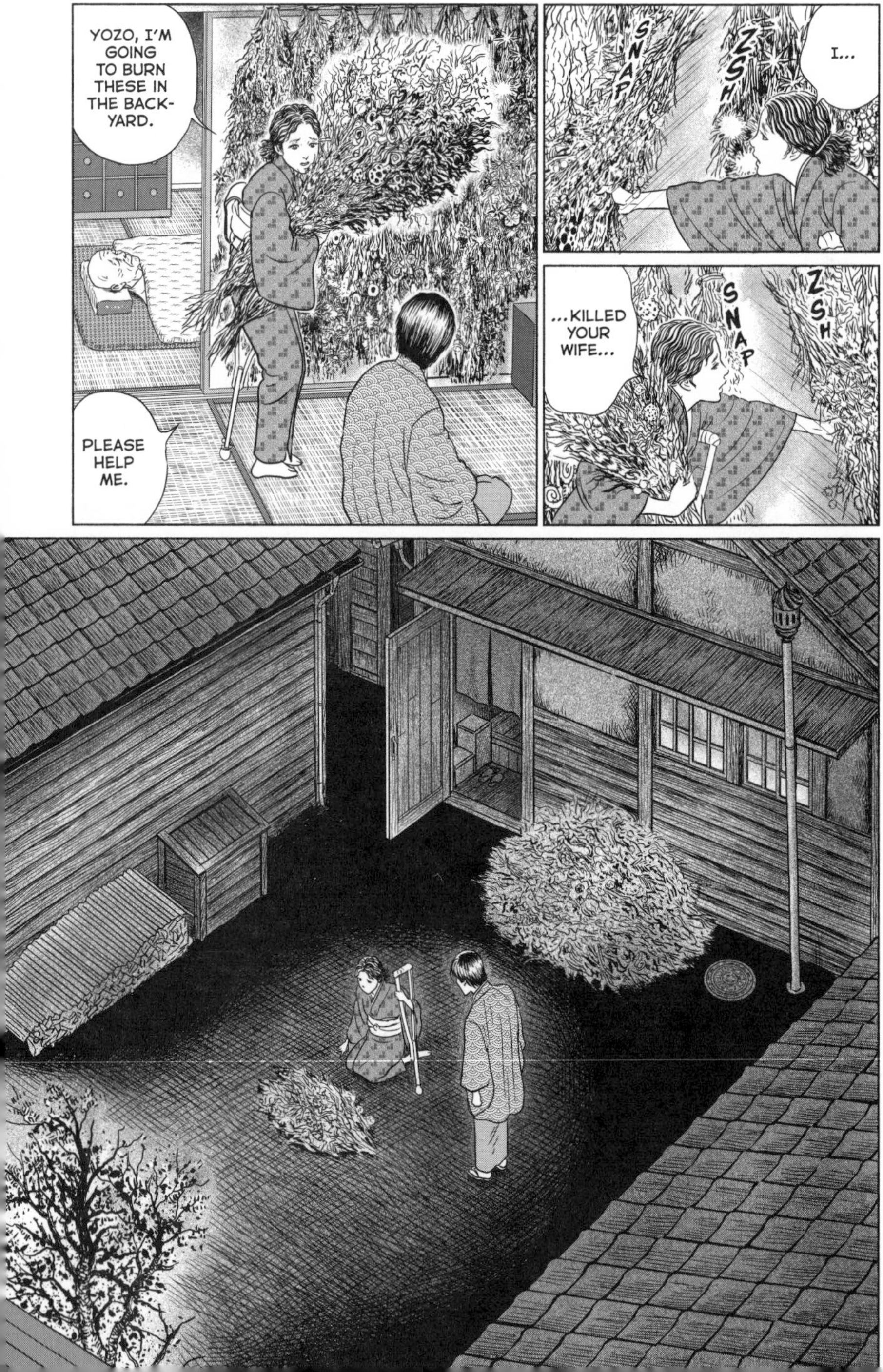
I...
ZSH
SNAP
ZSH
SNAP
...KILLED YOUR WIFE...
YOZO, I'M GOING TO BURN THESE IN THE BACK-YARD.
PLEASE HELP ME.

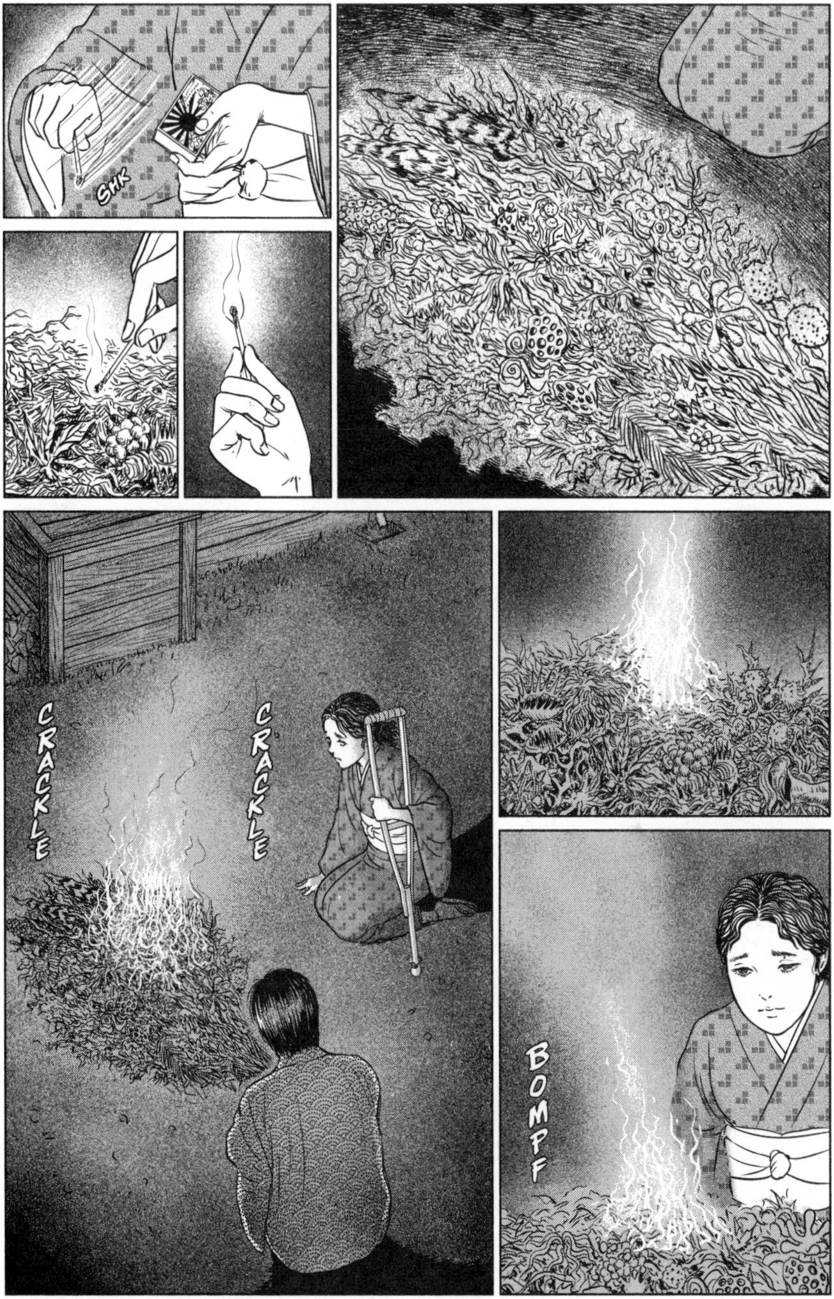
SHK
BOMPF
CRACKLE
CRACKLE

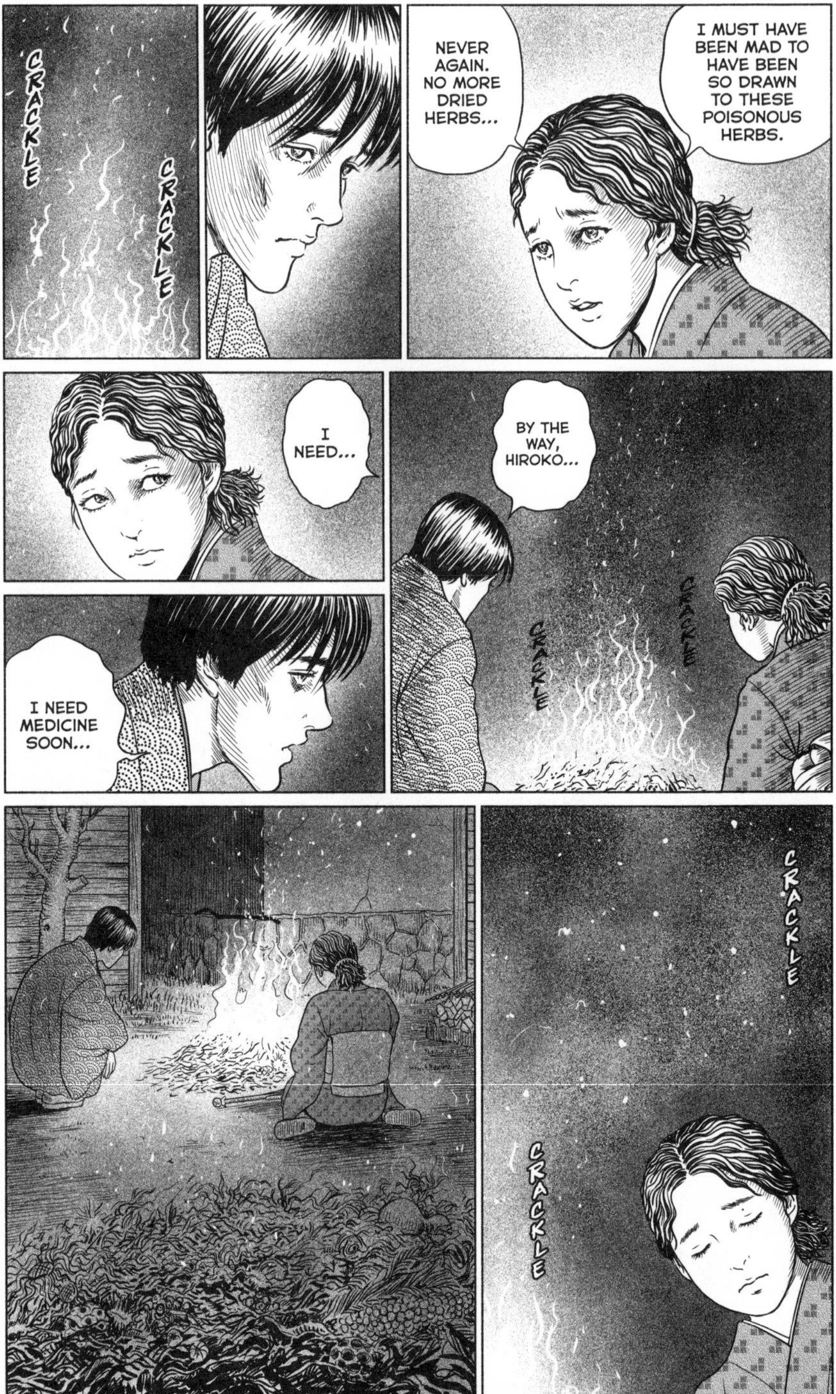
I MUST HAVE BEEN MAD TO HAVE BEEN SO DRAWN TO THESE POISONOUS HERBS.
NEVER AGAIN. NO MORE DRIED HERBS...
CRACKLE
CRACKLE
BY THE WAY, HIROKO...
CRACKLE
CRACKLE
I NEED...
I NEED MEDICINE SOON...
CRACKLE
CRACKLE

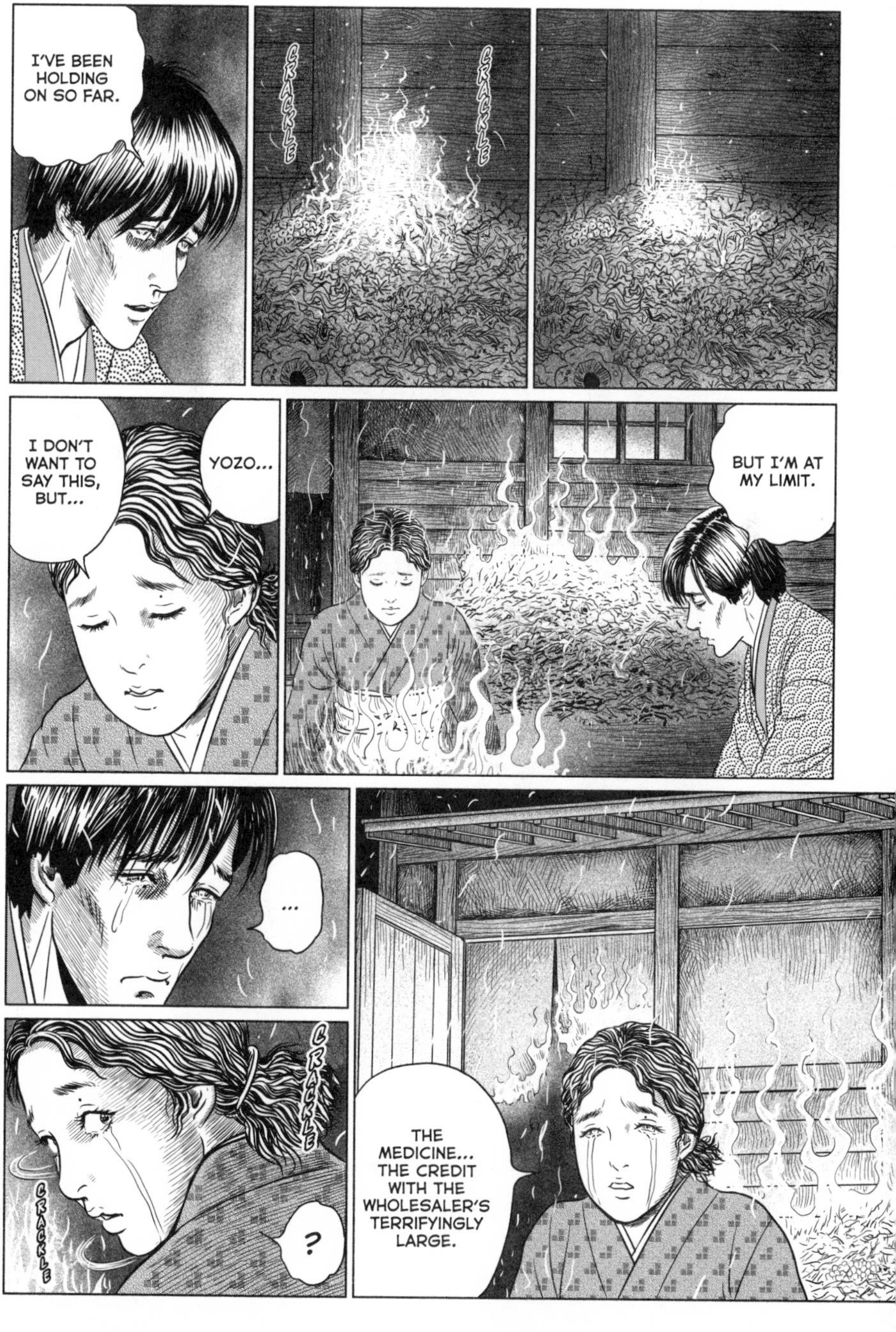
CRACKLE
CRACKLE
I'VE BEEN HOLDING ON SO FAR.
BUT I'M AT MY LIMIT.
YOZO...
I DON'T WANT TO SAY THIS, BUT...
THE MEDICINE... THE CREDIT WITH THE WHOLESALER'S TERRIFYINGLY LARGE.
...
CRACKLE
?
CRACKLE

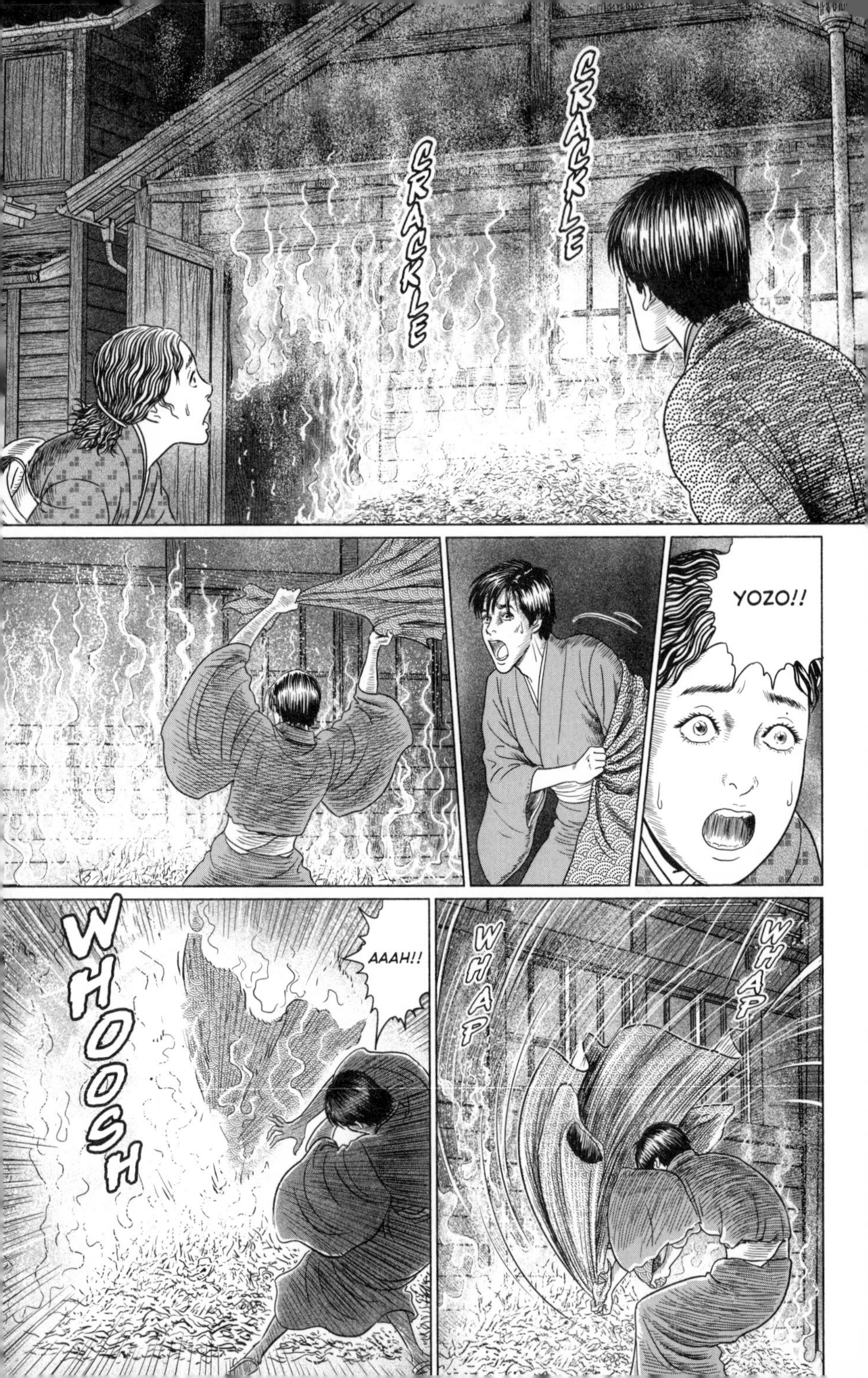
CRACKLE
CRACKLE
YOZO!!
WHAP
WHAP
AAAH!!
WHOOSH

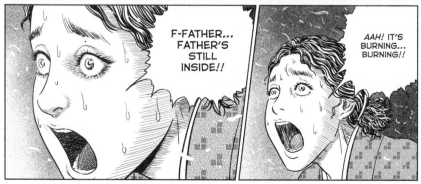

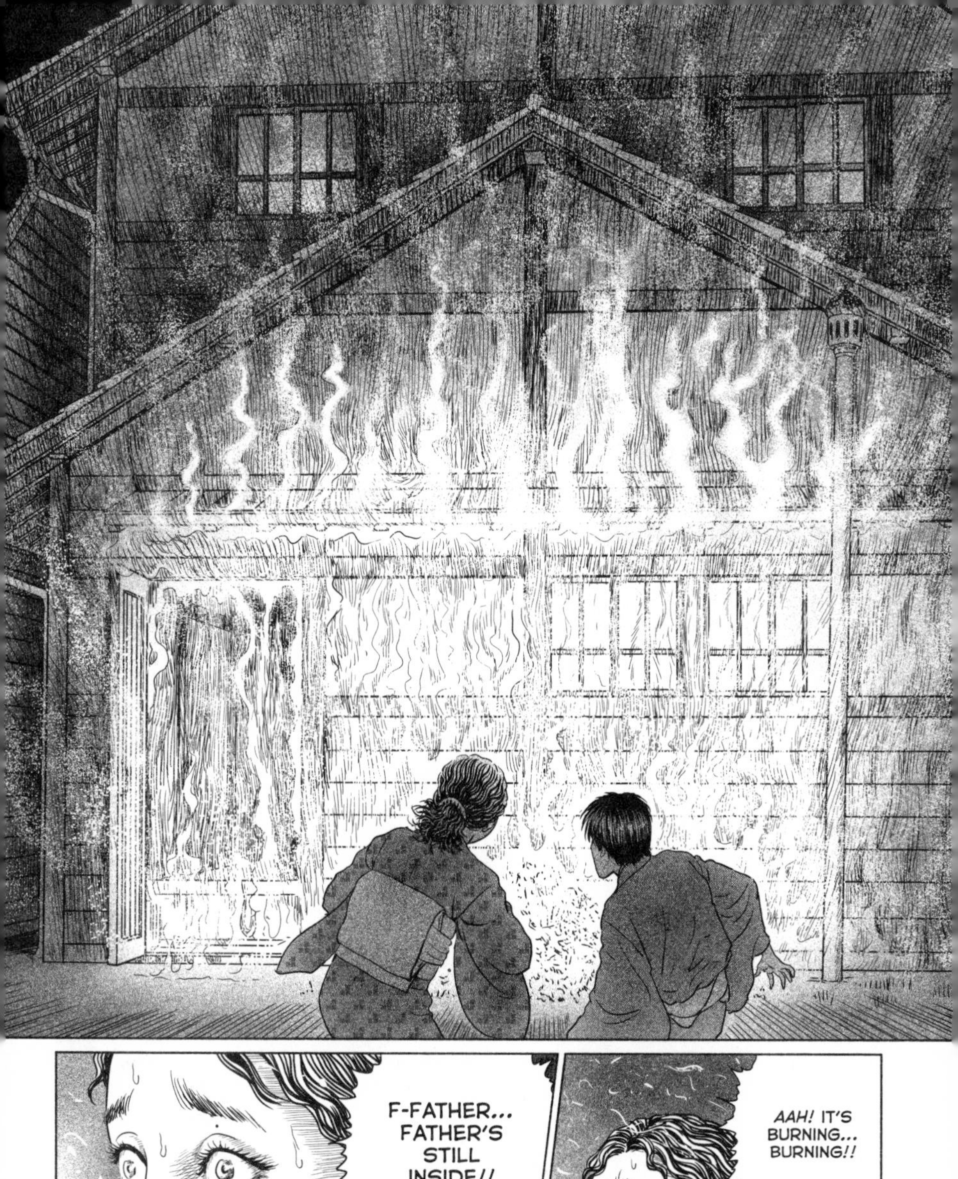
AAH! IT'S BURNING... BURNING!!
F-FATHER... FATHER'S STILL INSIDE!!

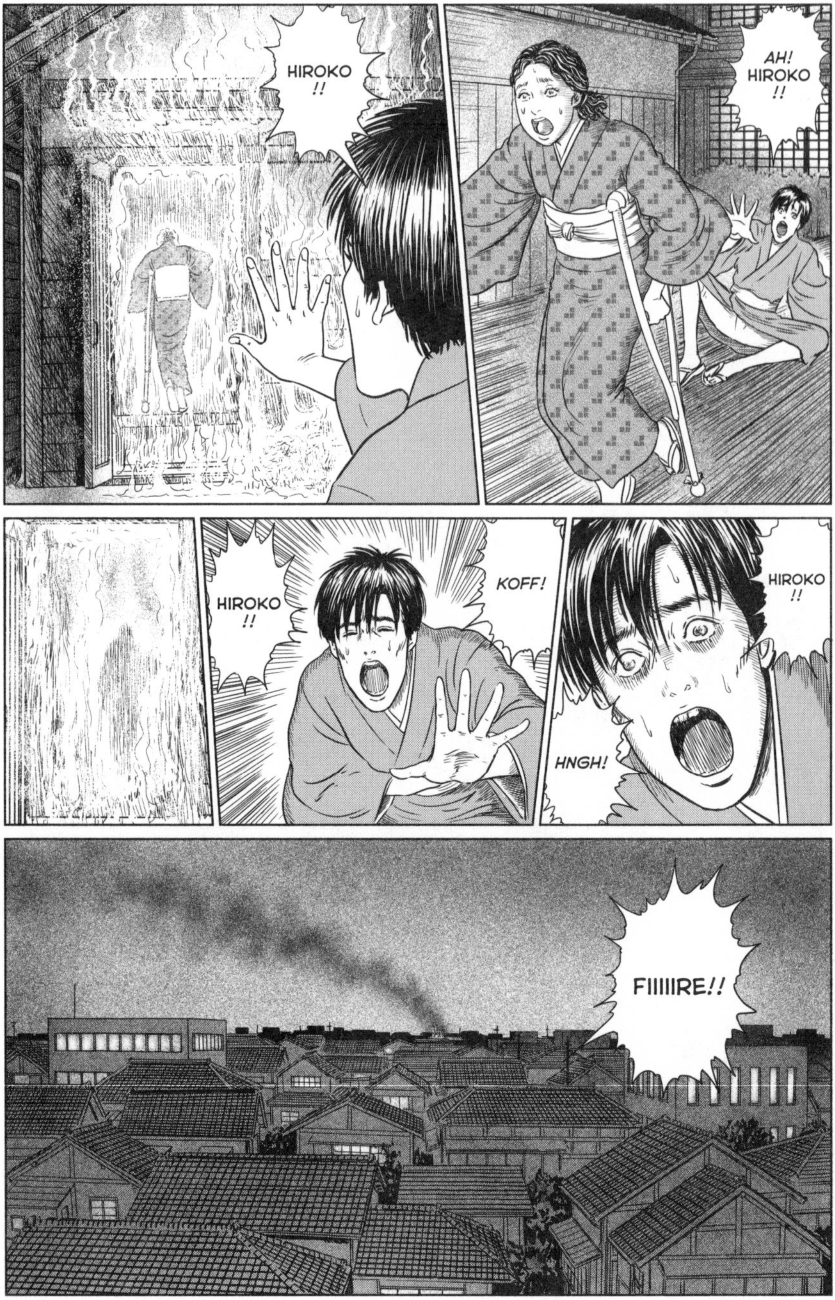
AH! HIROKO !!
HIROKO !!
HIROKO !!
HNGH!
KOFF!
HIROKO !!
FIIIIIRE!!

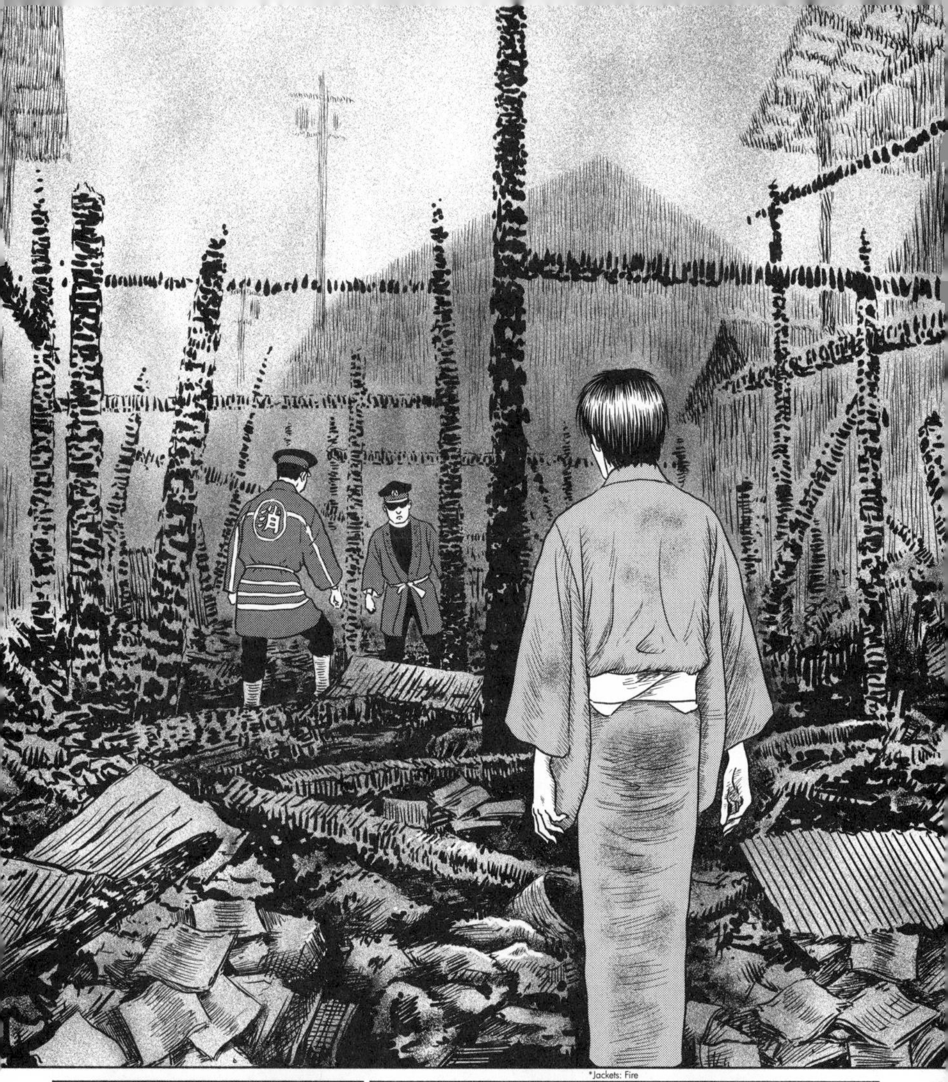

*Jackets: Fire

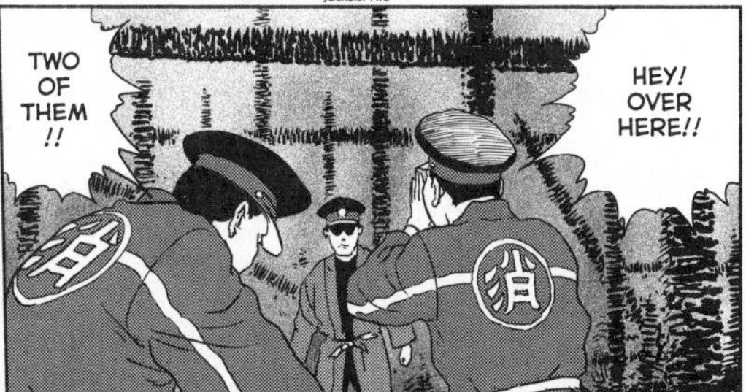
HEY! OVER HERE!!
TWO OF THEM!!

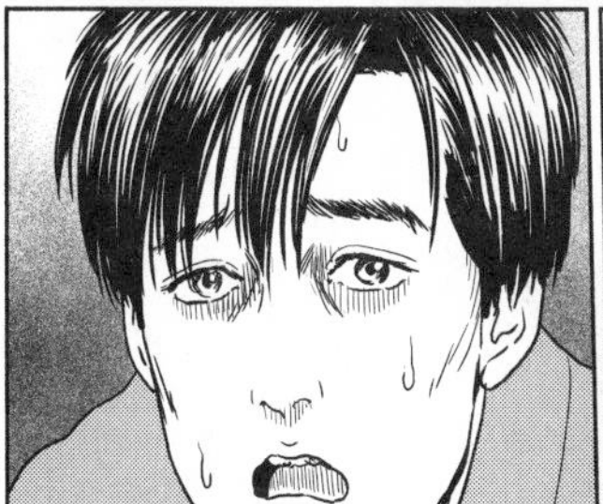

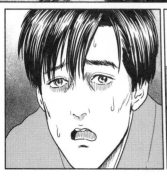

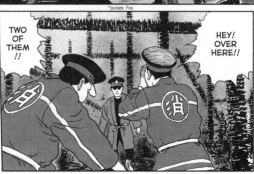

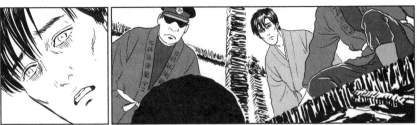

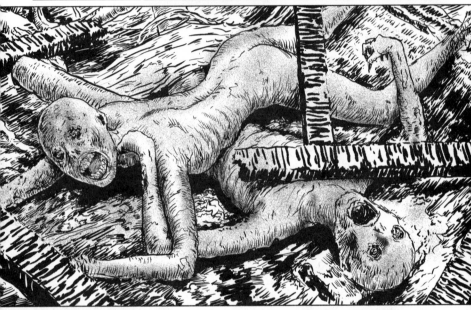

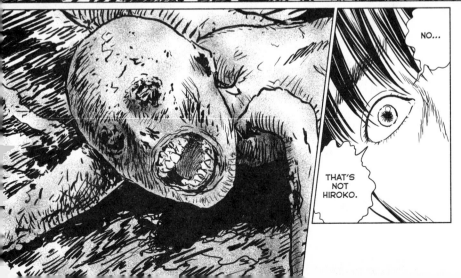

NO...

THAT'S
NOT
HIROKO.

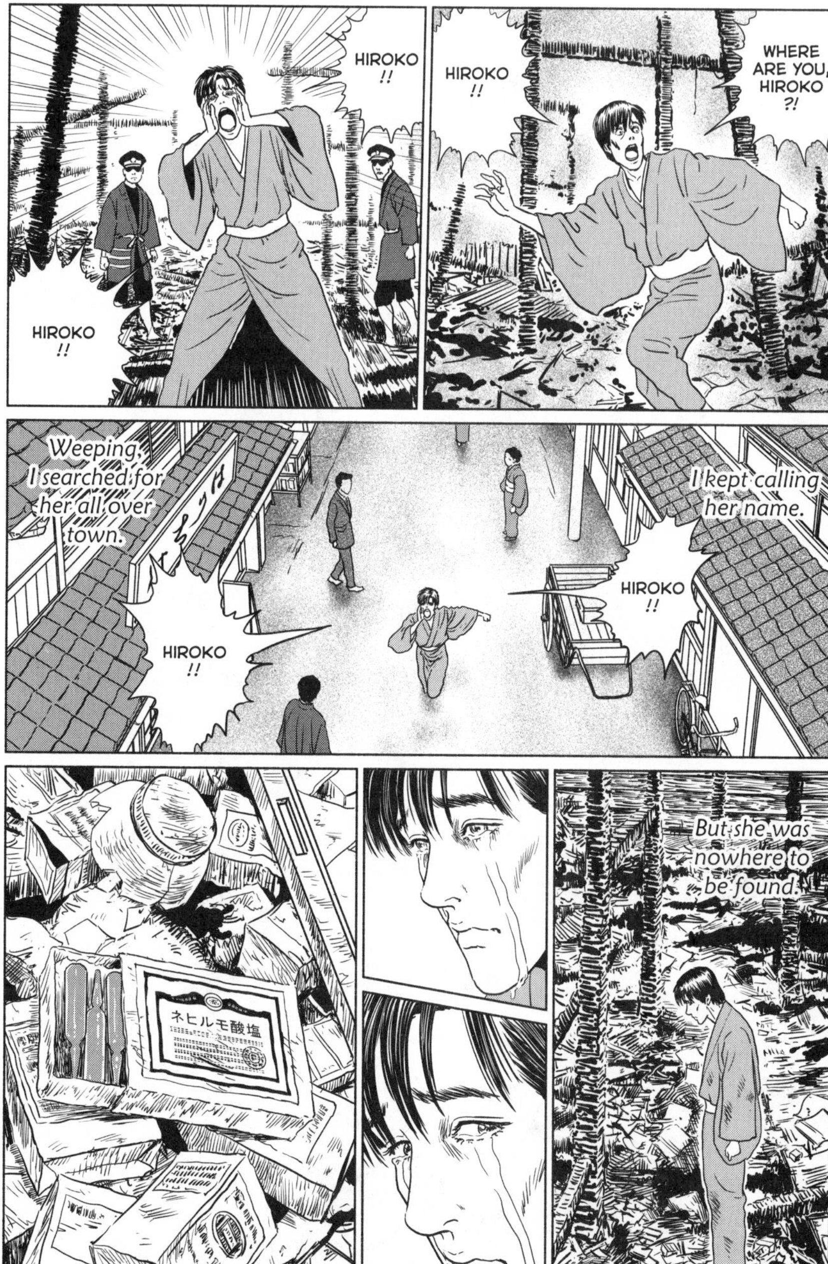
WHERE ARE YOU, HIROKO ?!
HIROKO !!
HIROKO !!
HIROKO !!
I kept calling her name.
Weeping, I searched for her all over town.
HIROKO !!
HIROKO !!
But she was nowhere to be found.
ネヒルモ酸塩

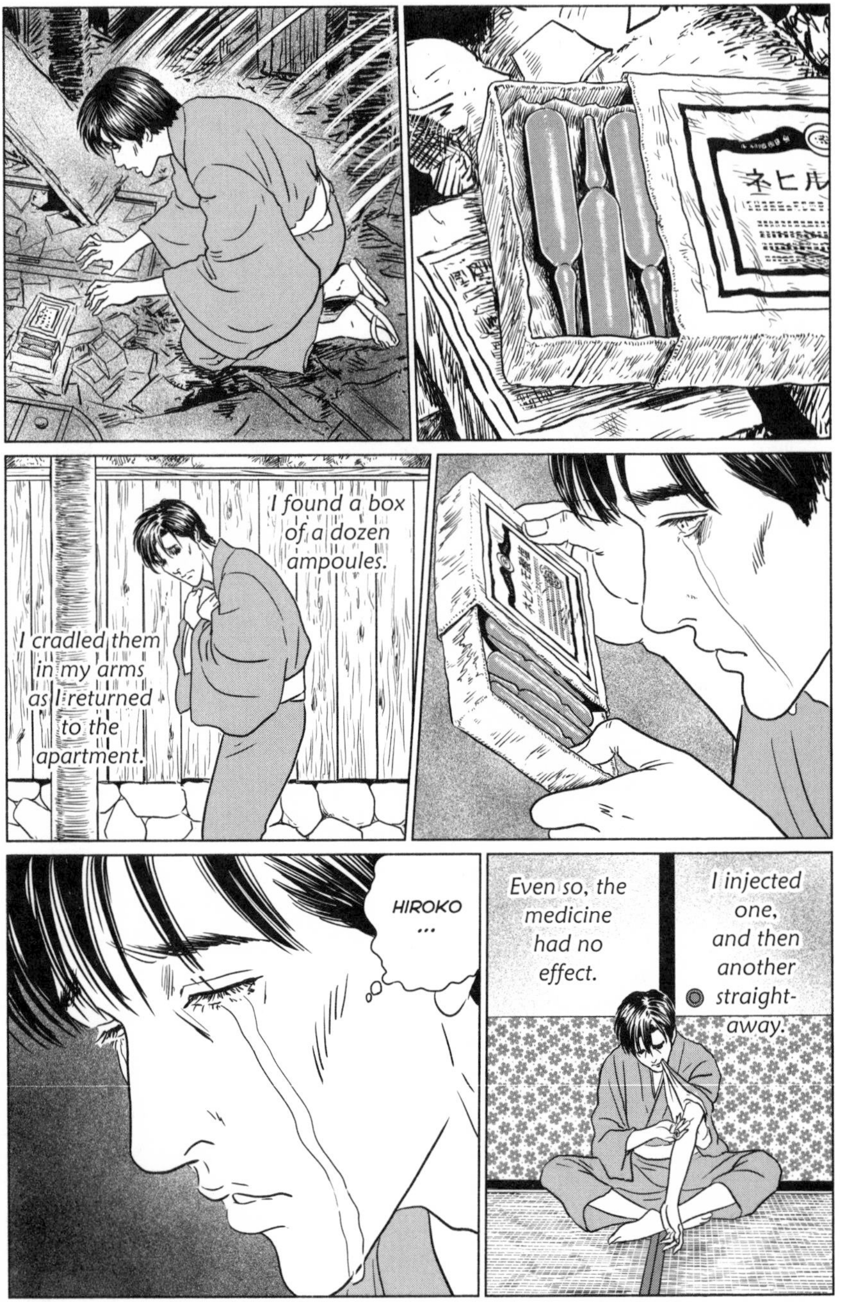
I found a box of a dozen ampoules.
I cradled them in my arms as I returned to the apartment.
I injected one, and then another straight-away.
Even so, the medicine had no effect.
HIROKO ...

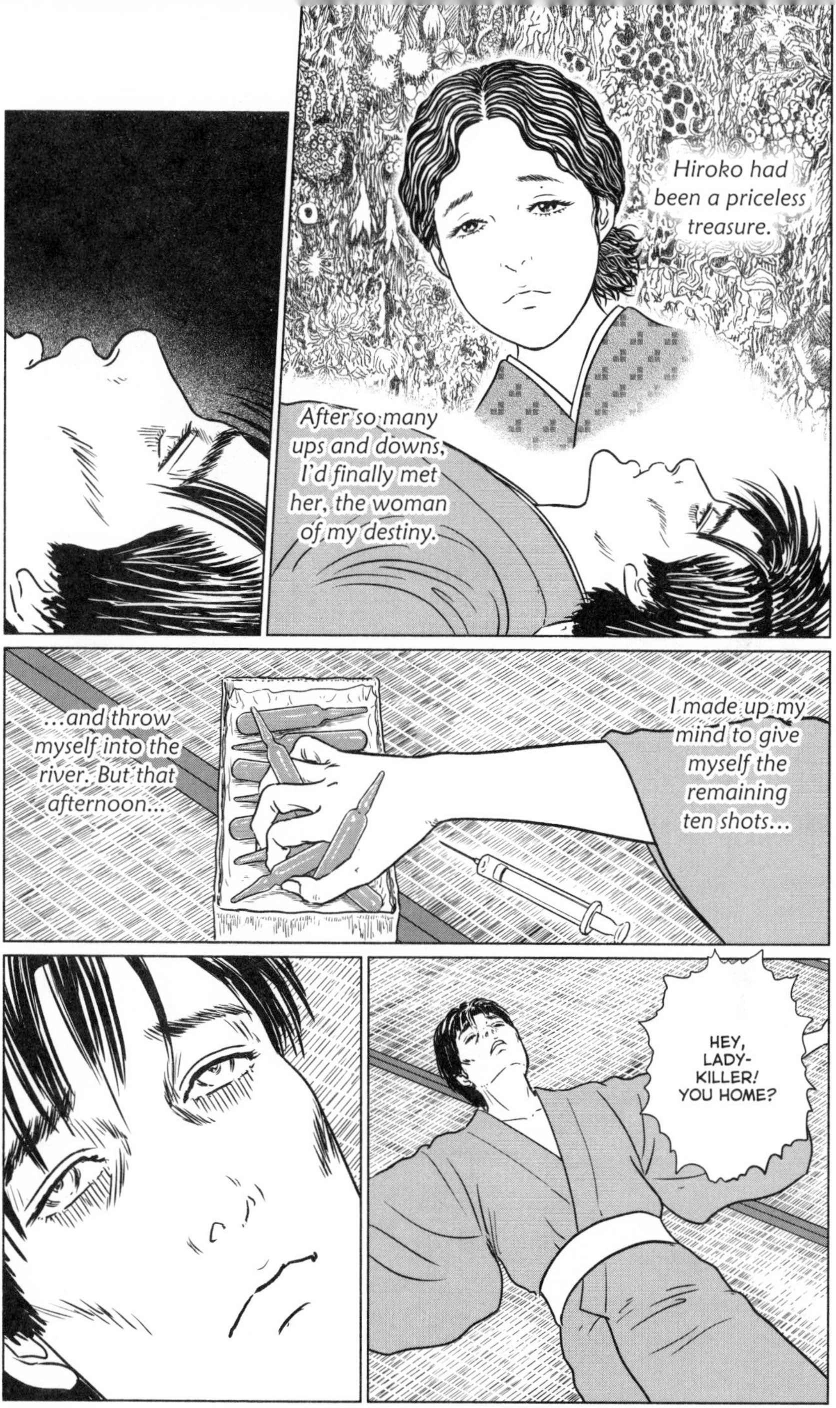
Hiroko had been a priceless treasure.
After so many ups and downs, I'd finally met her, the woman of my destiny.
I made up my mind to give myself the remaining ten shots...
...and throw myself into the river. But that afternoon...
HEY, LADY-KILLER! YOU HOME?

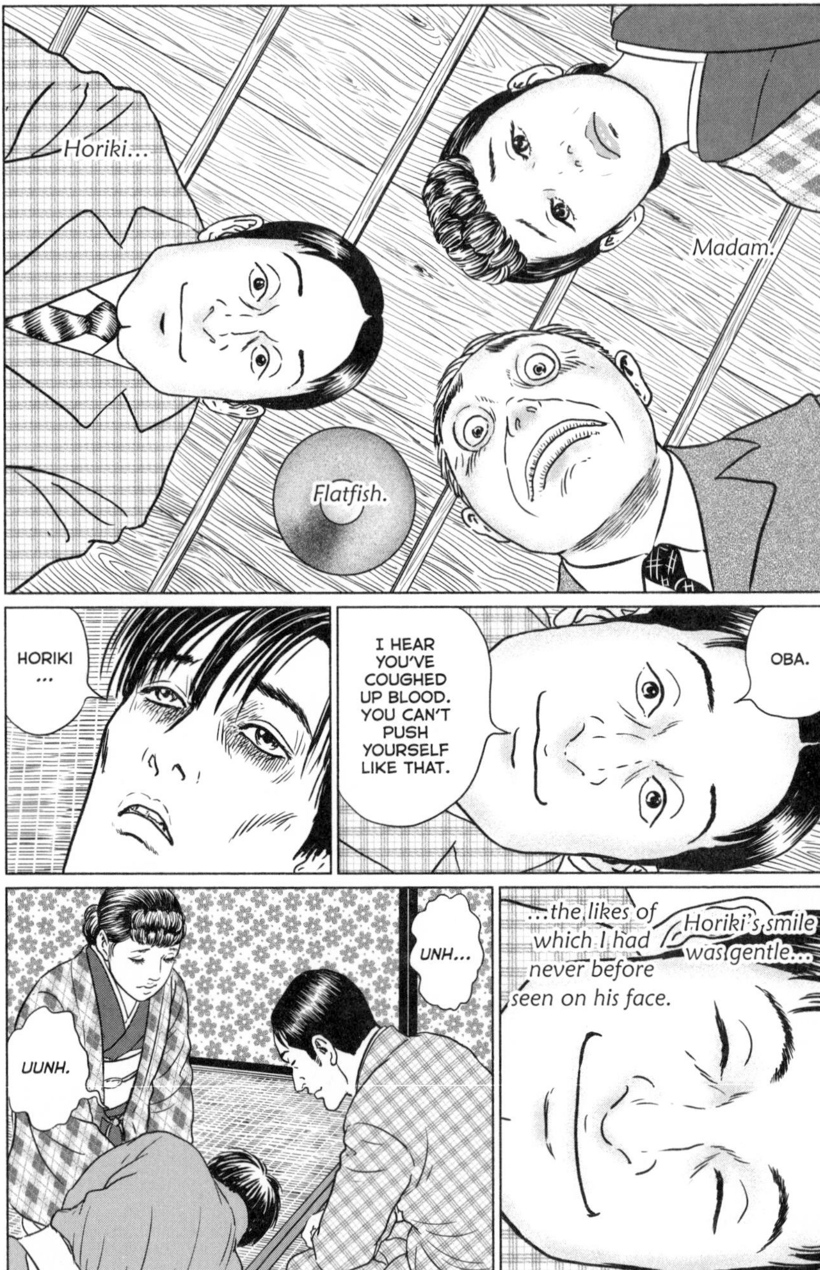
Madam.
Horiki...
Flatfish.
OBA.
I HEAR YOU'VE COUGHED UP BLOOD. YOU CAN'T PUSH YOURSELF LIKE THAT.
HORIKI ...
Horiki's smile was gentle...
...the likes of which I had never before seen on his face.
UNH...
UUNH.

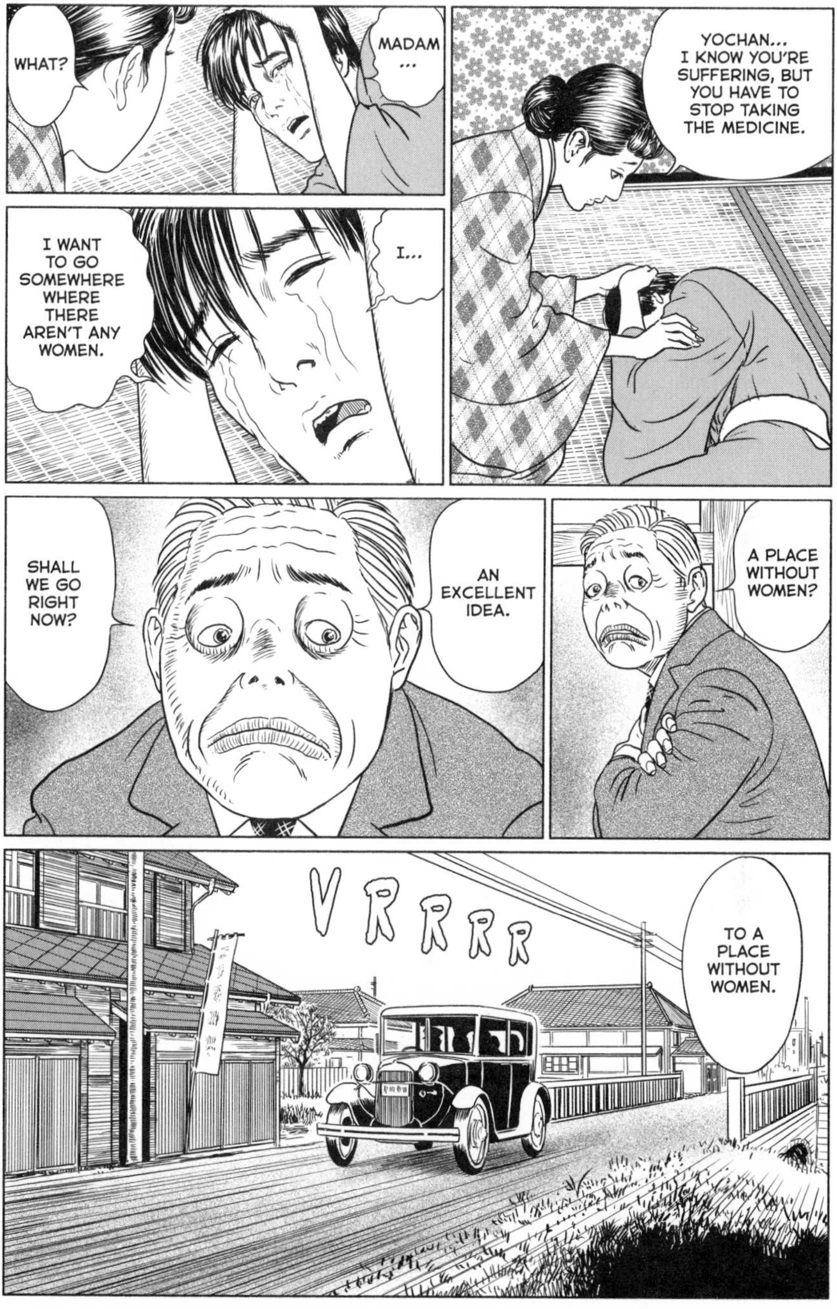
YOCHAN... I KNOW YOU'RE SUFFERING, BUT YOU HAVE TO STOP TAKING THE MEDICINE.
MADAM ...
WHAT?
I...
I WANT TO GO SOMEWHERE WHERE THERE AREN'T ANY WOMEN.
A PLACE WITHOUT WOMEN?
AN EXCELLENT IDEA.
SHALL WE GO RIGHT NOW?
TO A PLACE WITHOUT WOMEN.
VRRRR

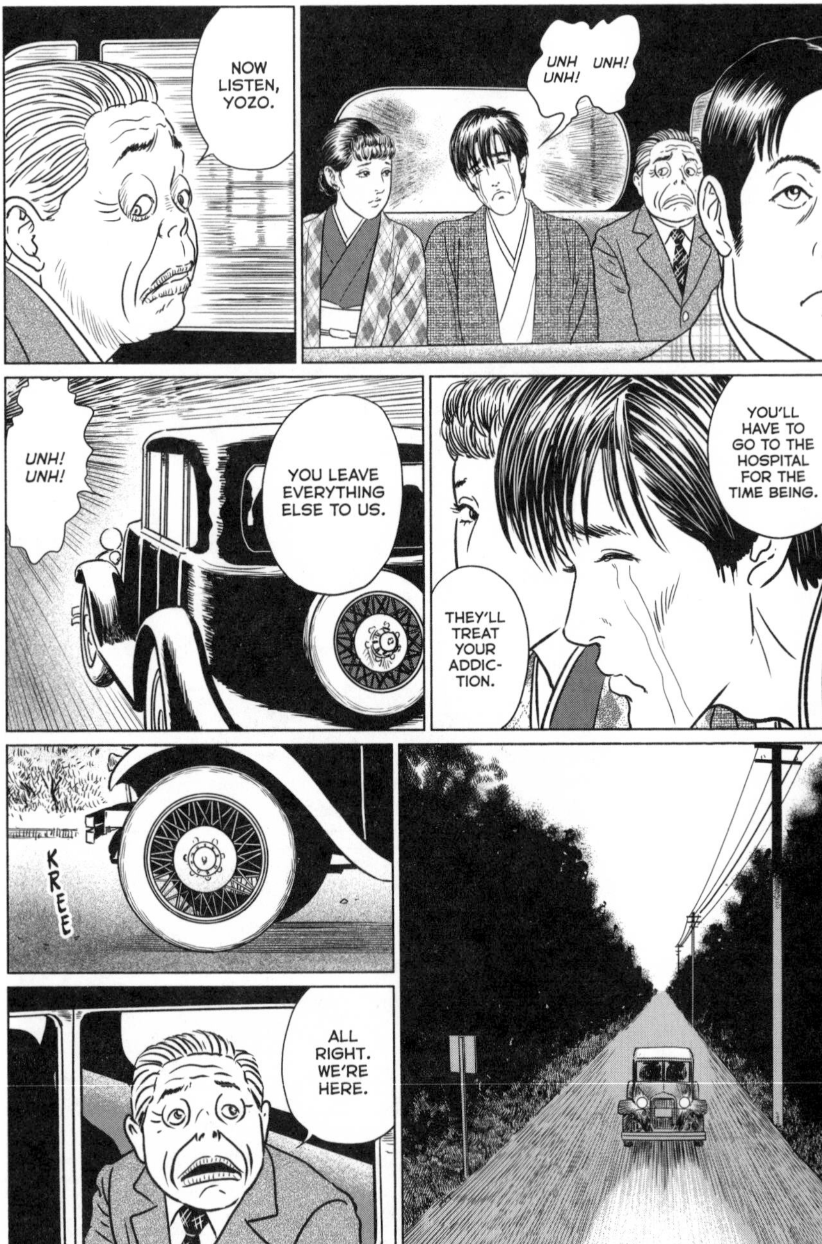
UNH UNH! UNH!
NOW LISTEN, YOZO.
YOU'LL HAVE TO GO TO THE HOSPITAL FOR THE TIME BEING.
THEY'LL TREAT YOUR ADDICTION.
YOU LEAVE EVERYTHING ELSE TO US.
UNH! UNH!
KREE
ALL RIGHT. WE'RE HERE.

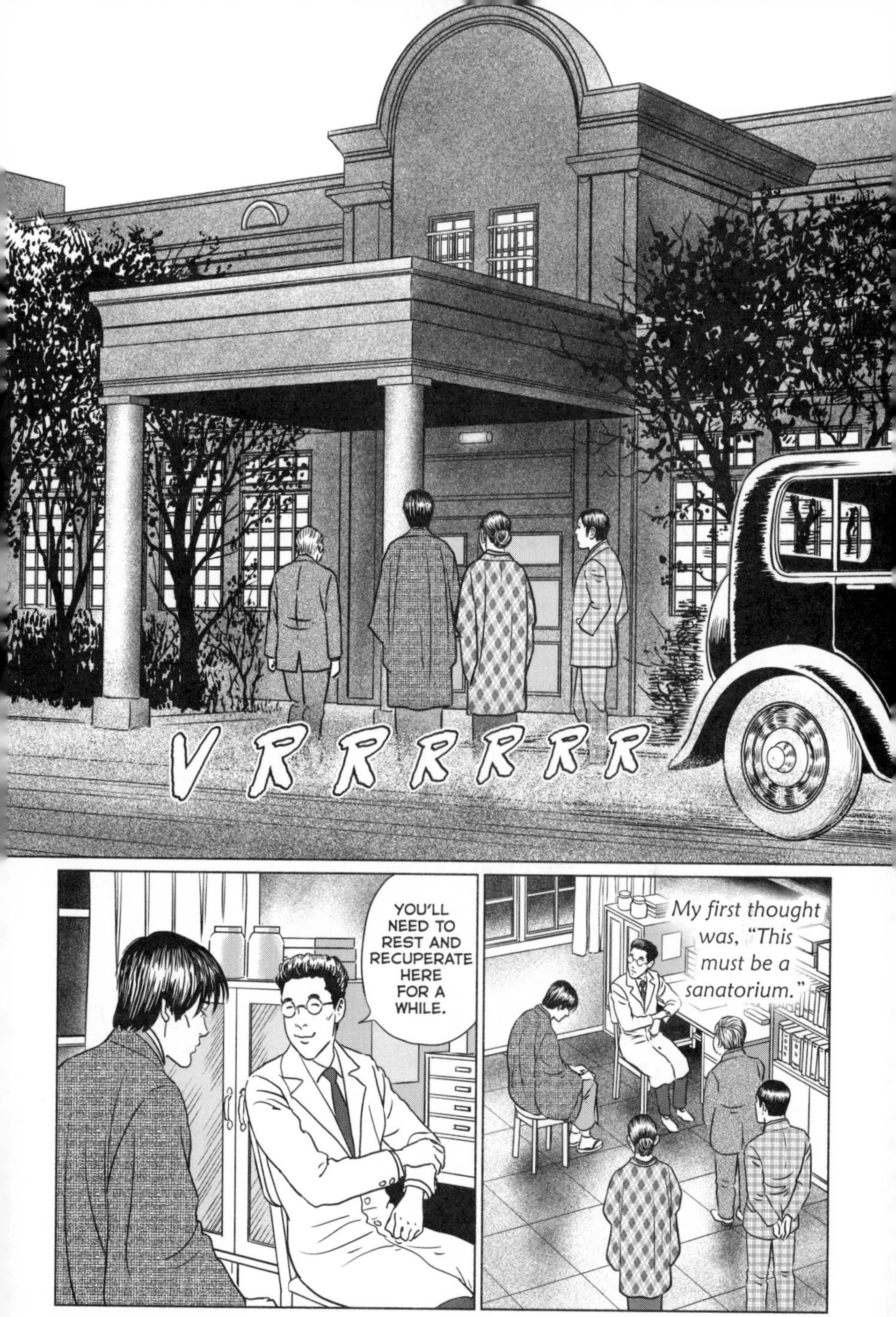
VRRRRRR
My first thought was, "This must be a sanatorium."
YOU'LL NEED TO REST AND RECUPERATE HERE FOR A WHILE.

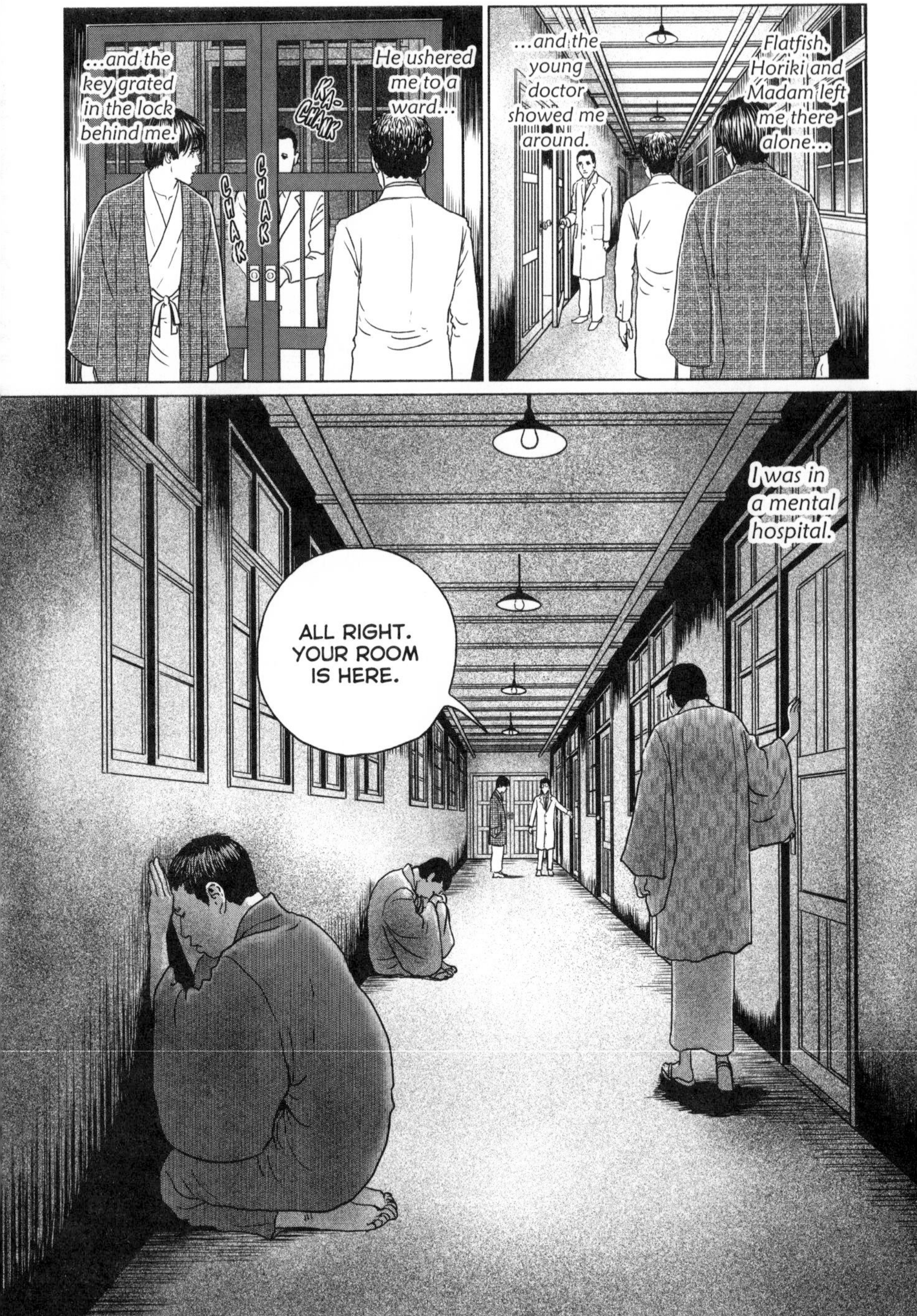
Flatfish, Horiki and Madam left me there alone...
...and the young doctor showed me around.
He ushered me to a ward...
KA-CHAK
CHAK
CHAK
...and the key grated in the lock behind me.
I was in a mental hospital.
ALL RIGHT. YOUR ROOM IS HERE.

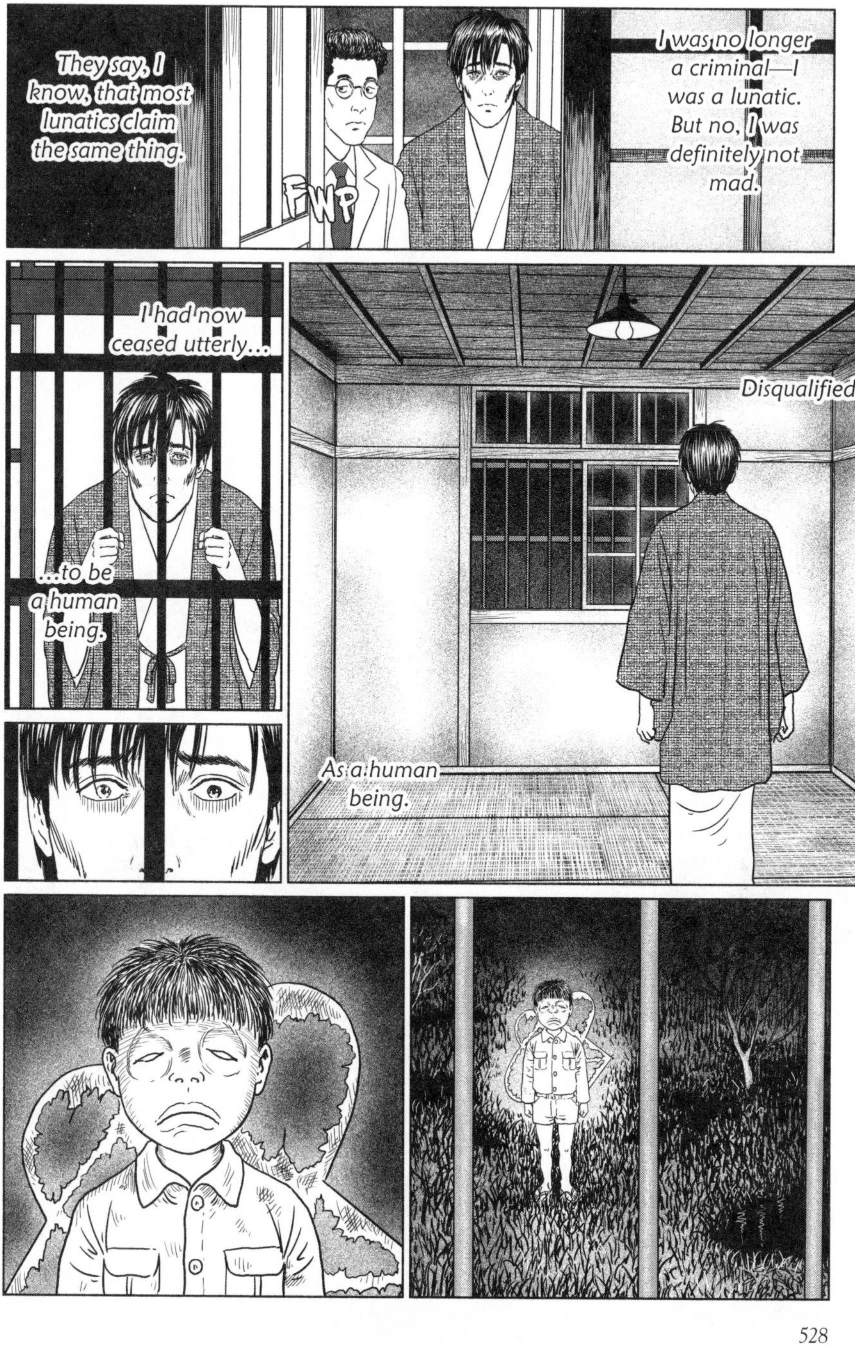
I was no longer a criminal—I was a lunatic. But no, I was definitely not mad.
They say, I know, that most lunatics claim the same thing.
FWP
Disqualified.
As a human being.
I had now ceased utterly...
...to be a human being.

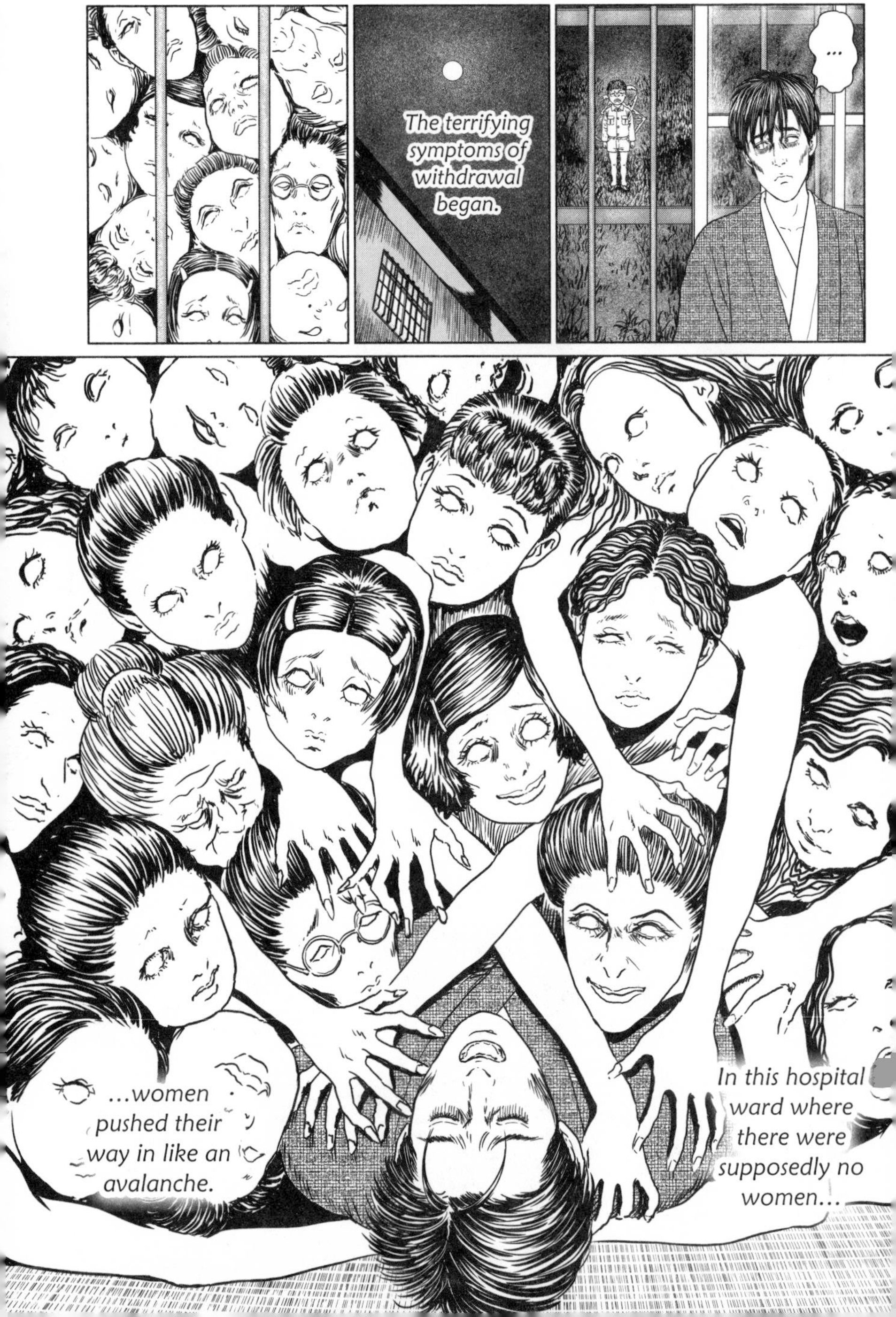
…
The terrifying symptoms of withdrawal began.
In this hospital ward where there were supposedly no women…
…women pushed their way in like an avalanche.

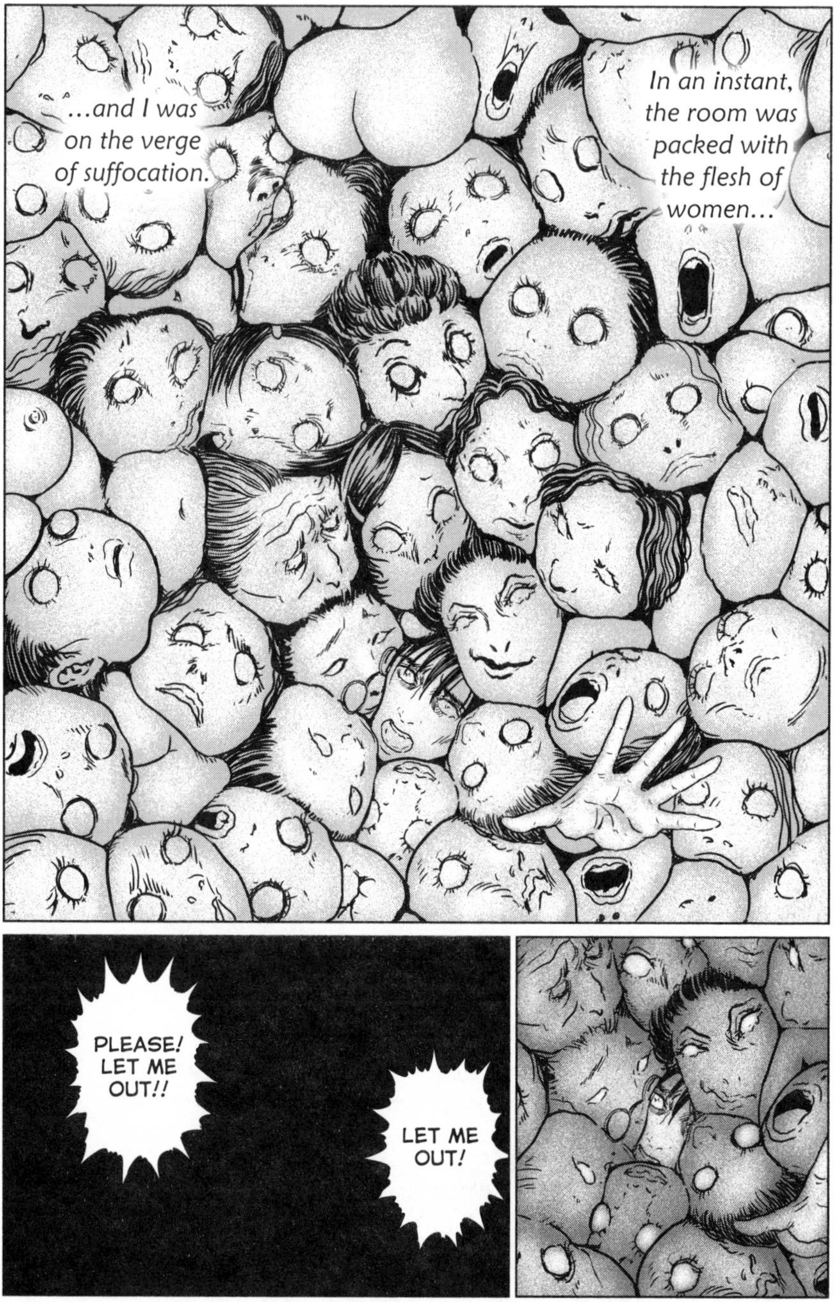
In an instant, the room was packed with the flesh of women…
…and I was on the verge of suffocation.
PLEASE! LET ME OUT!!
LET ME OUT!

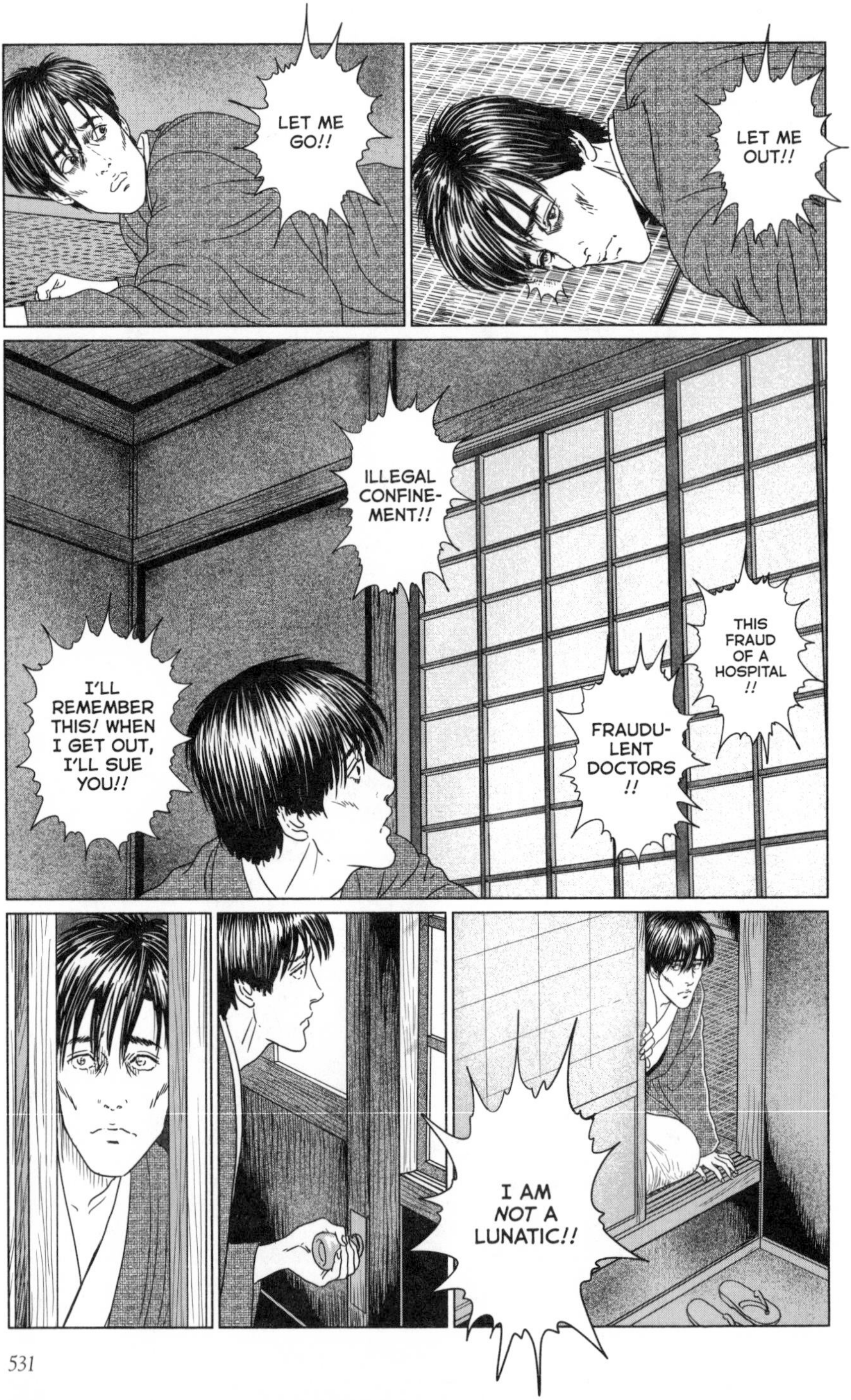
LET ME OUT!!
LET ME GO!!
ILLEGAL CONFINEMENT!!
THIS FRAUD OF A HOSPITAL!!
FRAUDULENT DOCTORS!!
I'LL REMEMBER THIS! WHEN I GET OUT, I'LL SUE YOU!!
I AM *NOT* A LUNATIC!!

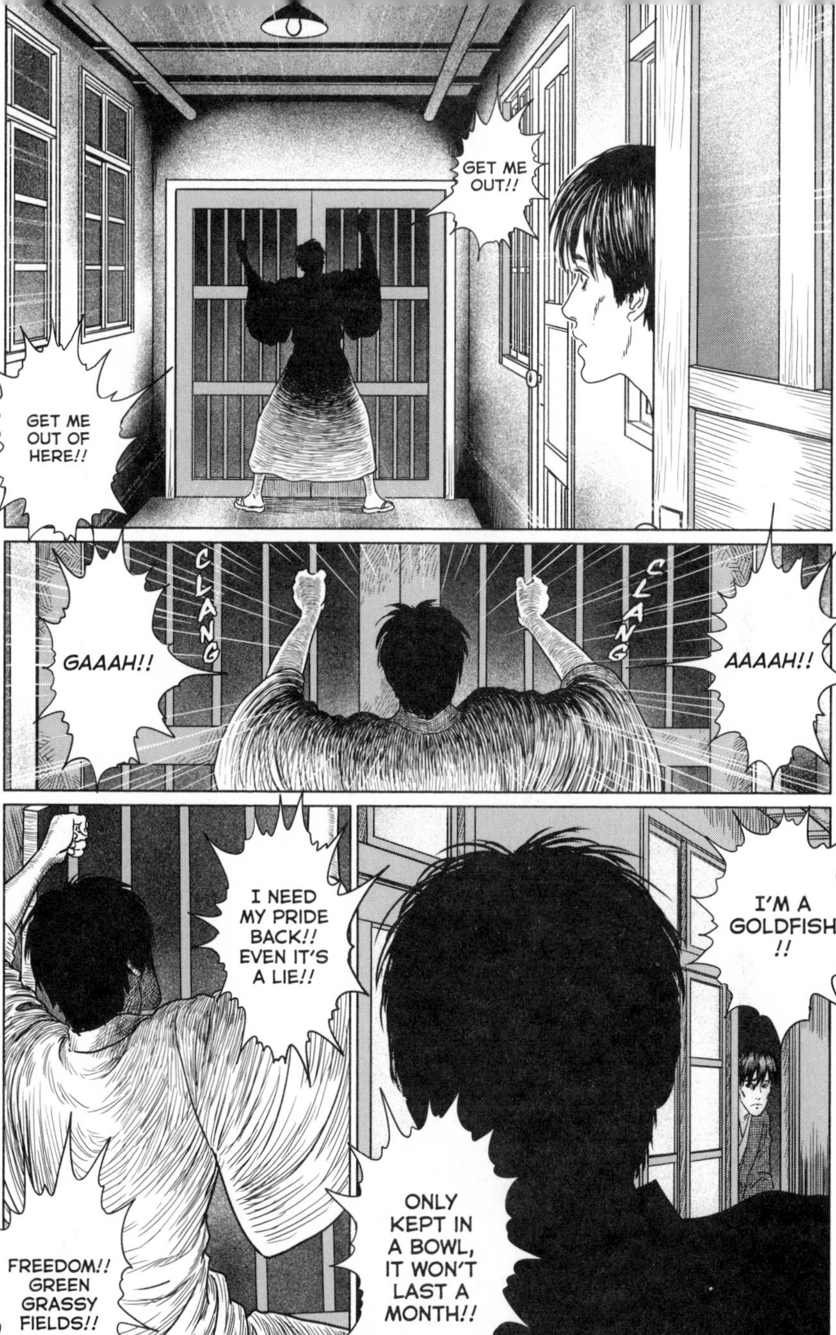
GET ME OUT!!
GET ME OUT OF HERE!!
CLANG
AAAAH!!
CLANG
GAAAH!!
I'M A GOLDFISH!!
ONLY KEPT IN A BOWL, IT WON'T LAST A MONTH!!
I NEED MY PRIDE BACK!! EVEN IT'S A LIE!!
FREEDOM!! GREEN GRASSY FIELDS!!

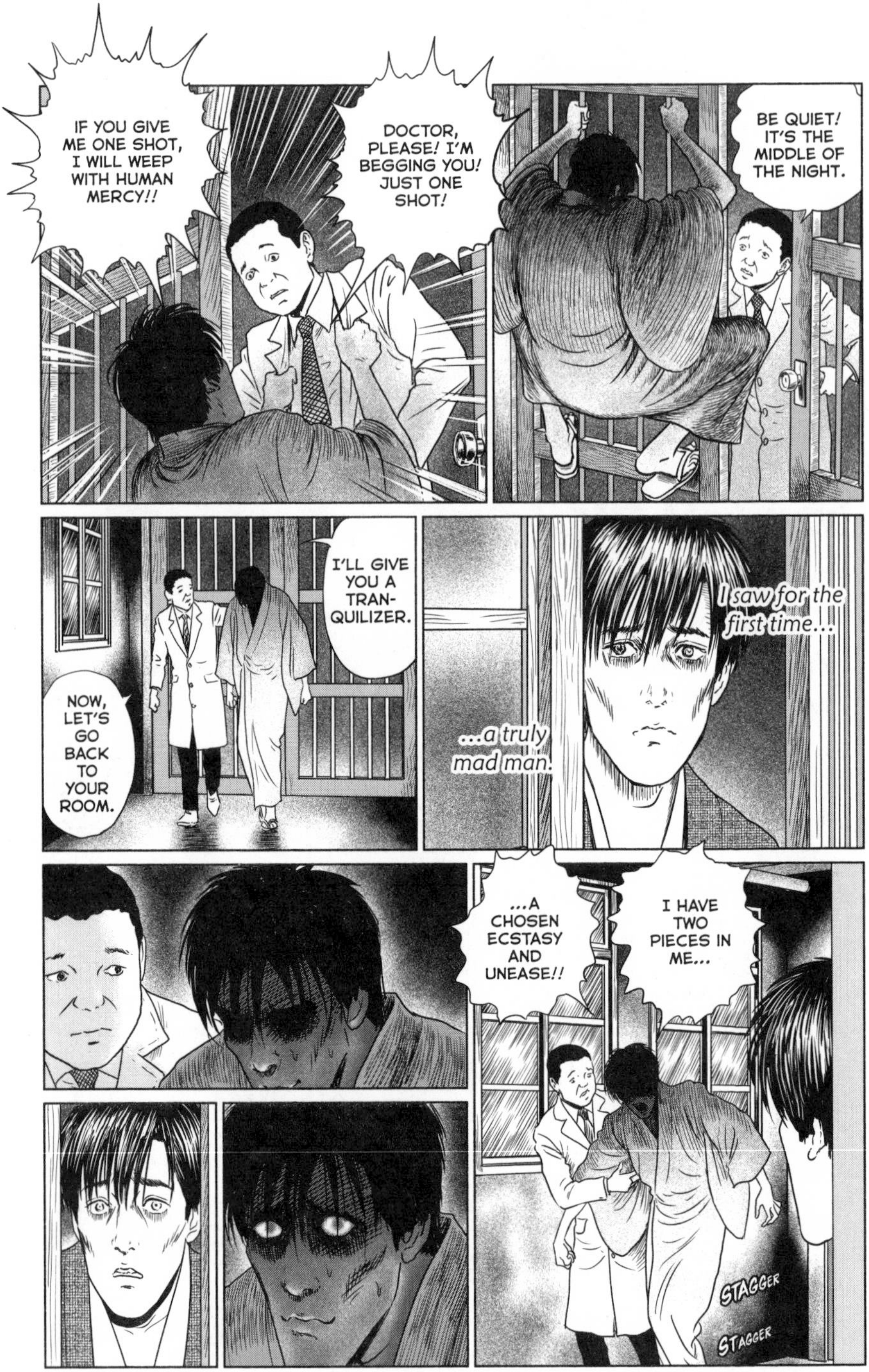
BE QUIET! IT'S THE MIDDLE OF THE NIGHT.
DOCTOR, PLEASE! I'M BEGGING YOU! JUST ONE SHOT!
IF YOU GIVE ME ONE SHOT, I WILL WEEP WITH HUMAN MERCY!!
I saw for the first time...
...a truly mad man.
I'LL GIVE YOU A TRAN-QUILIZER.
NOW, LET'S GO BACK TO YOUR ROOM.
I HAVE TWO PIECES IN ME...
...A CHOSEN ECSTASY AND UNEASE!!
STAGGER
STAGGER

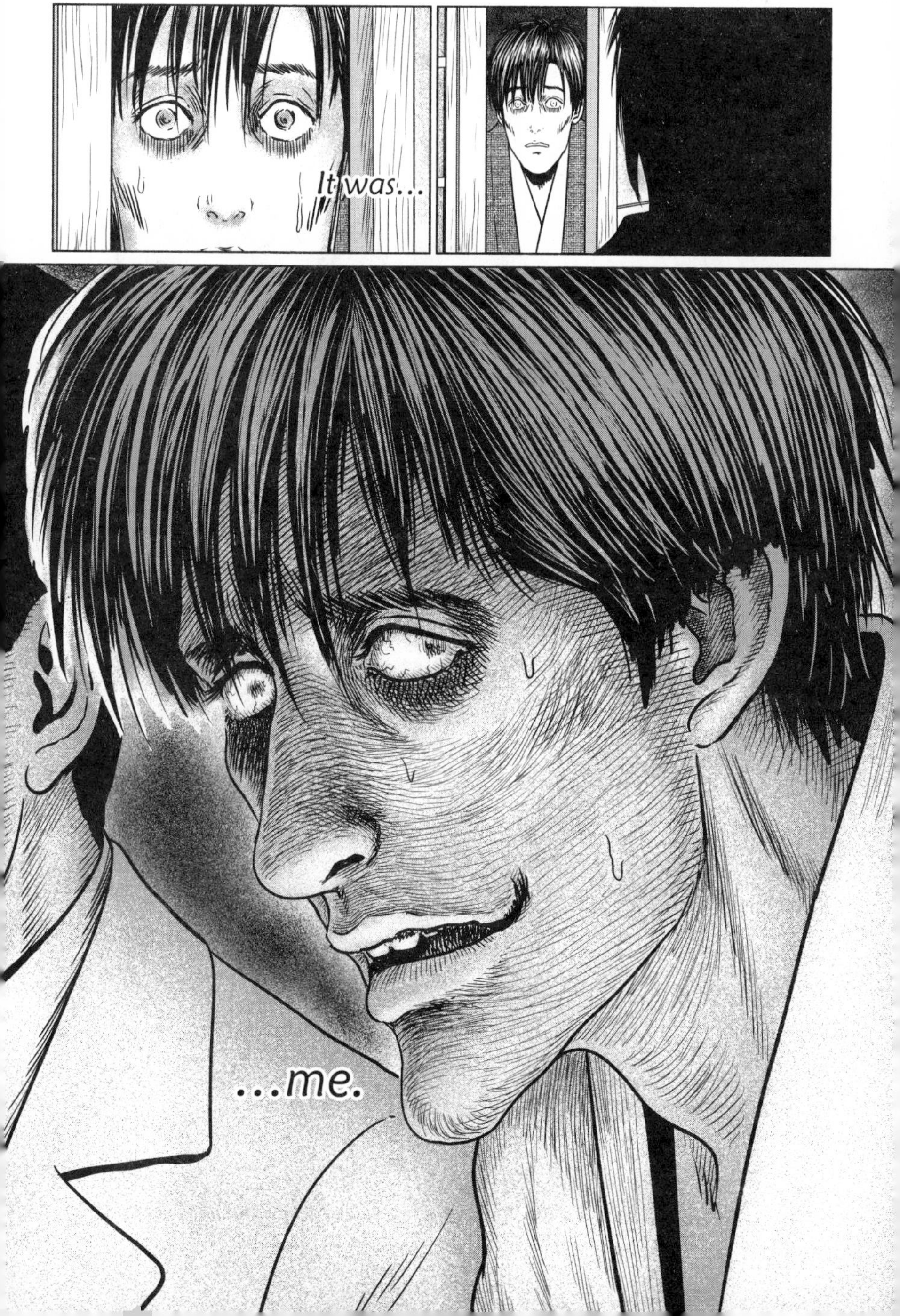
It was...
...me.

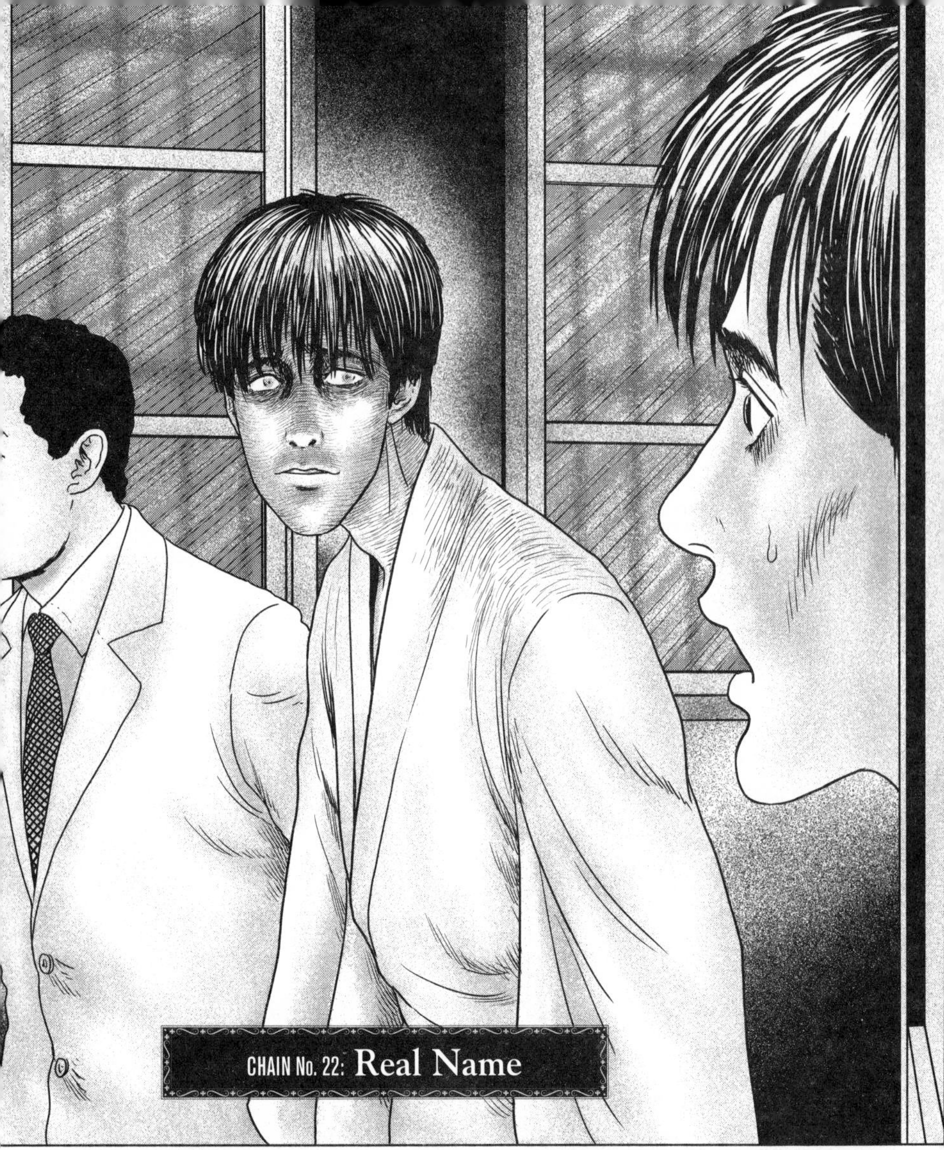
CHAIN No. 22: Real Name

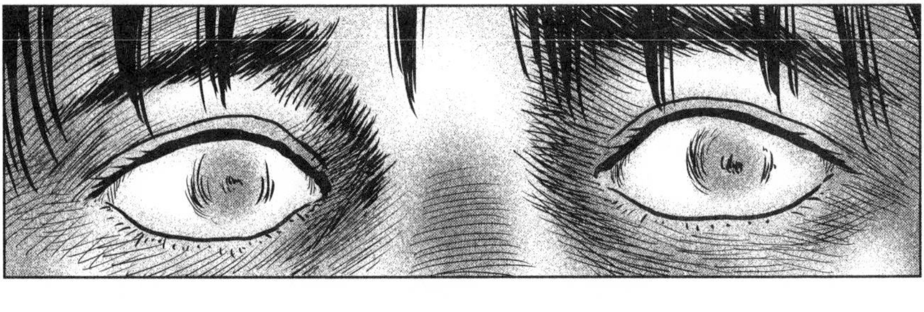

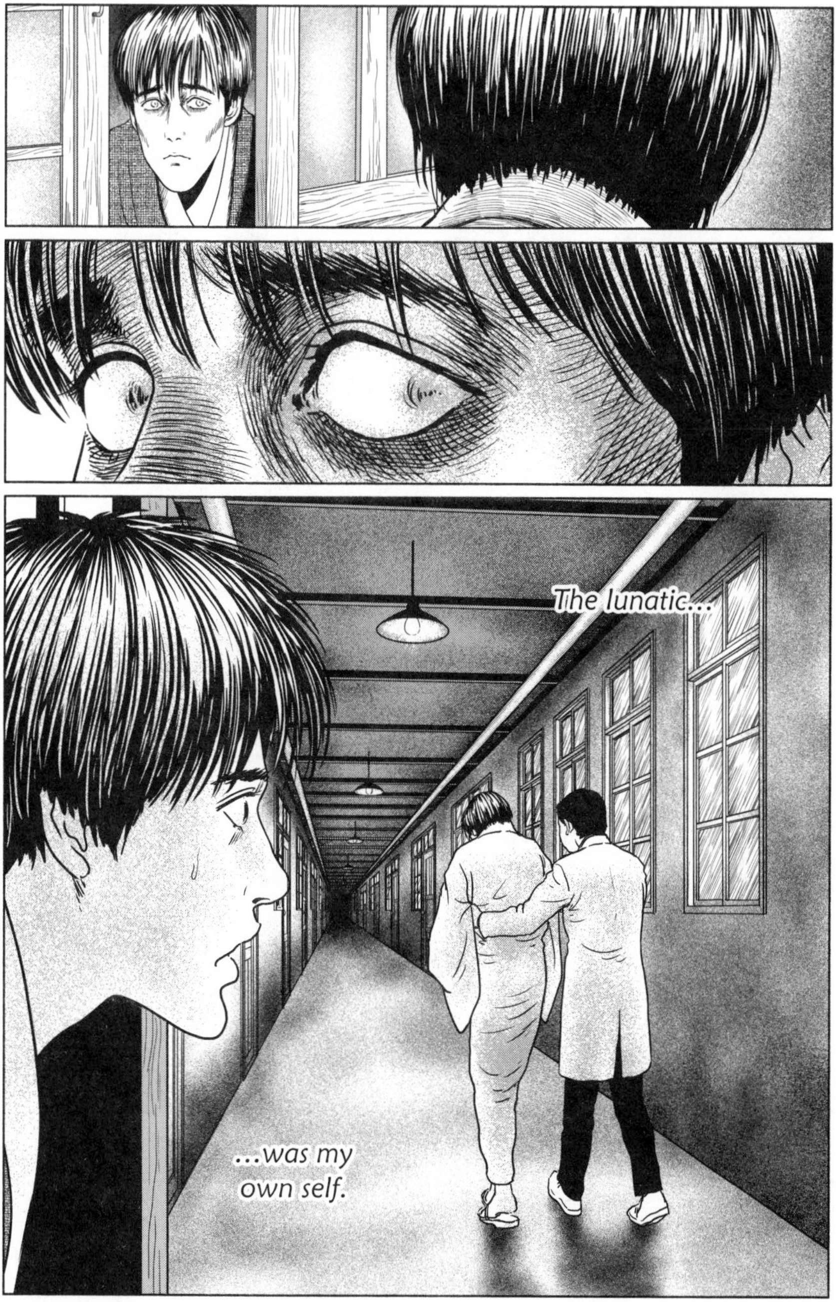
The lunatic...
...was my own self.

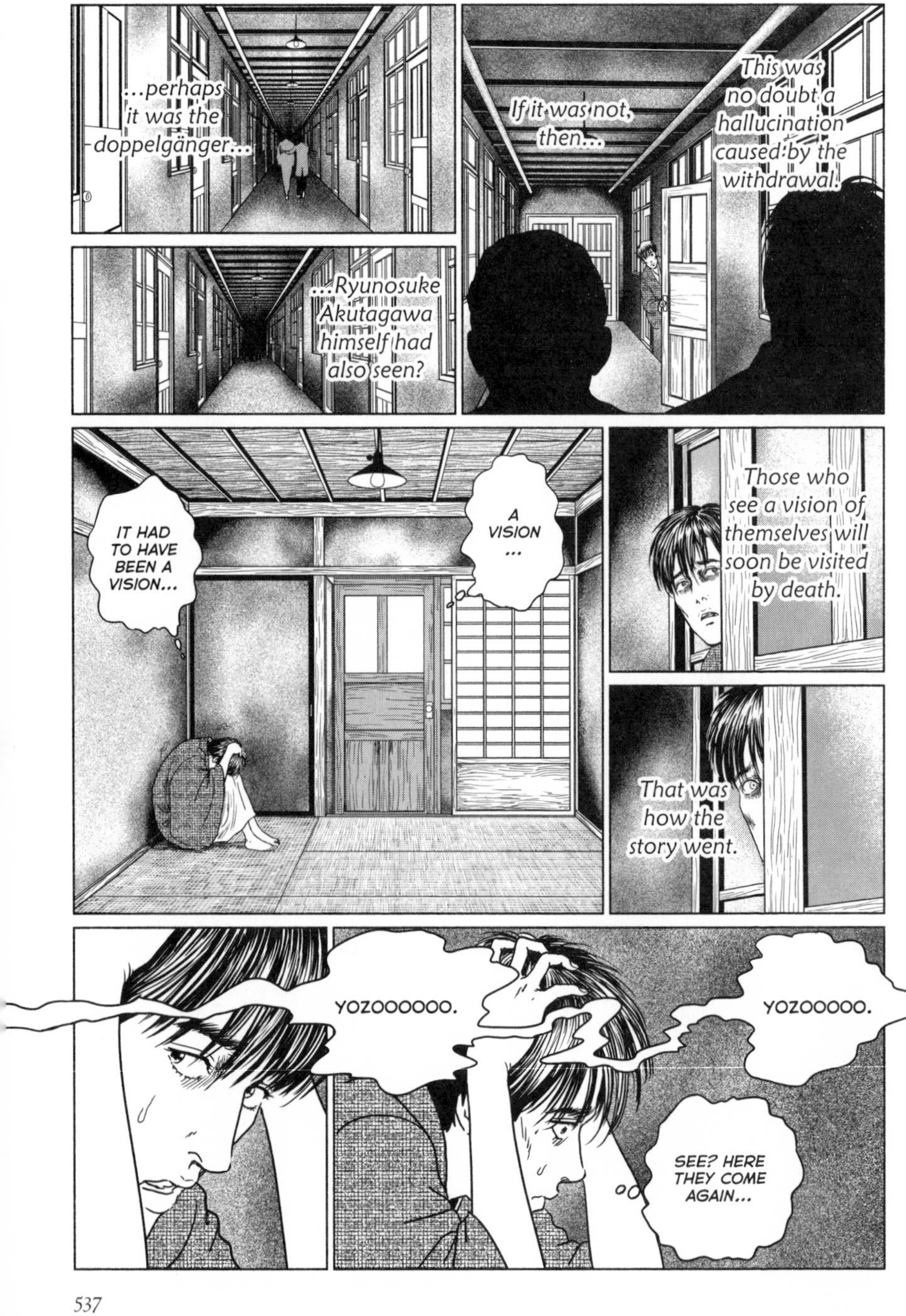
This was no doubt a hallucination caused by the withdrawal.
If it was not, then...
...perhaps it was the doppelgänger...
...Ryunosuke Akutagawa himself had also seen?
Those who see a vision of themselves will soon be visited by death.
That was how the story went.
A VISION ...
IT HAD TO HAVE BEEN A VISION...
YOZOOOOO.
SEE? HERE THEY COME AGAIN...
YOZOOOOOO.

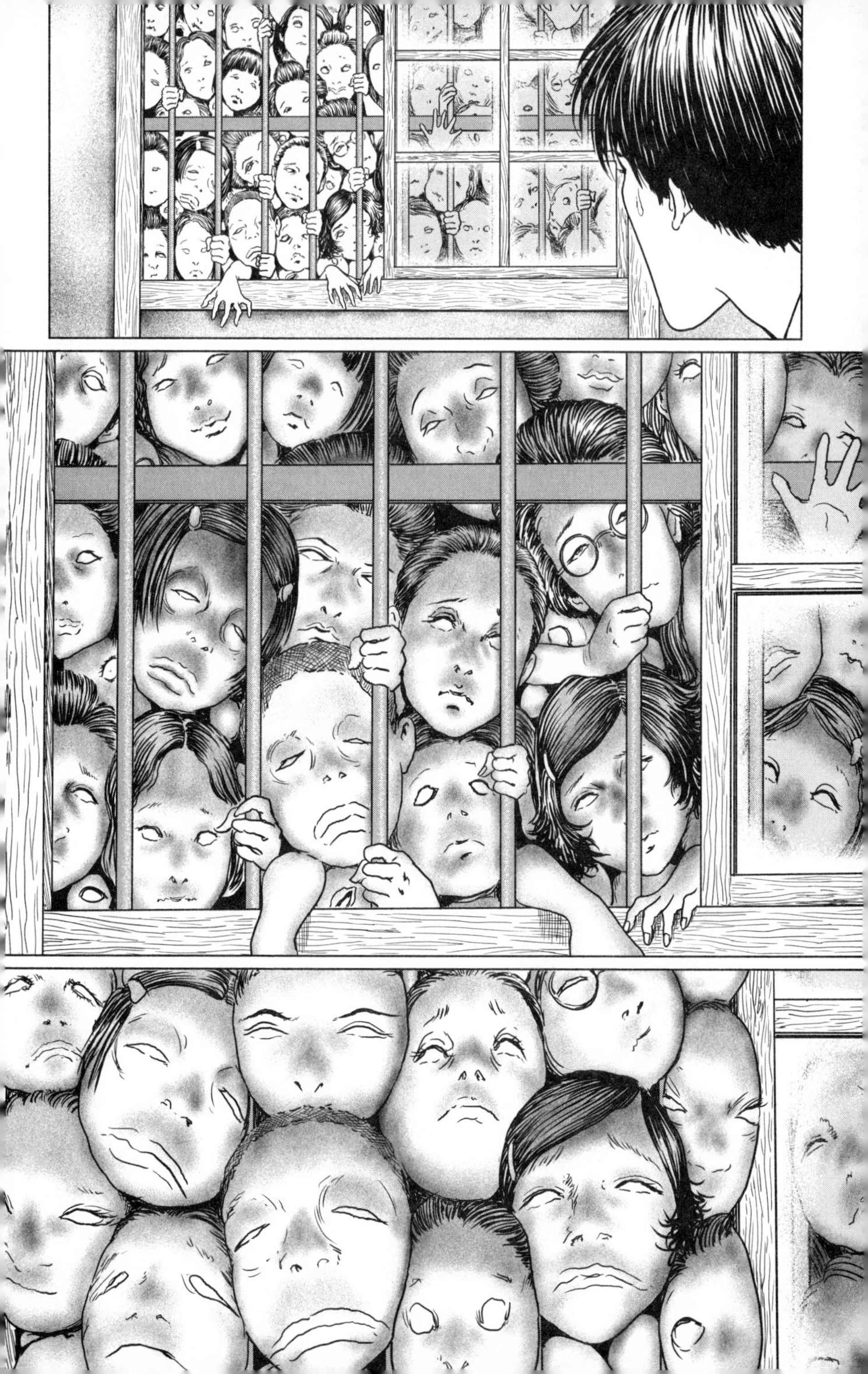

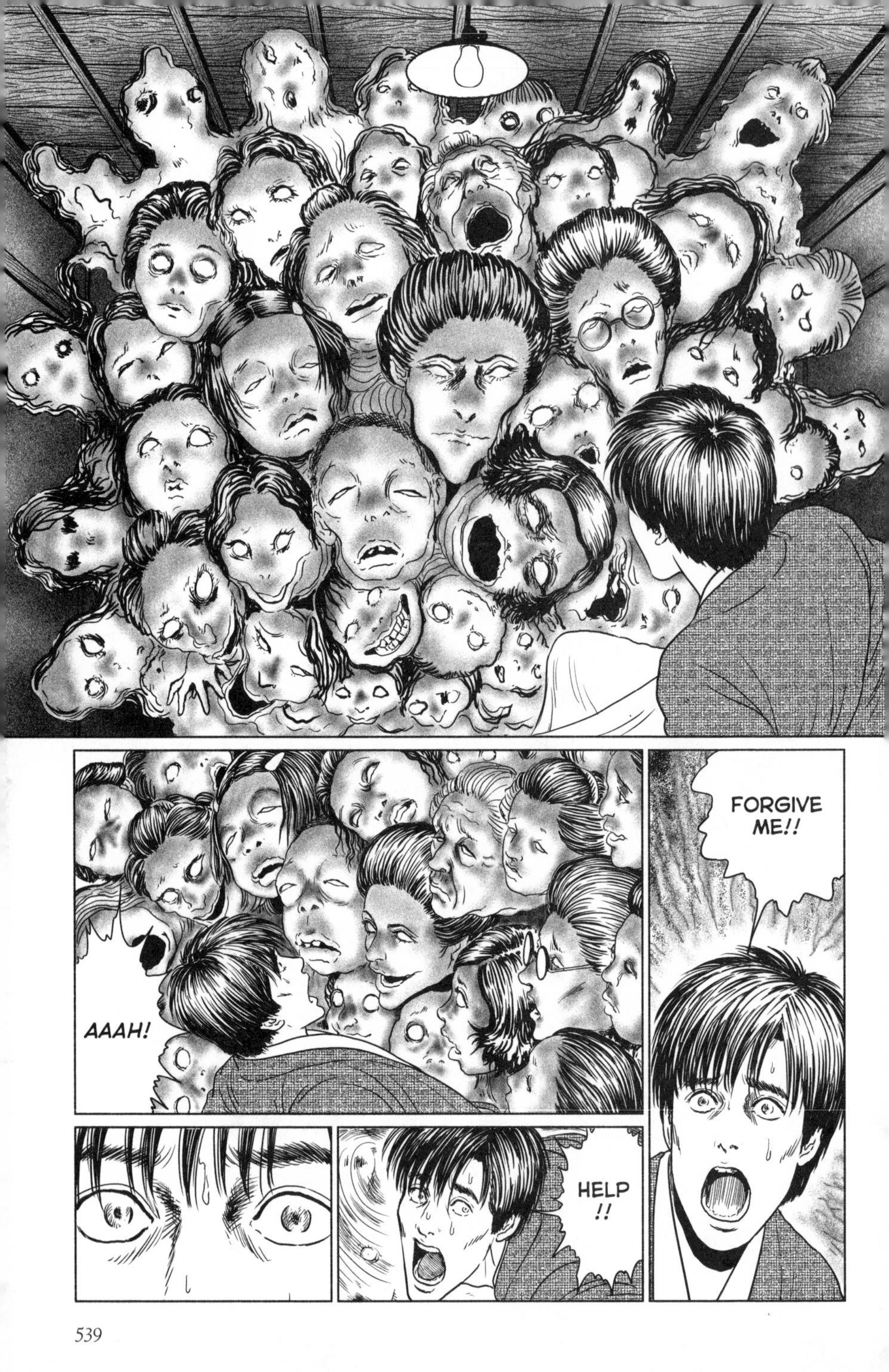
FORGIVE ME!!
AAAH!
HELP !!

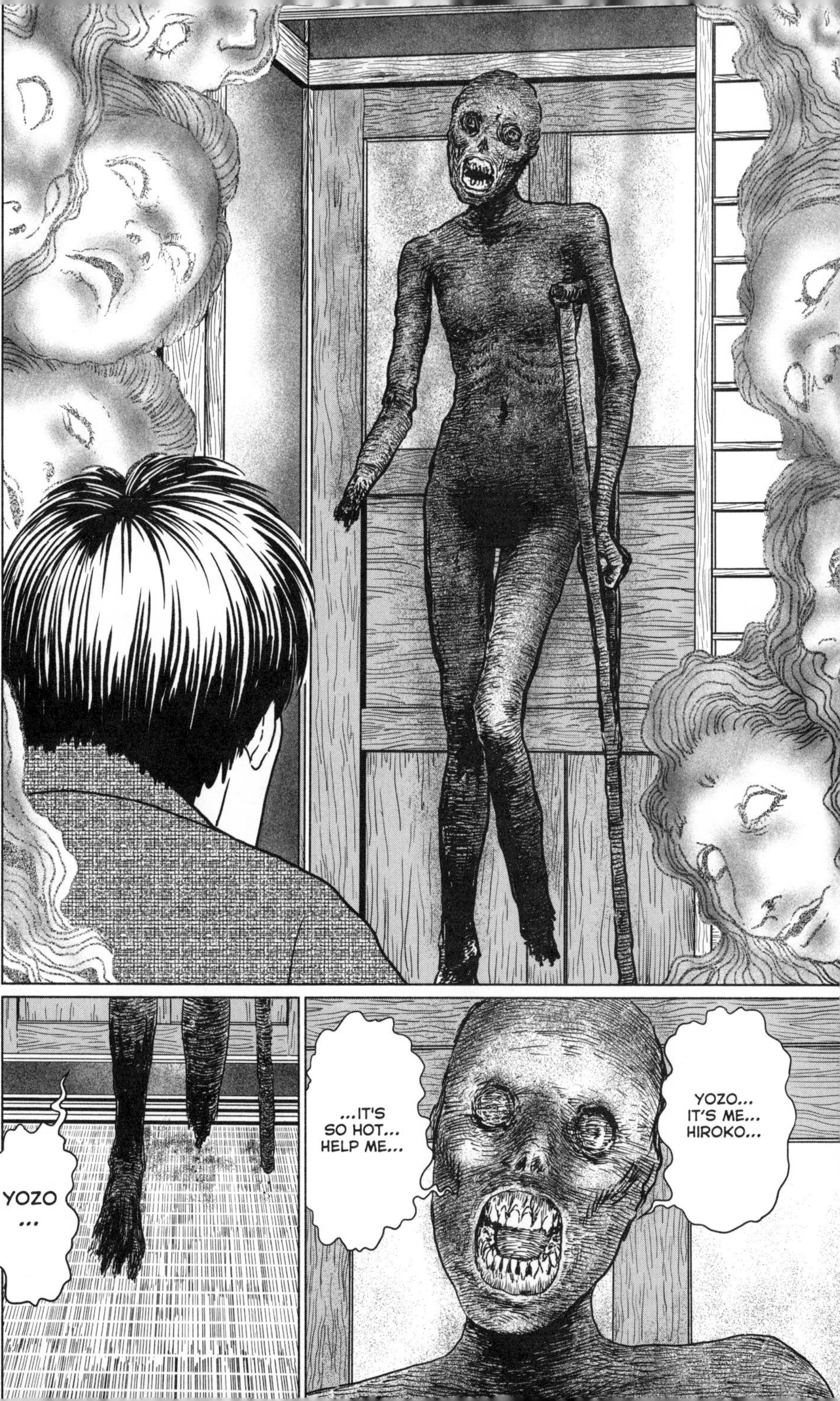
YOZO... IT'S ME... HIROKO...
...IT'S SO HOT... HELP ME...
YOZO ...

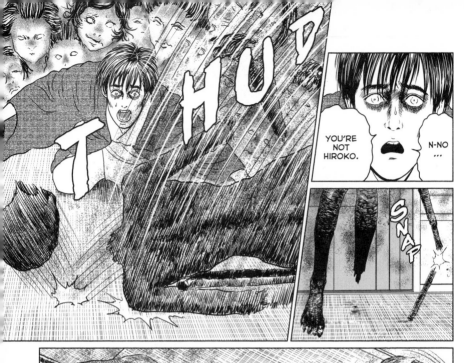

YOU'RE NOT HIROKO.

N-NO ...

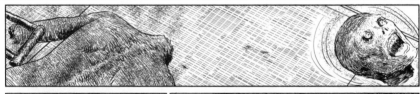

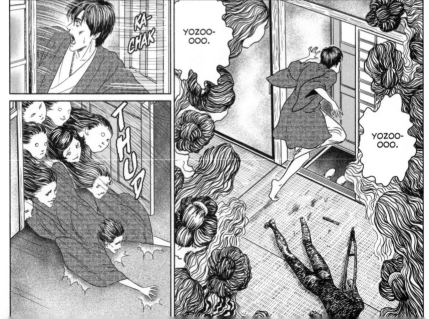

YOZOO-OOO.

YOZOO-OOO.

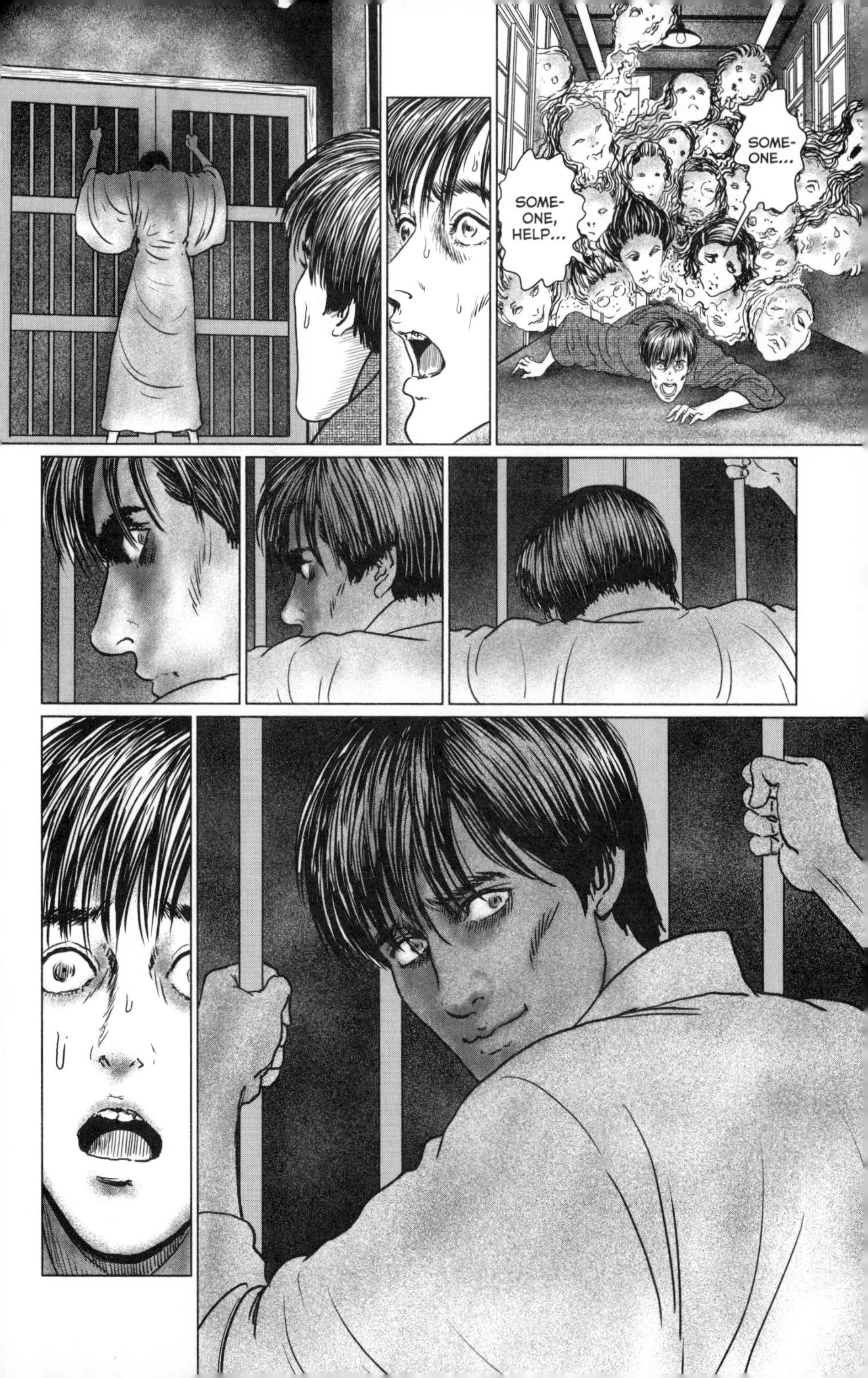
SOME-ONE...
SOME-ONE, HELP...

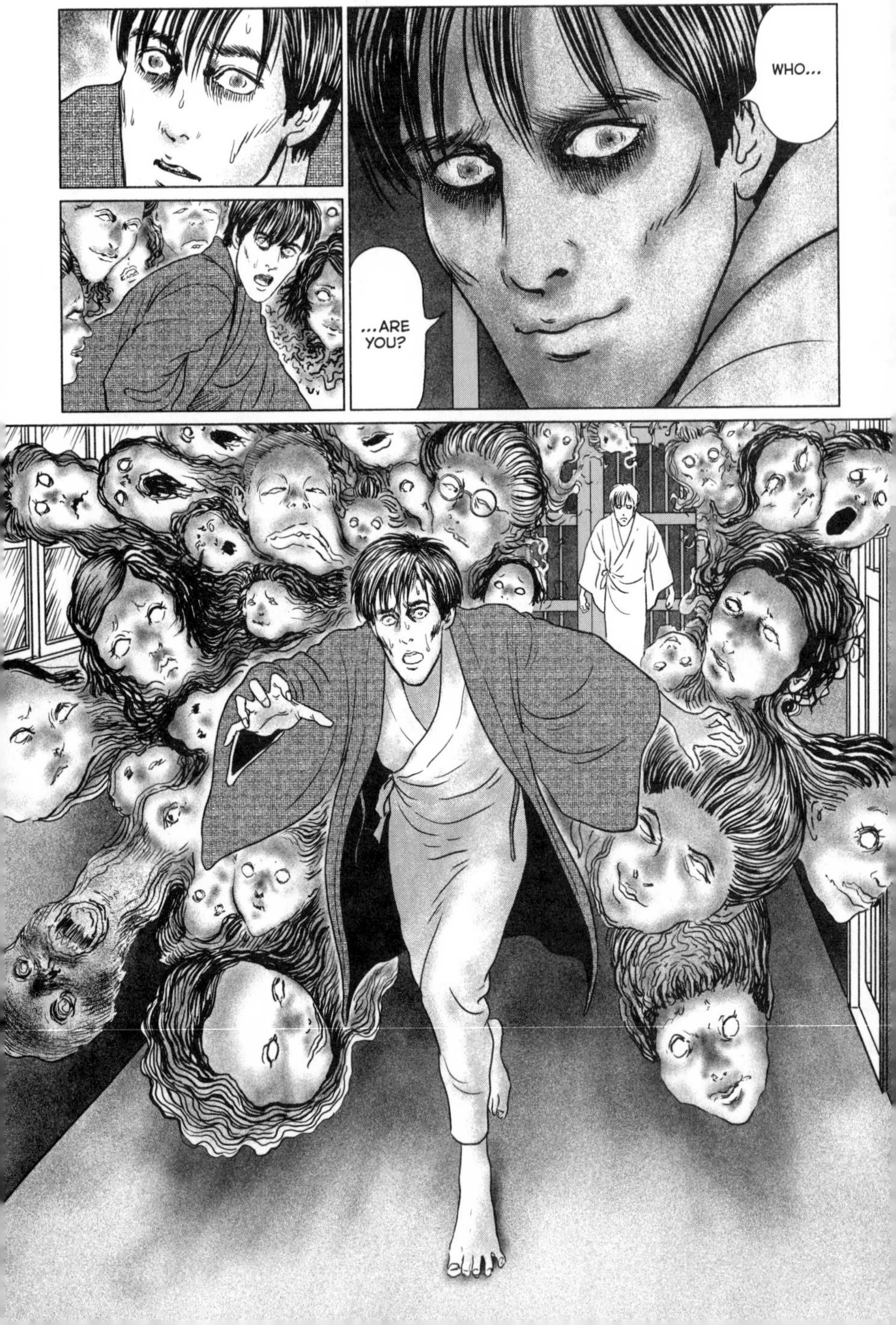
WHO...
...ARE YOU?

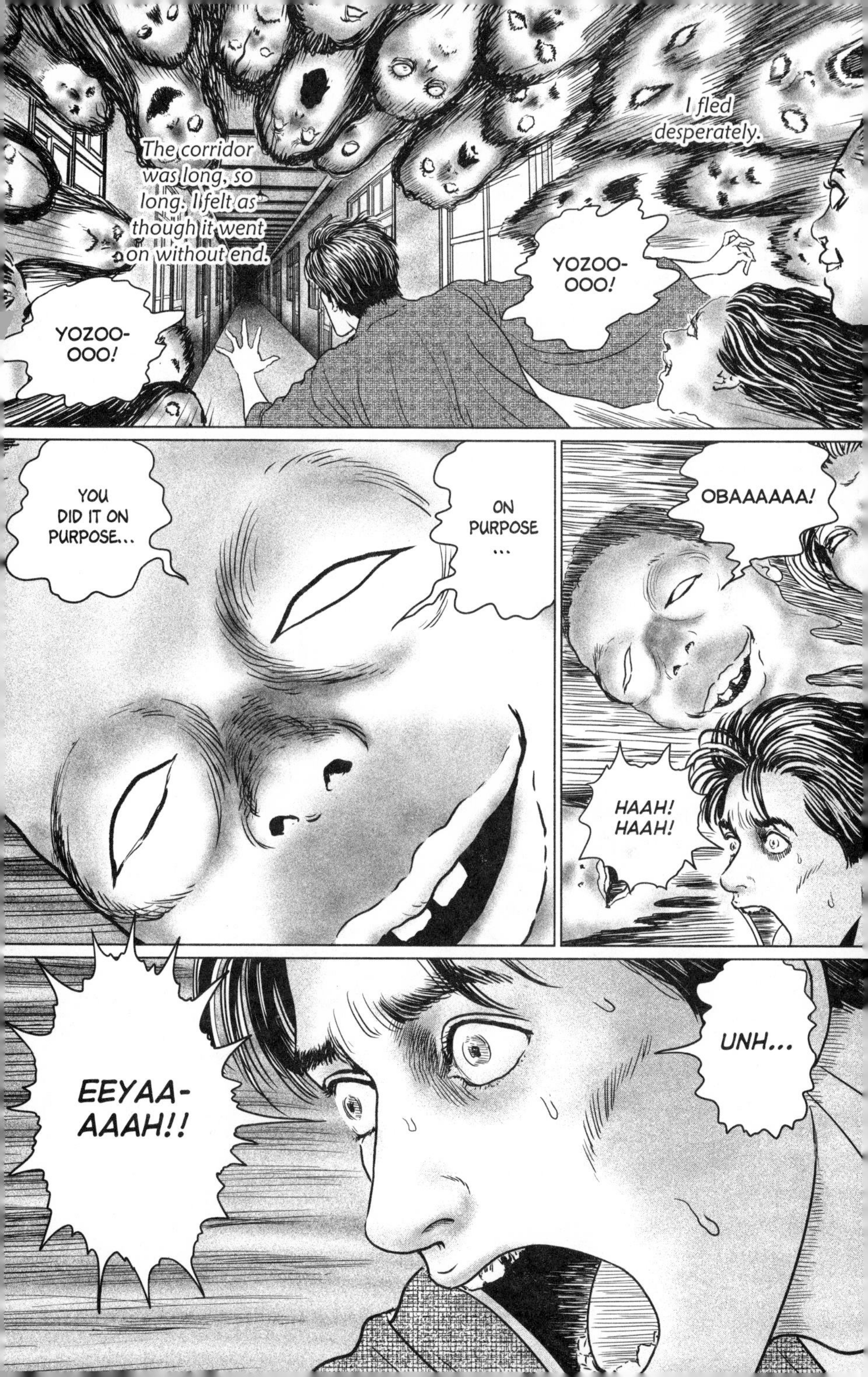
I fled desperately.
The corridor was long, so long. I felt as though it went on without end.
YOZOO-OOO!
YOZOO-OOO!
OBAAAAAA!
HAAH! HAAH!
ON PURPOSE ...
YOU DID IT ON PURPOSE...
UNH...
EEYAA-AAAH!!

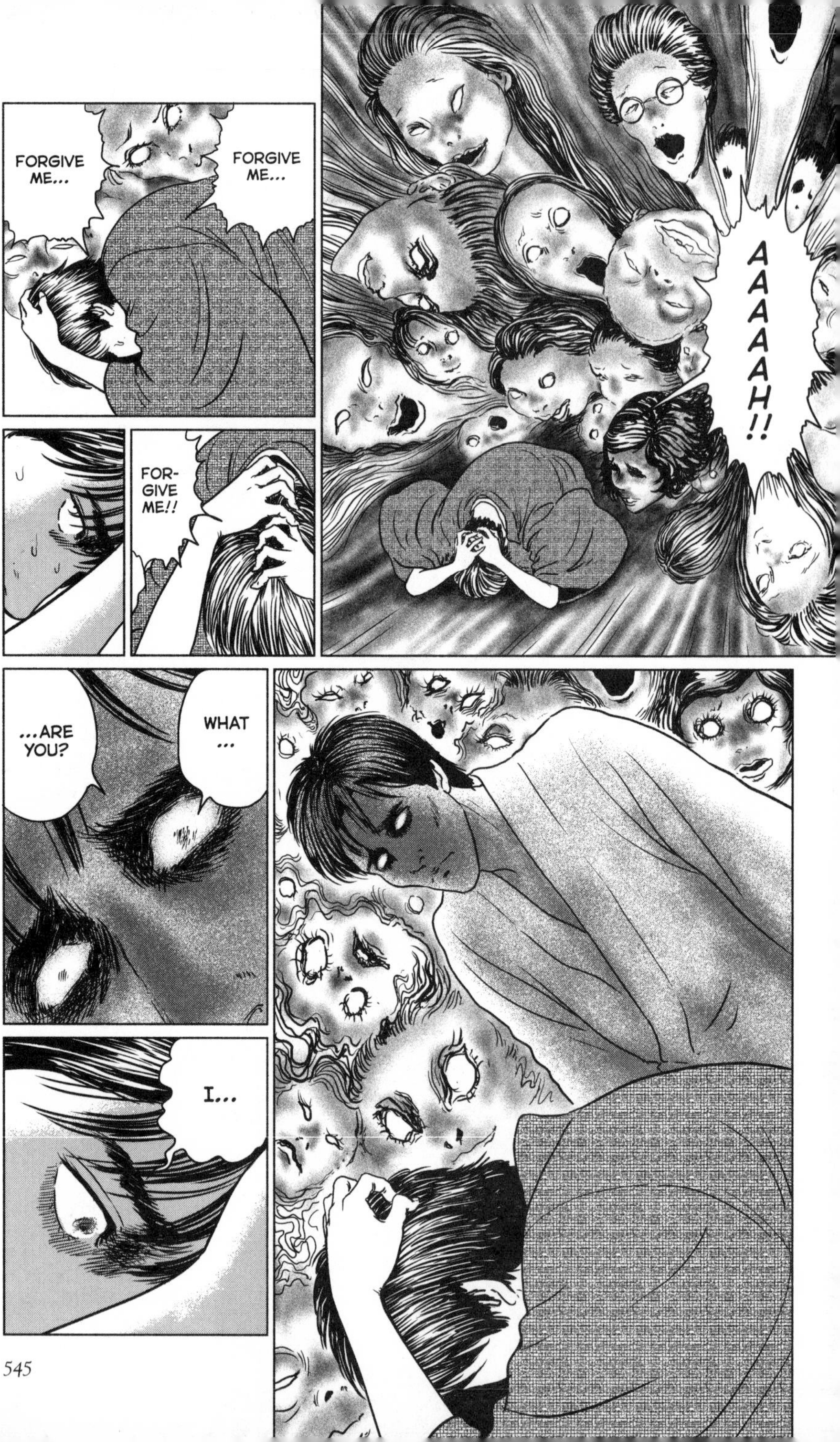
AAAAAAH!!
FORGIVE ME...
FORGIVE ME...
FOR-GIVE ME!!
WHAT...
...ARE YOU?
I...

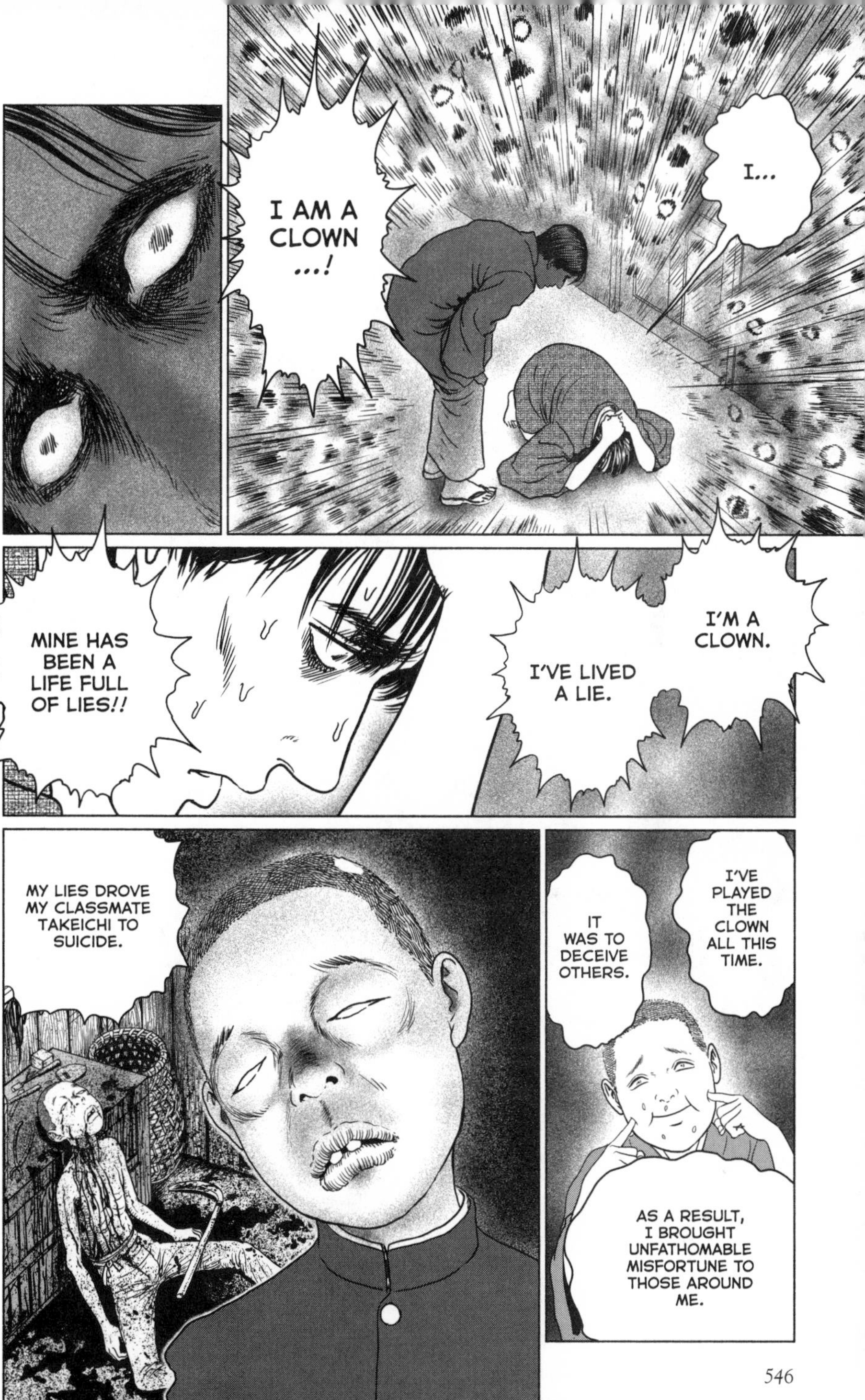
I...
I AM A CLOWN ...!
I'M A CLOWN.
I'VE LIVED A LIE.
MINE HAS BEEN A LIFE FULL OF LIES!!
I'VE PLAYED THE CLOWN ALL THIS TIME.
IT WAS TO DECEIVE OTHERS.
AS A RESULT, I BROUGHT UNFATHOMABLE MISFORTUNE TO THOSE AROUND ME.
MY LIES DROVE MY CLASSMATE TAKEICHI TO SUICIDE.

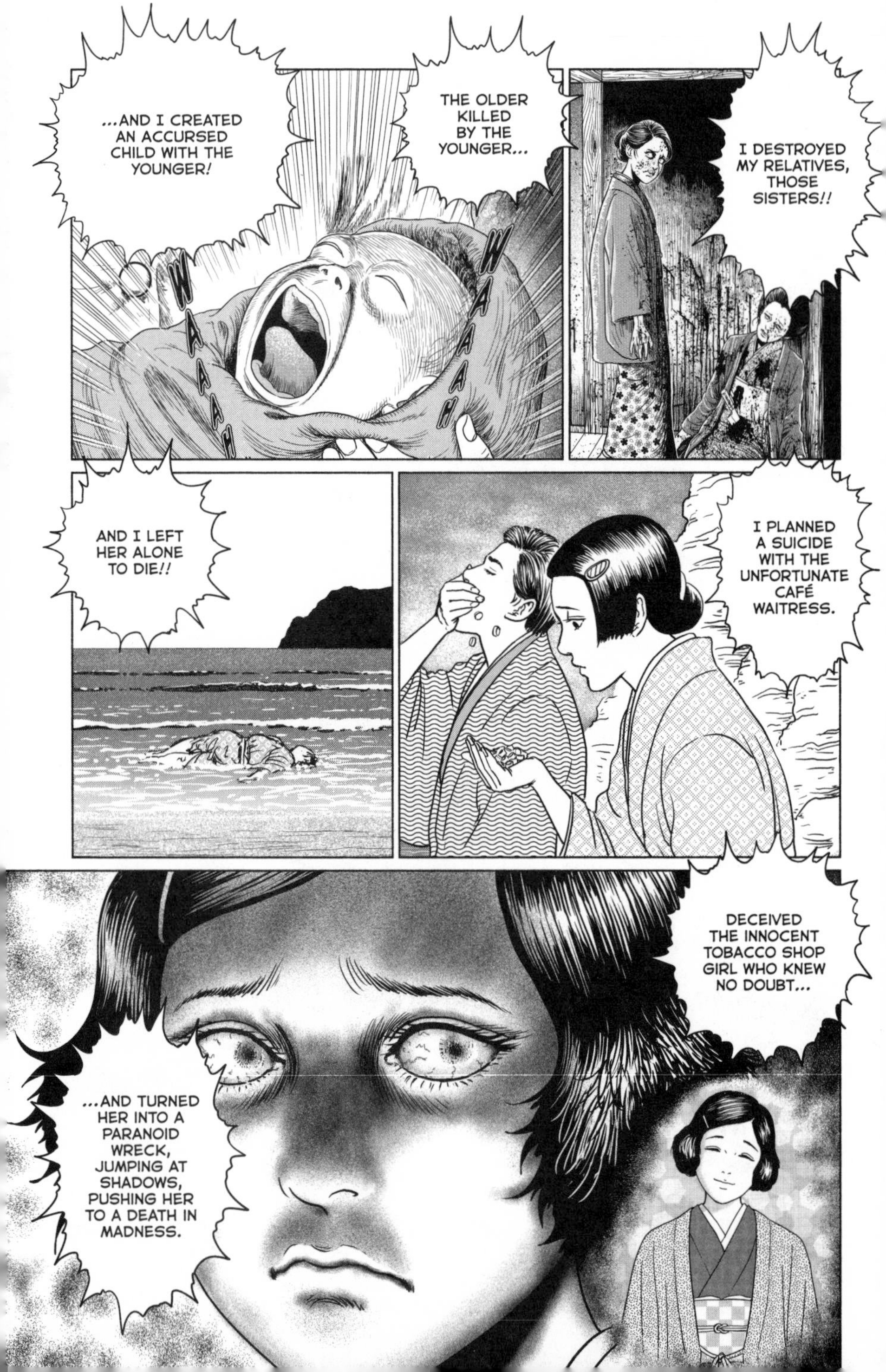
I DESTROYED MY RELATIVES, THOSE SISTERS!!
THE OLDER KILLED BY THE YOUNGER...
WAAAAH
...AND I CREATED AN ACCURSED CHILD WITH THE YOUNGER!
WAAAAH
I PLANNED A SUICIDE WITH THE UNFORTUNATE CAFÉ WAITRESS.
AND I LEFT HER ALONE TO DIE!!
DECEIVED THE INNOCENT TOBACCO SHOP GIRL WHO KNEW NO DOUBT...
...AND TURNED HER INTO A PARANOID WRECK, JUMPING AT SHADOWS, PUSHING HER TO A DEATH IN MADNESS.

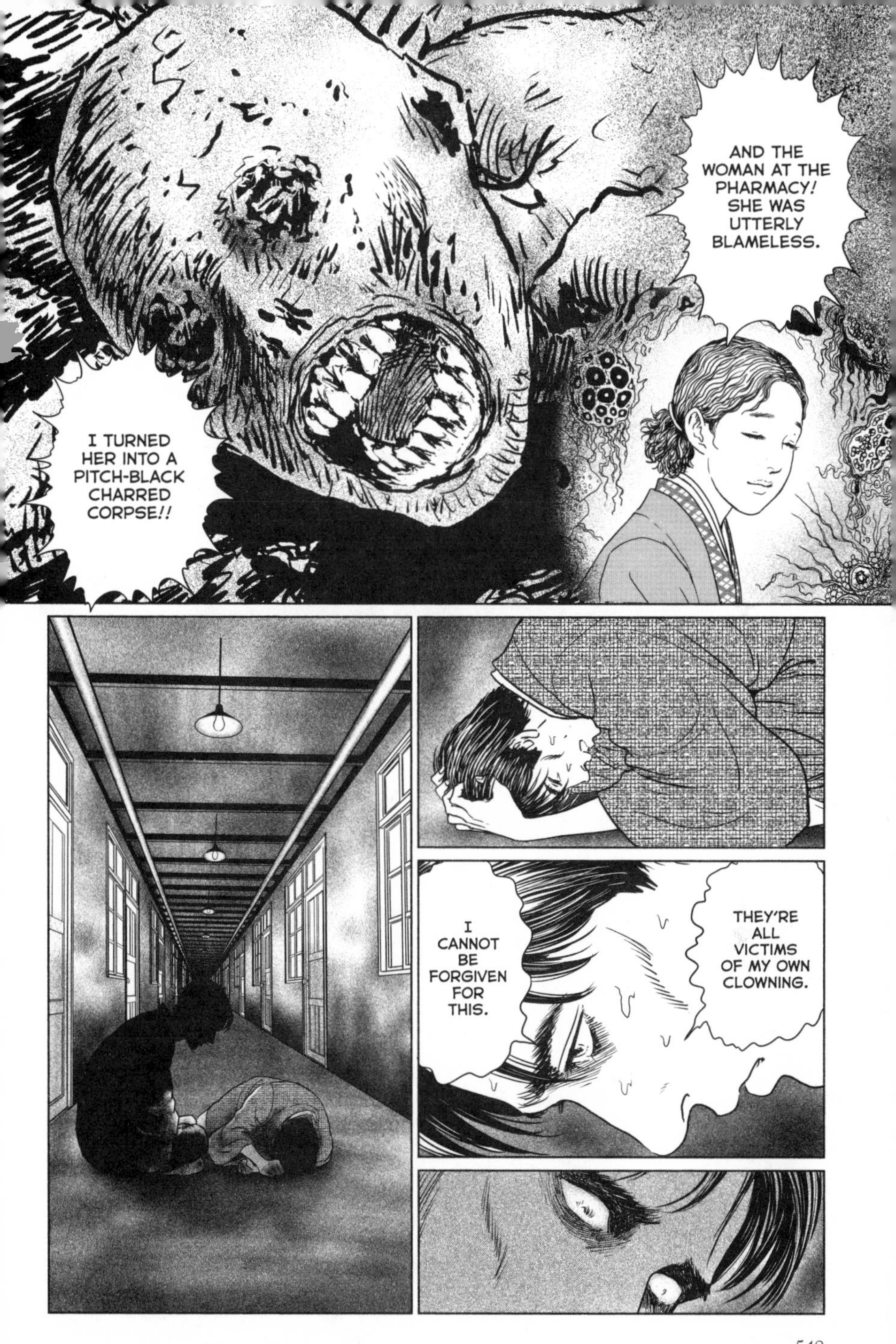
AND THE WOMAN AT THE PHARMACY! SHE WAS UTTERLY BLAMELESS.
I TURNED HER INTO A PITCH-BLACK CHARRED CORPSE!!
THEY'RE ALL VICTIMS OF MY OWN CLOWNING.
I CANNOT BE FORGIVEN FOR THIS.

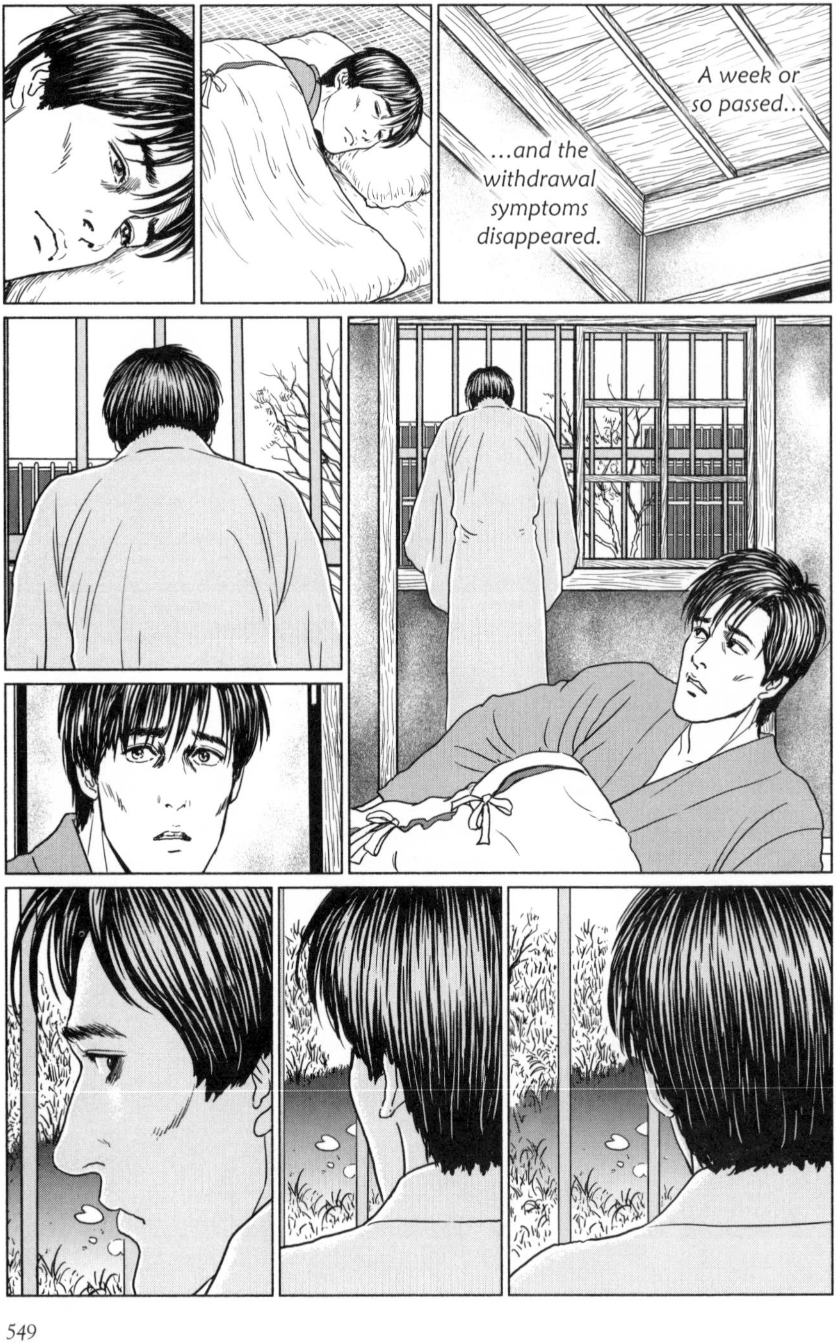
A week or so passed...
...and the withdrawal symptoms disappeared.

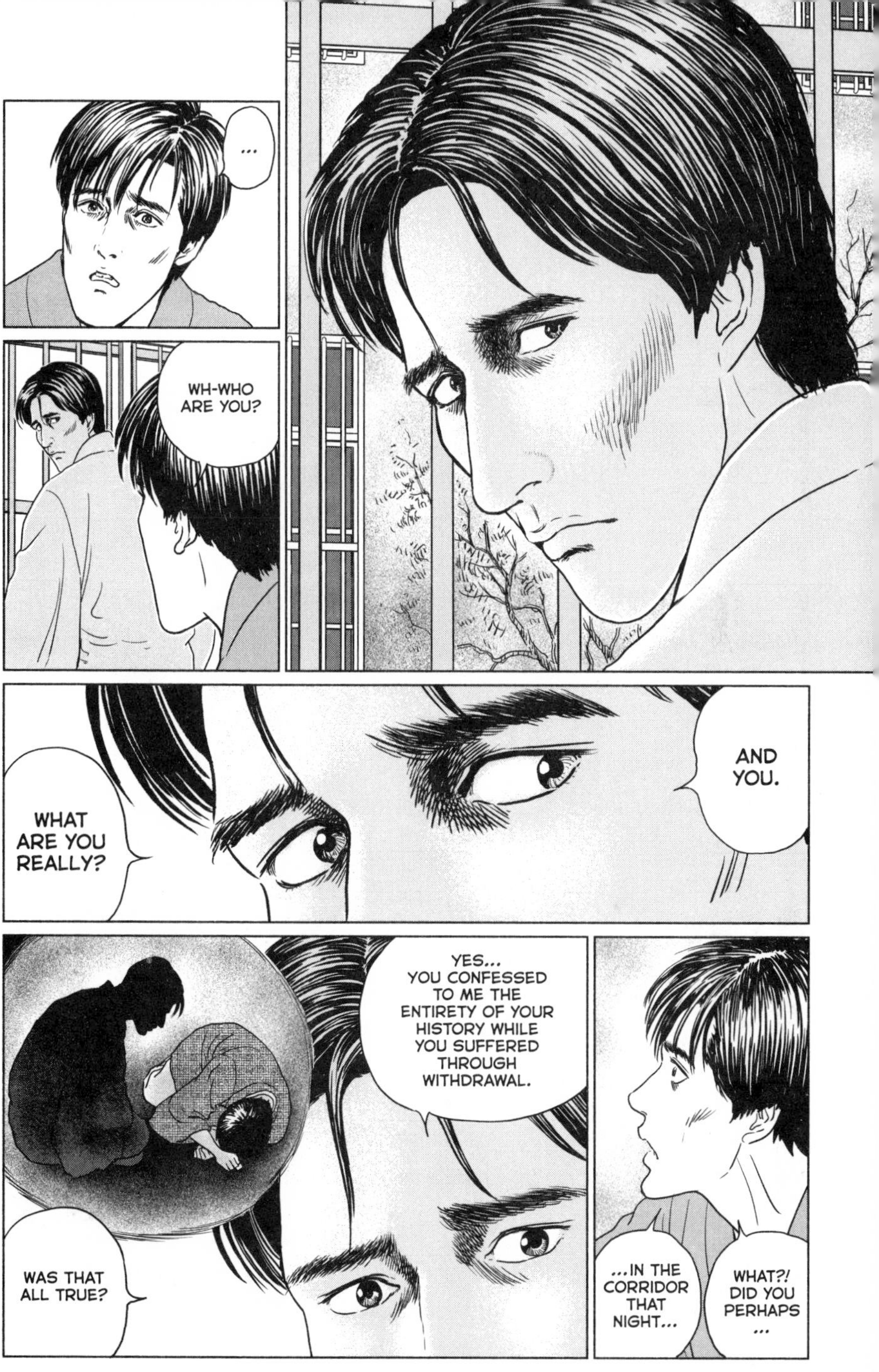
...
WH-WHO ARE YOU?
AND YOU.
WHAT ARE YOU REALLY?
WHAT?! DID YOU PERHAPS ...
...IN THE CORRIDOR THAT NIGHT...
YES... YOU CONFESSED TO ME THE ENTIRETY OF YOUR HISTORY WHILE YOU SUFFERED THROUGH WITHDRAWAL.
WAS THAT ALL TRUE?

*Yozo Oba

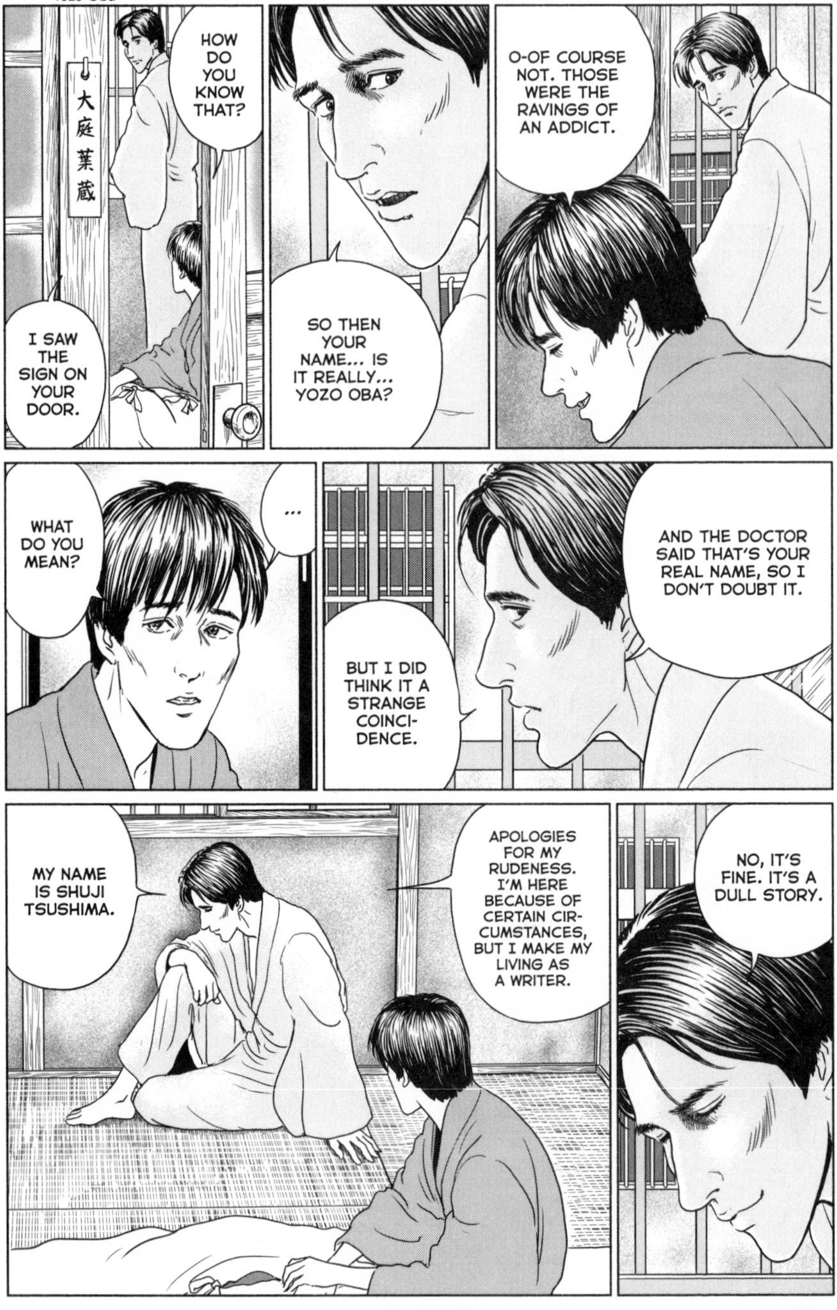
O-OF COURSE NOT. THOSE WERE THE RAVINGS OF AN ADDICT.
SO THEN YOUR NAME... IS IT REALLY... YOZO OBA?
HOW DO YOU KNOW THAT?
大庭葉蔵
I SAW THE SIGN ON YOUR DOOR.
AND THE DOCTOR SAID THAT'S YOUR REAL NAME, SO I DON'T DOUBT IT.
BUT I DID THINK IT A STRANGE COINCIDENCE.
...
WHAT DO YOU MEAN?
NO, IT'S FINE. IT'S A DULL STORY.
APOLOGIES FOR MY RUDENESS. I'M HERE BECAUSE OF CERTAIN CIRCUMSTANCES, BUT I MAKE MY LIVING AS A WRITER.
MY NAME IS SHUJI TSUSHIMA.

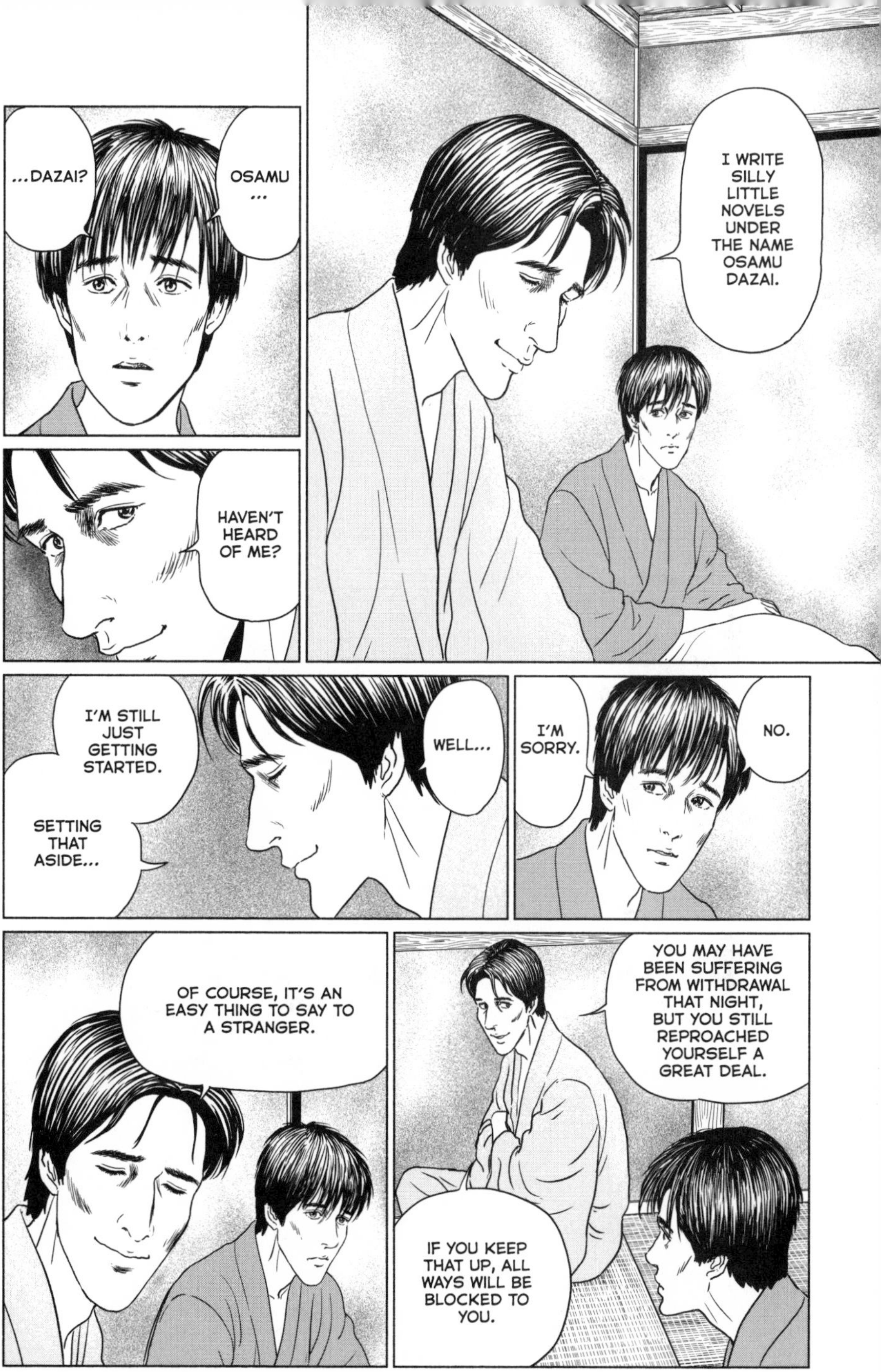
I WRITE SILLY LITTLE NOVELS UNDER THE NAME OSAMU DAZAI.
OSAMU ...
...DAZAI?
HAVEN'T HEARD OF ME?
NO.
I'M SORRY.
WELL...
I'M STILL JUST GETTING STARTED.
SETTING THAT ASIDE...
YOU MAY HAVE BEEN SUFFERING FROM WITHDRAWAL THAT NIGHT, BUT YOU STILL REPROACHED YOURSELF A GREAT DEAL.
IF YOU KEEP THAT UP, ALL WAYS WILL BE BLOCKED TO YOU.
OF COURSE, IT'S AN EASY THING TO SAY TO A STRANGER.

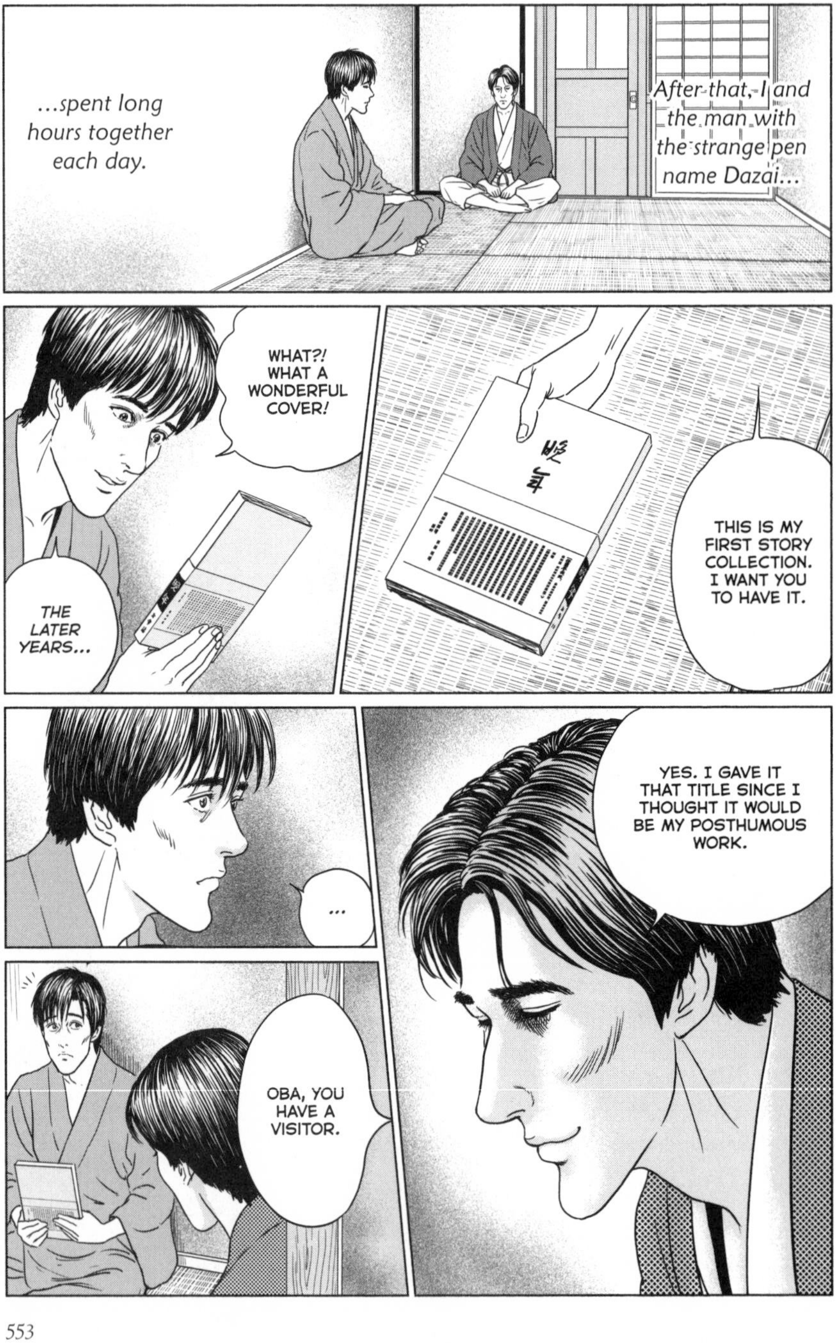
After that, I and the man with the strange pen name Dazai…
…spent long hours together each day.
THIS IS MY FIRST STORY COLLECTION. I WANT YOU TO HAVE IT.
WHAT?! WHAT A WONDERFUL COVER!
THE LATER YEARS…
YES. I GAVE IT THAT TITLE SINCE I THOUGHT IT WOULD BE MY POSTHUMOUS WORK.
…
OBA, YOU HAVE A VISITOR.

*Visiting Room

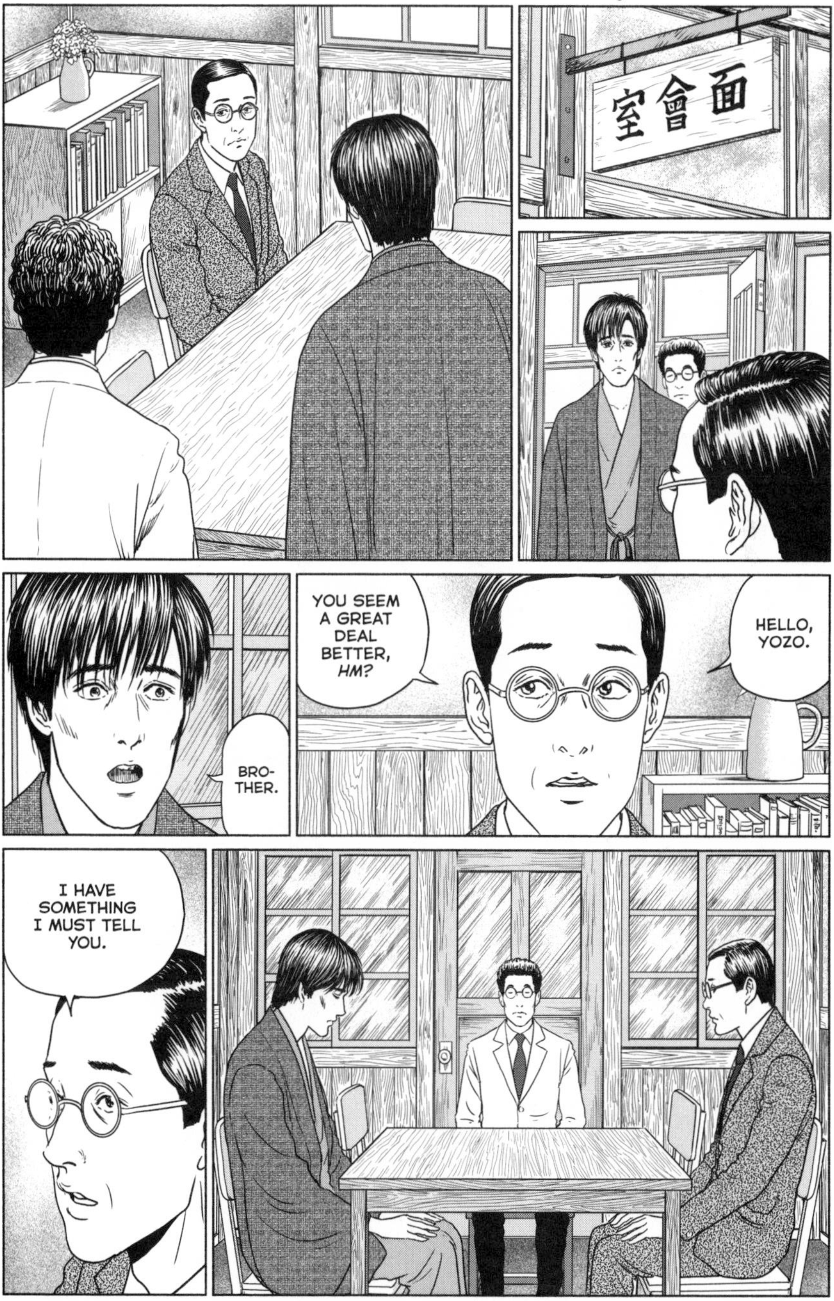
面會室
HELLO, YOZO.
YOU SEEM A GREAT DEAL BETTER, *HM?*
BRO-THER.
I HAVE SOMETHING I MUST TELL YOU.

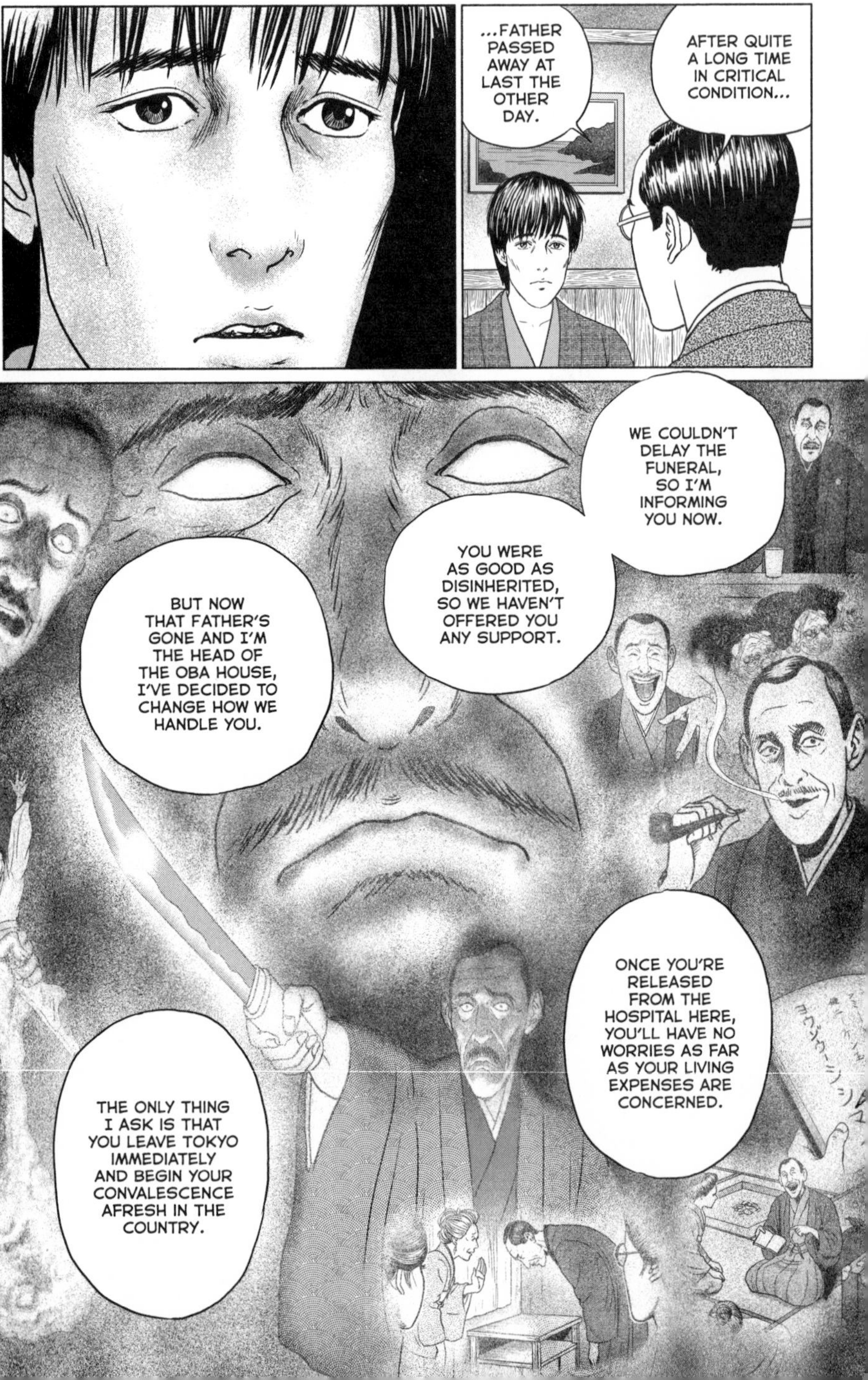
AFTER QUITE A LONG TIME IN CRITICAL CONDITION...
...FATHER PASSED AWAY AT LAST THE OTHER DAY.
WE COULDN'T DELAY THE FUNERAL, SO I'M INFORMING YOU NOW.
YOU WERE AS GOOD AS DISINHERITED, SO WE HAVEN'T OFFERED YOU ANY SUPPORT.
BUT NOW THAT FATHER'S GONE AND I'M THE HEAD OF THE OBA HOUSE, I'VE DECIDED TO CHANGE HOW WE HANDLE YOU.
ONCE YOU'RE RELEASED FROM THE HOSPITAL HERE, YOU'LL HAVE NO WORRIES AS FAR AS YOUR LIVING EXPENSES ARE CONCERNED.
THE ONLY THING I ASK IS THAT YOU LEAVE TOKYO IMMEDIATELY AND BEGIN YOUR CONVALESCENCE AFRESH IN THE COUNTRY.

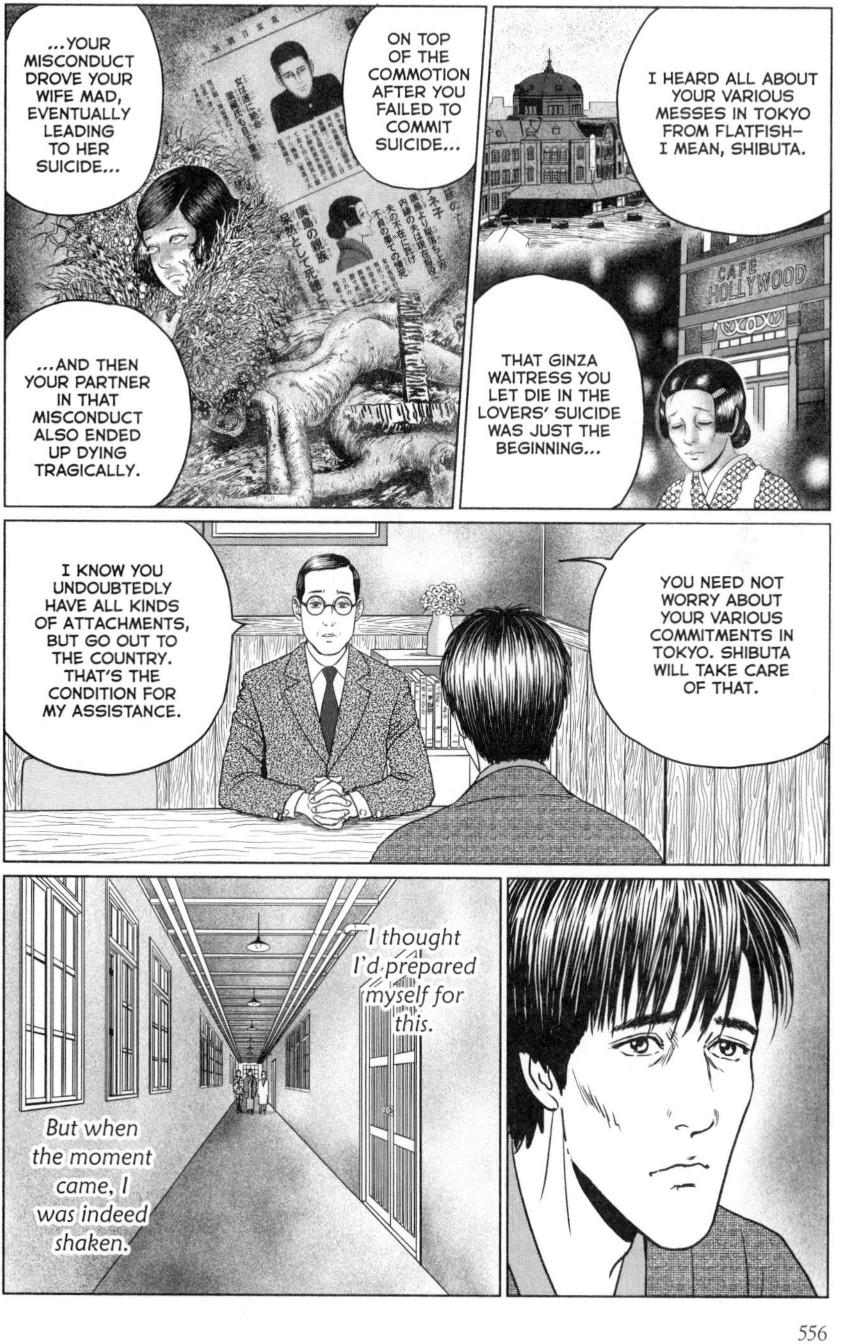
I HEARD ALL ABOUT YOUR VARIOUS MESSES IN TOKYO FROM FLATFISH– I MEAN, SHIBUTA.
CAFE HOLLYWOOD
THAT GINZA WAITRESS YOU LET DIE IN THE LOVERS' SUICIDE WAS JUST THE BEGINNING...
ON TOP OF THE COMMOTION AFTER YOU FAILED TO COMMIT SUICIDE...
...YOUR MISCONDUCT DROVE YOUR WIFE MAD, EVENTUALLY LEADING TO HER SUICIDE...
...AND THEN YOUR PARTNER IN THAT MISCONDUCT ALSO ENDED UP DYING TRAGICALLY.
YOU NEED NOT WORRY ABOUT YOUR VARIOUS COMMITMENTS IN TOKYO. SHIBUTA WILL TAKE CARE OF THAT.
I KNOW YOU UNDOUBTEDLY HAVE ALL KINDS OF ATTACHMENTS, BUT GO OUT TO THE COUNTRY. THAT'S THE CONDITION FOR MY ASSISTANCE.
I thought I'd prepared myself for this.
But when the moment came, I was indeed shaken.

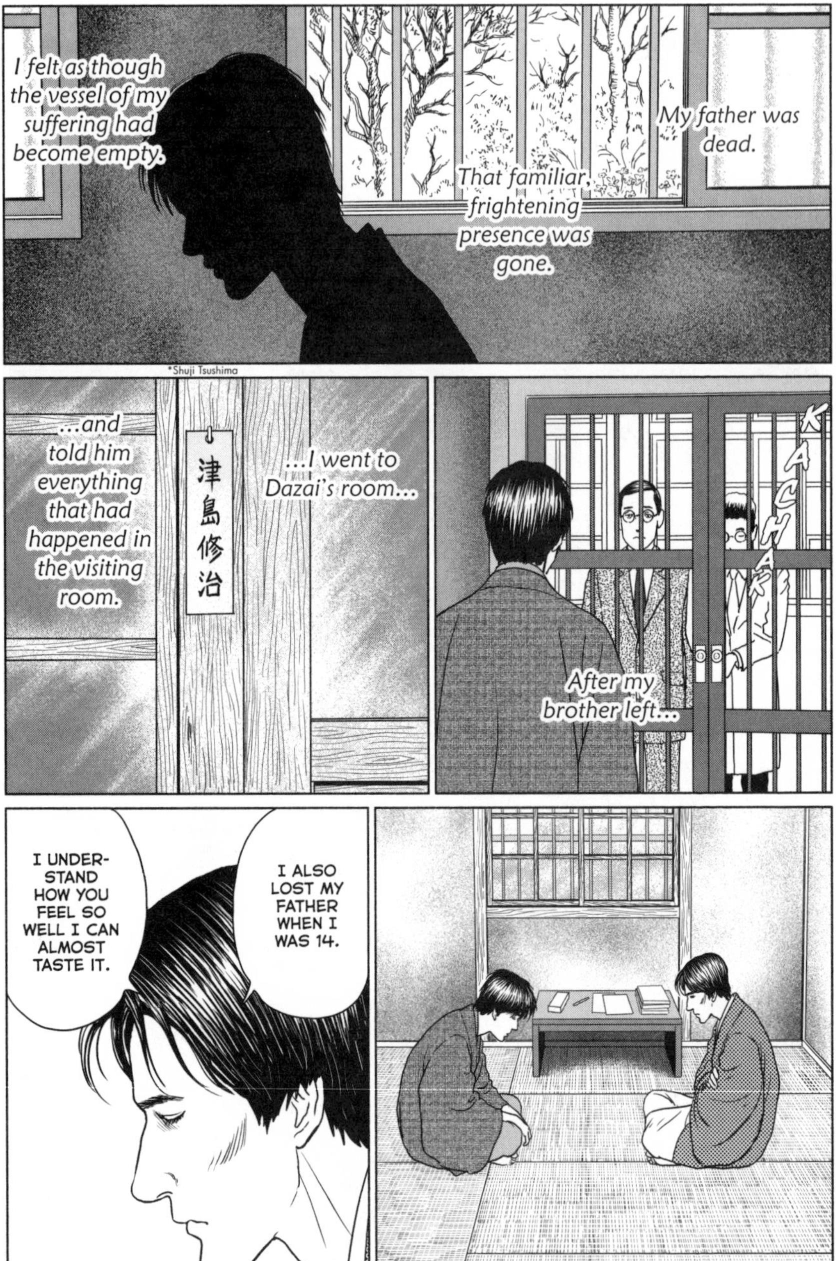
My father was dead.
That familiar, frightening presence was gone.
I felt as though the vessel of my suffering had become empty.
KACHAK
After my brother left...
...I went to Dazai's room...
津島修治
...and told him everything that had happened in the visiting room.
I ALSO LOST MY FATHER WHEN I WAS 14.
I UNDER-STAND HOW YOU FEEL SO WELL I CAN ALMOST TASTE IT.
*Shuji Tsushima

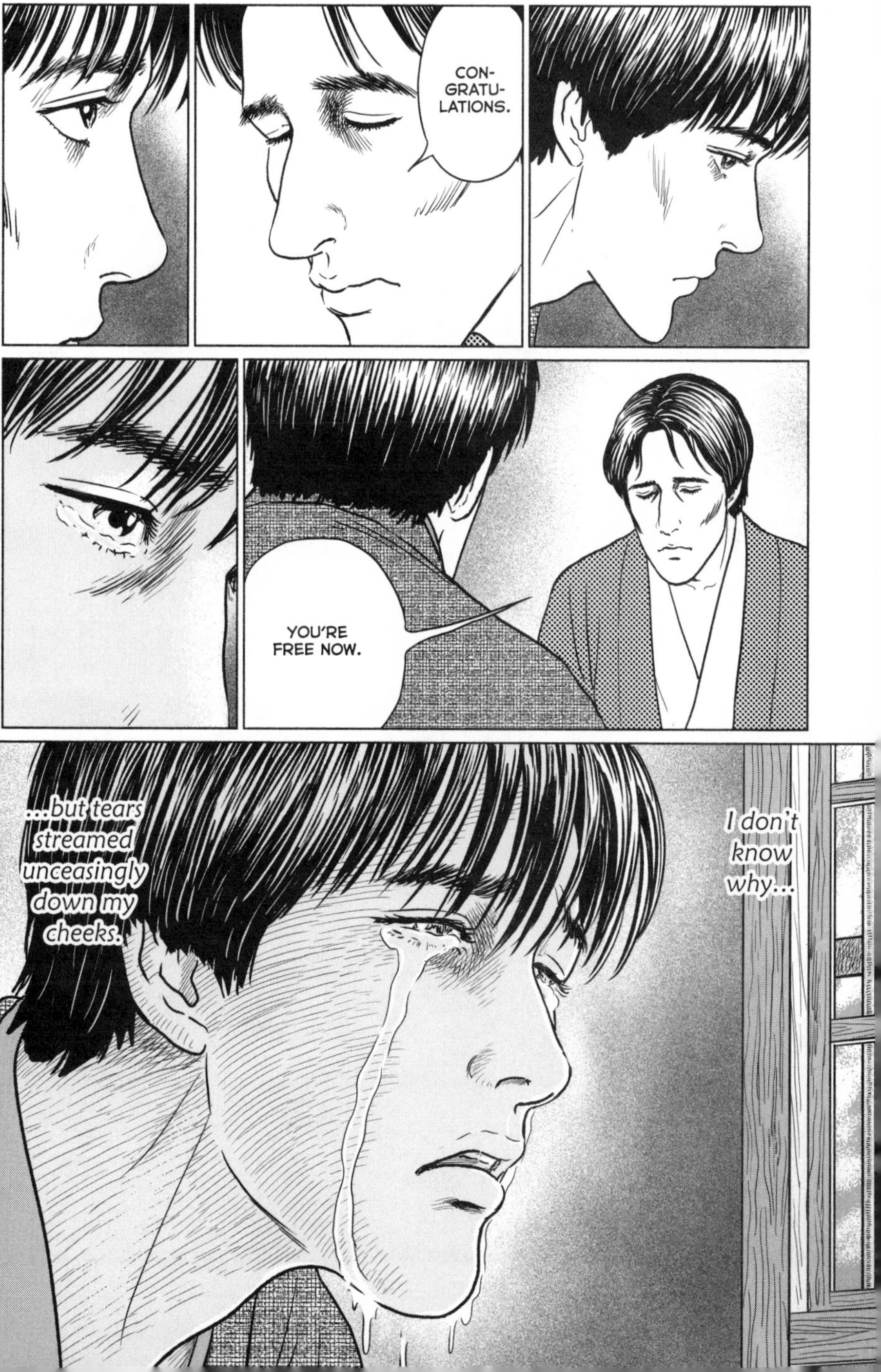
CON-GRATU-LATIONS.
YOU'RE FREE NOW.
I don't know why...
...but tears streamed unceasingly down my cheeks.

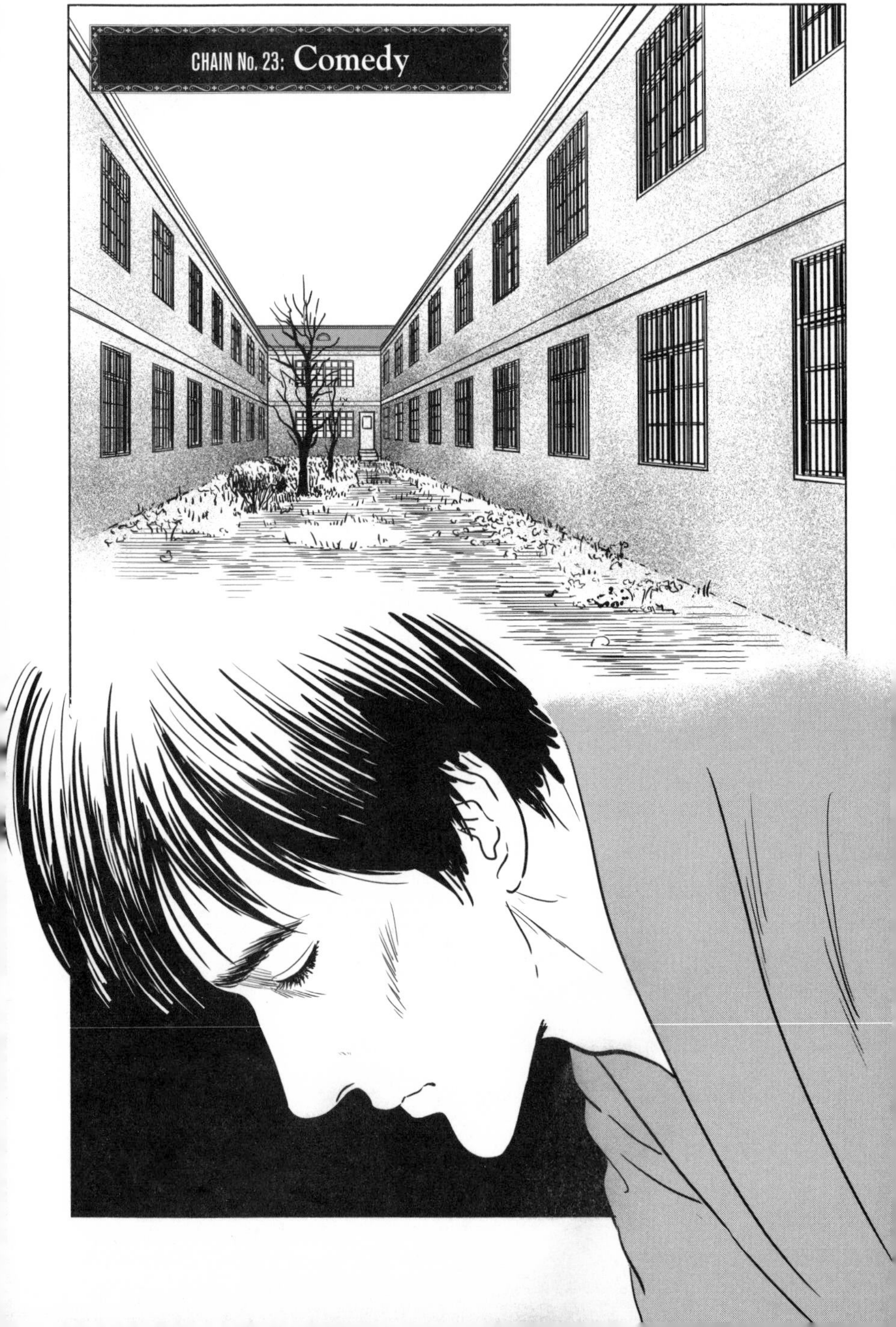
CHAIN No. 23: Comedy

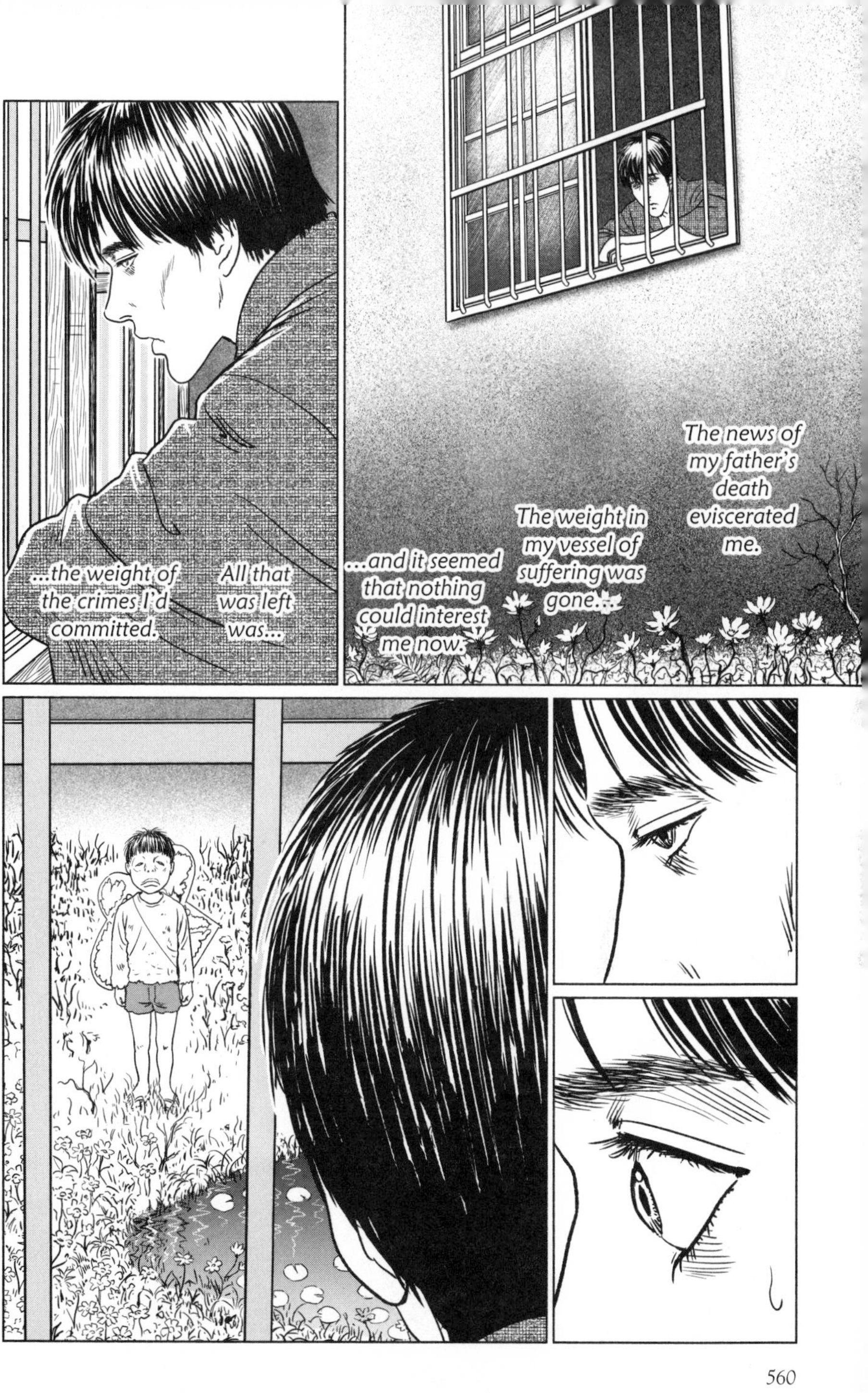
The news of my father's death eviscerated me.
The weight in my vessel of suffering was gone...
...and it seemed that nothing could interest me now.
All that was left was...
...the weight of the crimes I'd committed.

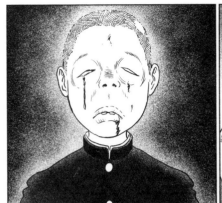
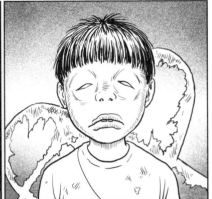
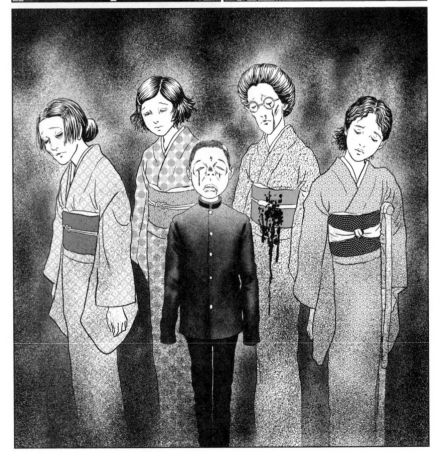

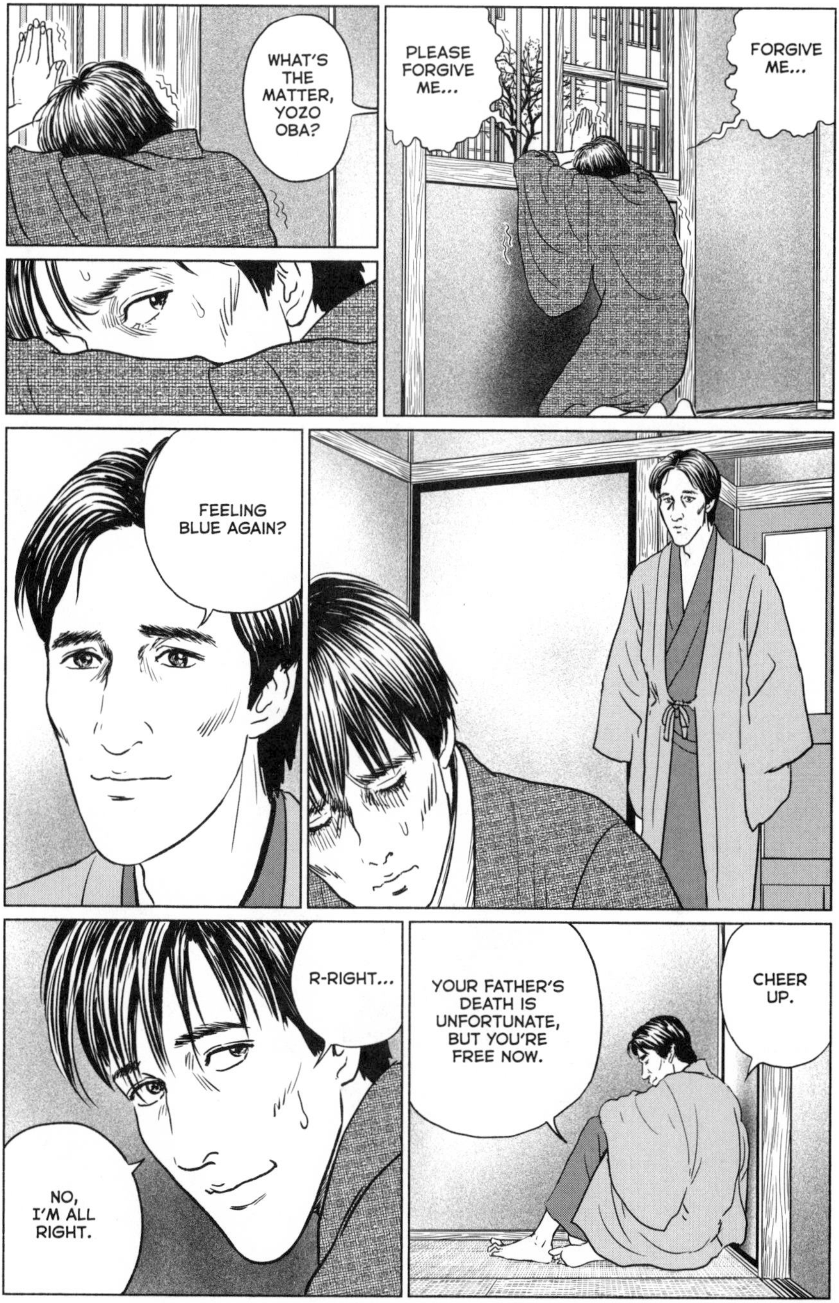
FORGIVE ME...
PLEASE FORGIVE ME...
WHAT'S THE MATTER, YOZO OBA?
FEELING BLUE AGAIN?
CHEER UP.
YOUR FATHER'S DEATH IS UNFORTUNATE, BUT YOU'RE FREE NOW.
R-RIGHT...
NO, I'M ALL RIGHT.

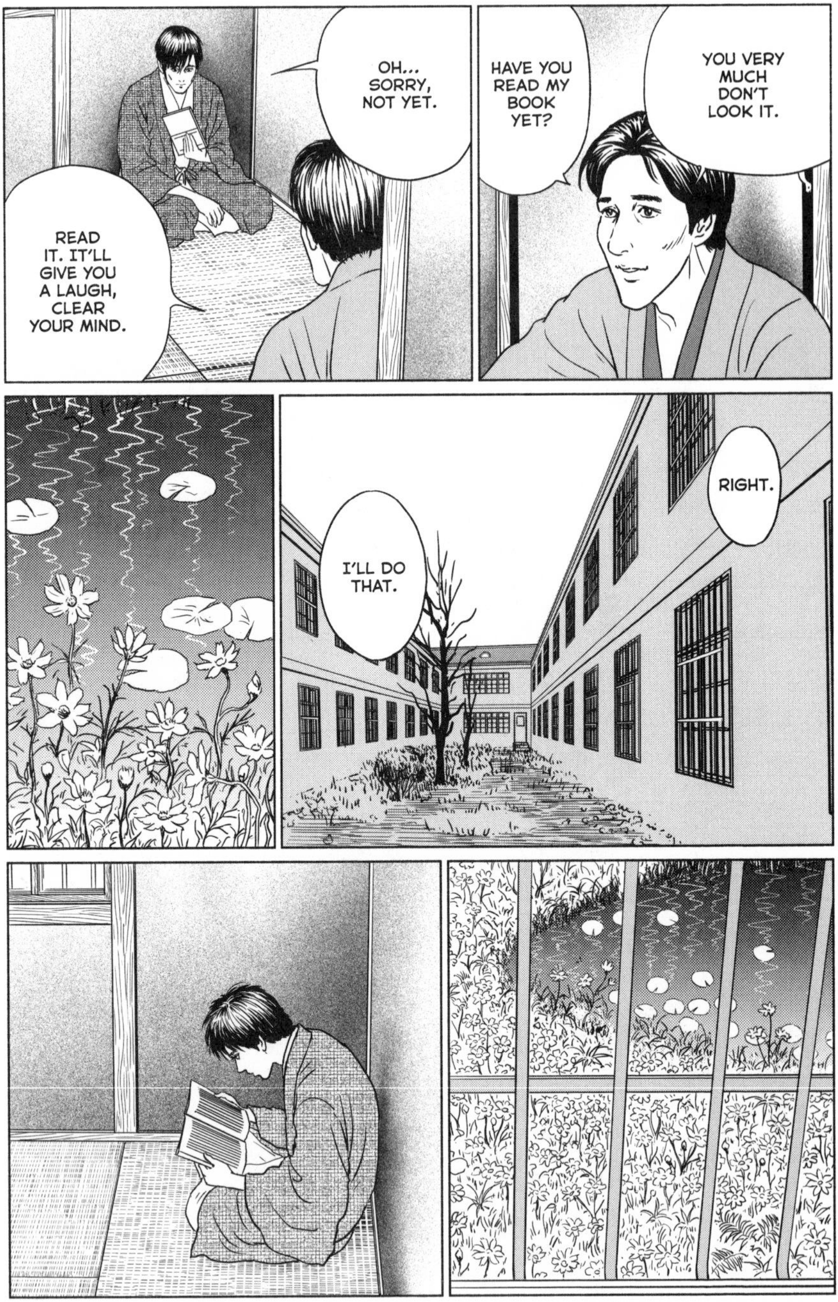
YOU VERY MUCH DON'T LOOK IT.
HAVE YOU READ MY BOOK YET?
OH... SORRY, NOT YET.
READ IT. IT'LL GIVE YOU A LAUGH, CLEAR YOUR MIND.
RIGHT.
I'LL DO THAT.

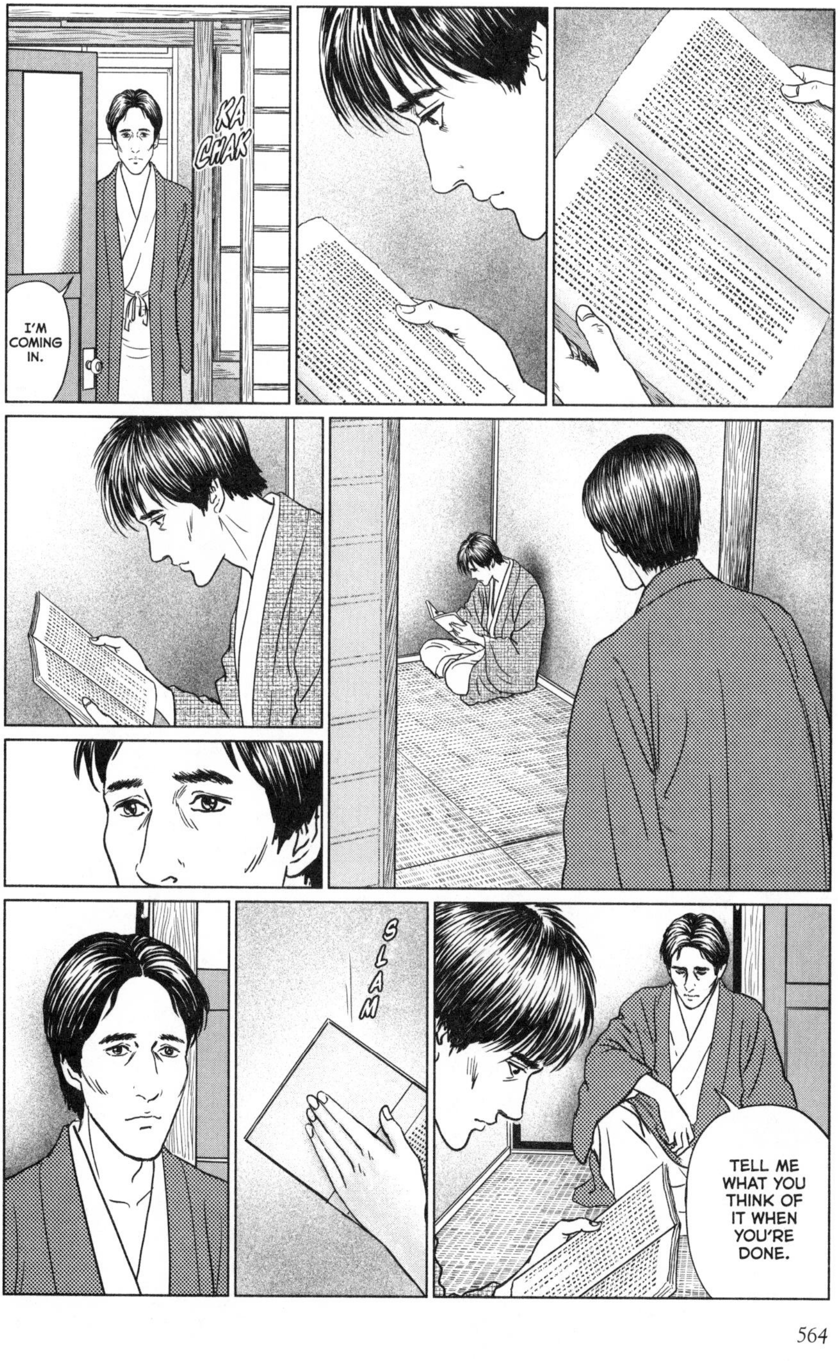
KA CHAK
I'M COMING IN.
TELL ME WHAT YOU THINK OF IT WHEN YOU'RE DONE.
SLAM

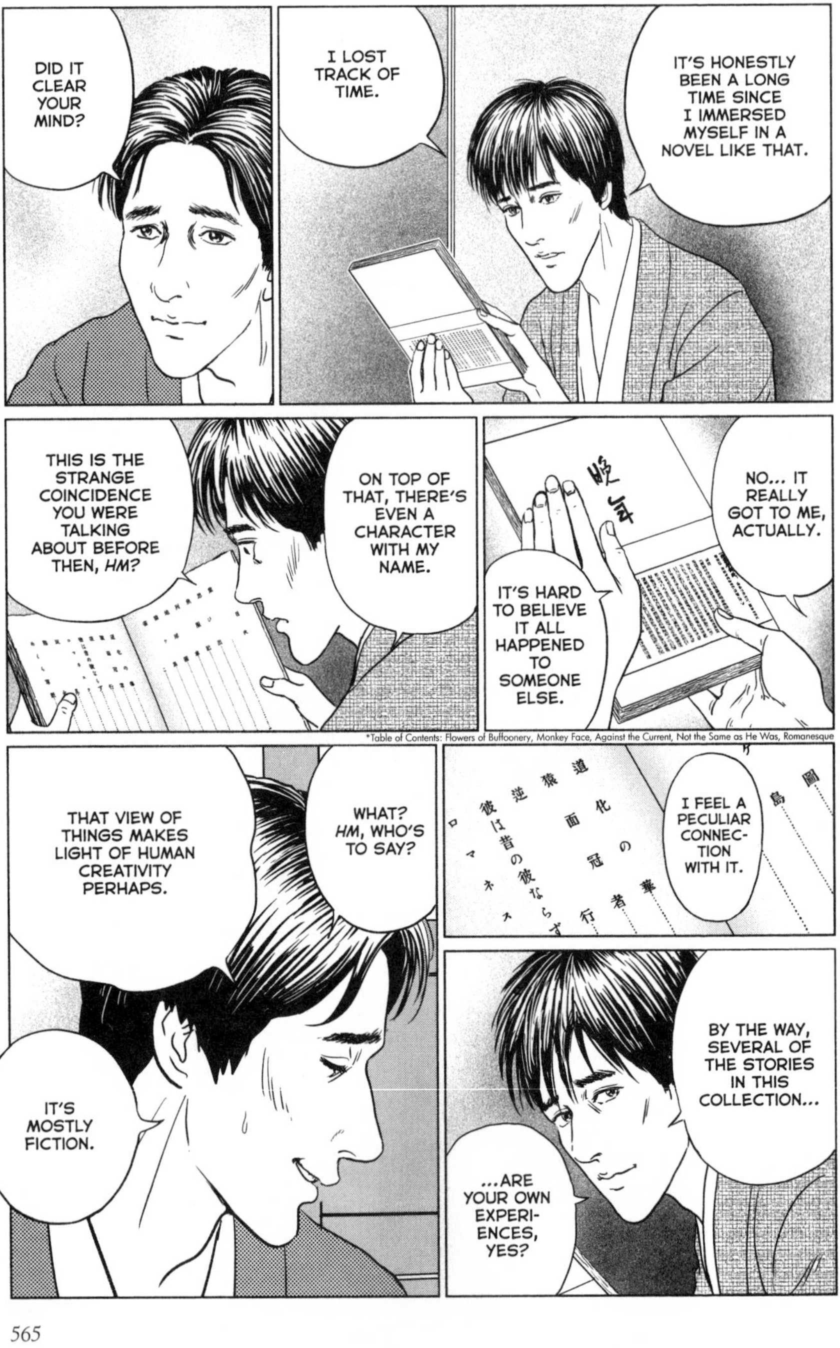
IT'S HONESTLY BEEN A LONG TIME SINCE I IMMERSED MYSELF IN A NOVEL LIKE THAT.
I LOST TRACK OF TIME.
DID IT CLEAR YOUR MIND?
NO... IT REALLY GOT TO ME, ACTUALLY.
晩年
IT'S HARD TO BELIEVE IT ALL HAPPENED TO SOMEONE ELSE.
ON TOP OF THAT, THERE'S EVEN A CHARACTER WITH MY NAME.
THIS IS THE STRANGE COINCIDENCE YOU WERE TALKING ABOUT BEFORE THEN, *HM*?
*Table of Contents: Flowers of Buffoonery, Monkey Face, Against the Current, Not the Same as He Was, Romanesque
I FEEL A PECULIAR CONNECTION WITH IT.
道化の華
猿面冠者
逆行
彼は昔の彼ならず
ロマネスク
BY THE WAY, SEVERAL OF THE STORIES IN THIS COLLECTION...
...ARE YOUR OWN EXPERIENCES, YES?
WHAT? *HM*, WHO'S TO SAY?
THAT VIEW OF THINGS MAKES LIGHT OF HUMAN CREATIVITY PERHAPS.
IT'S MOSTLY FICTION.

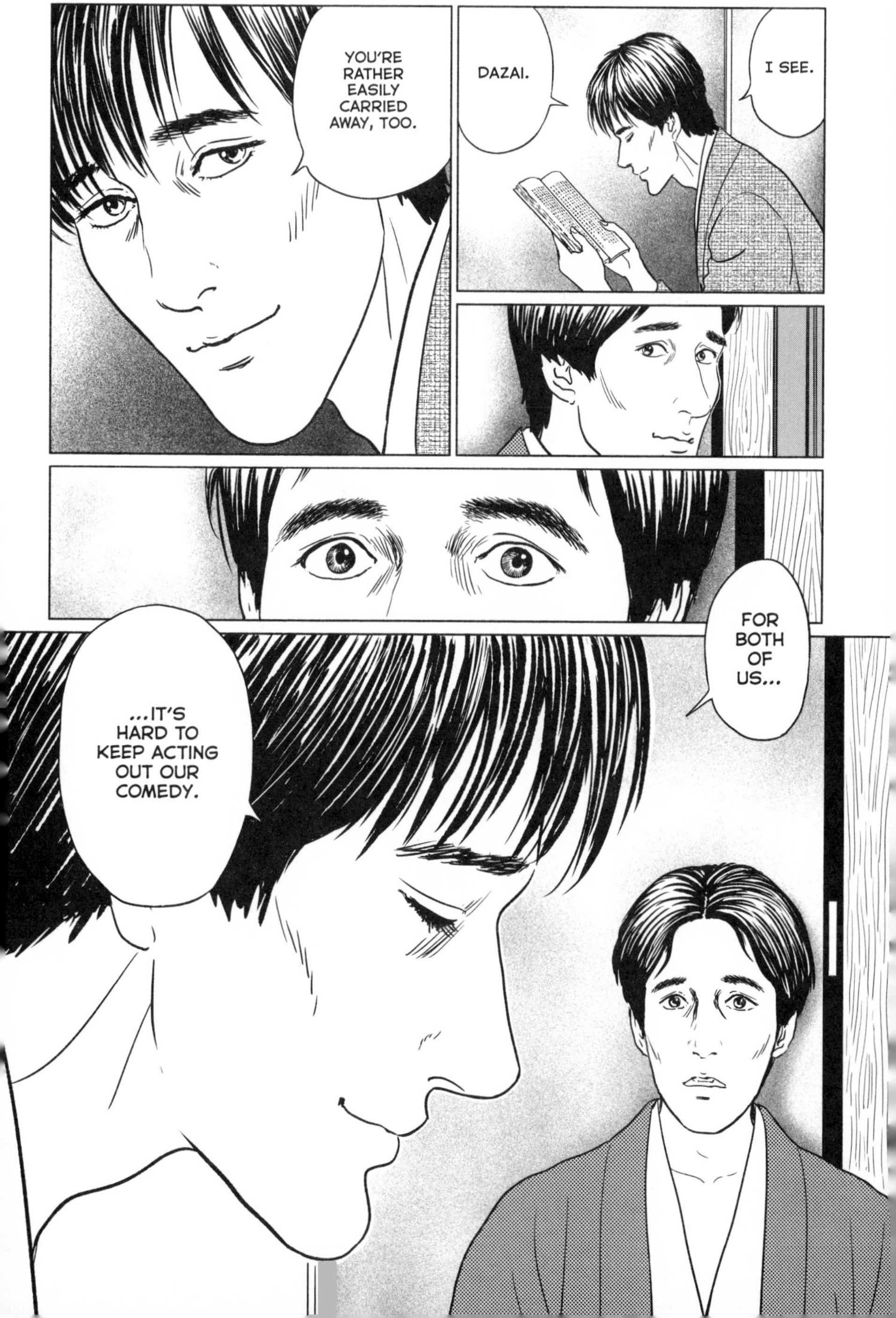
I SEE.
DAZAI.
YOU'RE RATHER EASILY CARRIED AWAY, TOO.
FOR BOTH OF US...
...IT'S HARD TO KEEP ACTING OUT OUR COMEDY.

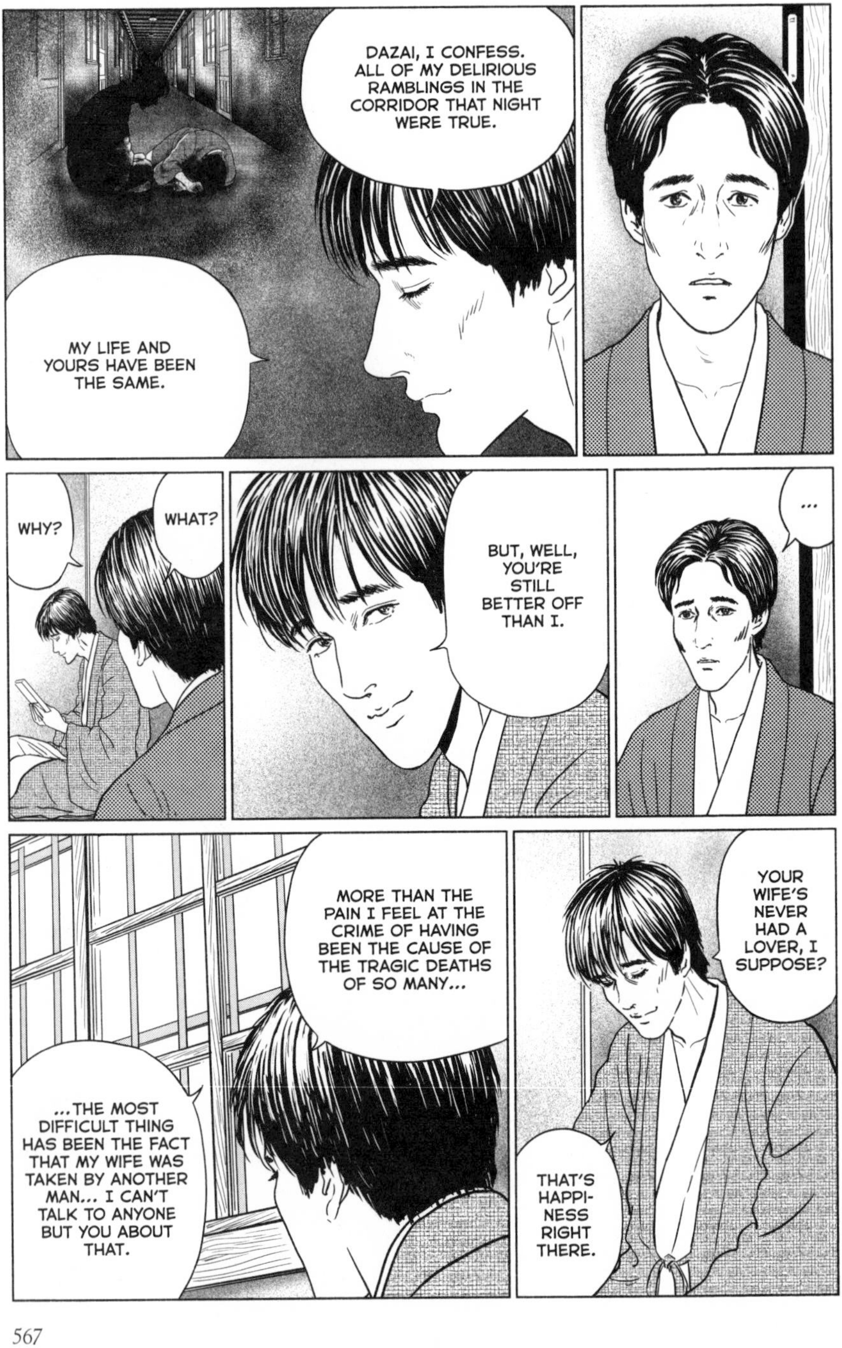
DAZAI, I CONFESS. ALL OF MY DELIRIOUS RAMBLINGS IN THE CORRIDOR THAT NIGHT WERE TRUE.
MY LIFE AND YOURS HAVE BEEN THE SAME.
...
BUT, WELL, YOU'RE STILL BETTER OFF THAN I.
WHAT?
WHY?
YOUR WIFE'S NEVER HAD A LOVER, I SUPPOSE?
THAT'S HAPPI-NESS RIGHT THERE.
MORE THAN THE PAIN I FEEL AT THE CRIME OF HAVING BEEN THE CAUSE OF THE TRAGIC DEATHS OF SO MANY...
...THE MOST DIFFICULT THING HAS BEEN THE FACT THAT MY WIFE WAS TAKEN BY ANOTHER MAN... I CAN'T TALK TO ANYONE BUT YOU ABOUT THAT.

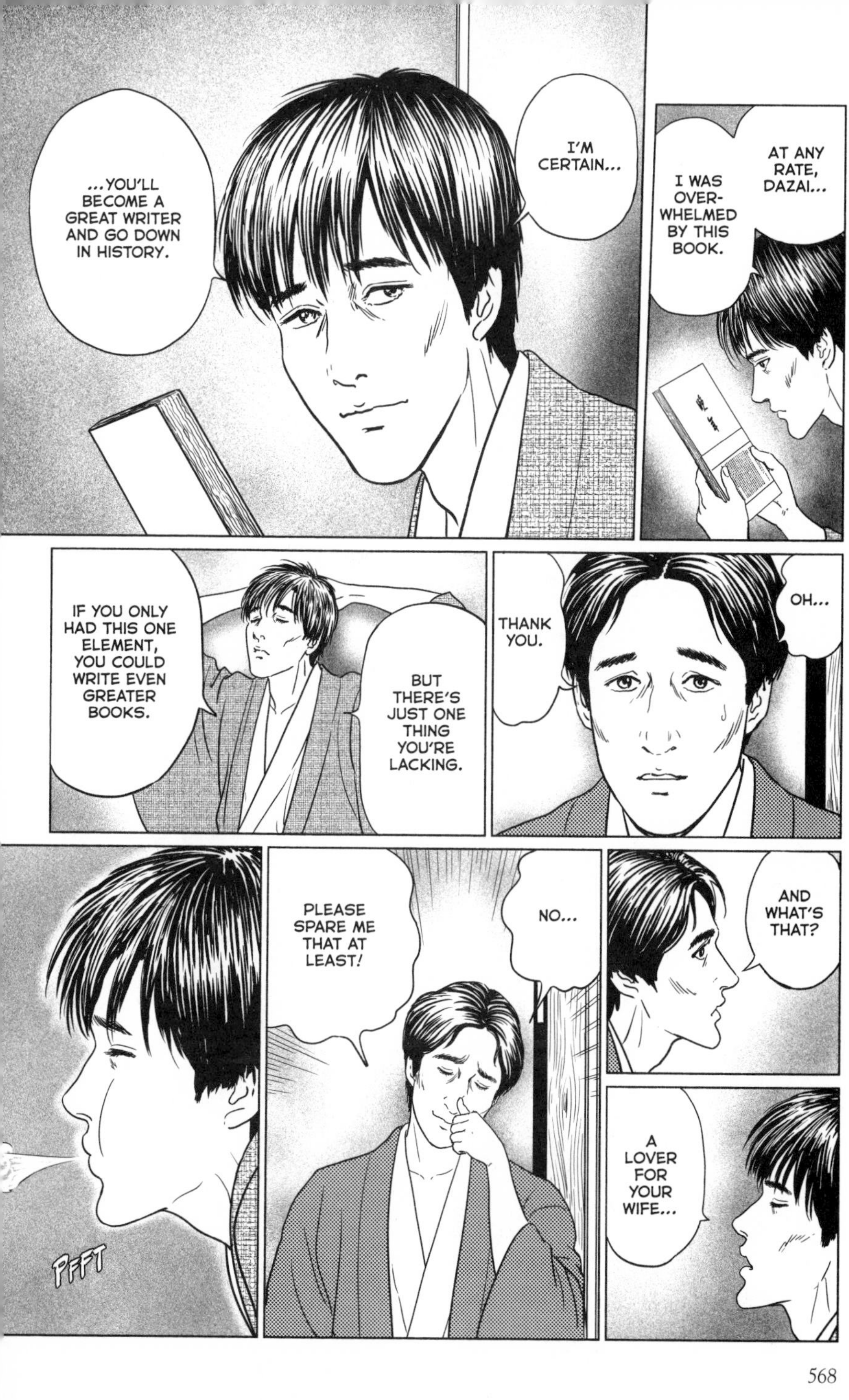
AT ANY RATE, DAZAI...
I WAS OVER-WHELMED BY THIS BOOK.
I'M CERTAIN...
...YOU'LL BECOME A GREAT WRITER AND GO DOWN IN HISTORY.
OH...
THANK YOU.
BUT THERE'S JUST ONE THING YOU'RE LACKING.
IF YOU ONLY HAD THIS ONE ELEMENT, YOU COULD WRITE EVEN GREATER BOOKS.
AND WHAT'S THAT?
A LOVER FOR YOUR WIFE...
NO...
PLEASE SPARE ME THAT AT LEAST!
PFFT

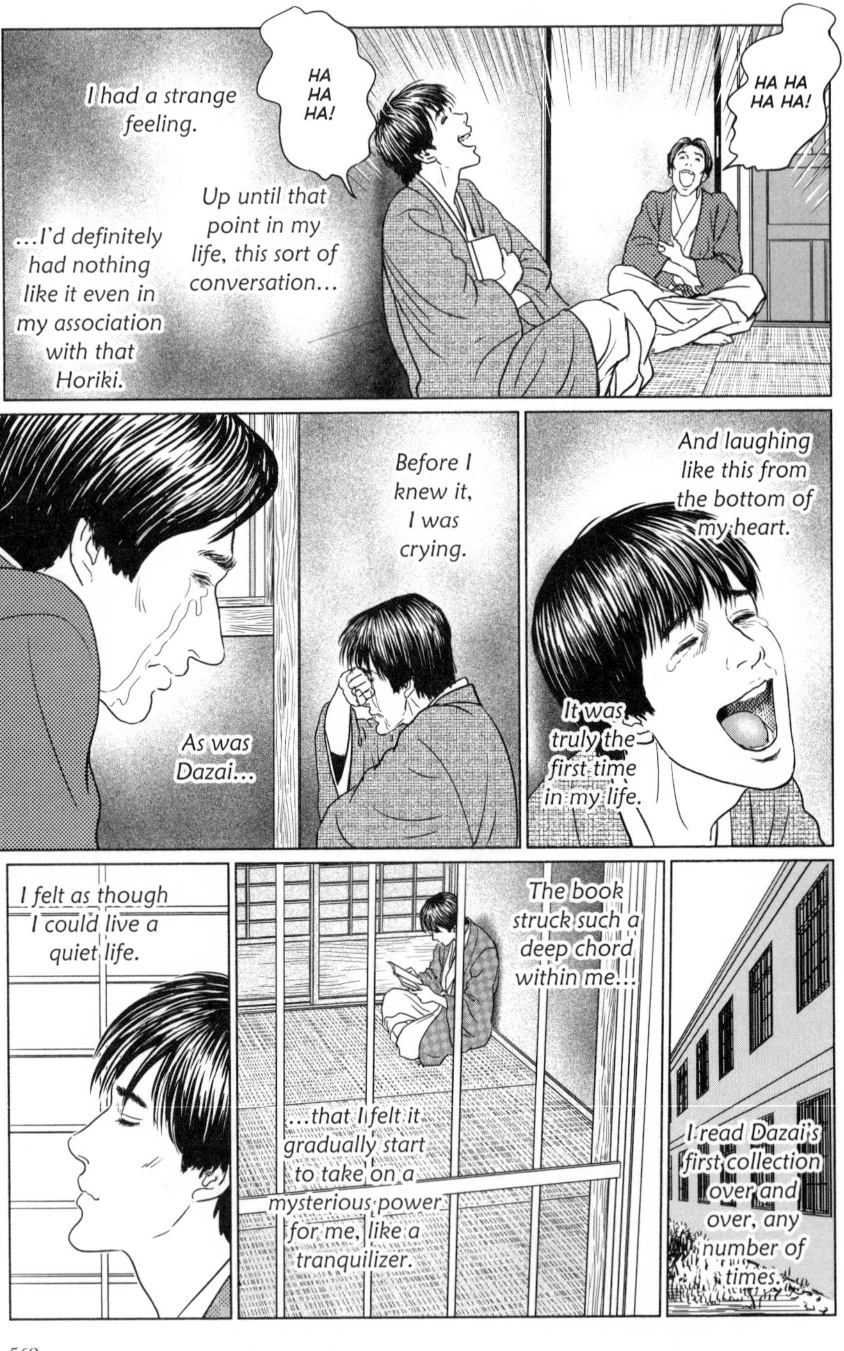
HA HA HA HA!
HA HA HA!
I had a strange feeling.
Up until that point in my life, this sort of conversation…
…I'd definitely had nothing like it even in my association with that Horiki.
And laughing like this from the bottom of my heart.
It was truly the first time in my life.
Before I knew it, I was crying.
As was Dazai…
I read Dazai's first collection over and over, any number of times.
The book struck such a deep chord within me…
…that I felt it gradually start to take on a mysterious power for me, like a tranquilizer.
I felt as though I could live a quiet life.

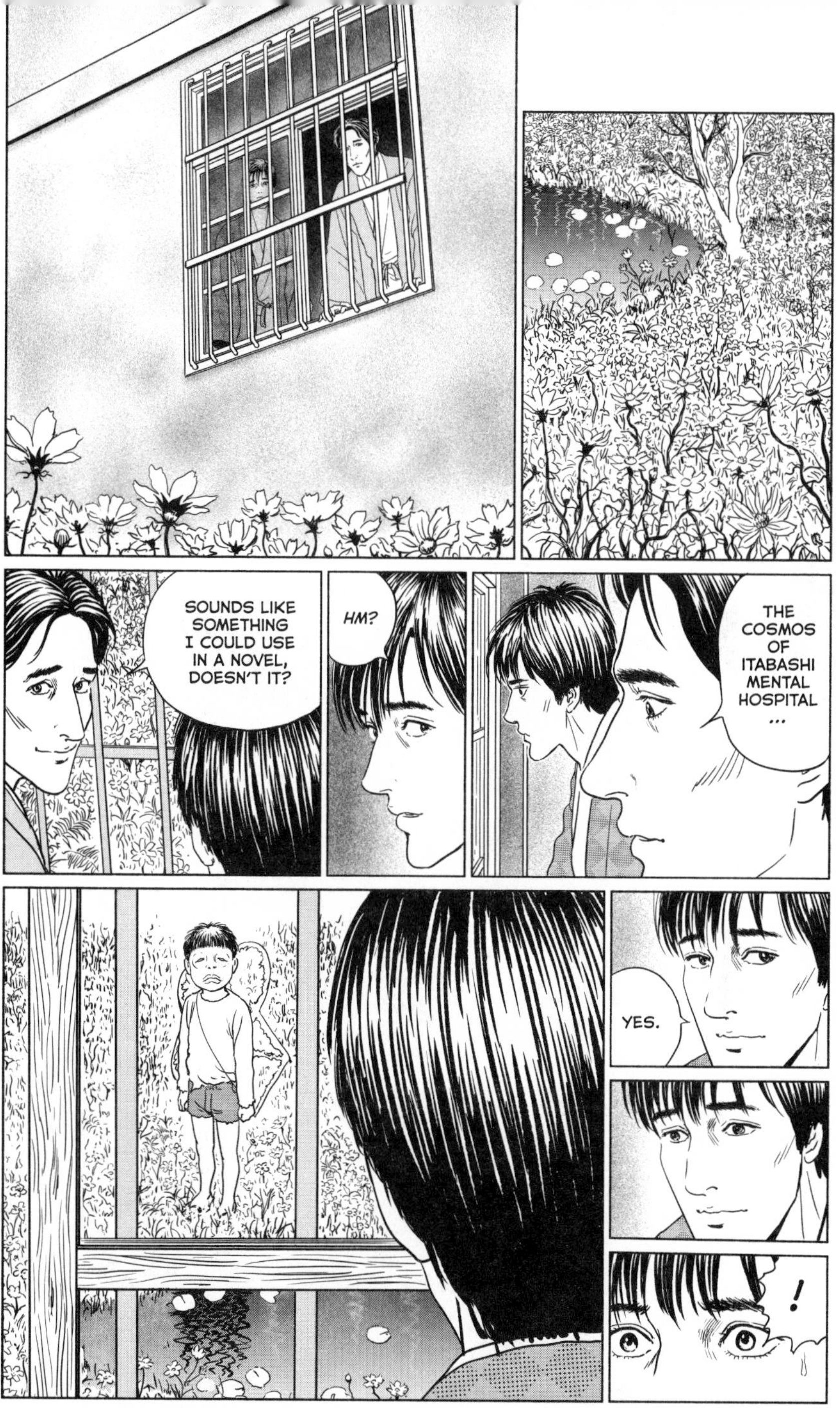
THE COSMOS OF ITABASHI MENTAL HOSPITAL ...
HM?
SOUNDS LIKE SOMETHING I COULD USE IN A NOVEL, DOESN'T IT?
YES.
!

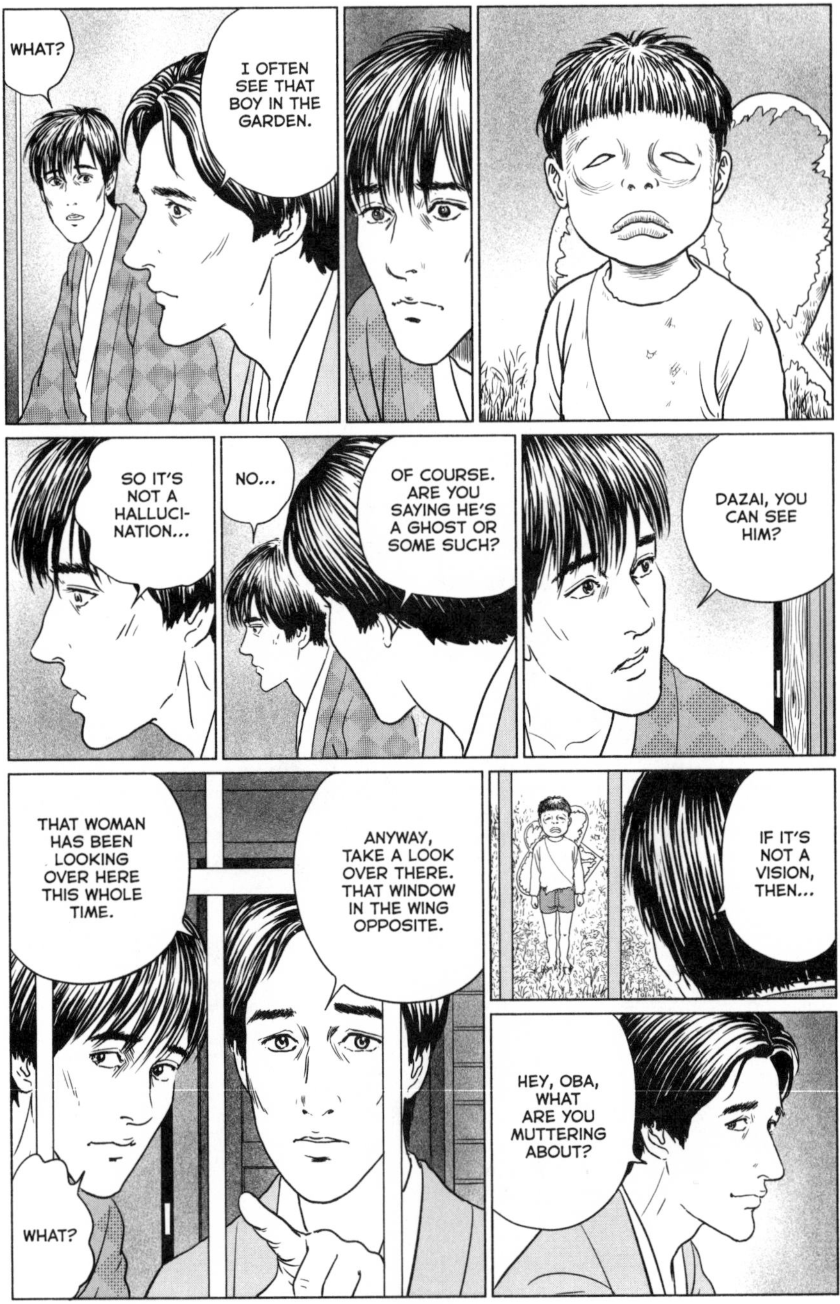
I OFTEN SEE THAT BOY IN THE GARDEN.
WHAT?
DAZAI, YOU CAN SEE HIM?
OF COURSE. ARE YOU SAYING HE'S A GHOST OR SOME SUCH?
NO...
SO IT'S NOT A HALLUCI-NATION...
IF IT'S NOT A VISION, THEN...
HEY, OBA, WHAT ARE YOU MUTTERING ABOUT?
ANYWAY, TAKE A LOOK OVER THERE. THAT WINDOW IN THE WING OPPOSITE.
THAT WOMAN HAS BEEN LOOKING OVER HERE THIS WHOLE TIME.
WHAT?

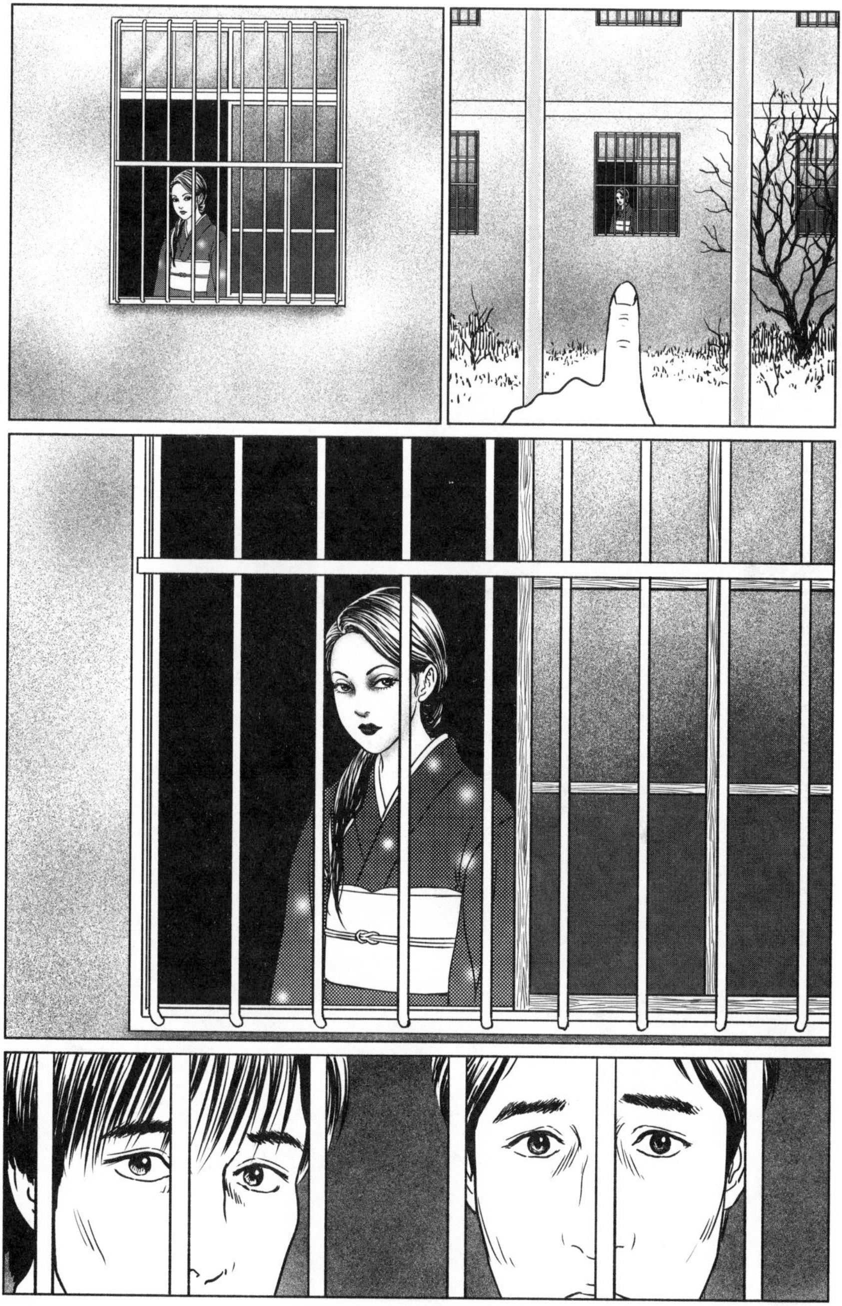

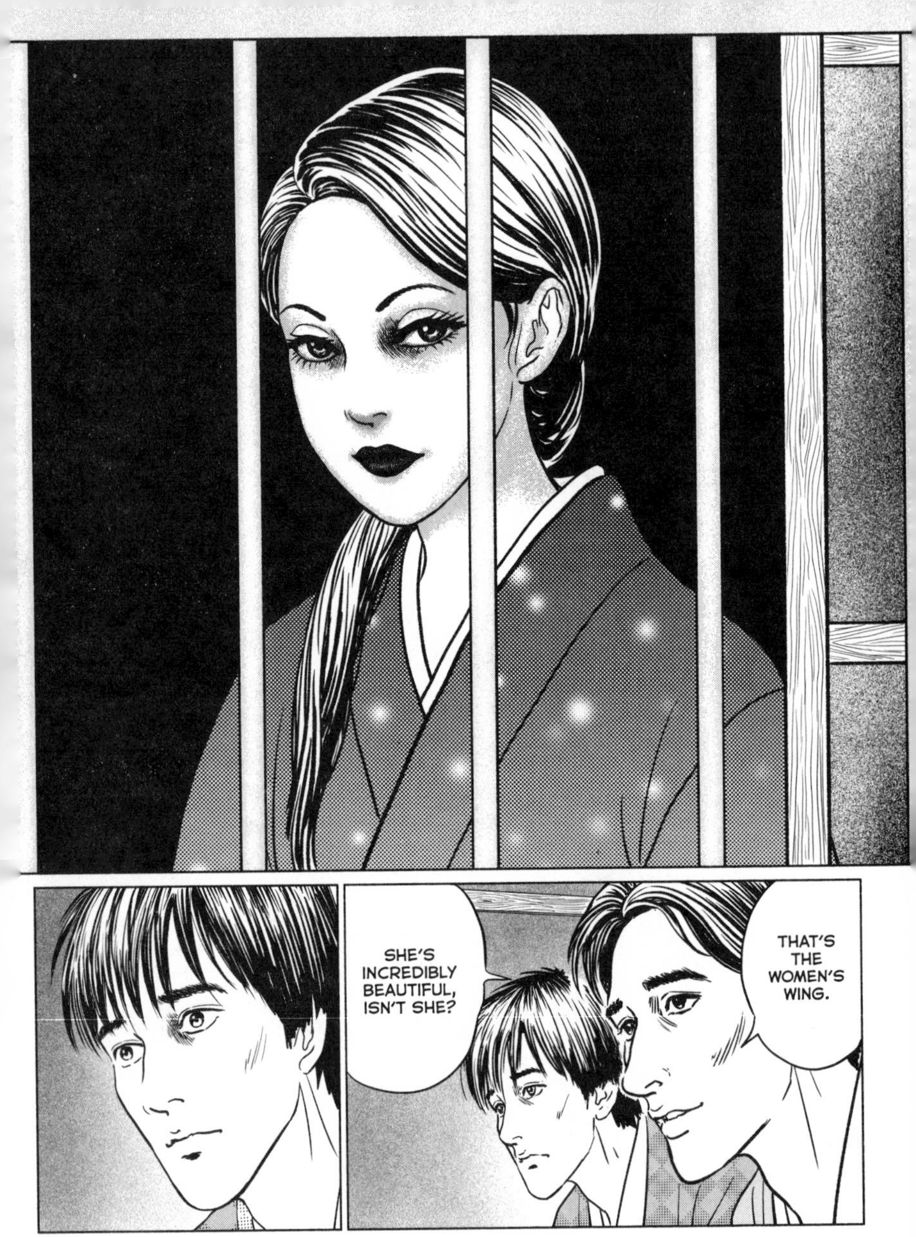
THAT'S THE WOMEN'S WING.
SHE'S INCREDIBLY BEAUTIFUL, ISN'T SHE?

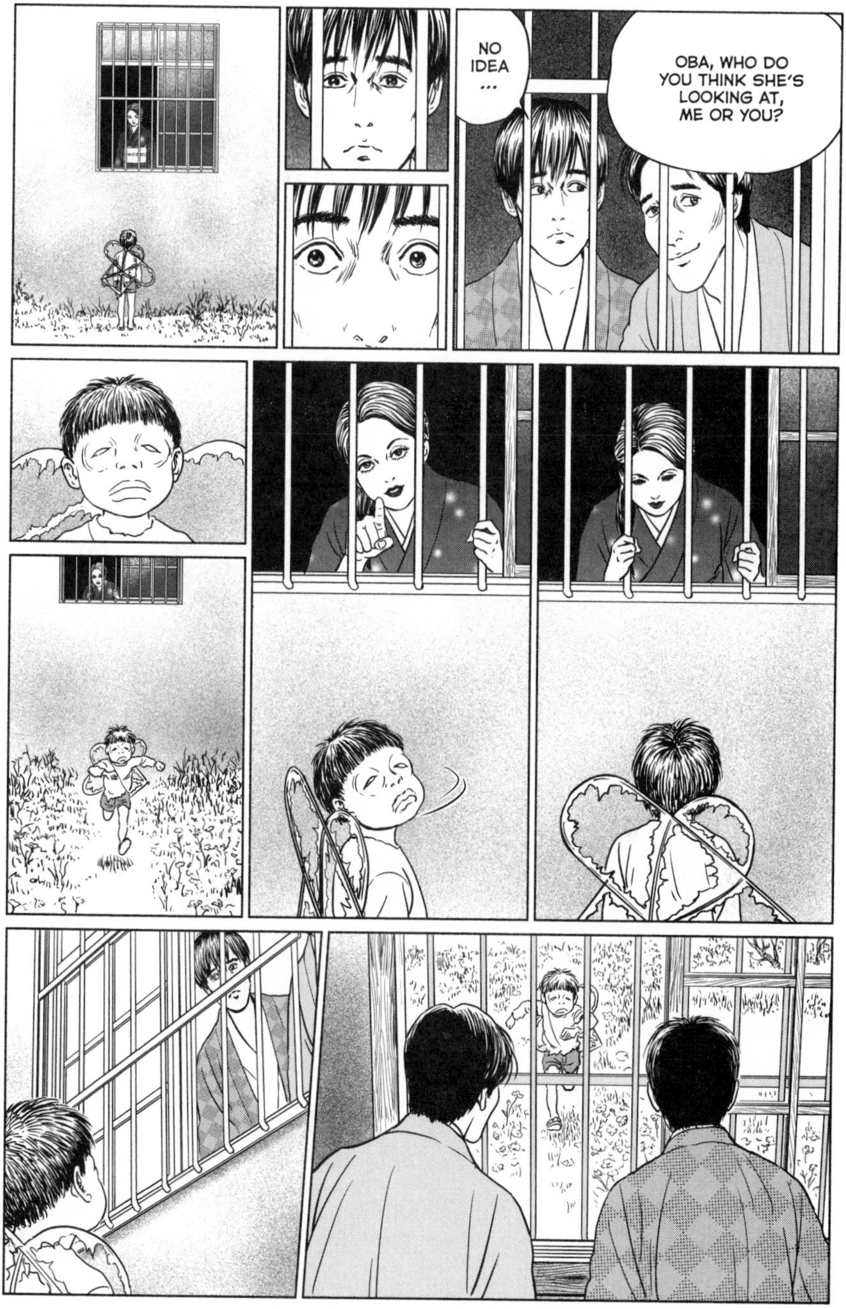
OBA, WHO DO YOU THINK SHE'S LOOKING AT, ME OR YOU?
NO IDEA...

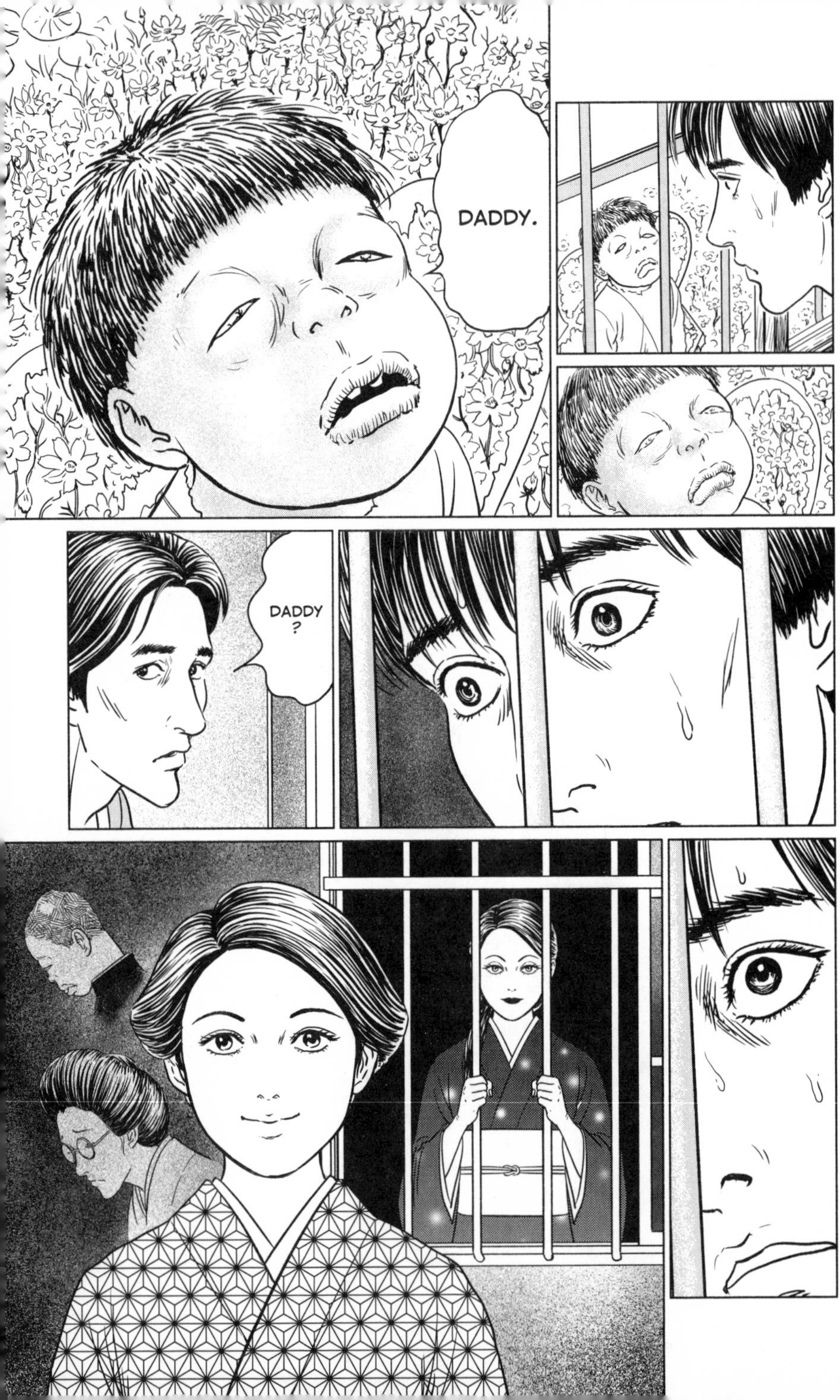
DADDY.
DADDY
?

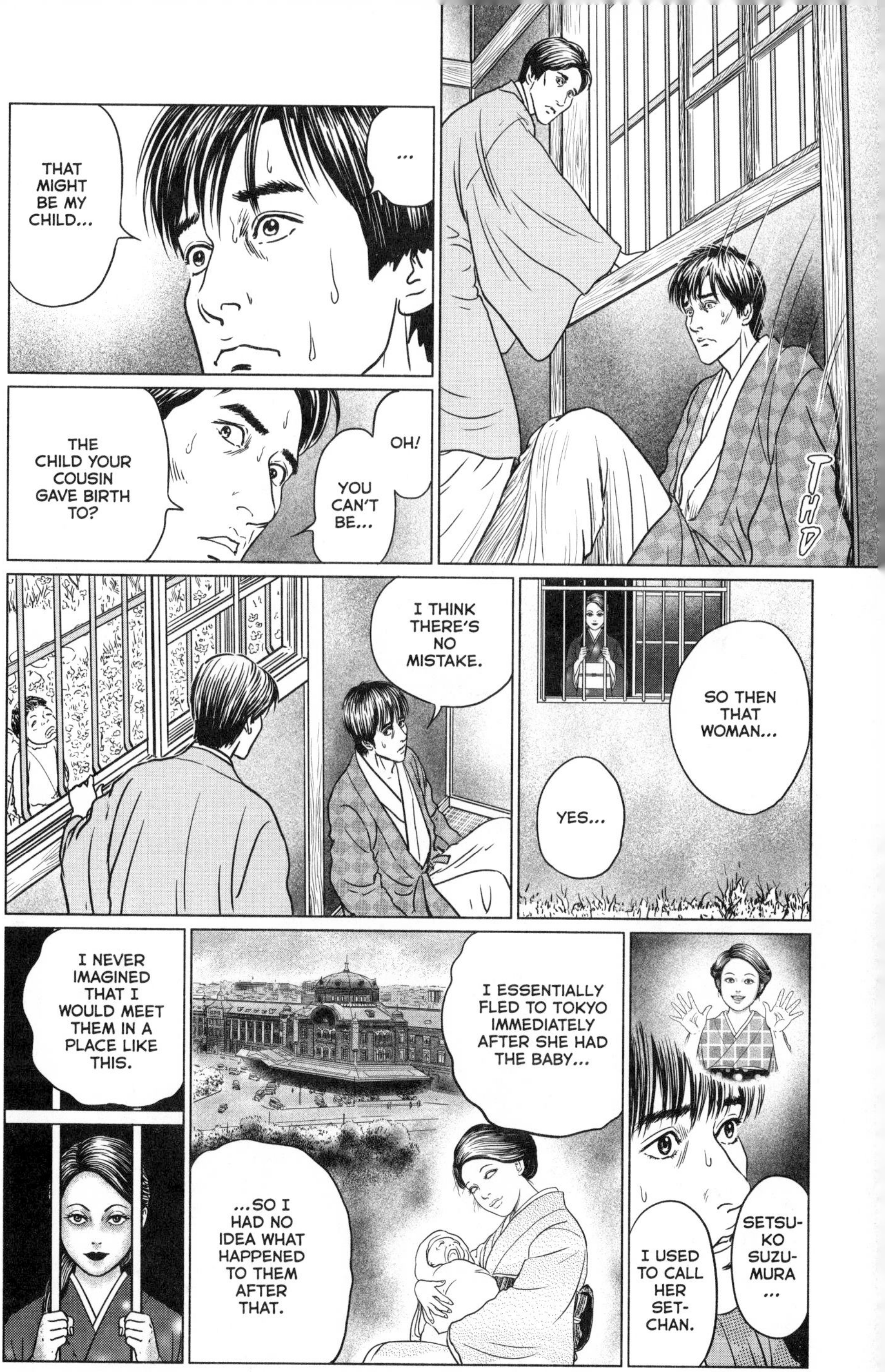
THD
...
THAT MIGHT BE MY CHILD...
OH!
YOU CAN'T BE...
THE CHILD YOUR COUSIN GAVE BIRTH TO?
SO THEN THAT WOMAN...
YES...
I THINK THERE'S NO MISTAKE.
SETSU-KO SUZU-MURA...
I USED TO CALL HER SET-CHAN.
I ESSENTIALLY FLED TO TOKYO IMMEDIATELY AFTER SHE HAD THE BABY...
...SO I HAD NO IDEA WHAT HAPPENED TO THEM AFTER THAT.
I NEVER IMAGINED THAT I WOULD MEET THEM IN A PLACE LIKE THIS.

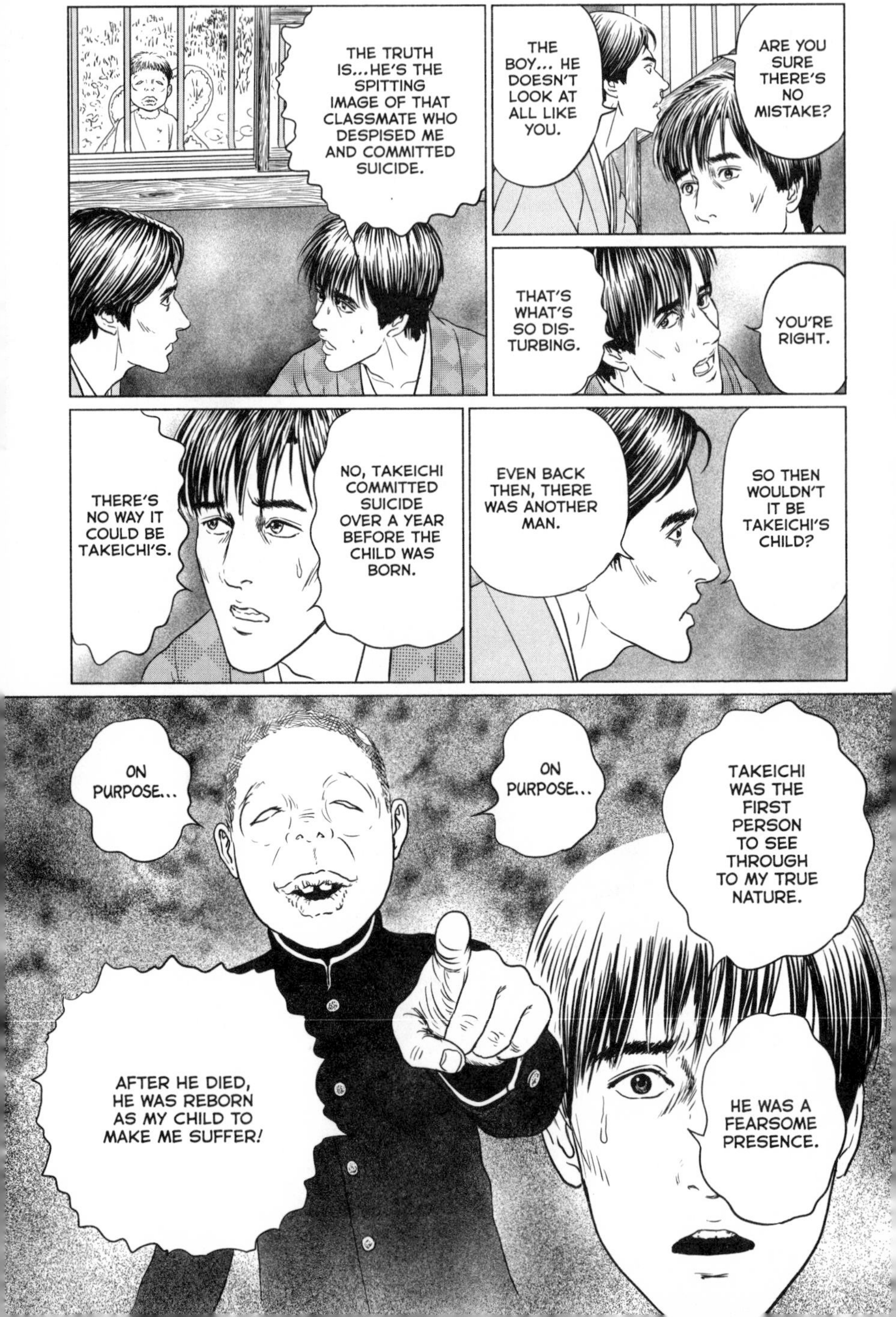
ARE YOU SURE THERE'S NO MISTAKE?
THE BOY... HE DOESN'T LOOK AT ALL LIKE YOU.
YOU'RE RIGHT.
THAT'S WHAT'S SO DIS-TURBING.
THE TRUTH IS...HE'S THE SPITTING IMAGE OF THAT CLASSMATE WHO DESPISED ME AND COMMITTED SUICIDE.
SO THEN WOULDN'T IT BE TAKEICHI'S CHILD?
EVEN BACK THEN, THERE WAS ANOTHER MAN.
NO, TAKEICHI COMMITTED SUICIDE OVER A YEAR BEFORE THE CHILD WAS BORN.
THERE'S NO WAY IT COULD BE TAKEICHI'S.
TAKEICHI WAS THE FIRST PERSON TO SEE THROUGH TO MY TRUE NATURE.
ON PURPOSE...
ON PURPOSE...
HE WAS A FEARSOME PRESENCE.
AFTER HE DIED, HE WAS REBORN AS MY CHILD TO MAKE ME SUFFER!

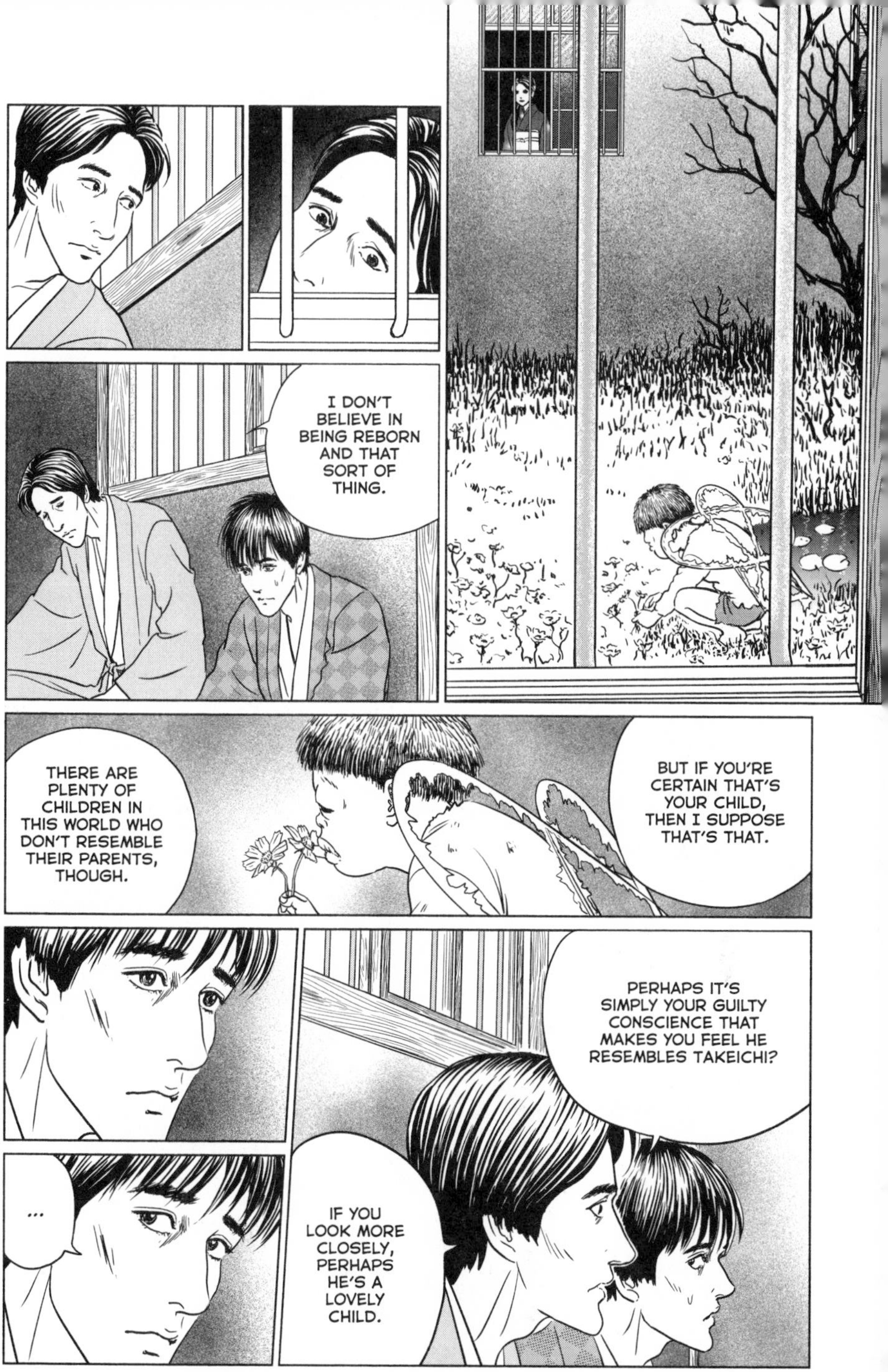
I DON'T BELIEVE IN BEING REBORN AND THAT SORT OF THING.
BUT IF YOU'RE CERTAIN THAT'S YOUR CHILD, THEN I SUPPOSE THAT'S THAT.
THERE ARE PLENTY OF CHILDREN IN THIS WORLD WHO DON'T RESEMBLE THEIR PARENTS, THOUGH.
PERHAPS IT'S SIMPLY YOUR GUILTY CONSCIENCE THAT MAKES YOU FEEL HE RESEMBLES TAKEICHI?
IF YOU LOOK MORE CLOSELY, PERHAPS HE'S A LOVELY CHILD.
...

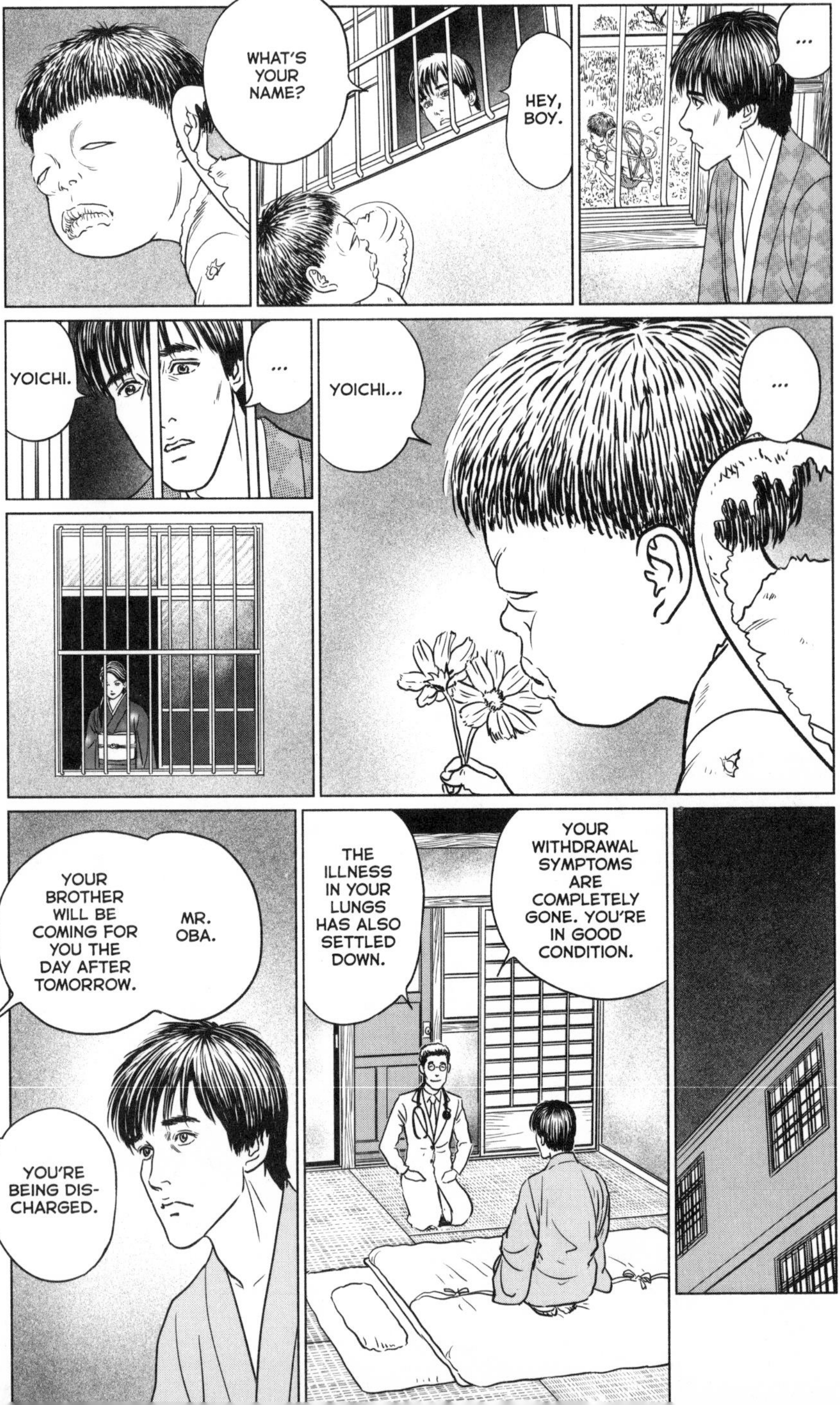
...
HEY, BOY.
WHAT'S YOUR NAME?
...
YOICHI...
...
YOICHI.
YOUR WITHDRAWAL SYMPTOMS ARE COMPLETELY GONE. YOU'RE IN GOOD CONDITION.
THE ILLNESS IN YOUR LUNGS HAS ALSO SETTLED DOWN.
MR. OBA.
YOUR BROTHER WILL BE COMING FOR YOU THE DAY AFTER TOMORROW.
YOU'RE BEING DIS-CHARGED.

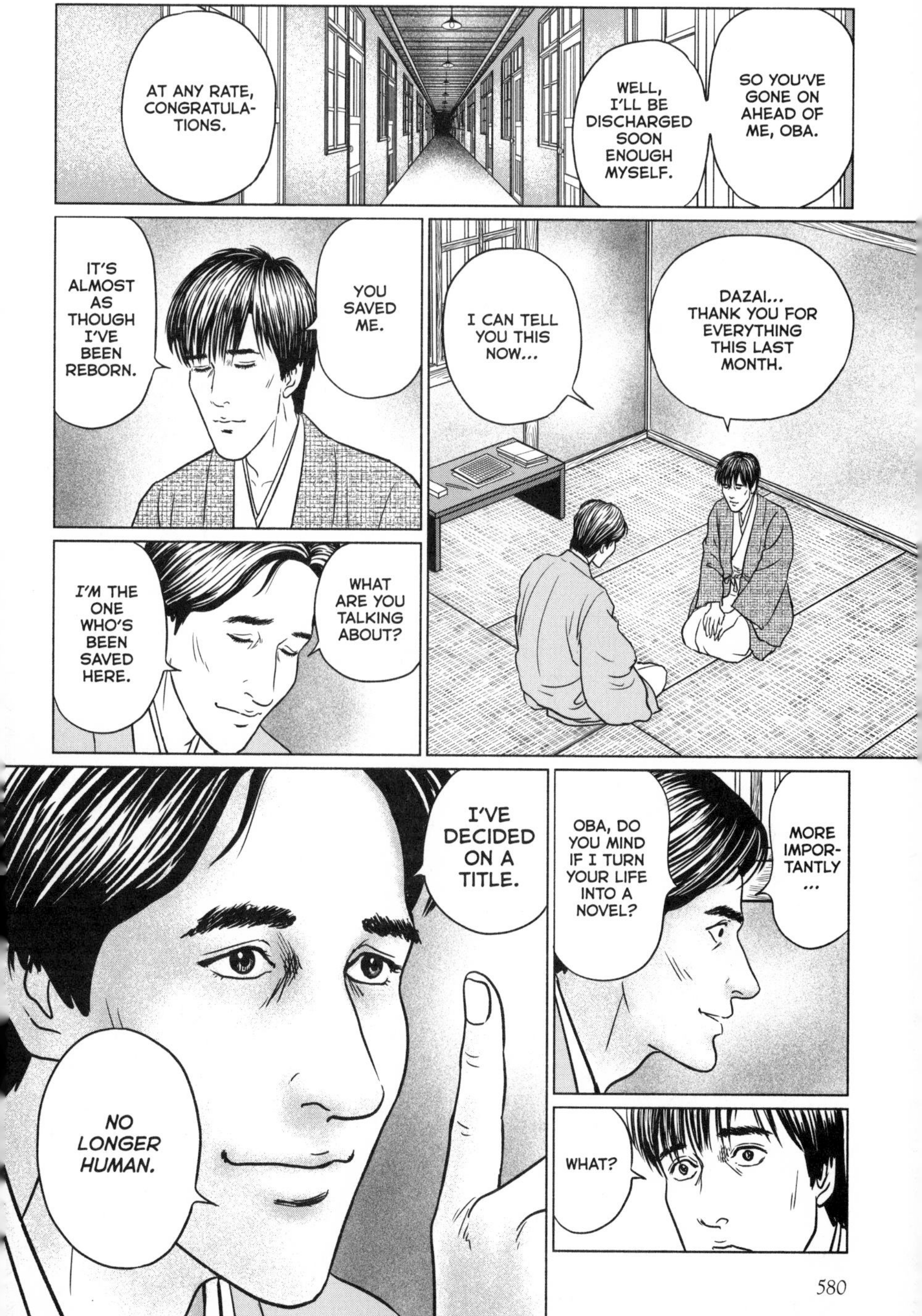
SO YOU'VE GONE ON AHEAD OF ME, OBA.
WELL, I'LL BE DISCHARGED SOON ENOUGH MYSELF.
AT ANY RATE, CONGRATULATIONS.
DAZAI... THANK YOU FOR EVERYTHING THIS LAST MONTH.
I CAN TELL YOU THIS NOW...
YOU SAVED ME.
IT'S ALMOST AS THOUGH I'VE BEEN REBORN.
WHAT ARE YOU TALKING ABOUT?
I'M THE ONE WHO'S BEEN SAVED HERE.
MORE IMPORTANTLY...
OBA, DO YOU MIND IF I TURN YOUR LIFE INTO A NOVEL?
WHAT?
I'VE DECIDED ON A TITLE.
NO LONGER HUMAN.

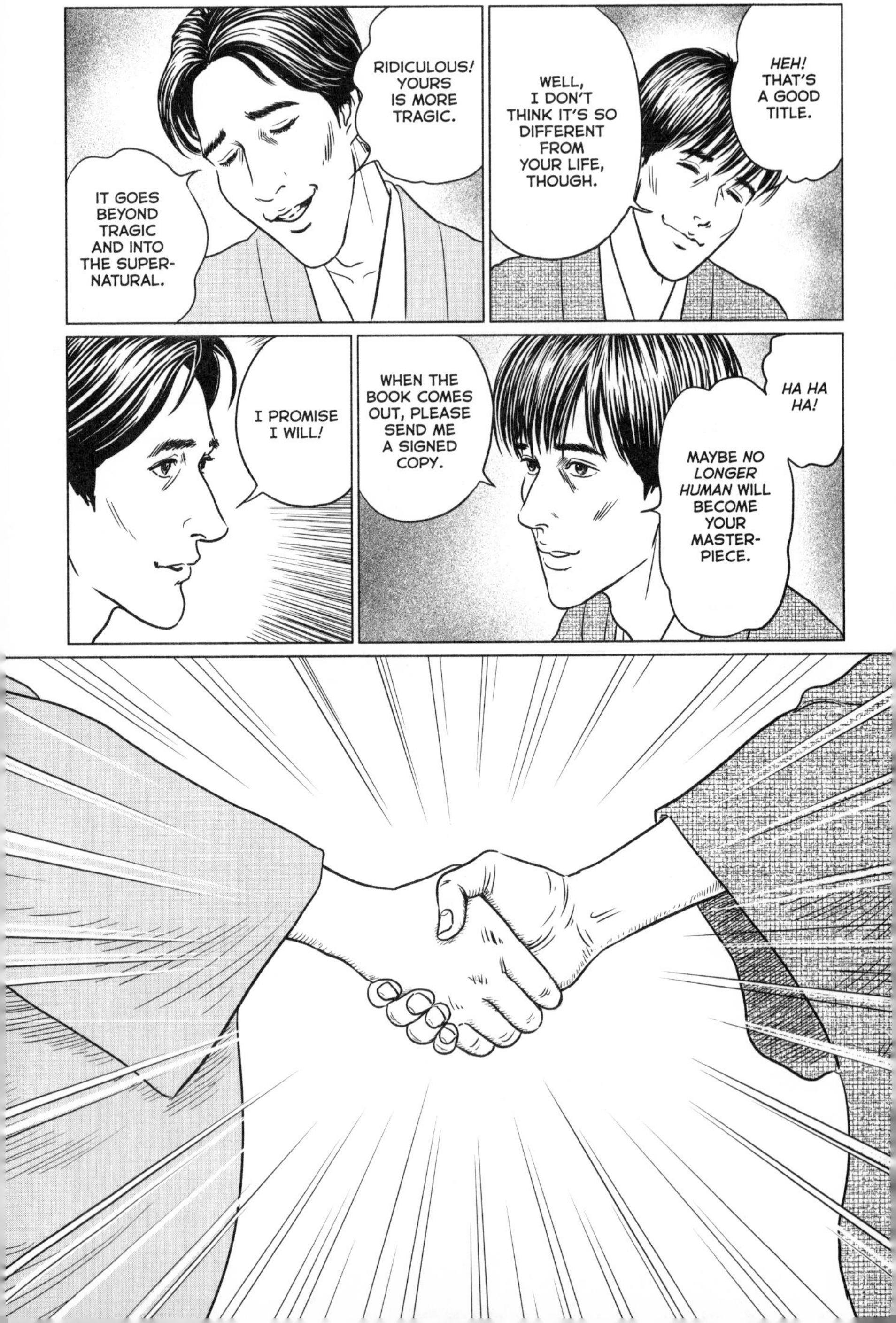
HEH! THAT'S A GOOD TITLE.
WELL, I DON'T THINK IT'S SO DIFFERENT FROM YOUR LIFE, THOUGH.
RIDICULOUS! YOURS IS MORE TRAGIC.
IT GOES BEYOND TRAGIC AND INTO THE SUPER-NATURAL.
HA HA HA!
MAYBE *NO LONGER HUMAN* WILL BECOME YOUR MASTER-PIECE.
WHEN THE BOOK COMES OUT, PLEASE SEND ME A SIGNED COPY.
I PROMISE I WILL!

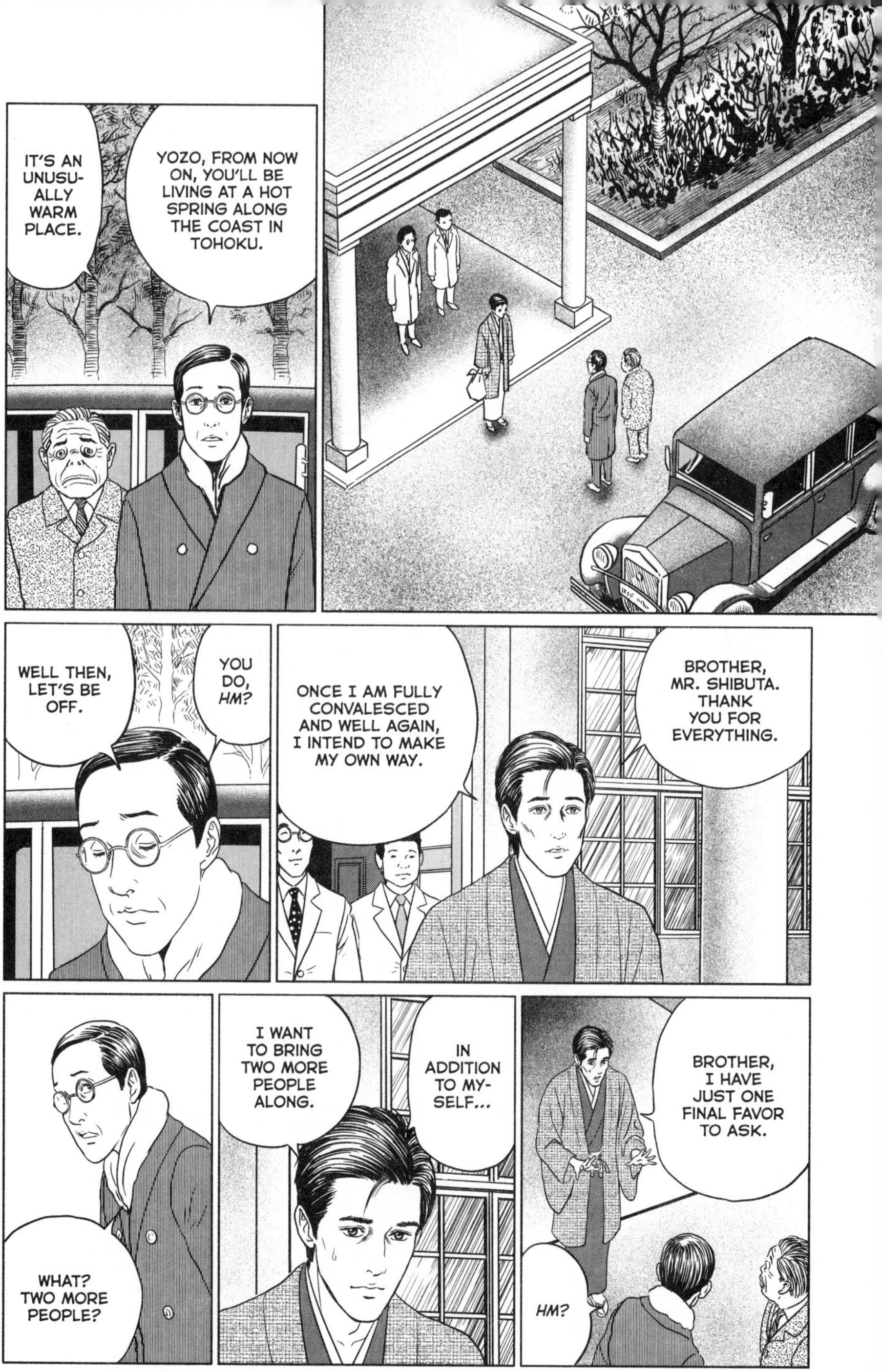
YOZO, FROM NOW ON, YOU'LL BE LIVING AT A HOT SPRING ALONG THE COAST IN TOHOKU.
IT'S AN UNUSUALLY WARM PLACE.
BROTHER, MR. SHIBUTA. THANK YOU FOR EVERYTHING.
ONCE I AM FULLY CONVALESCED AND WELL AGAIN, I INTEND TO MAKE MY OWN WAY.
YOU DO, *HM?*
WELL THEN, LET'S BE OFF.
BROTHER, I HAVE JUST ONE FINAL FAVOR TO ASK.
HM?
IN ADDITION TO MYSELF...
I WANT TO BRING TWO MORE PEOPLE ALONG.
WHAT? TWO MORE PEOPLE?

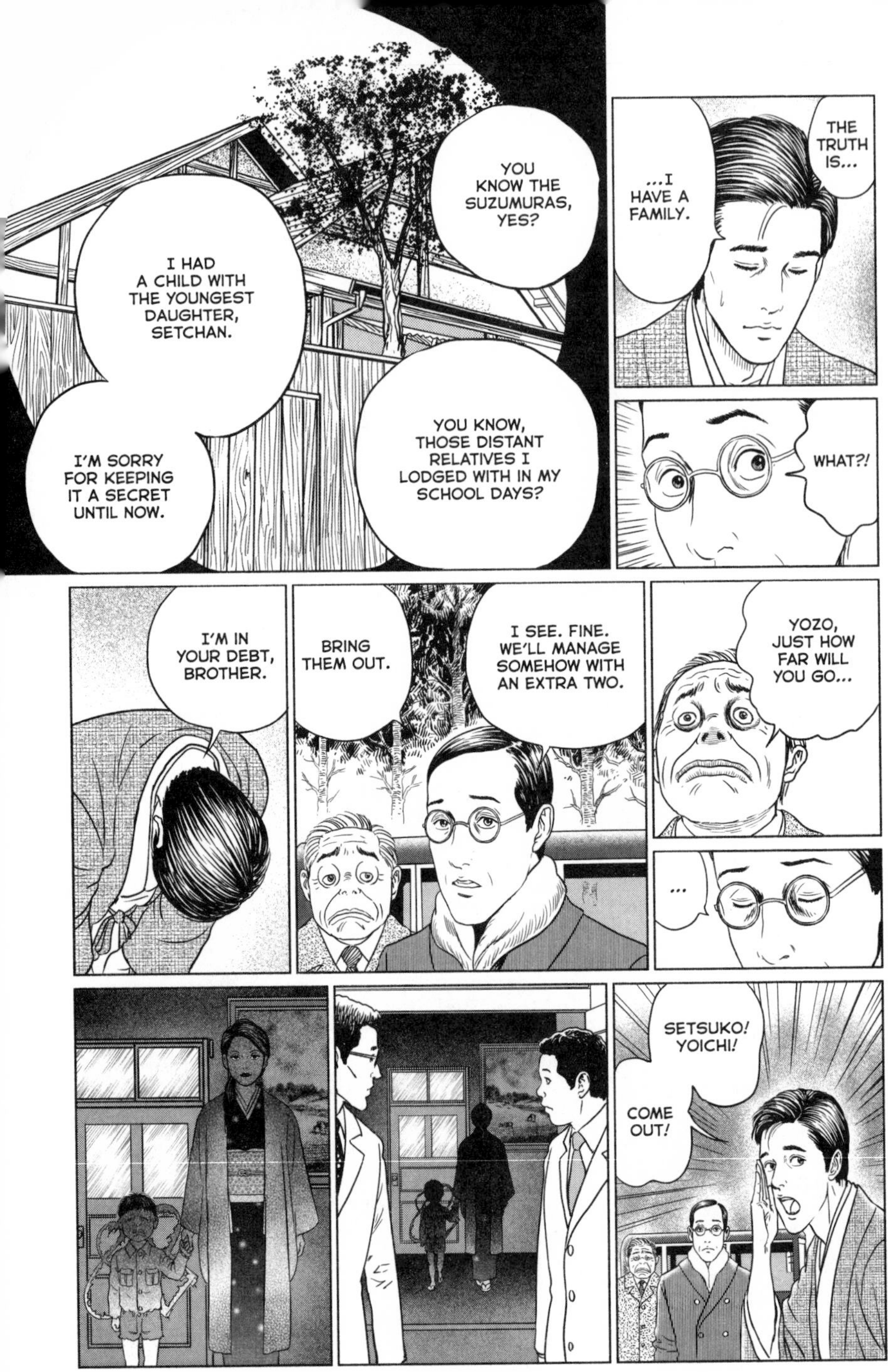
THE TRUTH IS...
...I HAVE A FAMILY.
WHAT?!
YOU KNOW THE SUZUMURAS, YES?
I HAD A CHILD WITH THE YOUNGEST DAUGHTER, SETCHAN.
YOU KNOW, THOSE DISTANT RELATIVES I LODGED WITH IN MY SCHOOL DAYS?
I'M SORRY FOR KEEPING IT A SECRET UNTIL NOW.
YOZO, JUST HOW FAR WILL YOU GO...
...
I SEE. FINE. WE'LL MANAGE SOMEHOW WITH AN EXTRA TWO.
BRING THEM OUT.
I'M IN YOUR DEBT, BROTHER.
SETSUKO! YOICHI!
COME OUT!

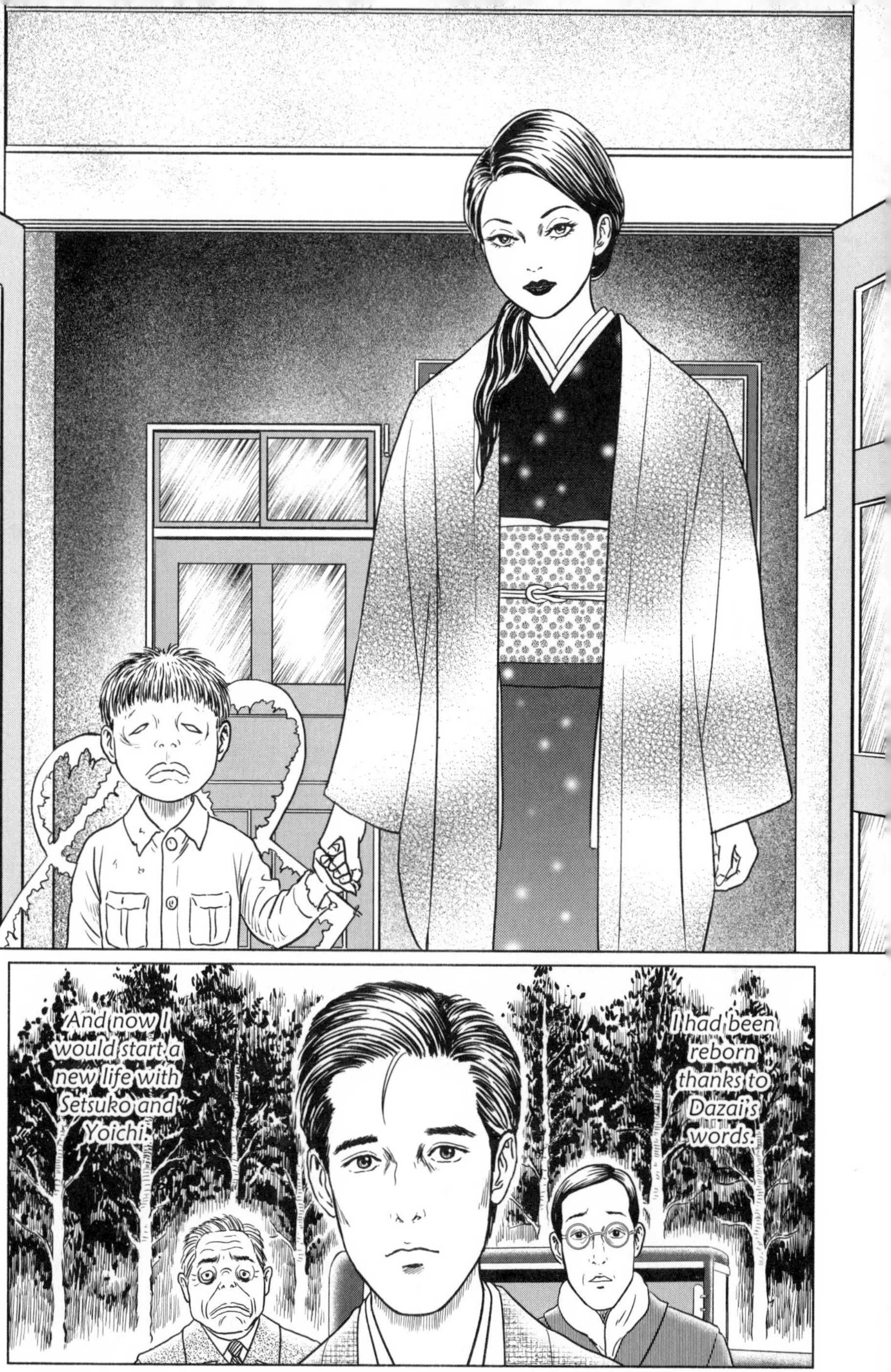
I had been reborn thanks to Dazai's words.
And now I would start a new life with Setsuko and Yoichi.

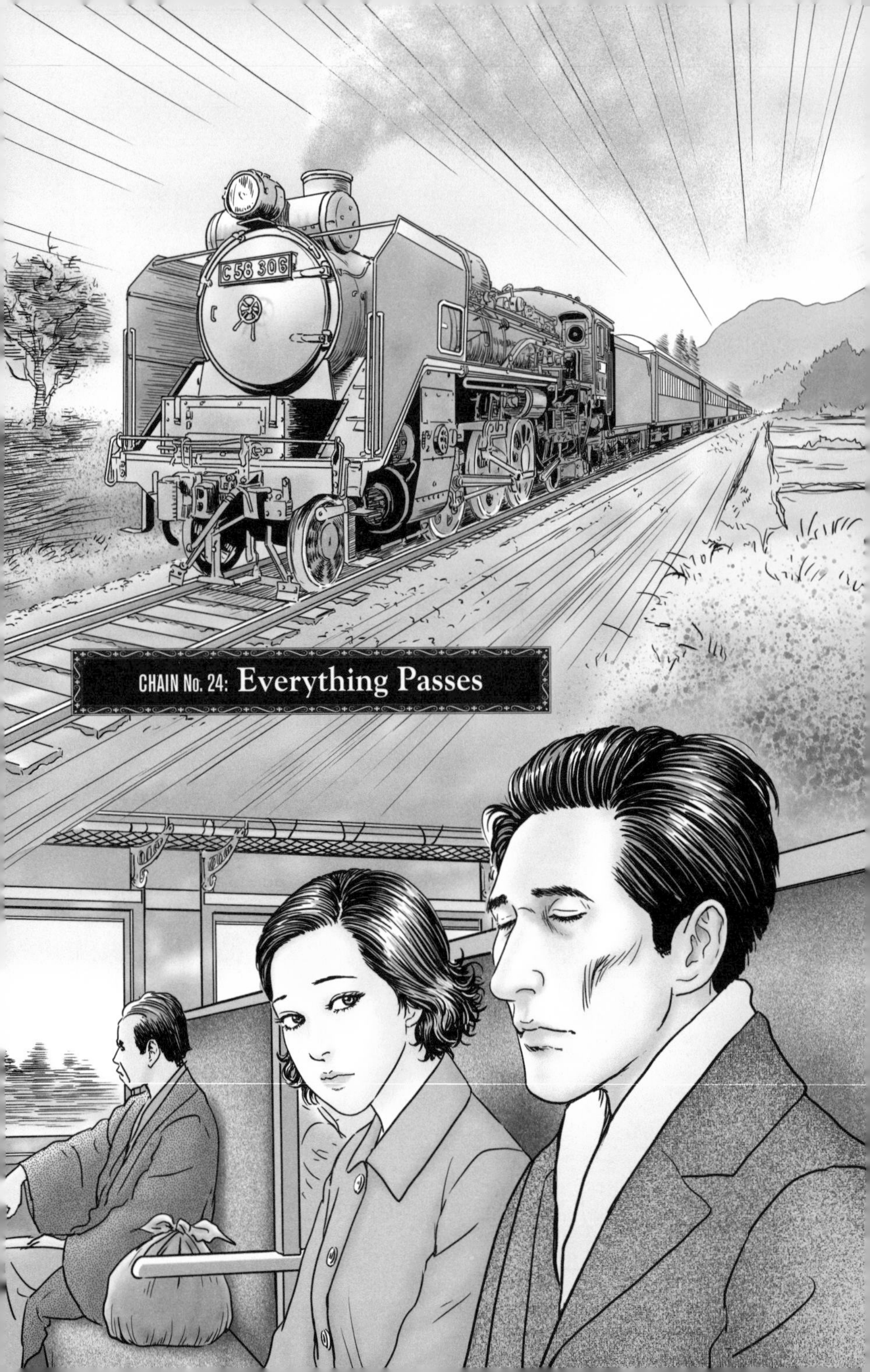
C58 306
CHAIN No. 24: Everything Passes

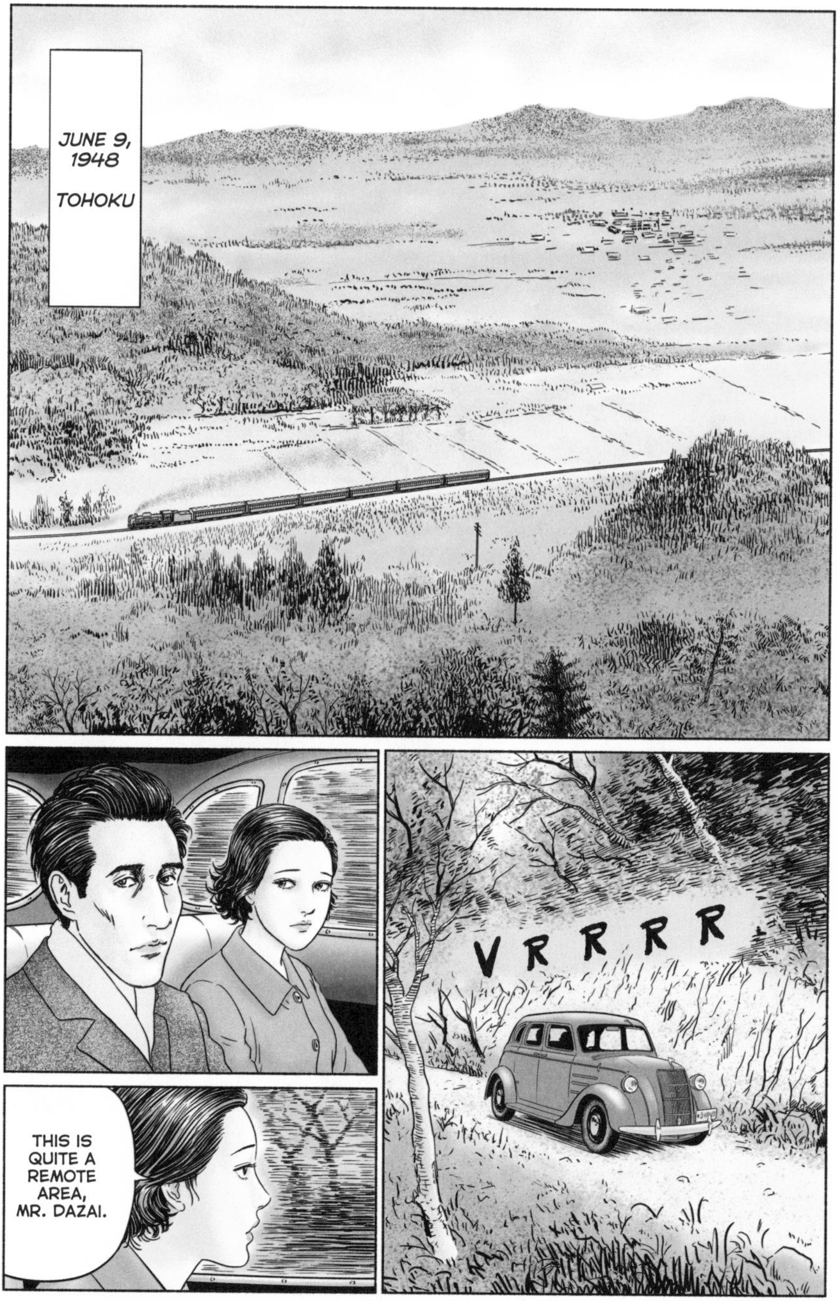
JUNE 9, 1948
TOHOKU
VRRRR
THIS IS QUITE A REMOTE AREA, MR. DAZAI.

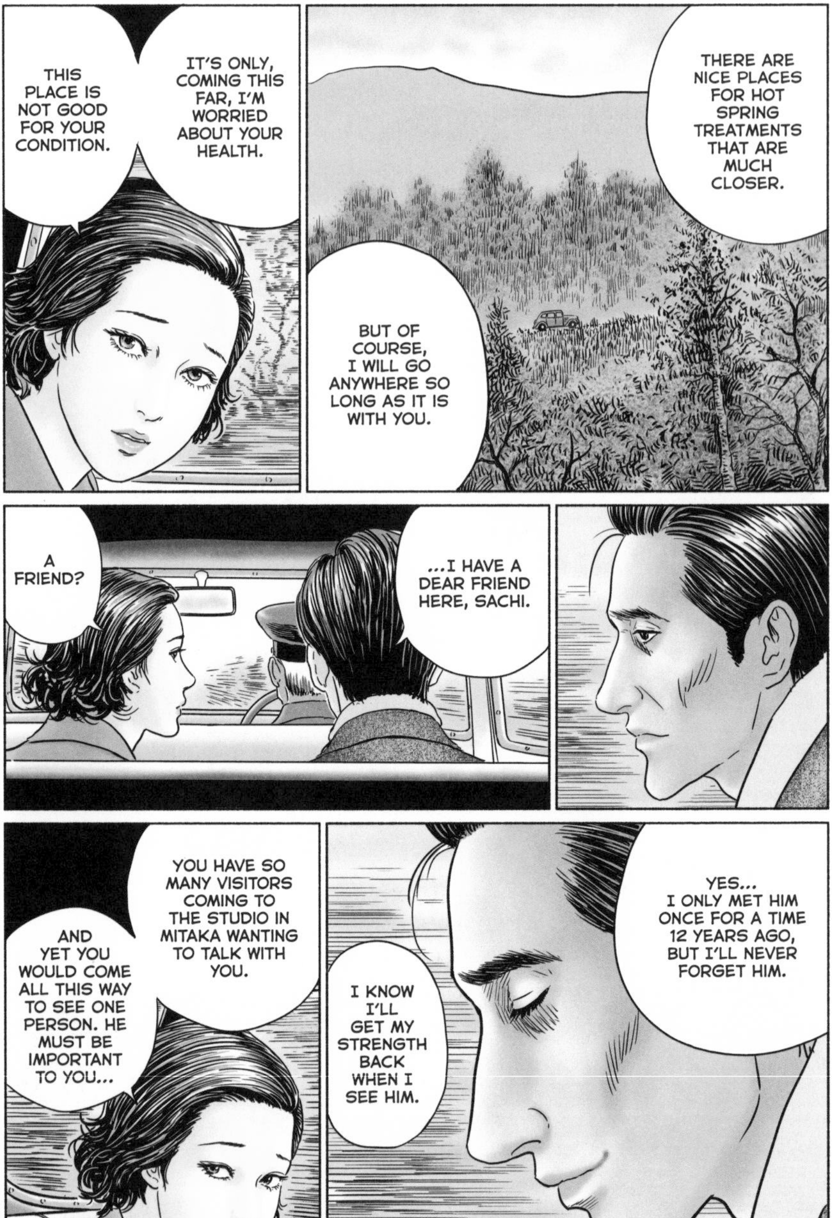
THERE ARE NICE PLACES FOR HOT SPRING TREATMENTS THAT ARE MUCH CLOSER.
BUT OF COURSE, I WILL GO ANYWHERE SO LONG AS IT IS WITH YOU.
IT'S ONLY, COMING THIS FAR, I'M WORRIED ABOUT YOUR HEALTH.
THIS PLACE IS NOT GOOD FOR YOUR CONDITION.
...I HAVE A DEAR FRIEND HERE, SACHI.
A FRIEND?
YES... I ONLY MET HIM ONCE FOR A TIME 12 YEARS AGO, BUT I'LL NEVER FORGET HIM.
I KNOW I'LL GET MY STRENGTH BACK WHEN I SEE HIM.
YOU HAVE SO MANY VISITORS COMING TO THE STUDIO IN MITAKA WANTING TO TALK WITH YOU.
AND YET YOU WOULD COME ALL THIS WAY TO SEE ONE PERSON. HE MUST BE IMPORTANT TO YOU...

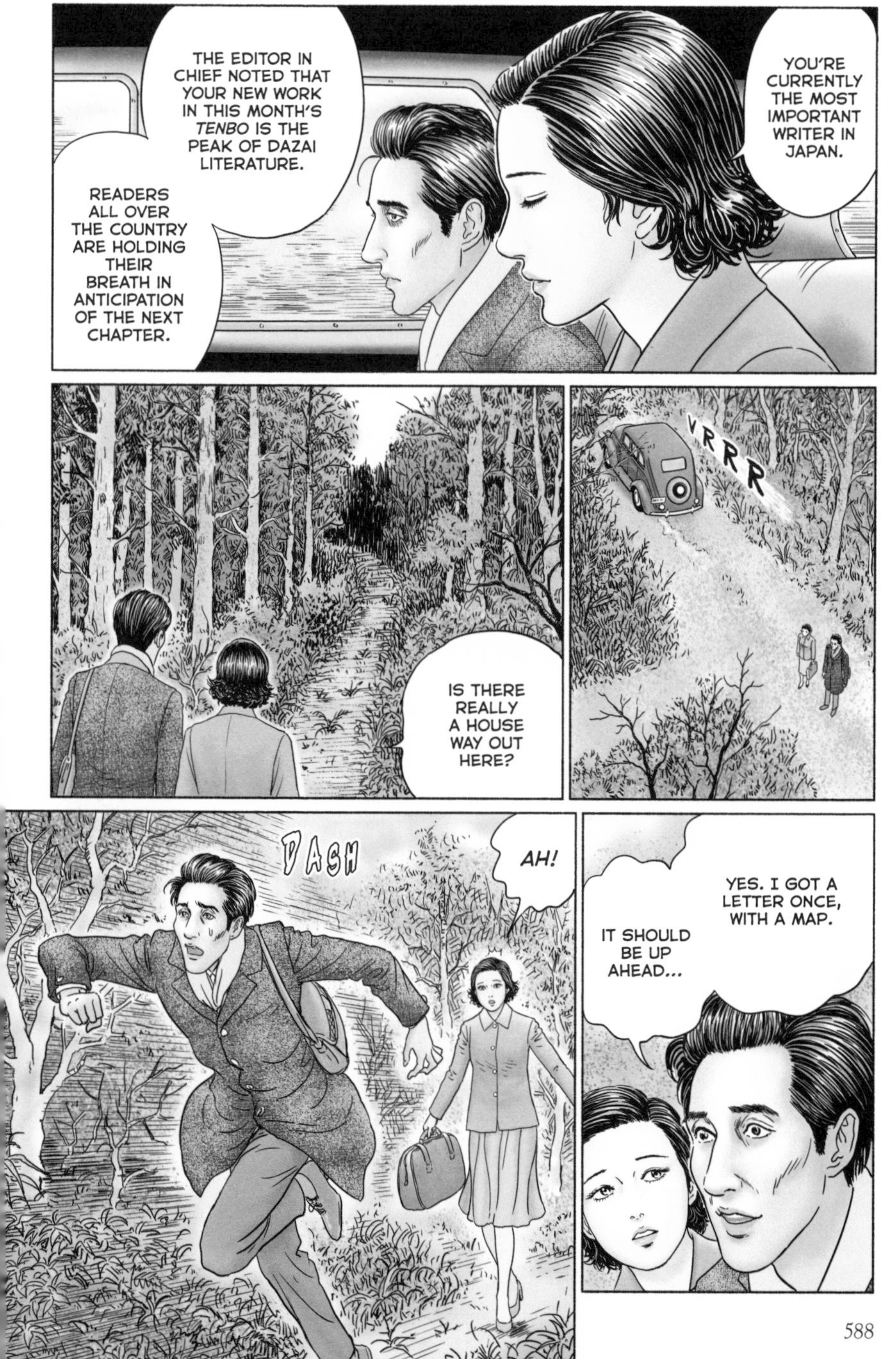
YOU'RE CURRENTLY THE MOST IMPORTANT WRITER IN JAPAN.
THE EDITOR IN CHIEF NOTED THAT YOUR NEW WORK IN THIS MONTH'S *TENBO* IS THE PEAK OF DAZAI LITERATURE.
READERS ALL OVER THE COUNTRY ARE HOLDING THEIR BREATH IN ANTICIPATION OF THE NEXT CHAPTER.
VRRRR
IS THERE REALLY A HOUSE WAY OUT HERE?
YES. I GOT A LETTER ONCE, WITH A MAP.
IT SHOULD BE UP AHEAD...
AH!
DASH

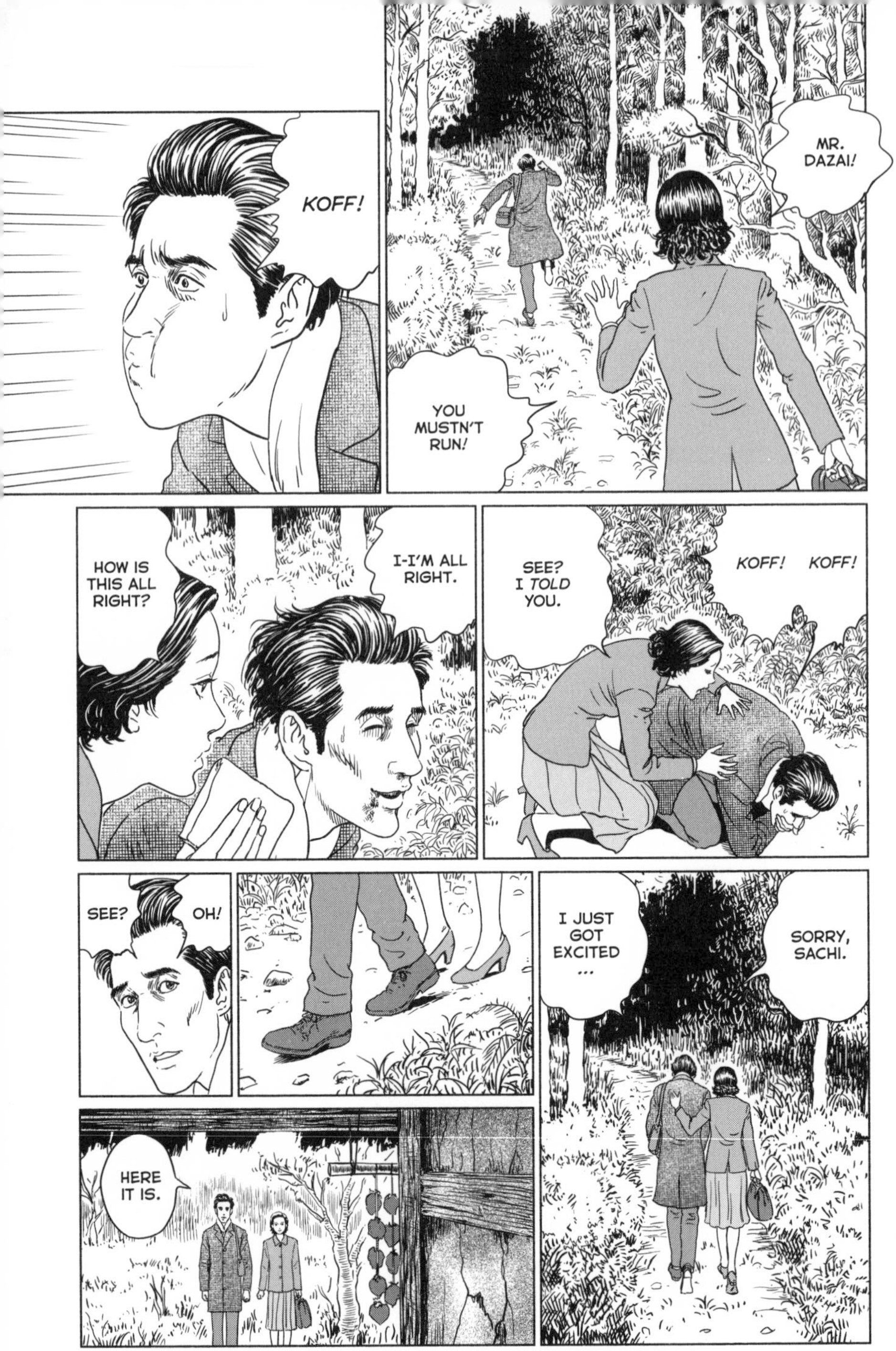
MR. DAZAI!
YOU MUSTN'T RUN!
KOFF!
KOFF! KOFF!
SEE? I TOLD YOU.
I-I'M ALL RIGHT.
HOW IS THIS ALL RIGHT?
SORRY, SACHI.
I JUST GOT EXCITED ...
OH!
SEE?
HERE IT IS.

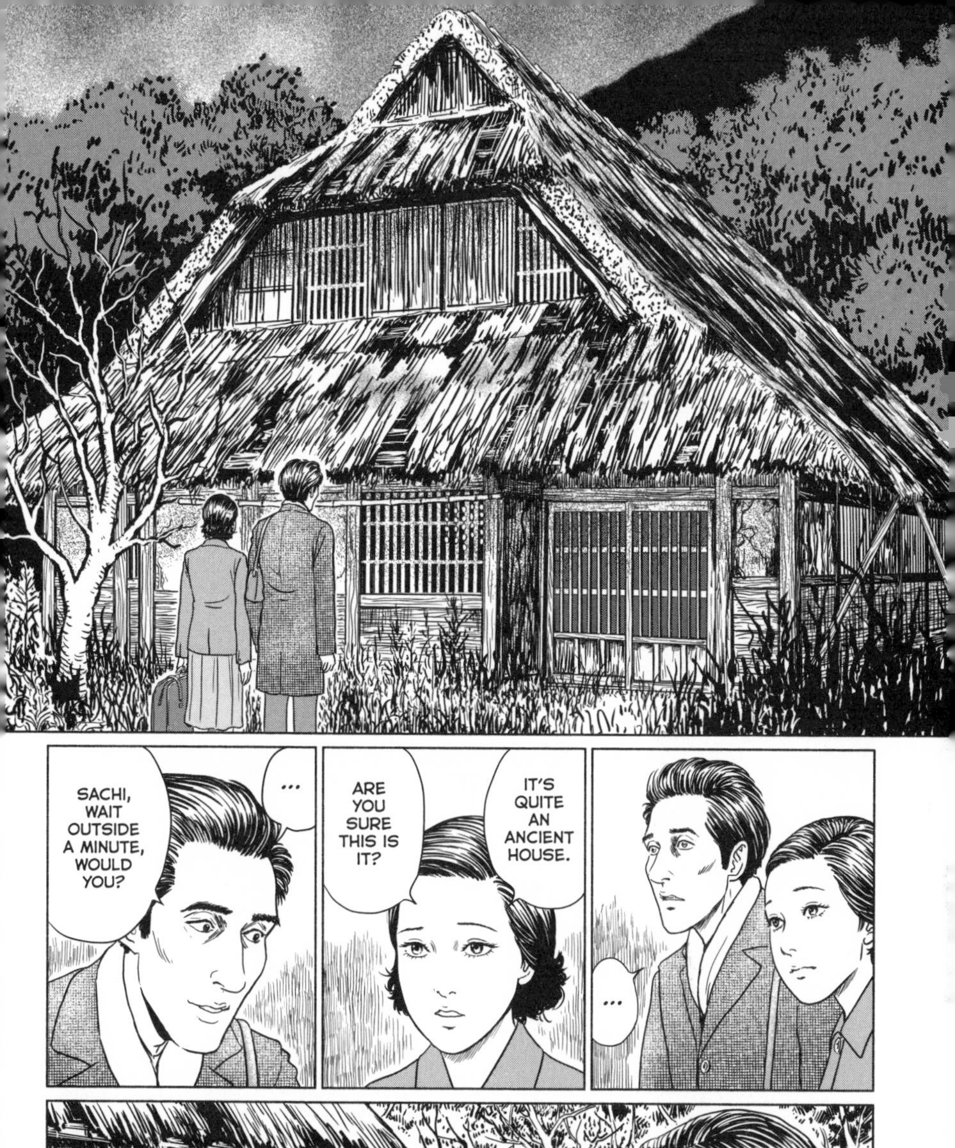
...
IT'S QUITE AN ANCIENT HOUSE.
ARE YOU SURE THIS IS IT?
...
SACHI, WAIT OUTSIDE A MINUTE, WOULD YOU?

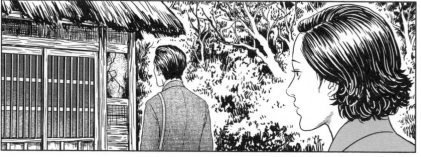

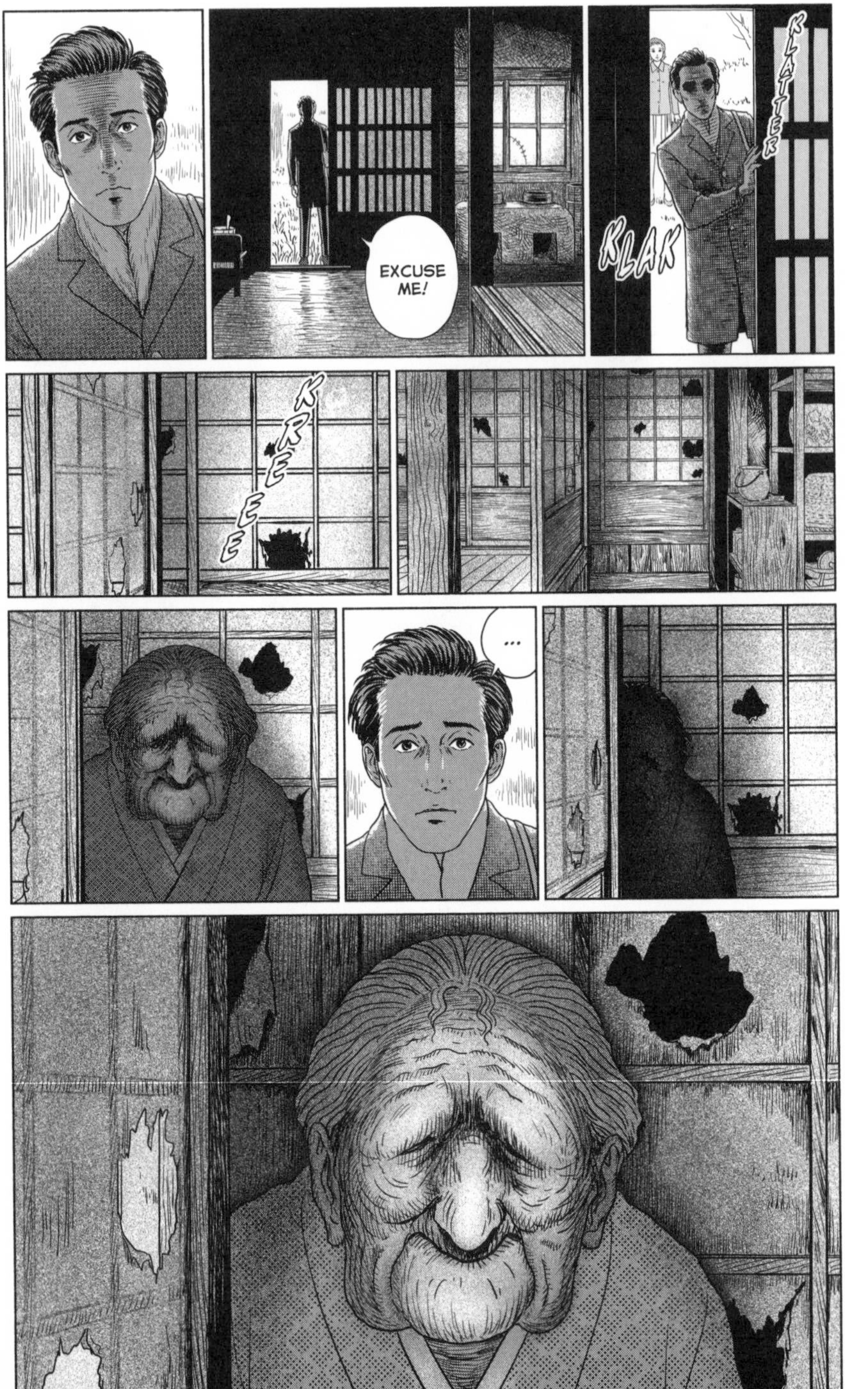
KLATTER
KLAK
EXCUSE ME!
KREEEE
...

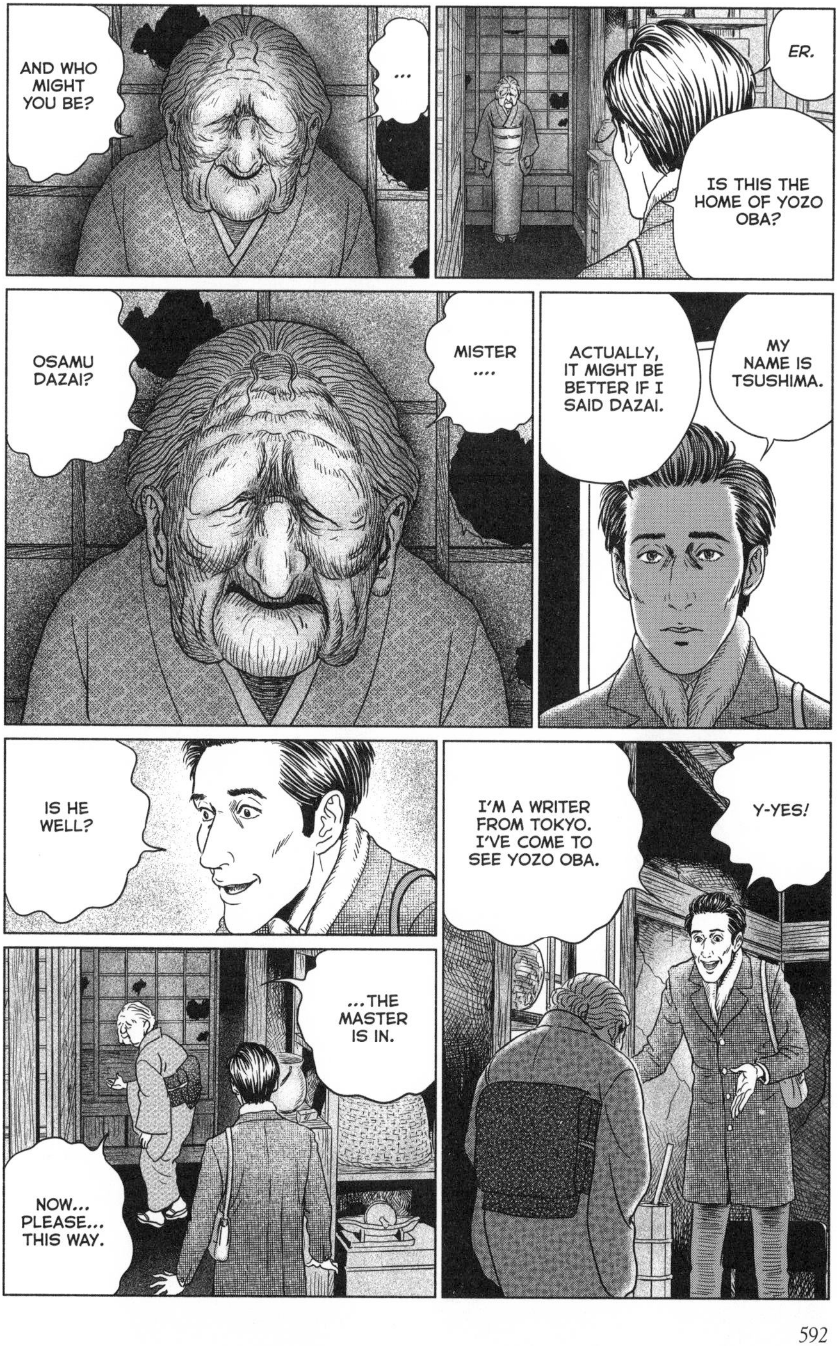
ER.
IS THIS THE HOME OF YOZO OBA?
...
AND WHO MIGHT YOU BE?
MY NAME IS TSUSHIMA.
ACTUALLY, IT MIGHT BE BETTER IF I SAID DAZAI.
MISTER ....
OSAMU DAZAI?
Y-YES!
I'M A WRITER FROM TOKYO. I'VE COME TO SEE YOZO OBA.
IS HE WELL?
...THE MASTER IS IN.
NOW... PLEASE... THIS WAY.

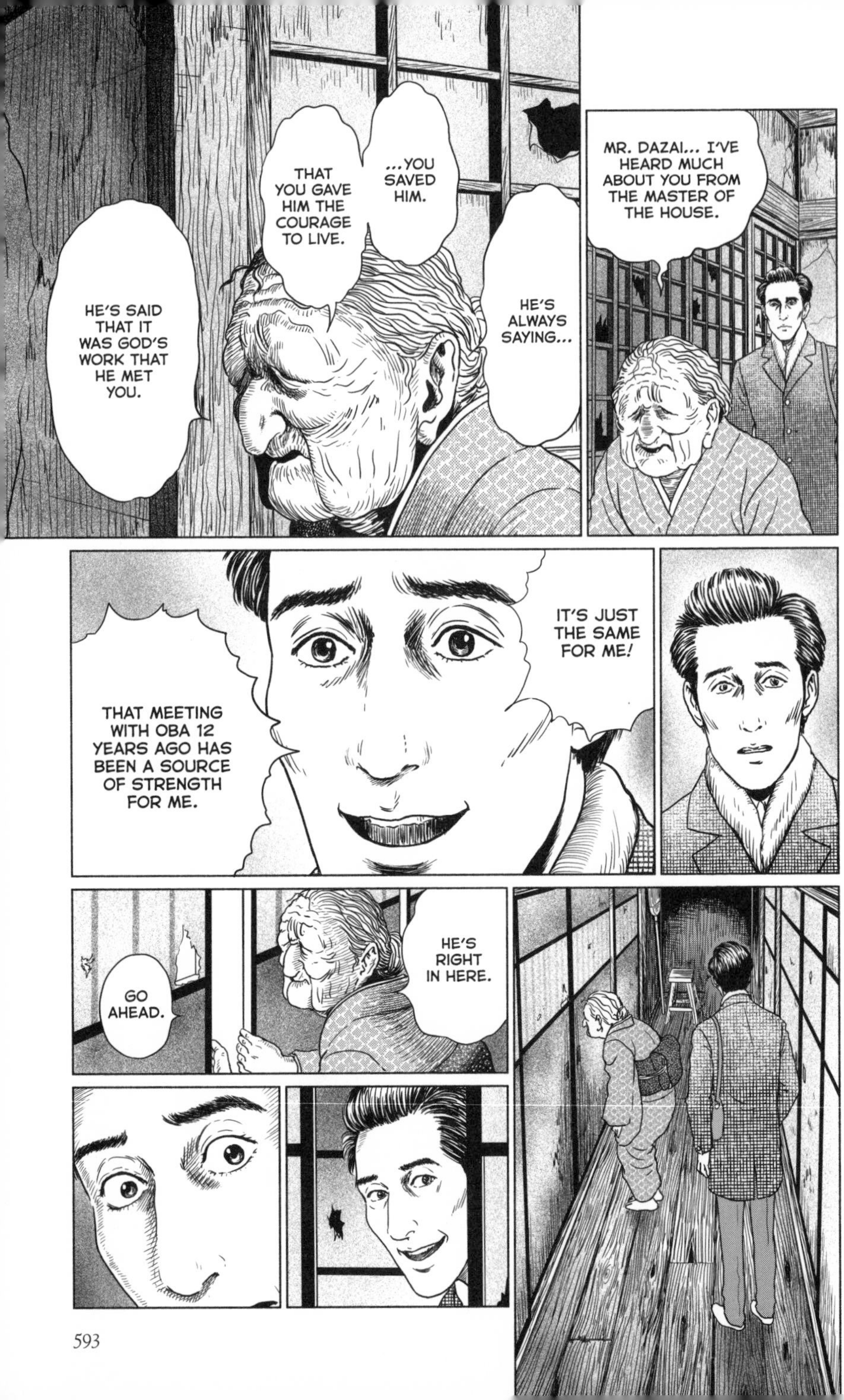
MR. DAZAI... I'VE HEARD MUCH ABOUT YOU FROM THE MASTER OF THE HOUSE.
HE'S ALWAYS SAYING...
...YOU SAVED HIM.
THAT YOU GAVE HIM THE COURAGE TO LIVE.
HE'S SAID THAT IT WAS GOD'S WORK THAT HE MET YOU.
IT'S JUST THE SAME FOR ME!
THAT MEETING WITH OBA 12 YEARS AGO HAS BEEN A SOURCE OF STRENGTH FOR ME.
HE'S RIGHT IN HERE.
GO AHEAD.

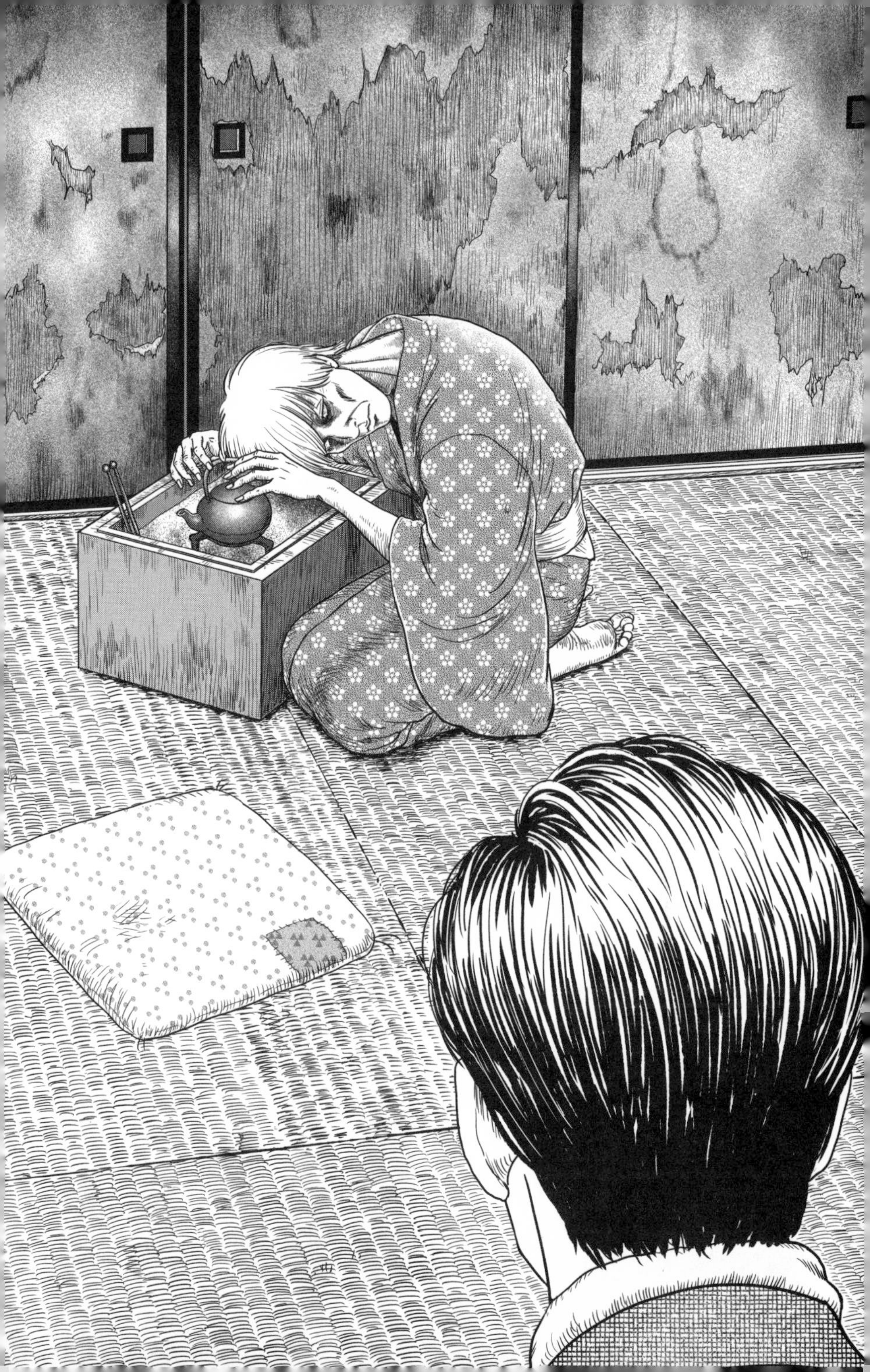

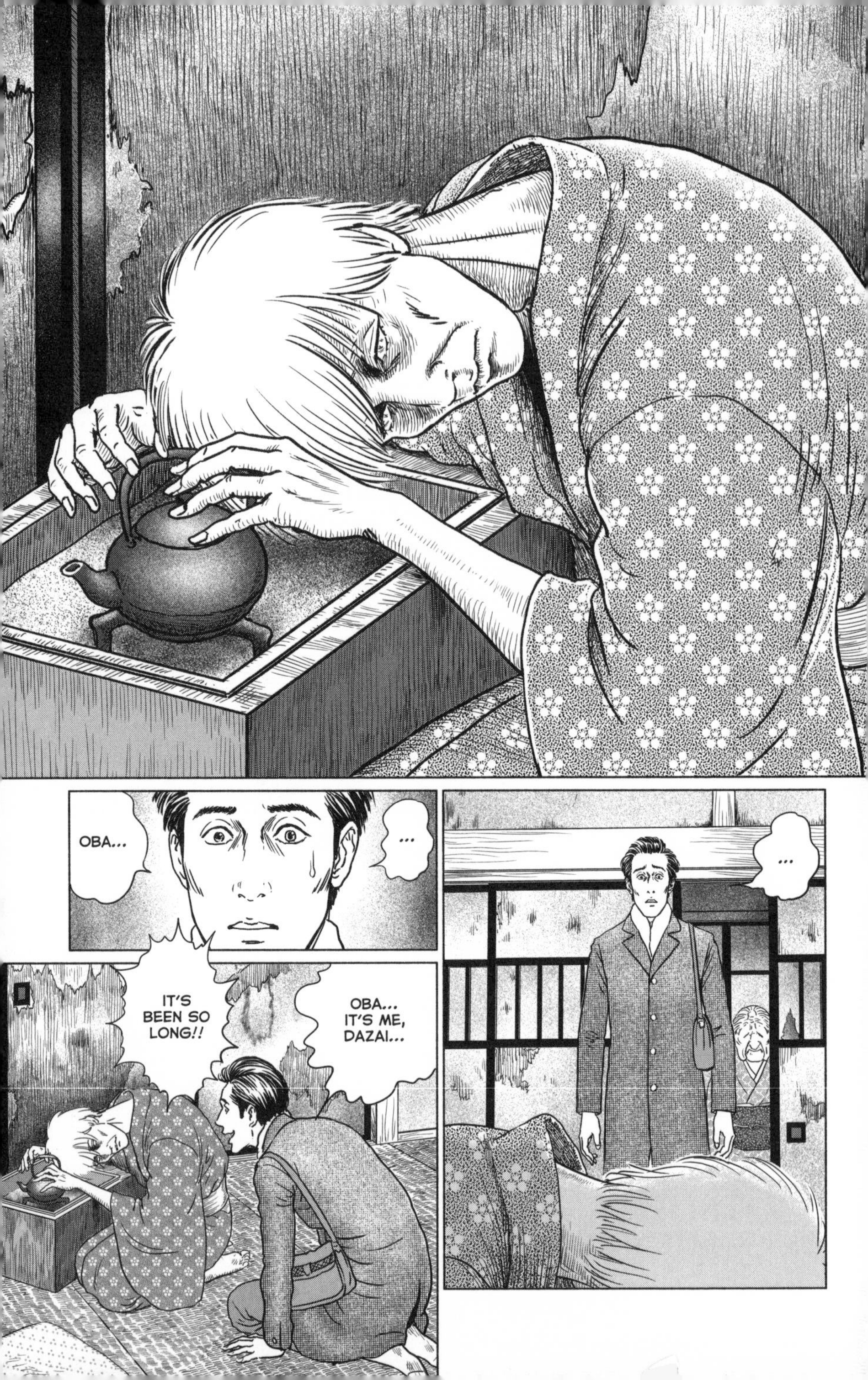
...
...
OBA...
OBA... IT'S ME, DAZAI...
IT'S BEEN SO LONG!!

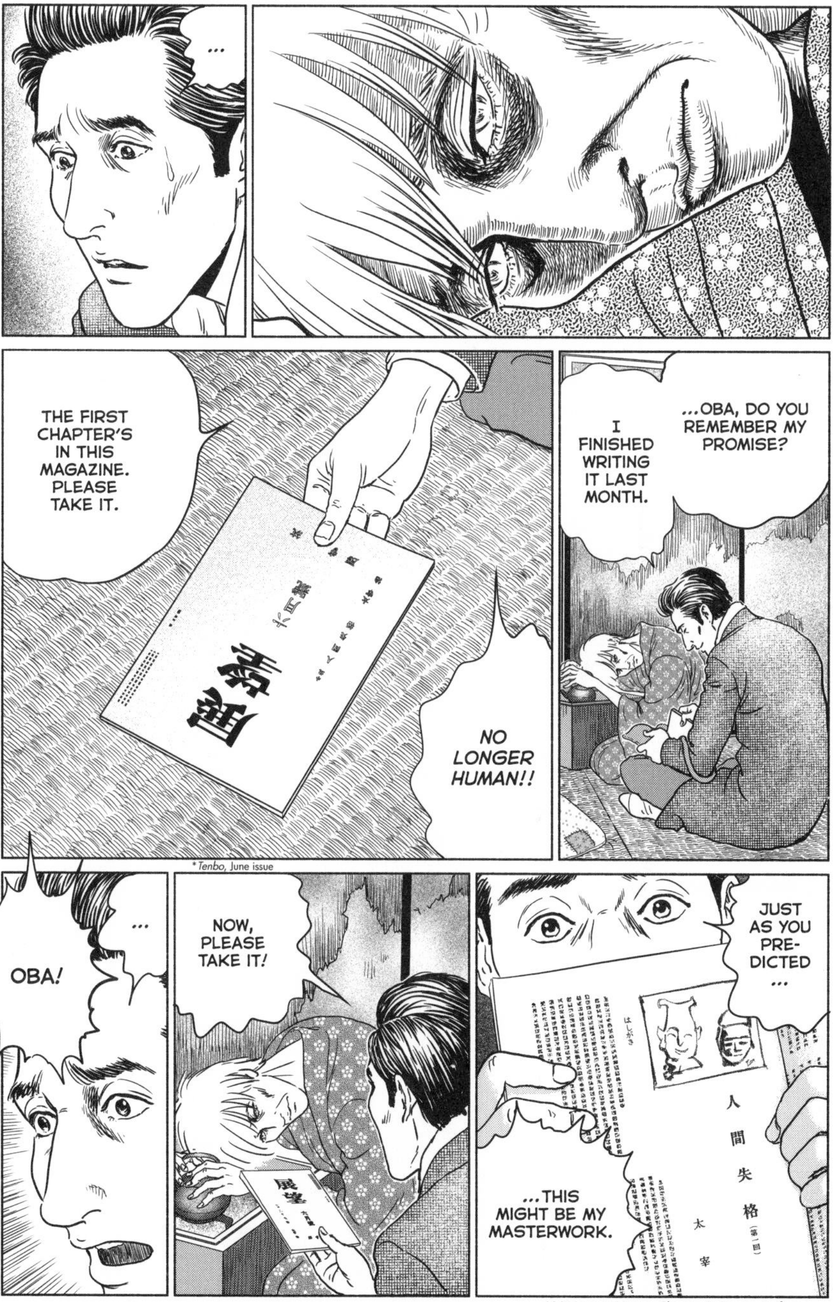
...
...OBA, DO YOU REMEMBER MY PROMISE?
I FINISHED WRITING IT LAST MONTH.
THE FIRST CHAPTER'S IN THIS MAGAZINE. PLEASE TAKE IT.
NO LONGER HUMAN!!
JUST AS YOU PRE-DICTED...
人間失格
(第一回)
太宰
...THIS MIGHT BE MY MASTERWORK.
NOW, PLEASE TAKE IT!
展望
...
OBA!

*Tenbo, June issue

*No Longer Human Chapter 1, Dazai, Preface

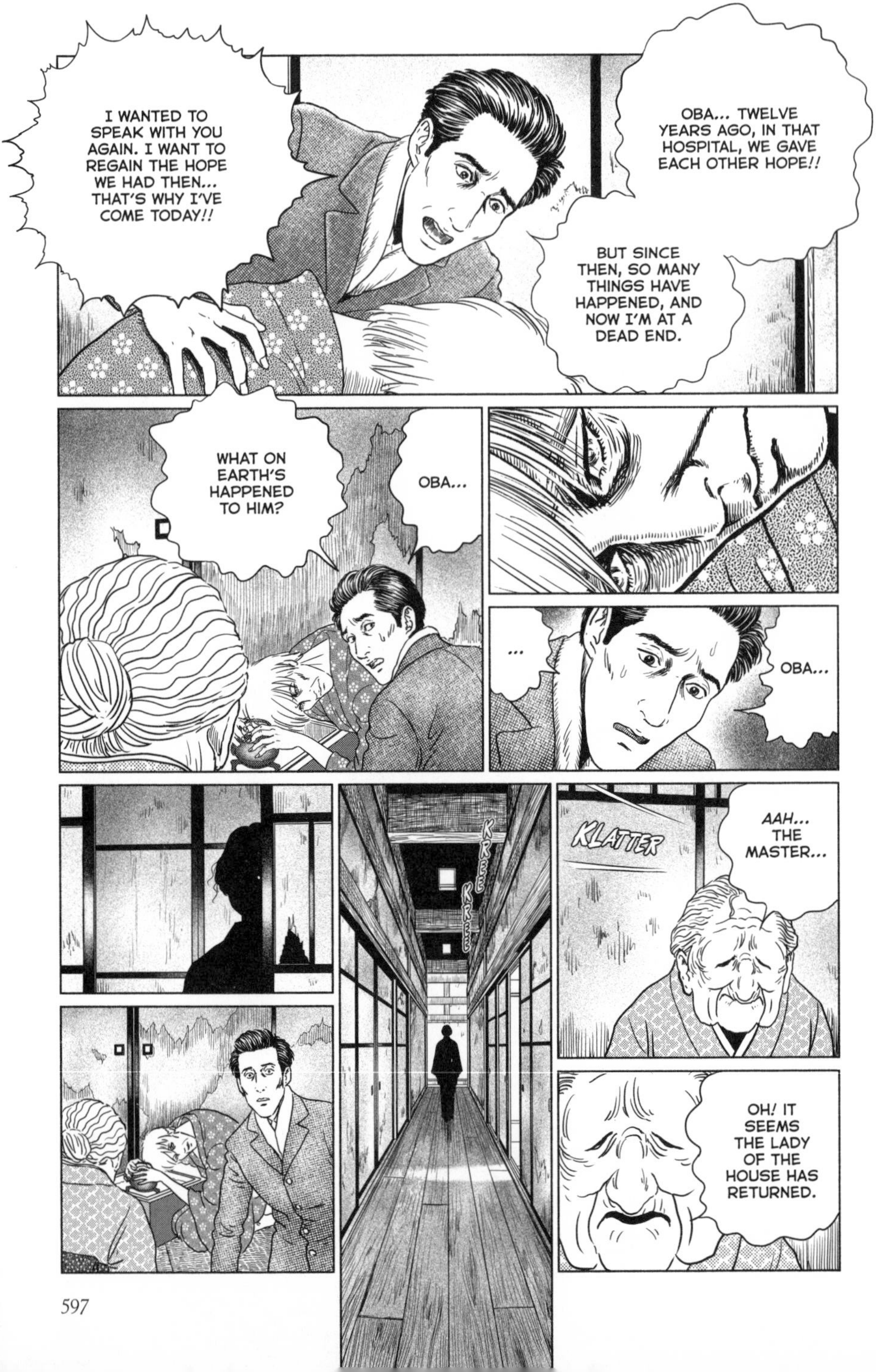
OBA... TWELVE YEARS AGO, IN THAT HOSPITAL, WE GAVE EACH OTHER HOPE!!
BUT SINCE THEN, SO MANY THINGS HAVE HAPPENED, AND NOW I'M AT A DEAD END.
I WANTED TO SPEAK WITH YOU AGAIN. I WANT TO REGAIN THE HOPE WE HAD THEN... THAT'S WHY I'VE COME TODAY!!
OBA...
...
OBA...
WHAT ON EARTH'S HAPPENED TO HIM?
AAH... THE MASTER...
KLATTER
OH! IT SEEMS THE LADY OF THE HOUSE HAS RETURNED.
KREE
KREE

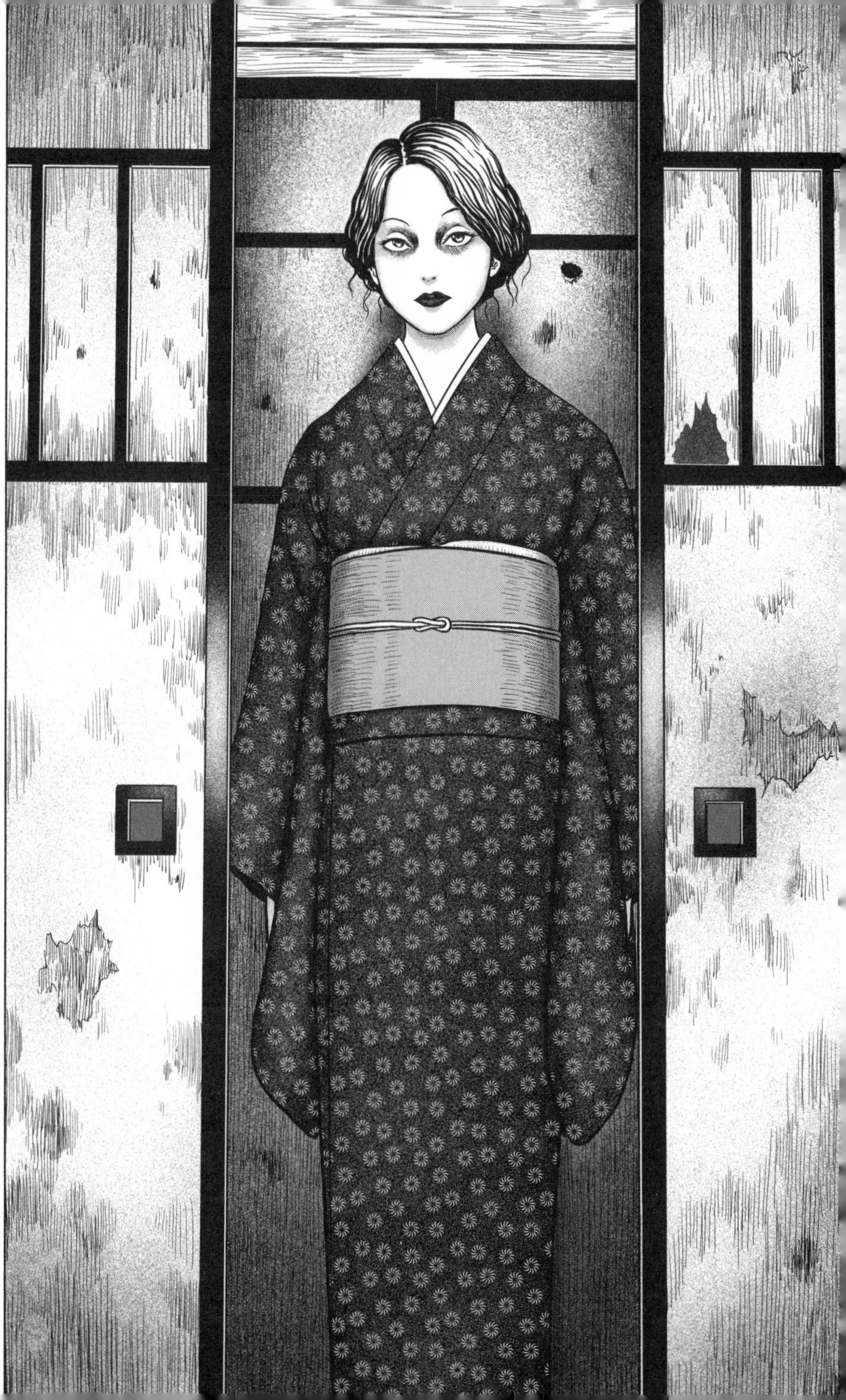

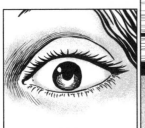

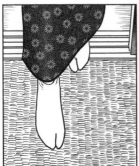

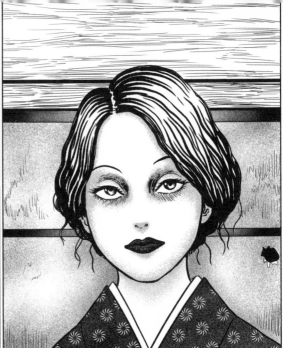

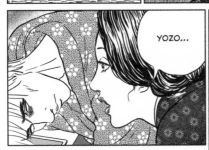

YOZO...

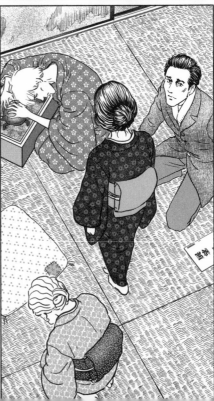

...THERE'S A BEAUTIFUL WOMAN STANDING OUTSIDE.

RIGHT NOW...

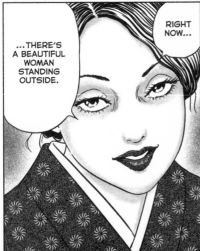

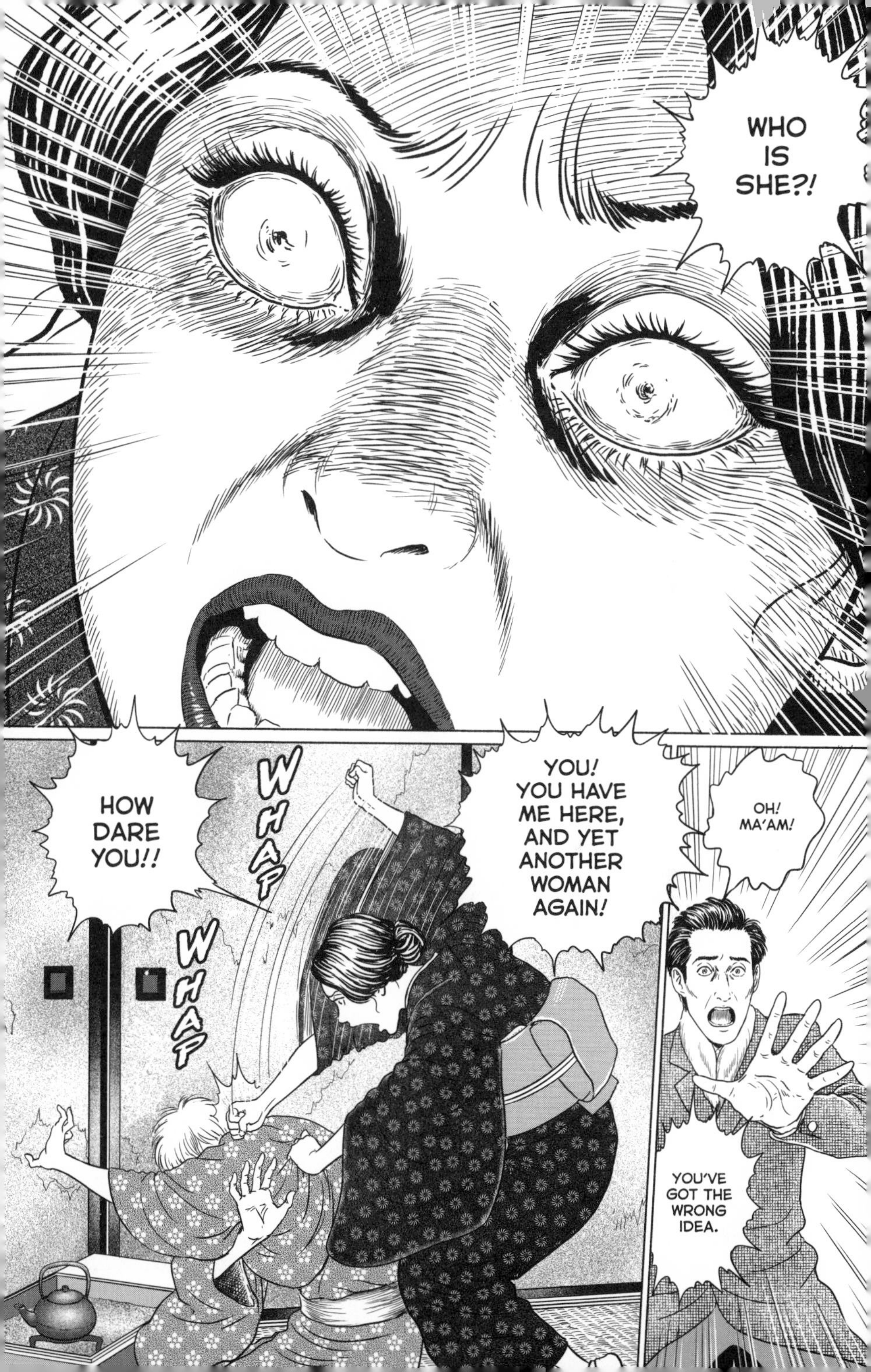
WHO IS SHE?!
OH! MA'AM!
YOU'VE GOT THE WRONG IDEA.
YOU! YOU HAVE ME HERE, AND YET ANOTHER WOMAN AGAIN!
HOW DARE YOU!!
WHAP
WHAP

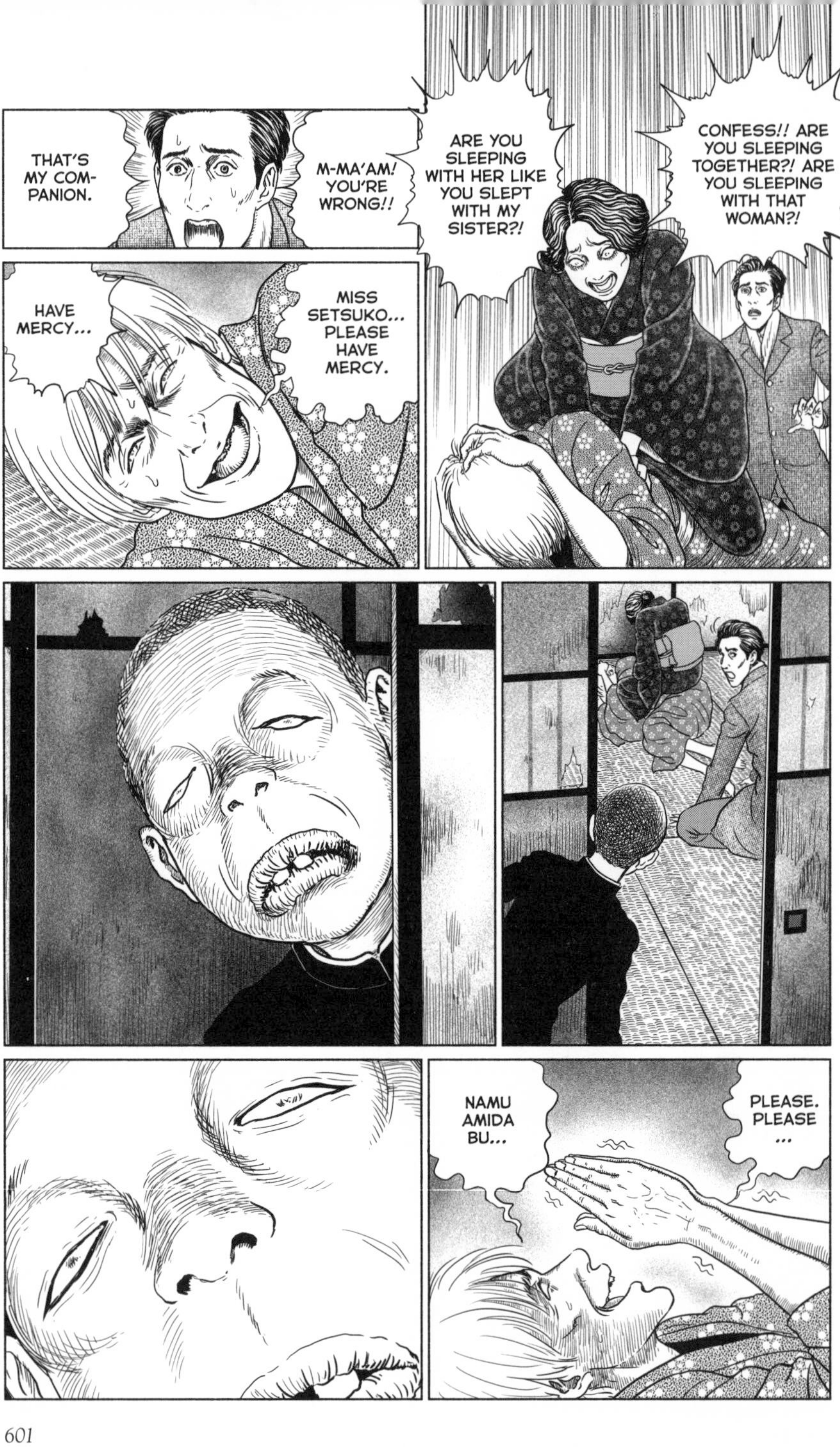
CONFESS!! ARE YOU SLEEPING TOGETHER?! ARE YOU SLEEPING WITH THAT WOMAN?!
ARE YOU SLEEPING WITH HER LIKE YOU SLEPT WITH MY SISTER?!
M-MA'AM! YOU'RE WRONG!!
THAT'S MY COMPANION.
MISS SETSUKO... PLEASE HAVE MERCY.
HAVE MERCY...
PLEASE. PLEASE ...
NAMU AMIDA BU...

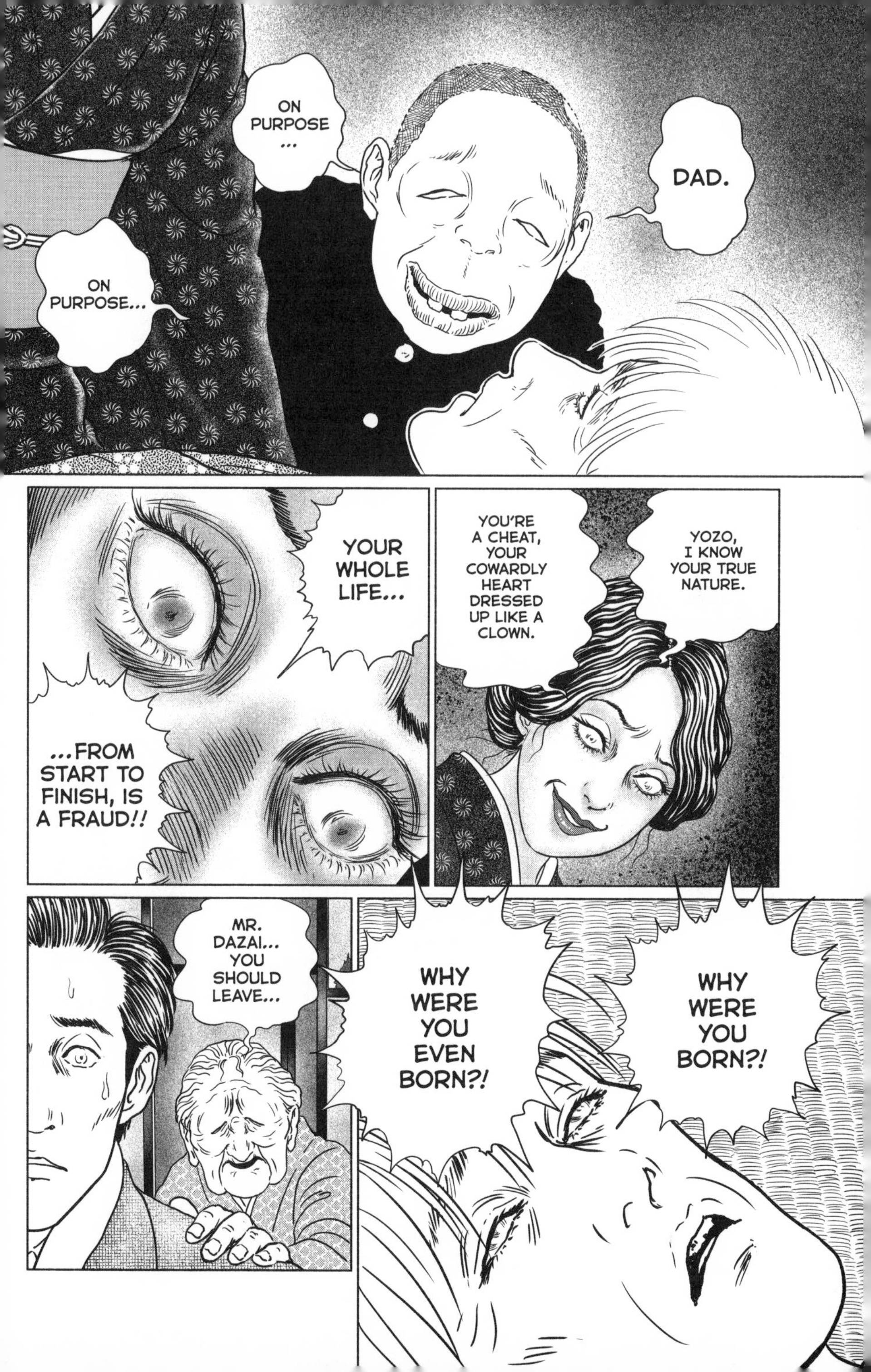
DAD.
ON PURPOSE ...
ON PURPOSE...
YOZO, I KNOW YOUR TRUE NATURE.
YOU'RE A CHEAT, YOUR COWARDLY HEART DRESSED UP LIKE A CLOWN.
YOUR WHOLE LIFE...
...FROM START TO FINISH, IS A FRAUD!!
WHY WERE YOU BORN?!
WHY WERE YOU EVEN BORN?!
MR. DAZAI... YOU SHOULD LEAVE...

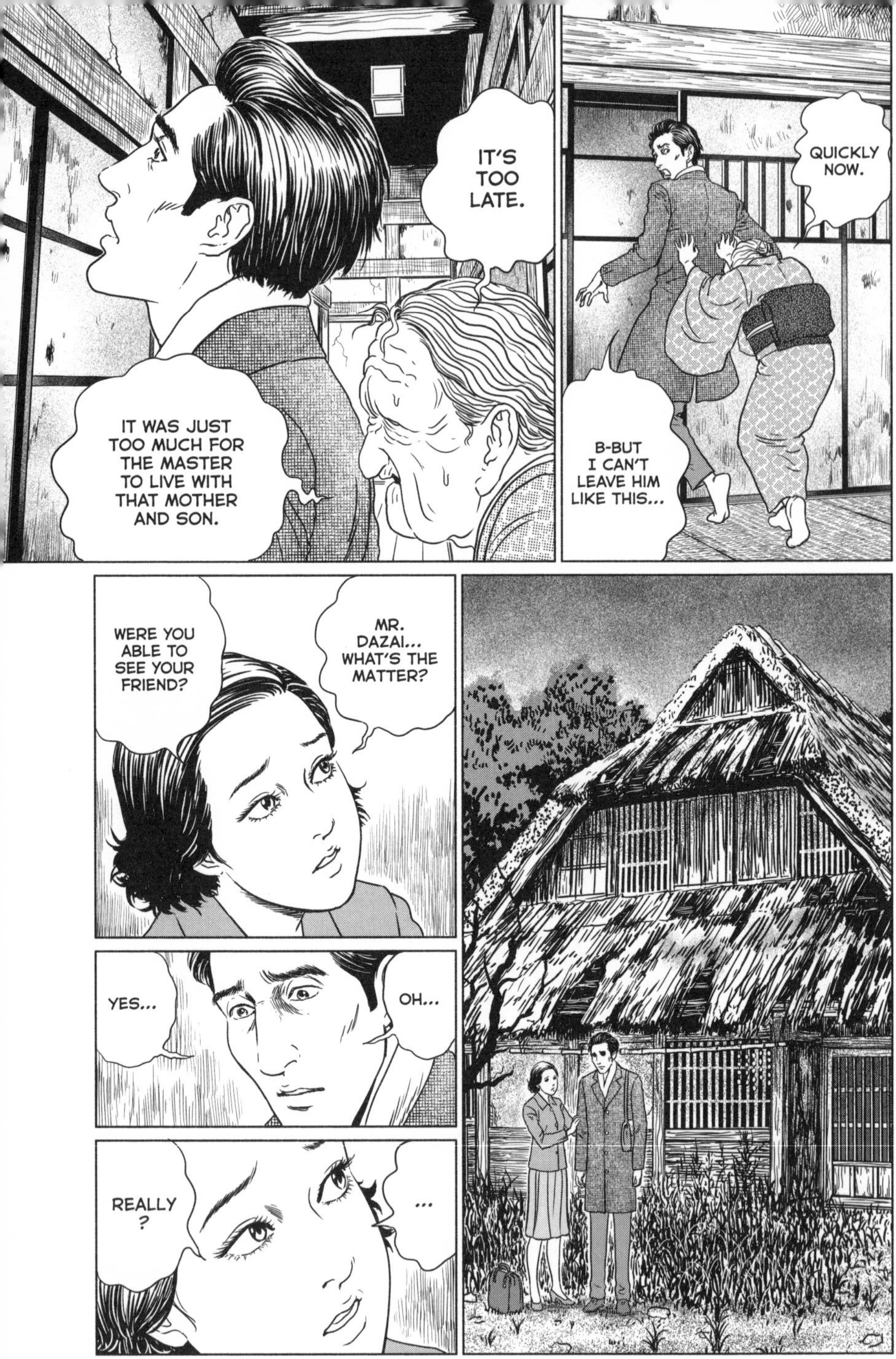
QUICKLY NOW.
B-BUT I CAN'T LEAVE HIM LIKE THIS...
IT'S TOO LATE.
IT WAS JUST TOO MUCH FOR THE MASTER TO LIVE WITH THAT MOTHER AND SON.
MR. DAZAI... WHAT'S THE MATTER?
WERE YOU ABLE TO SEE YOUR FRIEND?
OH...
YES...
...
REALLY?

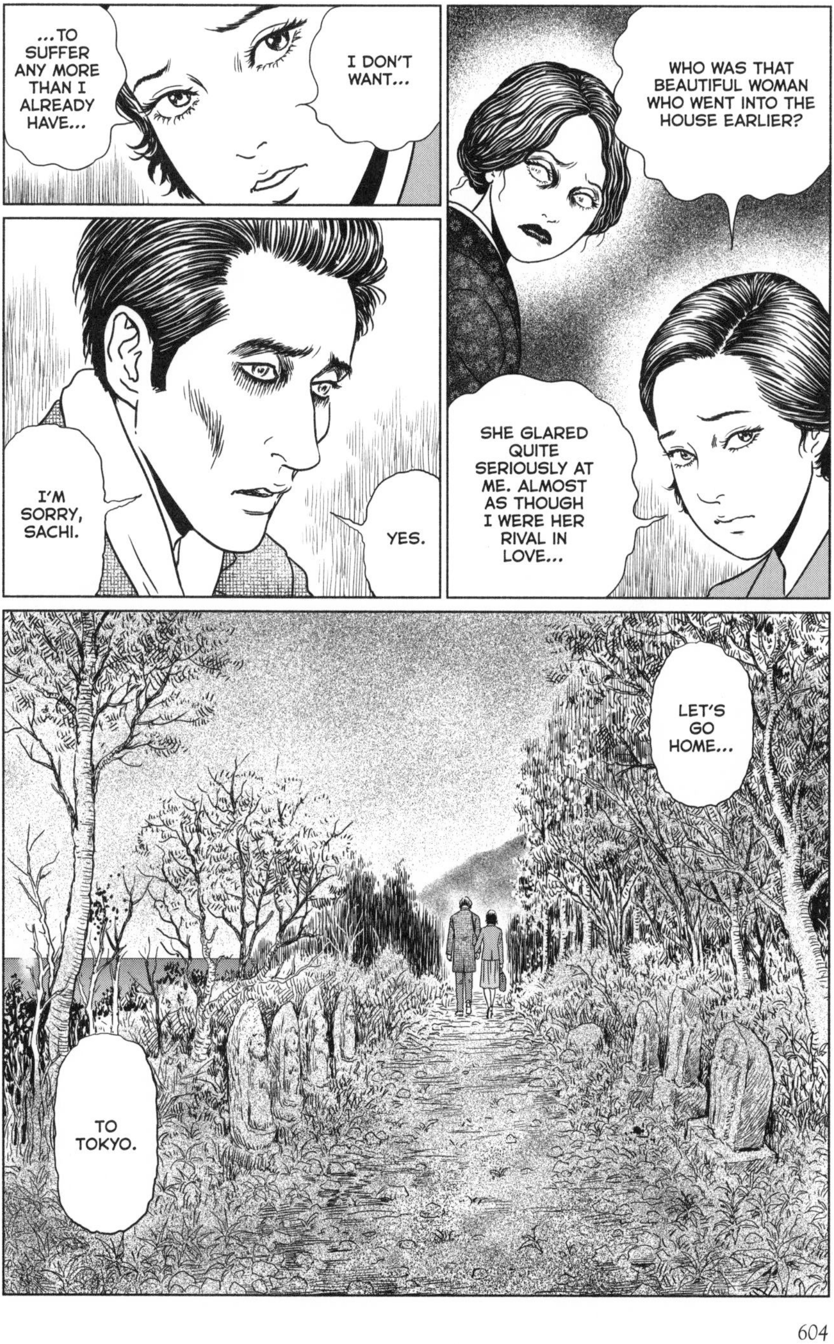
WHO WAS THAT BEAUTIFUL WOMAN WHO WENT INTO THE HOUSE EARLIER?
SHE GLARED QUITE SERIOUSLY AT ME. ALMOST AS THOUGH I WERE HER RIVAL IN LOVE...
I DON'T WANT...
...TO SUFFER ANY MORE THAN I ALREADY HAVE...
I'M SORRY, SACHI.
YES.
LET'S GO HOME...
TO TOKYO.

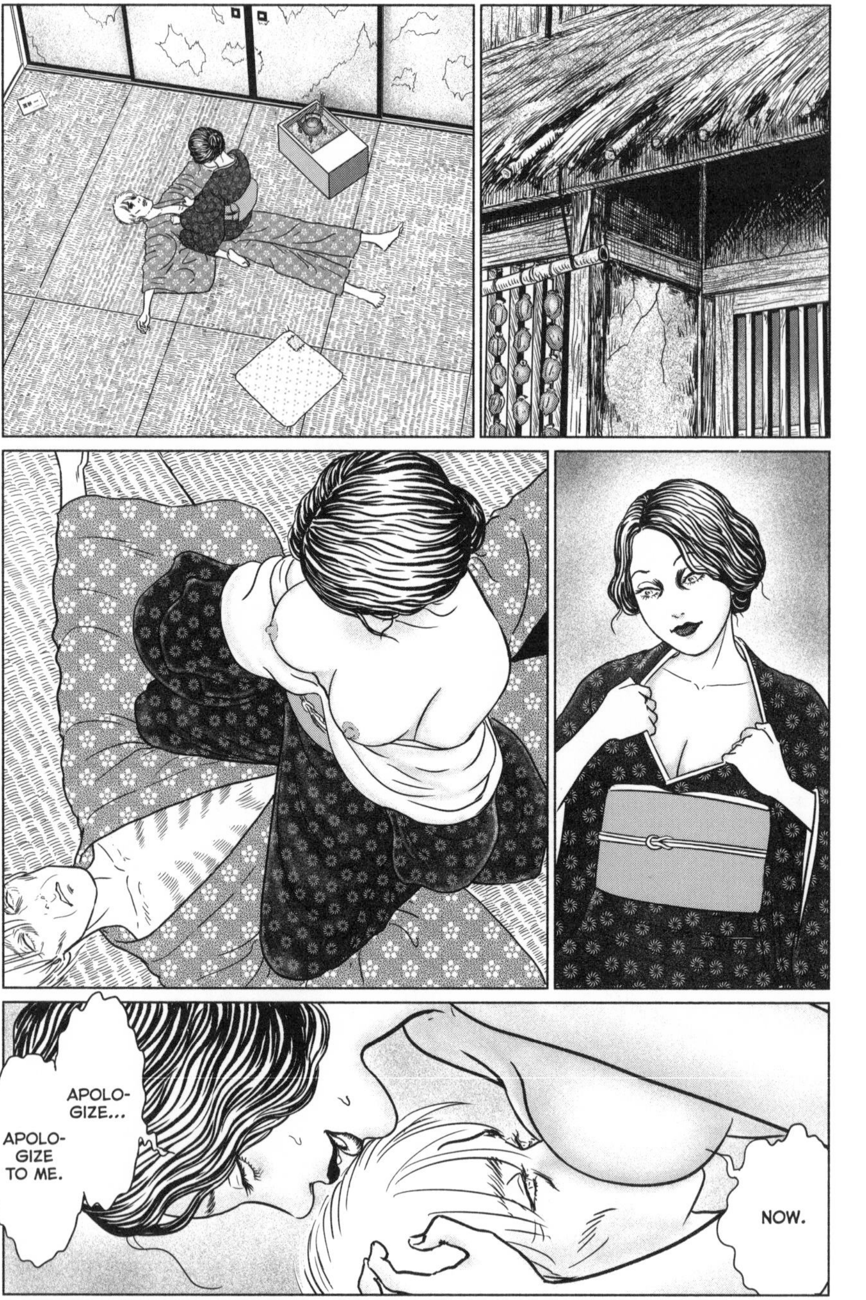
APOLOGIZE... APOLOGIZE TO ME.
NOW.

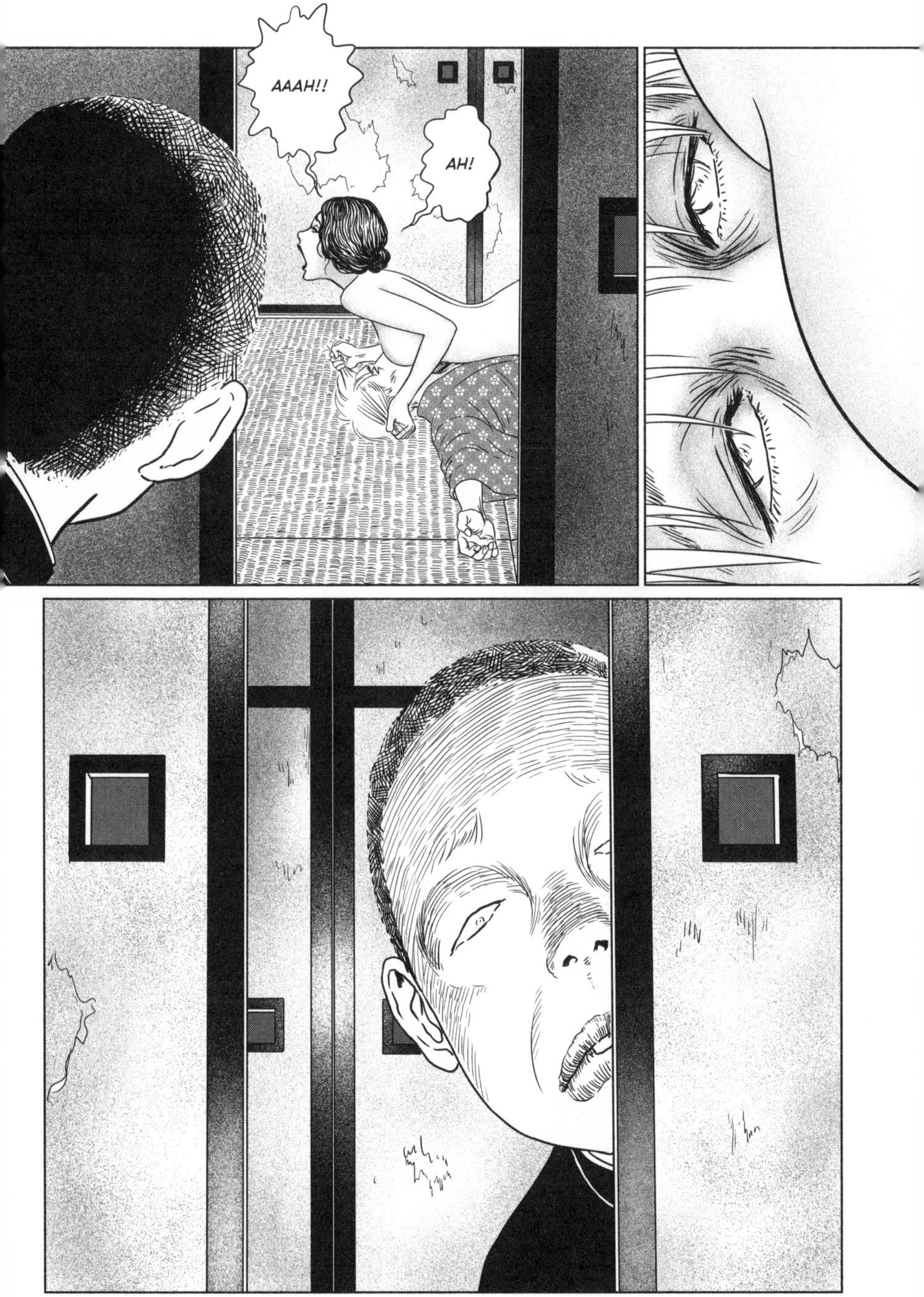
AAAH!!
AH!

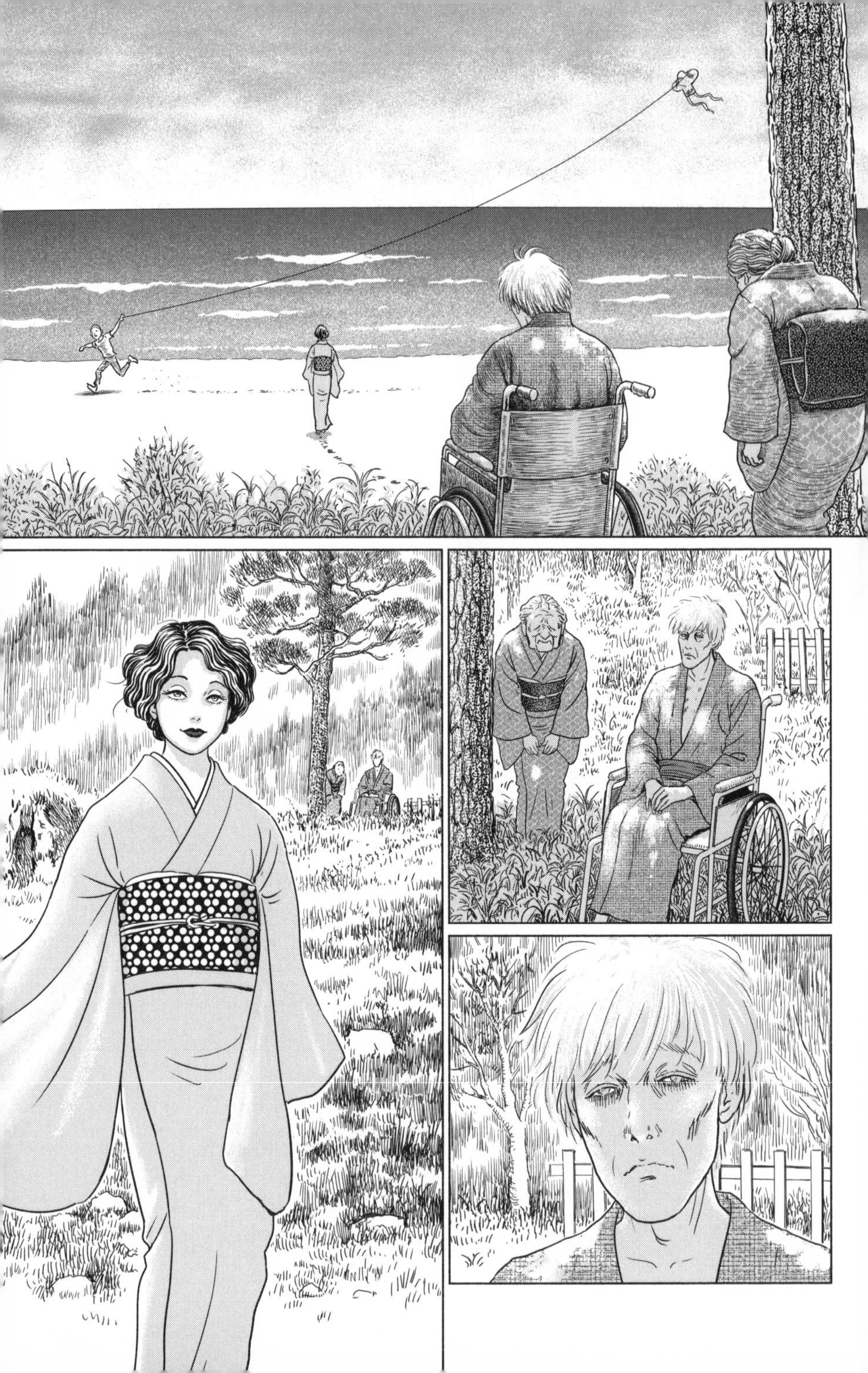

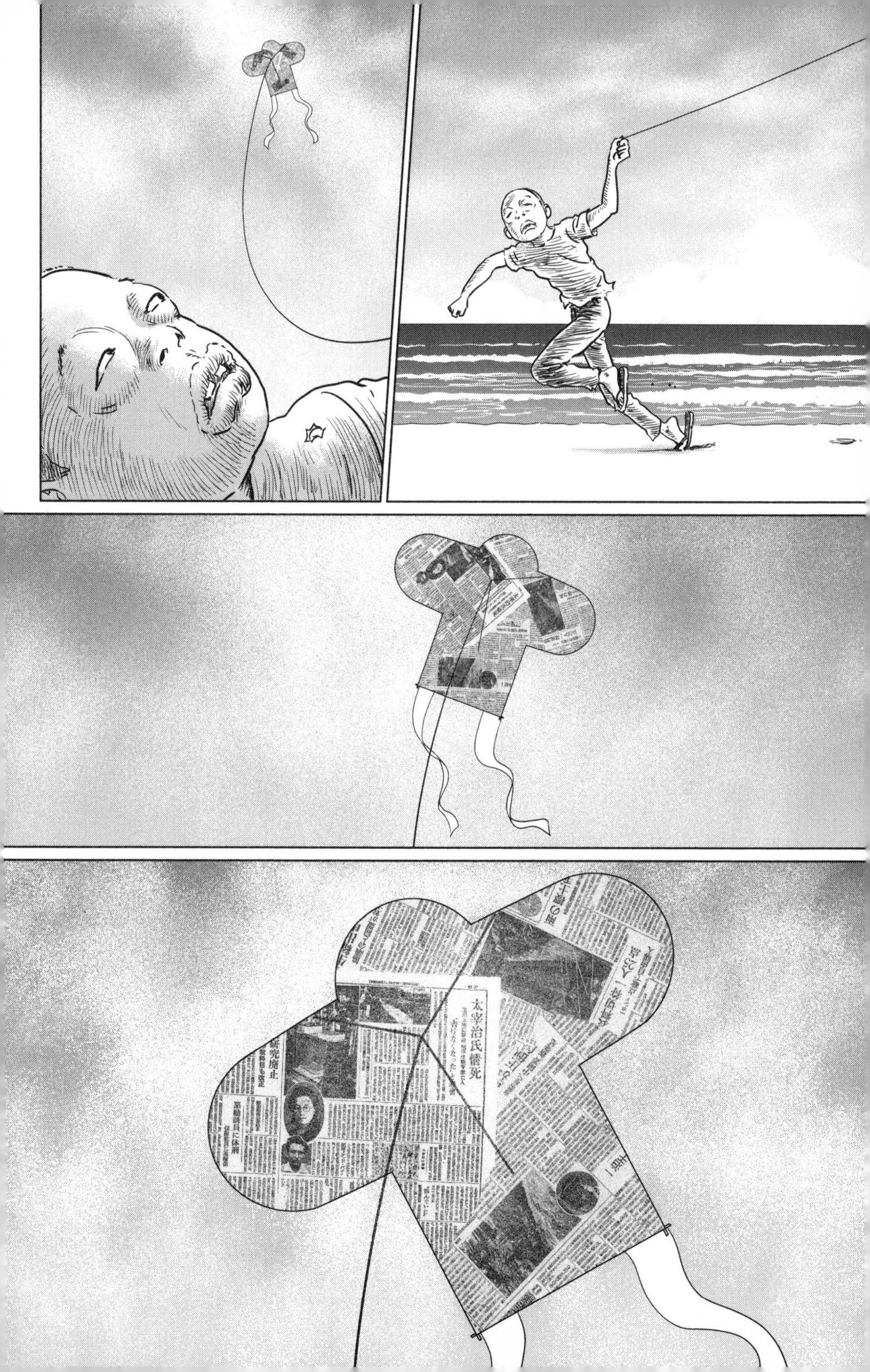
太宰治氏情死
研究廃止

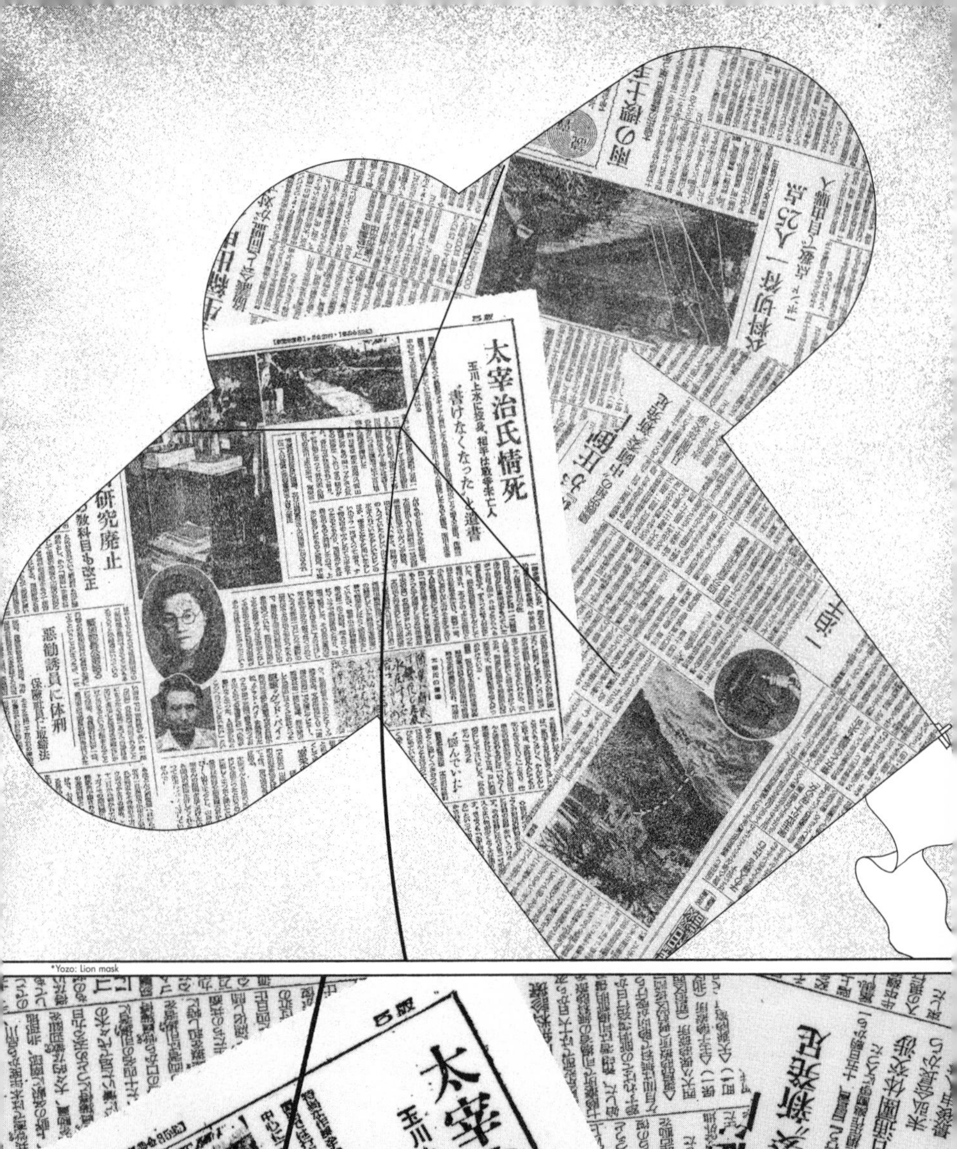
太宰治氏情死
玉川上水に投身、相手は戦争未亡人
"書けなくなった"と遺書

*Yozo: Lion mask

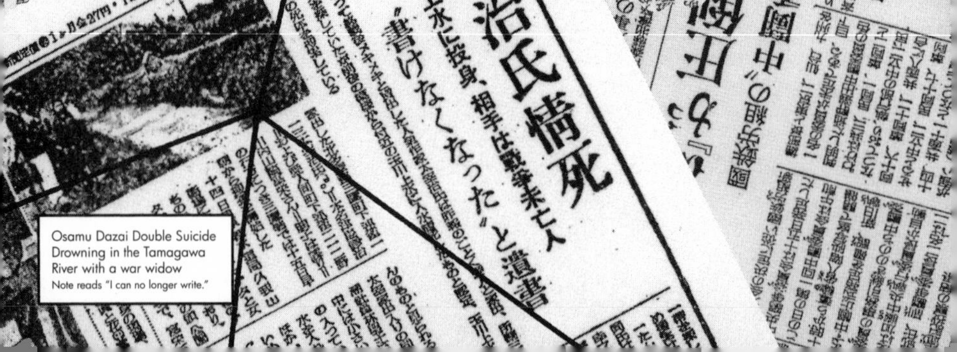
太宰治氏情死
玉川上水に投身、相手は戦争未亡人
"書けなくなった"と遺書
Osamu Dazai Double Suicide
Drowning in the Tamagawa
River with a war widow
Note reads "I can no longer write."

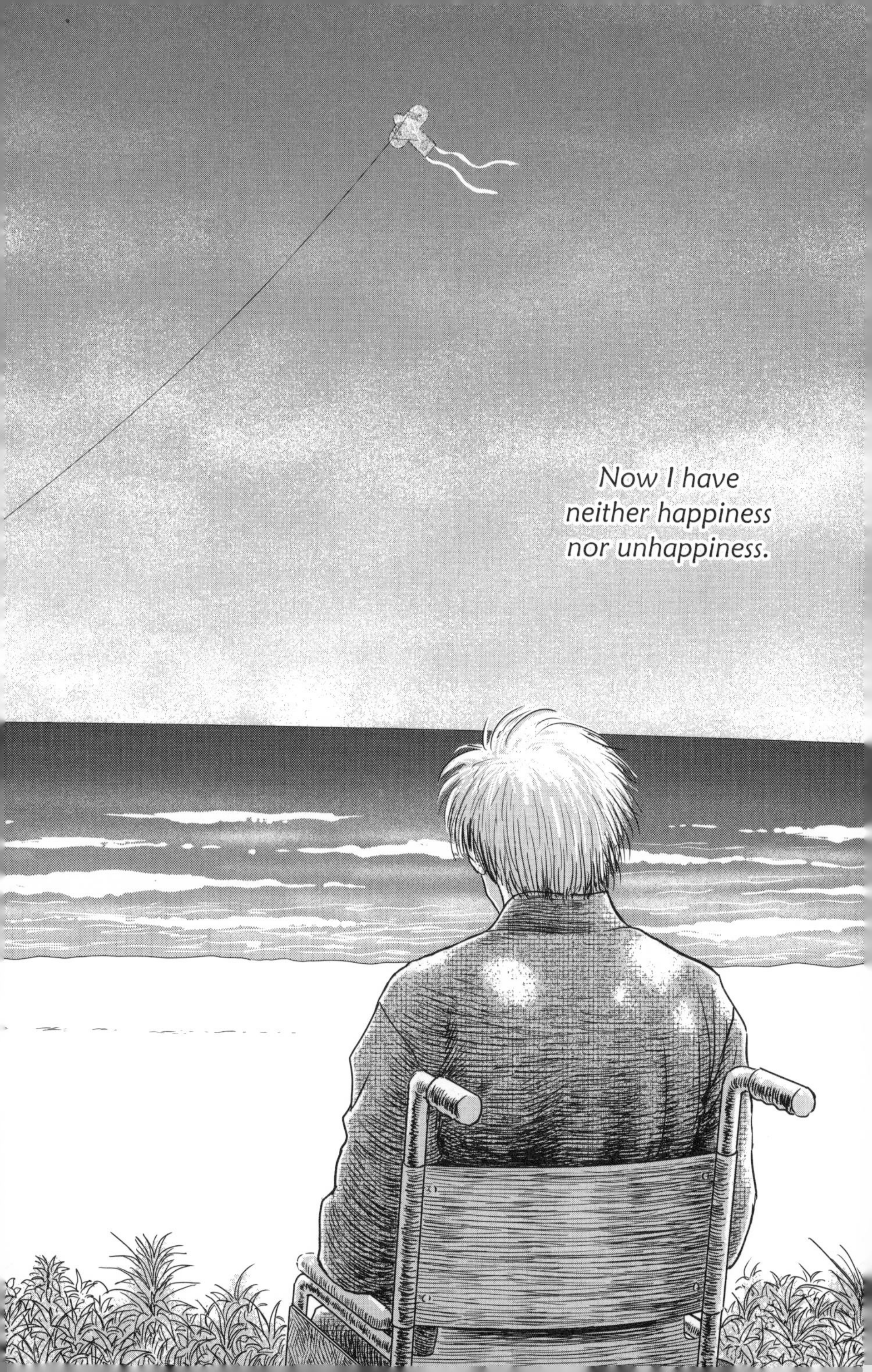
Now I have neither happiness nor unhappiness.

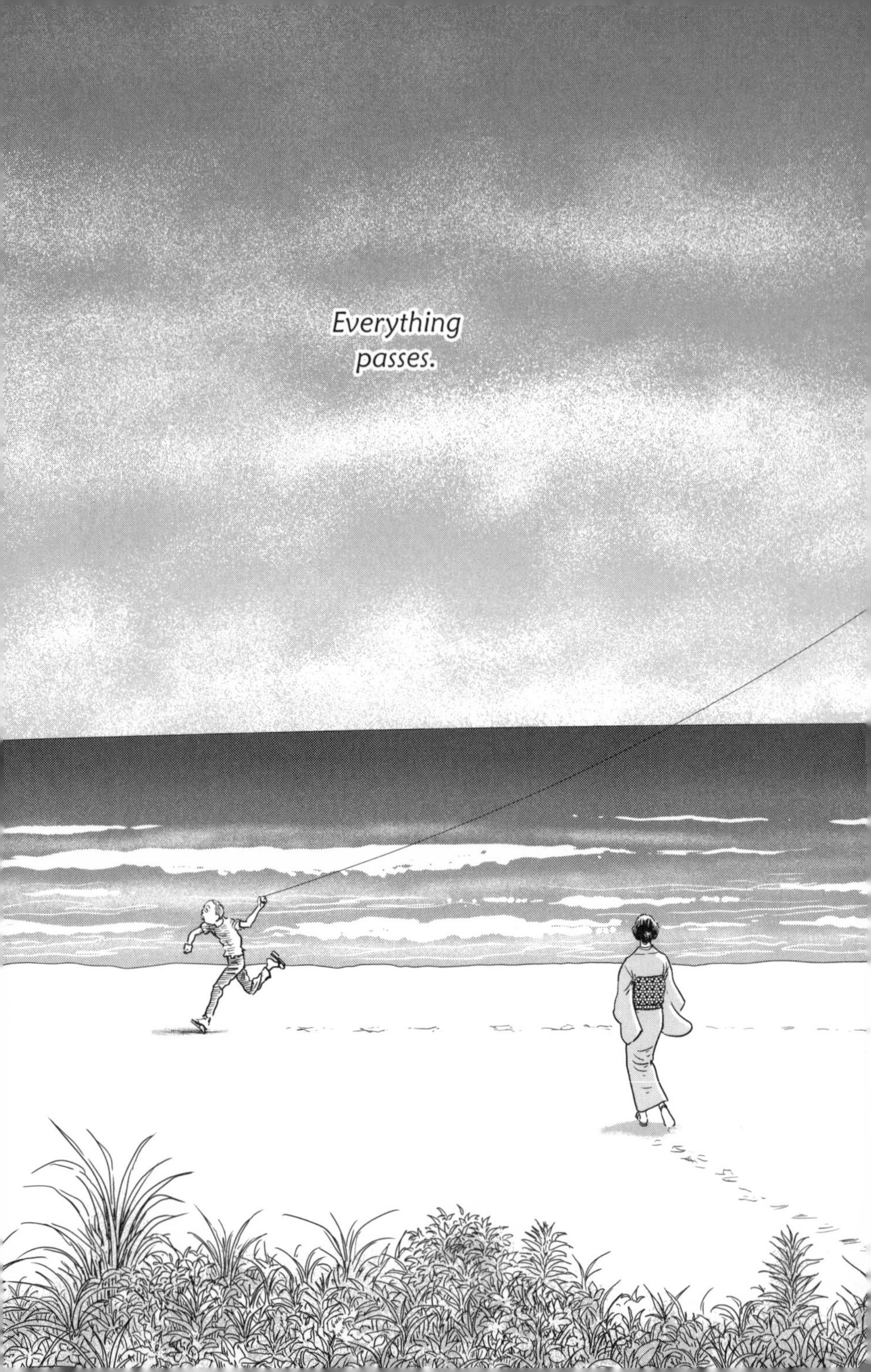
Everything passes.

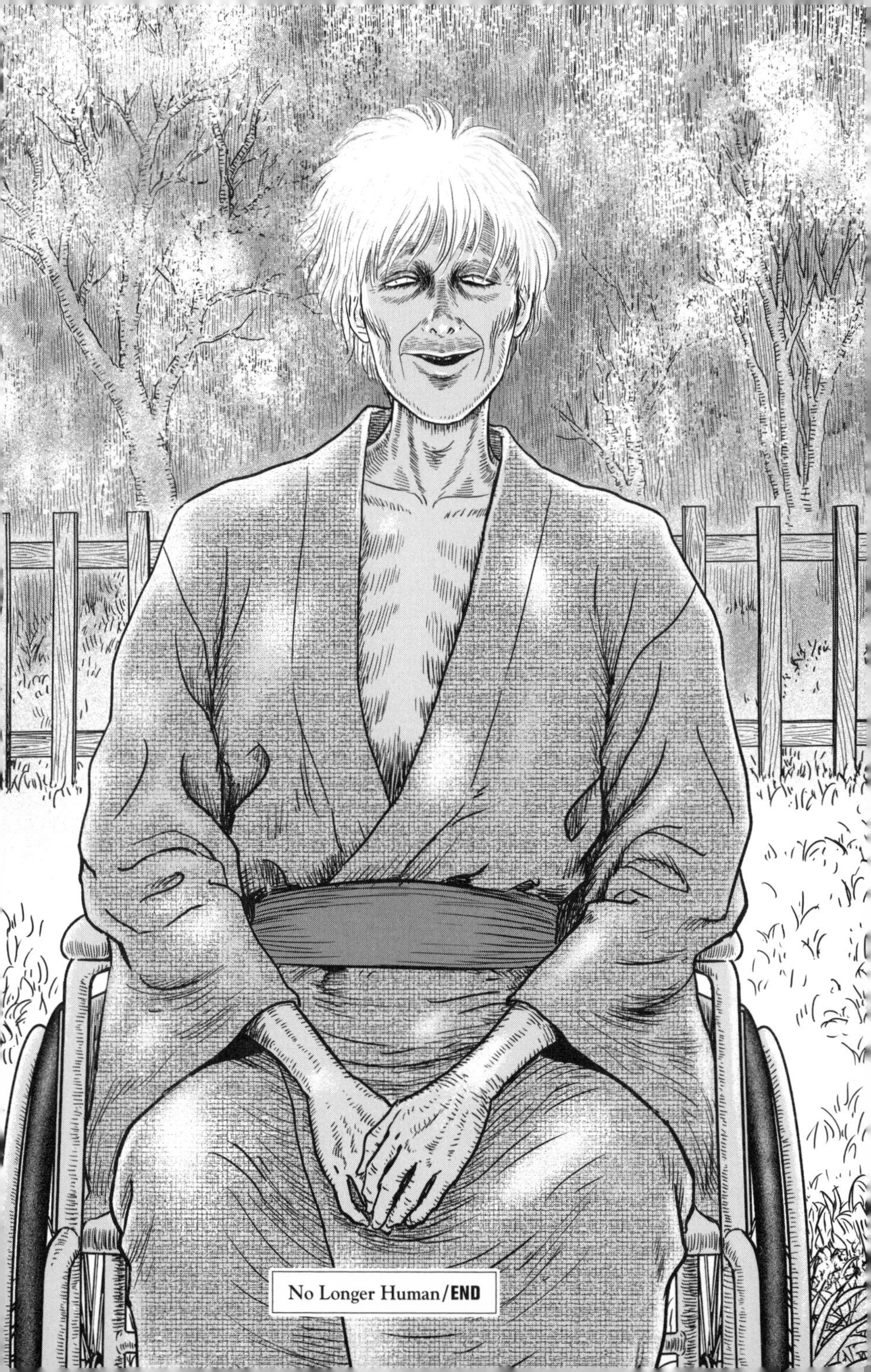
No Longer Human/END

PG. 195 TRANSLATION

TOKYO DAILY MORNING NEWSPAPER (SUNDAY)

Assemblyman Oba's brother* attempts a lovers' suicide

(via phone from Kamakura) The younger brother in the wealthy family of Assemblyman Oba in Kanaki-cho, Kita Tsugaru County, Aomori Prefecture, resident at Senyukan in Tokyo's Hongo district, Yozo (21), planned to commit suicide with a woman on the coast at Koshigoe at approximately 5:00 p.m. on the 29th. (Photo: Mr. Yozo Oba)

Woman dead, Oba in critical condition

Yesterday morning around 8:00 a.m., a local fisherman discovered Oba in anguish. He was taken to Shichirigahama's Aomatsu Clinic and received care. He was in critical condition, but is expected to survive. According to the Kamakura Police investigation, the woman was Tsuneko Abe (23), a hostess at Cafe Hollywood at the back of Jujiya Music Shop in Ginza.

Woman was Ginza hostess Tsuneko Abe

Eloped to Tokyo from Hiroshima

Common-law husband currently in prison

As a result of infidelity with husband's absence as a pretext, double lovers' suicide

The woman's whereabouts were at first unknown, but a week after the incident, her corpse was discovered washed up onto shore. (Photo: Tsuneko Abe)

Dumbfounded Hiroshima relatives confront the body

The woman's common-law husband is currently serving time for fraud. The Abe family from Hiroshima faced the body in shock and confirmed it was indeed Tsuneko. Both the man and woman in this case took the sedative Calmotin and planned to commit suicide together, but the reason and other factors are still not clear.

Express from the Oba house

The Oba family was surprised at the telegram, and a member of the family rushed to Kamakura on a train departing at 1:00 p.m. According to Assemblyman Oba, "We received notice that Yozo had disappeared, and we were concerned that something might have happened to him, but we never dreamed that he would do a thing like this. This is truly troubling, even if we don't know the true cause."

[AD] Mouth freshener and disinfectant

Oral hygiene Nioou

Before going out/After meals

**Editorial Note: By this time in the story, Yozo's brother had succeeded to their father's seat in the Diet.

BIBLIOGRAPHY

Dazai, Osamu. *Ningen Shikkaku* (No Longer Human). Shinchosha, Iwanami Shoten.

Dazai, Osamu. "Kyoko no Haru" (False Spring), *Nijusseiki Kishu* (A Standard-Bearer of the Twentieth Century). Shinchosha.

Dazai, Osamu. "Humanlost," *Nijusseiki Kishu* (A Standard-Bearer of the Twentieth Century). Shinchosha.

Dazai, Osamu. "Doke no Hana" (Flowers of Buffoonery), *Dazai Osamu Collection 1*. Chikuma Shobo.

Inose, Naoki. *Pikaresuku: Dazai Osamu Den* (Picaresque: A Life of Osamu Dazai). Bungeishunju.

Nakano, Kiichi. *Osamu Dazai: Shujii no Kiroku* (Osamu Dazai: His Doctor's Record). Hobunkan.

Matsumoto, Yuko. *Koi no Hotaru: Yamazaki Tomie to Dazai Osamu* (Fireflies of Love: Tomie Yamazaki and Osamu Dazai). Kobunsha.

The Museum of Modern Japanese Literature, ed. *Zusetu: Dazai Osamu* (Explanatory Diagram: Osamu Dazai). Chickuma Shobo.

Bessatsu Taiyo: Dazai Osamu. (Taiyo Magazine Special Edition: Osamu Dazai) Heibonsha.

Shincho Nihon Bungaku Album: Dazai Osamu (Shincho Japan Literature Album: Osamu Dazai). Shinchosha.

Komatsu, Ken'ichi. *Dazai Osamu to Tabisuru Tsugaru* (Traveling Tsugaku with Osamu Dazai). Shinchosha.

Pola Cultural Institution, ed. *Bakumatsu Ishin Meji Taisho Bijincho* (Beauty Portraits in End of Edo, Meiji and Taisyo periods). Shinjinbutsu Oraisha.

Fujimori, Terunobu, Hatsuta, Toru, and Fujioka Yoshiyasu. *Gen'ei no Tokyo: Taisho Showa no Machi to Sumai* (Illusions in Tokyo: Towns and Lives in Taisho and Showa periods). Kashiwa Shobo.

Harashima, Hiroshi. *Tokyo Konjaku Sampo* (Tokyo Walk: Past and Nowadays). Chukyo Shuppan.

Iguchi, Etsuo, and Ikuta, Makoto. *Tokyo konjaku Aruku Chizu-cho* (Working Maps: Past and Nowadays in Tokyo). Gakken Publishing.

Iguchi, Etsuo, and Ikuta, Makoto. *Kamakura Yokohama Shonan Konjaku Aruku Chizu-cho* (Working Maps: Past and Nowadays in Kamakura, Yokohama and Shonan). Gakken Publishing.

Mizuma, Masanori. *Hitome de Wakaru Senzen Nihon no Shinjitsu* (The Truth of Japan at a Glance–Pre WW2). PHP Institute.

Mizuma, Masanori. *Hitome de Wakaru Taisyo Showa Shoki no Shinjitsu* (The Truth of Japan at a Glance– Taisho and early Showa). PHP Institute.

Kondo,Yu. *Noh Byoin wo Meguru Hitobito* (People Surrounding a Psychiatric Hospital). Sairyusha.

Transportation Museum, ed. *Eki no Rekishi: Tokyo no Taminaru* (Histoy of Train Stations: Terminals in Tokyo). Kawade Shobo Shinsha.

Yamaguchi, Masato. *Tokyo Eki Monogatari* (Tokyo Station Story). Icarus Shuppan.

Yamagami, Shosuke, ed. *Furusato no Ayumi Kita Tsugaru* (The course of Hometown History– Kita Tsugaru). Tsugaru Shobo.

Adachi, Tatsuro. *Ikki ni Manabi Naosu Nihonshi, Kindai-Gendai Jitsuyohen* (Relearning Japanese History Instantly–Modern to Present, Practical Use). Toyo Keizai Shinsha.

Ogawa, Mineo, and Arakawa, Yoshio. *Yomigaeru Tohokuhonsen, Jobansen* (Reviving Tohoku Main Line and Joban Line). Gakken Publishing.

Tokunaga, Masuo, collection, Matsumoto, Ken'ichi, ed. *Zenkoku Joki Kikansha Haichihyo* (National Placement List for Steam Engines). Icarus Publishing.

Saito, Toshihiko. *Sakka Dazai Osamu no Tanjo* (Novelist Osamu Dazai's Birth). Iwanami Shoten.

Yamakawa, Ken'ichi. *Dazai Osamu no Onna tachi* (Osamu Dazai's Women). Gentosha.

Yomiuri Newspaper Archives, June 16, 1948 issue and June 17, 1948 issue.

Asahi Newspaper Archives, June 16, 1948 issue.

NO LONGER HUMAN

Story & Art by Junji Ito
Original Novel by Osamu Dazai

NINGEN SHIKKAKU Vol. 1-3
by Junji ITO
© 2017 Junji ITO
From the novel *No Longer Human* by Osamu DAZAI.
All rights reserved.
Original Japanese edition published by SHOGAKUKAN.
English translation rights in the United States of America, Canada, the United Kingdom,
Ireland, Australia and New Zealand arranged with SHOGAKUKAN.

NO LONGER HUMAN, by Osamu Dazai, translation by Donald Keene, copyright ©1958 by
New Directions Publishing Corp. Reprinted by permission of New Directions Publishing Corp.

Translation & Adaptation: Jocelyne Allen
Touch-Up Art & Lettering: James Dashiell
Cover & Graphic Design: Adam Grano
Editor: Masumi Washington

Printed in the U.S.A.

Published by VIZ Media, LLC
P.O. Box 77010
San Francisco, CA 94107

10 9 8 7 6 5 4
First printing, December 2019
Fourth printing, October 2021

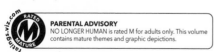
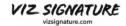
vizsignature.com

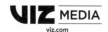
viz.com